HANDBOOK OF CLINICAL RESEARCH AND PRACTICE WITH ADOLESCENTS

Recent titles in the
Wiley Series on Personality Processes
IRVING B. WEINER, *Editor*
University of South Florida

Handbook of Clinical Research and Practice with Adolescents *edited by Patrick H. Tolan and Bertram J. Cohler*
Internalizing Disorders in Children and Adolescents *edited by William M. Reynolds*
Handbook of Clinical Child Psychology (Second Edition) *edited by C. Eugene Walker and Michael C. Roberts*
Assessment of Family Violence: A Clinical and Legal Sourcebook *edited by Samuel M. Turner, Karen S. Calhoun, and Henry E. Adams*
Psychological Disturbance in Adolescence (Second Edition) *by Irving B. Weiner*
Prevention of Child Maltreatment: Developmental and Ecological Perspectives *edited by Diane J. Willis, E. Wayne Holden, and Mindy Rosenberg*
Interventions for Children of Divorce: Custody, Access, and Psychotherapy (Second Edition) *by William F. Hodges*
The Play Therapy Primer: An Integration of Theories and Techniques *by Kevin John O'Connor*
Adult Psychopathology and Diagnosis (Second Edition) *edited by Michel Hersen and Samuel L. Turner*
The Rorschach: A Comprehensive System. Volume II: Interpretation (Second Edition) *by John E. Exner, Jr.*
Play Diagnosis and Assessment *edited by Charles E. Schaefer, Karen Gitlin, and Alice Sandgrund*
Acquaintance Rape: The Hidden Crime *edited by Andrea Parrot and Laurie Bechhofer*
The Psychological Examination of the Child *by Theodore H. Blau*
Depressive Disorders: Facts, Theories, and Treatment Methods *by Benjamin B. Wolman, Editor, and George Stricker, Co-Editor*
Social Support: An Interactional View *edited by Barbara R. Sarason, Irwin G. Sarason and Gregory R. Pierce*
Toward a New Personology: An Evolutionary Model *by Theodore Millon*
Treatment of Family Violence: A Sourcebook *edited by Robert T. Ammerman and Michel Hersen*
Handbook of Comparative Treatments for Adult Disorders *edited by Alan S. Bellack and Michel Hersen*
Managing Attention Disorders in Children: A Guide for Practitioners *by Sam Goldstein and Michael Goldstein*
Understanding and Treating Depressed Adolescents and Their Families *by Gerald D. Oster and Janice E. Caro*
The Psychosocial Worlds of the Adolescent: Public and Private *by Vivian Center Seltzer*
Handbook of Parent Training: Parents as Co-Therapists for Children's Behavior Problems *edited by Charles E. Schaefer and James M. Briesmeister*
From Ritual to Repertoire: A Cognitive-Development Approach with Behavior-Disordered Children *by Arnold Miller and Eileen Eller-Miller*
The Practice of Hypnotism. Volume 2: Applications of Traditional and Semi-Traditional Hypnotism; Non-Traditional Hypnotism *by Andre M. Weitzenhoffer*
The Practice of Hypnotism. Volume 1: Traditional and Semi-Traditional Techniques and Phenomenology *by Andre M. Weitzenhoffer*
Children's Social Networks and Social Supports *edited by Deborah Belle*
Advances in Art Therapy *edited by Harriet Wadeson, Jean Durkin, and Dorine Perach*
Psychosocial Aspects of Disaster *edited by Richard M. Gist and Bernard Lubin*
Handbook of Child Psychiatric Diagnosis *edited by Cynthia G. Last and Michel Hersen*
Grief: The Mourning After—Dealing with Adult Bereavement *by Catherine M. Sanders*
Problem-Solving Therapy for Depression: Theory, Research, and Clinical Guidelines *by Arthur M. Nezu, Christine M. Nezu, and Michael G. Perri*
Peer Relationships in Child Development *edited by Thomas J. Berndt and Gary W. Ladd*
The Psychology of Underachievement: Differential Diagnosis and Differential Treatment *by Harvey P. Mandel and Sander I. Marcus*
Treating Adult Children of Alcoholics: A Developmental Perspective *by Stephanie Brown*
Innovative Interventions in Child and Adolescent Therapy *edited by Charles E. Schaefer*
Delusional Beliefs: Interdisciplinary Perspectives *edited by Thomas F. Oltmanns and Brendan A. Maher*

HANDBOOK OF CLINICAL RESEARCH AND PRACTICE WITH ADOLESCENTS

Editors

PATRICK H. TOLAN
AND
BERTRAM J. COHLER

A WILEY-INTERSCIENCE PUBLICATION

JOHN WILEY & SONS, INC.
New York • Chichester • Brisbane • Toronto • Singapore

In recognition of the importance of preserving what has been
written, it is a policy of John Wiley & Sons, Inc., to have
books of enduring value published in the United States
printed on acid-free paper, and we exert our best efforts
to that end.

Copyright © 1993 by John Wiley & Sons, Inc.

All rights reserved. Published simultaneously in Canada.

Reproduction or translation of any part of this work
beyond that permitted by section 107 or 108 of the
1976 United States Copyright Act without the permission
of the copyright owner is unlawful. Requests for
permission or further information should be addressed to
the Permission Department, John Wiley & Sons, Inc.

This publication is designed to provide accurate and
authoritative information in regard to the subject
matter covered. It is sold with the understanding that
the publisher is not engaged in rendering legal, accounting,
or other professional services. If legal advice or other
expert assistance is required, the services of a competent
professional person should be sought. *From a Declaration
of Principles jointly adopted by a Committee of the
American Bar Association and a Committee of Publishers.*

Library of Congress Cataloging-in-Publication Data

Handbook of clinical research and practice with adolescents / edited
 by Patrick H. Tolan & Bertram J. Cohler
   p.   cm. — (Wiley series on personality processes)
  Includes bibliographical references and index.
  ISBN 0-471-61333-9 (cloth : alk. paper)
  1. Adolescent psychology. 2. Adolescent psychopathology.
 3. Adolescent psychotherapy. I. Tolan, Patrick H. II. Cohler,
 Bertram J. III. Series.
   [DNLM: 1. Adolescent Psychology. 2. Behavior Therapy—in
 adolescence. 3. Mental Disorders—in adolescence. WS 462 H2363]
 RJ503.H273 1993
 616.89'022—dc20
 DNLM/DLC
  for Library of Congress   92-5603
                                                            CIP

Printed in the United States of America

10 9 8 7 6 5 4 3 2 1

To my father, Francis Tolan
(P.H.T.)

To my wife, Anne Cohler
(B.J.C.).

For their support of our work and enriching of our spirits. We miss them daily.

Contributors

Patrick H. Tolan, Ph.D.
Associate Professor of Psychology and
  Psychiatry
University of Illinois at Chicago and,
Director of Research,
Institute for Juvenile Research
Chicago, Illinois

Bertram J. Cohler, Ph.D.
Professor of Human Development,
  Psychiatry, and Education
University of Chicago Chicago, Illinois

Steven Abell, Ph.D.
Senior Staff
The Sonia Shankman Orthogenic School
University of Chicago Chicago, Illinois

Thomas Berndt, Ph.D.
Professor
Department of Psychological Sciences
Purdue University Lafayette, Indiana

Andrew M. Boxer, Ph.D.
Assistant Professor
Department of Psychiatry
Northside Program University of Chicago
Chicago, Illinois

David C. Clark, Ph.D.
Associate Professor of Psychology and
  Psychiatry
Rush-Presbyterian/St. Luke's Medical Center
Chicago, Illinois

Catherine A. Crosby, J.D.
Student
Department of Psychology
University of Virginia
Charlottesville, Virginia

Leslie Davis, Ph.D.
Research Associate
Institute for Juvenile Research
University of Illinois at Chicago
Chicago, Illinois

Patricia A. H. Dyk, Ph.D.
Assistant Professor
Department of Sociology
University of Kentucky
Lexington, Kentucky

Julie Elmen, Ph.D.
Post-Doctoral Research Fellow
Department of Behavioral Science
University of Chicago
Chicago, Illinois

Robert M. Galatzer-Levy, M.D.
Faculty
Chicago Institute for Psychoanalysis
Chicago, Illinois

James Garbarino, Ph.D.
President
Erikson Institute
Chicago, Illinois

Nancy G. Guerra, Ph.D.
Assistant Professor of Psychology
University of Illinois at Chicago
Chicago, Illinois

Gilbert Herdt, Ph.D.
Professor of Human Development and
  Psychology
University of Chicago
Chicago, Illinois

Floyd Irvin, Ph.D.
Staff Psychologist
Department of Psychiatry
Humana/Michael Reese Hospital
Chicago, Illinois

Charles M. Jaffe, M.D.
Faculty, Chicago Institute for Psychoanalysis
Lecturer, Department of Psychiatry
Northwestern University Medical School
Chicago, Illinois

Betty M. Karrer, M.A.
Director, Family Systems Program
Institute for Juvenile Research
University of Illinois at Chicago
Chicago, Illinois

Douglas Kleiber, Ph.D.
Chair of Recreational and Leisure Studies
University of Georgia
Athens, Georgia

Reed Larson, Ph.D.
Associate Professor of Human Development
  and Family Ecology
University of Illinois at Champaign
Champaign, Illinois

Rolf Loeber, Ph.D.
Associate Professor of Psychiatry,
  Psychology and Public Health
Western Psychiatric Institute & Clinic
Pittsburgh, Pennsylvania

Hector Machabanski, Ph.D.
Associate Dean of Students
Chicago School of Professional Psychology
Chicago, Illinois

Richard C. Marohn, M.D.
Faculty, Chicago Institute for Psychoanalysis
Clinical Professor, Department of
  Psychiatry/Behavioral Sciences
Northwestern University
Chicago, Illinois

Brent C. Miller, Ph.D.
Professor
Department of Family and Human
  Development
Utah State University
Logan, Utah

Hartmut B. Mokros, Ph.D.
Assistant Professor
Department of Communication
Rutgers University
New Brunswick, New Jersey 08903

Daniel Offer, M.D.
Professor
Department of Psychiatry/Behavioral
  Sciences
Northwestern University
Chicago, Illinois

Anne C. Petersen, Ph.D.
Dean, College of Health & Human
  Development
Pennsylvania State University
University Park, Pennsylvania

Mark A. Reinecke, Ph.D.
Director of Center for Cognitive Therapy
Department of Psychiatry
University of Chicago Medical School
Chicago, Illinois

N. Dickon Reppucci, Ph.D.
Professor
Department of Psychology
University of Virginia
Charlottesville, Virginia

Maryse H. Richards, Ph.D.
Associate Professor
Department of Psychology
Loyola University of Chicago
Chicago, Illinois

Katherine Ryan, Ph.D.
Private Practice
Oak Park, Illinois

Ritch C. Savin-Williams, Ph.D.
Associate Professor
Human Development and Family Studies
Cornell University
Ithaca, New York

Michele Scheinkman, Ph.D.
Lecturer, School of Social Service
  Administration
University of Chicago
Faculty, Chicago Center for Family Health,
Chicago, Illinois

Kathleen D. Schmid, Ph.D.
Assistant Professor
Department of Psychology
University of Maryland
College Park, Maryland

Edison Trickett, Ph.D.
Professor
Department of Psychology
University of Maryland
College Park, Maryland

Froma Walsh, Ph.D.
Professor of Social Work and Psychiatry
University of Chicago
Co-Director, Chicago Center for Family
  Health,
Chicago, Illinois

Roderick Watts, Ph.D.
Assistant Professor
Department of Psychology
DePaul University
Chicago, Illinois

Jerry F. Westermeyer, Ph.D.
Professor and Director of Clinical Training
Adler School of Professional Psychology
Chicago, Illinois

Series Preface

This series of books is addressed to behavioral scientists interested in the nature of human personality. Its scope should prove pertinent to personality theorists and researchers as well as to clinicians concerned with applying an understanding of personality processes to the amelioration of emotional difficulties in living. To this end, the series provides a scholarly integration of theoretical formulations, empirical data, and practical recommendations.

Six major aspects of studying and learning about human personality can be designated: personality theory, personality structure and dynamics, personality development, personality assessment, personality change, and personality adjustment. In exploring these aspects of personality, the books in the series discuss a number of distinct but related subject areas: the nature and implications of various theories of personality; personality characteristics that account for consistencies and variations in human behavior; the emergence of personality processes in children and adolescents; the use of interviewing and testing procedures to evaluate individual differences in personality; efforts to modify personality styles through psychotherapy, counseling, behavior therapy, and other methods of influence; and patterns of abnormal personality functioning that impair individual competence.

IRVING B. WEINER

University of South Florida
Tampa, Florida

Acknowledgments

Developing and completing an endeavor such as this requires the help, support, and patience of many people. We thank our students, colleagues, and professors for stimulating us and helping in the formation of ideas that guided this book's contents. We also thank the support staffs at DePaul University, University of Chicago, and the University of Illinois at Chicago for their numerous hours of aid. In particular, we are indebted to Joann Godbold for her conscientious work and our department heads who encouraged our pursuit of this goal. Herb Reich and the staff at Wiley provided patient and professional assistance. We thank our families for the time with us that they gave up so we could complete this work. Finally, and certainly most, we thank the authors for their creative, timely, and astute contributions. They complied with our requirements and requests gracefully and exceeded our expectations consistently. We hope they and the reader find the volume due credit to them.

P.H.T.
B.J.C.

Contents

Introduction: Clinical Research and Practice with Adolescents   1
    Patrick H. Tolan and Bertram J. Cohler

PART ONE   DEVELOPMENTAL ISSUES   3

1. Normality, Turmoil, and Adolescence   5
   Julie Elmen and Daniel Offer
   - Adolescent Turmoil   5
   - Understanding the Role of Turmoil in Adolescence   10
   - Help-Seeking Behavior Among Adolescents   13
   - Conclusions   16
   - References   16

2. Biological Development   21
   Maryse H. Richards, Steve N. Abell, and Anne C. Petersen
   - The Nature of Pubertal Change   21
   - The Effects of Pubertal Development on Psychological Adjustment   25
   - Direct Effects Model   25
   - The Mediated Effects Models   29
   - The Mediated Effects Models: Our Current Knowledge   31
   - Clinical Implications   38
   - References   40

3. Cognitive Development   45
   Nancy G. Guerra
   - Cognitive Development During Adolescence   45
   - Structural–Developmental Competencies   46
   - Social Information-Processing Skills   53
   - Conclusion   57
   - References   58

4. The Psychological Significance of Others in Adolescence:
   Issues for Study and Intervention   63
   Robert M. Galatzer-Levy and Bertram J. Cohler
   Psychoanalysis, Subjectivity, and the Self   64
   Clinical Psychoanalytic Theory and Study of the Self   67
   Protecting the Self: Psychoanalytic Psychotherapy with Adolescents   77
   Conclusion   85
   References   86

5. Sexuality   95
   Brent C. Miller and Patricia A. H. Dyk
   Sexual Development   96
   Patterns of Adolescent Sexual Intercourse   101
   Antecedents of Early Sexual Intercourse   106
   Nonconsensual Sex   111
   Summary and Conclusions   116
   References   119

6. Daily Experience of Adolescents   125
   Reed Larson and Douglas Kleiber
   Criteria for Evaluating Leisure Activities   126
   Sports   128
   Socializing   131
   Art, Music, Hobbies, and Youth Organizations   134
   Media Use   136
   Deviant Activities   139
   Conclusion   140
   References   142

PART TWO   CONTEXTS OF ADOLESCENT DEVELOPMENT   147

7. The Family Context of Adolescence   149
   Froma Walsh and Michele Scheinkman
   A Systemic Orientation to Health and Dysfunction   149
   The Family Life Cycle at Adolescence   150
   Dimensions of Family Functioning in Adolescence   154
   Common Problems of Adolescence in Family Context   160
   Family Therapy Approaches   167
   References   169

8. The School as a Social Context   173
   Edison J. Trickett and Kathleen Doherty Schmid
   Underlying Assumptions for an Ecologically Based Approach to
      Interventions in Schools   174
   Environmental Assessment: The School as a Social Context and Adolescent
      Behavior in Schools   176

An Ecological Perspective on Intervention   190
Ecologically Based Intervention—A Brief Example   196
Summary   198
References   198

9. Peer Relations and Friendships   203

Thomas J. Berndt and Ritch C. Savin-Williams

The Effects of Adolescent Friendships   204
Effects of Peer-Group Acceptance, Rejection, and Isolation   211
Open Questions and Intervention Possibilities   214
References   216

10. Adolescence and Diversity   221

Roderick Watts, Hector Machabanski, and Betty M. Karrer

Introduction   221
The Sociopolitical Perspective   224
The Cross-Cultural Perspective   227
The Population-Specific Perspective   235
The Ecological Perspective   239
Conclusion   243
References   243

11. Gay and Lesbian Youth   249

Andrew M. Boxer, Bertram J. Cohler, Gilbert Herdt, and Floyd Irvin

Homosexuality and the Developmental Perspective   250
Life-Course, Development, and Homosexuality in Adolescence   258
Problems of Method in Longitudinal Research on Adolescent Homosexuality   268
Clinical Services and the Development of Gay and Lesbian Youth   270
Conclusion   271
References   273

12. The Legal System and Adolescents   281

Catherine A. Crosby and N. Dickon Reppucci

Introduction   281
The Juvenile Justice System   282
Medical Decision Making and Adolescence   288
Voluntary and Involuntary Mental Health Services   298
Conclusion   301
References   302

PART THREE   PROBLEMS AND INTERVENTIONS   305

13. Antisocial Behavior   307

Patrick H. Tolan and Rolf Loeber

Definition of Terms and Parameters   307
Prevalence and Incidence   310
General Predictors of Antisocial Behavior   312
Patterns of Adolescent Antisocial Behavior   316
Prevention and Treatment   320
Conclusion   323
References   324

14. Depression and Suicidal Behavior   333

David C. Clark and Hartmut B. Mokros

Overview   333
Depression   335
Completed Suicide in Adolescence   341
Appendix   351
References   352

15. Schizophrenia   359

Jerry F. Westermeyer

Introduction   359
Schizophrenia: Current Concepts and Epidemiological Data   359
Current Concepts on the Etiology of Schizophrenia   362
Historical and Cultural Influences on Schizophrenia   363
Gender Differences in Schizophrenia   365
Prognosis in Schizophrenia: Early Onset versus Late Onset   366
The Natural Course of Schizophrenia over the Adult Life Cycle   368
Suicide and Mortality in Schizophrenia   371
Treatment of Schizophrenia   372
Conclusion   378
References   380

16. Outpatient Treatment of Mild Psychopathology   387

Mark A. Reinecke

Introduction   387
Developmental Considerations   388
Epidemiology of Mild Behavioral and Emotional Problems   390
A Brief History of Adolescent Psychotherapy   392
A General Development Approach to Therapy   393
The Effectiveness of Psychotherapy in Treating Adolescents   395
Methodological Considerations   397
Specific Findings   400
Guidelines from the Research for the Treatment of Adolescents   403
Conclusion   404
References   404

17. The Adolescent Psychotherapist: Research Consumer and Producer 411

Charles M. Jaffe and Katherine Ryan

Introduction   411
Using Research in a Psychotherapy   412
The Adolescent Psychotherapist as Researcher   416
Conclusion   423
References   423

18. Alternative and Preventive Interventions 427

Leslie Davis and Patrick H. Tolan

Introduction   427
Social Skills Training   429
Community-Based Alternatives   430
Health-Related Interventions   438
Academic-Related Interventions   443
Delinquency Intervention Alternatives   444
Conclusion   446
References   446

19. Residential Services 453

Richard C. Marohn

Introduction   453
Major Issues in Treatment Programming   457
Limitations and Complications—A Reiteration   462
Unresolved Problems and Needed Research   464
Conclusion   465
References   465

PART FOUR   POLICY ISSUES 467

20. Enhancing Adolescent Development Through Social Policy 469

James Garbarino

Introduction   469
Social Policy: What Is It?   469
A Teen in Trouble Is a Teen Who Has Been Hurt   474
The Challenge of Being Parent to an Adolescent   476
Adolescents as Social Weather Vanes: The Role of Ideology   480
A Community Orientation   481
What Is Our Commitment to Solving Adolescent Problems?   482
Policy Considerations in Developing Clinical Services for Adolescents
  in Trouble   483
References   486

21. Tomorrow's Adolescent: Life-Course, Psychopathology, and Prevention 489
   Bertram J. Cohler and Patrick H. Tolan
   Adolescence, Generation, and Life-Course   489
   Adolescence and Social Change   496
   Clinical Research and Intervention: Toward the 21st Century   509
   Conclusion   515
   References   518

Author Index 527

Subject Index 545

HANDBOOK OF CLINICAL
RESEARCH AND PRACTICE
WITH ADOLESCENTS

INTRODUCTION

Clinical Research and Practice with Adolescents

PATRICK H. TOLAN and BERTRAM J. COHLER

Adolescence, as a distinct developmental stage with incumbent specialized research and treatment concerns, has been garnering increased attention from researchers, trainers, and practitioners. Since the inception of psychological study of this age period, about 100 years ago, there has been a cultural and intellectual recognition of the teenage years as a critical period in development with a distinct cultural function. For those interested in the mental health of adolescents, this increasing attention has raised troubling questions about clinically derived common assumptions of characteristics of this age period and heretofore accepted research results (Offer, Ostrov, & Howard, 1984; Rutter, Graham, Chadwick, & Yule, 1976). As our knowledge about adolescence and the related clinical issues increases in amount and complexity, many fundamental assumptions are being revised and operational guidelines redrawn. However, rather than spurring an increased exchange and greater intimacy between research and practice, this developmental complexity has resulted in a schism between practice and research, such that information flows back and forth even less. In fact, there appears to be a calcifying split between clinical description of adolescence and data-based findings (Jaffe & Tolan, 1988). For example, although many clinical descriptions present a picture of adolescence as a normally tumultuous time of alienation, symptomatology, and rebellion, survey data present a different picture of turmoil as being unusual and meriting concern. Life-span developmental research on turmoil and more careful examination of the actual ebb and flow of reported adolescent concerns suggest that emotional lability is heightened in this age period, but not exclusively during this age period and not in such great contrast to other age periods (Czikszentmihalyi & Larson, 1984).

Despite findings such as these that suggest a need for more careful consideration of research and its relation to practice, the literature has become more and more distinctly geared to clinical or research audiences, and segregated scholarly groups have developed. The widening misunderstanding between groups has impeded the quality and utility of information derived from research and practice.

Such a schism is not good for practice, research, or, most importantly, the adolescents of our communities. This book is designed to be a force in the opposite direction—to illustrate the importance of relating research and clinical practice and give direction on how to do so. We attempt to shed some light on the disjuncture between these two views by providing an integrative summary of the currently available research on adolescent development, psychopathology, intervention, and policy issues. We also suggest some directions for further research work and applications of research findings to practice. The book has grown out of the recognition that disciplined thinking and thoughtful application are *both* necessary components to adequately serve adolescents' mental health needs. As we have stated elsewhere, we contend that integration of empirical data not only enhances clinical work with adolescents, but is critical for effective work (Jaffe & Tolan, 1988). Conversely, the clinical utility of research should be one criterion for judging its merit.

This book is meant to summarize useful information for the practicing clinician (broadly defined) as well as stimulation for the inquiring researcher. It is meant to serve as a state-of-the-field summary that offers unifying direction for application and for future study. To that end, the book's four Parts address four areas that are necessary considerations for researchers and practitioners.

Part One is concerned with a normative base of essential developmental pathways, transitions, and issues that can comprise a viable, multifactor, biopsychosocial model. The second Part focuses on contexts of adolescent development that constrain, modify, and promote in the course and meaning of adolescent development. Part Three reviews the common types of psychopathology in adolescence, using developmental and epidemiological bases. In the intervention chapters in that Part can be found a broad conception of clinical interventions, an overview of effects of intervention, the empirical validity of various interventions, and information on how to utilize research more intimately in psychotherapeutic interactions. This is in service of the need for an empirical base for clinical interventions and suggests that considerable advantage can be gained by protocol intervention trials research and prescriptive application of protocol for interventions. Part Four brings the policy dimension to bear on research and practice. One chapter focuses on suggestions for directing basic policy; another suggests a general perspective on research from a life-course perspective as a base for service policy. Some chapters focus on basic conceptual issues, some on theoretical synthesis, some on reviews of the extant empirical literature, and some on specific approaches to a given issue. As a whole, they provide a rich, multitextured portrayal of the multiple factors influencing the development and psychopathology of adolescents. We hope you find them interesting.

REFERENCES

Csikszentmihalyi, M., & Larson, R. (1984). *Being adolescent.* New York: Basic Books.

Jaffe, C., & Tolan, P. H. (1988). *Toward empathic understanding of adolescents: Integrating epidemiological data into clinical practice.* Unpublished manuscript.

Offer, D., Ostrov, E., & Howard, K. I. (1984). Epidemiology of mental health and mental illness among adolescents. In J. Call (Ed.), *Significant advances in child psychiatry.* New York: Basic Books.

Rutter, M., Graham, P., Chadwick, D. F. D., & Yule, W. (1976). Adolescent turmoil: Fact or fiction. *Journal of Child Psychology and Psychiatry, 17,* 35–36.

PART ONE

Developmental Issues

CHAPTER 1

Normality, Turmoil, and Adolescence

JULIE ELMEN and DANIEL OFFER

According to Hill (1983), five sets of psychosocial issues take on special importance during adolescence: (a) discovering and understanding the self as an individual (identity); (b) forming close and caring relationships with others (intimacy); (c) establishing a healthy sense of independence (autonomy); (d) coming to terms with puberty and expressing sexual feelings (sexuality); and (e) becoming a successful and competent member of society (achievement). These five psychosocial issues do not arise for the first time during adolescence, nor do they disappear with the transition to adulthood. However, development in each of these areas takes on special meaning during the adolescent years because of the extensive biological, psychological, and social changes taking place at this time and the potential implications of such "turmoil" for adolescents' functioning.

The prevalence of turmoil and the role it plays during adolescence, when youngsters are negotiating these issues, have long been discussed in the psychiatric literature. Some writers have emphasized the inevitability and necessity of turmoil at adolescence. Others have minimized its prevalence and warned parents and mental health professionals about the harmful consequences of not recognizing serious disturbance in adolescent youngsters and offering appropriate help. The lack of agreement among professionals about the range of behavior considered abnormal has complicated the issue. Inconsistencies abound among and between researchers and clinicians with regard to what is considered normal behavior during adolescence. Given the important implications—for mental health policy formation, psychiatric research agendas, and clinical practice—that the definition of normality and the role attributed to turmoil can have, it is important that the empirical base for understanding these concepts be provided.

In this chapter, we attempt to disentangle some of the issues and assumptions that have contributed to the disagreement about the meaning of normality and the role of turmoil during the adolescent years. In addition, findings from a recent study on help-seeking behavior among adolescents are offered as an empirical base for understanding these concepts.

ADOLESCENT TURMOIL

The earliest references to turmoil during adolescence were not based on empirical data and yet have been extremely influential in determining how parents, scholars, clinicians, and perhaps even youngsters themselves view adolescence. Thus, in attempting to define parameters of adolescent turmoil, it is necessary to consider the important influence of the earliest scholars as well as the empirical contributions of more contemporary writers.

G. Stanley Hall's (1904) conception of adolescence as a time of *"sturm und drang"* (storm and stress) is a product of his immersion in the nineteenth-century German romantic literary movement that emphasized idealism, romanticism, rebellion against established ways, and the expression of deep passions. Hall's biogenetic theory offers a functional explanation for adolescent turmoil. The theory assumes that, throughout an individual's development, the evolutionary development of the human race is relived. Hall outlined four stages: *infancy,* during which the child recapitulates the animal stage of evolutionary development; *childhood,* which corresponds to the cave-dwelling and hunting–fishing epoch of human history; *youth,* the preadolescent stage of development during which the child reenacts the life savagery but is predisposed to learn reading, writing, drawing, manipulation of numbers, languages, music, and other subjects, through routine practice and discipline; and *puberty,* the period of adolescence corresponding to the time in evolutionary development when the human race was in a turbulent, transitional stage, a time of great storm and stress. Hall saw puberty as a time of emotional maladjustment and instability, characterized by oscillating moods and turbulent family relationships. Indeed, he considered this emotional lability and rebelliousness necessary for the youngster to emerge out of adolescence as a mentally healthy individual. According to Hall, the end of adolescence symbolizes and recapitulates the beginning of human civilization, for only then is the youth capable of higher, more completely human traits.

Anna Freud (1946, 1958), contrary to Hall, held that the growing individual was not impervious to environmental influences, despite the importance of biology in the determination of developmental change. She provided in her writings an elaborate description of the stage of adolescence and the changes in the psychic structure of the pubertal child. Freud's overall description of adolescence as a time of internal conflict, psychic disequilibrium, and erratic behavior is not at odds with Hall's description. Hall was somewhat vague about suggesting a cause for this pattern, saying that it had something to do with the sudden appearance of sexual feelings, which, he felt, could temporarily disable the brain. Freud offered a more specific explanation of the role of sexuality in adolescent turmoil. She attributed it to the reappearance at puberty of sexual conflicts that had previously occurred during the first five or six years of life. In a sense, what is relived or recapitulated, according to Freud's psychoanalytic theory of adolescent upheaval, is not part of human genetic history, but is, instead, the significant aspects of the individual's own earlier relationships to his or her parents.

Later psychoanalytic theorists elaborated Freud's perspective (Blos, 1962; Erikson, 1968), but retained the attribution of turmoil to an upsurge in impulses and saw turmoil as desirable. However, both Blos and Erikson made the separation and identity development of the adolescent the central process underlying adolescent turmoil.

Hall and Freud saw the clinical implications of their perspective as a view of turmoil as being expectable and to be tolerated by parents. It was not to be interfered with, so as not to disrupt the inevitable and necessary course of adolescent development. Parents, in essence, were subjected to the emotional upheaval and rebellion of their children, but the parent–adolescent relationship was not seen as an important determinant or component of turmoil at adolescence. Rather, Hall (1904), Freud (1958), and even the more contemporary psychoanalytic writers (e.g., Blos, 1962; Erikson, 1968) viewed parent–adolescent conflict primarily as a result of adolescent difficulties, needs, or developmental changes.

Such concepts led to two clinical confusions. First, failure to be rebellious or difficult was labeled as pathological. Second, because severe difficulties during the adolescent years were considered signs of normal healthy development, serious problems were often not recognized as such and not treated (Petersen, 1988).

During the late 1960s and 1970s, studies of adolescents appeared that refuted widely held notions. All of these studies suggested that a substantial proportion of adolescents experienced no significant psychological difficulties whatsoever. Douvan and Adelson (1966) concluded, based on interviews with adolescents, that the degree of conflict between adolescents and their parents is exaggerated:

The normative adolescent tends to avoid overt conflict with his family. Now this is not to say that conflict is not present; but it is largely unconscious conflict, those under-surface resentments which do not necessarily liberate or enlarge the personality, but which, paradoxically, increase the child's docility toward his parents. Even when we do find overt conflict one senses that it has an "as if" quality to it, that it is a kind of war game, with all the sights and sounds of battle but without any blood being shed. More often than not the conflicts will center on trivia, on issues of taste—clothing, grooming, and the like. (p. 352)

Similarly, a study of middle-class families of adolescent boys, conducted by Bandura and Walters (1959), found that the boys had adopted their parents' values and standards of conduct and saw their parents as supportive influences rather than as adversaries. Bandura (1964) noted several reasons for the persistence of the image of adolescence as a time of rebellion, inner turmoil, and parent–adolescent conflict. The first reason was *overinterpretation of superficial signs of nonconformity*. According to Bandura, adolescents frequently display idiosyncratic fashions and interests that are tagged as signs of disgruntlement, but "such fads, however, are not confined to adolescent age groups" (p. 93). Second, the *mass media sensationalism* often portrays the typical adolescent as deviant.

Third, there is a *generalization from samples of deviant adolescents*. Bandura pointed out that many theories of adolescents were based on extrapolations made by mental health professionals who saw primarily the most troubled adolescents. Fourth, he noted that there was *inappropriate generalization from cross-cultural data*. Some writers cite cross-cultural data as evidence of the discontinuity of adolescent development in American society. However, as stated by Bandura and Benedict (1938), cross-cultural studies have demonstrated that extraordinary distress and conflicts are not inherent to adolescence, but rather vary by culture. Fifth, Bandura suggested that there was an *overemphasis of the biological determination of heterosexual behavior*. He contended that adolescent sexuality and related frustrations, conflicts, or anxieties are governed more by social conditioning than biological drives. Sixth, *reliance on state theories of personality development* have promoted the view that adolescence is a stage that suddenly appears at pubescence, and just as suddenly disappears when adulthood is reached. It is viewed as a sudden event rather than as part of a life-span development process. Finally, he noted the *self-fulfilling prophecy* of labeling teenagers as by nature rebellious, unpredictable, and wild, which then encourages adolescents to behave this way. Thus, much of the turmoil seen in American adolescents could be attributed to influences other than developmental intrusions.

Offer and Offer (1975b) also provided evidence (based on a sample of boys) challenging the notion of adolescence as a time of inevitable psychological turmoil. They specified the developmental routes followed by a group of 73 boys studied over an 8-year period, identifying the following three different psychological growth patterns.

1. Continuous Growth (23% of the total group). The young males in this group progressed throughout adolescence and young adulthood with a sense of self-assurance as they looked toward meaningful and fulfilling adult lives. These subjects had favorable

genetic and environmental backgrounds. They had mastered earlier developmental stages without major problems and had an order to their lives that could be interrupted without resulting in symptomatology or chaotic behavior. The value system of the subjects in the Continuous Growth group dovetailed with that of their parents, although the parents seemed able to allow them to create their own individual lives outside of the household. None of the boys in this group had received psychotherapy or was thought by the researchers to need treatment.

2. Surgent Growth (35% of the total group). Developmental spurts characterized the pattern of growth of the subjects in this subgroup, even though they generally functioned as adaptively as those in the first group. For the young males in the Surgent Growth group, "there was more concentrated energy directed toward mastering developmental tasks than was obvious for members of the Continuous Growth group. At times these subjects would be adjusting very well, integrating their experiences and moving ahead, and at other times they seemed to be stuck at an almost premature closure and unable to move forward. A cycle of progression and regression is more typical of this group than the Continuous Growth group. The defenses used, anger and projection, represent more psychopathology than the defenses used by the first group" (p. 131). One of the major differences between subjects in the Continuous and Surgent Growth groups was the higher incidence of problems and traumas in the genetic and/or environmental backgrounds of the boys in the Surgent Growth group, who were more likely to have been affected by separation, death, or severe illness. In addition, relationships with parents were somewhat strained by conflicts of opinions and values.

3. Tumultuous Growth (21% of the total group). The youngsters placed in this group were similar to the adolescents so often described in the psychiatric, psychoanalytic, and social science literature. Inner turmoil that resulted in behavioral problems both at home and at school was characteristic of the boys in this group. The difficulties in their life situations outweighed the satisfactions, and a relatively high percentage of this group had overt clinical problems and underwent psychotherapy. Although family bonds were present for these boys, as for the boys in the other two groups, they tended to be from less stable backgrounds—more of them had parents with overt marital conflict or a history of mental illness. The adolescents in the Tumultuous Growth group experienced more psychological pain than did the others, but were no less well adjusted as a group in terms of overall functioning within their own environmental settings than were those in the other two groups.

This longitudinal study of boys suggests that continuity between generations and continuity of coping styles exist throughout the transition to young adulthood. Changes in levels of functioning and changes in emotional tone were relatively rare from 14 to 22 years of age. This study, and others like it, provide empirical direction for five basic questions in clinical practice and research with adolescents. The first is the issue of rate of psychopathology. Rutter, Graham, Chadwick, and Yule (1976) reported that 22% of 14- to 15-year-olds in their Isle of Wight sample had clinical level symptoms. Offer and Offer (1975a) and others (Graham & Rutter, 1973; Leslie, 1974; Masterson, 1967; Offer, Ostrov, & Howard, 1987) have confirmed a prevalence rate of about 20%. This rate is comparable to those found for adults (Uhlenhuth, Balter, Mellinger, Chisin, & Clinthorne, 1983). Similarly, these adolescent studies report about 20% of their sample is symptom- or stress-free, as has been found with other age samples (Bjornsson, 1974). Another important question these studies address is the extent to which adolescent psychotherapy rates represent continuing problems from childhood and arising problems will continue to adulthood. Rutter (1980) estimated that about one-half of adolescent disorders represent continuing childhood disorders. He noted that three types of disorder pathways can be identified: (a) those that decrease or do not change in prevalence from childhood to adolescence (e.g., nocturnal enuresis for 2.9% of 15-year-old males and 1.5% of same-age females vs. close to 6% and 4% respectively for 10-year-olds), (b) those that show increases in adolescence (e.g., suicide, drug abuse), and (c) those that have changing features at adolescence (e.g., Attention Deficit Disorder with Hyperactivity). Overall, Graham and Rutter (1973) found that a cohort of 15-year-olds had a slightly higher overall rate of psychiatric symptoms than they did at 10 years old.

The third area of interest these studies can comment on is the persistence of adolescent psychopathology. Studies have suggested that adolescent disturbances are fairly stable, with stability increasing as the severity of symptoms and the extent of symptomatology increase (Weiner & Del Gaudio, 1976). Although this overall pattern fluctuates with specific types of problems, the available longitudinal studies support this conclusion (Masterson, 1967).

Overall, these findings suggest that adolescence is not a time of "normal" psychiatric symptoms, and that clinical-level symptoms are not more prevalent during this age group than at any other time in life. Symptoms may vary a bit in their etiological and diagnostic meaning during this developmental period (Rutter, 1980), but their appearance is as serious as in other periods and reflects more than developmental stress. The extent to which these overall rates are meaningful for all adolescents, or whether more specific rates based on gender, urbanicity, socioeconomic status, and ethnicity are required, remains unclear.

Another pertinent question is whether today's adolescents are more disturbed than those of previous generations. There is a tendency to assume that the current group of teenagers is more disturbed than the last. A study comparing adolescent self-image across the 1960s, 1970s, and 1980s (Offer, Ostrov, & Howard, 1989a) found a curvilinear effect for these three decades. The adolescents of the 1960s seemed the healthiest (less turmoil). However, the 1980s adolescents were healthier than the 1970s adolescents.

The fifth question is whether disturbance/turmoil in adolescents leads to treatment. According to a study (Offer & Spiro, 1987) of a subsample of college students who had participated in a 1983 epidemiological investigation of emotional disturbance and help-seeking behavior among adolescents, the percentage of disturbed adolescents who go on to college remains the same as the percentage in high school—about 20% are emotionally disturbed. This same finding has emerged in other studies (e.g., Schuckit, Halikas, Schuckit, McClure, & Rimmer, 1973). Surprisingly, only about 20 to 30% of college students in need of mental health care actually receive it (Rimmer, Halikas, Schuckit, & McClure, 1978; Whitley, 1979). According to one study of high school students, only 41% who were assigned both a diagnosis and a rating of impairment had received any kind of clinical attention (Whitaker et al., 1990). Thus, although it seems adolescence is not necessarily a time of greater psychopathology prevalence, it appears that disturbed adolescents are conspicuously poor at getting the mental health care they need (Myers et al., 1984; Tolan, Ryan, & Jaffe, 1988).

These epidemiological data and the survey and interview research conducted by Douvan and Adelson (1966), Bandura and Walters (1959), and Offer and Offer (1975a), as well as findings from related work (e.g., Grinker, Grinker, & Timberlake, 1962), have changed the nature of adolescent research and clinical practice. However, even in the face of evidence to the contrary, adolescence has continued to be characterized by many parents, researchers, and practitioners as a period of tumultuous psychological development. The accompanying psychoanalytic notion (Blos, 1967; Erikson, 1968; Freud, 1958; Parsons, 1949) that the parent–adolescent relationship is always a stormy and conflictual one, and that this kind of relationship is basically healthy, has died an equally slow death. Needless to say, the line separating adolescent inner turmoil and parent–adolescent conflict is often and unavoidably obscure. For decades, mental health professionals have used the term "adolescent turmoil" to refer to interpersonal conflict between adolescents and their parents, as well as to describe psychologically disturbed adolescents.

Along with these changes in understanding adolescent turmoil has come the realization that processes of development must be studied as interactions between the individual and other people and contexts (Petersen, 1988). Specific to turmoil, studies have focused heavily on the importance of family relationships, particularly conflict in them, in the examination of adolescent mental health.

Amplifying the sentiments of Douvan and Adelson (1966), Bandura (1964), and Offer and Offer (1975b), and drawing on investigations in which parents or adolescents were questioned about actual conflicts or disagreements, Montemayor (1983), in his review of research on parent–adolescent conflict behavior, argued that the inevitability of tumultuous family relationships at adolescence is not grounded in empirical research. He concluded that, ". . . while the idea of parent–adolescent stress remains alive in the minds of many parents of adolescents and therapists" (p. 85), the old "*sturm und drang*" view of parent–adolescent relations has not been validated empirically. Montemayor reminded us, however, that conflict is an important part of any relationship, and that satisfactorily resolving differences is necessary to maintaining a relationship. In addition, he suggested that moderate levels of conflict between adolescents and their parents may be a normal part of family relations during this time, as adjustments and renegotiations between parents and their children occur with respect to, for example, autonomy and identity issues (see Walsh & Scheinkman, this volume).

Severe parent–adolescent conflict, on the other hand, appears to be associated with serious adolescent problem behavior. High levels of conflict are associated with adolescents' running away (Blood & D'Angelo, 1974), involvement in religious cults (Ullman, 1982), teenage pregnancies (McKenry, Walter, & Johnson, 1979), drug abuse (McCubbin, Needle, & Wilson, 1985), and development of psychiatric disorders (Rutter et al., 1976). How does one know when to consider parent–adolescent conflict severe or problematic? The emotion most often associated with interpersonal conflict is anger. Five criteria for problematic anger identified by Novoco (1978) have been adapted by J. Hall (1987) to apply to problematic parent–adolescent conflict. According to Hall, anger is a problem when it (a) is too frequent; (b) is too long-lasting; (c) is too intense; (d) leads to aggression; or (e) disturbs work or relationships. Undoubtedly, adolescence is not without its challenges for youngsters or their parents, but much of the more recent work has focused on the *nature* of conflict among adolescents and their families (e.g., Hill, Holmbeck, Marlow, Green, & Lynch, 1985a, 1985b; Montemayor, 1983, 1986; Smetana, 1988; Steinberg, 1981, 1987, 1988) and how best to deal with it (e.g., Alexander, 1973; Blackman & Silberman, 1975; Robin, 1979; Schenck & Schenck, 1978) rather than saying it does or does not exist for the average adolescent.

UNDERSTANDING THE ROLE OF TURMOIL IN ADOLESCENCE

The task of defining turmoil at adolescence is arduous, given the pervasive use of the word to describe both troubled and healthy adolescents, as well as both typical and troubled parent–adolescent relationships. Indeed, there persists a strong association of the term "adolescence" with the term "turmoil" for many clinicians and others in our culture (Rabichow & Sklansky, 1980). Anna Freud's (1958) discussion exemplifies this:

I refer to the difficulty in adolescent cases to draw the line between normality and pathology . . . adolescence constitutes by definition an interruption of peaceful growth which resembles in appearance a variety of other emotional upsets and structural upheavals. The adolescent manifestations come close to symptom formation of the neurotic, psychotic or dissocial order and merge almost imperceptibly into borderline states, initial, frustrated or fully fledged forms of almost all the mental illnesses. Consequently, the differential diagnosis between the adolescent upsets and true pathology becomes a difficult task. (p. 267) . . . I take it that it is normal for an adolescent to behave for a considerable length of time in an inconsistent and unpredictable manner; to fight his impulses and to accept them; to ward them off successfully and to be overrun by them; to love his parents and to hate them; to revolt against them and to be dependent on them; to be deeply ashamed to acknowledge his mother before others and, unexpectedly, to desire heart-to-heart talks with her. . . . While an adolescent remains inconsistent and unpredictable in his behavior, he may suffer, but he does not seem to me to be in need of treatment. I think that he should be given time and scope to work out his own solution. Rather, it may be his parents who need help and guidance so as to be able to bear with him. There are few situations in life which are more difficult to cope with than an adolescent son or daughter during the attempt to liberate themselves. (pp. 275–276)

More current views of normality during adolescence usually generalize about adolescent turmoil from clinical samples. However, some contemporary writers have stressed the importance of relying on empirical data rather than on theoretically based assertions, when attempting to clarify how a certain generation of adolescents looks with respect to normality and disturbance (Tolan, Jaffe, & Ryan, 1990). In this vein, Offer, Ostrov, and Howard (1981) provided empirical evidence on how mental health professionals view normal adolescents. The question that prompted the study was whether the "old" theories are still in force in light of "new" data refuting them. That is, do mental health professionals see normal adolescents as having mood swings and poor interpersonal and family relationships, a view emphasized by much of the psychiatric, psychoanalytic, psychological, and social science theory about normal adolescents? Or, do they see normal adolescents as relatively tension-free, happy, quiet, and involved in secure and satisfying family relationships? The findings of this study suggested that mental health professionals had not caught up in their conceptual perspectives with what behavioral scientists have empirically discovered. That is to say, the professionals studied believed that normal adolescents have a particularly hard time in dealing with their moods, with interpersonal and family relationships, and with confusion about future vocational and educational goals, whereas the study's data, collected from 407 normal, mentally healthy adolescents, indicated that this was not the way normal adolescents feel about themselves.

A recent study (Swedo & Offer, 1991), based on similar questions, examined pediatricians' conceptions of the normal adolescent. The findings of this study indicated that pediatricians also have a negatively skewed view of the self-image of the normal adolescent. The authors noted that this has important diagnostic and treatment implications:

Believing that the typical adolescent "feels sexually behind," the physician might delay needed anticipatory guidance about sexual activity. Similarly, the perspective of the typical adolescent as self-blaming and sad might preclude the accurate diagnosis of depression. Assuming that normal adolescent interactions with family and peers are troubled could result in unnecessary interventions, or conversely, in missing truly pathological relationships. Finally, the physician's negative impressions of the adolescent's coping skills could prevent the pediatrician from allowing the teen sufficient control over his own treatment. (p. 9)

The results of both of these investigations highlight the fact that health professionals, who are actively involved in clinical work with adolescents, have a problem in conceptualizing the self-image of normal, mentally healthy youngsters. The answer to the major question raised by the findings of these studies—how well can clinicians accurately diagnose adolescent difficulties when the line between normality and disturbance is unclear—appears to be "Not very well."

In addition to the cultural and professional beliefs that persist about adolescent turmoil, our concepts of normality may mitigate against viewing adolescent turmoil as abnormal. Competing conceptions of normality, and criteria for distinguishing mental health and normality from psychological disorder, have been discussed for at least the past three centuries. The definition of normality carries important implications for social issues, clinical practice, and mental health policy formation (Frances, Widiger, & Sabshin, 1990). Offer and Sabshin (1966) have outlined five distinct, yet overlapping, perspectives on normality that have emerged during the past century. The first is *the absence-of-pathology model* (or normality as health), which defines disorder by the presence of symptomatology, physical signs, and/or laboratory abnormalities, and health or normality as the absence of these. Within this model, a healthy person is one who is "reasonably free of undue pain, discomfort, disability, distress, disadvantage, and other features of disorder" (Frances et al., 1991). In this perspective, health refers to a reasonable rather than an optimal state of functioning. Thus, normality is equated with health, and health is seen as a nearly universal phenomenon. The second perspective, *the utopia model,* which is favored by psychoanalysts, is complementary to the first perspective in that it tends to result in the identification of a minority of persons as healthy. This may be attributed to the fact that health is equated with the ideal and utopic functioning that few individuals ever achieve. According to this second perspective, the typical or average individual falls considerably short of the ideal and is therefore seen as pathological. The third perspective, *the statistical model,* relies heavily on the average level of functioning in its definition of normality; that is, both extremes of a bell-shaped curve are deviant. This model has shown itself to be problematic in that the average is relative to an arbitrary and possibly abnormal population. A fourth perspective, *the systems model,* is transactional. The emphasis in this model is on normality as the result of the individual's changing and adapting as part of a social system that also fluctuates over time. Patterns of adjustment and disturbance are examined longitudinally with respect to transactions between the person and the social system. A fifth model, *the pragmatic model,* appears to be somewhat simplistic but is nonetheless considered useful by some practitioners. Mental disorders from this perspective are nothing more and nothing less than the conditions treated by clinicians. Proponents of this model have pointed out that defining normality is an evaluative task, and that this evaluation must be relative to the society and its citizens.

All of the models that have offered a definition of normality can be criticized for one reason or another. For example, Kendell (1975) suggested that the utopia model is problematic in that the healthy functioning described within this model is almost impossible to attain, and that the pragmatic model does not even try to provide a thoughtful conception of what normality is. None of the models is very useful in offering specific and practical guidelines for distinguishing abnormality from normality. Even so, the systems model, with its focus on normality as a transactional system, may be a particularly useful perspective from which to study and treat adolescents because adolescence is a phase of the life span requiring considerable adaptation to simultaneous ongoing changes across multiple systems (biological, cognitive, affective, and social). The systems or transactional perspective is also useful as a model of normality during adolescence because it highlights the difficulty and complexity of defining normality for adolescents as a group and makes it necessary to define normality vs. disturbance for each individual adolescent based on that individual's temperament and unique life experiences, as well as on the interaction of the person and the social system over time. Perhaps more than at any other time during the life span, one individual at adolescence is as unique in his or her normality as another is unique in his or her disturbance.

Within the current view of psychopathology during adolescence, turmoil can be viewed narrowly (for example, in terms of clinical depression or similar psychiatrically recognized disorders). A wider net also can be cast to include those adolescents who may not be clinically disturbed but are having considerable difficulties "getting through" their adolescent years. Rutter et al. (1976) discussed findings from their Isle of Wight study, in which data were collected from adolescents via a psychiatric interview:

There can be no doubt from these findings that many 14–15 year olds experience quite marked feelings of affective disturbance which could well be described as "inner turmoil." Although only a small minority appeared clinically depressed, many more reported feelings of misery which were often accompanied by self-deprecation and ideas of reference and occasionally even by suicidal thoughts. Of course, that still leaves half the group who did not experience such inner turmoil. But the findings show that inner experiences of misery and deprecation are very common. (p. 42)

Similarly, Masterson (1967) reported that depression and anxiety were as common in "normal" adolescents as in his patient sample, suggesting substantial feelings of distress even in youngsters without psychiatric disorders. It is probably the case that some personality disorders diagnosed in adolescence represent normal transitory developmental processes rather than true personality pathology, but there will always be those adolescents for whom an Axis II diagnosis marks the onset of a lasting pattern of personality dysfunction (Bernstein, Cohan, Schwab-Stone, Velez, & Siever, 1990). Although the waters are murky when it comes to distinguishing adolescent misery from incipient personality pathology, either could fall under the guise of adolescent turmoil and both may require professional mental health care.

Thus, evidence suggests that adolescence is not a time that is endogenously tumultuous or that clinical symptoms during that stage have different meanings from their appearance at other times. However, there is little detailed information about specific prevalence of mental health problems during adolescence (Tolan et al., 1990) and even less about pathway parameters of psychopathology. In any case, there is a clear need to better link adolescents in turmoil to mental health services (Tolan et al., 1988) and to provide a stronger empirical link between normal and problematic adolescent development.

HELP-SEEKING BEHAVIOR AMONG ADOLESCENTS

We now present some findings from an epidemiological study of urban and suburban high school students as an example of one such needed link. The study had two major objectives: (a) through interviews and psychological testing, to determine the extent of emotional disturbance among adolescents in three midwestern high schools; (b) to assess what kinds of mental health services the adolescents in these communities were utilizing. In addition, the type of social support the adolescents were obtaining from nonprofessionals (i.e., peers, parents, and so on) was to be examined.

Methodology

To carry out this study, three high schools in a large metropolitan area in the midwest were identified. Of these three high schools, two were located in the suburbs and one within the city. One suburban school (School 1) was upper-middle-class and was 89% White. The other suburban school (School 2) was middle-class and 88% White. The urban high school (School 3) was 98% Black. From each school, a complete list of juniors and seniors was obtained and random samples were drawn. Table 1.1 presents the breakdown of race and sex by school. Fifty-nine percent of the adolescents were living with both biological parents, and 24% were living with only their biological mother. The mean age was 17, with 98% of the sample between 16 and 18 years of age.

Table 1.1 Sample Studied in Three Midwestern High Schools*

Subject	Suburban Teenagers		Urban Teenagers		Total
	Male	Female	Male	Female	
White	126	136	0	0	261
Black	6	7	101	99	213
Other	13	7	3	0	23
Total	145	149	104	99	497

*Two suburban high schools, N = 294; one urban high school, N = 203; total adolescents studied in 1987, N = 497.
Note: From "To Whom Do Adolescents Turn for Help?" Offer, et al., 1991.

Subjects were administered a battery of self-reports. The instruments included the following:

1. The *Offer Self-Image Questionnaire (OSIQ)* (Offer, Ostrov, & Howard, 1989b), a multidimensional self-image questionnaire.
2. The *Delinquency Checklist (DCL)* (Short & Nye, 1957), a self-report inventory concerning the extent to which the adolescent has engaged in delinquent behaviors. The 38 items are presented with five response categories ranging from 1 = "never" to 5 = "very often." In this study, the DCL was presented in two time frames. The adolescents were asked about delinquent behaviors that had occurred in the past 2 weeks and those that had happened during the past year. After standard score transformations, a lower score on this scale indicated more delinquent behavior.
3. The *Symptom Checklist (SCL-90)* (Derogatis, 1977), a demographic questionnaire of 39 items such as racial background, mobility, parents' marital status and education, and students' employment.
4. The *Mental Health Utilization Questionnaire (MHUQ)* (Verhoff, Douvan, & Kulka, 1981), comprised of 53 items exploring the extent to which the adolescent has felt the need to use various kinds of treatment programs.
5. A *semistructured interview* directed at the adolescent's feelings, hopes and wishes, perceived problems, and methods of coping. After the interview, coding schemes were developed and applied.

The Adolescent Emotional Disturbance Assessment (AEDA) was then developed as an index of emotional disturbance and turmoil in adolescents. It is a composite of three separate assessments of different aspects of an adolescent's psychological makeup (described separately above):

1. The Offer Self-Image Questionnaire (OSIQ)—disturbance on the OSIQ was defined as scoring one standard deviation below the mean of the normative group (i.e., 35 or below) on at least one of the three following scales: Emotional Tone (or mood), Family Relationships, and Emotional Health (or psychopathology);
2. The Delinquency Checklist (DCL) (one standard deviation below mean);
3. The Symptom Checklist (SCL) (one standard deviation below mean).

A disturbed adolescent was defined as an adolescent who showed disturbance on any one of these three measures.

Using a broad definition of disturbance, the findings indicated that 39% of all adolescents studied in this sample (198 out of 497) showed some emotional disturbance. The rate of disturbance was slightly higher for female (41%) than for male adolescents (37%). A narrower, more clinically comparable definition that uses stricter psychiatric criteria gives a lower rate of disturbance (22%) (Offer, Howard, Schonert, & Ostrov, 1991). This lower rate is in agreement with other epidemiological studies of adolescents. The broader definition of disturbance was used because the focus of the study was on help seeking among adolescents, irrespective of how mild or severe the symptomatology might be.

Mental Health Care

The data indicated that, in the past year, 16.7% of a relatively representative sample of urban and suburban 17-year-olds had at least one visit to a mental health professional. In the suburban high schools, the rate was 24.5%; in the urban high school, 5.4% of the teenagers had had at least one visit to a mental health professional. The urban statistics are similar to the national statistics (Taube, Burns, & Kessler, 1984). Suburban mental health care is considerably more concentrated and available. Utilization of mental health services for adolescent males was 10.0%; for adolescent females, it was 23.8%. Therefore, the same 2:1 ratio of adolescent females to adolescent males, found by other investigators in national studies, was obtained in this sample.

Of the disturbed teenagers, 30.3% utilized mental health services, compared to 8.0% of the nondisturbed teenagers. Using a broad definition of disturbance, more adolescents sought mental health services; however, only a minority of disturbed teenagers sought and obtained mental health care. One implication of these results is that many disturbed adolescents are not receiving treatment. Even in the suburban communities, two-thirds of the disturbed adolescents had not received any treatment in the previous year. The data showed that 40% of the disturbed suburban teenagers had never obtained any mental health treatment. Among disturbed inner-city adolescents, the results were even more compelling. In that community, 95% of the disturbed adolescents had not received treatment in the past year, and 79% had never received any treatment at all. These findings have strong implications for the effective use of mental health resources: it is clear that, among the subjects here, most of the disturbed adolescents were not receiving mental health care (see Table 1.2).

The adolescent help-seeking survey showed that 78% of all suburban adolescents knew where to obtain mental health services, whereas 58% of urban teenagers knew where to go if they needed mental health care. Would teenagers go to a mental health professional if they believed they needed help? Compared to 68% of urban adolescents, 84% of suburban adolescents said that they would obtain help for emotional problems. That is, the urban adolescents were less likely than the suburban adolescents to seek mental health services for emotional problems. Mental health service is not only an economic issue; it is probably also a class distinction. The distribution of psychiatric services tends to be more heavily suburban than urban.

Adolescents, like most people, receive much of their emotional support from nonprofessionals. In our survey, the adolescents were asked to indicate to whom they would turn for emotional support (Table 1.3). Most of the teenagers indicated that they would turn to their friends before they would turn to their parents. Very few said they used teachers as an emotional resource, and one-third said they sought support from siblings. There was an inverse relation between disturbance and closeness to parents. Those adolescents with

Table 1.2 Adolescent Help-Seeking Survey (N = 497)

Service	Used Past Year	Currently Using	Know Where to Go
Alcholol/Drug abuse program	2.4%	.2%	61.2%
Teenage drop-in center	3.0	1.8	37.2
Crisis hotline	2.2	0.0	43.5
Mental health professional	16.7	6.2	69.6
School counselor	35.2	6.2	92.2
Clergy	5.6	.4	67.0

Table 1.3 Social Support for an Emotional Problem

When you have an emotional problem, do you discuss it with a _____?

	DM	NDM	DF	NDF
Friend	70%	69%	91%	88%
Parent	28	62	43	63
Sibling	36	43	42	45
Teacher	9	4	10	12
				N = 497

DM = Disturbed males
NDM = Nondisturbed males
DF = Disturbed females
NDF = Nondisturbed females
Note: "To Whom Do Adolescents Turn for Help?" Offer, et al., 1991.

emotional problems (who presumably could use help from their parents the most) were less likely than their less mentally healthy peers to turn to their parents for help. Not surprising was the finding that female adolescents relied on their friends for emotional support considerably more than did adolescent males. Adolescent girls are more interested in their social world and appear to be able to utilize it more effectively when necessary (Offer, Ostrov, & Howard, 1982). In general, disturbed adolescents, both male and female, are more isolated socially and use their social network less. That is to say, the adolescents who need help most get it least, and perhaps this is part of their disturbance.

CONCLUSIONS

Persistent low self-esteem, depression, and other disturbances are unusual in adolescence. Most teenagers are well-adjusted and cope effectively with the biological, psychological, and social changes that are a part of adolescence. They relate well to their families and peers, and they learn to live within the parameters of their communities. Some adolescents have transient problems, and still others are deeply disturbed and do not grow out of their problems. The truly disturbed adolescents—particularly those who do not receive help—probably will continue to be disturbed throughout adulthood. It is possible that offering support and encouraging these adolescents to accept help might save them years of anguish and emotional suffering. Many of them are probably too shy and withdrawn to ask for help, or too lonely, quiet, and depressed to seek out intervention. One definition of loneliness is a yearning for others that goes unfulfilled. The evidence strongly suggests that most adolescents in need of help are not receiving it. Offering a helping relationship to a disturbed adolescent may yield a surprisingly receptive response. To enhance the adolescent experience, the researcher and the mental health practitioner must work toward the goal of merging the knowledge and experience each has gained. Epidemiologic, longitudinal developmental, and clinic use studies, as well as attempts to trace other clinically relevant phenomena among general adolescent populations, are needed. Only then will the role of turmoil and the definition of normality during adolescence be more fully understood.

REFERENCES

Alexander, J. (1973). Defensive and supportive communication in family systems. *Journal of Marriage and the Family, 35,* 613–617.

Bandura, A. (1964). The stormy decade: Fact or fiction? *Psychology in the Schools, 1,* 224–231.

Bandura, A., & Walters, R. (1959). *Adolescent aggression.* New York: Ronald.

Benedict, R. (1938). Continuities and discontinuities in cultural conditioning. *Psychiatry, 1,* 161–167.

Bernstein, D., Cohan, P., Schwab-Stone, M., Velez, C., & Siever, L. (1990, May). Paper presented at the American Psychiatric Association meetings. New York City.

Bjornsson, S. (1974). Epidemiological investigations of mental disorders of children in Reykjavik, Iceland. *Scandinavian Journal of Psychology, 15,* 244–254.

Blackman, G., & Silberman, A. (1975). *Modification of child and adolescent behavior* (2nd ed.). Belmont, CA: Wadsworth.

Blood, L., & D'Angelo, R. (1974). A progress research report on value issues in conflict between runaways and their parents. *Journal of Marriage and the Family, 36,* 486–491.

Blos, P. (1962). *On adolescence: A psychoanalytic interpretation.* New York: Free Press.

Blos, P. (1967). The second individuation process of adolescence. In *Psychoanalytic study of the child, Vol. 15.* New York: International Universities.

Derogatis, L. (1977). *SCL-90R manual.* Baltimore, MD: Clinical Psychometrics Research Unit, Johns Hopkins School of Medicine.

Douvan, E., & Adelson, J. (1966). *The adolescent experience.* New York: Wiley.

Erikson, E. (1968). *Identity: Youth and crisis.* New York: Norton.

Frances, A., Widiger, T., & Sabshin, M. (1991). Psychiatric diagnosis and normality. In D. Offer & M. Sabshin (Eds.), *Normality: Context and theory* (pp. 3–39). New York: Basic Books.

Freud, A. (1946). *The ego and the mechanism of defence.* New York: International Universities.

Freud, A. (1958). *Adolescence: Psychoanalytic study of the child, Vol. 13.* New York: Academic.

Graham, P., & Rutter, M. (1973). Psychiatric disorder in the young adolescent: A follow-up study. *Proceedings of the Royal Society of Medicine, 66,* 58–61.

Grinker, R., Sr., Grinker, R., Jr., & Timberlake, I. (1962). Mentally healthy young males (homoclites). *Archives of General Psychiatry, 6,* 311–318.

Hall, G. S. (1904). *Adolescence: Its psychology and its relations to physiology, anthropology, sociology, sex, crime, religion, and education, Vols. 1, 2.* New York: Appleton-Century-Crofts.

Hall, J. (1987). Parent–adolescent conflict: An empirical review. *Adolescence, 22*(88), 767–789.

Hill, J. (1983). Early adolescence: A research agenda. *Journal of Early Adolescence, 3,* 1–21.

Hill, J., Holmbeck, G., Marlow, L., Green, T., & Lynch, M. (1985a). Pubertal status and parent–child relations in families of seventh-grade boys. *Journal of Early Adolescence, 5,* 31–44.

Hill, J., Holmbeck, G., Marlow, L., Green, T., & Lynch, M. (1985b). Pubertal status and parent–child relations in families of seventh-grade girls. *Journal of Early Adolescence, 14,* 301–316.

Kendell, R. (1975). *The role of diagnosis in psychiatry.* Oxford: Blackwell Scientific Publications.

Leslie, S. A. (1974). Psychiatric disorder in the young adolescents of an industrial town. *British Journal of Psychiatry, 125,* 113–124.

Masterson, J. (1967). *The psychiatric dilemma of adolescence.* London: Churchill.

McCubbin, J., Needle, R., & Wilson, M. (1985). Adolescent health risk behaviors: Family stress and adolescent coping as critical factors. *Family Relations, 34,* 51–62.

McKenry, P., Walter, L., & Johnson, C. (1979). Adolescent pregnancy: A review of the literature. *Family Coordinator, 28,* 16–28.

Montemayor, R. (1983). Parents and adolescents in conflict: All families some of the time and some families most of the time. *Journal of Early Adolescence, 3,* 83–103.

Montemayor, R. (1986). Family variation in parent–adolescent storm and stress. *Journal of Adolescent Research, 1,* 15–31.

Myers, J., Weissman, M., Tischler, G., Holzen, C., Leaf, P., Orvaschel, M., Anthony, J., Boyd, J., Burke, J., Kramer, M., & Stolzman, R. (1984). Six-month prevalence of psychiatric disorders in three communities. *Archives of General Psychiatry, 41,* 959–967.

Novoco, R. (1978). Anger and coping with stress. Cognitive–behavioral interventions. In J. P. Foreyt & D. T. Rathjen (Eds.), *Cognitive behavior therapy.* New York: Plenum Press.

Offer, D., & Offer, J. (1975a). *From teenage to young manhood: A psychological study.* New York: Basic Books.

Offer, D., & Offer, J. (1975b). Three developmental routes through normal male adolescence. In S. C. Feinstein (Ed.), *Annals of Adolescent Psychiatry, Vol. IV.* New York: Aronson.

Offer, D., Ostrov, E., & Howard, K. (1981). The mental health professional's concept of the normal adolescent. *Archives of General Psychiatry, 38*(2), 149–152.

Offer, D., Ostrov, E., & Howard, K. (1982). Family perceptions of adolescent self-image. *Journal of Youth and Adolescence, 11,* 281–291.

Offer, D., Ostrov, E., & Howard, K. (1989a). Adolescence: What is normal? *American Journal of Diseases of Children, 143,* 731–736.

Offer, D., Ostrov, E., & Howard, K. (1989b). The Offer Self-Image Questionnaire for Adolescents. Chicago: Michael Reese Hospital.

Offer, D., & Sabshin, M. (1966). *Normality: Theoretical and clinical concepts of mental health.* New York: Basic Books.

Offer, D., & Spiro, R. P. (1987). The disturbed adolescent goes to college. *Journal of the American College Health Association, 35,* 209–214.

Parsons, T. (1949). The social structure of the family. In R. Anshen (Ed.), *The family: Its function and destiny.* New York: Harper.

Petersen, A. (1988). Adolescent development. *Annual Review of Psychology, 39,* 583–607.

Rabichow, H., & Sklansky, M. (1980). *Effective counseling of adolescents.* Chicago: Follett.

Rimmer, J., Halikas, J., Schuckit, M., & McClure, J. (1978). A systematic study of psychiatric illness in freshman college students. *Comp. Psychiatry, 19,* 249–252.

Robin, A. (1979, April). *A controlled evaluation of problem-solving communication training with parent–adolescent conflict.* Paper presented at the annual meeting of the Eastern Psychological Association, Philadelphia, PA.

Rutter, M. (1980). *Changing youth in a changing society.* Cambridge, MA: Harvard University Press.

Rutter, M., Graham, P., Chadwick, O., & Yule, W. (1976). Adolescent turmoil: Fact or fiction? *Journal of Child Psychology and Psychiatry, 17,* 35–56.

Schenk, Q., & Schenck, E. (1978). *Pulling up roots.* Englewood Cliffs, NJ: Prentice-Hall.

Schuckit, M., Halikas, J., Schucket, J., McClure, J., & Rimmer, J. (1973). Four-year prospective study on the college campus. *Disabilities of the Nervous System, 4,* 320–324.

Short, J., & Nye, F. (1957). Reported behavior as a criterion of deviant behavior. *Social Problems, 5,* 207–213.

Smetana, J. (1988). Concepts of self and social convention: Adolescents' and parents' reasoning about hypothetical and actual family conflicts. In M. Gunnar (Ed.), *21st Minnesota symposium on child psychology.* Hillsdale, NJ: Erlbaum.

Steinberg, L. (1981). Transformations in family relations at puberty. *Developmental Psychology, 17,* 833–840.

Steinberg, L. (1987). The impact of puberty on family relations: Effects of pubertal status and pubertal timing. *Developmental Psychology, 23,* 451–460.

Steinberg, L. (1988). Reciprocal relation between parent–child distance and pubertal maturation. *Developmental Psychology,*

Swedo, S., & Offer, D. (1991). The pediatrician's concept of the normal adolescent. *Journal of Adolescent Health, 18,* 6–10.

Taube, C. A., Burns, B. J., & Kessler, L. (1984). Patients of psychiatrists and psychologists in office-based practice: 1980. *American Psychologist, 39,* 1435–1447.

Tolan, P., Jaffe, C., & Ryan, K. (1990). *The clinical implications of adolescent epidemiological research.* Unpublished manuscript, University of Illinois at Chicago, Department of Psychiatry. (Available from the senior author.)

Tolan, P. H., Ryan, K., & Jaffe, C. (1988). Adolescents' mental health service use and provider, process, and recipient characteristics. *Journal of Clinical Child, 17,* 228–235.

Uhlenhuth, E. H., Balter, M. B., Mellinger, G. D., Chisin, I. H., & Clinthorne, J. (1983). Symptom checklist syndromes in the general population: Correlations with psychotherapeutic drug use. *Archives of General Psychiatry, 40,* 1167–1173.

Ullman, C. (1982). Cognitive and emotional antecedents of religious conversion. *Journal of Personality and Social Psychology, 43,* 183–192.

Verhoff, J., Douvan, E., & Kulka, R. A. (1981). *The inner American.* New York: Basic Books.

Weiner, I. B., & Del Gaudio, A. C. (1976). Psychopathology in adolescence: An epidemiological study. *Archives of General Psychiatry, 33,* 187–193.

Whitaker, A., Johnson, J., Shaffer, D., Rapoport, J. L., Kalikow, K., Walsh, B. T., Davies, M., Braiman, S., & Dolinsky, A. (1990). Uncommon troubles in young people. *Archives of General Psychiatry, 47,* 487–496.

Whitley, J. (1979). Mental health of college students. *Journal of the American College Health Association, 28,* 92–95.

CHAPTER 2

Biological Development

MARYSE H. RICHARDS, STEVEN ABELL, and ANNE C. PETERSEN

The most exciting and anxiety-producing aspect of adolescence is change. Puberty is both a change and, for most youngsters, the entrance to this transitional period of life. Thus, in attempts to understand individual development during this life period, puberty has acquired a position of great importance.

This chapter addresses the role of puberty in the life changes of an adolescent. We first describe the biological changes that constitute puberty and then discuss the effects of puberty on the adolescent's psychological functioning. Theory and knowledge derived from recent research are included. Lastly, we address the implications of our present knowledge for clinical practice.

THE NATURE OF PUBERTAL CHANGE

Several dimensions of puberty help us to understand its role in development and its possible effect on adolescent emotional well-being (Richards & Petersen, 1987). First, it is a *near universal experience;* every person who survives childhood is transformed physically.*
The fact that puberty always occurs during adolescence makes it a convenient and fairly reasonable "explanation" for many adolescent behaviors, even when puberty alone may not be the full explanation (Richards & Petersen, 1987).

Second, puberty is a *gradual process,* not one event. It involves more or less continuous change over time, from a physically immature organism to a mature one with full reproductive potential (Grumbach, Grave, & Mayer, 1974). The fact that it occurs gradually, over several years, has implications for understanding its impact. The hormonal system needed to produce pubertal change actually develops prenatally. Functioning of the system, however, is suppressed in most individuals from shortly after birth until about seven years of age, when the system is gradually released from suppression and hormonal increases begin. The start and finish of this whole process vary from individual to individual, depending on many factors. Figure 2.1 displays the gradual hormonal swings, across childhood (Petersen & Taylor, 1980).

The authors wish to thank Grayson Holmbeck for his editorial comments on an earlier draft of this manuscript, and Paul Crowe for his assistance with the final version.

*Exceptions to this rule occur in certain circumstances of disease or hormonal or genetic anomalies (Money & Ehrhardt, 1972).

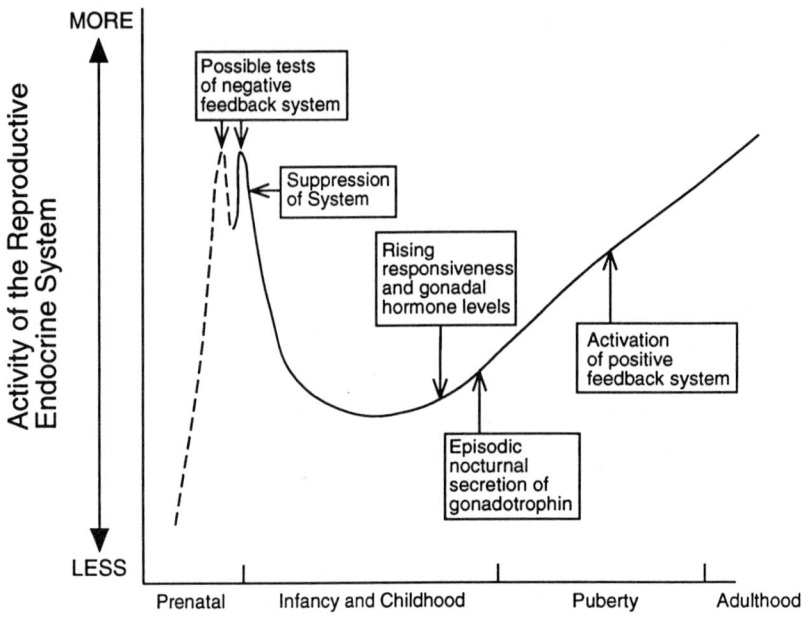

Figure 2.1 Schematic illustration of changes in the reproductive system from prenatal to mature status. Reproduced with permission from "Pubertal Development as a Cause of Disturbance: Myths, Realities, and Unanswered Questions" by A. C. Petersen, 1985, *Genetic, Social, and General Psychology Monographs, 111,* 205–232.
Note: Numbers beneath bar graphs refer to the mean age for each Tanner stage. The bars extend a standard deviation beyond the mean age of the events (bars without numbers) or the mean age of the Tanner stages (bars with numbers).

Third, the hormonal changes of puberty encompass *more than one endocrine system.* Each of these systems influences different aspects of pubertal growth, producing asynchrony among them. Thus, pubertal changes will occur at different times, with variations from individual to individual. Increasing levels of estrogens, androgens, and progestins, among others, characterize pubertal endocrine change. In addition to their effects on timing, the hormones appear to affect the behavior of the child differently, depending on the hormone system and gender. Adrenal androgens stimulate what appears to be the first endocrine event of puberty, adrenarche (Grumbach, Richards, Conte, & Kaplan, 1977); gonadotropins stimulate the gonads to produce mature gametes (sex cells) and secrete sex steroids, a process leading to gonadarche. The sex steroids (androgens, estrogens, and progestins) are responsible for the sexual maturation of the tissues. The concentration of each of these hormone groups increases during puberty, with androgens reaching higher concentrations in boys, and estrogens, progestins, and most adrenal hormones reaching higher concentrations in girls. Gonadotropins increase to about the same level in girls and boys (Nottelmann et al., 1987).

These increasing hormone levels lead to the changes in physiology and appearance that we commonly associate with puberty. These changes begin, on the average, at age 11 in girls and at age 12 in boys (Lee, 1980; Tanner, 1962). They include the development of secondary sex characteristics—penis and testicle development in boys, breast development and changes in the labia and vagina in girls, and axillary (underarm) and pubic hair growth in both boys and girls. Other changes include the initiation of beard growth in boys and the increased growth of hair on other parts of the body in both sexes. Glandular changes occur: The apocrine (sweat) glands, particularly those under the arm, begin to produce a characteristic odor, and the activity of the sebaceous (oil) glands increases, sometimes leading to a temporary overproduction of oil, which results in acne.

Rapid gains in height and weight occur at this time, with girls usually beginning their growth spurts about 1½ to 2 years prior to boys (Bock et al., 1973; Lee, 1980; Thissen, Bock, Wainer, & Roche, 1976). The growth pattern typically involves a spurt that is associated with an increased rate of bone growth, followed by slower but continuing growth and then the cessation of growth. Growth ceases when the ends of the growing bones reach and fuse with the joints, leaving no room for further growth.

The development of these secondary sex characteristics is due primarily to increasing levels of the two endocrine groups, estrogens and androgens. One of the major androgens is testosterone and one of the major estrogens is estradiol. Testosterone is responsible for the growth of the penis, prostate gland, and seminal vesicles in boys. Testosterone, along with other androgens, causes the development of body hair in both sexes. Pubic hair tends to appear concurrently with the growth of the penis, but axillary hair generally appears when pubic hair growth is relatively well-advanced. A sequential maturation of testosterone receptors in body tissue may explain this growth differential (Brook, 1981). Breast development results from an increase in estradiol levels and the maturation of estradiol receptors. Estradiol also promotes growth of the uterus and vagina and the development of the accessory vaginal exocrine glands. When critical levels of estradiol are attained, along with the development of the whole cycle, menarche occurs (Petersen, 1980). Menarche marks the beginning of the menstrual cycle, which is caused by approximate monthly fluctuations in hormones accompanied by monthly shedding of the uterine lining. This, like other endocrine changes, is gradual, and the cycles are initially anovulatory in most individuals (i.e., no ovulation occurs).

The adolescent growth spurt occurs through a synergism between the sex steroids (e.g., androgen, estrogen) and growth hormones (Tanner, 1974). Growth in the vertebral column and the width of the shoulders and hips is caused primarily by sex steroids. In contrast, growth of the legs is largely dependent on growth hormones. Voice change, which is particularly marked in males, appears due to testosterone secretion. Striking changes in body composition, which includes lean body mass, skeletal mass, and body fat, as well as body fat distribution, occur at puberty and are related to sex hormones. Estrogens are responsible for the feminine pattern of fat distribution; endogenous testosterone secretion appears to prevent this pattern in males. The sex differential in muscle strength appears to be caused by different levels and reception of testosterone (Frealy & Luttge, 1982).

Although these various changes describe a typical sequence of puberty, they may vary considerably among normal individuals. As indicated above, endocrine levels increase first. Breast and genital changes follow and are usually the first somatic manifestations. The time of *peak* (fastest) growth in height occurs relatively late in the process, as does menarche, which typically occurs just after the time of peak velocity in growth. On the average, the entire process takes about 4 years. Figure 2.2 shows the patterns of these changes for boys and girls, according to the work of Lee (1980) in studying American children. The patterns are very similar to those found by Tanner (1974) in studies of British adolescents.

As Figure 2.2 suggests, however, rather large individual differences describe the timing and sequence of these various changes (Eichorn, 1975; Tanner, 1972). For example, although breast growth is usually the first visible pubertal change in girls, in certain individuals, pubic hair appears earlier than breast growth. Even greater individual differences appear in the amount of time required

24 Biological Development

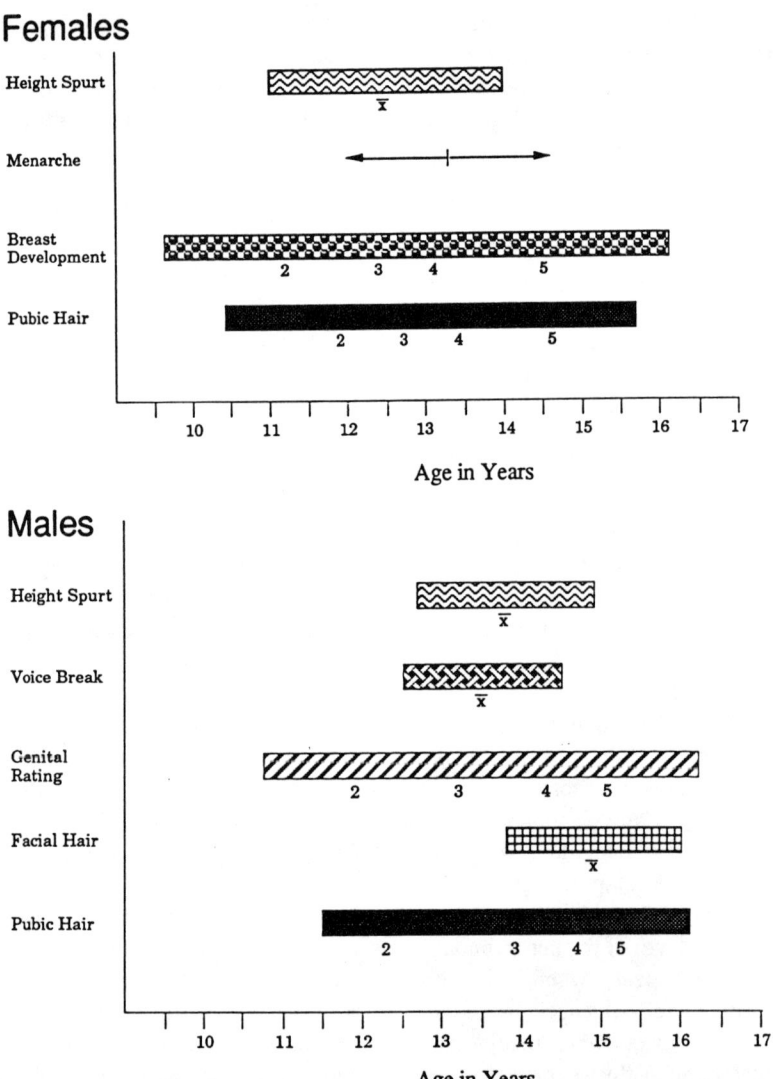

Figure 2.2 The sequence of pubertal events for an average American girl (upper chart) and boy (lower chart). Created from a table in "Normal Ages of Pubertal Events Among American Males and Females" by P. A. Lee, 1980, *Journal of Adolescent Health Care, 1*, 26–29.

for pubertal maturation. In some individuals, the entire set of pubertal changes occurs within a relatively short period of time, with the changes in various characteristics occurring in a near synchronous fashion; in others, the pubertal process can extend over several years. The age at which the somatic changes of puberty first appear varies widely among both boys and girls; hence, some youngsters may still be prepubertal when others of the same age have completed puberty (Lee, 1980).

Because of variations in the timing of puberty and the duration of maturation, somatic changes can, under normal circumstances, occur anywhere between the ages of 9 and 19 in the United States today (although those individuals who become pubertal at age 9 would not be those who are still pubertal at age 19).

Furthermore, in males, some changes, such as increases in height or in the amount of body hair, can continue into the early 20s.

In summary, puberty appears to be a universal process involving dramatic changes in size, shape, and appearance. The extent of the intra- and interindividual variations in the timing and duration of the pubertal process has important psychological consequences. These bodily transformations are expected to shift the ways adolescents view themselves. Puberty, more than any other change during adolescence, signals impending adult status. This change in status begins to affect self-perceptions. Thus, biological change can stimulate or elicit change in a number of psychological dimensions.

THE EFFECTS OF PUBERTAL DEVELOPMENT ON PSYCHOLOGICAL ADJUSTMENT

How does pubertal development affect psychological adjustment among adolescents? The answer to this complex question depends on a number of dimensions. First, pubertal development consists of hormonal changes, the physically apparent changes just described, and the timing of these changes relative to the timing experienced by one's peers. Second, psychological adjustment encompasses a variety of variables, including psychopathology, dating behavior, school adjustment, and perceptions of the self, to name a few. To confuse things further, type of school, sex of child, and grade in school have all been found to be important variables in this research (e.g., Simmons & Blyth, 1987). It is important to keep these complexities in mind as we proceed through the theory and research.

Although the physical changes of puberty are manifestations of hormone level, a long delay (months to years) may occur between the initial change in hormone level and the consequent physical changes. In addition, although pubertal stages increase with hormone levels, the relationship is not exact (Nottelmann et al., 1987). Lastly, the effects of both hormones and somatic change on psychological functioning depend on age, gender, and various contextual factors, such as the number of other changes experienced by a particular individual (Petersen & Ebata, 1987; Simmons, Burgeson, Carlton-Ford, & Blyth, 1987). For example, girls, but not boys, who are early maturers and have started dating, experience the lowest self-image (Simmons & Blyth, 1987).

The first question that has to be addressed is whether puberty affects psychological functioning at all. If so, how much? Assuming for a moment that it does affect functioning, which aspect of puberty is influencing? Is it internally driven, coming from the biochemical changes experienced within? Or, is it essentially externally driven, based on the responses of others to the changes manifested by the adolescent? In subtler forms, is this latter influence directed by internalized cultural attitudes?

DIRECT EFFECTS MODEL

The first model that attempts to answer these questions links the psychological effects directly to the physiological sources. Within this approach, nonbiological influences, such as historical change and cultural values, are either ignored or considered unimportant. Changes in psychological states and phases of psychological development are believed to be directly linked to pubertal changes in hormone levels (Kestenberg, 1967a,b), and dramatic increases in sexual and aggressive impulses are considered to be direct effects of fluctuating hormone levels (A. Freud, 1946, 1958). In addition to the direct link between puberty and its effects, this perspective assumes that a normative developmental disturbance occurs at adolescence, with specific phases to the process (Kestenberg, 1967a,b, 1968). This perspective has been called the Direct Effects Model (Petersen & Taylor, 1980).

Although it is a commonly held belief that pubertal change directly affects behavior, only in the past few years has any research specifically examined this belief. Until recently, methodological difficulties with hormone research impeded the process of examining direct hormone effects. Several studies (e.g., Smith, Udry, & Morris, 1985; Susman et al., 1985) provide evidence that some hormones may enhance certain behaviors during adolescence. For example, higher androgen levels are related to greater frequency of sexual behavior in boys. However, the relations are usually not simple ones; for example, in girls, greater frequency of sexual behavior is dependent on an interaction between higher hormone levels and a best friend's sexual behavior (Udry, Talbert, & Morris, 1986). In certain instances, it appears that it is not the hormone itself that affects the emotional state of the adolescent. For example, the *rapid increase* of estradiol itself appears to cause a temporary heightening of

Table 2.1 The Summary of the Research on Pubertal Hormones and Psychological Variables

Authors	N	Ages		Psychological Variable	p<
Sex Steroids in Girls					
		Higher Estrogens			
Inoff-Germaine et al. (1988)	30	9–14	⇧	Expresses modulated anger	.05
			⇧	Defiance towards mother	.05
			⇧	Defiance towards father	.05
			⇧	Shows anger toward mother	.05
Udry & Talbert (1988)	99	8th, 9th, & 10th graders	⇧	Ideal self	.01
		Higher Testosterone			
Udry & Talbert (1988)	99	8th, 9th, & 10th graders	⇧	Heterosexuality	.01
Urdy, Talbert, & Morris (1986)	73	8th, 9th, & 10th graders	⇧	Ever masturbated	.01
			⇧	Masturbated last month	.05
			⇧	Think about sex	.05
			⇧	Want/plan to have sex in the next year	.05
		Higher Progesterone			
Udry & Talbert (1988)	99	8th, 9th, & 10th graders	⇧	Exhibition	.001
			⇧	Aggression	.001
			⇩	Abasement	.01
			⇩	Self-control	.001
Udry, Talbert, & Morris (1986)	73	8th, 9th, & 10th graders	⇩	Ever masturbated	.05
Gonadotropins in Girls					
		Higher Luteinizing Hormone			
Susman et al. (1985)	52	9–14	⇩	Number of hours spent with friends	.01
Nottelmann et al. (1987)	52	M = 11.99 years	⇧	Self-image problems	.05

Table 2.1 (*continued*)

Authors	N	Ages	Psychological Variable	p<
Udry, Talbert, & Morris (1986)	73	8th, 9th, & 10th graders	⇩ Want/plan to have sex in the future	.05
Higher Follicle Stimulating Hormone				
Susman et al. (1985)	52	9–14	⇧ Psychopathology	.01
			⇧ Sad affect	.01
Inoff-Germaine et al. (1988)	30	9–14	⇧ Is explosive	.05
Adrenal Androgens in Girls				
Higher Androstenedione				
Inoff-Germaine et al. (1988)	30	9–14	⇧ Tries to dominate mother and father	.001
			⇧ Shows anger towards father	.01
Nottelmann et al. (1987)	52	M = 11.99 years	⇧ Self-image problems	.05
Udry, Talbert, & Morris (1986)	73	8th, 9th, & 10th graders	⇧ Want/plan to have sex in the next year	.01
Udry & Talbert (1988)	99	8th, 9th, & 10th graders	⇩ Self-confidence	.01
Higher Dehydroepiandrosterone Sulfate				
Nottelmann et al. (1987)	52	M = 11.99 years	⇩ Internalizing and externalizing behavioral problems	.05
Udry, Talbert, & Morris (1986)	73	8th, 9th, & 10th graders	⇩ Want/plan to have sex in the next year	.01
Higher Estradiol				
Susman et al. (1987)	56	9–14	⇩ Delinquent behavior	.001
Higher Testosterone				
Nottelmann et al. (1987)	56	M = 12.72 years	⇩ Self-image problems	.05
			⇩ Internalizing and externalizing behavioral problems	.05
Udry, Billy, Morris, Groff, & Raj (1985)	102	8th, 9th, & 10th graders	⇧ Have had sexual intercourse	.01
			⇧ Having any sexual outlet in the last month	.01
			⇧ Have masturbated	.01
			⇧ Report feeling "turned on"	.05
			⇩ Not intending to have sexual intercouse in next year	.01
			⇩ Think about sex less often than daily	.05

Table 2.1 (*continued*)

Authors	N	Ages	Psychological Variable	p<
Inoff-Germaine et al. (1988)	30	10–14	⇩ Express modulated anger	.001
Higher Testosterone—Estradiol Radio (T/E2)				
Susman et al. (1985)	56	9–14	⇩ Psychopathology	.05
			⇩ Sad affect	.05
Inoff-Germaine et al. (1988)	30	10–14	⇩ Express modulated anger	.05
Higher Testosterone—Estradiol Binding Globulin				
Inoff-Germaine et al. (1988)	30	10–14	⇩ Expresses modulated anger	.05
Susman et al. (1987)	56	9–14	⇩ Sad affect	.05
			⇩ Impulse control	.05
Gonadotropins in Boys				
Higher Luteninizing Hormone				
Inoff-Germaine et al. (1988)	30	10–14	⇧ Expresses modulated anger	.05
Susman et al. (1987)	56	9–14	⇧ Rebelliousness	.01
Higher Follicle Stimulating Hormone				
Susman et al. (1985)	56	9–14	⇧ Number of dates	.05
			⇧ Hours spent with friends	.05
Susman et al. (1987)	56	9–14	⇩ Rebelliousness	.05
Adrenal Androgens in Boys				
Higher Androstenedione				
Susman et al. (1985)	56	9–14	⇧ Psychopathology	.05
			⇧ Interest in dating	.01
Susman et al. (1987)	56	9–14	⇧ Sad affect	.05
			⇧ Delinquent behavior	.01
Nottelmann et al. (1987)	56	M = 12.72 years	⇧ Self-image problems	.05
			⇧ Internalizing and externalizing behavioral problems	.05
Higher Dehydroepiandrosterone				
Susman et al. (1987)	56	9–14	⇩ Impulse control	.05
			⇧ Rebelliousness	.05

depression and psychopathology in girls (Warren & Brooks-Gunn, 1989).

Table 2.1 summarizes the effects of hormone level increases on specific behaviors and affective states within early to middle adolescence. Hormones included in Table 2.1 all increase with pubertal development (Susman et al., 1987). Table 2.1 addresses only the singular effects of hormones, by providing an overview of how certain types of hormones tend to produce changes in a particular direction; it does not capture the complexity of the relationships. Within both genders, increments in the steroids testosterone and estrogen are associated with fewer behavior problems, more sexuality, and more positive ideal self (Nottelmann et al., 1987; Susman et al., 1987; Udry & Talbert, 1988). In contrast, higher estradiol in girls is associated with more angry and deviant behavior (Inoff-Germain et al., 1988) and higher levels of the steroid progesterone appear to contribute to behavior problems among females (Udry et al., 1986; Udry & Talbert, 1988).

The effects of the two remaining hormone groups appear to be generally deleterious to both boys and girls. Individual effects indicate that increments in gonadotropins and adrenal androgens are generally associated with more psychopathology, problem behaviors, lower emotional tone, and greater sexuality (Table 2.1).

In trying to sort out the findings emerging from the literature, it appears that it is not increasing or fluctuating hormones alone that affect the emotional states of adolescents. Instead, the interaction of the hormone with a more socially based aspect of change, such as pubertal stage or chronological age, may contribute to teenagers' behavior problems. For example, a very young adolescent boy with high hormone levels or an older adolescent boy with low hormone levels may experience more rebelliousness or aggression (Nottelmann et al., 1987). The major conclusion to be drawn from the current research is that it remains difficult to disentangle the effects of hormones from the effects of physical changes and age. Although evidence exists for the positive effects of steroids and the negative effects of gonadotropins and adrenal androgens on a child's emotional and behavioral functioning, the direct effects model needs further investigation.

THE MEDIATED EFFECTS MODELS

A second grouping, called *Mediated Effects Models* or *Indirect Effects Models,* proposes that the psychological effects of puberty are mediated by complex relations of intervening variables and/or moderated by contextual factors (Petersen & Taylor, 1980). The intervening variables consist of psychological factors, such as level of ego or object relations development; the contextual factors are those that are exogenous to the personality, such as the type of school a child attends or the grade he or she is in. In particular, this grouping concerns the type of response others, like parents, teachers, and peers, have to the physically changing child and the culturally shared meaning of these changes for the child. (Figure 2.3 displays both models.)

The bulk of our knowledge is about the psychological and behavioral correlates of pubertal status and the timing of pubertal development. The visible somatic changes (e.g., height spurt) are much easier to measure than are hormone levels, which necessitate such intrusive methods as repeatedly drawing blood samples from the children.

The timing of puberty may affect emotional adjustment in three different ways. A fourth explanation focuses on the general status effects of puberty. First, the timing of pubertal development relative to one's peers may have meaning for a young adolescent based on the individual's internal "social clock." Neugarten (1969, 1979) developed the notion that people have an internal sense of when certain life events should occur. If people are somewhat earlier or later than others in experiencing an event (for example, completing school), they

Direct Effects Model

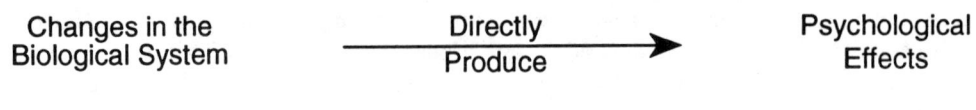

Mediated Effects Models

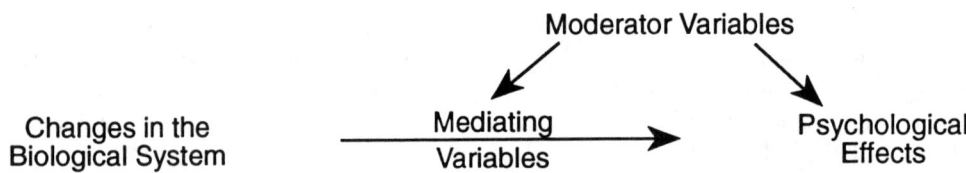

Figure 2.3 The Direct Effects and Mediated Effects Models. Reproduced with permission from "Early Adolescents' Perceptions of Their Physical Development" by M. H. Tobin-Richards, A. M. Boxer, & A. C. Petersen, 1983, in J. Brooks-Gunn & A. C. Petersen (Eds.), *Girls at Puberty: Biological and Psychosocial Perspectives*. New York: Plenum Press.

may feel they are "off-time." Also known as the *deviance hypothesis* (Clausen, 1975; Petersen & Taylor, 1980), this theory states that early or late maturing adolescents may be considered socially deviant from their peers and may suffer as a consequence of this view. For example, Silbereisen, Petersen, Albrecht, and Kracke (1989) found a relationship among maturational timing, peer rejection, and occurrence of problem behaviors. A relatively strong need for conformity, which is characteristic of young adolescents (Constanzo & Shaw, 1966), contributes to the salience of this theory of deviance and social clocks in pubertal timing. Two groups that may be at particular risk for being socially deviant in timing are girls who are the earliest maturers of their whole cohort and boys who mature much later than all the boys and girls in their cohort. For example, adolescent girls who developed faster than their peers, even though they had greater self-esteem, reported more contacts with deviant peers and engaged in a greater number of problem behaviors with greater frequency (Silbereisen et al., 1989).

Second, differences between early and late pubertal developers may be a function of the amount of time available for the completion of the psychological development of latency before puberty (Peskin, 1973; Peskin & Livson, 1972). Ego development and the opportunity to engage in latency activities, such as certain types of play, exemplify this. At the same time, the opposite may be true: additional time provided for the developmental tasks of adolescence may, by the end of adolescence, profit the early developers (Peskin, 1973; Peskin & Livson, 1972).

A third perspective, which integrates aspects of the first two, focuses on the importance of pubertal change for *social status* (e.g., Meyer, 1982; Opler, 1971). For example, in many societies, pubertal markers are used to signify attainment of adult status (Paige & Paige, 1982). In our own society, the status change is not so direct, but it is clear that adult size and appearance (and, presumably, reproductive maturity) lead to expectations for more mature behavior (Jones & Bayley, 1950; Mussen & Bouterline-Young, 1964). (See Conger & Petersen, 1984, for a review.) The attainment of an adultlike body is seen as ushering in significant changes in meanings of the social role for the adolescent and the perceptions of the adults and peers who share his or her world. Socially shared expectations, responses, and fantasies associated with this stage of physical maturation are viewed as influencing the adolescent's social prestige, role behaviors, social adaptation, and self-concept. Thus, it is hypothesized that a young adolescent with a mature body will experience a different environment and this experience will then influence his or her psychological functioning in a manner quite different from an age peer whose body still appears childlike. For example, significant others may react differently to pubertal boys and girls as they mature physically, stimulating a shift in socially shared aspects of their self-concepts. The visual and apparent changes of puberty have been found to influence patterns of family interaction (Hill & Holmbeck, 1987; Lynch, 1981; Steinberg, 1981, 1988a,b) and alter peer relations (Savin-Williams, 1979), particularly with regard to patterns of intimacy (Douvan & Adelson, 1966) and heterosocial behavior (Simmons, Blyth, Van Cleave, & Bush, 1979).

A fourth and final perspective is that of *general social norms,* which appear to mediate the effects of pubertal development on psychological development in ways other than timing. Social norms for what is considered attractive appear to be a significant force. During adolescence, a person's overall self-evaluation or self-image is strongly related to viewing one's body as attractive, and this association is stronger for females than it is for males (e.g., Kavrell & Jarcho, 1980; Lerner & Karabenick, 1974). A sex difference emerges at puberty in general body image satisfaction, with females feeling less satisfied than males (e.g., Rosenberg & Simmons, 1975; Tobin-Richards, Boxer, & Petersen, 1983). Additionally, more positive attributions are made about attractive relative to unattractive women; attractiveness does not differentiate attributions made about men to the same degree (e.g., Hill & Lando, 1976).

Although all four perspectives—the deviance or social clock theory, the stage termination theory, the social status, and the general social norms theory—have been supported by research, the picture is complicated by a number of important aspects in an adolescent's life. Examples include the grade a child is in, the type of community and school under study, and the sex of the child. Thus, these theories help us to understand the effects of puberty on psychological functioning, but the individual circumstances and characteristics of each child must be included in this understanding (Lerner, 1985).

THE MEDIATED EFFECTS MODELS: OUR CURRENT KNOWLEDGE

We now turn to several of the more consistent findings from this area of research. Our list is not comprehensive, but it provides a general picture of the present state of knowledge. Although pubertal development will be discussed as it affects many aspects of psychological functioning, our focus will be somewhat biased toward the clinically relevant perceptions of the self, particularly body image and feelings of attractiveness.

Off-Time Maturation

The first general finding is that deviant timing of pubertal development appears to produce some negative effects, particularly for early maturing girls. From our own research, we found that early maturing girls typically began to menstruate in the fifth grade (Petersen, 1983) and displayed behaviors that indicated distress about and attempts to deny their altered pubertal status.

One illustrative example is a girl who would not wear a bra but instead insisted on wearing several layers of T-shirts and sweatshirts to conceal the presence of her breasts. Somewhat consistent with this example are our results from another analysis of the same children over time and from a separate study of sixth-through-ninth-grade girls. We found that late maturers reported the least psychopathology, early maturers the most, and on-time maturers an intermediate level (Petersen & Crockett, 1985). In a separate study (Rierdan & Koff, 1985), off-time girls (i.e., postmenarcheal sixth graders and premenarcheal ninth graders) were found to display the highest scores on an anorexia nervosa and depression inventory.

When we studied seventh and eighth graders together, interesting sex differences, similar to earlier results reported by Gross and Duke (1980), emerged for boys and girls. For boys, pubertal change is experienced positively (Tobin-Richards et al., 1983). The relationship between pubertal change and self-perceptions is linear, with early maturing boys generally experiencing the highest body image, feelings of attractiveness, and self-image. Late maturing boys are lowest on these dimensions, with boys of average timing falling in between. Gross and Duke also found that late maturing boys receive more negative academic evaluations from parents and teachers.

For girls, the picture is entirely different. The girls who are maturing at about the same time as everyone else feel most attractive and positive about their bodies. Late maturers have just slightly less positive self-views. As we have described, early maturing girls score *much* lower on these dimensions (Tobin-Richards et al., 1983). This is consistent with the findings by Rierdan and Koff (1985), discussed above. Additionally, early maturing girls were also more worried and more likely to dislike menstruation (Stubbs, Rierdan, & Koff, 1989). These contrasting patterns for boys and girls are shown in Figure 2.4. For girls, the pattern was consistently obtained for

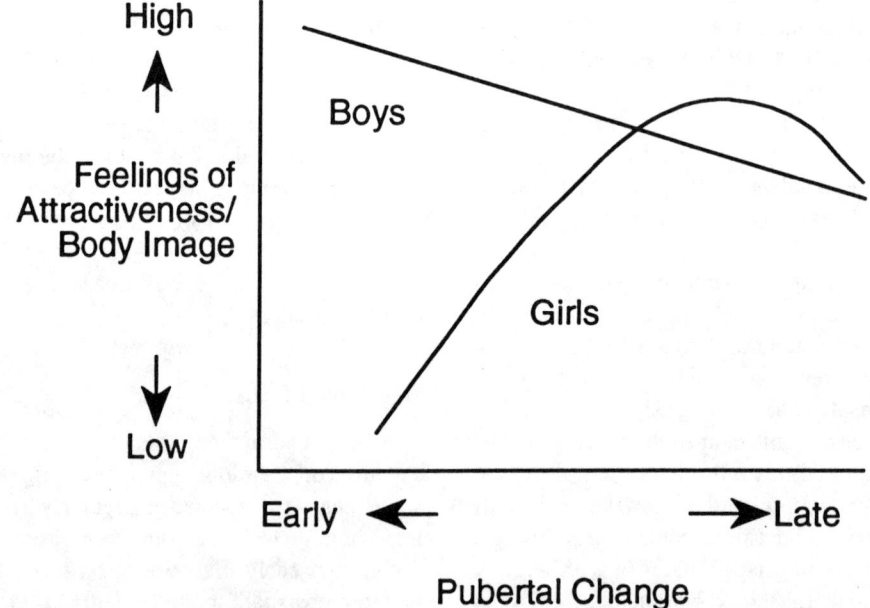

Figure 2.4 The relationship of pubertal change to body image and feelings of attractiveness. Reproduced with permission from "Early Adolescents' Perceptions of Their Physical Development" by M. H. Tobin-Richards, A. M. Boxer, & A. C. Petersen, 1983, in J. Brooks-Gunn & A. C. Petersen (Eds.), *Girls at Puberty: Biological and Psychosocial Perspectives*, New York: Plenum Press.

all indicators of pubertal change except breast development; in this case, more breast development was seen as positive.

Breast Development and the Sexualized Meaning of Puberty

Two culturally valued ideals in body shape may be influencing the young adolescent girl's feeling about herself. The positive attitudes associated with more advanced breast development (larger breasts) contrast with the cultural ideal of a prepubertal look (smaller breasts). The full-bodied, large-breasted, "sexy" look representative of the figures displayed in both popular and pornographic media emphasizes a more mature body with particular focus on large breasts. This may explain why a girl with breast development tends to feel more positive about her physical self than a girl who is more flat-chested (Tobin-Richards et al., 1983). In one study, breast growth was associated with positive body image, positive peer relations, and superior adjustment (Brooks-Gunn & Warren, 1988).

Interestingly, little research has been conducted on breast development (Brooks-Gunn, 1987; Brooks-Gunn & Warren, 1988). This research indicates that different pubertal events (especially observable versus unobservable) may play differential roles in young female adolescents' self-definition and social status. Based on exploratory research, Rosenbaum (1979) concluded that because of the relative absence of visibility and mobility of female genitalia, breasts occupy an inordinate degree of psychic space for adolescent girls. Interviews with adolescent girls revealed that all body parts, except for breasts, are desired to be small and unobtrusive, and that big breasts are valued for their appeal to boys. Rosenbaum wrote: "Thus, breasts were seen as the most consciously sexualized body parts, symbols of the maturing sexuality of the girl" (p. 245). Young adolescent girls, particularly premenarcheal seventh graders, appear to be more preoccupied with breast development than postmenarcheal seventh graders, as demonstrated in the production by the premenarcheal group of figures drawn with more explicit breasts (Rierdan & Koff, 1980). Additional support for this concern was the sex difference found in our research on a Body Image Scale item: "When others look at me they must think that I am poorly developed." Girls tend to endorse this item more than boys (Tobin-Richards et al., 1983). As an example of this preoccupation, girls frequently reported being teased about their breast development by family members, which was an unpleasant experience for them (Brooks-Gunn, 1987). There is some evidence that a cultural preoccupation with breasts never allows a woman to become completely unaware of her breast shape and size relative to cultural ideals (Ayalah & Weinstock, 1979).

Girls' Weight

The third important finding is that weight, especially in Western countries, has consistently emerged as very important to a girl's sense of her own attractiveness and to perceptions of her body (Faust, 1983; Richards, Boxer, Petersen, & Albrecht, 1990; Simmons, Blyth, & McKinney, 1983; Tobin-Richards et al., 1983). The heavier a girl is, or perceives herself to be, the more dissatisfied she is with both her weight and her figure. A strong cultural value to be tall and slim may contribute to these feelings and self-perceptions (Faust, 1983). A prepubertal image of being long-legged and lithe has been emphasized in the media, creating an idealized body image that a postpubertal girl cannot attain.

This strong cultural pressure appears to mediate the effects of pubertal development on psychological well-being. McCarthy (1989) has proposed that the cultural ideal of thinness for women causes the greater depression rates found for women and that this sex difference emerges at puberty. Simmons et al. (1983) report that early developers are significantly less satisfied with their weight, compared to late developers. When weight is controlled for, the difference in reported satisfaction disappears.

Consistent with Simmons's findings, our data indicate that, as girls mature physically, they become increasingly dissatisfied with their weight and perceive themselves as more overweight (Richards, Boxer et al., 1990). This effect is connected with maturation: most girls become dissatisfied with their weight as they mature, with early maturing girls reporting dissatisfaction earlier. Boys do not share these negative perceptions and feelings.

When weight and eating concerns were examined in relation to young adolescent daily experience and psychological adjustment, eighth- and ninth-grade girls were found to report more of these concerns than younger girls and boys (Richards, Casper, & Larson, 1990). The older girls who reported extreme weight and eating concerns also reported other signs of emotional maladjustment, therefore possibly placing themselves at risk for developing an eating disorder. Younger girls and all the boys appeared to be protected from this difficulty. When pubertal development was studied in relation to the same weight and eating concerns, girls who were early developers, as well as girls who *perceived* themselves to be earlier in their development, were found to report more weight and eating worries (Brodie & Richards, 1987). Eating-disordered behavior has been found to be heightened in pubertal girls in early development (Attie & Brooks-Gunn, 1989) and in early developing girls with premenopausal mothers (Paikoff, Brooks-Gunn, & Carlton-Ford, 1991). Perceptions of early puberty and actual early development may contribute to the early adolescent precursors of eating disorders among girls.

Simultaneous Transitions

The fourth finding of importance is that children experiencing simultaneous transitions, one of which may be pubertal development, are at the highest risk for emotional problems and negative self-perceptions. School change and the initiation of dating, when occurring with pubertal development, are two changes that have diminished self-esteem in girls (Blyth, Simmons, & Zakin, 1985; Simmons et al., 1979) and grade point averages and extracurricular participation in boys and girls (Simmons & Blyth, 1987). Facing multiple life changes simultaneously appears to have deleterious effects on young adolescents. Of even more concern is the conclusion (Simmons & Blyth, 1987) that negative consequences from this early adolescent experience appear to continue into high school, particularly in the academic arena and especially for girls. When these children attempt to cope with one set of changes by turning to a more familiar and comfortable sphere, they find that it is changing as well, and they have no place in which to withdraw and recover.

School change typically occurs prior to seventh grade, the same age at which most girls are mid- to late-pubertal (Petersen & Crockett, 1985); in contrast, most boys at this age are still prepubertal. Therefore, girls must begin dealing with several simultaneous changes while boys typically need to deal with only school change. These results may contain important implications for preventive interventions. The well-being of young adolescents, particularly girls, may be enhanced if they remain in elementary school during this period when so much else is changing.

Contextual Influence

Related to this last set of findings is the fact that type of school and community is important to how an adolescent negotiates pubertal development. We have found community differences in girls' responses to pubertal changes related to weight gain (Robin-Richards, Petersen, & Boxer, 1983). For our study, we randomly sampled two suburban school districts that represented two different communities similar in social class.

Boys from both communities and girls from one community reported similar satisfaction with their weight and feelings of attractiveness (Figure 2.5). In the other

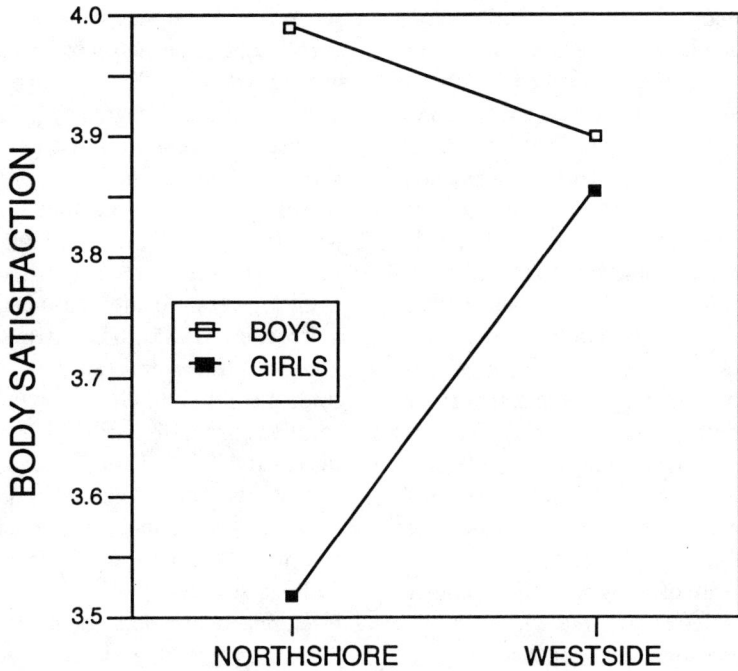

Figure 2.5 Body satisfaction by community and sex. Reproduced with permission from "The Relationship of Weight to Body Image in Pubertal Girls and Boys from Two different Communities" by M. H. Richards, A. M. Boxer, A. C. Petersen, & R. Albrecht, 1990, *Developmental Psychology, 26,* 313–321.

community, however, girls were dissatisfied with their weight, felt that they were overweight, and perceived themselves as unattractive. These differences persisted even when we controlled for actual weight in our analyses (Richards, Boxer et al., 1990). These girls, like many others in our society, hold standards of thinness that are unrealistic for postpubertal girls. We also noted that these girls were less active in sports and other school activities, compared to the girls from the other community and to the boys (Browning, 1983). Not only does this mean that they were less likely to exercise regularly, but, more importantly, it may mean that they had fewer experiences through which to develop their identities and their sense of self. Instead, they focused excessively on appearance. We think that these results have implications for understanding the recent increases in such eating disorders as anorexia nervosa and bulimia. Excessive control of one's body, an important element of eating disorders, may be reduced when other areas of control are available.

Community differences in girls' body perceptions appeared to be linked to two aspects of the communities that also differed; girls reported different levels of after-school activities, especially different feelings about athletics, and different levels of peer acceptance. Although it is unclear what characteristics of these communities promoted these perceptions, these findings indicate that, when certain aspects of a community are viewed as more available, the adolescent experiences the physical self differently (Richards, Boxer et al., 1990).

The following is an example from research by Richards (1984) of how pubertal timing can be mediated. Jenny exemplifies an early maturing girl who had made a reasonable adjustment about a year and a half after she began puberty. During the onset of puberty, during sixth grade, she had appeared somewhat listless and depressed. By the end of seventh grade, she impressed her interviewer as being much more cheerful and self-confident. Her improved emotional demeanor could be attributed to her better-than-average peer relations and her active athletic involvement. Relative to her peers, she perceived her friendships to be more satisfying and more intimate, and she felt very accepted by her peer group. In addition, she was involved in basketball, volleyball, track, and cheerleading. She was somewhat more satisfied with her weight than most girls and perceived it to be average. Satisfying, supportive friendships, a sense of being well-liked, and development in athletics, an area where she felt competent (which may contribute to her general comfort with her weight), all probably contributed to her positive self-esteem both in terms of her body and her overall self. She told the following story for a semistructured projective picture of a young adolescent girl looking at herself in the mirror. It includes a number of the themes discussed above.

Um, this girl just got out of the shower and she feels good 'cause she, um, is all clean and she was just playing basketball outside and she, um, she was hot so now she feels better. And, um, she was, um, talking to her friends 'cause she thought that she looked like, was overweight or something and her friends said that she didn't, that she wasn't overweight. So now she is just looking to see if she was overweight. [And what's she feeling?] She, um, agrees with her friends who think she's not overweight. [And how does it end?] Um, she feels better about herself.

Blyth et al. (1985) found that an early maturing girl in a K–6 school was more satisfied with her height and weight than a similar girl in a K–8 school. They stated that the early maturing sixth-grade girl in a K–6 school may see herself as looking more like an adult than her peers (which may be a desirable state) but at the same time may not be subject to pressure to act older than her age. Inherent to a K–8 school may be greater pressures to date, to engage in social activity, and to experiment with drugs and alcohol.

The general finding that pubertal effects are specific rather than global is consistent with the fact that grade-in-school has emerged as an important contextual variable (Petersen & Crockett, 1985). The fifth set of findings delineates the importance of knowing what grade a child is in. Grade, by creating a major reference group for children in our current society, establishes a set of norms by which to evaluate the self. Much of a child's life is organized by grade, including much of how and with whom a child spends time. The pattern of findings suggests that the effects of pubertal development are dependent on what grade a child is in and that this dependency may be due at least partially to the pubertal status of one's classmates.

Families

For both boys and girls, pubertal development appears to coincide with increased adolescent autonomy, greater parent–child conflict, and greater emotional distance (Hill & Holmbeck, 1987; Papini, Datan, & McCluskey-Fawcett, 1988; Steinberg, 1987, 1988a,b). The most frequently reported areas of family conflict include mundane issues such as time management and room care, as well as adolescent concerns such as sexual behavior, choice of friends, and the consumption of alcoholic beverages (Papini & Sebby, 1988). The transformations in family relations are not consistent across all types of families (Anderson, Hetherington, & Clingempeel, 1989). Physical appearance emerges as a common area of conflict for girls, but apparently not for boys. Parents may focus on the appearance of a daughter as they develop concerns about the possible ramifications of her burgeoning sexuality and as she experiments with more adultlike dress.

Parent–child conflict seems to be greatest during the period known as transpuberty, when the physiological changes of pubertal development are at their peak. During this period, adolescents may begin to assert behavioral autonomy in a number of areas, with parents sometimes reacting by making efforts to reassert their authority. Possibly as a result of this struggle, both adolescents and their parents report increased emotional distance (Steinberg, 1987) and more intense family conflicts over self-regulation (Papini, Clark, Barnett, & Savage, 1989) during the period of transpuberty. Hill and Holmbeck (1987) report that the increased conflict and decreased emotional closeness of this period occur across socioeconomic groups.

In most families, the conflict appears to occur primarily between the adolescent and his or her mother (Hill & Holmbeck, 1987; Papini & Sebby, 1988; Steinberg, 1987); mothers tend to report different degrees of conflict, depending on the child's sex and chronological age. For boys, early development appears to cause more intense mother–son conflict. For girls, physical maturation, regardless of timing, contributes to mother–daughter conflict (Steinberg, 1987). Steinberg (1987) suggested that conflict may be enhanced by earlier pubertal development. This would explain the findings for girls, who typically enter puberty at a younger age than do boys. It appears that the earlier family disturbance may continue beyond the time of puberty for early developing girls, placing them at risk for later problems (Hill, Holmbeck, Marlow, Green, & Lynch, 1985).

Part of the difficulty for families with early maturing girls may be the parents' response to their daughters' early sexuality. This response, perhaps unconscious, may be enacted with restrictions on the pubertal girls' freedoms, with parents becoming concerned with protecting their daughters (Katz, 1979). It has been suggested that sexual maturity is at this time more a concern than a joy to parents (Brooks-Gunn & Matthews, 1979). The way in which parents act on such concerns, however, is not clear. Restrictions on dating do not seem to be a factor: chronological age was found to predict dating behavior, but level of physical maturation was not (Dornbusch, Carlsmith, Gross, Rosenberg, & Duke, 1981). In addition, parents' personal responses to young adolescents' physical development may be mediated by their life-cycle position and experience of aging (Rossi, 1980). As adolescents become more adultlike in appearance, parents may be more likely to identify with their offspring. Thus, enhanced similarity between parent and child, triggered by the adultlike appearance of the child, may stimulate new feelings of competition, envy, and attraction in the parent, all of which can cause discomfort and anxiety in both the younger and older generations.

Why mothers, more than fathers, tend to report a greater increase in conflict and a greater decrease in closeness is not entirely clear. In families with traditional sex roles, adolescents may perceive a status difference between their parents and may find it easier to question the authority of the mother, whose status is generally lower. More probably, mothers are more available and do more of the disciplining (Montemayor, 1986), and hence are more likely to be involved in parent–child conflicts. Mothers are then drawn into conflicts by default (Hill & Holmbeck, 1987; Steinberg, 1987).

Such parent–child conflicts usually are short-lived, however, because the increased tension generally does not last beyond the period of transpuberty. In most cases, tension subsides naturally as family members adjust to the adolescent's altered status and greater behavioral and emotional autonomy.

Most families appear to negotiate this temporary turmoil without any damaging effects. When family problems at adolescence are more acute and more serious, they generally reflect a situation that needs clinical attention (Rutter, Graham, Chadwick, & Yule, 1976). Clinicians might watch for both overcontrolling parents and neglectful or distant parents, especially in the case of the early maturing girl. Problems can arise both from parents' overresponding to a daughter's or son's physical maturation or underreacting when their physically mature children are engaging in deviant behaviors.

Perceptions of Puberty

The seventh and final set of findings to be discussed has to do with perceptions of puberty. Psychoanalytic clinicians have known for some time that it is not always the reality of a situation that is important; instead, the perception of reality forms the basis of the treatment. Similarly, research suggests that one's perceptions of timing—that is, perceptions of being early, on time, or late relative to one's peers—may predict psychological functioning and self-perceptions better than does actual pubertal change. Analyses from our research reveal that subjective timing does not completely correspond with actual pubertal timing, and that perceptions of being early, on time, or late predict satisfaction with the body and development as well as, if not better than, objective timing does (Tobin-Richards et al., 1983; Wilen, 1980). Consistent with these analyses, Rierdan and Koff, in three different studies (Rierdan & Koff, 1985; Rierdan, Koff, & Stubbs, 1989; Stubbs et al., 1989), found that subjective timing was significantly related to menarcheal experience, but objective timing was not. Girls who experienced themselves as early remembered a more negative menarche than girls who experienced themselves as on time or late.

Fine (1988) argued that, by ignoring girls' perceptions, feelings, beliefs, and attitudes about sex, we do not allow girls a sense of empowerment, which is essential to healthy development. As a consequence of this denial of subjective experience (which includes desire), high rates of teenage pregnancies, school dropouts, and female victimizations continue. Adolescent vulnerability is increased whenever adolescents' subjective experience is suppressed, whether their subjective experience pertains to sexuality or the changes related to puberty. It may be more clinically relevant to focus on the subjective experience of pubertal timing than on the actual timing.

This pertains equally to adolescent boys' subjective experience. Just as we, as a society, assume that adolescent girls have no sexual desires, we also assume that adolescent boys are constantly interested and willing to be sexual (Zilbergeld, 1978). Pubertal development is intrinsically linked to sexuality. It is as important to provide teenage boys the chance to discuss fears and anxieties about their physical changes and sexuality as it is to give teenage girls a chance to discuss their sexual feelings and desires.

Our discussion has been more focused on the consequences of pubertal development among girls than among boys. This reflects the literature to some extent; a few more studies have been conducted on girls. To a greater extent, this focus on girls has been perpetuated by a belief that problem behavior and psychological turmoil, both of which become more pronounced in girls during adolescence, are caused by puberty. In addition, the consequences of puberty seem more complicated for girls than for boys. Concerns about puberty seem more straightforward among boys; they appear to revolve around sexual, athletic, and leadership abilities. Although perhaps more clear-cut, boys' concerns are of no less importance than girls' concerns, and the clinician needs to stay alert to their appearance.

CLINICAL IMPLICATIONS

The fact that all adolescents go through puberty remains extremely important. The adjustments in self-perceptions that accompany the physical changes include changes in interactions with family, friends, the opposite sex, and peers in general. For example, the *social stimulus value* of pubertal change is extremely important. Adult size and shape serve as the signal of adult status and lead to expectations that the adult-appearing person will behave like an adult. The risk here is that the adult-appearing individual is probably immature psychologically, socially, and cognitively (Petersen & Crockett, 1985).

Our culture does not prepare or allow individuals to be more fully mature in all ways, except for the physical, until many years have passed from the time of puberty. Young people are subjected to pressure to behave the way adults do—in both healthy and unhealthy ways—but usually lack the experience and ego development that allow individuals to make mature choices.

Currently, our society lacks a culturally shared acknowledgment of the transition from physical immaturity to physical maturity. Hence, there is no culturally bound support system to aid the child with the challenges of adjusting to a very different body. In fact, our society virtually ignores the whole pubertal process, almost pretending that it does not occur.

In many cultures, "rites of passage" emphasize the importance of the physical changes and validate the psychological stress attached to the transition. The ambivalence felt by and about the pubertal child is often concretely expressed through the various aspects of the rites of passage. They function to acknowledge the significance of the change in its multifaceted qualities and, thus, they create an important and effective support for the child. Acknowledging pubertal change appears to have a positive impact on adolescent females. Brooks-Gunn and Ruble (1980) found that girls whose fathers were openly told about the girls' onset of menses reported fewer negative attitudes and less severe menstrual symptoms.

We have argued elsewhere (Richards & Petersen, 1987) that pubescent adolescents, especially off-time adolescents, might gain psychologically from community recognition of their physical change. Pubertal adolescents could participate in a brief series of activities involving education about the physical changes, such as an opportunity to talk with a group of same-sex children of the same physical age about the feelings and thoughts stimulated by puberty. This could occur through a retreat or through their schools. Upon return to the community, a dinner shared with family and friends could celebrate the transition.

In particular, the opportunity to discuss feelings and fantasies about what is happening to them and about the consequences to friendships, family, and activities might alleviate tension connected with the change. A limited rite of passage would serve to validate the importance of the physical changes for the young adolescent and acknowledge the stress involved. The rite would create peer group support, which may be especially needed by early or late developers. In particular, strategies for special groups could be shared; for example, early developing girls could be encouraged to minimize the number of other changes experienced at the same time or be helped to understand the effects of multiple changes and to handle the interconnected strain. Additionally, community recognition might benefit parents, who could support each other in facing their children's inevitable growth and change.

Although "puberty rites" in the form of discussion groups cannot eradicate the dysfunction of socially derived expectations and opportunities from the physical transformations of puberty, these rites can acknowledge the importance and the strain of these changes for the child, the family, and, to a lesser extent, the community. This acknowledgment might function in itself as an important support, particularly for those who face unusual stress associated with puberty.

A second important implication of this research is that body image disturbance, as well as psychological disturbance in general, emerges most frequently in special groups, particularly in groups that are experiencing multiple changes or extremes relative to the larger reference group. For example, a young adolescent girl who shifts from elementary school to junior high in the midst of the pubertal process may report a lot of novel attention from older boys. The clinician should stay alert to the possible negative effects of multiplying stresses on this girl's mental health. The change from sixth to seventh grade for early developing girls can be stressful if it means a shift from an elementary school to a junior high. The simultaneity of the changes leads the child into potential emotional "danger zones." Further research will reveal whether these effects are consistently ameliorated by keeping children in the same school until they are older.

The last recommendation comes out of the finding of heightened dissatisfaction with weight, which occurs with pubertal development in girls. This dissatisfaction may form the precursor to the eating disorders of older adolescents (Richards, Casper, & Larson, 1990). There is a preliminary indication that when girls participate in structured activities, such as athletic programs designed for girls as well as for boys, girls do not suffer as much from our culturally pervasive preoccupation with weight (Richards, Boxer et al., 1990). It is suggested that clinicians evaluate the activities of their young clients, particularly girls, and encourage those who are uninvolved to become active in after-school activities for the junior high-aged child. In this situation, a girl may come to define herself in terms of her capacities rather than only her physical appearance, which should contribute to better self-esteem. In addition, physical exercise, in moderation, can aid in regulating body weight, without the young adolescent girl resorting to addictive dieting and other unhealthy eating habits.

In conclusion, puberty, although always involving psychological adjustment to change, does not necessarily lead to emotional difficulties. It will most likely involve heightened, but temporary, family conflict and distance between the adolescent and parents. In addition, in certain circumstances, for a girl, early development, multiple simultaneous changes, heightened concerns about weight, and dieting may signal problems; late development in a boy may signal comparable difficulties. Further clinical assessment may be needed in these cases. In general, though, puberty itself calls for a response like that to any other life transition: supportive concern and attention by others to the subjective experience of the child.

REFERENCES

Anderson, E., Hetherington, E., & Clingempeel, W. (1989). Transformations in family relations at puberty: Effects of family context. *Journal of Early Adolescence, 9,* 310–334.

Attie, I., & Brooks-Gunn, J. B. (1989). Development of eating problems in adolescent girls: A longitudinal study. *Developmental Psychology, 25,* 70–79.

Ayalah, D., & Weinstock, I. J. (1979). *Breasts: Women speak about their breasts and their lives.* New York: Summit Books.

Blyth, D. A., Simmons, R. G., & Zakin, D. F. (1985). Satisfaction with body image for early adolescent females: The impact of pubertal timing within different school environments. *Journal of Youth and Adolescence, 14,* 207–225.

Bock, R. D., Wainer, H., Petersen, A., Thissen, D., Murray, J., & Roche, A. F. (1973). A parameterization for individual human growth curves. *Human Biology, 45,* 63–80.

Brodie, S. K., & Richards, M. H. (1987, April). *The effects of pubertal timing on body-image and eating attitudes.* Paper presented at the Biennial Conference of the Society for Research in Child Development, Baltimore, MD.

Brook, C. G. (1981). Endocrinological control of growth at puberty. *British Medical Bulletin, 37,* 281–285.

Brooks-Gunn, J. (1987). Pubertal processes and girls' psychological adaptation. In R. M. Lerner & T. Foch (Eds.), *Biological–psychosocial interaction in early adolescence* (pp. 1223–155). Hillsdale, NJ: Erlbaum.

Brooks-Gunn, J., & Matthews, W. S. (1979). *He and she.* Englewood Cliffs, NJ: Prentice-Hall.

Brooks-Gunn, J., & Ruble, D. N. (1980). Menarche: The interaction of physiology, cultural, and social factors. In A. J. Dan, E. A. Graham, & C. Beecher (Eds.), *The menstrual cycle: A synthesis of interdisciplinary research* (pp. 141–159). New York: Springer.

Brooks-Gunn, J., & Warren, M. (1988). The psychological significance of secondary sexual characteristics in nine-to-eleven-year-old girls. *Child Development, 59,* 1061–1069.

Browning, M. M. (1983). *Children's and teacher's experience in two junior high schools.*

Unpublished manuscript, Committee on Human Development, University of Chicago.

Clausen, J. A. (1975). The social meaning of differential physical and sexual maturation. In S. E. Dragastin & G. H. Elder (Eds.), *Adolescence in the life cycle: Psychological change and social context* (pp. 25–47). Washington, DC: Hemisphere.

Conger, J. J., & Petersen, A. C. (1984). *Adolescence and youth: Psychological development in a changing world* (3rd ed.). New York: Harper & Row.

Constanzo, P. R., & Shaw, M. E. (1966). Conformity as a function of age level. *Child Development, 37,* 967–976.

Dornbusch, S. M., Carlsmith, J. M., Gross, R., Rosenberg, A., & Duke, P. (1981). Sexual development, age, and dating: A comparison of biological and social influences upon one set of behaviors. *Child Development, 52,* 179–185.

Douvan, E., & Adelson, J. (1966). *The adolescent experience.* New York: Wiley.

Eichorn, D. H. (1975). Asynchronizations of adolescent development. In S. E. Dragastin & G. H. Elder, Jr. (Eds.), *Adolescence in the life cycle: Psychological change and social context* (pp. 81–96). Washington, DC: Hemisphere.

Faust, M. S. (1983). Alternative constructions of adolescent growth. In J. Brooks-Gunn & A. C. Petersen (Eds.), *Girls of puberty: Biological, psychological, and social perspectives* (pp. 105–125). New York: Plenum Press.

Fine, M. (1988). Sexuality, schooling, and adolescent females: The missing discourse of desire. *Harvard Educational Review, 58,* 29–40.

Frealy, M. J., & Luttge, W. G. (1982). *Human endocrinology: An interactive text.* New York: Elsevier.

Freud, A. (1946). *The ego and the mechanisms of defense.* New York: International Universities Press.

Freud, A. (1958). Adolescence. *Psychoanalytic Study of the Child, 16,* 225–278.

Gross, R. T., & Duke, P. M. (1980). The effect of early versus late physical maturation on adolescent behavior. *Pediatric Clinics of North America, 27,* 71–77.

Grumbach, M. M., Grave, G. D., & Mayer, F. E. (Eds.). (1974). *The control of the onset of puberty.* New York: Wiley.

Grumbach, M. M., Richards, H. E., Conte, F. A., & Kaplan, S. L. (1977). Clinical disorders of adrenal function and puberty: An assessment of the role of the adrenal cortex in normal and abnormal puberty in man and evidence for the ACTH-like pituitary adrenal androgen stimulating hormone. In M. Seno (Ed.), *The endocrine function of the human adrenal cortex (Serono Symposium).* New York: Academic Press.

Hill, J. P., & Holmbeck, G. (1987). Familial adaptation to biological change during adolescence. In R. M. Lerner & T. T. Foch (Eds.), *Biological-psychosocial interactions in early adolescence.* Hillsdale, NJ: Erlbaum.

Hill, J. P., Holmbeck, G. N., Marlow, L., Green, T. M., & Lynch, M. E. (1985). Menarcheal status and parent–child relations in families of seventh-grade girls. *Journal of Youth and Adolescence, 14,* 301–317.

Hill, M. K., & Lando, M. A. (1976). Physical attractiveness and sex-role stereotypes in impression formation. *Perceptual and Motor Skills, 43,* 1251.

Inoff-Germain, G., Arnold, G. S., Nottelmann, E., Susman, E., Cutler, G. B., & Choursos, G. (1988). Relation between hormone level and observational measures of aggressive behavior of young adolescents in family interactions. *Developmental Psychology, 24,* 129–139.

Jones, M. C., & Bayley, N. (1950). Physical maturing among boys as related to behavior. *Journal of Educational Psychology, 41,* 129–148.

Katz, P. (1979). The development of female identity. *Sex Roles, 5,* 155–178.

Kavrell, S. M., & Jarcho, H. (1980, September). *Self-esteem and body image in early adolescence.* Paper presented at the annual meeting of the American Psychological Association, Montreal.

Kestenberg, J. (1967a). Phases of adolescence with suggestions for a correlation of psychic and hormonal organizations. Part I: Antecedents of adolescent organizations in childhood. *Journal of the American Academy of Child Psychiatry, 6,* 426–463.

Kestenberg, J. (1967b). Phases of adolescence with suggestions for a correlation of psychic and hormonal organizations. Part II: Prepuberty, diffusion, and reintegration. *Journal of the American Academy of Child Psychiatry, 6,* 577–614.

Kestenberg, J. (1968). Phases of adolescence with suggestions for a correlation of psychic and hormonal organization. Part III: Puberty growth, differentiation, and consolidation. *Journal of the American Academy of Child Psychiatry, 7,* 108–151.

Lee, P. A. (1980). Normal ages of pubertal events among American males and females. *Journal of Adolescent Health Care, 1,* 26–29.

Lerner, R. (1985). Adolescent maturational changes and psychosocial development: A dynamic interactional perspective. *Journal of Youth and Adolescence, 14,* 355–386.

Lerner, R. M., & Karabenick, S. A. (1974). Physical attractiveness, body attitudes, and self-concept in late adolescence. *Journal of Youth and Adolescence, 3,* 7–16.

Lynch, M. E. (1981). *Paternal adrogyny, daughters' physical maturity level, and achievement socialization in early adolescence.* Unpublished doctoral dissertation, Cornell University, Ithaca, NY.

Meyer, J. W. (1982, December). *Cultural links between gender roles and identity.* Paper presented at a conference on pubertal and psychosocial change, sponsored by the Social Science Research Council Subcommittee on Child Development in Life-Span Perspective, Tucson, AZ.

Money, J., & Ehrhardt, A. A. (1972). *Man and woman, boy and girl.* Baltimore, MD: Johns Hopkins University Press.

Montemayor, R. (1986). Family variation in parent–adolescent storm and stress. *Journal of Adolescent Research, 1,* 15–31.

Mussen, P. H., & Bouterline-Young, H. (1964). Personality characteristics of physically advanced and retarded adolescents in Italy and the United States. *Vita Humana, 7,* 186–200.

Neugarten, B. L. (1969). Continuities and discontinuities of psychological issues into adult life. *Human Development, 12,* 121–130.

Neugarten, B. L. (1979). Time, age, and the life-cycle. *American Journal of Psychiatry, 136,* 887–894.

Nottelmann, E. D., Susman, E. J., Blue, J. H., Inoff-Germain, L. D., Dorn, L. D., Loriaux, D. L., Cutler, G. B., & Chourson, G. P. (1987). Gonadal and adrenal hormone correlates of adjustment in early adolescence. In R. M. Lerner & T. Foch (Eds.), *Biological–psychosocial interactions in early adolescence* (pp. 303–325). Hillsdale, NJ: Erlbaum.

Opler, M. K. (1971). Adolescence in cross-cultural perspective. In J. G. Howells (Ed.), *Modern perspective in adolescent psychiatry* (pp. 152–179). Edinburgh: Oliver & Boyd.

Paige, K. M., & Paige, J. M. (1982). *The politics of reproductive ritual.* Berkeley: University of California Press.

Paikoff, R. L., Brooks-Gunn, J., & Carlton-Ford, S. (1991). Effect of reproductive status changes on family functioning and well-being of mothers and daughters. *Journal of Early Adolescence, 11,* 201–220.

Papini, D., Clark, S., Barnett, J., & Savage, C. (1989). Grade, pubertal status, and gender related variations in conflictual issues among adolescents. *Adolescence, 24,* 977–987.

Papini, D. R., Datan, N., & McCluskey-Fawcett, K. A. (1988). An observational study of affective and assertive family interactions during adolescence. *Journal of Youth and Adolescence, 17,* 477–486.

Papini, D. R., & Sebby, R. A. (1988). Variations in conflictual family issues by adolescent pubertal status, gender, and family member. *Journal of Early Adolescence, 8,* 1–15.

Peskin, H. (1973). Influence of the developmental schedule of puberty on learning and ego development. *Journal of Youth and Adolescence, 1,* 273–290.

Peskin, H., & Livson, M. (1972). Pre- and postpubertal personality and adult psychological functioning. *Seminars in Psychiatry, 4,* 343–353.

Petersen, A. C. (1980). Puberty and its psychosocial significance in girls. In A. J. Dan, E. A. Graham, & C. P. Beecher (Eds.), *The menstrual cycle: Synthesis of interdisciplinary research* (pp. 45–55). New York: Springer.

Petersen, A. C. (1983). Menarche: Meaning of measures and measuring meaning. In S. Golub (Ed.), *Menarche* (pp. 63–76). New York: Heath.

Petersen, A. C. (1985). Pubertal development as a cause of disturbance: Myths, realities, and unanswered questions. *Genetic, Social, and General Psychology Monographs, 111,* 205–232.

Petersen, A. C., & Crockett, L. (1985). Pubertal timing and grade effects on adjustment. *Journal of Youth and Adolescence, 14,* 191–206.

Petersen, A. C., & Ebata, A. T. (1987). Developmental transitions and adolescent problem behavior: Implications for prevention and intervention. In X. Hurrelmann & F. X. Kaufmann (Eds.), *The limit and potential of social intervention* (pp. 167–184). Berlin & New York: deGruyter/Aldine.

Petersen, A. C., & Taylor, B. (1980). The biological approach to adolescence: Biological change and psychological adaptation. In J. Adelson (Ed.), *Handbook of adolescent psychology* (pp. 117–155). New York: Wiley.

Richards, M. H. (1984). *Effects of pubertal development on perceptions of the self.* Doctoral dissertation, University of Chicago, 1984. Dissertation Abstracts International.

Richards, M. H., Boxer, A. M., Petersen, A. C., & Albrecht, R. (1990). Relations of weight to body image in pubertal girls and boys from two communities. *Developmental Psychology, 26,* 313–321.

Richards, M. H., Casper, R. C., & Larson, R. (1990). Weight and eating concerns among pre- and young adolescent boys and girls. *Journal of Adolescent Health Care, 11,* 203–207.

Richards, M. H., & Petersen, A. C. (1987). Biological theoretical models of adolescent development. In V. B. Van Hasselt & M. Hersen (Eds.), *Handbook of adolescent psychology* (pp. 34–52). Trowbridge, England: Pergamon Press.

Rierdan, J., & Koff, E. (1980). The psychological impact of menarche: Integrative vs. disruptive changes. *Journal of Youth and Adolescence, 9,* 49–58.

Rierdan, J., & Koff, E. (1985). Timing of menarche and initial menstrual experience. *Journal of Youth and Adolescence, 14,* 237–244.

Rierdan, J., Koff, E., & Stubbs, M. L. (1989). Timing of menarche, preparation, and initial menstrual experience: Replication and further analyses in a prospective study. *Journal of Youth and Adolescence, 18,* 413–427.

Rosenbaum, M. (1979). The changing body image of the adolescent girl. In M. Sugar (Ed.), *Female adolescent development* (pp. 234–252). New York: Brunner/Mazel.

Rosenberg, F., & Simmons, R. G. (1975). Sex differences in the self-concept in adolescence. *Sex Roles: A Journal of Research, 1,* 147–159.

Rossi, A. S. (1980). Life-span theories in women's lives. *Signs, 6,* 4–32.

Rutter, M., Graham, P., Chadwick, O. F. D., & Yule, W. (1976). Adolescent turmoil: Fact or fiction? *Journal of Child Psychology and Psychiatry, 17,* 35–36.

Savin-Williams, R. (1979). Dominance hierarchies in groups of early adolescents. *Child Development, 50,* 923–935.

Silbereisen, R., Petersen, A., Albrecht, H., & Kracke, B. (1989). Maturational timing and the development of problem behavior: Longitudinal studies in adolescence. *Journal of Early Adolescence, 9,* 247–268.

Simmons, R. G., & Blyth, D. A. (1987). *Moving into adolescence: The impact of pubertal change and school.* Hawthorne, NY: Aldine/deGruyter.

Simmons, R. G., Blyth, D. A., & McKinney, K. L. (1983). The social and psychological effects of puberty on white females. In J. Brooks-Gunn & A. C. Petersen (Eds.), *Girls at puberty: Biological and psychosocial perspectives* (pp. 229–272). New York: Plenum Press.

Simmons, R. G., Blyth, D. A., Van Cleave, E. F., & Bush, D. M. (1979). Entry into early adolescence: The impact of school structure, puberty, and early dating on self-esteem. *American Sociological Review, 44,* 948–967.

Simmons, R. G., Burgeson, R., Carlton-Ford, S., & Blyth, D. A. (1987). The impact of cumulative change in early adolescence. *Child Development, 58,* 1220–1234.

Smith, E., Udry, J. R., & Morris, N. M. (1985). Pubertal development and friends: A biosocial explanation of adolescent sexual behavior. *Journal of Health and Social Behavior, 26,* 183–192.

Steinberg, L. D. (1981). Transformations in family relations at puberty. *Developmental Psychology, 7,* 833–840.

Steinberg, L. (1987). Impact of puberty on family relations: Effects of pubertal status and pubertal timing. *Developmental Psychology, 23*(3), 451–460.

Steinberg, L. (1988a). Pubertal maturation and parent–adolescent distance: An evolutionary perspective. In G. Adams, R. Montemayor, &

T. Gullotta (Eds.), *Advances in adolescent development.* Beverly Hills, CA: Sage.

Steinberg, L. (1988b). Reciprocal relation between parent–child distance and pubertal maturation. *Developmental Psychology, 24,* 122–128.

Stubbs, M., Rierdan, J., & Koff, E. (1989). Developmental differences in menstrual attitudes. *Journal of Early Adolescence, 9,* 480–498.

Susman, E., Inoff-Germain, G., Nottelmann, E. D., Loriaux, D. L., Cutler, G. B., & Chrousos (1987). Hormones, emotional depositions, and aggressive attributes in young adolescents. *Child Development, 58,* 1114–1134.

Susman, E., Nottelmann, E. D., Inoff-Germain, G., Dorn, L., Cutler, G., Loriaux, D. L., & Chrousos, G. (1985). The relation of relative hormonal levels with physical development and social–emotional behavior in young adolescents. *Journal of Youth and Adolescence, 14,* 245–264.

Tanner, J. M. (1962). *Growth at adolescence.* Oxford: Blackwell.

Tanner, J. M. (1972). Sequence, tempo, and individual variation in growth and development of boys aged twelve to sixteen. In J. Kagan & R. Coles (Eds.), *Twelve to sixteen: Early adolescence* (pp. 1–24). New York: Norton.

Tanner, J. M. (1974). Sequence and tempo in the somatic changes in puberty. In M. M. Grumbach, G. D. Grave, & F. E. Mayer (Eds.), *Control of the onset of puberty* (pp. 448–470). New York: Wiley.

Thissen, D., Bock, R. D., Wainer, H., & Roche, A. F. (1976). Individual growth in stature: A comparison of four growth studies in the USA. *Annals of Human Biology, 3,* 529–542.

Tobin-Richards, M. H., Boxer, A. M., & Petersen, A. C. (1983). Early adolescents' perceptions of their physical development. In J. Brooks-Gunn & A. C. Petersen (Eds.), *Girls at puberty: Biological and psychosocial perspectives* (pp. 127–154). New York: Plenum Press.

Tobin-Richards, M. H., Petersen, A. C., & Boxer, A. M. (1983, April). *The significance of weight to feelings of attractiveness in pubertal girls.* Paper presented at the meeting of the Society for Research in Child Development, Detroit.

Udry, J. R., Billy, J. D. G., Morris, N. M., Groff, T. R., & Raj, M. H. (1985). Serum androgenic hormones motivate sexual behavior in adolescent boys. *Fertility and Sterility, 43,* 90–94.

Udry, J. R., & Talbert, L. M. (1988). Sex hormone effects on personality in puberty. *Journal of Personality and Social Psychology, 54,* 291–295.

Udry, J. R., Talbert, L. M., & Morris, N. (1986). Biosocial foundations for adolescent female sexuality. *Demography, 23,* 217–227.

Warren, M., & Brooks-Gunn, J. (1989). Mood and behavior at adolescence: Evidence for hormonal factors. *Journal of Clinical Endocrinology and Metabolism, 69,* 77–83.

Wilen, J. B. (1980, June). *The timing of pubertal changes and its psychological correlates.* Paper presented at the Annual Conference on the Psychology of Adolescence, Michael Reese Hospital and Medical Center, Chicago.

Zilbergeld, B. (1978). *Male sexuality.* New York: Bantam Books.

CHAPTER 3

Cognitive Development

NANCY G. GUERRA

COGNITIVE DEVELOPMENT DURING ADOLESCENCE

Both the research literature and popular views of adolescent development have stressed the central role of self-awareness and the search for individual identity (Erikson, 1968; Marcia, 1980). This search for identity has been linked with the hedonism and rebellion so typical of teenagers and corresponds to increases in problem behaviors such as school truancy, running away from home, and substance abuse (Achenbach & Edelbrock, 1981). Although much has been written about the developmental tasks of adolescence and the corresponding behaviors typical of the adolescent, less emphasis has been placed on careful analysis of the adolescent's emerging cognitive system. Because the process of establishing one's identity and understanding one's role in the larger social system depends heavily on the individual's thought processes, our understanding of adolescent development must be informed by a careful analysis of cognitive changes occurring during this period.

This chapter reviews cognitive growth during adolescence as related to the development of adaptive social behavior and the prevention and treatment of adolescent problem behavior.

A major focus is on *social cognition*—how individuals think about themselves, others, and social relations. The development of social cognition is clearly related to the development of impersonal, nonsocial cognition, but it has been treated increasingly as a distinct field of investigation (Damon, 1983; Selman, 1980; Shantz, 1975). Accordingly, a great deal of recent developmental research has focused on the cognitive bases of social behavior (Dodge, 1986; Dodge & Crick, 1990; Eron, 1987; Huesmann, 1988; Rothbaum & Weisz, 1989; Slaby & Guerra, 1988). In addition, a corresponding clinical literature has highlighted the utility of cognitive–behavioral interventions for treating a variety of adolescent disorders, including depression (Clarke & Lewinsohn, 1989; Reynolds & Coats, 1986; Wilkes & Rush, 1988; Winnett, Bornstein, Cogswell, & Paris, 1987) and serious antisocial behavior (Feindler, 1987; Guerra & Slaby, 1990; Hains & Hains, 1988).

Both the developmental and clinical literature will be discussed, utilizing a framework that focuses on two interrelated but distinct areas of social cognition: (a) structural–developmental competencies and (b) social information-processing skills. The primary focus of the structural–developmental approach has been to examine developmental changes in how children organize or structure social knowledge. This approach draws primarily on Piaget's stage model of cognitive development (Piaget, 1932/1965) translated into several different domains of social knowledge, including moral reasoning (Kohlberg, 1969), the nature of social rules and conventions (Turiel, 1978, 1982), conceptions of friendship (Selman, 1980), and self-understanding (Damon & Hart, 1982). On the other hand, information-processing models focus less on the organizational characteristics of social-cognitive understanding, and more on those cognitive processes related to the acquisition, storage, and retrieval of social information, particularly as applied to solving interpersonal problems (Dodge, 1986; Huesmann, 1988; Slaby & Guerra, 1988; Spivack & Shure, 1974). In addition, recent applications of social information-processing models have stressed the importance of the content as well as the process of thought (Slaby & Guerra, 1988), including beliefs about the self (Bandura, 1989), beliefs about appropriate standards for behavior (Huesmann, Guerra, Miller, & Zelli, 1990; Slaby & Guerra, 1988), beliefs about the consequences of one's actions (Guerra, 1989; Guerra & Slaby, 1989; Perry, Perry, & Rasmussen, 1986), and beliefs about causality (Guerra, Huesmann, & Zelli, 1990; Rothbaum & Weisz, 1989; Rubin & Krasnor, 1986).

STRUCTURAL–DEVELOPMENTAL COMPETENCIES

Descriptive research using structural–developmental models has sought to identify sequentially emerging stages in how children structure knowledge about their social world. In general, these approaches have relied extensively on Piaget's (1932/1965) stage model of cognitive development. Although Piaget's theory was primarily concerned with intellectual development, he also studied the relation between children's stages of cognitive development and their social understanding, particularly in the area of moral reasoning.

Stages of Cognitive Development

According to Piaget, one of the earliest building blocks of children's cognitive development is the scheme. A scheme refers to the child's internal representation of an activity. For example, babies have relatively simple schemes, such as sucking and grasping. With development, schemes become more diverse and sophisticated. New information is modified to fit existing schemes through the process of assimilation; existing schemes may change to fit new realities through the process of accommodation. These schemes are organized to form integrated mental structures. During certain critical times, existing schemes are no longer able to accommodate new information, resulting in disequilibration. Restoring equilibrium involves replacing the existing mental structure with a qualitatively different, more advanced structure representing a new and distinct stage of cognitive development.

It is assumed that these stages follow an invariant sequence across all individuals and social conditions. Piaget postulated four stages of cognitive development: (a) the sensorimotor period (birth to about 2 years); (b) the preoperational period (approximately 2 to 7 years); (c) the concrete operational period (approximately 7 to 11 years); and (d) the formal operational period (approximately 11 through adulthood). These ages are only vague indicators of general cognitive levels. In addition, because there is some debate over whether all individuals reach the formal operational period (Elkind, 1974), a discussion of both concrete and formal operations is relevant to our understanding of adolescent cognitive development.

At about age 7, children enter the stage of concrete operations. According to Piaget, this period is characterized by the ability to perform logical mental operations on concrete and familiar events. Rather than focusing only on the most obvious aspect of a stimulus typical of the preoperational stage, concrete operational children are now able to "decenter" and consider several relevant dimensions. In the social domain, this corresponds to a shift from an egocentric perspective, wherein children have difficulty appreciating others' viewpoints, toward an increasing ability to understand others' perspectives and an emerging ability to coordinate self and others' perspectives. Children also begin to evaluate actions in terms of underlying intentions and motives rather than focusing solely on outcome information (Ferguson & Rule, 1980; Piaget, 1932/1965). For example, during this cognitive stage, a child whose toy has been damaged by another child might try to find out why this happened and might consider the effect of retaliation on the other child. In addition, a more advanced concrete thinker might consider the effect of retaliation on both the other child *and* on their relationship, although this does not typically occur before age 10.

Concrete operational children are also able to theorize about the physical and social world. They can make guesses and anticipate what might happen. They may consider, for example, what would happen if they said something mean to another child. However, it is important to recognize that concrete operational children are able to apply these mental operations to concrete events that are testable within their realm of immediate experience. The ability to deal with abstract, hypothetical situations is beyond the realm of this stage.

The formal operations period is thought to begin around age 11. This stage is characterized by the ability to engage in formal reasoning on an abstract level. Children can imagine hypothetical events, draw hypotheses from their experiences, and use both deductive and inductive reasoning to systematically explore existing and potential relationships. The shift from egocentric thinking continues, and children are increasingly more able to coordinate multiple perspectives. Furthermore, this cognitive stage is associated with an emerging metacognitive ability. Individuals are now more aware of their own thought processes and are able to think about and monitor their thoughts (Flavell, 1985).

Thus, the passage from concrete to formal operations, which typically occurs during adolescence, involves a shift from reasoning based on the most obvious or probable variables to reasoning based on the full awareness of all possible variables and the relations between them. This passage is not an all-or-none phenomenon; it proceeds along three substages. In substage 1, which usually occurs at around ages 10 to 13, children become capable of inversing relations, but not of considering all abstract possibilities. In substage 2, beginning around ages 13 to 14, children become capable of ordering triads of propositions or relations. Substage 3 represents true formal thought, based on the consideration of all possibilities, and does not emerge until ages 15 to 16.

There has been considerable debate in the literature about the precise relation between developmental changes in thinking about physical and logical tasks and developmental changes in social cognition (Damon, 1983; Keating & Clark, 1980; Tomlinson-Keasey & Keasey, 1974). In general, social–cognitive theories based on structural–developmental models have borrowed heavily from Piaget's stage theory of cognitive development and have proposed corresponding developmental sequences in children's understanding in a number of different social domains. Logical stages typically have been viewed as necessary but not sufficient prerequisites for equivalent stages in social reasoning. Three areas of social cognition that have clinical significance in the area of adolescent development are moral reasoning, social perspective taking, and self-understanding.

Moral Reasoning

Elaborating on Piaget's (1932/1965) two-stage theory of moral development, Kohlberg (1969) proposed a six-stage invariant sequence of development in moral reasoning. Each stage is believed to represent a qualitative transformation in reasoning that reflects movement toward more mature reasoning based on universal principles of justice. A person's stage of moral development is determined by his or her reasoning about hypothetical moral dilemmas.

The first two stages represent *preconventional* thinking, with morality defined in terms of external consequences to self. Individuals at the first stage of moral reasoning focus on the physical consequences of an action and seek to avoid punishment. At stage 2, judgments shift toward general satisfaction of one's needs, and reciprocity takes the form of "You scratch my back and I'll scratch yours." However, at both stages, actions are judged by their consequences rather than by the actor's intent. These stages typify the reasoning of young children, although they may persist into adolescence and adulthood.

The third and fourth stages represent *conventional* reasoning, with morality determined by considerations of others' opinions and maintenance of the social order. Stage 3 has been termed the "good boy, nice girl" orientation, because good behavior depends largely on whether others approve. Stage 4 reasoning reflects a "law and order" orientation: moral decisions are based on respect for rules, authority, and the social order. Individuals who display conventional reasoning also consider an actor's intent. In general, Kohlberg held that individuals must attain Piaget's concrete operational stage before they can reason at the conventional level. Thus, this form of reasoning begins to emerge during middle childhood and early adolescence. Kohlberg and his colleagues have found that most adolescents reason at stages 2, 3, and 4, and rarely progress to stage 5 thinking before early adulthood.

The fifth and sixth stages represent *postconventional* morality, because individuals who reason at these stages evaluate actions in terms of moral principles that have validity apart from the persons or society holding them. At stage 5, reasoning shifts from a law and order orientation to a social contract orientation, whereby individual rights supersede authority, and actions are evaluated in terms of the greatest good for the greatest number of people. Stage 6 reasoning invokes a consideration of universal ethical principles, whereby decisions are made on the basis of what would be fair for a person regardless of what position he or she is in. Kohlberg also claimed that formal operations are necessary, though not sufficient, prerequisites for postconventional morality, and there is some research evidence to support this claim (Lee, 1971). That is, formal operational thinking enables the individual to realize that any individual's or society's definition of right and wrong is just one of any number of possibilities.

Research indicates that adolescents are certainly capable of going beyond moral judgments based purely on avoiding punishment. However, levels of moral reasoning tend to stabilize in late adolescence. Most typically, the highest stage of moral reasoning reached by adolescent males is stage 4, and adolescent females level off at stage 3 (Holstein, 1976; Kohlberg & Kramer, 1969), although this gender difference may indicate that females are simply less likely than males to invoke a morality of rights and justice (Gilligan, 1977, 1982). Nevertheless, the broad range of stages of reasoning that characterize adolescents may limit the utility of stage models of moral reasoning for understanding adolescent development. Research in social perspective taking focuses on a more specific domain of cognition that has been investigated in children and adolescents.

Social Perspective Taking

An interest in social role taking goes back to the early writings of James Baldwin (1906) and George Herbert Mead (1934). More recently, Selman and his colleagues (Brion-Meisels & Selman, 1984; Selman, 1971, 1976, 1980; Selman & Byrne, 1974) have taken a cognitive–developmental approach to the study of the child's emerging ability to take the perspective of another and coordinate it with his or her own perspective. They have proposed an invariant sequence of five stages in social perspective taking, beginning at an egocentric level (about age 3 to 6) where the perspectives of self and others are undifferentiated, and progressing through a series of stages involving increasingly complex abilities to coordinate the perspectives of self and others. Progression through these five stages is evaluated in terms of four social domains: individual concepts, friendship concepts, peer group concepts, and parent–child concepts. These domains provide the specific content for examining developmental changes in social understanding.

Parallel with the emergence of concrete operational thinking, the preadolescent at Selman's third stage (around age 7 to 12) becomes able to put his or her own viewpoint aside and take the perspective of another person. The child is thus aware that other people may have quite different feelings and thoughts. In addition, the preadolescent is aware that one can experience two opposing emotions (such as pleasure and displeasure) toward the same person or thing. However, perspective taking at this level is based on a two-way reciprocity; it is sequential but not yet simultaneous.

During early adolescence (around age 10 to 15), the child moves into Selman's fourth stage, that of mutual perspective taking. Adolescents can now step outside of both their own and others' perspective and assume the perspective of a neutral third-party observer. This ability allows the adolescent to step outside of a social interaction and simultaneously and mutually consider the perspective of both self and others. As observers, adolescents are also more able to see themselves as both actor and object.

The final stage in Selman's sequence occurs between late adolescence and adulthood. In this stage of societal perspective taking, the individual moves to a more abstract level of coordinating all possible third-person perspectives. Perspective taking moves from a process of coordinating perspectives within a social interaction to coordinating the perspectives of members of a larger social system.

The adolescent's developing cognitive abilities to take the perspective of another, to step outside of a relationship and evaluate it, and to coordinate perspectives within a social group have significant implications for both social competence and problem behavior. Social relationships during adolescence shift from sharing common activities with friends to belonging to social groups held together by shared thoughts, feelings, and values (O'Brien & Bierman, 1988; Savin-Williams & Berndt, Chapter 9 of this volume). Effective group membership may partially hinge on the adolescent's emerging social perspective-taking abilities. Developmental lags in perspective-taking skills may also promote involvement in antisocial activities where one's own interests are pursued without consideration of the effects of such actions on others. Empirical support for this position is derived from studies that have demonstrated deficits in social perspective-taking skills in populations of both emotionally disturbed children in a special clinic school (Selman, 1976) and incarcerated delinquent youth (Chandler, 1973).

Thus, in terms of understanding other people, relationships, and social groups, the cognitive shift from concrete to formal operations enables the adolescent to consider and coordinate multiple perspectives, and to construct his or her social world from both existing and potential experiences. Concurrent with this more complex understanding of others are several related shifts in self-understanding.

Self-Understanding

Although an extensive literature exists in the area of self-concept development (see Wylie, 1979 for a review), the majority of these studies have focused on the development of self-esteem—individuals' positive or negative feelings about themselves. Relatively few studies have examined developmental changes in how individuals construe and organize their self-understanding in relation to their emerging cognitive abilities.

Nevertheless, it is possible to describe some ontogenetic patterns in the development of self-understanding during childhood and adolescence. Perhaps the most frequently replicated finding is the shift from the concrete and physicalistic self-conceptions of early childhood to the more abstract, subjective, and psychological self-conceptions that emerge during adolescence (Barenboim, 1980; Bernstein, 1980; Damon & Hart, 1982; Montemayor & Eisen, 1977; Secord & Peevers, 1974; Wood, 1978). Studies generally have not attempted to link these shifts with corresponding changes in cognitive stages, but this shift is clearly in line with general cognitive changes from concrete to abstract thinking.

Another important development during adolescence is an increased striving for a unified self-definition. For instance, during the late elementary years, children may be aware that they have separate intentions that can exist simultaneously, but they rarely recognize the relations among these intentions. Rather, this disparity is resolved by holding separate notions of self. In contrast, the older adolescent recognizes that the self is comprised of a network of complex and interconnected intentions, and attempts to integrate these various intentions into a unified self-definition.

For example, in a related study of adolescent conceptions of the "self-system," Bernstein (1980) asked 10-, 15-, and 20-year-olds to list the ways they act with different people and to put these statements together in a unifying statement about themselves. Clear age-related trends were noted. Ten-year-olds simply repeated past statements about themselves. Fifteen-year-olds were able to recognize that their actions were sometimes discrepant or contradictory and often referred to feeling like "two different people." However, 20-year-olds were able to provide unifying statements about themselves, recognizing the discrepancies in their actions but organizing them into a self-system according to a set of unifying principles.

As the adolescent attempts to reconcile these contradictions, the self also becomes an object of increased attention. This self-consciousness has been linked with two characteristic beliefs of adolescents: the personal fable and the imaginary audience (Elkind, 1967). The personal fable refers to the adolescent's belief that he or she is unique and that no one has ever had the same feelings or thoughts. One can imagine a teenage girl who thinks that her mother "couldn't possibly understand" how she feels upon breaking up with her boyfriend, even though her mother, like most adults, has been in the same situation. For some adolescents, this belief extends into their thinking about high-risk behaviors, whereby they may see themselves as immune to ordinary dangers. The imaginary audience refers to the belief that other people are just as preoccupied with the adolescent's appearance and behavior as he or she is, and is reflected in public self-consciousness. The importance of the imaginary audience has been found to be more evident in girls than boys and to peak during early adolescence and decline with increasing age (Peterson, 1982). Delinquent youth have also been found to express more concern over the imaginary audience than their less delinquent peers (Anolik, 1981).

The development of self-understanding during adolescence is also marked by a struggle to recognize and integrate both the potential and the limits of personal agency. Developmental research has revealed an increasing awareness of the self's volitional powers (Greenberger, 1984; Harter, 1983; Montemayor & Eisen, 1977; Secord & Peevers, 1974). However, adolescents also realize that the mind's volitional powers are limited and that unconscious mental processes can influence one's actions. Private self-consciousness thus increases as the adolescent attempts to develop a more complex, sophisticated notion of personal agency.

This increase in private self-consciousness also can lead to increased psychological turmoil. For instance, heightened self-awareness has been linked with a variety of depressive symptoms when individuals are unable to adhere to their private standards (Carver & Scheier, 1981; Fenigstein, 1979; Wicklund,

1975). In contrast, adolescents may attempt to avoid the task of reconciling their conflicting motives, standards, and behavior, and actively refrain from self-reflection. This may be accomplished by various types of rebellious activities, including being unwilling to reveal themselves to others (Elkind & Bowen, 1979), joining highly structured groups such as gangs, and participating in a variety of thrill-seeking activities.

Thus, self-understanding during adolescence progresses from a conception of a global mental self with somewhat discordant and even mysterious mental processes to a view of an internally consistent and organized self, with discordant but integrated processes. This task requires a significant amount of self-reflection. Because of cognitive limitations, the younger adolescent has more difficulty differentiating his or her own identity from both physical characteristics and the opinions of others, and demonstrates a heightened public self-consciousness. However, the older adolescent is more capable of self-reflection, and private self-consciousness increases. This increasing systematization of the self is related to the formalization of cognitive reasoning skills that occurs during adolescence, and developmental lags in the emergence of these cognitive skills may interfere with achieving an integrated conception of the self.

Critique of Stage Models

Before reviewing clinical interventions derived from structural–developmental theories, it is important to discuss some of the major criticisms of stage models of social–cognitive development. Five relevant concerns can be identified. First, stage models imply discontinuity in development, in that any two stages are qualitatively different from each other in their organization. Yet, if one observes the development of children's thinking, it appears to change gradually over time, with considerable continuity from day to day (Damon, 1983). Second, the contention that children progress through stages in an invariant sequence has also been questioned. Studies have demonstrated "stage skipping" (Holstein, 1976) and regression to lower-level reasoning (Holstein, 1976; Kuhn, 1976). Third, studies have repeatedly demonstrated considerable variability in cognitive performance within individuals. A particular child typically does not display the same stage of reasoning across both situations and domains (Eisenberg-Berg, 1979; Larson & Kurdek, 1979).

Related to this lack of cognitive consistency is a fourth concern, the "judgment/action" discrepancy; that is, predicting children's behavior from their level of reasoning in any given domain is often quite difficult. Stages may be seen as representing an ideal standard of cognitive competence, whereas behavior depends on a wide range of individual and situational influences. Finally, there is some doubt about the universality of higher stages of cognitive development. For instance, moral reasoning at stages 4 and 5 is observed most frequently among males in Western industrialized nations. Noting that adolescent and adult women typically invoke stage 3 reasoning, Gilligan (1977, 1982) questioned whether women's moral reasoning actually reflects a different moral orientation, one that focuses on social responsibility and relationships rather than individual rights.

Cognitive–Behavioral Interventions Based on Structural–Developmental Models

A substantial body of literature has investigated the relation between "developmental lags" in progression through stages of social reasoning and adolescent problem behavior. Many of these studies have focused on the contribution of deficits in moral reasoning and social perspective taking to aggressive and delinquent behavior. For instance, numerous studies have demonstrated a negative relation between antisocial behavior and stages of moral reasoning (Bear & Richards, 1981) and stages of social perspective taking (Chandler, 1973; Feffer, 1970). Although the relation is often a modest one, there does appear to be reasonable consistency between antisocial behavior and developmentally immature moral reasoning and social perspective taking (for reviews, see Blasi, 1980 and Jurkovic, 1980).

Accordingly, interventions have been designed to promote advances in reasoning stages among adolescents with behavior problems. These interventions generally are conducted at either the classroom or small-group level. Moral education programs most frequently involve guided dilemma discussions designed to arouse cognitive disequilibrium. This type of program has been found to be most effective when individuals are exposed to reasoning that is one stage above their own level (" + 1 stage" method) (Arbuthnot & Faust, 1981; Cochrane & Manley-Casimir, 1980; Rest, 1973). This method can work well in the average high school classroom, because less troubled adolescents will usually display moral reasoning stages approximately one-half to one stage higher. In addition, adolescents who show at least some beginning formal operational thought appear to profit more from such training (Faust & Arbuthnot, 1978; Walker, 1980).

In a recent intervention that examined both changes in moral reasoning stage and changes in behavior problems, Arbuthnot and Gordon (1986) reported advances in moral reasoning stage and improvement on multiple behavioral measures. Thirty-five male and 13 female students (seventh through tenth grades) who had been nominated by teachers as being "behavior disordered" participated in a 16- to 20-week, small-group, guided dilemma discussion program (one 45-minute session per week) using the " + 1 stage" method. When compared with a matched no-treatment control group, experimental participants demonstrated significant long-term (1-year follow-up) improvements in moral reasoning stage, frequency of disciplinary referrals, tardiness, and grades.

Selman and his colleagues (Selman, 1980; Selman, Brion-Meisels, & Lavin, 1982; Selman & Demorest, 1984) have utilized both dyadic and small-group approaches to enhance the perspective-taking skills and improve the social behaviors of clinically referred adolescents. Using a range of activities, including guided dilemma discussions, role playing, and structured activities, the adolescent is led to realize developmentally feasible goals. In terms of social perspective taking, the emphasis is on Selman's fourth stage, whereby the individual is encouraged to take the role of an independent third-party observer. In addition to structural–developmental competencies, emphasis has also been placed on teaching specific functional strategies in order to make effective decisions and solve interpersonal problems. Improvements in both social perspective-taking skills and social behavior have been demonstrated.

In a frequently cited study, Chandler (1973) enhanced the perspective-taking skills of incarcerated delinquent teenage boys by having them develop, portray, act out, videotape, and critique brief skits about events relevant to people their age. The trainers were graduate students in psychology whose primary responsibility was to ensure that the skits depicted real-life situations and provided a role for every participant, and that each participant (five boys per group) had an opportunity to act out every role. Relative to matched placebo and attention control groups, those in the treatment group demonstrated significant improvements in social perspective-taking skills. Furthermore, they demonstrated significant reductions in recidivism for a period of 18 months following the intervention.

Although interventions focused on increasing structural–developmental competencies generally have been successful in improving adolescents' abilities to consider the effect of their actions on others, several researchers have questioned whether these abilities themselves are sufficient to foster the development of socially competent behavior (Urbain & Kendall, 1980). For example, it is only too easy to imagine how knowledge about the thoughts and feelings of others could enable an individual to be a more clever delinquent, a possibility that Chandler (1973) has acknowledged. A moral orientation that emphasizes an understanding that it is wrong to harm or hurt others would be likely to enhance the utilization of perspective-taking skills for prosocial ends. However, adolescents must still translate their social–cognitive understanding into specific strategies for making decisions and solving social problems in order to manage their social worlds effectively.

SOCIAL INFORMATION-PROCESSING SKILLS

In contrast to an emphasis on the organization of knowledge seen in structural–developmental models, a somewhat separate line of research has focused on the cognitive processes involved in solving social problems. This type of research has flourished over the past two decades, drawing on an earlier interest in the domain of social intelligence as well as a long tradition of research in impersonal problem solving (Davis, 1966; Newell & Simon, 1972). Instead of treating social competence as a unitary domain (which earlier notions of social intelligence had not been successful in doing), information-processing models conceptualized social competence as dependent on a set of separate yet interrelated skills in processing social information. Two areas of social information processing that are related to adolescent social behavior are interpersonal cognitive problem solving and cognitive self-control.

Interpersonal Cognitive Problem Solving

One of the first theoretical models in this area was articulated by D'Zurilla and Goldfried (1971), who outlined a multistep process of interpersonal cognitive problem solving. According to this model, an individual must first identify a situation as problematic. Second, he or she must generate a variety of possible alternative solutions. Next, the individual must evaluate the consequences of previously generated solutions and decide on an optimal response. Finally, the person must enact the chosen strategy. An individual who was deficient in these cognitive skills was believed to be at risk for a range of psychological problems.

However, D'Zurilla and Goldfried were interested in adult social competence and psychological adjustment and did not address developmental issues nor did they apply their model to children's social behavior. This task was begun in the 1970s by Spivack, Shure, and their colleagues (Shure & Spivack, 1978; Spivack, Platt, & Shure, 1976; Spivack & Shure, 1974). In addition to the skills outlined in D'Zurilla's model (recognizing situations as problematic, generating solutions, articulating consequences, and enacting an optimal strategy), Spivack and Shure emphasized the importance of the child's ability to think through step-by-step means to reach a specific problem-solving goal (means–ends thinking) and to identify causal relations in human motivation (causal thinking).

Developmental studies have demonstrated an increase in social problem-solving skills from childhood through adolescence (Marsh, 1982). Furthermore, numerous studies have found a relation between skill deficits and behavior problems (Richard & Dodge, 1982; Spivack & Shure, 1974). From a developmental perspective, there is some evidence to suggest that, for young children, alternative-solution thinking is the cognitive skill that best predicts behavioral adjustment, and that the remaining cognitive skills gain importance during middle childhood and adolescence (Platt & Spivack, 1973).

Since Spivack and Shure began their intervention research with young children, much of the emphasis of their training programs (and programs that immediately followed) was on improving children's abilities to generate a range of alternative solutions to problematic social situations in order to increase socially competent behavior. However, although some studies reported increases in alternative-solution thinking and corresponding decreases in behavior problems (Spivack & Shure, 1974), other studies failed to confirm these findings (Elardo & Cooper, 1977). More recently, researchers have begun to articulate more elaborate theoretical models that describe how cognition operates to modify behavior in social situations.

For example, based on research with elementary school-age children, Dodge and his colleagues (Dodge, 1980, 1986; Dodge & Coie, 1987; Dodge & Frame, 1982; McFall & Dodge, 1982) have formulated a five-step sequential model of social information processing. According to this model, prior to generating solutions, deciding on an optimal response, and enacting that response (steps 3, 4, and 5), an individual must first encode social cues (step 1) and interpret those cues (step 2). A significant amount of empirical evidence supports the relation between biases and deficits in processing information at some or all of the steps and problem behavior in children, particularly aggression (Dodge & Frame, 1982; Dodge & Newman, 1981; Richard & Dodge, 1982). One of the most frequently replicated findings is the tendency of elementary school-age aggressive children to attribute hostile intent to peers under conditions of ambiguity (Dodge, 1980; Dodge & Coie, 1987; Guerra & Slaby, 1989; Nasby, Hayden, & dePaulo, 1979).

Recent studies have extended these findings to adolescents. For instance, a hostile attributional bias has been found to characterize aggressive and aggressive/delinquent adolescents (Slaby & Guerra, 1988), particularly those delinquents who display interpersonally hostile and angry (i.e., reactive) aggression (Dodge, Price, Bachorowski, & Newman, 1990). Aggressive and aggressive/delinquent adolescents have also been found to be more likely than their less aggressive counterparts to adopt hostile goals, and less likely to seek additional information, generate alternative solutions, choose nonaggressive solutions, and generate consequences for behaving aggressively (Slaby & Guerra, 1988).

Beyond the discrete skills involved in processing social information, attention has been directed toward the general organizations or structures of knowledge that guide such processing. Because of the vast array of information that individuals must process quickly in real-life social encounters, they often make use of shortcuts or heuristics (Kahneman & Tversky, 1973). For instance, Huesmann (1988) has proposed that social behavior is controlled to a great extent by cognitive "scripts" learned during a person's early development. A script is a representation in memory of a specific sequence of actions corresponding to a familiar social event (Schank & Abelson, 1977).

Scripts can serve as guides for behavior to the extent that an individual possesses a stable cognitive representation of the script, enters a social interaction that contains elements evoking the script, and retrieves the script from memory. To illustrate this, one might imagine a teenage girl who frequently gets into arguments with her mother about her choice of friends. She might expect that every time she brings a certain type of friend to her house, her mother will get angry and a fight will ensue. Thus, she has a cognitive representation of an event sequence involving bringing friends to her house when her mother is home. When she enters the context that evokes the script (bringing a new friend home and seeing her mother), the scripted behavior (arguing) may unfold in a somewhat automatic manner.

Unfortunately, relatively little empirical research has investigated the relation between cognitive scripts and children's social behavior. However, the concept of scripts highlights the role of the content of thought as well as the process of thinking in mediating behavior. This focus on the content of thought is consistent with recent studies that have investigated the relation between specific beliefs and social behavior. Of particular relevance to social information processing are beliefs that serve both to motivate and to inhibit social behavior (Bandura, 1986).

For example, a belief that a specific behavior will lead to a desired outcome can serve to motivate a person to behave accordingly. If the belief is strong enough, it may also interfere with consideration of other response options. In the domain of aggressive behavior, aggressive adolescent boys have been found to be more likely than their less aggressive peers to believe that aggression increases status and self-esteem (Bandura, 1973; Slaby & Guerra, 1988). When confronted with a situation in which aggression is a possible response, this belief may motivate aggressive boys to behave aggressively and preclude consideration of other responses and other consequences, particularly when the consequence is highly valued. Teaching these boys merely to generate a variety of nonaggressive responses would be meaningless if they continued to believe that aggression (and only aggression) would lead to a highly desired consequence. Thus, in addition to focusing on the specific cognitive skills involved in social information processing, it is also important to consider how an individual's belief system serves to guide such processing.

Cognitive Self-Control

To the extent that social information processing is aided by the use of cognitive shortcuts or heuristics, individuals should respond to problematic social situations in a relatively automatic fashion. In contrast, under conditions where active social cognition is required (e.g., novel situations) or desired (e.g., interventions designed to alter cognitive scripts), attention must be directed toward the self-control processes that individuals use to regulate cognition and behavior.

Although these self-control processes are clearly related to interpersonal cognitive problem-solving skills, they have frequently been studied separately, partly because an interest in cognitive self-control processes developed from a distinct research tradition in verbal mediation. This research tradition was spearheaded by the work of Luria (1961) and Vygotsky (1962). Luria's work was significant because it highlighted the role of language in regulating overt motor behavior in young children. Vygotsky emphasized the role of internalized "private" speech in the self-regulation of overt behavior. Subsequent empirical evidence indicated that this capacity for private speech develops rapidly during middle childhood (around ages 7 to 10) (for a review, see Kohlberg, Yaeger, & Hjertholm, 1968).

There is also evidence that failure to develop age-appropriate, private, self-guiding speech can lead to behavioral problems such as withdrawal or aggression. For example, elementary school-age aggressive boys have been found to display more immature private speech than their less aggressive counterparts, independent of their verbal intellectual skills (Camp, Blom, Hebert, & Van Doorninck, 1977). Experimentally induced increases in private speech have also been found to relate significantly to improved peer ratings of social status in two isolated third-grade girls (Gottman, Gonso, & Schuler, 1976).

Because of the marked increase in private speech occurring during the early elementary school years, most research has focused on young children. Relatively few studies have investigated the relation between private speech and problem behavior during adolescence. However, drawing on studies that indicate a relation between impulsivity and problem behavior during childhood and adolescence (e.g., Finch & Nelson, 1976), several social–cognitive interventions for adolescents have incorporated self-instructional training methods. These methods (e.g., Meichenbaum & Goodman, 1971) are designed to increase adolescents' use of self-reflective speech to mediate overt behaviors, particularly to inhibit angry or aggressive responses (Feindler, Ecton, Kingsley, & Dubey, 1986; Feindler, Marriott, & Iwata, 1984; Guerra & Slaby, 1990).

Critique of Information-Processing Models

Several important concerns regarding social information-processing models have emerged. One major criticism is that such models are not intrinsically developmental and have not systematically investigated developmental changes. As Dolgin (1986) noted, most studies have investigated age-related differences across relatively narrow age ranges. These age differences generally have been small, but these findings should not be taken as evidence that differences in cognitive capacity across childhood and adolescence are unimportant. Although there may be relatively little change in basic information-processing capacity (Siegler, 1983), there are significant advances in knowledge base, strategy use, cognitive capacities, and metacognitive abilities (Flavell & Wellman, 1977). Furthermore, processes that are highly important at one developmental period may be less significant at other ages.

Another criticism concerns the role of affect in mediating both information processing and behavior. Although an individual's current emotional state typically influences the probability of an affect-consistent response (e.g., being angry would increase the likelihood of an aggressive response; being happy would increase the likelihood of a prosocial response), information-processing skills generally are evaluated without reference to the specific relations between affective and cognitive processes. The work in cognitive self-control is relevant because it highlights the need for affect regulation so that orderly cognitive processing can occur. Nevertheless, social information-processing models generally have not emphasized an integration of affective and cognitive processes.

Finally, investigators have focused on a relatively narrow range of information-processing biases and beliefs that influence social behavior. For example, although aggressive children have been found to display a bias toward attributing hostile intent to others under ambiguous circumstances (Dodge, 1980, 1986), many other biases and beliefs may play an important role in mediating aggressive behavior. In a similar fashion, different sets of biases and beliefs may characterize other types of behavior typical of adolescents, such as risk taking, rebelliousness, and depression. Systematic investigations of the range of cognitive correlates of such behaviors will surely enhance the effectiveness of cognitive–behavioral interventions designed to change such behaviors.

Cognitive–Behavioral Interventions Derived from Social Information-Processing Models

Interventions based on structural–developmental models have focused on facilitating an individual's progression to higher stages of cognitive reasoning; the information-processing approach has relied on training individuals in general cognitive skills for dealing with a range of problematic social situations. The information-processing approach also stands in contrast with social skills training, which often emphasizes the acquisition of discrete behavioral responses in relevant situations (e.g., how to resist peer pressure, how to initiate a conversation).

Social competence during adolescence has been linked with the ability to solve a range of normal everyday problems (Offer, 1969). Similarly, deficits in information-processing skills related to solving interpersonal problems have been linked with adolescent problem behaviors, particularly aggression and delinquency (Dodge et al., 1990; Guerra & Slaby, 1990; Slaby & Guerra, 1988). Most interpersonal cognitive problem-solving interventions have been conducted with elementary school-age children. In general, interventions with adolescents have been conducted with individuals who demonstrate more extreme forms of problem behaviors, typically institutionalized psychiatric patients or incarcerated juvenile delinquents.

For example, Feindler et al. (1986) trained institutionalized psychiatric male adolescents in a range of interpersonal cognitive problem-solving skills, with a particular emphasis on cognitive self-control via self-instructional methods for controlling anger. Following 12 one-hour small-group sessions, treated subjects evidenced decreases in hostile verbalizations during standardized role-play assessments and decreases in aggressive behaviors when compared to a no-treatment control group.

Sarason and Ganzer (1973) provided 14 one-hour sessions to small groups of incarcerated adolescent male delinquents. The focus of the groups was on teaching participants to think about socially appropriate responses to typical problem situations, either through a modeling or group discussion format. Much emphasis was placed on generating alternative solutions and considering consequences. In contrast with a no-treatment control condition, both modeling and discussion groups evidenced more positive attitudes, improvement in social behavior, and lower recidivism for 2 to 3 years following the intervention.

More recently, Guerra and Slaby (1990, 1991) developed a 12-session (one hour per session) social problem-solving intervention for incarcerated male and female adolescent delinquents. The focus of this program was to increase participants' social information-processing skills and to modify beliefs that support the use of aggression across a range of situations. The information-processing skills were derived from Dodge's (1986) 5-step model, with particular emphasis on searching for relevant information prior to making hostile intent attributions. Standard attitude change techniques were used to modify two sets of beliefs: normative beliefs about aggression (e.g., aggression is OK if you just "go crazy" with anger) and response–outcome expectancies (e.g., victims don't suffer). When compared to adolescents in an attention control group, treated youth evidenced gains in social problem-solving skills and decreases in endorsement of beliefs supporting aggression. Furthermore, significant decreases in aggressive, impulsive, and inflexible behavior were found.

In general, one of the driving forces behind cognitive problem-solving interventions has been the belief that training individuals at the level of discrete covert processes that can be applied across a range of social situations will be more likely to "build in" generalization as a part of the treatment (Urbain & Kendall, 1980). Thus, the emphasis has not been on changing "what" the child knows, but on improving "how" he or she comes to know it. However, as Guerra and Slaby (1990) pointed out, the content of thought in the form of an individual's social beliefs is also important in mediating social information processing and influencing social behavior. In particular, research with adolescents has pointed to a range of beliefs about the self (e.g., personal fable), beliefs about others (e.g., imaginary audience), and beliefs about appropriate standards of behavior that should be considered in designing treatment programs to prevent adolescent problem behavior and to foster the development of social competence.

CONCLUSION

Normative cognitive development during adolescence is characterized by specific changes in structural–developmental competencies and information-processing skills. As applied to the social domain, these cognitive changes have a marked influence on the teenager's personal and social worlds. To the extent that adolescent problems and psychopathology are related to developmental lags and maladaptive beliefs, clinical interventions may benefit from the incorporation of specific cognitive–behavioral techniques.

Changes in structural–developmental competencies (i.e., *how* adolescents organize and structure knowledge) are characterized by a shift from concrete to abstract thinking. This transformation is evident in several aspects of the adolescent's intra- and interpersonal understanding. In terms of *self-understanding,* changes are seen in self-definition, personal agency, and public and private self-consciousness. There is a marked shift in self-definition from concrete and physicalistic self-conceptions to subjective and psychological self-conceptions. In addition, adolescents display an intensified striving for a unified self-definition (Bernstein, 1980). There is an increased focus on the powers and limits of personal agency and a corresponding increase in private self-consciousness. This focus on the self also has been linked with tendencies to overestimate one's importance to others (imaginary audience) and to exaggerate one's uniqueness (personal fable).

Changes in interpersonal understanding are characterized by a shift from egocentric thought, whereby others' viewpoints are not understood, toward an increasing ability to consider others' perspectives and to coordinate self and others' perspectives. In the domain of *social perspective taking,* adolescents should now be able to step outside of their own and others' perspectives and assume the role of a neutral third-party observer. In the domain of *moral reasoning,* adolescents are developing the capacity to consider the effects of their actions both on others and on the larger social system.

In addition to structural–developmental competencies, adolescents must translate this social–cognitive understanding into specific information-processing strategies for personal development and social interaction. *Social information-processing skills* have been found to increase with development (Marsh, 1982) and to predict behavioral adjustment. These skills include the ability to search for and interpret social cues, generate alternative solutions, decide on an optimal response, and enact the chosen response in problematic social situations. These skills also rely on a certain degree of *cognitive self-control,* the ability to inhibit hostile or inappropriate social responding.

Adolescent social competence can be promoted by providing activities that foster cognitive development in these areas, in terms of both general enhancement activities and specific clinical interventions. An important focus of such efforts should be on helping adolescents work toward a unified self-definition while becoming less sensitive to both self-doubt and the opinions of others. Understanding the perspective of others can be helpful in establishing meaningful social relationships and in promoting prosocial behavior. Finally, teaching teenagers the cognitive skills necessary to inhibit impulsive behavior and solve social problems can provide a solid foundation for effective social interactions.

REFERENCES

Achenbach, T. M., & Edelbrock, C. S. (1981). Behavioral problems and competencies reported by parents of normal and disturbed children aged four through sixteen. *Monographs of the Society for Research in Child Development, 46,* 1–82.

Anolik, S. A. (1981). Imaginary audience behavior and perceptions of parents among delinquent and nondelinquent adolescents. *Journal of Youth and Adolescence, 10,* 443–454.

Arbuthnot, J., & Faust, D. (1981). *Teaching moral reasoning: Theory and practice.* New York: Harper & Row.

Arbuthnot, J., & Gordon, D. A. (1986). Behavioral and cognitive effects of a moral reasoning development intervention for high-risk behavior-disordered adolescents. *Journal of Consulting and Clinical Psychology, 54,* 208–216.

Baldwin, J. M. (1906). *Social and ethical interpretations in mental development.* New York: Macmillan.

Bandura, A. (1973). *Aggression: A social learning analysis.* Englewood Cliffs, NJ: Prentice-Hall.

Bandura, A. (1986). *Social foundations of thought and action.* Englewood Cliffs, NJ: Prentice-Hall.

Bandura, A. (1989). Human agency in social cognitive theory. *American Psychologist, 44,* 1175–1184.

Barenboim, C. (1980). The development of person perception in childhood and adolescence: From behavioral comparisons to psychological constructs to psychological comparisons. *Child Development, 52,* 129–144.

Bear, G. G., & Richards, H. C. (1981). Moral reasoning and conduct problems in the classroom. *Journal of Educational Psychology, 73,* 644–670.

Bernstein, R. M. (1980). The development of the self-system during adolescence. *Journal of Genetic Psychology, 136,* 231–245.

Blasi, A. (1980). Bridging moral cognition and moral action: A critical review of the literature. *Psychological Bulletin, 88,* 1–45.

Brion-Meisels, S., & Selman, R. (1984). Early adolescent development of new interpersonal strategies: Understanding and intervention. *School Psychology Review, 13,* 278–291.

Camp, B. W., Blom, G. E., Hebert, F., & Van Doorninck, W. J. (1977). "Think Aloud": A program for developing self-control in young aggressive boys. *Journal of Abnormal Child Psychology, 5,* 157–169.

Carver, C. S., & Scheier, M. F. (1981). *Attention and self-regulation: A control-theory approach to human behavior.* New York: Springer-Verlag.

Chandler, M. (1973). Egocentrism and antisocial behavior: The assessment and training of social perspective-taking skills. *Developmental Psychology, 9,* 326–332.

Clarke, G., & Lewinsohn, P. M. (1989). The coping with depression course: A group psychoeducational intervention for unipolar depression. *Behaviour Change, 6,* 54–69.

Cochrane, D. B., & Manley-Casimir, M. (1980). *Development of moral reasoning: Practice approaches.* New York: Praeger.

Damon, W. (1983). The nature of social–cognitive change in the developing child. In W. F. Overton (Ed.), *The relationship between social and cognitive development* (pp. 103–141). Hillsdale, NJ: Erlbaum.

Damon, W., & Hart, D. (1982). The development of self-understanding from infancy through adolescence. *Child Development, 53,* 841–864.

Davis, G. (1966). Current status of research and theory in human problem-solving. *Psychological Bulletin, 66,* 36–54.

Dodge, K. A. (1980). Social cognition and children's aggressive behavior. *Child Development, 51,* 162–170.

Dodge, K. A. (1986). A social information-processing model of social competence in children. In M. Perlmutter (Ed.), *Minnesota symposia on child psychology: Vol. 18* (pp. 77–125). Hillsdale, NJ: Erlbaum.

Dodge, K. A., & Coie, J. D. (1987). Social information-processing factors in reactive and proactive aggression in children's peer groups. *Journal of Personality and Social Psychology, 53,* 1146–1158.

Dodge, K. A., & Crick, N. R. (1990). Social information-processing bases of aggressive behavior in children. *Personality and Social Psychology Bulletin, 16,* 8–22.

Dodge, K. A., & Frame, C. M. (1982). Social cognitive biases and deficits in aggressive boys. *Child Development, 53,* 620–635.

Dodge, K. A., & Newman, J. P. (1981). Biased decision-making processes in aggressive boys. *Journal of Abnormal Psychology, 90,* 375–379.

Dodge, K. A., Price, J. M., Bachorowski, J., & Newman, J. P. (1990). Hostile attributional biases in severely aggressive adolescents. *Journal of Abnormal Psychology, 99,* 385–392.

Dolgin, K. G. (1986). Needed steps for social competence: Strengths and present limitations of Dodge's model. In M. Perlmutter (Ed.), *Minnesota symposia on child psychology: Vol. 18* (pp. 127–135). Hillsdale, NJ: Erlbaum.

D'Zurilla, T. J., & Goldfried, M. R. (1971). Problem-solving and behavior modification. *Journal of Abnormal Psychology, 78,* 107–126.

Eisenberg-Berg, N. (1979). Development of children's prosocial moral judgment. *Developmental Psychology, 15,* 128–137.

Elardo, P. T., & Cooper, M. (1977). *Project AWARE: A handbook for teachers.* Menlo Park, CA: Addison-Wesley.

Elkind, D. (1967). Egocentrism in adolescence. *Child Development, 38,* 1025–1034.

Elkind, D. (1974). Recent research on cognitive development in adolescence. In S. E. Dragastin & G. H. Elder, Jr. (Eds.), *Adolescence in the life cycle: Psychological change and social context* (pp. 49–61). Washington, DC: Hemisphere.

Elkind, D., & Bowen, R. (1979). Imaginary audience behavior in children and adolescents. *Developmental Psychology, 15,* 38–44.

Erikson, E. (1968). *Identity: Youth and crisis.* New York: Norton.

Eron, L. (1987). The development of aggressive behavior from the perspective of a developing behaviorism. *American Psychologist, 42,* 435–442.

Faust, D., & Arbuthnot, J. (1978). Relationship between moral and Piagetian reasoning and the effectiveness of moral education. *Developmental Psychology, 14,* 435–436.

Feffer, M. (1970). A developmental analysis of interpersonal behavior. *Psychological Review, 77,* 197–214.

Feindler, E. L. (1987). Clinical issues and recommendations in adolescent anger-control training. *Journal of Child and Adolescent Psychotherapy, 4,* 267–274.

Feindler, E. L., Ecton, R. B., Kingsley, D., & Dubey, D. R. (1986). Group anger-control training for institutionalized psychiatric male adolescents. *Behavior Therapy, 17,* 109–123.

Feindler, E. L., Marriott, S. A., & Iwata, M. (1984). Group anger control training for junior high school delinquents. *Cognitive Therapy and Research, 8,* 299–311.

Fenigstein, A. (1979). Self-consciousness, self-attention, and social interaction. *Journal of Personality and Social Psychology, 37,* 75–86.

Ferguson, T. J., & Rule, B. G. (1980). Effects of inferential set, outcome, severity, and basis for responsibility on children's evaluations of aggressive acts. *Developmental Psychology, 16,* 141–146.

Finch, A. J., Jr., & Nelson, W. M. (1976). Reflection–impulsivity and behavior problems in emotionally disturbed boys. *Journal of Genetic Psychology, 128,* 271–274.

Flavell, J. H. (1985). *Cognitive development.* Englewood Cliffs, NJ: Prentice-Hall.

Flavell, J. H., & Wellman, H. M. (1977). Metamemory. In R. V. Kail, Jr., & J. W. Hagen (Eds.), *Perspectives on the development of memory and cognition.* Hillsdale, NJ: Erlbaum.

Gilligan, C. (1977). In a different voice: Women's conceptions of the self and morality. *Harvard Educational Review, 47,* 481–517.

Gilligan, C. (1982). *In a different voice: Psychological theory and women's development.* Cambridge, MA: Harvard University Press.

Gottman, J., Gonso, J., & Schuler, P. (1976). Teaching social skills to isolated children. *Journal of Abnormal Child Psychology, 4,* 179–197.

Greenberger, E. (1984). Defining psychosocial maturity in adolescence. In P. Karoly & J. Steffen (Eds.), *Adolescent behavior disorders: Foundations and contemporary concerns* (pp. 54–81). Lexington, MA: Heath.

Guerra, N. G. (1989). Consequential thinking and self-reported delinquency in high school youth. *Criminal Justice and Behavior, 16,* 440–454.

Guerra, N. G., Huesmann, L. R., & Zelli, A. (1990). Attributions for social failure and aggression in incarcerated delinquent youth. *Journal of Abnormal Child Psychology, 18,* 347–356.

Guerra, N. G., & Slaby, R. G. (1989). Evaluative factors in social problem solving by aggressive boys. *Journal of Abnormal Child Psychology, 17,* 277–289.

Guerra, N. G., & Slaby, R. G. (1990). Cognitive mediators of aggression in adolescent offenders: 2. Intervention. *Developmental Psychology, 26,* 269–277.

Guerra, N. G., & Slaby, R. G. (1991). *Viewpoints: A cognitive–behavioral training program for aggressive adolescents.* Manuscript submitted for publication.

Hains, A. A., & Hains, A. H. (1988). Cognitive behavioral training of problem-solving and impulse-control with delinquent adolescents. *Journal of Offender Counseling, Services, & Rehabilitation, 12,* 95–113.

Harter, S. (1983). Developmental perspectives on the self-system. In E. M. Hetherington (Ed.), *Handbook of child psychology: Vol. 4, Socialization, personality, and social development* (pp. 275–386). New York: Wiley.

Holstein, C. B. (1976). Irreversible, stepwise sequence in the development of moral judgment: A longitudinal study of males and females. *Child Development, 47,* 51–61.

Huesmann, L. R. (1988). An information-processing model for the development of aggression. *Aggressive Behavior, 14,* 13–24.

Huesmann, L. R., Guerra, N. G., Miller, L., & Zelli, A. (1990, June). *Mitigating the development of aggression in young children by changing their cognitions.* Paper presented at the International Society for Research on Aggression, Banff, Alberta, Canada.

Jurkovic, G. J. (1980). The juvenile delinquent as a moral philosopher: A structural–developmental perspective. *Psychological Bulletin, 88,* 709–727.

Kahneman, D., & Tversky, A. (1973). On the psychology of prediction. *Psychological Review, 80,* 237–251.

Keating, D. P., & Clark, L. V. (1980). Development of physical and social reasoning in adolescence. *Developmental Psychology, 16,* 23–30.

Kohlberg, L. (1969). Stage and sequence: The cognitive–developmental approach to socialization. In D. A. Goslin (Ed.), *Handbook of socialization theory and research* (pp. 347–480). Chicago: Rand McNally.

Kohlberg, L., & Kramer, R. B. (1969). Continuities and discontinuities in childhood and adult moral development. *Human Development, 12,* 93–120.

Kohlberg, L., Yaeger, J., & Hjertholm, E. (1968). Private speech: Four studies and a review of theories. *Child Development, 39,* 691–736.

Kuhn, D. (1976). Short-term longitudinal evidence for the sequentiality of Kohlberg's early stages of moral judgments. *Developmental Psychology, 12,* 162–166.

Larson, S., & Kurdek, L. A. (1979). Intratask and intertask consistency of moral judgment indices in first-, third-, and fifth-grade children. *Developmental Psychology, 15,* 462–463.

Lee, L. C. (1971). The concomitant development of cognitive and moral modes of thought: A test of selected deductions from Piaget's theory. *Genetic Psychology Monographs, 83,* 93–146.

Luria, A. (1961). *The role of speech in the regulation of normal and abnormal behaviors.* New York: Liveright.

Marcia, J. E. (1980). Identity in adolescence. In J. Adelson (Ed.), *Handbook of adolescent psychology.* New York: Wiley.

Marsh, D. T. (1982). The development of interpersonal problem-solving among elementary-school children. *Journal of Genetic Psychology, 140,* 107–118.

McFall, R. M., & Dodge, K. A. (1982). Self-management and interpersonal skills learning. In P. Karoly & H. Kanfer (Eds.), *Self-management and behavior change: From theory to practice* (pp. 353–392). Elmsford, NY: Pergamon Press.

Mead, G. H. (1934). *Mind, self, and society.* Chicago: University of Chicago Press.

Meichenbaum, D., & Goodman, J. (1971). Training impulsive children to talk to themselves: A means of developing self-control. *Journal of Abnormal Psychology, 77,* 115–126.

Montemayor, R., & Eisen, M. (1977). The development of self-conceptions from childhood to adolescence. *Developmental Psychology, 13,* 314–319.

Nasby, W., Hayden, B., & dePaulo, B. M. (1979). Attributional bias among aggressive boys to interpret unambiguous social stimuli as displays of hostility. *Journal of Abnormal Child Psychology, 89,* 459–468.

Newell, A., & Simon, H. A. (1972). *Human problem solving.* Englewood Cliffs, NJ: Prentice-Hall.

O'Brien, S. F., & Bierman, K. L. (1988). Conceptions and perceived influence of peer groups: Interviews with preadolescents and adolescents. *Child Development, 59,* 1360–1365.

Offer, D. (1969). *The psychological world of the teenager.* New York: Basic Books.

Perry, D. G., Perry, L. C., & Rasmussen, P. R. (1986). Cognitive social learning mediators of aggression. *Child Development, 57,* 700–711.

Peterson, C. (1982). The imaginary audience and age, cognition, and dating. *Journal of Genetic Psychology, 140,* 317–318.

Piaget, J. (1965). *The moral judgment of the child.* New York: Free Press. (Original work published 1932.)

Platt, J. J., & Spivack, G. (1973). Studies in problem-solving thinking of psychiatric patients: Patient-control differences and factorial structure of problem-solving thinking. *Proceedings of the 81st Annual Convention of the American Psychological Association, 8,* 461–462.

Rest, J. R. (1973). The hierarchical nature of moral judgment: A study of patterns of comprehension and preference of moral stages. *Journal of Personality, 41,* 86–109.

Reynolds, W. M., & Coats, K. I. (1986). A comparison of cognitive–behavioral therapy and relaxation training for the treatment of depression in adolescents. *Journal of Consulting and Clinical Psychology, 54,* 653–660.

Richard, B. A., & Dodge, K. A. (1982). Social maladjustment and problem solving in school-aged children. *Journal of Consulting and Clinical Psychology, 50,* 226–233.

Rothbaum, F., & Weisz, J. R. (1989). *Child psychopathology and the quest for control.* Newbury Park, CA: Sage.

Rubin, K. H., & Krasnor, L. R. (1986). Social–cognitive and social–behavioral perspectives on problem solving. In M. Perlmutter (Ed.),

Minnesota symposia on child psychology: Vol. 18 (pp. 1–68). Hillsdale, NJ: Erlbaum.

Sarason, C. U., & Ganzer, V. J. (1973). Modeling and group discussion in the rehabilitation of juvenile delinquents. *Journal of Counseling Psychology, 20,* 442–449.

Schank, R. C., & Abelson, R. (1977). *Scripts, plans, goals and understanding.* Hillsdale, NJ: Erlbaum.

Secord, P., & Peevers, B. (1974). The development and attribution of person concepts. In T. Mischel (Ed.), *Understanding other persons.* Oxford: Blackwell.

Selman, R. (1971). The relation of role-taking to the development of moral judgment in children. *Child Development, 42,* 79–91.

Selman, R. (1976). Toward a structural analysis of developing interpersonal relations concepts: Research with normal and disturbed preadolescent boys. In A. Pick (Ed.), *Tenth annual symposium on child psychology.* Minneapolis: University of Minnesota Press.

Selman, R. (1980). *The growth of interpersonal understanding.* New York: Academic Press.

Selman, R., Brion-Meisels, S., & Lavin, D. (1982). Troubled children's use of self-reflection. In F. Serafica (Ed.), *Social cognitive development in context* (pp. 62–99). New York: Guilford Press.

Selman, R., & Byrne, D. F. (1974). A structural-developmental analysis of levels of role-taking in middle childhood. *Child Development, 45,* 803–806.

Selman, R., & Demorest, A. (1984). Observing troubled children's interpersonal negotiation strategies: Implications of and for a developmental model. *Child Development, 55,* 288–304.

Shantz, C. U. (1975). The development of social cognition. In E. M. Hetherington (Ed.), *Review of child development research, Vol. 5.* Chicago: University of Chicago Press.

Shure, M. B., & Spivack, G. (1978). *Problem-solving techniques in childrearing.* San Francisco, CA: Jossey-Bass.

Siegler, R. (1983). Information processing approaches to development. In J. H. Flavell & E. M. Markman (Eds.), *Cognitive development: Vol. 3.* In P. Mussen (Ed.), *Carmichael's manual of child psychology* (4th ed.). New York: Wiley.

Slaby, R. G., & Guerra, N. G. (1988). Cognitive mediators of aggression in adolescent offenders: 1. Assessment. *Developmental Psychology, 24,* 580–588.

Spivack, G., Platt, J. J., & Shure, M. B. (1976). *The problem-solving approach to adjustment.* San Francisco, CA: Jossey-Bass.

Spivack, G., & Shure, M. B. (1974). *Social adjustment of young children: A cognitive approach to solving real-life problems.* San Francisco, CA: Jossey-Bass.

Tomlinson-Keasey, C., & Keasey, C. B. (1974). The mediating role of cognitive development in moral judgment. *Child Development, 45,* 291–298.

Turiel, E. (1978). Social regulations and domains of social concepts. *New directions for child development, 1,* 45–75.

Turiel, E. (1982). *The development of social knowledge.* New York: Cambridge University Press.

Urbain, E. S., & Kendall, P. C. (1980). Review of social–cognitive problem-solving interventions with children. *Psychological Bulletin, 88,* 109–143.

Vygotsky, L. S. (1962). *Thought and language.* Cambridge, MA: MIT Press.

Walker, L. (1980). Cognitive and perspective-taking prerequisites for moral development. *Child Development, 51,* 131–139.

Wicklund, R. A. (1975). Objective self-awareness. In R. L. Berkowitz (Ed.), *Advances in experimental social psychology: Vol. 8* (pp. 233–277). New York: Academic Press.

Wilkes, T. C., & Rush, A. J. (1988). Adaptations of cognitive therapy for depressed adolescents. *Journal of the American Academy of Child and Adolescent Psychiatry, 27,* 381–386.

Winnett, R. L., Bornstein, P. H., Cogswell, K. A., & Paris, A. E. (1987). Cognitive–behavioral therapy for childhood depression: A levels-of-treatment approach. *Journal of Child and Adolescent Psychotherapy, 4,* 283–286.

Wood, M. E. (1978). Children's developing understanding of other people's motives for behavior. *Developmental Psychology, 14,* 561–562.

Wylie, R. C. (1979). *The self concept: Theory and research on selected topics: Vol. 2* (rev. ed.). Lincoln: University of Nebraska Press.

CHAPTER 4

The Psychological Significance of Others in Adolescence: Issues for Study and Intervention

ROBERT M. GALATZER-LEVY and BERTRAM J. COHLER

From the outset, the contribution of psychoanalysis to the study of the adolescent decade has been marked by controversy. From Freud's first detailed statement regarding the psychobiological changes accompanying adolescence in the "Three Essays on the Theory of Sexuality (1905a)" and his study of an 18-year-old adolescent girl in the case of "Dora" (1905b), application of classical psychoanalytic perspectives to the study of the adolescent decade suggested the significance of presumed biological changes as the primary factors leading to increased libidinal intensity, enhanced effort to rework the infantile neurosis marking the transition from early to middle childhood, and the inherent psychological conflict believed to mark the adolescent decade (P. Blos, 1967, 1989; Deutsch, 1967; A. Freud, 1936, 1965).

Contemporary perspectives (Brooks-Gunn & Petersen, 1984; Csikszentmihalyi & Larson, 1984; Offer, Offer & Ostrov, 1975; Offer, Ostrov & Howard, 1981; Petersen, 1988; Petersen & Taylor, 1980) question the significance of this emphasis on adolescence as a time of turmoil engendered largely by maturational forces. This more traditional view does not acknowledge the interplay of experience and biology across the course of development; just as maturational factors may influence experience of self and others, experience influences these same maturational forces. Further, the drive perspective regarding psychological development across the adolescent decade makes assumptions regarding the significance of the concept of drive in psychoanalysis that have been challenged by contemporary reconsideration of Freud's metapsychology (Galatzer-Levy & Cohler, 1990a; Swanson, 1977; Wallerstein, 1977). Focus on conflict, including drive alteration associated with pubertal development, appears to provide rather limited understanding of personality development and change across the years of adolescence.

In the first place, questions have been raised from within psychoanalysis itself, regarding the significance of drive theory for understanding personality. Clinical and counted-data approaches to the study of pubertal development have questioned Freud's initial formulation regarding the interplay of hormonal changes and both personality and behavior during adolescence (Petersen, 1988). In the second place, traditional libidinal perspectives do not allow recognition of the complex interplay between person and society that is so evident in adolescence (Csikszentmihalyi & Larson, 1984; Dornbusch, 1989). Finally, this perspective on the adolescent decade fails to recognize the manner in which, across the course of life, persons make psychological use of others in the maintenance of morale and the preservation of a sense of personal consistency and integration. Indeed, although recognizing the significance of such factors as sexuality, even sexual gratification must be understood as related to the place of the real (or imagined) partner for the experience of vitality and continuity of self.

This chapter explores the additional contributions toward study and intervention across the adolescent decade that have been realized, within psychoanalysis, from a shift of emphasis on the self, as exemplified by such theorists as Winnicott (1953, 1960/1965, 1988), Khan (1963/1974a, 1964/1974b), Sander (1962, 1969, 1975), Stechler and Kaplan (1980), Stern (1985, 1989), G. Klein (1976), and Heinz Kohut and his associates (Kohut, 1971, 1975/1985, 1977, 1984; Kohut & Wolf, 1978). This chapter reviews the concept of self and the psychologically essential other within contemporary psychoanalysis; considers normative and clinical study from the perspective of this psychology of self; and discusses the significance of psychology of the self, additionally informed by normative study of self in adolescence, in constructing a psychoanalytically informed approach to intervention across the adolescent decade.

PSYCHOANALYSIS, SUBJECTIVITY, AND THE SELF

Shifting perspectives regarding psychoanalytic study of adolescence parallel changes more generally in the application of psychoanalysis to the study of motivation and psychological development (Cohler, 1987, 1989; Galatzer-Levy & Cohler, 1990b). Careful study of the influences on Freud's early work, prior to the early 1890s, when Freud first began to explore the concept of motivated awareness, suggests that the works of Charles Darwin, James Hughlings Jackson (an English neurologist), and Ernest Hackel (a German biologist) were formative intellectual influences governing his approach to study of mental life quite apart from his clinically/observationally founded study of intention as realized in word and deed (Bernfeld, 1941, 1951; Jackson, 1969; Ritvo, 1990; Stengel, 1963; Sulloway, 1979).

From Neuroscience to Study of Subjectivity in Psychoanalysis

Drawing largely on his early neuroscience study, Freud sought to extend the philosophy of science derived from the emerging physiological psychology pioneered by Helmholtz and Brücke to study of mental life through the construction of a "metapsychology" referring to a "realm beyond consciousness" (Freud, 1898/1985a). This metapsychology—deliberately a play on Aristotle's discussion of metaphysics, which Freud had read with Brentano in 1873–1874 (Bernfeld, 1951)—initially had three defining points of view referring to intensity, direction, and expenditure of force (Freud, 1915/1958). These defining perspectives were later expanded by Rapaport and Gill (1959) to include both genetic (past coequal in the present) and (reality) adaptive perspectives as well as those earlier postulated to refer to drive.[1] Particularly in the United States after the Second World War, following the logic of positive science inspired by Karl Popper (1959) and the methods of experimental psychology, research programs were undertaken at the Menninger Foundation, Yale University, New York University, and elsewhere, devoted to "empirical" tests of metapsychological

---

[1]Freud was acutely aware of both the promise and problems inherent in the construction of a general theory of motivation. Indeed, citing Goethe, as he frequently did at times when he found himself at the limits of his understanding, he observed (1937/1964, p. 225):

> [If] we are asked by what methods and means [the instinct is brought into the harmony of the ego] we can only say: "We must call the witch to our help after all"—the witch metapsychology. Without metapsychological speculation and theorizing—I had almost said "phantasying"—we shall not get another step forward.

points of view (Gardner, Holzman, Klein, Linton, & Spence, 1959; Gardner, Jackson, & Messick, 1960; G. Klein, 1970; Rapaport, 1961/1967a, 1960/1967b). With few exceptions, this research program has contributed little of significance in understanding wish and intent, beyond the contributions from general experimental psychology (Fisher & Greenberg, 1977, 1978; G. Klein, 1976).

In a series of cogent, carefully argued essays posthumously published, George Klein (1976) reviewed the contributions of metapsychology, including its most recent reincarnation as ego psychology. Klein suggested that all of the ego functions carefully delineated by Rapaport, Hartmann, and their colleagues could be more parsimoniously understood as basic psychological processes that have long been the province of experimental psychology and are most appropriately studied using traditional laboratory procedures. Reviewing the current status of ego psychology, Klein concluded that it was little more than a catalog of functions and mechanisms in no way different from the mechanistic psychology that Freud initially eschewed. Further, assumptions of a now discredited drive psychology (Wallerstein, 1977) are hidden within implicit assumptions prevalent in ego psychology. Klein suggested that ego psychology straddles concepts of explanation and mechanism and fails to provide an adequate basis for a psychoanalytic theory of motivation. As Klein (1976) observed:

Freud's metapsychology is not distinctively psychoanalytic. Moreover, it reduces human behavior to a conceptual domain which requires a kind of observational datum different from that available in the analytic situation . . . metapsychology throws overboard the fundamental intent of the psychoanalytic enterprise—that of unlocking meanings. (p. 49)

Gill (1976) made the same point regarding metapsychology, noting the extent to which Freud's metapsychology is neither science nor psychology. Indeed, reflecting "unbridled speculation" (p. 102), Gill maintained that metapsychology has no place within psychoanalysis as a psychology of intention. As Klein (1976) noted:

It was the genius of Freud that brought [problems of meaning] back squarely into the psychologists' concern; he developed a taxonomy and a code for deciphering the meanings of personal relationships in their conscious and unconscious aspects. Psychoanalysis imputes meaning to behavior by showing the significance of myth in our life, those inner phantoms of fantasy which render objects significant, and which lead us to establish and react to relationships. (p. 53)

Klein referred to this contribution of psychoanalysis to experience-near study of wish and intent as the "clinical" theory, and contrasted this clinical theory with metapsychology or psychoanalysis as a general psychology. Holzman (1985), Wallerstein (1986, 1987), and others criticizing this renewed emphasis on the clinical theory have lamented Klein's distinction between this clinical theory, which they understand to refer to "curative" aspects of the psychoanalytic process itself, and the ego-psychological perspective on psychoanalysis as a general psychology with broad explanatory power in the study of human behavior.

Critics of Klein's distinction between these two types of theory in psychoanalysis misunderstand the concept of "clinical" as used by Klein in his portrayal of the clinical theory within psychoanalysis, and disregard his detailed critique of the concept of theory as used within both ego psychology and psychoanalysis more generally. Klein and others have questioned the value of psychoanalysis understood as a general psychology (Gill, 1976; Klein, 1976; Ricoeur, 1977; Schafer, 1976, 1983). Klein (1976) observed not only that ego psychology is little more than general experimental psychology, but also that the premier contribution of psychoanalysis concerns study of meanings as enacted in the relationship between analysand and analyst. These enactments, together with the means used by persons in order to protect themselves against enhanced awareness, are accessible to systematic study (Edelson, 1988).

It is important to differentiate between Klein's concept of "clinical" theory, as contrasted with metapsychology and "theory of technique," or technical strategies for intervention within psychoanalysis and psychodynamic psychotherapy as practiced by the journeyman therapist. While acting in the analysand's best interests in the conduct of practice, the therapist's focus on technique has little relevance to the clinical theory within psychoanalysis, which is concerned with the "experience-near" perspective for study and makes use of evidence obtained from the experience of enactments within the psychoanalytic setting, as contrasted with the "experience-distant" realm of the psychological experiment. Evidence obtained from the experience-near realm involves such issues as those means characteristically used to protect oneself against painful feelings, and the nature of attributions of others, enacted anew between analyst and analysand. No other forum except the clinical interview (and the analogous structure of the life-history research interview) is able to provide this unique information regarding lives over time.

Gill (1976), Klein (1976), and Galatzer-Levy and Cohler (1990a) have shown that it is important to differentiate between Freud's scientific world-view, reflected in metapsychology, and clinically informed and detailed observations regarding wish and intent, reflected in meanings attributed to a person and an event. Although some critics within psychoanalysis (Holzman, 1985; Wallerstein, 1986, 1987) have called this approach anti-intellectual, half a century of study devoted to advocacy of psychoanalysis as a general psychology has shown the limitations inherent in the view of psychoanalysis as a natural science. Indeed, Freud's particular understanding regarding the foundations of explicitly stated intents in implicit wishes has played a central role both in psychology and the arts and sciences more generally. Galatzer-Levy and Cohler (1990a) have suggested that Freud's adherence to this scientism was principally a statement of his intellectual world-view rather than a substantive contribution to understanding intention.

Clarification regarding the nature of Freud's contributions to the study of lives has emerged in tandem with two other intellectual currents within the human sciences: (a) a concern with the means by which persons make meanings in their own lives, including attributions regarding the psychological significance of others; and (b) an accompanying focus on the study of person or self rather than of function or mechanism, in understanding continuity and change in lives over time. Focus on intersubjectivity (Stern, 1985) and on study of self and personal integrity has emerged and reflects increasing appreciation of what Klein (1976) labeled the "clinical" theory within psychoanalysis.

Empathy and Intersubjectivity

Freud's metapsychology—and the effort at construction of a general psychology on which it is based—reflects Freud's scientific world-view and is largely lacking in content (Galatzer-Levy & Cohler, 1990a; Gill, 1976; Klein, 1976). The findings claimed to issue out of this scientific world-view may be accounted for largely in terms of experimental psychology (Klein, 1976): psychoanalytic explanations do not add to these findings a significance beyond that provided by experimental and developmental psychology. Indeed, these normative contributions reflect what Kohut (1959/1978, 1971, 1977) termed the contradiction between experience-distant and experience-near perspectives. The experience-distant perspective is based on observation apart from the meaning of the relationship between observer and observed; the experience-near perspective focuses on the joint construction of meaning among the participants.

This experience-near realm has been portrayed by Trevarthan (1980, 1989; Trevarthan & Hubley, 1978), Atwood and Stolorow (1984), Stolorow, Brandcraft, and Atwood (1987), and Stern (1985) as intersubjectivity. Atwood and Stolorow (1984) observed that inclusion of the different worlds of observer and observed within a common frame of reference provides both a unique opportunity for psychoanalytic study of social life and a bridge between the intrapersonal and the interpersonal. Following Trevarthan and Hubley (1978) and Trevarthan (1989), Stern (1985) further noted that the effort to share experiences regarding events and things—shown by joint attention, shared intention, and affective states' interaffectivity—reflects an essential task of development and leads to emergence of the capacity for relatedness over the first year of life. Realization of enhanced intersubjectivity not only facilitates completion of psychological development, but also is essential as the foundation of empathy, or the capacity for social understanding as reflected both in normative study and the psychoanalytic process.

Based both on developmental study and clinical observation, Stern (1985, 1989) posited that the child's "subjective experience of the observable event" (1985, p. 119) results from the unique life-experiences of each partner in the relationship. These experiences start at birth and occur as short-lived episodes of assistance with regulation and attunement. By the second half of the first year of life, the caretaker and the child have fashioned a relationship based on reciprocally shared intents and feelings. Attunement permits the baby to match his or her own state with that of others, providing the foundation for the subsequent capacity to both use the care provided by others and offer care to other persons.

Stern's study of the development of intersubjectivity was consistent with Winnicott's (1953, 1960/1965) observation that children create an intermediate, transitional space between self and caretaker which, over time, increases the child's capacity for self-regulation. Stern's study was also consistent with the formulations of psychological development posited by Kohut and his colleagues, suggesting that infants experience the caretaker's regulation of their inner states in the same manner in which they experience self-regulation (Cohler, 1980). Stern described a matrix of reciprocity that enhances self-regulation and is concerned less with the child–caretaker tie than with the child's *experience* of the relationship and its connection with the capacity for self-regulation, vitality, and creativity (G. Klein, 1976; Sander, 1975; Stechler & Kaplan, 1980; Winnicott, 1953).

Kohut (1959/1978, 1971, 1977) maintained that psychoanalysis represents a mode of study using the method of empathy, or vicarious introspection, which may be contrasted with the experience-distant mode of experimental laboratory study. In the experience-near mode, the observer uses his or her own psychological processes in understanding the other from *within* the field of observation that constitutes the observer and the observed; in the experience-distant mode, this "inappropriate" method is ruled out in favor of a perspective from without this relationship. As Kohut (1975/1985) observed, the issue is not whether these observations are at some point transformed into counted data but the perspective from which these observations are carried out.

CLINICAL PSYCHOANALYTIC THEORY AND STUDY OF THE SELF

Accompanying clarification of the place of metapsychology within psychoanalysis, there has been renewed interest in both the clinical theory and the experiential world within psychoanalysis. This shift may be observed in the current interest in the concept of "self" within psychoanalysis. Most recently associated with the work of Kohut and his associates (Kohut, 1971, 1977, 1984; Kohut & Wolf, 1978; Wolf,

1988), this particular study of the sense of personal integrity is but one of several approaches within psychoanalysis that are concerned with persons and lives rather than with functions and mechanisms (Khan, 1963/1974b; Klein, 1976; Winnicott, 1953, 1960).

Psychoanalytic Perspectives on the Self

Bettelheim (1983) observed that much of the problem with psychoanalysis, including the earlier shift away from study of experience, is founded in the translation itself, including Strachey and Jones's preference for the experience-distant Latinate term *ego* rather than the more introspective and experience-near term *I* as the best translation of the German term *Ich*. Kernberg (1982) supports the Editors of the *Standard Edition,* but others have argued that self may be a better translation for this term than ego (Gedo, 1979; Hartmann, 1950; Kernberg, 1982; Laplanche & Pontalis, 1973; Meissner, 1986; Richards, 1982a,b). The Editors of the *Standard Edition* (Strochey & Editors, 1921/1961, p. 8; 1923/1955, pp. 7–8) noted that they sometimes rendered *Ich* as self, in an effort to distinguish Freud's different uses of the term. Schafer's (1976, 1980, 1983) concept of the active self may be more consistent with Freud's thinking than the terms employed in the *Standard Edition.*

The Self

The concept of ego development is subtly merged into issues of the self and identity in adolescence. Contemporary psychoanalysis recognizes three distinct concepts—ego, identity, and self—which have been used in overlapping fashion. In contemporary usage, the ego refers to that part of the psychic organization that functions to regulate and integrate the various internal and external forces that are operative on the individual, including processes of knowing about, acting on, and protecting against the internal and external worlds. Identity refers to the experience of who one is in the world. It is the internal experience corresponding to the social role. It need not be the same as the social roles that others define. The nature of identity is highly dependent on the individual's society. For example, in some societies, ancestry is a very important aspect of identity; in others, it is unimportant.

The self is a more problematic concept. Initially conceptualized as a mental representation of one's own person in its various dimensions (Hartmann, 1939/1958, 1950), the term self has been variously used to describe the core experience of one's own being (Khan, 1963/1974b, 1964/1974a; Winnicott, 1953, 1960/1965) and to characterize that part of the person in which continuity over time and space results in a feeling of intactness and being a person.[2] Problems in the large social psychological and psychoanalytic literature concerned with the concept of self reflect both the subtlety and the importance of this problem. Kohut (1984) reiterated that his concept of the self was based on what he believed to be an immediately available experience of being or having a self.

The difficulty of achieving conceptually clear separation of these three concepts (ego, identity, and self) calls attention to their intimate interconnection in psychological reality. Bettelheim (1983), among others, observed that Freud's vigorous German prose incorporated images that are much closer to affective experience than the language his translators used in the *Standard Edition.* Freud's *"das Ich,"*—literally, "the I"—became a new English technical term, "the ego." Freud's original language evokes a far wider and more ambiguous group of ideas than his translators' language. In particular, it summons images from all three concepts—ego, identity, and self. Clinically, Federn (1926, 1928, 1934, 1943) was the first to observe the intimate interconnection of

---

[2] We will not review here the extremely large literature on the concept of self in psychoanalysis and its relationship to concepts in the social sciences, human development, religion, and literature. However, it should be observed that concepts of the self and attempts to understand the core nature of the referent of terms like self, soul, and first-person pronouns has been the subject of wide-ranging discourse in widely dispersed cultures for at least four millennia.

disturbed ego functions and self-feeling. In psychotic disorders, the interconnection among disturbed self-representation, disturbed object relations, and disturbances of ego function has been well documented in a large variety of contexts (Kernberg, 1975, 1982, 1988). However, the question of the primacy of these aspects of personality, together with their interrelationship, is the subject of continuing debate.

Other attempts to connect the experience of self-pathology, ego dysfunction, and disturbed identity have consistently demonstrated close correlations among these aspects of the personality, but have failed to provide convincing explanations for this correlation. For example, Kernberg (1975, 1988) proposed that people who are confronted with unusually strong aggressive drives and are capable of using the defense mechanisms of splitting and projection fail to develop cohesive representations of the self and object world, which, in turn, further exacerbates the intensity of the urges against which the individual defends. Though plausible, this hypothesis is difficult to explore beyond the already observed relationship of these clinical phenomena in adult patients.

The interrelationship of the experience and identity of the self is so strong that a group of psychologists (Baldwin, 1899; Mead, 1934) and their followers in interpersonal psychiatry (Sullivan, 1953) conceptualized the self as the product of experienced social roles. Galatzer-Levy (1988) proposed that the self and ego may be related in the same manner as a list of statements forming an executed instruction set is related to a computer program. Changes in the representation (self, list/computer program) result directly in changes in operation (ego, executed program).

Contemporary Psychoanalytic Perspectives Regarding the Self

Problems apparent in the translation of such terms as ego and id reflect lack of clarity regarding the contribution of experientially relevant concepts within psychoanalysis. The term self is perhaps the most readily confused of these concepts and may be too easily viewed as a psychosocial or interpersonal construct. Understood more generally within psychoanalysis as experienced coherence, continuity, or personal integrity (Gedo, 1977; Stechler and Kaplan, 1980; Klein, 1976; Pine, 1990; Wolf, 1988), the psychoanalytic construct of self refers to an intrapersonal or subjective state or agency leading to an enhanced sense of personal spontaneity and wholeness (Winnicott, 1960/1965).

Concern with differentiation between the realms of the interpersonal and the intrapsychic or intrapersonal was central in the efforts of Hartmann (1950) and Jacobson (1964) to clarify the concept of self. Together with Richards (1982a), these pioneering theoreticians viewed the self as including the ego, the sense of being the subject (versus the object) of experience, the bodily self, and the sense of being a whole individual person. Even recognizing these efforts, Meissner (1986) remained uneasy with Hartmann's (1950) equation of "self" and "person" and viewed "person" as a social rather than an intrapsychologic term. Further, as both Meissner (1986) and Gedo (1979, 1981) observed, Jacobson's (1964) view of the concept of self fosters an inconsistent understanding of the self. Jacobson (1964) viewed the self as an intrapsychic function resulting from experiences or representations of others (as contrasted with actual experiences with others) (Sandler & Rosenblatt, 1962). Jacobson also maintained that the self constitutes both a structure in the ego, serving as the repository of experience of an active sense of personal integration and coherence (Klein, 1976), and a structure containing the ego.

Perhaps the greatest concern with the concept of self in psychoanalysis has been evident in the contributions of Kohut and his collaborators (Basch, 1981, 1983a,b; Goldberg, 1982, 1988; Kohut, 1971, 1977, 1984; Kohut & Wolf, 1978; Tolpin & Kohut, 1980/1990; Wolf, 1988). In a series of clinical and theoretical papers, these clinical investigators explored the role of the experience of others for the emergence of personal vitality and capacity for smoothing tensions. Similar in many respects to the discussions of both Winnicott (1953, 1960, 1960/1965), and Khan (1964/1974a), Kohut and his associates coined the term Self Psychology for a clinical and developmental theory stressing intertwined poles of grandiosity, idealization, and appreciation of talents and skills.

Central to this clinical–developmental theory is assumption of the infant's experience of vitality from earliest infancy. A sense of agency and effectance (White, 1963) from earliest childhood facilitates the emergence of coherence and continuity within space and time and reflects a complex developmental line. This line begins with the parent's image of the infant's physical and historical coherence, and continues in the infant's experience of ever more organized and differentiated positions in life, through the child's discovery of an essential psychological self associated with, but differentiated from his or her body, to subsequent variation in the experience of personal integrity or coherence within ever increasing contexts of self within society.

The Contributions of Kohut and His Associates

The formulation of self emerging from Self Psychology is of a person embedded in a complex matrix of meanings. These include the capacity for self-soothing and the appropriate use of others as a source of comfort and are formed by the experience of others who are more or less able to provide solace during critical times of psychological distress. The "good enough" parent provides a context in which the young child is first able to experience soothing of tensions, which facilitates emergence of a sense of self as vital and effective (Cohler, 1980). Too often, self is defined largely in terms of psychopathology or an absence or impairment in one's sense of wholeness and well-being (Wolf, 1988). Particularly in the work of Kohut and his associates, such self states as grandiosity, fragmentation, emptiness, or a sense of being overburdened or overstimulated all become ways of understanding self in terms of its impairment. It is important to understand the implications of Self Psychology for development of the self beyond those instances in which the child experiences the caregiving environment as failing in intrinsic ways and leading to significant impairment.

Clinical study within this tradition, together with normative developmental study (Sander, 1962, 1964, 1969, 1975; Stern, 1985, 1989), suggests that limitations in the capacity for experiencing self-soothing are first attributed by the child to his or her own actions; only later is the child able to differentiate between his or her initiative and the actions of others on the child's behalf. This perspective on the development of self contrasts with that of Mahler and her colleagues (Mahler, Pine, & Bergman, 1975), who stressed development from an unrelated, "autistic" state, through a confusional symbiosis in which the baby experiences mother and self as one, toward enhanced psychological autonomy. Kohut (1971) observed that Mahler's method of study and formulation of the development of self represents an experience-distant perspective from without the baby's emerging subjectivity (Stern, 1985), rather than the experience-near perspective characteristic of psychoanalysis.

Further, as Kohut and his associates have observed, the separation–individuation approach to psychological development pioneered by Mahler and her colleagues (Mahler et al., 1975) emphasizes individualism rather than enhanced relatedness as the outcome of personality development across the years of early childhood. This lonely individualism contrasts with the reality of the continuing psychological use of others as a source of affirmation and support across the course of life. Beginning with earliest infancy, we turn to others for comfort and support during times of distress. Variations in the ability to experience solace and to realize continuing and sustaining comfort reflect variations in the vitality and sense of coherence of self. Persons seek ties with others who will provide them with solace at times of crisis and vitality at times of depletion. Kohut referred to these others who are experienced as part of self in terms of the concept of "selfobject" ties. Stern (1985) referred to a similar concept of the emerging psychological use of others as "evoked companions"; Galatzer-Levy and Cohler (1993) prefer the term "evoked other" or "essential other" as a means for describing continued psychological use of others (as well as realization of tangible support and assistance) across the course of life.

Perspectives such as those formulated by Kohut and his colleagues, G. Klein (1976), Stechler and Kaplan (1980), Winnicott (1953), Khan (1963/1974b, 1964/1974a), A. Green (1975), and others, all point in the direction of a new understanding of the development of subjectivity based on experience-near or empathic modes of observation. This perspective focuses on the concept of person, rather than function and mechanism, and is concerned with the process by which we come to experience the world as coherent and congruent over long periods of time, even when confronted with unexpected adversity. Experience-near issues such as agency or activity, attribution of particular meanings to experience, and use of time in particular ways, replace more experience-distant and mechanistic concern with presumed functions and mechanisms, which are more the province of experimental psychology than a human science concerned with the origins and significance of wish and intents enacted with others over long durations.

Adolescence and the Concept of the Self

Toward the end of the 19th century, Lord Kelvin, the British physicist, observed that science owed more to the steam engine than the steam engine owed to science. As we near the end of the 20th century, something similar might be said of the relationship between the adolescent and psychological understanding of the self. Psychoanalytic theory and technique owe more to the adolescent than adolescents owe to psychoanalysis. Many of Freud's early cases (Breuer & Freud, 1893–1895; Freud, 1905b) involved psychoanalytic and psychotherapeutic experiences with adolescent hysterics. Freud's patient, Dora, seems to have benefited little from the clinical encounter with Freud (Deutsch, 1957). However, Freud and his successors learned a vast amount from Dora's struggles, including those evoked anew within incompletely analyzed transference enactments. Freud gained enhanced understanding of the mechanisms of hysteria. Erikson (1964) used the exploration of the reasons of Freud's failure as data in his reformulation of the adolescent process. More recently, a "minor industry" has emerged in the reinterpretation of this particular case (Begel, 1982; Buckley, 1989; Decker, 1982; Delacour, 1986; Gabel, 1985; Glenn, 1986; Hare-Mustin, 1983; Jennings, 1986; Kanzer, 1980; Kohon, 1984; Krohn & Krohn, 1982; Langs, 1976; Lewin, 1973; Meissner, 1986; Muslin & Gill, 1978; Rogow, 1978; Slipp, 1977). Particularly in the exploration of the development of the self, adolescent patients have provided the raw data from which theoretical formulations have been derived. Although Heinz Kohut's seminal work in Self Psychology was based primarily on psychoanalytic experiences with adults, Kohut, early on, applied and amplified his thinking in discussion of adolescent psychopathology (Elson, 1987). In return for their contribution to understanding the self, adolescents have been rewarded with clearer conceptualizations of the self and related concepts that have provided more sophisticated therapeutic approaches to adolescent patients.

Freud chose to understand adolescence as the psychological response to pubertal changes. In particular, he viewed the adolescent process as a reworking of Oedipal struggles under the force of intensified sexual impulses (Freud, 1905a). This perspective has been expanded more recently (Laufer, 1968, 1989; Laufer & Laufer, 1984) while continuing to emphasize biological changes of puberty as equivalent to the psychological changes of adolescence.

Puberty forces a reshaping of the adolescent's psychological world; that which could only be fantasized prior to puberty now becomes physically possible.

Maturation of the body is not the only metamorphosis associated with puberty. At least in technologically advanced societies, puberty is associated with the transformation in the cognitive (Piaget & Inhelder, 1968) and moral (Kohlberg & Gilligan, 1971) capacities, reflected in formal operations. These phenomena, along with new modes of defense, were characterized by analysts as aspects of ego development (A. Freud, 1936/1966). Clinically, the interconnection among the experience of self, ego functioning, and identity is nowhere more evident than among adolescents. That adolescents have been the object of so much psychoanalytic investigation concerning the development of the self is consistent with the preoccupations of adolescents themselves and of the larger society regarding adolescents.

Unlike younger children, adolescents regularly refer to themselves as potential sources of the psychological suffering for which they come for treatment. Younger children characteristically describe external circumstances or failures of interaction, such as lack of friends or difficulties in school, as the sources of their difficulties. In contrast, adolescents characteristically either describe some personal difficulty as the problem or, alternatively, present the difficulty as an external problem with such vigor as to make it readily apparent that they are defending against the idea of the trouble arising in themselves. The characteristic complaint "My parents don't understand" refers to the centrality of the self in the adolescent's difficulty and simultaneously denies the adolescent's contribution to this difficulty.

Adolescents, including those who are not patients, are often preoccupied by discussions of themselves and their sense of self. In noting the conversation of adolescent friends and acquaintances, Gottman (Ginsberg & Gottman, 1986; Gottman, 1986; Gottman & Mettetal, 1986) found it necessary to introduce several new coding categories that had been unneeded to describe conversations during earlier periods of childhood, in order to encompass the very large part of adolescent discourse that centers on the self and identity.

Adults' fantasy of adolescence, which is not infrequently adopted by adolescents themselves, includes the image of adolescence as a period when the experience of self and identity is elaborated (Kett, 1977). In 19th- and 20th-century literature, this is epitomized by the massive production of *bildungs romans*—descriptions of the struggles of adolescents to find their true selves, usually in the context of a society experienced in falsifying this experience. In this social fantasy of adolescence, youngsters are seen as having extraordinary freedom to enact and explore possible identities, based on their combination of physical maturity and phase-appropriate lack of an adult responsibility that would tie them to material and moral necessities. Adolescents in our society receive two very strong messages. First, they are expected not to undertake committed positions "prematurely." Marriage, leaving school, taking full-time employment, and pregnancy are regarded as undesirable because they foreclose opportunities for the development of the self. At the same time, adolescents are urgently encouraged to select their definitive adult roles early on, so that they may efficiently pursue training toward those goals. Adolescents who fail to proceed in a linear fashion through a sequence of steps leading to a desirable identity are also regarded as being in great difficulty.

The fantasy that adolescents enjoy continued freedom, including lack of constraints regarding definitive identity, is also represented in the adult culture's holding on to the artifacts of adolescents in attempts to maintain the right to further self-development. The artifacts of the "culture of narcissism" are largely found in its continued attachment to cultural materials associated with adolescence (Lasch, 1977). It is not surprising that Self Psychology, the first psychoanalytic psychology that permits the systematic exploration of the development of the self, should find wide applications to adolescents.[3]

Self Psychology as developed by Kohut and his followers centers on three major concepts. The mode of observation employed is empathic comprehension of the subjective experience of the analysand (Kohut, 1959/1978). Empathy in this context refers to a process of "vicarious introspection" in which the observer comprehends complex mental states of another by attempting to picture what it is like to be in the other's place. This position contrasts with objective observation, which regards patients' reports as data to be interpreted for the purpose of understanding the underlying and hidden psychological mechanisms that determine its production (Galatzer-Levy & Cohler, 1990a; Hartmann, 1927). Within this empathic observational framework, the self is a term used to refer to the experience commonly expressed as "self," "me," or "I," which ordinarily is cohesive over time and place.

Kohut suggested that maintenance of self-experience is the preeminent motivating factor in human psychology (Kohut, 1984). Kohut's major discovery was that the experience of the self commonly requires the psychological presence of other people who function in a fundamental fashion to support the experiences of continuity, cohesiveness, and vigor. Early in development, the physical embodiments of these "selfobjects" are necessary for the person's psychological well-being. Nontraumatic failures of these selfobject functions result in the person's taking on the capacity to do some of the things that the selfobject did for the person independent of the presence of the selfobject. The selfobject function is gradually differentiated from inadvertent elements present in the person who serves this function. This process of "transmuting internalization" (Kohut, 1971) is the basis on which psychic structure develops.

The selfobject may function in the physical absence of the person who embodies this function through the person's capacity to evoke the selfobject. Kohut asserted that, normatively, selfobjects whose function is obvious in infancy continue to function across the course of life. However, he did not elaborate on the nature of these functions in their normal development beyond infancy. Several workers have begun to describe ordinary selfobject functioning across the course of life (Galatzer-Levy & Cohler, 1990b; Galatzer-Levy & Cohler, In Press; Wolf, 1980, 1982; Wolf, Gedo, & Terman, 1972). The selfobject is an intrapsychic phenomenon, not an interpersonal one. Certain of its aspects obviously derive from perceptions of interpersonal relations; from the psychological experiences of others, not their material presence; and from the psychological experience of being taken care of and responded to, not the concrete external interactions that are of interest here. Kohut (1971, 1977, 1984) explored selfobject functioning in depth. When allowed to develop transferences unimpeded by premature interpretation of the defensive function of these transferences,[4] persons with disorders of the

---

[3]It is also not surprising that it is the product of the 1960s, when society was dominated by the developmental concerns of adolescents, and discourse about the self pervaded sociological, psychological, and even religious discourse (Watts, 1966).

[4]The clinical phenomena that Kohut observed were long known to psychoanalysts. Patients commonly reported unrealistic idealization of the analyst or feelings that the analyst must respond to them in certain ways—with approval, camaraderie, or shared feeling—in order for the patient not to be greatly distressed. However, most earlier analysts understood these attitudes toward the analyst as reflecting attempts to disguise less acceptable underlying motives (Curtis, 1985). For example, idealization was understood as hiding denigrating feelings from the patient and analyst and also as setting up the analyst to a standard that must inevitably lead to his or her fall. ("The bigger they are, the harder they fall.") It was Kohut's contention that the assumption that all transferences of this work reflected primarily such defensive operation led to that interpretation to patients which, acting like any inexact interpretation (Glover, 1931), resulted in distortion of the emerging transference. If such premature interpretation were not made, so that the analyst could develop a more accurate picture of the function of these transferences, Glover claimed, they were often revealed to be not primarily defensive but, rather, direct expressions of intense psychological needs.

self developed transference-like responses. These responses were characterized by the following experience: when the needed selfobject function was missing, experiences of fragmentation of the self or derivatives thereof emerged, either in symbolic form or in the form of self-protective operations, and were designed to avoid experiences of impending fragmentation.

One characteristic of the ordinary development of the selfobject world is its expansion across the course of life. Kohut (1984) recognized the need for phase-appropriate responsive selfobjects throughout development but gave only the briefest descriptions of those functions. The infant's mothering selfobject more or less encompasses the psychological world. Although siblings and the father may play a role in early psychological life, only in the second year of life do second others (Herzog, 1982; Lacan, 1968) provide a distinctively new type of selfobject function. The selfobjects of the Oedipal phase, usually embodied in the same persons as the earlier selfobjects, are of a new psychological type that includes a differentiated gender and a fantasy of the relationship between others that does not include the child itself.

The selfobject world broadens further as the young child begins to go to school; it now includes peers and teachers, who support the experience of self through an extension of twinship and idealizing relations respectively. In the ordinary selfobject environment of the adolescent self are friends with whom elaborated profound relations often develop (Galatzer-Levy & Cohler, 1990b); mentors, who may be teachers in the formal sense; somewhat older individuals who are especially admired for certain capacities (e.g., young adult military leaders); people who respond to the adolescent's sexual body—partners and potential partners; and an ever widening circle, in the larger culture, of images that embody ideals such as historical figures, political leaders, entertainers, athletes, and fictional characters. Elaboration of selfobject functioning continues to develop across the course of life.

Adolescents may encounter difficulty in finding adequate selfobjects, for a variety of reasons. First, psychopathology or trauma earlier in life may lead to massive anxiety or pessimism about the possibility of finding adequate selfobjects, and the youngster may attempt to protect against repetition of painful experiences by rejecting possibilities for selfobject relationships. Many youngsters respond by adopting an attitude of tough, depressed, pseudo-independence. Second, the urgency of selfobject needs may be so great that intense emergency attachments that are ill suited to the youngster's developmental needs are formed.

A gay 17-year-old high school student, desperately in need of a caring response from an adult, met and became intensely involved with an older man who enthusiastically mirrored him so long as the boy enacted the role of a needy infant. The role did not fit well with the youngster's current psychological needs or with his further development, but he accepted it in return for the much needed selfobject function. The relationship precluded the search for more adequate selfobjects.

Third, the environment may be impoverished regarding appropriate selfobjects. Youngsters who have unusual talents or interests that are different from the majority, or whose environments are severely limited by political or economic circumstances, may find it nearly impossible to find appropriate selfobjects. Burnt-out teachers of ghetto youth, for example, rarely have the energy to notice or respond to intellectually bright youngsters from backgrounds of poverty and so cannot serve the much needed functions of idealizable and mirroring selfobjects. Not uncommonly, these three sources of failure of the selfobject environment occur in concert.

The new selfobject needs of the adolescent may lead to the disintegration of stable configurations of mutual selfobject function within the family. Characterological styles that could be adopted by the entire family in a mutually supportive fashion when children were younger may fail to support adolescent development. This failure can greatly disturb the way these methods of coping work for parents and siblings, so that an adolescent's breakdown in the face of these failures can precipitate manifest difficulty in the entire family (Galatzer-Levy, 1985).

A 19-year-old boy sought treatment during college because to him, the professors seemed to be engaged in endless discourse that was designed to cover over rather than clarify important problems. He came from a religious family that adopted selective elements of orthodoxy. Some of the family's beliefs in mystical happenings were woven into a highly inconsistent set of beliefs used to support several family members in avoiding a sense of meaninglessness and triviality about their lives. This muddled religiosity was commonly invoked to evade real disagreements among family members by obscuring the issues. The patient's angry demands for clarity, and confrontations about the inadequacy of the family's precarious religious stances, led first to even more irrational and fanatical religious practice and then to significant depression in his father and a sibling.

Many difficulties arise when adolescents are unable to find adequate selfobjects. For example, the need for idealizable selfobjects in a non-responsive milieu may lead either to despair and depression or, more commonly, to the adoption of available selfobjects that are less than optimal to support growth. For example, in an environment where the great mythic resources of the complex culture are relatively unavailable to poorly educated and culturally deprived youth, the idealization of figures who embody a sense of invulnerable power and access to erotic pleasure is common. The "superfly figures" so idealized by some Black ghetto adolescents reflect the choice of much needed figures of idealization in the absence of adequate, more sophisticated, and growth-promoting idealizable selfobjects.

A particular type of selfobject commonly observed among adolescents might be called "developmental assistance." They become vigorously engaged, often with an experience of utter commitment, but in the full realization, on some level, that the selfobjects are transient in nature and serve specifically to achieve some developmental task. Teachers, lovers, and friends may all be regarded as developmental assistance in this regard. The very avowal of the anticipated continuity of relationships that are predictably transient reflects the adolescents' preconscious awareness of the role of these relationships in promoting personal development rather than constituting a stably needed aspect of the environment. Thus, it is common for quite intense love affairs to end with the close of the academic year. The very intensity of these experiences sometimes leads to their confusion with the qualitatively different, stable configurations that are required by an endangered self. Far from promoting growth, these experiences often interfere with the individual's capacity to explore new possibilities.

Adolescents generally idealize their therapist and/or demand overt mirroring responses, with particular intensity. They also commonly react against and defend against awareness of these positions. These common adolescent processes are often mistaken for the archaic selfobject transferences first described by Kohut. Although they may represent such transferences, they more commonly represent an aspect of the adolescent's capacity to become profoundly engaged with individuals needed for the further development of an essentially already vigorous and coherent self. Confusion about the difference between ordinary and developmentally appropriate use of selfobjects during adolescence and superficially similar archaic selfobject needs has led to an overdiagnosis of pathology of self in adolescents in certain psychiatric centers.

Across cultures, the transition from the status of child to that of adult is perhaps the most widely recognized transition occurring in the life span, and it is widely associated with specific ritual processes (van Gennep, 1908/1960). Only birth and death are more enshrined in ritual. These processes characteristically involve a period, from several hours to more than a decade, during which the child enters into a special liminal state, where, isolated from society at large, he or she is not subject to the rules governing either child or adult roles but may be set other stringent requirements. The child emerges from this "rite of passage" into adult status. The adequacy of the ritual process might reasonably be judged by its capacity to support the internal psychological transformations as well as the social movement of an individual from one state to the other. Where magical and supernatural elements have largely been divorced from the ritual process and traditional ritual has been relegated to semihumorous nostalgia or empty form, the rites for the passage from childhood to adulthood have lost their force. The entire adolescent period may then be viewed as a socially defined ritual process supporting the transformation from childhood to adulthood (Kett, 1977).

The social role of teenagers can be regarded as a liminal state between childhood and adulthood that allows for serious playfulness in adult roles with the end in mind of working through the various newly adopted adult positions. Teenagers are expected to play at adult sexual relations. They are deviant either if they fail to involve themselves in such play or if they extend the play "too far" by engaging in sexual acts regarded as the right of adults only, by committing themselves to relationships, or by having children before the socially prescribed time. Similarly, many adolescents are expected to play at adult vocational roles by taking after-school or summer jobs independent of economic necessity. Again, adolescents are regarded as deviant if they are too much or too little like adults—if they either fail to become somewhat "responsible" in work or if they too early assume a full-time career.

Although an adolescent phase and corresponding social support were described as long ago as the classical era in Greece, only in the late 19th century did the specific adolescent phase of development emerge for any but a small minority of young people. Special groups of individuals planning to enter a monastic life might have been permitted a "period between the walls" (Erikson, 1959) before deciding to enter a religious vocation, but teenage apprentices were limited by their financial wherewithal from participating in the full benefits of adult life, and yet were otherwise regarded as adults. The emergence of a large-scale youth movement (Laqueur, 1962; Wohl, 1979) in Germany signaled the appearance of a mass culture of individuals in an in-between state that was ambivalently supported by society. One determinant of this ambivalent support is the need of technological societies for workers with much more formal education than is required in an agrarian or even an early industrial society.

The maintenance of student status into the late 20s and even the early 30s, as required for high-level technological jobs, helped to normalize a continued intermediate status for these much needed students. At the same time, the need to decrease the population of underemployed and unskilled laborers added to the humane basis for child labor laws and for laws extending compulsory education, which excluded at least younger teenagers from the work force. The extension of formal education supports a longer moratorium period but limits the opportunities available to youngsters. Often, the socially normative prolongation of this intermediate developmental phase tries the psychological resources of relatively healthy individuals who want to get on with adulthood earlier in their lives, and supports the psychopathology of young people who are unable to move out of psychological adolescence.

To work effectively with adolescents, the clinician needs to be aware of the function of society in the individual adolescent's psychological life. The same societal and institutional configurations that provide one adolescent with a playground that supports the fullest development of the self may be an institutionalized interference with another youngster's equally valid attempts to adopt an adult identity. For a particular adolescent, the environment may be actually impoverished with regard to available selfobjects. Therapists, who generally have successfully traversed an extended educational process (psychoanalytic training is the longest training course in our society, commonly continuing into the fifth decade), need to work through the meaning of the institution of adolescence and prolonged adolescence in order to accurately understand the psychology of youngsters with regard to these institutions.[5]

PROTECTING THE SELF: PSYCHOANALYTIC PSYCHOTHERAPY WITH ADOLESCENTS

Although adolescence is usefully regarded as a social construction characteristic of late 19th- and 20th-century western society rather than an inherent psychological response to biological development, people engaged in this period of life do share certain common psychological configurations, in depth. Clinical work with adolescents is characterized by the typical ways in which youngsters protect themselves from psychological distress. The ego psychology term, defense mechanism, emphasizes the avoidance of awareness of unconscious conflict. Consistent with a Self Psychology point of view, which emphasizes the person's experience-near efforts to maintain an integrated and invigorated experience of the self, as well as other viewpoints that focus on the adaptive function of defense across the course of life (Vaillant, 1977, 1986), a clinical self-psychological approach includes helping the patient to understand his or her efforts and specific means of avoiding damage to the self.

This approach contrasts with the implicitly pejorative ego psychology connotation that defense mechanisms are inevitably an attempt to get away from painful psychological realities (Brandchaft, 1985; Kohut, 1984; Oremland, 1985; Shane, 1987a, 1978b; Tolpin, 1985). This shift may appear to be a mere semantic trick, the formalization of ordinary tact, or another effort to move away from painful psychological realities by sugar-coating them; however, it is far more. It reflects a profound change in the therapist's attitude toward patients' efforts at self-protection. When the patient is seen as undertaking the reasonable task of trying to avoid potentially damaging psychological pain, rather than trying to avoid, in almost cowardly fashion, recognition of psychological "truth," a very different ambience emerges in the work between therapist and patient.[6]

A 16-year-old patient regularly spoke so rapidly and forcefully that the therapist found it hard to get a word in. Often, when the therapist started to speak, the patient interrupted him in midsentence. Interpretation to the effect that the patient feared hearing what the therapist had to say, if anything, intensified the behavior, as did references to the patient's fear of being influenced by the therapist, although there was much material that made these interpretations plausible. But when the therapist spoke of the importance to the patient of having a sense of being in charge of herself, and how alive and effective she felt when words flowed from her, the patient not only agreed but was far more comfortable allowing the therapist to speak.

Especially in work with adolescents, an appreciative attitude toward the patient's attempt to maintain a sense of cohesion and integrity in

---

[5]It seems no accident, for example, that Erik Erikson, whose personal search for identity involved a very prolonged period of remaining outside the normative institutions of society, was the first proponent of the developmental utility of such a period in life and carefully differentiated it from severe psychopathology (Roazen, 1976).

[6]This change in position is consistent with the shifting world-view of psychoanalysis, which no longer includes the idea of an absolute and positivist truth modeled on the 19th-century view of scientific reality that is implicit in Freud's writings and avowed in his ideals. The shift has been to a view that includes the appreciation of multiple structurings of "reality" consistent with the newer epistemologies of science, even in the "hard" sciences, and a widening vision of the possibilities for the appreciation of human psychologies (Galatzer-Levy & Cohler, 1990a).

the face of many sources of internal and external difficulty is useful. It results in a sense of collaborative effort, of being accurately understood and having a capacity to reexamine, reevaluate, and possibly modify characteristic modes of defense. This collaboration between adolescent patient and physician, which is essential for clinical psychoanalysis, can be effective, but it rarely occurs when the therapist adopts a pejorative attitude toward these much needed operations.

This is particularly important because adolescents commonly employ modes of self-protection that cause the therapist considerable distress. Fostering the therapeutic process can be particularly difficult when the therapist does not understand what is going on. The adolescent proclivity for enactment has been universally noted, although it has probably been somewhat overrated because of the way it stands out in the awareness of society, parents, and therapists. The circular argument is often made that, because adolescents are more prone to action than children are, their drives must have increased with puberty, and their increased action orientation is explained by the intensification of the drives. In this view, adolescence is a psychological response to an overwhelming of preexisting defenses by an upsurge of libidinal and aggressive drives. Adolescence is viewed as a kind of normative "actual" neurosis (Fenichel, 1945). The physiological changes of puberty are associated with shifts in the consciously wished-for gratifications of young people. Whether the adolescent's wishes are, in some primary sense, more intense than those of a younger child is questionable.

A different version of a similar concept is that, with the intensification of genital urges in particular, the adolescent is thrown into a new edition of the Oedipal situation (Freud, 1905a; Reich, 1932). The shape of the situation is largely determined by the social prohibition on full erotic development (Bernfeld, 1923), which therefore requires particularly intensified defensive operations. In fact, the situation is, in a sense, more problematic than the difficulties of the Oedipal phase proper, because now the adolescent has a body capable of enacting the fantasized wishes (Laufer & Laufer, 1984). Another group of ideas emphasizes the adolescent's need for activity as a defensive operation against (a) a longed-for passive position secondary to a process of separation–individuation, which is reengaged during adolescence (Blos, 1967), or (b) passive homosexuality stimulated by pro-Oedipal male longings for the father (Blos, 1989). Both these points of view would predict that normal adolescence would be characterized by turbulence; yet, studies of normal adolescence, though limited in depth, indicate that many apparently healthy adolescents do not experience this time of life as particularly turbulent, nor are they particularly prone to gross enactments (Offer & Sabshin, 1984).

It is more accurate to say that there are significant groups of adolescents who seem to use action more extensively than they did during middle childhood and who subsequently seem to give up this adolescent mode. When it does occur, adolescent action becomes either problematic or psychologically significant, and generally centers around issues of sex and violence. Both these matters may be influenced by the adolescent's perception of community expectations communicated through the media, peers, and parents (often in the form of prohibitions). Youngsters who are trying to figure out the psychological significance of their physically mature bodies are commonly informed of a normative expectation about what they will do with them. Social expectations, although not the sole determinant of the decision to use action, may directly shape the effects of such action. Dramatic instances include the difference between boys who grow up in communities where fighting is ordinarily done with fists and boys involved in the gang violence and weapons of the inner city.

With regard to both sex and violence, the adolescent bears the burden of fantasies of adult society. For example, although hardly limited by the demand for realism, the very popular Teenage Mutant Ninja Turtles of 1989 and 1990, like most super heroes, are violent (if lovable) adolescents. The intended audience for these characters is not adolescents but elementary school-aged and younger children. The notion of adolescence as a time of jocose violence represents part of the community's norms for this age.

The function of sexuality in adolescent psychology is often obscured for both patient and therapist, who simplify it into some notion of intense physiological urge. Freud (1905a) and Anna Freud (1936) believed that the enormous plasticity and possibility of delay of gratification of sexual urges accounted for the possibility for rich psychological developments derived from them. Freud comprehended adolescence as a period when new developments were driven by the intensification of these urges. We believe that an exploration of the phenomenology of sexual experience in adolescence suggests that intense wishes for sexual release are not the major driving cause for much adolescent sexual activity; rather, the activity serves several other functions that can be rationalized as based on the wish for physical gratification. Many of these functions center around the experience of the self. Kohut (1971) pointed out how the eroticization of narcissistic needs resulted in enormously intense wishes for and urgent carrying out of sexual activity. The transformation of a wish to be mirrored, or idealized, into a wish for a concrete sexual act that embodies the psychological operations results in an inordinate intensification of and increased significance for these acts.

Kohut's concept of the eroticization of narcissistic concerns is particularly helpful in thinking about adolescence. Adolescent sexual activity and fantasy center largely on narcissistic issues. The capacity for sexual function rather than sensuous pleasure is the main concern of many adolescents. As Laufer and Laufer (1984) emphasized, the "central masturbation fantasy," a fantasy that tells a recurrent story in only slightly varying form, condenses many psychological concerns of the adolescent. The adolescent may support a sense of worth based on the idea that one is valuable because of a physically mature body, and so expend much energy on development and appreciation of the body. This can be done in many ways—through masturbation;[7] through activities involving dress athleticism; or through interpersonal but narcissistically determined sexual relations with people whose main goals may include being mirrored as sexually desirable and effective, being in a relationship with an idealized and physically admirable person, or gaining the admiration of the community of other adolescents by virtue of being so engaged. The use of sexuality to express love and tenderness toward another, rather than as an aspect of one's self embodied in another person, usually progressively emerges across the adolescent years (Sklansky, 1977), although important narcissistic elements in sexual activity remain present throughout the course of life.

Clinically, the interrelationship among physiological tension, narcissistic needs, and engagements with another person out of love or hate can only be appreciated through detailed examination of the specific meaning of sexual activity to the individual. The fantasies accompanying sexual activity, which are usually carefully guarded by the adolescent, reveal much about inner psychological life in a relatively undisguised form. When adolescents are ashamed of masturbation, it is usually because of the fantasies that accompany it. Clinically,

---

[7]Nowhere is manifest behavior a poorer guide to internal psychological processes than in sexual behavior. Masturbation, for example, can be a psychologically narcissistic act or can have other people as its major psychological focus (Baker, 1984; Bernstein, 1962, 1975, 1983; Coen & Bradlow, 1984; Francis, 1968; Glenn, 1969; Halpert, 1973; Isay, 1975; Kernberg, 1988; Laufer, 1968, 1976; Novick & Novick, 1972; Wermer & Levin, 1967). It is only through the analysis of the conscious and unconscious fantasies that accompany masturbation in adolescence (or lead to abstention, as noted by A. Freud (1936/1966)) that its psychological function can be determined.

when sexuality has a driven compulsive or addictive quality that is largely independent of sensuous pleasure, it is likely that the function of the activity is to attempt to keep the experience of the self intact or to produce a feeling of an alive and vigorous self (Reich, 1960).[8]

As already noted, identity, in all its dimensions, is a central support of the self. In many contexts, sexual identity is an important part of overall identity, and acting as expected of one's gender becomes very important. A variety of activities—athletics, gender-related dress, activities with same-sex and opposite-sex contemporaries (hanging out with the guys, and dating), as well as overtly sexual activity—contribute to sexual identity in adolescence. When, for whatever reason, the adolescent does not engage in "respectable" sexual activity, this source of support for the self is jeopardized. The sexually inhibited adolescent may experience particular mortification and concern about sexual identity when living in a world where sexual activity is expectable.

Gay and lesbian adolescents have a complex psychological problem in this regard (Boxer & Cohler, 1989; Herdt, 1989; Martin, 1982; Schneider, 1989; Troiden, 1989; see also Chapter 11 of this volume). Manifestly homosexual behavior has many origins (Green, 1987; Isay, 1989; Socarides, 1989), including disorders of the self (Goldberg, 1975). Whatever the genesis of these wishes, adolescents with strong homosexual feelings are confronted with major challenges in establishing an identity. Because ubiquitous homosexual impulses in adolescence are ordinarily dealt with in our society through homophobic reaction formation, the young adolescent homosexual commonly finds his or her sexual impulses referred to exclusively in pejorative terms. Words like "cocksucker," "faggot," or "dike," are generally used to communicate overall unworthiness and to specifically attack the gay adolescent by their very use.

The gay liberation movement has altered some of the legal problems facing homosexuals and has affected the manifest attitudes of a segment of the adult population, but most non-homosexual adolescents in our society remain as profoundly homophobic as ever. Indeed, the variety of issues regarding consolidation of their own personal and sexual identity (Erikson, 1958, 1968) leads homosexuality to be a particular threat to adjustment. The possibility of forming a positive gay identity is open to some adolescents who may find exposure to positive aspects of the gay community, or at least a context for their homosexuality, through services directed at them, through an increasing literature that portrays gay individuals in a positive light, or through the more ready contracts that are available, at least in urban areas, for gay people (Gerstel, Feraios & Herdt, 1989; see also Chapter 11 of this volume). However, even this support has its price. The need for some identity may be so strong that the adolescent may foreclose the complex search for a sexual identity consistent with his or her overall psychology, because of the urgency of finding some sexual identity. For this reason, we regard interventions like Hetrick and Martin's (1987) modeling of a positive image of homosexuality by therapists as not the optimal approach to this issue. Their approach makes it extremely difficult for the adolescent to use the therapy as a safe environment for exploring the meaning of sexual impulses.[9]

---

[8] In classical psychoanalysis, compulsive sexuality was seen as resulting from intense castration anxiety (Fenichel, 1945; Freud, 1909). It was an attempt to concretely demonstrate genital intactness. Indeed, this understanding, as far as it goes, seems to be applicable to many people, including adolescents engaged in compulsive sex. However, the question of why genital intactness should be so urgent for certain people remains unanswered. When the experience of the self includes notions that overvalue genitals as the essence of one's being or as the sole source of life-giving stimulation, then the threat of genital loss or damage takes on a dimension far beyond simple loss of pleasure.

[9] A variety of therapeutic interventions with adolescents exploit adolescents' ordinary and pathological needs for idealizable selfobjects to achieve therapeutic goals. These methods range from the deliberate seduction of adolescents into a situation in which the therapist has sufficient power to undertake other types of work (Aichorn, 1925/1935) or assumes a directly educational position (Ashway,

Violence

There are so many indications that destructiveness is a recurrent human motive that, in the latter part of his life, Freud (1920/1955) took the point of view, later elaborated by M. Klein (1923/1975a, 1927/1975b, 1937/1975c, 1945/1975d) that destructiveness itself is a primary human motive. Ample historical evidence supports this view, as does widespread mythical representation of primal destructiveness, such as the god Shiva in Hinduism (Avalon, 1913; Hopkins, 1968; Vidyarnave Bhattacarya, 1914). Both Freud and Klein discussed the intimate relationship of external violence and wishes for death and consequent peace, which Freud referred to as the Nirvana principle. This association is common in apocalyptic ideas in which periods of cosmic turmoil and violence result in a purified universe in which calm is all-pervasive (Segal, 1983). The destructive fantasies of narcissistic rage often have a similar character. By destroying everything, perfect order and calm will once again be reestablished.

Violence commonly plays a role similar to that of sexual action in relation to the experience of the adolescent's self. Whether enacted or limited to fantasy, violence often produces a sense of personal integration and purpose that is not achievable in other ways. It introduces a sense of total, if temporary, engagement and a loss of often painful self-consciousness.[10] Violence carries with it an opportunity for the display of good bodily functioning as well as the mastery of trauma through making active what was previously experienced passively.

Kohut (1971) observed states of narcissistic rage, which he ascribed to responses to the fear of fragmentation or depletion of the self. Narcissistic rage may be an acute or chronic state. Like eroticized narcissistic needs, it is commonly rationalized as an instrumental response to external realities or as justified vengefulness consistent with some moral order.[11] Narcissistic rage, like enacting eroticized narcissistic wishes, only finds transient

---

1980; Hetrick & Martin, 1987) to the quite common, informal indoctrination of patients to the therapist's values. Such interventions may lead to more adaptive behavior, but they interfere with the opportunity to use the therapeutic situation to explore personal reality and to find solutions that integrate the patients' various goals in ways that are most fitting to themselves. Indoctrinating adolescent patients may seem desirable to therapists for many reasons, but, in general, it is done at an enormous price to the unique contribution that a therapist can make to a patient's life. Self Psychology is sometimes misunderstood. Idealization and mirroring processes are transferences in the analysis of self-disorders, i.e., the patient's construction in the context of a benign but neutral therapist's ordinary courteous dealing with the patient. The therapist takes no active measures in this regard, beyond ordinary interpretation and noninterference with the patient's development of whatever transference may emerge (Kohut, 1971).

[10]Self-consciousness and shame are characteristic features of affects associated with disturbances in the experience of the self. Like many aspects of good functioning, the ordinary experience of the self is not a prominent part of awareness, as Basch (1981) has observed. Consciousness is a special mental state whose function is to solve problems that the individual finds unsolvable by ordinary automatic mechanisms that are virtually always outside of awareness. For example, one only thinks about the mechanisms of walking if for some reason the normal capacity to walk is disturbed. This is not contrary to Freud's observation of a dynamic unconscious in which, in order to reduce anxiety, the person actively bars certain matters from awareness.

[11]The role of chronic narcissistic rage in political and international affairs, in which adolescents play such a significant role, cannot be overestimated. In his psychologically convincing portrait of the internal world of the politically oppressed and exploited, Fanon (1963) averred that chronic states of rage that arise from humiliation and feelings of lack of empowerment (in Kohut's terminology, narcissistic rage) are directed against the self. Thus, a cyclic historical and personal process is set in motion, in which the rage of the endangered self of the oppressed is turned against the self, further weakening the self structure. Fanon argued that the resolution of these chronic rages is essential for the psychological recovery of victims of oppression. He believed that the only adequate psychological resolution of these states came from enacted violent responses. Without concurring with the latter conclusion, the authors agree that the internal sense of relief from painful states of chronic rage anticipated through violence is a common feature of the experience of chronically narcissistically injured people and can lead to vendettas and ethnic and nationalistic hatreds that are important determinants of history.

relief through enactment, because it fails to solve the problem of the endangered self. However, the sense of identity associated with viewing oneself as a violent individual, an avenger, or an avatar of violence is a stable and valuable support for the experience of the self. It may be a major reason for delinquents' reluctance to give up this important dimension of personal identity.

Although commonly rationalized as instrumental aggression, the experience of narcissistic rage is altogether distinct from that of simple aggression. In instrumental aggression, people expend as little energy as possible to achieve a desired goal. In contrast, narcissistic rage is characterized by an all-encompassing sense of destructiveness. Richard III, in his opening monologue, clearly states that his intentions are universally destructive:

But I, that am not shaped for sportive tricks
Nor made to court an amorous looking-glass;
I, that am rudely stamped, and want love's majesty
To strut before a wanton ambling nymph;
I, that am curtailed of this fair proportion
Cheated of feature by dissembling Nature
Deformed, unfinished, sent before my time
Into this breathing world, scarce half made up,
And that so lamely and unfashionable
That dogs bark at me as I halt by them—
Why I, in this weak piping time of peace,
Have no delight to pass away the time,
Unless to see my shadow in the sun
And descant on mine own deformity.
And therefore, since I cannot prove a lover
To entertain these fair well-spoken days,
I am determined to prove a villain
And hate the idle pleasures of these days.

The supposed goal of gaining personal power is only a thin disguise and a secondary concern providing a rationalizing motivation for destructiveness.

The Therapist's Reaction to Action

Whether action is of a sexual or violent nature, it invites the therapist to take something other than an interpretive stance. In addition to providing extraordinarily convincing and concrete expression of narcissistic needs and wishes, action engages the environment, including the therapist, with an intensity that is impossible using other means. The mobilization of the therapist to action that is reciprocal to the patient's actions is an aspect of ordinary responsiveness. The adolescent commonly succeeds in evoking parental and societal actions that help in the management of psychological distress and the support of development. Often, this is done in such a manner that the adolescent can maintain a sense of independence or even of being imposed on, by using these sources of psychological support. It is common for adolescents to feel relief when reasonable parental prohibitions are imposed. An adolescent may protest these prohibitions, but they deliver the youngster from the internal and external conflicts that would confront him or her in the absence of the prohibition.

As with all psychological processes, the dysfunction of this type of selfobject function of adolescence brings that function into sharp focus. In *Romeo and Juliet* (Muslin, 1982), the protagonists are confronted with a host of failed selfobjects. The central values of the community in which these adolescents try to develop center around a meaningless familial feud. Thus, the values that might inform action cannot support personal integrity in any but trivial ways. Both their families and civil authorities are ineffectual and ambivalent about regulating adolescent destructive and sexual behavior. The parents are unconcerned with the psychological welfare of the children but instead see them principally as tools to be used toward parental goals. Peers, while far more sympathetic, provide no organizing and regulating structure but can only act as collaborators in the enactment of shared fantasies. The nurse and the friar, representative of common sense and intellect, have so weakly engaged these characteristics in themselves that they cannot fail to tragically muddle the use of these qualities in their interactions with Romeo and Juliet. Repeatedly, the youngsters, through their actions, should provoke caring and reasonable interventions, but they are always met with selfobject failure.

This characteristic of action that evokes intense and needed responses from the environment, including the therapist, is a central aspect of "externalization," a psychological process first discussed as a defense against unacceptable unconscious wishes but more usefully understood as a typically adolescent way of meeting a variety of psychological needs. Often, in work with adolescents, apparently external factors become central to the therapy. Parents and teachers may intrude themselves into the treatment, apparently interrupting or interfering with treatment. "Realistic" difficulties in terms of peers and school commonly come to play a prominent role in the treatment. Careful examination of these situations often reveals that what appears to be an external event, unrelated to the adolescent's psychology and in fact out of his or her control, was commonly unconsciously arranged by the adolescent and serves a function of both expressing some aspect of the adolescent's wish and disguising from both patient and therapist the adolescent's active role in its creation (Galatzer-Levy, 1986).

Careful work with the patient can often clarify that the supposedly external event represents some aspect of his or her internal life (for instance, the arguing of parents representing two sides of the child's own internal conflict about a situation). It can often be shown that the adolescent has artfully but in no mysterious way created the external event that now seems so out of his or her control. Typical transference-related examples of such phenomena involve announcements that the child must miss or discontinue therapy because the parent has scheduled some other activity at the times of the appointments. Careful investigation often indicates that the patient has given not particularly subtle messages to the parent to the effect that the treatment is unimportant.

Therapeutically meaningful understanding of such defensive operations includes not only the very essential first step of recognizing their presence and function, but recognizing also that the youngster has succeeded in eliciting the cooperation of the environment for the purpose of protecting himself or herself from psychological distress. This involves a normative and desirable capacity, an appreciation of which is not only likely to enrich the therapist's understanding of the occurrence but also to communicate to the youngster the therapist's understanding of the value and abilities that are involved in such operations. Rather than being the enemy of the "gang beneath the couch," the therapist becomes the patient's ally in establishing more sophisticated and flexible uses of selfobject functions available in the environment, without imposing on the adolescent unrealistic and, we believe, antidevelopmental demands for a kind of psychological independence. Although this independence is the ideal reflected in certain contemporary psychoanalytic theories (Mahler, Pine & Bergman, 1975; Settlege, Curtis, Lozoff, Silberschatz, & Simburg, 1988) as well as the common American ideals of independence from sources of psychological support, it does not constitute a particularly useful, healthy, or supportable model of ordinary psychological well-being. The therapist faced with an adolescent whose enmeshment with external figures may seem maladaptive should not be asking why the youngster is so dependent on others for support and comfort, but rather why the others chosen for this support integrate so poorly into the rest of the adolescent's life and make such inflexible demands on the adolescent as a condition for the support.

Parental involvement with adolescents is commonly misunderstood from the perspective that views adolescence as a normative period of continued separation. Parents commonly continue to serve as embodiments of ideals, as sources of enthusiastic support, and as protectors from psychological as well as material dangers. Midadolescents may loudly demand freedom, but, generally, they cooperate well in allowing the parent to set limits on behavior. The parent in this context saves the youngster the experience of internal conflict that would arise were he or she to directly confront the contradiction between some of his or her wishes and values. On a manifest level, this cooperation may even be demonstrated in adolescents' direct requests that they be given the excuse of parental prohibition to help them avoid some unpleasant situation.

Parents willingness in and comfort with engaging in this selfobject function will be highly influenced by the parents' own psychological needs and views of adolescence. Much parental frustration with adolescence arises because of the relatively rapidly changing needs of the adolescent with regard to selfobject functions. The youngster who one day is enraged at the parent for intrusive control may the next day be equally infuriated by what is perceived as parental indifference. The intensity of the adolescent experience and its relative instability commonly place extraordinary demands on parental empathic capacities and may lead to defensive rigidity in various directions with regard to the youngster.

In addition, as mentioned earlier, in our society, adolescents are the object of intense community transference—including from their own parents, who may regard them as embodying uncontrollable sexuality or aggression or, alternatively, as epitomizing the hope for the future. Particularly parents who grew up as part of the youth culture of the 1960s may so idealize adolescence as to unrealistically expect the youngsters to embody their own ideals from that period or to enact their own frustrated desires. The point of view of Self Psychology is useful in untangling these complexities because it does not deny the appropriateness of intense parental engagement in the developing adolescent's life, but rather emphasizes the complex nature of the mutual selfobject functions that parents and child fill for each other. These include, from the parents' side, the vicarious enlivening associated with their own renewed engagement with issues first confronted in their own adolescence (Anthony, 1970). The idea of carrying on into the future parental ambitions and the promise of the enlargement of the family through eventual marriage and procreation is perfectly ordinary for both the adolescent and the parents.[12]

The therapist who does not appreciate these legitimate wishes for the adolescent to fill selfobject needs of the parents is very likely to precipitate unnecessary conflicts between himself or herself and the parents. This does not mean that the therapist's role is to educate the adolescent to the legitimacy of parental demands; it simply means that, in work with parents, the trauma involved in (a) recognizing that the child is in difficulty and (b) tolerating changes from habitual modes of functioning that serve as psychological supports for the parents must be appreciated and worked on with teenagers and their families.

Countertransference

The analyst's or therapist's irrational responses to the patient are a particular problem for the therapist working with the adolescent. Freud (1910/1957, 1915/1958) suggested that transferences to the patient, an inevitable but unfortunate contaminate of the psychoanalytic method, should be minimized by virtue of the analyst's meticulous self-scrutiny. However, contemporary perspectives suggest that countertransference is a major source of information regarding the analysand's experience of self and others (Racker, 1968) and that it may be especially useful in work with more disturbed patients (Boyer, 1989; Burke & Cohler, 1992; Goldberg, 1979; Kernberg, 1975, 1987). The place of countertransference in therapeutic work remains controversial (Blum, 1986; Tyson, 1986). Skolnikoff (1990) suggested that, as with any intense engagement with

---

[12]The role of mothers in the pregnancies of their adolescent children tends to be underplayed and underestimated. In certain communities, it is a normative expectation that a child, on leaving the house, will replace herself with a new baby. Although the parental position may be manifestly opposed to adolescent pregnancies, the wish for grandchildren should not be underestimated in this regard nor necessarily regarded as pathological.

another human being, powerful unconscious processes are stimulated in the therapist during work with patients and that these processes are essential to the understanding of the patient but, more importantly, reflect a kind of engagement necessary for therapeutic work.

In work with adolescents, recognition of the analyst's own responses reciprocal to those of the adolescent patient is essential for therapeutic progress to take place. Countertransference may be both the "royal road" (Freud, 1900) and the major pitfall in work with adolescents. Because, as discussed earlier, the adolescent's ordinary use of the selfobject function of adults includes using them to externalize conflictual and difficult internal states, it is common in work with adolescents for the therapist to find himself or herself impelled to take up one side or another of a conflictual situation. For example, the patient's actions may seem to put the patient in such grave danger that the analyst believes that he or she must act in an educative, superego-, or egolike role toward the patient.[13]

A brilliant undergraduate student believed he was wasting his time in highly intellectual undergraduate studies that failed to address the urgent problems of his life. He correctly understood that his therapist was dedicated to intellectual pursuits. He presented his antieducational position in the form of highly coherent arguments supplemented with numerous citations from the books and articles he constantly read. The therapist felt strongly that the patient was "a natural" at academic thinking and pointed this out to him, repeatedly suggesting that the university clearly fit in with his native way of thinking about things. Consciously conforming to the therapist's supposedly superior knowledge of his psychology, the patient continued with his studies while continuing to protest against them. The situation was only clarified when, recognizing that he was engaged in a countertransference enactment, the therapist assumed a more neutral stance with respect to the patient's mode of being himself and at the same time helped the patient understand how he succeeded in making his internal conflict about going to college into an interpersonal conflict between himself and his therapist, in which the patient felt no internal strife.

CONCLUSION

The emergence of a concept of self within a clinical psychoanalytic framework permits the exploration of an issue that has been central to human psychology, particularly the psychology of adolescence, since time immemorial. Kohut's discovery that selfobject transference permits a window into the self function solves the problem, recognized by Freud, of the seeming unavailability of narcissistic issues within the transference neurosis (Freud, 1911). Armed with this new tool, self psychologists have begun the systematic exploration of the self and its functions. In recent years, these ideas have begun to be joined with ideas of life-course developmental psychology to produce an increasingly coherent psychoanalytic vision of the self in its development.

Adolescents, who are ordinarily concerned with issues about the self, have provided an exceptional laboratory for the understanding of the self and the characteristic modes that individuals employ in the maintenance of the experience of cohesion and vigor of the self.

---

[13]Therapists of adolescents and other action-prone individuals (Gedo, 1979) have advocated various active measures to provide these patients with educational experiences that will lead to their moral development and to their more realistic management of day-to-day affairs in the world. In certain instances, such interventions may indeed prove useful, but therapists should be aware that the temptations to make such interventions, especially when accompanied by a sense of urgency or emergency on the part of the therapist, commonly represent an aspect of externalization. Even when the therapist enacts the assigned role in such a situation, as, for example, when an actively suicidal youngster is hospitalized, it is useful to be aware, at the time, of the process that is occurring and more useful still to devote considerable energies to helping the patient understand what has occurred. In the case of hospitalization, it easily becomes a chronic position in the patient's mind that the hospitalization was entirely the result of external forces, an idea that is used to avoid the painful acknowledgment of the maladaptive functioning which, while it might have been responded to better than through hospitalization, was indeed the product of the patient's own actions.

In turn, these studies have led to increasingly clear ideas about therapeutic processes with adolescents—not only those with pathology of the self but those engaged in the ordinary vicissitudes of self-development that occur during these years.

The appreciation that ordinary development in adolescence is best described in terms of an enrichment and enlargement of the selfobject world, rather than, at best, the subsidiary process of separation–individuation, leads the therapist of adolescents to a more empathic (because more accurate) understanding of the patients' difficulties. When there is an implicit demand in the therapist's or patient's mind for adolescence to be a process by which the individual becomes "independent" of the sources of support and solace that are ordinarily available to people, it is not surprising that the patient responds with reluctance and distress. Similarly, when the processes of defense and "resistance" are understood as protective measures against the disturbance of the cohesive and vigorous self rather than attempts to avoid a "reality" that is morally and pragmatically valued, patients are far less likely to experience the therapeutic process as an attack on their personal integrity. Self Psychology opens opportunities for an enriched understanding of adolescents and their more successful treatment.

REFERENCES

Abend, S. M., Porder, & Willick, M. (1983). *Borderline patients: Psychoanalytic perspectives.* New York: International Universities Press.

Aichorn, A. (1935). *Wayward youth.* New York: Viking Press. (Original work published 1925.)

Anthony, E. J. (1970). The reactions of parents to adolescents and to their behavior. In E. J. Anthony & T. Benedek (Eds.), *Parenthood: Its psychology and psychopathology* (pp. 307–324). Boston: Little, Brown.

Ashway, J. A. (1980). The changing needs of female adolescents. *Adolescent Psychiatry, 8,* 482–498.

Atwood, G., & Stolorow, R. (1984). *Structures of subjectivity: Explorations in psychoanalytic phenomenology.* Hillsdale, NJ: Analytic Press.

Avalon, A. (Pseud.) (1913). Woodruffe, Sir Geye (Trans.) *Hymns to the goddess.* London: Luzac and Company.

Baker, R. (1984). Treatment of a patient with necrophilic fantasies in adolescence. *International Journal of Psychoanalysis, 65,* 283.

Baldwin, A. (1899). *Social and ethical interpretations in mental development* (2nd ed.). New York: Macmillan.

Basch, M. (1981). Selfobject disorders and theory: A historical perspective. *Journal of the American Psychoanalytic Association, 29,* 337–352.

Basch, M. (1983a). The concept of "self": An operational definition. In B. Lee & G. Noam (Eds.), *Developmental approaches to the self* (pp. 7–58). New York: Plenum Press.

Basch, M. (1983b). Some theoretical and methodological implications of self psychology. In A. Goldberg (Ed.), *The future of psychoanalysis* (pp. 431–442). New York: International Universities Press.

Basch, M. (1989). The teacher, the transference, and development. In K. Field, B. Cohler, & G. Wool (Eds.), *Learning and education: Psychoanalytic perspectives* (pp. 771–788). Madison, CT: International Universities Press.

Begel, D. M. (1982). Three examples of countertransference in Freud's Dora case. *American Journal of Psychoanalysis, 42,* 163–169.

Bernfeld, S. (1923). Ueber eine typishe Form der maenlichen Peurtaet. *Imago, 9,* 169–188.

Bernfeld, S. (1941). Freud's earliest theories on the school of Helmholtz. *Psychoanalytic Quarterly, 13,* 341–362.

Bernfeld, S. (1951). Sigmund Freud, M.D., 1882–1885. *International Journal of Psychoanalysis, 32,* 204–217.

Bernstein, I. (1962). Dreams and masturbation in an adolescent boy. *Journal of the American Psychoanalytic Association, 10,* 289–302.

Bernstein, I. (1975). Integrative aspects of masturbation. In I. Marcus & J. Francis (Eds.), *Masturbation from infancy to senescence* (pp. 53–76). New York: International Universities Press.

Bernstein, I. (1983). Masochistic pathology and feminine development. *International Review of Psychoanalysis, 15,* 467–486.

Bettelheim, B. (1983). *Freud and man's soul.* New York: Knopf.

Blos, P. (1967). The second individuation process of adolescence. *Psychoanalytic Study of the Child, 22,* 162–186.

Blos, P. (1989). The place of the adolescent process in the analysis of the adult. *Psychoanalytic Study of the Child, 44,* 3–18.

Blum, H. P. (1986). Countertransference and the theory of technique: Discussion. *Journal of the American Psychoanalytic Association, 34,* 309–328.

Boxer, A. M., & Cohler, B. (1989). The life course of gay and lesbian youth: An immodest proposal for the study of lives. *Journal of Homosexuality, 17,* 315–355.

Boyer, L. B. (1989). Countertransference and technique in working with the regressed patient: Further remarks. *International Journal of Psychoanalysis, 70,* 701–714.

Brandchaft, B. (1985). Resistance and defense: An intersubjective view. In A. Goldberg (Ed.), *Progress in self psychology* (pp. 88–96). New York: Guilford Press.

Breuer, J., & Freud, S. (1955). Studies in hysteria. In J. Strachey (Ed. and Trans.), *Standard Edition of the Complete Psychological Works of Sigmund Freud.* (Original work published 1893–1895) London: Hogarth Press.

Brooks-Gunn, J., & Petersen, A. (1984). Problems in studying and defining pubertal events. *Journal of Youth and Adolescence, 13,* 181–196.

Buckley, P. (1989). Fifty years after Freud: Dora, the Rat-Man, and the Wolf-Man. *American Journal of Psychiatry, 146,* 1394–1403.

Burke, N., & Cohler, B. (1992). Countertransference and psychotherapy with the anorectic adolescent. In J. Brandell (Ed.), *Countertransference in child and adolescent psychotherapy* (pp. 163–189). New York: Aronson.

Coen, S., & Bradlow, P. (1984). Mirror masturbation. *Psychoanalytic Quarterly, 53,* 267–285.

Cohler, B. (1980). Developmental perspectives on the psychology of self in early childhood. In A. Goldberg (Ed.), *Advances in self psychology* (pp. 69–115). New York: International Universities Press.

Cohler, B. (1987). Approaches to the study of development in psychiatric education. In S. H. Weissman & R. J. Thurnblad (Eds.), *The role of psychoanalysis in psychiatric education: Past, present and future* (pp. 225–269). Madison, CT: International Universities Press.

Cohler, B. (1989). Psychoanalysis and education: Motive, meaning and self. In K. Field, B. Cohler, & G. Wool (Eds.), *Learning and education: Psychoanalytic perspectives* (pp. 11–84). New York: International Universities Press.

Cohler, B. & Taber, S. (1993). Residential college and the transition from adolescence to young adulthood. In J. Sanders and J. Goldstein (Eds.) *Residential Treatment for Children and Adolescents.* New York: Haworth Press (In Press).

Csikszentmihalyi, M., & Larson, R. (1984). *Being adolescent.* New York: Basic Books.

Curtis, H. (1985). Clinical perspectives of self-psychology. *Psychoanalytic Quarterly, 54,* 339–378.

Decker, H. S. (1982). The choice of a name: "Dora" and Freud's relationship with Breuer. *Journal of the American Psychoanalytic Association, 30,* 113–136.

Delacour, S. (1986). Sigmund Freud's "Dora": A case of mistaken identity. 24–31.

Deutsch, F. (1957). A footnote to Freud's "Fragment of an analysis of a case of hysteria." *Psychoanalytic Quarterly, 26,* 159–167.

Deutsch, H. (1967). *Selected problems of adolescence, with emphasis on group formation.* New York: International Universities Press.

Dornbusch, S. (1989). The sociology of adolescence. *Annual Review of Sociology, 15,* 233–259.

Edelson, M. (1988). *Psychoanalysis: A theory in crisis.* Chicago: University of Chicago Press.

Elson, M. (Ed.). (1987). *The Kohut seminars.* New York: Norton.

Erikson, E. (1959). *Young man Luther.* New York: Norton.

Erikson, E. (1964). *Insight and responsibility.* New York: Norton.

Erikson, E. (1968). *Identity: Youth and crisis.* New York: Norton.

Fanon, F. (1963). *The wretched of the earth* (preface by Jean-Paul Sartre; C. Farrington, Trans.). New York: Grove Press.

Federn, P. (1926). Some variations in ego-feeling. *International Journal of Psychoanalysis, 7,* 434.

Federn, P. (1928). Narcissism in the structure of the ego. *International Journal of Psychoanalysis, 9,* 401.

Federn, P. (1934). The analysis of psychotics. *International Journal of Psychoanalysis, 15,* 209.

Federn, P. (1943). Psychoanalysis of psychoses, I–III. *Psychoanalytic Quarterly, 17.*

Fenichel, O. (1945). *The psychoanalytic theory of neurosis.* New York: Norton.

Fisher, S., & Greenberg, R. (1977). *The scientific credibility of Freud's theory and therapy.* New York: Basic Books.

Fisher, S., & Greenberg, R. (1978). *The scientific evaluation of Freud's theory and therapy: A book of readings.* New York: Basic Books.

Francis, J. (Reporter). (1968). Panel: Masturbation. *Journal of the American Psychoanalytic Association, 16,* 95–112.

Freud, A. (1965). *Normality and pathology in childhood: Assessments of development.* New York: International Universities Press.

Freud, A. (1936/1966). *The ego and the mechanism of defense* (rev. ed.). New York: International Universities Press.

Freud, S. (1895/1966). Project for a scientific psychology. In J. Strachey (Ed. and Trans.), *The standard edition of the complete psychological works of Sigmund Freud* (Vol. 1, pp. 295–387). London: Hogarth Press.

Freud, S. (1897/1985). Letter of February 13, 1896. In J. M. Masson (Ed. and Trans.), *The complete letters of Sigmund Freud to Wilhelm Fliess, 1887–1904* (pp. 277–278). Cambridge, MA: Harvard University Press.

Freud, S. (1897/1985). Letter of May 2, 1897 (including Draft L). In J. M. Masson (Ed. and Trans.), *The complete letters of Sigmund Freud to Wilhelm Fliess, 1887–1904* (pp. 239–243). Cambridge, MA: Harvard University Press.

Freud, S. (1898/1985). Letter of March 10, 1898. In J. M. Masson (Ed. and Trans.), *The complete letters of Sigmund Freud to Wilhelm Fliess, 1887–1904* (pp. 301–302). Cambridge, MA: Harvard University Press.

Freud, S. (1897/1985). Letter of September 21, 1987. In J. M. Masson (Ed. and Trans.), *The complete letters of Sigmund Freud to Wilhelm Fliess, 1887–1904* (pp. 263–267). Cambridge, MA: Harvard University Press.

Freud, S. (1905b/1953). Fragment of an analysis of a case of hysteria. In J. Strachey (Ed. and Trans.), *The standard edition of the complete psychological works of Sigmund Freud* (Vol. 7, pp. 3–124). London: Hogarth Press.

Freud, S. (1905a). Three essays on the theory of sexuality. In J. Strachey (Ed. and Trans.), *The standard edition of the complete psychological works of Sigmund Freud* (Vol. 7, pp. 130–243). London: Hogarth Press.

Freud, S. (1909). Notes upon a case of obsessional neurosis. In J. Strachey (Ed. and Trans.), *The standard edition of the complete psychological works of Sigmund Freud* (Vol. 10, pp. 153–318). London: Hogarth Press.

Freud, S. (1910/1957). The future prospects of psycho-analytic therapy. In J. Strachey (Ed. and Trans.), *The standard edition of the complete psychological works of Sigmund Freud* (Vol. 11, pp. 140–151). London: Hogarth Press.

Freud, S. (1900). The Interpretation of Dreams. *The standard edition of the complete psychological works of Sigmund Freud* (Vols. 4–5). London: Hogarth Press, 1953.

Freud, S. (1911). Psycho-analytic notes on an autobiographical account of a case of paranoia (*dementia paranoides*). In J. Strachey (Ed. and Trans.) *The standard edition of the complete psychological works of Sigmund Freud* (Vol. 12, pp. 3–82). London: Hogarth Press.

Freud, S. (1915/1958). Observations on transference love (further recommendations on the technique of psychoanalysis III). In J. Strachey (Ed. and Trans.), *The standard edition of the complete psychological works of Sigmund Freud* (Vol. 12, pp. 157–171). London: Hogarth Press.

Freud, S. (1937/1964). Analysis terminable and interminable. In J. Strachey (Ed. and Trans.), *The standard edition of the complete psychological works of Sigmund Freud* (Vol. 23, pp. 209–254). London: Hogarth Press.

Gabel, S. (1985). Sleep research and clinically reported dreams. Can they be integrated? Dora, revisited. *Journal of Abnormal Psychology, 30,* 185–205.

Galatzer-Levy, R. (1985). The analysis of an adolescent boy. *Adolescent Psychiatry, 12,* 336–360.

Galatzer-Levy, R. (1986). *What psychoanalysis can learn from computer science.* Paper presented at the Research Seminar, Chicago Institute for Psychoanalysis.

Galatzer-Levy, R. (1988). On working through—A model from artificial intelligence. *Journal of the American Psychoanalytic Association, 36,* 125–151.

Galatzer-Levy, R., & Cohler, B. (1990a). The developmental psychology of the self and the changing world-view of psychoanalysis. *Annual For Psychoanalysis, 17,* 1–44.

Galatzer-Levy, R., & Cohler, B. (1990b). *From adolescence to young adulthood, a transformation of the self-object world.* Manuscript submitted for publication.

Galatzer-Levy, R., & Cohler, B. (In Press). *The essential other.* New York: Basic Books.

Gardner, R., Holzman, P., Klein, G., Linton, H., & Spence, D. (1959). *Cognitive control: A study of individual consistencies in cognitive behavior.* New York: International Universities Press.

Gardner, R., Jackson, D., & Messick, S. (1960). *Personality organization in cognitive control and intellectual abilities.* New York: International Universities Press.

Gedo, J. (1977). Notes on the psychoanalytic management of archaic transference. *Journal of the American Psychoanalytic Association, 25,* 787–803.

Gedo, J. (1979). *Beyond interpretation: Toward a revised theory of psychoanalysis.* New York: International Universities Press.

Gedo, J. (1981). *Advances in clinical psychoanalysis.* New York: International Universities Press.

Gerstel, C., Feraios, A., & Gerdt, G. (1989). Widening circles: An ethnographic profile of a youth group. *Journal of Homosexuality, 17,* 75–92.

Gill, M. (1976). Metapsychology is not psychology. In M. Gill & P. Holzman (Eds.), *Psychology versus metapsychology: Psychoanalytic essays in memory of George S. Klein.* New York: International Universities Press.

Ginsberg, D., & Gottman, J. (1986). Conversations of college roommates: Similarities and differences in male and female friendships. In J. Gottman and J. G. Parker (Eds.), *Conversations of friends* (pp. 241–291). Cambridge, England: Cambridge University Press.

Glenn, J. (1969). Testicular and scrotal masturbation, *International Journal of Psychoanalysis, 50,* 353–362.

Glenn, J. (1986). Freud, Dora, and the maid: A study of countertransference. *Journal of the American Psychoanalytic Association, 34,* 591–606.

Glover, E. (1931). The therapeutic effect of inexact interpretation. *International Journal of Psychoanalysis, 12,* 397–411.

Goldberg, A. (1975). A fresh look at perverse behavior. *International Journal of Psychoanalysis, 56,* 335–342.

Goldberg, A. (1982). The self of psychoanalysis. In B. Lee (with collaboration of K. Smith) (Ed.), *Psychosocial theories of the self* (pp. 3–22). New York: Plenum Press.

Goldberg, A. (1988). Experience: Near, distant and absent. In A. Goldberg (Ed.), *A Fresh look at psychoanalysis: The view from Self Psychology* (pp. 84–95). Hillsdale, NJ: Analytic Press.

Goldberg, L. (1979). Remarks on transference–countertransference in psychotic states. *International Journal of Psychoanalysis, 60,* 347–356.

Gottman, J. (1986). The observation of social process. In J. Gottman & J. Parker (Eds.), *Conversations of friends* (pp. 51–102). Cambridge, England: Cambridge University Press.

Gottman, J., & Mettetal, G. (1986). Speculations about social and affective development: Friendship and acquaintanceship through adolescence. In J. Gottman & J. Parker (Eds.), *Conversations of friends* (pp. 192–239). Cambridge, England: Cambridge University Press.

Green, A. (1975). The analyst: Symbolization and the absence in the analytic setting. *International Journal of Psychoanalysis, 56,* 1.

Green, R. (1987). *The "sissy boy" syndrome.* New Haven, CT: Yale University Press.

Halpert, E. (1973). On a form of masturbation: The use of water. *Journal of the American Psychoanalytic Association, 21,* 526.

Hare-Mustin, R. T. (1983). An appraisal of the relationship between women and psychotherapy: 80 years after the case of Dora. *American Psychologist, 38,* 593–601.

Hartmann, H. (1964). Understanding and explaining. In H. Hartmann (Ed.) *Essays in ego psychology* (pp. 369–404). New York: International Universities Press. (Original work published 1927.).

Hartmann, H. (1939/1958). *Ego psychology and the problem of adaptation* (D. Rapaport, Trans.). New York: International Universities Press.

Hartmann, H. (1950). Comments on the psychoanalytic theory of the ego. In H. Hartmann, *Essays on ego psychology* (pp. 113–141). New York: International Universities Press.

Herdt, G. (1989). Gay and lesbian youth, emergent identities, and cultural scenes at home and abroad. *Journal of Homosexuality, 17*, 1–42.

Herzog, J. (1982). On father hunger: The father's role in the modulation of aggressive drive and fantasy. In S. Cath, A. Gurwith, & J. M. Ross (Eds.), *Father and son: Developmental and clinical perspectives* (pp. 163–174). Boston: Little, Brown.

Hetrick, E., Martin, A. D. (1987). Developmental issues and their resolution for gay and lesbian adolescents. *Journal of Homosexuality, 14*, 25–43. (special issue)

Holzman, P. (1985). Psychoanalysis: Is the therapy destroying the science? *Journal of the American Psychoanalytic Association, 33*, 725–770.

Hopkins, T. (1968). The social teaching of the Bhagavata Purana. In M. Singer (Ed.), *Krishna: Myths, rites, and attitudes*. Chicago: University of Chicago Press.

Isay, R. (1975). Influence of the primal scene on sexuality of the early adolescent. *Journal of the American Psychoanalytic Association, 23*, 535–553.

Isay, R. (1989). *Being homosexual: Gay men and their development*. New York: Farrar, Straus & Giroux.

Jackson, S. (1969). The history of Freud's concepts of regression. *Journal of the American Psychoanalytic Association, 14*, 743–784.

Jacobson, E. (1964). *The self and the object world*. New York: International Universities Press.

Jennings, L. (1986). The revival of "Dora": Advances in psychoanalytic theory and technique. *Journal of the American Psychoanalytic Association, 34*, 607–635.

Kanzer, M. (1980). Visual communication in the psychoanalytic situation. *International Journal of Psychoanalysis, 61*, 249–258.

Kernberg, O. F. (1975). Further contributions to the treatment of narcissistic personalities: A reply to the discussion by Paul H. Ornstein. *International Journal of Psychoanalysis, 56*, 245–247.

Kernberg, O. F. (1982). Self, ego, affects, and drives. *Journal of the American Psychoanalytic Association, 30*, 893–917.

Kernberg, O. F. (1987). Projection and projective identification: Developmental and clinical aspects. *Journal of the American Psychoanalytic Association, 35*, 795–819.

Kernberg, O. F. (1988). Clinical dimensions of masochism. *Journal of the American Psychoanalytic Association, 36*, 1005–1029.

Kett, J. (1977). *Rites of passage: Adolescence in America: 1790 to the present*. New York: Basic Books.

Khan, M. (1974a). Ego distortion, cumulative trauma and the role of reconstruction in the analytic situation. In M. Khan, *The privacy of the self* (pp. 59–68). London: Hogarth Press. (Original work published 1964.)

Khan, M. (1974b). The principle of cumulative trauma. In M. Khan, *The privacy of the self* (pp. 42–59). London: Hogarth Press. (Original work published 1963.)

Klein, G. (1970). *Perception, motives and personality*. New York: Knopf.

Klein, G. (1976). *Psychoanalytic theory: An exploration of essentials*. Madison, CT: International Universities Press.

Klein, M. (1975a). Early analysis. In M. Klein, *Love, guilt and reparation and other works, 1921–1945*. New York: Delacorte Press/Seymour Lawrence. (Original work published 1923.)

Klein, M. (1975b). Criminal tendencies in normal children. In M. Klein, *Love, guilt and reparation and other works, 1927–1945* (pp. 170–185). New York: Delacorte Press/Seymour Lawrence. (Original work published 1927.)

Klein, M. (1975c). Love, guilt and reparation. In M. Klein, *Love, guilt and reparation and other works, 1927–1945* (pp. 344–369). New York: Delacorte Press/Seymour Lawrence. (Original work published 1937.)

Klein, M. (1975d). The Oedipus complex in the light of early anxieties. In M. Klein, *Love, guilt and reparation and other works, 1927–1945* (pp.

370–419). New York: Delacorte Press/Seymour Lawrence. (Original work published 1945.)

Kohlberg, L., & Gilligan, C. (1971). The adolescent as a philosopher: The discovery of the self in the post-conventional world. *Daedalus, 100,* 1051–1086.

Kohon, G. (1984). Reflections on Dora: The case of hysteria. *International Journal of Psychoanalysis, 65,* 75–84.

Kohut, H. (1971). *The analysis of the self: A systematic approach to the psychoanalytic treatment of narcissistic personality disorders.* New York: International Universities Press.

Kohut, H. (1977). *The restoration of the self.* New York: International Universities Press.

Kohut, H. (1978). Introspection, empathy and psychoanalysis: An examination of the relationship between mode of observation and theory. In P. Ornstein (Ed.), *The search for the self: Selected writings of Heinz Kohut, 1950–1978* (Vol. 1, pp. 205–232). New York: International Universities Press. (Original work published in 1959.)

Kohut, H. (1984). *How does psychoanalysis cure?* Chicago: University of Chicago Press.

Kohut, H. (1985). Self Psychology and the sciences of man. In C. Strozier (Ed.), *Self Psychology and the humanities: Reflections on a new psychoanalytic approach by Heinz Kohut* (pp. 73–94). New York: Norton. (Original work published 1975.)

Kohut, H., & Wolf, E. (1978). The disorders of the self and their treatment: An outline. *International Journal of Psychoanalysis, 59,* 413–425.

Krohn, A., & Krohn, J. (1982). The nature of the Oedipus complex in the Dora case. *Journal of the American Psychoanalytic Association, 30,* 555–578.

Lacan, J. (1968). *The Languages of the self* (A. Wilden, Trans.). Baltimore, MD: Johns Hopkins University Press.

Langs, R. (1976). The misalliance dimension in Freud's case histories: I. The case of Dora. *International Journal of Psychoanalytic Psychotherapy, 5,* 301–317.

LaPlanche, J., & Pontalis, J. B. (1973). *The language of psychoanalysis.* New York: Norton.

Laqueur, W. (1962). *Young Germany: A history of the German youth movement.* London: Routledge & Kegan Paul.

Lasch, C. (1977). *Haven in a heartless world: The family besieged.* New York: Basic Books.

Laufer, M. (1968). The body image, the function of masturbation, and adolescence: Problems of ownership of the body. *Psychoanalytic Study of the Child, 23,* 114–137.

Laufer, M. (1976). The central masturbation fantasy, the final sexual organization, and adolescence. *Psychoanalytic Study of the Child, 31,* 297–316.

Laufer, M. (1986). Adolescence and psychosis. *International Journal of Psychoanalysis, 67,* 367–372.

Laufer, M. (1989). Adolescent sexuality: A mind/body continuum. *Psychoanalytic Study of the Child, 44,* 281–292.

Laufer, M., & Laufer, M. E. (Eds.). (1984). *Adolescence and developmental breakdown.* New Haven, CT: Yale University Press.

Lewin, K. K. (1973). Dora revisited. *Psychoanalytic Review, 60,* 519–532.

Mahler, M., Pine, F., & Bergman, A. (1975). *The psychological birth of the human infant.* New York: Basic Books.

Martin, A. D. (1982). Learning to hide: The socialization of the gay adolescent, *Adolescent Psychiatry, 10,* 52–65.

Mead, G. (1934). *Mind, self and society.* Chicago: University of Chicago Press.

Meissner, W. (1981). Notes on the psychoanalytic psychology of the self. *Psychoanalysis and Contemporary Thought, 1,* 233–248.

Meissner, W. (1986). Can psychoanalysis find its self? *Journal of the American Psychoanalytic Association, 34,* 379–400.

Muslin, H. (1982). Romeo and Juliet: The tragic self in adolescence. *Adolescent Psychiatry, 10,* 106–117.

Muslin, H., & Gill, M. (1978). Transference in the Dora case. *Journal of the American Psychoanalytic Association, 26,* 311–328.

Novick, J., & Novick, K. (1972). Beating fantasies in children. *International Journal of Psychoanalysis, 53,* 237–242.

Offer, D., Offer, J. B., & Ostrov. E. (1975). *From teenage to young manhood: A psychological study.* New York: Basic Books.

Offer, D., Ostrov, E., & Howard, K. (1981). *The adolescent: A psychological self-portrait.* New York: Basic Books.

Offer, D., & Sabshin, S. (1984) Adolescence: Empirical Perspective. In D. Offer & S. Sabshin (Eds.), *Normality and the life cycle.* New York: Basic Books.

Oremland, J. (1985). Kohut's reformulations of defense and resistance as applied in therapeutic psychoanalysis. In A. Goldberg (Ed.), *Progress in Self Psychology* (pp. 97–105). New York: Guilford Press.

Petersen, A. (1988). Adolescent development. *Annual Review of Psychology, 39,* 583–607.

Petersen, A., & Taylor, B. (1980). The biological approach to adolescence: Biological change and psychosocial adaptation. In J. Adelson (Ed.), *Handbook of the psychology of adolescence* (pp. 117–155). New York: Wiley.

Piaget, J., & Inhelder, B. (1969). *The psychology of the child* (H. Waver, Trans.). New York: Basic Books.

Pine, F. (1990). *Drive, ego, object, and self: A synthesis for clinical work.* New York: Basic Books.

Popper, K. (1959). *The logic of scientific discovery.* London: Hutchinson.

Racker, H. (1968). *Transference and countertransference.* New York: International Universities Press.

Rapaport, D. (1967a). The conceptual model of psychoanalysis. In M. Gill (Ed.), *The collected papers of David Rapaport* (pp. 405–431). New York: Basic Books. (Original work published 1951.)

Rapaport, D. (1967b). On the psychoanalytic theory of motivation. In M. Gill (Ed.), *The collected papers of David Rapaport* (pp. 853–915). New York: Basic Books. (Original work published 1961.)

Rapaport, D., & Gill, M. (1959). The points of view and assumptions of metapsychology. *International Journal of Psychoanalysis, 40,* 153–162.

Reich, W. (1932). *Der Einbruch der sexualmoral.* Berlin: Sexpol Verlag.

Richards, A. (Reporter). (1982a). Panel: Psychoanalytic theories of the self. *Journal of the American Psychoanalytic Association, 30,* 717–733.

Richards, A. (1982b). The superordinate self in psychoanalytic theory. *Journal of the American Psychoanalytic Association, 30,* 939–957.

Ricoeur, P. (1977). The question of proof in Freud's psychoanalytic writings. *Journal of the American Psychoanalytic Association, 25,* 835–872.

Ritvo, L. (1990). *Darwin's influence on Freud: A tale of two sciences.* New Haven, CT: Yale University Press.

Roazen, P. (1976). *Erik H. Erikson: The power and limits of a vision.* New York: Free Press.

Rogow, A. A. (1978). A further footnote to Freud's "Fragment of an analysis of a case of hysteria." *Journal of the American Psychoanalytic Association, 26,* 330–356.

Sander, L. (1962). Issues in early mother–child interaction. *Journal of the American Academy of Child Psychiatry, 2,* 141–166.

Sander, L. (1964). Adaptive relationships in early mother–child interaction. *Journal of the American Academy of Child Psychiatry, 3,* 221–263.

Sander, L. (1969). Regulation and organization in the early infant caretaker system. In R. Robertson (Ed.), *Brain and early behavior.* (pp. 311–333). London: Academic Press.

Sander, L. (1975). Infant and caretaking environment: Investigation and conceptualization of adaptive behavior in a system of increasing complexity. In E. J. Anthony (Ed.), *Explorations in child psychiatry* (pp. 129–166). New York: Plenum Press.

Sandler, J., & Rosenblatt, B. (1962). The concept of the representational world. *Psychoanalytic Study of the Child, 17,* 128–145.

Schafer, R. (1976). *A new language for psychoanalysis.* New Haven, CT: Yale University Press.

Schafer, R. (1980). Action language and the psychology of the self, *The annual of Psychoanalysis, 8,* 83–92.

Schafer, R. (1983). *The analytic attitude.* New York: Basic Books.

Schneider, M. (1989). Sappho was a right-on adolescent: Growing up lesbian. *Journal of Homosexuality, 17,* 111–130.

Segal, H. (1983). Some clinical implications of Melanie Klein's work: Emergence from narcissism. *International Journal of Psychoanalysis, 64,* 269–280.

Settlege, C., Curtis, J., Lozoff, M., Silberschatz, G., & Simburg, E. (1988). Conceptualizing adult development. *Journal of the American Psychoanalytic Association, 36,* 347–369.

Shane, E. (1987a). Varieties of psychoanalytic experience: I. *Psychoanalytic Inquiry, 7,* 199–240.

Shane, E. (1987b). Varieties of psychoanalytic experience: II. *Psychoanalytic Inquiry, 7,* 241.

Sklansky, M. (1977). The alchemy of love: Transmutation of the elements in adolescents and young adults. *Annual for Psychoanalysis, 5,* 77–104.

Skolnikoff, A. (1990). The emotional position of the analyst in the shift from psychotherapy to analysis. *Psychoanalytic Inquiry, 10,* 107–118.

Slipp, S. (1977). Interpersonal factors in hysteria: Freud's seduction theory and the case of Dora. *Journal of the Academy of Psychoanalysis, 5,* 359–376.

Socarides, C. (1989). *Homosexuality: Psychoanalytic therapy.* New York: Aronson.

Stechler, G., & Kaplan, S. (1980). The development of the self. *Psychoanalytic Study of the Self, 35,* 85–105.

Stengel, E. (1963). Hughlings Jackson's influence in psychiatry. *British Journal of Psychiatry, 109,* 348–355.

Stern, D. (1985). *The interpersonal world of the infant: A view from psychoanalysis and developmental psychology.* New York: Basic Books.

Stern, D. (1989). The representation of relational patterns: Developmental considerations. In A. Sameroff & R. Emde (Eds.), *Relationship disturbances in early childhood: A developmental approach* (pp. 52–68). New York: Basic Books.

Stolorow, R., Brandcraft, B., & Atwood, G. (1987). *Psychoanalytic treatment: An intersubjective approach.* Hillsdale, NJ: Analytic Press.

Strachey, J., & Editors. (1961a). Editor's annotation: Civilization and its discontents. *The standard edition of the complete psychological works of Sigmund Freud* (Vol. 21, pp. 65–66). London: Hogarth Press.

Strachey, J., & Editors. (1961b). Editor's note: The ego and the id. *The standard edition of the complete psychological works of Sigmund Freud.* (Vol. 19). London: Hogarth Press.

Strachey, J. & Editors. (1961c). Editor's annotation: Remarks on the theory and practice of dream interpretation. *The standard edition of the complete psychological works of Sigmund Freud* (Vol. 19, p. 133). London: Hogarth Press.

Sullivan, H. (1953). *The interpersonal theory of psychiatry.* New York: Norton.

Sulloway, F. (1979). *Freud, biologist of the mind.* New York: Basic Books.

Swanson, D. (1977). A critique of psychic energy as an explanatory concept. *Journal of the American Psychoanalytic Association, 25,* 603–634.

Tolpin, P. (1985). The primacy of the preservation of self. In A. Goldberg (Ed.), *Progress in Self Psychology* (Vol 1, pp. 83–87). New York: Guilford Press.

Tolpin, M., & Kohut, H. (1990). The disorders of the self: The psychopathology of the self. In S. Greenspan & G. Pollock (Eds.), *The course of life, II: Early childhood* (pp. 229–254). New York: International Universities Press. (Original work published 1980.)

Trevarthan, C. (1980). The foundations of intersubjectivity: Development of interpersonal and cognitive understanding in infants. In D. Olson (Ed.), *The social foundation of language and thought: Essays in honor of Jerome Bruner* (pp. 316–342). New York: Norton.

Trevarthan, C. (1989). Origins and directions for the concept of infant intersubjectivity. *SRCD Newsletter,* Autumn, pp. 1–4.

Trevarthan, C., & Hubley, P. (1978). Secondary intersubjectivity: Confidence, confiders, and acts of meaning in the first year. In A. Lock (Ed.), *Action, gesture and symbol.* New York: Academic Press.

Troiden, R. R. (1989). The formation of homosexual identities. *Journal of Homosexuality, 17,* 43–73.

Tyson, R. L. (1986). Countertransference evolution in theory and practice. *Journal of the American Psychoanalytic Association, 34,* 251–274.

Vaillant, G. (1977). *Adaptation to life.* Boston: Little, Brown.

Vaillant, G. (1986). *Empirical studies of ego mechanisms of defense.* Washington, DC: American Psychiatric Association Press.

Van Gennep, A. (1960). *The rites of passage* (M. B. Vizedom & G. L. Caffee, Trans.). Chicago: University of Chicago Press. (Original work published 1908.)

Wallerstein, R. (1977). Psychic energy reconsidered—introduction. *Journal of the American Psychoanalytic Association, 25,* 529–536.

Wallerstein, R. (1986). Psychoanalysis as a science: Response to new challenges. *Psychoanalytic Quarterly, 55,* 414.

Wallerstein, R. (1987). Psychoanalysis, psychoanalytic science, and psychoanalytic research.

Journal of the American Psychoanalytic Association, 57, 3–30.

Wermer, H., & Levin, S. (1967). Masturbation fantasies: Their changes with growth and development. *Psychoanalytic Study of the Child, 22,* 315–328.

White, R. W. (1983). *Ego and reality in psychoanalytic theory.* New York: International Universities Press.

Winnicott, D. W. (1953). Transitional objects and transitional phenomena. In *Collected papers: Through pediatrics to psychoanalysis* (pp. 229–242). New York: Basic Books.

Winnicott, D. (1960). The theory of the parent–infant relationship. *International Journal of Psychoanalysis, 41,* 585–595.

Winnicott, D. W. (1965). Ego distortion in terms of the true and the false self. In D. W. Winnicott, *The maturational process and the facilitating environment* (pp. 140–152). New York: International Universities Press. (Original work published 1960.)

Winnicott, D. W. (1988). *Human nature.* New York: Schocken Press.

Wohl, R. (1979). *The generation of 1914.* Cambridge, MA: Harvard University Press.

Wolf, E. (1980). Tomorrow's self; Heinz Kohut's contribution to adolescent psychiatry. *Adolescent Psychiatry, 8,* 41–50.

Wolf, E. (1982). Adolescence; Psychology of the self and selfobjects. *Adolescent Psychiatry, 10,* 171–181.

Wolf, E. (1988). *Treating the self: Elements of clinical Self-Psychology.* New York: Guilford Press.

Wolf, E., Gedo, J., & Terman, D. (1972). On the adolescent process as a transformation of the self. *Journal of Youth and Adolescence, 1,* 257–272.

CHAPTER 5

Sexuality

BRENT C. MILLER and PATRICIA A. H. DYK

Immense changes occur in human sexuality during the second decade of life. In many respects, humans are sexual beings from birth, but adolescence is a period when sexuality takes on different meanings and manifestations than before. This chapter is about sexuality during adolescence, and about the usual and unusual patterns of sexual development and behavior during this period of rapid growth and change.

Pubertal development is popularly associated with the emergence of sexuality, but human sexual interest and behavior begin much earlier than puberty.[1] Prenatally and shortly after birth, reflexive penile and clitoral erections occur (Langfeldt, 1981). Infants less than a year old are capable of orgasm (Kinsey, Pomeroy, & Martin, 1948), and many parents observe their infants touching and (apparently) deriving pleasure from their sex organs (Martinson, 1980). It is abundantly evident that sexual curiosity, genital stimulation, and overt or covert sex play are commonplace before pubescence in many if not all human cultures and in most primate species (Currier, 1981; Ford & Beach, 1951). Freud's notion of a preadolescent latency stage characterized by a lack of sexual interest is not supported by research (Goldman & Goldman, 1982).

As compared with the sexuality of younger children, however, there is a dramatic increase in sexual interest and behavior during pubescence (Diepold & Young, 1979; Dreyer, 1982). In the life course, puberty marks the point of most rapid sexual development. Changes in biology, such as hormonally linked sex drive (Higham, 1980), have been among the most frequent explanations given for this phenomenon. Secondary sexual characteristics, also under the control of pubertal hormones, serve as both latent and manifest signals to the individual, and to others, of the adolescent's sexual interest and readiness.

Although biology establishes the potential for sexual behavior, cross-cultural data have demonstrated that sociocultural factors determine how that potential will be expressed (Gagnon & Simon, 1973). Stated more explicitly, societies constrain "the age, gender, legal, and kin relationships between sexual actors, as well as setting limits on the sites of

---

Appreciation is expressed to Gerald Adams and Roger Graves for providing feedback on a previous version of this chapter.

[1] The following three paragraphs are adapted from Savin-Williams (1987).

behavior and the connections between sexual organs" (1973, p. 4).

Social institutions, especially the family and religion, play key roles in socializing, shaping, and constraining individual sexual behavior throughout life. DeLamater (1981, p. 264) has argued that social institutions control sexual behavior in three ways. First, they provide a specific perspective about sexuality that defines the norms for individual sexual conduct. Second, those who occupy institutional roles use the normative perspective on sexuality in interactions with individuals as the basis for informal controls. Third, social institutions often have formal sanctioning systems that constrain behavior through fear of these sanctions.

The Christian religion has had a major influence on sexual norms and behavior in North America; other religious traditions have influenced sexuality elsewhere. Christianity traditionally viewed many kinds of physical pleasure as questionable if not sinful, and sexual activity was explicitly defined as reproductive or procreational (LoPiccolo & Heiman, 1977). These basic beliefs have been elaborated into more specific norms and taboos, including those prohibiting the sexual activity of children, masturbation, homosexuality, and sodomy, perhaps because these forms of sexual behavior have no reproductive potential. Relatedly, the Christian tradition has also defined marriage as the acceptable context for reproductive intercourse, effectively prohibiting premarital and extramarital sexual relationships (DeLamater, 1981). During the 20th century, however, there has been a marked shift toward separating sexual behavior from its reproductive matrix (Freedman & Demilio, 1988).

The family always influences individual sexuality subtly, and sometimes overtly, by conveying to children a perspective about sexuality. In addition to socialization, some have argued that the family plays the key role in regulating sexual behaviors. All societies expect sexual activity to occur within marriage, and a major social function of marriage is to regularize access to a sexual partner (Davis, 1976; DeLamater, 1981). Within human cultures, sexual activities are evaluated in terms of their effect on the family as an institution; that is, rules about sexual conduct are subordinate to the family. If premarital intercourse is viewed as undermining marriage and the family, it is disapproved; if premarital sex is viewed as contributing to or at least not threatening marriage, it is relatively accepted.

In summary, the importance of cultural norms and social controls in shaping sexual patterns is apparent. Because sexuality has multiple dimensions, there are many ways of understanding sexuality in general, and adolescent sexuality in particular. Insights from biology, including pubertal development and hormonal influences, are key bases of understanding sexuality among adolescents. The psychological principles of cognition, learning, and identity formation are likewise necessary elements in understanding adolescents' sexuality.

SEXUAL DEVELOPMENT

This section begins with a brief description of major biological changes, but it emphasizes the psychosocial dimensions of sexual development. (See Chapter 2 for a more complete discussion of the hormonal and physical changes associated with adolescence.)

Biological Changes[2]

"Puberty is characterized by a sudden onset of hormone flow from the hypothalamus and pituitary gland, which triggers a complex set of biological and psychological responses manifested in extremely rapid growth and development" (Rosen & Weinstein, 1988).

Key pubertal changes in boys are the development of secondary sex characteristics, such

---

[2]This section is adapted from Rosen and Weinstein (1988).

as the initial growth of pubic hair; growth of the testes and scrotum; and a general body growth spurt that begins at about age 13, continues for 2 to 3 years, and then slows to adulthood. First ejaculation, achieved by masturbation or nocturnal emission (a wet dream), is common during this time, and it can be a source of anxiety and confusion to the uninformed male adolescent. Nocturnal emissions, often accompanied by erotic dreams, occur during the REM stage of sleep and can be repeated four to five times during one night.

For girls, hormonal changes trigger breast development and the appearance of pubic hair, the first signs of female sexual maturity. The onset of sexual maturation in girls usually occurs about 2 years earlier than it does in boys; this difference in onset tends to perpetuate the physical and emotional separation between boys and girls of the same age. Menarche, the onset of menstruation, usually occurs shortly after the physical growth spurt, but it is not a definite indication of reproductive maturity. Initial menstrual cycles are usually sporadic and irregular, and early cycles generally occur without ovulation. A regularized menstrual cycle takes about a year to achieve.

Sexual Orientation

Being attracted to persons of the same or opposite sex takes on greater importance when sexual arousal begins to accelerate during adolescence. Sexual orientation or preference is an especially salient issue for ambivalent or homosexually inclined adolescents (Herdt, 1988). Powerful social pressures, norms, and identity feelings surround this aspect of sexuality (Rematedi, 1987). The large majority of adolescents become heterosexual, but there is significant variation in attraction toward partners of the same or opposite sex. The most widely quoted statistics for males are (Kinsey, Pomeroy, & Martin, 1948):

Exclusively homosexual throughout life: 4%

Homosexual for 3 years or more between the ages of 16 and 55: 8% to 10%

Some overt homosexual experience to the point of orgasm between adolescence and old age: 37%.

More recent estimates based on population surveys are that about 20% of adult men in the United States had sexual contact to orgasm with another man at some time in life; 6.7% had such contact after age 19; and about 2% had such a homosexual contact in the previous year (Fay, Turner, Klassen, & Gagnon, 1989).

In 1970, the Kinsey Institute for Sex Research conducted a study of nearly 1,000 homosexual men and women in the San Francisco Bay area, along with nearly 500 heterosexuals for comparison (Bell, Weinberg, & Hammersmith, 1981). The focus of the study was on the origin and development of sexual orientation or sexual preference.[3] The conclusions about the development of sexual orientation are summarized as follows:

1. By the time boys and girls reach adolescence, their sexual preference is likely to be already determined, even though they may not yet have become sexually very active.

2. Homosexuality is indicated or reinforced by sexual feelings that typically occur 3 years or so before "advanced" homosexual activity begins, and these feelings, more than homosexual activities, appear to be crucial in the development of adult homosexuality.

3. Homosexual men and women are not particularly lacking in heterosexual experiences during their childhood and adolescent years. They are distinguished from their

---

[3]Although they titled their work *Sexual Preference*, we agree with the authors that this term is somewhat problematic. "Preference" implies a choice between alternatives, and it is not at all clear that people make this choice. As the authors stated: "We do not mean to imply that a given sexual orientation is the result of a conscious decision" (Bell et al., 1981, p. 222).

heterosexual counterparts, however, in finding such experiences unsatisfying.
4. Among both men and women, there is a powerful link between gender nonconformity and the development of homosexuality.
5. Respondents' identification with their opposite-sex parents while they were growing up appears to have no significant impact on whether they become heterosexual or homosexual.
6. For both male and female respondents, identification with the parent of the same sex appears to have a relatively weak connection to the development of sexual orientation.
7. For both men and women, poor relationships with fathers seemed more important than whatever relationships they may have had with their mothers.
8. Insofar as we can identify differences between male and female psychosexual development, gender nonconformity appears somewhat more salient for males than for females, and family relationships are more salient for females than for males.

From this major study and a variety of other sources (Ellis & Ames, 1987), the evidence is compelling that there are strong continuities between a person's childhood and adolescent sexual feelings (and to a lesser extent, behaviors), and his or her adult sexual orientation. These data can be interpreted in at least two different ways. The childhood-to-adulthood continuity in homosexual feelings and behavior can be interpreted, paraphrasing Bell et al. (1981, p. 187), as reflecting an extraordinarily strong conditioning effect that "tracks" people into homosexuality. In other words, situations that produce homosexual arousal, that make one feel sexually different, and/or that include genital homosexual experiences teach a boy or girl to respond homosexually.

An alternative explanation is that gradually more intense and focused sexual feelings and behavior simply reflect the emergence of a deep-seated propensity toward either homosexuality or heterosexuality, which begins to emerge during childhood and continues into adulthood. In other words, considerable evidence (Ellis & Ames, 1987) suggests that there may be a biological predisposition to be homosexual or heterosexual, and during childhood and adolescence this basic sexual orientation becomes increasingly evident.

In summary, the evidence is quite clear that adolescence is a crucial time in establishing sexual orientation. Although most adolescents are attracted to members of the opposite sex, some are aroused by and attracted to members of their own sex. This development of sexual orientation is, apparently, the result of a pattern of feelings and reactions within the child that cannot be traced back to a single social or psychological root. Indeed, homosexuality may arise from biological precursors. "For males in particular, sexual orientation as a rule evolves relatively early in life (very often, before the teenage years) and in general is relatively impervious to whatever occurs subsequently" (Bell et al., 1981, p. 222).

Psychosocial Development

A broader conceptualization about the development of sexuality in adolescence has been offered by Sarrel and Sarrel (1979, 1981). Based on clinical interviews with over 4,000 Yale University students over a decade, they suggested that adolescents go through a gradual sexual development which they have termed *"sexual unfolding."* Although the term "unfolding" suggests the activation of a scripted biological program, Sarrel and Sarrel have described a process that involves a realization of sexual response capacity, recognition of sexual preferences, and development of the capacity for sharing sexual pleasure in a loving relationship. The sequence and timing of puberty, sexual interaction, and other factors, combined with physical and emotional development and prior sexual experiences, determine the course of the unfolding process for each individual. Sarrel and Sarrel identified nine processes of sexual unfolding that usually occur during adolescence.

1. *An evolving sense of body—toward a body image that is gender-specific and fairly free of distortion (particularly about the genitals).* One of the tasks of adolescence is to become comfortable with one's maturing body. By understanding their bodily changes, adolescents may be saved embarrassment or anxiety provoked by ignorance or mistaken notions about their genitals. To accomplish this, it is important that an adolescent learn the facts about his or her own genital development, have opportunities to express concerns about pubertal changes, and gradually become comfortable with looking at and touching the genitals.

2. *The ability to overcome or modulate guilt, shame, fear, and childhood inhibitions associated with sexual thoughts and behavior.* Sex still remains one of the most difficult subjects for North American adolescents and parents to discuss. Although sex might be discussed more by younger than older generations of parents, much of the communication still focuses on prohibitions or warnings. Masturbation is often discouraged from early childhood. As an individual matures and begins to experiment sexually, he or she becomes more comfortable with a range of sexual activities. It becomes the task of the maturing adolescent to determine what is appropriate for him or her.

3. *A gradual loosening of primary emotional ties to parents and siblings.* As children mature, they experience a gradual process of separating from parents and developing a primary attachment to an age-mate. Problems are most likely to arise when an adolescent has a very dependent or ambivalent attachment to the parents, or when parental attitudes toward sex have been so restrictive that sexual behavior engenders feelings of disloyalty or fear of retaliation from the parents.. Developing a sense of independence from family in one's sexuality may be related to other aspects of life. For example, what may present as a sexual problem to the clinician may be a broader issue of dependence/independence.

4. *Learning to recognize what is erotically pleasing and displeasing and being able to communicate this to one's partner.* Many people consider sex to be a natural function but confuse "natural" with "automatic." Satisfying sexual interaction involves learning over time the type of touching and stimulation that is pleasing to oneself and one's partner and the ability to communicate this information. Although it may be difficult to verbalize one's preferences, not to communicate them can lead to emotionally or physically painful sexual experiences that may develop into a serious dysfunction such as a phobic anxiety associated with sexual situations.

5. *Resolution of conflict and confusion about sexual orientation.* Adolescents who become homosexual or bisexual often experience a long struggle in understanding their primary orientation, and their focus on sexual preference sometimes delays other aspects of sexual development. Several experiences may cause individuals, primarily males, to wonder about their sexual orientation. These include early or preadolescent same-sex play experiences; delayed sexual maturation and onset of sexual behavior; more satisfaction from self-stimulation compared to intercourse; remaining a virgin; or sexual inadequacy.

6. *An increasingly satisfying sexual life, free of sexual dysfunction or compulsion, and including, for the majority, satisfying autoeroticism.* Common sexual dysfunctions among adolescents include impotence, never experiencing an orgasm, or premature ejaculation. Left untreated, these dysfunctions will impair the unfolding process and can lead to a permanent impairment or a variety of psychological and interpersonal problems.

7. *A growing awareness of being a sexual person and of the value of sex in one's life, including options such as celibacy.* Late adolescence is a period of questioning and restructuring values, sexual values included. Individuals sometimes go through a period of experimentation or "casual sex" as a part of this process. Many young women indicate that problems arise with casual sex in that the experience is not satisfying or they become too emotionally involved in spite of a desire to have "no strings attached." Developing and understanding one's own value system and how one's sexuality is related to values is an important step in sexual unfolding.

8. *Becoming responsible about oneself, one's partner, and society, for example, using contraception and not using sex to exploit another person.* The decision to use contraception represents a level of ego development in which one recognizes that one's actions may result in an unwanted pregnancy. The ability of a couple to discuss, plan, and support one another in the decision to contracept might indicate a higher level of maturity and psychological intimacy.

9. *An increasing ability to experience eroticism as one aspect of intimacy with another person, to recognize that not all eroticism occurs in an intimate relationship, but that this fusion of sex and love is possible.* There appears to be an erosion of prescribed sex-role behaviors for males and females in sexual relationships, allowing more freedom for a couple to communicate honestly with each other. When emotional closeness, mutual caring, vulnerability, and trust are blended with eroticism, the result can be a relationship that can be sexually intimate.

The Cumulative Nature of Sexual Behaviors

In addition to, or perhaps in concert with, the more general psychological "unfolding" described by Sarrel and Sarrel from their clinical interviews, there is a large amount of survey research data to support the assertion that there is a normative developmental pattern in the sequence of adolescent heterosexual behaviors. This is not to say that the order is invariant, but that a sequence is discernible. Couples usually share less intimate behaviors first, such as touching, embracing, and kissing, then move on to moderately intimate behaviors, such as fondling and petting, and subsequently engage in more intimate behaviors that include sexual intercourse. The number of stages or behaviors delineated varies from study to study, but a developmental pattern is evident and shows increasing participation by age from less to more intimate behavior.

For example, among White junior and senior high school students in one Michigan community in the early 1970s, a large majority of males and females had held hands, embraced, and kissed; a moderate percentage had engaged in petting above and below the waist; and a much smaller percentage had experienced coitus (Vener & Stewart, 1974). The same pattern of most widespread experience with less sexually intimate behavior was evident within each year of age for both males and females.

Another way of inferring a developmental sequence of sexual behaviors is to calculate the average age when each behavior was first experienced. Randomly sampled 18-to-24-year-old students and nonstudents in Madison, Wisconsin, retrospectively reported the age at which they engaged in nine sexual behaviors (DeLamater & MacCorquodale, 1979). The sequence of their reports ranged from necking through French kissing, breast fondling, genital manipulation, to sexual intercourse.

The Guttman scaling technique or scalogram analysis has been used to quantify the cumulative nature of sexual behaviors. The coefficient of reproducibility measures how well respondents' most extreme scores in an ordered sequence predict their total response patterns. In the Wisconsin data described above, the coefficient of reproducibility was .98; in other words, knowing the most intimate sexual behavior that respondents had engaged in allowed the prediction of their less intimate behavior 98% of the time. Similar coefficients of reproducibility were obtained with a more recent volunteer sample of Australian teenagers and young adults (McCabe & Collins, 1984), using a sequence of 12 sexual behaviors.

A more sophisticated analysis of the sequence of sexual behaviors among younger adolescents was based on both cross-sectional scalogram analysis techniques and longitudinal linking of individual sexual behavior over a 2-year-period (Smith & Udry, 1985). In the student body of a junior high school, in which students were ages 12 to 15 at round one, strong evidence was found among White adolescents for a developmental sequence from necking, feeling breasts through clothing, feeling breasts without clothing, feeling female sex organs directly, feeling penis directly, to intercourse. This sequence of behaviors produced high coefficients of reproducibility (.97) and scalability (.75) for White males and females, but not for Blacks. Among Black males and females, a greater percentage indicated that they had had intercourse as compared to any of the unclothed petting behaviors. The investigators concluded that White and Black adolescents appear to have different normative expectations regarding intercourse, with Whites typically engaging in a longer sequence of behaviors prior to having intercourse, and Blacks being more likely to have intercourse with fewer precoital behaviors.

In summary, sexual development is a gradual process that accelerates and becomes more differentiated during the second decade of life. These changes are set in motion by hormones that activate the adolescent growth spurt and the development of secondary sexual characteristics. Sexual development also includes elements of psychological "unfolding" in terms of understanding and accepting one's sexuality, and establishing one's sexual orientation. These inner changes are usually accompanied by increasing sexual behaviors and experiences that are propelled by biology and social expectations. By the mid- to late teens, most adolescents will have experienced a fairly predictable sequence of sexual behaviors, usually including having had sexual intercourse.

PATTERNS OF ADOLESCENT SEXUAL INTERCOURSE

Prevalence and Trends

Our specific focus on heterosexual intercourse in this section represents a belief that it is among the most important adolescent sexual behaviors that need to be understood. Several compelling issues, including unwanted pregnancy (Hayes, 1987), sexually transmitted diseases (Bell & Hein, 1984), and the AIDS epidemic (Hein, 1988), cannot be addressed without accurate knowledge about intercourse behavior.

Table 5.1 shows percentages, by age, of female adolescents who reported having had sexual intercourse; data are from the early 1970s through the late 1980s. Two trends are of interest in these data. The more obvious trend is apparent from reading down any column in Table 5.1: as age increases, there is a higher percentage of female adolescents who have experienced sexual intercourse. Second, reading across the table for any given age shows a trend toward increasing sexual intercourse experience in recent years. Sexual intercourse experience among female adolescents increased most markedly during the 1970s, plateaued in the early 1980s (Hofferth, Kahn, & Baldwin, 1987), and appears to have risen again in the middle 1980s.

Table 5.2 shows both male and female sexual intercourse experience by age and race in 1983–1984. Relatively similar percentages of White and Hispanic adolescents reported sexual intercourse experience; slightly higher percentages of Hispanic males than White males were sexually experienced, but lower percentages of Hispanic females than White

Table 5.1 Percentages of Never Married Females Who Have Had Sexual Intercourse: U.S. National Sample Surveys, 1971–1986

Age	Year of Survey					
	1971[a]	1976	1979	1982[b]	1983–1984[c]	1986[d]
12						7%
13					3.3%	10
14					8.4	9
15	14.8%	18.9%	22.8%	17.0%	17.6	22
16	21.8	30.0	39.5	29.0	33.2	42
17	28.2	46.0	50.1	41.0	50.9	53
18	42.6	56.7	63.0	58.6	67.6	—
19	48.2	64.1	71.4	72.0	—	—
Average	30.4	43.4	49.8	44.9	—	24
N	2,739	1,452	1,717	1,157	5,450	486

[a]1971–1979 data are from the National Surveys of Young Women (Zelnik & Kantner, 1980).
[b]1982 data are from the National Survey of Family Growth (reported in Hofferth, Kahn, & Baldwin, 1987, table 1).
[c]1983–1984 data are from the National Longitudinal Surveys of Youth (Mott & Haurin, 1988, table 1). Figures are the percentages who reported sexual intercourse prior to the next year of age.
[d]1986 data are from Harris & Associates (1986), table 1.1.

females had had intercourse. Black adolescents of both sexes were much more likely than their White or Hispanic counterparts to have had sexual intercourse at each year of age. Although there is some evidence of a decline in the double standard (Bell et al., 1981), it is evident that, within each race, males are still more likely than females of the same age to report sexual intercourse experience.

As was true for Table 5.1, the strongest pattern in Table 5.2 is the increasing percentage of intercourse experience by age. Although increasing sexual experience by age is intuitively expected, it is worthwhile to look more closely at the circumstances associated with first sexual intercourse.

The Transition to Having Sexual Intercourse

Limited research has been done about first intercourse experiences. In the mid-1980s, it could still be accurately stated that relatively little was known about the context of first

Table 5.2 Cumulative Percentages of Adolescents Who Had Sexual Intercourse Prior to Given Ages, by Gender and Race, 1983–1984

Age	Males				Females			
	Total	White	Black	Hispanic	Total	White	Black	Hispanic
14	10.2%	6.8%	30.4%	9.9%	3.3%	3.2%	4.9%	2.0%
15	17.2	12.5	44.3	18.3	8.4	7.9	12.5	6.1
16	29.1	23.5	61.4	31.8	17.6	16.6	24.2	15.2
17	48.4	43.3	78.6	49.9	33.2	31.3	45.7	28.5
18	64.8	60.8	87.3	68.0	50.9	49.2	64.2	42.3
19	78.2	75.5	93.5	80.3	67.6	66.2	79.1	58.4
N	5,396	3,219	1,362	815	5,450	3,230	1,365	855

Note: Adapted from Mott & Haurin, 1988, table 1.

premarital sexual intercourse, in spite of the significance of the event both to the individual and to society (Zelnik & Shah, 1983). Only recently has it been possible to answer questions such as: Under what circumstances do adolescents have their first sexual intercourse experience? Where and with whom does first sexual intercourse occur?

The Zelnik and Kantner surveys of young women (1980) included questions about the first sexual intercourse experience; in the 1979 survey, similar questions were asked of a sample of 17-to-21-year-old males. In the samples of young women, the age at first intercourse averaged 16.4 in 1971, 16.1 in 1976, and 16.2 in 1979. In the 1979 survey data, Black females were nearly a year younger than White females when they first had intercourse (15.5 vs. 16.4), and Black males were about a year and a half younger than White males when they first had intercourse (14.4 vs. 15.9). (See Table 5.3.) These large differences, between races, in early intercourse experiences are not significantly reduced by controlling for social, economic, or educational variables and appear to be largely attributable to a normative contextual effect (Furstenberg, Morgan, Moore, & Peterson, 1987).

In the 1979 Zelnik and Kantner survey, respondents were asked the age of their first sexual partner. The average age of young women's first partners was 19 (19.2 among Whites and 18.4 among Blacks); in other words, a female's first sexual partner tended to be about 3 years older than she was. Males' first sexual partners were also older than they were at the time of their first intercourse experience, but by less than a year (on the average, older female partners were 16.4 and males averaged 15.7 years of age at first intercourse). The older sexual partners of both sexes were rarely a great deal older; only 9% of young women and 3% of young men reported that their first sexual experience was with a partner age 23 or older.

The large majority of young women were in an ongoing relationship with the male with whom they first had sexual intercourse. In the 1979 Zelnik and Kantner data (see Table 5.4), 55% were going steady, 24% were dating, and 9% were engaged to their partner when they first had intercourse; the remaining 11% said that their first intercourse experience occurred with "a friend" or someone whom they had met only recently. Young Black females were more likely than Whites to say that they had been just dating their first sexual partners (33% vs. 22%) and were less likely than Whites to say that they had been going steady (47% vs. 58%).

The above data are of particular interest when viewed in combination with young women's reports of where their first intercourse took place. Over 75% said that their first sexual experience occurred in the home of their partner, in their own home, or in the home of a friend, and these percentages were similar for Blacks and Whites. Among those whose first sexual experience did not take place in a home, Blacks were more likely to say that it happened in a hotel/motel and Whites were more likely to say that it occurred in a car (Zelnik & Shah, 1983).

The relationship between males and their first female sexual partner tends to be

Table 5.3 Mean Age of Respondent and Partner at First Sexual Intercourse

	Female			Male		
	Total	White	Black	Total	White	Black
Respondent	16.2	16.4	15.5	15.7	15.9	14.4
Partner	19.0	19.2	18.4	16.4	16.6	15.2
N	938	479	459	682	400	282

Note: Adapted from Zelnik & Shah, 1983, table 1.

Table 5.4 Percentage Distribution of Women Aged 15 to 19 and of Men Aged 17 to 21, by Relationship with Their First Sexual Partner, According to Race

Relationship with First Partner	Women			Men		
	Total (N = 936)	White (N = 478)	Black (N = 458)	Total (N = 670)	White (N = 396)	Black (N = 274)
Engaged	9.3%	9.6%	8.2%	0.6%	0.5%	1.0%
Going steady	55.2	57.6	46.5	36.5	39.2	21.9
Dating	24.4	22.2	32.6	20.0	20.2	19.0
Friends	6.7	6.0	9.4	33.7	30.2	52.4
Recently met*	4.4	4.6	3.3	9.3	9.9	5.7
Total	100.0	100.0	100.0	100.0	100.0	100.0

Note: From Zelnik & Shah, 1983, table 2.

*Among women, this category includes a small number who reported some other relationship.

characterized by less commitment than is the case among females. Among the males, 36% said that they were going steady, 34% said that their first partner was "a friend," and 10% said that they first had intercourse with someone they "recently met." Black male adolescents were much more likely than Whites to first have had intercourse with a friend (52% vs. 32%) and were less likely to have been going steady (22% vs. 39%).

Perhaps the most striking aspect of the first sexual experience is its apparent spontaneity—for most adolescents, first sexual intercourse is not planned. In 1979, only 17% of young women and 23% of men said that they had planned their first act of intercourse (Zelnik & Shah, 1983). Similarly, in a 1986 survey, 65% of sexually experienced males and females said that their first intercourse "just happened" (Harris & Associates, 1986). This might be because intercourse tends to occur in a progressive sequence of dyadic behaviors, as previously described.

Frequency of Intercourse and Number of Partners

It is also of interest to know how often adolescents have intercourse and with how many different partners. Data are very limited on these questions. Tabulations in the 1982 National Survey of Family Growth on the frequency of sexual intercourse among 15-to-19-year-old unmarried females who were sexually experienced showed that 18% had not had intercourse in the 3 months prior to the interview, 16% said about once a month, 25% said 2 to 3 times a month, 20% said once a week, and another 20% said more than twice a week or daily (Hofferth, 1987). Younger teens, aged 15 to 17, were somewhat less likely than older teens (18 to 19 years old) to have had sexual intercourse twice a week or more, and a 3-month span of no sexual intercourse was more common among Whites (20.7%) than among Blacks (9.5%).

Data on the number of premarital partners of sexually experienced adolescent females come from the National Surveys of Young Women (Zelnik, 1983). The average number of sexual partners was 2.9 in 1976 and 2.6 in 1979. In 1971, over 60% reported having had intercourse with only one partner; in the 1979 survey, those who reported having sexual experience with only one partner had declined to just under half (49%). A little over one-third (35%) reported intercourse experience with two or three partners, 8% reported four or five partners, and 8% reported having six or more partners.

Contraceptive Use by Adolescents

In spite of prevalent sexual intercourse among adolescents, researchers have repeatedly found that they are slow to adopt contraception.

About half of unmarried females aged 15 to 19 in 1982 reported using some method of contraception at first intercourse; about two-thirds of unmarried teens exposed to the risks of unintended pregnancy report currently using a contraceptive method (Bachrach & Mosher, 1984; Pratt, Mosher, Bachrach, & Horn, 1984). Among young women 15 to 24 who made their first family planning visit to a doctor or clinic in 1982, only 17% came before having intercourse; another 10% came within a month after first intercourse. For those waiting longer to seek contraception, the median delay between dates of first intercourse and first visit was just less than two years (Mosher & Horn, 1988). Many of these young women probably used nonmedical methods, at least some of the time, but, in the late 1980s, about 20% of sexually active adolescents did not use contraception of any kind (Moore & Peterson, 1989; Sonenstein, Pleck, & Ku, 1989).

Because the first intercourse episode usually "just happens," the most often used contraceptive methods for first intercourse are the "male methods," withdrawal and condoms (Zelnik & Shah, 1983). Unfortunately, the failure rates for these and other nonmedical methods are high, particularly among adolescents (Jones & Forrest, 1989). Recent data suggest that a dramatic increase in condom use occurred in the late 1980s. Sonenstein et al. (1989) compared data for males aged 17 to 19, interviewed in 1979, with similar data for males in 1988. Condom use had more than doubled, from 20% to 54% at first intercourse and from 21% to 58% at most recent sex. No increase in the use of effective female methods was reported by these young men; an overall increase in the use of contraception was entirely identified with increased condom use. Data collected from female adolescents in the 1988 National Survey of Family Growth corroborate the recent increase in condom use (Bachrach, 1989).

There are many reasons why American adolescents are slow to adopt contraception and are relatively ineffective in its use (Byrne & Fisher, 1983). The complexity of this behavior is an important problem for both clinical practice and research. At the most basic level, the adolescent has to admit that he or she is or will be sexually active. This acceptance or planfulness is often difficult, perhaps because of value ambivalence and limited future perspective-taking ability. The adolescent also has to understand that sexual intercourse leads to pregnancy and that methods of contraception can prevent pregnancy. Further, the possibility that pregnancy could occur must be personalized, and the adolescent must believe that this would be a negative event. For adolescents who recognize that they are or will be sexually active, who realize that pregnancy is possible, who do not want a pregnancy, and who feel that birth control can reduce the likelihood of pregnancy, another set of issues must be considered. The many perceived costs—psychological, familial, relationship, economic, health—to the adolescent of obtaining and using a method of birth control must be weighed against the perceived risks and costs of pregnancy. When these complex issues have been weighed and an adolescent decides to use birth control, there must be reasonable accessibility to implement the decision. Moreover, most methods, once selected, require repeated decisions and actions with every act of sex. Given the complexity of this process, it should be no surprise that most adolescents default to using male methods—or nothing, to begin with. Some gradually become effective contraceptors, but some never use contraception at all.

In summary, the majority of adolescents have experienced sexual intercourse by their mid- to late teens. First sexual intercourse occurs sooner among males than females and sooner among Blacks than other races. Although this appears to be more true for females than males, both sexes tend to be in a relationship with their first sexual partner, who tends to be older and already sexually experienced. The data are very consistent that first sexual intercourse "just happens" without being planned. This spontaneity is related to the fact that about half of first intercourse experiences are totally without the use of any contraception. As teens accept their own sexual activity, most of them make a gradual transition to using contraception. In the late 1980s, survey data showed a near doubling of the use of condoms among adolescents, although about one in five continued to play sexual roulette, using no contraception at all.

ANTECEDENTS OF EARLY SEXUAL INTERCOURSE

Individual Factors

Biological Factors

There is strong evidence that early pubertal development (e.g., age at menarche for girls, level of pubertal development for boys) is associated with early initiation of sexual activity. This finding appears to hold, net of other factors and using various measures of sexual activity, from masturbation to intercourse, including the frequency of such activity (Billy & Udry, 1985; Westney, Jenkins, Butts, & Williams, 1984; Zabin, Smith, Hirsch, & Hardy, 1986; Zelnik & Kantner, 1980).

Several researchers have sought to answer the question whether heterosexual interaction was governed by an individual's level of sexual maturation or chronological age. Dornbusch et al. (1981) found that individual levels of sexual maturation add very little to explained variance in dating, after age is taken into account. Thus, they concluded that social pressures based on behavior considered appropriate at various ages, and not maturation, determine the onset of dating in adolescence. Further research by Zabin et al. (1986) revealed that age of puberty exerts an influence separate from that of normative patterns; when the age is low, it applies a downward pressure on the age of sexual onset. As age of puberty increases, the cultural influence of social norms, as opposed to the individual developmental timetable, becomes stronger.

A study by Udry, Billy, Morris, Groff, and Raj (1985) found strong evidence for the hormonal basis of sexual motivation and behavior in adolescent males. Information was obtained from ninth- and tenth-grade boys on pubertal development, sexual motivation, sexual behavior, and levels of serum androgenic hormones (from blood samples). In an analysis of sexual intercourse and masturbation that included age, pubertal development (Tanner scale), and hormonal levels, only the hormonal influences (especially testosterone) retained their effects.

In a comparable study of eighth- to tenth-grade females (Udry, Talbert, & Morris, 1986), it was found that hormonal levels have weak effects on sexual behavior but stronger effects on motivation. In an analysis including age, pubertal development, and hormonal levels, only the hormonal influences retained their effects on certain aspects of sexual behavior and motivation. These researchers concluded that, because sexual motivation is not reflected in females' behavior to the extent that it is among males, sexual behavior of females is influenced to a greater extent by social controls.

Further research by Udry (1988) revealed an interaction between hormonal and sociological variables. However, pubertal development remains the only strong predictor of the timing of the transition to coitus (Udry & Billy, 1987).

The initiation of sexual behavior, including coitus, of early adolescent males is strongly differentiated by the effects of male hormones (androgens), but the effects of social controls, if they exist, are so uniform that they do not have explanatory power in microanalysis. Sexual motivation and noncoital sexual behavior of early adolescent white females are substantially influenced by androgens, but their coital behavior is primarily differentiated by social control processes, not hormones. (pp. 841–855)

Although there appears to be a strong relationship among hormonal levels, pubertal development, and sexual activity, social–psychological factors do intervene in determining when an adolescent will initiate sexual activity. Also, there appear to be gender differences in the biological factors influencing sexual behavior.

Psychosocial Factors

Cognitive and emotional development often lag behind pubertal development in adolescence. Although teens may be physiologically capable of sexual and reproductive behavior and even have knowledge about their developmental changes, they may lack the cognitive and behavioral skills necessary to choose a course of action and understand its long-term consequences and implications. Zabin, Hirsch, Smith, and Hardy (1984) reported that the majority of adolescents had values and attitudes consistent with responsible sexual conduct, but not all were able to translate these attitudes into personal behavior. Of the sexually experienced teens, 83% cited a best age for first intercourse as being older than the age at which they initiated coitus.

Several personality measures have been found to be associated with early onset of sexual intercourse. Jessor, Costa, Jessor, and Donovan (1983), in their 10-year longitudinal study, found that adolescents who placed a higher value on and expectation for independence and a lower value on and expectation for academic achievement, who were more socially critical, and who were more tolerant of deviance and less religious, experienced intercourse earlier than their peers.

Miller, Christensen, and Olson (1987) found that the relationship between self-esteem and permissive sexual attitudes and behaviors was mediated by personal attitudinal permissiveness. Self-esteem was found to be positively related to sexual intercourse experience among adolescents who believed that premarital sex was usually or always right, and negatively related to sexual intercourse among those who believed it was wrong. Whether self-esteem influences sexual behavior or sexual behavior influences self-esteem remains unclear.

Social Factors

Culture

Because the culture or society in which one grows up affects the individual through membership or residence in particular groups, communities, and neighborhoods, it is important to consider these factors as antecedents to an adolescent's sexual behavior. An individual's race, social class, and religion represent various influences on his or her values and attitudes, including those regarding sexuality. The school affects the educational and socialization experiences and levels of achievement of the adolescent.

Research has demonstrated that one of the most important factors differentiating early from later initiators of sexual activity is race. There are large Black–White differences in levels of sexual activity in the raw data, and these differences do not disappear when controls for other factors, including poverty status, are introduced (Zelnik & Kantner, 1980; Zelnik, Kantner, & Ford, 1981). There is evidence for some important differences in attitudes between Blacks and Whites. Blacks appear to be more sexually permissive than Whites (greater tolerance for sexual activity outside a marital relationship), rate marriage as less important than do Whites, and perceive a greater tolerance in their neighborhoods for an out-of-wedlock birth (Moore, Simms, & Betsey, 1986b). In a recent study, Furstenberg et al. (1987) tested three hypotheses for the racial differences in the prevalence and timing of sexual behavior. The results offer limited support for a demographic composition argument and stronger support for a contextual subgroup argument. Blacks in a predominantly Black school were much more likely to report ever having intercourse than Blacks in racially integrated schools.

Religion has been found to be an important differentiator of early versus later initiators of sexual intercourse. The tendency to be devout and observant of religious custom and teaching is more important than any specific affiliation. However, the highest level of premarital intercourse occurs among those with no religious affiliation (Zelnik et al., 1981). Young women 15 to 19 who said religion was important to them and who attended church more frequently were less likely to have reported having had sexual intercourse (see also Forste & Heaton, 1988). Several studies (Miller & Olson, 1988; Thornton & Camburn, 1987) have found that adolescents who were members of churches that teach that sexual intercourse before marriage is always wrong were significantly less likely to report having had sexual intercourse, compared to those affiliated with other denominations.

The research findings show few regional differences in the probability of sexual activity; however, there do appear to be rural–urban factors. Teens living in urban centers have indicated more permissive attitudes toward sex than teens living in either the suburbs or rural areas (Coles & Stokes, 1985). Hogan and Kitagawa (1985) also cited the importance of neighborhood for sexual activity. They reported that Black females 15 to 19 living in a poverty area of Chicago had a much higher rate of initial sexual intercourse than peers not living in a poverty area.

Family

Probably the most important influence on early development is the family of origin. Many aspects of the family can affect sexual behavior: (a) parental characteristics (education, family background, parents' sexual experience, age at marriage and at first birth); (b) family configuration (number of parents, children, and extended family members); (c) family experiences (communication, divorce, remarriage); and (d) attitudes, values, and norms of family members (Miller & Jorgensen, 1988).

Parents' level of education and their aspirations for their children play a significant role in influencing adolescents' attitudes and behavior (Miller & Sneesby, 1988). Research has shown that the more years of education completed by the parents, the less likely their teens are to be sexually active (Forste & Heaton, 1988; Zelnik et al., 1981). This may be explained by the finding that better educated parents (usually an indication of higher socioeconomic status) tend to set more goals, put a higher value on achievement, and value work more than play. Low educational goals and poor educational achievement are associated with greater sexual activity among both adolescent boys and girls (Miller & Sneesby, 1988). Teens who score well on intelligence tests, are academically motivated, and do well in school are less likely to initiate sexual activity at a young age (Hayes, 1987). Chilman (1980a,b) also suggested that, especially for girls, a focus on educational achievement (thereby pleasing parents and teachers) may inhibit interest in boys or may make girls less interesting to boys.

Another parental characteristic associated with adolescents' sexual behavior is the mother's adolescent sexual experience. Research (Newcomer & Udry, 1984) has shown a strong relationship between the mother's sexual and fertility experience as a teenager and that of her daughter. The earlier the mother's first sexual experience and first birth, the earlier the daughter's experience. Based on their research, these authors suggested that this association is due to a biological relationship between the sexual maturation of mother and daughter rather than social factors.

Several studies have shown that adolescents—daughters, in particular—from single-parent families are more likely to begin sexual intercourse at young ages than their peers from two-parent families (Forste & Heaton, 1988; Hayes, 1987; Newcomer & Udry, 1983), and adolescents whose mothers remarry have more permissive sexual attitudes and experience (Thornton & Camburn, 1987). Rodgers (1983) reported that, in a sample of southern eighth to tenth graders, in addition to living with a single parent, having older brothers was related to early adolescent sexual intercourse experience. Miller et al. (1987), in a study of western high school students, failed to replicate the older-brother effect but did replicate the effect of parents' marital status. Miller and Bingham (1989), using a nationally representative sample, found that teenage young women who have been raised by a single parent are more likely to have nonmarital sexual intercourse than young women from intact marriages.

Several reasons have been given for the higher rates of sexual activity among teenagers who have been or are now living in single-parent households. Parental control seems to be more consistent in two-parent homes (Dornbusch et al., 1985). Single mothers are more likely to work full-time than are mothers in two-parent households, which may inhibit their ability to supervise their children's activities. Single parents may be dating and their sexual behavior may have a role-model effect. Also, it has been shown that both adolescents and parents who have experienced divorce have more permissive attitudes about having sexual intercourse outside of marriage (Thornton & Camburn, 1987).

Several other family characteristics have been shown to be factors in explaining adolescent sexual behavior. Hogan and Kitagawa (1985) found that family size was a related variable. When other factors such as socioeconomic status were controlled, daughters in very large families (more than five children) were more likely than those in smaller families to initiate sexual activity early.

A number of studies have focused on the sexual socialization process within the family and have sought to understand the relationship between familial communication regarding sex and adolescent sexual attitudes and behaviors. Findings indicate a somewhat ambiguous relationship among these variables, which may be attributable to the difficulty in adequately tapping the family processes and the time order of the variables of interest.

In a study of mother–daughter communication, Fox and Inazu (1980) reported that, although mothers and daughters reported discussions of sex-related topics, they differed in terms of how comfortable they felt with each other, what roles each played in initiating discussions, and whether they desired more frequent discussions in the future. Higher frequencies of current communication were associated with more responsible patterns of daughters' sexual behavior. Furstenberg, Moore, and Peterson (1985) reported that the ability to discuss sex with parents was associated with a lower prevalence of sexual intercourse among a nationally representative sample of 15- and 16-year-old teens. Papini, Farmer, Clark, and Snell (1988), in their study of the familial and individual developmental factors influencing sexual disclosure between parents and adolescents, found that adolescent sexual disclosure to parents was strongly associated with adolescent perception of the openness and adaptiveness of the family context.

On the other hand, Newcomer and Udry (1984), studying seventh to ninth graders longitudinally, reported that prior communication with mothers was not related to subsequent sexual behavior. Kahn, Smith, and Roberts (1984) reported that parent–teen communication had an effect on the sexual activity of sons but not that of daughters. Boys who discussed a larger number of sexual topics with their fathers were more likely to engage in premarital sexual behaviors, but increased communication with their mothers yielded opposite results; discussions between mothers and sons were associated with a lower incidence of intercourse among sons. Sexual activity of teens appeared to be unaffected by whether parents discouraged premarital sex, conveyed a more lenient attitude, or said nothing at all.

There are many plausible explanations for these contradictory findings. There are large differences in the samples studied, and, in the correlational analyses, it is often impossible to tell whether parental communication preceded or followed adolescents' sexual behavior. Other explanations of the divergent findings are the variety of communication measures used and a possible interaction effect of parents' attitudes or values on the relationship between their communication and adolescent sexuality. For example, Moore, Peterson, and Furstenberg (1986) found little support in their total sample for the hypothesis that parent–teen communication discourages adolescent sexual behavior. However, when their sample was partitioned based on the parents' traditional versus moderate-to-liberal values, daughters of traditional parents who had communicated about sex were found to be less likely to have had sexual intercourse.

In another study examining the relationship between parent–child communication about sexuality and similarity of attitudes between adolescents and their parents, Fisher (1985) found that the correlation between parents' and children's attitudes was high for early adolescents and low for middle adolescents. Only among the late adolescents was there a significant difference in the correlations between the sexual attitudes of parents and their children as a function of family communication level; the attitudes of adolescents and parents in the high communication group were highly correlated and the attitudes of adolescents and parents in the low communication group were not significantly correlated. Middle adolescents had significantly more permissive sexual attitudes than early and late adolescents.

Miller, McCoy, Olson, and Wallace (1986) found a curvilinear relationship between adolescents' perceptions of parental strictness and rules and the adolescents' sexual attitudes and behaviors. Sexual activity and permissiveness were highest among adolescents whose parents were least strict, lowest among those who said that their parents were moderately strict, and intermediate among teens who perceived their parents as being very strict. Home environments that were very liberal or very conservative were associated with a higher incidence of adolescent sexual experience. In a recent study, Baker, Thalberg, and Morrison (1988) revealed that parental behavioral norms accounted for 5% of the variance in whether adolescents had experienced intercourse. Fathers' approval of their children's sexual activity was the variable that accounted for the greatest amount of the variance.

Other researchers (Fox, 1981; Hepburn, 1983) noted that various forms of communication are operating within the family and that many parents indirectly teach sexual attitudes and values through discussions of and comments on the behavior of other people.

Peers

Adolescence is a time when the influence of the family often declines and the influence of the peer group increases. As reported by adolescents in a poll by Harris and Associates (1986), social pressure was identified as the chief reason why so many of their peers did not wait to have sexual intercourse until they were older. Both boys and girls cited social pressure more than other factors for initiating sexual activities, but girls (73%) mentioned it more than boys (50%) did. However, some researchers (Newcomer, Gilbert, & Udry, 1980) have concluded that sexual behavior and attitudes are more closely related to what adolescents perceive as the behavior and values of their peers rather than what is really going on. Until recently, it has been difficult to assess the degree of peer influence because, in most studies, the adolescent has reported on his or her own behavior as well as his or her friends' attitudes and behavior, without independent validation.

Recent research has attempted to better test the peer influence hypothesis through longitudinal studies. In selected schools, students who filled out questionnaires identified friends by a code. With all adolescents in these schools participating in the study, matches could be made between teens and their best friends. Because the data were collected at several time points, peer influences could be examined over time. Using this technique, Billy and Udry (1985) found evidence that the sexual behavior of White girls was influenced by the behavior of their best male and female friends; that is, those who were virgins at the first time point were more likely to experience intercourse between waves of the survey if they had sexually experienced friends when the study began. In contrast, rather than being influenced by friends' behavior, White males appeared to pick their friends on the basis of sexual activity. Blacks appeared neither to be influenced by friends' sexual behavior nor to pick their friends on that basis (Billy, Rodgers, & Udry, 1984; Billy & Udry, 1985). Thus, the evidence for the peer influence hypothesis varies by race and sex.

In summary, many studies have helped to document the various individual and social antecedents of adolescent sexual behavior. These range from individual differences in biological development and hormonal levels to the social-cultural contexts established by race and religion. Peer and family influences are also important in timing the transition to sexual intercourse. Not all adolescents' sexual transitions are gradual or voluntary, however, as discussed below.

NONCONSENSUAL SEX

Nonconsensual or coercive sexual acts are perpetrated against the victim's will, without consent, or in an aggressive, exploitative, or threatening manner. Some adolescents are sexual victims, and some adolescents are sexual offenders.

Sexual Victimization of Adolescents

Adolescents have been noted to be at risk for sexual victimization (rape or sexual assault) by various predators, including peers (Ageton, 1981), adult acquaintances (Finkelhor, 1979), family members (Lystad, 1982), and strangers (National Crime Survey, 1981).

Since the 1970s, the definition of rape has been expanded from vaginal penetration against a female's will to include "statutory and attempted rape as well as completed rape and any other criminal sexual assault, whether homosexual or heterosexual, that involves the use or the threat of force, including coercion and bribery of children" (Burgess, 1985, p. 2). Although in most cases females are victims and males are perpetrators, there are cases of males being raped. Because of an expanded understanding of the damage caused by all forms of sexual victimization, clinical researchers have broadened the concept of sexual assault to include more subtle forms of sexual pressure and exploitation of either sex.

Recent studies about the antecedents of rape confirm the importance of sex-role learning, traditional dating patterns, and adherence to rape myths (Burt, 1980; Koss & Oros, 1982). Females associate femininity with softness, nonassertiveness, and dependence on men and are socialized to be alluring yet sexually unavailable. Males are conditioned to be strong, powerful, aggressive, and the initiators in sexual situations. Goodchilds, Zellman, Johnson, and Giarrusso (1988) found that male and female respondents agreed with the belief that force is "all right" under certain circumstances and is most acceptable when a girl "leads a boy on" or gets him sexually aroused.

Acquaintance rape has been found to occur with disturbing frequency among adolescents. Acquaintance rape, particularly dating rape, takes place in the context of normal adolescent social activities, unlike rape by strangers. The full extent of acquaintance rape and sexual exploitation is not known. Even acquaintance rape with obvious force is rarely reported. Assaults involving deception or trickery are even less likely to be talked about and are unlikely to be reported to the authorities or anyone else. Adolescents can be taken advantage of because of their fear of getting into trouble, their inexperience and lack of information about sexuality, or their own needs, along with outside pressures to enter the adult world of love and romance. Teens may have heard that rape is a violent, not a sexual crime. But they are more likely to encounter rape in situations of sexual bargaining than in interactions that seem overtly violent to them.

Ageton (1985a), based on teenage sexual assault data from the National Youth Survey (NYS, a nationally representative sample of 1,700 youths 11 to 17 years in the first of 5 years of study), reported that the typical adolescent sexual assault is committed by a boyfriend or acquaintance of approximately the same age and occurs during a date. Most sexual assaults among teenagers do not involve physical violence or the use of a weapon. The kind of force typically used is verbal pressure. Drinking or drug use by the offender often plays a part in the assault. Most of the assaults occur in the victim's home, the offender's home, or a vehicle. An unstable home environment, involvement in delinquent behavior, and membership in a delinquent network increase the risk of being sexually assaulted. However, adolescents who are involved in delinquent activities are not the only victims of sexual assault.

Based on interviews of sexual assault victims (172 incidents for the period 1978 to 1980), Ageton (1985a) noted an increase in use of physical force as girls became older. This may be attributed to the greater mobility and freedom of older adolescent girls, as well as their association with older males. These factors increase the likelihood that they will confront more serious physical pressure (such as beating, choking, or injury from a weapon) to engage in sex. However, the vast majority of the interviewed assault victims offered verbal or physical resistance or both; because of efforts of the victim or other factors, most of the assaults were not completed.

In an effort to better understand adolescents' attitudes toward sexuality and rape, as well as behavioral expectations, perceptions, and norms about dating, Goodchilds et al. (1988) interviewed 432 adolescents (14 to 18) in Los Angeles. When asked, "Is it okay for a boy to hold a girl down and force her to have sexual intercourse?", 82% of the youths said it was *never* all right. However, when they were presented with a series of questions describing nine different situations (all depicting rape), only 34% said force was not acceptable in any of these circumstances. Force was seen as most acceptable "when a girl gets a guy excited" (not okay: females, 58%; males, 49%) and least acceptable "when a guy spends a lot of money on a girl" (not okay: females, 88%; males, 61%). A significantly higher percentage of females (44%) as compared to males (24%) rejected the use of force across all nine circumstances.

Gender differences were also noted in responses to situational cues. The adolescents were asked: "If a guy and a girl go to the guy's house alone when there is nobody home, does that mean the guy wants to have sex or the girl wants to have sex?" The other situations included going to a park or beach at night, going to a party where there were drugs or a party where the couple took drugs, and going somewhere together after meeting for the first time in a public place. Male respondents perceived the situations as "sexier" than females. Both males and females viewed males as wanting sex more than females. These findings are consistent with Burt's (1980) report that people with stereotypic views of gender roles are more likely to view some rapes as legitimate sexuality. Thus, the fact that males and females attribute different meanings to the same behaviors and contexts is of particular concern in light of the findings that adolescents seem relatively accepting of forced sex in certain circumstances.

Recent efforts have been directed at trying to influence knowledge and attitudes associated with sexual assaults. Naylor, Tolan, and Wilson (in press) report that their workshop for college students had an immediate and at least a short-term impact on rape knowledge, some specific attitudes about rape, perceptions of rape responsibility and rapists, and accurate labeling of sexual assaults. Men also reportedly changed their behavior, reporting a reduction in sexually coercive practices between pretesting and post- and follow-up testing.

Stringer and Rants-Rodriguez (1987) have written a sexual assault information booklet for male teenagers that could be useful in sexual assault prevention programs. Topics covered include sex-role expectations, assertiveness skills, sexual harassment, differences between sexual behavior and sexual exploitation, evaluating and setting personal limits, and the shared responsibility of saying and hearing "no." Additionally, the results of Ageton's study have been compiled into a research report for adolescents (Ageton,

1985b) that answers common questions about sexual assault and offers advice on how to prevent sexual victimization.

It is difficult to obtain accurate statistics regarding adolescent sexual victimization. Because there is not a centralized national or state recording system, adolescents are often included in adult statistics, and many adolescents are reluctant to report sexual assault.

The National Crime Survey (1981), a household survey to identify crimes that are not reported to official agencies, indicated that sexual victimization occurred in 1979 at the rate of 2.5 cases per 1,000 females aged 12 to 15, and at the rate of 5.7 cases per 1,000 females aged 15 to 19. However, Finkelhor (1979), in his survey of college-age students, found that 19.2% of the women students reported a childhood sexual encounter with an adult (mean age of exposure 10.2, with 63% not previously having reported the incident). In the sample, 8.6% of the male students had experienced a childhood sexual encounter with an older person (mean age 11.2, with 73% not previously having reported the incident).

More specific data about nonvoluntary sexual intercourse during childhood and adolescence have recently been reported from the third wave of the National Survey of Children (Moore, Nord, & Peterson, 1989). Of all sample youth aged 18 to 22 in 1987, 7% responded "yes" to the question "Was there ever a time when you were forced to have sex (sexual intercourse) against your will, or were raped?" Among White females, however, nearly 12% reported having been forced to have sex, as compared to 7% of Black females, 6% of Black males, and 2% of White males. Nonvoluntary sex is quite rare among males younger than age 12, but among females such experiences are likely to occur during both childhood and adolescence.

Further analyses—limited because of sample size to the subset of data for White females—revealed that a number of family and individual characteristics were strongly related to having nonvoluntary sexual intercourse. Heavy parental drinking, parental drug use, parental smoking as a teenager, physical/emotional/mental limitation of the child, childhood poverty, and having lived apart from both parents at age 15 or younger were all significant variables in a cumulative model to predict sexual abuse. Only 5.4% of young women with no risk factors reported nonvoluntary sexual intercourse, but the proportions rose to 9.4% among young women who had one risk factor, 25.5% among those with two risk factors, and 67.8% among those with three or more risk factors in their background.

Victim Response

Developmental Implications

Sexual victimization can disrupt the adolescent's development, producing serious effects in both the short and long term. Because a major developmental task of adolescents is gaining a sense of identity or self-definition (Erikson, 1968), a sexual assault may be an ego-shattering experience, engendering feelings of extreme helplessness and raising questions about sexual identity. A female may also be worried about pregnancy or develop an acute sense of vulnerability. A male may be confused about his gender identity or develop fears of homosexuality when he is molested or raped by another male.

An adolescent's recovery from sexual assault is greatly influenced by his or her level of maturity, psychosocial functioning prior to the incident, coping and personality styles, and social support. Adolescents who conceal the experience are left to their own internal resources to work through the healing process. Because sexual assault is highly stressful, adolescents may lack the resources to resolve and overcome such stress by themselves. Their relationship to the perpetrator, along with parental attitudes and support, are primary factors in recovery.

Response Patterns

To assist adolescent victims of sexual assault, the typical response patterns associated with attacks by strangers and nonstrangers need to be understood. Williams and Holmes (1981) reported the responses of stranger-rape victims to be fear, anxiety, apprehension, and confusion. Ageton's (1981) findings about reactions to nonstranger attacks were similar in kind but different in degree; they included guilt, embarrassment, depression, and a sense of betrayal. It has gradually become apparent that the large majority of rapes are perpetrated by someone the victim knows, and that rape by an acquaintance or intimate is usually more traumatizing than rape by a stranger.

The psychological consequences of experiencing a sexual assault appear to be varied and depend on individual personality traits and social supports available to the victim. This variability has made it difficult to delineate precise diagnostic criteria for a postabuse syndrome (Finkelhor & Browne, 1986). However, Burgess and Holmstrom (1974), Gelinas (1983), and Browne and Finkelhor (1986) have all made substantial contributions to understanding the experience of sexual abuse victims.

Burgess and Holmstrom (1974) described a two-phased rape trauma syndrome. The acute phase, lasting from days to weeks, is characterized by disorganization of daily activities, disruption of essential functions, a variety of somatic reactions, and intense emotions. The second phase is a long-term reorganization during which the victim must reorder his or her life in light of the event. Most victims continue to experience rape-related symptoms (e.g., intrusive thoughts about the attack, development of phobic behaviors) that tend to decrease as the person who was victimized overcomes fear and anxiety.

In contrast to acquaintance and date rape among age-mates, incest usually refers to sexual intercourse between persons who are so closely related that they are forbidden by law to marry. Incestuous adult–child sexual activity most commonly occurs between a daughter and the male in the caretaking role (e.g., father, stepfather, mother's boyfriend). However, the extent of remarriage among American families also brings the issue of sibling incest to greater prominence. With the increasing number of blended families, stepsiblings of differing ages, and foster children, where biological ties are absent, the issue of intrafamilial sexual contact between brothers and sisters takes on new significance (Kempe & Kempe, 1984).

Relying primarily on clinical data from female victims of intrafamilial abuse, Gelinas (1983) suggested a typical symptom picture, which she termed "traumatic neurosis." Similar to other forms of posttraumatic stress disorder, this pattern includes intrusive memories associated with intense affect and vivid recall, which tend to alternate with denial of the event(s). Untreated, this syndrome is likely to produce chronic depression, guilt, poor self-esteem, and a sense of powerlessness.

Gradual social and psychological withdrawal is a characteristic reaction to incest and may be particularly pronounced when the victim has been pledged to secrecy and has kept the secret through a period of repeated sexual encounters. Quite often, older adolescents will try to remove themselves from incestuous situations by running away. In other cases, the reaction is intense unfocused anxiety, especially among early adolescents.

In their literature review, Browne and Finkelhor (1986) argued that a distinction must be made between initial effects (within the first 2 years of an incest incident) and longer-term effects. The most prominent symptoms shown in the studies reviewed by Browne and Finkelhor were depression, self-destructive behavior, anxiety and isolation, low self-esteem, a tendency toward revictimization, and substance abuse.

Behavioral Indicators of Sexual Victimization

Because so many cases of adolescent sexual assault are not disclosed by the victims, professionals need to be alert to the behavioral indicators of sexual victimization.

Burgess and Holmstrom (1974) identified the following symptoms that may be observed in adolescents who have not reported their rape to anyone and thus have not been able to psychologically or emotionally resolve the incident:

1. Increasing signs of anxiety as an interview progresses, such as long periods of silence, block on associations, minor stuttering, or physical distress;
2. Marked behavioral changes, such as irritability, avoidance of interaction with men, or changes in school behavior;
3. Sudden onset of phobic reactions and fear of being alone, going outside, or being inside;
4. Sudden loss of self-confidence and self-esteem, a self-blame attitude, paranoid feelings, dreams of violence, or nightmares.

Sgroi (1982) enumerated a more detailed list of behavioral indicators that might suggest that a young person is the subject of ongoing sexual abuse.

Adolescents who have been pressured into sexual activity by an adult often find it difficult to end the abuse or to disclose it. The offender often tries to persuade the victim to cooperate or consent to the sexual relationship by bribing or rewarding the adolescent with attention, affection, approval, money, gifts, treats, or good times.

Adolescent Sex Offenders

An adolescent sex offender is a youth, from puberty to the legal age of majority, who commits any sexual act with a person against the victim's will, without consent, or in an aggressive, exploitative, or threatening manner. Until recently, adolescent sexual offenses often had been characterized as sexual experimentation, curiosity, or a normal expression of aggression in adolescent males. Juvenile courts, in an effort to avoid stigmatizing the adolescent, often took the position that these offenses were less serious than those committed by adults. However, in light of recent findings (Groth, Longo, & McFadin, 1982) that most incarcerated adult sex offenders began committing sexual crimes in early adolescence, the adolescent perpetrator is being taken more seriously (National Adolescent Perpetrator Network, 1988).

Offense and Victim Characteristics

In the United States, about 20% of all rapes and about 30% to 50% of all cases of child sexual abuse can be attributed to adolescent offenders (Davis & Leitenberg, 1987). In a review of the Uniform Crime Reports during the late 1970s, Fehrenbach, Smith, Monasterky, and Deisher (1986) reported that adolescents accounted for 30% of all rapes. Abel, Mittelman, and Becker (1985) reported that, in a large sample of adolescent perpetrators, their deviant sexual pattern was established during their teenage years.

In nearly two-thirds of these offenses, younger children (under 10) are the victims, with the vast majority being acquaintances or relatives of the offender (Fehrenbach et al., 1986; Wasserman & Kappel, 1985). There are generally more female than male victims, but the proportion of female victims is less when the victims are children and greater in non-contact offenses, where most victims are adolescents or adults (Fehrenbach et al., 1986). Wasserman and Kappel (1985) reported that 75% of the offenses occurred in a home. Fehrenbach et al. (1986) reported that, for male offenders, 40% of rapes of young children and 47% of cases of indecent liberties took place during baby-sitting. For the eight female offenders in that study, 63% of their offenses took place during baby-sitting.

Offender Characteristics

The vast majority of adolescent sex offenders are males; females account for less than 5% of the offenses (Fehrenbach et al., 1986). Brown, Flanagan, and McLeod (1984) reported that 64% of sexual offenses were committed by White adolescents and 24% by

Black adolescents. Davis and Leitenberg (1987) found that these adolescents were often characterized as having low self-esteem, coming from an unstable or poor family environment, and lacking appropriate social skills and/or social competence. Adolescent sex offenders more frequently have a history of being physically abused than other groups of male adolescents (Van Ness, 1984). Contrary to the notion that sexual offenses stem from a lack of sexual experience, adolescent sex offenders claim to have had more sexual experiences, including consensual ones, than do other adolescents (Becker, Cunningham-Rathner, & Kaplan, 1986; Groth, 1977).

Clinicians have suggested several individual factors that may have etiological significance in distinguishing adolescent sex offenders from other adolescents: feelings of male inadequacy; low self-esteem; fear of rejection by and anger toward women; atypical erotic fantasies; poor social skills; or having been sexually abused. However, because of the paucity of research comparing offenders with nonoffenders on these characteristics, it is difficult to conclude which of these factors are unique to the adolescent sex offender, which are shared with other delinquents, and which are shared with the general population of adolescents.

There is also a need for more information comparing the characteristics of adolescent and adult offenders. It may not be appropriate to categorize adolescent male aggressiveness exactly along the lines drawn for adults. However, to ignore adolescent offenders is to ignore the possibility of pedophilic or otherwise deviant sexuality that may persist into and throughout adulthood (Costell, 1980). As Bolton and MacEachron (1988) point out, adolescence might be the developmental period during which treatment could be most effective. At present, our knowledge of risk factors and our identification of both male and female victims and perpetrators and of effective treatment modalities are marginal. Future efforts by researchers and clinicians are needed to improve our understanding of deviant adolescent sexuality.

SUMMARY AND CONCLUSIONS

The second decade of life is a critical period in the development of human sexual behavior. Stimulated by elevated hormonal secretions, and usually beginning about age 12 or 13, adolescents undergo major changes in sexual interest, arousal, appearance, and activity. These biologically driven changes are shaped considerably by social influences, especially by the family, the peer group, and religion. Most adolescents are in a continual state of defining their own sexual identity as part of the larger process of identity formation.

There is a well-documented trend over the past two decades toward increasing proportions of North American adolescents having sexual intercourse. As the 1990s began, roughly half of all females and two-thirds of all males in the United States had had intercourse by the end of their 16th year. Males are more likely than females, and Blacks are more likely than Whites and Hispanics, to have had intercourse at each year of adolescent age. Among both males and females, regardless of race, the first sexual experience usually takes place in a home with a dating or steady partner who is slightly older.

There is considerable evidence for a sequential or cumulative developmental pattern in adolescent heterosexual behavior, especially among White adolescents. During the second decade of life, most individuals initiate heterosexual relationships with touching and kissing and then proceed with the same or different partners through light and heavy petting to having sexual intercourse. Young Black adolescents appear to be more likely than Whites to experience coitus before petting. Other exceptions to the gradual developmental pattern occur when individuals have intercourse without other precoital activities (as, perhaps, in cases of incest, rape, and prostitution).

Data about the frequency of intercourse and number of partners are very limited. Among unmarried sexually experienced female adolescents, over one-third have had intercourse less than once a month or less; almost half (46%) report intercourse between two and four times per month; and about one in five (19.6%) report having intercourse more than once a week. About half of sexually experienced female adolescents have had intercourse with only one partner, but the average number of partners is between two and three. Comparable recent data for males are just now becoming available through the National Survey of Adolescent Males.

Some adolescents are at considerably greater risk from their sexual behavior than others. Adolescents whose sexual activities are especially precocious, those who are promiscuous, and those who are involved in nonvoluntary sexual relationships are most likely to require clinical attention. Homeless adolescent females are at especially high risk of precocious sexual activity (Hein et al., 1978). Female adolescents are much more likely to have had nonvoluntary sexual experiences if they live apart from their parents; have physical or mental limitations; have parents who smoke, drink, and use drugs; and live in a family that is poor (Moore et al., 1989).

Recognition that a majority of adult sexual offenders began assaults when they were teenagers or even younger has rapidly led to specialized early intervention approaches for juvenile sex offenders. Given the prevalence of sexual abuse and its apparent early onset, this is clearly an important area for further research and clinical refinement. Research priorities suggested by the National Adolescent Perpetrator Network (1988) include:

1. More basic information about the "normal" nature and course of sexual knowledge, attitudes, and behavior;
2. Improved ability to discriminate the nature of a sexual offense that might have arisen from experimentation/curiosity, from delinquent/antisocial syndrome, or from a proto- or fully paraphiliac disorder;
3. Identification of malleable causal variables for proto- and fully paraphiliac disorders;
4. Development, refinement, and evaluation of targeted treatments;
5. Testing of the effectiveness of perpetration prevention programs aimed at reducing cognitive acceptance of violent or exploitative sexuality and at preventing sexual offenses.

Sexually transmitted diseases (STDs), AIDS, and unwanted pregnancy also bring adolescents to the attention of concerned applied professionals. Homosexual and bisexual relations and the sharing of needles for IV drug use are, by far, the behaviors that account for the majority of adult HIV transmission in the United States. Adolescents are at risk of AIDS through these behaviors, but they are also at risk because of their increasing rate of heterosexual intercourse (especially unprotected intercourse) and their sexual relations with those who engage in the higher-risk activities.

In 1990, adolescents constituted less than 1% of all those who had been diagnosed as having AIDS. This fact might lead to a sense of complacency about adolescents and AIDS and cause adolescents to be overlooked in AIDS prevention programs (Brooks-Gunn, Boyer, & Hein, 1988; Flora & Thoresen, 1988). However, because of the long latency period between infection with the HIV virus and the diagnosis of AIDS, the problem of HIV infection among adolescents is more serious than it appears. Young adults, from their mid-20s to mid-30s, are most commonly diagnosed with AIDS. Because the average latency period is 8 to 10 years between becoming infected with the HIV virus and being diagnosed as having AIDS, many of those in their 20s who are diagnosed as having AIDS are likely to have become infected while they were adolescents (Haffner, 1987). Further, a greater proportion of adolescents than adults with AIDS are female (18% vs. 9%), and more adolescents than adults were infected with the HIV virus through heterosexual contact (9% vs. 4%) (Goldsmith, 1988).

The picture of other STDs among adolescents in the United States is one way of gaining a perspective that might be applicable to understanding AIDS in this population. When the prevalence of various STDs for national data is plotted by age, using those who are sexually active as the denominator for each age group, it is shown that adolescents aged 15 to 19 have the highest rates of gonorrhea, syphilis, chlamydia, and hospitalization for pelvic inflammatory disease (Bell & Hein, 1984). Although not as many adolescents as older individuals are sexually active, adolescents who are having sexual intercourse are at greater risk for these STDs than those who are older. There are many possible explanations for this finding, including the myth of personal invulnerability common to youth, and the adolescent's less developed future-time perspective, which could make it harder to connect today's sexual encounter with tomorrow's STD. The bottom line from pregnancy and STD data suggests that adolescents, especially younger adolescents, are less likely than those who are older to use contraceptives and are, therefore, exposed to the risks of unprotected intercourse.

The meaning of "risk" and "unprotected intercourse" has taken on new meanings since the beginning of the AIDS epidemic. Protection from risk of pregnancy has been a dominant concern, and sexually active older adolescents often have relied on the pill. But oral contraceptives, and most other methods of contraception, which can be highly effective for preventing pregnancy, provide no protection against the spread of the HIV virus. At the beginning of the 1980s, about half of all teenagers did not use any contraception the first time they had sexual intercourse (Zelnik & Shah, 1983), and this percentage has fallen very slowly. Younger adolescents are even less likely to use a contraceptive at first intercourse, and they remain less likely to initiate use even after being sexually active for a year or more. Among those who use any contraceptive method, the male methods of condom use and withdrawal are most common at first intercourse. Withdrawal has little preventive value; condoms provide some protection against both pregnancy and STDs, including AIDS. Data from the mid-1980s showed some improvement in adolescents' attitudes and knowledge regarding condoms and AIDS, but less change in behavior (DiClemente, Zorn, & Temoshok, 1986; Kegeles, Adler, & Irwin, 1988). However, there is more encouraging nationally representative evidence that condom use among teenagers increased dramatically in the late 1980s (Sonenstein et al., 1989).

As suggested above, there are several reasons to be concerned about the potential for HIV infection to become widespread among adolescents: the increase in adolescent sexual intercourse in recent years; the high rate of "unprotected" sexual activity; and the unknown extent of activity of adolescent "sexual adventurers" (Sorenson, 1973), who have sex frequently and with multiple partners, and who might be especially likely to form a bridge from the highest-risk populations of young adult male gay/bisexuals and IV drug users. Risk reduction among teenagers poses special challenges to health professionals. In particular, it would seem to be incumbent on those who counsel with adolescents to expand their focus such that adolescents better protect themselves from the risks of both unwanted pregnancy and STDs—HIV in particular. Relatedly, research is needed to address the difficult issues of how best to bring about behavior changes among adolescents for whom levels of cognitive development and the myth of invulnerability probably pose special problems (Miller, Card, Parkoff, & Peterson, 1992).

Our understanding of "normative" adolescent sexual development and behavior has increased greatly during the past two decades, and major research efforts aimed at acquiring knowledge about adolescent sexuality are continuing. Still, some fundamental information is just now becoming available; for example, results of the first national survey of adolescent male sexual behavior were disseminated in 1989–1990. It is clear that more basic and applied research is needed to provide the knowledge base about adolescent sexuality that is necessary for effective clinical interventions and prevention programs.

REFERENCES

Abel, G. G., Mittelman, M., & Becker, J. V. (1985). Sex offenders: Results of assessment and recommendations for treatment. In H. H. Ben-Aron, S. I. Hucker, & C. D. Webster (Eds.), *Clinical criminology: Assessment and treatment of criminal behavior* (pp. 212–240). Toronto: M & M Graphics.

Ageton, S. S. (1981). *Sexual assault among adolescents: A national survey.* NIMH Final Report, National Technical Information Service, Springfield, VA.

Ageton, S. S. (1985a). *A research report for adults who work with teenagers: Facts about sexual assault.* Boulder, CO: Behavioral Research Institute.

Ageton, S. S. (1985b). *A research report for teenagers: Facts about sexual assault.* Boulder, CO: Behavioral Research Institute.

Bachrach, C. (1989). Personal communication.

Bachrach, C., & Mosher, W. (1984). Use of contraception in the United States, 1982. Advance data from *Vital and Health Statistics, Vol. 102.*

Baker, S. A., Thalberg, S. P., & Morrison, D. M. (1988). Parents' behavioral norms as predictors of adolescent sexual activity and contraceptive use. *Adolescence, 23,* 265–282.

Becker, J. V., Cunningham-Rathner, J., & Kaplan, M. S. (1986). The adolescent sexual perpetrator: Demographics, criminal history, victims, sexual behavior and recommendations for reducing future offenses. *Journal of Interpersonal Violence, 1,* 431–445.

Bell, A. P., Weinberg, M. S., & Hammersmith, S. K. (1981). *Sexual preference: Its development in men and women.* Bloomington: Indiana University Press.

Bell, T., & Hein, K. (1984). The adolescent and sexually transmitted diseases. In K. Holmes, P. A. Mardh, P. S. Sparling, & P. J. Wiesner (Eds.), *Sexually transmitted diseases* (pp. 73–84). New York: McGraw-Hill.

Billy, J. O. G., Rodgers, J. L., & Udry, J. R. (1984). Adolescent sexual behavior and friendship choice. *Social Forces, 62,* 653–678.

Billy, J. O. G., & Udry, J. R. (1985). Patterns of adolescent friendship and effects on sexual behavior. *Social Psychology Quarterly, 48,* 27–41.

Bolton, F. G., Jr., & MacEachron, A. E. (1988). Adolescent male sexuality: A developmental perspective. *Journal of Adolescent Research, 3,* 259–273.

Brooks-Gunn, J., Boyer, C. B., & Hein, K. (1988). Preventing HIV infection and AIDS in children and adolescents. *American Psychologist, 43,* 958–964.

Brown, E. J., Flanagan, T. J., & McLeod, M. (Eds.). (1984). *Sourcebook of criminal justice statistics, 1983.* Washington, DC: Bureau of Criminal Justice Statistics.

Browne, A., & Finkelhor, D. (1986). Initial and long-term effects: A review of the literature. In D. Finkelhor (Ed.), *A sourcebook on child sexual abuse.* Newbury Park, CA: Sage.

Burgess, A. W. (1985). *The sexual victimization of adolescents.* National Center for the Prevention and Control of Rape, U.S. Department of Health and Human Services, NIMH, Rockville, MD.

Burgess, A. W., & Holmstrom, L. L. (1974). Rape trauma syndrome. *American Journal of Psychiatry, 131,* 981–986.

Burt, M. R. (1980). Cultural myths and supports for rape. *Journal of Personality and Social Psychology, 38,* 215–230.

Byrne, D., & Fisher, W. A. (1983). *Adolescents, sex, and contraception.* Hillsdale, NJ: Erlbaum.

Chilman, C. S. (1980a). Toward a reconceptualization of adolescent sexuality. In C. S. Chilman (Ed.), *Adolescent pregnancy and childbearing: Findings from research* (NIH Publication No. 81-2077). Washington, DC: U.S. Government Printing Office.

Chilman, C. S. (1980b). Social and psychological research concerning adolescent childbearing: 1970–1980. *Journal of Marriage and the Family, 42,* 793–803.

Coles, R., & Stokes, G. (1985). *Sex and the American teenager.* New York: Harper & Row.

Costell, R. M. (1980). The nature and treatment of male sex offenders. In B. Jones (Ed.), *Sexual abuse of children: Selected readings* (OHDS Publication No. 78-B0161). Washington, DC: National Center on Child Abuse and Neglect.

Currier, R. L. (1981). Juvenile sexuality in global perspective. In L. L. Constantine & F. M. Martinson (Eds.), *Children and sex: New findings,* new perspectives (pp. 9–19). Boston: Little, Brown.

Davis, G. E., & Leitenberg, H. (1987). Adolescent sex offenders. *Psychological Bulletin, 101,* 417–427.

Davis, K. (1976). Sexual behavior. In R. K. Merton & R. Nisbet (Eds.), *Contemporary social problems* (pp. 219–261). New York: Harcourt Brace Jovanovich.

DeLamater, J. (1981). The social control of sexuality. *Annual Review of Sociology, 7,* 263–290.

DeLamater, J., & MacCorquodale, P. (1979). *Premarital sexuality: Attitudes, relationships, behavior.* Madison: University of Wisconsin Press.

DiClemente, R. J., Zorn, J., & Temoshok, L. (1986). Adolescents and AIDS: A survey of knowledge, attitudes and beliefs about AIDS in San Francisco. *American Journal of Public Health, 76,* 1143–1145.

Diepold, J., Jr., & Young, R. D. (1979). Empirical studies of adolescent sexual behavior: A critical review. *Adolescence, 16,* 45–64.

Dornbusch, S. M., Carlsmith, J. M., Bushwall, S. J., Ritter, P. L., Leiderman, H., Hastorf, A. H., & Gross, R. T. (1985). Single parents, extended households, and the control of adolescents. *Child Development, 56,* 326–341.

Dornbusch, S. M., Carlsmith, J. M., Gross, R. T., Martin, J. A., Jennings, D., Rosenberg, A., & Duke, P. (1981). Sexual development, age and dating: A comparison of biological and social influence upon one set of behaviors. *Child Development, 52,* 179–185.

Dreyer, P. (1982). Sexuality during adolescence. In B. Wolman (Ed.), *Handbook of developmental psychology.* Englewood Cliffs, NJ: Prentice-Hall.

Ellis, L., & Ames, M. A. (1987). Neurohormonal functioning and sexual orientation: A theory of homosexuality–heterosexuality. *Psychological Bulletin, 101,* 233–258.

Erikson, E. H. (1968). *Identity: Youth and crisis.* New York: Norton.

Fay, R. E., Turner, C. F., Klassen, A. D., & Gagnon, J. H. (1989). Prevalence and patterns of same-gender sexual contact among men. *Science, 243,* 338–348.

Fehrenbach, P. A., Smith, W., Monasterky, C., & Deisher, R. W. (1986). Adolescent sex offenders: Offender and offense characteristics. *American Journal of Orthopsychiatry, 56,* 225–233.

Finkelhor, D. (1979). *Sexually victimized children.* New York: Free Press.

Finkelhor, D., & Browne, A. (1986). The traumatic impact of child sexual abuse: A conceptualization. *American Journal of Orthopsychiatry, 55,* 530–541.

Fisher, T. D. (1985). An exploratory study of parent–child communication about sex and sexual attitudes of early, middle, and late adolescents. *The Journal of Genetic Psychology, 147,* 543–557.

Flora, J. A., & Thoresen, C. E. (1988). Reducing the risk of AIDS in adolescents. *American Psychologist, 43,* 965–970.

Ford, C. S., & Beach, F. A. (1951). *Patterns of sexual behavior.* New York: Harper & Row.

Forste, R. T., & Heaton, T. B. (1988). Initiation of sexual activity among female adolescents. *Youth and Society, 19,* 250–268.

Fox, G. L. (1981). The family's role in adolescent sexual behavior. In T. Ooms (Ed.), *Teenage pregnancy in a family context: Implications for policy.* Philadelphia: Temple University Press.

Fox, G. L., & Inazu, J. K. (1980). Patterns and outcomes of mother–daughter communication about sexuality. *Journal of Social Issues, 36,* 7–29.

Freedman, E., & Demilio, J. (1988). *Intimate matters: A history of sexuality in America.* New York: Harper & Row.

Furstenberg, F. F., Jr., Moore, K. A., & Peterson, J. L. (1985). Sex education and sexual experience among adolescents. *American Journal of Public Health, 75,* 1331–1332.

Furstenberg, F. F., Morgan, S. P., Moore, K. A., & Peterson, J. L. (1987). Race differences in the timing of adolescent intercourse. *American Sociological Review, 52,* 511–518.

Gagnon, J. H., & Simon, W. (1973). *Sexual conduct: The social sources of human sexuality.* Chicago: Aldine.

Gelinas, D. J. (1983). The persisting negative effects of incest. *Psychiatry, 46,* 312–332.

Goldman, R., & Goldman, J. (1982). *Children's sexual thinking.* Boston: Routledge & Kegan Paul.

Goldsmith, M. (1988). Stockholm speakers on adolescents and AIDS: Catch them before they catch it. *Journal of the American Medical Association, 260,* 258.

Goodchilds, J., Zellman, G. L., Johnson, P. B., & Giarrusso, R. (1988). Adolescents and their perception of sexual interaction. In A. W. Burgess (Ed.), *Rape and sexual assault,* Vol. 2. New York: Garland.

Groth, N. A. (1977). The adolescent sexual offender and his prey. *International Journal of Offender Therapy and Comparative Criminology, 21,* 249–254.

Groth, N. A., Longo, R. E., & McFadin, J. B. (1982). Undetected recidivism among rapists and child molesters. *Crime and Delinquency, 128,* 450–458.

Haffner, D. (1987). *AIDS and adolescents: The time for prevention is now.* Washington, DC: Center for Population Options.

Harris, L., & Associates, Inc. (1986). *American teens speak: Sex, myths, TV, and birth control* (The Planned Parenthood Poll). New York: Author.

Hayes, C. D. (Ed.). (1987). *Risking the future: Adolescent sexuality, pregnancy, and childbearing: Vol. 1.* Washington, DC: National Academy Press.

Hein, K. (1988). *AIDS in adolescence: A rationale for concern.* Working paper. New York: Carnegie Council on Adolescent Development.

Hein, K., Cohen, M. I., Marks, A., Schonberg, S. K., Meyer, M., & McBride, A. (1978). Age at first intercourse among homeless adolescent females. *Journal of Pediatrics, 93,* 147–148.

Hepburn, E. H. (1983). A three-level model of parent–daughter communication about sexual topics. *Adolescence, 18,* 523–534.

Herdt, G. (1988, March). *The Chicago Youth Project: Coming-out processes as an anthropological rite of passage.* Paper presented at the Biennial Meeting of the Society for Research on Adolescence, Alexandria, VA.

Higham, J. (1980). Variations in adolescent psychohormonal development. In J. Adelson (Ed.), *Handbook of adolescent psychology* (pp. 472–494). New York: Wiley.

Hofferth, S. L. (1987). Initiation of sexual intercourse. In S. L. Hofferth & D. C. Hayes (Eds.), *Risking the future: Adolescent sexuality, pregnancy, and childbearing: Vol. 2.* Washington, DC: National Academy Press.

Hofferth, S. L., Kahn, J. R., & Baldwin, W. (1987). Premarital sexual activity among U.S. teenage women over the past three decades. *Family Planning Perspectives, 19*(2), 46–53.

Hogan, D. P., & Kitagawa, E. M. (1985). The impact of social status, family structure, and neighborhood on the fertility of Black adolescents. *American Journal of Sociology, 90,* 825–855.

Jessor, R., Costa, F., Jessor, L., & Donovan, J. E. (1983). Time of first intercourse: A prospective study. *Journal of Personality and Social Psychology, 44,* 608–626.

Jones, E., & Forrest, J. (1989). Contraceptive failure in the United States: Revised estimates from the 1982 National Survey of Family Growth. *Family Planning Perspectives, 21* 103–109.

Kahn, J. R., Smith, K. W., & Roberts, E. J. (1984). *Family communication and adolescent sexual behavior.* Unpublished manuscript, American Institutes for Research.

Kegeles, S. M., Adler, N. W., & Irwin, C. E. (1988). Sexually active adolescents and condoms: Changes over one year in knowledge, attitudes and use. *American Journal of Public Health, 78,* 460–461.

Kempe, R. S., & Kempe, C. H. (1984). *The common secret: Sexual abuse of children and adolescents.* New York: Freeman.

Kinsey, A. C., Pomeroy, W. B., & Martin, C. E. (1948). *Sexual behavior in the human male.* Philadelphia: Saunders.

Koss, M. P., & Oros, C. J. (1982). Sexual experience survey: A research instrument investigating sexual aggression and victimization. *Journal of Consulting and Clinical Psychology, 50,* 455–457.

Langfeldt, T. (1981). Sexual development in children. In M. Cook & K. Howels (Eds.), *Adult sexual interest in children.* London: Academic Press.

LoPiccolo, J., & Heiman, J. (1977). Cultural values and the therapeutic definition of sexual function and dysfunction. *Journal of Social Issues, 33,* 166–183.

Lystad, M. (1982). Sexual abuse in the home: A review of the literature. *International Journal of Family Psychiatry, 3,* 13–31.

Martinson, F. M. (1980). Childhood sexuality. In B. B. Wolman & J. Money (Eds.), *Handbook of human sexuality* (pp. 29–59). Englewood Cliffs, NJ: Prentice-Hall.

McCabe, M. P., & Collins, J. K. (1984). Measurement of depth of desired and experienced sexual involvement at different stages of dating. *The Journal of Sex Research, 20,* 377–390.

Miller, B. C., & Bingham, C. R. (1989). Family configuration in relation to the sexual behavior of female adolescents. *Journal of Marriage and the Family, 50,* 499–506.

Miller, B. C., Card, J. J., Paikoff, R. L., & Peterson, J. L. (Eds.). (1992). *Preventing adolescent pregnancy: Model programs and evaluations.* Newbury Park: Sage.

Miller, B. C., Christensen, R., & Olson, T. D. (1987). Self-esteem in relation to adolescent sexual attitudes and behavior. *Youth and Society, 19,* 93–111.

Miller, B. C., & Jorgensen, S. R. (1988). Adolescent fertility-related behavior and its family linkages. In D. M. Klein & J. Aldous (Eds.), *Social stress and family development.* New York: Guilford Press.

Miller, B. C., McCoy, J. K., Olson, T. D., & Wallace, C. M. (1986). Parental discipline and control attempts in relation to adolescent sexual attitudes and behavior. *Journal of Marriage and the Family, 48,* 503–512.

Miller, B. C., & Olson, T. D. (1988). Sexual attitudes and behavior of high school students in relation to background and contextual factors. *Journal of Sex Research, 24,* 194–200.

Miller, B. C., & Sneesby, K. R. (1988). Educational correlates of adolescents' sexual attitudes and behavior. *Journal of Youth and Adolescence, 17,* 521–530.

Moore, K. A., Nord, C. W., & Peterson, J. L. (1989). Non-voluntary sexual activity among adolescents. *Family Planning Perspectives, 21,* 110–114.

Moore, K. A., & Peterson, J. (1989). *The consequences of teenage pregnancy: Final report.* Washington, DC: Child Trends.

Moore, K. A., Peterson, J. L., & Furstenberg, F. F. (1986). Parental attitudes and the occurrence of early sexual activity. *Journal of Marriage and the Family, 48,* 777–782.

Moore, K. A., Simms, M. C., & Betsey, C. L. (1986). *Choice and circumstance.* New Brunswick, NJ: Transaction Books.

Mosher, W. D., & Horn, M. C. (1988). First family planning visits by young women. *Family Planning Perspectives, 20* 33–40.

Mott, F. L., & Haurin, R. J. (1988). Linkages between sexual activity and alcohol and drug use among American adolescents. *Family Planning Perspectives, 20*(3), 128–136.

National Adolescent Perpetrator Network. (1988). Preliminary report from the National Task Force on Juvenile Sex Offending, 1988. *Juvenile and Family Court Journal, 39*(2), 1–67.

National Crime Survey. (1981). *Criminal victimization in the United States, 1979.* Washington, DC: U.S. Department of Justice.

Naylor, K. E., Tolan, P. H., & Wilson, M. (in press). *Diminishing sexual assault in a college population.* Manuscript submitted for publication.

Newcomer, S. F., Gilbert, M., & Udry, J. R. (1980, September). *Perceived and actual same-sex peer behavior as determinants of adolescent sexual behavior.* Paper presented at the annual meeting of the American Psychological Association, New York, NY.

Newcomer, S. F., & Udry, J. R. (1983). Adolescent sexual behavior and popularity. *Adolescence, 18,* 515–522.

Newcomer, S., & Udry, R. (1984). Mothers' influence on the sexual behavior of their teenage children. *Journal of Marriage and the Family, 46,* 477–485.

Papini, D. R., Farmer, F. L., Clark, S. M., & Snell, W. E., Jr. (1988). An evaluation of adolescent patterns of sexual self-disclosure to parents and friends. *Journal of Adolescent Research, 3,* 387–401.

Pratt, W., Mosher, W., Bachrach, C., & Horn, M. (1984). Understanding U.S. fertility: Findings from the National Survey of Family Growth, Cycle III. *Population Bulletin, 39,* 1–43.

Rematedi, G. (1987). Homosexual youth: A challenge to contemporary society. *Journal of the American Medical Association, 258,* 222–225.

Rodgers, J. L. (1983). Family configuration and adolescent sexual behavior. *Population and Environment, 6,* 73–83.

Rosen, E., & Weinstein, E. (1988). Adolescent sexuality counseling. In E. Weinstein & E. Rosen (Eds.), *Sexuality counseling: Issues and implications.* (pp. 36–37) Pacific Grove, CA: Brooks-Cole.

Sarrel, L. J., & Sarrel, P. M. (1979). *Sexual unfolding: Sexual development and sex therapies in late adolescence.* Boston: Little, Brown.

Sarrel, L. J., & Sarrel, P. M. (1981). Sexual unfolding. *Journal of Adolescent Health Care, 2,* 93–99.

Savin-Williams, R. C. (1987). An ethological perspective on homosexuality during adolescence. *Journal of Adolescent Research, 3,* 283–302.

Sgroi, S. M. (1982). *Handbook of clinical intervention in child sexual abuse.* Lexington, MA: Heath.

Smith, E., & Udry, J. R. (1985). Coital and noncoital sexual behaviors of White and Black adolescents. *American Journal of Public Health, 75,* 1200–1203.

Sonenstein, F., Pleck, J. H., & Ku, L. C. (1989). Sexual activity, condom use, and AIDS awareness among adolescent males. *Family Planning Perspectives, 21* 152–158.

Sorenson, R. E. (1973). *Adolescent sexuality in contemporary America.* New York: World Publishers.

Stringer, G. M., & Rants-Rodriguez, D. (1987). *So what's it to me? Sexual assault information for guys.* Renton, WA: King County Rape Relief.

Thornton, A., & Camburn, D. (1987). The influence of the family on premarital sexual attitudes and behavior. *Demography, 24,* 323–340.

Udry, J. R. (1988). Biological predispositions and social control in adolescent sexual behavior. *American Sociological Review, 53,* 709–722.

Udry, J. R., & Billy, J. O. G. (1987). Initiation of coitus in early adolescence. *American Sociological Review, 52,* 841–855.

Udry, J. R., Billy, J. O. G., Morris, N. M., Groff, T. R., & Raj, M. H. (1985). Serum androgenic hormones motivate sexual behavior in adolescent human males. *Fertility and Sterility, 43,* 90–94.

Udry, J. R., Talbert, L., & Morris, N. M. (1986). Biosocial foundations for adolescent female sexuality. *Demography, 23,* 217–230.

Van Ness, R. (1984). Rape as instrumental violence: A study of youth offenders. *Journal of Offender Counseling Services and Rehabilitation, 9,* 161–170.

Vener, A. M., & Stewart, C. S. (1974). Adolescent sexual behavior in middle America revisited: 1970–1973. *Journal of Marriage and the Family, 36,* 728–736. f Wasserman, J. S., & Kappel, S. (1985). *Adolescent sex offenders in Vermont.* Burlington: Vermont Department of Health.

Westney, O. E., Jenkins, R. R., Butts, J. D., & Williams, I. (1984). Sexual development and behavior in Black preadolescents. *Adolescence, 19,* 557–568.

Williams, J. E., & Holmes, K. A. (1981). *The second assault: Rape and public attitudes.* Westport, CT: Greenwood Press.

Zabin, L. S., Hirsch, M. B., Smith, E. A., & Hardy, J. B. (1984). Adolescent sexual attitudes and behavior: Are they consistent? *Family Planning Perspectives, 16*(4), 181–185.

Zabin, L. S., Smith, E. A., Hirsch, M. B., & Hardy, J. B. (1986). Ages of physical maturation and first intercourse in Black teenage males and females. *Demography, 23,* 595–605.

Zelnik, M. (1983). Sexual activity among adolescents: Perspective of a decade. In E. R. McAnarney (Ed.), *Premature adolescent pregnancy and parenthood.* New York: Grune & Stratton.

Zelnik, M., & Kantner, J. F. (1979). Reasons for nonuse of contraception by sexually active women aged 15–19. *Family Planning Perspectives, 11* 289–296.

Zelnik, M., & Kantner, J. F. (1980). Sexual activity, contraceptive use, and pregnancy among metropolitan-area teenagers: 1971–1979. *Family Planning Perspectives, 12* 230–237.

Zelnik, M., Kantner, J., & Ford, K. (1981). *Sex and pregnancy in adolescence.* Beverly Hills, CA: Sage.

Zelnik, M., & Shah, F. K. (1983). First intercourse among young Americans. *Family Planning Perspectives, 15* 64–70.

CHAPTER 6

Daily Experience of Adolescents

REED LARSON and DOUGLAS KLEIBER

One of the fundamental challenges many teenagers face is that of simply getting through the day: crawling out of bed and going through the day's activities while maintaining a belief that it is all worthwhile. The demands of school, hassles from parents, the cross-currents of peer relationships, and numerous other frustrations associated with their rapidly changing and barely controllable lives loom as obstacles and threats to their internal sense of well-being. How do adolescents get through the day? How do they maintain a positive attitude and a sense of buoyancy and optimism about life?

On these questions, psychiatry and clinical psychology have much to learn from the study of nondisturbed adolescents—most of whom seem to survive the frustrations and stress of teenage life without turning to maladaptive or deviant behaviors as a means to cope. Other chapters in this volume address adjustment to school and the family; we focus on adjustment in the free time that remains, the discretionary time that fills 40% to 50%

This research was partially supported by NIMH grant no. MH38324 awarded to the first author.

of adolescents' waking hours (Csikszentmihalyi & Larson, 1984; Larson & Richards, 1989).

Drawing on work in the area of leisure studies and on our own investigations of teenagers' daily experience, we examine the role of free-time activities in helping adolescents get through the day. We argue that activities chosen in the context of free time play a critical role in teens' immediate emotional adjustment by providing enjoyment and absorption.

In addition, we consider the significance of free-time activities to adolescents' long-term development. For younger children, the developmental value of play is generally accepted: childhood play is an important means of coming to know the world and learning to get along with others (Bruner, Jolly, & Sylva, 1976; Erikson, 1963; Piaget, 1962). Yet, after childhood, the developmental character of play or the free-time activities that take its place are often disregarded or devalued, especially in the clinical field. It is our position that these activities provide important opportunities for the development of self-direction, self-expression, and motivated involvement. Free-time activities such as socializing, sport, playing a musical instrument, or even, in some cases, deviant activities, provide a transitional link between the spontaneous play of childhood and the more disciplined activities of adulthood.

Freely chosen activities vary considerably in terms of both their emotional and developmental potential. Free time can be spent in ways that erode or contribute to personal well-being or are neutral in their impact. We therefore begin this chapter by developing a set of criteria for evaluating free-time activities, drawing on those that have evolved in leisure studies and developmental theory. Having established these criteria, we then review evidence on four of the most common adolescent free-time choices: playing sports, socializing, art/music/youth organizations, and media use. We will also consider deviant activities as a special category of leisure. We examine how each contributes to immediate well-being and to longer-term development and mental health.

CRITERIA FOR EVALUATING LEISURE ACTIVITIES

The Problem of Leisure

Modern concern with how young people spend their time has its origins in child labor laws and other changes in the late 19th century that created an unprecedented amount of free time for young people. In Victorian morality, idle time was seen as wasted time, and idleness put a youth at risk of greater vices. Reformers created supervised and well-structured recreational activities, such as the YMCA, YWCA, Boy Scouts, and Girl Scouts, as a way of filling time and as "a tool for furthering social, intellectual and moral development" (Goodale & Godbey, 1988, p. 112). In keeping with a Puritan heritage of utilitarianism, they distrusted leisure itself and did not promote self-directed, spontaneous activity in childhood.

The philosophical dilemma discovered by these reformers was that, to legitimize recreation as a developmental activity, they were forced to use many of the methods of industrialism—such as goal setting, specialization, and incremental improvement through mastery of technique—even though their stated objective was to counteract the industrial system that utilized them (Goodale & Godbey, 1988). Even as the study of leisure became an academic discipline in the middle part of this century, this dilemma did not go away, but rather has come to be seen as fundamental. Personal freedom, initiative, and self-expression are now recognized as central to the developmental and adjustment value of leisure, yet questions are repeatedly raised about the desirability and "dangers" of this freedom, particularly for adolescents. A growing body of research demonstrates the importance of the subjective qualities of leisure, such as perceived freedom and intrinsic motivation, to quality of life and adjustment (for a review, see Iso-Ahola, 1980). Still, theorists struggle with the paradoxical supposition that adolescents need to be guided to make the best use of these opportunities. Hence, teachers, social agencies, and all who deal with youth encounter tension between the costs of social control—suppression of autonomy and of innovation—and the liabilities of relinquishing it—excessively individualistic or antisocial activities. This tension, of course, describes the individual-versus-society dialectic faced in any developmental context (Buss, 1979), but it is the context of leisure, more than any other, that presupposes the individual's ability to act responsibly and affords him or her the opportunity to do otherwise (Kelly, 1981).

Enjoyment and Challenge

A theoretical advance that shows a partial way out of this dilemma is a model of enjoyment developed by Csikszentmihalyi (1975). This model has attracted the attention of leisure scholars by specifying the conditions that lead to an optimal leisure experience. Csikszentmihalyi demonstrates that enjoyment, which he differentiates from pleasure, occurs in contexts of personal challenge when a person experiences his or her skills as well matched to the demands of the situation. The state of enjoyment or "flow" is not merely a state of positive affect (indeed, positive affect is not always a major component); rather, its distinctive feature is deep involvement, enrapt attention, a total focusing of the mind's energies on the challenges of the activity at hand.

It follows that structure (in the form of challenge) and the positive qualities of leisure (such as the experience of enjoyment and freedom) need not be seen as opposites but may instead complement each other. An adult's provision of structure to an adolescent, if it creates challenges, does not contradict but rather may facilitate initiative, self-expression, and an optimal state of experience. If the adolescent is able to internalize the challenges and reinterpret them in terms of his or her own meaning system, they are likely to be a stimulus to enjoyable involvement. By the same token, when a teenager gets involved in a free-time activity on his or her own, it is important to ask whether he or she experiences challenge and enjoyment.

Two additional properties of enjoyment are important to note. Along with the experience of enrapt attention, people who are enjoying themselves also experience diminished awareness of other things in their lives; they lose track of time and become detached from mundane reality (Csikszentmihalyi, 1975). This suggests why an enjoyable leisure activity can be cleansing and restorative: it distracts one from things going on in one's life and wipes the slate clean. Csikszentmihalyi's model also suggests that enjoyment can be a stimulus to self-expansion and growth. Enjoyment involves a process of pitting one's skills against challenges, and, as these challenges are met, fresh and often more difficult challenges must be found requiring development of further skills.

Enjoyment and challenge, then, provide a first criterion for evaluating free-time experience in adolescence. A teenager who has at least one activity that is absorbing enough to engage his or her interest will find it easier to get through the day. Enjoyment itself, however, is not a sufficient criterion for evaluating the merit of free-time activities. One could certainly imagine that the game of "mailbox baseball," in which a "batter" in a moving car takes swings at rural mailboxes, might fulfill the conditions for enjoyment, and a few "innings" might restore one's spirits after taking "flak" from teachers all day. But the development of skills to meet the challenges of this "sport" only moves an adolescent away from healthy accommodation to society. Enjoyment is a criterion for immediate well-being and is an indication of potential for skill development; however, we need other criteria for evaluating the skills involved and the ultimate value of a leisure activity for long-term adjustment and development.

The Development of Instrumentality

Such broader criteria are provided by Robert Havighurst's recently revived concept of "developmental tasks." Havighurst (1966) identified specific developmental issues faced at six life-course periods; in adolescence, for example, a person must develop expressive competencies, achieve emotional independence from adults, and shape a personal identity. This idea of developmental tasks has been revived within action theory, which emphasizes the role of the individual in setting his or her own tasks—albeit within the general requirement of accommodating to society (Silbereisen, Eyferth, & Rudinger, 1986). In the language of Lerner and Busch-Rossnagel (1981), individuals are "producers of their own development." This framework suggests that individuals achieve direction and control over their lives by having experiences of setting goals, acting on them, and evaluating progress toward their achievement.

Oerter (1986) has argued that it is only in the course of self-appropriated activity that an adolescent can engage in this process of setting approximate goals and assessing his or her developmental status in relation to personal standards. In school, Oerter argues, this kind of self-determination is curtailed. Likewise, economic imperatives appear to restrict and discourage freedom in the workplace. Dittmann-Kohli (1986) found that even after 1 to 2 years on a job, teenagers had not learned to take advantage of the opportunities for personal initiative that were readily available. Free-time activities, Oerter asserts, offer the best opportunities for deliberate self-development, self-determined experimentation, and self-evaluation. Furthermore, if the activity at least loosely resembles adult activities, we might anticipate carryover.

The adolescent is able to say, "This is what I like doing," "This is what I do that is appreciated by the wider world," and "This is what I like to do that is connected to what society says I should be doing."

Elsewhere, we have coined the term "transitional activities" to refer to adolescent activities that meet both of the above criteria by being enjoyable and self-motivating while generating challenges consistent with development into adulthood (Kleiber, Larson, & Csikszentmihalyi, 1986; Larson, Ham, & Raffaelli, in press). Such activities perpetuate desirable aspects of childhood play in being pleasurable, expressive, and intrinsically motivating, but they anticipate the meaning systems, reward structures, and intentional, directed effort associated with mature ego functioning.

The presence of these opportunities within an activity does not necessarily mean an adolescent will take them. Free-time activities can be enjoyable or boring; they can be used constructively or squandered. Therefore, we need to turn to empirical data to evaluate what adolescents typically experience in different activities and how often teenagers actually take advantage of the opportunities that are available. We also can examine whether participation in a given activity is related to developmental growth in any general sense.

Operationalizing the Criteria

The best means of assessing enjoyment during free-time activities is to interrupt people during these activities and ask them about their subjective state. In one study with senior high school (SHS) students and a second with junior high school (JHS) students, we did just that (Csikszentmihalyi & Larson, 1984; Larson & Richards, 1989). Using a procedure called the Experience Sampling Method, we had these students carry electronic pagers during their daily lives and asked them to fill out reports on their subjective experience when they received signals. Because the signals occurred randomly, the reports provided a representative sample of how these teenagers spent their time and how they felt engaging in different activities. The data we consider here deal with the times these signals were received during leisure activities. We give particular attention to the students' reports on four subjective dimensions of enjoyment: affect, motivation, attention, and challenge. We refer to the groups from the two studies as the JHS sample and the SHS sample.*

Although we have good data on immediate enjoyment of activities, there has been little empirical research, unfortunately, on the second criterion. Few data are available on whether activities stimulate adolescents to formulate and follow through on personal challenges; hence, this part of the activity analysis that follows will be largely speculative. We can, however, bring in longitudinal evidence on the long-term correlates of different activity choices that is suggestive of how well each prepares teens for psychological adjustment and membership in adult society.

SPORTS

For centuries, sports have been promoted as a desirable way for youth to spend time. Sports were seen by reformers at the turn of the century as "an ideal means of integrating the young into the work rhythms and social demands of a

---

*Both of these samples are composed of White middle-class and lower-middle-class teenagers who were randomly selected, with stratification by grade, sex, and residential area. The first study included 75 students from all four grades in a large high school. The second included 483 fifth-to-ninth graders from six schools in two communities. Except where indicated, for this later study, we report data only on the 201 seventh and eighth graders.

dynamic and complex urban–industrial civilization, ... the means through which the young developed specific skills, moral tendencies and social values" (Cavallo, 1981, pp. 2–3). Among the enduring assumptions was that strength of body was consistent with strength of mental and moral faculties.

Such a rationale notwithstanding, adolescents themselves generally need little more justification for participation in sports than that it is fun and that it captures the attention of others in their social worlds. In a study of the recreational sport involvement of 90,000 Michigan children between the ages of 5 and 16, over 85% of both boys and girls indicated at least some involvement in bicycling and swimming (Fountain, 1978). Basketball followed these two sports for males at 82%, and kickball, roller skating, and softball followed for girls at more than 72% each. Of the 35 different sports listed, 17 were done by over 50% of the boys and 13 involved at least 50% of the girls. Much of these data reflect the play patterns of late childhood, with about half of the activities showing a decline beginning in early adolescence. A more conservative estimate for older adolescents is suggested in data on 402 juniors and seniors from two midwestern high schools (Kleiber & Roberts, 1989). In an examination of only school-sponsored extracurricular activities, 57% of the boys and 21% of the girls indicated involvement in one of 13 sports.

Time budget data obtained from our two time-sampling studies indicated that sports and related physical activities (such as dance and calisthenics) fill about 5.6% of waking hours among JHS-aged adolescents and 3.4% among SHS-aged students, with boys accounting for roughly two-thirds of this time (Csikszentmihalyi & Larson, 1984; Kirshnet, Ham, & Richards, 1989). Sports participation is somewhat more common among higher socioeconomic status students and students who do better in school (Otto & Alwin, 1977). We also found that depressed boys and girls are much less involved in sport than nondepressed peers (Larson, Raffaelli, Richards, Ham, & Jewell, in press; Merrick, 1989).

Consistent with its reputation, participation in sports stands out as one of the most enjoyable parts of adolescents' lives. When our students carrying pagers were signaled during sports involvement, they reported levels of affect, motivation, and attention that were much more positive than at other times (Csikszentmihalyi & Larson, 1984; Kirshnet et al., 1989). Figure 6.1 shows the average subjective states reported by our JHS and SHS samples during sports, using a z-score scale in which 0.00 corresponds to each person's average report and a unit of 1.00 corresponds to each person's standard deviation. One can see on this graph that the experience of sports is one of favorable affect and positive involvement. However, the subjective feature that most differentiates sports from other leisure activities is the experience of challenge; indeed, sports are more like studying or taking a test in the level of challenge reported (Kleiber et al., 1986).

Chalip, Csikszentmihalyi, Kleiber, and Larson (1984) broke these SHS data down further, contrasting experience in informal sports (such as playing "pick-up" basketball in a park) and formal, adult-organized sports. They found the former to be related with the experience of greater openness, freedom, joking, and positive feelings; the latter was associated with higher concentration and a closer identification with group goals. These findings confirm that informal sports are more playlike in the experience they engender, and that formal sports represent the choice to pursue goals that are structured within an adult-governed system. Nevertheless, it is important to reiterate that overall affect and motivation were found to be very positive in both settings. Even though an adolescent may become frustrated by not performing well or temporarily depressed by losing, the modal experience of sports is that of enjoyment. Other recent studies, employing differing methodologies, confirm that physical activity and exercise reduce anxiety and depression (Brown &

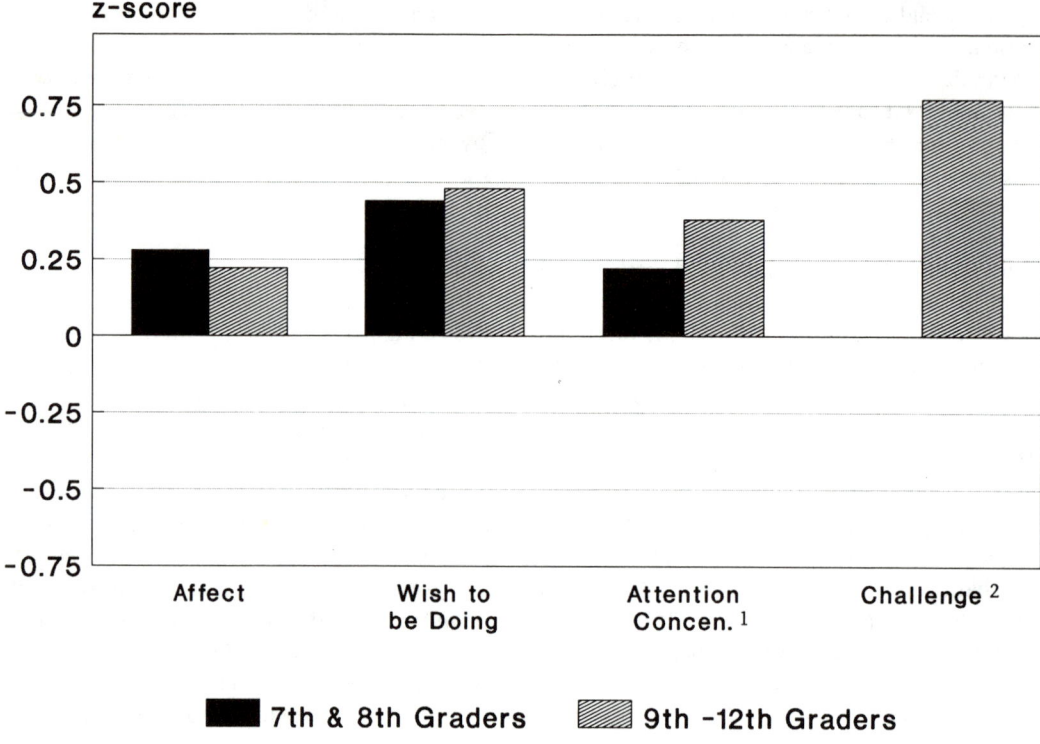

¹For the younger sample, this item was "attention"; for the older sample, it was "concentration."
²This item was not used in the study with the younger sample.

Figure 6.1 Reported average subjective states for sports.

Siegel, 1988; Morgan, 1979; Morgan & Goldston, 1987). In short, for the typical teenager, participating in sports has a direct effect on immediate mental health. But what about more enduring effects?

To the extent that the challenges of sport are self-chosen and are superseded by greater self-chosen challenges, a compelling argument can be made for their value in the enhancement of competence and development of instrumentality. Such is the case for informal sports and for organized sports for some individuals. However, to the extent that the challenges are defined externally—in terms of winning, as often happens in formal, adult-organized teams—a youth's sense of success is subject to the relative abilities of opponents and the sport becomes a zero-sum game; for every "winner" there is a "loser." The importance given to winning differs among people, and these differences are related to age, athletic experience, and gender, among other things (Duda, in press). It is not inevitable that defeat has a deflating effect on perceived competence and self-esteem. There is increasing emphasis, in applied sport psychology and coaching practice, on the value of personal goal setting, task involvement, effort, and improvement (Danish, Kleiber, & Hall, 1987). Establishing performance goals (e.g., four rebounds, no turnovers) enables youth to stay focused on the activity, rather than on their opponents or the outcome of a contest, and has been shown to enhance motivation, performance, and the quality of the experience (Locke, Sarri, Shaw, & Latham, 1981). In short, there has been a deliberate effort to reconstruct youths' experience of sport in a manner consistent with the developmental criteria we have described above.

One might also imagine sports to be a useful vehicle for identity development. Being an athlete or even a skill specialist (e.g., pole vaulter) provides tangible behavioral evidence of what one is, and the popularity of sport involvement validates that identity socially. Studies of adolescent social status find no more popular roles in high school than that of athlete (Coleman, 1961; Eitzen, 1976), but there is very little evidence on the impact of sport on identity development, and what little there is suggests a possible negative effect. Using Lovinger's ego development measures, Malmisur (1976) found college athletes to be significantly behind nonathletes in terms of ego development—they were "stuck," as it were, in a level of conventionality. It also appears that those athletes who do not diversify their interests into other activities do not fare well in the long run (Spady, 1970). A narrow focus on sports is associated with adjustment problems subsequent to "retiring" from sport involvement (Hill & Lowe, 1974). One interpretation of these data is that sport involvement may be especially valuable in beginning the identity formation process but runs the risk of contributing to identity foreclosure (Marcia, 1980)—becoming fixated in an identity narrowly limited to physical skills and anchored in sport values, which, especially in this country, are exceedingly conservative and conventional (Kleiber, 1983; Kleiber & Roberts, 1987; Sage, 1978).

Despite these limitations and dangers, two relatively common patterns may make sport developmentally useful. The first case is the child who is otherwise disenfranchised or "at risk" and finds in sport a means for self-betterment. The popularity of athletic involvement integrates athletes more securely into supportive social systems and may provide social and even academic advantages that those not involved in sports are denied (Otto & Alwin, 1977). Although the negative correlation between delinquency and sport involvement is partly due to a socioeconomic confound, it does appear that sport sometimes deters antisocial behavior (for reviews, see Hendry, 1978; Landers & Landers, 1978). As a mechanism of self-advancement and social integration, sport has a celebrated place in the annals of the American dream (Nixon, 1984). Athletes from disadvantaged backgrounds are sometimes the victims of exploitation, left with few usable skills when their sport involvement ends (Edwards, 1976); but in the course of adolescence, it is clear that sport can be a primary source of social integration for some individuals.

The second, and not mutually exclusive, pattern is that of the adolescent who develops from sport useful habits, motivational orientations, and ego skills that generalize to other domains of life. This pattern is "transitional" in the more psychological sense referred to earlier: it provides a link between the enjoyable and expressive play of childhood and the disciplined demands of adulthood. The freedom to participate identifies sport as a leisure activity; the application of effort and concentration and the demand for persistence to improve skills give it a worklike character that is comparable to other demanding situations that an adolescent faces increasingly in the transition to adult life. Indeed, although it is not clear what the cause-and-effect mechanisms are, sport involvement in high school is correlated with academic achievement and greater educational aspirations (e.g., Hanks & Eckland, 1976). Thus, although the athlete identity is limiting in the ways discussed earlier and must alternately be transcended for further maturation, it may afford a relatively compelling preliminary identity structure for one whose competence and autonomy are not being validated in other ways (Danish, 1983).

SOCIALIZING

In the past, idle time spent with friends was seen to lead teenagers into a life of banal conversation, languor, conformity, and amorality (Payot, 1904). Yet, "hanging out" is adolescents' free-time activity of first choice. Asked how they would prefer to spend their leisure time, a majority of teenagers say "partying" (Hedin & Simon, 1980). This idealized state of group fusion, of deindividuation, occupies the pinnacle of adolescent free-time preferences. One-on-one talk, whether in person or on the phone, also rates highly as a preferred activity (Youniss & Smollar, 1985).

The leisure category of "socializing" is perhaps the most difficult to make generalizations about; it includes an enormous variation, from rowdy bacchanals to quiet and intimate self-analysis with one friend. Evaluation of the time teens spend socializing ultimately depends on whom they talk with, what they talk about, and how they talk about it, all of which must be considered in terms of long-term meanings and relationships. Most of these factors have not been adequately studied. The reader is referred to Chapter 9 of this volume for a more thorough discussion of the broader topic of peer relationships. Here, we try to focus on the activity of socializing in itself.

Socializing, the most frequent free-time activity of high school students, accounts for 16.0% of waking hours—10.1%, if we include only talking with friends (Csikszentmihalyi & Larson, 1984). Raffaelli and Duckett (1989) showed that this percentage represents a substantial increase over preadolescent rates of socializing, particularly for girls, who appear to spend more time socializing than boys (Youniss & Smollar, 1985). Overall, the data suggest little difference in rates of socializing between working-class and middle-class teens. Larson, Raffaelli, et al. (1990) (see also Merrick, 1989) found that early adolescent depressed boys, but not depressed girls, engaged in substantially less socializing than controls.

On the average, the experience of socializing is one of positive affect and intrinsic motivation, although the levels of motivation are below those for sports (Figure 6.2). The JHS students reported levels of "attention" during socializing that were comparable to those reported during sports; however, the SHS students reported "concentration" and "challenge" that were below the mean. This suggests that, although enjoyable, talk with friends may often be impulsive and unstructured rather than effortful and disciplined. The SHS students also reported that the feedback they got from their companions was positive and supportive and that the talk typically was more "joking" than "serious." Elsewhere, we have proposed that the dynamics of interactions with friends resemble those of a positive feedback system (Larson, 1983). Whether talking with a close chum or bantering in a group, friends tend to reinforce what each other says. Typically, companions build on what is said before, with each speaker taking the topic further, in a more probing, intimate, or perhaps zany direction.

In the structure of the school day, socializing is intermixed with classwork. Adolescents exchange quick words with friends between classes and see them at lunch, during study halls, and at the end of the day. Analyses of teens' moods suggest that these interludes provide a boost from the low motivation and boredom of schoolwork; students get recharged for the next class (Csikszentmihalyi & Larson, 1984). For older adolescents, socializing is the primary activity on Friday and Saturday nights. It includes partying, driving around, and dating—activities that provide the emotional climax of the week. The agenda for Friday and Saturday nights is one of losing oneself in a state of *communitas* with friends, experiencing a state of flow in which all else is forgotten and the slate is wiped clean to begin another week. Sometimes this works out, sometimes it does not. There are variations among teens in the access they have to this kind of experience. Those without access, those who are alone on Friday or Saturday night, experience the obverse of *communitas,* profound loneliness (Larson, Csikszentmihalyi, & Graef, 1982).

It is clear, then, that talk is important to teenagers' immediate well-being, to getting through the day. What about its contribution to sustained mental health and long-term development? On this question, we are reduced to more speculative evidence.

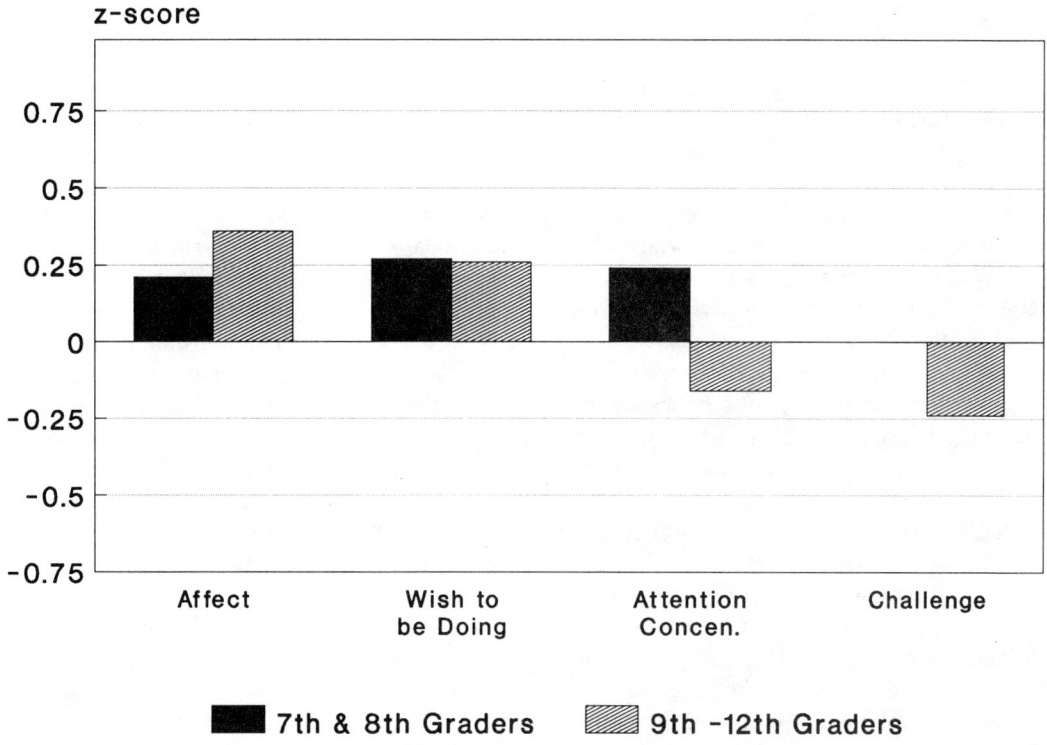

Figure 6.2 Reported average subjective states for socializing.

First, it is relevant that, from style of dress to rules about fighting, the world of peers is a highly structured domain (Argyle, 1986), and success within this world depends on how well a teenager takes on the challenge of acting strategically within the given constraints (Elkind, 1980). Teenagers do not experience high challenges on a moment-to-moment basis, but the demands on them may still be there. Thus, even in deviant peer groups, a member must learn to fashion his or her behavior within an evolving set of norms. Sherif and Sherif (1964) argue that this adaptation requires maturity and psychological sophistication.

Second, it is relevant that much one-on-one talk, particularly among girls, is talk about self and relationships (Raffaelli & Duckett, 1989; Youniss & Smollar, 1985). The majority of teens report that close friends try to understand them and do understand them more than their parents (Youniss & Smollar, 1985). As such, talk with friends provides a potential forum for self-understanding (Parker & Gottman, in press) and for understanding the dynamics of reciprocity necessary for mutual relationships (Douvan & Adelsen, 1966; Youniss, 1980). Even argument and conflict with friends are potentially beneficial if they lead to clarification of self vs. other boundaries and stimulate a process of analysis and relationship renegotiation (Youniss, 1980). Indeed, teenagers report learning more from their friends than from their parents (Youniss & Smollar, 1985) and demonstrate more advanced interpersonal reasoning, which Youniss (1980) suggests eventually is transferred to parental and other relationships.

Third, many of the developmental goals that teenagers spontaneously set for themselves have to do with interpersonal relationships

(Dreher & Oerter, 1986). Emotional autonomy from the family is a very common developmental task for which peer relations provide a bridge. Learning self-control or learning to cope with the eccentricities of others are other examples. Socializing with friends, then, is a context in which teens are actively striving to better themselves. It is a forum for agentic action and the outcomes may encourage or discourage their attempts to take control of other parts of their lives.

When authors have been critical of friends, the peer group, not one-on-one interactions, is usually their target. Conformity pressures from peers may undermine agentic self-determination, although it also should be noted that these pressures are typically prosocial, not antisocial (Brown, Clasen, & Eicher, 1986). Furthermore, the positive feedback dynamics of peer groups are liable to run out of control. When they are caught up in enjoyment and in the relaxing of superego controls that Freud (1921/1960) saw as inherent in group processes, the challenges of having more fun can potentially lead teenagers into deviant activities that they would never consider doing on their own (Larson, 1983).

Ultimately, it is too simplistic to ask whether talk itself is a factor in long-term development. There are certainly examples of socially isolated adolescents (Bertrand Russell, Albert Einstein) who grew up to be mature and adequately adjusted adults. As a gross generalization, however, it is worth noting that peer acceptance or rejection in childhood and adolescence is one of the best predictors of adult mental health (Parker & Asher, 1987). Although this is hardly proof that social interaction per se promotes mental health, programs that train children and adolescents in social skills appear to bring improvements in overall mental health (Wanlass & Prinz, 1982). Curiously, the goal of these programs is often to teach children to focus their attention and identify challenges in peer interaction—essentially, to learn to enjoy them.

ART, MUSIC, HOBBIES, AND YOUTH ORGANIZATIONS

Confronting the burgeoning expanse of adolescent free time, early reformers promoted hobbies, the arts, and youth clubs as means to protect teens from idleness. Within American secondary schools, extracurricular activities—school publications, student government, drama clubs, band, and orchestra—were developed as "laboratories for training in citizenship" that would stimulate the learning of initiative, cooperation, and leadership (Roemer, Allen, & Fretwell, 1926; Terry, 1930). Outside of school, Ys, 4H clubs, church youth groups, and a subculture of music lessons, hobbies, and other home activities emerged with the objective of promoting constructive use of leisure time. All of these activities were seen as prototypic and anticipatory of adult activities. As such, they represented a deliberate attempt to create transitional activities.

Current data indicate that many teenagers are involved in at least one organization or activity of this kind, but the average amount of time they devote to them is relatively small. In Kleiber and Roberts's (1989) study of two midwestern high schools, 37% of high school juniors and seniors reported at least one nonsport extracurricular activity. Our time budget data indicated that the average high school student spends only 1.8% of waking hours, or approximately 2 hours a week, in working at a hobby, playing music, or participating in an organization (Csikszentmihalyi & Larson, 1984). For JHS-aged teenagers, we obtained a similar estimate (Larson & Richards, 1989). Other research suggests that participation in these kinds of activities, particularly when they involve a club or organization, is not equally distributed, but is more common in smaller schools (Barker & Gump, 1964), among students of higher socioeconomic status (Hanks & Eckland, 1978; Hendry, 1983) who have more positive self-concepts (Yarmouth & Gauthier, 1978), do better in school (Hansley, Lupkowski, & Edind, 1986), and are more favorably disposed to school and adult society (Hendry, 1983). Further, young people perceive organizations to be controlled by cliques (Hedin & Simon, 1980; Long, Buser, & Jackson, 1977); hence, participation for many is limited by their social group membership or the lack thereof.

Although these activities are not successful in engaging a substantial amount of adolescent free time, they are successful in creating positive involvement for the teens who are engaged. Unfortunately, our research provided too few data points to examine experiential states during participation in organizations. But, when paged during arts and hobbies, our adolescents—particularly the SHS-aged adolescents—reported high levels of motivation, attention, and challenge. (See Figure 6.3.) For the SHS students, motivation and concentration were two-thirds of a standard deviation unit above average; challenge was a full standard deviation above the mean. Thus, although these activities do not raise affect, they are very engaging.

In addition to being absorbing, these activities provide rich opportunities for development of instrumentality. Participants to extracurricular activities report them to be significant to personal growth (Hedin & Simon, 1980; Long et al., 1977). Both school and nonschool activities often have the quality of "serials" (Little, 1983): they provide individuals with the opportunity to set goals, launch long-term projects, and monitor the cumulative success or failure of their actions. Consider, for example, the initiative exercised by a particular 17-year-old who has developed an extensive collection of baseball cards by trading with other, mostly

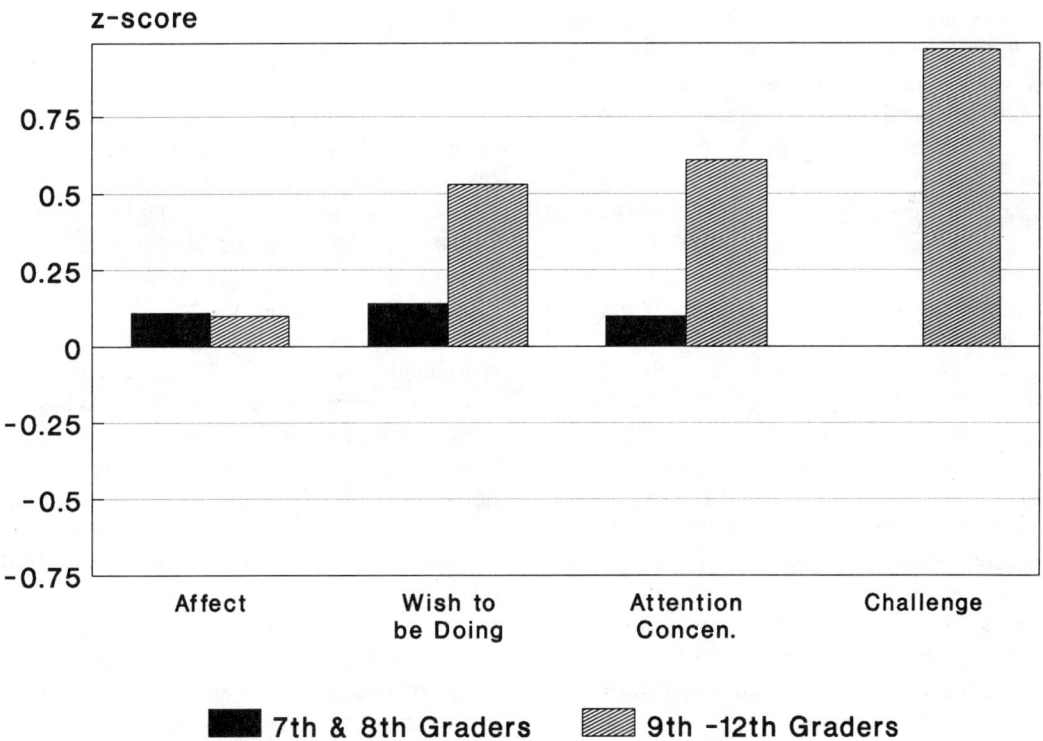

Figure 6.3 Reported average subjective states for arts, hobbies, and creative activities.

adult, collectors. Baseball cards may seem juvenile to some observers, but this boy has had the experience of pursuing long-term aspirations, weathering the strains of commerce, displaying the trophies of his labor before others, and perhaps even reflecting on the meaning (or meaninglessness) of his accomplishments. His hobby has provided numerous opportunities for personal development that would not have been available in school or at a job. A teenager who builds a computer in the basement has an opportunity to learn about his or her own qualities of discipline and creativity. A teen who chooses to participate in a neighborhood service group learns to regulate his or her commitment to a moral cause in relation to others.

Confirmation that adolescents use and learn from these opportunities is provided by short-term and long-term longitudinal research. In a study in which random assignment was used to select ninth-grade students for a 10-week "community service project," participants, when compared with controls, showed less alienation, less isolation, and lower rates of discipline referrals both during and after the project (Calabrese & Schumer, 1986). Similarly, in an assessment of 27 experiential learning programs in secondary schools, Hedin and Conrad (1981) found significant changes, relative to controls, in measures of participants' self-esteem, moral reasoning, social and personal responsibility, empathy, and attitudes toward adults and the community. In a long-term study, Spady (1970) found that participation in extracurricular activities in secondary school was correlated with later fulfillment of college educational goals. Hanks and Eckland (1978) found that extracurricular participation in high school predicted voluntary association participation and voting at age 30, independently of education, occupation, and income. Studies of political activists also show a pattern of continuity between adolescent and adult involvement (DeMartini, 1983) similar to the pattern found for involvement in the arts (Bloom, 1986).

It is difficult to be confident that these studies have adequately separated all the variables affecting these youths' development, and it is regrettable that research has not isolated different activities and different types of involvement. It is fair to surmise, however, that, for many teenagers, these kinds of activities become a part of their personal narratives. In adulthood, these adolescent experiences with hobbies or organizations are identified as significant influences on their lives (Hildreth, Richard, & Burts, 1986). The ribbon-winning 4H project, the work on a school yearbook, the memories of playing jazz piano alone in the house, become significant parts of a person's life story and thus of his or her ego resources and sense of self. In short, these activities meet the criteria of transitional activities, providing enjoyment within a context of developmental challenges.

MEDIA USE

Technology has created a succession of new media for home entertainment and each has been derided as a poor influence on youth, beginning with early concerns about children who spent too much time reading books. Television has unleashed the largest outcry, but there is also much current concern about the effects of rock music, music videos, and arcade games. Although it is undeniable that these media, particularly TV, are a major part of children's lives, research in this area has recently shifted away from this "effects tradition," which pictures youth as passive victims of media, toward interpretive analyses of each medium's text and a "uses and gratifications" approach, which recognizes that each child takes an active role in choosing and interpreting what is presented.

Among the different media, television is the most frequently chosen among all adolescent age groups. Our time sampling data suggested that TV accounts for 12.9% of time in JHS but this quantity diminishes in SHS, accounting for only 7.2%. With age, there is also a shift to adult programs and toward watching TV more often alone (Larson, Kubey, & Colletti, 1989). Nonschool reading is relatively stable across this age period, accounting for 1% to 2% of time. Music, in contrast to TV, increases substantially from 1% in fifth and sixth grades to 2–3% in ninth grade, an increase that is more marked if we include times when music is an accompaniment to another activity (2% to 5–6%). Although they have now been around for a decade or more, music videos, VCR use, and video games all account for less than .5% of time (Kubey & Larson, in press).

Choice of media varies with the adolescent. TV watching is more frequent among family-oriented youth (Larson & Kubey, 1983), those who are less popular within the peer group (Coleman, 1961; Hendry & Patrick, 1977), and depressed youth (Merrick, 1989). Reading is more common among solitary teenagers, and music listening is more common among those who are more involved with peers (Larson et al., 1989). In a longitudinal study, Roe (1983) effectively demonstrated that characteristics of a person are more likely to be a cause, rather than a result, of heavy media use. He found, for example, that heavy music listening does not precede teens' doing less well in school; rather, teens who do less well in school turn to music, perhaps as a means of reinforcing an identity that diverges from normative values. We mut be careful, therefore, about using correlational data to jump to the conclusion that TV and music are harmful.

What is striking in the daily experience of all these media is that teens report they want to

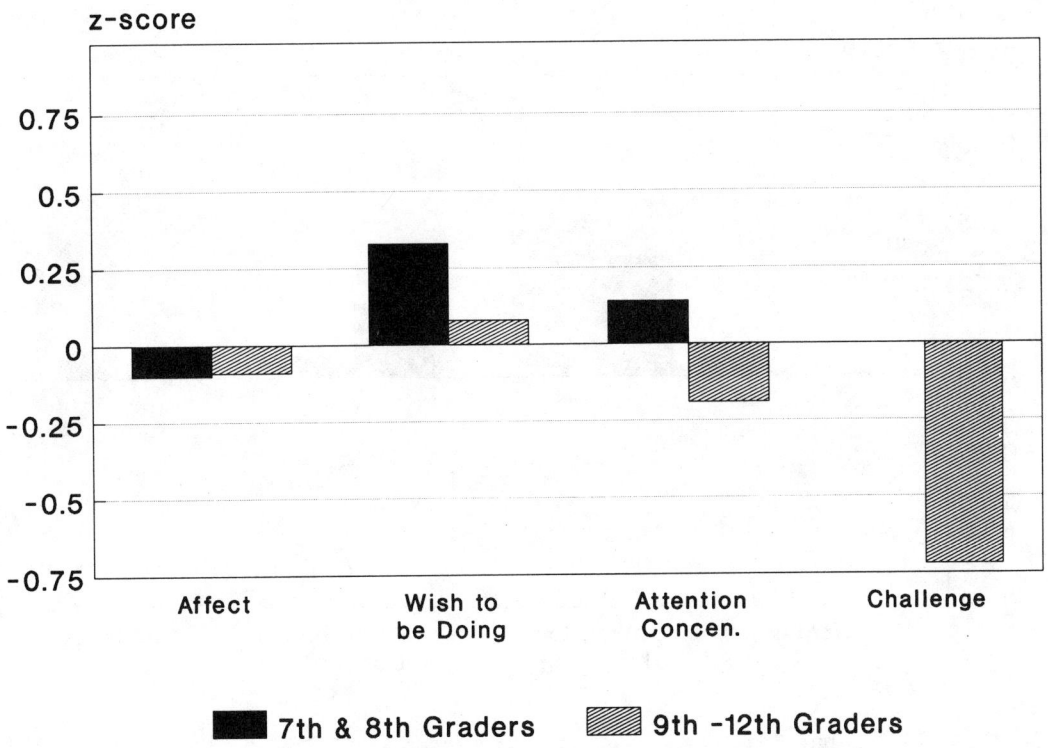

Figure 6.4 Reported average subjective states for watching television.

be attending to them: scores for motivation are high. Other aspects of their subjective states, however, tell a different story. While watching TV, JHS and SHS adolescents report feeling less happy, less alert, more passive, and more bored than at other times (Larson, et al., 1989; Larson & Kubey, 1983). For the JHS-aged teenagers, a wish to be in the activity (motivation) and attention are above the norm, but this absorption appears to diminish by the SHS age (Figure 6.4). More importantly, it is apparent that this absorption occurs with no challenge: self-ratings of challenge during TV viewing were extremely low. Unfortunately, these two studies did not ask participants whether they felt relaxed, a distinguishing quality of TV experience among adults (Csikszentmihalyi & Kubey, 1981). It is possible that the numb and passive feeling state associated with TV is a needed respite from the intensity of adolescent life. However, one would hope that other, more challenging forms of relief would be available.

Listening to music, in contrast to watching TV, brings more features of enjoyment (Figure 6.5). Although most music listening is done in the privacy of the bedroom—typically, a low-energy context—the reported feelings are excitement, freedom, and a sense of control (Larson & Kubey, 1983). Overall affect is relatively low, particularly among girls (Larson et al., 1989), but intrinsic motivation, attention, and challenge are high. The moving lyrics of ballads and the hard-driving beat of rock appear to stimulate a level of personal involvement that is lacking in TV watching. A teenager may be lying face-down on her bed, but her mind is alive and active, thinking about friends, school, or the future.

TV, then, might be thought of as a drug that is used to bring adolescents down, and music a

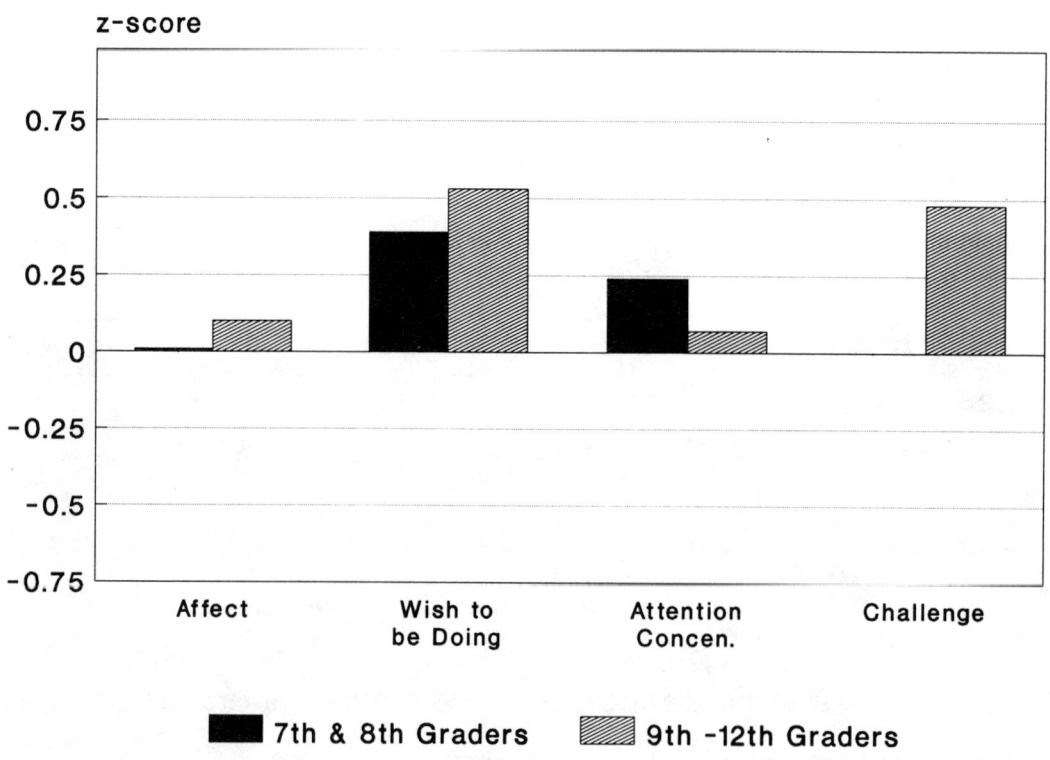

Figure 6.5 Reported average subjective states for listening to music.

drug that pumps them up. Apparently, TV also acts as a distraction in tense families, allowing teenagers and their parents to avoid direct conflict (Rosenblatt & Cunningham, 1976). It may also stimulate family interaction and reinforce family solidarity (Lull, 1980). Both TV and music also provide a common frame of experience that is a basis of conversation with friends, a vernacular of personalities and events to be talked about at the lunch table. Indeed, one often finds savvy teachers (or psychotherapists) who draw on TV or music to maintain a common language with their students.

All media, of course, are major sources of information and symbols that adolescents may use for good or ill. The question is: How do they use these? Does media use provide a context for long-term development? For TV, the answer has to be no. It remains debatable whether heavy TV watching causes poorer schoolwork, but there is no evidence that it promotes good schoolwork (Hendry & Patrick, 1977; Roe, 1983), and the majority of evidence suggests that TV violence can promote aggressive behavior (Rubenstein, 1983). Teenagers do not name TV as a conscious influence on their lives (McCormack, 1984), and their relatively passive and vacant state while watching TV would seem to exclude the possibility of this being a vehicle for the formulation of personal goals.

Music, by contrast, may sometimes be a vehicle for conscious self-construction. The content and semiotics of music often relate to a specific peer culture (punk, disco, heavy metal), but the majority of music listening is done alone at home, often in a bedroom, accompanied by fantasy or self-reflection. In this context, autonomous thinking may be as likely as indoctrination into a musical credo. A majority of teenagers (71%) can name a song that has had an influence on how they think about an important issue, and 81% say that music is an important part of their lives (Leming, 1987). For the average teenager, music probably serves as a medium of symbols, feelings, and impulses that help with separation from the world of parents and other adults (Larson & Kubey, 1983). For many teens, music's content and energy, and the excuse it provides to lie on one's bed and reflect, may provide raw materials for work on the issue of autonomy and on other given and self-defined developmental tasks.

DEVIANT ACTIVITIES

Drug use, delinquency, and other deviant activities should also be examined as free-time activities, because they emerge out of expressive interests (Anson, 1977; Reimer, 1981; Richards, Berk, & Foster, 1979) and are reported by a large number of teenagers. Recent data indicated that 57% of high school seniors had tried an illicit drug, 36% had tried a drug other than marijuana, and 92% reported use of alcohol ("Patterns," 1987). Delinquent actions are reported by more than half of all boys (Rutter & Giller, 1984).

Our Experience Sampling data confirmed that the immediate states associated with drug and alcohol use are quite positive (Larson, Csikszentmihalyi, & Freeman, 1984). Particularly during alcohol use, which occurs most often in the context of parties, teens report positive affect, arousal, and motivation. Reported attention and challenge, however, are low, suggesting that the experience associated with substance use is better described as pleasure than as enjoyment. Csikszentmihalyi (personal communication) made the interesting observation that subjective states during marijuana use are a mirror image of those reported during schoolwork (Figure 6.6). This comparison suggests that this drug serves as a symbolic antidote to the intense concentration, control, and boredom of school.

In the case of drug use, the motive of escape has been acknowledged for many years. To that extent, drug use may be seen as having some adaptive value in the face of stressful life circumstances. In the initial stages, at least, drugs and alcohol becomes addictive precisely because the subjective states they induce help a

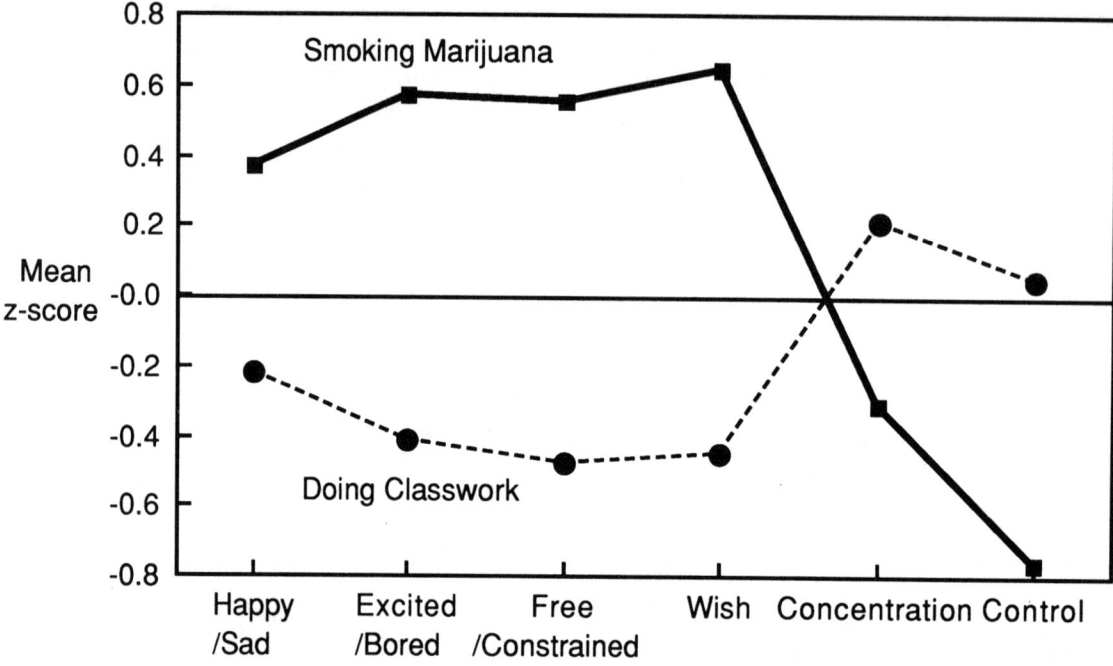

Figure 6.6 Reported subjective states when using marijuana and doing classwork.

person get through the day. However, the absence of challenges and the deliberate relinquishing of control suggest that neither alcohol use nor drug use is likely to provide a forum for agentic, long-term learning experiences.

Curiously, a stronger case can be made for the developmental value of delinquent activities, although recognizing the harm they may cause others. Elsewhere, we have argued that enjoyment of deviant activities involves a hierarchy of challenges that requires a development of particular talents (Csikszentmihalyi & Larson, 1978). Participation in a deviant group, as we pointed out earlier, requires development of skills within a demanding set of norms (Sherif & Sherif, 1964). Furthermore, it is increasingly recognized by developmentalists that acting up can be individuating at the same time that it is reactionary (Silbereisen et al., 1986). Thus, it affords an opportunity akin to self-determination and self-regulation. Although these may be short-term effects with additional negative concomitants, the developmental orientation of such behavior needs to be recognized within intervention efforts aimed at curbing them (Tolan, 1988).

Substance use and delinquency, like other free-time activities are, at the least, ways of filling time and of obtaining positive experiences that, for whatever reason, are not regarded by an adolescent as obtainable through any other activity.

CONCLUSION

The thesis we have advanced in this chapter is that leisure activities play an important role in adolescents' lives and deserve more attention from mental health professionals, in practice and research. First, they fill a sizable chunk of time: 40% of waking hours for the high school group that we studied and close to 50% for the younger adolescents. Second, and more importantly, they are regular and predictable sources of pleasure and enjoyment in adolescents' daily lives. Sports, socializing with friends, involvement in a club, or getting drunk provide the high points in teenagers' experience. They are what teenagers look forward to, what gets them out of bed in the morning, and what sustains them through weeks when school stress or family tensions fill life with dread. Lacking these free-time activities, it is safe to predict, many "normal" teens would be on clinical rolls.

Third, beyond immediate mental health, we have argued that these free-time activities often provide a forum for development of instrumentality. Because of their relative freedom from constraint and coercion, they provide an opportunity for exercise of initiative, expression of personal interest, self-formulation of goals, and the learning that comes from long-term investment in a self-defined project. Other parts of adolescents' lives demand accommodation—to school assignments, to parental rules, to the requirements of a job; free-time activities, as the heir of childhood play, provide opportunities for assimilation into the adolescent's *own* structures and the elaboration of these structures in terms of a personally meaningful construction of the world.

Across the activities we have discussed, sports and art/hobbies/organizations stand out as the most consistent forum for immediate adjustment and positive development. They are associated with active enjoyment and provide clear opportunities for the development of skills that are most likely to be useful in adulthood. Socializing is an activity over which adults have less influence and, as such, is more liable to be empty or to take the form of meaningless gossip, goofing around, or regressive childhood play. Yet, because many of adolescents' developmental tasks involve social relationships, we believe that, for many youths, even this regressive play may be an important forum for experimentation and learning. TV, although not established by evidence as either a positive or negative influence, is clearly a major time filler, and thus its worth rests on what else a teen might be doing; for the majority of youth, there are certainly more enjoyable and engaging activities. Listening to music, we have argued, provides a context of solitary reflection that is typically more engaging and challenging, and more developmentally meaningful than TV. All of these generalizations need to be seen as such, and the ultimate question is how a specific free-time activity is experienced and used by a specific adolescent.

Unfortunately, although leisure activities clearly are important to the adjustment and development of "normal" teenagers, clinicians have been slow to be concerned with them. In fact, the recently burgeoning literature on adolescent depression and related adolescent disorders has shown little interest in the ecology of this population's daily lives, with the important exception of research on their social relationships. Little data exist on how adolescents in different clinical categories fill their free time and how these uses of time are interrelated with their psychopathology. Regrettably, recreational therapy, which deals with this part of adolescents' lives, has been cast as a subprofessional discipline that mainly fills patients' time in between "serious" therapy.

What little research there is indicates that disturbed individuals are less involved in the more favorable types of free-time experiences we have described—sports, social interaction, and organizations—and spend more time watching TV. The absence of meaningful uses of free time for these youths represents not only a handicap in their daily efforts to get through the day, but also a developmental deprivation, the absence of a large category of experience that is important to the psychological development of most teens. Drug use and delinquency may in some cases represent attempts to fill time and find the same kind of enjoyment that others find in more prosocial activities.

Responding to these types of concerns, deVries (1987) called for more research on the daily experience associated with psychopathology. He suggested that treatment of various disorders requires knowledge based on "thick description" of patients' daily lives.

We propose that this is particularly true in adolescence, when adult habits and patterns of time use are being formed. We need to know more about the daily scenarios that make up the lives of depressed, anxious, conduct-disordered, or drug-dependent teenagers. How do they spend their free time? How do the activities and events in their lives affect their experiential state? What inhibits them from participation in the types of leisure activities that play such a constructive role in the lives of other teens?

REFERENCES

Anson, R. (1977). Recreation deviance. *Journal of Leisure Research, 8,* 177–180.

Argyle, M. (1986). Social behavior problems in adolescence. In R. K. Silbereisen, K. Eyferth, & G. Rudinger (Eds.), *Development as action in context* (pp. 55–86). New York: Springer-Verlag.

Barker, R., & Gump, P. (1964). *Big school, small school: High school size and student behavior.* Stanford, CA: Stanford University Press.

Bloom, B. (1986). *Developing talent in young people.* New York: Ballantine.

Brown, B. B., Clasen, D., & Eicher, S. (1986). Perceptions of peer pressure, peer conformity dispositions, and self-reported behavior among adolescents. *Developmental Psychology, 22,* 521–530.

Brown, J., & Siegel, J. (1988). Exercise as a buffer of life stress: A prospective study of adolescent health. *Health Psychology, 7,* 341–353.

Bruner, J., Jolly, A., & Sylva, K. (1976). *Play: Its role in development and evaluation.* New York: Basic Books.

Buss, A. (1979). *A dialectical psychology.* New York: Wiley.

Calabrese, R., & Schumer, H. (1986). The effects of service activities on adolescent alienation. *Adolescence, 21,* 675–687.

Cavallo, D. (1981). *Muscles and morals: Organized playground and urban reform. 1880–1920.* Philadelphia: University of Pennsylvania Press.

Chalip, L., Csikszentmihalyi, M., Kleiber, D., & Larson, R. (1986). Variations of experience in formal and informal sport. *Research Quarterly for Exercise and Sport, 55,* 109–116.

Coleman, J. (1961). *The adolescent society.* New York: Free Press.

Csikszentmihalyi, M. (1975). *Beyond boredom and anxiety.* San Francisco: Jossey-Bass.

Csikszentmihalyi, M., & Kubey, R. (1981). Television and the rest of life: A systematic comparison of subjective experience. *Public Opinion Quarterly, 45,* 317–328.

Csikszentmihalyi, M., & Larson, R. (1978). Intrinsic rewards in school crime. *Crime and Delinquency, 24,* 322–335.

Csikszentmihalyi, M., & Larson, R. (1984). *Being adolescent.* New York: Basic Books.

Danish, S. (1983). Musings about personal competence. The contribution of sport, health and fitness. *American Journal of Community Psychology, 11,* 221–240.

Danish, S., Kleiber, D., & Hall, H. (1987). Enhancing motivation in the context of sport. In M. Maehr & D. Kleiber (Eds.), *Enhancing motivation,* Vol. 5 (pp. 211–238). Greenwich, CT: JAI Press.

DeMartini, J. (1983). Social movement participation: Political socialization, generational consciousness, and lasting effects. *Youth and Society, 15,* 195–223.

deVries, M. (1987). Investigating mental disorders in their natural settings. *Journal of Nervous and Mental Disease, 175,* 509–513.

Dittmann-Kohli, F. (1986). Problem identification and definition as important aspects of adolescents' coping with normative life tasks. In R. K. Silbereisen, K. Eyferth, & G. Rudinger (Eds.), *Development as action in context* (pp. 19–38). New York: Springer-Verlag.

Douvan, E., & Adelsen, J. (1966). *The adolescent experience.* New York: Wiley.

Dreher, D., & Oerter, R. (1986). Children's and adolescents' conceptions of adulthood: The changing view of a crucial developmental task. In R. K. Silbereisen, K. Eyferth, & G. Rudinger (Eds.), *Development as action in context* (pp. 109–120). New York: Springer-Verlag.

Duda, J. (in press). Goal perspectives and behavior in sport and exercise settings. In C. Ames & M. Maehr (Eds.), *Advances in motivation and achievement: Vol. 6* (pp. 81–116). Greenwich, CT: JAI Press.

Edwards, H. (1976). *Sociology of sport.* Homewood, IL: Dorsey Press.

Eitzen, D. S. (1976). Sport and social status in American public secondary education. *Review of Sport and Leisure, 1,* 139–155.

Elkind, D. (1980). Strategic interactions in early adolescence. In J. Adelson (Ed.), *Handbook of adolescent psychology* (pp. 432–446). New York: Wiley.

Erikson, E. (1963). *Childhood and society* (2nd ed.). New York: Norton.

Fountain, C. D. (1978). *Sex and age differences in the recreational sport participation of children.* Unpublished master's thesis, Michigan State University, East Lansing.

Freud, S. (1960). *Group psychology and the analysis of the ego* (J. Strachey, Trans.) New York: Bantam. (Original work published 1921)

Goodale, T., & Godbey, G. (1988). *The evolution of leisure.* State College, PA: Venture Publishing.

Hanks, M., & Eckland, B. (1976). Athletics and social participation in the educational process. *Sociology of Education, 49,* 271–294.

Hanks, M., & Eckland, B. (1978). Adult voluntary associations and adolescent socialization. *The Sociological Quarterly, 19,* 481–490.

Hansley, P., Lupkowski, A., & Edind, E. (1986). The risk of extracurricular activities in education. *High School Journal, 69,* 110–119.

Havighurst, R. (1972). *Developmental tasks and education* (3rd ed). New York: D McKay.

Hedin, D., & Conrad, D. (1981). National assessment of experiential education: Summary and implications. *Journal of Experiential Education,* Fall, 6–20.

Hedin, D., & Simon, P. (1980). *Minnesota youth poll: Youth's views on leisure time, friendship and youth organizations.* St. Paul, MN: Center for Youth Development and Research.

Hendry, L. (1978). *School, sport and leisure.* London: Lepus Books.

Hendry, L. (1983). *Growing up and going out: Adolescents and leisure.* Aberdeen, Scotland: University of Aberdeen Press.

Hendry, L., & Patrick, H. (1977). Adolescents and television. *Journal of Youth and Adolescence, 6,* 325–336.

Hildreth, G., Richard, S., & Burts, D. (1986). Sex-role attitudes of senior high school 4-H members regarding careers and employment. *Journal of Adolescent Research, 1,* 267–276.

Hill, P., & Lowe, B. (1974). The inevitable metathesis of the retiring athlete. *International Review of Sport Sociology, 9,* 5–29.

Iso-Ahola, S. (1980). *The social psychology of leisure and recreation.* Dubuque, IA: Brown.

Kelly, J. (1981). Leisure interaction and the sound dialectic. *Social Forces, 60,* 304–322.

Kirshnet, C., Ham, M., & Richards, M. (1989). The sporting life. *Journal of Youth and Adolescence,* 18(6), 601–616.

Kleiber, D. (1983). Sport and human development: A dialectical interpretation. *Journal of Humanistic Psychology, 23,* 76–95.

Kleiber, D., Larson, R., & Csikszentmihalyi, M. (1986). The experience of leisure in adolescence. *Journal of Leisure Research, 18,* 165–176.

Kleiber, D., & Roberts, G. (1987). High school play: Putting it to work in organized sport. In J. Block & N. King (Eds.), *School play* (pp. 193–218). New York: Garland.

Kleiber, D., & Roberts, G. (1989). *Extracurricular activity, academic orientation and personal development among high school students.* Unpublished manuscript, University of Illinois, Urbana-Champaign.

Kubey, R., & Larson, R. (1990). The daily use and experience of television and new video media among children and young adolescents. *Communications Research,* 17 (1), 107–130.

Landers, D., & Landers, D. (1978). Socialization via interscholastic athletics: Its effect on delinquency. *Sociology of Education, 51,* 299–301.

Larson, R. (1983). Adolescents' daily experience with family and friends: Contrasting opportunity systems. *Journal of Marriage and the Family, 45,* 739–750.

Larson, R., Csikszentmihalyi, M., & Freeman, M. (1984). Alcohol and marijuana use in adolescents' daily lives: A random sample of experiences. *The International Journal of the Addictions, 19,* 367–381.

Larson, R., Csikszentmihalyi, M., & Graef, R. (1982). Time alone in daily experience: Loneliness or renewal? In L. A. Peplau & D. Perlman (Eds.), *Loneliness: A sourcebook of research, theory, and therapy.* New York: Wiley.

Larson, R., Ham, M., & Raffaelli, M. (1989). The nurturance of motivated attention in the daily experience of children and adolescents. In C. Ames & M. Maehr (Eds.), *Advances in motivation and achievement: Vol. 6.* (pp. 45–80) Greenwich, CT: JAI Press.

Larson, R., & Kubey, R. (1983). Media use in the ecology of adolescent life. *Youth and Society, 15,* 13–31.

Larson, R., Kubey, R., & Colletti, J. (1989). Changing channels: Early adolescent media choices and shifting investments in family and friends. *Journal of Youth and Adolescence,* 18(6), 583–600.

Larson, R., Raffaelli, M., Richards, M., Ham, M., & Jewell, L. (1990). The ecology of depression in childhood and early adolescence: A profile of daily psychological states. *Journal of Abnormal Psychology, 99* (1), 92–102.

Larson, R., & Richards, M. (Eds.) (1989). The changing life space of early adolescence [special issue]. *Journal of Youth and Adolescence,* 18(6), 501–626.

Leming, J. (1987). Rock music and the socialization of moral values in early adolescence. *Youth and Society, 18,* 363–383.

Lerner, R., & Busch-Rossnagel, N. (Eds.) (1981). *Individuals as producers of their development.* New York: Academic Press.

Little, B. (1983). Personal projects: A rationale and method for investigation. *Environment and Behavior, 15,* 273–309.

Locke, G., Sarri, L., Shaw, K., & Latham, G. (1981). Goal setting and task performance, 1969–1980. *Psychological Bulletin, 90,* 125–152.

Long, R., Buser, R., & Jackson, M. (1977). *Student activities in the seventies.* Reston, VA: National Association of Secondary School Principals.

Lull, J. (1980). Family communication patterns and the social uses of television. *Communication Research, 7,* 319–334.

Malmisur, M. (1976). Ego development of a sample of college football players. *Research Quarterly, 47,* 140–153.

Marcia, J. (1980). Identity in adolescence. In T. Adelson (Ed.), *The handbook of adolescent psychology* (pp. 159–187). New York: Wiley.

McCormack, J. (1984). *Formative life experiences and the channeling of adolescent goals.* Unpublished doctoral dissertation, University of Chicago.

Merrick, W. (1989). *Dysphoric moods in normal and depressed adolescents.* Unpublished doctoral dissertation, University of Chicago.

Morgan, W. (1979). Anxiety reduction following acute physical activity. *Psychiatric Annals, 9,* 141–147.

Morgan, W., & Goldston, S. (1987). *Exercise and mental health.* Washington, DC: Hemisphere Publishing.

Nixon, H. (1984). *Sport and the American dream.* New York: Leisure Press.

Oerter, R. (1986). Developmental tasks through the lifespan: A new approach to an old concept. In P. Baltes, L. Featherman, & R. Lerner (Eds.), *Lifespan development and behavior: Vol. 7* (pp. 233–269). Hillsdale, NJ: Erlbaum.

Otto, L., & Alwin, D. (1977). Athletics, aspirations and attainments. *Sociology of Education, 50,* 102–113.

Parker, J., & Asher, S. (1987). Peer relationship and later personal adjustment: Are low-accepted children at risk? *Psychological Bulletin, 102,* 357–389.

Parker, J., & Gottman, J. (1989). Social and emotional development in a relational context. In T. Berndt & G. Ladd (Eds.), *Peer relationships in child development* (pp. 95–131). New York: Wiley.

Patterns of drug use. (1987). *ISR Newsletter* (University of Michigan), *15,* pp. 3–4.

Payot, J. (1904). *The education of the will* (Smith Jelliffe, Trans., 1910). New York: Funk & Wagnalls.

Piaget, J. (1962). *Play, dream and imitation in childhood.* New York: Norton.

Raffaelli, M., & Duckett, E. (1989). We were just talking . . .: Conversations in early adolescence. *Journal of Youth and Adolescence,* 18(6), 567–582.

Reimer, J. (1981). Deviance as fun. *Adolescence, 16,* 39–43.

Richards, P., Berk, R., & Foster, B. (1979). *Crime as play: Delinquency in a middle-class suburb.* Cambridge, MA: Ballinger.

Roe, K. (1983). *Mass media and adolescent schooling: Conflict or co-existence?* Stockholm: Almqvist & Wiksell.

Roemer, J., Allen, C. F., & Fretwell, E. (1926). *Extra-curricular activities in junior and senior high school.* New York: Heath.

Rosenblatt, P., & Cunningham, M. (1976). Television watching and family tensions. *Journal of Marriage and the Family, 38,* 105–111.

Rubinstein, E. (1983). Television and behavior: Research conclusions of the 1982 NIMH report and their policy implications. *American Psychologist, 38,* 820–825.

Rutter, M., & Gillner, H. (1984). *Juvenile delinquency: Trends and perspectives.* New York: Guilford Press.

Sage, G. (1978, October). American values and sport: Formation of a bureaucratic personality. *Leisure Today,* pp. 10–12.

Silbereisen, R. K., Eyferth, K., & Rudinger, G. (Eds.) (1986). *Development as action in context.* New York: Springer-Verlag.

Sherif, M., & Sherif, C. (1964). *Reference groups.* Chicago: Henry Regnery.

Spady, W. (1970). Lament for the letterman: Effect of peer status and extracurricular activities on goal and achievement. *American Journal of Sociology, 75,* 680–702.

Terry, P. (1930). *Supervising extra-curricular activities.* New York: McGraw-Hill.

Tolan, P. H. (1988). Delinquent behaviors and male adolescent development: A preliminary study. *Journal of Youth and Adolescence, 17,* 413–427.

Wanlass, R., & Prinz, R. (1982). Methodological issues in conceptualizing and treating childhood isolation. *Psychological Bulletin, 92,* 39–55.

Yarworth, J., & Gauthier, W. (1978). Relationship of student self-concept and selected personal variables to participation in school activities. *Journal of Educational Psychology, 70,* 335–344.

Youniss, J. (1980). *Parents and peers in social development.* Chicago: University of Chicago Press.

Youniss, J., & Smollar, J. (1985). *Adolescent relations with mothers, fathers, and friends.* Chicago: University of Chicago Press.

PART TWO

Contexts of Adolescent Development

CHAPTER 7

The Family Context of Adolescence

FROMA WALSH and MICHELE SCHEINKMAN

This chapter addresses the importance of the family context for understanding adolescent dysfunction and for promoting healthy development. Grounding our discussion in a family systems orientation and a family life cycle framework, we focus on the life challenges and tasks of families with adolescents, examining the structural reorganizations and intergenerational issues that facilitate or impede developmental passage. We explore family dynamics that are commonly associated with symptoms in the adolescent and describe family therapy approaches that have been found effective. Throughout, our discussion will be informed by advances in family systems theory and research.

A SYSTEMIC ORIENTATION TO HEALTH AND DYSFUNCTION

Over the past 30 years, family systems theory has emerged as a major approach to understanding healthy functioning and the formation, maintenance, and resolution of individual and family problems. Although the influence of the family in adolescent development has long been recognized, a systemic orientation is distinguished by the view of the family as an interactional unit.

Traditionally, clinical family assessment presumed a parental causal role in the origin and development of adolescent problems, particularly in early childhood mothering. In attributions of deficiency in personality and parenting style, mothers were most often blamed as noxious influences in the child's development. Scant attention was given to paternal contributions, to the complex network of family relationships, or to biological and social factors (Walsh & Scheinkman, 1989).

With the study and treatment of whole families, attention shifted from questions of origin to ongoing transactions that spark and maintain individual disturbance. Since the system can not be understood simply by summing up the characteristics of its individual members or various dyads, it is necessary to attend to family organization, communication processes, and shared belief systems.

A bio-psycho-social perspective considers the mutual influences of individual, family, and larger social systems. A circular view of causality recognizes the ways in which children affect parents as well as being influenced by them. Marital dysfunction can be a source of adolescent distress in many cases; in others, it may result from the stress of coping unsuccessfully with a child's problems. In fact, couples research at different life cycle stages has found marital satisfaction to be lowest with children in adolescence. The added stress of a child's chronic disorder, or death, increases the risk for marital conflict and divorce (Walsh & McGoldrick, 1991).

An ecological view is required to appreciate how the child and family are embedded in more inclusive systems, from schools and courts to the community and larger culture. Because the family mediates between the child and the social world, mental health professionals and other child advocates are at least one ecological level removed from the child (Combrinck-Graham, 1988). In forming an individual relationship with an adolescent, the child's ecology is violated if the family is not involved in the process. Further, because family attachments are fundamental and ecological systems are delicately balanced, an attempt to remove a child from an undesirable, or even abusive, family situation may have unintended and destructive consequences for the child or other family members. Instead, every attempt should be made to engage and strengthen the family as the child's primary resource system.

Given the operation of multiple influences, deterministic assumptions of linear causality are reductionistic and erroneous. Because the same origin may lead to different outcomes and the same outcome may result from different origins, it is a "genetic fallacy" (Watzlawick, Beavin, & Jackson, 1967) to confuse origin with significance in determining outcome. The same stressor may be disabling to a vulnerable child or family while those more resilient are able to master the challenge. The influence of any event is mediated by many variables—most importantly, the family's organizational patterns and coping response.

It is not surprising that researchers have found no one-to-one correlation between an individual's presenting problem or psychiatric diagnosis and a single pattern of family dysfunction (Grigg & Friesen, 1989; Walsh, 1988a). Thus, it would be erroneous to type or label a family by the diagnosis of a dysfunctional adolescent member. For example, just as no single pattern has been found to distinguish all families—or all mothers—with a schizophrenic offspring (Walsh, 1988b), labels such as "schizophrenic families" or "schizophrenogenic mother" carry faulty attributions of parental blame and fail to recognize the diversity of family styles and levels of functioning. Problems in adolescence may be primarily biologically based, as in schizophrenia, or may largely result from social or economic pressures. Therefore, the interaction of influences involving the child, the family, and larger social systems must be carefully assessed in any adolescent disorder.

Recent research and conceptualization of normal family processes have provided a valuable perspective for rebalancing the clinical field's skewed focus on family pathology (Walsh, 1982, 1988). Family evaluation must include a careful appraisal of the strengths and resources, as well as the deficits and conflicts, of each family in relation to developmental and environmental challenges.

THE FAMILY LIFE CYCLE AT ADOLESCENCE

A systemic view of history takes into account the epigenesis of family processes as the family moves forward in time over the generations and over the course of the family life cycle (McGoldrick & Walsh, 1983). From this perspective, life change events are not regarded as discrete events that determine certain outcomes, but rather as stressful change processes that pose adaptive challenges for the family system.

The perspective of the family as a system moving through time (Minuchin, 1974) is crucial to understanding the emotional problems that adolescents and other family members develop as they progress together through the life cycle. Symptoms and dysfunction are assessed in the context of family development, in relation to each family's legacies from past experiences, to their present challenges, and to future expectations. In the systemic framework developed by Carter and McGoldrick (1980, 1988), the family life cycle is viewed as a complex transactional process involving at least three generations that influence one another from past to present and in ongoing reciprocal interaction. The normative (i.e., typical) course and phases can be identified and the salient issues and tasks predicted for each successive stage in the family life cycle.

Transition to each new stage involves structural reorganization and the renegotiation of relationship rules and roles (Hoffman, 1988). These periods are characterized by a temporary disequilibrium in the family system, when family stability and continuity are threatened by pressures for change. Family stress is generally highest at such points; members are likely to feel a sense of loss, confusion, and anxiety. Symptoms are likely to appear when there is an interruption or dislocation in the unfolding family life cycle—a signal that the family is having difficulty in making the transformation (Haley, 1980; Solomon, 1973). Such distress is not necessarily an indication of long-standing family pathology. Transitions are likely to be more complicated when they intersect with unresolved issues from earlier nodal points and previous generations (Carter & McGoldrick, 1988). When an adolescent problem is presented, it is useful to explore the same issue and family transition in both parents' own adolescence.

One member's change affects roles and relationships of all family members and the functioning of the family as a unit. The entry to adolescence requires a renegotiation of parent–child roles, rules, and authority (Ackerman, 1980). With the launching of the last child, an entire reorganization of the family unit takes place: parents shift from a two-generational to a couple household, from parental to marital focus, and from triad to dyad (Walsh, 1988).

Tasks of Adolescence

Adaptations in family organization are required to meet the tasks of adolescence. They transform the family from a unit geared to protect and nurture young children to one that prepares them to enter the world of adult responsibilities and commitments (Garcia-Preto, 1988).

The physiological and psychological changes that occur with puberty challenge the child's sense of self and initiate a long process of experimentation and internal reorganization. The family must accommodate to this process while, at the same time, continuing to provide a strong base for the testing and consolidation of these changes. In an interactional study of early adolescence, Steinberg (1981) observed increasing conflict between adolescent boys and their mothers at the onset of puberty. This heightened conflict subsided over a year's time, not because of modifications in the adolescent's behavior but, rather, because of accommodations by the mother as she backed off and loosened control. Changes in the adolescent–father pattern were different; they were characterized by increased paternal assertiveness and adolescent deference. We should note, however, the gender-based differential regarding power and dominance communicated in the juxtaposition of such transactions.

Three major tasks of adolescence—identity clarification, sexuality, and separation—have been discussed by Garcia-Preto (1988; Garcia-Preto & Travis, 1985) in relation to the concomitant family challenges and tasks. Although initiated by the biological and cognitive changes in the child, these tasks are also highly influenced by the ways the family and social community construe and connote them.

Identity Clarification

The task of identity clarification involves the process of differentiation of self from the family and the exploration of new relationships and a place in the social world. As adolescents begin to construct their own ideas and beliefs about life, they question and challenge values and rules at home, at school, and in the community. They especially evaluate their parents more critically. As they integrate many parental characteristics, they discard those beliefs and attributes that they view as negative or inconsistent with the values of their peers. They seek adults and ideas to model, but they fear losing their own tenuous sense of self by adopting others' beliefs or life-style.

Research by Hauser et al. (1984) has shown that family interactions emphasizing warmth, acceptance, and understanding tend to support higher levels of ego development and identity clarification in the adolescent. The absence of such positive interactions and the presence of their negative counterparts—devaluing, indifference—are associated with diminished levels of adolescent ego development.

Differences in male and female development and the ways gender identities are structured have been reconsidered in the conceptual work of Gilligan (1982) (Gilligan et al., 1989), and others, and that of family theorists such as Goldner (1989) and Hare Mustin (1989). Traditionally, during adolescence, girls have been socialized to be affiliative, caregiving, and dependent on relationships for their identities and well-being; boys have been taught to value competition and to strive for separation and autonomy. Because gender is an integral aspect of self-identify, same-sex parent–child relationships during adolescence strongly affect the process of gender identification. The child's perception of gender relations in the parents' marriage also shapes expectations. The powerful influences of other adults in the family relationship network should be appreciated, especially grandparents, aunts, uncles, and stepparents, who offer a variety of models for identification. Adolescents' feelings about being male or female are linked to the ways in which gender roles are constructed in the family and larger community. With recent social changes has come a reconsideration of traditional gender-based role expectations that have constrained identity development by maintaining an imbalance of power and status, devaluing qualities labeled "feminine" or activities deemed "women's work," and limiting the full range of self-expression, relatedness, and life pursuits for men and women (McGoldrick, Anderson, & Walsh, 1989).

As adolescents strive to clarify their identities, the family is also struggling to maintain its coherence and continuity in the face of change (Falicov, 1988). As parental authority is challenged or relaxed and the family boundaries become more permeable, the family's sense of integrity may seem more tenuous. Garcia-Preto and Travis noted:

In the midst of massive transformation, a reasonable degree of stability is necessary if the family is to be the protective haven the adolescent will periodically require. It is obviously difficult and confusing for the family to be both the target of rebellion and a sanctuary. (1985, p. 26)

Nevertheless, for the emergence of a strong sense of self in the adolescent, considerable family energy must be directed to providing a sense of safety and acceptance in the family, in order to buffer the anxiety, confusion, and disappointment likely to accompany new experiences in the world. For successful individuation, the family must be both strong and flexible, striving for a balance of power that allows for experimentation and yet provides protection.

Research by Campbell, Adams, and Dobson (1984) found evidence that a moderate degree of family connectedness, reflected through shared affection and an acceptance of individuality, provides the foundation and security for the adolescent's process of searching for self-defined commitments. In contrast, weak affectionate bonding with parents and poor communication levels reflected by rejection or psychological withdrawal provide an insecure or constricted base for self-exploration.

Sexuality

Coping with adolescent sexuality is a family matter. As adolescents struggle individually to integrate sexual feelings and thoughts and to learn skills for interpersonal expression of sexuality, the ways in which the family experiences and connotes sexuality have important effects. When the adolescent's sexuality is denied, misconstrued, or rejected by parents, the development of a positive sexual self-concept is potentially impaired and there is risk of sexual inhibitions or dysfunctional sexual activity. The family's intergenerational legacy, parental beliefs, and past experiences with sexuality influence their expectations and the ways in which they approach and establish rules for the adolescent. Parents who had benign sexual experiences at home and with peers during their adolescent years are more likely to provide a similar experience for their children. Where parents suffered traumatic experiences with sexuality, there is greater risk for pattern replication of sexual abuse, severe inhibitions, or teen pregnancy.

The literature on adolescent sexuality has focused on family influences in the development of adolescent sexual expression, activity, and attitudes, with less attention to the reciprocal influences. Combrinck-Graham (1988) proposed that the adolescent's sexuality propels a major renegotiation of boundaries between the child and all other family members:

At each level of expression of adolescent sexuality, we can see the figurative closing of the door, from the modesty that accompanies physical changes, to the privacy of plans and fantasies at the cognitive level, to the conduct of experimentation and exploration outside the family. The youth may close the door, but it also happens that other family members, too, increase the privacy boundaries. (p. 116)

When this door closes on the adolescent's sexuality, a new boundary is formed, which has repercussions throughout the family system. A loving bond between father and daughter may suddenly change as the daughter's budding sexuality leads her to push him away. Sometimes, the father is the one who becomes stimulated or uncomfortable and distances himself. In either case, the unacceptability of incestuous impulses between parent and child can easily transform a previously easy relationship into conflict or alienation. This new distance between father and daughter may lead him to place new demands on his wife, or turn to an affair, thereby creating tension or a need for renegotiation within the marital subsystem.

Separation

With the onset of adolescence, a child's membership status in the family alters dramatically. The dependent attachments to parents and participation in family life diminish as autonomy and directedness outside the family increase. During the separation process, parents may experience a sense of loss when they are no longer valued and needed in the same way. Dependency and counterdependency between the adolescent and family present an oscillating dynamic (Garcia-Preto & Travis, 1985). A constant struggle between autonomy and control can generate confusion and conflict when the family must cope with sudden outbursts of intense and inconsistent feelings. Fears of abandonment are easily aroused for adolescents; their parents, who are contending with their own midlife identity issues and the increasing dependency of their elders, are at a heightened vulnerability for feeling exploited or rejected.

In American culture, which values independence and autonomy, leaving home has been regarded as the rite of passage from adolescence to adulthood. Although they experience feelings of loss, most parents welcome this turning point. The so-called "empty nest syndrome" is not the norm, but rather may be symptomatic of a problem marriage (Walsh, 1988a). Recent economic conditions have, in fact, created new stresses for families by delaying the launching process and forcing many fledglings to return to the nest. It is important not to confuse leaving home with a cutoff of family attachments and dependencies. Despite a preference for separate residences, intergenerational connectedness continues throughout the family life cycle (Cohler & Geyer, 1982). What is required at separation in renegotiation and rebalancing of those relationships.

Social Context of Adolescent Developmental Tasks

These developments occur in the context of the larger social world, which has become increasingly complex and diverse. With the dramatic social changes in recent years, it has become increasingly difficult to determine what family life-cycle patterns are normal—either typical or functional. Transformations in family structure and roles, and accompanying ambiguities, are themselves sources of stress for family members who lack models for the challenges they are confronting.

Moreover, economic and social pressures confronting adolescents and their families have strained even well-functioning families. Environmental perils, from the immediacy of such problems as AIDS to the ever present nuclear threat, pose new risks to survival for today's youth (Garcia-Preto, 1988). Deteriorating economic and social conditions for increasing numbers of lower-income families have ravaged family stability and contributed to the alarming rise in teen pregnancy, school dropout, drug abuse, violent crime, and suicide. Thus, clinical assessment and intervention cannot be restricted to the interior of the family, but must also address critical social concerns.

DIMENSIONS OF FAMILY FUNCTIONING IN ADOLESCENCE

A conceptual framework for the assessment of family and marital functioning has been developed to plan interventions that strengthen the family system as presenting problems are resolved (Walsh, in press). By integrating empirical findings from leading investigations of normal families, attributes of well-functioning families can be distinguished from those of dysfunctional family systems. The functionality of family patterns—that is, how well they work—varies in relation to each family's life challenges and resources. Family styles that promote the health and growth of members at certain phases in the life cycle, as in early childhood, may be dysfunctional for meeting the demands of other stages, particularly adolescence. Here, we examine key variables in family functioning that involve structural reorganizations and intergenerational relationships and assess their connection to family developmental tasks at adolescence.

Organizational Patterns in Adolescence

The functioning of any family must be considered in terms of how effectively it organizes its structure and available resources to master life challenges of adolescence.

Adaptability is one of the chief requisites for well-functioning family systems (Olson, 1988). It involves a balance between maintaining a stable structure and allowing for flexibility in response to the developmental and environmental challenges. Whereas high structure and more rigid rules and controls may facilitate effective family functioning and the welfare of small children at an earlier phase in the family life cycle, increasing flexibility and tolerance for change are required as children move through adolescence. At the extremes, overly rigid organization or chaotic disorganization tend to be highly dysfunctional and associated with symptomatic behavior in adolescents. Clinical interventions that promote structured flexibility can be most helpful. Families need to bend considerably to meet adolescents' needs for greater autonomy and self-control while providing a clear and consistent structure (Steinberg, 1981).

Cohesion

The other central dimension of family organization is cohesion (Olson, 1988). Families must balance needs for closeness and connectedness with a respect for separateness and individual differences. Here, too, the balance shifts as families enter the phase of adolescence. In families with small children, members pull inward, in a system pattern termed "centripetal." When adolescence begins, family organization typically shifts to a more "centrifugal" pattern, with decreasing proximity and more emphasis on differentiation of adolescent members (Combrinck-Graham, 1985).

Because issues of identity, sexuality, and separation are salient in adolescence, it is crucial to assess family cohesion more specifically in terms of individual, generational, and family-unit boundaries.

Individual Boundaries

Well-functioning families are respectful of individual boundaries even when members are very close. At the extreme of enmeshment, families are intolerant of adolescent needs for separate time, space, and privacy. Enmeshed families are poorly differentiated; they have difficulty acknowledging and accepting individual needs and differences, which threaten parental well-being or the family's very survival. In such cases, adolescent identity formation is blocked, there is little sense of self, or a distorted, rigid role assumption is made, based on parental needs and projections.

At the other extreme of disengagement, family cohesion may be so fragmented that members feel disconnected from one another; they lack mutual caring or support. Serious problems of child abuse and neglect are more likely to occur in disengaged families and contribute to antisocial, delinquent behaviors in adolescence.

Generational Boundaries

In well-functioning families, generational boundaries are clear. Rights and responsibilities differentiate parents from children. Rules must be renegotiated as children enter and progress through adolescence; increasing privilege and freedom are balanced by increased responsibility and self-control. Although adolescents are allowed greater voice in determining their own life choices and their participation in family life, parental leadership and authority are, nevertheless, exercised consistently and firmly. If a parental coalition is weak or a single parent lacks support to exercise effective leadership, adolescent dysfunction is more likely to occur. Where generational boundaries are blurred by the child's assuming a parentified caretaker role or by a matelike function for a parent, the child's development is likely to be derailed to the extent that role demands are pervasive and inappropriate.

Modulating parental authority is essential to accomplish tasks of identity clarification. Clear expectations and limits are required to respond to the adolescent's dependency needs, while, at the same time, a flexible willingness to modify family rules respects the striving for independence. At one extreme, if parental guidance and control are too lax, a risk for self-harm results. At the other extreme, authoritarian controls inhibit development.

Family–Community Boundaries

Well-functioning families are characterized by a clear sense of the family as a unit with permeable boundaries connecting the family with the community. Adolescents enjoy increasing freedom to come and go, and to spend time with friends, both at home and away from the family. At launching, young adults can leave home and pursue their own life directions and commitments without cutting off relationships with parents. In enmeshed families, the boundary around the family unit may be drawn too tightly, isolating the family from social support and impeding the launching process. In such overly centripetal systems (Stierlin, 1979), adolescent separation is blocked by loyalty ties, overdependence on parents, or concerns for parental well-being or the survival of the marriage. In overly centrifugal systems, adolescents are propelled out of the family or bolt from home in a flight for independence. Because differentiation of self must occur in relation to significant others, attempts to separate and achieve independence through emotional or geographical distance only result in a pseudo-autonomy, which crumbles with family contact and can become problematic in other intimate relationships.

Communication Processes

The *"sturm und drang"* theory of heightened conflict in families of adolescents has not been supported in research. Montemayor (1983), in his review of numerous studies of conflict between adolescents and their parents, concluded that there is considerable variability in the degree of conflict experienced. All families do conflict some of the time, but some families are in conflict most of the time. Healthy families are distinguished by clear, direct communication and the ability to acknowledge and resolve conflict. More dysfunctional families get caught up in cycles of criticism, blaming, and scapegoating that block empathy and problem-solving. With adolescents, parental communication can become overly focused on adolescent compliance with rules and responsibilities as adolescents withdraw or become silent or secretive. Cycles of pursuer-distancer can ensue. Showing interest in the adolescent as a person can facilitate more open communication and trust.

Intergenerational Patterns

In family assessment, the entire multigenerational system should be evaluated. Events at one generational level, or between two generations, affect all others, regardless of household boundaries or geographical distances. Too often, when an adolescent problem is presented, the family assessment focuses narrowly on the household unit, overlooking the grandparental generation and, in divorced and remarried families, failing to assess the impact of other significant relationships or their loss.

Tracking significant events and changes in the multigenerational family life cycle provides valuable information for the assessment of adolescent dysfunction and the formulation of treatment objectives, including the determination of which members and parts of the family system to involve in the therapeutic process. It is most useful to note linkages between the timing of symptoms and both current and past critical events that have disrupted or are threatening the family system (Walsh, 1983). A genogram (McGoldrick & Gerson, 1985) and family time line are useful to schematize system patterns and focal points for intervention. They aid the clinician in visualizing, ordering, and clarifying information of potential relevance to presenting symptoms and problem resolution.

Current Stresses in the Multigenerational System

Adolescent development often coincides with parents' midlife transitions, when they reevaluate their marriage, career commitments, and life goals. It also typically interacts with changes in parental roles and relationships with aging grandparents (Walsh, 1988c). Clinicians need to assess powerful emotional triangles, cutoffs, and pattern replications in the multigenerational system to understand how the reverberations from a change in one part of the system may impact on other relationships. Most common triangles involve an adolescent and both parents or an adolescent, a parent, and a grandparent.

It is crucial to assess recent and anticipated stresses in the system at the time of adolescent symptom onset and treatment request. Frequently, a sharp decline in school performance and truancy by a teenage son follows a job loss by the father. In one case, a suicide attempt was made by a 14-year-old girl on the same night as her father's third job loss in a year. The father's failure to sustain employment was especially devastating for this family. Both parents had grown up in poverty that had fragmented their families. A cornerstone of their marital vows had been the determination to provide adequately for their children in order to hold their family together. As the father's self-esteem as provider was shattered, his drinking increased and marital conflict escalated to the point of violence and threat of family breakup (Walsh, 1983).

Stressful changes in the extended family also need to be explored. Most parents of adolescents are confronting the declining functioning and loss of their aging parents and other significant family members. Behavior problems in an adolescent may be an expression or displacement of concurrent stresses elsewhere in the family system, as the following case illustrates:

> Mrs. A. requested psychiatric treatment for her teenage son, stating that she feared that her son "needed to be institutionalized" because his behavior was unmanageable. She had been feeling increasingly helpless in dealing with her son's uncontrollable behavior over the past six months. A family system assessment revealed that, eight months before, the maternal grandmother, who had a deteriorating Alzheimer's condition, had moved in with the family. Mrs. A. tearfully described her mounting difficulty in caring for her mother at home. She was alarmed by her mother's increasing loss of control of functioning and felt helpless in dealing with her. When asked whether institutionalization had been considered, she replied that it was "out of the question" and had never been discussed; she had promised her father on his deathbed, a year earlier, that she would always take care of her mother.

A systemic view of the problem situation also requires inquiry into the functioning of the marital relationship and any contributions to the dilemma from the other spouse's family of origin. In this case, the husband had distanced from the family since the arrival of his mother-in-law and was unable to be supportive to his wife or facilitative in solving the caregiving problem. Discussion of his genogram revealed that, at his own mother's illness, he had left all caretaking to his sister. The current situation stirred up lingering guilt and a belief that his failure to assume more responsibility for his mother's care had contributed to her early death.

Traditional gender-role socialization reinforces such an imbalance in marital functioning at midlife: women are expected to assume primary responsibility for caregiving to their own—and their husband's—aging family members, while men tend to withdraw from those uncomfortable socioemotional demands and painful feelings concerning loss (McGoldrick et al., 1989; Walsh & McGoldrick, 1991).

This case underscores the importance of exploration of current and past relationships in the extended family network. Feeling alone in a burdensome and conflictual dilemma, Mrs. A. had become increasingly focused on struggles with her son over his swings between irresponsible dependency and defiance of her authority. In a vicious cycle, the harder she tried to control him, the more reckless and unmanageable he became. Family intervention was directed to shifting the peripheral position of the father/husband for more spousal support: first, for shared involvement in exploring institutionalization and other alternatives for the grandmother's care, and, second, for a more balanced coparental role with their son, particularly in managing issues of control and autonomy.

Multigenerational Legacies

The legacy of past experiences, and the myths surrounding them, extends over many generations. Family life-cycle transitions are especially likely to reactivate past unresolved conflicts and losses, because each generation has had to confront the challenges of passage through successive stages. Even though particular circumstances may be different, current developmental challenges are likely to evoke feelings and reactions associated with the same transition point in the past, and to affect a family's style and ability to confront and master current tasks. In fact, many families function well until they reach a critical point in the life cycle at which complications arose a generation earlier. One father began to have serious problems with his teenage son despite a good prior relationship. The father's loss of his own father at age 14 blocked his ability to relate to his son, once the son surpassed the same age.

Past nodal events and relationship changes in the three-generational field should be tracked, with particular attention to the following transition points (Walsh, 1983):

1. Stressful changes, a generation earlier, at the same point in developmental passage or at the same age as the symptomatic child;
2. Stressful changes, especially losses, that concurred with a major developmental transition of the symptomatic child, particularly birth or entry into adolescence.

Adolescents' autonomy, independence, and sexuality may reactivate old emotional issues and catalyze shifts in relationships across generations. For example, moves toward greater independence are more likely to stir fears of loss and rejection in parents if, during their own adolescence, they rejected their own parents. Not uncommonly, father–son conflict flares up at precisely the point in adolescence when the parent had fought with his own father. Similarly, a teen may run away from home at the same age a parent had left home in conflict.

The possible replication of patterns across the generations should also be considered in concerns about sexuality. A single parent brought her 16-year-old daughter for therapy with heightened concern that her daughter was going to become pregnant. A battle ensured in which the mother attempted unsuccessfully to control her social activities as the daughter stayed out later and later, refusing to reveal her whereabouts. A brief exploration of the family system, using a genogram to sketch relationship patterns, revealed that the mother had become pregnant at 16 with this daughter, and that she, herself, had been conceived when her own mother was the same age.

It was important to help mother and daughter discuss these "coincidences" openly and to positively connote the mother's intrusive and controlling behavior as attempts to protect her daughter from the life struggles she had experienced. Although it is possible that a parent may, in part, wish unconsciously for a child to repeat a pattern, family therapists find it more helpful to reinforce the positive side of ambivalence. In this case, it was helpful to attribute benign intentions to the mother's behavior, to credit her with caring for her child's well-being, and to support her in helping her daughter to experience a different outcome.

In making covert connections explicit, the therapist does so in a way that helps both the mother and the daughter view historical patterns in an evolutionary, systemic frame. Understanding for the context and consequences of the mother's earlier experiences is increased without blaming her as the cause of presenting problems. The therapeutic task is to work with the mother and daughter to differentiate the present from the past—in effect, to prevent history from repeating itself. Some sessions may involve other children in the family, who become heirs to the legacy when they reach the same developmental crossroad. Sons and daughters will have different patterns of identification to work through. Family members cannot change the past, but it need not determine their future. They can work together to make changes in the present and reshape their relationships.

Often, an adolescent's reckless behavior is an attempt to differentiate and gain autonomy by defying parental control. This function of self-destructive behavior can be deconstructed by pointing out that the behavior increases the risk that he or she will be like the father or mother, repeating his or her life of misfortune. Therapy can be focused on helping the adolescent to differentiate and assume more autonomy by handling sexuality more responsibly and charting a different life course.

Family Belief Systems

A family's approach and response to stress events are influenced strongly by the family belief system and the meanings attached to the event, with both immediate and long-term ramifications. Reiss (1981) contended that such pivotal experiences set in motion major family reorganizations and alterations of belief systems that influence future problem-solving styles and abilities. Reiss demonstrated that each family's actions in a new situation are shaped by that family's paradigm, or basic premises for viewing and approaching life events. A family's paradigm is an enduring structure of shared beliefs, convictions, and assumptions about the social world that evolve from past experiences and their social context. This set contributes to the family's perception of events, the meanings ascribed, and expectations about their likely consequences. Catastrophic expectations can contribute to systemic rigidity (a reluctance to change established patterns) or to symptoms that express the distress and may function to restore family homeostasis.

The meaning of symptoms for a particular family should always be explored, as the following case illustrates:

Tommy, age 14, was seen with his family, who were concerned about his recent decline in school grades and his stealing. When asked what was of most concern, the father replied: "Stealing. He's been stealing the money, small change, that my wife has been saving under our mattress for a trip she wants to take in three years to Las Vegas for our twentieth wedding anniversary."

The interview revealed that the father had been laid off when his factory closed and was unable to find other steady employment. The mother's father, unemployed, had deserted her family when she was young, forcing her mother onto welfare to support the family. When asked the legacy of that experience, the mother replied: "I live in constant fear that we won't have enough money and our family will just fall apart."

Husband: "My wife needs a lot of security. So do my kids."

Wife: "That's why, when Tommy took this money, it hurt so much. It felt like he robbed us of our security."

In the family belief system, the catastrophic fear of family dissolution was held covertly by all members, but never discussed. The emotional shock wave of heightened insecurity generated by the father's unemployment was expressed by the son, who was strongly identified with his father.

Adolescent Dysfunction and Adaptation in Divorced and Remarried Families

With the recent dramatic changes in family structure, a growing majority of children can be expected to live in a single-parent household at some period of their development, and most will make another transition to a remarried family system. Assertions that divorce is inevitably pathogenic for children and that a remarried family is a poor substitute for an intact one have been based on cultural idealization of the nuclear family and on research with disturbed families in treatment (Walsh, 1991). Rather, an accumulating body of research finds a wide range of response to divorce and remarriage, with some parents and children doing poorly, but with most adapting reasonably well over time and many functioning at a high level (Hetherington, 1988, 1989).

Gender differences have been found in a child's long-term adjustment to divorce and remarriage. In numerous studies, boys have been found to have more difficulty with divorce but to adjust more readily in remarriage, whereas girls do far better postdivorce but more often find remarriage problematic. Following divorce, boys tend more to externalize distress in aggressive, noncompliant, antisocial behavior and inflexibility. In single-parent households, boys show more conflict in relationships with their mothers and their siblings. After the initial postdivorce turmoil, girls are more likely to function as well as children in intact families. In the single-parent household, they tend to develop closer relationships with their mothers and to draw together with siblings. Largely because of the closer mother–daughter bond, girls are more likely to regard a new stepparent as an intruder on the family unit. Conversely, a stepfather tends to buffer previous mother–child conflict for boys.

The developmental stage of a child at the time of divorce and at remarriage is a major factor in adaptation. Younger children adjust more readily and successfully to both transitions than do older children. Preadolescent and adolescent offspring are likely to have the most difficulty with remarriage. Adaptation to remarriage appears to be more complicated at this stage because the tasks of forming a cohesive remarried family unit are in opposition to the adolescent's thrust toward autonomy and independence. Teenagers are likely to balk at expectations for family togetherness and attachment to a new stepparent at a time when they are investing energies in outside activities and peer relationships. Additionally, because children in single-parent families grow up more quickly, they are likely to bristle around control issues with a new stepparental authority. Furthermore, as issues of sexuality come to the fore, adolescents may be uncomfortable with a parent's new sexual relationship and with their own relationship to a stepparent and stepsiblings of the opposite sex. Confusion may arise around expression of affection—or alarm about feelings of attraction and intimacy. Because men commonly remarry to considerably younger women, complicated feelings of rivalry and a blurring of generational boundaries may occur for a teenage daughter who has a youthful stepmother. In later adolescence, as children begin thinking about leaving home, they may be more accepting of a stepparent as someone to take care of their single parent in their absence.

A number of mediating family variables have been found to either adversely affect or buffer the stress of divorce and remarriage transitions. Children fare most poorly when they are drawn into persistent conflict between their parents or when the noncustodial parent cuts off contact and support. Child adjustment is best when biological parents can cooperate in coparenting and the noncustodial parent maintains reliable contact and support. In remarriage, the complicated network of relationship requires flexibility for children to maintain their relationships with both biological parents and with extended families as new steprelationships develop (Walsh, 1991).

COMMON PROBLEMS OF ADOLESCENCE IN FAMILY CONTEXT

From a systems perspective, adolescent symptoms are viewed as particular ways in which the adolescent and family cope with stresses that accompany family reorganization in normal development. Difficulties in family reorganization may be expressed through a variety of symptoms, from anorexia or substance abuse to such problems as runaway behavior or school failure. While a systemic assessment requires that we address the total ecology of the adolescent, our present focus is on the role the family may play in the development, maintenance, and treatment of dysfunction. In this section, we describe dysfunctional family patterns that are often associated with common adolescent problems; in each situation, we outline major therapeutic goals.

Eating Disorders

Anorexia nervosa and bulimia are life-threatening problems that have become increasingly frequent for adolescent girls in recent years. This increase, especially in the incidence of bulimia, has generated concern about the factors that contribute to the onset and perpetuation of eating disorders. Although extensive data-based research is still in preliminary stages, investigators concur that eating disorders are multidetermined (Johnson, 1985).

Anorexia is most common for girls during puberty, when issues of sexuality and autonomy come to the fore; the onset of bulimia is typically later, around the period of leaving home, going to college, and establishing oneself as a separate adult. Although the two syndromes differ in symptomatology and timing in the family life cycle, they both often occur in family contexts in which parents have difficulty making the necessary adjustments to the tasks of separation and individuation required by normal development. Hilde Bruch (1963) first linked anorexic symptoms to the patient's struggle for autonomy and identity within a family that stifled these qualities. Later observations by family therapists (Minuchin, Rosman, & Baker, 1978; Liebman, R., Sargent, J., & Silver, M., 1983; Schwartz, Barrett, & Saba, 1985) supported the view that families of anorectics and bulimics are organized in ways that limit and shape their identities. Bruch emphasized early relations between mother and child; family systems therapists, however, have focused on the influence of current family interactions. They contend that the "noxious" family context can be restructured to remove obstacles to competent functioning so that underdeveloped parts of the adolescent's personality can be activated and nurtured as the total organization of the family changes (Schwartz, 1988).

A major contribution to the understanding and treatment of eating disorders was made by Minuchin and his colleagues (Minuchin et al., 1978), who identified a constellation of characteristics in families of anorectics and developed a family therapy model explicitly designed to correct these family malfunctions. Later studies of bulimia (Schwartz et al., 1985) found the same family constellation, in addition to other factors, in nearly all bulimic cases observed. The child's symptoms and the dysfunctional family patterns were viewed reciprocally, with each influencing the development and functioning of the other.

This systemic approach to families of anorectics first developed from the research of Minuchin, Rosman, and their colleagues, with families of diabetic and asthmatic children. Irrespective of the child's metabolic vulnerability to diabetes or asthma, certain transactional patterns appeared to be associated with symptom exacerbation. At the same time, the group was studying cases of anorexia nervosa and observed that, although a physical predisposition could not be demonstrated, similar transactional processes were evident. They identified four general structural and functional characteristics typical of families with anorectic adolescents (Minuchin et al., 1978):

1. *Enmeshment*—an extreme form of proximity and intensity in family interactions in which family members are overinvolved with one another. In these families, excessive togetherness and intrusiveness into each other's feelings and thoughts result in a blurring of interpersonal boundaries at the individual, subsystem, and family levels.

2. *Overprotectiveness*—the very high degree of concern that family members have for each other's welfare. In these families, the parents' overprotective style tends to retard the adolescent's development of autonomy, competence, and activities outside the safety of the family. The children, in turn, also feel great responsibility for protecting the family.

3. *Rigidity*—the tendency of the family to maintain the status quo in situations that require flexibility and change. For example, when the child reaches adolescence and the family is required to renegotiate rules to allow for greater autonomy, such issues don't even surface in these families.

4. *Conflict avoidance*—the pattern by which the family denies the existence of problems and is highly invested in consensus and harmony. Some psychosomatic families disagree openly, but constant interruptions and subject changes obfuscate any conflictual issue before it reaches salience.

In addition to the four general characteristics, a fifth variable was considered to be the key factor supporting the particular psychosomatic symptom in the child—the way in which the child becomes involved as a regulator of parental conflict. Three interactional patterns were seen as methods these families tend to use to cope with conflict: (a) *triangulation,* a pattern that occurs when the spousal dyad becomes split in opposition or conflict and the child cannot express himself or herself without siding with one parent against the other; (b) *stable parent–child coalition,* in which the symptomatic child moves into a relatively stable alliance with one parent against the other; (c) *detouring,* a pattern in which the spousal dyad is ostensibly united; open marital conflict is avoided or quickly submerged by the parents' uniting around concern for or blaming of the sick child.

Based on these observations, Minuchin et al. (1978) developed a model of intervention aimed at changing the family patterns that maintain symptoms. The goal of therapy is to transform the total system so that the family can meet its members' needs for both autonomy and support without recurrence of symptoms in the anorectic child or any other family member. In order to sustain lasting changes, the family must be restructured and helped to generate alternative transactional patterns in addition to eliminating the anorectic symptoms.

The structural family therapy model for anorexia aims at the following short- and long-term goals:

1. *Symptom remission.* Given that anorexia is a life-threatening syndrome, the initial objective is to alleviate symptoms so that the child begins to eat and regain weight. This is done by a combination of behavioral and family therapy interventions, such as a "family lunch session" in which the therapist joins the family for a meal, to observe and challenge the way the family handles the patient's refusal to eat.
2. *Forming the therapeutic system.* The therapist facilitates the formation of the therapeutic system by joining the family and assuming leadership *before* initiating the process of change. This is done by recognizing family strengths—respecting hierarchies and values, supporting family subsystems, and confirming individual members in their sense of self. The therapist assumes leadership in establishing the rules for the therapeutic system, controlling the flow of transactions, supporting family members, and suggesting views of reality that offer alternatives and hope.
3. *Challenging realities.* By this process, the therapist questions the family's portrayal of the child as "sick" and the rest of the family as uninvolved bystanders. The problem is redefined in interactional terms while maintaining support.
4. *Challenging enmeshment.* This is done by supporting the hierarchical organization of the family in which the parents are more clearly in charge, as well as by reinforcing individual and subsystem boundaries.
5. *Challenging overprotection.* The therapist gently confronts instances of overprotectiveness that occur in the session.
6. *Challenging conflict avoidance.* The therapist highlights and escalates differences of opinion between two family members, while blocking the intrusion of a third member who attempts to diffuse the conflict. Most importantly, the therapist helps the conflicting dyad to effectively negotiate and resolve their conflict.
7. *Challenging rigidity.* Repeated therapeutic attempts are made to alter the family's imperviousness to change by interventions such as assignment of tasks aimed toward greater flexibility.
8. *Challenging conflict detouring.* This is achieved by interventions aimed at strengthening the parent–child boundaries.

These guidelines may be useful with many families, but it should be kept in mind that recent research (Grigg & Friesen, 1989) supports the view of Garfinkel and Garner (1982) that no one family pattern is unique to anorexia nervosa. A variety of family relationship patterns may play secondary roles to environments that predispose children to anorexia nervosa as well as maintain the symptom.

Adolescent Runaways

Unlike adolescents with eating disorders, who tend to be female, middle-class, and members of somewhat typical families, adolescent runaways cut across ethnic, socioeconomic, and family types. The number of male and female runaways is reported to be roughly equal. In spite of this diversity, Lappin and Covelman (1985) identified four common characteristics of family functioning that they saw as implicated in the runaway process: (a) dysfunctional hierarchy; (b) triangulation of the adolescent runaway; (c) conflict avoidance; and (d) parental collusion in the runaway process. Because the first three characteristics are common to many families with troubled children, they are not considered sufficient conditions to produce adolescent runaways. The fourth characteristic, parental collusion in the runaway process, is thought to account for this particular symptom choice (Lappin & Covelman, 1985).

In families with runaway adolescents, there is evidence that the generational hierarchy is reversed (Lappin & Covelman, 1985; Mirkin, Raskin, & Antogini, 1984). Both male and female adolescents in single- and two-parent families tend to have a parentified role, overfunctioning as surrogate parents to their own parents or as peers to one or both parents.

Often, the parents in these families have chronic, unresolved marital problems. Marital conflict is usually played out in the parental arena, triangulating the adolescent. In some families, conflict between the parents is overt, and the triangulation occurs as the adolescent becomes the focus of parental discord. In a typical pattern, one parent is closely allied with the child and the other parent is more peripheral. In such cases, the allied parent becomes increasingly more critical of the spouse for being too harsh, too demanding, or emotionally unresponsive to the adolescent. Such criticism further escalates the position of the peripheral parent, who becomes increasingly more harsh, demanding, or unresponsive. In other families, conflict between parents is covert and they present a united front in their concern about the child. Therapeutic exploration, however, reveals the unity to be more apparent than real, masking significant unresolved marital differences. In both cases, marital conflict is detoured through the adolescent in ways in which the focus on the adolescent serves to stabilize the couple's relationship. Even in divorced families, triangulation occurs when the adolescent operates as a go-between for parents who are highly conflictual or have cut off contact. The child functions to maintain the connection between the parents.

Frequently, in families with runaway adolescents, conflicts between the parents have existed for many years without resolution. Consequently, the family lives in an imploded state of tension with periodic outbursts of violence or sexual abuse. Although the runaway act may seem arbitrary or impulsive to an outside observer, at a family systems level it may occur at an explosive moment in the interactional sequence in the family. As spousal conflicts heat up to a level where family members see them as a threat to the family unit, the act of running away forces the parents to refocus on the child. As the parents unite in their concern over the runaway child, marital conflict deescalates. In this sense, the runaway behavior functions as a mechanism of family conflict control (Lappin & Covelman, 1985).

Hierarchy violations, parental triangulation of the adolescent, and conflict avoidance are processes common to many dysfunctional families with symptomatic children. In trying to understand the specific choice of symptom of runaway behavior, Lappin and Covelman (1985) found evidence of a parental collusion in the runaway process itself. This collusion often takes one of the following three forms:

1. A cross-generational coalition. As the child takes care of one parent and becomes a confidante, he or she becomes aware that the parent desires to run away or leave the marriage, but at the same time is unable to do so. Given the imploded family tension, the adolescent's runaway act is a metaphor for the adolescent's overidentification with the parent. In other cases, it may express

the wish of an overburdened single parent to take flight from an intolerable situation.

2. An isomorphic process between the adolescent and the parental behavior, rather than a coalition between parent and child. In these families, the parent is frequently stressed and emotionally isolated and becomes more and more disengaged from parental responsibilities. The parent may leave the home for hours or days at a time, leaving the children to fend for themselves. One mother took a two-day vacation, only checking in on the phone. Within a few days of her return, her 13-year-old son ran away (Lappin & Covelman, 1985, p. 351). These families tend to function toward the disengaged end of continuum. The therapeutic task is one of mobilizing parental concern while helping parents to meet their own needs more appropriately.

3. A role as scapegoat for all of the family problems, with messages communicated that everything would be fine if the adolescent were not there. This situation can also occur in newly remarried families, when the parental anxiety and conflict around normal difficulties in the formation of the new family are denied in order to sustain the fantasy of an ideal relationship and avoid another "failed marriage." The adolescent is more likely triangulated if caught in a loyalty bind with the noncustodial parent, unable to accept the new stepparent.

Any family can temporarily experience the difficulties described above. However, when these patterns become rigidly embedded, families will have difficulty meeting the tasks required by adolescent development to support separation, individuation, and age-appropriate autonomy. An adolescent who feels responsible for either taking care of or rescuing a parent will not have the energy necessary to move into the world of his or her peers. One of the first therapeutic operations is to challenge instances of dysfunctional hierarchy. On one side, the adolescent needs to be blocked from maintaining the dysfunctional position in the family. On the other side, parents needs to be helped to rely on each other and on the therapist for support, so that the parental task of nurturing and guiding the adolescent can be realized. When marital conflicts are revealed, therapeutically one must deal with them at the level in which they are presented, by initially joining with parents to resolve the child-focused problem. The therapist can work with the parents to resolve their differences around parenting the adolescent rather than attempting initially to deal directly with underlying marital issues. Even in divorced families, the therapeutic goal is to remove the adolescent from a triangulated position while helping parents reduce conflict.

Adolescent Addiction and Substance Abuse

Substance abuse often starts in adolescence and is tied to the normal process of experimenting with new behaviors, becoming self-assertive, developing extrafamilial relationships, and leaving home (Stanton & Todd, 1982). Adolescents become most vulnerable to substance abuse when they enter high school and wish to experiment and, at the same time, are most vulnerable to peer pressure and other social systems. Kandel, Treinman, Faust, and Single (1976), based on their research, found in some cases, frequent drug use is primarily social and influenced by peers, but, in many cases, drug use is contingent more on the quality of parent–adolescent relationships than on other factors.

A variety of extrafamilial factors can trigger the onset of substance abuse—loss of a girlfriend or boyfriend, difficulties in school, peer problems, the values and mores of a particular community, the economic and social conditions of poverty, and a sense of hopelessness about future life options. The physiological cycle of addiction itself must always be taken into account.

In looking at addiction not only as a physiological predisposition, Stanton and Todd (1982) underscored the role of the family in the long-term maintenance of an addiction, even when the family operates mainly to accentuate or attenuate the impact of external forces and/or physiological vulnerabilities. These authors described, among others, the following common characteristics of families of addicts:

1. There is evidence of a high frequency of multigenerational chemical dependency in these families, particularly alcohol abuse, in addition to other addictionlike behaviors such as gambling. Such practices provide modeling for children and can develop into family "traditions." Such patterns are typically denied or distorted in family communication.
2. Compared with members of other dysfunctional families, addicts are more likely to form strong extrafamilial relationships and to retreat to them following family conflict, even if only briefly. The illusion of independence is greater in these families because the addicts have a subculture to which they can relate.
3. Families of addicts often characterize themselves as close, showing a great deal of nurturant but infantilizing relationships.
4. Addicts' families show a preponderance of traumatic death themes, particularly untimely and violent deaths. Loss issues of unresolved mourning or cut-off relationships are commonly connected to separation difficulties and to the substance abuser's self-destructive behavior. (Coleman, 1991).
5. Acculturation and parent–child cultural disparity can play an important role in the maintenance of an addiction. Various research findings show that the rate of addiction for offspring of people who migrated from either another country or other parts of the United States was three times higher than the rate for immigrants themselves.

In addition to describing these predisposing factors, which may contribute to addiction, Stanton and Todd (1982) proposed a systemic homeostatic model that explains the addiction process in functional terms as part of a cyclical process involving three or more individuals, commonly the addict and two parents. Their model does not deal extensively with the etiology of drug addiction, but rather with current family functioning and the ways in which family operations maintain adolescent substance abuse.

As in other adolescent problems, the two life-cycle transitions—first, reaching adolescence, and, later, separating and leaving home—are particularly salient in the development of addiction in the young person. (Haley, 1980; Stanton & Todd, 1982). In the model suggested by Stanton and Todd, drug addiction is seen as related to an intense fear of separation experienced by the whole family, in response to the adolescent's attempts to individuate. Drug taking typically starts as a paradoxical solution for the family's dilemma of whether the adolescent is to become independent. By taking drugs, the adolescent can be simultaneously close and distant, "in" and "out," competent and incompetent, relative to the family of origin. This process of "pseudo-individuation" is maintained by cyclical processes within the family. The adolescent's symptoms are both system-maintained and system-maintaining. Very much like the anorectic or the runaway child, the addict is seen as a regulator of family conflict and/or as having a protective function in the maintenance of family homeostasis:

At times the equilibrium of this interpersonal system (the parental system) is threatened, such as when discord between the parents is amplified to the point of impending separation. When this happens the addict becomes activated, his behavior changes, and he creates a situation that dramatically *focuses the attention upon himself*. This behavior can take a number of forms. For example, he may lose his temper, come home high, commit a serious crime, or overdose on drugs. Whatever its form, however, this action allows the parents to shift focus from their marital conflict to a parental overinvolvement with him. In effect, the movement is from an unstable dyadic interaction (e.g., parents alone) to a more stable triadic interaction (parents and addict). By focusing on the problems of the addict, no matter how severe or life-threatening, the parents choose a course that is apparently safer than dealing with long-standing marital conflicts. Consequently, after the marital crisis has been successfully avoided, the addict shifts to a less provocative stance and begins to behave more competently. This is a new step in the sequence. As the addict demonstrates increased competence, indicating that he can function independently of the family—for example, by getting a job, getting married, enrolling in a methadone program, or detoxifying—the parents are left to deal with their previously unresolved conflicts. At this point in the cycle, marital tensions increase and the threat of separation arises. The addict then behaves in an attention-getting or self-destructive way, and the dysfunctional triadic cycle continues. (Stanton & Todd, 1982, pp. 22–23)

This major goal of therapy with younger substance abusers and their families is to transform the family system, improving the parents' ability to work together in an undivided manner and, at the same time, modulating the ways in which family members deal with each other. The objective is to bolster the family hierarchy while increasing flexibility to respond more appropriately to developmental needs and the vicissitudes of life.

Even with the older adolescent who may be living away from home, it is essential to engage families in the therapeutic process where they have not been able to traverse the separation–individuation process but instead have become stuck in a cycle in which the addict remains inappropriately tied to the parents. By convening the whole family, the therapist can more easily help members achieve healthier differentiation and autonomy. Thus, parental control is reinstated and then gradually relaxed as the adolescent assumes greater responsibility and control for his or her own life course. In cases where unresolved mourning issues are blocking separation or contributing to self-destructive behavior, these losses need to be addressed (Walsh & McGoldrick, 1988, 1991).

The immediate goal of therapy is to deal with the triad composed of the addict and both parents (or a parental surrogate, such as the maternal grandmother). Involvement of siblings in sessions is also important in the initial phase. Absent siblings can behave homeostatically and undercut in-session accomplishments; getting their direct input is thus very helpful. Siblings can also help to support the addict in more appropriate self-assertion. They provide a useful alternative focus and prevent exclusive attention to the addict (Stanton & Todd, 1982).

Suicide

Any number of problems in living, or larger social concerns, may contribute to an adolescent's self-destructive behavior or actual decision to commit suicide. Frequently, an adolescent suicide signals the pain of family fragmentation and a need for family reconciliation (Gutstein, 1991). When a suicide attempt occurs, it is crucial to explore a possible connection to other unresolved losses in the family system (Landau-Stanton & Stanton, 1985; Walsh & McGoldrick, 1988, 1991). A 12-year-old boy was hospitalized following an attempted suicide. The boy and his family were at a loss to explain the episode and made no mention of an older brother. Family assessment revealed that the boy was born shortly before the death of an elder son at the age of 12. The younger son grew up attempting to take the place of the brother he had never known, in order to relieve his parents' sadness. The father, who could not recall the date or events surrounding the death, wished to remember his first son "as if he were still alive." The boy cultivated his appearance to resemble photos of his brother. Only when asked about his brother did the boy reply that he had attempted suicide to join his "12-year-old brother in heaven." The timing corresponded to his reaching (and surviving) the age of his brother's death and to his concern, with his growth spurt at puberty, that he was changing from the way he was "supposed" to look. Therapy focused on enabling the boy and his parents to relinquish his surrogate position and to move forward with his own development.

In the aftermath of any suicide, all family members need help, even those who are apparently functioning well. The death of a child, particularly from suicide, is generally the most painful of losses and has long-term effects. Where painful mourning issues are not dealt with, parents are at high risk of marital breakdown. Siblings may become dysfunctional or assume a replacement function. Parents may become overly vigilant of surviving children. When a suicide occurs, the parents can be devastated by questions of responsibility—especially the mother, whose primary role centers on the protection and well-being of children. Issues concerning blame and guilt need to be carefully explored as the family is helped to move on with their lives. It is crucial that the shame surrounding a suicide not prevent the family from carrying out valuable mourning rituals, especially a funeral; otherwise, the family is left isolated from social support (Walsh & McGoldrick, 1988, 1991).

When adolescent suicide is associated with other traumatic losses in the family, therapy should be directed to the exploration and facilitation of open family communication, rituals, and support around unresolved mourning issues. Recent research (Walsh & McGoldrick, 1989) dispels the myth that there is an ideal grief process or a progression of stages, or that traumatic losses, especially suicide, can ever be completely resolved. Clinicians need to respect the variety of ways in which families may experience this process over time while helping them support one another.

FAMILY THERAPY APPROACHES

Family therapy is not simply a therapeutic modality in which all family members are treated conjointly. A family systems approach is distinguished less by who is in the room and more by how the clinician attends to the relationship system in problem formulation and treatment planning. Therapeutic interventions are aimed at interrupting dysfunctional family patterns in which symptomatic behavior is embedded. Grounded in a set of assumptions about the interplay of individual and family processes, therapy may involve individual sessions with an adolescent, combined with direct work with the parental unit, the sibling subsystem, and key extended family members.

Family therapy is not a unitary practice model, any more than is individual therapy. Approaches differ mainly in their focus on various aspects of family functioning, in assumptions about the goals of therapy and how change occurs, and in utilization of particular strategies and techniques (Walsh, 1983b). (For an extensive review of family process and outcome studies, see Gurman, Kniskern, & Pinsof, 1988.)

A number of approaches to family therapy have been found to be particularly useful with problems in adolescence (Breunlin, Breunlin, Kearns, & Russell, 1988). A structural–strategic approach is particularly effective with many adolescent problems, as illustrated above. With this approach, the major goals of intervention are to shift dysfunctional organizational patterns and unblock immediate impasses in the interactional process so that the adolescent can gradually separate and leave home without alienation or breaking away from the family (Fishman, 1988). Family therapy with adolescents promotes a progressive renegotiation of the parent–child bond and generational boundaries; the asymmetrical organization of earlier childhood takes on a more symmetrical mutuality in adulthood. The added integration of behavioral and communication techniques has been shown to be particularly effective with delinquents, despite the heterogeneity of this population (Patterson & Brodsky, 1976; Patterson, Reid, Jones, & Conger, 1975; Stuart, 1971; Tolan, Cromwell, & Brasswell, 1986). Tolan and Mitchell (1989) advocated a multilevel structural–strategic approach, combining concurrent individual and family sessions, at least in the beginning of therapy.

The Functional Family Therapy approach developed by Alexander and his colleagues (Alexander & Parsons, 1982; Alexander, Barton, Schiavo, & Parsons, 1976) has been found to be highly effective with adolescent behavior problems. Recent research by Alexander, Waldron, Barton, and Mas (1989) examined different strategies in initiating the family intervention process with delinquent adolescents. They found that setting a positive therapeutic context can elicit nonblaming attributions in conflicted families. Where negative interactions are entrenched, use of such techniques as positive connotation and relabeling probably requires repeated application. They cautioned that, because negative events are more salient than positive ones for these clinical families, problem-focused interventions may exacerbate negative attributions and behaviors, and, consequently, heighten resistance to therapeutic change. In contrast, approaches that prescribe a more positive, nonblaming relational focus facilitate positive change.

Psychodynamically oriented and Bowen approaches are useful for more intensive exploration and resolution of past conflicts and losses in the multigenerational system that block or distort current relationships. These approaches are also of particular value, where parental death, divorce, or adoption has occurred, in coaching an adolescent to explore and integrate a lost relationship with a biological parent.

The therapeutic choice may vary in emphasis on past or present and in the extent of attention to multigenerational relationships. Regardless of the particular approach, it is useful to take into account the interplay of past, present, and future in family life-cycle passage and adolescent development.

We share with Combrinck-Graham (1989) the basic premise that the family is a child's primary resource system. Even when families are severely distressed or hard to reach, their crucial contribution to improving the well-being of their children should be promoted in any treatment plan. Family therapy is based on the assumption that problems presented by an individual can most effectively be treated by mobilizing family resources to resolve problems and promote healthy development. Where family interaction processes have contributed to symptom development or maintenance, alteration of dysfunctional relationship patterns is crucial.

Thus, the often asked question, "When is family therapy indicated?", requires reframing from a systems perspective. When problems are conceptualized interactionally, an individual's problems cannot be understood or changed apart from the context in which they occur and the functions they may serve. Individual change cannot be expected to be sustained, without symptoms appearing elsewhere in the system, unless the system changes. Likewise, where larger systems impact detrimentally on individual and family well-being, as in poverty, racism, and sexism, interventions must take those influences into account. Thus, the question of indications becomes a question of context: "What is the symptom-maintaining context of a specific problem in a particular family and how can it most effectively be altered?"

A respect for the mutuality of influences also requires that a clinician assess the impact of adolescent behavior—and of larger systems' stressors—on the family. It is a disservice to families to base indications for family therapy on linear assumptions that the family is *the cause* of an adolescent's problem or the *real* problem behind individual symptoms. Family therapy is indicated whenever a child or family is in distress and when an adolescent's dysfunctional behavior is embedded in family interactional patterns. Even when the primary source of distress lies outside the family, as in the rape of a teenage girl, the family may not know how to be helpful or provide optimal support. Moreover, other members are bound to be affected, even apparently asymptomatic siblings, and need attention to their distress. Most importantly, families should be involved in some way in the treatment of any adolescent problem because the family is the most valuable potential resource that can be mobilized to promote a child's healthy functioning and development.

REFERENCES

Ackerman, N. (1980). The family with adolescents. In E. Carter & M. McGoldrick (Eds.), *The family life cycle: A framework for family therapy.* New York: Gardner Press.

Alexander, J., Barton, C., Schiavo, R., & Parson, B. (1976). Systems-behavioral intervention with families of delinquents: Therapist characteristics, family behavior, and outcome. *Journal of Consulting and Clinical Psychology, 44,* 656–664.

Alexander, J., & Parsons, B. (1982). *Functional family therapy: Principles and procedures.* Carmel, CA: Brooks/Cole.

Alexander, J., Waldron, H., Barton, C., & Mas, C. H. (1989). The minimizing of blaming attributions and behaviors in delinquent families. *Journal of Consulting and Clinical Psychology, 57,* 19–24.

Breunlin, D., Breunlin, C., Kearns, D., & Russell, W. (1988). A review of the literature on family therapy with adolescents 1979–1987. *Journal of Adolescence, 11,* 309–334.

Bruch, H. (1963). Psychotherapeutic problems in eating disorders. *Psychoanalytic Review, 50,* 43.

Campbell, E., Adams, G., & Dobson, W. (1984). Familial correlates of identity formation in late adolescence: A study of the predictive utility of connectedness and individuality in family relations. *Journal of Youth and Adolescence, 13,* 509–525.

Carter, E., & McGoldrick, M. (1980). *The family life cycle: Framework for family therapy.* New York: Gardner Press.

Carter, B., & McGoldrick, M. (1988). *The changing family life cycle: Framework for family therapy* (2nd ed.). Boston: Allyn & Bacon.

Cohler, B., & Geyer, S. (1982). Psychological autonomy and interdependence within the family. In F. Walsh (Ed.), *Normal family processes.* New York: Guilford Press.

Coleman, S. (1991). In F. Walsh & M. McGoldrick (Eds.), *Living beyond loss.* New York: Norton.

Combrinck-Graham, L. (1985). A developmental model for family systems. *Family Process, 24,* 139–150.

Combrinck-Graham, L. (1988). Adolescent sexuality in the family life spiral. In C. Falicov (Ed.), *Family transitions: Continuity and change.* New York: Guilford Press.

Combrinck-Graham, L. (1989). *Children in family contexts: Perspectives on treatment.* New York: Guilford Press.

Falicov, C. (1988). *Family transitions: Continuity and change over the life cycle.* New York: Guilford Press.

Fishman, H. C. (1988). *Treating troubled adolescents: A family therapy approach.* New York: Basic Books.

Garcia-Preto, N. (1988). Transformation of the family system in adolescence. In B. Carter & M. McGoldrick (Eds.), *The changing family life cycle.* Boston: Allyn & Bacon.

Garcia-Preto, N., & Travis, D. (1985). In M. Mirkin & S. Koman (Eds.), *Handbook of adolescents and family therapy.* New York: Gardner Press.

Garfinkel, P., & Garner, D. (1982). *Anorexia nervosa: A multi-dimensional perspective.* New York: Brunner/Mazel.

Gilligan, C. (1982). *In a different voice.* Cambridge, MA: Harvard University Press.

Gilligan, C., Lyons, N., & Hanmer, T. (Eds.) (1989). *Making connections: The relational worlds of adolescent girls at Emma Willard School.* Cambridge, MA: Harvard University Press.

Goldner, V. (1989). Generation and gender: Normative and covert hierarchies. In M. McGoldrick, C. Anderson, & F. Walsh, *Women in families: A framework for family therapy.* New York: Norton.

Grigg, D., & Friesen, J. (1989). Family patterns associated with anorexia nervosa. *Journal of Marital and Family Therapy, 15,* 29–42.

Gurman, A., Kniskern, D., & Pinsof, W. (1988). Research on marital and family therapy. In S. Garfield & A. Bergin (Eds.), *Handbook of psychotherapy and behavior change* (2nd ed.) New York: Wiley.

Gutstein, S. (1991). Adolescent suicide: The loss of reconciliation. In F. Walsh & M. McGoldrick (Eds.), *Living beyond loss: Death in the family.* New York: Norton.

Haley, J. (1980). *Leaving home.* New York: McGraw-Hill.

Hare Mustin, R. (1989). The problem of gender in family therapy theory. In M. McGoldrick, C. Anderson, & F. Walsh, *Women in families: A framework for family therapy.* New York: Norton.

Hauser, S., Powers, S., Noam, G., Jacobson, A., Weiss, B., & Follansbee, D. (1984). Familial contexts of adolescent ego development. *Child Development, 55,* 195–213.

Hetherington, M. (1989). Marital transitions: A child's perspective. *American Psychologist, 44,* 303–312.

Hoffman, L. (1988). The family life cycle and discontinuous change. In B. Carter & M. McGoldrick, *The changing family life cycle: Framework for family therapy* (2nd ed.) Boston: Allyn & Bacon.

Johnson, C. (1985). The etiology of bulimia: A bio-psycho-social perspective. *The Annals of Adolescent Psychiatry* (Vol. 13).

Kandel, D., Treinman, D., Faust, R., & Single, E. (1976). Adolescent involvement in legal and illegal drug use: A multiple classification analysis. *Social Forces, 55,* 438–458.

Landau-Stanton, J., & Stanton, M. D. (1985). Treating suicidal adolescents and their families. In M. Mirkin & S. Koman (Eds.), *Handbook of adolescents and family therapy.* New York: Gardner Press.

Lappin, J., & Covelman, C. (1985). Adolescent runaways: A structural family therapy perspective. In M. Mirkin & S. Koman (Eds.), *Handbook of adolescents and family therapy.* New York: Gardner Press.

Liebman, R., Sargent, J., & Silver, M. (1983). A family systems orientation to the treatment of anorexia nervosa. *Journal of the American Academy of Child Psychiatry, 22,* 134–139.

McGoldrick, M., Anderson, C., & Walsh, F. (1989). *Women in families: A framework for family therapy.* New York: Norton.

McGoldrick, M., & Gerson, R. (1985). *Genograms in family assessment.* New York: Norton.

McGoldrick, M., & Walsh, F. (1983). A systemic view of family history and loss. In M. Aronson (Ed.), *Group and family therapy: 1983.* New York: Brunner/Mazel.

Minuchin, S. (1974). *Families and family therapy.* Cambridge, MA: Harvard University Press.

Minuchin, S., Rosman, B., & Baker, L. (1978). *Psychosomatic families: Anorexia nervosa in context.* Cambridge, MA: Harvard University Press.

Mirkin, M., Raskin, P., & Antogini, F. (1984). Parenting, protecting, and preserving: Mission of the female runaway. *Family Process, 23,* 63–74.

Montemayor, R. (1983). Parents and adolescents in conflict: All families some of the time and some families most of the time. *Journal of Early Adolescence, 3,* 83–103.

Olson, D. H. (1988). *The circumplex model.* New York: Haworth Press.

Quinn, W. H., Newfield, N., & Protinsky, H. (1985). Rites of passage in families with adolescents. *Family Process, 24,* 101–111.

Patterson, G., & Brodsky, G. (1976). A behavior modification program for a child with multiple problem behaviors. *Journal of Child Psychology and Psychiatry, 7,* 277–295.

Patterson, G., Reid, J., Jones, R., & Conger, R. (1975). *A social learning approach to family intervention: Families with aggressive children* (Vol. 1). Eugene, OR: Castalia.

Reiss, D. (1981). *The family's construction of reality.* Cambridge, MA: Harvard University Press.

Schwartz, R. (1988). Families and eating disorders. In F. Walsh & C. Anderson (Eds.), *Chronic disorders and the family.* New York: Haworth Press.

Schwartz, R., Barrett, M. J., & Saba, G. (1985). Family therapy for bulimia. In P. Garner & P. Garfinkel (Eds.), *Handbook for the psychotherapy of anorexia nervosa and bulimia.* New York: Guilford Press.

Solomon (1973). A developmental conceptual premise for family therapy. *Family Process, 12,* 179–188.

Stanton, M. D., & Todd, T. (1982). *The family therapy of drug abuse and addiction.* New York: Guilford Press.

Steinberg, L. (1981). Transformations in family relations at puberty. *Developmental Psychology, 17,* 833–840.

Stierlin, H. (1979). Separating parents and adolescents: A perspective on running away, schizophrenia, and waywardness. New York: Quadrangle.

Stuart, R. (1971). Behavioral contracting within the families of delinquents. *Journal of Behavior Therapy and Experimental Psychiatry, 2,* 1–11.

Todd, T. C. (1985). Anorexia nervosa and bulimia: Expanding the structural model. In M. Mirkin & S. Koman (Eds.) *Handbook of adolescents and family therapy.* New York: Gardner Press.

Tolan, P., Cromwell, R., & Brasswell, M. (1986). Family therapy with delinquents: A critical review of the literature. *Family Process, 25,* 619–649.

Tolan, P., & Mitchell, M. (1989). Families and the therapy of anti-social and delinquent behavior. In P. Tolan (Ed.), *Multi-systemic structural–strategic interventions for child and adolescent behavior problems* [Special issue], *Journal of Psychotherapy and the Family, 6,* 29–48.

Walsh, F. (1982). Conceptualizations of normal family functioning. In F. Walsh (Ed.), *Normal family processess.* New York: Guilford Press.

Walsh, F. (1983a). The timing of symptoms and critical events in the family life cycle. In H. Liddle (Ed.), *Clinical implications of the family life cycle.* Rockville, MD: Aspen Publications.

Walsh, F. (1983b). Family therapy: As systemic orientation to treatment. In A. Rosenblatt & D. Waldfogel (Eds.), *Handbook of clinical social work.* San Francisco: Jossey-Bass.

Walsh, F. (1988a). The clinical utility of normal family research. *Psychotherapy, 24,* 496–503.

Walsh, F. (1988b). New perspectives on schizophrenia and families. In F. Walsh & C. Anderson (Eds.), *Chronic disorders and the family,* New York: Haworth Press.

Walsh, F. (1988). The family in later life. In B. Carter & M. McGoldrick (Eds.), *The changing family life cycle.* Boston: Allyn & Bacon.

Walsh, F. (1991). Promoting healthy functioning in divorced and remarried families. In A. Gurman & D. Kniskern (Eds.), *Handbook of family therapy* (rev. ed.). New York: Brunner/Mazel.

Walsh, F., & McGoldrick, M. (Eds.) (1991). *Living beyond loss: Death in the family.* New York: Norton.

Walsh, F. & Scheinkman, M. (1989). (Fe)Male: The hidden gender dimension in models of family therapy. In M. McGoldrick, C. Anderson, & F. Walsh (Eds.), *Women in families: A framework for family therapy.* New York: Norton.

Watzlawick, P., Beavin, J., & Jackson, D. (1967). *Pragmatics of human communication.* New York: Norton.

CHAPTER 8

The School as a Social Context

EDISON J. TRICKETT and KATHLEEN DOHERTY SCHMID

The thesis of the present chapter is that the school is not simply a site where interventions by mental health professionals can occur. Instead, the school is viewed as a resource in developing remedial and preventive efforts to aid adolescents. Although adolescents often bring into the school troubles that originate outside of the school, the supervision of these difficulties and the way they are dealt with involve aspects of the local school culture, its definitions of maladjustment, and its resources for aid. Through its approach to dealing with adolescents, the school can unintentionally exacerbate ongoing problems or, as some see it, create them (Sedlak, Wheeler, Pullen, & Cusick, 1986).

During the past 20 years, it has become increasingly clear that schools, through their structures and processes, do indeed affect a wide range of student outcomes. Initial studies were more likely to focus on solely academic criteria, but more recent work has examined how specific school processes affect a wide range of student variables, including social functioning, post secondary school plans, employability, social attitudes, and behavioral adjustment. Examples of this broadened emphasis are found in studies that examine how principal leadership style and school organizational structure affect student outcomes (Good & Weinstein, 1986), the relationship of school size and available roles to student participation and school satisfaction (Glass, Cohen, Smith, & Filby, 1982), and how teaching style influences student interest in and mastery of course content (Brophy, 1986). (For additional findings and summary statements on school effects, see Linney & Seidman, 1989; Rutter, 1983; Rutter, Maughan, Mortimore, Ouston and Smith, 1979.)

Findings such as these highlight the importance of the school as a setting that influences the adolescent in a variety of ways. They further suggest that interventions in schools per se can have broad consequences for the lives of adolescents. The task for the outside interventionist is to work collaboratively with the school to enhance its ability to be a positive resource for its students. Doing so, however, requires knowledge about how the school context affects behavior and a commitment to developing interventions that build on what the school has to offer. This, in turn, requires a perspective on the school as a social context that can sharpen research questions and intervention options and can serve as a guide for the kinds of roles professionals may play in the intervention process.

The purpose of this chapter is to outline one perspective that is useful in this task—an ecological perspective on the schools, adolescent behavior in schools, and intervention. Although many different definitions of ecology are currently evolving (e.g., Barker, 1968; Bronfenbrenner, 1979; Moos, 1979), the metaphor of choice for the present chapter is the ecological analogy first articulated by Kelly (1968, 1971, 1986; Kelly & Associates, 1979) and extended by his colleagues (e.g., Mills & Kelly, 1972; Trickett, 1984, 1987; Trickett & Birman, 1989; Trickett, Kelly, & Todd, 1972; Trickett, Kelly, & Vincent, 1985; Trickett & Mitchell, in press; Trickett & Todd, 1972). This approach has served as a heuristic for research and intervention across a variety of settings and research areas, and represents a distinctive framework for assessment and intervention in settings such as schools (Kelly & Associates, 1979; Kelly & Hess, 1987; Trickett et al., 1972; Trickett & Birman, 1989; Trickett & Todd, 1972).

The ecological metaphor itself derives from field biology, in which the entire biological community is the object of study and the unit of analysis. The image is one of looking at a community in terms of its discrete parts and how those parts work together to form a whole. To understand the functioning of any one part, the larger context must be considered. Thus, the ecological mind-set is that of the naturalist (Kelly, 1971), exploring both the overall nature of the school environment and how its components affect the functioning of individuals.

In later sections of this chapter, the specific principles derived from this metaphor will be applied to enhance understanding of (a) the school as a social context, (b) individual behavior in the social context, and (c) the school as a context for intervention. First, however, discussion is directed at highlighting some of the broad underlying assumptions of an ecological approach for intervention.

UNDERLYING ASSUMPTIONS FOR AN ECOLOGICALLY BASED APPROACH TO INTERVENTIONS IN SCHOOLS

The broad focus of ecologically based intervention is to embed interventions in an understanding of the social context and the individual's relation to it. Thus, both the substance of the intervention (what it is) and the process by which it is developed (how it comes to be) are shaped by the requirements of the setting and are not superimposed by outside professionals. In this section, the intent is to provide a broad overview of assumptions that orient interventionists to ecologically based intervention in the school setting. Three broad aspects of this type of approach are considered: (a) the fundamental importance of environmental assessment, (b) the development of a collaborative intervention style, and (c) the creation of an empowering intervention.

The Fundamental Importance of Environmental Assessment

Within an ecological perspective, behavior is seen as a transaction between the environment and the individual. As such, assessment of the environment becomes a critical tool for the ecologically based intervention. Conceptualized as an ongoing, multilevel evaluation of the school culture, environmental assessment can include evaluating the environmental characteristics that contribute to problems, the resources of the setting, the organizational openness to change, or the systemic changes as a result of intervention.

The creation of activities and time to undertake environmental assessment is an important task. Sarason, Levine, Goldenberg, Cherlin, and Bennett (1966), for example negotiated a time span in their consultation with schools where their primary task, before providing any specific service, was to get to know the school and allow school personnel to get to know the interventionists. Others have provided examples of working in schools, over time, to expand traditional individually based intervention approaches to include multilevel interventions that address systems and environmental influences as well (e.g., Medway & Nagle, 1982).

Much will be said later in the chapter about specific kinds of questions that might be asked in environmental assessment. For now, the goals are (a) to suggest the primacy of understanding the nature of the school context in designing, implementing, and evaluating interventions and (b) to emphasize the value of creating time and activities for this type of assessment.

Developing a Collaborative Intervention Style

Ecologically based intervention rests on the value of a collaborative relationship between the interventionist and members of the school. The spirit of the collaborative intervention involves two emphases: (a) a shared concern for the school as a setting and (b) the notion of differential rather than unidirectional expertise. Collaboration evokes the image of working as colleagues on an issue of mutual importance; it suggests that school personnel will be concerned about translating the school culture to the interventionist so the work can proceed in a culture-congruent way, and that the interventionist will demonstrate an eagerness to understand and learn from the experience of school personnel.

Although the specifics of the collaboration are expected to vary across schools, a number of approaches proposed in the consultation literature are relevant to its spirit. Communication in a collaborative relationship, for example, is characterized by nonhierarchical professional-to-professional exchanges (Caplan, 1970; Meyers, 1981; Parsons & Meyers, 1984). The interventionist does not assume an authoritative role, but instead, presents ideas and formulations in a tentative manner that allows their acceptance or rejection. Active involvement by those in the setting is encouraged by valuing their participation, respecting their opinions, and promoting their collaboration in aspects of the intervention (O'Neill & Trickett, 1982; Parsons & Meyers, 1984).

An additional aspect of the collaborative process is the notion of differential expertise of different parties. The psychological knowledge, research expertise, and knowledge of local programs of the interventionist become integrated with the educational expertise, knowledge of the school culture, and personal qualities of school personnel. The explicit understanding is that, if the intervention is to influence the school as well as the adolescent, the specific professional skills of the interventionist are not enough; rather, active and authentic collaboration with school personnel is necessary. This is not only because school personnel have specialized knowledge about the school and the adolescent that the outside interventionist does not have, but also because collaboration supports the value of creating empowering interventions.

Creating an Empowering Intervention

The previous two sets of activities—environmental assessment and the development of collaborative relationships—are preconditions for this third topic. Because the goal of ecologically based interventions is to strengthen the school as a social context for the development of adolescents, interventions are intended to empower school personnel to become more effective in dealing with current and future situations. Unless the intervention affects the setting in an empowering way, it carries no positive long-term systemic consequences. Thus, the goal of the intervention is to use the knowledge and trust gained through the development of collaborative processes to create an intervention that builds on and strengthens individuals and/or structures in the local setting. Empowerment here is intended to include such factors as an increased belief that future problems can be solved, the development of new norms for dealing proactively with issues, and the creation of new settings in the school for the expression of conflict and its potential resolution.

The fundamental assumptions of ecologically based intervention then focus on how the nature of the school context and the interventionist's relationship to the school can serve to strengthen the school as a setting for the development of the adolescent. With this orientation in mind, this chapter describes a series of ecological processes that carry implications for how to examine more specifically (a) the social context of the school and adolescent behavior in that context, and (b) the intervention in the social context of the school.

ENVIRONMENTAL ASSESSMENT: THE SCHOOL AS A SOCIAL CONTEXT AND ADOLESCENT BEHAVIOR IN SCHOOLS

The specifics of the ecological metaphor lie in the elaboration of four ecological principles: adaptation, cycling of resources, interdependence, and succession. In this section of the chapter, each is outlined to guide ecological assessment of (a) schools as social contexts and (b) individual behavior in those contexts. Selected research studies have been incorporated into the discussion as a means of concretizing the assessment process.

The Adaptation Principle

In field biology, the adaptation principle refers to the mutually interactive way in which organisms and their host settings adapt to each other. Of the four ecological principles, this principle provides the broadest heuristic for understanding behavior, referring both to the nature of the social context in which individuals find themselves and to the processes individuals use in negotiating these contexts. It thus calls attention to (a) social context characteristics that create the conditions for adaptive behavior and (b) individual qualities that affect coping in these contexts.

The School as a Context for Individual Adaptation

The school environment conveys a certain environmental press (Murray, 1938), which forms the context for adolescent coping. To understand behavior, one must understand the context in which it occurs. Recent descriptions of high school culture (Boyer, 1983; Cusick, 1983; Goodlad, 1984; Lightfoot, 1983) have captured the regularity of schooling practices across institutions. As described by these studies, a common organizational structure around scheduling routines, specialized subjects, monitored attendance, and demands for order converges to create a similar role for students across high schools. Because of these broad role similarities, there are common threads of student experience across schools. Students must deal with authority issues, develop increasing self-discipline around academic matters, and cope with a formal structure of rules and regulations that constrain their behavior.

Nonetheless, these studies have also noted subtler variations among and within schools as to how daily routines are implemented. Policies and norms surrounding student behavior differ across schools, and discipline, while an issue in every school, may take quite different forms and have different meaning in different schools. Thus, the specific ways in which schools carry out educational tasks converge to form a particular context that impacts student coping and behavior.

Within the ecological perspective, four aspects of school culture will be explored as a framework for assessing differences in specific school contexts: structures, norms, attitudes, and policies.

ORGANIZATIONAL STRUCTURES. The concept of school structures implies both a macro and micro view of how the school is organized. The macro level focuses on the organizational layout of the school per se. Trickett and his colleagues (Gruber & Trickett, 1986; Trickett, 1991; Trickett, McConahay, Phillips, & Ginter, 1985) have described one such layout in their research on alternative and traditional public schools. The structure of the alternative school contrasted with the traditional high schools in its emphasis on shared decision making—allowing students to influence the design of their curricula and giving teachers autonomy in classroom practices.

Such overall differences in organizational structure were, in turn, reflected at the more micro level of specific programs, events, and settings. The alternative school, for example, included a Policy Council, which served as a teacher–student–parent decision-making group, and a Community Orientation Program, which placed students in the community to learn from lawyers, mental health professionals, or beauticians. These structures were not available to students in the traditional schools. These differences in macro and micro structures significantly affected the experience of adolescents attending the different schools. Compared to controls attending more traditional schools, students in the alternative school reported greater affection toward teachers, greater overall school satisfaction, greater interracial tolerance, and a greater likelihood of pursuing postsecondary education. Thus, the different organizational structures created different contexts for coping which, in turn, affected school outcomes of psychological and social importance.

The assessment of schools in terms of their macro and micro structures provides the interventionist with a broad conception of the adaptive demands placed on adolescents. It allows an investigation of how the school creates the conditions for certain outcomes and behaviors through the kinds of opportunities its structures provide. Such an analysis also highlights what potentially relevant structures are missing and need to be created to serve the needs of adolescents.

NORMS. Structures embody certain general norms, or expectations, about what kinds of attitudes and behavior are valued, discouraged, or ignored. The specific content of these norms may differ from school to school and, of course, among subgroups of adolescents or adults within any particular school (Gottlieb, 1975). Of particular relevance to mental health professionals are norms around classroom behavior and definitions of deviance.

Norms around classroom behavior can be assessed in a number of ways. One way is through the use of measures such as the Classroom Environment Scale (CES) (Trickett & Moos, 1973), which taps aggregate student perceptions of what high school classrooms are like. The CES surveys classroom organizational structure, interpersonal relationships, and the emphasis placed on learning goals through competition and sticking to academic concerns. The scale has been used to show that different types of schools (e.g., urban, rural, vocational, private vs. public) create different kinds of normative classroom environments (Trickett, 1978; Trickett & Moos, 1979; Trickett, Trickett, Castro, & Schaffner, 1982). The normative environments, in turn, create different kinds of environmental presses on adolescents in these different types of schools (Moos, 1979; Moos & Trickett, 1987).

Norms around the definition of deviance constitute another example of how contexts, rather than the individual qualities of adolescents per se, affect the interpretation of behavior. Increasingly, for example, it has been suggested that "subjective" (Ysseldyke & Algozzine, 1982) or "judgmental" (U.S. Department of Health, Education, and Welfare, n.d.) learning problems such as mild mental retardation, emotional disturbance, and learning disabilities represent social constructions rather than "problems" located in individuals. Reschly (1987) advocated that these types of disorders, in contrast to medically or "objectively" defined problems, be defined as social systems disorders:

It is highly likely that the classification of learning disability and mild mental retardation would not exist if we did not have compulsory attendance laws and nearly universal public education between the ages of approximately 5 and 17. Social system model handicaps . . . are best understood as a function of the demands and expectations placed upon students in a highly technological society, particularly the demands and expectations for the development of abstract thinking and literacy skills. (p. 40)

Evidence for this perspective is found in the research literature. Thus, rates of learning disabilities have been found to vary greatly from state to state, while rates for more "objectively" defined disorders such as physical handicaps are consistent across states (Edgar & Hayden, 1985). Rates of diagnosis of nonobjective disorders have been linked to sociocultural factors (Gelb & Mizokawa, 1986; Tucker, 1980), referral procedures (Pugach, 1985), availability of personnel, and even the manner of information presentation (Huebner, 1988). Norms, then, provide environmental standards that frame the meaning of individual behavior in that context.

ATTITUDES. Attitudes reflect the more individualized perspectives of administrators, teachers, and peers in the school. For example, certain teachers may be known as sympathetic to varied subgroups of students, "easy in their grading habits and definitions of deviance, or "tough, but fair" in their attitudes toward schoolwork. These individual variations may or may not coincide with the broader norms of the school, but they become part of the school culture that adolescents must negotiate.

The importance of attitudes is well illustrated in the two following contrasting examples. Here, the issue involves how the school responds to an influx of foreign-born students. First, an elementary school principal describes a program to work with culturally diverse individuals in a heretofore 100% Anglo school:

We came to the conclusion that our goal must be to offer these children (newly arrived Cambodian immigrants) the best education possible, and also, and probably even more importantly, to make them feel that they are wanted, that they were welcome in this school and this land; that this school was a building full of friends, not just a brick and mortar place where they would learn. So we went on a crusade of teaching every child in the school about Cambodian children that were coming. . . . We implemented an anti-prejudice program . . . every child is immediately paired up with a buddy, and that buddy is responsible for that new child for one week. We try to pair them up according to where they live, so that they can come to school together and go home together. . . . Every Cambodian child that came into the school was immediately given a buddy, and that buddy introduced them to friends in the school, sat with them at lunchtime, and showed them around. (National Coalition of Advocates for Students (NCAS), 1988, p. 85)

In contrast, the following teacher's description of another school, a metropolitan high school, suggests a totally opposite possibility:

In general the reception given to immigrant children was so negative and hostile that many of them were so turned off to their new society that they were never able to learn to speak English. Bilingual students were called animals, garbage, jerks, idiots by many teachers . . . and this unprofessional and inhumane treatment was condoned by administration. (NCAS, 1988, p. 60)

In these examples, administrator and teacher attitudes toward foreign-born students contributed to creating very different environments. In assessing the school and the problems of concern, individual attitudes are important to understand. They can be contributing to the problem or be part of its solution.

POLICIES. Policies reflect those codified aspects of the school culture that provide rules and criteria for defining successful adaptation to school. Policies aid in defining both *how* things are done and *what* things are done, in terms of regulating student behavior, providing accountability for teachers, and protecting the rights of all involved with the school.

School discipline policy can serve as an example of the importance of understanding school policies as part of an overall assessment of the school culture. Because many adolescents who come to the attention of mental health professionals in schools are seen as disciplinary problems or truants, such policies are often of great impact. Current wisdom around school discipline is, as Knoff (1987) contended, that "the development of a well-defined, school-wide policy may be the best preventive program available to encourage appropriate school behavior" (p. 125). By specifying appropriate and inappropriate behavior and the disciplinary consequences for violating the rules, students can respond to the clear expectations and develop prosocial behavior.

However, what constitutes appropriate and inappropriate behavior is not always easy to decide, nor is what constitutes appropriate punishment. Different groups of parents, teachers, and students may arrive at different conclusions. In addition, policies around a variety of aspects of school life are perceived and interpreted differently by subgroups of students. When current policies involving bilingual education are discussed, it is clear that different constituencies believe that they will result in different outcomes. Not all policies involve such vivid contrasts in political and pedagogical ideology, but an assessment of school policies and their implications for adolescents represents an important aspect of the assessment of the school as an ecological niche.

In summary, structures, norms, attitudes, and policies represent a broad roadmap for understanding and assessing what adolescents must adapt to in schools. They supply a general orientation to the culture of the school (Sarason, 1971), and their evaluation provides a means for assessing the school as a differentiated yet integrated social context that impacts on behavior.

Adolescent Adaptation in the School Context

Although the structures, norms, attitudes, and policies of schools provide a social context that exerts pressure on adolescents to adapt to its ways, adolescents, within the ecological perspective, are not assumed to be passive recipients of their environment. Rather, they actively interpret and cope with it, using their available repertoire of cognitive and behavioral skills. The following two statements represent examples of how the adaptation principle stimulates thinking about adolescent coping in schools: (a) school adaptation reflects the sociocultural embeddedness of the individual; and (b) behavior that is adaptive in one setting may be maladaptive in another.

ADAPTATION AND SOCIOCULTURAL EMBEDDEDUESS. Individual behavior is embedded in a sociocultural matrix. An ecological perspective on individual adaptation begins with the notion of the sociocultural embeddedness of individuals. By that we mean that the world view and coping styles that adolescents bring to high school reflect the accumulated socialization influences of social and cultural forces operating over time. An understanding of the adolescent's sociocultural context allows the interventionist to address more critically how school demands interact with adolescent perspectives to influence behavior.

Matute-Bianchi's (1986) description of Mexican-descent and Japanese-American high school students illustrates how a sociocultural perspective on adolescents illuminates their school experience. In this ethnographic investigation, the author interviewed minority students in an agricultural-suburban California community to determine how familial attitudes, school attitudes, and beliefs about the future were related to school performance. One group of Mexican-descent adolescents was described as courteous and well-behaved. They perceived high school to be a necessary stepping-stone to college and higher-status jobs. Parental limit setting and support emphasized going to school and doing well. Likewise, participation in the Mexican-American school organization aided the formation of an ethnic identity that viewed achievement as a positive goal.

Other Mexican-descent students experienced a conflict between school demands and cultural identification, and remained outside the mainstream:

[These students] appear to resist certain features of the school culture, especially the behavioral and normative patterns required for scholastic achievement. . . . To adopt these cultural features—that is, to participate in class discussions, to carry books from class to class, to ask the teacher for help in front of others, to expend effort to do well in school—are efforts that are viewed derisively, condescendingly, and mockingly by other Chicanos. Hence, to adopt such features presents these students with a forced-choice dilemma. They must choose between doing well or being Chicano. From this perspective, it is not possible or legitimate to participate in both the culture of the dominant group, that is, school culture, and in Chicano culture. . . . Hence, school policies and practices are viewed as forces to be resisted, subverted, undermined, challenged, and opposed. (Matute-Bianchi, 1986, p. 254)

A final group, the Japanese-Americans, were perceived as coming from socialization experiences that placed an emphasis on achievement. Like the first group of Mexican-descent students, these students and their families believed high school to be an important precursor to college and future success. However, the future orientation of these students was more differentiated. Familial and outside connections provided a context that encouraged students to seek out specialized high school experiences that would lead to their acceptance at specific, high-status schools.

These comparisons highlight how adolescent sociocultural context interacts with school experiences, even within the same school. They further suggest that multiple sources of influence, including both family and school characteristics, affect school adaptation. Some specific implications are found in the next topic.

ADAPTIVE/MALADAPTIVE BEHAVIOR. Behavior that is adaptive in one context may be maladaptive in another. It is clear from the preceding example that adolescents must negotiate a variety of social contexts, such as family, school, and peer groups, which themselves vary in terms of their adaptive requirements. Because these contexts require different behavior, a behavior that is adaptive in one context may be maladaptive in another. This suggests that one aspect of the assessment process should focus on how different contexts push or pull adolescents in different ways.

There are times, however, when adolescents experience conflict from competing sets of adaptive requirements within the same setting. Such was the case with the Mexican-descent group torn between obedience to peer-group norms and appropriate school behavior. Consider another example, reported in Trickett (1984):

The following example was told to me by a teacher in a racially mixed inner city alternative school. The student body was, at that time, 60% white, 40% black, and the staff 90% white. The school was not strict in terms of rules and regulations; students would often hang out in the halls rather than attending class. Among the "regulars" who hung out was a 19-year-old black student, who drove a new Lincoln to school, dressed and acted like "Superfly," and always carried an obvious roll of bills. During the school day, he would hang out in the halls or outside of the building. His situational adaptation was to play it cool, an option made available because of the particular norms of the school. After school was over, and his peers had left, however, he would return to school for tutoring in reading by one of his teachers. It was the teacher's hunch that adapting to school in the normative sense of going to class, etc. was seen as conflicting with his highly valued street image. However, he also knew he needed to learn to read. His way of adapting was not to adjust to the behavioral expectations of the school by going to class, to avoid overt school behavior which conflicted with his peer group or street image, yet find a way to learn those school-related skills he felt necessary. (pp.271–272)

From this example comes the following conclusion about the assessment of adaptive behavior: the range of behavior exhibited by adolescents in any particular setting may vary widely from normative expectations and still be adaptive for the adolescent, depending on the perceived demands of the other social contexts he or she must negotiate. It is this kind of contextualized approach to understanding adolescent behavior in schools that is highlighted by the ecological metaphor.

In sum, the adaptation principle promotes a global focus on the nature of the school context and the ways individual qualities interact with this context. Three additional principles—cycling of resources, interdependence, and succession—will now be considered, as a means of examining more focused aspects of the school as a social context and the adolescent in that context.

Cycling of Resources

In field biology, the principle of cycling of resources refers to the way in which communities maintain and distribute resources. Applied to human communities, it evokes an image of strength, potential, and, indeed, hope for positive change through developing resources in the community.

The School as a Resource

A resource perspective on the school as a social context focuses on the search for those aspects of the school that can provide energy, ideas, structures, and occasions that can facilitate improved problem solving. Elsewhere (Kelly, 1987; Trickett, Kelly, & Vincent, 1985), people, settings, and events have been nominated as different kinds of potential resources in the school environment.

PEOPLE AS RESOURCES. An ecological perspective on people as resources focuses on both the formal and informal roles adopted by individuals in the service of the school and its students. We begin with the formal roles of principal, teachers, and mental health professionals and conclude with informal potential resources—individuals operating outside of their formal role requirements, and peer groups. Assessing the formal and informal resource network sets the stage for indigenous and empowering interventions.

Principal The formal role of today's high school principal is enormous. Harris and Dawes (1988) outlined almost 300 pages of tasks confronting the principal. This myriad of tasks, plus a powerful role in sanctioning any outside intervention, makes the principal a potentially key resource for adolescents, the school as an organization, and the interventionist. With respect to adolescents, for example, the principal is often called on to intervene in crisis situations such as a student on the verge of dropping out or a recurrent discipline issue (Weinstein, 1982). How the principal handles this aspect of the role is an important signal about his or her orientation to the ways adolescents are treated in the school.

With respect to the school more generally, the principal serves a linkage function to the broader community, which may be critical in developing external resources. The principal's potential impact is exemplified in one of Lightfoot's (1983) descriptions of excellent high schools. Of a school principal, he said the following:

[H]e also seems to think of his role at Carver as largely external. He has an ambitious vision and he expects that the resources for executing his plan will be found in the connections he creates with sources of power and influence far beyond the poor Black community. So much of his energy and intellect is spent making and sustaining these connections, moving outward and away from Carver. (p. 41)

A primary concern for the interventionist involves the way in which the principal supports and can become a resource for the proposed intervention. Principals generally have a keen sense of how the school operates and what kind of ideas can and cannot be implemented. Their support is often critical for initiating an intervention and for ensuring that it lasts.

Teachers The teacher has been characterized as the "immediate transmitter, contact, and instrument of schooling" (Murphy, 1987, p. 455). In addition to formal instruction, teachers provide students with help in other aspects of their lives. A recent study of public and special education high school teachers, for example, suggests teachers spend a good deal of time outside of class providing students with other types of help (Schmid et al., 1989). Because of this potent combination of formal and informal influence, teachers can be powerful resources for the development and continuity of interventions.

Various examples have been reported of how teachers have been involved as resources in interventions. Thus, teachers are often used to detect and manage classroom behavior problems early, before there is a need for formal referral (Graden, Casey, & Bonstrom, 1985). Teacher task forces have been used to work proactively to improve the school environment (Weinstein, 1982). Specific teachers develop significant informal relationships with various subgroups of students who are often not involved in the more ongoing life of the school.

The interventionist is concerned about assessing both the formal and informal connections that teachers have with students. In addition, teachers who are not currently involved in ongoing programs may have energy, ideas, and talents that are looking for a means of expression. The specific resource value of teachers depends on the kinds of problems to be solved, but an assessment of their connections and talents provides a useful set of data for integrating teacher resources into the intervention.

Mental health professionals Guidance counselors and mental health professionals such as school psychologists have had long-standing roles in the provision of resources to students. Although their job descriptions (Phye & Reschly, 1979) and training would seem to make them perfect resources to manage school problems, understaffing and administrative and service demands placed on mental health personnel often jeopardizes the delivery of timely and adequate services (Gibson, Mitchell, & Higgins, 1983; Phye & Reschly, 1979). Nonetheless, the institutional mandate of these professionals to provide such services plus their understanding of the kinds of issues facing adolescents in the school make them important sources for understanding the school and its resources. Indeed, freeing them up from such tasks as clerical work and scheduling (Gysbers & Moore, 1981; Medway & Nagle, 1982) may itself represent a useful intervention goal.

Other school personnel and "weak ties"
The principal, teachers, and in-school mental health personnel represent formal resources who, in different ways and in different settings, can be involved in the development and implementation of intervention activities. In addition to resources that evolve from formal roles, there are resources inherent in individuals who, because of personal style, serve latent organizational roles in dealing with the varied problems of adolescents. For example, it is not uncommon for adolescents defined as deviant by the dominant school culture to find subtle though real support from adults who are also not in the mainstream of school life.

One aspect of a consultation project reported elsewhere (Cherniss, Trickett, D'Antonio, & Tracy, 1982) exemplifies the value of understanding this process of informal support. A human relations-oriented drug education program was implemented using a group of teachers and guidance counselors selected by the school for their reputation as individuals who related well with adolescents. One particular guidance counselor was pointedly omitted from the selection because of his reputation as an unorthodox counselor who spent a great deal of time with students not officially assigned to him. Many of these students were minority students marginally involved in the school. This counselor argued vehemently for his inclusion in the training program precisely because of these informal contacts. He asserted that no other counselor was adequately connected to this segment of the school population. The original selection process had not seen this informal aspect of his role as a resource. His eventual inclusion, however, proved to be very beneficial for this group of minority students. Thus, the search for resources should not be limited to a focus on formal role nor to individuals who represent dominant values in the school culture.

The outside networks of students and adults are also potential resources for the development of an intervention. Called "weak ties" (Granovetter, 1973) in the social network literature, the out-of-school networks of school adults, peers, and the interventionist may serve as resources for the proposed intervention. The broader the interventionist's knowledge of school personnel representing different ideologies, races, and outside interests, the greater the breadth of potential resources to be tapped.

Peers The peer group can also serve as a resource for intervention. Through norms about acceptable behavior, sex, schoolwork, and help seeking, peers can serve a powerful role in designing interventions, and knowledge of peer-group norms and behaviors unearths important pieces of contextual data.

Evidence for the potentially positive role of peers during adolescence comes from literature on social support and from literature that demonstrates the effectiveness of peer interventions during this phase of the life span. Some studies, for example, have found greater perceived peer support to be associated with better school attendance and higher grade point averages (Barone, Deandreis, & Trickett, in preparation). For younger groups, peer tutoring has been shown to be an effective medium for increasing academic achievement (Gerber & Kauffman, 1981; Miller & Petersen, 1987). Evidence also suggests peers can play an important role in reducing tobacco, alcohol, and marijuana use (Botvin & Dusenbury, 1987).

Not all findings, however, point to the positive role of students as resources. In some studies, peer support has been associated with negative school outcomes, such as lower grade point averages, more school absences, and greater substance use (Cauce, Felner, & Primavera, 1982; Vaux, 1981). From an ecological perspective, such findings demonstrate the importance of assessing specific peer group norms before touting the positive role that peers may play as resources. (See Epstein, 1983, for an excellent example of the complex role of peer groups in affecting adolescent school outcomes.)

SETTINGS AS RESOURCES. Individuals, predictably, can be seen as resources. An ecologically based approach to intervention further suggests the value of assessing social settings as resources. Settings, in this usage, correspond to Barker's (1968) notion of a time- and space-bound entity with specific goals and functions, such as student government, the teachers' lounge, or the PTA. An analysis of current settings is not restricted to a differentiated picture of where and how the school functions to accomplish its tasks; it allows an analysis of what opportunities for adolescent development or organizational problem solving are present and what potential settings are missing.

Curricular settings, for instance, cn be categorized in terms of the amounts and types of resources they provide for students—available types of regular classroom instruction, special education services, specialized placements, therapies, and so on. These types of resources vary from setting to setting (Biklen, 1988) and their assessment will allow the interventionist to give careful consideration to how they might be brought to bear on the problem at hand. Extracurricular activities can also be important resources for students. Student government, athletic programs, and interest clubs can provide opportunities for students to gain skills, experiment with role structures, and enhance self-esteem (Newman & Newman, 1987).

How an assessment of settings can enhance intervention is described by Torrance (1982). In this example, a new setting was developed to enhance the self-esteem and commitment of a young boy with a history of vandalism:

The principal, the janitor, the teachers all worked on the problem of John, the vandal. . . . He was reported as being the culprit of many a weekend shambles at our school, but no one could prove anything. . . . The consensus, as a result of brainstorming, was that John did not feel he belonged. The problem was how to make him feel he did belong.

He was appointed by the Student Council (in which he could never be an officer, because of their strict code of grades and behavior) to be chairman of the lunchroom committee. He organized a team of boys; they spent half of their noon recess cleaning, moving tables, and helping the janitor. He began to notice litter which collected in certain windy corners of the schoolyard. His "gang" cleaned it up. He helped park cars for Back-to-School Night. . . . Happily, as John became part of the school, the vandalism became less and less. (p.486)

In assessing settings as resources, then, it is important for the interventionist not only to consider existing settings, but also to keep an eye out for potential settings that can be created in service of problem resolution. This type of analysis helps sharpen issues in adolescent–school transactions by breaking down the complex school environment into discrete parts. Setting-specific analysis and determination of setting needs can then follow.

EVENTS AS RESOURCES. Events in school signify important aspects of the school culture; like settings, they can serve as resources for both understanding and intervention. The themes of occasions highlight concerns in the broader school culture, and their atmosphere often allows informal interaction that is less role-bound than the interaction that may occur in the school's more ongoing settings. For example, the interventionist can learn about aspects of school personnel and adolescents that do not emerge in ongoing school life.

The role and value of events are demonstrated in the following description of a school that hosted its State's Special Olympics. Teachers, students, and parents worked collaboratively, provided a valuable service, made connections in the community, and enhanced students' sense of self-worth. The event's multifaceted nature is captured in this narrative:

One of the first stories Mastruzzi (the principal) tells me is about Kennedy's hosting of New York State's Special Olympics last year. From all over the state, thousands of handicapped athletes and their escorts arrived to compete against each other in the Olympic Games. For eighteen months, Mastruzzi and his staff planned and worked on this gala event. Although the races were the central event, there were also extravagant satellite events—a big parade, an evening of disco dancing, a fireworks display over the river, and games organized for participants who were not competing. Terrance Avenue, the street leading up to the school, was temporarily renamed with a street sign that read "Special Olympics." Hundreds of students, teachers, and parents volunteered their services; the event was extensively covered by the local media; and politicians and celebrities came to offer support and gain visibility. The film students at Kennedy documented the happenings through film and video, producing an inspiring short that brought tears to the eyes of faculty viewers when they saw it several months later. As he recounts the details, Mastruzzi beams with pride. He admits to liking the public relations and the community service aspects and feels glad Kennedy has the facilities to accommodate an event of this great magnitude. But his passion seems to be reserved for the kids as he reminds me of the Special Olympic motto "You are all winners." "I believe that is true for all the kids here at Kennedy. . . ." (Lightfoot, 1983, p. 62–63)

An event such as this provides a culminating point of school energies directed at bolstering self-worth and the value of all persons. The Special Olympics not only allowed an opportunity to provide service but also placed a landmark in the school's history that could be looked back on with pride.

Interventions can take the form of events that serve as catalysts for future activity. Vincent (1987) described one such event: a collaboratively structured meeting between the teachers and administrators of two schools that were about to merge. One agenda item for this "getting to know you" event was the planning of future steps to reduce between-school tensions. In like manner, Trickett and Birman (1989) describe the development of an in-service training meeting around the issue of international student adaptation to a U.S. high school. Themes from the meeting fed into future planning efforts. Thus, besides serving an immediate intervention goal, the design of events can aid in future planning and serve to validate the feelings of those involved in the intervention. Events then become vehicles for collaboration and empowerment.

Resource Perspective on Individuals

A resource perspective on student behavior in schools suggests (a) an emphasis on the strengths and competencies adolescents possess and (b) a need to understand students' attitudes toward resource use. Even among those adolescents who come to the attention of school personnel because of perceived deficits in school adaptation, there are settings, roles, and relationships where a positive identity is affirmed and supportive networks are generated. The search for adolescent competence, then, focuses on those places, roles, and people that bring out the best in the adolescent's coping repertoire. Such a perspective reinforces the importance of assessing individual behavior within a larger life space than the school. However, even within the school, it is unusual to find *no* settings where the adolescent is coping effectively. For example, in reviewing a year's worth of referrals in one predominantly blue-collar high school, O'Neill and Trickett (1973) found *no* student referred for psychological testing who was not seen by at least one of his or her teachers as coping adequately in class.

The subtleties of searching out adolescent competence are well illustrated in how adolescents from varying cultural backgrounds cope with the norms and demand characteristics of U.S. high schools. Often, the clash between the adolescent's culture of origin and the school context can mask the resourcefulness of the adolescent and lead to a misinterpretation of adolescent behavior. In one study, for example, Evans, Mantilla, and Royal (1987) described the case of a 14-year-old boy from El Salvador who was believed to be disinterested in school because he sometimes fell asleep in class. This particular youth had an unusual—indeed, chilling—history. He had been recruited for the army in El Salvador at age 8 and, at age 12, made his way alone from there to the Washington, DC, area. He had to support himself by working after school until 11 P.M., five days a week. He would then do his homework, sleep briefly, and come to school. Being an undocumented alien, he did not speak English well and had not confided the particulars of his situation to school personnel. This lack of knowledge prevented school personnel from appreciating both the dynamics of his in-school behavior and the extraordinary resources he showed in his out-of-school life.

A resource perspective on adolescents also directs attention to how students perceive and are willing to use interpersonal resources available to them from peer, adult, or family relationships. Tolsdorf (1976) and others (Iscoe, 1989; Vaux, 1988) have conceptualized and refined "network orientation," or an individual's willingness to use interpersonal resources. A nonaffiliative network orientation is characterized by a belief that help from others is unavailable, inadequate, or not to be trusted. An affiliative orientation, in contrast, is characterized by a greater willingness to use interpersonal resources. Individuals with this type of more affiliative orientation have been found to engage in more supportive interactions, to perceive support more positively, and to have greater resources (Vaux & Wood, 1987).

In a further refinement of this construct, Iscoe (1989) has found adolescent network orientation to vary, depending on whether the potential sources of support were family members, friends, or important nonfamily adults. Thus, assessment of a student's orientation to help from different reference groups, in addition to evaluation of strengths within the individual, becomes an important component of a resource perspective on the student in the school setting.

The Principal of Interdependence

In contrast to the cycling of resources principle, which alerts the interventionist to the manifest and latent resources of the school and the individual, the interdependence principle focuses on the nature of the connections among different components of the school and the individual's relationship to varied school contexts. The basic premise of the interdependence principle is similar to a basic tenet of systems theory (Von Bertallanfy, 1973): in a system, everything is connected to everything else.

Interdependence and the School Context

The interdependence principle suggests that connections exist among the structures, norms, attitudes, and policies that embody the social climate of the school. Further, it suggests that events and dynamics at one level of the system will impact what happens at another. Various aspects of the assessment process are implied by this principle, including (a) the nature and strength of connections among component parts of the school, and (b) the congruence among system components.

THE NATURE AND STRENGTH OF CONNECTIONS AMONG COMPONENT PARTS. The interdependence principle suggests that parts of a social system are connected; however, not all connections are of equal strength. Thus, changes in one aspect of the school do not radiate equally to all other aspects of the school. Trickett (1991) provides an example of how an alternative school changed significantly in its organizational structure and dynamics without any change in student perception of the classroom environment during this same time. In this instance, during a 3-year period shortly after the school began, a variety of efforts to tighten up the school were made: policies became more clearly articulated, expectations for student behavior and attendance became clearer and more broadly shared, and governance of the school become more efficient. During each of the years when these organizational developments were occurring, students reported on their perception of their classroom experience using the Classroom Environment Scale (Trickett & Moos, 1973). No significant changes in perceived classroom environment were reported during this time.

Assessing the strength of connections among component parts of the school alerts the interventionist to the ways in which a proposed intervention may be expected to affect the broader school context. Different types of interventions affect different parts of the school. Further, some interventions might affect only a few aspects of the school, while others may be more pervasive. For example, a change in the referral process may cause change in teacher behavior and in the structure of the helping services, but would not necessitate a fundamental reexamination of how deviance was defined. On the other hand, a significant increase in the number of foreign-born, non-English-speaking students in a school may sharpen the importance of understanding how the very definition of deviance is linked to cultural values and difficulties arising from lack of ability to speak English. Understanding the pervasive issues facing this population may indeed result in a broad-based examination of how both the curriculum and behavioral expectations of students are culture-bound. Such an assessment may result in changes that impinge on many aspects of school life.

CONGRUENCE OF CONNECTIONS Congruence of connections involves the degree to which the varied school settings the adolescent must negotiate daily operate in accordance with similar or differing values and norms. Perhaps the most common example involves the different demands that different classrooms place on students. Consultants in schools are familiar with the situation where students, leaving an exciting and energizing class for a boring and rigidly structured one, become unusually restless and are prone to being seen as bothersome in the latter class. Such differences in behavioral norms represent one example of how the congruence of setting demands is an important part of the assessment process.

Another concern is the issue of the congruence between intention at one level of the school system and impact at another. For example, it is not unusual to find that a new policy to improve the quality of education, while reasonable in itself, can inadvertently backfire. The Effective Schools Program (Edmonds, 1983), currently receiving national attention, stresses the creation of school environments that focus on various correlates of academic achievement, such as a safe learning environment, improved parent–school relationships, and high expectations for students. One school in which we are currently working is implementing such a program. Of particular concern to school personnel is the potential negative impact of increasing expectations for students without providing additional resources to help them fulfill the expectations. The worry is that more academically marginal students will view school as an even more difficult and punishing place. Similar concerns have been voiced by others (McDill, Natriello, & Pallas, 1986).

In general, the discussion of the interdependence principle and schools clarifies that interventions are not likely to impact only on those for whom they are intended. Further, the nature of the impact varies as a function of the degree of congruence among affected aspects of the school. Knowledge of the interdependencies that exist among people, policies, norms, and structures can inform both the design and evaluation of interventions.

The Interdependence Principle and Adolescent–School Transactions

Applied to the individual, the interdependence principle focuses on how adolescent behavior in the school setting reflects the joint contributions of persons and environments. The assessment implications include the gathering of data on individuals in multiple rather than single settings and the value of assessing the ways in which the settings of importance to the adolescent are themselves interdependent.

The importance of multiple setting assessment was highlighted in a useful paper by Moos and Fuhr (1982). Beth, a 15-year-old girl, was referred for school underachievement, dropping out, and depression. Rather than seeking to formulate Beth's problems as a reflection of intrapsychic stress, the authors began with some questions about how family, school, and parent work environments contributed to the girl's problems. Beth was asked to complete the Classroom Environment Scale (described earlier) to reflect both real and ideal perceptions of the classroom. The girl and her parents all completed real and ideal forms of the Family Environment Scale, a comparable scale for family social climate. Finally, both parents completed the Work Environment Scale, to examine how these environments might contribute to the identified problem. The results are summarized as follows:

Mr. and Mrs. B. were highly committed to and satisfied with their jobs and described their relationship to each other quite favorably. They both worked hard, enjoyed considerable responsibility, and were interested in pursuing their professional careers and obtaining higher level managerial positions. In contrast, Beth was very critical of both home and school. Although the family status quo was satisfactory for Mr. and Mrs. B., in view of their demanding work environments, it did not meet Beth's need for parental warmth and support, expression of feelings, or sense of belongingness that emerges from shared participation in family activities. Considering Beth enjoyed reading for pleasure and liked to engage in intellectual and cultural pursuits, and recalling that the major difference between real and ideal class descriptions involved affiliation, we concluded her school problems derived primarily from interpersonal and social factors, rather than academic factors.

Beth's "school problems" seemed to have their roots in her relationship to her parents. Beth's parents worked long and demanding hours, were physically and emotionally drained at the end of each day, and did not take sufficient time to understand and fulfill her emotional needs adequately. (pp. 118–119)

Based on this conceptualization of the problem, intervention plans were then made to change environmental contributors to the problem. Thus, an assessment that focused on the interdependence of the adolescent with multiple settings provided intervention implications both for the adolescent and the systems of which she was a part.

The case of Beth highlights a second implication of the interdependence principle and individual behavior: individual behavior in part reflects not only the interdependence of the individual with multiple settings but the relationship among the settings themselves. Bronfenbrenner (1979), in his influential book *The Ecology of Human Development*, called this level of influence the mesosystem. Using as an example the relationship between home and school as an influence on the developing child, Bronfenbrenner discussed how such factors as the nature and amount of contact between the home and school may influence the adolescent's school experience through information exchange, action plans, or more subtle attitude changes on the part of the family or school personnel.

At a more specific level, Power and Bartholomew (1987) have identified various patterns that characterize the interaction between family and school. For example, the *collaborative* relationship is characterized by open communication between family and school and an appropriate demarcation of roles and boundaries between parents and teachers; the *avoidant* relationship is characterized by distance between parents and teachers and results in a lack of communication and common goals across home and school. Each of these different types of relationships affects the potential problem facing adolescents and the kinds of interventions that may help. Thus, the interdependence principle applied to the individual highlights the transactional nature of behavior by suggesting the value of assessing individual behavior in multiple settings and the relationship of those settings to each other.

The Principle of Succession

The principle of succession in field biology focuses on how biological communities change over time as a function of internal and external influences. New forms and new adaptations succeed old ones as patterns useful in prior circumstances become dysfunctional under current ecological conditions and are replaced. Applied to schools and adolescents, the succession principle likewise emphasizes their development or evolutionary aspects. Both historical and anticipatory perspectives are included. The historical aspect focuses attention on those contextual influences that make the current school or adolescent more understandable as a function of institutional or individual history. Further, it defines the present as an evolving rather than a static state. The anticipatory aspect heightens the role that hopes and aspirations play in shaping settings, individuals, and interventions. Here, future orientation becomes a proactive force in assessment and intervention.

The Succession Principle and the School

The historical emphasis of the succession principle, most broadly conceived, draws attention to how the educational goals and social climate of the school have evolved and are reflected in its current structures, norms, attitudes, and policies. In sum, it focuses on institutional history. The assessment of institutional history is of both general and specific relevance to the interventionist. On a general level, such an understanding clarifies what, over time, the local culture has come to see as valued, appropriate, and supportable. Elsewhere, Kelly (1970) used the distinction between "gossamer" and "grit" to highlight that, in social contexts, some norms and values are peripheral while others are central to the local culture. Interventions that run counter to the "grit" of the setting are themselves at-risk, and only the historical approach to the school can clearly ferret those out. On a more specific level, a focus on the history of how problems have come to be defined and dealt with can, in like manner, inform the interventionist about the school's prior experience with interventions. Such data are critical in designing interventions that do not simply replicate past failures.

The succession principle further reinforces the notion that who and what schools nominate as problems are influenced by the larger zeitgeist. (See Sarason, 1983, for an elaboration.) Twenty years ago, for example, many high schools were coping with social unrest and student power movements (e.g., Ochberg & Trickett, 1970; Wittes, Chesler, & Crowfoot, 1975). The dynamics of activism and activists assumed priority and students who were not doing well academically but were not causing trouble were less likely to receive attention. Today, with the national push for academic excellence and accountability, academic nonachievers and disengaged youth are more likely to receive scrutiny and intervention. Thus, because there is a link between current social context and the definition of problems, the definition of deviance is further contextualized by attention to the succession principle.

The succession principle also draws attention to the fact that schools, as organizations, go through different stages or phases at different times. Various authors have proposed taxonomies for these stages. Kurpius (1985), for example, describes four phases: development, maintenance, decline, and crisis. Each phase is characterized by different goals and behaviors, which influence the setting's responsiveness to change. During the development phase, for example, energy and motivation for change are often high, while decline is characterized by a decrease in morale and little ability to develop the energy necessary for change. Others (e.g., Perkins, Nieva, & Lawler, 1983; Reinharz, 1984) have proposed similar frameworks.

The overall implication, however, is the importance of understanding that schools have institutional histories and go through phases or cycles that have implications for assessment and intervention on behalf of adolescents. For example, interventionists might capitalize on the high energy and openness during a school's evolution or growth period to create outward-looking programs or goals. However, were the school in a phase of crisis, emphasis might shift to internal conflict resolution and morale building, because school personnel would be expected to be preoccupied by internal issues and have little energy available for new program initiatives.

Finally, the succession principle includes an anticipatory component. Schools are not only influenced by their histories but by their hopes. Coping and hoping thus become important facets of the assessment process. Coping focuses on the structures, policies, and practices schools have developed to anticipate their future development. How well schools prepare for anticipated events—changing student populations in urban areas, the impact of changing household composition on home-school communication, and the implications, for academically marginal students, of increased expectations of student achievement—influence both schoolwide and individual problems.

Hoping focuses on the way in which current school culture and practices reflect what the school wants itself and its students to become. Such aspirations may be embodied in norms around achievement and deviance, themes communicated to parents via newsletters, and the energy the school puts into post-high-school planning for its graduates. Interventions that not only solve current problems but do so in a way that enhances the school's aspirations for itself are a priority. How individuals define "making the school a better place" thus becomes a relevant assessment task stemming from the succession principle.

The Succession Principle and the Adolescent

At an individual level, attention to the succession principle can help contextualize the adolescent's history and hopes. Much has already been said about how cultural background, family, and community contexts over the life cycle form an important aspect of the assessment process. From this series of transactions with various ecological systems, over time, comes the world view the adolescent brings to the school. Examples have been given, particularly with respect to foreign-born students in U.S. schools, about the potential for misinterpretation of adolescent behavior when the adolescent's sociocultural background is either ignored or distorted. The succession principle underscores sensitivity to how prior contexts influence the adolescent. Both history and hopes are emphasized.

The sociocultural perspective highlighted by the succession principle not only allows both the interventionist and school personnel to develop a contextual understanding of the behavior of others. It promotes the notion they, too, have, as a consequence of their own niche in the social order, developed values, preferences, and attitudes that are culture-bound. This awareness, in turn, increases the understanding of how interventions, often implicitly, flow from cultural assumptions about normality, appropriate behavior, and the skills necessary for success in the dominant culture. The succession principle cannot resolve these issues of value; rather, by reminding professionals that we all reflect a sociocultural history, it allows a more purposeful examination of how the helping process itself is embedded in a sociocultural context.

AN ECOLOGICAL PERSPECTIVE ON INTERVENTION

Prior sections of the chapter have outlined how an ecological perspective can be used to assess both the school as a social context and the adolescent in that context. If schools are to be strengthened through the design and implementation of interventions for adolescents, then knowledge of the school culture becomes as important as knowledge of the adolescent. The assessment of individual behavior as it is linked to the school context will often elucidate targets for intervention that affect the school as well as the adolescent—a needed change in policy; in-service training to educate teachers about cultural pluralism; renewed efforts to increase parental involvement with the school or to improve the adolescent's study skills and career aspirations. By focusing on the individual in context and the context itself, the ecological metaphor is intended to serve both the adolescent and the school.

Yet, successful intervention rests not only on identifying appropriate targets for change, but also on a simultaneous evaluation of what resources can be brought to bear on the proposed change. Here, the *process* of developing interventions becomes central, for, if the school is to benefit, it must be empowered as a consequence of the intervention. The search for resources and the emphasis on collaboration thus anchor the spirit of the intervention strategy. Various implications for intervention have already been mentioned. The intent of this final section is to discuss specific intervention processes and goals that flow from the four ecological principles previously described.

Adaptation and Intervention

Earlier, we discussed the adaptation principle as the broadest of the four ecological processes, the one that focuses most generally on the school context and the adolescent in that context. Its relevance to intervention processes and goals is likewise broad. Two implications of this premise are explored more fully here: (a) coupling the intervention with the host environment and (b) attending to the potential systemic implications of individually defined problems.

Coupling with the Host Environment

In the broadest sense, the spirit of the ecological metaphor is to design collaborative interventions specifically tailored to the particular setting where they occur. Where specific intervention technologies are concerned, they are adapted to the setting; the setting is not adapted to the technologies. This means getting to know what the setting is like, developing trusting relationships with relevant individuals and groups in the setting, and demonstrating commitment to the setting through the way the work is carried out.

By concentrating on setting characteristics as the context within which the intervention is designed, the ecological metaphor stresses the importance of involving setting members in shaping the setting in ways that are useful to them. The goal is to couple the intervention with the host environment in such a way that is has support, credibility, and what we have called elsewhere "constituent validity" (Trickett, 1991) or authenticity in the eyes of those whose setting it affects.

The intended consequence of this approach is not only to develop useful immediate programs or projects, however. The hope is that, through attending carefully to the process of developing such interventions, their effects will endure beyond the intervention itself. This is not a new hope; indeed, much of the early justification of mental health consultation expressed this goal. The contribution of the ecological metaphor is to specify a number of processes and topics that feed into system impact.

Although relatively little intervention work in schools has adopted this perspective, a few studies have begun to use research designs that address some of these issues. Graden and her colleagues (Graden et al., 1985), for example, monitored the degree to which an outside intervention became incorporated into the ongoing workings of the school over time. In a series of studies, referrals for special education evaluation and placement were examined one year prior to, during, and one year after implementation of a program to provide prereferral consultation to teachers. The inclusion of the postimplementation year, when outside personnel were no longer involved, was seen as an indicant of how well the program had been incorporated into the school setting.

In another study, Botvin and Dusenbury (1987) conducted a series of investigations to ensure that a drug diversion program initially run by outside interventionists could be run by teachers. In the first stage of this study, outside personnel conducted a drug prevention program in the school setting. Evaluation data suggested that the program was effective in reducing drug use. In order to check whether the program could be implemented using the resources within the school, a second stage of the study was conducted. Teachers implemented the project, and outcomes were evaluated. Findings suggested that the program could be equally well implemented by either group, thus increasing the confidence that the intervention could sustain itself once the outside interventionists left (see also Kelly & Hess, 1987). In sum, much is yet to be learned about how interventions can be coupled with schools in such a way that they can be incorporated into ongoing school life when the interventionist leaves. Attention to how this process occurs is clearly critical if interventions are intended to be empowering over the long run.

Systemic Implications of Individually Defined Problems

A second broad implication of the adaptation principle is a view of each instance of individual behavior in schools as reflecting on some aspect of the school environment. This stance reaffirms the notion that behavior is transactional and its sources seldom lie only in the adolescent who is defined as the problem. Because the context gives meaning to the behavior and defines it as appropriate or deviant, individual behavior tells us something about the context. An inquiry based on the kinds of situational assessment strategies previously mentioned can unearth the connections of behavior to the immediate environment. This is not to imply that adolescents transport no issues from setting to setting, or that, in general, the responsibility for adolescent behavior rests with the school and not the adolescent. Rather, the spirit is to use each instance of individually defined problems as an inroad to learning more about the culture of the school.

Even when individually defined problems are clearly the result of individual difficulties or traits, person-level interventions offer the opportunity for augmenting individual treatment with environmental changes that may affect the targeted student as well as other students. Snapp and Davidson (1982) offered two good examples of how a contextually oriented approach to individual cases paved the way for environmental change. In one instance, a young adolescent was referred to the school superintendent for possession of drugs. Subsequent examination of the problem suggested that drug use was a growing problem at the school. Rather than simply deal with this student through long-term suspension, the school psychologist, in unison with counselors, developed an intervention directed at reducing drug use among the boy and his peers. The student was allowed to return to school on the contingency that he and his friends would no longer use drugs at school. The individual problem was seen as an instance of a broader problem. In another case, a student served by multiple agencies became a partial stimulus for the formation of a school–community liaison group directed at improving communication and referral procedures between the school and outside service providers. Thus, even in cases where the focus is on individual change, system factors may be enhanced by considering the individual as, in part, reflecting system issues.

Cycling of Resources and Intervention

The adaptation principle suggests the broad goals and processes of intervention; the cycling of resources focuses on how the intervention is developed and assessed in terms of its resource potential for the school. Kelly (1987) stated two principles underlying the spirit of the resource perspective: (a) "The ecological paradigm advocates the conservation and management of resources" (p. 9), and (b) "The activating qualities of persons, settings, and events, are emphasized" (p. 11).

Conservation and Management of Resources as an Intervention Goal

The first principle, in addition to reaffirming the importance of assessing the school in terms of its resource potential, adopts an environmental criterion for gauging the success of the intervention. If the school as a social context is itself strengthened, then the intervention has accomplished its task. The emphasis on conservation reminds the interventionist that interventions in social settings *use* setting resources, which are often in short supply. Interventions thus involve resource exchange. The management-of-resources goal highlights the need to develop processes to integrate persons, settings, and events into the intervention plan.

How resources are combined depends on the ecology of the particular context and the problem around which resources are mobilized. In the previously discussed paper on an ecological approach to psychological testing (O'Neill and Trickett, 1973), interventions with individual adolescents varied depending on their own resources and those of the school and community. For some, teachers trusted by the adolescents were involved; for others, network members outside the school, such as local ministers, aided the effort.

Searching for Resources as an Intervention Process

The second principle focuses on the ongoing search for resources in the school through attending to "activating qualities." "By 'activating qualities,'" wrote Kelly (1987), "the ecological paradigm refers to such qualities as personal initiative, volunteering to help another (setting) member, spontaneous acts of providing information, bringing into the organization new ideas, expressing energy and enthusiasm for an idea, acknowledging and validating others' initiatives, etc." (pp. 11–12). Knowledge of formal and informal resources in the setting provides a guide for who and what may be incorporated into an intervention plan. This plan, in essence, creates the blueprint for new resources in the school.

An example of this process is found in Cherniss et al., (1982). Their work took place in a high school serving a racially mixed, predominantly blue-collar population. The student government was comprised of mostly White students who were active in school functions and academically successful. In the process of getting to know the school, it was discovered that a number of students, mostly Black, cared about improving the school but felt excluded from its ongoing life. The concerns of this group represented a latent resource that was not being tapped by the school.

The authors collaborated with the student government to create a School Effectiveness Committee, comprised of student government members and members of the more marginal groups. This committee met for over a year as an action organization, identifying and dealing with issues that had not come to the attention of the student government. It increased school awareness of the concerns of more marginal members and validated their perspectives and carings about the school. The identification of latent resources was transformed into a new setting for both students and school.

A resource perspective, then, focuses on how to define and mobilize resources in the creation of interventions. It advocates a commitment to assessing intervention impact in terms of its resource value to the school, and intends to create resources that will last after the intervention ends. Such resources can include persons with new skills and understandings, settings not previously available, and events that provide spinoffs for future problem solving.

The Interdependence Principle and Intervention

As defined earlier, the interdependence principle asserts the importance of considering interconnections between parts of the system. Several aspects of the interdependence principle are relevant to the processes and goals of intervention. They include (a) assessing the congruence between the proposed intervention and the local context of the school; (b) actively searching for positive and negative side effects; and (c) developing processes for monitoring feedback from relevant school personnel.

Congruence Between Proposed Intervention and the School

The first intervention implication focuses on how the proposed intervention fits into the overall culture of the school in terms of its processes and its intent. Although it may seem unnecessary to discuss the notion that proposed interventions should be congruent with the school culture, intervention literature suggests otherwise. The predictable issues facing interventions that run counter to widely accepted norms and values were nicely described by Corbett, Firestone, and Rossman (1987) in their analysis of the responses of three high schools to various changes in curriculum and discipline policy. Changes that challenged highly regarded or "sacred" norms met with open resistance, whereas changes that were more consonant with the school norms were more readily incorporated. Thus, in one school where quality classroom instruction was seen as paramount, introduction of new teaching techniques to improve learning was widely accepted. In another school, new mandates for competency testing for departing students required instructional energy that ran counter to faculty emphasis on autonomy and specialization. Antagonism between staff and administrators ensued and compliance took place only under mandate.

The complexities of these types of changes are eloquently summarized by the authors:

Essentially, our discussion should put the issues of resistance to planned change in a new perspective. It seems likely that change of any magnitude at all will touch norms deeply rooted in the school's culture. Managing change requires more than artfully adjusting the process to minimize barriers and maximize incentives. The normative content of the changes must also be considered. Change redefines what is and ought to be in a school. Attacks on existing definitions, especially those that concern professional purpose, engender resistance and opposition. As seen (at one of the schools), behavioral changes can be implemented, but at a considerable cost to morale and productive staff relationships and without internalizing the norms necessary for change to last. Managing change, like politics, is the art of the possible. But it requires knowing what changes are inherently compatible with the local culture and which ones are not, and which ones can be repackaged to fit existing norms.

Such knowledge comes from understanding individual schools and is not easily gained at the higher levels of the educational system where policies are generated. There is a tendency from above to view schools as empty vessels that can be filled and refilled according to changing public concerns and reform agendas. This tendency rests on the assumption that schools are value-free, easily adjusted organizations. This, of course, is far from the case. Schools not only teach values but also have a value structure embedded in them.

. . . It is sometimes appropriate and necessary to attempt to change aspects of a school's culture. Some of the changes studied in the three high schools were misguided not only because they challenged sacred norms, but also because the challenge went unrecognized. If changes are to be successful, then initiators must understand how the culture will accept the proposed innovation and where the culture itself needs modification. (pp. 56–57)

Actively Searching for Side Effects

It is axiomatic that interventions carry with them unanticipated consequences (Argyris, 1970; Kelly, 1987). The significance of this issue validates the basic premise of the interdependence principle: because aspects of the school are themselves interconnected, interventions that directly affect certain aspects of the system ripple across other aspects, thus yielding indirect consequences. That such consequences are often labeled "unanticipated" highlights both the complex nature of social systems and the relative lack of conceptual attention to the interdependence in the local ecology when implementing interventions.

The active search for side effects can take numerous forms. For example, in evaluating the effects of interventions, multiple outcome variables may be employed. These may include both positive and negative outcomes and may cut across individuals and settings. Maher and Bennett (1984) provided an example of this approach. They advocated a sequential evaluation process that examines broad learning environment and behavioral variables both before and after educational intervention. Others have suggested the use of "consumer" surveys to tap reactions of intervention participants, as well as of those who might be indirectly impacted by the intervention, as a means of identifying potentially unintended side effects (Maher & Kruger, 1985).

The active search for side effects serves a variety of functions for the ecologically oriented interventionist. First, it demonstrates a caring about the school over and above the impact of the intervention on those individuals directly affected by it. Second, it promotes the development of collaborative processes with school personnel so that such effects can be noted. Where negative, these effects can be minimized in terms of impact; where positive, they can be capitalized on as a new resource for the setting. Thus, the search for side effects can have both content and process benefits for the interventionist and the school.

Developing Processes for Monitoring Feedback

This aspect of the interdependence principle is broader than the creation of collaborative processes to detect side effects. The intent is to create, between interventionist and school, an interdependence that clarifies both the fundamental nature of the collaboration and, more specifically, the accountability of the interventionist to the school.

Multiple purposes are served by the proactive development of accountability structures and processes. In addition to affirming collaborative intent, the involvement of the school personnel promotes empowerment and opens channels for both formal and informal interactions. By so doing, it increases the chance that proposed interventions will be fully discussed ahead of time in terms of their implications for different aspects of the school. This, in turn, increases the possibility that they can be structured in a way that is most useful to the school.

Such feedback mechanisms can take a variety of forms. Kelly and Associates (1979) created, in various schools, paid positions for school personnel who served not only as in-house coordinators of activities but also as providers of guidance about how research should proceed. Further, the principal of one of the schools was invited to contribute a chapter to the book, reporting the research, in which he outlined the varied costs and benefits of the research collaboration from the perspective of the school. Trickett and Gibson (1980) reported the development of groups of citizens and mental health service providers in four regions of Maryland, to provide input on what data should be gathered and how results should be interpreted around issues of the community support needs of the chronically mentally disabled. The mechanisms themselves may take varied forms, but their overall intent is to promote collaboration and accountability in the intervention process.

Intervention and the Succession Principle

Applying the succession principle to intervention practices in schools requires the interventionist to consider historical and anticipatory trends in that setting. Consideration of these issues provides a framework for designing and implementing interventions that show respect for the traditions and folkways of both the individual and the school. It can provide an antidote to making quick and acontextual judgments about either the behavior of the adolescent or the attitudes and policies enforced by school personnel. In this regard, two final points bear mention: (a) assessing prior intervention efforts in the school, and (b) the importance of working with schools over time.

Assessing Prior Intervention Efforts

Previously, we discussed the value of understanding institutional history more generally as part of the assessment process. Here, the focus is more specifically tied to institutional history surrounding past intervention efforts in the school. In assessing the usefulness of newly proposed interventions, school members understandably draw on their past experience with other change efforts. This history affects how they process the interventionist and what concerns they have about being involved in the intervention.

In one school where we have been recently working, for example, both the principal and teachers have felt bombarded during recent years by a variety of imposed programs from administrative leaders. These programs had a short life: they were implemented without adequate preparation of school personnel and then were withdrawn when a new idea appeared. Often, teachers were forced to meet in multiple committees with unclear agendas, to carry out these imposed programs. It was not surprising, then, that we, as outsiders who had been invited to enter the school by the principal rather than the teachers, found that the teachers resisted any intervention that "required more work of them." Regardless of the possible value of the collaboration, the teachers' history with interventions coming from the outside made them skeptical about both their value and the credibility of outsiders who proposed them. Under these ecological conditions, the intervention task focused on the development of a group of teachers interested in designing their own interventions. The history of prior interventions can become a useful source of knowledge for the interventionist.

A Longitudinal Time Perspective on the Interventionist–School Relationship

This topic focuses on the advantages of a long-term relationship between the interventionist and the school. In advocating the value of sustained contact between interventionist and school over a period of time, the ecological perspective is affirming that (a) it takes time to develop an understanding of the school and a trusting collaborative relationship with school personnel; (b) interventions themselves can have an evolutionary trajectory, with initial efforts leading to subsequent work that builds on the initial intervention; and (c) the overarching concern is to strengthen the school as a setting, in terms of its resources for problem solving. The image is of a relationship that can deepen and diversify as new events unfold in the school, as new resources become available to the interventionist, and as the positive side effects of early interventions are used to develop new initiatives.

Such a longitudinal perspective can enhance both theory and impact. With respect to theory, much has been written about both schools and intervention, but minimal data are available on many of the questions raised by an ecological perspective. How do schools create resources for problem solving? How do school characteristics interact with adolescents of varying cultural backgrounds to influence educational and psychological outcomes? What characterizes the different phases schools go through, and how do those phases affect the implementation of interventions? Can interventions, over time, affect how schools define and deal with deviance? These and other ecologically based questions require longitudinal time frames, multiple methods of inquiry, and ongoing relationships. Such data form the generative base for designing interventions of use to adolescents *and* schools.

A similar set of questions arises with respect to the impact of interventions themselves. We have few natural histories of interventions implemented in schools (see however, Smith & Keith, 1971). More frequently, programs and their effects are reported in terms of their impact on the individual program recipients, not the settings where the programs were implemented. An ecological approach to intervention *starts* with the concern for school impact and focuses on how technologies can mesh with different kinds of school cultures to achieve school as well as individual impact. The process by which interventions can evolve into school resources is in need of elaboration through example. Thus, the ecological principle of succession suggests that a longitudinal perspective on the interventionist–school relationship is both conceptually and pragmatically valuable.

ECOLOGICALLY BASED INTERVENTION—A BRIEF EXAMPLE

The preceding sections have outlined an ecological perspective on schools, adolescents, and intervention, and have used varied examples of research and intervention to illustrate aspects of the ecological perspective. The intent here is to provide a brief synopsis of a particular intervention based on an ecological approach, in order to highlight certain of its distinctive characteristics. More full-blown case studies are available elsewhere (Kelly & Hess, 1987), but the present report outlines how an ecological mind-set translates into intervention activities and goals.

The project involved the development of a long-term relationship with a public high school that was serving as a site for a research project on the role of social networks in school adaptation. One aspect of the relationship with the school involved the development of a quid pro quo in exchange for their collaboration in the research. The vehicle for this collaboration was a graduate course taught by one of the authors (EJT). Called "Research as Intervention," the course was based on an ecological perspective and was designed to couple social science methodology and data-gathering skills with preventive intervention goals. More specially, the course involved working with public schools on problems they deemed important. Our task was to learn about how a problem was expressed in the school environment and develop collaborative processes to address it.

Several steps in this process reflected the values and assumptions of the ecological metaphor. The first step, collaboration with school personnel about the definition of the problem, involved a variety of meetings with the principal and guidance counselors about the issues they faced for which we had some potential expertise to contribute to the collaboration. The primary issue emerging from these discussions involved how to cope with the increasing number of foreign-born students who were entering the school. These, students, primarily from Central and South America, the Caribbean, and Southeast Asia, represented a wide range of cultural and linguistic backgrounds, prior educational histories, and reasons for immigrating to the United States.

Rather than be pressed into the role of providing direct service for these students, we negotiated for a broader perspective: assessment of how these students were experiencing the school and how the school was processing these students. Our belief was that only by generating such knowledge of student–school transactions could we design appropriate interventions. Environmental reconnaissance was thus at the core of the process.

Three ecological guidelines influenced how this reconnaissance process was conducted: (a) building an empowering relationship with various groups in the school; (b) developing a multilevel conception of the issues facing foreign-born students and school personnel; and (c) assessing the school's manifest and latent resources. With respect to building empowering relationships, our emphasis was to ensure that various groups in the school knew about our agenda, understood that it resulted from a collaborative process, and felt that their perspectives were represented in data gathering. Included in these interviews were administrators, teachers who held a variety of views about foreign-born students, and students, both foreign-born and U.S. born.

In these various interviews, we probed for how school structures, norms, attitudes, and policies impacted on both the student and teacher experience. This allowed us to develop the ways in which various levels of ecological influence contributed to the issues surrounding foreign-born students. We found that family circumstances, school system placement policies, and teacher norms about "appropriate" classroom behavior all contributed to an understanding of the ecology of these students. The importance of developing the multilevel understanding was at least twofold. First, it provided a basis for counteracting the person-blame attributions of some teachers who did not understand either the cultural norms or the social circumstances of many of the students; second, it generated a variety of potential intervention options ranging from the provision of individual services to discussions of school system policy. All these levels of intervention seemed justified on the basis of our data.

Throughout the course of these interviews, we were consciously on the lookout for those persons, settings, and events that could be resources to the students and the school. While certain individuals, such as the ESOL (English for Speakers of Other Languages) teachers, were among the obvious resources, other teachers were found who were not publicly acknowledged as caring about this group of students. Further, we could not always predict on a seemingly rational basis who had energy to work with these students and who did not. The librarian showed great interest and an initiative that was unknown to most other teachers in the school; the psychology teacher was manifestly disinterested in issues facing foreign-born students. Settings such as the International Club and events such as the annual International Dinner were also explored to see how their resource value might be increased.

Translating the Data into an Intervention

As a consequence of these varied activities, we developed a broad range of data about the issues facing both students and the school. The next step involved translating our knowledge into an intervention. In conjunction with the principal and the ESOL teachers, we decided that the most beneficial short-term strategy was to develop an in-service training session with the teachers. This meeting would have three goals, suggested by our inquiry as important: (a) helping teachers understand the implications of cultural pluralism for student behavior in the classroom; (b) promoting a richer and more complex picture of the difficulties facing foreign-born students, thereby fostering a stronger systemic commitment to them; and (c) providing a forum where teachers could share with one another the thoughts that they had shared with us.

The processes involved in creating the in-service training likewise reflected our concern with empowerment through collaboration. The ESOL teachers agreed to assume primary responsibility for structuring the in-service training, because they had insider knowledge of both the issues facing these students and the teacher culture around what worked and what did not. Further, their involvement would heighten other teachers' awareness of them as resources for their colleagues in dealing with these students.

The first decision about the in-service training was to develop a small group format. In a school with over 130 teachers, this seemed essential if discussion and sharing of experiences were the goals. Each group followed the same procedure. The session began with one of the ESOL teachers addressing the group in Arabic, a language no other teacher spoke. The intent was to place the teachers immediately in the position of so many of the foreign-born students, who were not able to understand what they were supposed to do in the classroom. Another ESOL teacher then showed a videotape of ESOL students at the school discussing their school experiences. Coming from students who were known to many of the teachers, these comments rang true and caused considerable discussion about classroom management and behavior issues that teachers felt unable to understand or deal with. Finally, the graduate students, who themselves represented different minority groups, spoke about what they had learned from interviewing teachers and students during the year. They fed back to the teachers the results of the teacher interviews, and presented contrasting portraits of Asian, Hispanic, and Black foreign-born students in terms of the cultures they came from and their impressions of the school.

The final meeting brought all the teachers together with the principal and the countywide director of placement and guidance for foreign-born students. Many policy-related questions had been raised, and discussion was lively. Most importantly, this aspect of the in-service training was intended both to provide a larger context of support for the teachers and to promote a commitment to caring about the foreign-born students. The principal voiced support for the collaboration between us and the school and stated an intent to push for additional external resources in the future.

The preceding description neither represents the end of the intervention story in this particular high school nor adequately represents all the activities conducted during the relevant time period (see Trickett and Birman, 1989). However, it is intended to provide a sampling of how the concepts presented in this chapter guided our activities. Thicker, richer descriptions of such work are needed to amplify further the distinctiveness of the ecological approach.

SUMMARY

The intent of this chapter has been to provide the contours of an ecological perspective on school, adolescents in schools, and interventions designed to be useful to both. Four ecological processes have been elaborated as relevant to this task. The school as a social context represents an important site for the work of mental health professionals. The impact of that work is magnified when efforts are made to aid schools in their efforts to help adolescents in addition to providing service to adolescents themselves. Doing so requires both a framework for assessing the school as a social context and intervention goals involving system impact. The ecological metaphor is intended to stimulate thought and activity around these issues.

REFERENCES

Argyis, C. (1970). *Intervention theory and method: A behavioral science view.* Reading, MA: Addison-Wesley.

Barker, R. (1968). *Ecological psychology.* Stanford, CA: Stanford University Press.

Barone, C., Deandreis, A., & Trickett, E. (in preparation). *A longitudinal study of high school transition: Social problem solving, life stress and social support as predictors of adjustment.* University of Maryland, College Park.

Biklen, D. (1988). Myth of clinical judgment. *Journal of Social Issues, 44,* 127–140.

Botvin, G., & Dusenbury, L. (1987). Life skills training: A psychoeducational approach to substance-abuse prevention. In C. Maher & J. Zins (Eds.), *Psychoeducational interventions in the schools* (pp. 46–65). New York: Pergamon Press.

Boyer, E. (1983). *High school: A report on secondary education in America.* New York: Harper & Row.

Bronfenbrenner, U. (1979). *The ecology of human development.* Cambridge: Harvard University Press.

Brophy, J. (1986). Teacher influences on student achievement. *American Psychologist, 41,* 1069–1077.

Caplan, G. (1970). *Theory and practice of mental health consultation.* New York: Basic Books.

Cauce, A., Felner, R., & Primavera, J. (1982). Social support in high risk adolescents: Structural components and adaptive impact. *American Journal of Community Psychology, 14,* 417–428.

Cherniss, C., Trickett, E., D'Antonio, M., & Tracy, K. (1982). Involving students in organizational change in a high school. In J. Alpert (Ed.)., *Psychological consultation in educational settings* (pp. 108–142). San Francisco: Jossey-Bass.

Corbett, H., Firestone, W., & Rossman, G. (1987). Resistance to planned change and the sacred in school cultures. *Educational Administration Quarterly, 23,* 36–59.

Cusick, P. (1983). *the egalitarian ideal and the American high school.* New York: Longman.

Edgar, E., & Hayden, A. (1985). Who are the children special education should serve and how many children are there? *Journal of Special Education, 18,* 523–539.

Edmonds, R. (1983). *Programs of school improvement: an overview.* Washington, DC: National Institute of Education.

Epstein, J. (1983). The influence of friends on achievement and affective outcomes. In J. Epstein & N. Karweit (Eds.), *Friends in school: Patterns of selection and influence in secondary schools* (pp. 177–200). New York: Academic Press.

Evans, A. C., Mancilla, Y., & Royal, J. (1987). *Transcultural transitions: An ecological study of interracial high school students.* Paper presented at the meeting of the Eastern Psychological Association, Arlington, VA.

Gelb, S., & Mizokawa, D. (1986). Special education and social structure: The commonality of "exceptionality." *American Educational Research Journal, 23,* 543–557.

Gerber, M., & Kauffman, J. (1981). Peer tutoring in academic settings. In P. Strain (Ed.), *The utilization of classroom peers as behavior change agents.* New York: Plenum Press.

Gibson, R., Mitchell, M., & Higgins, R. (1983). *Development and management of counseling programs and guidance services.* NY: Macmillan.

Glass, G., Cohen, L., Smith, M., & Filby, N. (1982). *School class size: Research and policy.* Beverly Hills, CA: Sage.

Good, T., & Weinstein, R. (1986). Schools make a difference: Evidence, criticisms, new directions. *American Psychologist, 41,* 1090–1097.

Gooden, W. (1975). *The relationship between race, personality, and satisfaction in an alternative high school.* Unpublished manuscript, Yale University.

Goodlad, J. (1984). *A place called school.* New York: McGraw-Hill.

Gottlieb, B. (1975). The contribution of natural support systems of primary prevention among four social subgroups of adolescent males. *Adolescence, 10,* 207–219.

Graden, J., Casey, A., & Bonstrom, O. (1985). Implementing a prereferral intervention system: Part II. The data. *Exceptional Children, 51,* 487–496.

Granovetter, M. (1973). The strength of weak ties. *American Journal of Sociology, 78,* 1360–1380.

Gruber, J., & Trickett, E. (1986). Can we empower others? The paradox of empowerment in the governing of an alternative public school. *American Journal of Community Psychology, 15,* 353–372.

Gysbers, N., & Moore, E. (1981). *Improving guidance programs.* Englewood Cliffs, NJ: Prentice-Hall.

Harris, G., & Dawes, R. (1988). *The business management and service tasks of the school principalship.* Springfield, IL: Thomas.

Huebner, E. S. (1988). Bias in teachers' special education decisions as a function of test score reporting format. *Journal of Educational Research, 81,* 217–220.

Iscoe, E. (1989). *A measure of adolescent network orientations by reference groups.* Poster presented at the annual meeting of the American Psychological Association, New Orleans.

Kelly, J. (1968). Towards an ecological conception of preventative interventions. In J. W. Carter (Ed.), *Research contributions from psychology to community mental health* (pp. 76–100). New York: Behavioral Publications.

Kelly, J. (1970). Antidotes for arrogance: Training for community psychology. *American Psychologist, 25,* 524–531.

Kelly, J. (1971). Qualities for the community psychologist. *American Psychologist, 26,* 897–903.

Kelly, J. (1986). Context and process: An ecological view of the interdependence of practice and research. *American Journal of Community Psychology, 14,* 581–589.

Kelly, J. (1987). An ecological paradigm: Defining mental health consultation as a prevention service: In J. Kelly & R. Hess (Eds.), *The ecology of prevention: Illustrative mental health consultation* (pp. 1–36). New York: Haworth Press.

Kelly, J. G. (1979). *Adolescent boys in high school: A psychological study of coping and adaptation.* Hillsdale, NJ: Erlbaum.

Kelly, J., & Hess, R. (Eds.). (1987). *The ecology of prevention: Illustrative mental health consultation.* New York: Haworth Press.

Knoff, H. (1987). School-based interventions for discipline problems. In C. Maher & J. Zins (Eds.), *Psychoeducational interventions in the schools* (pp. 118–140). New York: Pergamon Press.

Kurpius, D. (1985). Consultation interventions: Successes, failures, proposals. *Counseling Psychologist, 13,* 368–389.

Lightfoot, S. (1983). *The good high school.* New York: Basic Books.

Linney, J., & Seidman, E. (1989). The future of schooling. *American Psychologist, 44,* 336–340.

Maher, C., & Bennett, R. (1984). *Planning and evaluating education services.* Englewood Cliffs, NJ: Prentice-Hall.

Maher, C., & Kruger, L. (1985). Best practices in evaluating educational programs. In A. Thomas & J. Grimes (Eds.), *Best practices in school psychology* (pp. 275–285). Columbus, OH: Association of School Psychologists.

Matute-Bianchi, M. (1986). Ethnic identities and patterns of school success and failure among Mexican-descent and Japanese-American students in a California high school: An ethnographic analysis. *American Journal of Education, 95,* 233–255.

McDill, E., Natriello, G., & Pallas, A. (1986). A population at risk: Potential consequences of tougher school standards for student dropouts. *American Journal of Education, 94,* 135–181.

Medway, F., & Nagle, R. (1982). Improving discipline in a high school. In J. Alpert (Ed.), *Psychological consultation in educational settings* (pp. 143–173). San Francisco: Jossey-Bass.

Meyers, J. (1981). Mental health consultation. In J. Conoley (Ed.), *Consultation in schools: Theory, research, practices* (pp. 35–56). Hillsdale, NJ: Erlbaum.

Miller, J. & Petersen, D. (1987). Peer-influenced academic interventions. In C. Maher & J. Zins (Eds.), *Psychoeducational interventions in the schools* (pp. 81–100). New York: Pergamon Press.

Mills, R., & Kelly, J. (1972). Cultural adaptation and ecological analysis: Analysis of three Mexican villages. In S. Golann & C. Eisdorfer (Eds.), *Handbook of community mental health* (pp. 157–205). New York: Appleton-Century-Crofts.

Moos, R. (1979). *Evaluating educational environments.* San Francisco: Jossey-Bass.

Moos, R., & Fuhr, R. (1982). The clinical use of social ecological concepts: The case of an adolescent girl. *American Journal of Orthopsychiatry, 52,* 111–122.

Moos, R., & Trickett, E. (1979). Determinants of classroom environments. In R. Moos (Ed.), *Evaluating educational environments* (pp. 159–182). San Francisco: Jossey-Bass.

Moos, R., & Trickett, E. (1987). *Classroom environment scale manual* (2nd ed.). Palo Alto, CA: Consulting Psychologists Press.

Murphy, J. (1987). Educational influences. In V. Hasselt & M. Hersen (Eds.), *Handbook of adolescent psychology* (pp. 442–457). New York: Pergamon Press.

Murray, H. (1938). *Explorations in personality.* New York: Oxford University Press.

National Coalition of Advocates for Students (NCAS). (1988). *New voices: Immigrant students in U.S. public schools.* Boston: Author.

Newman, B., & Newman, P. (1987). The impact of high school on social development. *Adolescence, 22,* 525–534.

Ochberg, F., & Trickett, E. (1970). Administrative responses to racial conflict in a high school. *Community Mental Health Journal, 6,* 470–482.

O'Neill, P., & Trickett, E. (1973). *Ecological considerations in psychological testing.* Paper presented at the annual convention of the American Psychological Association, Montreal, Canada.

O'Neill, P., & Trickett, E. (1982). *Community consultation.* San Francisco: Jossey-Bass.

Parsons, R., & Meyers, J. (1984). *Developing consultation skills.* San Francisco: Jossey-Bass.

Perkins, N., Nieva, N., & Lawler, E. (1983). *Managing creation: The challenge of building new organizations.* New York: Wiley.

Phye, G., & Reschly, D. (Eds.). (1979). *School psychology: Perspectives and issues.* New York: Academic Press.

Power, T., & Bartholomew, K. (1987). Family–school relationship patterns: An ecological assessment. *School Psychology Review, 16,* 498–512.

Pugach, M. (1985). The limitations of federal special education policy: The role of classroom teachers in determining who is handicapped. *Journal of Special Education, 19,* 123–137.

Reinharz, S. (1984). Alternative settings and social change. In K. Heller, R. Price, S. Reinharz, & A. Wandersman (Eds.), *Psychology and community change* (2nd ed.) (pp. 286–336). Chicago, IL: Dorsey Press.

Reschly, D. (1987). Learning characteristics of mildly handicapped students: Implications for classification, placement and programming. In M. Wang, M. Reynolds, & H. Wolberg (Eds.), *Handbook of special education* (pp. 35–58). New York: Pergamon Press.

Rutter, M. (1983). School effects on pupil progress: Research findings and policy implications. *Child Development, 54,* 1–29.

Rutter, M., Maughan, B., Mortimore, P., Ouston, J., & Smith, A. (1979). *Fifteen thousand hours.* Cambridge, MA: Harvard University Press.

Sarason, S. (1971). *The cultural of the school and the problem of change.* Boston: Allyn & Bacon.

Sarason, S. (1983). *Schooling in America: Scapegoat and salvation.* New York: Free Press.

Sarason, S. B., Levine, M., Goldenberg, I. I., Cherlin, D., & Bennett, E. M. (1966). *Psychology in community settings.* New York: Wiley.

Schmid, K., Schatz, C., Walter, M., Shidla, M., Leone, P., & Trickett, E. (1989). *Providing help: Characteristics and correlates across three groups of teachers.* Paper presented at annual Teacher Educators for Children with Behavioral Disorders Conference, Tempe: AZ.

Sedlak, M., Wheeler, C., Pullin, D., & Cusick, P. (1986). *Selling students short.* New York: Teachers College Press.

Smith, L., & Keith, P. (1971). *Anatomy of an educational intervention: An organizational analysis of an elementary school.* New York: Wiley.

Snapp, M., & Davidson, J. (1982). Systems interventions for school psychologists: A case study approach. In C. Reynolds & T. Gutkin (Eds.), *The handbook of school psychology* (pp. 858–870). New York: Wiley.

Tolsdorf, C. (1976). Social networks, support, and coping: An exploratory study. *Family Process, 15,* 407–417.

Torrance, E. (1982). Identifying and capitalizing on the strengths of culturally different children. In C. Reynolds & T. Gutkin (Eds.), *The handbook of school psychology* (pp. 481–500). New York: Wiley.

Trickett, E. (1978). Towards a social–ecological conception of adolescent socialization: Normative data on contrasting types of public schools. *Child Development, 49,* 408–414.

Trickett, E. (1984). Towards a distinctive community psychology: An ecological metaphor for training and the conduct of research. *American Journal of Community Psychology, 12,* 261–279.

Trickett, E. (1987). Consultation as a preventative intervention. In J. Kelly & R. Hess (Eds.), *The ecology of prevention: Illustrative mental health consultations* (pp. 187–204). NY: Haworth Press.

Trickett, E. (1991) *Living an idea: Empowerment and the evolution of an alternative high school.* Brookline, MA: Brookline Books.

Trickett, E., & Birman, D. (1989). Taking ecology seriously: A community development approach to individually-based interventions. In L. Bond & B. Compas (Eds.), *Primary prevention in the schools.* Hanover, NH: University Press of New England.

Trickett, E. J., & Gibson, M. J. (1980). *The community support project: Final report on needs assessment, education, and the participatory planning process*. Unpublished manuscript. University of Maryland, College Park.

Trickett, E., Kelly, J., & Todd, D. (1972). The social environment of the high school: Guidelines for individual change and organizational development. In S. Golann & C. Eisdorfer (Eds.), *Handbook of community mental health* (pp. 331–406). New York: Appleton-Century-Crofts.

Trickett, E., Kelly, J., & Vincent, T. (1985). The spirit of ecological inquiry in community research. In D. Klein & E. Susskind, *Knowledge building in community psychology* (pp. 283–333). New York: Praeger.

Trickett, E., McConahay, J., Phillips, D., & Ginter, M. (1985). Natural experiments and the educational context: The environment and effects of an alternative inner-city public on adolescents. *American Journal of Community Psychology, 13*, 617–643.

Trickett, E., & Mitchell, R. (in press). An ecological metaphor for research and intervention in community psychology. In M. S. Gibbs, J. Lachenmeyer, & J. Sigal (Eds.), *Community psychology: Theoretical and empirical approaches*. New York: Wiley.

Trickett, E., & Moos, R. (1973). The social environment of junior high and high school classrooms. *Journal of Educational Psychology, 65*, 93–102.

Trickett, E. J., & Moos, R. N. (1979). Determinants of classroom environments. In R. H. Moos, *Evaluating educational environments*. San Francisco: Jossey-Bass. 159–182.

Trickett, E., & Todd, D. (1972). The assessment of the high school culture: an ecological perspective. *Theory into Practice, 11*, 28–37.

Trickett, E., Trickett, P., Castro, J., & Schaffner, P. (1982). The independent school experiences: Aspects of the normative environment of single-sex and co-ed secondary schools. *Journal of Educational Psychology, 74*, 375–381.

Tucker, J. (1980). Ethnic proportions in classes for the learning disabled: Issues in nonbiased assessment. *Journal of Special Education, 14*, 93–105.

U. S. Department of Health, Education, and Welfare (n.d). *Directions of elementary and secondary school districts and schools in selected districts: School year 1978–79, Volume 1*. Washington, DC: U.S. Government Printing Office.

Vaux, A. (1981). *Psychological, health, and behavioral consequences of adolescent life stress and social support*. Paper presented at the Western Psychological Association meeting, Los Angeles, CA.

Vaux, A. (1988). *Social support: Theory, research, and intervention*. New York: Praeger.

Vaux, A., & Wood, J. (1987). Social support resources, behavior, and appraisals: A path analysis. *Social Behavior and Personality, 15*, 107–111.

Vincent, T. (1987). Two into one: An ecological perspective on school consultation. In J. Kelly & R. Hess (Eds.), *The ecology of prevention: Illustrating mental health consultation* (pp. 113–149). New York: Haworth Press.

Von Bertalanfy, L. (1973). *General systems theory: Foundations, development, aspirations*. New York: Braziller.

Weinstein, R. (1982). Establishing a mental health team in a middle school. In J. Alpert (Ed.), *Psychological consultation in educational settings* (pp. 85–107). San Francisco: Jossey-Bass.

Wittes, G., Chesler, J., & Crowfoot, D. (1975). *Student power: Practice and promise*. New York: Citation Press.

Ysseldyke, J., & Algozzine, B. (1982). *Critical issues in special and remedial education*. Boston: Houghton Mifflin.

CHAPTER 9

Peer Relations and Friendships

THOMAS J. BERNDT and RITCH C. SAVIN-WILLIAMS

Forming and maintaining satisfying relationships with peers is a central developmental task of adolescence. Adolescents who have close friendships and are accepted by peers typically are high in self-esteem, socially skilled, and academically successful (Berndt, 1988; Savin-Williams & Berndt, 1990). Adolescents who lack supportive friendships or who are rejected by many of their peers show poor psychological, social, and academic adjustment (Berndt, 1989; Parker & Asher, 1987).

Theorists and researchers have long assumed that relationships with peers have important effects on adjustment in adolescence (e.g., Sullivan, 1953; Youniss, 1980). During the 1980s, researchers began to distinguish among different aspects of peer relationships. They made the sharpest distinction between the qualities of an adolescent's close friendships and the adolescent's acceptance by a larger group of peers in a school or other setting. Both friendships and peer-group acceptance acquire special significance during adolescence. Time spent with friends increases between childhood and adolescence; time spent with family members decreases. Adolescents typically interact more often with friends than with parents or other adults (Csikszentmihalyi & Larson, 1984).

Acceptance by peers is important even in childhood. Nevertheless, adolescents are more aware than younger children of peer-group influence and more likely to describe themselves as belonging to a specific group (Crockett, Losoff, & Petersen, 1984; O'Brien & Bierman, 1988).

The connection between the qualities of adolescents' friendships and their peer-group acceptance is not always a close one (Feltham, Doyle, Schwartzman, Serbin, & Ledingham, 1985; McGuire & Weisz, 1982). Moreover, variations in friendships are likely to affect adolescents' adjustment in different ways and via different processes than do variations in peer-group acceptance (Parker & Asher, 1987). For this reason, issues related to friendships and to peer acceptance are discussed in different sections of the chapter. The first section addresses two sets of issues concerning friendship: (a) the influence of having *friends* with particular characteristics (e.g., friends who use drugs or receive high grades), and (b) the influence of having *friendships* with particular qualities (e.g., friendships in which there is a high level of intimate self-disclosure). The second section is concerned with the consequences of a lack of acceptance in the peer group and with the mechanisms leading to these consequences.

A few studies of adolescents' peer relationships cannot be classified neatly as focusing on friendships or on peer-group acceptance. Rather, these studies focus on age changes in the structure of the peer group itself. The classic study of this type was done by Dunphy (1963) with Australian teenagers in social clubs and organizations. He identified two major changes in the structure of peer groups from early to late adolescence. First, adolescents move from same-sex cliques to mixed-sex cliques and, eventually, to a loosely connected network of dating couples. Second, adolescents move from relatively small and intimate cliques that include peers with similar interests and values to larger and more diverse crowds.

To the best of our knowledge, no other investigator has replicated Dunphy's (1963) study using his method of participation observation and his measures. Still, there is no doubt that most adolescents become more interested in members of the opposite sex as they grow older. They also spend more time either in mixed-sex groups or with dating partners. These age trends are less relevant to this chapter, however, than to Chapter 5 of this volume (Miller & Dyk), on adolescent sexuality. Most of the research reviewed in this chapter addresses primarily or exclusively with same-sex, non-romantic peer relationships.

Dunphy's (1963) hypothesis that adolescents shift from close-knit cliques to larger and more diverse crowds has been examined by a few researchers (e.g., Shrum & Cheek, 1987). This shift occurs as adolescents move from small, neighborhood-based elementary schools to larger junior and senior high schools. As adolescents spend more time with large groups of peers and less time with their family, they may seek a sense of belonging in same-sex cliques. As they develop greater autonomy in late adolescence, their small clique may seem less rewarding than participation in a larger crowd. The research on adolescent crowds is limited, however, and has been recently reviewed by Brown (1989, 1990), so we do not discuss it extensively.

A central theme in our chapter should be mentioned at the beginning. Perhaps the most important and controversial question about adolescent peer relationships is their net effect on adolescents' behavior and development. As already mentioned, several theorists have suggested that peer relationships can contribute positively to adolescents' adjustment (Berndt, 1988). By contrast, other theorists have suggested that peer influence can lead to a lack of motivation to achieve in school (Coleman, 1961), delinquent behavior (Bronfenbrenner, 1970; Steinberg & Silverberg, 1986), and drug use (Downs, 1987).

Many studies indicate that sweeping claims about the positive or negative influence of peers on adolescents are either overstated or inaccurate. One objective of this chapter is to clarify the conditions in which peers have a positive influence versus a negative influence on adolescents' behavior and adjustment. The evidence on this issue is not entirely consistent, however, and some specific questions have not been investigated fully. The limitations in the research literature are highlighted in the third and final section of the chapter. Questions that could set the agenda for future research are noted. In addition, the implications of current knowledge about peer relationships for intervention with troubled adolescents are explored.

THE EFFECTS OF ADOLESCENT FRIENDSHIPS

When parents or other adults talk about the effects of adolescents' friendships, they often mean the effects on an adolescent of having peers with certain characteristics as friends. For example, they regard a peer who drinks beer or smokes cigarettes as a potentially bad influence on an adolescent. They regard a peer who receives good grades and studies hard before tests as a potentially good influence.

Adolescents are affected by the characteristics of their friends, just as children and adults are. Nevertheless, this perspective on the effects of friendship is both limited and incomplete. Most theories of adolescent friendship focus not on the attitudes and behaviors of friends, but on the features of these friendships (Berndt, 1989; Youniss, 1980). The theories refer, for example, to the consequences of intimate friendships in which ideas are freely shared.

To fully understand the effects of friendship, both perspectives must be considered. We focus first on the influence of friends' attitudes and behaviors. Then we examine the effects of variations in the features of adolescents' friendships.

The Influence of Friends' Characteristics

Researchers have often estimated the magnitude of friends' influence from the similarity between adolescents and their friends on specific attitudes or behaviors (Ide, Parkerson, Haertel, & Walberg, 1981). These researchers have assumed that friends become more similar over time as a result of their interactions with each other. If friends' similarity is indeed a consequence of their influence on each other, then the degree of similarity among friends can be used as an index of the amount of influence they have had on each other.

Adolescents are similar to their friends on many characteristics, from their grades and educational aspirations to their use of marijuana, their church attendance, and their frequency of dating (Cohen, 1977; Ide et al., 1981; Kandel, 1978b). Nevertheless, this similarity should not be attributed entirely to influence. Kandel (1978a) pointed out that similarity is often a basis for friendship selection. For example, adolescents typically choose friends who are the same age, sex, and race as themselves. Because adolescents cannot influence each other's age, sex, and race, friends' similarity on these characteristics must be attributed to selection rather than influence.

Adolescents may also select friends on the basis of similarities in attitudes and behaviors. If friends' similarity on a particular measure of attitudes or behavior is assessed at only one time, judging to what degree this similarity is due to selection rather than influence is impossible. If friends' similarity is assessed at two or more times, then friends' influence on each other can be estimated from the increase in their similarity over time. In more technical terms, friends' influence can be evaluated adequately with longitudinal designs but not with cross-sectional designs. Only longitudinal designs provide the data necessary to determine the relative contributions of selection and influence to friends' similarity.

Kandel (1978a) was among the first investigators to report longitudinal data on friends' similarity. At the beginning and the end of a school year, Kandel assessed the similarity between adolescents and their best friends in educational aspirations, marijuana use, minor delinquency, and political orientations (e.g., liberal vs. conservative). She found an increase over time in friends' similarity that could be attributed partly to the friends' influence on each other. The increase in similarity could also be attributed partly to adolescents' ending friendships with dissimilar peers and selecting new friends who were similar to themselves. By examining both the changes in adolescents' attitudes and behaviors and the changes in their friendships, Kandel determined that the increase in friends' similarity during the year was due about as much to friendship selection as to friends' influence.

More recent longitudinal studies have shown that friends influence a wide range of attitudes and behaviors during adolescence. As a result of their interactions, friends become more similar in their attitudes toward school and their achievement in school (Epstein, 1983). In addition, influence processes contribute to an increase in the similarity of friends' sexual behavior, although this effect is more obvious for White females than for White males or Black adolescents of either sex (Billy & Udry, 1985). Friends also influence adolescents' use of alcohol, cigarette smoking, and other behaviors relevant to adolescents' social and academic life (Chassin, Presson, Montello, Sherman, & McGrew, 1986; Cohen, 1977; Downs, 1987; Fisher & Baumann, 1988).

Only a few investigators have followed Kandel's (1978a) lead and examined the relative contributions of selection and influence to friends' similarity. In one of the most comprehensive investigations, Fisher and Baumann (1988) reported that friends' similarity in cigarette smoking and in alcohol use depended more on selection than on influence. These findings imply that researchers who try to judge influence from similarity at just one time, which is still a common practice (see Ide et al., 1981), are likely to overestimate the influence of friends.

The issue of selection versus influence has practical implications as well. Parents may overestimate the influence of friends on their sons' and daughters' behavior, just as researchers may. Parents may believe, for example, that their son or daughter started using drugs because he or she felt compelled to conform to friends who used drugs. In reality, their adolescent may have been using drugs for some time, and merely found a group of friends who used them too. Thus, friends do not always deserve the blame they receive for adolescents' problem behaviors. Moreover, trying to reduce problem behaviors by limiting adolescents' involvement with their supposedly undesirable friends may have less impact than changing the attitudes and behaviors that led adolescents to choose those friends.

Three other conclusions about friends' influence are suggested by recent longitudinal studies. First, influence in a close friendship group is a mutual process. Each adolescent influences his or her friends and is, in turn, influenced by them (Downs, 1987). As a result of this process, friends become more similar. By contrast, writers who emphasize the negative effects of friends' influence (Coleman, 1961; Steinberg & Silverberg, 1986) suggest that friends often pressure adolescents to engage in antisocial behaviors such as cheating or vandalism. Adolescents then react to the pressure by conforming to their antisocial friends. The outcome of friends' influence, in this view, is a net shift by adolescents toward less desirable behavior.

Because influence among friends is a mutual process, using the metaphor of an individual conforming in the face of pressure from a group is highly misleading. Moreover, the assumption that friends' influence is predominantly in a negative direction should be questioned. When adolescents are asked directly about their peers' influence on them (Brown, Clasen, & Eicher, 1986), they report that peers exert more pressure toward good conduct than toward misconduct.

Broad claims that friends' influence is either positive or negative in direction are likely to be inaccurate. Friends' influence may be either positive or negative, depending on who the friends are. For example, Ball (1981) found negative effects of friends' influence on children and adolescents in the lowest academic tracks in schools. In these tracks, friends' influence contributed to disruptive behavior and a lack of interest in school. In the highest academic tracks, by contrast, there were positive effects of friends' influence. Students in these tracks often discouraged their friends' disruptive behavior and encouraged them to aim for high grades.

The most likely outcome of friends' influence may be an increase in friends' similarity without a shift in their average position. For example, when adolescents choose friends with grades higher than their own, their grades are likely to rise and the friends' grades are likely to fall (Epstein, 1983). If the rise and fall are equally great (i.e., there is as much influence of low-scoring adolescents on their high-scoring friends as vice versa), then the average of the adolescents' and the friends' grades will not change.

Under certain conditions, friends' influence may produce shifts in their average position. After a group discussion, friends may make decisions more or less extreme than the average of the independent decisions they made before the discussion. Adolescents may decide, for example, to engage in delinquent acts after talking with friends, even if each adolescent was initially unwilling to perform these acts. Such shifts in the average position of group members are not always toward undesirable behaviors. Shifts toward socially desirable decisions can also occur (Berndt, 1984). Unfortunately, the conditions that lead to shifts in a particular direction are not well understood.

The second conclusion suggested by recent longitudinal studies qualifies the previous one. Although influence is a mutual process, not all adolescents have equal influence on their friends; not all adolescents are equally influenced by their friends. The leaders of adolescent friendship groups have more influence on the behavior of other group members than do lower-status adolescents (Savin-Williams, 1987). Attributes of individuals that contribute to leadership—attributes such as athletic ability, intelligence, and physical attractiveness—should increase an adolescent's influence on his or her friends.

There is less evidence on the characteristics of adolescents most susceptible to friends' influence. Most researchers have examined a rather different question, the characteristics of adolescents most responsive to the *negative* influence of friends. Based on the results of two cross-sectional studies, Berndt (1979) suggested that conformity to friends who encourage antisocial behavior peaks around ninth grade or 15 years of age. Berndt's findings were replicated, in part, by Brown et al. (1986) and by Steinberg and Silverberg (1986) in their cross-sectional studies. More recently, Chassin et al. (1986) used longitudinal data to test the hypothesis that friends' influence on cigarette smoking is greater in late adolescence (grades 8 to 11) than in early adolescence (grades 6 and 7). Their analyses suggested that friends' influence on adolescents' cigarette smoking changed little with age. These results weaken claims that conformity to friends on socially undesirable behaviors changes significantly during adolescence (see also Epstein, 1983).

Willingness to engage in antisocial behaviors with peers is greater among adolescents whose parents are permissive, inconsistent in discipline, and unlikely to monitor or supervise their behavior (Snyder, Dishion, & Patterson, 1986; Steinberg & Silverberg, 1986). Snyder and his colleagues proposed that deficiencies in parenting make adolescents more likely to select deviant peers as friends. When their parents are inept in monitoring and disciplining them, adolescents are not likely to develop good social skills and are likely to form antisocial attitudes. These characteristics repel most of their peers. As a result, these adolescents gravitate toward deviant peer groups.

In a longitudinal study of adolescents' marijuana use, Kandel and Andrews (1987) examined the effects of parents' and friends' influence over time. Their results suggested that high susceptibility to negative peer influence is an outcome of a causal chain that begins with problems in parenting, continues with selection of friends who engage in deviant behaviors, and ends with the accentuation of deviant behavior through the mutual influence of friends on each other.

The hypothesized causal sequence contrasts sharply with the view that peers pull adolescents away from parents into deviant behavior. Indeed, recent research supports the claim of Condry and Siman (1974) that parents more often push adolescents toward deviant peers—because of neglect or other failures in parenting—than peers pull adolescents away from parents. No doubt some adolescents with well-intentioned, responsive parents are drawn into deviant peer groups and are heavily influenced by their peers. Yet, more often, problems in parenting set the stage for involvement with peers whose behavior is undesirable.

A third conclusion that can be drawn from recent research concerns sex differences in influence. In a few cross-sectional studies (Berndt, 1979; Brown et al., 1986; Steinberg & Silverberg, 1986), boys seemed more willing than girls to conform to friends who encouraged them to engage in socially undesirable behaviors. Some researchers have drawn the conclusion that girls are more resistant to peer pressure than are boys (Steinberg & Silverberg, 1986). There is an alternative interpretation of the findings, however. Boys evaluate antisocial behaviors less negatively than girls do (Berndt, 1979), so they may be more willing than girls to engage in these behaviors even when not pressured to do so by peers. In short, the sex differences in previous studies may tell us more about boys' and girls' standards for behavior than about their susceptibility to friends' influence.

When friends' influence has been judged from increases in their similarity over time, the evidence regarding sex differences has been mixed. Some researchers (Fisher & Baumann, 1988; Kandel, 1978), did not report analyses for the two sexes separately. Other researchers found that friends had more influence on girls than on boys (Billy & Udry, 1985; Davies & Kandel, 1981). In other studies, sex differences were absent or were not consistent across measures (Chassin et al., 1986; Epstein, 1983). Taken together, the data suggest no reliable differences in friends' influence on adolescent boys and girls.

One major limitation of the research on friends' influence is a lack of attention to the features of these friendships. Hypotheses about peer pressure (Steinberg & Silverberg, 1986) imply that these friendships are based more on coercion than on mutual respect. Although coercive behavior occasionally occurs in adolescents' friendship groups, influence usually takes more positive forms, such as approval for living up to the norms of the group (Savin-Williams & Berndt, 1990). Moreover, friends' influence may be strongest when friendships are based on mutual trust and shared goals (Hallinan, 1983). If this hypothesis is correct, variations in friends' influence depend partly on variations in the features of adolescents' friendships.

Friendship Features

Adolescents are aware of the variations in their friendships. When adolescents describe their friendships, they provide a range of comments that researchers have categorized in different ways (Berndt, 1986a; Youniss, 1980).

Features of Adolescents' Friendships

Four categories of comments have received the greatest attention from theorists and researchers. First, adolescents describe friendships as intimate relationships. Friends talk with each other about personally important topics they would not discuss with anyone else. Sullivan (1953) emphasized the positive effects of these intimate conversations on the development of adolescents' self-concepts and their understanding of other people. (See also Youniss, 1980.) Berndt (1989) proposed that intimate friendships give adolescents the kind of support that has been shown to help adults cope with stressful events.

Adolescents view friendships as intimate relationships more often than younger children do (Berndt, 1986a, 1988). Moreover, the intimacy of friendships increases during adolescence (Sharabany, Gershoni, & Hofman, 1981). Often, but not always, adolescent girls emphasize the intimacy of their friendships more than do adolescent boys (Buhrmester & Furman, 1987; Sharabany et al., 1981).

Second, adolescents assume that friends behave prosocially toward each other. They say that a friend will loan you money, will help you with homework, or will let you borrow things. Sullivan (1953) and Youniss (1980) suggested that sensitivity to a friend's needs and desires increases markedly in the preadolescent and adolescent years. This increase in sensitivity can be seen more clearly in friends' actual behavior than in their comments about their relationships (Berndt, 1986b). When commenting on their friendships, girls refer to prosocial behavior roughly as often as do boys (Berndt, 1986a). Sex differences in boys' and girls' actual behavior toward friends vary across studies, but the differences are usually nonsignificant (Berndt, 1986b).

Third, adolescents recognize that conflicts occur in friendships. Friends fight, disagree with each other, and violate each other's expectations about how a friend should behave. Until recently (Hartup, 1989), few theorists paid much attention to friends' conflicts. This neglect may reflect a belief that conflicts simply illustrate the opposite of a good friendship. Thus, when the features of a good friendship have been defined, the features of a poor friendship have been implicitly defined.

Adolescents themselves recognize a distinction between the positive and the negative features of friendships. One analysis of eighth graders' comments about their friendships revealed separate factors for positive and negative features (Berndt & Perry, 1986). The separation of the two factors indicated that some eighth graders had friendships with many positive features and many conflicts; other eighth graders had friendships with many positive features and few conflicts.

Adolescents report conflicts with friends roughly as often as younger children do; girls report roughly as many conflicts with friends as boys do (Berndt, 1986a). These data cannot be considered conclusive because they are based on reports about friendships rather than observations of friends' behavior. Still, they suggest that management of conflicts with friends is important throughout childhood and adolescence.

Fourth, adolescents say that friends spend a considerable amount of time with each other. They hang around together at school, talk on the phone, and go places together. The frequency of friends' interaction is not emphasized in most theories and is a dubious indicator of friendship because these interactions could be negative or positive. Therefore, research on this feature of friendship is not discussed further.

Adolescents mention other features of friendship besides the four mentioned thus far. They refer, for example, to the loyalty and faithfulness of friends. Adolescents express more concern about the loyalty and faithfulness of friends than younger children do; girls are especially likely to express concern about a friend's disloyalty or unfaithfulness (Berndt, 1986a). Previous research suggests that girls have more exclusive friendship groups than boys do (Eder & Hallinan, 1978). Moreover, girls are more likely than boys to limit the size of their friendship groups (Berndt & Hoyle, 1985). This exclusiveness may explain girls' special concern about the unfaithfulness of a friend. That is, girls may worry more than boys about a friend leaving them because girls expect the friend to join another small and exclusive friendship group that is not open to them.

Further research on the specific features of adolescents' friendships should continue. This research may reveal adolescents' ideas about friendship or patterns of interactions with friends that are important but poorly understand. Currently, however, the evidence suggests that the most significant variations in friendships can be captured by measuring two broad and overlapping dimensions, one for positive features and one for negative features or conflicts (Berndt & Perry, 1986).

Effects of Friendship Features

Correlational designs have been used in virtually all studies of the effects of friendship features during adolescence. In one study (Kurdek & Sinclair, 1988), seventh and ninth graders who perceived their friends as supportive reported fewer psychological and school-related problems than those with less supportive friendships. In another study, sixth graders who reported little emotional support from friends also seemed more depressed, especially if they lived in single-parent families (Feldman, Rubenstein, & Rubin, 1988). Adolescents who described their friendships more positively had higher self-esteem than other adolescents, in several studies (Mannarino, 1976; McGuire & Weisz, 1982; Townsend, McCracken, & Wilton, 1988). The correlations of friendship perceptions with self-esteem and other indicators of adjustment were comparable for boys and girls in studies that reported these data (e.g., Feldman et al., 1988).

In a recent study with multiple measures of adjustment, Perry (1987) found that eighth graders who had positive perceptions of their friendship group also had higher self-esteem, greater confidence about their social acceptance by peers, higher perceived athletic and scholastic competence, and lower loneliness.

This study also included measures of negative friendship features. Eighth graders who reported more conflicts in the friendship groups had lower self-esteem, lower scholastic competence, and greater loneliness and anxiety than adolescents who had fewer conflicts with friends.

Perry (1987) cautioned that the correlations between the friendship and adjustment measures might reflect a negative affectivity bias (Watson & Clark, 1984). Self-report measures of psychological adjustment often assess people's affect toward themselves and their world. Those people who respond more negatively to one measure are likely to respond similarly to other measures. Self-report measures of friendship features may be influenced by the same bias. Adolescents who view themselves negatively might view their friendships negatively, too. Thus, correlations between self-report measures of friendship and adjustment do not clearly demonstrate an effect of friendships on adjustment. On the contrary, the evidence for a negative affectivity bias implies that friendships do not affect adjustment. Rather, adolescents' perceptions of their friendships and their perceptions of themselves derive from a fundamentally positive or negative attitude toward life.

To limit the impact of the negative affectivity bias, researchers have examined the relations of adolescents' perceptions of their friendships to measures of adjustment not derived from self-reports. For example, Cauce (1986) reported that seventh graders who viewed their friendships as emotionally supportive were more popular with peers and had more positive reputations with peers. Mannarino (1976) found that sixth graders with a close, stable friendship like that described by Sullivan (1953) were more altruistic toward their partners in a modified Prisoner's Dilemma Game than sixth graders who lacked such a friendship. Other researchers have replicated these findings and shown relations of adolescents' reports on their friendship to measures of social inference, classroom behavior, and academic achievement (Cauce, 1986; McGuire & Weisz, 1982; Miller & Berndt, 1987).

A few investigators have examined the relations of adolescents' friendships to clinical assessments of their psychological problems. Emotionally disturbed 8 to 13 years old reported fewer positive interactions and more negative interactions with friends than did children in the same age group who showed few signs of psychopathology (Bierman & McCauley, 1987). When interacting with friends, well-adjusted adolescents expressed more positive affect and were rated by observers as more socially competent than were adolescents with conduct disorders or serious problems of anxiety and withdrawal (Panella & Henggeler, 1986).

The evidence for correlations between measures of friendship and adjustment not derived from self-reports is reassuring. Nevertheless, these correlations do not prove that the qualities of adolescents' friendship affect their adjustment, because no correlation by itself is proof of a cause–effect relation between two constructs. Hypotheses about cause–effect relations can be tested more definitively in longitudinal studies. In a study of the transition to junior high school, Berndt (1989) found that adolescents who described their best friendships most positively at the beginning of seventh grade became more popular between the beginning and the end of the school year. Supportive friendships contributed to acceptance in the peer group.

Another reason for caution in drawing conclusions about the effects of friendship is the lack of consistency in the research data. Predictions of a positive correlation between supportive friendships and self-esteem have not always been confirmed. In one large-scale interview study (Giordano, Cernkovich, & Pugh, 1986), there was no relation of friends' support to measures of adolescents' delinquent behavior, but delinquents did report more conflicts with friends than did nondelinquents. Occasionally, researchers have reported negative correlations between measures of friendship and adjustment. In one study (Hirsch &

Reischl, 1985), reports of friends' support were negatively (but not significantly) related to the self-esteem of adolescents with depressed and arthritic parents.

Despite the inconsistencies in the research findings, the weight of the evidence suggests that problems in friendships are often part of a broader syndrome of poor adjustment. Whether adolescents' friendships have a direct impact on their psychological and social adjustment is less clear. Strategies for investigating the effects of friendship more directly are discussed at the end of this chapter.

EFFECTS OF PEER-GROUP ACCEPTANCE, REJECTION, AND ISOLATION

In addition to their relationships with friends, adolescents have less close relationships with other adolescents in their classrooms, schools, and neighborhoods. Mead (1934) argued that through the process of social communication people come to understand and evaluate themselves from the vantage point of significant others. In adolescence, these significant others almost always include peers. Acceptance by peers can enhance psychosocial resilience through its effects on adolescents' sense of interpersonal competence, security, and belonging (Rutter, 1987). A lack of acceptance by peers can create or reinforce self-doubt and hamper development. Research has shown that "poorly accepted children stand a greater chance than others of developing later life difficulties and, therefore, should be considered a group at risk" (Parker & Asher, 1987, p. 357). Before asking how they are at risk and why, an examination of measures of peer-group acceptance and status is necessary.

Categories of Social Status in the Peer Group

Researchers usually assess adolescents' social status by asking groups of peers to name the adolescents whom they most like and those whom they most dislike. Nominations are often restricted to same-sex peers within the same classroom, or peers in the same grade. Adolescents are then classified into groups based on the nominations they receive from their peers. In one frequently used classification system (Coie, Dodge, & Coppotelli, 1982), five groups are distinguished. *Popular* adolescents are liked by many of their classmates and disliked by few of their classmates. In other words, they receive many positive nominations and few negative nominations. *Rejected* adolescents receive few positive nominations and many negative nominations. *Neglected* adolescents receive few positive or negative nominations; few (or no) classmates strongly like or strongly dislike them. *Controversial* adolescents receive many positive and many negative nominations. Finally, *average* adolescents do not fall into any of the more extreme groups.

Most researchers have focused on the differences among popular, rejected, and neglected adolescents. Both rejected and neglected adolescents are unpopular, but only rejected adolescents are disliked by many of their classmates. Neglected adolescents seem neither objectionable nor attractive to their classmates. To clarify the distinctive characteristics of popular, rejected, and neglected adolescents, the adolescents in these social-status categories are often compared with average adolescents. Researchers have paid less attention to adolescents in the controversial group, because most samples indicate only a small number of these adolescents. Moreover, researchers have found more distinctive correlates of classification in the two unpopular status groups, those for rejected and neglected adolescents.

Peer Rejection

Adolescents who are rejected by their peers often have severe adjustment problems. Compared to average or popular adolescents, rejected adolescents are more hyperactive, aggressive, obsessive-compulsive, and delinquent (Coie & Dodge, 1983; East, Hess, & Lerner, 1987;

Feltham et al., 1985; French & Waas, 1985). In addition, rejected adolescents are more likely to show poor scholastic performance and to drop out of high school before graduation (Coie & Dodge, 1983; East et al., 1987; Parker & Asher, 1987).

Rejected adolescents are vulnerable to psychological stress, according to East and her colleagues (1987), because they lack peer support and acceptance. They may feel embarrassed and angry because of their peers' dislike of them, and these emotions may lead to further hostility and withdrawal. This self-perpetuating cycle may explain why rejected status has a significant degree of stability over time, even after the transition to a new school (Coie & Dodge, 1983). Stability is not absolute, however. In one major study (Coie & Dodge, 1983), only about half of the students who were in the rejected-status group during one school year were in the same group a year later.

Not all rejected adolescents behave in the same way. French and Waas (1985) identified five distinct behavioral patterns that can lead to peer rejection: (a) antagonism toward authorities, (b) social withdrawal combined with hostility, (c) seriously disturbed behavior patterns, (d) aversive and domineering behavior toward peers, and (e) appropriate social behavior but severe mental or physical disabilities. Whether rejected adolescents exhibiting the different behavioral patterns are at risk for different outcomes is not yet known.

Olweus (1978, 1987) approached the question of rejected status from a different perspective. He studied two unpopular groups of adolescents, bullies and whipping boys. As the label implies, bullies are aggressive, impulsive, and antisocial. They often harass other adolescents. Whipping boys can be either provocative solicitors of attacks or passive victims of attacks. Provocative solicitors are often bullies as well. They pick fights, ridicule others, or behave in ways that are irritating to peers. Passive victims withdraw rather than fight back when attacked. They are insecure, lonely, and so sensitive that they seem to invite attacks. There is no comparable study of female bullies, but Savin-Williams (1987) studied early adolescent groups in which one girl was known by her peers as a "bitch." The girls who were given this label had many characteristics of male bullies. In particular, they were aggressive and relied on physical force or ridicule to get what they wanted.

Peer Neglect

Not all forms of unpopularity with peers have such clearly negative correlates a peer rejection. Adolescents in the neglected status group are not popular; few of their classmates say that they strongly like them. These adolescents are not rejected, either, because few of their classmates say that they strongly dislike them. Neglected status is rarely associated with maladjustment or negative long-term consequences. On parent and teacher ratings of behavior and personality, neglected children and adolescents differ little from average-status adolescents (French & Waas, 1985). Neglected adolescents have few friends at school and are often shy and solitary, but they are not necessarily lonely (Asher & Wheeler, 1985; Coie et al., 1982; Dodge, 1983; East et al., 1987). Moreover, neglected adolescents are not especially likely to drop out of high school, become adult criminals, or be diagnosed as mentally ill in adulthood (Parker & Asher, 1987).

The shyness and social withdrawal often associated with neglected status may have benefits as well as costs for adolescents. Csikszentmihalyi and Larson (1984) emphasized the importance of the distinction between solitude and loneliness. Solitude can give adolescents an opportunity to relax, to restore inner equilibrium, and to express their individuality in creative pursuits. Adolescents report feeling more free, intrinsically motivated, and able to concentrate when by themselves than when with other people.

Loneliness, by contrast, is associated with solitude but adds an unpleasant feeling to it.

Lonely adolescents and adults are often anxious, depressed, alienated, self-conscious, and introspective. They feel inferior to others, believe they cannot control the events in their lives, have poor social skills, and suffer from medical problems such as high blood pressure and indigestion (Csikszentmihalyi & Larson, 1984; Goswick & Jones, 1982; Marcoen, Goossens, & Caes, 1987; Peplau & Perlman, 1982).

Some neglected adolescents apparently avoid the problems of loneliness because they take the opportunity to develop their individuality during times of solitude. Other neglected adolescents may suffer more from their relative social isolation. They may be depressed or emotionally detached, or may experience other mental health problems (East et al., 1987). Neglected status may have negative outcomes only if coupled with loneliness. Research is needed to test this hypothesis.

Peer Status: Causes, Effects, and Processes

Most researchers have tentatively assumed that low peer status has negative effects on adolescents, yet they often acknowledge that low status may result from preexisting problems in adolescents' adjustment (Parker & Asher, 1987). For example, adolescents may be rejected by peers because they have poor social skills. Their poor social skills may explain why their adjustment in adulthood is poor.

Still, stating questions about peer status in such an either/or fashion is probably unwise. Variations in adolescent peer status may have their origins in childhood but still have effects of their own. Peer rejection, for example, may result partly from problems in parent–child relationships (Putallaz, 1987). The experience of rejection by peers may contribute independently to maladjustment. Prolonged peer rejection could lead adolescents to view themselves and their world negatively. In particular, being disliked by many classmates could increase adolescents' inclination to dislike school and to drop out as soon as possible (Parker & Asher, 1987).

The task of identifying the causes and effects of variations in peer status remains to be tackled by researchers. As they begin this task, they will need to examine more carefully the processes by which variations in peer status influence adolescents' adjustment and vice versa.

One facet of peer interactions that is likely both to communicate and to reinforce an adolescent's low status in the peer group is ridicule. Many observers of adolescent groups have discussed the negative effects of ridicule on self-esteem and other aspects of adjustment (Brown & Lohr, 1987; Eder, 1987; Savin-Williams, 1987). Their observations suggest that ridicule is a nearly universal phenomenon in the peer groups of adolescent boys and girls.

Ridicule must be distinguished from verbal teasing by peers. Although the two may be similar in their verbal content, they differ in their meaning to adolescents (Eder, 1987). Teasing describes playful, humorous verbal interactions that express interpersonal attraction, group solidarity, and positive feelings. Thus, teasing is an indication of peer acceptance. Ridicule, by contrast, is a negative form of humor that communicates hostility, anger, and dislike; it is an indication of peer rejection.

The distinction between teasing and ridicule is often overlooked, even by adolescents themselves. For example, "ritual insulting" is readily understood by working-class African-American and White adolescent girls as a form of teasing. Middle-class White girls are intimidated by this behavior, however, because they perceive it as ridicule (Eder, 1986; Schofield, 1982).

Direct evidence on the contrasting consequences of teasing and ridicule is scarce, but some evidence is suggestive. Early adolescents who report more positive experiences with peers, including experiences of "fun and joking with kids," also report less depression, lower anxiety, and higher self-worth than early adolescents who report more negative peer experiences, including ridicule (Kanner, Feldman, Weinberger, & Ford, 1987). More research is needed, not only on teasing and ridicule but also on other facets of adolescents' interactions that are linked to peer status.

OPEN QUESTIONS AND INTERVENTION POSSIBILITIES

The most significant unanswered question about adolescent peer relationships is how they affect adolescents' adjustment. Virtually all theories focus on the consequences of close friendships or acceptance by peers (Berndt, 1989; Sullivan, 1953; Youniss, 1980). By contrast, most empirical studies focus either on the characteristics or on the correlates of peer relationships. There is little definitive information about the effects on adolescents of variations in their peer relationships.

To investigate the influence of peer relationships, researchers will need to draw on many different research designs. Longitudinal designs have clarified the effects on adolescents of making friends with peers who show particular types of behavior. Researchers who examine the effects of variations in friendship features and in peer acceptance should make more use of these designs because they help to disentangle causes and effects. Long-term, prospective studies with large samples are especially needed. Previous research with follow-back designs has indicated that many maladjusted adults had poor relationships with peers during childhood and adolescence. However, the findings do not prove that most children with poor peer relationships have problems in adulthood (Parker & Asher, 1987). Prospective studies would document the prevalence of problems in peer relationships and, more importantly, would attempt to explain why some adolescents with problematic relationships continue to have problems in adulthood and others do not.

Experimental designs can also be valuable. Although researchers cannot ethically manipulate adolescents' friendships, they can examine the effects of interactions with friends under experimental conditions. For example, friends' influence and friends' support often occur during discussions among friends. Experimental designs can be employed to evaluate the effects of discussions with friends on adolescents' own attitudes and behavior (Berndt, 1984).

Correlational designs have not exhausted their usefulness, especially as a valuable first step in examining the antecedents of variations in friendships and peer-group acceptance. As noted earlier, correlational designs have been used to explore the influence of parent–child relationships on peer-group acceptance (Putallaz, 1987). They could also be used to examine the influence of parent–child relationships on the features of adolescents' friendships (Gold & Yanof, 1985).

In addition, researchers could use correlational designs to investigate the relations between adolescents' acceptance in the peer group and the features of their closest friendships. Some investigators have suggested that peer acceptance and friendship features are largely independent (McGuire & Weisz, 1982). Other investigators have found significant correlations between peer acceptance and friendship (Cauce, 1986). Clarification of this issue would help to integrate the research on these two facets of adolescents' peer relationships.

Finally, recent ethnographic data on adolescents' relationships with peers are in short supply (but see Eder, 1986; Savin-Williams, 1987). Most researchers have used structured interviews, standardized questionnaires, or observations under controlled conditions to assess adolescents' friendships. These methods have demonstrated advantages, but they have only limited ability to explore relationships in depth or to illustrate how these relationships function in their natural settings. Ethnographic data are especially needed on the relationships of adolescents who have problems in adjustment, such as delinquent behavior and drug abuse.

Also needed is a replication and extension of Dunphy's (1963) study of age changes in the structure of adolescents' peer groups. The replication should be done in a variety of settings, including urban, suburban, and rural areas, with adolescents who vary in sex, ethnicity, and social class. This research may show more variety than uniformity in adolescents' transitions from same-sex cliques to mixed-sex groups and dating relationships. Some cliques may not disappear during adolescence but, instead, may maintain their intimacy and exclusiveness. Eder (1985) suggested that elite cliques may show this kind of continuity. Some adolescents never belong to a clique and perhaps never become central members of crowds. The origins and consequences of these individual differences deserve more careful study.

Even more important than an increase in the range of research strategies is an expansion of theoretical perspective. Two gaps in previous research are most critical. First, researchers have given little attention to the processes responsible for the effects of peer relationships. There is little direct evidence about how friends influence each other, how adolescents with supportive friendships interact with each other, or how variations in peer status are manifested in adolescents' behavior toward each other. Researchers are forced to speculate about the reasons for relations between measures of peer relationships and adjustment, with little idea about the mediating links between them.

Second, few theorists or researchers have considered the possible connections between the influence of particular friends and the effects of friendship features. As noted earlier, Hallinan (1983) is a conspicuous exception. She argued that friends' influence should be greatest when these friendships are based on trust and a perception of shared goals. Cauce and Gonzales (1989) carried this argument a step further by suggesting that supportive friendships can have negative effects if an adolescent's friends have undesirable attitudes and values. In short, these writers proposed that support from friends can magnify the influence of the friends' attitudes and behavior, for good or for ill.

There is a plausible alternative hypothesis. Most theorists who emphasize the positive effects of supportive friendships (Berndt, 1989; Youniss, 1980) would argue that support from friends is always beneficial. Thus, when an adolescent has a supportive friendship with a peer whose behavior is deviant, the positive effects of support partly or wholly counteract the negative influence of the friend's deviant behavior. Empirical tests of this hypothesis and the opposing hypothesis—that support amplifies the influence of friends' characteristics—would have important implications for theories of friends' influence.

Tests of the opposing hypotheses would also be relevant for interventions that attempt to alter the effects of peer influence. Barrett, Simpson, and Lehman (1988) suggested that drug-abuse intervention programs are most effective when adolescents have least contact with drug-using peers. The authors concluded, therefore, that adolescents who use drugs should be encouraged to develop relationships with peers who do not use drugs. As indicated earlier, most adolescents who regularly use drugs have friends who do the same. Thus, in effect, these investigators are proposing that interventions with drug-using adolescents cannot succeed unless these friendships are broken up.

Interventions need not be based on breaking up old friendships. Instead, adults could try to change the qualities and norms of the deviant friendship groups. Vorrath and Brendtro (1974) devised an intervention program based on "positive peer culture." In this program, adults try to alter deviant behavior patterns by increasing adolescents' concern for others, including their concern for their friends. Adults also try to increase friends' mutual trust and support. By showing deviant adolescents the benefits of trusting, supportive friendships, adults can bring about more general changes in adolescents' values and conduct.

Thus far, positive peer culture programs have been implemented mainly in total institutions, such as reform schools. These programs are similar in important respects, however, to interventions designed to improve children's friendships and increase their acceptance by peers. The central goal of most interventions is to increase the social skills of children and adolescents who either lack friends or are rejected by many of their peers. For example, the target children or adolescents are encouraged to initiate positive interactions with peers, to resolve conflicts nonaggressively, and to think about the interpersonal consequences of their behavior before acting (Ladd & Mize, 1983). These interventions are most successful when (a) they focus on skills or abilities that particular children or adolescents clearly need to master, and (b) they work to ensure the maintenance of the trained skills after the intervention ends.

One drawback of social skills interventions is that they change the individual but not the peer group as a whole. By contrast, Kohlberg and his coworkers (e.g., Kohlberg & Higgins, 1987) attempted to implement Just Communities in high schools. The teachers and students who join these communities agree to abide by principles of mutual respect and concern for other members of the community. Support for one another and the avoidance of overt rejection of other community members are mandated. This form of total-context intervention may be a valuable complement to programs focusing on individuals.

Finally, perhaps the most glaring omission in past research on adolescence has been evidence on the changes in the effects of peer relationships. There are inconsistent findings regarding the strength of friends' influence during early, middle, and late adolescence. There is almost no evidence on possible changes, during adolescence, in the impact of supportive friendships and the consequences of popularity or rejection by peers. With increasing age, adolescents may place a higher value on time spent apart from peers, in creative solitude (Csikszentmihalyi & Larson, 1984). Peer status may also become less important as dating relationships become more significant to adolescents.

Still, peer relationships are likely to retain their significance throughout adolescence. Regardless of their age, adolescents should always benefit from having friends whose own attitudes and behaviors are socially desirable, from having friendships that are supportive and not often marred by conflicts, and from being well-accepted (even if not extremely popular) in the peer group. Conversely, adolescents are likely to be negatively affected by having friends whose attitudes and behavior are socially undesirable, having friendships lacking in emotional support or frequently threatened by conflict, and being rejected by peers. The task of clinicians and researchers is to identify and implement strategies that increase the number of adolescents who have good peer relationships and reduce the number who have problematic relationships.

REFERENCES

Asher, S. R., & Wheeler, V. A. (1985). Children's loneliness: A comparison of rejected and neglected peer status. *Journal of Consulting and Clinical Psychology, 53,* 500–505.

Ball, S. J. (1981). *Beachside comprehensive.* Cambridge, England: Cambridge University Press.

Barrett, M. W., Simpson, D. D., & Lehman, W. E. (1988). Behavioral changes of adolescents in drug abuse intervention programs. *Journal of Clinical Psychology, 44,* 461–473.

Berndt, T. J. (1979). Developmental changes in conformity to peers and parents. *Developmental Psychology, 15,* 608–616.

Berndt, T. J. (1984). The influence of group discussions on children's moral decisions. In J. C. Masters & K. L. Yarkin-Levin (Eds.), *Boundary areas in social and developmental psychology* (pp. 195–219). New York: Academic Press.

Berndt, T. J. (1986a). Children's comments about their friendships. In M. Perlmutter (Ed.), *Cognitive perspectives on children's social and behavioral development* (pp. 189–212). Hillsdale, NJ: Erlbaum.

Berndt, T. J. (1986b). Sharing between friends: Contexts and consequences. In E. C. Mueller & C. R. Cooper (Eds.), *Process and outcome in peer relationships* (pp. 105–127). New York: Academic Press.

Berndt, T. J. (1988). The nature and significance of children's friendships. In R. Vasta (Ed.), *Annals of child development: Vol. 5* (pp. 155–186). Greenwich, CT: JAI Press.

Berndt, T. J. (1989). Obtaining support from friends in childhood and adolescence. In D. Belle (Ed.), *Children's social networks and social supports* (pp. 308–331). New York: Wiley.

Berndt, T. J., & Hoyle, S. G. (1985). Stability and change in childhood and adolescent friendships. *Developmental Psychology, 21,* 1007–1015.

Berndt, T. J., & Perry, T. B. (1986). Children's perceptions of friendships as supportive relationships. *Developmental Psychology, 22,* 640–648.

Bierman, K. L., & McCauley, E. (1987). Children's descriptions of their peer interactions: Useful information for clinical assessment. *Journal of Clinical Child Psychology, 16,* 9–18.

Billy, J. O. G., & Udry, J. R. (1985). The influence of male and female best friends on adolescent sexual behavior. *Adolescence, 20,* 21–32.

Bronfenbrenner, U. (1970). Reaction to social pressure from adults versus peers among Soviet day school and boarding school pupils in the perspective of an American sample. *Journal of Personality and Social Psychology,*

Brown, B. B. (1989). The role of peer groups in adolescents' adjustment to secondary school. In T. J. Berndt & G. W. Ladd (Eds.), *Peer relationships in child development* (pp. 188–215). New York: Wiley.

Brown, B. B. (1990). Peer groups and peer cultures. In S. S. Feldman & G. R. Elliott (Eds.), *At the threshold: The developing adolescent.* Cambridge, MA: Harvard University Press.

Brown, B. B., Clasen, D. R., & Eicher, S. A. (1986). Perceptions of peer pressure, peer conformity dispositions, and self-reported behavior among adolescents. *Developmental Psychology, 22,* 521–530.

Brown, B. B., & Lohr, M. J. (1987). Peer group affiliation and adolescent self-esteem: An integration of ego identity and symbolic interaction theories. *Journal of Personality and Social Psychology, 52,* 47–55.

Buhrmester, D., & Furman, W. (1987). The development of companionship and intimacy. *Child Development, 58,* 1101–1113.

Cauce, A. M. (1986). Social networks and social competence: Exploring the effects of early adolescent friendships. *American Journal of Community Psychology, 14,* 607–628.

Cauce, A. M., & Gonzales, N. (1989). *But is it good for schoolwork? Peer social support and academic achievement.* Paper presented at the AERA.

Chassin, L., Presson, C. C., Montello, D., Sherman, S. J., & McGrew, J. (1986). Changes in peer and parent influence during adolescence: Longitudinal versus cross-sectional perspectives on smoking initiation. *Developmental Psychology, 22,* 327–334.

Cohen, J. M. (1977). Sources of peer group homogeneity. *Sociology of Education, 50,* 227–241.

Coie, J. D., & Dodge, K. A. (1983). Continuities and changes in children's social status. A five year longitudinal study. *Merrill Palmer Quarterly, 29,* 261–282.

Coie, J. D., Dodge, K. A., & Coppotelli, H. (1982). Dimensions and types of social status: A cross-age perspective. *Developmental Psychology, 18,* 557–570.

Coleman, J. S. (1961). *The adolescent society.* New York: Free Press.

Condry, J., & Siman, M. L. (1974). Characteristics of peer- and adult-oriented children. *Journal of Marriage and the Family, 36,* 543–554.

Crockett, L., Losoff, M., & Petersen, A. C. (1984). Perceptions of the peer group and friendship in early adolescence. *Journal of Early Adolescence, 4,* 115–181.

Csikszentmihalyi, M., & Larson, R. W. (1984). *Being adolescent.* New York: Basic Books.

Davies, M., & Kandel, D. B. (1981). Parental and peer influences on adolescents' educational plans: Some further evidence. *American Journal of Sociology, 87,* 363–387.

Dodge, K. A. (1983). Behavioral antecedents of peer social status. *Child Development, 54,* 1386–1399.

Downs, W. R. (1987). A panel study of normative structure, adolescent alcohol use and peer alcohol use. *Journal of Studies on Alcohol, 48,* 167–175.

Dunphy, D. (1963). The social structure of urban adolescent peer groups. *Sociometry, 26,* 230–246.

East, P. L., Hess, L. E., & Lerner, R. M. (1987). Peer social support and adjustment of early adolescent peer groups. *Journal of Early Adolescence, 7,* 153–163.

Eder, D. (1985). The cycle of popularity: Interpersonal relations among female adolescents. *Sociology of Education, 58,* 154–165.

Eder, D. (1986). Serious and playful disputes: Variation in conflict talk among female adolescents. In A. D. Grimshaw (Ed.), *Conflict talk: Sociolinguistic investigations of arguments in conversations*. Cambridge, England: Cambridge University Press.

Eder, D. (1987). *The role of teasing in adolescent peer group culture*. Paper presented at the Conference on Ethnographic Approaches to Children's Worlds and Peer Cultures, Trondheim, Norway.

Eder, D., & Hallinan, M. T. (1978). Sex differences in children's friendships. *American Sociological Review, 43*, 237–250.

Epstein, J. L. (1983). The influence of friends on achievement and affective outcomes. In J. L. Epstein & N. L. Karweit (Eds.), *Friends in school* (pp. 177–200). New York: Academic Press.

Feldman, S. S., Rubenstein, J. L., & Rubin, C. (1988). Depressive affect and restraint in early adolescents: Relationships with family structure, family process and friendship support. *Journal of Early Adolescence, 8*, 279–296.

Feltham, R. F., Doyle, A. B., Schwartzman, A. E., Serbin, L. A., & Ledingham, J. E. (1985). Friendship in normal and socially deviant children. *Journal of Early Adolescence, 5*, 371–382.

Fisher, L. A., & Baumann, K. E. (1988). Influence and selection in the friend–adolescent relationship: Findings from studies of adolescent smoking and drinking. *Journal of Applied Social Psychology, 18*, 289–314.

French, D. C., & Waas, G. A. (1985). Behavior problems of peer-neglected and peer-rejected elementary-age children: Parent and teacher perspectives. *Child Development, 56*, 246–252.

Giordano, P. C., Cernkovich, S. A., & Pugh, M. D. (1986). Friendships and delinquency. *American Journal of Sociology, 91*, 1170–1202.

Gold, M., & Yanof, D. S. (1985). Mothers, daughters, and girlfriends. *Journal of Personality and Social Psychology, 49*, 654–659.

Goswick, R. A., & Jones, W. H. (1982). Components of loneliness during adolescence. *Journal of Youth and Adolescence, 11*, 373–383.

Hallinan, M. T. (1983). Commentary: New directions for research on peer influence. In J. L. Epstein & N. Karweit (Eds.), *Friends in school* (pp. 219–231). New York: Academic Press.

Hartup, W. W. (1989). Behavioral manifestations of children's friendships. In T. J. Berndt & G. W. Ladd (Eds.), *Peer relationships in child development* (pp. 46–70). New York: Wiley.

Hirsch, B. J., & Reischl, T. M. (1985). Social networks and developmental psychopathology: A comparison of adolescent children of a depressed, arthritic, or normal parent. *Journal of Abnormal Psychology, 94*, 272–281.

Ide, J. K., Parkerson, J., Haertel, G. D., & Walberg, H. J. (1981). Peer group influence on educational outcomes: A quantitative synthesis. *Journal of Educational Psychology, 73*, 472–484.

Kandel, D. B. (1978a). Homophily, selection, and socialization in adolescent friendships. *American Journal of Sociology, 84*, 427–436.

Kandel, D. B. (1978b). Similarity in real-life adolescent friendship pairs. *Journal of Personality and Social Psychology, 36*, 306–312.

Kandel, D. B., & Andrews, K. (1987). Processes of adolescent socialization by parents and peers. *International Journal of the Addictions, 22*, 319–342.

Kanner, A. D., Feldman, S. S., Weinberger, D. A., & Ford, M. E. (1987). Uplifts, hassles, and adaptational outcomes in early adolescents. *Journal of Early Adolescence, 7*, 371–394.

Kohlberg, L., & Higgins, A. (1987). School democracy and social interaction. In W. M. Kurtines & J. L. Gewirtz (Eds.), *Moral development through social interaction* (pp. 000–000). New York: Wiley.

Kurdek, L. A., & Sinclair, R. J. (1988). Adjustment of young adolescents in two-parent nuclear, stepfather, and mother-custody families. *Journal of Consulting and Clinical Psychology, 56*, 91–96.

Ladd, G. W., & Mize, J. (1983). A cognitive-social learning model of social-skill training. *Psychological Review, 90*, 127–157.

Mannarino, A. P. (1976). Friendship patterns and altruistic behavior in preadolescent males. *Developmental Psychology, 12*, 555–556.

Marcoen, A., Goossens, F. A., & Caes, P. (1987). Loneliness in pre- through late adolescence: Exploring the contributions of a multidimensional approach. *Journal of Youth and Adolescence, 16*, 561–577.

McGuire, K. D., & Weisz, J. R. (1982). Social cognition and behavior correlates of preadolescent chumships. *Child Development, 53*, 1478–1484.

Mead, G. H. (1934). *Mind, self and society.* Chicago: University of Chicago Press.

Miller, K. E., & Berndt, T. J. (1987). *Adolescent friendship and school orientation.* Paper presented at a conference of the Society for Research in Child Development, Baltimore, MD.

O'Brien, S. F., & Bierman, K. L. (1988). Conceptions and perceived influence of peer groups: Interviews with preadolescents and adolescents. *Child Development, 59,* 1360–1365.

Olweus, D. (1978). *Aggression in the schools: Bullies and whipping boys.* Washington, DC: Hemisphere.

Olweus, D. (1987). Bully/victim problems among school children in Scandinavia. In J. P. Myklebust & R. Ommundsen (Eds.), *Psykologprofesjonen mot ar 2000* (pp. 345–413). Oslo: Universitetsforlaget.

Panella, D., & Henggeler, S. W. (1986). Peer interactions of conduct-disordered, anxious-withdrawn, and well-adjusted Black adolescents. *Journal of Abnormal Child Psychology, 14,* 1–11.

Parker, J. G., & Asher, S. R. (1987). Peer relations and later personal adjustment: Are low-accepted children at risk? *Psychological Bulletin, 102,* 357–389.

Peplau, L. A., & Perlman, D. (Eds.) (1982). *Loneliness: A sourcebook of current theory, research, and therapy.* New York: Wiley.

Perry, T. B. (1987). *The relation of adolescent self-perceptions to their social relationships.* Unpublished doctoral dissertation, University of Oklahoma, Norman.

Putallaz, M. (1987). Maternal behavior and children's status. *Child Development, 58,* 324–340.

Rutter, M. (1987). Psychosocial resilience and protective mechanisms. *American Journal of Orthopsychiatry, 57,* 316–331.

Savin-Williams, R. C. (1987). *Adolescence: An ethological perspective.* New York: Springer-Verlag.

Savin-Williams, R. C., & Berndt, T. J. (1990). Friendships and peer relations. In S. S. Feldman & G. R. Elliott (Eds.), *At the threshold: The developing adolescent.* Cambridge, MA: Harvard University Press, pp. 277–307.

Scholfield, J. W. (1982). *Black and White in school: Trust, tension, or tolerance?* New York: Praeger.

Sharabany, R., Gershoni, R., & Hofman, J. W. (1981). Girlfriend, boyfriend: Age and sex differences in intimate friendships. *Developmental Psychology, 17,* 800–808.

Shrum, W., & Cheek, N. H. (1987). Social structure during the school years: Onset of the degrouping process. *American Sociological Review, 52,* 218–223.

Snyder, J., Dishion, T. J., & Patterson, G. R. (1986). Determinants and consequences of associating with deviant peers during preadolescence and adolescence. *Journal of Early Adolescence, 6,* 29–43.

Steinberg, L., & Silverberg, S. B. (1986). The vicissitudes of autonomy in early adolescence. *Child Development, 57,* 841–851.

Sullivan, H. S. (1953). *The interpersonal theory of psychiatry.* New York: Norton.

Townsend, M. A. R., McCracken, H. W., & Wilton, K. M. (1988). Popularity and intimacy as determinants of psychological well-being in adolescent friendships. *Journal of Early Adolescence, 8,* 421–436.

Vorrath, H. H., & Brendtro, L. K. (1974). *Positive peer culture.* Hawthorne, NY: Aldine.

Watson, D., & Clark, L. A. (1984). Negative affectivity: The disposition to experience aversive emotional states. *Psychological Bulletin, 96,* 465–490.

Youniss, J. (1980). *Parents and peers in social development.* Chicago: University of Chicago Press.

CHAPTER 10

Adolescence and Diversity

RODERICK WATTS, HECTOR MACHABANSKI, and BETTY M. KARRER

INTRODUCTION

The purposes of this chapter are to highlight the significance of human diversity in adolescent research and treatment and to describe a range of concepts and methods relevant to work in this area. Although a special emphasis will be on the application of these ideas to adolescents from non-White ethnic populations in the United States, the perspectives we consider will aid in the understanding of European-Americans as well. Of particular interest for this review are the psychologically and socially important aspects of human diversity that include race and ethnicity, gender, class, and sexual orientation.

Before we begin a review of the areas of interest, it is important to understand why it is now, more than ever, essential that we develop a psychology of human diversity. Population projections for the early 21st century indicate that diversity will be one of the most salient aspects of the U.S. population. By that time, upward of 1 in 4 people in this country will be African American, Latin American,* or Asian American. By 2010, almost one-third of U.S. children and work-force entrants will be Latin American or Black and only about 20% will be European American males (U.S. Bureau of the Census, 1989). Despite these dramatic future demographic shifts and the significant range of human diversity already apparent, we do not yet have a general theory in psychology that addresses human diversity. Moreover, psychologically and socially meaningful dimensions of the human experience, such as gender, race, ethnicity, social class, sexual orientation, age, and disability, are not typically integral parts of psychological theories. If dominant models of psychological theory and application equitably served the needs of all young people in society, there would be little reason to challenge current thinking; but this is not the case. Indeed, many psychological theories and practices have contributed to the stigma certain populations of adolescents experience. When human diversity attributes are the focus of study, too often the methods and interpretations frame differences in terms of superiority or inferiority, with the European

---

*No wholly satisfactory term is available to describe all the indigenous peoples of Mexico, Central and South America, the Spanish-speaking people of the Caribbean, and their descendants in the United States. Therefore, we refer to specific nationalities when possible and use the term "Latin American" to describe these groups collectively.

American male's perspective as the point of reference. For example, research on women often "emphasize[s] how women differ from men and use[s] these differences to support the norm of male superiority" (Hare-Mustin & Marecek, 1988, p. 455). In the clinical area, there is a persistent bias against members of lower social classes (Sutton & Kessler, 1986), and psychological assessments assign disproportionate numbers of Black youngsters to "special education" (Ogbu, 1978).

Philosophy and Values: Toward a Psychology of Diversity with Adolescents

What is a "psychology of human diversity," and how can it contribute to adolescent research and treatment? In answer to the former question we would say that a psychology of diversity has a number of defining characteristics. Philosophically, it is allied with social constructivism (Gergen, 1985; Watzlawick, 1984) because the human diversity perspective is consistent with the notion that reality emerges from a "social consensus process" (Unger, Draper, & Pendergrass, 1986). Consequently, an understanding of our social, psychological, and environmental contexts is necessary for a science of human behavior. Cultural relativism, or, more broadly, *human relativism,* is also a central tenet of the human diversity perspective. In other words, no one population defines, or should impose, a standard of goodness on other populations. A value on relativism can be fulfilled through a pluralistic approach to human differences. Pluralism calls for the creation of settings and an approach to treatment that permits people to retain their distinctiveness or to have a just role in decisions that will affect their distinctiveness. Thus, pluralism cannot exist without shared power and influence. According to the educational literature (Stent, Hazard, & Rivlin, 1973), pluralism is a state of equity, mutual respect, and interdependence among several populations that form a single society. In pluralism, each group retains distinctive institutions, patterns of value, behavior, appearance, or language, while a common social structure exists to bind groups together. According to Farley (1988), "[U]nder pluralism there exists one society made up of a number of distinct parts. In contrast to the melting pot, the pluralist model is often compared to a *mosaic:* one unit made up of many distinct parts" (p. 151; author emphasis).* Thus, the pluralistic social scientist views human diversity as an inherently valuable human resource to be preserved and enhanced through psychological theory, research, and practice.

Psychologists and other mental health professionals who treat adolescents are in a unique position to promote pluralism because they frequently treat adolescents and their families during the developmental stage, when identity, including cultural identity, is a salient concern. As Harrison, Wilson, Pine, Chan, and Buriel (1990) pointed out, the family plays a pivotal role in transmitting the cultural identities that maintain cultural distinctiveness. Minority children are "oriented toward the family group as a source of information regarding their ethnic identity and culture. . . . Parents of successful children emphasized ethnic pride, self-development, awareness of racial barriers, and egalitarianism in their socialization practices" (p. 355). Consequently, *cultural identity development* should receive the same attention as the more general notions of identity. As Erickson noted (Phinney, 1989), members of an "oppressed and exploited minority" are at risk of internalizing negative stereotypes about their group and a negative identity.

The mental health professional who intervenes in a family system of a subcultural group must first respond to the expressed needs of the client, but the therapist makes

---

*We recognize that other authors (e.g., Berry, Katlin & Taylor, 1977) define pluralism more as we would define separatism and, as such, view it as undesirable. They prefer the term "multiculturalism." We chose pluralism because our concerns are broader than culture and because pluralism highlights our concern with power sharing.

choices about how she or he understands the presenting problem. A pluralistic approach requires that an intervention recognize and affirm cultural values and distinctiveness. Thus, the therapist would attend to such variables and even initiate their exploration.

A psychology of human diversity also contributes to adolescent research and treatment through a deceptively simple idea: distinctive behavior in a population reflects its members' culturally influenced adaptation to environmental resources and constraints. This formulation of human behavior has the advantage of encouraging "why" as well as "what" questions. In clinical settings, "what" questions are used to identify an adolescent's behavior, make a diagnosis, and devise a treatment. For example "what" is the diagnosis, "what" is the problem behavior. "Why" questions emerge from a consideration of culture and adaptation; for instance, why is this adolescent selecting this behavior over others? Lambert, Weisz, and Knight (1989) provided an illustration of this analytical method in their cross-cultural study of Jamaican and U.S. adolescents. Based on a review of clinical data in both countries, they concluded that "characteristics of a culture (e.g., values, expectancies, and childrearing practice) may suppress the development of certain types of child behavior and foster . . . others" (p. 470). They found that Jamaicans tended to have more "over-control" disorders (e.g., fearfulness, sleep problems, somaticizing) and fewer of the "under-control problems" (e.g., fighting, disobedience, stealing) typical of U.S. youth. When the "what" of adolescent behavior is put in the "why" context of adaptation and culture, the treatment provider working with members of nondominant cultures is faced with some new questions: How is treatment success defined? Is it bringing the adolescent in line with the norms of his or her culture of origin, or is conformity with dominant cultural norms the criterion for success? As society is currently structured, those who adopt dominant European American cultural norms are less stigmatized. Nonetheless, a treatment provider who encourages a Jamaican youth here in the United States to do more acting-out and less acting-in may exacerbate the child's problems while undermining the family's transmission of cultural values. Such actions also encourage assimilation to the dominant cultural norm.

Pragmatic solutions to this dilemma and to the problems of cultural identity formation are not easy to devise, but it is clear that a value on human diversity is inconsistent with interventions that promote the loss of an adolescent's cultural heritage. One solution to the problem of culture loss, considered in this chapter, is a bicultural or multicultural identity that permits an adolescent to participate in other cultural settings without relinquishing her or his culture of origin. *In a truly pluralistic society, however, biculturality is not a one-way street; members of the majority culture must be competent in other cultures as well.*

Key Paradigms in a Psychology of Human Diversity

Our approach to this topic is organized around four perspectives in psychology that are quite different in emphasis but equally relevant to a psychology of human diversity. Some are relevant because they permit differences to be viewed as strengths rather than deviations from a norm. Others are included because they offer new alternatives for specific research and intervention activities. The first perspective we will consider is the *sociopolitical approach* (Prilleltensky, 1989); where psychological well-being is seen as a function of social equity. Interventions emphasize social change and the analysis of social processes from the viewpoint of the oppressed. But the role that injustice and other sociopolitical factors play in mental health and behavior accounts for only a portion of population and ethnic variation. A fuller understanding and an affirmation of population differences are needed. This need leads to the second perspective: the *population-specific psychologies*

(PSPs). PSPs offer a detailed understanding of a population (e.g., women, Asian Americans, gays) with minimal use of comparative methods. The basic supposition is that each population has a distinctive history, culture, or world view that is best understood through a psychology specific to the population.

Such a comprehensive understanding of distinctive groups is essential, but it is not the best way to illuminate similarities and differences among groups. Moreover, in a multicultural society, cross-population research and intervention are inevitable. This need for methods that are applicable to a range of populations provides the rationale for the third perspective, the *cross-cultural perspective*. The search for psychological "universals" and variations in their cultural expression are key questions in cross-cultural research.

Integrating these seemingly disparate perspectives may seem impossible at first glance. However, each of these perspectives can be understood as a special case of ecological psychology because the notion of person–environment interdependence is essential to each one. *Ecological psychology* (Trickett, Kelly, & Todd, 1972) unites the other perspectives through its focus on the context of human behavior. Its emphasis on the role of the environment in human behavior and on the use of indigenous personal and environmental resources in interventions is consistent with the sociopolitical perspective, while its attention to culture as an aspect of the psychosocial environment is consistent with population-specific and cross-cultural perspectives. In addition, the central role accorded environmental resources and the adaptation process reduces the "person blame" conclusions that often accompany the use of trait-based theories and research (Caplan & Nelson, 1973).

Relevant to all the areas of our review are the systematic forms of discrimination based on an abuse of power and on an ideology of superiority held by the powerful. Racism and sexism are two of the most frequently discussed "-isms," but homophobia (D'Augelli, 1989) and ageism (Kimmel, 1988) produce victims as well. Although ageism is seldom considered a problem for the young, preventing all 15-year-olds from driving or working, regardless of maturity and solely on the basis of age, is typical of the prejudicial, categorical policies that characterize all the other forms of discrimination. The impact of systematic discrimination will be considered throughout this review.

THE SOCIOPOLITICAL PERSPECTIVE

Because of the health and mental health consequences of social inequity (Albee, 1982; Bulhan, 1988; McCord & Freeman, 1990), adherents of the sociopolitical perspective study the inequitable distribution of power and its social consequences; the ways in which dominant-group psychology serves the powerful; and strategies for social change. Insight is gained through an understanding of the historical, political, and economic context of power. Two of the essential concepts for consideration here are ideology and oppression. Ideology was defined by Beyer (1981) as "relatively coherent sets of beliefs that bind some people together and that explain their worlds in terms of cause-and-effect relations" (quoted in Weiss & Miller, 1987). Ideology is self-serving; Berger and Luckmann (1966) highlighted this characteristic: "When a particular definition of reality comes to be attached to a concrete power interest, it may be called an ideology" (quoted in Weiss & Miller, 1987). At the disciplinary level, ideology is a useful concept for critiquing the role psychology plays in social control and in serving the interests of the dominant culture. (King, Moody, Thompson, & Bennett, 1983; Prilleltensky, 1989; Wallston, 1981). In the United States, for example, the dominant culture views individual initiative and character as the keys to success and the "American Dream" (Katz, 1985). This value is ideological in the sense that it deflects attention away from society's systematic impediments to success, such as racism and sexism. As such, it serves the interests of the powerful, who benefit from the current social order. Psychological theories and research often serve these power interests by focusing on individuals rather than social systems. For example, psychologists frequently define "Juvenile delinquency" in terms of personal deficiencies—cognitive deficits, abnormal personality, moral development deficits, and so on (Binder, 1988). Social systems analysis is relegated to sociology. From the sociopolitical perspective, these and other person-centered formulations that fail to implicate social processes reflect dominant-group interests and ideology.

An ideology rationalizes the use of power, and the unjust exercise of power results in oppression. The use of these three concepts—ideology, power, and oppression—may help to shed new light on important issues in adolescence. Bulhan (1988) is one of the few U.S. psychologists who have examined oppression at length. He describes oppression as "any relation, process or condition by which an individual or group violates the physical, social and/or psychological integrity of another person or group." This violation affects "one's space, time, energy, mobility, bonding, and identity" (Bulhan, 1988). Albee (1982) vividly illustrated the relationship among ideology, power, and oppression. He reviewed how the ideology of the early 1900s shaped the racist and sexist development of intelligence testing and related theory. He also showed the contribution psychology made to the oppression of European immigrants and people of color. Echos of these ideas can be heard in current policies on intelligence testing, the educational placement of Black children and adolescents and the issue of gender differences in mental ability remain politically and professionally controversial.

Racism, sexism, and similar social aberrations are special cases of oppression; they represent *systematic* discrimination justified by an ideology of superiority. Based on work by Jones (1972), Dovidio and Gaertner's (1986) definition of institutional racism highlighted its systemic properties: "[Institutional racism is] the intentional or unintentional manipulation or toleration of institutional policies . . . that unfairly restrict the opportunities of particular groups of people" (p. 3). Equally relevant is the notion of cultural racism, defined by Jones (1986) as "the maintenance and functioning of opportunity structures . . . predicated on certain values of individuality, future-orientation, . . . which define appropriate inputs . . . . If a person does not or cannot operate within this framework, he or she is obliged to operate within another . . . or is at a disadvantage within the majority context" (p. 293).

These definitions aid our understanding of policies that impede the use of mental health services by people of color. Rogler, Malgady, Costantino, and Blumenthal (1987), in their discussion of culturally sensitive mental health services, noted that the "underutilization" of mental health services by Latin Americans is due, in part, to the *types* of services available. Thus, if an agency's policies only provide for treatment modalities based on European American needs and sensibilities (i.e., cultural racism), policy makers share the responsibility for "underuse." This policy responsibility extends beyond merely increasing access to or modifying traditional services; it also includes an awareness of racist, sexist, and ethnocentric biases that impede the development of alternative interventions.

Moving down to the clinical level, the concepts of ideology and oppression may provide an alternative perspective on child abuse that links the sociopolitical and psychological levels of the problem. Anecdotally, family therapists have already made some of these linkages: A boss uses institutional power against a male worker and the worker returns home to use physical power against his wife, who in turn abuses their child. The child may then abuse the family dog, who in turn bites the mail carrier! Research findings on the link between wife battering and child abuse (Stark & Flitcraft, 1988) support this multileveled model of abuse and the notion of a downward movement of oppression.

Oppression is also an alternative way of understanding certain instances of "depression" or "adjustment" reactions. The Latin root of *oppression,* "to press," is the same as the root for *depression.* The only difference is in the prefixes: "op-" means against, and "de-" means down. This similarity invites the hypothesis that depressed adolescents may, in certain instances, be said to be suffering from oppression. For instance, the DSM-III-R (American Psychiatric Association, 1987) Dysthymia diagnosis includes feelings of hopelessness and low self-esteem, which are the emotional components of subjugation and low personal power. Similarly, the animal model of learned helplessness that is frequently cited as an analog to human depression (Seligman, 1975) may also be considered a model of oppression and its consequences.

In work with families, the concepts of ideology and oppression also have applications in the area of parenting behavior and parent–adolescent conflict. Viewing parenting attitudes as "parenting ideology" better highlights the "concrete power interests" associated with parenting style. Parents seek to maintain parental power while shaping adolescent behavior in accordance with parental and societal ideals. Although developmental psychologists and family theorists recognize the important process of reworking unilateral (i.e., parent → child) power relationships during adolescence, there is little information about the dynamics of power and hierarchical relations in families (Feldman & Gehring, 1990). The concept of ideology, with its focus on a coherent set of attitudes that serve a specific power interest, may be a useful way of integrating the notions of parental power and parenting style in the hierarchical context of the family.

The concept of oppression is potentially useful wherever the dynamics of power are involved. For example, parents exercise their power and control in the areas identified by Bulhan: Adolescents can be controlled by confinement to the home (space), appropriation of their personal time for chores (time and energy), and curfews or social restrictions (mobility), to name a few. Thus, oppressive control in family systems may parallel oppressive control in social systems. Unfortunately, there is no research, to our knowledge, that attempts to validate these dimensions of oppression or the linkages among various levels of analysis. Are those who suffer the worst societal oppression more or less oppressive in their parental roles than less oppressed parents? Is oppression associated with a distinct constellation of psychological symptoms, such as depressive symptoms? If so, there may be a need to view the causes of depression as a continuum ranging from depression caused by external antecedents (oppression and ecological factors) to depression caused by internal antecedents (biological or psychological factors).

Empowerment: The Antidote for Oppression

Ideology cannot be eliminated, nor is it inherently evil. It is only a problem when it rationalizes an unjust exercise of power. Although it cannot be eliminated, it should be recognized, analyzed, and critically evaluated. (We will have more to say about this critiquing process in the section on the population-specific perspective.) Oppression, on the other hand, can be eliminated. However, when abuse is reframed as oppression, intervention goals and methods change as well. To consider these changes, we turn to the sociopolitical tradition of psychology, where *empowerment* has emerged as the sociopolitical "treatment" of choice for oppression and the related conditions of powerlessness, alienation, and anomie (Rappaport, 1977). Zimmerman and Rappaport (1988) defined empowerment as "a combination of self-acceptance and self-confidence, social and political understanding, and the ability to play an assertive role in controlling resources and decisions in one's community" (p. 726).

Zimmerman and Rappaport's definition, like the concept of oppression, is useful because it spans levels of analysis. At the clinical level, assertive communication constitutes a form of personal empowerment. Research on power and authority in families suggests that an adolescent's assertiveness plays a significant role in family dynamics as he or she becomes more independent and the parent–adolescent balance of power shifts (Feldman & Gehring, 1990). Moreover, research on empowerment-related interventions indicates that feelings of empowerment are associated with a variety of positive psychological effects (Fairweather, 1979; Zimmerman & Rappaport, 1988).

Simmons and Parsons's (1983) empowerment intervention is one of the few research efforts to directly demonstrate the concept's potential with adolescents. Their intervention was based on Solomon's (1976) strategy of empowerment, which emphasizes the provision of information, alternatives, and resources. This approach was combined with locus-of-control learning theory, "with the expectation that successful empowerment would lead to a stronger sense of personal control over life events and greater perceived competence to reach life goals" (p. 918). The aims of these authors' multisession Life Choices workshop were "increasing the girls' self-esteem, developing an awareness of future role alternatives, and strengthening a sense of personal control or internality over life events" (p. 917). Curiously, the authors did not link the interventions to sexism, despite the fact that all the participants were girls.

Both the successes and the failures of Simmons and Parsons's intervention are instructive. These authors succeeded in significantly raising internal locus of control and perceived competence in a variety of areas from pre- to posttesting and in comparison with controls. Though exploratory, these results demonstrate the value of empowerment interventions for adolescents. However, this success was limited to the "working-class" girls. "Underclass" girls in the investigation showed no positive changes; in fact, the investigators speculate, the program may have had a negative effect on this group. These mixed findings should remind us of the influence of class and other within group differences on program outcome.

THE CROSS-CULTURAL PERSPECTIVE

Cross-cultural psychologists seek to understand both unique and universal cultural attributes, their influence on behavior, and the dynamics of intercultural contact. Unlike the sociopolitical perspective, the cross-cultural approach takes no a priori position on the external validity of psychological concepts traditional to U.S. psychology. Indeed, much of the work in cross-cultural psychology is concerned with methods of determining the usefulness of specific concepts across cultures and populations. Although cross-cultural psychologists usually have no explicit and consistent ideological stance aside from cultural relativity, research efforts are much more likely, in actual practice, to seek validation of dominant-group psychological concepts on nondominant groups than vice versa (Jahoda, 1980).

The influence of the cross-cultural perspective on theories of adolescence has a long history. As early as 1929, theories of adolescent development were being influenced by anthropologists, most notably Margaret Mead's (1949) classic study of Samoan youth. A comprehensive review of all the concepts and methods of cross-cultural psychology is well beyond the scope of this chapter, so we will limit our review to a few ideas that are especially pertinent: Emic and Etic methodologies, culture, the psychological process of acculturation and related concepts, and culture as an identity issue of adolescence.

The Emic–Etic distinction in research methods, originated by Pike (1966) and further developed by others (Berry, 1988) is the most useful place to begin. The Emic approach focuses on the study of a specific culture from its own vantage point. Insofar as possible, this method strives to be noncomparative and nonjudgmental. Investigators immerse themselves in the culture under study and work to develop an outlook identical to the group's native members. Participant observation and ethnographic techniques reflects this strategy. These noncomparative, culture-specific methods are akin to the ones used in the population-specific psychologies reviewed in the next section. We will use the more intuitively appealing term "internal research" to describe the Emic method.

In contrast, the Etic (i.e., "external") approach analyzes behavior from an intellectual position outside the system. External researchers use comparative methods in their effort to construct and verify cultural universals. Research strategies focus on group comparisons and cross-cultural construct validation. A priori concepts are essential because they build the corpus of "universal" concepts. The use of a priori concepts requires the investigators to strive for objectivity. This minimizes distortions that may influence the evaluation of the concepts.

Internal and external methods have strengths and weaknesses. Examples of both can be found in the research on "overcontrolled" and "undercontrolled" behavior conducted by Lambert et al. (1989). Lambert and his colleagues assumed that the issue of "control" was the universal issue at the heart of clinical symptoms such as somatization (overcontrol of psychological distress) or fighting (undercontrol). They predicted that overcontrolling cultures would produce more adolescents having anxiety, sleep, and somatic problems than cultures more tolerant of expressiveness. The findings supported their predictions: Thai adolescents suffered from more overcontrol problems whereas U.S. youth suffered from more undercontrol problems. On the fact of it, Lambert et al.'s findings illustrate the value of the external method for understanding the role of culture in adolescent behavior. However, their application of universal concepts may be misleading. The notion of "control" as an organizing concept may be culture-bound rather than culturally universal, despite its apparent usefulness. Viewing emotions as something to control (i.e., restrain) may be in itself cultural. In an alternative perspective, White and Parham (1990) saw "emotional vitality" as a recurrent psychological theme in African American culture. Their work suggests that Blacks are concerned with *channeling* rather than controlling emotions. For example, the call-and-response interplay heard in some Black churches is a ritualized interchange that governs or channels emotional expression. The structure of this interplay permits participants to express themselves intensely while enjoying the security of agreed-on boundaries and protocols for behavior. External investigators seeking only to validate the control notion may overlook the importance of these ritual structures for channeling in favor of a classification of the emotional expression itself.

In contrast, internal investigators avoid this pitfall by exploiting an instrument neglected by the external investigators: the investigators themselves. Internal investigators use personal reactions, feelings, and observations to better understand the context as well as the content of phenomena. Thus, the validity of the research depends on the quality of the investigator-as-instrument. Internal investigators have problems communicating discoveries to outsiders, because unique experiences cannot be communicated precisely with a generic, scientific language.

The Concept of Culture

Of all the Etic concepts, *culture* is the most basic to cross-cultural psychology. Yet it remains among the most difficult to define. The definition of culture by Kroeber and Kluckhohn (1954) is one of the most frequently cited:

Culture consists of patterns, explicit and implicit, of and for behaviour acquired and transmitted by symbols, constituting the distinctive achievement of human groups, including their embodiments in artifacts; . . . culture systems may, on the one hand be considered as products of action, on the other as conditioning elements of further action. (quoted in Jones & Block, 1984, p. 59)

The appeal of this general concept has led to its application in a variety of settings and for a number of populations, where widely shared patterns of behavior exist. For instance, Fasick (1984) used the concept of youth culture to describe the socializing influences of peers: "The crucial characteristic of youth culture is the irrelevance of the tastes, orientations and activities that make up adult life—with the exception of sexual behavior, drinking and drug use. [The core of youth culture is] sports, language, music, clothing, dating and 'hacking about'" (p. 151). Fasick argued that youth culture provides an opportunity for middle-class adolescents to develop *behavioral* autonomy, relative to their parents, in the areas noted above. Behavioral autonomy is the freedom to experiment with new behaviors that are not a threat to core social values. He contended that, in general, this is relatively harmless experimentation, not to be confused with attempts to achieve *value* autonomy.

Fasick saw youth culture as a less important means for developing autonomy among the upper and lower classes because of a higher and lower degree (respectively) of parental control. Among upper-class families, parents frequently usurp adolescent leisure time and use it to extend the adult socialization process. This socialization process occurs in highly structured leisure-time experiences like extracurricular private-school activities, special clubs, and so on. In the lower classes, the lack of adequate child care, other conditions that reduce parental supervision, and the availability of fewer structured leisure activities give young people many more options for autonomy beyond ordinary youth culture. Unfortunately, according to Fasick, many of these options include opportunities for the value autonomy associated with dropping out of school and with membership in crime-prone adolescent subcultures (gangs, etc.). These examples illustrate the value of culture as a general concept to describe the dynamics of large groups that share values, patterns of behavior, or systems of meaning.

Although culture arises from the dynamics of large groups, it manifests itself on a variety of levels. Keesing (1974) conceived of culture not only as a shared biological and social phenomenon, but also as a personal system that each individual uses in knowing, interpreting, and elaborating about the world. Thus, thinking culturally helps in avoiding the pitfalls of an exclusive focus on intrapsychic dynamics and personal behaviors. This psychosocial view includes the cause, development, and social reinforcement of cultural patterns of behavior.

High-Context and Low-Context Cultures

Hall (1976) organized cultures into two categories: high context and low context. The two differ in the extent to which context and circumstances are used to establish meaning. In the high-context Asian, African American, and Latin American cultures, circumstances determine meaning. Nonverbal communication, the behavior setting's characteristics (Barker & Associates, 1978), the social status of the participants, past experience, and process variables are essential for establishing meaning. In low-context cultures (e.g., Anglo, German, Swiss), what Hall called the "code" is central to meaning. The code is the data—the words, the content, and the explicit aspects of a transaction. In reality, this typology is oversimplified because a single culture may be high-context in some areas and low-context in others, but we will illustrate how the idea offers a useful way of understanding cultural differences.

The concept of high-context communication can be illustrated in a parent's attempt to interpret a child's crying behavior. The parent obtains relatively little information from the crying itself, which Hall called the data or code in the transaction. Instead, the parent relies on context to establish meaning: her or his past experience about distress under similar circumstances, how long it has been since the child ate or was changed, and so on. After childhood, cultures differ in their reliance on context to convey meaning. For example, Anglo-Americans (as distinct from their more high-context southern European counterparts) are near the low-context end of the continuum. This cognitive style is associated with a preference for content-centered communication, linear processes of reasoning that stress logic, counting, reductionist analytical methods, and a strong distinction between self and other. Consequently, one would expect parents using this style to rely increasingly on content for understanding. In contrast, high-context peoples emphasize patterns and gestalt, synthesis, intuitive methods, symbolic imagery, metaphor, qualitative analysis, and minimal self–other distinction. These parents should continue their reliance on context. The high- and low-context notions are analogous to the "field dependence" and "field independence" orientations measured by the Rod and Frame Test (Cole & Scribner, 1974). Field independence is the ability to reduce complex stimuli into simpler parts, or to be uninfluenced by context. Historically, cross-cultural researchers viewed this as evidence of *advanced* psychological development (Witkin, 1967). However, this attribution of superiority to low-context styles of knowing is ethnocentric and unjustified (Hall, 1976). Ramirez's (1983) term "field sensitive" is preferable to "field dependent" because it better conveys how the two styles are simply different.

The concept of context and field usage has implications for both research and treatment. In the research area, it has implications for measurement. Survey methods require the respondent to produce responses that are stripped of their context and in reduced, elemental form. In contrast, the highly contextual life-history methods developed by Ramirez (1983), which will be detailed later, rely on extensive, minimally structured interviews as a source of data. The client controls the process and, in effect, creates a context for understanding. This method seems more consistent with the phenomenology of high-context cultures than an investigator-driven question-and-answer method. In the area of adolescent treatment, Hall's work suggests that the context of treatment requires as much attention as the content. Thus, a therapeutic alliance is not built solely through the disclosure of data and empathetic responses. It also depends on the perceived attributes of the professional— part of the context of treatment. Sue and Zane (1986), based on their work with Asian Americans, called these contextual variables "credibility." Status is part of credibility, and it is also one of the key contextual variables noted by Hall. According to Sue: "At least two factors are important in enhancing credibility: ascribed and achieved status. *Ascribed status is one's position or role that is assigned by others . . .* achieved credibility refers more directly to therapists' skills" (emphasis added, p. 163). Similarly, Gibbs's (1980) work in school consultation suggested that it is more important to establish an interpersonal context for Black clients than for White clients. Blacks value an interpersonal orientation that "focuses on the process rather than the content of the interactions, both verbal and nonverbal . . . ." Whites tend to focus on the consultant's "instrumental competence"—his or her degree of effectiveness in task-related activities. Just as many Asian Americans are attuned to status issues in establishing credibility, Gibbs argues that many African Americans ". . . attempt to place the consultant in a social status hierarchy, along an ideological spectrum, or [they] evaluate the consultant's previous professional experiences." European Americans are also concerned with credibility. Presumably, to establish the consultant's qualifications, they rely less on the client–consultant interpersonal context and more on code: résumés, the recommendations of others, and the consultant's task performance. For Asian and African Americans (and members of other high-context cultures), the interpersonal context is a particularly important prerequisite for task-related activities and intimacy.

The role of context in psychological interventions, as defined by Hall, Gibbs, and others, is intriguing but underresearched. A clearer understanding of the process of context formation is needed. How does context formation differ from self-disclosure? What are the signs that a shared context exists? Are there cultural differences in the development of intimacy? Future research must address these questions.

Acculturation and Acculturative Stress

Although it is important to understand the cultural context of human behavior, in a multicultural society it is also essential to understand the dynamics of intercultural contact. *Acculturation* is a term that describes this contact and the range of possible outcomes. When two cultural groups interact, a range of political, social, and psychological changes occur, and, as Berry (1984) described, the outcomes can fall into four categories:

- Assimilation (the nondominant group renounces its distinctiveness and is absorbed);
- Separation (the nondominant group fully retains its unique characteristics and has little contact with the dominant group);
- Integration (some distinctiveness remains, but the group becomes an integral component of the mainstream);
- Marginalization (members have few connections with their cultural origins but do not join the dominant group).

Yinger (1985) described several processes that promote assimilation: amalgamation (biological intermixing), psychological identification, and integration. This latter notion, integration, has had a confusing history in the literature and in the popular mind. Integration or "structural pluralism" (Pettigrew, 1988) exists when many groups are represented, with equal status, at all levels of the social structure. For example, Jews are nearly integrated in U.S. society, although anti-semitism continues to persist. In contrast, separation, or "cultural pluralism" (Pettigrew, 1988), is the maintenance of cultural homogeneity. Separation requires that group members scrupulously adhere to their unique traditions and shun contact with outsiders in order to maintain their distinctiveness. True cultural pluralism is uncommon in the United States, but the Hasidic Jews (viewed as an ethnic group) and the Amish are two examples. Native Americans' reservations are not good examples of cultural pluralism because they are largely a consequence of segregation (imposed separation).

In the United States, people who are not White males (namely, White women and people of color) have not, as a group, assimilated, integrated, or separated. This brings us to a fourth outcome of acculturation, noted by Berry, Trimble, and Olmedo (1986) and known as *marginalization*. Marginalization exists for a large proportion of these populations, for two reasons: (a) sexism, racism, and ethnocentric attitudes have prevented them from gaining the social acceptance needed for assimilation or integration (the other alternative, separation, has not been accomplished on a large scale); and (b) marginalization has occurred because many members of the population have rejected, been turned against, or know little of, their culture of origin. Without the acceptance of the dominant culture or positive identity with a culture of origin, a person risks marginalization. As a group, African Americans provide an example of marginalization. Unlike Europeans who immigrated to the United States, Africans arrived through the slave trade and experienced the systematic disparagement and destruction of their cultural traditions. Consequently, many Blacks have spurned or are unaware of their cultural history, while racism precludes assimilation or integration into the European American population. Moreover, according to Pettigrew (1988), African Americans are burdened by their lingering social status as a caste group (i.e., slaves) rather than an ethnic group. The notion of caste is also useful for describing the restricted social mobility of White women because of continuing sex-based prejudices.

With respect to adolescents, gang-related antisocial behavior, delinquency, and perhaps even substance abuse may be aggravated by marginalization, just as these problems are associated with the related concept of alienation. Future research should explore links between the two ideas. For example, Keniston (1965) regarded one component of marginalization, termed the "explicit rejection of traditional American culture," as a form of alienation. In the research literature, Paulson, Lin, and Hanssen (1980) attempted to link childhood socialization to adolescent alienation by comparing "anti-establishment" and "establishment" oriented youth. Their data suggested that the recall of family harmony was negatively related to later alienation. In the area of substance abuse, Gary and Berry's (1984) research found that African American adolescents who scored high on a racial consciousness measure (i.e., those who were not marginalized) were less likely to be drug abusers than their low-consciousness counterparts. Similarly, research on alienation hints at associations among alienation, adolescent deviance, and substance abuse (Aultman & Wellford, 1977; Covington, 1982; Simon, 1986), although the nature and strengths of these links remain debatable. Nonetheless, alienation, marginalization, and the process of cultural "transfer" during adolescence are important themes to consider in diagnosis and treatment.

The preceding discussion on acculturation highlights the complex intercultural dynamics that adolescents from nondominant populations must negotiate as they acculturate. The risk of marginalization, the one unqualified negative outcome, depends on a variety of variables inside and outside of the adolescent's family. In the United States, acculturation has traditionally meant dissolving into the national "melting pot" through assimilation, at least for those who qualified. More recently, "salad bowl" pluralism and mutual cultural accommodation have gained favor, which permits significant populations in the social mix to retain their distinctiveness while contributing to the whole. Assimilation pressures remain, however, and they have important implications for ethnic minority adolescents and their families. For instance, the pervasive and glamorous portrayal of certain values of the majority culture in the media (e.g., unbridled materialism) makes it a potentially more powerful force for the development of *new* behaviors in a Native American youngster who recently left a reservation than in a European American youngster whose culture produced these media images. Consequently, the Native American youngster's absorption of dominant cultural values may become more than a bid for *behavioral autonomy* as described by Fasick (1984); The pervasiveness of dominant-culture values and rewards may lead the adolescent to develop an identity based on dominant cultural values. Fasick contended that value autonomy is a much greater departure from family norms than behavioral autonomy and it carries greater risk for serious family conflict.

Family conflict and adolescent development in this context raise a number of complex questions. In treatment interventions, for example, should the focus be on contracting to treat what seems to be a conduct disorder, or should equal attention be given to exploring the stress and conflicts arising from acculturation or from intrafamilial differences in the rate of acculturation? In preventive interventions that include skill building, is it important to identify and build skills indigenous to the client's culture? How does the use of interventions developed for European Americans affect the acculturation of those who are not part of that culture? These are important questions. As new programs are developed and disseminated nationally by sponsors such as the National Institute of Mental Health, it is especially important that we evaluate the impact of packaged interventions that are not "culturally tuned" for people of color.

The conflicts associated with acculturation are also associated with acculturative stress. Severe acculturative stress is related to psychological conflict, social disintegration, domestic violence, and so on (Berry et al., 1986). According to Berry and Kim (1988), acculturative stress can occur during any of the five phases of acculturation: precontact, contact, conflict, crisis, or adaptation. The seriousness of the symptoms depends on the attendant circumstances. If, for example, a Chicano adolescent girl had troubled relationships with her peers during the precontact phase and her experiences in the contact phase are associated with cultural isolation (e.g., she is the lone Chicano student in the high school), there may be intense pressures to behave in accordance with dominant-culture norms in order to adapt to the new setting. The student may attempt to adapt by assimilating. However, if assimilation is contrary to the family's cultural values, the conflict can spread to the family system. Alternatively, the student may shun other students, refuse to assimilate, and thereby lose the benefits of social support. In this latter scenario, there is a complex interaction between family cultural values and the adolescent's negotiation of the school setting. As indicated by Berry's model, the stress may become chronic if the student is marginally successful in reconciling the demands of parents and school, or her personal resources may prove grossly inadequate and lead to a crisis.

An understanding of acculturation is especially important in work with immigrant families and adolescents, because of the high rates of behavioral disorders associated with the stresses of sociocultural disruption (Szapocznik, Scopetta, & King, 1978). Although differences in rates must be scrutinized carefully for cross-cultural validity (Good & Good, 1986), disruption-associated disorders are predictable from the stressful life events model of psychological distress. The hypothesis that behavioral disturbances are associated with acculturative stress is also supported by the research of Szapocznik et al. (1978). They found that differences between parents and children in their rates of acculturation increased the likelihood of clinically significant family conflict: "Further, the model predicts that the most severe intra-family differences in behavioral acculturation occur between young males and their mothers, suggesting that the most severe intrafamily conflicts should occur between these family members" (p. 116).

The solution they proposed for this conflict contradicts democratic models of family structure. At least for Cuban families, Szapocznik and his colleagues (1978) recommended restoration and support of the traditional hierarchical family structure, where harmony is valued over individual freedom. Aponte's (1974) *ecological–structural family therapy* is their treatment of choice. This high-context approach to treatment is consistent with Ramirez's (1983) mestizo psychology:

The mestizo world view stresses the importance of ecology . . . it had its origins in the native peoples of the Americas . . . . Indian cultures view the person as an open system which both affects and is affected by his or her surroundings. Harmony with the environment, both physical and social, is thus of primary concern in psychological adjustment. (p. 8)

The psychological distress associated with acculturation also calls for caution when using symptoms as a basis for determining treatment and diagnosis for those who do not identify with European American culture. Moreover, the context of the behavior should be as influential on formulation and treatment as the behavior itself. If diagnoses are an inevitable part of practice, new categories may be needed— including, perhaps, Adjustment Reaction to Acculturation.

Acculturation and acculturative stress are important areas for service providers to consider when working with adolescents in nondominant cultures. As we noted, they have implications for assessment and intervention activities. Further information on this topic, especially as it applies to cross-cultural research, is available in Berry et al. (1986).

Population and Cultural Identity

The various acculturation alternatives just discussed interact with cultural identity and values; that is, the process of acculturation affects and is influenced by the extent to which an individual identifies with his or her culture of origin. Therefore, the concept of identity also warrants attention in the development of culturally sensitive theories and intervention.

The concept of identity has been applied to several attributes of human diversity: gender (Hare-Mustin & Marecek, 1988), racial (Helms, 1990), and gay and lesbian (Ponse, 1978) research. Understanding specific ethnic identities and values is also a concern of population-specific psychologies. Among cross-cultural psychologists, it is the part of a general model of culture that addresses the psychological aspects of cultural-group membership. The conceptualization and measurement of identity are important in all these areas because, presumably, something psychological binds the members of a population and serves to define them as a distinctive group.

Examples of the significance of identity for both the family and the adolescent can be seen in an analysis of Korean childrearing by Yu and Kim (1983). They described the differences between traditional Korean parenting and parenting in the United States. Unlike many of their European American counterparts, a Korean child may sleep in the same room as the parents until 5 years of age, and parents engage in other behavior that maintains a strong interdependency between child and family. Moreover, Confucian values on harmonious social relations, propriety, and the patriarchal family structure serve to promote obedience and conformity among the children. In a U.S. context, where autonomy and *personal* identity are seen as the developmental milestones for adolescents, a youngster raised in a traditional Korean household may be subject to conflicting expectations and desires. Yu and Kim identified three distinct acculturation alternatives for Koreans under these circumstances:

1. A "full Korean identity," in which they identify solely with their culture of origin;
2. A Korean American identity, in which they synthesize the two cultures into a new pattern that presumably includes the best of both—These Korean American young people are bicultural and are competent in both cultures;
3. A "full American identity," in which they reject the Korean culture in favor of the dominant culture.

The full Korean alternative is the counterpart to the separatist option described earlier (Berry et al., 1986), and the full American alternative corresponds to the assimilation option. However, the Korean American alternative reveals an additional choice. This approach is known by various authors as biculturalism (e.g., Szapocznik, Kurtines, & Fernandez, 1980) or double consciousness (DuBois, 1961).

Some authors may differentiate biculturalism further, noting that the newly acquired cultural knowledge can be internalized or remain instrumental. As an example of instrumental acquisition, a Puerto Rican immigrant may speak English at school with her European American classmates, but at home, and with other Puerto Ricans, she may speak Spanish exclusively. Thus, knowledge of a new culture is viewed as a means to interact with that culture, not as an integral part of the self. At present, we have virtually no information on the long-term stability of the bicultural option (e.g., does it decay in monocultural environments?) or its mental health implications (Harrison et al., 1990). No one, to our knowledge, has studied bicultural European American adolescents. These are important areas for future research.

Naditch and Morrissey (1976) implicated cultural identity in the high rate of mental illness they found among immigrant Cuban adolescents. They hypothesized that the high rate was partially a function of devaluation of their culture on the mainland and the subsequent impact on their cultural identity. Ethnic identity for Blacks (also known as racial identity or consciousness) is associated with a variety of behavioral, affective, and cultural predispositions. Some empirical research has found racial identity attitudes to be related to preference for counselor's race (Parham & Helms, 1981), self-esteem (Parham & Helms, 1985a), affective states (Parham & Helms, 1985b), and cultural values (Carter & Helms, 1987), while remaining unrelated to socioeconomic status (Carter & Helms, 1988; Watts & Carter, 1990).

Would "identity enhancement" prove a useful clinical intervention? Oler (1989) has argued that identity issues often require special attention in therapy with African Americans. His strategy for addressing racial identity is based on an assessment of the client's level of identity development. In the area of prevention, there are a number of cultural socialization programs for African American adolescents (Oliver, 1989; Warfield-Coppock, 1990). These programs promote a positive cultural identity and racial pride, while inoculating youngsters against racism. One example is the *Simba* ("young lions") program, which has chapters across the country, serving Black boys and adolescents (Kunjufu, 1986). As yet, there is little research evidence to indicate the effect of these programs, but the existing evidence is encouraging (Ferguson, 1990) and there is some indication that racial identity is associated with psychological well-being (Helms, 1990; Phinney, 1989). These and other cultural socialization strategies may help marginalized youngsters draw on their culture of origin as a source of social or psychological support (Berry & Kim, 1988).

Considering ethnic identity as a variable in mental health invites several interesting questions. Are low self-esteem and alienation in an adolescent who rejects his or her ethnic heritage just ordinary variants of identity formation, or is this distress a result of a steady diet of negative cultural stereotypes on television and elsewhere, and negative social reinforcement in the dominant culture? Should a therapist use conventional strategies for enhancing self esteem, or should ethnic identity be targeted for enhancement?

THE POPULATION-SPECIFIC PERSPECTIVE

Some of the more prominent examples of population-specific psychologies (PSPs) are the psychology of women, Chicano psychology, Black (Afrocentric) psychology, and Asian American psychology. Since their emergence, terms like "Anglo," "European American," "middle class," and "male" have become a common part of psychology's vocabulary. These modifiers have helped to increase our awareness of the cultural and social underpinnings of psychology. Katz (1985) specified some of these imbedded perspectives, stating that "White culture serves as a foundation for counseling theory, research, and practice" (p. 615). As examples, she noted some 15 categories of White culture that define the European American world view: rugged individualism, competition, and Protestant work ethic, among others. These social and cultural values, according to Katz, pervade the reasoning, goals, and valued activities in counseling. Her work illustrates how the PSPs have contributed to psychology theory by stimulating a closer examination of psychology's cultural backdrop. It challenges the idea that one psychology is appropriate for all, regardless of social, historical, or cultural context.

The outlook of PSPs sometimes overlaps with that of the sociopolitical perspective because PSP theorists frequently concern themselves with oppressed populations. PSPs are distinct from theories in the sociopolitical area in that the PSP adherents seek to articulate a world view that is specific to its particular members (e.g., Belenky, Clinchy, Goldberger, & Tarule, 1986; Ramirez, 1983). The specificity is typically based on gender, race, sexual orientation, age, or ethnicity. Thus, there are two principal ingredients in population-specific psychologies and they are present in varying proportions: culture or world view, and the dynamics of oppression.

Critique and Creativity: Revising Existing Ideas and Creating New Ones

In PSPs, critique is important because it reveals the cultural bias or ideology implicit in a theory or investigation. For theorists who believe that sexism, ethnocentrism, and racism have limited traditional psychology's usefulness with White women and people of color, critique becomes an intellectual test of the cross-cultural validity of theories and methods. Sue (1981) noted three versions of antidiversity research in the literature that can be identified through critique: (a) models that understand distinctive attributes of nondominant populations as psychopathology; (b) genetic- or constitutional-deficiency models for explaining population differences; and (c) cultural deficit models for explaining differences. Each of these explanations for differences tends to undermine efforts to understand differences as part of human diversity and as potential social assets. A critique based on these questions, in conjunction with culture-specific knowledge, is a useful method for assessing the value of psychological research and theory. Moreover, all psychologists would benefit from a critical examination of their own attitudes, research, theory, clinical formulations, and favorite sources of information in terms of these three areas.

On the treatment level, critique means a willingness to be *self*-critical. A treatment provider who is sensitive to the influence of his or her own world view strives to maintain a consensus of meaning between the family and therapist (Karrer, 1989). To Karrer, this means questioning clinical understanding by regularly asking the family what their view is about the presenting problems, the solutions, the content of therapy, and the therapeutic relationship. For example, the therapist might ask: "What do you think about what I just said? About what I just did? What do *you* mean by 'intimate'? By 'respect'?" The more dissimilar the cultural background of the family and therapist, the greater the possibilities for miscommunication. In addition to these low-context methods of maintaining congruence, the treatment provider can become more sensitive to contextual phenomena like eye contact, body language, proximity preferences, and so forth (Ivey, 1988).

Effective critique also includes a social constructivist perspective. An understanding of the roles that history, class, and culture play in scholarly activity will help us to be more circumspect when acting on our "facts." As Myrdal (quoted in Albee, 1982) observed:

> Now we all know that when we look back at any earlier era, we regularly find that not only popular discussion but also the work of social scientists were biased in the sense that their approach was influenced by dominating national or group interests in the society they were part of. However, like contemporary social scientists today, they were firmly convinced that their analysis and inferences were founded simply upon their observations of facts. (p. 157)

Creativity is the other side of the critique–creativity coin. New theories and methods must be created to replace flawed ones. The most radical approach to creativity is to create a wholly new psychology from a *tabula rasa*. Theorists using this approach begin anew with a set of principles and methods derived directly from the study of the population of interest, or from the population's underlying philosophy and values. Ramirez's mestizo psychology (1983), Nobles' African (Black) psychology (Nobles, 1986), and work by a number of White women (e.g., Wallston, 1981) are prominent examples of this approach.

As noted earlier, Ramirez (1983) described a number of methodologies inspired by or consistent with the *mestizo** world view. Two are The Multiple Autobiography in a Single Family (MASF), and its outgrowth, The Family

---

*Ramirez (1983) described the "Mestizo" world view as a egalitarian amalgamation of Native American, Latino, and European cultures; it is based on the unique experiences of peoples in the Americas rather than the experiences of Europeans in Europe, which, he argued, is the foundation of the dominant perspectives in psychology.

History Questionnaire (FHQ). Both are high-context, qualitative assessment tools. In the case of the MASF:

> . . . Each member of the family tells his own life story in his own words. [Sessions are audiotaped.] . . . The independent versions of the same incidents given by the various members provide a built-in check upon the reliability and validity of much of the data . . . unskilled, uneducated, and even illiterate persons can talk about themselves . . . in an uninhibited, spontaneous and natural manner . . . [It reduces] investigator bias because the accounts are not put through the sieve of a middle-class North American mind. . . . (Lewis, 1961, pp. xi, xii, and xxi; quoted in Ramirez, 1983, p. 76)

Unpublished research by Ramirez, Diaz-Guerrero, Hernandez, and Iscoe (1982) suggests that this and the similar but more structured FHQ provide useful information on family coping effectiveness and the use of religion, schools, and community agencies in coping with life crises.

The MASF and FHQ complement the treatment approach called for by Zayas and Bryant (1984), based on their work with Puerto Rican adolescents. They emphasize empathy and congruence with the family's values, expectations, and natural coping style. Their approach calls for similarly detailed, high-context assessment methods as a prerequisite for intervention. Other methods conceptualize the notion of social networks more broadly to include the support functions of activities, objects, and events—for example, attending church, singing Mexican songs, or praying the rosary (Ramirez, 1983). Investigators referred to this expanded support network as the "webwork."

All of these methods are creative alternatives to the investigator-controlled, content-oriented, and reductionistic methods typical of most assessment instruments. Despite their potential for increasing ethnic validity, understanding the extensive, detailed, qualitative data resulting from such methods can be daunting. To fully use the data, inductive and intuitive methods are needed. A number of methods have been used since antiquity to aid the understanding of complex ideas, including metaphors, symbolic imagery, myths, and fables. One clinical example is Costantino, Malagady, and Rogler's (1986) innovative *Cuento* (folktale) therapy with children, where complex ideas are organized around a story line. Methods for using metaphor and symbolic imagery as heuristic tools for the organization of complex data deserve much more attention in the study of adolescents.

Other PSP authors contend that intellectual knowledge and ethnically valid methods are not sufficient for professional competence. Jacobson (1988) has argued that competent cross-cultural work with adolescents requires the therapist to have (or gain) *personal* experience with his or her client's culture. Ideally, the therapist would be knowledgeable about the characteristics of culture as they exist in the client's community. This knowledge would give the therapist a more intuitive sense of workable interventions. Short of these measures, Jacobson recommends a professional network that includes people experienced in the client's culture.

There are other innovative approaches to population-specific psychology that depart less from traditional methods. A notable example is Jones's (1986) TRIOS theory of Black personality: he identifies *T*ime perception, *R*hythm, *I*mprovisation, *O*ral tradition, and *S*pirituality as key elements of Black personality. Rather than create a new psychology, he developed this culture-specific personality theory, based in part on African cultural values. His work suggests that the most effective treatment of African Americans recognizes these cultural values as assets and builds on them. As part of his discussion of time, he details the differences between the Afrocentric Present Temporal Perspective (PTP) and the Eurocentric Future Temporal Perspective (FTP):

> For persons responsive to a present time perspective, the future is a consequence of continued survival or existence. Therefore, to secure a positive

future, one need only maintain a positive outcome in the present. For persons following a future time perspective, the future "follows from" successfully attaining proximal goals that have been judged to bear definable relations to the future. Thus it is the valence of the future goals that drives present behavior. Said differently, *the present drives the future for PTP, while the future drives the present for FTP* (author emphasis, p. 35).

The work of other population-specific psychologists suggests that Latin Americans and certain European ethnic groups are more present-centered as well (Hall, 1976; Szapocznik et al., 1980). Ethnographic research by Kochman (1981) also supports the idea of time perspective differences. Jones notes the adaptive value of PTP for Blacks because of racism's potential for blocking the rewards that result from the delay of gratification; whereas Kochman emphasizes the African and African American cultural underpinnings of PTP. From a cultural perspective, European Americans prefer a clock-referenced notion of time for defining the boundaries of events; in African American and Latin American cultures, clock time is defined by, and subservient to, real events. In other words, ethnic Blacks and Latin Americans prefer to fit clock time to events; European Americans prefer to fit events to clock time.

Cultural differences in time perspective can cause significant miscommunication in treatment situations. A high-ethnic African American adolescent who reveals sensitive material just before a session ends may be offended by a non-bicultural European American therapist's insistence that the session "end on time." If the client views the therapist's insistence as callousness (rather than a cultural difference), the therapeutic alliance could be undermined. Meanwhile, the therapist may focus on an interpretation of the client's timing: Why was this material brought up five minutes before the session ended? The validity of the therapist's interpretation rests on the assumption that client and therapist are working from a common conception of time.

Clients who do not subscribe to Anglo-American notions of time may also question the traditional weekly treatment session that is scheduled without regard for real events. A client might ask: "What if I need you on Tuesday, but our session isn't scheduled until Friday, and by time Friday comes I have other things I need to do?" Clock-oriented therapists sometimes view an event-oriented approach to help seeking as a crisis orientation that is part of the client's problem. A diversity-sensitive view entertains the possibility that the orientations are simply different. An understanding of different time orientations requires a reexamination of psychodynamic interpretations of "tardiness" and no-shows. A valid interpretation depends on a common orientation toward time. Moreover, both research and treatment professionals who operate exclusively on clock-time are subject to frustration or negative countertransference as they repeatedly deal with "late" or "no-show" clients.

One diversity-conscious solution to differences in time perspective among adolescents is "drop-in" treatment. Drop-in treatment does not make assimilation a prerequisite for treatment; it permits clients to use services as they experience a need for them. Ecologically, athletic facilities, shopping malls, and popular restaurants are important settings for teenagers. Establishing drop-in centers near enough to these facilities to make access easy, but far enough away to minimize clients' fears of encountering peers, is one option. Although drop-in services are frequently offered in community-based agencies, they are often eschewed by larger agencies and state-run facilities. Efforts to make the drop-in approach workable logistically and more widely available for adolescents are indicated.

Although the population-specific perspective offers a range of new insights for adolescents' treatment and research, it includes some shortcomings as well. One is the tendency to create parallel psychologies ad infinitum. The desire to abandon the notion that "one psychology fits all" can lead to a multitude of separate psychologies and isolated groups of social scientists. For example, is there a need for a Puerto Rican, a Chicano, *and* a Cuban psychology, or will a general Latin American psychology suffice? "Asian" is used as a collective term, but Vietnamese, Chinese, Japanese, and other Asian nationalities are distinct in their complex histories, international conflicts, and alliances. On the other hand, Asians share a cultural and biological history that includes Confucianism, Buddhism, and race. The situation is similar for Latin Americans. Multiple psychologies are also an issue for Whites; there are a variety of differences among U.S., and European, psychologies (Moghaddam, 1987). A combination of merit and the sociopolitical salience of a population (and its psychologists) will probably determine which psychologies survive. In any case, a plethora of distinct psychologies has implications for psychology training, research, and practice.

THE ECOLOGICAL PERSPECTIVE

At the broadest level of analysis is the ecological perspective. It uses concepts from the study of natural environments to understand human behavior in its social and environmental contexts. The ecological perspective, unlike many traditional psychological theories, emphasizes the relationship between humans and their settings. The ecological psychologist is similar to his or her cross-cultural counterpart because the cultural elements of the environment receive special attention (Trickett, Watts, & Birman, 1991). Ecological psychology is also similar to sociopolitically oriented psychology because oppressive features of the environment, like sexism or racism, are seen as potent determinants of an adaptive strategy (Trickett et al., 1991). However, in ecological psychology, the focus is not necessarily on social change or intercultural processes. A school is an example of a setting where ecological features like *adaptation, cycling of resources, succession, and interdependence* are the focus of assessment and intervention (Trickett et al., 1972; Trickett & Schmid, Chapter 8 of this volume).

For ethnic minority adolescents, a number of issues can be understood from an ecological perspective. At the highest level of ecological analysis, defined by Bronfenbrenner (1979) as the macrosystem, the relevant variables are sociopolitical: national and state political institutions and their policies, the national media, and the socioeconomic forces that produce ethnic stratification (Noel, 1985). At the next level, the exosystem, are the metropolitan areas, communities, their associated institutions, and regional organs of communication. At the exosystem level, ethnic minority populations ". . . have suffered from discrimination and racism, yet they have formed communities, social institutions and other organizations for adapting and adjusting to these ecological challenges" (Harrison et al., 1990, p. 348). These organizations, which include research and educational institutions, are the prime resources that must be tapped in devising self-sustaining ecological interventions. A great deal of ecologically oriented research and intervention occurs at this level—frequently in schools.

All too often, mental health researchers and practitioners in the exosystem obtain outside (macrosystem) grants for funding short-term demonstration or research projects with minimal attention to devising ways of sustaining services when the projects end. Moreover, because resources for research and intervention are often awarded on the basis of macrosystem priorities, projects are shaped by national views of local problems and by questions of theoretical interest. The resulting lack of attention to local definitions of problems has spurred an interest among ecological psychologists in the host–investigator research relationship (e.g., Kelly, 1986). Cross-cultural "internal" methods are also useful for combating undue external biases at this level by helping service providers to adopt an insider's view of the local ecosystem.

The next level is the mesosystem, where the immediate neighborhood, local social networks, and extended family are located. Prestby and Wandersman (1985) and their colleagues have done a great deal of important work on citizen participation through research and consultation with block organizations. "Rites of passage" and other locally based cultural socialization programs for adolescents are at this level. In addition, antisocial gang behavior, teenage prostitution, the drug trade, and other street-based social problems that plague low-income people are at this level (although the causes for these problems can be found at the upper levels!). Despite these examples, ecological research and intervention at this level with adolescents are not often reported in the literature. The lack of formal institutional structures like schools or human service agencies seems to be one of the impediments.

The last level of analysis is the microsystem, where the family and household reside. This is the traditional focus for clinical interventions. Yet, even at this level, it is important to view behavior and circumstances in the context of the other three levels, to keep pathology in context. For example, the traditionally strong family system among Latin Americans and Asians may grow even stronger as a result of difficult circumstances at other ecological levels, and, based on an individualist norm for European American culture (Katz, 1985), such a family risks being seen as excessively "enmeshed." Similarly, complex, blended African American families that arise in response to the need for able adult resources in single-parent families (Harrison et al., 1990) create what some might label "chaotic" family systems.

The contribution of the ecological approach to the other models we have reviewed is its multileveled, comprehensive approach emphasizing adaptation, resources, and interdependence. Its focus on the interplay between the person and environment complements the PSPs while avoiding the PSPs' tendency to posit cultural traits that operate independently of specific environmental circumstances. It also incorporates the sociopolitical focus on systemic variables and the differences-as-diversity value found in cross-cultural psychology. In sum, the ecological perspective provides a general framework or umbrella under which all the other perspectives can be linked.

Additional Implications for Adolescent Research and Intervention

To facilitate an integration of the perspectives presented in this chapter, their key elements are summarized in Table 10.1. The perspectives range from the very specific (the population-specific) to the very general (the ecological). We will now illustrate how the concepts can work together by applying them to problems in adolescent research and intervention.

Human Diversity and Research with Adolescents

The first step for the diversity-conscious researcher is to delineate the ecosystem that includes both the investigator and the research host. Typically, this is the mesosystem. A thorough assessment is key. How is the research *institution* viewed by those in the host environment? Have the two settings had contact in the past? The history of contact will influence the process of entry and the dynamics of implementation. The successful use of the ecological method hinges on collaboration, especially the collaborative development of research objectives. In the case of adolescents, this means parents, institutional officials, and the adolescents themselves (Trickett & Birman, 1988).

Often, an ecological analysis will reveal an unjust pattern of resource allocation, and the behavior patterns will reflect efforts to adapt to adverse circumstances. This is especially true in segregated, impoverished environments. For example, an investigator interested in studying gang violence must consider his or her project's likely impact on the social conditions that contribute to gang behavior. Is the research a direct contribution to a solution? Based on the sociopolitical approach, a diversity-conscious investigator values methods that produce social change as well as knowledge. Consequently,

Table 10.1 A Summary of Human Diversity Perspectives

Aspects of Research or Practice	Perspective				
	Sociopolitical	Cross-Cultural	Population-Specific	Ecological	
Central concepts	Power, oppression, ideology, and social change	Culture, high/low context, acculturation, and identity	Specific identities, specific "-isms," specific patterns of distinctiveness in population attitudes, behavior, etc.	Settings, adaptation, interdependence, cycling of resources, succession, hosts	
Valued research or intervention questions	Those that identify the systematic abuse of power, its impact on individuals, and methods to combat it	Those that permit universal or unique dimensions of culture, and their implications, to emerge	Those that reveal distinctive population-specific attributes in a nonpejorative way	Those that clarify the links between behavior and environment: Competencies rather than deficits are stressed	
Valued methods	Those based on equity; those that produce social change as well as knowledge and critical analysis	External (Etic) research to determine cultural universals, and internal (Emic) research to understand uniqueness	Critiquing methods to rebut racist, sexist, etc., research; methods based on the population's own unique world view	Host-focused methods emphasizing collaborative relationships; intensive ecological assessment	
Preferred intervention strategies	Solidarity building, political education, empowerment, and policy	Change agents who have the training and experience needed to work across cultures	Empowerment that aids the development of population consciousness and group esteem; change agents who are group members	Structural changes in the built-in social environment that alter interactions; interventions sustained by native resources	
Orientation to human diversity	Diversity requires intergroup equity, pluralism, and social change	Diversity requires intergroup understanding and sensitivity	Diversity requires intragroup knowledge, esteem, and empowerment	Diversity is a resource that must be assessed, valued, and strengthened in successful interventions	

studying problems in impoverished environments requires action-research methods.

The gang violence example may include racial as well as socioeconomic elements. Because they are human diversity issues, race and culture play a role in the research effort as well. If the investigator is from a different racial and ethnic background, the cross-cultural components noted in Table 10.1 are important, especially the investigator's choice of internal and external methods and his or her cross-cultural training and experience. Although cross-cultural methods are essential for multicultural research, research with a homogeneous population benefits from leadership by investigators who identify with, and are members of, the target population. Population-specific psychologies are the best sources of theory and method.

Appropriate knowledge and technique are not sufficient to ensure diversity-conscious research. Those espousing these ideas must have the power to influence the research process. Issues of power and equity are sociopolitical.

Human Diversity and Professional Practice

In the area of adolescent treatment and intervention, a psychology of human diversity allows the possibility that there may be sufficient population distinctiveness to warrant a population-specific psychology. The value on pluralism supports the psychologies of women, gays and lesbians, Chicanos, and other populations. These population-specific psychologies have led to further fruitful specialization, such as the recent book *Black Adolescents* (Jones, 1989).

Paralleling the issues raised for researchers, the diversity-conscious service provider must locate himself or herself and the client in an ecological system. The ecological approach calls for intervention questions that focus on the person–environment interface rather than on either alone. Thus, a troubled adolescent is best understood in the context of the troubling situation rather than in the context of the treatment room. Home visits, observation, assessment of peer networks, and similar methods are consistent with this perspective. The ecological perspective also values interventions that are sustainable by indigenous resources; interventions requiring ongoing involvement by professionals may strain or disrupt the ecosystem. For example, training coaches and parents to recognize and manage the minor adjustment problems adolescents experience would be preferable to establishing a new role in the mesosystem for professionals, such as a new school counselor.

Whenever a population has not achieved socioeconomic equity, a diversity-conscious assessment and intervention must reflect that fact. For example, a psychologist receives a referral to treat a 14-year-old African American "learning disabled" girl who is disruptive in class and threatens her teacher. The diversity-conscious psychologist first completes an ecological (mesosystem) analysis of the girl's school and school system, and finds that they have conditions similar to those of many inner-city schools nationally, as reported by Murray and Fairchild (1989):

For Blacks in integrated or desegregated schools, the policy to maintain the provision of inferior education has been insured by institutional practices of mandatory administration of culturally-biased standardized testing . . . , counseling placements, tracking and ability categorization . . . , bigoted textbooks . . . , and inferior curricula . . . . large cities have regularly decreased the amount of funding per pupil in several of their public schools as a function of the proportionate increase of the Black student population . . . . Per-pupil-expenditures . . . [are also] significantly related to academic achievement . . . . (p. 235)

Based on this analysis, inner-city education is a macrosystem problem. Therefore, is it ethical for a psychologist to acknowledge the validity of this assessment and treat only the presenting problem? From both ecological and sociopolitical perspectives, an appropriate intervention cannot be limited to the girl and her microsystem. Working with the girl's problem behavior, and thereby deflecting attention from the systemic problems at the school, cannot be considered a success. In this setting, defining success as the elimination of problem behavior in individuals reduces the psychologist's role to one of a firefighter who extinguishes a blaze in an already condemned building. A more diversity-conscious intervention would include efforts to assess aspects of the school that contribute to behavior problems and to collaborate with parents, policy makers, and similar resources. Unfortunately a sociopolitical analysis of most schools would reveal few roles for psychologists that encourage systems change.

Cross-cultural and population-specific strategies would be helpful in identifying issues of racial identity, marginalization, cultural patterns of difference, and intercultural conflict that may contribute to the youngster's problems in the classroom setting. These perspectives are also needed to ensure effective client–provider communication.

CONCLUSION

In this chapter, we consolidated concepts from a variety of areas relevant to human diversity. One purpose was to highlight concepts and techniques for working with young people of color. Another purpose was to begin identifying key elements for a psychology of diversity that benefits all members of our multicultural society. The essence of a psychology of human diversity is simple: Mutable human thought and behavior is a function of historical, cultural and social conditioning in interaction with the environment. Rather than a denial of the role of heredity, this is an affirmation of the interdependence of people and their physical and psychological environments. It requires professionals to constantly ask themselves: Does a single norm of virtue underlie my work? Are my actions promoting a one-way accommodation to dominant cultural norms by only encouraging members of ethnic minorities to be bicultural? Are my methods essential for quality research, or are they a function of a cultural tradition? Is it best to treat all people the same, or is it better to treat people differently and in accordance with their needs and values?

These questions may seem quixotic in a society that rewards behavior that fits dominant cultural norms, research that generates at least interval data, and "equal treatment." However, bowing to these pressures without reflection only complicates the transition to a pluralistic society that, for moral and demographic reasons, is inevitable in our future.

REFERENCES

Albee, G. (1982). The politics of nature and nurture. *American Journal of Community Psychology, 10*, 4–28.

American Psychiatric Association. (1987). *Diagnostic and statistical manual of mental disorders* (3rd ed. rev.). Washington, DC: Author.

Aponte, H. (1974, March). Psychotherapy for the poor: An eco-structural approach to treatment. *Delaware Medical Journal*, 1–7.

Aultman, M. G., & Wellford, C. F. (1977). Towards an integrated model of delinquency causation: An empirical analysis. *Sociology and Social Research, 63*, 316–327.

Barker, R. G. (1978). *Habitats, environments and human behavior.* San Francisco: Jossey-Bass.

Belenky, M., Clinchy, B., Goldberger, N., & Tarule, J. (1986). *Women's ways of knowing: Development of self, voice, and mind.* New York: Basic Books.

Berger, P. L., & Luckmann, T. (1966). *The social construction of reality.* New York: Doubleday.

Berry, J. (1984). Cultural relations in plural societies: Alternatives to segregation and their socio-psychological implications. In M. Brewer & N. Miller (Eds.), *Groups in contact.* New York: Academic Press.

Berry, J. W. (October, 1988). Human diversity: A cross-cultural perspective. Paper presented at a conference on "Human Diversity: perspectives on people in context." Department of Psychology, University of Maryland, College Park.

Berry, J. W., Katlin, R., & Taylor, D. (1977). *Multiculturalism and ethnic attitudes in Canada.* Ottawa: Government of Canada.

Berry, J. W., & Kim, U. (1988). Acculturation and mental health. In P. R. Dasen, J. W. Berry, & N. Sartorius (Eds.), *Health and cross-cultural psychology: Vol. 10. Cross-cultural research and methodology series* (pp. 207–238). Newbury Park, CA: Sage.

Berry, J. W., Trimble, J. E., & Olmedo, E. L. (1986). Assessment of acculturation. In W. Lonner & J. Berry (Eds.), *Field methods in cross-cultural research,* (pp. 290–325). Beverly Hills, CA: Sage.

Beyer, J. M. (1981). Ideologies, values, and decision-making in organizations. In P. C. Nystrom & W. H. Starbuck (Eds.), *Handbook of organizational design* (pp. 166–202). New York: Oxford University Press.

Binder, A. (1988). Juvenile delinquency. In M. Rosenzweig & L. Porter (Eds.), *Annual review of psychology: Vol. 39* (pp. 253–282). Palo Alto, CA: Annual Reviews.

Bronfenbrenner, U. (1979). *The ecology of human development.* Cambridge: Harvard University Press.

Bulhan, H. (1988). *Franz Fanon and the psychology of oppression.* New York: Plenum Press.

Caplan, N., & Nelson, S. (1973). The nature and consequences of psychological research on social problems. *American Psychologist, 28,* 199–211.

Carter, R. T., & Helms, J. E. (1987). The relationship of Black value-orientations to racial attitudes. *Measurement and Evaluation in Counseling and Development, 17,* 185–195.

Carter, R. T., & Helms, J. E. (1988). The relationship between racial identity attitudes and social class. *Journal of Negro Education, 57,* 22–30.

Cole, M., & Scribner, S. (1974). *Culture and thought* (pp. 82–83). New York: Wiley.

Costantino, G., Malagady, R., & Rogler, L. (1986). Cuento therapy: A culturally sensitive modality for Puerto Rican children. *Journal of Youth and Adolescence, 54,* 639–645.

Covington, J. (1982). Adolescent deviation and age. *Journal of Youth and Adolescence, 11,* 329–344.

D'Augelli, A. (1989). Lesbians' and gay men's experiences of discrimination and harassment in a university community. *American Journal of Community Psychology, 17,* 317–321.

Dovidio, J. F., & Gaertner, S. L. (Eds.) (1986). *Prejudice, discrimination and racism.* New York: Academic Press.

DuBois, W. E. (1961). *The souls of Black folk.* New York: Fawcett.

Fairweather, G. (1979). Experimental development and dissemination of an alternative to psychiatric hospitalization: Scientific methods for social change. In R. Munoz, L. Snowden, & J. Kelly (Eds.), *Social and psychological research in community settings* (pp. 305–342). San Francisco: Jossey-Bass.

Farley, J. (1988). *Majority–minority relations.* Englewood Cliffs, NJ: Prentice-Hall.

Fasick, F. A. (1984). Parents, peers, youth culture and autonomy in adolescence. *Adolescence, 19,* 143–157.

Feldman, S. S., & Gehring, T. M. (1990). Changing perceptions of family cohesion and power across adolescence. In R. E. Muuss (Ed.), *Adolescent behavior and society* (4th ed.) (pp. 145–155). New York: McGraw-Hill.

Ferguson, R. (1990). *The case for community-based programs that inform and motivate Black male youth.* Urban Institute Research Publication. Available from the Urban Institute, Washington, DC.

Gary, L., & Berry, G. (1984). Some determinants of attitudes toward substance abuse in an urban ethnic community. *Psychological Reports, 54,* 539–545.

Gergen, K. (1985). The social constructionist movement in modern psychology. *American Psychologist, 40,* 266–275.

Gibbs, J. T. (1980). The interpersonal orientation in mental health consultation: Toward a model of ethnic variations in consultation. *Journal of Community Psychology, 8,* 195–207.

Good, B. J., & Good, M. D. (1986). The cultural context of diagnosis and therapy: A view from medical anthropology. In M. Miranda & H. Kitano (Eds.), *Mental health research and practice in minority communities* (pp. 1–27). (DHHS Publication No. ADM 86-1466). Washington, DC: U.S. Government Printing Office.

Hall, E. T. (1976). *Beyond culture.* Garden City, NY: Doubleday/Anchor.

Hare-Mustin, R. T., & Marecek, J. (1988). The meaning of difference: Gender theory, postmodernism, and psychology. *American Psychologist, 43,* 455–464.

Harrison, A. O., Wilson, M. N., Pine, C. J., Chan, S. Q., & Buriel, R. (1990). Family ecologies of ethnic minority children. *Child Development,* 61, 347–362.

Helms, J. E. (1990). An overview of racial identity theory. In J. E. Helms (Ed.), *Black and White racial identity: Theory, research, and practice.* Stamford, CT: Greenwood Press.

Ivey, A. E. (1988). *Intentional interviewing and counseling: Facilitating client development* (2nd ed.). Belmont, CA: Brooks/Cole.

Jacobson, F. M. (1988). Ethnocultural assessment. In L. Comas-Diaz & E. F. Griffith (Eds.), *Clinical guidelines in cross-cultural mental health* (pp. 135–148). New York: Wiley.

Jahoda, G. (1980). Theoretical and systematic approaches in cross-cultural psychology. In H. Triandis & J. Draguns (Eds.), *Handbook of cross-cultural psychology: Vol. 6* (pp. 69–141). Boston: Allyn & Bacon.

Jones, J. M. (1972). *Prejudice and racism.* Reading, MA: Addison-Wesley.

Jones, J. M. (1986). Racism: A cultural analysis of the problem. In J. F. Dovidio & S. L. Gaertner (Eds.), *Prejudice, discrimination and racism.* New York: Academic Press.

Jones, J. M. & Block, C. B. (1984). Black cultural perspectives. *The Clinical Psychologist, 37*(2), 58–62.

Jones, R. (1989). *Black Adolescents.* Berkeley, CA: Cobb & Henry.

Karrer, B. (1989). The sound of two hands clapping. In G. Saba, B. Karrer, & K. Hardy (Eds.), *Minorities and family therapy.* New York: Haworth Press.

Katz, J. H. (1985). The sociopolitical nature of counseling. *The Counseling Psychologist, 13,* 615–624.

Keesing, R. M. (1974). Theories of culture. In B. Siegel (Ed.), *Annual review of anthropology: Vol. 3* (pp. 73–98). Palo Alto, CA: Annual Reviews.

Kelly, J. G. (1986). Context and process: An ecological view of the interdependence of practice and research. *American Journal of Community Psychology,* 14, 573–605.

Keniston, K. (1965). *Social change and youth in America.* Garden City, NY: Doubleday/Anchor.

Kimmel, D. (1988). Ageism, psychology and public policy. *American Psychologist, 43,* 175–178.

King, L., Moody, S., Thompson, O., & Bennett, M. (1983). Black psychology reconsidered: Notes toward curriculum development. In J. Chunn, P. Dunston, & F. Ross-Sheriff (Eds.), *Mental health and people of color.* Washington, DC: Howard University Press.

Kochman, T. (1981). *Black and White styles in conflict.* Chicago: University of Chicago Press.

Kroeber, A., & Kluckhohn, C. (1952). Culture: A critical review of concepts and definitions. Papers of the Peabody Museum of American Archaeology and Ethnology, Harvard University, 57(1).

Kunjufu, J. (1986). *Countering the conspiracy to destroy Black boys: Vol. 2.* Chicago: African American Images.

Lambert, M. C., Weisz, J. R., & Knight, F. (1989). Over- and undercontrolled clinic referral problems of Jamaican and American children and adolescents: The culture general and the culture specific. *Journal of Consulting and Clinical Psychology,* 57, 467–472.

Mead, M. (1949). *Coming of age in Samoa.* New York: Mentor Books.

Moghaddam, F. M. (1987). Psychology in the three worlds: As reflected by the crisis in social psychology and the move toward indigenous Third-World psychology. *American Psychologist,* 42, 912–920.

McCord, C., & Freeman, H. P. (1990). Excess mortality in Harlem. *New England Journal of Medicine,* 322, 173–177.

Murray, C., & Fairchild, H. (1989). Models of Black adolescent underachievement. In R. Jones (Ed.), *Black Adolescents.* Berkeley: Cobb & Henry.

Naditch, M., & Morrissey, R. (1976). Role stress, personality, and psychopathology in a group of immigrant adolescents. *Journal of Abnormal Psychology,* 85, 113–118.

Noel, D. L. (1985). A theory of the origin of ethnic stratification. In N. R. Yetman (Ed.), *Majority and minority* (pp. 109–120). Boston: Allyn & Bacon.

Ogbu, J. U. (1978). *Minority education and caste: the American system in cross-cultural perspective.* New York: Academic Press.

Oler, C. (1989). Psychotherapy with Black clients' racial identity and locus of control. *Psychotherapy, 26,* 233–241.

Oliver, W. (1989). Black males and social problems: Prevention through Afrocentric socialization. *Journal of Black Studies 20,* 15–39.

Parham, T. A., & Helms, J. E. (1981). The influence of Black students' racial identity attitudes on preferences for counselor's race. *Journal of Counseling Psychology, 28,* 250–257.

Parham, T. A., & Helms, J. E. (1985a). Attitudes of racial identity and self-esteem: An exploratory investigation. *Journal of College Student Personnel, 26,* 143–146.

Parham, T. A., & Helms, J. E. (1985b). Relation of racial identity attitudes to self-actualization and affective states of Black students. *Journal of Counseling Psychology, 32,* 431–440.

Paulson, M. J., Lin, T., & Hanssen, C. (1980). Family harmony: An etiologic factor in alienation. In R. E. Muuss (Ed.), *Adolescent behavior and society: A book of readings* (3rd ed.). New York: Random House.

Pettigrew, T. (1988). Integration and pluralism. In P. A. Katz & D. A. Taylor (Eds.), *Eliminating racism: Profiles in controversy* (pp. 19–29). New York: Plenum Press.

Phinney, J. (1989). Stages of ethnic identity development in minority group adolescents. *Journal of Early Adolescence, 9,* 34–49.

Pike, K. (1966). *Language in relation to a unified theory of the structure of human behavior.* The Hague, The Netherlands: Mouton.

Ponse, B. (1978). Emergence of identity as the research problem. In *Identities in the lesbian world* (pp. 49–85). Westport, CT: Greenwood Press.

Prestby, J. E., & Wandersman, A. (1985). An empirical exploration of a framework of organizational viability: Maintaining block organizations. *Journal of Applied Behavioral Science, 21,* 287–305.

Prilleltensky, I. (1989). Psychology and the status quo. *American Psychologist, 44,* 795–802.

Ramirez, M. (1983). *Psychology of the Americas: Mestizo perspectives on personality and mental health.* New York: Pergamon Press.

Ramirez, M., Diaz-Guerrero, R., Hernandez, M., & Iscoe, I. (1982). Coping with life stress in families: A cross-cultural comparison. Unpublished manuscript.

Rappaport, J. (1977). *Community psychology: Values, research and action.* New York: Holt, Rinehart and Winston.

Rodriguez, A. M. (1987). Institutional racism in the organisational setting: An action–research approach. In J. W. Shaw (Ed.), *Strategies for improving race relations: The Anglo-American experience* (pp. 128–148). Manchester, U.K.: Manchester University Press.

Rogler, L. H., Malgady, R. G., Costantino, G., & Blumenthal, R. (1987). What do culturally sensitive mental health services mean? *American Psychologist, 42,* 565–570.

Seligman, M. (1975). *Helplessness.* San Francisco: Freeman.

Simmons, C. H., & Parsons, R. J. (1983). Developing internality and perceived competence: The empowerment of adolescent girls. *Adolescence, 18,* 917–922.

Simon, D. R. (1986). Alienation and alcohol abuse: The untested dimensions. *Journal of Drug Issues, 16,* 339–356.

Solomon, B. (1976). *Black empowerment: Social work in oppressed communities.* New York: Columbia University Press.

Stark, E., & Flitcraft, A. (1988). Women and children at risk: A feminist perspective on child abuse. *International Journal of Health Services, 18,* 97–118.

Stent, M., Hazard, W., & Rivlin, H. (1973). *Cultural pluralism in education: A mandate for change.* New York: Appleton-Century-Crofts.

Sue, D. W. (1981). *Counseling the culturally different: Theory and practice.* New York: Wiley.

Sue, S., & Zane, N. (1986). Therapists' credibility and giving: Implications for practicing and training in Asian-American communities (pp. 157–174). In M. Miranda & H. Kitano (Eds.), *Mental health research and practice in minority communities* (pp. 1–27) (DHHS Publication No. ADM 86-1466). Washington, DC: U.S. Government Printing Office.

Sutton, R. G., & Kessler, M. (1986). National study of the effects of clients' socioeconomic status on clinical psychologists' professional judgments. *Journal of Consulting and Clinical Psychology, 54,* 275–276.

Szapocznik, J., Kurtines, W., & Fernandez, T. (1980). Bicultural involvement and adjustment in Hispanic-American youths. *International Journal of Intercultural Relations, 4,* 353–365.

Szapocznik, J., Scopetta, M., & King, O. (1978). Theory and practice in matching treatment to the special characteristics and problems of Cuban immigrants. *Journal of Community Psychology, 6,* 112–122.

Trickett, E., & Birman, D. (1988). *Taking ecology seriously: A community development approach to individually-based preventive interventions in schools.* Unpublished manuscript, University of Maryland, College Park.

Trickett, E., Kelly, J., & Todd, D. (1972). The social environment of the high school: Guidelines for individual change and organizational development. In S. Golann (Ed.) *Handbook of community mental health* (pp. 331–406). Englewood Cliffs, NJ: Prentice-Hall.

Trickett, E., Watts, R., & Birman, D. (1991). *Human diversity and community psychology: Still hazy after all these years.* Manuscript submitted for publication.

Unger, R., Draper, R., & Pendergrass, M. (1986). Personal epistemology and personal experience. *Journal of Social Issues, 42,* pp. 67–79.

U.S. Bureau of the Census. (1989). *Statistical Abstract of the United States* (109th ed.). Washington, DC: U.S. Government Printing Office.

Wallston, B. S. (1981). What are the questions in psychology of women? A feminist approach to research. *Psychology of Women Quarterly, 5,* 597–617.

Warfield, N. (1990). *Afrocentric theory and application, Volume 1: Adolescent rites of passage.* Washington, DC: Baobab Associates.

Watts, R., & Carter, R. (1991). *Psychological aspects of racism in organizations.* Manuscript submitted for publication.

Watzlawick, P. (Ed.) (1984). *The invented reality: Contributions to constructivism.* New York: Norton.

Weiss, R. M., & Miller, L. E. (1987). The concept of ideology in organizational analysis: The sociology of knowledge or the social psychology of beliefs? *Academy of Management Review, 12,* 104–116.

White, J., & Parham, T. (1990). *The psychology of Blacks.* Englewood Cliffs, NJ: Prentice-Hall.

Witkin, H. (1967). A cognitive style approach to cross-cultural research. *International Journal of Psychology, 2,* 233–250.

Yinger, J. M. (1985). Ethnicity. In R. Turner & J. Short (Eds.), *Annual review of sociology: Vol. 11* (pp. 151–180).

Yu, K. H., & Kim, L. C. (1983). The growth and development of Korean-American children. In G. H. Powell (Ed.), *The psychosocial development of minority group children.* (pp. 147–158). New York: Brunner Mazel.

Zayas, L., & Bryant, C. (1984). Culturally sensitive treatment of adolescent Puerto Rican girls and their families. *Child and Adolescent Social Work Journal, 1,* 235–253.

Zimmerman, M., & Rappaport, J. (1988). Citizen participation, perceived control, and psychological empowerment. *American Journal of Community Psychology, 16,* 725–750.

CHAPTER 11

Gay and Lesbian Youth

ANDREW M. BOXER, BERTRAM J. COHLER, GILBERT HERDT, and FLOYD IRVIN

It doesn't bother me that I am gay. I don't know why shrinks should get so upset about it. What bothers me is that people should have such a hard time believing it. This is a new time and society has to learn to accept us as no different from anyone else. My roommate and friends understand that; my biggest problem is with my parents and my high school teachers who never understood that teenagers can be gay but no different from anyone else.

First-year college student

Concern with the mental health of the gay and lesbian adolescent has led to increased study of this issue across the past two decades.[1] This study, in turn, reflects heightened awareness within society, including that among adolescents themselves, regarding diversity of sexual orientation and life-style (Boxer, Levinson, & Petersen, 1989; Petersen, 1985; Petersen & Boxer, 1982). Initial study of the meanings of sexuality constructed by adolescents has provided important findings regarding the impact of pubertal change on adjustment across the adolescent decade. These findings show that issues of body changes, and accompanying increased awareness of sexual wishes, pose problems for all adolescents. Further, reflecting larger social changes, adolescents are increasingly aware of possible life-styles associated with sexuality and intimacy and may be more acceptant and understanding regarding these issues than the generation of their parents.

As one student observed, we have in large measure failed (a) to recognize a significant shift in attitudes toward sexual orientation, and (b) to differentiate between expectable struggles with sexuality in adolescence and the particular problems of stigma and stereotype additionally posed for the gay and lesbian

---

A portion of this chapter appeared in the *Journal of Homosexuality, 17,* 1989. The authors wish to thank Judith Cook and Bernice Neugarten, whose unique intellectual and personal contributions to the study of person and life-course helped to make this chapter possible. Support for the findings reported in this study was made possible by a grant from the Spencer Foundation to Gilbert Herdt. The authors are grateful to Horizons Community Services and, in particular, to members of the Youth Group participating in Horizons program, for the opportunity to observe the youth support group and interview group members. We are particularly grateful to the group for their willingness to share their experiences with the project staff.

[1]In the present chapter, the terms gay and lesbian are used to refer to homosexuality among boys and girls and men and women. Some investigators (Murray, 1984) use these terms interchangeably without sufficient recognition of the very different significance of homosexuality for men and women (Herdt, 1990).

adolescent—problems that compound issues of adjustment posed by the adolescent decade. Self-definition of oneself as gay or straight may be less of a psychological issue than the social implications posed by this self-definition. The gay and lesbian life-style among adolescents self-identified as experiencing nearly exclusively homoerotic wishes provides a life-style option that offers a positive resolution for the dual problem of the increased psychological distress accompanying pubertal change and the stigma attached by society to this life-style option.

Much of the additional turmoil previously reported as associated with adoption of a homosexual orientation in adolescence was a consequence of stigma and social stereotyping. Reduction of prejudice and increased acceptance and expression of a wish for same-gender intimacy have been accompanied by lessened psychological distress among gay and lesbian adolescents. Study of gay and lesbian adolescents in a milieu acceptant of their sexual orientation suggests that their effort to make sense of pubertal changes and to come to terms with increasing awareness of sexual wishes does not differ from the personal struggles of their heterosexual counterparts.

Both historically and cross-culturally, formation of intense, intimate ties with others of the same gender, sometimes including satisfaction of sexual wishes as well, has been common in adolescence. Some young people ultimately rely exclusively or nearly exclusively on a homosexual orientation continuing on into their adult years. Little is known regarding determinants of exclusive or nearly exclusive preference for a sexual orientation involving others of the same gender, or of factors influencing choice of a homosexual orientation into adulthood, or of the mental health and well-being of gay and lesbian adolescents as contrasted with their heterosexual counterparts. The present chapter reviews evidence from other studies and from a continuing study of gay and lesbian teenagers in Chicago (Boxer, 1990; Boxer, Cook, & Herdt, 1990; Gerstel, Feraios, & Herdt, 1989; Herdt, 1990). The focus is on findings from these studies and, particularly, problems associated with method of study, which must be resolved in order to begin to answer questions regarding the place of sexual orientation as a factor related to adjustment and morale during adolescence.

HOMOSEXUALITY AND THE DEVELOPMENTAL PERSPECTIVE

Homosexuality has been the subject of much developmental analysis but little prospective longitudinal research, particularly across age groups or life stages (Morin, 1977; Watters, 1986). Such lacunae have also been noted in the study of sexuality in general. To the extent that the findings of developmental research have had an impact on either social theory or clinical practice, they have served primarily to provide what is believed to be scientific verification of particular assumptions regarding the origins of homosexual behavior in early childhood. So far, this use of a developmental perspective results from combining both longitudinal and retrospective findings, rendering the developmental perspective as a problematic "history of confusion" and a confusion of "histories." Investigators employing a developmental paradigm have been principally focused on linking various derivatives of early experience (e.g., maternal and paternal identification), including aspects of infancy and early childhood, to adult homosexual behavior. This line of inquiry, then, represents concern with causality and delineation of continuities through functions and mechanisms presumed to give rise to emergent adult forms of homosexuality.

Longitudinal Study and Emergence of Sexual Orientation

The only longitudinal study explicitly aimed at developmental understanding of homosexuality has been reported by Green (1987). This work implicitly followed an earlier line of developmental research, which attempted to link aspects of childhood sex-role interests and identifications to adult gender roles and sexual orientation (Bieber et al., 1962; Chang & Block, 1960; Gebhard, Gagnon, Pomeroy, & Christensen, 1965; Holeman & Winokur, 1965). Developmental hypotheses elaborated in Green's (1987) study are concerned with whether and how gender identity precedes the emergence and development of sexual orientation, albeit in a clinically constituted sample. The predominant paradigm of Green's study is child-centered; its major emphasis is on longitudinal changes in gender-role-atypical "sissy males" (a term employed by Green to describe a constellation of atypical behaviors, i.e., a syndrome) and on examining parent and child variables that predict adult homosexuality.

A major problem of method apparent in Green's study is the quite different sources of data employed for childhood and adult measurements. Although there are statistically significant correlations between some child and adult variables, overall they account for little explained variance. The sample selection procedures themselves precluded examination of homosexual individuals who did not manifest effeminate behavior in early childhood. (For a critical review of these issues, see De-Cecco, 1987.[2]) Because of the selection criteria, this study of males represents one subtype of homosexuality and likely excludes many others. Green's work is not, in contrast to the focus of our discussion, primarily concerned with gay or lesbian identity development and the life-course of youth subsequent to adolescence. The focus on origins and causes in this line of research meant that Green was unable to provide more detailed description and understanding of the life-course subsequent to childhood.

Kagan and Moss's (1962) analysis of 25 years of longitudinal data from the Fels Research Institute in Ohio was actually one of the first contemporary reports on personality and gender-role development from childhood to adulthood that employed both longitudinal design and complex methods of data analysis. This study employed ratings of home visits and laboratory observations across several points in early and middle childhood, together with detailed assessment of personality in adulthood. High correlations were reported, particularly, between boys' childhood and adult gender-role behaviors and interests. The Fels report, with its numerous variables, has been criticized as maximizing chance relationships and, similar to the Green (1987) study, reflecting largely cultural definitions of gender roles and personality traits, rather than genuine aspects of continuity or change in such attributes over time.

Aside from these studies, the bulk of the developmental research on homosexuality is retrospective and based on adults' reconstructions of their childhood. Causal inferences made from retrospective data are highly problematic, because adults' self-representations and understandings are infused with current cultural constructs and ideologies.[3] Additionally, recent findings in family research suggest that influences within families are bidirectional (Bell & Harper, 1977; Boxer, Cook, & Cohler, 1986; Cohler & Geyer, 1982; Cook, 1988; Cook & Cohler, 1986; Hagestad, 1981). Causal inferences typically only consider the *forward direction of effects* in socialization, from parent to child. The concept of *reciprocal socialization* (Cook & Cohler, 1986) specifies that children influence parents in as many (but different) ways as parents influence children. A growing corpus of research provides

---

[2]Green's (1987) study illustrates our earlier point regarding the difficulties with changing theoretical perspectives within the history of a longitudinal study. The original purpose for initiating this work, as he has indicated (Green, 1987), was to understand the development of transsexualism.

[3]It is not surprising to learn that culturally defined attributes of behaviors such as sex-role definitions are so important in organizing adult personality. Internalization of the situation is a major determinant of personal expression, as recognized by symbolic interactionist perspectives in social science (Cooley, 1902; Janowitz, 1966; Strauss, 1964).

evidence that, across the family life cycle, children, from infancy throughout adulthood, actively socialize their parents in diverse ways, from behavioral discipline strategies to political values (Bugental & Shennum, 1984; Cook & Cohler, 1986; Dawson & Prewitt, 1969; Troll & Bengtson, 1982).

Because of this disproportionate focus on development in childhood, the early development of gay men is still the focus of much attention. There is little comparable research on lesbians, and existing studies raise questions as to whether there are parallel factors operating for women (Ponse, 1978; Sophie, 1985/1986).[4] Based on newer and more refined studies of adults, gay men's early development is now being reinterpreted employing an *implicit* concept of reciprocal socialization. Isay (1985, 1986, 1987), for example, on the basis of detailed clinical case studies, suggests that adult gay men report the lack of close bonds with their fathers in childhood because of defensive distortions of their early erotic attachments to their fathers. A normal developmental issue of these men's childhood years, Isay posits, is the cross-gender behavioral characteristics such boys manifest in order to acquire and maintain the attraction and attention of their fathers. The primary supposition is that the father or father surrogate, not the mother, becomes the main object of the child's sexual attention.

While supporting Green's findings regarding cross-gender childhood behavior, Isay posits (1987) that sexual orientation precedes the development of gender identity. Silverstein (1981), based on interviews with a nonclinical sample of adult gay men, has also maintained that the absent/distant father relationship, reported by the majority of his sample of 190 males, was a result, not a cause, of the adult men's homosexuality. Bell, Weinberg, and Hammersmith (1981) have similarly, on the basis of retrospective reports, called attention to the strong manifestations of early childhood cross-gendered behavior as reported by adult male homosexuals. Harry's (1982) recent study of "gay children grown up" makes similar conclusions about childhood effeminacy. All four authors, then, suggest that sexual orientation is a biological, or at least very early emergent phenomenon, and that it sets the course of many different aspects of later development, at least in the samples studied.

Retrospective and Prospective Perspectives in Longitudinal Study

More recent studies discussing the early development of gay men, with the exception of Green's (1987), were focused on adults who were asked to retrospect backward in time. We therefore may know more about remembered childhoods than about the experienced adult present. As a result, we must be very wary of the influence of cultural conceptions of homosexuality/"inversion" on the reconstructed life history (Herdt, 1989). The developmental models emphasizing causal linkages in adult homosexuality are employing a system of explanation and generalization based on descriptive, narrative modes of understanding, ordering the material of life histories into a coherent account.

Past and Present in Study of Lives Over Time

Retrospective and prospective data may render quite different life histories. The origin of this confusion is commonly attributed to Freud, although he himself pointed out:

So long as we trace the development from its final outcome backwards, the chain of events appears continuous, and we feel we have gained an insight which is completely satisfactory or even exhaustive. But if we proceed the reverse way, if we start from the premises inferred from the analysis and try to follow these up to the final result, then we no longer get the impression of an inevitable sequence of events which could not have been otherwise determined. We notice at once that there might have

---

[4]It is unfortunate to note that this new line of research has primarily been directed to the study of males, a circumstance that follows the earlier historical masculine bias of developmental research (see, e.g., Chodorow, 1978; Gilligan, 1982).

been another result, and that we might have been just as well able to understand and explain the latter. (Freud, 1920/1955, p. 167).

It is particularly interesting to note that, despite recent conclusions of a number of developmental and personality researchers (Brim & Kagan, 1980; Cohler, 1981; Gergen, 1982; Neugarten, 1977, 1979) on the lack of continuity across the life cycle, most developmental research on homosexuality has focused on examining continuities related to sexual orientation between childhood and adulthood. In contrast, there is a paucity of accumulated data regarding the experience of individual change and the impact of life events through the life-course. Thus, with fixed concern on childhood, little attention has been devoted to studying either adolescence or adulthood as other than an *outcome* of childhood; experiences *across* the life-course have been virtually ignored. We would do well, it appears, to now apply to adolescence what Neugarten (1969) said over 20 years ago about the study of adulthood:

We shall not understand the psychological realities of adulthood by projecting forward issues that are salient in childhood—neither those issues that concern children themselves, nor those that concern child psychologists as they study cognitive development and language development and the resolution of the Oedipal. (Neugarten, 1969, p. 121)

Livson and Peskin (1980), in their comprehensive review of adolescent longitudinal research, commented:

In both the theoretical and empirical underpinnings of birth-to-maturity longitudinal study, the adolescent years may have been unduly hidden or homogenized in the grist of consistencies over time, weakening their psychosocial and psychobiological claim to status as a separate phase. (Livson & Peskin, 1980, p. 64)

While recognizing the value of longitudinal research in understanding the influences of childhood on the subsequent life-course, the emphasis on childhood causation has focused research on the demonstration of continuity. This presumes that development proceeds in a linear manner, with future attainments or changes directly associated with those of past years. Several investigators have recently called this presumption into question (Cohler, 1981, 1982; Gergen, 1982; Kagan, 1980; Weinberg, 1984), noting the limitations associated with linear assumptions regarding development. Gergen (1982) has suggested that the course of development is largely unpredictable, subject to chance. A major task across the course of life is to make "sense" of such chance events, weaving these events into a narrative that provides meaning and coherence.

Life-Course and Personal Narrative

From this perspective, the most interesting question in longitudinal research involves the factors influencing the maintenance of an internally consistent account of the course of life at different life-cycle positions (Cohler, 1982). Understanding the manner in which persons maintain a sense of self-cohesiveness and identity remains a key problem in the study of lives. Together with the experience of particular normative and eruptive events, these developmental factors contribute to successive *revisions* of the person's own narrative of the life-course, resulting in significant alterations over time in the subjective account of a life history. Such revisions include alterations in the remembered past and the anticipated future, so as to provide a sense of continuity of the life as a whole.

It is important to remember that every adult retrospectively develops a picture of what his or her parents were like (Cohler, 1980). This picture of one's parents fluctuates across the life cycle: adolescents expectedly view their parents in terms of distantiation, autonomy, and dependency (Greene & Boxer, 1986; Montemayer, 1986; Steinberg & Silverberg, 1986), whereas many older persons view their parents in highly idealized terms (Lieberman & Falk, 1971; Prosen, Martin, & Prosen, 1972).

Across the life-course, persons' self-representations are redefined in relation to dimensions of the past, present, and future in differing ways, depending on their life-course position (Back & Gergen, 1963; Boxer & Cohler, 1980; Butler, 1963; Cohler & Boxer, 1984; Lens & Gailly, 1980; Revere & Tobin, 1980/1981). The relativity of time itself colors differential perceptions of experience as a function of the individual's life-cycle position. For an adolescent, one year out of sixteen will seem longer than one year out of eighty for an octogenarian (Janet, 1877).

The process by which the personal narrative is successively reconstructed, from childhood to old age, is similar in some respects to the writing of history; discrete events are significant only as they become part of a narrative that is understood as coherent and makes sense to readers at a particular time (Ricoeur, 1977). Just as there is a shift over time in the interpretation of historical events, similar shifts can be observed across the life-course, both in the narration of personal events and in the interpretation provided for the relationship among these events (Cohler, 1982).

Because of these complexities of reminiscence, the study of individuals' remembered past is likely to result in different "developmental histories" than the *prospective,* longitudinal study of their lives through time. Predictive and interpretive approaches may each make an important contribution to the developmental study of lives (Cohler, 1987). However, it is necessary to differentiate these two perspectives in order to fully understand the transformations and changes that constitute human development. Predictive studies have the virtue, at least in theory, of being verifiable in terms of external criteria beyond the coherence of a narrative itself. In an effort to provide verifiable findings, predictive studies, concerned with "a laws and instances ideal of explanation" (Geertz, 1983, p. 19), are unable to account for many aspects of the life history that may be most important in understanding such characteristics as resilience, vulnerability, personal success, and achievement. They fail to include shifting meanings attributed to past experiences across the course of life as determinants of present adjustment. Interpretive studies are critical, as Geertz (1983) has stated, "for connecting action to its sense rather than behavior to its determinants" (p. 34).

Event and Cohort: Toward Definition of Gay and Lesbian Youth

In few areas of study of the life-course are the problems of the phenomenon to be studied, and the time at which study takes place, so inextricably intertwined as in the study of gay youth. Prior to the late 1960s, discussion of a gay or lesbian life-style was largely taboo. Although some pioneering reports such as those of Evelyn Hooker (1956, 1965) provided information regarding pathways into what is now regarded as the homosexual life-style, the few extant reports regarded same-gender sexual preference as evidence of impaired mental health. The very tabooed nature of the subject provided both the foundation for reports of personal distress accompanying homosexual wish and action and the content of delusions among particularly suspicious psychiatric patients. It was unthinkable that adolescents might already have self-identified as nearly exclusively homosexual or that such self-definition might be largely independent of mental illness.

Historical Context and the Process of "Coming Out"

Sociohistorical events played a significant role in altering the significance of homosexuality for personal adjustment in adolescence and adulthood. Across the 1960s, accompanying increased recognition of the legitimate values and norms of other minority groups, men and women with same-gender sexual orientation gained increased recognition within a pluralistic culture. In 1969, a protest against police brutality during a raid on a gay bar, the Stonewall in New York, consolidated the diverse interests of gay and lesbian groups (Herdt, 1989). Investigation of this event mobilized sentiment in favor of increased tolerance within the larger community. Extension of civil liberties to the gay and lesbian community began at that time.

Over the intervening years, symbolic urban communities have emerged which are characterized by homogeneity in life-style, residence, and services. Publications such as *Advocate* and *Christopher Street* have further legitimated identity as gay or lesbian and have offered timely and accurate information on subjects ranging from legal issues to AIDS. Indeed, the tragedy associated with AIDS has further strengthened ties within the gay community; informal support services devised by caring community members have provided at least some care and assistance parallel with that which is usually provided for ill and infirm family members.

The label "gay" or "lesbian" *adolescent* appears to represent a unique emergence in history. It seems unlikely that past groups of "pre-Stonewall" youth would have labeled themselves gay or lesbian, let alone had the same opportunities for organized, collective socializing or socialization that some do today. Thus, this aspect of the life-course—self-identification as gay or lesbian during adolescence—may be a unique developmental process found only in current cohorts of some homosexual youth and may carry different consequences for later life-course development. For that reason alone, studies of gay and lesbian youth are a timely occurrence.

Legal and social protection won over the past several decades has enabled urban and suburban adolescents to seek understanding of their particular life-style through peer counseling and other informal support groups. Even public high schools in more sophisticated communities have provided staff and support services for gay and lesbian adolescents. However, little is known about the "career pathways" into a consolidated identity and gay or lesbian life-style among these teenagers with long-term homoerotic orientations, or about the impact on adult adjustment of different routes into a gay or lesbian identity in adolescence. Evidence that problems are posed for these gay and lesbian adolescents can be found in a number of popular articles appearing in homosexual publications such as *Advocate, Christopher Street, New York Native,* and *Village Voice.*

Homosexuality in Adolescence

Recognition of the gay and lesbian life-style as one that is socially acknowledged and legally protected has provided the circumstances in which urban adolescents who were predisposed to intimate relations with others of the same gender found support for this life-style. The issue of adolescent homosexuality, one of the most sensitive social problems of our time, is little studied because of its taboo subject matter. Stereotyped views of adolescent sexuality, often reflecting attributions of their parents, portray teenagers as necessarily predisposed to heterosexuality. Adolescent homosexuality is presumed to reflect psychopathology and to be caused by sexual abuse resulting from adults' taking advantage of young people who were still uncertain of their own sexual orientation or constitutional vulnerability. This view is consistent with the beliefs, prevalent since the Enlightenment, that childhood is a time of particular psychological vulnerability, and that children need a protected and measured environment if they are to grow into resilient adults. It is much more difficult for family and school to accept the possibility of a group of adolescents who early recognize their homosexual orientation and who seek a consistent life-style in the same manner as their heterosexual counterparts.

Little systematic study has been reported regarding presumed origins of sexual orientation. About 10% of adolescents self-define themselves as primarily or exclusively attracted to others of the same gender, but the origins of this attraction are not clear. There does not appear to be any single, sovereign explanation for the origins of homosexuality in adolescence.

Herdt (1992) has noted the variation in the expression of same-gender ties based on intimacy and desire, which abounds in our own and other cultures. Considering the "varieties" of homosexuality and the variety of meanings constructed out of the same-gender sexual orientation, there seems to be little value in trying to find a common origin of homosexuality. For example, it is assumed that specific early-life circumstances or an adverse life situation must determine adolescent and adult same-gender sexual orientation. Bieber and Bieber (1962) had argued for a characteristic family pattern determining homosexuality in men: the father was cold and distant while the boy was growing up, and failed to interfere in the mother's overt seductiveness. Other attributions of cause include childhood sexual abuse and constitutional bisexuality, although the issue of constitutional (biologically determined) homosexuality is a difficult one to prove.

Although there is little comparative longitudinal study of children who later differ in their adolescent sexual orientation, observational study of a group of adolescent gay boys and lesbian girls does not support the Bieber and Bieber hypothesis (Boxer, 1990). Continuing study by Herdt and Boxer, (1993) does not support a hypothesis of childhood sexual abuse and neglect.[5] Regardless of stigma, stereotyping, and possible peer rejection, some adolescent boys and girls find the gay or lesbian sexual orientation to be personally compelling and satisfying. The American Academy of Pediatrics conservatively estimates there to be 3 million homosexually inclined youth (Sladkin, 1983). Recognizing this social issue, it is necessary to study the impact of homosexuality on personality development and adjustment into the adult years, and to find ways of providing gay and lesbian adolescents with the means to realize satisfying relationships with others.

Although they lack the cross-sequential design essential in studying issues of adolescent sexuality and personal adjustment, findings reported by Boxer (1990) show that, in a milieu lacking in stigma and stereotyping, gay and lesbian teens report little specific difficulty associated with selection of same-gender rather than other-gender patterns of sexual satisfaction. More than half of the gay and lesbian youth in Boxer's (1990) study of homosexuality in adolescence reported marked satisfaction from their relationships. Less than one-fifth of these adolescents reported that "coming out" within the context of a homosexual encounter proved to be a source of psychological distress. Reports of initial attraction to others of the same gender varied from early childhood to adolescence itself. A small number of gay boys reported being frightened by the realization that their sexual fantasies were becoming focused on other men, but this was not generally a problem for these boys or girls.

Lesbian girls and gay boys reported first same-sex fantasies at about the same age (between 11 and 12), but boys reported fantasies that were more explicitly sexual than those of girls, which were more generally focused on closeness and sharing. Gay boys began their homosexual experience at an earlier age (13) than girls, who began their first homosexual experience at about age 15. A small number of gay boys and lesbian girls reported homosexual fantasies but had not yet experimented with the expression of these sexual wishes within a relationship. First sexual experiences were overwhelmingly with a friend who was within three years of the age of the gay adolescent. A quarter of the boys and only about 10% of the girls in Boxer's (1990) study reported being the instigator of the sexual experience, deliberately planning to create a liaison. For most of the boys and girls in this study, the first homosexual experience emerged naturally within the course of a deepening friendship. For example, one 18-year-old gay adolescent boy reported:

It was beautiful. The sex wasn't planned. It was already a relationship. We'd just kissed and hugged

---

[5]Issues of definition posed problems for the study of the sexual abuse hypothesis. The classic pattern is that of an adult (usually a family member) using a child for sexual gratification. This is a quite different pattern from intimacy between friends, one of whom is still in high school and one of whom may be in college or working.

before. I'm romantic. The relationship lasted two years. It was very romantic. I'd go to his house. We'd go out for dinner.

Friendship was the most important element of the relationship for nearly half of the lesbian adolescent females but for only one-fifth of the gay adolescent males. Again, this is consistent with the culturally acknowledged roles of men (more concerned with sexual satisfaction) and women (more concerned in a relationship with issues of intimacy and caring).

It is important to note that the significance of cohort issues and same-gender sexual orientation may be different for gay boys and lesbian girls (Boxer, 1990). Within the present generation of gay adolescent boys, as more generally within our culture, previously stereotyped masculine interests and life-styles have become increasingly flexible. In the same way, it is more permissible than formerly for women to engage in active athletic competition such as basketball. The meanings of masculine and feminine in our own culture are presently being reconsidered with increasing interest in such concepts as psychological androgyny (Spence & Helmreich, 1978). Further, although the present discussion often treats issues of gay and lesbian youth as similar, there are many differences. The very definition of gender in our society leads to differences in the expression of sexual wishes among men and women. Cultural construction of sexuality leads men to seek more frequent and intense sexual pleasure than women. Issues of gender-defined activity and passivity in sexual relations and the reality of sexual differences must also be considered. Boxer (1990) reported that sexual pleasure is of primary significance among gay adolescent boys; their lesbian counterparts report sense of intimacy and caring to be primary in determining first same-sex experiences. A homosexual orientation may have clearly different consequences for the life-courses of gay men and lesbian women.

There is some suggestion that a lesbian sexual orientation may be a less encompassing and enduring definition of sexual orientation for women than for men in our society. Anecdotal reports of college women self-defined as lesbian suggest that some of these women, in time, may also marry and have children. Even if they remain committed to a lesbian sexual orientation, they are able to have children and may raise these children together with their lesbian partners. A heterosexual orientation either parallels or may replace the same-sex orientation of youth. Gay men in our culture are less likely to marry and have children than are their lesbian counterparts. Further, even if they seek to express their generativity (Erikson, 1950/1963) through care of foster children, the prevailing stigma and stereotyping, in which gay men are viewed as pernicious influences on the lives of boys and young men, may make it difficult in many states for gay men to adopt children. Finally, there is the pressing issue of AIDS, which is principally a disease among gay men. Increasingly, lesbian women have observed that the issue of AIDS further stigmatizes issues of homosexuality, among both men and women, and leads to nearly exclusive focus on social problems associated with homosexuality among men while neglecting the social problems of lesbian women.

Morale, Psychological Distress, and Homosexuality in Adolescence

From the mental health perspective, children need experience dosed in terms of their capacity to modulate tension. At the same time, as psychoanalysis has shown, instinctual forces are plastic and seek satisfaction in diverse ways (Freud, 1905). Further, sexuality itself is much more than instinctual satisfaction; it is a means of dealing with tension states and of expressing feelings of love and caring. To date, there has been little understanding of the basis of sexual orientation; however, a number of young people find same-gender persons particularly appropriate sources of caring and satisfaction.

Traditionally, within psychodynamic perspectives, this same-gender sexual preference has been understood either as a regressive response to the renewed conflict surrounding the renewed resolution of the nuclear (oedipal) wish with recurrence of sexual drives in adolescence (A. Freud, 1936/1946; Blos, 1967) or as evidence of archaic personality elements interfering with heterosexual adjustment.

Without doubt, some adolescents expressing confusion regarding sexual identity do reflect deficits in personality development. Among some of these young people, there may be pervasive difficulties in making friends, conflict with family, and recurrent substance abuse. Life-style becomes one more avenue in which rebellion may be expressed.[6] These more troubled adolescents must be differentiated from another group of young people who report being sexually attracted to others of the same gender from as early as they can recall explicit sexual awareness. Some of these young people recall same-gender sexual fantasies from their nursery years; others first became aware of such wishes just prior to adolescence. However, regardless of the time of first awareness of same-gender sexual preference, by midadolescence, these young people have chosen a life-style emphasizing same-gender sexual orientation even though they may have had little or no actual sexual experience with persons of the same or opposite gender.

When these young people adopt a gay or lesbian life-style, they show little of the explicit impairment in their ability for realizing close relationships with others that has been assumed in much of the mental health literature. They have a number of friends with whom they can talk about fears, hopes, and dreams, and they relate well to adults, family, and peers. In the majority of families where parents are able to accept the teenager's sexual orientation and provide support for the development of age-appropriate intimacy with same-gender peers, good relations are maintained within the family (Boxer, 1990). Where problems have arisen, they are primarily the consequence of stigma rather than of deficits in a capacity for closeness or for soothing of tension states. In the main, gay and lesbian adolescents do not fit stereotypes such as that of Green (1987), who has characterized many of these homosexual young people as effeminate. Again, cross-dressing and other transvestite behavior must be differentiated from the wishes and life-styles of these gay and lesbian adolescents; they are similar to their same-age peers in all but sexual orientation. Much of the psychopathology attributed to the gay adolescent is a consequence of the stereotyping and homophobic preoccupations of their peers, teachers, and parents, who do not understand the manner in which these gay and lesbian adolescents differ from others.

LIFE-COURSE, DEVELOPMENT, AND HOMOSEXUALITY IN ADOLESCENCE

The developmental study of adolescence, in general, is currently burgeoning.[7] Research on this phase of the life-course has come of age.

---

[6] In recent years, there has been much discussion of the urban runaway. As a consequence of conflict with family and community, these young people leave home without permission or advice, often finding their way to socially disorganized areas of such large cities as New York, Chicago, or Los Angeles. Stereotyped conceptions of the runaway life-style emphasize heavy use of drugs and both heterosexual and homosexual prostitution. Some of these runaway adolescents show personality disorganization and psychopathology (Coleman, 1989); others are simply fleeing from pervasive family patterns of neglect and abuse and may return after a period of protest marked by physical absence. Boyer (1989) has shown that at least some young men engaging in homosexual prostitution are seeking affirmation of their gay identity, using the only means they presently know for contacting persons of similar life-style. With increased acceptance of the gay and lesbian adolescent and provision of appropriate support systems, the use of homosexual prostitution as a pathway into a gay identity should diminish.

[7] The proliferation of adolescent research is evidenced by the recent formation of a new, interdisciplinary, adolescent research society (The Society for Research on Adolescence), new journal publications (e.g., *The Journal of Early Adolescence, The Journal of Adolescent Research*), the formation of policy-promoting bodies (The Carnegie Council on Adolescent Development; The Youth Policy Institute), and more thorough and specialized texts and handbooks for students and scholars (see, e.g., Adelson,

In partial consequence of the increasing attention directed to its study by interdisciplinary researchers, adolescence is now the focus of varying kinds of new public attention, from the drama of the humanities and popular journalism (Coons, 1987; Spacks, 1981) to the sway of blue-ribbon presidential commissions (see Coleman et al., 1974). An example of this concern is an issue of the *Journal of the American Medical Association* (1987) devoted to research on adolescent health concerns. None of this work has addressed the concerns of gay and lesbian youth.

However, the accumulating body of research findings on adolescence has been particularly useful in joining public health interventions with educational institutions in beginning to address national concerns regarding youth, such as teen pregnancy and parenting, substance abuse, school failure, and now, most recently, it is hoped, education about AIDS. Without a "remapping" of adolescent development (Herdt, 1989), the experience and needs of a significant group of youth cannot be understood and addressed.

Adolescence and Longitudinal Research

Recently, there has been increased interest in the study of lives from the perspective of the lifespan as a whole, rather than as based on cross-sectional studies of human development. This new focus may be traced, in large part, to the failure of much previous research to account for significant changes in personality and adjustment from childhood to adulthood (Cohler, 1982). The popular assumption, immortalized by Wordsworth, that "the child is the father of the man," has been questioned by life-course studies of adversity and resilience (Clarke & Clarke, 1976; Cohler, 1987; Kagan, 1980). Studies of both cognitive and affective development (Clarke & Clarke,

---

1980; Conger & Petersen, 1984; Kimmel & Weiner, 1985; Leigh & Petersen, 1986; Steinberg, 1985) as well as for parents (Lerner & Galambos, 1984).

1976; Kagan & Klein, 1973; Lennenberg, 1967; Schaffer, 1977) and of early childhood deprivation (Dennis, 1973; Rutter, 1972) all show that there may be remarkably little consistency between early childhood development and later adult outcomes. Longitudinal research all too often has been concerned with the demonstration of stability of lives over time and, perhaps for this reason, has failed to address the most interesting question: What conditions account for change in lives? As Baltes (1979) suggested (see also Kohlberg, Ricks, & Snarey, 1984), on the basis of a thorough review of developmental research, no single point in the life-cycle can claim such primacy for developmental change.

Longitudinal Study and Developmental Outcome

Longitudinal research on youth, both short-term prospective studies within the adolescent age period and longer-term studies following groups of youth into maturity, has examined various domains of adolescent experience. One of the earliest developmental investigations of adolescence, the Adolescent Growth Study, was pioneered at the Institute of Human Development (then the Institute of Child Welfare) at the University of California at Berkeley. This longitudinal project is one of the longest running and most comprehensive developmental studies of lives ever conducted on a nonclinical sample in this country. As an illustrative example, it demonstrates the inherent potential of such research efforts.

The Adolescent Growth Study (later renamed the Oakland Growth Study) was begun in 1931 by Harold E. Jones, Mary C. Jones, and Herbert Stolz on a sample of 212 fifth and sixth graders attending schools in Oakland, California. The initial questions of the investigators were directed to the experience of youth growing up; specifically, they focused on physical growth, personality development, and social relationships (Jones, 1940; Stolz & Stolz, 1951), examining the influences of biological, puberty-induced changes on psychological development (Jones, 1958; Jones & Mussen, 1958; Mussen & Jones, 1957).[8] Subsequent follow-ups of the sample were conducted when the study subjects were approximately 33 and 38 years old; recently, the study was merged with other long-term longitudinal samples to form one intergenerational panel of (now) middle-aged and older adults. Some of the study subjects' parents and children are included. It is an extremely unique data set, in both the range of data collected and the period of time covered across the life-course.

Some analyses conducted on the Berkeley data have attempted to relate specific aspects of adolescence to adult outcomes and adjustment (Peskin & Livson, 1981; see other recent analyses of the adult data in Eichorn, Clausen, Haan, Honzik, & Mussen, 1981). For example, Peskin and Livson (1981) examined both adolescent and adult data from this study and found that particular personal resources and modes of coping used during adolescence became salient once again and were further drawn on in midlife. It would not have been possible to examine these so-called "sleeper" effects without longitudinal observation.

The impact of sociocultural and historical events has also been investigated with various subsamples of these respondents. Elder's (1974) classic volume, *Children of the Great Depression*, and subsequent analyses building on its content (Elder, 1979, 1980; Elder, Downey, & Cross, 1986; Elder & Rockwell, 1979), examined the impact of the Depression on the lives of children and adolescents. Economic privation among members of the sample had differential effects on males and females, depending on whether the respondents were adolescents or children at the time of the economic loss. Erik Erikson and his colleagues (Erikson, Erikson, & Kivnick, 1986) tested the revised Eriksonian life-cycle model against the experiences of the oldest generation of parents (of the original study subjects), employing 50 years of archival data for their analyses.

Longitudinal Study and Pubertal Development

Despite their intensive focus, investigators conducting longitudinal research on adolescent development have typically not examined the sexual development of the respondents under investigation.[9] Livson and Peskin (1980) catalogued this work by major foci that included: (a) puberty-induced behavior; (b) consistency and change over time; (c) prediction of adaptation, psychopathology, and social deviance; (d) youth and school culture; (e) identity formation, sex-role identification, and vocational planning; (f) later separation and autonomy; (g) environmental and family stress; and (h) retrospection.

In spite of this neglect of sexuality, a number of important findings have emerged as a result of longitudinal research. Through examining the *course* of adolescence itself, more refined understanding is possible (Greene & Boxer, in press). For example, evidence suggests that multiple, simultaneous transitions can be particularly stressful for young adolescents (Coleman, 1980; Simmons, Blythe, Van Cleave, & Bush, 1979). One large study found that the convergence of school transitions, pubertal development, and new social relationships resulted in difficulties, particularly for

---

[8]This study also pioneered participant observational field methods applied to youth in intensive longitudinal efforts to document and understand growth and change over time. In the Adolescent Growth Study, a Club House was maintained by Institute Study staff near the study sample's school (Jones, 1940; Newman, 1946).

[9]Conversely, specialized investigations of adolescent sexuality ethnocentrically presume the heterosexuality of respondents, and usually do not situate the subject matter of sexuality in the context of other aspects of the respondents' lives (see Herdt, 1989). These investigations have been problem-focussed with the bulk of this work directed to teen pregnancy and parenthood (Coates, Petersen, & Perry, 1982; Dreyer, 1982). In addition, general surveys of adolescent sexual behavior (for a comprehensive review, see Dreyer, 1982) are typically only quantitative in approach and neglect the meaning of sexuality to adolescents, or the ways in which sexuality is related to other aspects of the adolescents' lives, such as their identity development (for an unusual exception to this, see D'Augelli & D'Augelli, 1979).

young adolescent girls. Longitudinal studies also suggest that, although puberty may be an important "developmental organizer" for youth, the experience of puberty and its psychological outcomes are strongly influenced/mediated by the social and cultural contexts in which adolescents live (Clausen, 1975; Petersen & Crockett, 1985).

The longitudinal perspective has modified earlier views of parent–youth conflict; although only a small percentage of adolescents experience severe turmoil and conflict with their families, many adolescents may experience time-limited perturbations in relations with fathers and mothers (Steinberg, 1981; Steinberg & Hill, 1978). Short-term longitudinal studies of adolescents' daily lives reveal that they may experience emotional highs and lows in different and perhaps more intense ways than adults (Csikszentmihalyi & Larson, 1984; Larson, Csikszentmihalyi, & Graef, 1980). Through the longitudinal method, it has been demonstrated that developmental trajectories through adolescence are quite variable. In one study of adolescent males (Offer, 1969; Offer & Offer, 1975), it was found that there were three developmental routes through the course of adolescence: continuous, surgent, and tumultuous growth patterns. The presumption of "raging hormones" resulting in a stormy and stressful adolescent phase appears to be a reality for only a small group of adolescents. This research questions models of adolescent development based on direct and linear effects (Petersen & Taylor, 1980), which assume that biological changes act directly on behavior without consideration of the psychosocial and cultural processes that mediate these changes.

Questions regarding the relations between pubertal change and psychosocial outcomes predominated some of the earliest concerns on adolescence, in G. Stanley Hall's (1904) pioneering work.[10] These relations are still the subject of much research (Boxer et al., 1989; Brooks-Gunn, Petersen, & Eichorn, 1985), particularly regarding the effects of pubertal timing on adolescent psychosocial development. There is marked interindividual variation both in the sequence of the appearance of such pubertal changes as secondary sex characteristics and in the time taken to complete this process of pubertal change (Tanner, 1971). Changes generally take place gradually over a number of years, and although, cumulatively, these changes have an impact on self-regard and expression of wish and intent, the impact is not nearly as dramatic as has been portrayed classically in psychodynamic formulations of adolescence (A. Freud, 1936/1946; Blos, 1967, 1979). The relationship between pubertal changes and psychosocial development is more complex and less linear than initially assumed. At the same time, most studies report self-esteem as more negative among younger than older adolescents (Simmons, Rosenberg, & Rosenberg, 1973), with a particularly marked drop in self-esteem more likely to continue into adulthood among girls than among boys (Petersen, 1981). To date, there has been little systematic comparative study of these issues of pubertal and psychological development among heterosexual and homosexual adolescents.

It is interesting to note that questions regarding pubertal status and psychological change in adolescence were echoed as an early concern of Alfred Kinsey and his associates (Kinsey, Pomeroy, & Martin, 1948). Kinsey viewed the onset of puberty and early adolescence as important turning points, at least for male homosexuality. In his cross-sectional sample, Kinsey found a high positive correlation between the earlier onset of puberty and the frequency of homosexuality during adolescence and later life. This high correlation was not found among the female respondents. Kinsey also linked this correlation into the fact that the occurrence of peak sexual activity for males was between the ages of 16 and 20; sexual behavior was thus viewed as reinforced by high sexual drives. Correlational data in the male sample (Kinsey et al., 1948, p. 317)

---

[10]For a comprehensive review of this literature, see Boxer & Petersen, 1986; Petersen & Taylor, 1980.

demonstrated that the earlier the onset of puberty, the greater the accumulated incidence of homosexual behavior.

Other associates of Kinsey have attempted to account for this relationship by positing a kind of environmental-conditioning hypothesis (Gebhard, 1965; Tripp, 1975). This quasi-theory states that boys who begin masturbating early build a "crucial" associative connection between maleness and male genitalia, and these in turn are linked to a set of sexually arousing and exciting associations. Tripp (1975) hypothesized that these associations build into an eroticism that is "ready" to extend itself to other male attributions and later to a same-sex partner. Thus, heterosexual interests are preempted. The retrospective, correlational data of Kinsey may have been demonstrating a spurious correlation or, though less likely, a result rather than a cause of sexual orientation.

It should be noted that, although there has been little longitudinal study of this issue, available findings do not suggest that aspects of pubertal timing are associated with a higher incidence of homosexuality among youth. Rather, across the adolescent epoch, homosexual teenagers become increasingly aware of being off-course regarding the gender of their erotic desires, rather than off-time in their pubertal development; largely as a consequence of social expectation, awareness of one's homosexual desires initiates a crisis of being "off-course" rather than off-time. All gays and lesbians, up to the present time, have experienced this discontinuity. What is different today is that adolescents currently coming out have the opportunity to integrate aspects of their sexuality with other components of their developing identities.

Developmental Continuities, Homosexuality, and the Study of Lives Over Time

Search for developmental continuities has implicitly characterized many investigations of adult homosexual men and women in which the focus has been on delineating childhood correlates of adult sexual orientation.[11] This preoccupation with continuity is in striking contrast to the discontinuities and changes that characterize the lives of many gay and lesbian adults, particularly when internalized societal expectations and early socialization experiences require strategies for dealing with the many cultural discontinuities experienced throughout the adult life-course (Bell et al., 1981; Bell & Weinberg, 1978; Cass, 1979, 1984; Humphreys & Miller, 1980; Martin, 1982; Minton & McDonald, 1983/1984; Troiden, 1979; Weinberg & Williams, 1974).

Continuity, Discontinuity, and the Life Story

Contemporary studies of lives have recognized the importance of providing a more complete ecology of the life-course, including: study of individuals' wishes and intents as shaped by development and maturation; aspects of social context; and, in particular, the historical circumstances that so dramatically affect the lives of persons within a specific generation or age-linked cohort (Cohler & Boxer, 1984). There is, consequently, increased interest in the study of factors that might be associated with individual differences in stability and change over time.

The determinants of continuity and discontinuity are also related to factors of vulnerability and resilience (Cohler, 1987). Of particular interest for the study of gay and lesbian youth are those qualities and features associated with the capacity to remain resilient when

---

[11]There are many different ways to examine continuity. Kagan (1980, 1981) has discussed three ways to infer continuity. The first regards hypothesizing the persistence of changeless elements beneath surface phenomena; a second is to uncover changing mechanisms that operate in different contexts across time. The third strategy rests on assuming that two or more events are related because some structural properties in an earlier event are found also in a later one. Alternatively, earlier events may lay the foundation for establishing conditions that result in a later event (Kagan, 1981).

confronted by adverse life circumstances. Such resilience has been identified as a characteristic of many older gay and lesbian adults, as a result of their having dealt with the adversity of various types of discrimination, homophobia, and other social stigmata throughout a significant portion of their lives (Berger, 1982; Kelly, 1977; Kimmel, 1978, 1980; Lee, 1987; Robinson, 1979; Weinberg & Williams, 1974). The study of resilience and coping requires consideration of the characteristics associated with particular life changes, as well as their timing and synchronization. These characteristics of events must be considered together with attributes of persons at particular points in the life-course. This predictive approach, based on information regarding the type of life change, the social context in which particular changes take place, and the developmental attributes of persons, must be complemented by a narrative or interpretive approach, which is concerned with the manner in which persons experience and interpret ("make sense" of) these life changes.

Little is known of the manner in which persons create a narrative that renders adversity coherent in terms of experienced life history, or the manner in which presently constructed meanings of life changes may be altered in order to maintain a sense of personal integration (Cohler, 1981, 1982, 1987). For some persons, the experience of adverse life events may be used as an explanation for failure to realize personal goals; for others, this misfortune becomes the impetus for increased effort in order to attain these goals. The value of an interpretive approach as a complement to the predictive one becomes even greater as a result of findings emerging from longitudinal studies (Emde, 1981; Jones, Bayley, MacFarlane, & Honzik, 1971; Kagan & Moss, 1962; Livson & Peskin, 1980; Moss & Sussman, 1980; Rutter, 1984), showing that lives are not as ordered and predictable over time as had previously been assumed. To the extent that lives show predictability, this order may be more a function of shared understanding regarding the linear organization of the expectable course of life in this culture, than of continuity reflected by data collected at multiple observation points. (For a more comprehensive review, see Anthony & Cohler, 1987; Cohler, 1987.)

The Life Story and the Transition into a Homosexual Life-Style

Over the past two decades, the process leading to the disclosure to oneself and others of a self-identity as gay or lesbian has been referred to as "coming-out" (of the closet) and, more recently, simply as "out" or "being out." The origin of this term is obscure; presumably, it was borrowed from debutantes' societal introduction. The concept was fully explicated in the work of Dank (1971), who referred to the fact of becoming homosexual; however, as Herdt (1992) observed, the concept is still not clear. Further, not only does it imply a process referring to a person rather than to a cohort across the course of life, but also it perpetuates Western concern with understanding the life-course in terms of stages for every transition from emergence into a homosexual identity (Troiden, 1988, 1989) to the study of death and dying. Introduction of stage and state models tends to impose artificial order on the life story and to reflect more on prevailing social expectations than on actual life experiences of those undergoing particular life transitions and adoption of new role identities (McCall & Simons, 1980).

Stage models tend to reify and simplify transitions in lives that have much more complexity, over time, than is reflected by the model. For example, in an otherwise sensitive portrayal of the assumption of a gay or lesbian identity, Troiden (1989) fails to consider the sequence by which gay and lesbian adolescents arrive at a self-definition as gay. However, as Boxer (1990) has shown, most homosexual adolescents go through a phase in their development in which they experiment with both heterosexuality and homosexuality before settling on a gay or lesbian sexual orientation. Boys appear more likely to experiment with homosexual relationships first, then to experiment with heterosexual relationships, and then to elect homosexuality; girls are more likely to elect homosexuality following heterosexual experimentation. Boxer's finding suggest that both gay and lesbian adolescents electing homosexuality found heterosexuality to be less personally rewarding and less personally meaningful and intense than homosexuality. Among lesbian girls, heterosexual intercourse was something that just "happened," but gay boys actively sought out heterosexual experiences and then compared their responses to gay and heterosexual experiences. It may be that the normative pressure toward heterosexuality in our society led these boys to "check out" heterosexuality, in an effort to convince themselves of the inevitability of their homosexual adjustment.

Herdt (1992) has argued for the significance of understanding the emergence into a homosexual identity of Van Gennep's (1912/1960) tripartite model of separation, liminality, and reaggregation. Van Gennep suggested that life-course transitions are marked by separation from the group, a period of time spent apart from the group learning new conceptions of one's role, and, finally, reunion with the larger group, with the new role conception learned and affirmed as a part of self. The concept of "coming-out," so often used in discussions of homosexuality in our own culture and in the literature on homosexuality (Plummer, 1975; Troiden, 1988, 1989), does not correspond in any ready manner to Van Gennep's portrayal of life-course transitions.

Studying a group of gay and lesbian adolescents attending coming-out groups, and struggling with issues related to the transition to a homosexual sexual orientation and life-style, Herdt (1992) found in Van Gennep's model of life transitions much that was relevant for understanding the process of becoming homosexual during the adolescent years. Adolescents in the groups observed by Herdt struggled, over a long time period, before coming to the gay and lesbian services center sponsoring the group. Willingness to enter the agency marked a first stage in the transition leading to separation from previously defined conceptions of oneself. Group members came to value the weekly meetings as a worthwhile time apart from the rest of the week, and the group as providing shelter and comfort before the inevitable return into the larger society for another week. All these issues of the transition into a homosexual life-style occur within a point in the course of life which, itself, is liminal. As Erikson (1959) observed, adolescence in our culture is inherently a time marked by liminality and by remaining apart from the larger society in order to arrive at a more clearly defined role identity.

Again, issues of acceptance, both by self and others, of the gay or lesbian life-style were a prominent feature of group discussions. Coming out involves, first, self-disclosure, then disclosure to friends and siblings, and, ultimately, disclosure to parents. Comparative study of the experience of coming out among boys and girls shows that boys find it somewhat more difficult to disclose their homosexuality than girls do. It is not likely that either gay and lesbian youth or their adult counterparts would discuss these issues in the workplace. There was little of the organized and emergent acceptance of oneself as homosexual in the manner portrayed by Troiden's (1989) four-stage model: (a) stressing sensitization to subsequent self-definition as homosexual; (b) struggling between dissonant homosexual wishes and efforts to view oneself as heterosexual; (c) assuming the identity of gay or lesbian; and (d) committing to the same-sex sexual orientation and life-style as legitimate. Rather, issues attendant on all three states—separation, liminality, and reunion—were expressed together and were facilitated by the liminality of the group, apart from the larger society. The fact that these states occurred within closer proximity than in societies studied by Van Gennep, in which initiation ceremonies occurred over periods of many weeks or months, made it possible to continually contrast a current transition with previous life or the lives of straight counterparts.

Life-Course Social Science and Study of Homosexuality in Adolescence

It is important that future research on homosexuality in adolescence be approached using the concepts and methods of life-course social science. Concepts of social timing, of careers and sequencing, and of transition into the gay or lesbian role-identity must be studied over time and across cohorts. These studies must span sociohistorical time periods that have dramatic impact on transitions across major life changes and transitions into and out of roles that are particularly salient at any one point in the course of life. Longitudinal, life-span investigations (employing both predictive and interpretive methodologies) will not only have an impact on our understanding of vulnerability, resilience, and well-being for gay and lesbian youth and adults, but will also carry important implications for models, methods, and theories within the social sciences for the study of lives (Lee, 1987). From the vantage point of the life-course, this section delineates some critical questions emerging from our current knowledge regarding gay and lesbian youth. Applications of the developmental paradigm to homosexuality, which have been primarily focused on causal inferences based on adult retrospections, are then briefly examined.

What happens to adolescents after they have traversed the coming-out phases as outlined by Troiden (1988)? After they come out to family members, how do gay and lesbian youth further negotiate their relationships with mothers and fathers during young adulthood and well after (Boxer, 1990; Boxer et al., 1990; Savin-Williams, 1988)? How will the differing life biographies and self-representations of "José" and "Pedro" in Mexico, elaborated by Carrier (1988), evolve as adults? How and in what form will the young lesbian discussed by Schneider (1988) create the life she desires as "normal and gay" (Schneider, 1988, p. 24)? More generally, what we do not yet know is how the experiences of gay and lesbian youth are evolving through the course of adolescence, how continuity and change are prefiguring their lives, and how resilience and vulnerability are at work. In short, little is yet known about how they experience their lives as they are living them, rather than as they *remember* them.

It is still not clear how the life experiences of present gay and lesbian youth may differ from those of gay and lesbian teenagers who have grown up in different settings and historical periods. In addition, there is a frequently asked and still unanswered question: How do gay and lesbian adolescents differ from their heterosexual peers? Is the normative adolescent "storm and stress" exacerbated among these youth?[12] It is important to be sensitized to variations in development as a function of cultural and ecological factors (Barker, 1968; Bronfenbrenner, 1977; Levine, 1973) or what used to be called the individual's "total life space" (Lewin, 1946/1964).

We are left, though, with the question of what happens to these youth over time and, especially, after initial coming out experiences. How will adulthood be affected by adolescent experiences within a particular cohort? More specifically, how will coming out in the current sociocultural and historical context shape expectations and hopes for the future? How will intimacy, sexual expression, and friendships develop within a cohort of youth coming of age during the AIDS crisis, knowing no other historical context of life experience? More specifically, how does a teenager's initial life adjustment to coming out relate to later outcomes, to patterns of achievement and cultural competence, to resilience and vulnerability, in young adulthood? How do those

---

[12]It should be noted that several decades of research on nonclinical samples of adolescents demonstrate that not all adolescents experience high levels of stress and turmoil and that there are multiple developmental pathways through adolescence (Douvan & Adelson, 1966; Kandel & Lesser, 1972; Offer & Offer, 1975).

who fall victim to physical or emotional abuse, because of their sexual orientation, negotiate relationships later in adult life? Does the specific context of individual socialization into gay and lesbian communities relate to patterns of successful aging and life satisfaction during middle and later life? What kinds of effects do gay- and lesbian-sensitive service providers have on the youth who make use of these, albeit limited, services?

The rise of AIDS both as an illness and as a historical context makes coming out in the 1980s unlike any other time in recent history. We tend to associate the current cultural ethos of AIDS only with individual life event/illness outcomes; it is also part of a general cultural and historical context for both male and female adolescents who are currently coming out. In the study of 202 gay and lesbian youth in Chicago (Herdt, Boxer, & Irvin, 1986), one gay male adolescent, Marc, gave this response to the question of how AIDS had affected his coming out:

It has politicized me. It forced me or sobered me. I came out at a critical time. Six months earlier if I had come out, I might have gone through a slutty period. In my case it wasn't an option. People I met were into getting serious, not just dating. The tone of the community was alerted and cautious. My sexual behavior didn't change. It's been consistent.

This young man's experience, inevitably, is both similar to and different from that of gay men who grew up 20 years or even 10 years earlier. In response to a question about his feelings regarding coming out, Marc said:

There was an awareness that things aren't always the way you are told they are. It's like being an expatriate in another country and you can view your own country from that distance. The isolation I experienced in being gay, and feeling there was no one to go to, resulted in my mustering up my own resources. Mustering up that fiber once was important.

His perceptions on his own development highlight the importance of examining the impact of historical and cultural changes on the course of lives. Marc discussed his relative ease, after some initial reticence, in being open with others about being gay. At the same time, he drew social support from certain "role colleagues" whom he had met at a gay and lesbian youth group—a circumstance quite different from any he would have encountered 10 years earlier. He is also aware of the danger and constraints that AIDS has created. A component of "danger to life" is associated with the expression of sexuality, but there is also an opportunity for the expression and consolidation of his gay identity. This cultural context of AIDS has differential effects on women as well, and may hold different meanings for them, as compared to males. One lesbian youth, Jana, in the Chicago project put it this way:

I'm concerned about it not only because males are getting it, but also because lesbians are getting it. . . . But a friend of mine died of AIDS. We were really close. He was like 17. When he died I didn't know much about it. It really did scare me. Friends would say he was a fag, that's why he died of AIDS. It still scares me but not as much as it did before. I'm more educated so I feel a lot better about it. It's hard with lesbians; how do you have safe sex? I'm not sure what lesbians can do. I'm about as safe as I can get.

Additionally, this cultural context becomes not only a fear of death and "plague," but also an adverse life event for those peers, like Jana, who may experience various aspects of loss, grief, and bereavement.

All existing studies of gay and lesbian youth (and of gay and lesbian adults as well) portray slices of experience at *one point in time,* rather than their construction or *development across time.* The questions we have delineated regarding the gay and lesbian life-course have either been neglected or have been investigated through the use of retrospective methods—a highly questionable procedure for the type of knowledge that is needed, and an approach that has been severely criticized for the distortions and biases that may result

(Ross, 1980; Spanier, 1976; Yarrow, Campbell & Burton, 1970). It is no surprise, then, that, up to the present time, our understanding of the development of gay and lesbian individuals across the entire life-course has been constructed using cross-sectional and retrospective findings, through which processes are inferred across stages or age groups. For example, in the development of gay or lesbian identity, current coming out schemas and ideal types are typically based on data gathered from respondents at one point in time, at varying phases of this process.

Study of the process of disclosing a homosexual life-style and sexual orientation must adopt the perspective pioneered in longitudinal research on the adult life-course. For example, longitudinal studies of the adult years, particularly those focusing on issues of intellectual decline with the advent of midlife, show that dramatically different interpretations arise from longitudinal study (following one group of persons over a number of years) as contrasted with cross-sequential studies based on comparative longitudinal study of persons who are a similar age but are examined at different points in their history (Schaie, 1965). Studies of intellectual development in adulthood were initially based on data collected at one point in time, from cross-sectional samples.

These findings were viewed as developmental sequences across different age groups, suggesting a general decrement in intellectual functioning across the latter half of life. However, longitudinal and cross-sequential analyses (Baltes, 1968; Schaie, 1965) of the same group of individuals across time demonstrated that, across age groups, such initial inferences regarding the decline in intelligence were erroneous. Cohort effects, such as that of educational level, were strongly associated with different groups (see Botwinick, 1977; Horn & Donaldson, 1980; Schaie, 1965), which resulted in the misinterpretation of cross-sectional data. Our understanding of intellectual development across the adult years is now quite different as a result of longitudinal studies.

The developmental psychology of the gay and lesbian life-course is, in consequence, largely a psychology of the *remembered past.* It now seems necessary to link studies of adulthood with those of adolescence, through prospective research rather than inference. Therefore, the study of contemporary cohorts of gay and lesbian youth provides the opportunity to begin systematic investigation of individuals at a critical transition phase of the life cycle and to trace their development into adulthood and beyond, to old age. This mapping of gay and lesbian life-span trajectories will no longer necessitate reliance on the *reconstructed past.* The resulting picture may be quite different from our current body of retrospective knowledge. For example, previous gender differences in age at first homosexual experience (see Troiden's review, 1989) may be a result of different cultural ideologies of men and women (in addition to historical changes). Relationship and connection have been identified as more salient cultural categories for many women, whereas autonomy and differentiation have been more important for men (Chodorow, 1978; Gilligan, 1982); this may affect the ways in which adult men and women reconstruct the memories of their adolescent sexual experiences. Longitudinal study of gay and lesbian youth may yield a different picture, with a narrower range of gender differences.

From a life-course point of view, the newly expanding visibility of gay and lesbian youth strongly suggests that the time has come to reassess certain key developmental concepts, including the coming out process itself, as well as the generalized concepts of gay and lesbian identity. These concepts, perhaps because they have been the first of more recent, developmentally informed investigations of homosexuality, now appear, ironically, to have a static and ahistorical timelessness that will ultimately render them meaningless, unless such factors as historical time, social structure, and the individual's position in the life-course are taken into account (Elder, 1975,

1980). In a historical overview of adolescent studies, Elder commented:

Adolescence is intimately linked to matters historical: the evolution of social age categories, the emergence of youth-related institutions, the impact of social change on lives. . . . In what sense can we presume to understand the psycho-social development of youth without systematic knowledge of their life course and collective experience in specific historical times? (Elder, 1980, p. 3,4).

For example, regarding the historical changes in gay and lesbian life-course trajectories, we may ask: Is coming out now as a 16-year-old adolescent in Chicago the same process as that for someone who came out in 1970 in San Francisco at age 40? Some researchers (Dank, 1971; Kimmel, 1978) have suggested that Stonewall is a critical historical marker distinguishing the manner of coming out for different "cohorts" of individuals. To a large extent, these processes have been studied independently of other life-span developmental issues. There is no doubt that, depending on the life-cycle position, the psychological issues are different. A middle-aged man must reconcile the time that has passed with the limited future time he has to live (Neugarten, 1967). An adolescent, on the other hand, is reckoning with the future in a new way (Greene, 1985, 1986) and must deal with the personal and social meanings of time and time mastery, looking forward toward the years that are yet to be lived.

Too often, we have presumed that creating a positive self-representation is the same for a middle-aged man or woman as it is for an adolescent or young adult (Cass, 1979, 1983/1984, 1984; Herek, 1985; Plummer, 1981; Weinberg, 1984).[13] Other research suggests significant differences in the coming out experiences among urban, suburban, and rural groups within the same historical period (reviewed in Herdt, 1989); see also Lynch, 1987; Murray, 1984; Troiden, 1988). More frequently overlooked is the question of how the individual's identity has evolved in the years subsequent to the initial coming out process.

PROBLEMS OF METHOD IN LONGITUDINAL RESEARCH ON ADOLESCENT HOMOSEXUALITY

The neglect and omission of sexuality in longitudinal research are likely traceable to several causes in addition to guiding assumptions of heterosexuality. The study of sexuality or any related phenomena in a group of legal minors presents numerous obstacles. Typically, researchers of adolescence draw their samples through school systems or other social institutions (summer camps, church groups, and so on). Many of these groups manifest strong resistance to investigation of a topic they perceive their constituency of parents will find unacceptable (Petersen, Tobin-Richards, & Boxer, 1983). In addition, ethical considerations and federal guidelines requiring informed consent by parents of study subjects make many investigators reticent to even enter into such research, and many parents may be suspicious of researchers' studying their children's sexuality. As Deisher (1988) indicated, the problems are compounded in the case of gay and lesbian youth. For example, many gay and lesbian youth have not come out to their parents and are therefore unwilling to have a parent sign a consent form.

We are aware that longitudinal research is no panacea; it can be a complex, time-consuming, and costly endeavor. The many complexities and methodological problems inherent in the use of longitudinal methods are probably further responsible for the paucity of such work to date. Primary considerations are the tracking and monitoring of respondents' whereabouts, and sample attrition. Many self-selection

---

[13]There are exceptions to this, such as Kimmel's (1978, 1980) studies of middle-aged and aging homosexual men, which examined certain developmental issues related to coming out as well as the individual's position in the life cycle, in the context of cultural and historical influences. (See also Berger, 1982; Kehoe, 1986; Robinson, 1979.)

processes may also be operating among respondents, because longitudinal studies require continued cooperation for participation in a number of examinations, interviews, tests, and so on. Maintaining a research alliance (Offer & Sabshin, 1967) with respondents is always important; however, with gay and lesbian youth, who may not have yet come out to many others, sensitivity and understanding are critical.

Developmentalists who study the life span have increasingly focused their attention on differentiating those behaviors that are age-related (and, in this sense, developmental) and those that may result from the impact of sociohistorical and cultural events (Baltes, 1968; Schaie, 1965; Schaie & Hertzog, 1982). Many studies are unable to differentiate cultural–environmental and maturational influences on developmental change. In other words, the components of age change, cohort differences, and environmental influences are typically confounded. Attempts to differentiate these effects are often lacking in current longitudinal work. One remarkable exception, disaggregating maturational and contextual effects, was the study of adolescent personality development conducted by Nesselroade and Baltes (1974). They examined 1,800 children born between 1954 and 1957; respondents were tested three times during a 2-year period. Developmental changes in personality were found to be more influenced by historical effects than by ontogenetic, age-related changes. However, the implications of this study have been directed largely to issues of method, rather than to substantive issues of defining particular sociohistorical forces that have an influence on the life-course of youth (see Boxer, Gershenson, & Offer, 1984; Cohler & Boxer, 1984).

A major problem to date has been the definition of the cohort to be studied (Kertzer, 1983; Nydegger, 1977; Rosow, 1978; Ryder, 1965). Although two groups of persons born as closely as one year apart may suffice as separate cohorts according to critics of longitudinal research, the definition of cohort to be used in a particular study depends, in large part, on the questions addressed by the research (Cohler & Boxer, 1984). The personal significance of particular historical circumstances is likely to be of greater critical importance in the very definitions that persons have of their own lives (Elder, 1974, 1975, 1980). However, it is an open question as to how exactly the concept of cohort functions among communities of gay and lesbian individuals over the life-course. While "pre" and "post" Stonewall have been identified as cohort markers, other events, including "pre" and "post" the AIDS crisis, are also likely to be salient. (See Murray, 1984, for a discussion of historical markers.)

From its very point of initiation, a longitudinal design guides a group of researchers on a given course, and, although it should be flexible enough to be subject to modifications, the consequences of any given research strategies may be felt 30 to 50 years later. As new measures come into existence, researchers question the use of old ones. In many longitudinal studies, continuity of data was favored, even when an instrument was found to be faulty or inaccurate. In addition, using one instrument to measure an attribute at several ages does not guarantee that the same process will be measured at each age level; nor do many investigators control for the practice effects of repeated measures. Longitudinal studies, with their accumulating data banks, do offer possibilities of reanalysis and reinterpretation of data within the limited perspectives available. In a 1971 analysis of the Berkeley longitudinal studies (Block, with Haan, 1971), it was noted that not even half of the data available had been subject to complete analysis. In an article written over 30 years ago (Jones, 1958), Harold Jones, co-founder and long-time director of the Oakland Growth Study, cited many pertinent issues that plagued his research design, but concluded: "If we wish, as we should, to achieve a body of developmental theory, we cannot eliminate developmental observation" (p. 98). The longitudinal method presents itself with a multitude of problems for the study of development, but the costs incurred appear to be worth every effort. Our current knowledge of development will only be advanced through the longitudinal study of change as it is occurring throughout people's lives.

CLINICAL SERVICES AND THE DEVELOPMENT OF GAY AND LESBIAN YOUTH

Developmental research has generally had a profound impact on the delivery of services to adolescents. Since Anna Freud's (1958) comment that adolescence was the "stepchild of developmental theory," more sophisticated and comprehensive understandings of adolescence have emerged in research, theory, and clinical services. Accompanying the recognition of adolescence as being distinctly different from both childhood and adulthood is the emerging idea that what is "normal" or expectable for an adolescent is different from what is normal or expectable for an adult (Offer, 1987; Offer & Sabshin, 1984). The longitudinal perspective on adolescence has had particularly important implications for mental health practitioners and service providers, in giving them a baseline in terms of which the origin, course, and treatment of psychological distress and disturbances may be evaluated. This perspective has been particularly useful in informing diagnosis and assessment of psychopathology during the adolescent years. The tendency among clinicians has been to base their understanding of problems characteristic of this decade on generalizations derived from small psychopathological samples (Offer, Ostrov, & Howard, 1981).

The use of findings from developmental research has led to the realization that not all adolescents must necessarily experience severe identity crises and accompanying turmoil. The view of inevitable turmoil during adolescence, held by many mental health professionals, has been questioned on the basis of several developmental studies (Csikszentmihalyi & Larson, 1984; Douvan and Adelson, 1966; Kandel & Lesser, 1972; Offer & Offer, 1975). Continued endorsement of this view by those working with adolescents sometimes makes it difficult for troubled teenagers to obtain care addressed to their particular concerns. Thus, major psychopathology may not always be differentiated by clinicians from concerns characteristic of the adolescent epoch. The needs of adolescents can only be addressed when service providers are informed by a broad understanding of development across the adolescent decade, including the complex interplay between maturational and personality processes, and the reciprocal impact of increasingly complex, socially defined expectations regarding major roles on self-conceptions and individual well-being.

However, conspicuously missing is a developmental understanding of what is "normative" and expectable for gay and lesbian youth growing up in our society today. In understanding the problems of this group, we should consider both the nature of life changes and the means by which adolescents cope more or less effectively with such changes. Some evidence suggests that gay and lesbian teenagers are "at risk" for adjustment problems such as drug abuse, sexually transmitted diseases, physical abuse, prostitution, and psychiatric disorders (Gibson, 1987; Kourany, 1987; Martin & Hetrick, 1987; Roesler & Deisher, 1972). For example, one developmentally informed series of studies of self-identified gay male adolescents (Remafedi, 1987a, 1987b) indicates that they are at high risk for physical and psychosocial dysfunction as a result of experiencing strong negative attitudes (e.g., homophobia) from parents and peers. In addition, some of these youth reported verbal abuse, physical assaults, and discrimination.

These studies raise important questions, but they are almost always based primarily on small, cross-sectional, opportunity samples of men. Existing studies (including those based on retrospective methods or on clinically constituted samples) support this hypothesis of higher risk, and yet no longitudinal, naturalistic investigations have been conducted to determine the validity of this point of view over time. Research is needed to determine, in other words, how gay and lesbian adolescents negotiate their life-course around school, family, and peer relations. It remains an open question as to what subsequently happens to those who are physically or emotionally abused by friends, family, or society-at-large. How do the teenager's initial resilience and vulnerability relate to subsequent coping processes and life experiences in young adulthood? This and other related questions, such as the impact of service providers on the adjustment of gay youth, can only be answered by following a group of youth across time, through repeated interviews and observations.

It is important that both the services provided for gay and lesbian adolescents and the study of adjustment across the adolescent decade among these youth include the family as well as the adolescent. Boxer (1990) and Boxer et al. (1990) provided important first findings regarding the manner in which gay and lesbian adolescents communicate their sexual orientation to their family. These findings point to a complex process of communication in the family, marked by continuing efforts of each generation to influence the other regarding health and life-style. Adolescents socialize their parents into new conceptions of sexuality, and parents often communicate particular concern regarding their offspring's use of condoms as a part of their sexual behavior.

Mothers of both gay and lesbian adolescents maintained a relationship with their offspring similar to the past relationship; unexpectedly, the father–daughter tie was more disrupted than that of fathers and sons. Muller (1987) reported that, where there was disruption of the mother's tie with offspring, this disruption more often occurred with daughters than with sons. In spite of the fact that the women's movement has provided a rhetoric of acceptance that ought to be useful in the father's acceptance of his daughter's sexual orientation and life-style, it appears that both parents have particular difficulty with their daughter's adoption of a homosexual orientation. This may be related to disruption of parental hopes for a grandchild. This issue, which posed problems for parents of both sons and daughters, may be more general in contemporary society because marriage occurs at ever later ages and many adults decide to postpone or abandon plans for parenthood. Again, only cross-sequential study using groups of both homosexual and heterosexual adolescents in more than one cohort, followed over time, will be able to resolve this issue of the role of expectation in the course of the relationships among generations within the family.

As we have emphasized, there is little existing research on the development of gay and lesbian individuals over time.[14] Such an effort would help answer questions regarding the outcomes of youth who may be at risk for various biological, social, and psychological stressors. The relationship between positive life satisfactions and successful aging can also be examined by repeated study of cohorts of youth moving into adulthood. AIDS is now an especially critical factor to be considered. The use of longitudinal methods would provide an ideal way of delineating the psychosocial impact of AIDS on youth coming of age during the current AIDS epidemic (Feldman, 1988; Millan & Ross, 1987). The needs of groups of lesbians and gay males can only be determined through assessment that examines changes in life-style, behavior, and development over time.[15]

CONCLUSION

The concept of life-course, which is socially structured, must be differentiated from such terms as life cycle or life span, which refer only to change over time, without consideration of the normative cultural element implicit in making sense of such change. It is

---

[14] One exception is a study by Lee (1987), who followed a group of middle-aged homosexual men for 4 years, examining aspects of adult development and aging.

[15] Some investigators have discussed the potential follow-up of adult respondents from their previous studies (e.g., McWhirter & Mattison, 1984; Silverstein, 1981).

clear that age as a chronological marker is of little significance for the study of the life-course, except as represented by the socially shared meanings attached to particular ages across the life cycle. Without such cultural and historical knowledge, age itself becomes an "empty" variable in the study of lives. It is precisely this social definition of the course of life that transforms the study of the life span or life cycle into the study of the *life-course*.

The present generation of gay and lesbian adolescents is confronting their sexuality and their relations with others in ways that are different from those of preceding generations. With the removal of at least some of the stigma attending prior generations of gay and lesbian youth, it is possible to study psychological stress, lowered morale, and psychological distress, which may be associated with selection of a particular sexual orientation and life-style, apart from stigma and stereotyping. Life-course study, emphasizing cross-sequential research designs evaluating the impact of generation, cohort, and place in the course of life, is essential in order to realize a revision of our current developmental understanding of gay and lesbian youth.

Study of the contemporary cohort of gay young men and lesbian young women, informed by life-course perspectives but necessarily retrospective and anecdotal, suggests the need for revision in our understanding of mental health and adolescent homosexuality. There seems to be little explicit impact on mental health, as a result of selection of a homosexual orientation, that is different from the impact experienced by heterosexual counterparts. To date, there has been little systematic comparative study of heterosexual and homosexual adolescents; however, findings from the study of several gay and lesbian adolescents in Chicago show that the overwhelming majority of these adolescents (more than 80 percent) report little psychological distress accompanying the first actual homosexual experience. Where stigma and stereotyping are reduced, homosexuality itself does not appear related to increased personal distress. Although clinicians encounter adolescents whose adjustment has been adversely affected by the possibility of a gay or lesbian sexual orientation and life-style, it is important not to generalize on the basis of this group of more troubled adolescents seeking mental health services.

Future studies will almost certainly lead to the remapping of gay and lesbian adult life-course trajectories. The developmental perspective can be a useful framework from which to examine the effects and interrelations of historical time and sociocultural contexts on individual development. This examination requires both quantitative and qualitative research strategies, to better understand a previously hidden and neglected group of youth. Many past research findings, which were based on cross-sectional samples and/or retrospective methods, may be radically altered by studying lives through time.

Young adults today must negotiate a complicated series of decisions concerning the sequencing of events in the transition to adulthood (Greene & Boxer, 1986). During late adolescence, school, career, and family-related decisions appear to be interwoven, and they make late adolescence and young adulthood a time in which there is often a pileup of role changes. Gay and lesbian adolescents are therefore faced with negotiating these decisions, as well as those involving the meaning, management, and expression of their sexuality. The construction of personal expectations and anticipations for the future life-course may be a unique developmental task for these youth. The first generation of gay and lesbian youth currently coming of age during the AIDS crisis are likely to become some of those with the longest life-time histories of a gay or lesbian identity. It is now time to embark, with them as consociates, in developmental studies that continue as they grow up, enter adulthood, and grow old.

Issues raised in this chapter question methods presently used to study gay youth, including: the validity of reliance on respondents' recollections regarding their childhood and adolescent experiences; inferences about developmental processes and outcomes made on the basis of cross-sectional samples; the time-specific, cohort-bound nature of many previous constructs and findings; and the persistent search for continuities between childhood gender behavior and adult sexual orientation. In consequence, the emerging body of theory is largely a developmental psychology of the remembered past. Strategies such as those suggested here for longitudinal, prospective research on homosexual adolescents—shifting attention from child-based, "causal" models to those of adolescent and adult-centered perspectives—may lead to important new understandings of the development of gay youth. Aimed at understanding life-changes and the developmental processes and course of negotiating them, longitudinal methods will more accurately reflect current experiences of gay and lesbian youth coming of age in a unique historical context. Findings from studies of the life-course have direct implications for modification of current developmental theories, particularly those that can inform gay- and lesbian-sensitive clinical services for all age groups.

REFERENCES

Adelson, J. (Ed.). (1980). *Handbook of adolescent psychology.* New York: Wiley.

Anthony, E. J., & Cohler, B. J. (Eds.) (1987). *The invulnerable child.* New York: Guilford Press.

Back, K., & Gergen, K. (1963). Apocalyptic and serial time orientations and the structure of opinions. *Public Opinion Quarterly, 27,* 427–442.

Baltes, P. H. (1968). Longitudinal and cross-sequential sequences in the study of age and generation effects. *Human development, 11,* 145–171.

Baltes, P. H. (1979). Life-span developmental psychology: Some converging observations on history and theory. In P. Baltes & O. G. Brim, Jr. (Eds.), *Life-span development and behavior: Vol. 2* (pp. 256–281). New York: Academic Press.

Barker, R. G. (1968). *Ecological psychology: Concepts and methods for studying the environment of human behavior.* Stanford, CA: Stanford University Press.

Bell, A. P., & Weinberg, M. S. (1978). *Homosexualities: A study of diversity among men and women.* New York: Simon & Shuster.

Bell, A. P., Weinberg, M. S., & Hammersmith, S. K. (1981). *Sexual preference: Its development in men and women.* Bloomington: Indiana University Press.

Bell, R. Q., & Harper, L. (1977). *Child effects on adults.* Hillsdale, NJ: Erlbaum.

Berger, R. M. (1982). *Gay and gray: The older homosexual man.* Urbana: University of Illinois Press.

Bieber, I., Dain, H., Dince, P., Drellich, M., Grand, H., Gundlach, R., Kremer, M., Rifkin, A., Wilbur, C., & Bieber, T. (1962). *Homosexuality: A psychoanalytic study of male homosexuals.* New York: Basic Books.

Block, J., with Haan, N. (1971). *Lives through time.* Berkeley, CA: Bancroft Books.

Blos, P. (1967). The second individuation process of adolescence. *Psychoanalytic Study of the Child, 22,* 162–187.

Blos, P. (1979). *The adolescent passage: Developmental issues.* New York: International Universities Press.

Botwinick, J. (1977). Intellectual abilities. In J. E. Birren & K. W. Schaie (Eds.), *Handbook of the psychology of aging* (pp. 580–605). New York: Van Nostrand Reinhold.

Boxer, A. M. (1990). Life course transitions of gay and lesbian youth: Sexual identity development and parent–child relationships. Unpublished doctoral dissertation, Committee on Human Development, The University of Chicago.

Boxer, A. M., & Cohler, B. J. (1980, November). *Personal time orientations and intergenerational conflicts in three-generation families.* Paper presented at the annual meetings of The Gerontological Society of America, San Diego, CA.

Boxer, A. M., Cook, J. A., & Cohler, B. J. (1986). Grandfathers, fathers, and sons: Intergenerational relations among men. In K. Pillemer & R. Wolf (Eds.), *Elder abuse: Conflict in the family* (pp. 93–121). Dover, MA: Auburn House.

Boxer, A. M., Cook, J., & Herdt, G. (1990). Double jeopardy: Identity transformations and parent–child relations among gay and lesbian youth. In K. Pillemer & K. McCartney (Eds.), *Parent–child relations across the life-span.* Hillsdale, NJ: Erlbaum.

Boxer, A. M., Gershenson, H. P., & Offer, D. P. (1984). Historical time and social change in adolescent experience. In D. Offer, E. Ostrov, & K. Howard (Eds.), *Patterns of adolescent self-image* (pp. 83–95). New directions for mental health services, Series No. 22. San Francisco: Jossey-Bass.

Boxer, A. M., Levinson, R. A., & Petersen, A. (1989). Adolescent sexuality. In J. Worrell & F. Danner (Eds.), *The adolescent as decision maker* (pp. 209–243). New York: Academic Press.

Boxer, A. M., & Petersen, A. C. (1986). Pubertal change in a family context. In G. K. Leigh & G. W. Petersen (Eds.), *Adolescence in families* (pp. 73–103). Cincinnati, OH: South-Western.

Boyer, D. (1989). Male prostitution and homosexual identity. In G. Herdt (Ed.), *Gay and lesbian youth* (151–184). New York: Harrington Park Press.

Brim, O. H., Jr., & Kagan, J. (1980). Constancy and change: A view of the issues. In O. G. Brim, Jr. & J. Kagan (Eds.), *Constancy and change in human development*. Cambridge, MA: Harvard University Press.

Bronfenbrenner, U. (1977). Toward an experimental ecology of human development. *American Psychologist, 32,* 513–531.

Brooks-Gunn, J., Petersen, A. C., & Eichorn, D. (Eds.). (1985). Timing of maturation and psychosocial functioning in adolescence. Part I and Part II (two special issues). *Journal of Youth and Adolescence, 14*(3), *14*(4).

Bugental, D. P., & Shennum, W. A. (1984). "Difficult" children as elicitors and targets of adult communication patterns: An attributional-behavioral transactional analysis. *Monographs of the Society for Research in Child Development, 205.*

Butler, R. (1963). The life review: An interpretation of reminiscence in the aged. *Psychiatry, 26,* 65–76.

Carrier, J. (1988). Gay liberation and coming out in Guadalajara, Mexico. *Journal of Homosexuality, 22,* 225–252.

Cass, V. C. (1979). Homosexual identity formation: A theoretical model. *Journal of Homosexuality, 4,* 219–235.

Cass, V. C. (1983/1984). Homosexual identity: A concept in need of definition. *Journal of Homosexuality, 9,* 105–126.

Cass, V. C. (1984). Homosexual identity formation: Testing a theoretical model. *Journal of Sex Research, 20,* 143–167.

Chang, J., & Block, J. (1960). A study of identification in male homosexuals. *Journal of Consulting and Clinical Psychology, 24,* 307–310.

Chodorow, N. (1978). *The reproduction of mothering: Psychoanalysis and the sociology of gender.* Berkeley: University of California Press.

Clarke, A., & Clarke, A. D. B. (Eds.) (1976). *Early experience: Myth and evidence.* New York: Free Press.

Clausen, J. A. (1975). The social meaning of differential physical and sexual maturation. In S. Dragastin & G. H. Elder, Jr. (Eds.), *Adolescence in the life cycle* (pp. 25–47). Washington, DC: Hemisphere.

Coates, T. J., Petersen, A. C., & Perry, C. (1982). *Promoting adolescent health: A dialog on research and practice.* New York: Academic Press.

Cohler, B. J. (1980). Developmental perspectives on the psychology of the self in early childhood. In A. Goldberg (Ed.), *Advances in self psychology* (pp. 69–115). New York: International Universities Press.

Cohler, B. J. (1987). Vulnerability, resilience, and the study of lives. In E. J. Anthony & B. J. Cohler (Eds.), *The invulnerable child* (pp. 363–424). New York: Guilford Press.

Cohler, B. J. (1981). Adult developmental psychology and reconstruction in psychoanalysis. In S. I. Greenspan & G. H. Pollock (Eds.), *The course of life: Vol 3. Adulthood and aging.* Washington, DC: DHHS, U.S. Government Printing Office.

Cohler, B. J. (1982). Personal narrative and life course. In P. Baltes & O. G. Brim, Jr. (Eds.), *Life-span development and behavior: Vol 4.* New York: Academic Press.

Cohler, B. J., & Boxer, A. M. (1984). Middle adulthood: Settling into the world—Person, time and context. In D. Offer & M. Sabshin (Eds.), *Normality and the life cycle* (pp. 145–203). New York: Basic Books.

Cohler, B. J., & Geyer, E. S. (1982). Psychological autonomy and interdependence within the family. In F. Walsh (Ed.), *Normal family process.* New York: Guilford Press.

Coleman, E. (1989). The development of male prostitution activity among gay and bisexual adolescents. In G. Herdt (Ed.), *Gay and lesbian youth* (pp. 131–149). New York: Harrington Park Press.

Coleman, J. C. (1980). *The nature of adolescence.* New York/London: Methuen.

Coleman, J. S., Bremner, R. H., Clark, B. R., Davis, J. B., Eichorn, D. H., Griliches, Z., Kett, J. F., Ryder, N. B., Doering, Z. B., & Mays, J. M. (1974). *Youth: Transition to adulthood. Report of the panel on youth of the President's Science Advisory Committee.* Chicago: University of Chicago Press.

Conger, J. J., & Petersen, A. C. (1984). *Adolescence and youth: Psychological development in a changing world.* New York: Harper & Row.

Cook, J. A. (1988, 37, 42–49). Who mothers the chronically mentally ill? *Family relations.*

Cook, J. A., & Cohler, B. J. (1986). Reciprocal socialization and the care of offspring with cancer and with schizophrenia. In N. Datan, A. L. Greene, & H. W. Reese (Eds.), *Life-span developmental psychology: Intergenerational relations* (pp. 223–243). Hillsdale, NJ: Erlbaum.

Cooley, C. H. (1902). *Human nature and the social order.* New York: Scribner.

Coons, N. (1987, June). Modern prom: A night to forget. *Chicago,* pp. 162–173.

Csikszentmihalyi, M., & Larson, R. (1984). *Being adolescent: Conflict and growth in the teenage years.* New York: Basic Books.

Dank, B. (1971). Coming out in the gay world. *Psychiatry, 34,* 180–197.

D'Augelli, A. & D'Augelli, J. (1979). Sexual development and relationship involvement: A cognitive developmental view. In R. Burgess & T. Huston (Eds.), *Social exchange in developing relationships* (pp. 307–349). New York: Academic Press.

Dawson, R. E., & Prewitt, K. (1969). *Political socialization.* Boston: Little, Brown.

De Cecco, J. P. (1987). Homosexuality's brief recovery: From sickness to health and back again. *The Journal of Sex Research, 23,* 106–129.

Deisher, R. (1988). Preface to the issue, "Gay and Lesbian Youth." *Journal of Homosexuality,* xiii–xv.

Dennis, W. (1973). *Children of Creche.* New York: Appleton-Century.

Douvan, E., & Adelson, J. (1966). *The adolescent experience.* New York: Wiley.

Dreyer, P. (1982). Sexuality during adolescence. In B. B. Wolman (Ed.), *Handbook of developmental psychology* (pp. 559–601). Englewood Cliffs, NJ: Prentice-Hall.

Eichorn, D., Clausen, J., Haan, N., Honzik, M. P., & Mussen, P. H. (1981). *Present and past in middle life.* New York: Academic Press.

Elder, G. H., Jr. (1974). *Children of the Great Depression.* Chicago: University of Chicago Press.

Elder, G. H., Jr. (1975). Age differentiation and the life course. In *Annual Review of Sociology* (pp. 165–190) Palo Alto, CA: Annual Reviews.

Elder, G. H., Jr. (1979). Historical change in life patterns and personality. In P. Baltes & O. G. Brim, Jr. (Eds.), *Life-span development and behavior: Vol. 2* (pp. 117–159). New York: Academic Press.

Elder, G. H., Jr. (1980). Adolescence in historical perspective. In J. Adelson (Ed.), *Handbook of adolescent psychology* (pp. 3–46). New York: Wiley.

Elder, G. H., Jr., Downey, G., & Cross, C. E. (1986). Family ties and life chances: Hard times and hard choices in women's lives since the 1930s. In N. Datan, A. L. Greene, & H. W. Reese (Eds.), *Life-span developmental psychology: Intergenerational relations* (pp. 151–183). Hillsdale, NJ: Erlbaum.

Elder, G. H., Jr. & Rockwell, R. W. (1979). Economic depression and postwar opportunities in men's lives: A study of life patterns and health. In R. G. Simmons (Ed.), *Research in community and mental health.* Greenwich, CT: JAI Press.

Emde, R. (1981). Changing models of infancy and the nature of early development: Remodeling the foundation. *Journal of the American Psychoanalytic Association, 29,* 179–219.

Erikson, E. (1959). *Identity and the life cycle.* New York: Norton.

Erikson, E. (1963). *Childhood and society.* New York: Norton.

Erikson, E. (1968). *Identity: Youth and crisis.* New York: Norton.

Erikson, E., Erikson, J., & Kivnick, H. (1986). *Vital involvement in old age.* New York: W.W. Norton.

Feldman, D. A. (1989). Gay youth and AIDS. *Journal of Homosexuality, 17,* 185–193.

Freud, A. (1946). *The ego and the mechanisms of defense,* New York: International Universities Press. (Original work published 1936)

Freud, A. (1958). Adolescence. *Psychoanalytic Study of the Child, 16,* 225–278.

Freud, S. ([1905] 1953). Three essays on the theory of sexuality. *Standard Edition, 7,* 130–243. London: Hogarth Press.

Freud, S. (1955). The psychogenesis of a case of homosexuality in a woman. In J. Strachey (Ed. and Trans.). *The standard edition of the complete psychological works of Sigmund Freud.* (Vol. 18, pp. 145–172). London: Hogarth Press. (Original work published 1920)

Gebhard, P. H. (1965). Situational factors affecting human sexual behavior. In F. A. Beach (Ed.), *Sex and behavior.* New York: Wiley.

Gebhard, P. H., Gagnon, J. H., Pomeroy, W. B., & Christensen, C. V. (1965). *Sex offenders: An analysis of types.* New York: Harper & Row.

Geertz, C. (1983). Blurred genres: The refiguration of social thought. In C. Geertz (Ed.), *Local knowledge* (pp. 19–35). New York: Basic Books.

Gergen, K. (1982). *Toward transformation in social knowledge.* New York: Springer-Verlag.

Gerstel, C., Feraios, A. J., & Herdt, G. (1989). Widening circles: An ethnographic profile of a youth group. *Journal of Homosexuality, 17,* 75–92.

Gibson, P. (1987). *Gay male and lesbian youth suicide.* Unpublished manuscript, San Francisco, CA.

Gilligan, C. (1982). *In a different voice: Psychological theory and women's development.* Cambridge, MA: Harvard University Press.

Green, R. (1987). *The "sissy boy" syndrome.* New Haven: Yale University Press.

Greene, A. L. (1985, March). *Great expectations: Age norms in expected future life events in mid and late adolescence.* Paper presented at the annual meeting of the Eastern Psychological Association, Boston, MA.

Greene, A. L. (1986). Future time perspective in adolescence: The present of things future revisited. *Journal of Youth and Adolescence, 15,* 99–113.

Greene, A. L., & Boxer, A. M. (1986). Daughters and sons as young adults: Restructuring the ties that bind. In N. Datan, A. L. Greene, & H. W. Reese (Eds.), *Life-span developmental psychology: Intergenerational relations* (pp. 125–149). Hillsdale, NJ: Erlbaum.

Hagestad, G. O. (1981). Problems and promises in the social psychology of intergenerational relations. In R. W. Fogel, E. Hatfield, S. B. Kiesler, & E. Shanas (Eds.), *Stability and change in the family* (pp. 11–46). New York: Academic Press.

Hall, G. S. (1904). *Adolescence: Its psychology and its relation to physiology, anthropology, sociology, sex, crime, religion and education.* New York: Appleton.

Hamburg, D. A. (1986). *Preparing for life: The critical transition of adolescence.* New York: Carnegie Corporation. (Reprinted from the 1986 Annual Report of the Carnegie Corporation of New York.)

Harry, J. (1982). *Gay children grown up.* New York: Praeger.

Herdt, G. (1981). *Guardians of the flutes.* New York: McGraw-Hill.

Herdt, G. (1989). Introduction: Gay and lesbian youth, emergent identities, and cultural scenes at home and abroad. *Journal of Homosexuality, 17,* 1–42.

Herdt, G. (1990a). *"Coming out" as a rite of passage.* Unpublished manuscript, Committee on Human Development, University of Chicago.

Herdt, G. (1992). "Coming out" as a rite of passage: A Chicago study. In G. Herdt (Ed.), *Gay culture in America* (29–67). Boston: Beacon Press.

Herdt, G., & Boxer, A. M. (1993). *Children of Horizons.* Boston: Beacon Press.

Herdt, G., Boxer, A. M., and Irvin, F. S. (1986). *Sexual orientation and cultural competence in Chicago.* Proposal for funding, submitted to Spencer Foundation, Chicago.

Herek, G. M. (1985). On doing, being, and not being: Prejudice and the social construction of sexuality. *Journal of homosexuality, 12,* 135–151.

Holeman, R. E., & Winokur, G. (1965). Effeminate homosexuality: A disease of childhood. *American Journal of Orthopsychiatry, 35,* 48–56.

Hooker, E. (1956). The adjustment of the male overt homosexual. *Journal of Projective Techniques, 21,* 30–35.

Hooker, E. (1965). Male homosexuals and their worlds. In J. Marmor (Ed.), *Sexual inversion: The multiple roots of homosexuality.* New York: Basic Books.

Horn, J. L., & Donaldson, G. (1980). Cognitive development in adulthood. In O. G. Brim, Jr. & J. Kagan (Eds.), *Constancy and change in human development* (pp. 445–529). Cambridge, MA: Harvard University Press.

Humphreys, L., & Miller, B. (1980). Identities in the emerging gay culture. In J. Marmor (Ed.), *Homosexual behavior: A modern reappraisal* (pp. 142–156). New York: Basic Books.

Isay, R. A. (1985). On the analytic therapy of homosexual men. *Psychoanalytic Study of the Child, 40,* 235–254.

Isay, R. A. (1986). The development of sexual identity in homosexual men. *Psychoanalytic Study of the Child, 41,* 467–489.

Isay, R. A. (1987, May). *Fathers and their homosexually inclined sons in childhood.* Paper presented at the annual meetings of the American Psychoanalytic Association, Chicago.

Janet, P. (1877). Une illusion d'optique interne [The illusion of the inner image]. *Révue philosophie, 1,* 497–502.

Janowitz, M. (Ed.). (1966). *W. I. Thomas on social organization and social personality.* Chicago: University of Chicago Press.

Jones, H. (1958). Problems of method in longitudinal research. *Vita Humana 1,* 93–99.

Jones, H. E. (1939). The adolescent growth study: I. Principles and methods; II. Procedures. *Journal of Consulting Psychology, 3,* 157–169; 177–180.

Jones, H. E. (1940). Educational research at the Institute of Child Welfare. *Journal of Educational Research, 34,* 158–159.

Jones, H. E. (1958). Problems of method in longitudinal research. *Vita Humana, 1,* 93–99.

Jones, M. C., Bayley, N., MacFarlane, J. W., & Honzik, M. (Eds.) (1971). *The course of human development: Selected papers from the longitudinal studies, Institute of Human Development, University of California, Berkeley.* Waltham, MA: Xerox College Publishing.

Jones, M. C., & Mussen, P. H. (1958). Self-conceptions, motivations, and interpersonal attitudes of early- and late-maturing girls. *Child Development, 29,* 491–501.

Kagan, J. (1980). Perspectives on continuity. In O. G. Brim, Jr. & J. Kagan (Eds.), *Constancy and change in human development.* Cambridge, MA: Harvard University Press.

Kagan, J. (1981). Issues in psychological development. In F. Schulsinger, S. A. Mednick, & J. Knop (Eds.), *Longitudinal research: Methods and uses in behavioral science* (pp. 66–92). Boston: Martinus Nijhoff.

Kagan, J., & Klein, R. (1973). Cross-cultural perspectives on early development. *American Psychologist, 28,* 947–961.

Kagan, J., & Moss, H. A. (1962). *Birth to maturity.* New York: Wiley.

Kandel, D., & Lesser, G. S. (1972). *Youth in two worlds.* San Francisco: Jossey-Bass.

Kehoe, M. (1986). Lesbians over 65: A triply invisible minority. *Journal of Homosexuality, 12,* 139–152.

Kelly, J. (1977). The aging male homosexual: Myth and reality. *The Gerontologist, 17,* 328–332.

Kertzer, D. I. (1983). Generation as a sociological problem. *Annual Review of Sociology, 9,* 125–149.

Kimmel, D. C. (1978). Adult development and aging: A gay perspective. *Journal of Social Issues, 34,* 113–130.

Kimmel, D. C. (1980). Life history interviews of aging gay men. *International Journal of Aging and Human Development, 10,* 239–248.

Kimmel, D. C., & Weiner, I. B. (1985). *Adolescence: A developmental transition.* Hillsdale, NJ: Erlbaum.

Kinsey, A. C., Pomeroy, W. B., & Martin, C. W. (1948). *Sexual behavior in the human male.* Philadelphia: Saunders.

Kohlberg, L., Ricks, D., & Snarey, J. (1984). Child development as a predictor of adaptation in adulthood. *Genetic Psychology Monographs, 110,* 91–173.

Kourany, R. F. C. (1987). Suicide among homosexual adolescents. *Journal of Homosexuality, 13,* 111–117.

Larson, R., Csikszentmihalyi, M., & Graef, R. (1980). Mood variability and the psychosocial adjustment of adolescents. *Journal of Youth and Adolescence, 9,* 469–490.

Lee, J. A. (1987). What can homosexual aging studies contribute to theories of aging? *Journal of Homosexuality, 13,* 43–71.

Leigh, G. K., & Petersen, G. W. (Eds.) (1986). *Adolescence in families.* Cincinnati, OH: South-Western.

Lennenberg, E. (1967). *Biological foundations of language*. New York: Wiley.

Lens, W., & Gailly, A. (1980). Extention of future time perspective in motivational goals of different age groups. *International Journal of Behavioral Development, 3*, 1–17.

Lerner, R. M., & Galambos, N. L. (Eds.) (1984). *Experiencing adolescents: A sourcebook for parents, teachers, and teens*. New York: Garland.

Levine, R. A. (1973). *Culture, behavior, and personality*. Chicago: Aldine.

Lewin, K. (1964). Behavior and development as a function of the total situation. In K. Lewin (Ed.), *Field theory in social science* (pp. 238–304). New York: Harper. (Original work published 1946)

Lieberman, M., & Falk, J. (1971). The remembered past as a source of data for research on the life-cycle. *Human Development, 14*, 132–141.

Livson, H., & Peskin, H. (1980). Perspectives on adolescence from longitudinal research. In J. Adelson (Ed.), *Handbook of adolescent psychology* (pp. 47–98). New York: Wiley.

Lynch, F. R. (1987). Non-ghetto gays: A sociological study of suburban homosexuals. *Journal of Homosexuality, 13*, 13–42.

Martin, A. D. (1982). Learning to hide: The socialization of the gay adolescent. *Adolescent Psychiatry, 10*, 52–65.

McCall, G., & Simmons, J. (1980). *Identities and interactions: An examination of human associations in everyday life*, rev. ed. New York: Free Press.

McWhirter, D. P., & Mattison, A. M. (1984). *The male couple: How relationships develop*. Englewood Cliffs, NJ: Prentice-Hall.

Millan, G., & Ross, M. W. (1987). AIDS and gay youth: Attitudes and life-style modifications in young male homosexuals. *Community Health Studies, 11*, 50–53.

Minnegerode, F. A. (1976). Age-status labeling in homosexual men. *Journal of Homosexuality, 1*, 273–276.

Minton, H. L., & McDonald, G. J. (1983/1984). Homosexual identity formation as a developmental process. *Journal of Homosexuality, 9*, 91–104.

Montemayor, R. (1986). Family variation in parent–adolescent storm and stress. *Journal of Adolescent Research, 1*, 15–31.

Morin, S. F. (1977). Heterosexual bias in psychological research on lesbianism and male homosexuality. *American Psychologist, 32*, 629–637.

Moss, H., & Sussman, E. (1980). Longitudinal study of personality development. In O. G. Brim, Jr. & J. Kagan (Eds.), *Constancy and change in human development*. Cambridge, MA: Harvard University Press.

Murray, S. O. (1984). *Social theory, homosexual realities*. New York: Gay Academic Union.

Mussen, P. H., & Jones, M. C. (1957). Self-conceptions, motivations and interpersonal attitudes of late- and early-maturing boys. *Child Development, 28*, 243–256.

Nesselroade, J., & Baltes, P. (1974). Adolescent personality development and historical change: 1970–1972. *Monographs of the Society for Research in Child Development, 39*, no. 154.

Neugarten, B. L. (1967). The awareness of middle age. In R. Owen (Ed.), *Middle age*. London: British Broadcasting Co. (Reprinted in B. Neugarten (Ed.). (1968). *Middle age and aging: A reader in social psychology* (pp. 93–98).) Chicago: The University of Chicago Press.

Neugarten, B. L. (1969). Continuities and discontinuities of psychological issues into adult life. *Human Development, 12*, 121–130.

Neugarten, B. L. (1977). Personality and aging. In J. E. Birren & K. W. Schaie (Eds.), *Handbook of the psychology of aging* (pp. 626–649). New York: Van Nostrand Reinhold.

Neugarten, B. L. (1979). Time, age, and the life cycle. *American Journal of Psychiatry, 136*, 887–894.

Newman, F. B. (1946). The adolescent in social groups: Studies in the observation of personality. *Applied Psychology Monographs, 9*, 1–94.

Nydegger, C. (1977, November). *Multiple cohort membership*. Paper presented at the annual meetings of Gerontological Society, San Francisco.

Offer, D. (1969). *The psychological world of the teenager: A study of normal adolescent boys*. New York: Basic Books.

Offer, D. (1987). In defense of adolescents. *Journal of the American Medical Association, 257*, 3407–3408.

Offer, D., & Offer, D. (1975). *From teenage to young manhood: A psychological study*. New York: Basic Books.

Offer, D., Ostrov, E., & Howard, K. (1981). The mental health professional's concept of the normal adolescent. *Archives of General Psychiatry, 38,* 149–152.

Offer, D., & Sabshin, M. (1967). Research alliance versus therapeutic alliance: A comparison. *American Journal of Psychiatry, 12,* 1519–1526.

Offer, D., & Sabshin, M. (Eds.). (1984). *Normality and the life cycle.* New York: Basic Books.

Peplau, L. A., Cochran, S., Rook, D., & Padesky, C. (1978). Loving women: Attachment and autonomy in lesbian relationships. *Journal of Social Issues, 34,* 7–27.

Peskin, H., & Livson, N. (1981). Uses of the past in adult psychological health. In D. Eichorn, J. Clausen, N. Haan, M. P. Honzik, & P. H. Mussen (Eds.), *Present and past in middle life* (pp. 153–181). New York: Academic Press.

Petersen, A. (1981). The development of the self-concept in adolescence. In D. M. Lynch, A. Norem-Heibeisen, & K. Gergen (Eds.). *The self-concept* (pp. 191–202). New York: Ballinger.

Petersen, A. C. (1985). Pubertal development as a cause of disturbance: Myths, realities, and unanswered questions. *Genetic, Social, and General Psychology Monographs 111,* 205–232.

Petersen, A. C., & Boxer, A. M. (1982). Adolescent sexuality. In T. J. Coates, A. C. Petersen, & C. Perry (Eds.), *Promoting adolescent health: A dialog on research and practice* (pp. 237–253). New York: Academic Press.

Petersen, A. C., & Crockett, L. (1985). Pubertal timing and grade effects. *Journal of Youth and Adolescence, 14,* 191–206.

Petersen, A. C., & Taylor, B. (1980). The biological approach to adolescence: Biological change and psychological adaptation. In J. Adelson (Ed.), *Handbook of adolescent psychology* (pp. 117–155). New York: Wiley.

Petersen, A. C., Tobin-Richards, M., & Boxer, A. M. (1983). Puberty: Its measurement and its meaning. *Journal of Early Adolescence, 3,* 47–62.

Plummer, K. (1975). *Sexual stigma: An interactionist account.* London: Routledge & Kegan Paul.

Plummer, K. (1981). Going gay: Identities, life cycles, and lifestyles in the male gay world. In J. Hart & D. Richardson (Eds.), *The theory and practice of homosexuality* (pp. 93–110). London: Routledge & Kegan Paul.

Plummer, K. (1989). Lesbian and gay youth in England. *Journal of Homosexuality, 22,* 195–224.

Ponse, B. (1978). *Identities in the lesbian world: The social construction of self.* Wesport, CT: Greenwood Press.

Prosen, H., Martin, R., & Prosen, M. (1972). The remembered mother and the fantasized mother: A crisis of middle age. *Archives of General Psychiatry, 27,* 791–794.

Remafedi, G. (1987a). Male homosexuality: The adolescent's perspective. *Pediatrics, 79,* 326–330.

Remafedi, G. (1987b). Adolescent homosexuality: Psychosocial and medical implications. *Pediatrics, 79,* 331–337.

Revere, V., & Tobin, S. (1980/1981). Myth and reality: The older person's relationship to his past. *International Journal of Aging and Human Development, 12,* 15–26.

Ricoeur, P. (1977). The question of proof in Freud's psychoanalytic writings. *Journal of the American Psychoanalytic Association, 25,* 835–872.

Robinson, M. K. (1979). *The older lesbian.* Unpublished master's thesis. California State University, Dominguez Hills.

Roesler, T., & Deisher, R. W. (1972). Youthful male homosexuality. *Journal of the American Medical Association, 219,* 1018–1023.

Rosow, I. (1978). What is a cohort and why? *Human Development, 21,* 65–75.

Ross, M. W. (1980). Retrospective distortion in homosexual research. *Archives of Sexual Behavior, 9,* 523–531.

Rutter, M. (1972). Relationships between child and adult psychiatric disorders: Some research considerations. *Acta Psychiatrica Scandinavica, 48,* 3–21.

Rutter, M. (1984). Continuities and discontinuities in socioemotional development: Empirical and conceptual perspectives. In R. Emde & R. Harmon (Eds.), *Continuities and discontinuities in development.* New York: Plenum Press.

Ryder, N. B. (1965). The cohort as a concept in the study of social change. *American Sociological Review, 30,* 843–861.

Savin-Williams, R. C. (1989). Parental influences on the self-esteem of gay and lesbian youth: A reflected appraisals model. *Journal of Homosexuality, 17,* 93–109.

Schaffer, R. (1977). *Mothering.* Cambridge, MA: Harvard University Press.

Schaie, K. W. (1965). A general model for the study of developmental problems. *Psychological Bulletin, 64,* 92–107.

Schaie, K. W., & Hertzog, C. (1982). Longitudinal methods. In B. B. Wolman (Ed.), *Handbook of developmental psychology.* Englewood Cliffs, NJ: Prentice-Hall.

Schneider, M. (1989). Sappho was a right-on adolescent: Growing up lesbian. *Journal of Homosexuality, 17,* 111–130.

Silverstein, C. (1981). *Man to man: Gay couples in America.* New York: Morrow.

Simmons, R. G., Blythe, D. A., Van Cleave, E. F., & Bush, D. M. (1979). Entry into early adolescence: The impact of school structure, puberty, and early dating on self-esteem. *American Sociological Review, 44,* 948–967.

Simmons, R., Rosenberg, M. F., & Rosenberg, M. C. (1973). Disturbance in the self-image at adolescence. *American Sociological Review, 38,* 553–568.

Sophie, J. (1985/1986). A critical examination of stage theories of lesbian identity development. *Journal of Homosexuality, 12,* 39–51.

Spacks, P. M. (1981). *The adolescent idea: Myths of youth and the adult imagination.* New York: Basic Books.

Spanier, G. B. (1976). Use of recall data in survey research on human sexual behavior. *Social Biology, 23,* 244–253.

Spence, J. T., & Helmreich, R. (1978). *Masculinity and femininity: Their psychological dimensions.* Austin: University of Texas Press.

Steinberg, L. (1981). Transformations in family relations at puberty. *Developmental Psychology, 17,* 833–840.

Steinberg, L. (1985). *Adolescence.* New York: Knopf.

Steinberg, L., & Hill, J. (1978). Patterns of family interaction as a function of age, the onset of puberty, and formal thinking. *Developmental Psychology, 14,* 683–684.

Steinberg, L., & Silverberg, S. B. (1986). The vicissitudes of autonomy in early adolescence. *Child Development, 57,* 841–851.

Stolz, H. R., & Stolz, L. M. (1951). *Somatic development of adolescent boys.* New York: Macmillan.

Strauss, A. (Ed.) (1964). *George Herberd Mead: On social psychology.* Chicago: University of Chicago Press.

Suggs, D. (1987, March 24). More than friends: Conversations with lesbian and gay youth. *Village Voice,* p. 18.

Tanner, J. M. (1971). Sequence, tempo, and individual variation in the growth and development of boys and girls aged twelve to sixteen. *Daedalus, 100,* 907–30.

Tripp, C. A. (1975). *The homosexual matrix.* New York: McGraw-Hill.

Troiden, R. (1979). Becoming homosexual: A model of gay identity acquisition. *Psychiatry, 42,* 362–373.

Troiden, R. R. (1988). "Homosexual identity development," *Journal of Adolescent Health Care, 9,* 105–113.

Troiden, R. (1989). The formation of homosexual identities, *Journal of Homosexuality, 22,* 43–74.

Troll, L., & Bengtson, V. L. (1982). Intergenerational relations throughout the life span. In B. Wolman (Ed.), *Handbook of developmental psychology.* Englewood Cliffs, NJ: Prentice-Hall.

Van Gennep, A. (1960). *Rites of passage.* Chicago: University of Chicago Press. (Original work published 1912.)

Weinberg, M. S., & Williams, C. J. (1974). *Male homosexuals: Their problems and adaptations.* New York: Oxford University Press.

Weinberg, T. S. (1983). *Gay men, gay selves: The social construction of homosexual identities.* New York: Irvington.

Weinberg, T. S. (1984). Biology, ideology, and the reification of developmental stages in the study of homosexual identities. *Journal of Homosexuality, 10,* 77–84.

Watters, A. T. (1986). Heterosexual bias in psychological research on lesbianism and male homosexuality (1979–1983), utilizing the bibliographic and taxonomic system of Morin. *Journal of Homosexuality, 13,* 35–58.

Yarrow, M. R., Campbell, J. D., & Burton, R. V. (1970). Recollections of childhood: A study of the retrospective method. *Monographs of the Society for Research in Child Development, 35* (serial no. 138).

CHAPTER 12

The Legal System and Adolescents

CATHERINE A. CROSBY and N. DICKON REPPUCCI

INTRODUCTION

In the past two decades, the legal system has begun to recognize the developmental category of adolescent as a legal entity that requires special treatment by the courts and legislatures. The overriding issue that has led to the legal separation of adolescents from children and adults has been the issue of capacity: Does the cognitive capacity of adolescents require the law to treat them more like children or more like adults? Are adolescents able to make decisions as competent as those of adults? Should the adolescent enjoy the same level of autonomy and individual determination as that enjoyed by adults or the same paternalistic protections afforded children? These and several related questions arise when one begins to study adolescents within the legal system.

This chapter examines the rights of adolescents within the legal system and the contribution that social science research has made and

can make to the understanding of the U.S. Supreme Court's extension and limitations of these rights. This examination focuses on three areas of legal rights of adolescents: (a) the juvenile justice system; (b) medical decision-making, especially in the context of the reproductive rights of adolescents; and (c) involuntary commitment and psychological counseling. These topics were chosen for their importance, timeliness, and relevance to practitioners of psychology.

Before addressing the substantive topics outlined above, two important qualifications must be stated. First, because this chapter is meant as a general review of the law as applied to adolescents and not a review of jurisdictional differences, the discussion focuses on U.S. Supreme Court case law and discusses state law only when relevant to an understanding of the law in general. Decisions of the Supreme Court are binding on all state and federal courts and, therefore, are the appropriate level of analysis for an overview of legal policy.

This focus, however, leads to the second qualification. The legal policies enunciated by the Supreme Court and reviewed in this chapter may reflect the ideal rather than the actual behavior of any individual court, mental health institution, or other relevant agency. As the

---

Parts of this chapter were originally written under a grant from the Virginia Treatment Center for Children. We gratefully acknowledge this support and the continued encouragement of the Center's Director, Dr. Robert Cohen. We also acknowledge the assistance and support of Dr. Michael Arthur in the writing of this chapter.

section on involuntary and voluntary mental health services illustrates, states also vary widely on the substance and procedures of their guiding legislation. The law may be interpreted or implemented to suit the purposes of the interpreter or implementer, and the resulting behavior, statute, or agency regulation may never be challenged in a court (see Abel, 1980). Therefore, clinicians must be aware of the reality of the legal system within which they are practicing and/or conducting research, as well as the Supreme Court's interpretation of the law that is reviewed in this chapter.

THE JUVENILE JUSTICE SYSTEM

History and Philosophy of the System

In 1899, Illinois created the first juvenile court. By 1917, all but three states had followed suit. These courts were a direct outgrowth of reformers' sense of outrage at the handling of children in the criminal courts (Wadlington, Whitebread, & Davis, 1983). The "Juvenile Court Philosophy" was based on a concept of individualized justice that encompassed five critical ideas:

1. A special court was needed for neglected, dependent, or delinquent children under the age of 16;
2. This court's purpose was to rehabilitate, not to punish, children;
3. All records and proceedings were to be confidential, in order to ensure that no stigma would result from a court appearance;
4. When incarcerated, children had to be separated from the corrupting influence of adult criminals;
5. All proceedings were to be informal.

Informality meant that the system was not to operate on a legal model, but rather on a medical model that would use techniques of the then fledgling "social and behavioral sciences to diagnose, treat and cure socially sick children" (Wadlington et al., 1983, p. 198).

The legal basis for the juvenile court resides in the *parens patriae* power of the state as legal guardian of the community and those citizens who are not competent to care for themselves. The juvenile court is empowered to substitute state control for parental control on the assumption that the state will act in the best interests of the child and that its intervention will enhance the child's welfare. Until *Kent v. United States*,[1] juvenile courts operated without legal oversight or monitoring. There was little or no recognition that the dual function of *parens patriae*—protection of the community and protection of the child—could lead to conflict of interest in denial of equal protection to the child (Worrell, 1985).

Structure of the Juvenile Justice System

In an effort to fulfill its special goals, the structure of the juvenile justice system differs from that of the adult criminal court. However, as the discussion on the development of legal rights for juveniles will illustrate, these structural differences may be more semantic than substantive.

The procedures of the juvenile court generally parallel the procedures in the adult criminal court.[2] A large proportion of juveniles are never arrested; instead, police release them with a warning. Upon arrest, the juvenile may be detained—*pretrial detention*—for up to 72 hours without a hearing. The juvenile may be released after this detention, with no formal proceedings pursued, although an informal agreement may be made among the probation officer, the parents, and the juvenile (Grisso & Conlin, 1984). Informal adjustments of this type are called *diversion*.[3]

---

[1] 383 U.S. 541 (1966).

[2] The constitutional issues that surround the juvenile court procedures will be discussed below, in the context of the legal rights of juveniles. For a discussion of the procedural issues in juvenile court and suggestions for reform, see Grisso & Conlin (1984).

[3] See Linney (1984) for a discussion of the deinstitutionalization of the juvenile justice system.

Once the juvenile has entered the system but prior to a finding of guilt, the court may remove the juvenile from the jurisdiction of the juvenile court by an *order of waiver or transfer* of the juvenile to the adult criminal court. The concept of transfer is based on the belief that some juveniles are inappropriate candidates for the services of the juvenile court. If a juvenile is transferred to adult court, the juvenile is treated as an adult for the purposes of the immediate case. In most states, the juvenile must be a certain age before he or she can be transferred, and most states require other criteria to be met before a juvenile can be transferred. Although these criteria vary from state to state, many states allow transfer only for certain types of offenses (e.g., murder, rape, arson), require a finding that the juvenile is not amenable to treatment, and/or require that the juvenile be found not insane or mentally retarded (Grisso & Conlin, 1984).[4]

If the state proceeds with the case, the juvenile's guilt or innocence of the offense(s) accused is determined by a judge in the *adjudication.* A juvenile can be adjudged either a juvenile delinquent or a status offender. A juvenile delinquent is a juvenile who has committed an offense that would be a crime if committed by an adult. A status offender is a juvenile who has committed an act that is an offense only by virtue of the age of the actor (e.g., truancy, promiscuity). Since the passage of the Juvenile Justice and Delinquency Prevention Act in 1974, states have increasingly diverted status offenders from the juvenile justice system (Linney, 1984); however, some states still adjudicate status offenders in the juvenile court. Therefore, for the purposes of this chapter, the term "juvenile offender" will include both juvenile delinquents and status offenders.

In the adjudication, the juvenile is represented by counsel and evidence is presented relevant to the offense(s). If the judge finds the juvenile guilty of the offense(s) beyond a reasonable doubt, the case proceeds to *disposition,* the sentencing phase of the juvenile court process. Juvenile court procedures in all states require that disposition be made at a hearing separate from the adjudication (Grisso & Conlin, 1984). During this proceeding, the court will decide whether rehabilitative services are necessary and, if so, which services are the best for this particular juvenile. Thirty-one states require the judge to choose the "least detrimental alternative" when deciding disposition (Grisso, Tomkins, & Casey, 1988). The court may hear testimony from psychologists, social workers, or probation officers as to the best disposition for the juvenile. In the juvenile court, the judge can also make an indeterminate disposition, which means that the juvenile is committed to the appropriate agency until he or she is "rehabilitated," without the length of that commitment specified.

Legal Rights of Adolescents in the Juvenile Justice System

In 1967, the profile of an adolescent's rights within the juvenile justice system changed drastically with the U.S. Supreme Court decision in *In re Gault.*[5] Prior to the Court's decision in *Gault,* the Court in *Kent v. United States*[6] had indicated that they had begun to question whether the juvenile court was trodding on the individual juvenile's rights while not fulfilling its goal of individualized justice: "[T]here may be grounds for concern that the child receives the worst of both worlds: that he gets neither the protection accorded to adults nor the solicitous care and regenerative treatment postulated for children."[7]

In *Gault,* the Court found that its concern expressed in *Kent* was well-founded and held that the juvenile was entitled to several of the constitutional protections afforded adults. The Court did not grant juveniles all the rights guar-

---

[4]See Va. Code § 16.1-269 (1988) for an example of a statutory scheme for transfer of a juvenile to adult court.

[5]387 U.S. 1 (1967).
[6]383 U.S. 541 (1966).
[7]*Id.* at 556.

anteed to adults but did grant juveniles the right of notice of charges, the right to counsel, the right to confront and cross-examine witnesses, and the right against self-incrimination.[8] The Court based its opinion on the grounds that the procedures accorded juveniles did not meet the constitutional standards of due process required by the Fourteenth Amendment. To reach this conclusion, the Court found that the juvenile court had failed in large part to fulfill is mission of individualized justice. Justice Fortas, in his opinion for the Court, rendered an indictment of the juvenile court:

[T]he highest motives and most enlightened impulses led to a peculiar system for juveniles, unknown to our law in any comparable context. The constitutional and theoretical basis for this peculiar system is—to say the least—debatable. And in practice . . . the results have not been entirely satisfactory. Juvenile Court history has again demonstrated that unbridled discretion, however benevolently motivated, is frequently a poor substitute for principle and procedure.[9]

Following their decision in *Gault,* the Court has continued to consider the constitutional protections to be accorded to juveniles within the juvenile justice system. Although in some of the post-*Gault* decisions the Court has extended the rights afforded to juveniles within the juvenile justice system, in others, it has limited this extension. Early cases of extension were *In re Winship,*[10] in which the Court found that due process required that juveniles be adjudicated guilty by a standard of proof of beyond a reasonable doubt, and *Breed v. Jones,*[11] in which the Court found that the Fifth Amendment protection against double jeopardy[12] applied to the trial of a juvenile in criminal court if an adjudication in juvenile court already had been made.[13]

In the area of interrogations, juvenile suspects have been treated like their adult counterparts. In *Miranda v. Arizona,*[14] decided one year before *Gault,* the Court held that, upon arrest, defendants must be made aware of their Fifth Amendment privilege against self-incrimination and their Sixth Amendment right to counsel due to the coercion inherent in the process of interrogation. Although the Supreme Court has not directly addressed the issue of the applicability of *Miranda* to juveniles, courts have uniformly held that it does apply (Wadlington et al., 1983). The important concern that surrounds the issue of juveniles and *Miranda* is the ability of juveniles to validly waive their *Miranda* rights. In *Fare v. Michael C.,*[15] the Court found that Michael C. had made a valid waiver of his rights and that his request to speak to his probation officer after being informed of his *Miranda* rights was not an invocation of his privilege against self-incrimination. The Court made this finding despite their own admonitions in *Gault* that juveniles are in need of special care when they are interrogated upon arrest.

Following the Court's decision in *Fare,* a well-controlled, informative study was conducted by Grisso (1980), who investigated the question of minors' capacity to waive *Miranda* rights. A valid waiver of *Miranda* rights must be made knowingly, intelligently, and voluntarily.[16] Grisso investigated the first two elements of knowing and intelligent, and operationalized

---

[8]The Court was presented with the issues of the right of appellate review and transcripts of the proceedings but chose not to render an opinion on these issues, stating that they were able to reverse the lower court's decision for other reasons.
[9]387 U.S. 1, 17–18 (1967).
[10]387 U.S. 358 (1970).
[11]421 U.S. 519 (1975).

[12]Double jeopardy is the legal concept that an individual cannot be tried twice for the same crime. See *Green v. United States,* 355 U.S. 184 (1957).
[13]But see *Swisher v. Brady,* 438 U.S. 204 (1978), in which the Supreme Court found constitutional a Maryland procedural rule that allowed a juvenile court judge to conduct a *de novo* hearing of a juvenile delinquency case after the case was heard and recommendations were made by a master.
[14]384 U.S. 436 (1966).
[15]442 U.S. 707 (1979).
[16]*Supra* note 14.

them, according to case law and legal commentary, as comprehension of the words and phrases of the *Miranda* warnings and an accurate perception of the function and significance of the rights. He employed a sample of three groups of juveniles aged 10 to 16—recent admittees to a juvenile detention center, residents of a boys' town, and residents of a boys' correctional school—and two groups of adults—ex-offenders and custodial and maintenance workers. Three different methods were used to measure comprehension of the words and phrases: participants (a) paraphrased the four *Miranda* warning statements, (b) gave definitions of six critical words, and (c) responded on a true–false test as to the accuracy of rewordings of the rights. Comprehension of the function and significance of the rights was measured in a structured interview.

Grisso assessed the ability of juveniles to comprehend their *Miranda* rights and their significance by a comparison between their results and absolute and adult standards of comprehension. Juveniles age 15 and younger failed to meet both standards. Grisso, therefore, concluded that juveniles should have a nonwaivable right to counsel based on their inadequate understanding of their rights. Furthermore, he argued that this rule should apply to juveniles over 15 as well because, even though they performed as well as the adult group, the level of understanding by adults was inadequate as measured against an absolute standard. The study's importance inheres both in its dissemination to legal scholars and judges by virtue of its publication in a legal journal, and in its sound methodology—its use of multiple measures, relevant samples, and comparison groups, and legally informed standards.

The Court has extended some constitutional protections to juveniles, but it has failed to extend others. The Court denied juveniles the right to a trial by jury in *McKiever v. Pennsylvania*.[17] Justice Blackmun, writing for a divided Court, found that the precedent established in *Gault* does not require that juveniles be accorded all of the procedural protections given to adults in criminal proceedings; the merits of guaranteeing each specific right to juveniles should be considered separately. The Court found that the reasons for guaranteeing a right to jury trial to juveniles were outweighed by the negative effects it would have on the purpose of the juvenile court as a system of individualized and informal justice.

More recently, in *Schall v. Martin*,[18] the Court found constitutional a New York statute that allows a juvenile to be held in a detention center for up to 72 hours prior to a hearing. The Court based its decision on the argument that the juvenile's interest in freedom from institutional restraint (i.e., detention) is substantial, but this interest is "qualified by the recognition that juveniles, unlike adults, are always in some form of custody."[19] Employing this line of reasoning, the Court found that a juvenile's liberty interest can be subordinated to the state's *parens patriae,* which is served by pretrial detention. Legal commentators have questioned the logic of this decision because it falsely equates parental and state custody and fails to acknowledge the limits placed on parents and the state in regard to juveniles' constitutional rights (Worrell, 1985). However, the Supreme Court has not overturned the *Schall* decision and the constitutional legitimacy of pretrial detention has been sustained.

The most recent issue before the Supreme Court in regard to juvenile offenders' constitutional rights is that of capital punishment. The issue of the death penalty for juveniles is unique because, as opposed to all of the previous constitutional issues considered, it involves a constitutional protection to be *given* to juveniles, because of their age, which is *not given* to adults similarly situated. The Supreme Court has found that capital punishment, in general, is not unconstitutional by virtue of the Eighth

---

[17]403 U.S. 528 (1971).

[18]467 U.S. 253 (1984).
[19]*Id.* at 265.

Amendment protection against cruel and unusual punishment when applied to adults,[20] although it may be unconstitutional when used in certain contexts such as in the case of rape.[21] The argument against capital punishment of juvenile offenders is that the Eighth Amendment prohibition against cruel and unusual punishment is violated when capital punishment is applied to juveniles. However, this argument has recently been rejected by a divided Supreme Court. In *Stanford v. Kentucky*,[22] the Court found "neither a historical nor a modern societal consensus forbidding the imposition of capital punishment on any person who murders at 16 or 17 years of age."[23]

Stanford v. Kentucky is significant both because of its rejection of the Eighth Amendment argument as applied to the capital punishment of juveniles and because of Justice Scalia's rejection of "socioscientific, ethicoscientific, or even purely scientific evidence"[24] as relevant to the decision of whether to execute juveniles. The majority specifically rejects psychological evidence on the emotional and cognitive development of adolescents that suggests that capital punishment fails to deter young offenders because they lack the cognitive and moral capacity of adults. They reject this evidence because it cannot demonstrate that "no 16-year-old is 'adequately responsible' or significantly deterred."[25] *Stanford* marks one of the few times that the Court has considered psychological evidence in juvenile jurisprudence and illustrates the tension between the field of psychology, which is based on assumptions of probability, and the field of law, which is based on assumptions of truth.

Psychological Research on the Juvenile Justice System

The juvenile justice system is based on a conception of adolescents as vulnerable and malleable individuals who need to be protected and rehabilitated (Mack, 1909). This conception has resulted in a system that has prevention and rehabilitation as its dual purposes. It has also resulted in a system that is based on individualized justice, which necessarily translates into discretionary decision making. This section provides a brief summary of the psychological research on the effectiveness of treatment with juvenile offenders and on discretion in juvenile justice decision making. Because this chapter focuses on adolescents in the legal system, primary and secondary prevention programs designed to target adolescents before they enter the juvenile justice system are not discussed. (For a review, see Burchard & Burchard (1987).)

Effectiveness of Treatment of Juvenile Offenders

Although the concept of treatment is one of the cornerstones of the juvenile court, the Supreme Court has not held that a right to treatment through the juvenile justice system exists. The best-known relevant case is *Willie M. v. Hunt*,[26] filed in a federal district court in North Carolina in 1979. This case raised the issue of a right to treatment for juveniles involuntarily committed to state institutions through the juvenile justice system but was never ruled on because the parties decided to settle the matter before the district court rendered its decision. The settlement resulted in an integrated service delivery system in North Carolina (Behar, 1985) but provided no answer to the question of right to treatment.

Few clear conclusions can be drawn from the research on the effectiveness of treatment of juvenile offenders. Among the issues that make a determination of effectiveness problematic are: the lack of an accepted definition of a

---

[20]See *Gregg v. Georgia*, 428 U.S. 153 (1976).
[21]*Coker v. Georgia*, 433 U.S. 584 (1977); see also *Enmund v. Florida*, 458 U.S. 782 (1982) (capital punishment for participation in robbery where an accomplice commits murder is unconstitutional); *Ford v. Wainwright*, 477 U.S. 399 (1986) (execution of insane is unconstitutional).
[22]57 U.S.L.W. 4974 (June 26, 1989).
[23]*Id.* at 4978.
[24]*Id.*
[25]*Id.*

---

[26]Civil No. C-C-79-294-M (W.D.N.C. 1980).

successful outcome, and the heterogeneity of the juvenile offender population (Arbuthnot, Gordon, & Jurkovic, 1987). Some evidence of the effectiveness of certain types of interventions, such as behavioral models (Cohen & Filipczak, 1971), cognitive problem-solving and skill development interventions (Serna, Schumaker, Hazel, & Sheldon, 1986), and family therapy (Barton, Alexander, Waldron, Turner, & Warburton, 1985), does exist. Positive effects of wilderness (Winterdyk & Roesch, 1981; Kelly & Baer, 1971) and restitution (Schneider, 1986) programs have been reported, but the extent of these positive effects is unclear. In general, interventions that (a) are guided by the needs of the individual juvenile, (b) incorporate interventions that improve family functioning, (c) include some behavioral methods, and (d) modify the juveniles' social networks appear to be the most promising. (For more information see Tolan & Loeber, Chapter 13 in this volume.)

Discretion in Juvenile Justice Decision Making

Few researchers have investigated the issue of discretion in the juvenile justice system, although the use of discretion is integral to the system's operation. Police often use their discretionary power not to arrest juveniles. Court intake officers may use their discretion to divert juveniles from the system, and judges may find a juvenile not amenable to treatment and transfer him or her to an adult criminal court. Once a juvenile is adjudicated in the juvenile court, his or her disposition is a product of the judge's discretion and can range from a short period of probation to incarceration in a secure juvenile institution. At each of the judge's discretionary points, he or she may be aided by recommendations from mental health professionals; however, the limited validity of diagnostic formulations and predictions creates the possibility for misuse of clinical information (Mulvey & Reppucci, 1988).

Studies on discretion in juvenile justice decisions have focused on standards used by juvenile justice personnel. One of the overriding issues concerns the ethical balances between the goals of treatment vs. retribution and the needs vs. the rights of the juvenile (Mulvey & Phelps, 1988). The balance struck between these competing interests has been assumed to influence how decisions are made in the system (Sosin, 1982). A well-controlled study by Grisso, Tomkins, and Casey (1988) has begun to examine what characteristics of juveniles and their families most influence judicial decisions. As a first step to answering the question of what standards are employed by juvenile justice personnel and how these standards affect their decisions, Grisso et al. derived a list of words and phrases describing the juvenile and familial factors considered by juvenile justice personnel from the juvenile codes of all 50 states, appellate opinions, empirical and nonempirical writings in social science and law, and interviews with juvenile court personnel. This list was reduced to 93 variables; juvenile court personnel ratings of 79 of these variables were subjected to a factor analysis, which revealed nine factors considered by juvenile court personnel:

1. Motivation to accept intervention;
2. Self-reliance;
3. Prior contacts with juvenile justice system;
4. Presence of serious mental disorder;
5. Family's caring and resource capability;
6. Opportunity for delinquent peer influence;
7. Unsocialized family;
8. Degree of behavioral compliance with legal settings;
9. Functioning in academic or work settings.

This study provides a strong starting point for investigating how these different factors affect juvenile court discretionary decisions and the efficacy of these factors in reaching functional decisions.

In an attempt to look beyond the individual case characteristics influencing discretionary decision making, Mulvey and Reppucci (1988) examined the hypothesis that the determination of amenability to treatment in juvenile offenders is influenced not only by the perceived characteristics of the juveniles but also by the ecological context of the service delivery network and the organizational context of the decision maker. A sample of 168 community mental health center, welfare, and juvenile court personnel from six different locales within a state rated (a) the amenability to treatment of juvenile offenders in four case vignettes and (b) the effectiveness of a variety of services for youth. Locales were chosen as being low, medium, or high along a continuum of service availability, and the effects of resource availability and agency type on these amenability judgments were examined. The clearest result was that personnel in low-resource locales saw more potential benefit from punishment than did personnel in high-resource locales, and court personnel consistently saw more potential benefit from punishment than did social service or mental health center personnel. Furthermore, although judgments regarding the potential benefit of services were not as direct, social service and mental health center personnel in medium-resource locales judged a youth's likelihood of benefiting from treatment as higher than their counterparts in high- and low-resource locales. For court personnel, judgments of a youth's benefit from services were directly related to resource availability. This evidence suggests that the contextual factors of resource availability and agency setting may have a significant systematic relationship to assessments of potential treatment outcomes. Thus, the traditional wisdom that the opinions of mental health professionals may be a method to counteract the biases of judges may provide far less of a safeguard against bias than has been idealized. In addition, these results support policy efforts to keep youth from being assessed by court personnel in order to avoid their entering institutions.

Unfortunately, most of the research in the area of discretionary decisions in the juvenile justice system suffers from methodological flaws such as skewed samples, a narrow range of variables studied, and lack of attention to the heterogeneity in the judgments, which may result in identical case outcomes (Grisso et al., 1988). In general, the limited research, including Tomkins's (1984) meta-analysis of studies of dispositional decisions and several studies on the relationship between juvenile and community characteristics and discretionary decisions in the juvenile justice system (Cohen & Kluegel, 1978; Mulvey & Reppucci, 1988; Scarpitti & Stephenson, 1971; Thomas & Cage, 1977), tends to support the conclusions that (a) different orientations toward the juvenile justice system exist and may influence discretionary decisions (Sosin, 1982); (b) race may have an effect on the likelihood of a juvenile's remaining in the juvenile justice system (Arnold, 1971; Westendorp, Brink, Roberson, & Ortiz, 1986); and (c) the relationship between the complainant and the juvenile may affect the outcome of the case (Dannefer, 1984).

MEDICAL DECISION MAKING AND ADOLESCENCE

The issue of competence overarches the area of medical decision making and adolescence. Is an adolescent competent to make his or her own medical decisions? The legal response is that some adolescents are competent in some situations for some types of procedures. The relevant legal issues are the concepts of informed consent and *parens patriae*. Although the complex issue of informed consent arises when the potential patient is an adult, it becomes more complicated when that patient is a minor. Part of this complication is inherent in the issue of *parens patriae,* which allows the state to intervene in situations in which such intervention would be prohibited if the patient were an adult.

This section outlines the issue of informed consent by adolescents and summarizes the psychological research regarding adolescents' capacity to consent to treatment. It then examines in some detail the issue of adolescent reproductive rights because the U.S. Supreme Court has involved itself in this debate and has rendered opinions on some of the issues involved. This examination highlights the conflict among the state's interest in the protection of the public health and of potential life, the parents' interest in family privacy and autonomy, and the adolescent's interest in individual privacy and autonomy.

Informed Consent by Adolescents

Informed consent is a legal doctrine in tort law[27] under which a doctor has an obligation to fully inform a patient as to the information necessary to make an informed and voluntary choice concerning treatment. If the doctor fails to obtain informed consent, he or she can be held liable for any damage suffered as a result of this failure.[28] In general, parental consent is required before a medical procedure can be performed on a minor (Wadlington, 1983).

As applied to adolescents, the doctrine of informed consent is complicated by the question of the adolescent's competence to render consent that is informed and voluntary. The requirements of competence to consent to treatment, however, have never been adequately outlined by the Court. Consequently, the concept of competence to consent has taken on several different definitions. The generally accepted legal definition states that competence to consent is an appreciation of "the nature, extent and probable consequences of the conduct consented to."[29] Meisel (1979) and Roth, Meisel, and Lidz (1977) derived from the literature four different standards of competence to consent. These standards range from very minimal to very stringent:

1. Evidence of a choice, which is simply the expression of a preference for one alternative;

2. Reasonable outcome, which is selection of an option that a hypothetical "reasonable person" might choose;
3. A reasonable decision-making process, which is choosing a preference by logical and rational steps;
4. Understanding.

Weithorn (1984) suggested that the last standard—understanding—may be defined as concrete factual understanding, abstract appreciation of consequences, or a "hypothesized capacity or ability rather than a skill that is measured in the decision-making situation" (p. 245).

Research on the Decision-Making Competence of Adolescents

The research on adolescents' and children's competence to make treatment decisions comprises a very small proportion of the large decision-making literature. One of the difficulties in studying the competence of adolescents to make treatment decisions is the ambiguity in the meaning of competence. Researchers have usually chosen an operationalization of competence that is uninformed or, at best, partially informed by the law (Weithorn, 1982). In most cases, they have compared the competence of adolescents to that of the average adult. This yardstick for competence is a stricter requirement than the law requires because, if legal competence were that of the average adult, all those adults who fall below the average would be found legally incompetent. Consequently, this operationalization is a greater level of competence than is required for informed consent.

Another complication is the difficulty in confirming the null hypothesis (Gardner, Scherer, & Tester, 1989). The studies are usually designed such that a failure to reject the null hypothesis supports the theoretical hypothesis that adults and adolescents do not differ in their competence. However, this failure to reject does not prove the null hypothesis.

---

[27]Tort law is the area of law that concerns wrongs committed by one entity against another.
[28]See *Canterbury v. Spence*, 464 F.2d 772 (1972).
[29]*Restatement (Second) of Torts*, Ch. 45, § 892A(2) (1979).

Gardner et al. (1989) stated that "a hypothesis of no difference is difficult to confirm because researchers can fail to find differences between groups by either asking the wrong questions or posing them in the wrong way. So a compelling demonstration that adolescents do not differ from adults would have many stringent requirements" (p. 899). Among the requirements would be a very large sample size, replication of findings, including replication in a naturalistic setting, and valid and various measures and methodologies (Gardner et al, 1989). As will become apparent from this review, these requirements have not been met.

In 1978, Grisso and Vierling reviewed the developmental and applied research on the competence of minors to consent to treatment and found no research that had directly addressed this issue. Therefore, they extrapolated from the relevant research on the cognitive, moral, and social development of children and concluded that "there is little evidence that minors of age 15 and above as a group are any less competent to provide consent than are adults" (p. 423).

Weithorn and Campbell's investigation (1982) was the first to compare the competence of adolescents to make treatment decisions to that of adults. Ninety-six subjects, equally divided among four age levels (ages 9, 14, 18, and 21),[30] were compared on four competency criteria scales derived from the competency standards outlined by Meisel and associates (Meisel, 1979; Roth, et al., 1977). These scales were Evidence of Choice, Reasonable Outcome, Rational Reasons, and Understanding, which was divided into two subscales of Rote Recall and Inference. Four different treatment scenarios concerning diabetes, epilepsy, depression, and enuresis were used to determine whether complexity, difficulty, and content affected competence to make a treatment decision.

Nine-year-olds were found to be significantly different from all other age groups on the scales of Rational Reasons and Understanding for all of the treatment dilemmas and on the Reasonable Outcome scale for the depression dilemma, because of their willingness to choose inpatient treatment. However, the 14-year-olds differed from the adult groups only on the scale of Rational Reasons for the epilepsy scenario, which the authors attributed to adolescents' concerns with body image and physical attractiveness. Weithorn and Campbell (1982) concluded that "minors age 14 were found to demonstrate a level of competence equivalent to that of adults, according to four standards of competency . . . and four hypothetical dilemmas" (p. 1595).

The investigators noted several limitations in their study. First, the participants were all healthy, White, middle-class, intelligent individuals, which limits the generalizability of the results to other populations, including the most relevant population—unhealthy individuals seeking treatment. Second, the decisions were hypothetical, with no real consequences for the participants. Treatment decisions made in naturalistic settings may be more competent because of increased motivation, or may be less competent because of stress on the decision maker.

Another criticism of this and similar studies concerns the use of a very young "adult" comparison group. Several have argued that an underestimation of the competence of minors may result, because this adult group is the most comfortable with technical and probabilistic questions; others have claimed that, because competence increases as people mature through experience, young adults may represent the least competent adults. Because the law assumes 18-year-olds are competent to make treatment decisions, they are an appropriate comparison group on the issue of legal competence.

Lewis and her colleagues studied the question of competence to make treatment decisions in situations where those decisions had

---

[30] The age groups were also equally divided between males and females, but no significant differences were found for sex on any of the scales.

real-life consequences for the participants. Lewis, Lewis, and Ifekwunigue (1978) investigated the ability of elementary school children to decide whether to participate in an actual swine-flu vaccination study. Very few age differences were found in the children's ability to elicit appropriate information and to weigh the benefits and risks; however, this finding is limited because the children's behavior was not compared to the behavior of adults: a hypothetical competent decision maker was used as the index of competence and may not have reflected the level of competence required by law. Also, the comparison was between classrooms, not individuals, which would tend to negate developmental differences attributable to the probable large within-class variability. In a similar study, Lewis, Lewis, Lorimer, and Palmer (1977) evaluated an elementary school program that allowed children ages 5 to 12 to make their own decisions on whether to seek treatment from the school nurse and what treatment option to choose. Although no control or comparison groups were used, the authors concluded that the children did make reasonable treatment decisions.

Lewis (1980) also investigated the decision-making process of women awaiting pregnancy test results; these women were potentially confronted with the decision of whether to terminate a pregnancy, carry the child to term, or put the child up for adoption. Lewis conducted a semistructured interview (N = 42) of minors (13 to 17 years old) and adults (18 to 25 years old) whom she compared on their knowledge of the law, number and type of persons consulted, and decision-reasoning as measured by a semistructured interview. The few age-related differences she found were attributed by Lewis to the different situations of pregnant minors versus pregnant adults; she cautioned that, although generalizable to the population of women who make pregnancy decisions, her findings were limited by the small sample size and methodological concerns.

Two very recent studies (Ambuel & Rappaport, 1992; Rowe, 1989) have also looked at the decision-making competence of adolescents in the context of pregnancy resolution. No support was found for the conclusion that minors are less competent than adults to consent to treatment. Ambuel and Rappaport (1989) investigated competence to render informed consent to abortion in a sample of women (N = 75)—young minors (ages 13 to 15), old minors (ages 16 and 17), and adults (ages 18 to 21)—who suspected an unplanned pregnancy. The participants were also grouped into those who considered abortion and those who did not.

Content analysis of the semistructured interviews revealed four dimensions of competence: volition, consideration of consequences, number of reasons considered (richness), and quality of the reasoning process. None of the minors who considered abortion was found to be significantly less competent than the adult comparison group. However, young minors who did not consider abortion were found to be significantly less competent than the older minors and the adults on all of the dimensions except richness. A regression analysis also found age to be a predictor of all of the dimensions except volition. The use of a large, diverse, and relevant sample that included an adult comparison group makes this study probably more ecologically valid than most of the prior research on competence to consent. The study does suffer from some of the problems in studying competence outlined above: the adult comparison group was only 1 to 3 years older than the oldest minor group, and the competence criteria, while multifaceted, may or may not reflect the criteria actually used to determine "maturity" by the courts.

Rowe (1989) employed a sample of 34 pregnant women (12 minors, 22 adults) and 35 never-pregnant women (13 minors, 22 adults) to assess competence to make decisions regarding abortion under the rational reasons and appreciation standards discussed above. She found no differences between the minors' and adults' level of competence on either standard nor in the number of abstract and concrete reasons employed when reaching a decision on a hypothetical unwanted teen pregnancy. She also found no significant differences in competence between the pregnant adults and minors in their own pregnancy decision, but this finding is merely suggestive, because of the small sample of pregnant minors. The strength of this study lies in its ecologically valid sample and its use of legally relevant standards of competence; however, its conclusions are limited by the small sample size, the use of a hypothetical decision-making vignette, and the use of retrospective data for the women's own pregnancy decisions. This study also could not address the prior findings of differences in the competence of younger minors and adults because the sample was comprised of generally older minors (average age = 16.5 years).

Another group of studies has looked at the competence of minors to make treatment decisions in psychotherapy. Belter and Grisso (1984) examined minors' ability to recognize rights violations and to protect their rights in psychotherapy. Although they did not investigate decision-making competency directly and employed a nonclinical sample of questionable generalizability to real psychotherapy settings, the results do not support the hypothesis that 15-year-olds are less able than 21-year-olds to recognize rights violations in a simulated counseling session. Nine-year-olds, on the other hand, were found to be significantly less able to identify rights violations.

Two other studies (Kaser-Boyd, Adelman, & Taylor, 1985; Kaser-Boyd, Adelman, Taylor, & Nelson, 1986) used clinical samples of children with learning and behavioral disorders to examine one element of children's competence to render informed consent in the context of psychotherapy: the ability to identify and understand the risks and benefits of psychotherapy. The results provided no support for the hypothesis that children are less competent than adults. However, both studies suffered from small sample sizes and the probable large within-group variances,[31] because of the somewhat arbitrary age group demarcations (ages 10 to 13 and ages 14 to 20). In addition, the age grouping is uninformative on legal competence because 18- and 19-year-olds—a group considered legally competent—are assumed not to vary from those aged 14 to 17—a group considered not legally competent.

Finally, Scherer and Reppucci (1988) examined the element of voluntariness in informed consent in situations in which adolescents' parents attempted to influence their treatment decision. The authors hypothesized that, as parental influence became more coercive, adolescents' confidence in their decisions in hypothetical treatment dilemmas would decrease, and this change would interact with the nature of the treatment dilemma. Forty participants (20 females and 20 males), ages 14 and 15, were presented with five different treatment vignettes (kidney donation, tonsillectomy, depression, enuresis, and wart removal). Each vignette was presented three times: the first time, no parental influence was included; the second time, a noncoercive influence by the parents was included; the third time, the parental influence was coercive. After each different treatment dilemma, the participant was asked what treatment was the best choice, why it was the best choice, and how, on a 10-point scale, he or she would rate his or her confidence or conviction in his or her choice. The investigators found that parental influence significantly affected the adolescent's level of confidence in his or her treatment decision; as parental influence became more coercive, the adolescent's confidence in his or her choice was diminished. However, confidence was found to be less susceptible to parental influence in the situations involving more grave treatment decisions, especially the kidney donation vignette. This finding suggests that many adolescents, although mindful of their parents' wishes, reserve the right to make treatment decisions on issues that may have significant consequences for them. Unfortunately, the sample, composed of all-White, predominantly middle- to upper-middle-class youth with an average IQ of 118, and the

---

[31] Within-group variances were not reported.

design did not allow for a conclusion regarding whether the adolescents actually would or did change their treatment decisions in response to parental influence.

In a follow-up study, Scherer (1989) used three of the vignettes (kidney donation, tonsillectomy, and wart removal) with a sample of 40 children (20 males, 20 females) ages 9 and 10, and a sample of 47 young adults (20 males, 27 females) ages 21 to 25, and compared their responses with those of the 40 adolescents in the original Scherer and Reppucci (1988) investigation. Scherer found no statistically significant differences among the three groups on the wart removal or tonsillectomy vignettes as a consequence of parental influence attempts. However, on the more serious kidney donation vignette, more young adults tended to be nonchangers than adolescents, and both young adults and adolescents were significantly more likely to be nonchangers than children. Thus, rather than a clear and consistent developmental trend in the expression of medical decision-making autonomy across decision-making contexts, no single voluntariness ability can be generalized to all types of medical situations. Furthermore, there is no conclusive evidence to presume that adolescents are incapable of a voluntary consent comparable to that of young adults.

In summary, the psychological research on minors' competence to make treatment decisions tends to support the conclusion that younger children (10 and under) are not as competent as adults to make treatment decisions, but does not support the conclusion that adolescents are less competent than adults to make treatment decisions. However, the lack of age differences generally found between adolescents and adults does not necessarily lead to the conclusion that adolescents are as competent as adults to make treatment decisions.[32] The research on adolescent treatment decision making is far from extensive and contains many methodological limitations, and the difficulty of proving the null hypothesis limits the conclusions that can be drawn. In the following discussion of adolescents' reproductive rights, the issues that arise illustrate the need to extend the current findings on competence to enable psychology to contribute effectively to the adolescent abortion debate.

Reproductive Rights of Adolescents

Three different processes have been the focus of the adolescent reproductive rights debate—sterilization, contraception, and abortion. Currently, abortion has taken the center stage because the legal status of the right to abortion for all women is in a state of flux. This section first provides a brief summary of the law on involuntary sterilization and then explores contraceptive rights of adolescents and the evolving state of adolescents' abortion rights.

Involuntary Sterilization

The issue of sterilization of competent individuals has not been considered by the Supreme Court. In general, "normal" adults have been found to have unrestricted freedom to seek sterilization of themselves; on the other hand, the freedom of "normal" minors to seek sterilization has been restricted by state legislation that prohibits sterilization until the minor has reached adulthood (Scott, 1984).[33] This legislation has been created to protect the adolescent's reproductive capacities until he or she is presumedly in a better position to make such a permanent reproductive decision (Scott, 1984).

Involuntary sterilization has become a controversial issue in the context of adolescents with disabilities. Fears of unwanted pregnancies and the inconvenience of the menstrual cycle may lead parents to seek sterilization of

---

[32]But see the American Psychological Association brief in *Thornburgh v. American College of Obstetricians and Gynecologists* (Bersoff, Malson, & Ennis (1985)) and *Hartigan v. Zbaraz and Charles* (Bersoff & Ogden (1987)), in which the authors argue that empirical research has confirmed the fact that most adolescents are competent to make treatment decisions including abortion decisions.

[33]See, for example, Mont. Code Ann. § 41-1-405(4) (1988) and Nev. Rev. Stat. § 129.030 (1986), which prohibit any sterilization of a minor.

an incompetent daughter.[34] Involuntary sterilization, therefore, differs from the other reproductive issues because it usually involves a determination of whether parents' request for the sterilization of their incompetent minor is in the best interests of that child, not whether the minor is competent to make a reproductive decision on his or her own.

The only Supreme Court decision to address the issue of involuntary sterilization is *Buck v. Bell*,[35] in which the Court upheld the constitutionality of Virginia's eugenics statute. Although the Court has not overturned its decision in *Buck*, the rejection of the eugenics movement and the increased recognition of rights of mentally retarded individuals (Melton & Scott, 1984) suggest that the Court would not follow its precedent in *Buck* in a future case. State case law after *Buck* has established standards that must be met before an involuntary sterilization is performed,[36] and most states have adopted legislation that outlines these criteria.[37] The criteria legislatures have instructed courts to consider include whether the individual is unlikely to develop mentally to a degree sufficient to allow making an informed sterilization decision;[38] whether the individual would be likely to procreate a child who would have a tendency toward serious disability;[39] whether the individual is likely to engage in sexual intercourse;[40] and whether alternative methods of contraception have been tried.[41] These laws illustrate the movement away from the eugenics focus on involuntary sterilization to a focus on *parens patriae*, in which the state interest is not protection of society but protection of the individual from a sterilization procedure not in his or her best interests (Melton & Scott, 1984).

Contraception

The Supreme Court recognized the right to contraception prior to its recognition of any constitutional right to abortion. In addition, it acknowledged a right to contraception that is broader than the right to abortion accorded adult women in the landmark *Roe v. Wade*[42] case. In *Griswold v. Connecticut*,[43] the Supreme Court struck down a state statute that prohibited the use of contraceptives by adults because it violated the right of privacy. This precedent in *Griswold* was reinforced in *Eisenstadt v. Baird*,[44] in which the Court found unconstitutional a Massachusetts law that restricted the sale of contraceptives to married couples. The holdings of *Griswold* and *Eisenstadt* have established a strict constitutional prohibition against state intrusion into adult contraceptive behavior.

Although the Court has clearly recognized an unqualified right to contraception for adults, the status of this right for adolescents is unclear. In the only Supreme Court case to consider the right to contraception for adolescents, *Carey v. Population Services International*,[45] the Court struck down a state statute that forbade the sale of contraceptives to minors under 16, even with parental permission. The holding in this case only applied to the constitutionality of a legislative ban on the sale of contraceptives to minors and does not address the issues of parental notification or a requirement of parental permission.

---

[34] Although parents may seek sterilization of an incompetent male child, the literature, common law, and legislation surrounding involuntary sterilization have concentrated on the female child because of the issues of pregnancy and menstruation.
[35] 274 U.S. 200 (1927).
[36] See *In re Hayes*, 93 Wash. 228 (1980); *In re Grady*, 85 N.J. 235 (1981).
[37] See, e.g., Ark. Stat. Ann. §§ 20-49-101 to 20-49-304 (1987); Conn. Gen. Stat. §§ 45-78p to 45-78z (1981); Ga. Code Ann. §§ 31-20-1 to 31-20-5 (1985); Minn. Stat. §§ 525-619(c) (Supp. 1990); N.C. Gen. Stat. § 35-36-50 (1984); Tenn. Code Ann. § 68-34-108 (1987).
[38] Va. Code Ann. § 54.1-2975 (1988).
[39] N.C. Gen. Stat. § 35-39(3) (1984).
[40] Or. Rev. Stat. § 436.225 (1987).

[41] Minn. Stat. § 252A.13, subd. 4 (1982).
[42] 410 U.S. 113 (1973).
[43] 381 U.S. 479 (1965).
[44] 405 U.S. 438 (1972).
[45] 431 U.S. 678 (1977).

Although the Court has not addressed the constitutionality of these restrictions of adolescents' contraceptive rights, the Court will most likely not reach these issues in the near future. First, most states allow free access to contraceptives by adolescents (Scott, 1984); therefore, the issue of restrictions on these rights is unlikely to arise. Second, enforcement of restrictive Department of Health and Human Services (DHHS) regulations on contraception access by adolescents, which required parental notification before prescription contraceptives were supplied to minors through federally funded family planning programs, was stopped by two federal district courts.[46] On appeal, the circuit courts upheld the finding of the lower courts that the regulations undermined the overall federal mandate of preventing unwanted pregnancies and births.[47] After receipt of the strongly worded opinions of the district and circuit courts, DHHS did not appeal to the U.S. Supreme Court and removed the offending regulations from the governing requirements of the family planning clinics (Boumil, 1988).

The courts in *Planned Parenthood* and *Heckler* did not base their decision on the constitutional right of adolescents to contraceptives without parental notification. However, their decisions made clear their belief that regulations restricting adolescents' access to contraceptives do not further the governmental interest in the prevention of unwanted teenage pregnancies but rather are detrimental to this interest. The broad holdings of *Griswold* and *Eisenstadt* and dicta[48] in the opinions of *Carey, Heckler,* and *Planned Parenthood* suggest that the Court may find the right to contraception to have greater constitutional protection than the right to abortion, because the state's interests in prohibiting contraception are minimal. In the case of abortion, as will be discussed below, the fetus's interests and the state's interests in potential life limit the individual's right to privacy. One legal commentator argues that parental notification requirements are unconstitutional because they impermissibly burden the adolescents' recognized right to privacy and they are not necessary to further any legitimate state interest (Hoffman, 1984).[49]

Abortion

In 1973, the Supreme Court established, in *Roe v. Wade,*[50] that the constitutional right to privacy encompasses a woman's decision to terminate a pregnancy, and this right is unqualified in the first trimester. *Roe* did not pertain specifically to adolescents, but, without this decision, the constitutionality of restrictions placed on adolescent abortions would have never come before the Court. Two forms of restriction on adolescent abortions have been considered by the Court: parental consent and parental notification. These restrictions, while facially unconstitutional and illogical when applied to adult women, illustrate the unique position of adolescents in the legal system. As stated by Justice Stevens in one of the two most recent adolescent abortion decisions:

[T]hree separate but related interests—the interest in the welfare of the pregnant minor, the interest of the parents, and the interest of the family unit—are relevant to the consideration of the constitutionality of the . . . parent notification [and consent] requirement.

The State has a strong and legitimate interest in the welfare of its young citizens, whose immaturity,

---

[46]*Planned Parenthood Federation v. Schweiker,* 559 F. Supp. 658 (D.D.C. 1983); *New York v. Schweiker,* 559 F. Supp. 354 (S.D.N.Y. 1983).

[47]*Planned Parenthood Federation of America, Inc. v. Heckler,* 718 F.2d 650 (D.C. Cir. 1983); *New York v. Heckler,* 718 F.2d 1191 (2d Cir. 1983).

[48]Dicta is a legal term referring to remarks or observations of a judge that are not essential to the decision of the immediate case.

[49]But see Boumil's (1988) argument that parents' rights to the care and management of their children require states to inform parents if their child seeks prescription contraceptives from a government-funded clinic.

[50]410 U.S. 113 (1973).

inexperience, and lack of judgment may sometimes impair their ability to exercise their rights wisely.[51]

The following section outlines the current constitutional status of restrictions on adolescent abortions.

Following the holding in *Roe*, the Court in *Planned Parenthood of Central Missouri v. Danforth*[52] found unconstitutional a statute that required parental consent to a minor's abortion. The Court found the adolescent's privacy interest to outweigh any state interest in protection of the family unit or parental authority: "[T]he State does not have the constitutional authority to give a third party an absolute, and possibly arbitrary, veto over the decision of the physician and his patient to terminate the patient's pregnancy, regardless of the reason for withholding the consent."[53] The Court left open the question of whether other forms of restriction might be constitutional.

In *Bellotti v. Baird*,[54] the Court partially answered this question when it held that a parental consent requirement was constitutional so long as the state provided an alternative to that consent. This case established the "mature minor/judicial bypass rule," which allows a female adolescent to bypass the need for parental consent if she can establish, in a judicial or administrative proceeding, that she is mature enough to make the abortion decision independently, or that an abortion would be in her best interests. Although the Court has continued to find constitutional statutes that require parental consent but allow for judicial bypass,[55] it has not established a standard for determination of an adolescent's maturity. This determination includes within itself a curious paradox: How can an adolescent who is not mature enough to make an independent abortion decision be mature enough to carry to term and raise a child?

The second type of restriction on adolescent abortion has been the requirement of parental notification. Parental notification survives the constitutional attack of *Danforth* because it does not provide parents with absolute veto power. In *H.L. v. Matheson*,[56] the Court upheld a state statute that required the physician to notify the parents or guardian before performing an abortion on a minor. The Court restricted its holding to the class of adolescents represented in that case—immature and unemancipated minors. It did not consider the issue of parental notification when the adolescent is found to be a mature minor.

In between the Court's adolescent abortion decisions of 1983 and the Court's most recent decisions, another case, *Webster v. Reproductive Health Services*,[57] was decided by the Court and affected all women's right to abortion. In this case, the Court found constitutional a Missouri statute that required viability testing and prohibited abortions performed by public employees and within public facilities. Although the decision did not apply specifically to adolescents, it could have grave consequences for generally indigent adolescents' access to abortions. The language of the public facilities definition found constitutional in *Webster* is broad enough to cover facilities built on land leased from the state.[58] The dissent recognized that this holding may result in the unavailability of abortions to many adult women; a similar point was made by the dissent in *Maher v. Roe*,[59] in which the majority upheld constitutional restrictions on public funding of

---

[51]*Hodgson v. Minnesota*, 110 S.Ct. 2926, 2941–2942 (1990).
[52]428 U.S. 52 (1976).
[53]*Id.* at 74.
[54]443 U.S. 622 (1979).
[55]*City of Akron v. Akron Center for Reproductive Health*, 462 U.S. 416 (1983); *Planned Parenthood of Kansas City, Missouri v. Ashcroft*, 462 U.S. 476 (1983); *Thornburgh v. American College of Obstetricians and Gynecologists*, 476 U.S. 747 (1986).

[56]450 U.S. 398 (1981).
[57]492 U.S. 490 (1989).
[58]*Id.* (Blackmun, J. dissenting).
[59]432 U.S. 464 (1977).

abortions. However, the *Webster* decision may have a greater impact on adolescents, who may be found less entitled to meaningful access to abortions because of their age.

In 1990, the Supreme Court rendered its most recent decisions regarding adolescent abortion. The opinions in *Hodgson v. Minnesota*[60] and *Ohio v. Akron Center for Reproductive Health*[61] are the products of an extremely divided Court. Before the Court in *Hodgson* was a Minnesota statute that required the notification of the parents of a minor seeking an abortion as well as a 48-hour waiting period after such notification and before the actual procedure. "Parents" is defined as *both* parents of the pregnant minor: "No exception is made for a divorced parent, a noncustodial parent, or a biological parent who never married or lived with the pregnant woman's mother . . . [except] 'if the second parent cannot be located through reasonably diligent effort.'"[62] The statute also included a judicial bypass clause very similar to the one discussed in *Bellotti*.

The outcome of the Court's decision in *Hodgson* was that the Minnesota statute survived constitutional scrutiny, but the judgment of the Court is not straightforward. The Court found that (a) the requirement of a 48-hour waiting period is constitutional, (b) the requirement of a two-parent notification is unconstitutional, but (c) the same "two-parent notification law with a judicial bypass alternative is constitutional."[63] This seemingly paradoxical judgment resulted from the divergent rationales used by the Justices and the concurrence of Justice O'Connor in all three of the holdings.

Justice Stevens, who delivered the opinion of the Court for holdings (a) and (b), stated that the 48-hour waiting period imposed only a minimal burden on the minor and "reasonably further[ed] a legitimate state interest in ensuring that the minor's decision is knowing and intelligent."[64] He was joined in this holding by five of the other Justices. He also found that the two-parent notification requirement was unconstitutional because it did not further any legitimate state interest:

The rationale for a parental consent or notification provision is that it supports the authority of a parent who is presumed to act in the minor's best interest and thereby assures that the minor's decision to terminate her pregnancy is knowing, intelligent, and deliberate. To the extent that such an interest is legitimate, it would be fully served by a requirement that the minor notify one parent.[65]

Justice O'Connor joined in this part of Justice Stevens's opinion, as did Justices Marshall, Brennan, and Blackmun. The latter Justices, however, based their rejection of the two-parent notification on the grounds that any notification requirement is unconstitutional, whether it is one- or two-parent notification.

Justices Kennedy, Rehnquist, White, and Scalia dissented from the second holding. They disagreed with the majority's finding that the two-parent notification requirement does not further a legitimate state interest: "A state pursues a legitimate end under the Constitution when it attempts to foster and preserve the parent–child relationship by giving all parents the opportunity to participate in the care and nurture of their children."[66] Joined by Justice O'Connor, these Justices formed the new majority holding that, assuming that the first holding is correct (which they were required to do), the judicial bypass procedure renders the notification statute constitutional. This decision is based on precedents that have allowed parental consent

---

[60]*Supra* note 51.
[61]110 S.Ct. 2972 (1990).
[62]*Supra* note 51, at 2931.
[63]*Id.* at 2970.
[64]*Id.* at 2944.

[65]*Id.* at 2945.
[66]*Id.* at 2963.

where a judicial bypass procedure is available, as well as the decision in *Matheson,* in which a notice requirement was found constitutional without a bypass procedure when applied to immature minors who would be best served by parental notice. The remaining four Justices dissented from this holding based on the rationale that this judicial bypass procedure, which three of these Justices believe is itself unconstitutional, cannot now render the two-parent notification requirement constitutional.

The second case, *Ohio v. Akron Center for Reproductive Services,*[67] concerned a parental notification statute that required notification of only one parent and provided a judicial bypass. At issue in this case was the adequacy of that bypass procedure. Justice Kennedy, writing for the six-person majority, found that the bypass procedure comported with the Court's precedents on parental notice and consent. He found that the four criteria for a bypass procedure outlined by the plurality in *Bellotti* were met; the procedure allowed the minor to show that she possessed the maturity necessary to make the decision in consultation with her doctor, without her parent's involvement, or that the abortion would be in her best interests, protected the minor's anonymity, and was expeditious. The dissenting Justices, Blackmun, Brennan, and Marshall, disagreed that the Ohio statute was constitutional on its face. They found that the *Bellotti* criteria were not met and that the statute's requirements (that the minor prove her case by clear and convincing evidence and that the minor's physician notify the parent) placed additional unconstitutional burdens on both the minor and her physician.

A consensus does not exist in the Supreme Court over the adolescent abortion issue. The lack of a definitive and strong majority opinion in these recent cases, as well as changes in the makeup of the Court and the creation of stricter state statutes in regard to abortion, signal that the final word on adolescent abortion has not been given. In addition, although the judicial bypass procedure is probably here to stay, the Court has still given no clear guidelines on how a judge is to determine whether a minor is mature enough to make the decision without parental involvement.

VOLUNTARY AND INVOLUNTARY MENTAL HEALTH SERVICES

We now turn to two topics in the area of mental health services and adolescents: (a) the rights of adolescents to seek psychological counseling without the permission and/or against the wishes of their parents and (b) the constitutionality of involuntary commitment of adolescents. Once again, competence is one of the main issues involved with adolescents and mental health. In the area of voluntary mental health services, the question is whether potential benefits of mental health services outweigh the possible incompetence of adolescents to make treatment decisions. However, in the area of involuntary commitment to an institution, the question has become whether the potential benefits of the services outweigh the constitutional right against deprivation of liberty without due process. The competence of the adolescent to make this treatment choice is generally assumed not to exist, and the issue is whether the "incompetent" adolescent's interests have been adequately protected.

Voluntary Mental Health Services

The issue of voluntary mental health services revolves around adolescents who seek mental health services without the permission or against the wishes of their parents. Although the Supreme Court has not addressed the question of a constitutional right of adolescents to seek mental health services that supersedes parental autonomy and authority, the Court's precedents on abortion and contraception suggest that adolescents may have a qualified right to seek psychological counseling without parental consent.

---

[67]*Supra* note 61.

Several state legislatures have created statutes that allow children, typically only those who have reached adolescence, to seek outpatient mental health services without the consent of their parents.[68] In addition, an even greater number of states provide for minors' admission to inpatient services without parental consent.[69] The reasoning that seems to underlie these statutes is that the potential benefits from the services, coupled with the fear that adolescents will not seek services if their parents must be informed, outweigh any parental rights to control the services provided to their children (Melton, 1978). Research by Melton (1980) on children's conceptions of their rights suggests that seventh grade children believe they should have a right to seek help from a doctor for mental health problems.

Some of the research discussed above in the context of medical decision making, although flawed methodologically, suggests that older adolescents may be capable of identifying and understanding the risks and benefits of psychotherapy and, therefore, may be competent to make mental health treatment decisions (Kaser-Boyd et al., 1985; Kaser-Boyd, et al., 1986). Some additional research by Adelman, Kaser-Boyd, and Taylor (1984) has addressed the effect of children's participation in consent to psychotherapy on the outcome of the therapy. Although this research also suffers from methodological flaws, such as a nonrandom sample and lack of attention to developmental issues, it suggests that minors' participation in the consent to psychotherapy has a positive relationship to treatment adjustment and outcome.

Involuntary Commitment of Adolescents

Involuntary commitment of adolescents means "voluntary" commitment to an institution by an adolescent's parents when the adolescent either objects or is unable to articulate a competent decision about commitment, or when the adolescent's opinion is unknown. This section studies commitment from the perspective of the adolescent's rights and, therefore, refers to this type of commitment proceeding as involuntary. Some courts, legislatures, and commentators equate the parents' wishes for commitment of their adolescent with those of the adolescent and, consequently, regard this form of commitment as voluntary.

Unlike voluntary mental health services, the issue of involuntary commitment of adolescents by their parents and guardians has been specifically addressed by the Supreme Court. In *Parham v. J.R.*,[70] the Supreme Court considered the constitutionality of a Georgia statute that allowed voluntary commitment of a juvenile to a mental hospital upon a parent's or guardian's application and a finding by the superintendent of the hospital that the juvenile was suitable for treatment. The Court found that juveniles do have an interest in being free of bodily restraint, which is protected under the Fourteenth Amendment and is implicated by "voluntary" commitment to a mental hospital. However, the Court also found that parents' interests are "inextricably linked" to those of their children:[71]

The law's concept of the family rests on a presumption that parents possess what a child lacks in maturity, experience, and capacity for judgment required for making life's difficult decisions. More important, historically it has recognized that natural

---

[68]See, for example, Colo. Rev. Stat. § 27-10-103 (Supp. 1988); Ga. Code Ann. § 88-503.1 (37-3-20) (Harrison 1982); Ill. Ann. Stat. ch. 91 para. 3-501 to 3-504; Md. Health Gen. Code Ann. § 20-104 (1987); N. C. Gen. Stat. § 90-21.5 (Supp. 1988); Tenn. Code Ann. § 33-6-102 (1984 Repl.); Va. Code Ann. § 54.1-2969 (1988).

[69]See, for example, Colo. Rev. Stat. § 27-10-103 (Supp. 1988); Kan. Stat. Ann. §§ 59-2905, 59-2907 (1987); Md. Health Gen. Code Ann. § 20-104 (1987); Mass. Gen. Laws Ann. ch. 123 § 10; Miss. Code Ann. § 41-21-103; N.Y. Mental Hyg. Law § 9.13 (McKinney 1988); S.C. Code Ann. § 44-17-310 (1984); Utah Code Ann. § 62A-12-228 (Supp. 1988); Wis. Stat. § 51.13 (1985–1986).

[70]442 U.S. 584 (1979).
[71]*Id.* at 600.

bonds of affection lead parents to act in the best interest of their children.⁷²

The Court concluded, therefore, that, although a risk of error does exist, an independent medical decision-making process by a neutral factfinder (e.g., a staff physician) to determine whether the child should be admitted is sufficient to meet due process requirements. Additionally, the Court found no reason to believe that children who are wards of the state and voluntarily committed by their social workers are in need of any greater protection than children "voluntarily" committed by their parents.

The dissent, authored by Justice Brennan, although in agreement with the majority that a precommitment hearing is not required by due process when the parent requests commitment, took issue with the majority's characterization of the commitment of juveniles by their parents or guardians as voluntary. Justice Brennan, citing the majority in *Danforth*, argued that the liberty interest of the child outweighs any interest in parental authority and family autonomy and, therefore, due process requires a formal, postadmission commitment hearing in which "the superintendent's determinations were reached through fair proceedings with due consideration of fairly presented opposing viewpoints."⁷³ Children committed by their state guardians, on the other hand, must be afforded a preadmission commitment hearing because the parental interests that mitigate against a preadmission hearing are no longer present.

Legal commentary prior to the Court's decision in *Parham* suggested the need for the Court to outline, in their impending decision, the constitutionally legitimate scope of parental authority (Note, 1978). Commentary after the Court's opinion strongly criticized the resultant majority's decision. This commentary consisted mainly of two criticisms: (a) the Court made several questionable psychological assumptions in the rationale for its decision, and (b) the Court's decision was incongruent with its recent precedents in the area of adolescent abortion, which had limited parental authority in areas that have significant impact on the adolescent.

Melton (1984) outlined 14 questionable assumptions on which the majority based their decision, stating that they were inconsistent with the facts developed during the *Parham* trial and current psychological knowledge. Several of these assumptions were based on an "idyllic view of the family" (p. 155). The Court also evidenced idyllic conceptions of the quality of care in mental hospitals and the validity and reliability of psychiatric diagnosis; these conceptions are incompatible with the evidence, which illustrates lack of reliability and validity of diagnosis. Melton also took issue with the Court's assumption that adversarial proceedings are harmful for the child and family; he pointed to the outcome data from the Mental Health Advocacy program in New Jersey, which suggest that an adversarial advocate for the child leads to greater consideration of more alternative, less restrictive placements.

In an article concerning the rise in admission rates of adolescents to mental hospitals, Weithorn (1988) argued that the *Parham* decision is inconsistent with trends in the Court's decisions to limit parental discretion in the face of the constitutional rights of their minor children. In the *Parham* decision, the Court strikes a balance in "stark contrast to the Court's decision in *Belotti v. Baird* . . . decided just two weeks after *Parham*" (p. 809). In *Belotti v. Baird*, the Court held that a parental consent requirement for an adolescent abortion is only constitutional if a mechanism is provided for a mature minor to bypass parental consent.⁷⁴ Also in contrast, on the same day as the *Parham* decision, the Court handed down its decision in *Fare*, in which the Court found juveniles competent to waive their *Miranda* rights. In addition,

---

⁷²*Id.* at 602.
⁷³*Id.* at 636.

⁷⁴See text accompanying notes 45 to 51.

Weithorn argued that the Court's balancing of the rights of the parents against those of the adolescent rests on untrue assumptions about the family, the potential harm of adversary proceedings, and the hospital staff's neutrality as factfinders. She stated that the latter assumption is questionable in light of the domination of for-profit psychiatric hospitals, which have a large economic state in admitting adolescents and have contributed to the rise in admission rates for juveniles.

Despite this criticism, the issue of involuntary commitment of adolescents by their parents and guardians has not come before the Supreme Court in the several years since the decision, and the precedent of *Parham* is unlikely to be overturned in the near future.

CONCLUSION

The law has created, in the areas of reproductive rights, mental health services, and juvenile justice, a very complex legal entity—the adolescent. The adolescent is a mutable legal creature who is both competent and incompetent, who is in need of paternal solicitation but is searching for independent autonomy, who is fighting both for and against constitutional rights. For the past two decades, the Supreme Court has been engaged in a dance of adolescent legal rights in which it moves forward two steps by creating greater constitutional protections in one area and then takes another step backward by outweighing the adolescent's interests with those of parents. The dance is further complicated by the perspective of the audience: Are those steps truly forward, are they backward, or do they possibly evidence no movement at all?

Either as a result of or in spite of this legal morass, the past 20 years have witnessed a dramatic increase in interest in the behavioral sciences and the law by psychologists, legal scholars, legislatures, and courts (Monahan & Walker, 1990). Recognition by lawmakers of the importance of understanding the extent of adolescents' competence when establishing legal policy has created a climate solicitous of psychological theory and research (Melton, 1983–1984). However, large gaps exist in psychology's knowledge of adolescent competence as evidenced by the lack of strong research on this topic. Other adolescent issues on which psychological investigation is critically necessary are custodial preference (Scott, Reppucci, & Aber, 1988), child witnesses (Goodman, 1984), and human experimentation (Weithorn, 1984).

In addition, the need for clinical services for adolescents involved in the legal system is critical. Any study of juvenile justice and mental health services for adolescents leads to the inevitable conclusion that these adolescents typically do not suffer from a single problem (Behar, 1985; Friedman, 1986; Knitzer, 1982). Juvenile offenders often suffer from serious behavioral or emotional disorders, and adolescents involuntarily committed by their parents are often also juvenile justice system recidivists. The issues involved in reproductive rights and adolescents also indicate that other mental health issues may be involved in these situations; for example, a young woman may be justifiably frightened by the legal requirement that she inform her parents of her decision to obtain birth control or an abortion if those parents are abusive.

The fact that adolescents suffer from multiple difficulties strongly suggests the need for coordinated systems of care that can adequately meet the mental health needs of this population (Inouye, 1988). More systems, such as that found in North Carolina as a result of the *Willie M.* litigation, should be implemented to provide a full continuum of care with linkages among different service providers and with flexibility in funding and decision making, to allow movement of the adolescent through the system as his or her needs change (Behar, 1985).

Adolescents are complicated creatures, and the legal, clinical, and research issues that surround them are resultantly complex. This chapter represents an initial step toward delineation of this intricate interface of psychology, the law, and adolescents.

REFERENCES

Abel, R. L. (1980). Redirecting social studies of law. *Law and Society Review, 14,* 805–829.

Adelman, H. S., Kaser-Boyd, N., & Taylor, L. (1984). Children's participation in consent for psychotherapy and their subsequent response to treatment. *Journal of Clinical Child Psychology, 13,* 170–178.

Ambuel, B., & Rappaport, J. (1992). Developmental trends in adolescents' psychological and legal competence to consent to abortion. *Law and Human Behavior, 16,* 129–154.

Arbuthnot, J., Gordon, D. A., & Jurkovic, G. J. (1987). Personality. In H. C. Quay (Ed.), *Handbook of juvenile delinquency* (pp. 139–183). New York: Wiley.

Arnold, W. R. (1971). Race and ethnicity relative to other factors in juvenile court dispositions. *American Journal of Sociology, 72,* 211–227.

Barton, C., Alexander, J. F., Waldron, H., Turner, C. W., & Warburton, J. (1985). Generalizing treatment effects of functional family therapy: Three replications. *American Journal of Family Therapy, 13,* 16–26.

Behar, L. (1985). Changing patterns of state responsibility: A case study of North Carolina. *Journal of Clinical Child Psychology, 14,* 188–195.

Belter, R. W., & Grisso, T. (1984). Children's recognition of rights violations in counseling. *Professional Psychology: Research and Practice, 15,* 899–910.

Bersoff, D., Malson, L., & Ennis, D. (1985). *In the Supreme Court of the United States: Thornburgh v. American College of Obstetricians and Gynecologists. Brief of amicus curiae, American Psychological Association in support of appellees.* (No. 85-495).

Bersoff, D., & Ogden, D. (1987). *In the Supreme Court of the United States: Hartigan v. Zbaraz and Charles. Brief of amicus curiae, American Psychological Association in support of appellees.* (No. 85-673).

Boumil, M. M. (1988). Dispensing birth control in public schools: Do parents have a right to know? *Seton Hall Law Review, 18,* 356–377.

Burchard, J., & Burchard, S. (Eds.) (1987). *Prevention of delinquent behavior.* Beverly Hills: Sage.

Cohen, H. L., & Filipczak, J. (1971). *A new learning environment.* San Francisco: Jossey-Bass.

Cohen, L., & Kluegel, J. (1978). Determinants of juvenile court dispositions: Ascriptive and achieved factors in metropolitan courts. *American Sociological Review, 43,* 162–176.

Dannefer, D. (1984), "Who signs the complaint?": Relational distance and the juvenile justice process. *Law and Society Review, 18,* 249–271.

Friedman, R. M. (1986). Major issues in mental health services for children. *Administration in Mental Health, 14,* 6–13.

Gardner, W., Scherer, D., & Tester, M. (1989). Asserting scientific authority: Cognitive development and adolescent legal rights. *American Psychologist, 44,* 895–902.

Goodman, G. S. (1984). The child witness: Conclusions and future objectives for research and legal practice. *Journal of Social Issues, 40,* 157–175.

Grisso, T. (1980). Juveniles' capacities to waive *Miranda* rights: An empirical analysis. *California Law Review, 68,* 1135–1166.

Grisso, T., & Conlin, M. (1984). Procedural issues in the juvenile justice system. In N. D. Reppucci, L. A. Weithorn, E. P. Mulvey, & J. Monahan (Eds.), *Children, mental health and the law* (pp. 171–193). Beverly Hills: Sage.

Grisso, T., Tomkins, A., & Casey, P. (1988). Psychosocial concepts in juvenile law. *Law and Human Behavior, 12,* 403–436.

Grisso, T., & Vierling, L. (1978). Minors' consent to treatment: A developmental perspective. *Professional Psychology, 9,* 412–427.

Hoffman, B. D. (1984). The squeal rule: Statutory resolution and constitutional implications—Burdening the minor's right of privacy. *Duke Law Journal, 1984,* 1325–1357.

Inouye, D. K. (1988). Children's mental health issues. *American Psychologist, 43,* 813–816.

Kaser-Boyd, N., Adelman, H. S., & Taylor, L. (1985). Minors' ability to identify risks and benefits of therapy. *Professional Psychology: Research and Practice, 16,* 411–417.

Kaser-Boyd, N., Adelman, H. S., Taylor, L., & Nelson, P. (1986). Children's understanding of risks and benefits of psychotherapy. *Journal of Clinical Child Psychology, 15,* 165–171.

Kelly, F. J., & Baer, D. J. (1971). Physical challenge as a treatment for delinquency. *Crime and Delinquency, 17,* 437–445.

Knitzer, J. (1982). *Unclaimed children.* Washington, DC: Children's Defense Fund.

Lewis, C. (1980). A comparison of minors' and adults' pregnancy decisions. *American Journal of Orthopsychiatry, 50,* 446–453.

Lewis, C. E., Lewis, M. A., & Ifekwunigue, M. (1978). Informed consent by children and participation in an influenza vaccine trial. *American Journal of Public Health, 68,* 1079–1082.

Lewis, C. E., Lewis, M. A., Lorimer, A., & Palmer, B. (1977). Child-initiated care: The use of school nursing services by children in an "adult-free" system. *Pediatrics, 60,* 499–507.

Linney, J. A. (1984). Deinstitutionalization in the juvenile justice system. In N. D. Reppucci (Ed.), *Children, mental health and the law* (pp. 211–231). Beverly Hills: Sage.

Mack, J. (1909). The juvenile court. *Harvard Law Review, 23,* 104–119.

Meisel, A. (1979). The "exceptions" to the informed consent doctrine: Striking a balance between competing values in medical decision-making. *Wisconsin Law Review, 1979,* 413–488.

Melton, G. B. (1978). Children's right to treatment. *Journal of Clinical Child Psychology, 7,* 200–202.

Melton, G. B. (1980). Children's concepts of their rights. *Journal of Clinical Child Psychology, 9,* 186–190.

Melton, G. B. (1983–1984). Developmental psychology and the law: The state of the art. *Journal of Family Law, 22,* 445–482.

Melton, G. B. (1984). Family and mental hospital as myths: Civil commitment of minors. In N. D. Reppucci, L. A. Weithorn, E. P. Mulvey, & J. Monahan (Eds.), *Children, mental health and the law* (pp. 151–167). Beverly Hills: Sage.

Melton, G. B., & Scott, E. S. (1984). Evaluation of mentally retarded persons for sterilization: Contributions and limits of psychological consultation. *Professional Psychology: Research and Practice, 15,* 34–48.

Monahan, J., & Walker, L. (1990). *Social science in law: Cases and materials* (2d ed.). Westbury, NY: Foundation Press.

Mulvey, E. P., & Phelps, P. (1988). Ethical balances in juvenile justice research and practice. *American Psychologist, 43,* 65–69.

Mulvey, E. P., & Reppucci, N. D. (1988). The context of clinical judgment: The effect of resource availability on judgments of amenability to treatment in juvenile offenders. *American Journal of Community Psychology, 16,* 525–545.

Note (1978). The mental hospitalization of children and the limits of parental authority. *Yale Law Journal, 88,* 186–216.

Roth, L. H., Meisel, A., & Lidz, C. W. (1977). Tests of competency to consent to treatment. *American Journal of Psychiatry, 134,* 279–284.

Rowe, K. (1989). *The competence of minors and adults to make reasoned decisions about abortion: An empirical investigation with legal policy implications.* Unpublished doctoral dissertation, University of Virginia, Charlottesville.

Scarpitti, R., & Stephenson, R. (1971). Juvenile court dispositions: Factors in the decision-making process. *Crime and Delinquency, 17,* 142–151.

Scherer, D. G. (1989). *The capacities of minors to exercise voluntariness in medical treatment decisions.* Unpublished doctoral dissertation, University of Virginia, Charlottesville.

Scherer, D. G., & Reppucci, N. D. (1988). Adolescents' capacities to provide voluntary informed consent. *Law and Human Behavior, 12,* 123–141.

Schneider, A. (1986). Restitution and recidivism rates of juvenile offenders: Results from four experimental studies. *Criminology, 24,* 533–552.

Scott, E. (1984). Adolescents' reproductive rights: Abortion, contraception and sterilization. In N. D. Reppucci, L. A. Weithorn, E. P. Mulvey, & J. Monahan (Eds.), *Children, mental health and the law* (pp. 125–150). Beverly Hills, CA: Sage.

Scott, E., Reppucci, N. D., & Aber, M. (1988). The role of the child's preference in custody proceedings. *Georgia Law Review, 22,* 1035–1078.

Serna, L. A., Schumaker, J. B., Hazel, J. S., & Sheldon, J. B. (1986). Teaching reciprocal social skills to parents and their delinquent adolescents. *Journal of Clinical Child Psychology, 15,* 64–77.

Sosin, M. (1982). Models of organization and commitment rates in juvenile courts. *Journal of Social Science Research, 4,* 35–50.

Thomas, C., & Cage, R. (1977). The effect of social characteristics on juvenile court dispositions. *Sociological Quarterly, 18,* 237–252.

Tomkins, A. (1984). *A study of postadjudication disposition decisions using the framework of social judgment theory.* Unpublished doctoral dissertation, Washington University, St. Louis, MO.

Wadlington, W. (1983). Consent to medical care for minors. In G. B. Melton, G. P. Koocher, & M. J. Saks (Eds.), *Children's competence to consent* (pp. 57–74). New York: Plenum Press.

Wadlington, W., Whitebread, C. H., & Davis, S. M. (1983). *Children in the legal system.* New York: Foundation Press.

Weithorn, L. A. (1982). Involving children in decisions affecting their own welfare: Guidelines for professionals. In G. B. Melton, G. P. Koocher, & M. J. Saks (Eds.), *Children's competence to consent* (pp. 235–260). New York: Plenum Press.

Weithorn, L. A. (1984). Children's capacities in legal contexts. In N. D. Reppucci, L. A. Weithorn, E. P. Mulvey, & J. Monahan (Eds.), *Children, mental health and the law* (pp. 25–55). Beverly Hills: Sage.

Weithorn, L. A. (1988). Mental hospitalization of troublesome youth: An analysis of skyrocketing admission rates. *Stanford Law Review, 40,* 773–838.

Weithorn, L. A., & Campbell, S. B. (1982). The competency of children and adolescents to make informed treatment decisions. *Child Development, 53,* 1589–1598.

Westendorp, F., Brink, K. L., Roberson, M. K., & Ortiz, I. E. (1986). Variables which differentiate placement of adolescents into juvenile justice or mental health systems. *Adolescence, 21,* 23–37.

Winterdyk, J., & Roesch, R. (1981). A wilderness experimental program as an alternative for probationers: An evaluation. *Canadian Journal of Criminology, 23,* 39–49.

Worrell, C. (1985). Pretrial detention of juveniles: Denial of equal protection masked by the *parens patriae* doctrine. *Yale Law Journal, 95,* 174–193.

PART THREE

Problems and Interventions

CHAPTER 13

Antisocial Behavior

PATRICK H. TOLAN AND ROLF LOEBER

The purpose of this chapter is to summarize the current research, based on our understanding of antisocial behavior and conduct problems in adolescence, in order to stimulate clinical practice and research. We consider antisocial behavior as a broad concept, rather than confining our focus to behavior captured by the DSM-III-R definition of the clinical syndrome of conduct disorder. In a broader context, antisocial behaviors can range from the merely obnoxious to the most legally and socially offensive acts. These acts are related by their antisocial impact and differentiated by the seriousness of the harm they impose. Thus, one can talk about a continuum of antisocial behavior involvement on how serious and extensive the behaviors exhibited by one individual are (Loeber, 1985; Lorion, Tolan, & Wahler, 1987).

This approach differs from a syndrome orientation that views antisocial behaviors as relatively interchangeable symptoms that, when occurring over a certain period in a sufficient variety, constitute a psychiatric disorder. Youths exhibiting such behavior are distinguished from those with other disorders—and those not exhibiting any syndrome—by the presence of a presumed underlying cause that generates the constellation of defining symptoms. Although the patterned serious antisocial behavior that coincides with conduct disorder is of particular interest, such behavior is best understood as part of a continuum of antisocial tendency present, to some degree, in almost all adolescents. Understanding the causes of juvenile antisocial behavior requires a broader perspective.

This chapter is organized into five sections: (a) the definition of useful parameters demarcating adolescents' antisocial behavior; (b) prevalence and incidence of antisocial behavior; (c) predictors of antisocial involvement; (d) patterns of adolescent antisocial behavior, highlighting three major pathways toward antisocial behavior; (e) promising prevention and treatment methods, and suggestions for improvements in clinical evaluation and research. In addition, the relation of antisocial behavior to co-morbid conditions will be discussed (e.g., Attention Deficit Hyperactivity Disorder and Depression). Most of this chapter concerns antisocial behavior in males, because antisocial behavior in females has been studied much less.

DEFINITION OF TERMS AND PARAMETERS

The problems that are the focus of this chapter are referred to by three different terms:

antisocial behavior, delinquency, and conduct disorder.

Antisocial acts are behaviors that "inflict physical or mental harm or property loss or damage on others, and which may or may not constitute the breaking of criminal laws" (Loeber, 1985; p. 6). Such acts, thus, share and are distinguished by being social problems as well as resulting in psychological distress.

In the present context, drug use is seen as a co-occurring problem of antisocial behavior. Although drug abuse/use can obviously occur as a symptom of depression or other disorders or as part of a pattern of general antisocial behavior, it can also occur by itself. Also, explanatory correlates of drug use are similar to those found for antisocial behavior (Huba & Bentler, 1982; Jessor & Jessor, 1977; Johnston, O'Malley, & Eveland, 1978; Robins & Ratcliff, 1979). However, there is evidence that drug abuse propensity can be distinguished from other patterns of antisocial behavior (Loeber & LeBlanc, 1990).

Delinquency refers to the more serious end of the continuum of antisocial behavior. Delinquent acts are those that, if brought to the attention of the police, would make the perpetrator liable for arrest. Delinquency as a descriptor emphasizes the criminologic/legal aspect of the behaviors. When committed by adolescents, most antisocial behaviors are illegal and therefore are delinquency. Those that are not delinquent are usually more innocuous (e.g., truancy) and tend to have limited prediction, discrimination, or utility for the planning of intervention (Tolan, 1988; Tolan & Thomas, 1988b). Therefore, the literature on delinquent behavior in adolescence is often the most pertinent to understanding the problem.

Conduct disorder refers to a psychiatric syndrome (within the larger category of "disruptive disorders") that is defined by the presence of at least three types of problem behavior (conduct) that are exhibited over at least a 6-month period (American Psychiatric Association, 1987). The central feature that distinguishes conduct disorders from other psychiatric disorders is a disturbance of behavior rather than a disturbance of thought or affective processes. Further, antisocial behavior is distinguished by whether it occurs when with peers only, or otherwise. As defined, conduct disorder identifies adolescents not necessarily exhibiting the more antisocial serious acts; however, in effect, adolescents assigned this diagnosis usually are those most involved in problem behavior. The diagnosis is usually applied to those exhibiting antisocial behavior in a patterned (sustained and repetitive) manner.

In summary, antisocial behavior represents the most general descriptor and has a large overlap with delinquent behavior and with conduct disorder. However, the overlap and the distinctions do not clarify meaningful differences in involvement in antisocial behavior.

Because involvement in antisocial behavior of some sort is almost universal among American adolescents (Elliot, Huizinga, & Menard, 1989; Tolan & Guerra, 1992; Tolan & Lorion, 1988), various levels of involvement must be distinguished. Further, because most adolescents' antisocial behavior is limited to less serious offenses over a few years, the type and duration of involvement (or chronicity) need to be considered (Blumstein, Farrington, & Moitra, 1985). Loeber (1982), Loeber and LeBlanc (1990), and, with some modification, Tolan (1990b); Tolan & Guerra, (1992) have defined several parameters distinguishing patterns of involvement. These parameters focus on three concerns: current level of involvement, duration of involvement, and rate of development of involvement.

Involvement

Three characteristics of current involvement have been found to have logical and empirical utility: frequency, seriousness, and variety. Frequency refers to overall level of involvement during a set time period (usually one year). It is the crudest measure of involvement because it fails to distinguish seriousness of acts or patterns of behavior. Seriousness of involvement can be defined either by the most serious act exhibited or the general level of seriousness based on some tallying of frequency of any acts weighted by seriousness. Both frequency and seriousness distinguish from the habitual serious offender those youngsters who have little involvement and cause only minor harm. Frequency and seriousness correlate with likelihood of arrest, chronicity of involvement, and poorer showing on a host of psychosocial predictors (Elliot, Huizinga, & Ageton, 1985; Tolan, 1988, 1990b). Versatility or the range of variety of types of offenses engaged in (e.g., acts against persons vs. acts against property, or vs. drugs and alcohol, or vs. status offenses) also has shown predictive and discriminative utility (LeBlanc, Cote, & Loeber, 1991; Loeber & LeBlanc, 1990; Tolan & Lorion, 1988). However, the utility of variety is limited because most adolescents committing antisocial acts engage in a large variety of acts, or what has been termed "cafeteria-style offending" (Klein, 1984, 1989). Type of offending has been found helpful in identifying adolescents whose antisocial behavior is limited to drug abuse or closely related crimes (Loeber, 1985).

Duration

Duration of involvement is usually distinguished by three parameters: initiation, desistance, and chronicity (or persistence). Initiation usually refers to the occurrence of any antisocial or delinquent act (Tolan, 1990). Earlier initiation in males seems to be a powerful predictor of likely patterns of involvement, including seriousness and chronicity (Farrington et al., 1990; Tolan, 1987b; Tolan & Thomas, 1988b). Early initiation is also a common characteristic of antisocial adolescents who fit the criteria of conduct disorder. In other words, boys with conduct disorders are the most likely to develop serious antisocial behavior in adolescence and to engage in such behavior chronically (Farrington, 1979; Moffitt, 1990).

Desistance is the opposite of initiation; it is the ending of engaging in a given antisocial act or antisocial behavior in general, and it is the least studied parameter of adolescent antisocial behavior. Predictors of desistance will be particularly valuable for secondary and tertiary prevention efforts (Elliot et al., 1989; Farrington & West, in press; LeBlanc, Cote, & Loeber, 1991; Mulvey & Phelps, 1988; Tolan, 1988).

Chronicity refers to the tendency to maintain antisocial behavior involvement (Tolan, 1990b). It usually refers to male adolescents who exhibit regular (and often serious) antisocial behavior across the adolescent years and into adulthood. Three well-replicated findings show why chronicity is a critical parameter of involvement. First, because most adolescents exhibit some antisocial behavior, merely considering current involvement will limit predictive accuracy and ability to target interventions. Second, even among adolescents exhibiting serious antisocial behavior, many desist in involvement shortly after adolescence. Adolescent chronicity differentiates the youths whose antisocial behavior persists into adulthood (Farrington & West, in press). Third, those most seriously and chronically involved are responsible for the majority of the delinquent behavior of their age cohort (Elliot et al., 1989; Wolfgang, Figlio, & Sellin, 1972).

Developmental Parameters

Identification of the parameters of development is important to understand the natural pathways to serious antisocial behavior and to distinguish common patterns of involvement (Tolan & Guerra, 1992). The most important parameters are onset, progression patterns, progression rate, and stabilization (Loeber & LeBlanc, 1990). Onset refers to the first occurrence of a given antisocial act or a given class of acts (e.g., assault with a deadly weapon, crimes against persons). Usually, onset is used to mark the development of increasingly serious acts or of diverse types of offenses. In turn, these parameters have been tied to greater chronicity (Tolan, 1990b; Tolan & Thomas, 1988a). Progression patterns refer to the predictable order of onset of involvement in different antisocial acts within a definable pathway. However, because few pathways have been identified to date and fewer have been adequately defined, actual specification of progression patterns, for the most part, remains to be done. One pattern that has had some replication among serious delinquents is the progression from lying to stealing to aggression against persons (LeBlanc et al., 1991; Loeber & LeBlanc, 1990). Another is the progression among conduct-disordered children from coercive behavior with parents to peer interactions (Patterson, 1982; Patterson, Capaldi, & Bank, 1991).

Progression rate refers to the rate at which an adolescent or group of adolescents advances through seriousness levels of antisocial behavior. It appears that early-onset adolescents not only begin their acts earlier but have a faster progression rate than late-onset adolescents (Tolan & Thomas, 1988a). Stabilizing refers to the consistency of level of involvement, usually the seriousness over time. For example, about 25% of the National Youth Survey sample showed intermittent involvement in the first 4 years of that study (Thomas & Tolan, 1988). Although similar to that of chronic, stable offenders, this group's crime seems more reactive to changes in familial and social factors. It is assumed that involvement patterns can be distinguished by degree of stability as well as level of stability.

At first glance, the defined parameters seem so numerous as to render implausible any clinically manageable understanding of antisocial behavior in adolescence based on them. However, researchers often refer to different parameters of antisocial behavior, and this variation affects how their results should be interpreted.

Such complexity seems necessary to develop a powerful and sensitive enough method of identifying antisocial behavior patterns. Further, when applied within a developmental framework and a subgroup/pathway distinguishing approach, these parameters can become important distinguishers of risk, propensity, likely outcome, and needed intervention (Boyle & Offord, 1990; Loeber & Stouthamer-Loeber, 1987). Our knowledge of specifics of these distinctions is only beginning, and most characteristics of patterns of involvement are far from verified. Nevertheless, we believe this approach will ultimately prove most effective for research and practice. We will use these parameters as a base for the rest of the chapter.

PREVALENCE AND INCIDENCE

Although always hard to estimate (because of the presumable reluctance of antisocial adolescents to be fully forthcoming about their activities), the level of antisocial behavior occurring among adolescents has been extensively studied. In fact, there is a voluminous literature on measuring antisocial behavior and the merits of various methods of estimate (cf. Elliot, Huizinga, & Ageton, 1985; Farrington, 1973; Klein, 1989). Rather than review here the issues involved, it is sufficient to note two main approaches, each of which has its merits and limitations (Elliot & Ageton, 1980). One approach consists of measuring antisocial and delinquent behavior distinct from the legal response to it; for this approach, self-reports and reports by others close to the adolescent are used (Loeber & LeBlanc, 1990; Lorion et al., 1987; Tolan, 1990b). The second approach consists of identifying the most serious offenders, using official records (e.g., arrest or court records).

The majority of available prevalence data has been drawn from self-reports. The National Youth Survey (NYS; Elliot et al., 1985, 1989) represents the best evaluation of overall rates in this country to date. Starting in 1976, it has followed a nationally representative sample (by age, gender, area of country, urbanicity, and race) of more than 1,500 youths over 8 waves (annual or biannual samplings). More localized surveys (e.g., Farrington & West, in press; Huizinga, 1986; Loeber et al.,

1986; Tolan, 1990b; LeBlanc et al., 1989) have been or are being conducted to build a more thorough and reliable epidemiological base for understanding patterns of involvement. From the NYS and other studies, several guiding estimates can be derived.

The overall rate of involvement in antisocial acts is high among adolescents: 87% of the NYS sample engaged in at least one delinquent act during adolescence. For the majority of these adolescents, delinquent activity was limited to a few minor offenses and persisted for only a short time, usually during midadolescence (Cohen, 1986; Elliot et al., 1989; Tolan, 1987a, 1988; Tolan & Guerra, 1992). When the focus is limited to serious patterned (repetitive) offending, the prevalence rate drops dramatically to about 8%, which appears to be consistent cross-nationally (Farrington & West, in press; Moffitt, 1989) and across studies within this country (Tonry, Ohlin, & Farrington, 1991; Wolfgang et al., 1972). Not surprisingly, this rate is commonly found for conduct disorder in males (Boyle & Offord, 1990).

Drug use estimates follow similar patterns. Over 90% of adolescents report trying alcohol by age 18, with about 45% reporting significant use in the past year; marijuana use shows similar rates. The percentage reporting "ever tried" more serious drugs drops off (Bachman, O'Malley, & Johnston, 1978; Elliot et al., 1989; Kandel, 1982). Approximately 20 to 25% of adolescents report use of more serious drugs "more than once at some time" during adolescence, with about 19% of those over 16 reporting such use in any one year (Elliot et al., 1989). Overall and specific drug use rates have dropped in recent years but still maintain rates close to those reported here.

Second, males have higher rates of antisocial behavior than females (about three times the female rate), with male offenders being more active than their female counterparts (having a mean offense rate that is usually three to four times that for females). The exceptions are larceny and theft, in which the difference in prevalence rate is less substantial. In the NYS sample, the mean rate for these offenses was actually higher for females (Elliot et al., 1989).

Prevalence rates for alcohol and marijuana use are somewhat higher for males, and male users report higher levels of use. However, it appears that the difference in prevalence is due to an earlier onset for male use; gender differences in percent of the population using alcohol are nonsignificant by age 16. For use of more serious drugs, gender differences appear to be increasing: males have gone from a prevalence rate about the same as that of females in the mid-1970s to a rate of 3-to-2 from 1983 data (the most recent NYS data published).

Third, urban residence is associated with higher prevalence and incidence of antisocial behavior. In contrast, socioeconomic status (SES) has been a less reliable correlate of antisocial behavior, although it is usually related to arrest rate (Elliot et al., 1989; Farnsworth, Thornberry, Lizotte, & Krohn, 1989; Tolan, 1988). Few ethnicity differences in prevalence are found, when SES and urbanicity are controlled. However, significant differences in incidence and seriousness levels have been found between Black and White groups (Elliot et al., 1985; Hindelang, Hirschi, & Weis, 1981).

Fourth, age correlates positively in adolescence with the overall prevalence of antisocial involvement; incidence shows a less clear pattern. The prevalence of serious offense with age shows a curvilinear relationship, with the peak prevalence at age 16. The age prevalence relation appears to shift at about ages 17 to 19, with prevalence rates dropping off rapidly beginning then. However, the incidence of those continuing does not drop off (Elliot, Dunford, & Huizinga, 1987; Farrington, 1986a). Both minor and serious drug use show a linear effect for adolescents, increasing with each successive year. The peak prevalence is later than for other crimes.

Fifth, age of initiation is related to frequency level, seriousness level, and chronicity of involvement (Farrington, et al., 1990; Patterson et al., 1991; Tolan, 1987a; Tolan & Thomas, 1988b; White, Moffitt, Earls, Robins, & Silva, 1990). Those starting earlier seem to make up the bulk of the serious, chronically offending group; those starting later tend to have more transient involvement (Tolan, 1987a,b).

Sixth, the most serious group of male offenders (the 8% of patterned offenders, those diagnosed as conduct-disordered) accounts for over half of the offenses committed by a cohort. In the NYS survey, this group committed, on the average, 11 serious offenses (FBI Index crimes) and 161 crimes overall each year (Elliot et al., 1989). As this finding suggests, seriousness correlates well with frequency. Further, it appears that, as these adolescents "graduate" to more serious offenses, they continue their less serious antisocial behavior. They are a very active, versatile, and persistent group; their activity starts early and quickly escalates to serious offenses (Dunford, Elliot, & Huizinga, 1983; Elliot et al., 1987; Loeber & LeBlanc, 1990; Tolan, 1987a,b). They follow, over time, one of the three major pathways of adolescent antisocial behavior outlined below.

GENERAL PREDICTORS OF ANTISOCIAL BEHAVIOR

In addition to the demographic correlates of involvement outlined above, there are several biopsychosocial variables that have been correlated with antisocial behavior (Loeber & Dishion, 1983; Quay, 1987b; Rutter & Giller, 1984). These relationships have been evaluated from longitudinal as well as cross-sectional studies. Overall, because numerous variables and constructs can be related to antisocial behavior, it is hard to identify the critical variables for prediction and intervention. Fortunately, results from several longitudinal studies and the recent publication of excellent reviews can provide some guidance (Farrington & West, in press; Henggeler, 1989; Kazdin, Bass, Siegel, & Thomas, 1989; Loeber & Dishion, 1983; Loeber & Strouthamer-Loeber, 1987; Quay, 1987a; Tonry et al., 1991). These should be consulted for extended discussions of the research to date and the accompanying methodological issues. All of these studies and reviews conclude that no single factor explains antisocial behavior, and, instead, a multivariate model is needed to adequately explain and direct intervention with antisocial behavior (Bronfenbrenner, 1979; Tolan, 1990a,b; Tolan & Lorion, 1988). Further, each review implies that risk is usually a dynamic interaction of the child and the environment: although general pathways based on predictable patterns of interaction between child and environment seem identifiable, the risk for a given child is less determinable (Tolan, 1990a). At present, there has been some good evaluation of the general utility of groups of predictors and identification of the necessary components of an adequate explanatory model. The promising components of such a model come from five classes of variables; inividual/constitutional; individual/psychological; familial; peer group/relations; and social/community. The nature of how these predictors/explainers interact with timing and the general developmental processes of children remains to be articulated (Boyle & Offord, 1990; Loeber, 1982, in press; Tonry et al., 1991).

Individual/Constitutional Variables

Individual/constitutional variables' contributions to antisocial behavior are among the most poorly understood and least studied to date. The largest body of evidence for a biological/temperamental influence comes from studies implicating hyperactivity as an important risk-heightening characteristic (Farrington et al., 1990; McGee, Williams, & Silva, 1984; Moffitt & Silva, 1988). This evidence falls within a general relating of temperament to antisocial behavior risk (Kazdin, 1990; Tonry et al., 1991). The other leading implicator of individual/constitutional influence is the finding that low intelligence (IQ) in males increases the risk for serious antisocial behavior (Moffitt, Gabrielli, Mednick, & Schulsinger, 1981; Quay, 1987b; West, 1982). However, the impact of these variables seems reactive to the social environment in which children's development takes place (Bachman, Johnston, & O'Malley, 1978; Moffitt et al., 1981; Sackett, Sameroff, Cairns, & Sujomi, 1981). Thus, the extent to which hyperactivity and intelligence reflect direct constitutional influences is undetermined to date. At least, it is evident that early difficult/antisocial/hyperactive behavior greatly increases risk for later serious antisocial behavior (see below) (Loeber & Stouthamer-Loeber, 1987; Moffitt, 1990; White et al., 1990).

In addition, three other types of individual/constitutional variables may be promising for understanding antisocial behavior risk:

1. The genetic correlations demonstrated by adoption and twin studies (Cadoret, Cairns, & Crowe, 1983; Mednick & Hutchings, 1978);
2. The argument that early results such as congenital abnormalities, perinatal complications, toxic exposures, and traumas or disease can increase risk of later antisocial behavior (Cloninger, Reich, & Guze, 1978; Werner & Smith, 1982);
3. Variances in normal physiological and biochemical processes of the brain for highly aggressive individuals (Brown, 1990; Tonry et al., 1991).

Utility of these general risk factors remains to be established and the implications for intervention are even less clear. It is likely that such markers are more useful in predicting very extreme patterns of involvement rather than general prevalence or incidence patterns.

Individual/Psychological Variables

The previously documented relationship of specific individual psychological factors to antisocial behavior has been criticized recently. In part, arguments rest on the outcomes of multivariate studies that suggest other variables overshadow the relationship (Tolan & Lorion, 1988). In addition, it is argued that individual psychological status is dependent on many of the same factors that influence antisocial behavior. Psychological status may be a co-variate of antisocial behavior rather than a cause (Donovan & Jessor, 1985). Thus, markers that used to be considered risk mediators—self-esteem, emotional stability, or presence of other symptoms—seem, at present, of questionable value. However, several constructs representing cognitive activity level and style relate to increased risk and seem to have prediction and intervention utility (Dishion, Loeber, Stouthamer-Loeber, & Patterson, 1984). First, antisocial children tend to utilize aggressive social cognitions in evaluating problems (Dodge, 1980; Dodge & Frame, 1982; Guerra, Tolan, Huesmann, Van Acker, & Eron, 1990; Huesmann, 1988; Huesmann & Eron, 1984). Second, antisocial children and adolescents tend to overlabel other individuals' behavior as motivated by aggression, and to apply aggressive responses to problem solving (Dodge & Somberg, 1987). Antisocial children are often less aware of the impact of such behavior on others (Guerra & Slaby, 1990) and are less able to take the perspective of others in social interactions (Guerra, Eron, Huesmann, Tolan, & Van Acker, 1991; Huesmann & Eron, 1984). Third, they evidence limited moral reasoning skills (Guerra & Slaby, 1989, 1990), and, fourth, their low social skills level is related to the risk for antisocial behavior (Tolan, Pentz, Aupperle, & Davis, 1990). Antisocial adolescents tend to have lower ability to generate competent social dilemma solutions, tend to have a less competent and less broad range of coping skills (Tolan, Blitz, et al., 1990), and utilize more direct (passive) as well as aggressive coping responses to stress (Tolan & Gorman-Smith, 1991). Thus, there appears to be a base for focusing on individual cognitive styles and skills for prediction and prevention.

Familial Variables

Familial factors have been consistently implicated in studies of antisocial behavior and appear to be among the most powerful predictors of risk (Loeber & Stouthamer-Loeber, 1986; Tolan, Cromwell, & Brasswell, 1986). Most well-established are the relationships of parental behavior management techniques. Poor monitoring, extensive use of coercive disciplinary methods, inconsistent discipline methods and behavioral expectations (between parents and by a parent across time), and the absence of positive parenting (e.g., parental attention and recognition of good behavior) all discriminate families of antisocial children and adolescents (Patterson, 1982, 1986). In addition, it appears that a harsh or negative emotional atmosphere within the family and poor family cohesion can increase antisocial behavior risk (Henggeler, 1989; Tolan, 1987a; Tolan, 1988). This has led several intervention researchers to place the family system (disciplinary style, emotional cohesion, problem-solving organization) at the center of intervention strategies (Guerra, Tolan, et al., 1990; Henggeler, 1989; Patterson, 1982, 1986; Tolan & Mitchell, 1989).

Peer Group/Relations Variables

Clinicians and researchers have long contended that peers influence delinquency and other antisocial behaviors (Parker & Asher, 1987). In the NYS, involvement with deviant and delinquent peers was the most powerful predictor of subsequent delinquency level. Similarly, peer drug-use level is a strong predictor of likelihood of using drugs and increasing seriousness of drug use (Kandel & Davies, 1982). However, most measures of peer influences and juveniles' antisocial behavior are not independent: the majority of delinquent behavior occurs in the company of peers (Erickson & Jensen, 1977). Yet, except for a few recent studies (e.g., Agnew, 1991), the processes of peer influence on antisocial behavior have not been closely studied (Gottfredson, 1987). We have little knowledge of how peers influence antisocial behavior risk. Some characteristics have shown strong predictive utility; for example, peer rejection has been shown to relate to aggressive behavior (Dishion, 1990; Huesmann, Lefkowitz, Eron, & Walder, 1984). Similarly, reported level of delinquent behavior by peers and percent of friends engaged in delinquent behavior have been correlated to self-reported delinquency in one sample (Tolan, Blitz, et al., 1990). Family relationship difficulties seem to heighten peer influence susceptibility (Patterson & Dishion, 1985). However, it remains to be investigated whether the process is that delinquent peers recruit naïve or at-risk peers to graduate to delinquency, whether mutually at-risk peers flock together, or whether the sum of their interpersonal deficits catalyzes antisocial behavior (Dishion, 1990). Tolan (1990b) summarized the probable peer influences as falling into three types: who one's friends are (Elliot et al., 1985)—having more delinquent friends increases risk; peer status negotiation skills (Dodge, 1980)—those less able to negotiate peer relations and attain adequate social status are more at risk; and personal relations skills such as intimacy, reciprocity, and dependability—those least able to access or develop such skills are most at risk (Parker & Asher, 1987).

Social/Community Variables

Social factors have long been considered important in the advent of antisocial behavior. More recently, social stress has been implicated in risk for delinquency (Patterson, 1986; Tolan, 1988; Vaux & Ruggerio, 1983). Those living with multiple and traumatic life transitions and experiences have a greater risk. Living in an environment of continuous personal danger, frequent traumatic events, and unstable living conditions, as many inner-city children do, is also likely to increase risk (Guerra et al., 1991; Seidman, 1991).

At least three level of social/community variables have shown importance in predicting risk. The first level is the immediate social network and structures, such as the interpersonal network and living conditions. Parental, peer, and sibling criminality have all been related to antisocial behavior (Rutter & Giller, 1984). Similarly, religious values and participation in neighborhood recreational and organized social activities have weak support as limiting risk (Fisher, 1991; see Davis & Tolan, Chapter 18 of this volume). The second level is the neighborhood/community in which the child resides—its demographic and social characteristics as well as the "sense of community" held by the child and by those around the child (Bursik, 1988). For example, Simcha-Fagan and Schwartz (1986) found a moderately strong relation between neighborhood organization and risk. Stability of antisocial behavior also related to risk. The third level is the larger social unit—the town, city, or other governmental unit. Communities vary by crime rates, and it is likely that a child's risk is related to where he or she lives. Regional differences and urban–rural–suburban differences have been documented (Elliot et al., 1985, 1989). However, refined elaboration of which community variables and what level of community are being referred to is still needed. Controversy about what are adequate measures of these constructs and what biases might distort their impact must be resolved if this need is to be filled (Tonry et al., 1991).

Constructing a Viable Explanatory Model

At present, in combination, these findings suggest that a multivariate model that combines individual social cognitive characteristics, family functioning (especially parental style and skill), peer relationship qualities, and social/community contextual influences is necessary and most promising for providing a general model of risk (Guerra et al., 1991; Loeber, in press; Tolan, 1990b; Tolan & Lorion, 1988; Tonry et al., 1991). Further, in some of these component areas, the specific processes are being identified. Individual constitutional factors also merit consideration. However, even with the narrowing of focus to these promising predictors, one is still faced with what seems like an unwieldy complexity in trying to develop viable model(s) for predicting, discriminating, and intervening with antisocial behavior. In part, this is related to the need for longitudinal data that adequately assess variables across the classes of promising predictors and can direct refinement. Obtaining these data is an enormous task because of factors such as a reluctance to participate, among those most active in antisocial behavior; the need for multiple sources/methods to have confidence in the data obtained; and the lack of well-developed and established measures of many of the constructs (Tolan, 1990b). However, several studies that are currently under way incorporate these methodological concerns and should, as a group, produce cross-validated refinements for prediction, classification, and intervention.

A second reason for difficulty in developing a variable model has been the limitations that occur in attempting to make direct comparison of studies that vary greatly in methods, subjects, and power. One tool that has aided such comparison is the Relative Improvement over Chance Index (RIOC; Farrington & Loeber, 1989). This index evaluates the extent to which a given predictor improves classification power compared to chance. Thus, predictors' importance can be "standardized" for construction of models and choice of variables to study. For example, when Loeber and Stouthamer-Loeber (1987) and Loeber and Dishion (1983) applied this index to review available studies, they reported that family functioning overall was the most powerful improvement and that having deviant peers provided the single most powerful improvement. Using RIOC, Tolan (1987a,b) found that age of initiation was the most powerful improver of prediction over chance level; family functioning was most important, once age of initiation was considered. The limitations of RIOC are that it is responsive to base rates and it can only consider already studied variables.

The third limitation in identifying the necessary variables and constructing a viable exploratory model is the recognition that there are probably several pathways to adolescent antisocial behavior. Two adolescents may arrive at the same level of involvement for very different reasons. Identification of common pathways and the variables that predict and discriminate them will permit construction of more refined, probably simpler, and certainly more clinically applicable models. At present, as we have mentioned above, there appear to be at least three pathways of involvement in serious antisocial behavior in adolescence, and at least two patterns (chronic and transient).

PATTERNS OF ADOLESCENT ANTISOCIAL BEHAVIOR

By tying prevalence and incidence trends to predictors of antisocial behavior, three primary pathways of involvement can be identified. These pathways are distinguished by the types of antisocial behavior exhibited, the predictors of involvement, and the sequence and constituents of development. However, prior to describing these pathways and their respective differences, it is important to note that they are probably more characteristic of chronically involved antisocial adolescents. The extent to which they fit a transient or intermittent pattern of involvement is unclear (Thomas & Tolan, 1988a). Drawing from evidence of previous studies, Tolan has suggested, as have others, the need to distinguish transient from chronically involved adolescents not only because of different antisocial impact and empirically defined differences in psychosocial predictors (Tolan, 1987a,b; Tolan & Lorion, 1988) and the role of biological factors (Moffitt & Silva, 1988), but also for the types of preventive and therapeutic efforts that are likely to be effective (Guerra et al., 1991; Henggeler, 1989; Kazdin, 1990; Tolan & Mitchell, 1989). For example, transient involvement seems best understood as an undesirable by-product of developmental consternation, which in turn seems related to cultural or population-affecting factors that exacerbate the difficulty of normal transitions of adolescence (Tolan, 1988, 1989). However, chronic involvement seems to represent a more extreme and clinically distinct pattern, with the adolescent antisocial behavior continuing an increasingly serious pattern of aggression (Dodge, 1980; Eron, 1987; Eron, Walder, & Lefkowitz, 1971; Huesmann & Eron, 1984; Loeber, 1982; Olweus, 1979) and coercive interpersonal actions (Patterson, 1982, 1986; Wahler & Dumas, 1989) that are established early in childhood. These differences suggest that transient antisocial behavior may be best understood as a general social problem in need of group-focused preventive efforts such as education, social skills training, or shifting group norms (Guerra et al., 1991; Tolan, 1988). The chronic group seems to need more intensive, targeted, and multicomponent approaches, such as intensive parent training combined with social cognitive/social skills training for the target child/children (Boyle & Offord, 1990; Guerra et al., 1991; Loeber, 1985; Tolan, 1988, 1990a).

Thomas and Tolan (1988) have suggested a third pattern of involvement: intermittent offending marked by fluctuations in level of involvement over time. In one year, an adolescent may be seriously involved and, in the next year, may show minor or no antisocial acts. Although minimally explored at this point, this group appears to have poor adjustment and familial and social conditions similar to those of the chronically involved, but the group is differentiated by what sparks the periodic involvement. The involvement seems to increase when familial and/or social crises erupt (Thomas & Tolan, 1988; Tolan, Blitz et al., 1990; Tolan & Guerra, 1992).

Within the chronically involved pattern, three pathways can be identified (Loeber, 1989). (An extensive argument of the rationale and empirical support for the three pathways described here are presented in Loeber (1989). Interested readers are referred there for further explication.) All of these pathways are marked by a characterized general progression in seriousness.

Antisocial behavior, in general, can be said to progress in the number of types of behaviors, graduating from merely obnoxious conduct problems to delinquency, from less serious acts to more serious acts (while continuing less serious acts), and from legal to illegal forms of substance use (Blumstein et al., 1985). For all pathways, the probability of graduation to the next step along any of these gradients is low—usually less likely than not. However, it is extremely unlikely that a given adolescent will progress to a given level unless he or she has previously reached the prior level. Thus, like the gateway theory of drug abuse (Jessor & Jessor, 1977; Robins, 1980), it appears that involvement at each step of a pathway is necessary to progress to the next stage (Loeber & LeBlanc, 1990). Targeting onset timing and patterns can be quite helpful in directing the timing and type of intervention that will be most profitable. With an adequate data base, it should be possible to establish onset, continuation, and progression probabilities of each pattern to guide preventive efforts (Farrington, Snyder, & Finnegan, 1988; Tolan, 1990b).

Pattern 1: Aggressive/Versatile Path

The aggressive/versatile path is probably the most common path among serious chronic offenders. It is characterized by a pattern of progression from aggressive conduct to violent offenses, with or without property offenses (Chaiken & Chaiken, 1982). Substance abuse frequently occurs but usually follows onset of other forms of serious antisocial behavior. Early initiation of antisocial behavior and other conduct problems is common; these children are often identifiable by kindergarten (White et al., 1990). Early onset of delinquent behaviors with rapid progression also differentiates this group. Property offending often precedes involvement in violent crimes (Chaiken & Chaiken, 1982).

Later, serious drug use may occur (Robins, Davis, & Wish, 1977; Robins & McEvoy, 1990; Vaillant, 1983). There is a trend of increasing overlap of aggressive/versatile delinquents and poly-drug users. In 1976, 16% of aggressive/versatile delinquents were poly-drug users. The percentage increased to 49% by 1980 and 70% in 1983. Conversely, 40% of poly-drug users were aggressive/versatile offenders (Elliot et al., 1989).

Violent crimes often start before age 16 (Chaiken & Chaiken, 1982). Across-setting aggression also is common (Loeber, 1982), and engagement in a variety of antisocial behavior occurs (Loeber & Schmaling, 1985a, 1985b; Loeber & Stouthamer-Loeber, 1987). They are often identified by several persons as problematic. For example, 87% of males and 82% of females with four or more arrests had high teacher ratings at ages 10 to 13 (Farrington & West, in press). Pulkkinen (1983) and Huesmann et al. (1984) found that most were identifiable by age 8 from peer ratings and were engaging in high-frequency aggression. It is likely that this group of highly aggressive children over-ascribes aggressive motives to others and resorts to aggressive solutions to interpersonal dilemmas (Dodge, 1980; Dodge & Frame, 1982; Farrington, 1986; Farrington & Hawkins, 1991; Huesmann, 1988; Huesmann et al., 1984; Huesmann & Eron, 1984; Olweus, 1979; Robins, 1978; Robins & Wish, 1977).

Moffitt (1988) and others (Farrington, Loeber, & Van Kammen, 1987; Prinz, Connor, & Wilson, 1981) report an elevated rate of Attention Deficit Disorder among this group. High rates of coercive interactions among their families differentiate these children (Patterson, 1982, 1986). Poor parental monitoring and ineffective discipline are other notable family characteristics (Laub & Sampson, 1988; Loeber & Stouthamer-Loeber, 1987; Patterson & Capaldi, 1990). This group tends to have higher arrest frequency than other delinquency groups (McCord, 1978; Langner, Gersten, Wills, & Simcha-Fagan, 1983).

In other words, their development is marked by multiple negative risk factors, and individual characteristics seem to be prominent discriminators (Loeber & LeBlanc, 1990; Tolan, 1990b). Their involvement is broad as to types of offending and includes serious patterned violent offending. There is little evidence of any effective preventive or treatment ventures for this group to date (Kazdin, 1987a, 1990; Lipsey, 1988). One apparent exception has been reported by Guerra and Slaby (1990). They worked to modify social cognition to increase the number and types of solutions to typical interpersonal dilemmas of incarcerated youths, with the goal of lessening their reliance on a few aggressive solutions. They were able to attain desired social cognitive changes, with the participants rated postintervention as less aggressive than controls. Although the recidivism rate was not lower, the time to recidivism was longer for the participants. Notably, an elaboration of this approach seems to have been less effective with a prevention effort in a general population, although changes in social cognitive processes were attained; at one year follow-up, no change in aggressive behavior was reported (Guerra, Huesmann, & Zelli, 1990). It may be that the effects are specific to an already established very serious group. However, this type of approach shows promise, as has been noted by others (Hawkins & Lam, 1987; Tremblay et al., 1991), and is currently being tested as part of a multicomponent prevention effort targeting high-risk children's social cognition in regard to aggression (Guerra, Tolan, et al., 1990; Guerra et al., 1991).

Pattern 2: Nonaggressive Path

This pattern of involvement is characteristic of those adolescents who tend to exhibit only property offenses (e.g., theft, vandalism, larceny). Their involvement is less versatile and usually less serious, but often as chronic as in the aggressive/versatile group. They usually begin their involvement with nonaggressive conduct problems. For example, early arrest for nonaggressive acts predicts property offense better than nonproperty offenses (Chaiken & Chaiken, 1984; Magnusson, Stattin, & Duner, 1983). They progress less rapidly to more serious forms of antisocial behavior and have a higher desistance rate than the versatile group. They are more likely to be transiently involved in delinquency, although many show chronic involvement. White-collar criminals and "career" thieves are thought to develop via this pathway (Loeber, 1985).

Hyperactivity is a less common antecedent for this group (Loeber, 1989). Unlike the versatile/aggressive group, many of them have good relationships with parents and peers. Much of their antisocial behavior occurs with peers. Also, although boys predominate, the difference in rate between males and females is less for this group (Elliot et al., 1989).

Pattern 3: Exclusive Substance Use Path

Adolescents who limit their antisocial behavior to substance use and related activities are less reliably identifiable by early aggression/conduct problems (Anthony, 1984; Huizinga & Elliot, 1981; Loeber, 1985; Tolan, 1990a; Vaillant, 1983). The most common prediction error is that many of those exhibiting risk characteristics do not, in fact, become drug users or otherwise antisocial (Robins, 1980). This group is characterized by low aggressiveness in childhood (Andersson & Magnusson, 1985; Kellam, Brown, Rubin, & Ensminger, 1983; McCord, 1981), but has early introduction to substances legal for adults (e.g., cigarettes and alcohol) and subsequent early progression to illegal substances (Brennan, Elliot, & Knowles, 1981; Jessor, Donovan, & Widmer, 1980; Kandel, 1982; Kandel & Faust, 1975; Yagamuchi & Kandel, 1984). This pattern seems to be the path to adult addiction/alcoholism, with involvement in other illegal activities usually related to maintaining the addiction (Van Kammen, Loeber, & Stouthamer-Loeber, 1990). This group differs from others in that substance use often precedes delinquency (Huizinga & Elliot, 1981; Newcomb & Bentler, 1988). Their drug use may lead to late-onset crime (Farrington, 1982; Farrington et al., 1990). They tend to show limited social skills (Fleming, Kellam, & Brown,

1981), and they are often characterized by early involvement in other adult activities, such as sexual relationships (Newcomb & Bentler, 1988). The extent of criminal activity and drug use is influenced by involvement with delinquent/drug-using peers (Elliot et al., 1989; Kandel & Faust, 1975), family drug use, social values and beliefs, and early age of introduction to "gateway drugs" (Newcomb & Bentler, 1988). They evidence precocious involvement in developmental challenges, yet lag social skills and ability to resolve appropriate developmental concerns (Newcomb & Bentler, 1988).

The promising interventions for drug-use treatment among adolescents appear to be (a) family-oriented, individual psychotherapy (Szapocznik, Kurtines, Foote, Perez-Vidal, & Hervis, 1983, 1986) and (b) family therapy that focuses on increasing positive emotional atmosphere and *then* on improving family problem-solving skills (such as monitoring skills, in-session change of interactions about discipline, and problem solving) (Lewis, Piercy, Sprenkle, & Trepper, 1990). For prevention, social skills and refusal skills training (Davis & Tolan, Chapter 18 of this volume; Tolan, Pentz, et al., 1990) and multicomponent community level, information provision, values influence, and media use have proven effective (Pentz et al., 1989). However, there is still a need to integrate the prediction and intervention literature, which have, to a large extent, existed independent of each other to date (Tolan, 1990a).

Co-Morbidity

An additional question regarding pathways of involvement is the role of other common psychopathologies. In particular, the relations of Attention Deficit Disorder and Depression to antisocial behavior have received much attention.

Several recent studies have suggested that antisocial behavior is a common outcome for attention deficit children. However, the coincidence rate and the overlap of antecedents of the two disorders are not yet clear (e.g., Offord, Sullivan, Allen & Abrams, 1979; Prinz et al., 1981; Schachar, Rutter, & Smith, 1981). Farrington et al. (1987) developed an index of hyperactivity, impulsivity, and attention deficit (HIA) and applied it to Farrington's London sample. They found that HIA level at ages 8 and 10 predicted offending, including chronic offending up to age 25. This was true independent of the presence of conduct problems at ages 8 and 10. Also, those with HIA *and* conduct problems had a higher likelihood of being convicted than those with only one of these problems. Moffitt (1990) reported similar findings, but elaborated the impact. She found that children who fit both the attention deficit disorder and conduct disorder diagnostic criteria started their antisocial behavior younger, were arrested earlier, and had a faster rate of antisocial development. Whether HIA features directly increase antisocial behavior levels or promote risk level because of increasing family difficulties, peer rejection, and social skills failures is unsettled at this point. Overall, these results suggest that hyperactive children are at high risk for antisocial behavior and that the risk is particularly heightened for these boys in the aggressive/versatile offending pathway. This finding implies that clinicians working with this group may want to incorporate, in their interventions, treatments found to be effective with hyperactive adolescents.

Another recent line of inquiry in co-morbidity that merits consideration is the overlap of depression and antisocial behavior. In the 1960s, the theory of antisocial behavior as "masked depression" was quite popular among clinicians (Cytryn & McKnew, 1972). However, no significant empirical support for this claim was available. Subsequent study of child and adolescent depression showed that the characteristics of depression in these age groups were generally the same as the symptoms of corresponding adult depression (see Clark & Mokros, Chapter 14 of this volume; Garber, 1984; Kandel, 1982). Recently, Masten (1988) noted that depression and delinquent behavior may coincide often enough to merit consideration as a distinct pathway. Tolan and colleagues (Tolan,

Fisher, Schwartz, & Thomas, 1990) found that, among three volunteer inner-city samples, an average of 10.09% of 12- to 18-year-old adolescents evidenced a clinically significant level of depressive symptoms *and* serious chronic delinquency. About one-third of the sample with above-average delinquency also scored at a clinically significant level of depression. Study of individual, family, and community correlates suggests that the depressed and delinquent subjects usually fared worse than either depressed-only or delinquent-only groups. However, it also appears that the depression and the delinquency were separate concerns; each had particular correlates (see Cytryn & McKnew, 1972, for a similar conclusion from a clinical sample). Family criminality related to delinquency but not depression; the percent of population under 18 in the census tract related to depression only; interpersonal trust related to delinquency level, and perceived dislike by peers related to the presence of depression.

These findings concur with the findings of others. For example, Patterson and Capaldi (1990) have identified peer rejection as a particularly important mediator of the development of depression. Cairns, Peterson, and Neckerman (1988) reported that violent youth have a higher-than-normal rate of suicide and depressive symptoms. Puig-Antich (1982) found that antisocial behavior was a strong component of three-quarters of adolescent suicides in his clinical sample/report. Together, these findings suggest that there is a depressed, antisocial group who substantially differ from nondepressed antisocial adolescents. However, further study is needed to determine whether their pathway leads to a particular type of involvement or merely represents two coinciding problems (depression plus an already identified pathway). Also, whether the depression precedes, co-emerges with, or is subsequent to the antisocial behavior needs to be determined. The distinguishing psychosocial predictors of this pattern also must be established. Only then can the design of meaningful treatment and prevention programs occur (Price, Cowen, Lorion, & Ramos-McKay, 1988).

PREVENTION AND TREATMENT

The history of prevention and treatment of antisocial behavior among adolescents has been marked by very limited effects and some evidence of harm (McCord, 1981). As with predictors of risk, a voluminous literature, of varying quality, has reported on an array of approaches. This volume and variation can impede evaluation and allow perpetual use of ineffective approaches (Gensheimer, Mayer, Gottschalk, & Davidson, 1986; Lipsey, 1988; Lorion et al., 1987). Design limitations often preclude confident interpretation of results. For example, Lipsey (1988), in his review of available studies, concluded that the effectiveness of interventions has been underestimated in several instances because of low dosage (limited time and intensity) and too few subjects. Further, similar to the prediction literature, there has been a resurgence of interest in interventions: new, more reliable, and potentially very important findings are emerging (Guerra et al., 1991). What can be concluded at this time from the literature may need to change rapidly. Therefore, our summary of recommended intervention approaches is presented with that qualification.

For treatment, two approaches appear most promising. Each has been the subject of considerable study that, in sum, suggests they can be effective with antisocial behavior (Feldman, Caplinger, & Wodarski, 1983; Lipsey, 1988), especially milder forms with earlier intervention. However, these conclusions must be understood within another general qualification: the success rate of treatment with antisocial behavior is quite low. Thus, it can be argued that preventive efforts should be strongly favored over later intervention, when serious antisocial behavior is already ingrained (Guerra, Tolan et al., 1990, 1991; Lorion et al., 1987; Price et al., 1988).

At the individual level, cognitive–behavioral training appears most effective (Arbuthnot & Gordon, 1986; Henggeler, 1989; Kazdin, 1985, 1987a,b, 1990; Michelson, 1987; Rutter & Giller, 1984). Such work has followed two lines; attempts to modify social reasoning (specific examples include attempts to improve moral reasoning (Guerra & Slaby, 1989)) increase awareness of the other's perspective (Allen, Leadbeater, & Aber, 1989), increase generation of prosocial solutions to interpersonal dilemmas (Huesmann, Guerra, Miller, & Zelli, in press), and increase frustration tolerance. For example, Lochman, Burch, Curry, and Lampron (1984) found that problem-solving training (alone or combined with contingency reinforcement of goal setting) resulted in reduced aggression and less disruptive classroom behavior in boys, lower rates of substance use, and higher esteem. Similar findings were reported by Kazdin et al. (1989).

One exception to this general conclusion can be found in the work of Shore and Massimo (1979) with adolescents. They applied a psychodynamic therapy that focuses on improving interpersonal relations and self-concept. They also provided practical aid in vocational, educational, and legal concerns. Although the quality of experimental control in their study was basic, they found at a 15-year follow-up that their clients evidenced less criminal activity than controls. This suggests that effective individual treatment needs to include direct practical advice and interpersonal relationship building, as well as cognitive training, modeling, and social skills rehearsal.

The other promising treatment approach focuses on the family interactions of antisocial adolescents (Tolan et al., 1986). The work identified with Alexander (Alexander & Parsons, 1982), Henggeler (Henggeler, 1982, 1989; Henggeler et al., 1986), Patterson (Patterson, 1982, 1986; Patterson et al., 1991), and Wahler (Wahler & Dumas, 1989) exemplifies this approach. All share a focus on improving parental behavior management skills (increase awareness of child's activities, decrease punitive and inconsistent disciplinary practices) and increasing a positive emotional atmosphere among family members. Most emphasize direct therapist intervention in family interactions, to redirect behavioral sequences, as well as education/training of parents to assure possession of requisite behavior management skills (Tolan & Mitchell, 1989).

Their relatively good outcomes suggest that family interventions should be the treatment of choice when dealing with antisocial behavior, unless otherwise indicated by case particulars (Lipsey, 1988; Tolan et al., 1986). At least, family systemic variables must be directly addressed in order to have any lasting impact on the child's behavior (Szapocznik & Kurtines, 1989). In particular, improving parental ability to monitor, direct, and discipline child behavior using consistent rules and reasonable expectations; and limiting reliance on only harsh or negative verbalizations and punishments are needed (Henggeler, 1982; Tolan & Mitchell, 1989). In addition, it seems important to consider how family social context may limit application of acquired skills outside the intervention meetings (Wahler & Dumas, 1989).

It is likely that the largest intervention impact (and perhaps a level necessary to realize any lasting impact) will only be realized when the individual skills development training is combined with family therapy (Tolan & Mitchell, 1989). It seems that a combination of individual skill, family organization, and behavior onsets management is necessary (Lipsey, 1988).

As mentioned above, the recalcitrance of antisocial behavior, once established, argues for development of prevention programs. In addition, the extensive legal, economic, and social costs of antisocial behavior justify early identification in order to provide prevention programs (Price et al., 1988; Tremblay et al., 1991). However, at present, the technology of prevention of antisocial behavior suffers the same limitations of low-power, low-dosage, single-component interventions that mar treatment studies. Further, prevention efforts raise complex legal and ethical dilemmas that can impede their study and application (Lipsey, 1988; Lorion et al., 1987; Mulvey & Phelps, 1988). A primary prevention approach could be advocated based on the almost universal prevalence of some antisocial behavior among adolescents and the apparent link of such behavior to this age period (Tolan, 1988; Weis & Sundstrom, 1981). Educational programs and social skills training approaches have been advocated as primary prevention, but there has not been empirical support for effects of such programs (Lorion et al., 1987; Tolan & Lorion, 1988).

At present, it appears that the potential risks (McCord, 1981) and documented benefits argue for a secondary prevention approach by targeting at-risk populations (Lorion et al., 1987). If a secondary prevention approach is used, targeting subjects based on risk assessment, then sophisticated risk identification methods and evidence of which intervention works with which risk group are needed (Guerra et al., 1991; Loeber & Stouthamer-Loeber, 1987; Tolan, 1990a; Tolan & Guerra, 1992). Available reviews suggest that prevention of serious antisocial behavior in adolescents will require, prior to adolescence, intervention composed of at least a combination of social cognitive/social skills training of the youth (problem-solving, peer-relations skills) with familial relations and behavior management skills (Gensheimer et al., 1986; Guerra et al., 1991; Guerra, Tolan et al., 1990; Henggeler, 1989; Kazdin, 1990), and administration over many months at least. How early intervention must occur to have an effect remains to be determined (Guerra, Tolan et al., 1990; Tonry et al., 1991).

However, although there is consensus of what are the most promising intervention approaches, few adequately documented prevention programs have altered the prevalence or level of involvement of youth at risk for serious patterned behavior (Burchard & Burchard, 1987; Guerra, Tolan et al., 1990). One promising exception is the work of Tremblay, LeBlanc, and their colleagues, in Montreal (LeBlanc & Frechette, 1989; Tremblay et al., 1991). They report that a program for highly disruptive boys identified in kindergarten, combining parent behavior management training with social skills, fantasy play, and television-watching training for the child, resulted in a lower rate of academic problems and disruptive behavior ratings by teachers and peers, and fewer reports of stealing and fighting. However, parental reports suggested a negative effect (mother's ratings of disruptiveness were higher for treatments than controls postintervention). Further reports from this study suggest that it will be important to consider the interaction between intervention and subjects' characteristics and circumstances (Tremblay et al., 1991). Similar interaction effects have been noted in other prevention studies (Kellam et al., 1991).

Guerra, Tolan, Huesmann, Van Acker, and Eron (1990; Guerra et al., 1991) recently began a multistage preventive intervention study to help answer the question of what are the requisite components and how can preventive intervention affect the prevalence of serious adolescent antisocial behavior among inner-city children and the eventual level of involvement of those most at risk. In addition, this study tests the advantages of "early-as-possible" intervention versus "critical-period" timing (just prior to adolescence) for affecting prevalence and involvement level. A third question addressed is the impact of an ecological or general prevention program on gains made by high-risk children in more intensive, targeted interventions. This study includes over 5,000 children in grades 2 through 6 at 16 schools. Four schools receive a general enhancement intervention that consists of social cognitive training of all children and instructional and behavior management training of all teachers. This is compared to a no-treatment control group of four schools and eight more intensively intervened-with schools. Four schools receive the general enhancement intervention; in addition, their high-risk students receive a peer intervention aimed to provide more intensive social cognitive training, with particular emphasis on peer interactions. Four schools receive the general enhancement plus the peer intervention components plus a family intervention aimed at modifying family skills and relation characteristics thought to affect antisocial behavior risk. Thus, the four groups represent increasing cost, breadth, intensity, and areas of life as targets of intervention. Similar studies are under way by other groups and, in combination, should provide a good map of intervention strategies and necessary components for serious antisocial behavior (Coie, 1990; Kellam et al., 1991).

CONCLUSION

Navigating the voluminous literature on the characteristics of adolescent antisocial behavior, its predictors and mediators, and the viable and promising intervention strategies, presents a formidable task for the earnest researcher, let alone the practicing clinician who wishes to integrate the material as a guide to ongoing work. However, the literature's empirical evidence of prevailing pathways and protocol interventions can be one of the best examples of how research can inform practice. As outlined here, several promising inroads into organizing and advancing our understanding of the problem and what is best to do about it have occurred or are under way. The first step is to locate the problem's occurrence within its social and developmental context; this volume is an attempt to do so (Tolan, 1990a). Second, the general patterns of involvement and the most promising predictors are being defined and our understanding of them is being refined to permit development of adequately complex and specific models to guide intervention targeting and component selection (Tolan & Guerra, 1992).

Third, the important characteristics of pathways to and patterns of such behavior are being articulated and evaluated (Elliot et al., 1989; LeBlanc, McDuff, et al., 1991; Loeber & LeBlanc, 1990; Tolan, 1990b; Tolan & Guerra, 1992). From this work, it appears that serious chronic antisocial behavior needs to be distinguished from transient and, usually, less serious behavior. However, the latter pattern, which still results in considerable harm to adolescents as well as to the communities they live in, needs study and amelioration (Tolan, 1988; 1990a).

Fourth, among the more serious and chronic adolescent offenders, there appear to be at least three meaningfully distinct patterns of involvement: aggressive/versatile; less serious/property; and drug and alcohol use. The timing and components of intervention seem to need to vary for each pattern. Fifth, the relations of differing types of antisocial behavior (e.g., drug use to aggressive acts) and of antisocial behavior to other types of psychopathology are being documented. In particular, the evidence, although meager to date, suggests that a co-morbidity model of cause and intervention is preferable to models that assume one is the precedent or cause for the other. For example, it appears that understanding how risk for depression and antisocial behavior are linked and interact is more useful than assuming one is a by-product of the other.

The sixth direction that can be obtained from the available literature is that intervention efforts should emphasize prevention over treatment, with secondary prevention most justified at present. However, this matter merits much more evaluation, and vigorous pursuit of promising treatment approaches as well as prevention programs are needed (Kazdin, 1990). The literature suggests that, whether applied as treatment or prevention, effecting social cognition and improving family functioning are requisite components. In addition, interventions aimed at improving peer relation skills and enhancing social resources seem important (Guerra, Tolan et al., 1990; Guerra et al., 1991). As we have indicated elsewhere (Loeber, 1989; Tolan, 1990b), programmatic study of causes, pathways of involvement, and multicomponent interventions are needed to refine these directions so that they can more confidently be applied with methods that make them more adequately articulated. Interested researchers are referred to the available reviews/overviews (e.g., Kazdin, 1990; Loeber, 1989; Rutter & Giller, 1984; Tonry et al., 1991) for further elaborations on suggestions for studies and methods that will help realization of that status. Interested clinicians are referred to similar overviews; they are sources for feeding data (observations) back to their research colleagues so that what is obtained from application can expedite the utility of research efforts (see Jaffe & Ryan, Chapter 17 of this volume).

REFERENCES

Agnew, R. (1991). The interactive effects of peer variables on delinquency. *Criminology, 29,* 47–72.

Alexander, J., & Parsons, B. V. (1982). *Functional family therapy.* Monterey, CA: Brooks/Cole.

Allen, J. P., Leadbeater, B., & Aber, J. L. (1990). The relationship of adolescents' expectations and values to delinquency, hard drug use and unprotected sexual intercourse. *Developmental and Psychopathology, 2,* 85–98.

American Psychiatric Association (1987). Diagnostic and Statistical Manual of mental disorders (3rd ed.-revised). Washington, DC: American Psychiatric Association.

Andersson, T., & Magnusson, D. (1985). *Aggressiveness in middle childhood and registered alcohol abuse in early adulthood.* Stockholm, Sweden: University of Stockholm.

Anthony, J. C. (1984). Young adult marijuana use in relation to antecedent misbehavior. *National Institute of Drug Abuse Monograph Series, 55,* 238–244.

Arbuthnot, J., & Gordon, D. A. (1986). Behavioral and cognitive effects of a moral reasoning development intervention for high-risk behavior-disordered adolescents. *Journal of Consulting and Clinical Psychology, 54,* 208–216.

Bachman, J. G., O'Malley, P., & Johnston, J. (1978). *Youth in transition: Vol. 6. Adolescence to adulthood: Change and stability in the lives of young men.* Ann Arbor: University of Michigan.

Blumstein, A., Farrington, D. P., & Moitra, S. (1985). Delinquency careers: Innocents, desisters, and persisters. In M. Tonry & N. Morris (Eds.), *Crime and justice: Vol. 6* (pp. 187–222). Chicago: University of Chicago Press.

Boyle, M. H., & Offord, D. R. (1990). Primary prevention of conduct disorder: Issues and prospects. *Journal of the American Academy of Child and Adolescent Psychiatry, 29,* 227–233.

Brennan, T., Elliott, D. S., & Knowles, B. A. (1981). *Patterns of multiple drug use: A discriptive analysis of static types and change patterns, 1976–1978. A report of the National Youth Survey* (Project Report No. 15). Boulder, CO: Behavior Research Institute.

Bronfenbrenner, U. (1979). *The ecology of human development: Experiments by nature and design.* Cambridge, MA: Harvard University Press.

Brown, G. L. (1990, September). *Biological contributions to aggressive behavior from a developmental perspective.* Paper presented to the McArthur Foundation Program on Human Development and Criminal Behavior, Madison, WI.

Burchard, J. D., & Burchard, S. N. (Eds.). (1987). *Prevention of delinquent behavior.* Newbury Park, CA: Sage.

Bursik, R. J., Jr. (1988). Social disorganization and theories of crime and delinquency: Problems and prospects. *Criminology, 26,* 519–551.

Cadoret, R. J., Cairns, C., & Crowe, R. R. (1983). Evidence for gene–environment interaction in the development of adolescent antisocial behavior. *Behavior Genetics, 13,* 301–310.

Cairns, R. B., Peterson, G., & Neckerman, H. J. (1988). Suicidal behavior in aggressive adolescents. *Journal of Clinical Child Psychology, 17,* 298–309.

Chaiken, M. R., & Chaiken, J. M. (1984). Offender types and public policy. *Crime and Delinquency, 30,* 195–226.

Chaiken, J. M., & Chaiken, M. R. (1982). *Varieties of criminal behavior.* Santa Monica, CA: Rand Corporation.

Cloninger, C. R., Reich, T., & Guze, S. B. (1978). Genetic–environmental interactions and antisocial behaviour. In R. D. Hare & D. Schalling (Eds.), *Psychopathic behaviour: Approaches to research* (pp. 225–237). Chichester, England: Wiley.

Cohen, J. (1986). Research on criminal careers: Individual frequency rates and offense seriousness. In A. Blumstein, J. Cohen, J. A. Roth, & C. A. Visher (Eds.), *Criminal careers and career criminals: Vol. 1* (pp. 242–291). Washington, DC: National Academy Press.

Coie, J. D. (1990). *Multisite prevention of conduct disorder.* NIMH Grant Proposal, R18 MH48043.

Cytryn, L., & McKnew, D. H. (1972). Proposed classification of childhood depression. *American Journal of Psychiatry, 129,* 63–69.

Dishion, T. J. (1990). The family ecology of boys' peer relations in middle childhood. *Child Development, 61,* 874–892.

Dishion, T. J., Loeber, R., Stouthamer-Loeber, M., & Patterson, G. R. (1984). Skill deficits and male adolescent delinquency. *Journal of Abnormal Child Psychology, 12,* 37–54.

Dodge, K. A. (1980). Social cognition and children's aggressive behavior. *Child Development, 53,* 162–170.

Dodge, K. A., & Frame, C. M. (1982). Social cognitive biases and deficits in aggressive boys. *Child Development, 53,* 620–635.

Dodge, K. A., & Somberg, D. R. (1987). Hostile attributional biases among aggressive boys are exacerbated under conditions of threats to self. *Child Development, 58,* 213–224.

Donovan, J. E., & Jessor, R. (1985). Structure of problem behavior in adolescence and young adulthood. *Journal of Consulting and Clinical Psychology, 53,* 890–904.

Dunford, F. W., Elliot, D. S., & Huizinga, D. (1983). *Characteristics of career offending: Testing four hypotheses* (Project Report No. 2 submitted to National Institute of Justice). Boulder, CO: Behavior Research Institute.

Elliot, D. S., & Ageton, S. S. (1980). Reconciling race and class differences in self-reported and official estimates of delinquency. *American Sociological Review, 45,* 95–110.

Elliot, D. S., Dunford, F. W., & Huizinga, D. (1987). The identification and prediction of career offenders utilizing self-reported and official data. In J. D. Burchard & S. N. Burchard (Eds.), *Prevention of delinquent behavior* (pp. 90–121). Beverly Hills, CA: Sage.

Elliot, D. S., Huizinga, D., & Ageton, S. S. (1985). *Explaining delinquency and drug use.* Beverly Hills, CA: Sage.

Elliot, D. S., Huizinga, D., & Menard, S. (1989). *Multiple problem youth: Delinquency, substance use, and mental health problems.* New York: Springer-Verlag.

Erickson, M. L. & Jensen, G. F. (1977). Delinquency is still group behavior! Toward revitalizing the group premise in the sociology of deviance. *Journal of Criminal Law and Criminology, 68,* 262–273.

Eron, L. D. (1987). The development of aggressive behavior from the perspective of a developing behaviorism. *American Psychologist, 42,* 435–442.

Eron, L. D., Walder, L. O., & Lefkowitz, M. M. (1971). *Learning of aggression in children.* Boston: Little, Brown.

Farnsworth, M., Thornberry, T. P., Lizotte, A. J., & Krohn, M. D. (1989, November). *Measuring social class and delinquency.* Paper presented at the annual meeting of the American Society of Criminology, Reno, NV.

Farrington, D. P. (1973). Self-reports of deviant behavior: Predictive and stable? *Journal of Criminal Law and Criminology, 64,* 99–110.

Farrington, D. P. (1979). Longitudinal research on crime and delinquency. In N. Morris & M. Tonry (Eds.), *Crime and justice: An annual review of research: Vol. 1* (pp. 289–348). Chicago: University of Chicago Press.

Farrington, D. P. (1986). Stepping stones to adult criminal careers. In D. Olweus, J. Block, & M. R. Yarrow (Eds.), *Development of antisocial and prosocial behavior* (pp. 359–384). New York: Academic Press.

Farrington, D. P., & Hawkins, J. D. (1991). Predicting participation, early onset and later persistence in officially recorded offending. *Criminal Behavior and Mental Health, 1,* 1–33.

Farrington, D. P., & Loeber, R. (1989). RIOC and phi as measures of predictive efficiency and strength of association in 2×2 tables. *Journal of Quantitative Criminology, 5,* 201–213.

Farrington, D. P., Loeber, R., Elliott, D. S., Hawkins, J. D., Kandel, D. B., Klein, M. W., McCord, J., Rowe, D. C., & Tremblay, R. E. (1990). Advancing knowledge about the onset of delinquency and crime. In B. B. Lahey & A. E. Kazdin (Eds.), *Clinical child psychology: Vol. 13* (pp. 283–342). New York: Plenum.

Farrington, D. P., Loeber, R., & Van Kammen, W. B. (1987). Long-term criminal outcomes of hyperactivity–impulsivity–attention deficit and conduct problems in childhood. In L. N. Robins & M. Rutter (Eds.), *Straight and devious pathways from childhood to adulthood* (pp. 62–81). New York: Cambridge University Press.

Farrington, D. P., Synder, H. S., & Finnegan, T. A. (1988). Specialization in juvenile court careers. *Criminology, 26,* 461–488.

Farrington, D. P., & West, D. J. (in press). The Cambridge Study in Delinquent Development: A long-term follow-up of 411 London males. In G. Kaiser & H. J. Kerner (Eds.), *Criminality: Personality, behaviour, life history*. New York: Springer-Verlag.

Feldman, R. A., Caplinger, T. E., Wodarski, J. S. (1983). *The St. Louis conundrum: The effective treatment of antisocial youths* (pp. 115–183). Englewood Cliffs, NJ: Prentice-Hall.

Fisher, A. (1991, June). *Community level influences on adolescent depression and delinquency*. Paper presented at the 3rd Biennial Meeting of the Society for Community Research and Action, Tempe, AZ.

Fleming, J. P., Kellam, S. G., & Brown, C. H. (1981). Early predictors of age at first use of alcohol, marijuana, and cigarettes. *Drug and Alcohol Dependence, 9*, 285–303.

Garber, J. (1984). Classification of childhood psychopathology: A developmental perspective. *Child Development, 55*, 30–48.

Gensheimer, L. K., Mayer, J. P., Gottschalk, R., & Davidson, W. S. (1986). Diverting youth from the juvenile justice system: A meta-analysis of intervention efficacy. In S. J. Apter & A. P. Goldstein (Eds.), *Youth violence: Program and prospects* (pp. 39–57). New York: Pergamon.

Gottfredson, G. D. (1987). Peer group interventions to reduce the risk of delinquent behavior: A selective review and a new evaluation. *Criminology, 25*, 671–714.

Guerra, N. G., Eron, L. D., Huesmann, L. R., Tolan, P. H., & Van Acker, R. (1991). *A cognitive/ecological approach to the prevention and mitigation of violence and aggression in urban minority youth*. Manuscript submitted for publication.

Guerra, N. G., Huesmann, L. R., & Zelli, A. (1990). Attributions for social failure and aggression in incarcerated delinquent youth. *Journal of Abnormal Child Psychology, 18*, 342–355.

Guerra, N. G., & Slaby, R. G. (1989). Evaluative factors in social problem solving by aggressive boys. *Journal of Abnormal Child Psychology, 17*, 277–289.

Guerra, N. G., & Slaby, R. G. (1990). Cognitive mediators of aggression in adolescent offenders: 2. Intervention. *Developmental Psychology, 26*, 269–277.

Guerra, N., Tolan, P., Huesmann, R., Van Acker, R., & Eron, L. (1990). *Preventing the emergence of serious antisocial behavior in high risk youth*. NIMH Grant Proposal, R18 MH48034.

Hawkins, J. D., & Lam, T. (1987). Teacher practices, social development, and delinquency. In J. D. Burchard & S. N. Burchard (Eds.), *Prevention of delinquent behavior* (pp. 241–274). Newbury Park, CA: Sage.

Henggeler, S. W. (Ed.) (1982). *Delinquency and adolescent psychopathology: A family ecological systems approach*. Littleton, MA: Wright-PSG.

Henggeler, S. W. (1989). *Delinquency in adolescence*. Beverly Hills, CA: Sage.

Henggeler, S. W., Rodick, J. D., Borduin, C. M., Hanson, C. L., Watson, S. M., & Urey, J. R. (1986). Multisystemic treatment of juvenile offenders: Effects on adolescent behavior and family interaction. *Developmental Psychology, 22*, 132–141.

Hindelang, M. J., Hirschi, T., & Weis, J. G. (1981). *Measuring delinquency*. Beverly Hills, CA: Sage.

Huba, G. J., & Bentler, P. M. (1982). A developmental theory of drug use: Derivation and assessment of a caused modeling approach. In B. P. Baltes & O. G. Brim, Jr. (Eds.), *Life-span development and behavior: Vol. 4* (pp. 141–203). New York: Academic Press.

Huesmann, L. R. (1988). An information-processing model for the development of aggression. *Aggressive Behavior, 14*, 12–24.

Huesmann, L. R., & Eron, L. D. (1984). Cognitive processes and the persistence of aggressive behavior. *Aggressive Behavior, 10*, 243–251.

Huesmann, L. R., Guerra, N. G., Miller, L. S., & Zelli, A. (in press). The role of social norms in the development of aggressive behavior. In A. Fraczek & H. Zumkley (Eds.), *Socialization and aggression*. New York: Springer-Verlag.

Huesmann, L. R., Lefkowitz, M. M., Eron, L. D., & Walder, L. O. (1984). Stability of aggression over time and generations. *Developmental Psychology, 20*, 1120–1134.

Huizinga, D. H. (1986). *Understanding Delinquency: A longitudinal multidisciplinary study of developmental patterns*. Grant Proposal (funded) to Office of Juvenile Justice and Delinquency Prevention.

Huizinga, D. H., & Elliott, D. S. (1981). *A longitudinal study of drug use and delinquency in a national sample of youth: An assessment of causal order.* Unpublished manuscript. Boulder, CO: Behavioral Research Institute.

Jessor, R., Donovan, J. E., & Widmer, K. (1980). *Psychosocial factors in adolescent alcohol and drug use: The 1980 National Sample Study, and the 1974-78 Panel Study.* Unpublished final report. Boulder, CO: University of Colorado.

Jessor, R., & Jessor, S. L. (1977). *Problem behavior and psychosocial behavior: A longitudinal study of youth.* New York: Academic Press.

Johnston, L. D., O'Malley, P. M., & Eveland, L. K. (1978). Drugs and delinquency: A search for causal connections. In D. B. Kandel (Ed.), *Longitudinal research on drug use.* New York: Wiley.

Kandel, D. B. (1982). Epidemiological and psychosocial perspectives on adolescent drug use. *Journal of the American Academy of Child Psychiatry, 21,* 328-347.

Kandel, D. B., & Davies, M. (1982). Epidemiology of depressive mood in adolescents: An empirical study. *Archives of General Psychiatry, 39,* 1205-1212.

Kandel, D. B., & Faust, R. (1975). Sequence and states in patterns of adolescent drug use. *Archives of General Psychiatry, 32,* 923-932.

Kandel, E., & Mednick, S. (1991). Perinatal complications predict violent offending. *Criminology, 29,* 519-529.

Kazdin, A. E. (1985). *Treatment of antisocial behavior in children and adolescents.* Homewood, IL: Dorsey Press.

Kazdin, A. E. (1987a). *Conduct disorders in childhood and adolescence: Vol. 9.* Beverly Hills, CA: Sage.

Kazdin, A. E. (1987b). Treatment of antisocial behavior in children: Current status and future directions. *Psychological Bulletin, 102,* 187-203.

Kazdin, A. E. (1990, June). *Prevention of conduct disorder.* Paper presented at the National Conference on Prevention Research, National Institute of Mental Health, Washington, DC.

Kazdin, A. E., Bass, D., Siegel, T., & Thomas, C. (1989). Cognitive–behavioral therapy and relationship therapy in the treatment of children referred for antisocial behavior. *Journal of Consulting and Clinical Psychology, 57,* 522-535.

Kellam, S. G., Brown, C. H., Rubin, B. R., & Ensminger, M. E. (1983). Paths leading to teenage psychiatric symptoms and substance use: Developmental epidemiological studies in Woodlawn. In S. B. Guze, F. J. Earls, & J. E. Barrett (Eds.), *Childhood psychopathology and development* (pp. 17-51). New York: Raven Press.

Kellam, S. G., Werthamer-Larsson, L., Dolan, L. J., Barown, C. H., Mayer, L. S., Rebok, G. W., Anthony, J. C., Laudolff, J., & Edelsohn, G. (1991). Developmental epidemiologically based preventive trials: Baseline modeling of early target behaviors and depressive symptoms. *American Journal of Community Psychology, 19,* 563-584.

Klein, M. W. (1984). Offense specialization and versatility among juveniles. *The British Journal of Criminology, 24,* 185-194.

Klein, M. W. (Ed.) (1989). *Cross-national research in self-reported crime and delinquency.* The Netherlands: Kluwer.

Langner, T. S., Gersten, J. C., Wills, T. A., & Simcha-Fagan, O. (1983). The relative role of early environment and early behavior as predictors of later child behavior. In D. F. Ricks & B. S. Dohrenwend (Eds.), *Origins of psychopathology.* New York: Cambridge University Press.

Laub, J. H., & Sampson, R. J. (1988). Unraveling families and delinquency: A reanalysis of the Gluecks' data. *Criminology, 26,* 355-380.

LeBlanc, M. (1985, November). *An integrated control theory of delinquent behavior: A validation 1976-1985.* Paper presented at the meeting of the American Society of Criminology, Palm Springs, CA.

LeBlanc, M., Cote, G., & Loeber, R. (1991). Temporal paths in delinquency: Stability, regression, and progression analyzed with panel data from an adolescent and a delinquent male sample. *Canadian Journal of Criminology, 8,* 23-44.

LeBlanc, M., & Frechette, M. (1989). *Male offending from latency to adulthood.* New York: Springer-Verlag.

LeBlanc, M., McDuff, P., Charlebois, P., Gagnon, C., Larrivee, S., & Tremblay, R. E. (1991). Social and psychological consequences at 10 years old, of an earlier onset of self-reported delinquency. *Psychiatry, 54,* 133-147.

Lewis, R. A., Piercy, F. P., Sprenkle, D. H., & Trepper, T. S. (1990). The Purdue Brief Family Therapy Model for adolescent substance abusers. In T. Todd & M. Selekman (Eds.), *Family therapy approaches with adolescent substance abusers* (pp. 121–151). Boston: Allyn & Bacon.

Lipsey, M. W. (1988). Juvenile delinquency intervention. In H. S. Bloom, D. S. Cordray, & R. J. Light (Eds.), *Lessons from selected programs and policy areas*. San Francisco: Jossey-Bass.

Lochman, J. E., Burch, P. R., Curry, J. F., & Lampron, L. B. (1984). Treatment and generalization effects of cognitive–behavioral and goal-setting interventions with aggressive boys. *Journal of Consulting and Clinical Psychology, 52*, 915–916.

Loeber, R. (1982). The stability of antisocial and delinquent child behavior: A review. *Child Development, 53*, 1431–1446.

Loeber, R. (1985). Patterns and development of antisocial child behavior. *Annals of Child Development, 2*, 77–116.

Loeber, R. (1987). The prevalence, correlates, and continuity of serious conduct problems in elementary school children. *Criminology, 25*, 615–642.

Loeber, R. (1988). Behavioral precursors and accelerators of delinquency. In W. Buihuisen & S. A. Mednick (Eds.), *Explaining crime* (pp. 51–67). Leiden, The Netherlands: Brill.

Loeber, R. (1989). Natural histories of conduct problems, delinquency, and associated substances use: Evidence for developmental progressions. In B. B. Lahey & A. E. Kazdin (Eds.), *Advances in clinical child psychology: Vol. 10* (pp. 73–124). New York: Plenum Press.

Loeber, R. (in press). Development and risk factors of juvenile antisocial behavior and delinquency. *Clinical Psychology Review*.

Loeber, R., & Dishion, T. J. (1983). Early predictors of male delinquency: A review. *Psychological Bulletin, 94*, 68–99.

Loeber, R., & Dishion, T. J. (1987). Antisocial and delinquent youths: Methods for their early identification. In J. D. Burchard & S. N. Burchard (Eds.), *Prevention of delinquent behavior* (pp. 75–89). Beverly Hills, CA: Sage.

Loeber, R., & LeBlanc, M. (1990). Toward a developmental criminology. In M. Tonry & N. Morris (Eds.), *Crime and justice: An annual review of research: Vol. 9* (pp.121–172). Chicago: University of Chicago Press.

Loeber, R., & Schmaling, K. B. (1985a). Empirical evidence for overt and covert patterns of antisocial conduct problems: A meta-analysis. *Journal of Abnormal Child Psychology, 13*, 337–352.

Loeber, R., & Schmaling, K. B. (1985b). The utility of differentiating between mixed and pure forms of antisocial child behavior. *Journal of Abnormal Child Psychology, 13*, 315–336.

Loeber, R., & Stouthamer-Loeber, M. (1986). Family factors as correlates and predictors of juvenile conduct problems and delinquency. In M. Tonry & N. Morris (Eds.), *Crime and justice: An annual review of research: Vol. 7* (pp. 29–149). Chicago: University of Chicago Press.

Loeber, R., Stouthamer-Loeber, M., Costello, A., & Farrington, D. P. (1986). "Progression in Antisocial and Delinquent Child Behavior." Grant Proposal (funded) to Office of Juvenile Justice and Delinquency Prevention.

Loeber, R., & Stouthamer-Loeber, M., (1987). The prediction of delinquency. In H. C. Quay (Ed.), *Handbook of juvenile delinquency* (pp. 325–382). New York: Wiley.

Lorion, R. P., Tolan, P. H., & Wahler, R. G., (1987). Prevention. In H. Quay (Ed.), *The handbook of juvenile delinquency* (pp. 383–416). New York: Wiley.

Magnusson, D., Stattin, H., & Duner, V. (1983). Aggression and criminality in a longitudinal perspective. In K. T. Van Dusen & S. A. Mednick Prospective studies of crime and delinquency (pp. 277–330). Boston: Kluwer-Nijhoff.

Masten, A. S. (1988). Toward a developmental psychopathology of early adolescence. In M. D. Levine & E. R. McAnarney (Eds.), *Early adolescent transitions* (pp. 261–278). Lexington, MA: Heath.

McCord, J. (1978). A thirty-year follow-up of treatment effects. *American Psychologist, 33*, 284–289.

McCord, J. (1981). Alcoholism and criminality. *Journal of Studies on Alcohol, 42*, 739–748.

McGee, R., Williams, S., & Silva, P. A. (1984). Background characteristics of aggressive, hyperactive, and aggressive–hyperactive boys.

Journal of the American Academy of Child Psychiatry, 23, 280–284.

Mednick, S. A., & Hutchings, B. (1978). Genetic and psychophysiological factors in asocial behavior. In R. D. Hare & D. Schalling (Eds.), *Psychopathic behavior: Approaches to research* (pp. 231–272). Chichester, England: Wiley.

Michelson, L. (1987). Cognitive–behavioral strategies in the prevention and treatment of antisocial disorders in children and adolescents. In J. D. Burchard & S. N. Burchard (Eds.), *Prevention of delinquent behavior* (pp. 275–310). Newbury Park, CA: Sage.

Moffitt, T. E. (1989). Accommodating self-report methods to a low-delinquency culture: A longitudinal study from New Zealand. In M. W. Klein (Ed.), *Cross-national research in self-reported crime and delinquency* (pp. 43–66). The Netherlands: Kluwer.

Moffitt, T. E. (1990). Juvenile delinquency and attention deficit disorder: Developmental trajectories from age 3 to 15. *Child Development, 61,* 893–910.

Moffitt, T. E., Gabrielli, W. F., Mednick, S. A., & Schulsinger, F. (1981). Socioeconomic, status, IQ, and delinquency. *Journal of Abnormal Psychology, 90,* 152–156.

Moffitt, T. E., & Silva, P. A. (1988). Self-reported delinquency, Neuropsychological deficit, and history of attention deficit disorder. *Journal of Abnormal Child Psychology, 16,* 553–569.

Mulvey, E. P., & Phelps, P. (1988). Ethical balances in juvenile justice research and practice. *American Psychologist, 43,* 65–69.

Newcomb, M. D., & Bentler, P. M. (1988). *Consequences of adolescent drug use.* Beverly Hills, CA: Sage.

Offord, D. R., Sullivan, K., Allen, N., & Abrams, N. (1979). Delinquency and hyperactivity. *Journal of Nervous and Mental Disorders, 167,* 734–741.

Olweus, D. (1979). Stability of aggressive reaction patterns in males: A review. *Psychological Bulletin, 86,* 852–857.

Parker, J. G., & Asher, S. R. (1987). Peer relations and later personal adjustment: Are low-accepted children at risk? *Psychological Bulletin, 102,* 357–389.

Patterson, G. R. (1982). *Coercive family process.* Eugene, OR: Castalia.

Patterson, G. R. (1986). Performance models for anti-social boys. *American Psychologist, 41,* 432–444.

Patterson, G. R., & Capaldi, D. M. (1990). A mediational model for boys' depressed mood. In J. Rolf, A. S. Masten, D. Cicchetti, K. H. Nuechterlein, & S. Weintraub (Eds.), *Risk and protective factors in the development of psychopathology* (pp. 141–163). New York: Cambridge University Press.

Patterson, G. R., Capaldi, D., & Bank, L. (1991). An early starter model for predicting delinquency. In D. J. Pepler & K. H. Rubin (Eds.), *The development and treatment of childhood aggression* (pp. 139–168). Hillsdale, NJ: Erlbaum.

Patterson, G. R., & Dishion, T. J. (1985). Contributions of families and peers to delinquency. *Criminology, 23,* 63–79.

Pentz, M. A., Dwyer, J. H., MacKinnon, D. P., Flay, B. R., Hansen, W. B., Wang, E. Y. I., & Johnson, A. (1989). A multicommunity trial for primary prevention of adolescent drug abuse. *Journal of the American Medical Association, 261,* 3259–3266.

Price, R. H., Cowen, E. L., Lorion, R. P., & Ramos-McKay, J. (1988). *14 ounces of prevention: A casebook for practitioners.* Washington, DC: American Psychological Association.

Prinz, R., Connor, P., & Wilson, C. (1981). Hyperactive and aggressive behaviors in childhood: Intertwined dimensions. *Journal of Abnormal Child Psychology, 9,* 191–202.

Puig-Antich, J. (1982). Major depression and conduct disorder in prepuberty. *Journal of the American Academy of Child Psychiatry, 21,* 118–128.

Pulkkinen, L. (1983). Search for alternatives to aggression in Finland. In A. P. Goldstein & M. Segall (Eds.), *Aggression in global perspective* (pp. 381–405). New York: Pergamon Press.

Quay, H. C. (Ed.). (1987a). *Handbook of juvenile delinquency.* New York: Wiley.

Quay, H. C. (1987b). Intelligence. In H. C. Quay (Ed.), *Handbook of juvenile delinquency* (pp. 106–117). New York: Wiley.

Robins, L. N. (1978). Sturdy childhood predictors of adult antisocial behavior: Replication from longitudinal studies. *Psychological Medicine, 8,* 611–622.

Robins, L. N. (1980). Epidemiology of adolescent drug use and abuse. In E. F. Purcell (Ed.), *Psychopathology of children and youth* (pp. 131–151). New York: Josiah Macy, Jr. Foundation.

Robins, L. N., & McEvoy, L. (1990). Conduct problems as predictors of substance use. In L. N. Robins & M. Rutter (Eds.), *Straight and devious pathways from childhood to adulthood* (pp. 182–204). New York: Cambridge University Press.

Robins, L. N., & Ratcliff, K. S. (1979). Risk factors in the continuation of childhood antisocial behavior into adulthood. *International Journal of Mental Health, 7,* 96–116.

Robins, L. N., & Wish, E. (1977). Childhood deviance as a developmental process: A study of 223 urban Black men from birth to 18. *Social Forces, 56,* 448–473.

Runyan, W. M. (1980). A stage–state analysis of the life course. *Journal of Personality and Social Psychology, 38,* 951–962.

Rutter, M., & Giller, H. (1984). *Juvenile delinquency: Trends and perspectives.* New York: Guilford Press.

Sackett, G. P., Sameroff, A. J., Cairns, R. B., & Sujomi, S. J. (1981). Continuity in behavioral development: Theoretical and empirical issues. In K. Immelmann, G. W. Barlow, & L. Petrinovich (Eds.), *Behavioral development.* Cambridge, MA: Harvard University Press.

Schachar, R., Rutter, M., & Smith, A. (1981). The characteristics of situationally and pervasively hyperactive children: Implications for syndrome definition. *Journal of Child Psychology and Psychiatry, 22,* 375–392.

Seidman, E. (1991). Growing up the hard way: Pathways of urban adolescents. *American Journal of Community Psychology, 19,* 173–205.

Shore, M. F., & Massimo, J. L. (1979). Fifteen years after treatment: A follow-up study of comprehensive vocationally-oriented psychotherapy. *American Journal of Orthopsychiatry, 49,* 240–245.

Simcha-Fagan, O., & Schwartz, J. (1986). Neighborhood and delinquency: An assessment of contextual effects. *Criminology, 23,* 667–703.

Szapocznik, J. I., Kurtines, W. M. (1989). *Breakthroughs in family therapy with drug-abusing and problem youth.* New York: Springer.

Szapocznik, J. I., Kurtines, W. M., Foote, F. H., Perez-Vidal, A., & Hervis, O. (1983). Conjoint versus one-person family therapy: Some evidence for the effectiveness of conducting family therapy through one person with drug-abusing adolescents. *Journal of Consulting and Clinical Psychology, 51,* 889–899.

Szapocznik, J., Kurtines, W. M., Foote, F. H., Perez-Vidal, A., & Hervis, O. (1986). Conjoint versus one-person family therapy: Further evidence for the effectiveness of conducting family therapy through one person with drug-abusing adolescents. *Journal of Consulting and Clinical Psychology, 54,* 395–397.

Thomas, P. J., & Tolan, P. H. (1988). *Continuous and discontinuous delinquents: Predictors and correlates.* Paper presented at the annual meeting of the American Society of Criminology, Chicago, IL.

Tolan, P. H. (1987a, November). *Age of onset and delinquency patterns, legal status, and chronicity of offending.* Paper presented at the annual meeting of the American Society of Criminology, Montreal, Quebec, Canada.

Tolan, P. H. (1987b). Implications of age of onset for delinquency risk identification. *Journal of Community Psychology, 15,* 47–65.

Tolan, P. H. (1988). Socioeconomic, family, and social stress correlates of adolescents' antisocial and delinquent behavior. *Journal of Abnormal Child Psychology, 17,* 317–332.

Tolan, P. H. (1989). Delinquent behaviors and male adolescent development: A preliminary study. *Journal of Youth and Adolescence, 17,* 413–427.

Tolan, P. H. (1990a). Family therapy, substance abuse, and adolescents: Moving from isolated cultures to related components. *Journal of Family Psychology, 3,* 454–465.

Tolan, P. H. (1990b). *Pathways of adolescent antisocial behavior.* NIMH Grant Proposal R01 MH45936.

Tolan, P. H., Blitz, C., Davis, L., Fisher, A., Schwartz, L., & Thomas, P. (1990, November). *Stress, coping, and development of adolescent delinquency.* Paper presented at the annual meeting of the American Society for Criminology, Baltimore, MD.

Tolan, P. H., Cromwell, R. E., & Brasswell, M. (1986). The application of family therapy to juvenile delinquency: A critical review of the literature. *Family Process, 25,* 619–649.

Tolan, P. H., Davis, L., & Blitz, C. (1989, November). *A stress, coping, and support model of delinquency: A first look.* Paper presented at the annual meeting of the American Society for Criminology, Reno, NV.

Tolan, P. H., Fisher, A., Schwartz, L., & Thomas, P. (1990, March). *Feeling bad vs. acting bad: Psychological differences in depressed and delinquent adolescents.* Paper presented at the biennial meeting of the Society for Research on Adolescence, Atlanta, GA.

Tolan, P. H., & Gorman-Smith, D. (1991, June). *Coping by urban youth: Critical dimensions for prevention.* Paper presented at the Third Biennial Conference on Community Research and Action, Tempe, AZ.

Tolan, P. H., & Guerra, N. (1992). *A developmental approach to adolescent antisocial behavior.* Manuscript submitted for publication. Available from the first author. University of Illinois at Chicago.

Tolan, P. H., Keys, C., Jason, L., & Chertok, F. (Eds.) (1990). Conversing about theories, methods, and community research. In P. H. Tolan, C. Keys, F. Chertok, & L. Jason (Eds.), *Research community psychology: The integration of theories and method* (pp. 3–8). Washington, DC: American Psychological Association.

Tolan, P. H., Keys, C., & Maton, K. (1990, August). *Research training in community psychology training programs.* Paper presented at the annual meeting of the American Psychological Association, Boston, MA.

Tolan, P. H., & Lorion, R. P. (1988). Multivariate approaches to the identification of delinquency-proneness in males. *American Journal of Community Psychology, 16,* 547–561.

Tolan, P. H., & Mitchell, M. E. (1989). Families and the therapy of antisocial and delinquent behavior. *Journal of Psychotherapy and the Family, 6,* 29–48.

Tolan, P. H., Pentz, M. A., Aupperle, D., & Davis, L. (1990). *Sixteen years of social skills training with adolescents: A critical review of trends, dimensions, and outcomes.* Unpublished manuscript. (Available from the first author.)

Tolan, P. H., & Thomas, P. J. (1988a). *Age of onset and delinquency participation, arrests, and persistence: Another look.* Paper presented at the annual meeting of the American Society of Criminology, Chicago, IL.

Tolan, P. H., & Thomas, P. J. (1988b). Correlates of delinquency participation and persistence. *Criminal Justice and Human Behavior, 15,* 306–327.

Tonry, M., Ohlin, L. E., & Farrington, D. P. (1991). *Human development and criminal behavior.* New York: Springer-Verlag.

Tremblay, R. E., McCord, J., Boileau, H., Charlebois, P., Gagnon, C., LeBlanc, M., & Larrivee, S. (1991). Can disruptive boys be helped to become competent? *Psychiatry, 54,* 148–161.

Vaillant, G. E. (1983). Natural history of male alcoholism. IV: Is alcoholism the cart or the horse to sociopathy? *British Journal of Addiction, 78,* 317–326.

Van Kammen, W. B., Loeber, R., & Stouthamer-Loeber, M. (1990). Substance use and its relationship to conduct problems and delinquency in young boys. *Journal of Youth and Adolescence, 20,* 399–414.

Vaux, A., & Ruggerio, M. (1983). Stressful life change and delinquent behavior. *American Journal of Community Psychology, 11,* 169–183.

Wahler, R. G., & Dumas, J. (1989). Family factors in childhood psychopathology: A coercion–neglect model. In T. Jacob (Ed.), *Family interaction and psychopathology* (pp. 381–428). New York: Plenum Press.

Weis, J. G., & Sundstrom, J. (1981). *The prevention of serious delinquency: What to do?* Washington, DC: Government Printing Office.

Werner, E. E., & Smith, R. S. (1982). *Vulnerable, but invincible: A longitudinal study of resilient children and youth.* New York: McGraw-Hill.

West, D. J. (1982). *Delinquency: Its roots, careers, and prospects.* London: Heinemann.

White, J. L., Moffitt, T. E., Earls, F., Robins, L., & Silva, P. A. (1990). How early can we tell? Predictors of childhood conduct disorder and adolescent delinquency. *Criminology, 28,* 507–533.

Wolfgang, M. E., Figlio, R. M., & Sellin, T. (1972). *Delinquency in a birth cohort.* Chicago: University of Chicago Press.

Yamaguchi, K., & Kandel, D. B. (1984). Patterns of drug use from adolescence to young adulthood: III. Predictors of progression. *American Journal of Public Health, 74,* 673–681.

CHAPTER 14

Depression and Suicidal Behavior

DAVID C. CLARK and HARTMUT B. MOKROS

The study of early-onset affective or mood disorders, as they are now referred to in the DSM-III-R (American Psychiatric Association, 1987), represents one of the most active areas of research in childhood psychopathology over the past decade. The distinction between childhood and adolescence is often not clearly drawn; many studies of children, in fact, include large subsamples of early adolescents, and studies that purport to study adolescents include youngsters as young as 11 years of age. Much of the research has been skewed toward the study of prepubertal children, with a relative neglect of adolescents. This neglect may reflect the implicit assumption that adolescents are adultlike in presentation and response, and, therefore, that research of adolescence is less critical than that of childhood. There is also a commonly held bias that experiences during infancy and early childhood are uniquely important in causing depression. This neglect is apparent in the development of research evaluation tools as well as the empirical investigation of topics ranging from epidemiology to treatment. In this review, we consider issues of definition, assessment and diagnosis, epidemiology, comorbidity, biological correlates, and treatment. Because of the relative rarity of bipolar disorders, the primary focus of discussion is depressive disorders. In addition, given the availability elsewhere of theoretical discussions (Beck, 1967; Kovacs, 1989; Puig-Antich & Gittelman, 1982; Rutter, Izard, & Read, 1986) and the current interest in suicide, we first overview the empirical data on adolescent depression and then turn our attention to suicide. Within the topic of depression, we focus more specifically on the less often considered biological data than on the commonly reviewed psychological findings.

OVERVIEW

The idea that depressive disorders may manifest themselves in youth has historically encountered considerable skepticism. Those whose theoretical orientation was psychoanalytic argued against the concept of clinical depression in childhood because of the lack of sufficiently elaborated superego structure (Rie, 1966). The implication following from this is that depression first appears in adolescence. Others argued that the commonality of depressive symptomatology in childhood suggests that such symptoms are properties of a normative and transient developmental course (Lefkowitz & Burton,

1978). This attitude is particularly pronounced with regard to adolescents because of the often assumed normality of storm and stress during this developmental phase.

Research over the past decade has clearly indicated that depression is experienced in youth and is not confined to mere symptom expressions of sadness as reactions to environmental stressors or developmental transitions (Puig-Antich, 1986). Although transitory experiences of negative mood are no doubt part of the fabric of existence, the important point demonstrated by this research is the tendency, in some children, for a syndromelike constellation of symptoms to concur with a negative mood state. Thus, vegetative features such as loss of appetite and sleep disturbance, behavioral expressions of psychomotor retardation or agitation and inabilities to concentrate and focus attention externally, and ideational experiences, including perceived hopelessness and morbid or suicidal preoccupations accompanying a dysphoric mood state, common in adults, also occur among adolescents. The added discovery that adolescents who experience such constellations of symptoms in consort with their depressed affective state have these experiences episodically, with identifiable parameters of symptom onset and offset, and are additionally psychosocially impaired during these episodes, strongly suggests the presence of a depressive disorder.

Thus, the current research orientation is the assumption of equivalence or continuity of affective disorders between adulthood and youth (Puig-Antich, 1986). Several lines of evidence support this assumption. First, although some age-related differences in phenomenology have been noted, these have been found to be minimal (Kovacs & Gatsonis, 1989; Mitchell, McCauley, Burke, & Moos, 1988; Ryan, Puig-Antich, Ambrosini et al., 1987). Diagnostic criteria used with adults are seen as applicable to youth and are routinely used in both research and clinical practice. Second, assessment of the adult relatives of affectively disordered youth indicates high rates of affective disturbance in these populations (e.g., Dwyer & DeLong, 1987; Puig-Antich, Goetz, Davis et al., in press; Strober et al., 1988). Third, at-risk studies indicate significantly elevated risks of affective disorder in the offspring of affectively disordered parents (e.g., Beardslee et al., 1988), with some evidence that offspring of unipolar parents are more prone to unipolar disorders (Weissman et al., 1987) and children of bipolar parents are more prone to bipolar disorders (Klein, Depue, & Slater, 1985). Fourth, biological correlates such as cortisol nonsuppression (e.g., Evans, Nemeroff, Haggerty, & Pederson, 1987), growth hormone secretion (Ryan et al., 1988), and sleep parameters (Lahmeyer, Poznanski, & Bellur, 1983) all show differences between normal and depressives in adolescent samples, and provide data consistent with results from adult studies. Fifth, longitudinal research on the natural course of illness indicates that, as in adults, affective disorders in youth are episodic; that is, once an index episode is experienced, risk of relapse is greatly elevated (Keller et al., 1988; Kovacs, Feinberg, Crouse-Novak, Paulauskas, & Finkelstein, 1984).

However, two types of observations argue against the view that mood disturbances in youth are early manifestations of adult-form mood disorder. First is the failure to establish treatment superiority of tricyclic antidepressants over placebo. To date, four double-blind placebo-controlled studies have been reported, with only one of these conducted with adolescents (Kramer & Feiguine, 1981), and all have failed to find evidence for the superiority of tricyclic medication over placebo, even when a placebo washout period was included in the study design (Geller, Cooper, McCombs, Graham, & Wells, in press). Second, the high rate of psychiatric comorbidity among youth diagnosed with a mood disturbance, together with increased risk of future nonaffective psychiatric morbidity following a depressive episode, suggests that mood disturbance in youth is a more insidious form of affective disorder than that seen in adults. Thus, although research is currently dominated by the view of equivalence between childhood and adult affective disorders, these findings question such a position.

Other objections to this working assumption of equivalence have been raised. Historically, the constructs of "masked depression" and "depressive equivalents" (e.g., Cytryn & McKnew, 1974; Glaser, 1967), now largely discarded, reflected the view that affective disturbance in childhood differed phenomenologically from what was seen in adults. More recently, proponents of the emergent field of developmental psychopathology (Cicchetti & Schneider-Rosen, 1984; Rutter et al., 1986) have challenged the continuity perspective's lack of a developmental perspective. A central objective of these researchers is reliance on rationally—rather than empirically—derived taxonomic classification (Achenbach & Edelbrock, 1984). They argue that nosology in childhood should be developed from data rather than fit to existing models. Although the logic of this position is compelling, little empirical evidence has been offered that argues against the continuity assumption (Kaslow, Rehm, & Siegel, 1984).

DEPRESSION

Assessment and Diagnosis

One of the prominent developments in the study of mental disorder over the past two decades has been the standardized diagnostic criteria and methods of assessment. These developments have increased definitional comparability by reducing criterion and information variance respectively.

The unstructured interview represents the traditional approach to clinical assessment. For research purposes, the unstructured interview is inadequate because of clear danger of incomplete evaluation, difference in approach to eliciting responses, lack of explicit criteria for establishing symptom presences, and danger that the interview will be unknowingly guided by both implicit and explicit predispositions of the clinician. These features mitigate against comparisons across patients, thereby limiting the generalizability of research.

Numerous instruments using either self-report or interview-based measures have been developed for the assessment of affective disorders. Most are variants of adult instruments, with modifications made in language and content to make them age-appropriate. By and large, these modifications have not been empirically guided. Self-report measures used with adolescents include the Beck Depression Inventory (BDI: Beck, 1967), the Depression Self-Rating Scale (Birelson, 1981), the Children's Depression Inventory (CDI: Kovacs, 1985a), the Children's Depression Scale (Lang & Tisher, 1978), the Peer Nomination Inventory (Lefkowitz & Tesiny, 1980), and the Reynolds Depression Rating Scale (Reynolds, 1983). Diagnostic interview measures include the Schedule for Affective Disorders and Schizophrenia, Children's Version (K-SADS: Puig-Antich, Chambers, & Tabrizi, 1983), the Diagnostic Interview for Children and Adolescents (DICA: Herjanic & Reich, 1982), the Diagnostic Interview for Children (DISC: Costello & Dulcan, 1985), and the Interview Schedule for Children (ISC: Kovacs, 1985b). Depression severity interview measures include the Children's Depression Rating Scale, Revised (CDRS-R: Poznanski, Freeman, & Mokros, 1985) and the Hamilton Rating Scale for Depression (Hamilton, 1960). In studies of adolescents, the most commonly used measures are the self-report BDI as a severity and screening measure, and the K-SADS and DICA for diagnostic purposes. Psychometric study of such instruments in regard to adolescents is scant. Thus, the reliability and the validity of these measures need further investigation.

Use of Cutoff Scores for Case Identification

Many studies have relied exclusively on self-report measures, with cases of depression identified on the basis of cutoff scores. Problematic with such use is the fact that a cutoff score does not indicate whether the essential symptom of depression, a dysphoric mood, is present. Moreover, cutoff scores, even when they have been validated against diagnostically defined cases, may vary considerably in accuracy because the sensitivity/specificity of an instrument in identifying a case is contingent on the base rate of disorder.

The impact of case identification difficulties on research findings is illustrated by the following. A Beck Depression Inventory (BDI: Beck, 1967) cutoff score of 16 has a reported sensitivity of 95% and a specificity of 86% in correctly classifying individuals as depressed or not depressed, according to DSM-III criteria (Beck, 1967). Kaplan, Hong, and Weinhold (1984), in an epidemiological study of adolescent depression, found that 8.6% of their sample scored above the cutoff of 16. Assuming that this figure of 8.6% represents an accurate estimate of the base rate of depression in this sample, and that the sensitivity/specificity data already cited are correct, relying on the Bayes Theorem, the probability is that an individual with a score above the cutoff score of 16 is, indeed, depressed. This probability would be 39%. In other words, if a treatment or intervention study identified depressed cases in this manner, then the majority of individuals with a high cutoff score would be misclassified (false positives). This would certainly compromise the assessment of treatment efficacy. Cases of depression defined exclusively on the basis of self-report cutoff scores are not equivalent to cases identified by means of diagnostic assessment.

Epidemiology

Research on the prevalence of depression in community samples of adolescents has largely relied on self-report instruments. Estimates of depression rates have varied considerably. This variation may in part be a function of differences in instrumentation as well as in cutoff score criteria used to define a case of depression. However, even when similar instruments and cutoff criteria have been used, considerable variation has been evident.

In one of the earliest systematic studies reported, Albert and Beck (1975) identified 33.3% of 63 seventh and eighth graders between the ages of 11 and 15 years as moderately depressed, and 3.2% as severely depressed, on the basis of responses to a shortened (13-item) form of the Beck Depression Inventory (BDI). Using the complete 21-item BDI in a study of 568 adolescents 14 to 17 years old, Teri (1982) identified moderate depression in 27% and severe depression in 5%. Kaplan et al. (1984) identified moderate depression in 7.3% of 385 adolescents 11 to 18 years old, and severe depression for an additional 1.3%. In a large sample of 2,875 adolescents 13 to 18 years old, including subjects from urban, suburban, and rural high schools, Reynolds (1983) identified moderate and severe depression in 18% of this sample using the BDI. Thus, across four studies using the BDI, prevalence rates of depression ranged from 8.6% to 36.5%, although severe depression was identified in less than 7% of subjects across all studies. By comparison, in the largest study reported to date, Kandel and Davies (1982) identified 18% of 8,206 adolescents 14 to 18 years old as "highly depressed." They based their assessment on a six-item self-report instrument derived from the Hopkins Symptom Checklist. Thus, considerable variability in estimates of depression exists on the basis of self-report. The differences must be considered in light of the characteristics of the samples assessed and the noncomparability of different cutoff scores. Although Strober, Green, and Carlson (1981) demonstrated that moderate-to-severe BDI depression scores converged with DSM-III depression diagnosis among adolescent psychiatric patients, without comparison of self-report and diagnostic assessment data for normal subjects, it is difficult to interpret the meaning of prevalence rates from self-report studies.

Fewer interview-based structured evaluations of depression have been conducted than self-report studies. Two recent studies have employed structured interviews to identify the prevalence of depressive disorders in adolescents according to DSM-III criteria. Deykin, Levy, and Wells (1987) studied the co-occurrence of depression, alcohol, and drug abuse in 424 students between the ages of 16 to 19 years and reported a 6.8% lifetime prevalence for major depressive disorder based on interviews using the Diagnostic Interview Schedule (DIS: Robins, Helzer, Croughan, & Ratcliff, 1981). Kashani et al. (1987) studied a group of 150 adolescents between the ages of 14 to 16 years and found a point-prevalence of 4.7% for major depressive disorder and 3.3% for dysthymic disorder, based on modified DICA interviews with the adolescents and their parents. When compared to the results of two large-scale studies of children 9 years of age (Kashani et al., 1983) and 11 years of age (Anderson, McGee, Williams, & Silva, 1987), the prevalence of major depression and dysthymic disorder shows a fourfold jump among the group 14 to 16 years old.

Demographic Correlates of Depressive Disorder

Data from self-reported depression studies such as those cited above have been viewed as both supporting and discounting the view that adolescence is a particularly turbulent developmental epoch. Kandel and Davies (1982), for example, concluded that the high rate of depression they identified (18%) supports the view that adolescence is, in fact, a time of storm and stress, and that considerable concern among professionals is warranted. Just the opposite conclusion was drawn by Kaplan et al. (1984); in the low rate of "severe" depression they identified (1.3%), they saw evidence indicating that the storm and stress notion of adolescence is a myth. Whether adolescent depression reflects a stormy developmental period, cannot, however, be adequately evaluated based on prevalence data alone. Minimally, comparison with data from other developmental periods is necessary to make such an argument. Kandel and Davies (1982), who reported such data, found that adolescents were significantly higher in self-ratings of dysphoria than a matched sample of parents. For example, when asked "During the past year, how often were you troubled by feeling unhappy, sad, or depressed?," 19.7% of adolescents reported they were much bothered, compared to 6.5% of their parents. This is consistent with the findings of Csikszentmihalyi and Larson (1984) using the Experience Sampling Method; in comparing adolescents and adults, they reported greater variability (greater range and frequency of both highs and lows) in adolescent ratings of moods.

In adults, research has consistently identified elevated rates of depression among females. This sex difference has not been identified in prepubertal children, but has been reported in several of the studies reviewed. The two largest sample studies (Kandel & Davies, 1982; Reynolds, 1983) both reported significant sex differences, as did Teri (1982) and Kashani et al. (1987). The latter, in fact, found that depression was five times more common among girls than boys. Two studies have not reported a sex difference (Albert & Beck, 1975; Kaplan et al., 1984). The lack of sex effect in these studies may reflect the fact that both studies included young adolescents who may, in fact, have been prepubertal.

Evaluation of the relationship of sociodemographic variables such as race, religion, socioeconomic status, and parental education to depression has failed to show any clear results in either prepubertal or adolescent samples. One study (Schoenbach, Kaplan, Wagner, Grimson, & Miller, 1983) reported a significant race effect, with Blacks higher than non-Blacks, and a significant effect of socioeconomic status, with lower status scores correlated with higher depression scores.

Interestingly, neither prevalence nor correlates of depression have been reported to vary across the adolescent years. This is also true in studies of prepubertal children. Thus, although there is a jump in depression from the prepubertal to the adolescent years, within these age spans no trend is apparent for increased incidence or severity of depression.

These studies certainly add to our understanding of the epidemiology of childhood mood disorders, but methodological shortcomings limit the generalizability of their results. Lack of uniformity in criteria, assessment, and procedures has produced some of the apparent problems. Identification of the population to which results generalize represents another problem. Samples of adolescents representative of the population-at-large need to be studied using uniform assessment, criteria, and subject recruitment procedures before any defendable conclusions about the epidemiology of depression in childhood and adolescence can be articulated.

Additionally, the above studies do not address an important question: Is there a secular increase in depression? For example, Shaffer and Fisher (1981) provided evidence of a threefold increase in adolescent suicide over the past 20 years, which does not appear to be simply an artifact of greater recognition. Klerman (1988) similarly argued that the age of onset of depression has been more predictable and the prevalence of depression during adolescence has been greater for the baby boom generation than among prior generations. In any identification, changes in base rates over time must be kept in mind.

Comorbidity

It appears that affective disorders in youth are, as a rule, accompanied by other psychiatric difficulties (Ryan et al., 1987). Indeed, researchers of childhood depression are now resigned to the view that a search for "pure depressions" is futile (Puig-Antich et al., in press). For example, Kashani et al. (1987) found that 100% of the depressed adolescents in their study qualified for an additional DSM-III diagnosis; Mitchell et al. (1988) found coexisting disorders in 86% of the adolescents they assessed with anxiety disorders. Anxiety disorders were the most common concurrent disorders in both studies. The importance of these findings was underscored by Keller et al. (1988), who reported that the risk of recurrent depression is greatly increased by the presence of coexisting psychiatric disorders. Deykin et al. (1987) found a strong interrelationship between alcohol and substance abuse and major depressive disorder, with alcohol abuse specific to major depressive disorder, but substance abuse related to other mental disorder as well. Interestingly, the onset of major depressive disorder almost always preceded alcohol and substance abuse when these diagnoses overlapped. Subjects with a history of alcohol or drug abuse were three times more likely to report a history of major depression than other adolescents, and the first episode of major depression usually preceded substance abuse by 4 years. Students with a history of major depression or of substance use disorder were more likely to report a history of suicidal behavior. A history of major depression showed a stronger association with suicidal behavior, although a history of substance use disorder had an independent association with suicidal behavior.

Christie et al. (1988) examined findings from the NIMH Epidemiological Catchment Area Program in five different cities as they applied to 4,778 persons aged 18 to 30 years old. They found that young adults who developed a major depression or anxiety disorder were twice as likely to develop a subsequent drug use disorder (but not alcohol abuse). These findings suggest that some adolescents begin using alcohol and/or illicit drugs to alleviate painful mood states, as has been contended by Paton, Kessler, and Kandel (1977). These substances are, of course, not effective palliatives. If this is so, such comorbidity introduces another layer of symptoms, impairment, complications, compromised judgment, and increased risk of violent death.

Two positions can be taken with regard to these high rates of codiagnosis. The first position is to accept that depression in youth is often accompanied by other difficulties, and therefore view early-onset affective disturbances as a particularly insidious variant of affective disorders. The second position suggests that the high levels of additional psychiatric difficulties bring into question the validity of the adult-based depression diagnosis in youth, and thereby challenges the assumption of equivalency between childhood and adult affective disorders (McGee & Williams, 1988). Thus, key questions for future research are: What constitutes a depressive disorder in youth? What is an appropriate time frame for predicting outcome (i.e., prognosis)? What should be the role of depression in nosology of adolescent psychopathology in general?

Psychosocial Markers

Although any number of psychological markers can be related to depression, few studies have identified markers that are specific to depression and not general to psychopathology, and even fewer studies have evaluated markers with a focus on adolescence. Most predictive research has focused on childhood (Rutter et al., 1986). In part, this latter focus has been perpetuated by findings suggesting that the psychosocial markers of depression risk and presence are relatively constant across childhood and adolescence. Prominent among these are parental affective disorder (Beardslee, Bemporad, Keller, & Klerman, 1983), low self-esteem (Mendelson, 1982), high sense of guilt (Harter, 1983), early loss (Brown, Harris, & Bifulco, 1986), behavior problems (Puig-Antich, 1982), poor cognitive control, and a tendency to attribute bad events to internal, stable, and global causes (Seligman & Peterson, 1986).

A developing body of literature suggests that adolescence is a time when gender differences emerge in psychological experience and characteristics (Gjerde, Block, & Block, 1988) and rates of depression (Kandel & Davies, 1982; Tolan, DeJesus, & Thomas, 1988). For example, Gjerde et al. (1988) reported that, among depressed late adolescents, females tended to be more introspective, self-defeating, rebellious, self-centered, easily upset, and concerned with adequacy, and less trusting and lower in self-liking, than their male counterparts. Depressed males were more self-indulgent, hostile, rebellious, negativistic, power-oriented, and reactive to minor frustrations, and less dependable, productive, ready to feel guilt, and self-insightful than depressed females.

Together, these two sets of findings on psychological markers suggest a need for some basic longitudinal developmental studies to trace the psychosocial predisposing and precipitating factors that mark depression across childhood and adolescence (Rutter, 1986). This seems a prerequisite to developing reliable and specific understanding of what constitutes the disorder across age groups and how its presenting form interacts with developmental stage.

Biological Markers

The search for biological markers of affective disorders has been the focus of enormous research interest recently (Fawcett & Kravitz, 1985), although the range and extent of such investigation in adolescence have been more limited than in either child or adult populations. Nevertheless, at least three biological markers—cortisol secretion, growth hormone secretion, and sleep parameters—have been investigated. In each case, they have produced results that distinguish depressed from nondepressed adolescents and show patterns similar to those found for adults.

Dexamethasone Suppression Test (DST)

The dexamethasone suppression test was developed by Carroll as a measure of hypothalamic–pituitary axis dysfunction. Early escape from cortisol suppression has been interpreted as a state marker of depressed episodes. Average sensitivity of 50% and specificity of 95% for the DST have been reported across adult studies (Fawcett & Kravitz, 1985). Poznanski and Mokros (1989) reviewed seven studies that reported DST data for depressed adolescents. Across these studies, sensitivity for major depressive disorder ranged from 25% (Robbins, Alessi, Yanchysyn, & Colfer, 1983) to 64% (Hsu et al., 1983). DST results were obtained across these studies from 130 adolescents with a diagnosis of major depressive disorder; 51 of these adolescents were identified as nonsuppressors, resulting in a cumulative sensitivity of 39%. Six of these seven studies included controls with a range in specificity from 81% (Ha, Kaplan, & Foley, 1984) to 100% (Robbins et al., 1983). Altogether, 163 adolescents were identified by Poznanski and Mokros (1989) as valid controls; of these, 139 were cortisol suppressors, for a cumulative specificity of 85%. Poznanski and Mokros reported that an analysis of these data showed a significant association between dichotomized DST results and depression diagnosis. In comparison to both child and adult data, the sensitivity of the DST among adolescent major depressives was lower; the specificity was higher than for children and comparable to what has been reported for adults.

Growth Hormone Secretion

Two studies have examined growth hormone secretion in adolescents. Elevated growth hormone secretion during sleep has been reported. In a study of nine adolescent depressives with matched controls, depressives were found to have elevated secretion during sleep (Kutcher et al., 1988), a pattern also identified in depressed children (Puig-Antich et al., in press). In a recent study, Ryan et al. (1988) found significant hyposecretion of growth hormone in response to a single dose of desipramine. Interestingly, a sizable proportion of effect variance was attributable to the presence of suicidal behavior during the depressive episode, a result that parallels findings with suicidal adults.

Sleep Studies

Depressed adults exhibit a number of abnormalities in sleep parameters, including abnormalities in rapid eye movement (REM), sleep stages (particularly decreased REM latency and increased REM density), and abnormalities in sleep architecture. The sensitivity and specificity of sleep parameters, as markers for cases of depression, have been found superior to the dexamethasone suppression test. In addition, it appears that changes in certain REM parameters following an initial dose of antidepressant medication may predict treatment response (Fawcett & Kravitz, 1985). Given these findings, it is surprising how few studies of sleep parameters among adolescent depressives have been reported.

Appelboom-Fondu, Kerkhofs and Menlewicz (1988) found that adolescents with major depressive disorders, when compared to adolescents with minor depression and normal controls, experienced reduced sleep efficiency and greater awakening. Lahmeyer et al. (1983) studied 13 adolescents between the ages of 11 and 19 years who met criteria for DSM-III unipolar depression and a control group of 13 adolescents matched by sex and age. The depressed group failed to differ from controls on various measures of sleep architecture associated with depression in adults, but did differ in REM latency and REM density. The depressed subjects evidenced shortened REM latency and increased REM density, although the REM latency was found to be correlated with age rather than severity of depression.

Treatment

Depressed adolescents are currently treated with a variety of approaches, including psychodynamic individual therapy, family therapy, social skills training, and cognitive therapy. Psychopharmacological interventions are becoming increasingly more common. Yet, within this vast armamentarium of treatment modalities, there is a clear and disturbing lack of knowledge as to what is effective and, among effective approaches, which is the best treatment for what specific types(s) of depression. As with other areas of research of affective disorders in youth, investigation of the treatment of adolescents, relative to prepubertal children, has been under-represented (Campbell & Spencer, 1988).

Psychotherapy

Many studies have evaluated the efficacy of psychotherapy in children and adolescents.

These were reviewed in two meta-analytic studies (Casey & Berman, 1985; Weitz, Weiss, Alicke, & Klotz, 1987; also see Reinecke, Chapter 16 of this volume). However, only three studies have specifically evaluated treatment of depression, and two of these focused on children. These studies identified subjects on the basis of cutoff scores on self-report measures which, as pointed out earlier, may result in considerable misclassification. Thus, a study of carefully diagnosed affectively disordered adolescents has not been conducted to date. In the only study of adolescents we are aware of, Reynolds and Coats (1986) compared cognitive-behavioral therapy and relaxation training to waiting-list controls in the treatment of 30 depressed adolescents identified by scores on three self-report depression measures originally administered to a sample of 800 children selected from the general population. Subjects in the two therapeutic conditions received 10 highly structured sessions over a 5-week period. In contrast to scores for waiting-list controls, depressed subjects showed a significant decline in their depression scores at posttreatment for both treatment conditions, although no difference was noted between treatment conditions. Differences between the treated and untreated groups were still evident at a 5-week follow-up after termination of treatment.

Pharmacotherapy

The effectiveness of antidepressant agents in depressed adults, the recognition of the phenomenological similarity between adults and children, plus the presence of positive affective disorder histories in families of depressed children have led to the increased adoption of pharmacological treatment strategies for children and adolescents, despite the lack of clear evidence of their utility. Clinical efficiency of tricyclic antidepressants has been reported in a number of open trial studies with both children and adolescents. In children, the strongest substantiation of clinical efficiency has come from studies of dose/plasma levels, although reports for adolescents (Ryan et al., 1986) show no relation. In the only double-blind placebo control study of tricyclic antidepressants among adolescents, Kramer and Feiguine (1981) found no significant advantage of a fixed dose of amitriptyline over placebo. The meager state of evidence supporting the efficacy of pharmacotherapy for youthful depression is surprising, given the phenomenological similarity between children and adults and the results of neuroendocrine studies of children and adolescents (Campbell & Spencer, 1988). Two reports indicate that adolescents who fail to respond to antidepressants do subsequently respond to monoamine oxidase inhibitors (Ryan et al., 1988; Ryan & Puig-Antich, 1987), and there is one report of successful response to lithium augmentation by nonbipolar adolescents who showed no response to antidepressants alone (Ryan & Puig-Antich, 1987). In general, however, controlled studies are lacking in this area. Given the potential complications associated with these psychopharmacological agents, one might conclude their utility remains in question.

COMPLETED SUICIDE IN ADOLESCENCE

Many people find it difficult to think about affective disorders as entities associated with serious impairment or debilitation. Many assume the experience of a person with major depression is not much different from the universal, tolerable experience of transient sadness. Another reason is that there is usually little physical evidence of depressive disorder (e.g., no bleeding, no inability to walk, no high bacteria counts). A third reason is that the lay public tends to assume that one can always avert or shrug off depressive disorder by dint of personal effort (e.g., by "whistling a happy tune," maintaining a "stiff upper lip," or discussing one's problems with family and friends). These misperceptions are compounded by the fact that there is no direct correlation between the severity of a depressive illness state and the degree of impairment manifested by the affected individual (Weissman & Paykel, 1974). Thus, one can be extremely ill with depression, but function relatively well; or one can be mildly depressed but show marked social, occupational, or school impairment. One indicator of the seriousness of major affective disorder is the fact that about 15% of all depressed patients eventually die by suicide (Miles, 1977). This figure does not include the greatly elevated incidence of physical and psychological wounds associated with nonlethal suicide attempts among depressed persons.

There are many different pathways to the endpoint of death by suicide. Completed suicide is almost always associated with the presence of a psychiatric disorder. Yet, most persons affected by the psychiatric disorders commonly associated with a suicidal death (i.e., major depression, alcoholism, and schizophrenia) never die by suicide and never make a suicide attempt. One must conclude that major affective disorders are not by themselves the cause of or explanation for suicide, but are almost always one critical factor in the suicide equation.

Completed Suicide, Attempted Suicide, and Life-Endangering Behavior

Although the remainder of this chapter focuses on the phenomenon of suicide completion by adolescents, the relationship of attempted (nonfatal) suicide to completed suicide should be briefly discussed. Dahlgren (1945) and Stengel (1964) were the first to argue that attempted and completed suicide are essentially different phenomena occurring in different but overlapping populations. Two types of evidence will suffice to underline the point. First, all large-sample studies of consecutive cases of suicide in a selected geographical area consistently show that a slight majority (about 60%) of all completers had never made a prior suicide attempt in their lifetime. Second, all long-term follow-up studies of patients who attempted suicide consistently show that only 7% to 10% ever go on to die by suicide. Linehan (1986) reviewed evidence showing that those who complete suicide and those who make nonfatal attempts are more different than alike, and documented the heterogeneity of the suicide-attempting population in a manner that should discourage future investigators from lumping different kinds of attempters together in monolithic samples.

There has been considerable speculation about a continuum of suicidal behavior, ranging from overt and conscious suicidal acts to subtle and perhaps unconscious examples of risk-taking or life-threatening behavior (e.g., illicit drug use, anorexia nervosa, use of guns and knives), but there has been little empirical evidence to support this perspective. Recently, Clark, Sommerfeldt, Schwartz, Hedeker, & Watel (in press) developed an inventory of physically dangerous behaviors with health- or life-endangering implications, and administered the inventory to a large sample of adolescents (264 psychiatric inpatients and 742 "normal" high school students) along with measures of depression severity (the Beck Depression Inventory) and history of suicide attempts. Three dimensions of physically reckless behavior emerged from a dichotomous full-information factor analysis of item response: (a) an interest in weapons and military dangers; (b) an interest in dangerous driving, almost always in the context of alcohol and drug use; and (c) an interest in cigarette smoking and "bad company." The first two dimensions showed no significant association with depression severity scores, patient status, diagnosis, or history of suicidal behavior. The third factor was associated with inpatient status and a history of suicide attempts. All three recklessness factors shared a significant positive relationship with histories of alcoholism and drug abuse/dependence. Perhaps the substance abuse implicit in the types of adolescent recklessness described here helps explain the enduring clinical impression that adolescent recklessness and suicidal tendencies are interrelated: about 15% of those treated for substance abuse ultimately die by suicide (Miles, 1977).

Epidemiology

2,245 adolescents die by suicide in the United States every year (National Center for Health Statistics, 1992). The suicide rate for older adolescents (i.e., 15 to 19 years old) has quadrupled between 1955 and 1988, reaching a peak in 1988 of 11.3 suicides per 100,000 adolescents per year. The suicide rate for the entire group aged 15 to 24 years reached its lowest point in this century during the 1940s and 1950s. Between 1955 and 1977, the youth suicide rate more than trebled, from 4.1 per 100,000 per year to 13.6 per 100,000 per year. Since this 1977 peak, youth suicide rates have hovered between 11.9 and 13.3 per 100,000 per year. The rate was 13.3 per 100,000 in 1988, the most recent year for which statistics are available (Fingerhut & Kleinman, 1988; National Center for Health Statistics, 1988, 1989). For context, it is important to note that: (a) the suicide rate for adults between the ages of 30 and 60 (15 to 16 per 100,000 per year) is consistently higher than recent youth suicide rate peaks; (b) the adult suicide rate has remained relatively level for the past 50 years, except for a modest decrease during World War II; and (c) the suicide rate for adults over the age of 65 years decreased sharply between the late 1930s and 1980, from almost 45 per 100,000 to 19 per 100,000. For the past decade, suicide has been the second or third leading cause of death for persons between ages 15 and 34. The leading cause of death has been accidental injury (preponderantly motor vehicle fatalities), followed at some distance by either suicide or homicide, depending on the year. Thus, these three types of violent death account for more than 75% of all youthful deaths in the United States each year (Centers for Disease Control, 1985).

Why did the adolescent suicide rate rise so steeply between 1955 and 1988? One might just as well ask why the elderly suicide rate dropped by a factor of 2.5 during an equivalent period. There are several competing epidemiological theories. Those focusing on "cohort/period effects" point to the rising incidence of affective disorder and substance use disorders, with earlier ages of onset, among the post-World War II "baby-boom" generation (Klerman, 1987; Murphy & Wetzel, 1980). Holinger and his colleagues, on the other hand, have shown that, as the fraction of the U.S. adult population in the age bracket of 15 to 24 years grows larger, the suicide rate for that group grows larger; but as the fraction in the older adult age bracket grows larger, the suicide rate for that group decreases (Holinger, 1987; Holinger & Offer, 1986). As a result, Holinger's model made specific predictions about suicide rates by age cohort for the next several decades: as the youthful sector of the population shrinks in the post-baby boom era, youth suicide rates will drop, and as the older adult sector of the population swells in the last years of this century, elderly suicide rates will also drop. From the point of initial predictions (1977–1978) through 1989, however, youth suicide rates have remained level or edged upward and elderly suicide rates have not shown any signs of decreasing (Fingerhut & Kleinman, 1988; National Center for Health Statistics, 1992).

Demographic Correlates

Within the adolescent years, the suicide rate increases with increasing age. Prepubertal and young adolescent children may be less vulnerable to suicide by virtue of their cognitive immaturity, which makes it more difficult for them to plan and implement lethal attempts. The suicide rate for boys is almost four times higher than for girls, and the suicide rate for White adolescents is about twice that for Black or Hispanic adolescents. The only U.S. minority groups evidencing a suicide rate higher than that for the White majority are some specific Native American tribes. The predominant methods of suicide used by U.S. adolescents are firearms (about 60% of cases for males and females alike) and hanging (20% of cases for males, 10% for females) (Shaffer & Fisher, 1981).

In a record review study of 100 adolescents who died by suicide in one populous county over a 25-month period, Grossman and colleagues (unpublished) reported that eight of the suicide victims had a parent in the law enforcement profession and eleven had a parent in the health professions (four had a physician parent, seven had a nurse parent). There are no reliable estimates of how many parents of living teenagers in that county work in law enforcement or in health care, but a suspicion is raised that both groups are overrepresented in this adolescent suicide sample. Of the eight suicide victims from law enforcement families, seven used their parents' service revolver to kill themselves. As a group, the children of law enforcement officers used firearms to kill themselves significantly more often than the remainder of the suicide victims.

Guns and Increased Suicide

Boyd and Moscicki (1986) showed that, between 1933 and 1982, the rate of "suicide by firearms" for those between 15 and 24 years old increased by 139%, while the corresponding rate for "suicide by all other means" increased by only 32%. The relatively dramatic increase in the "suicide by firearms" rate began in 1970 and is most apparent for males. The investigators also showed that, although the numbers of civilian firearms imported and exported have remained constant since 1969, domestic production of firearms has increased sharply. This has culminated in a 47% increase in the number of guns per U.S. citizen, so that by 1979 there were 75 guns in civilian hands for every 100 Americans. Estimates of the number of U.S. families owning firearms remained constant at about 50% for the period from 1959 to 1977, so the findings suggest that gun-owning households are accumulating larger numbers of guns. Boyd suggested that the increasing availability of firearms contributes to the increasing rate of youthful suicide.

Does the extraordinary availability of firearms in the United States augment youth suicide rates? Some argue that it does; others argue that those intent on suicide would simply switch to another method, resulting in no net change in numbers. There are no empirical studies that would help one estimate the potential life-saving benefits of increased gun controls, but an epidemiological study by Kellerman and Reay (1986) highlighted the extent of the problem. The investigators reviewed all firearms deaths occurring in one populous county for a 6-year period and identified cases occurring inside a home or dwelling where the firearm in question had been kept (398 cases, or 54% of all firearms deaths). When they classified each of these 398 cases according to the circumstances of the death, 2% were examples of homicide in self-protection, 3% were ruled "accidental," 10% were cases of criminal homicide, and the great majority (84%) were instances of suicide. Kellerman and Reay concluded that people keep guns in their home for self-protection, but that these same guns are used for suicide almost 40 times more often than they are used for self-protection.

Sloan, Rivera, Reay, Ferris, and Kellerman (1990) examined two adjacent metropolitan areas that are socioeconomically similar but have different policies about gun ownership, to estimate the impact of stricter handgun controls on local suicide rates. The two urban areas under scrutiny were King County, Washington, and Vancouver, British Columbia. In King County, there is a 7-day waiting period before a handgun may be purchased for use at home, and a 30-day period before a permit can be issued to carry a handgun as a concealed weapon in public. In Vancouver, handguns cannot be purchased for self-protection and concealed weapons cannot be carried in public. A comparison of sex- and age-adjusted suicide rates showed no significant differences between the two areas for the years 1985 through 1987, even though the rate of suicide by handgun was 5.7 times higher in King County than in Vancouver (rates of suicide by rifle or shotgun did not differ between the two areas). In the group aged 15 to 24 years, however, the rate of suicide by handgun was 1.4 times higher in King County than in Vancouver; this difference was almost entirely due to a higher rate (9.6 times) of suicide by handgun. The authors concluded that stricter handgun control measures might reduce the suicide rate for persons aged 15 to 24 years old, but would probably not result in a decrease in the overall suicide rate for all age groups combined. Sloan et al. (1990) speculated that the relationship between handgun availability and suicide rates is particularly relevant to adolescent suicide. They believe that youthful suicides capitalize on opportunity or impulse to a greater extent. (See Appendix.)

Psycho-Social Factors

Three factors often cited in regard to adolescent suicide are peer influence via cluster suicides, family history of suicide, and stress buildup.

Clusters and Pseudoclusters

A body of studies demonstrate that adolescent (but not adult) suicide rates increase significantly in the week following newspaper or television coverage of any suicide-related account, provided that the coverage is intense (i.e., front-page newspaper stories, several network evening news programs) and repeated for several days in a row (Kessler, Downey, Stipp, & Milavasky, 1989; Phillips, 1974; Phillips & Carstensen, 1986, 1988). This kind of obituary coverage is generally reserved for celebrities; examples in recent decades are Marilyn Monroe and the comedian Freddie Prinz. The precise mechanism by which contagion or imitation is facilitated remains to be described. There is considerable controversy about whether fictional made-for-TV movies about suicide, generally developed with the help of "expert" consultants and intended to prevent suicides in an educational manner, spur the same kind of imitation (Gould & Shaffer, 1986). Replication studies have generally failed to show their finding that television movies are associated with increased numbers of suicides, but none of these has retested Gould and Shaffer's observation of increased numbers of nonfatal suicide attempts following the airing of TV movies (Berman, 1988; Gould, Shaffer, & Kleinman, 1988; Phillips & Paight, 1987).

Three to six adolescent deaths by suicide in close geographic proximity, within the span of a few months, occur from time to time in any large population and, occasionally, in a small or geographically isolated population. School districts or townships intermittently become aware that two or more youthful suicides have occurred within a relatively short period of time, often accompanied by other cases of accidental deaths, suicide attempts, threats, and hospitalizations (Centers for Disease Control, 1988; Robbins & Conroy, 1983). In such situations, however, there is rarely any resource to fall back on for epidemiological ascertainment, because there is no common or shared definition of suicide clusters in the United States. Thus, there is a serious danger that those interested in studying the psychological mechanism at work in cluster suicides will spend previous energy, time, and research dollars examining the dynamics of pseudoclusters, because there is no scientific method for distinguishing between outbreaks that occur by chance (given the increasing base rate of adolescent suicide) and true clusters.

Using time–space clustering techniques, Gould, Wallenstein, and Kleinman (1990) found that 1% to 2% of all adolescent suicides in the United States during the period 1978 to 1984 may be attributed to cluster phenomena, but these techniques do not permit the investigator to determine whether specific, isolated outbreaks represent cluster phenomena. Gibbons, Clark, and Fawcett (in press) recently introduced a "Poisson mixture model" for assessing potential clusters of adolescent suicide, which can be applied to specific geopolitical units (i.e., a county, a school district, a hospital, a military base, or a Native American reservation). Using this model, they examined the monthly incidence rates of adolescent suicide for one large and populous U.S. county over the past 11 years and found no evidence of clustering, despite the fact that several clusters had been alleged by clinicians and the media during this period. They also demonstrated that as many as eight suicides could (occasionally) occur within that county in a single month by chance alone.

Brent et al. (1989) recently described a flurry of suicidal behavior occurring within a three-week period at a public high school, encompassing two deaths by suicide, seven suicide attempts, two suicidal gestures, six suicide threats, and 15 students with serious suicidal ideation. The investigators screened the entire student body during the second and third weeks of the cluster, to identify students experiencing difficulty. Of the students who were actively suicidal in the wake of the cluster, 47% were not identified by systematic screening, despite the fact that they sought treatment in medical or psychiatric facilities. Brent found that 75% of all actively suicidal students had a history of at least one major psychiatric disorder predating the cluster, and 62% of these had a history of affective disorder. Students who developed suicidal tendencies after the beginning of the cluster were likely to evidence a prior history of suicidal tendencies and a current episode of major depression. Close friends of suicide victims and those who attended the funerals of the suicide victims, on the other hand, were not more likely to evidence suicidal reactions than their classmates. Close friends of suicide victims who did develop suicidal tendencies were less likely to have any psychiatric history than nonfriends who developed suicidal tendencies. Although the presence of a major depressive disorder identified students vulnerable to suicidal tendencies in reaction to the suicidal behavior of other students, close involvement with the suicide victim (by virtue of a friendship or funeral attendance) did not seem to contribute.

Family History of Suicide

Suicides appear to cluster in some biological families (Egeland & Sussex, 1985; Farberow & Simon, 1969; Tsuang, 1983), but there are a number of mechanisms that might explain this phenomenon in addition to that of genetics (Wender et al., 1986). For example, Pitts and Winokur (1964) showed that 68% of 37 psychiatric inpatients with a family history of suicide had an affective disorder, and Roy (1983) showed that, of 243 psychiatric inpatients with a family history of suicide, 56% had a current primary depressive disorder and 84% had a history of major depressive disorder. These findings suggest the possibility that family members of a suicide victim are at greater risk for suicide because a genetic predisposition for *specific mental disorders* (e.g., mood disorders) runs in the family, and the latter predisposition is what raises the risk for suicide. This position is supported by a report from the NIMH Collaborative Study (Scheftner et al., 1988). Among 955 affectively disordered psychiatric patients and their 5,042 relatives aged 18 years and over, no association was observed between completed or attempted suicide in relatives and completed suicide by patients during a 5-year follow-up. The lack of any association between familial and patient suicide may be attributable to the fact that all the patients shared a history of major affective disorder; that is, once a background of affective disorder is common to all subjects, any unique relationship between familial and patient suicide disappears.

To reconcile the differences between their findings and those of previous studies, Scheftner et al. 1988) pointed out that their results were based on a 5-year follow-up study of the patients, while previous studies reporting a relationship between patient death by suicide and positive family history of suicide had been based on 12 or more years of follow-up (usually more than 30 years). Shorter follow-up periods mean that the average age of the first-degree relatives is younger, so the pool of relatives has necessarily traversed fewer years at risk for attempting or completing suicide. The implication is that, after one or two more decades pass, the cumulative pattern of deaths by suicide in the pool of patients and relatives defining Scheftner's sample may eventually yield a positive relationship. However, because the clinician rarely has 29 or 30 years of prospective information about the patient and the patient's family tree, Scheftner and colleagues doubt there is any clinical application to findings even if a positive relationship could eventually be demonstrated.

Psychosocial Stress

Although the part that acute life stress plays in completed adolescent suicide has not yet been addressed with adequate comparisons, with adequate instruments for assessing acute stressors, or with good control over the problem of informant memory decay with time (interviews typically take place weeks to months after the suicide event), it is an area deserving of careful attention and study. It is important to remember that the great majority of persons who die by suicide are in the midst of an episode of major mental disorder; these disorders are associated with a variety of severe stressors in the absence of a suicide event. Sometimes, the stressors play a precipitating role in the emergence of a psychopathological episode; or, the stressors are manifestations of symptomatic impairment or sequelae of the psychopathological process. One study of adult patients has shown, for example, that acutely depressed patients who died by suicide were not under more stress than other acutely depressed patients, whether that stress was defined objectively by the clinician or subjectively by the patient (Fawcett et al., 1987).

Contributions from Psychological Autopsy Studies

Psychological autopsy studies are a relatively unknown and yet quite useful way of understanding adolescent suicide and its correlates. This section focuses on this body of literature in some detail, to help integrate the epidemiologic and correlating factors literature. The first formal psychological autopsy study of completed suicide was reported by Robins, Murphy, Wilkinson, Gassner, and Kayes in 1959. The psychological autopsy method involves selecting a geographical unit (usually a county) and a time period for study, and then identifying all consecutive cases of completed suicide within that unit and that time frame. Knowledgeable surviving family members (as many as possible) of the suicide victim are interviewed using structured protocols. The goal is to reconstruct the psychological and psychiatric state of mind and the psychosocial situation of the suicide victim for a period of weeks to months preceding the death. Despite the confounds of informant bereavement, memory decay, and large discrepancies between informant accounts, this method can be quite helpful (Brent, 1989; Cowles, 1988).

Findings from adult psychological autopsy studies published in the United States, England, and Sweden show that 93% to 95% of persons who die by suicide met objective criteria for a mental disorder in the weeks preceding death. The most commonly associated disorders are major depression, alcohol and other substance abuse, and schizophrenia. Conversely, long-term follow-up mortality studies have consistently demonstrated that 15% of patients with major affective disorder, 15% of patients with alcoholism, and 10% of patients with schizophrenia ultimately die by suicide (Miles, 1977; Murphy, 1986). By comparison, only 1.4% of the U.S. general population dies by suicide each year. Thus, there is compelling evidence that suicide is rare in the absence of a major mental disorder.

Only four psychological autopsy studies of any size have examined completed suicide in adolescence. The major findings from these four (the Louisville, San Diego, Pittsburgh, and Gothenburg studies) are discussed in some detail below. Only the Louisville and Pittsburgh studies have employed comparison groups. None of the studies employed a comparison group of adolescents who died suddenly and violently (e.g., car-accident fatalities) to control for informant bereavement and memory decay.

Shafii and colleagues (Shafii, Carrigan, Whittinghill, & Derrick, 1985; Shafii, Steltz-Lenarsky, Derrick, Beckner, & Whittinghill, 1988) interviewed available family members, relatives, friends, teachers, counselors, ministers, and physicians for 20 to 24 (83%) of the persons aged 19 years or younger who died by suicide in Jefferson County, Kentucky, between 1980 and 1983. For a comparison group, they recruited 17 closest friends of the suicide victims, implicitly controlling for age, sex, race, education, socioeconomic status, and religious background. They found that suicide victims were more likely to evidence two or more mental disorders, usually a mood disorder and substance abuse. However, this may be an underestimate of differences because close friends of suicide victims show high rates of psychopathology and suicidal tendencies.

The first report on a large series of consecutive youthful suicides was from San Diego County for the years 1981 to 1983 (Fowler, Rich, & Young, 1986; Rich, Young, & Fowler, 1986). The investigators identified 133 consecutive cases of suicide by individuals younger than age 30. They conducted structured interviews with available family members, acquaintances, employers, and physicians. Of the sample, 53% evidenced a substance abuse disorder at the time of death; all but two of these substance abusers met DSM-III criteria for drug abuse. A relatively smaller proportion (39%) evidenced a mood disorder, and 16% evidenced major depression and a concomitant diagnosis of substance abuse. However, only 43% of the subjects were under age 20. Rich and colleagues concluded that, for those under age 30, completed suicide is associated with drug abuse more often than with any other mental disorder.

They further suggested that profiles of adult suicides developed over the past three decades do not describe youthful suicides well. Until the 1980s, base prevalence rates for drug abuse were much lower than those for the depressive disorders and alcoholism. Perhaps the association of suicide mortality with drug abuse had been masked in the past by the low rate of drug abuse, only to emerge more clearly in the study by Fowler, Rich, and Young (1986) because of its recency and because it is the first large-scale youth study. Shaffer (informal communication) has indicated that the substance abuse rate in his ongoing study of adolescent suicide victims in the New York City area is also quite high.

In the Pittsburgh study, Brent and colleagues used the psychological autopsy method to compare 27 consecutive adolescent suicide deaths in three Pennsylvania counties between 1984 and 1986 with 56 adolescents admitted to an inpatient psychiatric unit for suicidal attempts or ideation (Brent et al., 1988; Brent, Perper, & Allman, 1987). Brent's group typically interviewed two informants for each case: a parent and a peer or sibling for each suicide victim, and a parent and the patient for each inpatient. As structured interviews, they used the youth version of the SADS (Orvaschel & Puig-Antich, 1986) and a family history interview.

In five important ways, the adolescent victims differed from inpatients. The suicide victims were more likely to evidence a bipolar disorder (i.e., Major Depression and mania or hypomania) or a major affective disorder with a concomitant nonaffective disorder (e.g., anxiety disorder, conduct disorder), and to have guns in their homes. They were less likely to have had any contact with a mental health professional and to have been engaged in conflict with their parents. A third of those who died by suicide were legally intoxicated at the time of their death. Although 83% of suicide completers talked about their suicidal state of mind with others within a week of their death, half of those who communicated their intentions did so only to siblings or friends.

In both groups, 90% met criteria for at least one major psychiatric diagnosis, most commonly Major Depression. Their rates of alcohol and drug abuse disorders were similar. Twenty-two percent of the suicide victims had bipolar history. The two groups did not differ significantly by frequency of common precipitants (e.g., losses, disciplinary problems); history of mental illness prior to the current episode; history of suicidal threats, gestures, or attempts; family history of mental disorder or suicide; or frequency of exposure to models of suicide.

Brent and colleagues speculated that young persons with a major mood disorder and concomitant nonaffective disorder have a worse prognosis than peers with an uncomplicated mood disorder. Because the nonaffective disorder diverts attention from the mood disorder, these young persons are less likely to receive adequate treatment for the serious condition. In addition, the combination of affective and nonaffective disorders is more difficult to treat, more likely to lead to relapse, and associated with longer episodes. This may be particularly true when the mood disorder is bipolar. Only one-third of the adolescents who died by suicide in Brent's sample had ever seen a mental health professional; only 2 of the 27 suicide victims were receiving any psychological treatment close to the time of death; only 1 of the 6 bipolar patients had ever been diagnosed.

In a related study that examined coroners' records of adolescent suicide cases between 1960 and 1983, Brent et al. (1987) showed that (a) high blood-alcohol levels and suicide by firearms were strongly and positively correlated; (b) the "suicide by firearms" rate for youth increased faster than the corresponding rates for "suicide by other means," or for "accidental death by firearms"; (c) there was an increase (from 13% to 46%) in the incidence of positive blood-alcohol concentration findings among youthful suicide victims; (d) there was no change over time in the incidence of positive toxicology findings for drugs among youthful suicide victims (the rates of positive drug findings ranged between 10% and 17%); and (e) there was no increase in the proportion of suicide victims with symptoms of depression or with a history of mental health treatment. They concluded by hypothesizing that the epidemic increase in adolescent suicide may be the result of the increased prevalence of adolescent alcohol abuse. The precise role of alcohol in adolescent suicide and the processes of its influence remain unclear. Acute intoxication impairs judgment and sometimes promotes depression; each in turn may lower the threshold for suicidal behavior. Do suicide victims drink to lower their inhibitions and facilitate a planned suicide? Or does the fatal impulse emerge spontaneously during a drinking bout? These questions merit immediate consideration by researchers and clinicians.

Runeson (1989) identified all cases of suicide or death by undetermined causes in the population aged 15 to 29 years in Gothenburg, Sweden, between 1984 and 1987. There were 48 cases of suicide and 10 undetermined-cause deaths, which he reclassified as suicides. Face-to-face interviews were conducted, typically 9 weeks after the death, with at least one close relative (average of two, maximum of five) in all but one case. Sixteen percent of those who completed suicide were hospital inpatients, another 17% had received inpatient care, and another 10% had been in outpatient therapy within the most recent 6 months.

When Runeson classified the suicide victims by psychiatric diagnosis (more than one diagnosis was possible), 95% of the sample met criteria for an Axis I mental disorder and 34% met criteria for an Axis II personality disorder. Only one subject did not qualify for any diagnosis. The frequencies associated with the most prevalent diagnoses were: Major Depression 41%, Alcohol Use Disorder 31%, Borderline Personality Disorder 28%, Drug Use Disorder 16%, Schizophrenia 14%, and Adjustment Disorder with Depression Mood 12%. Of those with major depression, 17% also met criteria for Borderline Personality Disorder, and 12% of those with Major Depression were schizophrenic. There was virtually no overlap between the subsample with affective disorder and the substance-abusing subsample. Forty-eight percent of the substance-abusing subjects also met criteria for Borderline Personality Disorder. These two disorders were the most common coexisting Axis I and Axis II combination. In 52% of all cases, there was a positive family history for substance abuse. Runeson concluded that far too few suicide victims were receiving antidepressant medication for their Major Depression, particularly those with depression secondary to another disorder.

Considering the controversy about the relative parts that affective disorders and substance abuse play in adolescent suicide, it is important to note that there is little overlap in Runeson's sample between the 41% with Major Depression and the 47% with substance use disorders. The Swedish study dovetails with the San Diego study by Fowler et al. (1986) insofar as both reported high rates of substance abuse or dependence. Only 5% of Runeson's sample met criteria for bipolar affective disorder, compared to 22% of Brent's sample. Runeson reported a relatively low rate of concomitant affective and nonaffective disorders, unlike Brent and Shafii. Runeson and Brent both, however, emphasized how common it may be for parents and clinicians to overlook a secondary or concomitant diagnosis of Major Depression in a young person, and so fail to treat or undertreat depressive pathology posing a suicidal risk.

Preventing Suicides

Because accidental injury, homicide, and suicide are the three leading causes of death for adolescents, accounting for 75% of youthful deaths, there is a real likelihood that psychological and societal interventions can reduce the needless carnage. Whether programs will or should specifically target suicide or all three problems is unclear. Suicide prevention programs appear to attract persons who eventually die by suicide, but there is not yet any evidence that these programs have any direct effect on community suicide rates (Dew, Bromet, Brent, & Greenhouse, 1987). How else can our psychological knowledge be employed to reduce the numbers of adolescent deaths by suicide?

First, we must recognize that the existing knowledge base about suicide and suicidal behavior encompasses many gaps and holes, and offers only limited amounts of useful clinical information. Relatively little systematic study of adolescent suicide has occurred. It remains to be seen how much we can extrapolate from adult suicide studies to adolescents. Current epidemiological and nonspecific clinical profiles of adolescents at risk for suicide invariably classify too many as "high suicide risk" and miss a large percent of actual suicides. Available profiles do not help the clinician estimate whether a suicide is likely to occur in the next hour, the next day, the next week, the next month, or the next year, and current knowledge does not clarify what kinds of treatment interventions effectively reduce suicide risk. For all these reasons, continuing research is a necessary precondition for better intervention and prevention services.

Second, mental health professionals must take more responsibility for educating the general public about the existence and nature of mental disorders, and about the availability of efficacious treatment interventions for these disorders. Depressive illness, in particular, is probably not recognized by most laypersons as a distinct illness that can seriously compromise work and social functioning or lead to premature death. The layperson is particularly likely to deny the significance of an acute depressive illness when it appears in the context of readily identifiable life stress. The fact remains that 10% to 15% of patients treated for affective disorder, alcoholism, drug abuse/dependence, and schizophrenia will ultimately die by suicide. This markedly elevated risk of suicide applies to child and adolescent psychiatric patients as well as to adult patients (Kuperman, Black, & Burns, 1988). Despite these well-established facts, the evidence is that 95% of school-based adolescent suicide prevention programs in the United States report that their theoretical approach is patterned after the "stress model," wherein suicide is seen as a response to extreme stress, to which everyone is vulnerable (Garland, Shaffer, & Whittle, 1989). Only 4% subscribe to the view that suicide is typically the consequence of a mental disorder. In this way, school-based programs seem out of touch with current scientific knowledge.

Finally, policy efforts are needed—specifically, the relationship between gun availability and suicide rates in the United States deserves attention. No country in the world has a higher rate of suicide by firearms that the United

States. For the past 40 years, half the deaths by firearms in the United States each year have been attributable to suicide. In 1986, 64% of the men and 40% of the women who committed suicide shot themselves; similar percentages apply to cases of adolescent suicide. Although there is no evidence as yet of a direct causal relationship between gun availability and adolescent suicide, there are reasons for thinking that decisively restrictive gun control laws would reduce the adolescent (as well as the adult) suicide rate. By depriving persons in an acute suicidal crisis of a handy and lethal means for self-murder, and by introducing a greater time delay between the suicidal impulse and the identification of a suitable means for suicide, a proportion of those intent on suicide may outlive the crisis period and forego further attempts. Adolescents who complete suicide may be particularly prone to fluctuating suicidal intent and therefore to abandoning a suicidal decision once the storm of the acute suicidal crisis has passed.

APPENDIX

Loftin and colleagues (Loftin, McDowall, Wiersema, & Cottey, 1991) took advantage of a public experiment to estimate the potential effects of strict gun control legislation on local suicide rates. In 1976, the District of Columbia adopted one of the most restrictive handgun policies in the nation. Under the new law, the only citizens allowed to keep firearms were those who had already registered them under previous law, and who then re-registered them within 60 days of when the new law went into effect. After 60 days, all other handguns became illegal. Rifles and shotguns, however, could subsequently be registered if the applicant met specific criteria. The new law also required those owning registered guns to store them unloaded and disassembled, except for those using a gun to protect a place of business.

To examine the impact of the District of Columbia legislation on homicide and suicide rates, the investigators calculated four indices of death rates for the 1968 to 1987 period: the mean monthly number of gun-related homicides, the mean monthly number of gun-related suicides, the mean monthly number of homicides by other means, and the mean monthly number of suicides by other means. To test whether changes observed were specific to the District of Columbia (DC), the investigators calculated these four death rates separately for DC and for the surrounding metropolitan area (four counties in Virginia and two in Maryland). The 240-month observation period consisted of 105 months prior to the new, stricter gun control legislation and 135 months following. Thus the investigators could compare mean monthly totals before and after the law went into effect for an "interrupted time series analysis."

The results showed that both homicide and suicide rates by firearms decreased by about 25% after the new DC law went into effect. The adjacent counties showed no parallel decrease over the same time period. There was no compensatory increase in the rate of homicides or suicides by methods *other than guns* in the DC area—in fact, the rate of homicides and suicides by methods other than guns *dropped* slightly. Thus Loftin and colleagues conclude that the 1976 DC gun control legislation had the hoped-for and felicitous result: afterward, there were on average 47 fewer deaths by homicide or suicide each year in DC.

The investigators noted that the size and speed of the legislation effect is surprising, given the facts that: (a) basic social conditions were not altered, (b) those who had legally registered guns under previous law were permitted to keep them, and (c) of course guns continued to be available under less restrictive conditions in the counties immediately surrounding DC.

There is also data available from clinical studies suggesting that the availability of guns in homes has a direct impact on suicide risk. Brent and colleagues (Brent et al., 1991) studied consecutive cases of suicide by persons aged 19 years and younger in 28 western Pennsylvania counties during 1986, 1987, and 1988. Seventy-five percent of the 64 families contacted four months after the suicide consented to participate.

The investigators fashioned two comparison groups: adolescent psychiatric inpatients who were 13 to 19 years old and who had recently engaged in active suicidal behavior, and adolescent psychiatric inpatients who had *never* been suicidal (i.e., not even suicidal ideation with a plan or intent). These numbers allowed the investigators to match the 47 suicide completers to 47 "attempters" and 47 "psychiatric controls" for the analyses reported.

Brent and colleagues found that 69% of the completers and none of the attempters used guns to harm themselves. Eighty-five percent of the suicide victims who lived in homes where guns were stored used a gun to accomplish the suicide, but only eight percent of the suicide victims who lived in homes where no guns were stored used a gun to die. Guns were four times more likely to be stored in the homes of completers than attempters or psychiatric controls (handguns were five to six times more likely and long guns were three to four times more likely). More guns (handguns and long guns alike) were stored in the homes of suicide victims: an average of four guns were stored in the home of each completer, one in the home of each attempter, and two in the home of each psychiatric control. This difference persisted even after the effects of gender, county of residence, presence of a man in the household, history of inpatient treatment, and psychiatric diagnosis were taken into account.

Where both handguns and long guns were stored in the home of a suicide victim, the adolescent tended to choose the handgun, but 75% of the suicide victims who only had long guns available used a long gun to die. Nearly half of the firearms suicides in this series were attributable to long guns.

Guns can be stored under lock and key, separate from ammunition, together with ammunition, or loaded. For those homes storing at least one gun, there were no differences in the way guns were stored among the completers, attempters, or psychiatric controls. The way guns were stored had no impact on the likelihood that they would be used for suicide: the adolescent suicide victims were just as likely to access guns stored in a locked place and without ammunition as they were guns stored in an unlocked place and loaded.

Brent and colleagues concluded that "Good gun safety habits are not likely to be protective against suicide, insofar as firearms in the home are probably a risk factor for adolescent suicide, regardless of the manner of storage. Therefore, all guns must be removed from the home of an adolescent assessed to be at risk for suicide."

The problem of gun availability is not limited to parental ownership and storage in the home. The national school-based Youth Risk Behavior Survey (Centers for Disease Control, 1991) was designed to evaluate the prevalence of health-endangering behaviors among a representative sample of 11,631 U.S. students in grades nine through twelve from all 50 states, the District of Columbia, Puerto Rico, and the Virgin Islands. It was found that 20% of all students reported having carried a weapon in the past 30 days for self-protection. The weapons carried in order of frequency were knives or razors (55% of weapons), clubs (24%), and guns (21%). About 4% of all the high school students surveyed said they had recently carried a gun with them—usually a handgun—in the past 30 days. By extrapolation, this suggests that in any given month 525,800 U.S. high school students carry a gun on their person.

REFERENCES

Achenbach, T. M., & Edelbrock, C. S. (1984). Psychopathology of childhood. *Annual Review of Psychology, 35,* 227–256.

Albert, N., & Beck, A. T. (1975). Incidence of depression in early adolescence: A preliminary study. *Journal of Youth and Adolescence, 4,* 301–307.

American Psychiatric Association. (1987). *Diagnostic and statistical manual of mental disorders (3rd ed. rev.)*. Washington, DC: Author.

Anderson, J. D., Williams, S., McGee, R., & Silva, P. A. (1987). DSM-III disorders in preadolescent children. *Archives of General Psychiatry, 44,* 69–76.

Appelboom-Fondu, J., Kerkhofs, M., & Menlewicz, J. A. (1988). Depression in adolescents and young adults: Polysomnographic and neuroendocrine aspects. *Journal of Affective Disorders, 14,* 35–40.

Beardslee, W. R., Bemporad, J., Keller, M. B., & Klerman, G. L. (1983). Children of parents with a major affective disorder. *American Journal of Psychiatry, 140,* 825–844.

Beardslee, W. R., Keller, M. B., Lavori, P. W., Klerman, G. L., Dorer, D. J., & Samuelson, H. (1988). Psychiatric disorder in adolescent offspring of parents with affective disorder in a non-referred sample. *Journal of Affective Disorders, 15,* 313–322.

Beck, A. T. (1967). *Depression: Clinical, experimental, and theoretical aspects.* New York: Harper & Row.

Berman, A. L. (1988). Fictional depiction of suicide in television films and imitation effects. *American Journal of Psychiatry, 145,* 982–986.

Birelson, P. (1981). The validity of depressive disorder in childhood and development of a self-rating scale: A research report. *Journal of Child Psychology and Psychiatry, 22,* 73–88.

Boyd, J. H., & Moscicki, E. K. (1986). Firearms and youth suicide. *American Journal of Public Health, 76,* 1240–1242.

Brent, D. A. (1989). The psychological autopsy: Methodological considerations for the study of adolescent suicide. *Suicide and Life-Threatening Behavior, 19,* 43–57.

Brent, D. A., Kerr, M. M., Goldstein, C., Bozigar, J., Wartella, M., & Allan, M. J. (1989). An outbreak of suicide and suicidal behavior in a high school. *Journal of the American Academy of Child and Adolescent Psychiatry, 28,* 918–924.

Brent, D. A., Perper, J. A., & Allman, C. J. (1987). Alcohol, firearms, and suicide among youth. *Journal of the American Medical Association, 257,* 3369–3372.

Brent, D. A., Perper, J. A., Goldstein, C. E., Kolko, D. J., Allan, M. J., Allman, C. J., & Zelenak, J. P. (1988). Risk factors for adolescent suicide: A comparison of adolescent suicide victims with suicidal inpatients. *Archives of General Psychiatry, 45,* 581–588.

Brent, D. A., Perper, J. A., Allman, C. J., Moritz, G. M., Wartella, M. E., & Zelenak, J. P. (1991). The presence and accessibility of firearms in the homes of adolescent suicides: A case-control study. *Journal of the American Medical Association, 266,* 2989–2995.

Brown, G. W., Harris, T. O., & Bifulco, A. (1986). Long-term effects of early loss of parent. In M. Rutter, C. E. Izard, & P. B. Read (Eds.), *Depression in young people: Clinical and developmental perspectives* (pp. 251–290). New York: Guilford Press.

Campbell, M., & Spencer, E. K. (1988). Psychopharmacology in child and adolescent psychiatry: A review of the past five years. *Journal of the American Academy of Child and Adolescent Psychiatry, 27,* 269–279.

Casey, R. J., & Berman, J. S. (1985). The outcome of psychotherapy with children. *Psychological Bulletin, 98,* 388–400.

Centers for Disease Control (1985). *Suicide surveillance, summary: 1970–1980.* Atlanta, GA: U.S. Department of Health and Human Services.

Centers for Disease Control (1988). Cluster of suicides and suicide attempts—New Jersey. *Morbidity and Mortality Weekly Report, 37,* 213–216.

Christie, K. A., Burke, J. D., Regier, D. A., Rae, D. S., Boyd, J. H., & Locke, B. Z. (1988). Epidemiologic evidence for early onset of mental disorders and higher risk of drug abuse in young adults. *American Journal of Psychiatry, 145,* 971–975.

Cicchetti, D., & Schneider-Rosen, K. (Eds.) (1984). *Bringing child development to child depression.* New directions for child development, no. 26. San Francisco: Jossey-Bass.

Clark, D. C., Sommerfeldt, L., Schwarz, M., Hedeker, D., & Watel, L. (1990). Physical recklessness in adolescence: Trait or by-product of depressive/suicidal states? *Journal of Nervous and Mental Disease, 178,* 423–433.

Costello, A. J., & Dulcan, M. K. (1985). *DISC: Diagnostic Interview for Children.* Unpublished manuscript.

Cowles, K. V. (1988). Issues in qualitative research on sensitive topics. *Western Journal of Nursing Research, 10,* 163–179.

Csikszentmihalyi, M., & Larson, R. (1984). *Being adolescent: Conflict and growth in the teenage years.* New York: Basic Books.

Cytryn, L., & McKnew, D. H. (1974). Factors influencing the changing clinical expression of the depressive process in children. *American Journal of Psychiatry, 131,* 879–881.

Dahlgren, K. G. (1945). *On suicide and attempted suicide.* Lund, Sweden: A.-B. PH. Lindstedts University-Bokhandel.

Dew, M. A., Bromet, E. J., Brent, D., & Greenhouse, J. B. (1987). A quantitative literature review of the effectiveness of suicide prevention centers. *Journal of Consulting and Clinical Psychology, 55,* 239–244.

Deykin, E. Y., Levy, J. C., & Wells, V. (1987). Adolescent depression, alcohol and drug abuse. *American Journal of Public Health, 77,* 178–182.

Dwyer, J. T., & DeLong, G. R. (1987). A family history of twenty probands with childhood manic-depressive illness. *Journal of the American Academy of Child and Adolescent Psychiatry, 26,* 176–180.

Egeland, J. A., & Sussex, J. N. (1985). Suicide and family loading for affective disorders. *Journal of the American Medical Association, 254,* 915–918.

Evans, D. L., Nemeroff, C. B., Haggerty, G. G., & Pederson, C. A. (1987). Use of the dexamethasone suppression test with DSM criteria in psychiatrically hospitalized adolescents. *Psychoneuroendocrinology, 12,* 203–209.

Farberow, N. L., & Simon, M. D. (1960). Suicides in Los Angeles and Vienna—An intercultural study of two cities. *Public Health Reports, 84,* 389–402.

Fawcett, J., & Kravitz, H. (1985). New medical diagnostic procedures for depression. In E. E. Beckham & W. R. Leber (Eds.), *Handbook of depression: Treatment, assessment, and research* (pp. 445–513). Homewood, IL: Dorsey Press.

Fawcett, J., Scheftner, W. A., Clark, D. C., Hedeker, D., Gibbons, R. D., & Coryell, W. (1987). Clinical predictors of suicide inpatients with major affective disorders: A controlled prospective study. *American Journal of Psychiatry, 40,* 35–40.

Fingerhut, L. A., & Kleinman, J. C. (1988). Suicide rates for young people: Letter to the Editor. *Journal of the American Medical Association, 259,* 356.

Fowler, R. C., Rich, C. L., & Young, D. (1986). San Diego suicide study. II. Substance abuse in young cases. *Archives of General Psychiatry, 43,* 962–965.

Garland, A., Shaffer, D., & Whittle, B. (1989). A national survey of school-based, adolescent suicide prevention programs. *Journal of the American Academy of Child and Adolescent Psychiatry, 28,* 931–934.

Geller, B., Cooper, T. B., McCombs, H. G., Graham, D., & Wells, J. (in press). Double-blind placebo-controlled study of nortriptyline in depressed children using a "fixed plasma level" design. *Psychopharmacology Bulletin.*

Gibbons, R. D., Clark, D. C., & Fawcett, J. (1990). A statistical method for evaluating suicide clusters and implementing cluster surveillance. *American Journal of Epidemiology, 132* (Suppl.), S183–S191.

Gjerde, P., Block, J., & Block, J. (1988). Depressive symptoms and personality during late adolescence: Gender difference in the externalization–internalization of symptom expression. *Journal of Abnormal Psychology, 976,* 475–486.

Glaser, K. (1967). Masked depression in children and adolescents. *American Journal of Psychotherapy, 21,* 565–574.

Gould, M. S., & Shaffer, D. (1986). The impact of suicide in television movies: Evidence of imitation. *New England Journal of Medicine, 315,* 690–694.

Gould, M. S., Shaffer, D., & Kleinman, M. (1988). The impact of suicide in television movies: Replication and commentary. *Suicide and Life-Threatening Behavior, 18,* 90–99.

Gould, M. S., Wallenstein, S., & Kleinman, M. (1990). Time–space clustering of teenage suicide. *American Journal of Epidemiology, 131,* 71–78.

Ha, H., Kaplan, S., & Foley, C. (1984). The dexamethasone suppression test in adolescent psychiatric patients. *American Journal of Psychiatry, 141,* 421–423.

Hamilton, M. (1960). A rating scale for depression. *Journal of Neurosurgery and Psychiatry, 23,* 56–62.

Harter, S. (1983). Developmental perspectives on the self system. In E. M. Hetherington (Ed.), *Handbook of child psychology* (pp. 275–285). New York: Wiley.

Herjanic, B., & Reich, W. (1982). Development of a structured psychiatric interview for children: Agreement between child and parent on individual symptoms. *Journal of Abnormal Child Psychology, 10,* 307–324.

Holinger, P. C. (1987). *Violent deaths in the United States: An epidemiologic study of suicide, homicide, and accidents.* New York: Guilford Press.

Holinger, P. C., & Offer, D. (1986). Suicide, homicide, and accidents among adolescents: Trends and potential for prediction. *Advances in Adolescent Mental Health, 1,* 119–145.

Hsu, G. L., Molcan, K., Cashman, M. A., Lee, S., Lohr, J., & Hindmarsh, D. (1983). The dexamethasone suppression test in adolescent depression. *Journal of the American Academy of Child Psychiatry, 22,* 470–473.

Kandel, D. B., & Davies, M. (1982). Epidemiology of depressive mood in adolescence. *Archives of General Psychiatry, 39,* 1205–1212.

Kaplan, S. L., Hong, G. K., & Weinhold, C. (1984). Epidemiology of depressive symptomatology in adolescents. *Journal of the American Academy of Child and Adolescent Psychiatry, 23,* 91–98.

Kashani, J. H., Carlson, G. A., Beck, N. C., Hoeper, E. W., Corcoran, C. M., McAllister, J. A., Fallahi, C., Rosenberg, T. K., & Reid, J. C. (1987). Depression, depressive symptoms, and depressed mood among a community sample of adolescents. *American Journal of Psychiatry, 144,* 931–934.

Kashani, J. H., McGee, R. O., Clarkson, S. E., Anderson, J. C., Walton, L. A., Williams, S., Silva, P. A., Robins, A. J., Cytryn L., & McKnew, D. H. (1983). Depression in a sample of nine-year-old children. *Archives of General Psychiatry, 40,* 1216–1223.

Kaslow, N. J., Rehm, L. P., & Siegel, A. W. (1984). Social cognitive correlates of depression in children. *Journal of Abnormal Child Psychology, 12,* 605–620.

Keller, M. B., Beardslee, W., Lavori, P. W., Wunder, J., Dorer, D. L., & Samuelson, H. (1988). Course of major depression in non-referred adolescents: A retrospective study. *Journal of Affective Disorders, 15,* 235–243.

Kellerman, A. L., & Reay, D. T. (1986). Protection or peril? An analysis of firearm-related deaths in the home. *New England Journal of Medicine, 314,* 1557–1560.

Kessler, R. C., Downey, G., Stipp, H., & Milavasky, J. R. (1989). Network television news stories about suicide and short-term changes in total U.S. suicides. *Journal of Nervous and Mental Disease, 177,* 551–555.

Klein, D. N., Depue, R. A., & Slater, J. F. (1985). Cyclothymia in the adolescent offspring of parents with bipolar affective disorder. *Journal of Abnormal Psychology, 94,* 155–227.

Klerman, G. L. (1987). Clinical epidemiology of suicide. *Journal of Clinical Psychiatry, 48* (Suppl.), 33–38.

Klerman, G. L. (1988). The current age of youthful melancholia: Evidence for increase in depression among adolescents and young adults. *British Journal of Psychiatry, 152,* 4–14.

Kovacs, M. (1985a). The Children's Depression Inventory (CDI). *Psychopharmacology Bulletin, 21,* 991–994.

Kovacs, M. (1985b). The Interview Schedule for Children (ISC). *Psychopharmacology Bulletin, 21,* 991–994.

Kovacs, M. (1989). Affective disorders in children and adolescents. *American Psychologist, 44,* 209–215.

Kovacs, M., Feinberg, T. L., Crouse-Novak, M. A., Paulauskas, S. A., and Finkelstein, R. (1984). Depressive disorders in childhood: I. A longitudinal prospective study of characteristics and recovery. *Archives of General Psychiatry, 41,* 643–649.

Kovacs, M., & Gatsonis, C. (1989). Stability and change in childhood-onset depressive disorders: Longitudinal course as a diagnostic validator. In L. N. Robins & J. E. Barret (Eds.), *The validity of psychiatric diagnosis.* New York: Raven Press.

Kramer, A. D., & Feiguine, R. J. (1981). Clinical effects of amitriptyline in adolescent depression.

Journal of the American Academy of Child and Adolescent Psychiatry, 20, 636–644.

Kuperman, S., Black, D. W., & Burns, T. L. (1988). Excess mortality among formerly hospitalized child psychiatric patients. *Archives of General Psychiatry, 45,* 277–282.

Kutcher, S., Williamson, P., Silverberg, J., Marton, P., Malkin, D., & Malkin, A. (1988). Nocturnal growth hormone secretion in depressed adolescents. *Journal of the American Academy of Child and Adolescent Psychiatry, 27,* 751–754.

Lahmeyer, H. W., Poznanski, E. O., & Bellur, S. N. (1983). EEG sleep in depressed adolescents. *American Journal of Psychiatry, 140,* 1150–1153.

Lang, M., & Tisher, M. (1978). *Children's Depression Scale.* Melbourne: Australian Council for Educational Research.

Lefkowitz, M. M., & Burton, N. (1978). Childhood depression: A critique of the concept. *Psychological bulletin, 85,* 716–726.

Lefkowitz, M. M., & Tesiny, E. P. (1980). Assessment of childhood depression. *Journal of Consulting and Clinical Psychology, 48,* 43–50.

Linehan, M. (1986). Suicidal people: One population or two? In J. J. Mann & M. Stanley (Eds.), *Psychobiology of suicidal behavior* (pp. 16–30). New York: New York Academy of Sciences.

McGee, R., & Williams, S. (1988). Longitudinal study of depression in nine-year-old children. *Journal of the American Academy of Child and Adolescent Psychiatry, 27,* 342–348.

Mendelson, M. (1982). Psychodynamics of depression. In E. Paykel (Ed.), *Handbook of affective disorders* (pp. 140–161). New York: Guilford Press.

Miles, P. (1977). Conditions predisposing to suicide: A review. *Journal of Nervous and Mental Disease, 164,* 231–246.

Mitchell, J., McCauley, E., Burke, P. M., & Moos, S. J. (1988). Phenomenology of depression in children and adolescents. *Journal of the American Academy of Child and Adolescent Psychiatry, 27,* 12–20.

Murphy, G. E. (1986). Suicide and attempted suicide. In G. Winokur & P. Clayton (Eds.), *The medical basis of psychiatry* (pp. 562–579). Philadelphia: Saunders.

Murphy, G., & Wetzel, R. (1980). Suicide risk by birth cohort in the United States, 1949 to 1974. *Archives of General Psychiatry, 37,* 519–523.

National Center for Health Statistics. (1988). Advance report of final mortality statistics, 1986. *NCHS Monthly Vital Statistics Report, 37* (6) (Suppl.).

National Center for Health Statistics. (1989). Advance report of final mortality statistics, 1987. *NCHS Monthly Vital Statistics Report, 38* (5) (Suppl.).

National Center for Health Statistics. (1992). Advance report of final mortality statistics, 1989. *NCHS Monthly Vital Statistics Report, 40* (8) (Suppl. 2).

Orvaschel, H., & Puig-Antich, J. (1986). *Schedule for Affective Disorders and Schizophrenia for School-Age Children, Epidemiologic Version* (4th ed.). Unpublished manuscript. Pittsburgh, PA: Western Psychiatric Institute and Clinic.

Paton, S., Kessler, R., & Kandel, D. (1977). Depressive mood and adolescent illegal drug use: A longitudinal analysis. *Journal of Genetic Psychology, 131,* 267–289.

Phillips, D. P. (1974). The influence of suggestion on suicide: Substantive and theoretical implication of the Werther effect. *American Sociological Review, 39,* 340–354.

Phillips, D. P., & Carstensen, L. L. (1986). Clustering of teenage suicides after television news stories about suicide. *New England Journal of Medicine, 315,* 685–689.

Phillips, D. P., & Carstensen, L. L. (1988). The effect of suicide stories on various demographic groups, 1968–1985. *Suicide and Life-Threatening Behavior, 18,* 100–114.

Phillips, D. P., & Paight, D. J. (1987). The impact of televised movies about suicide: A replicative study. *New England Journal of Medicine, 317,* 809–811.

Pitts, F., & Winokur, G. (1964). Affective disorder: III. Diagnostic correlates and incidence of suicide. *Journal of Nervous and Mental Disease, 139,* 176–181.

Poznanski, E. O., & Mokros, H. B. (1989). *Mood disorders in children and adolescents: II. Biological markers, risk factors, longitudinal course and treatment.* Unpublished manuscript.

Poznanski, E. O., Freeman, L. N., & Mokros, H. B. (1985). Children's depression rating scale, revised. *Psychopharmacology Bulletin, 21*, 979–989.

Puig-Antich, J. (1982). Major Depression and conduct disorder in prepuberty. *Journal of the American Academy of Child Psychiatry, 21*, 118–128.

Puig-Antich, J. (1986). Psychobiological markers: Effects of age and puberty. In M. Rutter, C. E. Izard, & P. B. Reod (Eds.), *Depression in young people* (pp. 341–381). New York: Guilford Press.

Puig-Antich, J., Chambers, W. J., & Tabrizi, M. (1983). The clinical assessment of current depressive episodes in children and adolescents. Interviews with parents and children. In D. P. Cantwell & G. A. Carlson (Eds.), *Affective disorder in childhood and adolescence—an update* (pp. 157–179). New York: Spectrum.

Puig-Antich, J., & Gittelman, R. (1982). Depression in childhood and adolescence. In E.S. Paykel (Ed.), *Handbook of affective disorders* (pp. 379–392). New York: Guilford Press.

Puig-Antich, J., Goetz, R., Davies, M., Kaplan, T., Davies, S., Ostrow, L., Asnis, L., Twomey, J., Iyengar, S., Ryan, N. D. (1989). A controlled family history study of prepubertal major depressive disorder. *Archives of General Psychiatry, 46*, 406–416.

Reynolds, W. M. (1983). *Depression in adolescents: Measurement, epidemiology, and correlates.* Paper presented at the annual meeting of the National Association of School Psychologists, Detroit, MI.

Reynolds, W. M., & Coats, K. I. (1986). A comparison of cognitive behavioral therapy and relaxation training for the treatment of depression in adolescents. *Journal of Consulting and Clinical Psychology, 54*, 653–660.

Rich, C. L., Young, D., & Fowler, R. C. (1986). San Diego suicide study: I. Young vs. old subjects. *Archives of General Psychiatry, 43*, 577–582.

Rie, H. E. (1966). Depression in childhood: A survey of some pertinent contributions. *Journal of the American Academy of Child Psychiatry, 38*, 381–389.

Robbins, D. R., Alessi, N. E., Yanchysyn, G. W., & Colfer, M. V. (1983). The dexamethasone suppression test in psychiatrically hospitalized adolescents. *Journal of the American Academy of Child Psychiatry, 22*, 467–469.

Robbins, D. R., & Conroy, R. C. (1983). A cluster of adolescent suicide attempts: Is suicide contagious? *Journal of Adolescent Health Care, 3*, 253–255.

Robins, L. N., Helzer, J. E., Croughan, J., & Ratcliff, K. S. (1981). National Institute of Mental Health Diagnostic Interview Schedule: Its history, characteristics, and validity. *Archives of General Psychiatry, 38*, 381–389.

Robins, E., Murphy, G. E., Wilkinson, R. H., Gassner, S., & Kayes, J. (1959). Some clinical considerations in the prevention of suicide based on a study of 134 successful suicides. *American Journal of Public Health, 49*, 888–899.

Roy, A. (1983). Family history of suicide. *Archives of General Psychiatry, 26*, 971–974.

Runeson, B. (1989). Mental disorder in youth suicide: DSM-III-R Axes I and II. *Acta Psychiatrica Scandinavica, 79*, 490–497.

Rutter, M. (1986). The developmental psychopathology of depression: Issues and perspectives. In M. Rutter, C. E. Izard, & P. B. Read (Eds.), *Depression in young people: Clinical and developmental perspectives* (pp. 3–22). New York: Guilford Press.

Rutter, M., Izard, E. E., & Read, P. E. (Eds.) (1986). *Depression in young people: Clinical and developmental perspectives.* New York: Guilford Press.

Ryan, N. D., & Puig-Antich, J. (1987). Pharmacological treatment of adolescent psychiatric disorders. *Journal of Adolescent Health Care, 8*, 137–142.

Ryan, N. D., Puig-Antich, J., Ambrosini, P., Rabinovich, H., Robinson, D., Nelson, B., Iyengar, S., Twomey, J. (1987). The clinical picture of major depression in children and adolescents. *Archives of General Psychiatry, 44*, 854–861.

Ryan, N. D., Puig-Antich, J., Rabinovich, H., Ambrosini, P., Robinson, D., Nelson, B., & Novacenko, H. (1988). Growth hormone response to desmethylimipramine in depressed and suicidal adolescents. *Journal of Affective Disorders, 15*, 323–337.

Scheftner, W. A., Young, M. A., Endicott, J., Coryell, W., Fogg, L., Clark, D. C., & Fawcett, J. (1988).

Family history and five-year suicide risk. *British Journal of Psychiatry, 153,* 805–809.

Schoenbach, V. J., Kaplan, B. H., Wagner, E. H., Grimson, R. C., & Miller, F. T. (1983). Prevalence of self-reported depressive symptoms in young adolescents. *American Journal of Public Health, 73,* 1281–1287.

Seligman, M. E. P., and Peterson, C. (1986). A learned helplessness perspective on childhood depression: Theory and research. In M. Rutter, C. E. Izard, & P. B. Read (Eds.), *Depression in young people: Clinical and developmental perspectives* (pp. 223–249). New York: Guilford Press.

Shaffer, D., & Fisher, P. (1981). The epidemiology of suicide in children and young adolescents. *Journal of the American Academy of Child and Adolescent Psychiatry, 20,* 545–561.

Shafii, M., Carrigan, S., Whittinghill, J. R., & Derrick, A. (1985). Psychological autopsy of completed suicide in children and adolescents. *American Journal of Psychiatry, 142,* 1061–1064.

Shafii, M., Steltz-Lenarsky, J., Derrick, A. M., Beckner, C., & Whittinghill, J. R. (1988). Comorbidity of mental disorders in the postmortem diagnosis of completed suicide in children and adolescents. *Journal of Affective Disorders, 15,* 227–233.

Sloan, J. H., Rivara, F. P., Reay, D. T., Ferris, J. A. J., & Kellerman, A. L. (1990). Firearm regulations and rates of suicide: A comparison of two metropolitan areas. *New England Journal of Medicine, 322,* 369–373.

Stengel, E. (1964). *Suicide and attempted suicide.* Baltimore, MD: Penguin Books.

Strober, M., Green, J., & Carlson, G. (1981). Reliability of psychiatric diagnosis in hospitalized adolescents. *Archives of General Psychiatry, 38,* 141–145.

Strober, M., Morrell, W., Burroughs, J., Lampert, C., Danforth, H., & Freeman, R. (1988). A family study of bipolar I disorder in adolescence: Early onset of symptoms linked to increased familial loading and lithium resistance. *Journal of Affective Disorders, 15,* 255–268.

Teri, L. (1982). The use of the Beck Depression Inventory with adolescents. *Journal of Abnormal Child Psychology, 10,* 277–284.

Tolan, P. H., DeJesus, S., & Thomas, P. (1988). *Gender patterns in referral and mental health service use by adolescents.* Paper presented at the second biennial meeting of the Society for Research on Adolescence, Alexandria, VA.

Tsuang, M. T. (1983). Risk of suicide in the relatives of schizophrenics, manics, depressives, and controls. *American Journal of Clinical Psychiatry, 44,* 396–400.

Weissman, M. M., Gammon, G. D., John, K., Merikangas, K., Warner, V., Prusoff, B., Sholomskas, D. (1987). Children of depressed parents: Increased psychopathology and early onset of major depression. *Archives of General Psychiatry, 44,* 847–853.

Weissman, M., & Paykel, E. S. (1974). *The depressed woman: A study of social relationships.* Chicago: University of Chicago Press.

Wender, P. H., Kety, S. S., Rosenthal, D., Schulsinger, F., Ortmann, J., & Lunde, I. (1986). Psychiatric disorders in the biological and adoptive families of adopted individuals with affective disorders. *Archives of General Psychiatry, 43,* 923–929.

CHAPTER 15

Schizophrenia

JERRY F. WESTERMEYER

O time, thou must untangle this, not I,
It is too hard a knot for me t'untie.
William Shakespeare, *Twelfth Night*

INTRODUCTION

The timing, prognosis, and natural course of schizophrenia across the adult life cycle have suggested vital clues regarding its nature and treatment. Inherent in Kraepelin's "Dementia Praecox" (the first term coined for what is today known as schizophrenia) was the belief that the psychotic states, disordered thinking, and decline in functioning that characterize schizophrenia often became apparent in late adolescence or young adulthood (Kraepelin, 1919). "Dementia Praecox" implies a premature or early development of mental decline. Although schizophrenia may occur well into the life cycle, especially among women (Cohler & Ferrono, 1987), the clinical appearance of schizophrenia at the earliest stages of the adult life cycle has always been a distinguishing feature of this disorder.

This research was supported, in part, by Grant MH 26341 from the National Institute of Mental Health, and research grants from the John D. and Catherine T. MacArthur Foundation and the Irving B. Harris Foundation.

The purposes of this chapter are to explore the issues regarding the onset of schizophrenia in adolescence, to summarize the literature on prognosis and the natural course of schizophrenia across the adult life cycle, and to consider the implications of the timing and natural course of schizophrenia on treatment, etiology, and current social policy, especially for adolescents. In considering applied social policy, various types of therapies and community support programs for schizophrenia are presented, and current issues in planning services for individuals with schizophrenia are discussed.

SCHIZOPHRENIA: CURRENT CONCEPTS AND EPIDEMIOLOGICAL DATA

The precise cause and cure of schizophrenia are yet unknown. A life-cycle perspective of schizophrenia, with special emphasis on adolescence, may provide important information in understanding this disorder. As Gottesman (1989) suggested, a wealth of information for understanding a mental disorder is available from investigating its vital statistics, such as age of onset, gathered from epidemiological data.

There are many difficult problems in determining the vital statistics, such as the number and demographic characteristics, of individuals with schizophrenia. These problems include: (a) establishing criteria for schizophrenia; and (b) setting time frames of schizophrenia counts and determining the number of untreated schizophrenics.

A major shift in the definition of schizophrenia has occurred in recent years. The older conceptions (such as the DSM-II; American Psychiatric Association, 1968) of schizophrenia had their roots in the descriptive psychiatry of the 19th century. These concepts of schizophrenia did not contain explicit criteria; instead, they provided a general description that allowed considerable individual judgment in defining schizophrenia. For example, the DSM-II definition of schizophrenia is as follows:

. . . a group of disorders manifested by characteristic disturbances of thinking, mood and behavior. Disturbances in thinking are marked by alterations of concept formations which may lead to misinterpretations of reality and sometimes to delusions and hallucinations, which frequently appear psychologically self-protective. Corollary mood changes include ambivalent, constricted and inappropriate emotional responsiveness and loss of empathy with others. Behavior may be withdrawn, regressive and bizarre. (American Psychiatric Association, 1968)

It was noticed by various investigators that the definition of schizophrenia varied widely by geographical location, and that the European concept of schizophrenia appeared to be more narrow (classifying fewer patients as schizophrenic) than the American concept of schizophrenia (Professional Staff of the U.S.–U.K. Cross-National Project, 1974). In brief, critics maintained that schizophrenia could not be reliably rated, and that the same patients diagnosed schizophrenic in one location may be given a different diagnosis in another location.

To correct this and other problems, the more modern Research Diagnostic Criteria (RDC: Spitzer, Endicott, & Robins, 1978), DSM-III, and DSM-III-R (American Psychiatric Association, 1980, 1987) diagnostic systems established reliable exclusion and inclusion criteria for schizophrenia in the 1970s and 1980s. These new criteria (like those of the older description of the DSM-II) were primarily based on the assessments of symptoms at hospitalization, although the DSM-III also allowed for a multiaxial system to assess personality factors, medical status, prehospital adjustment, and precipitating stress. Inclusion criteria are identifiable behaviors or symptoms that a person must have to be diagnosed schizophrenic. The presence of typical "schizophrenic symptoms" such as hallucinations, delusions, and thought disorders provided the defining symptoms for inclusion into schizophrenics. Exclusion criteria are identifiable behaviors or symptoms that would remove persons from a schizophrenic classification.

Currently, there is no single defining symptom in the DSM-III-R inclusion criteria of schizophrenia. Rather, there are several different symptoms of importance, one or more of which must be present for a DSM-III-R diagnosis of schizophrenia. This is also true of the closely related Research Diagnostic Criteria (RDC: Spitzer, Endicott, & Robins, 1978). The minimum inclusion criteria for a DSM-III-R diagnosis of schizophrenia require the presence, among other features (e.g., impaired functioning), of the following severe psychotic or psychoticlike symptoms in category A, B, or C for at least one week (American Psychiatric Association, 1987):

A: Two of the following:
1. delusions (any),
2. hallucinations (any),
3. incoherence or marked loosening of associations,
4. catatonic behavior or
5. flat or grossly inappropriate affect.

B: Bizarre delusions.
C: Hallucinations (not depressed or elated).

In establishing *exclusion* criteria, the new diagnostic systems borrowed heavily from the prognostic literature on DSM-II schizophrenia.

For example, the presence of an affective syndrome, previously considered to mark "good prognosis" DSM-II schizophrenia, removed or excluded patients from schizophrenia under the new DSM-III-R and RDC criteria. Consequently, the DSM-III, RDC, and DSM-III-R *narrowed* the scope of schizophrenia and classified fewer patients as "schizophrenic" than the DSM-II, because a number of patients have an affective syndrome in combination with psychotic symptoms and are classified as nonschizophrenic by these new systems (Westermeyer & Harrow, 1984). The DSM-III-R, DSM-III, and RDC systems also *enlarged* the scope of other nonschizophrenic, psychotic disorders. Patients classified as schizophrenic by the DSM-II are now often classified as bipolar disorders, schizoaffective disorders, and psychotic depressive disorders by the new diagnostic systems. Proponents of these new systems maintain that the various mental disorders may now be reliably assessed.

A second problem in determining the epidemiological rate of schizophrenia involves various time frames for schizophrenic counts. Epidemiologists generally use *several* time frames for prevalence estimates (Gottesman & Shields, 1982). These include: (a) *point prevalence,* which includes those persons who meet the illness criteria at one point in time; (b) *period prevalence,* which includes those persons who meet the illness criteria for a specific time period (e.g., 1 month, 6 months, 1 year, etc.); (c) *lifetime prevalence,* which includes those people *now alive* who meet the illness criteria at any time during their life; and (d) *lifetime morbid risk,* which includes the lifetime prevalence rate above, an estimate of persons likely to develop the illness, and persons within a cohort with the illness who have died and cannot be counted.

The prevalence rates also may include an estimate of untreated cases, which is a major problem in epidemiology (Gottesman & Shields, 1982). Individuals may meet the illness criteria for a mental disorder and yet not be treated by hospitals or other service agencies, and so may be less likely than treated individuals to be counted by epidemiologists. Nevertheless, Gottesman and Shields pointed out that a large percentage of schizophrenics (80%) are eventually treated. This is a much higher rate of treatment than for most other mental disorders because of the severe symptoms associated with schizophrenia.

Because many individuals experience time-limited or episodic symptoms, the rates for the above time frames will vary. For example, many schizophrenics would not be included in point prevalence rates if they were not symptomatic at that particular point in time and could not give accurate information on past symptom episodes or treatment. Therefore, lifetime morbid risk or expectancy is the most inclusive or accurate time frame for assessing schizophrenic rates.

It has been difficult to determine the precise treated and untreated lifetime morbid expectancy of schizophrenia and other mental disorders. A recent landmark epidemiologic study, the NIMH Epidemiologic Catchment Area Program (ECA) found that the 1-month prevalence rate for schizophrenia was 1.5% (Regier et al., 1988). The ECA study employed a sample with a fivefold increase over previous American studies and utilized the Diagnostic Interview Schedule (DIS), a modern diagnostic questionnaire specifically designed for use by lay interviewers. However, the ECA study did not employ *exclusion* criteria for determining DSM-III rates of illness. Therefore, it is not surprising that the 1.5% 1-month prevalence rate for schizophrenia reported by the ECA study is slightly higher than the 1% schizophrenia prevalence rate reported by others (Gottesman & Shields, 1982). Currently, it is estimated that there are about 2.5 to 3 million schizophrenics in the United States.

For many individuals, the first onset of schizophrenia occurs in late adolescence or early adulthood. Indeed, DSM-III criteria, presented in 1980, eliminated from schizophrenia persons who had their first onset over age 45 (American Psychiatric Association, 1980). However, Cohler and Ferrono (1987), Gottesman and Shields (1982), and others have pointed out that first onset of schizophrenia is possible late in the adult life cycle. The DSM-III-R, the later modification of DSM-III, corrected the age criterion for schizophrenia; it now may occur at any point in the life cycle (American Psychiatric Association, 1987).

Although schizophrenia may occur throughout adulthood (and rare forms of childhood schizophrenia exist), the average age of onset in schizophrenia is about 21 to 28 years for males and about 26 to 33 years for females (depending on diagnosis and other factors). Those are the ages of first hospitalization for psychosis for schizophrenia; the actual onset age for both males and females is unknown at present and is a subject for further research.

CURRENT CONCEPTS ON THE ETIOLOGY OF SCHIZOPHRENIA

The precise cause, or etiology, of schizophrenia remains a mystery. Despite progress over the past few decades in identifying contributing factors, it is generally assumed that (as with most other mental disorders) numerous factors play a role in the etiology of schizophrenia.

Thus, current theories of schizophrenia are couched in diathesis-stress, vulnerability, or systems processes that share a common viewpoint in allowing a variety of genetic, biochemical, developmental, and sociocultural factors to be explored on the cause, course, and treatment of schizophrenia (Grinker & Westermeyer, 1984; Harrow & Marengo, 1986; Zubin & Spring, 1977). These theories suggest that there is a vulnerability to schizophrenia inherent in a proportion of the population. This vulnerability may be genetic or polygenetic in nature (Gottesman & Shields, 1982) and may be associated with the biochemistry of the brain in different ways. The biochemistry associated with schizophrenic abnormalities may implicate certain areas of the brain and/or the neurotransmitter dopamine (Carlsson, 1988; Weinberger, 1987; Weinberger, Berman, & Chase, 1988). This inherent or basic vulnerability to schizophrenia may be "triggered" by a stress associated with an event or a particular developmental phase such as adolescence.

Although the precise factors involved in the "vulnerability" and "triggering stress" may be quite varied and the interactions involved may be quite complicated, this general theoretical orientation has proven attractive to many because it would appear to accommodate both (a) the heterogeneity in schizophrenic symptoms at one point in time and (b) the considerable diversity observed across the course of schizophrenia. Research conducted to date on schizophrenia seems to indicate that there is no single cause to explain all forms of this complex disorder and that multiple factors enter into its nature and expression.

The diathesis-stress, vulnerability, or systems theories provide heuristic models that emphasize the area-separateness of various factors (e.g., genetic, biochemical, sociocultural, developmental) and the potential for the interaction of these diverse influences in complex ways. At this stage of our understanding, such models seem to offer the best approaches to the schizophrenia phenomenon. Thus, investigators from various disciplines may pursue their line of inquiry without a scientific reductionism or relativism impeding their research efforts.

Several types of factors (often biological in nature) may be investigated under the "vulnerability" category. To illustrate one viewpoint, Weinberger (1987) presented interesting hypotheses on psychosis and age of onset across the life cycle. He mapped the association of age to characteristics of psychopathology for various disorders, such as Alzheimer's disease and psychotic depressive disorders. In terms of schizophrenia, he noted:

The existence of a critical period of vulnerability for the expression of schizophreniform psychosis suggests that the neural systems mediating this behavior reach a functional peak during this period (i.e. late adolescence or early adulthood). This may relate to hormonal influences on central nervous systems physiology or, more simply, the natural course of the ontological development of psychosis-related systems. . . . It may also reflect developmental changes in systems that normally inhibit or modulate the psychosis-related system. (Weinberger, 1987, pp. 662–663)

In addition, research on thought disorder in schizophrenia suggests that deficits in the highest levels of thinking or executive mental powers are involved (Harrow & Quinlan, 1985). As noted by Weinberger (1987), it is at the earliest phases of adulthood, when the highest forms of metathought are coming on line in human cognitive abilities, that the severe mental disorder that often characterizes schizophrenia begins to manifest itself. The involvement of the highest levels of thinking in schizophrenia may implicate certain regions of the brain in this disorder (Benes, 1989; Weinberger, 1987).

In terms of a "triggering stress," developmental, social, and cultural factors, in addition to other types of biological and social factors, may be included in a schizophrenic pathogenesis. For example, adolescence involves major transitions to achieve adulthood. A variety of these new "stresses" may play a part in triggering psychotic episodes.

Transitions may include new relationships and intimacies, leaving home for the first time, pubertal changes, and new careers (Holzman & Grinker, 1974). The basic tasks for adolescents and young adults include separating from parental figures, completing their education and entering the job market, and forming relationships with significant others. All have counterparts related to schizophrenia. In particular, issues of identity at this time are often based on being able to find and hold a job, which, in turn, facilitates financial and psychological independence as well as career development.

The concept of "off-time" events in schizophrenia, advanced by Cohler and associates (Cohler & Ferrono, 1987), may exacerbate adjustment for schizophrenics, especially adolescents. Cohler and his colleagues suggest that individuals carry within themselves a cognitive map of the life cycle indicating when certain events, such as marriage, retirement, or completion of education, are "on time" or expected to take place relative to other members of a similar age cohort (Cohler & Boxer, 1984). These expectations are socially and culturally shared, and problems may be associated with "off-time" events, that is, when expected events are early or late or do not occur. With regard to schizophrenia, there may be disruptions, such as dropping out of school or leaving jobs or relationships, at an important developmental phase. An extended mental illness in late adolescence or early adulthood may result in lost educational and social skills that are crucial to gain access to the job market.

Schizophrenics tend to be "off time" in several areas relative to others of their age. For schizophrenic adolescents, the illness is in its earliest phases, and depression and frustration may be particularly severe because they may find themselves suddenly "off time." The initial manifestation of schizophrenia often provides a particularly keen shock to individuals who have never experienced a mental disorder. Severe depression may occur as the person realizes the potentially debilitating nature of schizophrenia. The first occurrence of severe mental illness may require an extensive reworking of the cognitive map or the expectations a person has set for his or her career and other achievements.

HISTORICAL AND CULTURAL INFLUENCES ON SCHIZOPHRENIA

The historical and cultural context may interact with the person and the developmental period (adolescence) in having an impact on various mental illnesses, including schizophrenia. Lin and Kleinman (1988) have recently reviewed the literature on cross-cultural follow-up studies in schizophrenia. They addressed several issues of prevalence of schizophrenia in different cultures and the hypothesis that outcome for schizophrenics in non-Western countries is better than outcome for schizophrenics in more developed, Western countries.

Lin and Kleinman concluded that the schizophrenia prevalence rate of 1% is fairly stable across different countries and cultures and that the majority of follow-up studies conducted in developing, non-Western countries show a better outcome for schizophrenics than the outcome for schizophrenics reported in Western countries.

Lin and Kleinman maintained that the best empirical evidence for the cross-cultural difference in schizophrenic outcome currently available in the literature is based on The International Pilot Study of Schizophrenia (IPSS), sponsored by the World Health Organization, which explored outcome for about 1,200 schizophrenics from 9 different countries (Sartorius, Jablensky, & Shapiro, 1978; WHO, 1979). The IPSS found that the prognosis of schizophrenia is better in lesser developed countries than in the developed Western countries.

Nevertheless, there are several methodological problems of cross-cultural outcome studies, and various mediating factors may account for the differences observed across cultures (Lin & Kleinman, 1988). For example, the individuals most biologically vulnerable to a variety of disorders may be selected out of the population by early death in less developed countries. Whereas 50% of individuals may die before age 5 in some developing countries, about 96% of individuals may reach age 18 in developed countries such as the United States. The high death rate in many developing countries may select out those individuals who are susceptible to poor outcome in schizophrenia.

Other potential mediating factors for better outcome among schizophrenic patients in developing countries include a variety of psychosocial or stress factors: family and social support, stigma, the role assigned to the sick, self-attribution, and different skills and abilities for work roles. Often, the sociocultural environment in developing countries resembles the therapeutic climate recommended for schizophrenia in developing countries. In particular, an extended family (in contrast to a nuclear family) appears better equipped to provide continuous emotional support. There are more potential caretakers in the extended family and, in such families, there may be a better variety of employment niches for disabled persons. Indeed, the types of employment common in less developed countries would be less stressful and less likely to require complex skills and cognitive abilities that may be beyond the capacity of many schizophrenics. Persons with schizophrenia may easily fulfill social and performance roles in an extended family. The psychological and social supports available in an extended family may also forestall psychotic episodes.

Lin and Kleinman (1988) suggested that future cross-cultural studies need to explore specific linkages between various factors and outcomes, to resolve some of the competing explanations, and that the finding of better outcome for schizophrenics in less developed countries than in more developed Western countries is the single most important issue in cross-cultural studies.

In addition to cross-cultural differences, it has been suggested that historical (or cohort) differences have had an impact on schizophrenia. Important cohort differences have been documented for developmental issues in studies of the effects of the Great Depression era on children (Elder, 1974), and in changes for successive cohorts in rates of suicide (Holinger, Offer, & Zola, 1989; Murphy & Wetzel, 1980). It has also been noted that the period of adolescence may be a relatively new developmental phase in history (Demos & Demos, 1969).

Although there is evidence of cross-cultural influence in schizophrenia, there are several problems in establishing a historical or cohort effect for schizophrenia. The major problem is that schizophrenia was not systematically defined before the early 20th century; hence, it is difficult to actually assess prevalence rates.

Despite this difficulty, Hare (1989) and Cooper and Sartorius (1977) have suggested that schizophrenia is a recent illness in human history. According to Cooper and Sartorius (1977), the increase in schizophrenia in the 20th century coincided with the rise of industrialization and medical advances that made it possible for vulnerable children to live longer and develop schizophrenia. Similar reasoning involving mortality is mentioned by Lin and Kleinman (1988) as one possible factor for the better outcome of schizophrenics in lesser developed countries.

Hare (1988) proposed that schizophrenia, if it is a recent illness, may be caused by infection and immunity problems. If its pattern is like that of other infectious illnesses, there may be less severe forms of the illness over successive cohorts, as natural resistance is built up or milder forms of the illness emerge. If true, Hare suggests, schizophrenia will be milder and will decrease in the future, especially among those who may have the severest forms of the illness, such as early-onset or adolescent schizophrenia.

GENDER DIFFERENCES IN SCHIZOPHRENIA

Several gender differences in schizophrenia have been noted in recent years, and these differences may pertain to the etiology and treatment of schizophrenia (Angermeyer, Kuhn, & Goldstein, 1990; Goldstein & Tsuang, 1990; Haas, Glick, Clarkin, Spencer, & Lewis, 1990). Traditionally, it has been suggested that equal percentages of males and females become schizophrenic. Recent data, however, have indicated that, when modern, narrow concepts of schizophrenia are used (e.g., DSM-III, DSM-III-R, and RDC), a greater percentage of males than females will be diagnosed schizophrenic than in the older, broader DSM-II concept of schizophrenia (Lewine, Burbach, & Meltzer, 1984; Westermeyer & Harrow, 1984, 1987). This shift may occur because the new diagnostic systems *exclude* from a diagnosis of schizophrenia patients with a full affective syndrome, and, because women are more likely to manifest affective syndromes than men (Weissman & Klerman, 1977), women are more likely than men to be excluded from a classification of schizophrenia by the DSM-III.

The most consistent finding of gender differences in schizophrenia involves age of onset. Extensive research has shown that first hospital admission in schizophrenia on average occurs earlier in men than in women. Angermeyer and Kuhn (1988) suggested that this difference is because psychosis typically occurs earlier in men than in women, and *not* because men have a shorter period between symptom onset and hospitalization. In reviewing other disorders, these authors also suggested that the gender differences in age of onset may be unique to schizophrenic spectrum disorders. They found no such gender differences in nonpsychotic affective disturbance or in manic disorders. The few studies on schizoaffective disorders indicate that there may be a gender difference in age of onset for this disorder (Angermeyer & Kuhn, 1988).

Theorists have also posited that female schizophrenics have a better premorbid history and better outcomes than male schizophrenics (Goldstein, 1988; Goldstein & Tsuang, 1990; Salokangas, 1983). Many studies have shown that women have better prehospital adjustment than men, which may be closely associated to the later age of onset consistently observed for women (Rosen, Klein, Levenstein, & Shanian, 1968). In addition, gender effects on outcome have been stronger in schizophrenia than in the affective disorders (McGlashan & Bardenstein, 1990; Westermeyer, Harrow, & Marengo, 1989). Nevertheless, the recent literature on gender differences in schizophrenic outcome has been mixed (Angermeyer et al., 1990; Loyd, Simpson, & Tsuang, 1985) and gender appears to have more of an effect on rehospitalization rates and role functioning than on clinical symptoms (Haas et al., 1990). Gender differences have been more likely in broadly defined samples of schizophrenics and less likely in narrowly defined samples of schizophrenics. A certain number of women diagnosed schizophrenic in the past (i.e., DSM-II) and currently reclassified as nonschizophrenic (i.e., DSM-III) have shown good outcomes (Westermeyer & Harrow, 1984, 1987).

Explanations for gender difference in schizophrenia encompass biological and social or developmental factors. For example, Weinberger (1987) proposed that the later onset of schizophrenia for women than for men may be because, in normal development, dopamine activity peaks later in women than in men. From another perspective, Seeman and associates (Seeman, 1983; Seeman & Lang, 1990) suggested that the hormone estrogen in women modifies symptoms in schizophrenia and may (at least until menopause) account for observed gender differences in schizophrenia.

From a social developmental perspective, theorists such as Zigler (Zigler, Glick, & Marsh, 1979) have said that men may experience more stress than women in young adulthood. For example, men may have greater expectations than women to leave home and become independent in late adolescence and early adulthood. In heterosexual relationships, men may have greater expectations than women to be assertive and to assume occupational roles to provide for the financial well-being of others. Although changing sex roles are the highlight of our sociocultural setting over the past few decades, it is possible that young women may not have the same types of stress or expectations as young men. Nevertheless, when one looks at the multiple—and, at times, opposite—types of functioning and roles that many young women are expected to fill in our society, one can see a possibility that young women may face equal or even greater stresses than men (Gove & Herb, 1974; Tolan, 1988). This issue of contrasting stresses for young men and women is important and is open to further research.

PROGNOSIS IN SCHIZOPHRENIA: EARLY ONSET VERSUS LATE ONSET

Because schizophrenia traditionally has been considered a poor outcome disorder, predictors of schizophrenic remission have received much attention over the years. An early onset (often encompassing the adolescent years) has been shown to be a poor prognostic sign in schizophrenia (Rosen et al., 1968; Rosen, Klein, & Gittelman-Klein, 1969; Westermeyer & Harrow, 1986; Zigler & Levine, 1981; Zigler & Phillips, 1961). Table 15.1 presents data on this issue from the Chicago Follow-up Study (Grinker & Harrow, 1987; Harrow, Westermeyer, Silverstein, Strauss & Cohler, 1986); it shows age at first hospitalization and 2-year outcome for 65 RDC schizophrenics.

Results indicate that schizophrenics who have a first hospital admission in their teenage years (i.e., 17 to 19) are less likely to have a good outcome than schizophrenics who were older at *first* hospitalization. Schizophrenics with an adolescent onset showed a small percentage with favorable or good outcome, and well over half of this group showed a poor overall outcome at follow-up. In contrast, schizophrenics who were 20 years of age or over at first hospital admission showed over 20% with good outcome, and less than half of this group showed poor overall outcome at follow-up.

These data, and research reported by others (Rosen, Klein, & Gittelman-Klein, 1971; Zigler & Levine, 1981) indicate that an early onset in schizophrenia, especially during the adolescent years, is an ominous prognostic sign. Several theorists in human development

Table 15.1 Age at First Hospital Admission and Overall Outcome at a Two-Year Follow-Up Among 65 Schizophrenics

	Overall Outcome		
Age at Onset	Good	Moderate Impairment	Poor
Late adolescence: 17 to 19 years	1(4%)	8(32%)	16(64%)
Early adulthood: 20 to 31 years	9(22.5%)	14(32.5%)	18(45%)

have pointed out that chronological age, in itself, provides little explanatory information (Cohler & Boxer, 1984). The importance of chronological age is based on its association to other biological or developmental factors. For example, there may be different types of schizophrenia, and one type may be associated with biochemical processes that normally occur in late adolescence. Benes (1989) has suggested that certain areas of the brain implicated in schizophrenia may show changes in myelination during late adolescence. It is possible that individuals who are vulnerable to specific types of biochemical changes in the brain at adolescence may have a severe "dose" of schizophrenia, which may be easily triggered by mild stress or strain. In contrast, a schizophrenic episode that first occurs in later stages of the life cycle may indicate a biochemically milder form of mental illness requiring a great stress or strain to manifest itself.

From another theoretical perspective, persons (especially adolescents) experiencing psychotic symptoms at an early age may not have had the opportunity to develop social and educational skills to overcome the disruption (Strauss, Kokes, Carpenter, & Ritzler, 1978; Zigler et al., 1979; Zigler & Phillips, 1961). This theoretical orientation toward psychopathology is sometimes referred to as the "developmental" perspective. Older persons (or persons beyond the adolescent years) may have been more able than adolescents to establish social relationships and work and educational skills before being hospitalized. They would have reached a developmental level, prior to illness, at which they would have already acquired social, occupational, and interpersonal maturation that aids them in overcoming most mental disorders, or life stress in general. Proponents of this position maintain that the same developmental prognostic items (e.g., marriage, education, age, and work history, which assess social or work developmental levels) predict outcome across a range of mental disorders (Strauss et al., 1978; Zigler et al., 1979).

Another perspective (e.g., systems, vulnerability, or diathesis-stress theories discussed above) would maintain that all of the above theoretical orientations are true to some extent, and that they operate in a reciprocal, interactive fashion (Harrow & Westermeyer, 1987; Westermeyer & Harrow, 1986). From this perspective, an early onset may be the result of a biochemical or genetically more severe form of mental disorder in interaction with an environmental stress or event in developmentally less mature individuals. In turn, the illness itself prevents the individual from acquiring further educational or social skills.

The following case histories may illustrate the above processes. A late-onset schizophrenic (Mr. A) is compared to an early-onset or adolescent schizophrenic (Mr. B).

Case History: Mr. A was first hospitalized at the age of 27. As an adolescent, he had several friends and dated regularly. He was a good student and excellent athlete, and graduated from a major midwestern college. Upon graduation, he worked for 2 years in the Peace Corps, but returned feeling depressed. He obtained a job as a professional and worked until 3 months prior to his first hospitalization. In the 6 months preceding this first hospitalization, Mr. A began a new relationship with a woman, began using drugs, and his apartment became a counterculture meeting place. He impulsively quit his job, and his behavior became bizarre just prior to hospitalization. He hovered in corners, claimed to be God, threatened to kill his girlfriend, and was unable to perform basic tasks such as feeding himself.

Mr. A showed vast improvement during his 9 months of hospitalization. His psychotic symptoms remitted during this time with the aid of neuroleptics and individual therapy. Five follow-ups over the next 16 years found him free of psychotic symptoms and working full-time as a professional. By the fifth follow-up, he was married, with two children, and owned his own home. He was never rehospitalized again, and had not taken medications or been in therapy since his first and only hospitalization.

Case History: Mr. B's first hospitalization occurred at age 19, after his first year in college, although he appeared to have experienced psychotic symptoms (delusions) during his early adolescent years. As an adolescent, he found himself socially isolated and quite anxious when in the company of others. In spite of a high intelligence, he was a poor student and felt he "can't concentrate." The immediate precipitant for his first hospitalization was a rejection by a girl he met on two occasions. At that time, he felt people were plotting against him, and he experienced multiple ideas of reference. Five follow-ups over the next 15 years revealed persistent delusions, hallucinations, and severe thought disorder. Mr. B spent much of the time in long-term hospitalizations and halfway houses because his parents could not tolerate his destructive behavior (e.g., breaking furniture, psychotic speech) in their home. At the fifth follow-up, he was 34 years of age and had never held a job. He had resided in a halfway house for the past 7 years.

The case histories of Mr. A and Mr. B are prototypes of a good prognosis later-onset schizophrenic (Mr. A) and a poor prognosis early- (or adolescent) onset schizophrenic (Mr. B).

Age at first hospitalization significantly correlated with several other poor prognostic signs in the Chicago Follow-up Study. Younger schizophrenics were more likely than older schizophrenics to be single at hospitalization, to have few years of education, to have a poor work history, and to have experienced a gradual onset of illness (Westermeyer, 1982). Ironically, younger patients (Mr. B) appeared to be more chronic at hospitalization than older, later-onset patients (Mr. A).

Mr. A is typical of good prognosis schizophrenics. He had an excellent educational and work history. Although he had experienced some limited prehospital difficulties and had not married by the time of his hospitalization, he had good social relationships and sustained heterosexual relationships during his adolescence and young adulthood. Thus, Mr. A was able to find work and reinstate friendship and social activities immediately after hospitalization. The possibility of subsequent psychotic episodes may have been minimized by his commitment to work and a social network.

In contrast, the relatively early schizophrenic onset characteristic of Mr. B was quite disruptive to his education, social relationships, and career development. Chronic unemployment is stressful for most adults, and the social supports that are a positive resource to most adults were absent for Mr. B.

Nevertheless, aside from social, educational, and work skills acquired prior to hospitalization, Mr. B may have a more severe type of schizophrenia than Mr. A. (It also should be noted that Mr. B's maternal uncle and paternal grandmother were chronic schizophrenics.) For unknown reasons, Mr. A's psychosis remitted after a few months' duration. Despite strong doses of medications, Mr. B's psychosis has endured over a 15-year period.

THE NATURAL COURSE OF SCHIZOPHRENIA OVER THE ADULT LIFE CYCLE

The overwhelming majority of studies exploring outcome in a range of mental disturbances have found that schizophrenics have a poorer outcome than other types of diagnostic disorders (Harrow, Grinker, Silverstein, & Holzman, 1978; Marneros, Diester, Rohde, Steinmeyer, & Junemann, 1989; McGlashan, 1984; Opjordmoen, 1988; Tsuang, Woolson, & Fleming, 1979; Westermeyer, Harrow, & Carone, 1987). Two recent, detailed reviews (McGlashan, 1988; Westermeyer & Harrow, 1988) have documented schizophrenic course and outcome in comparison to other disorders. Unfavorable course and outcome for schizophrenia, in comparison to other disorders, extend across a variety of severe symptoms, work and social functioning, and rehospitalization.

When using a similar criterion of *complete or total* recovery (Stephens, 1978; Vaillant, 1978a), there is fairly good agreement, among the various outcome studies of schizophrenia, that the recovery rate ranges from about 14% to about 30%, depending on whether broad or narrow concepts of schizophrenia are used, and depending on treatment, sociocultural factors, chronicity, and other prognostic factors. There is also fairly good agreement that most schizophrenics do not experience a completely unfavorable outcome that requires *continuous* hospitalization (Westermeyer & Harrow, 1988, 1990).

Thus, most schizophrenics improve from their flagrant psychosis at hospital admission, but many continue to show persistent and less intense psychosis (Harrow, Carone, & Westermeyer, 1985), and others still show moderate difficulties, episodic symptoms, or revolving-door rehospitalization at follow-up. Despite the fact that most schizophrenics improve to the point where they may reside in the community without hurting themselves or others, the great majority of schizophrenics still show a relatively negative outcome when compared to other mental disorders or to "normal" persons, with persistent or episodic psychopathology and major difficulties in working and loving across the life cycle. About 50% to 75% may be unemployed at any one time (Bleuler, 1978, Vaillant, 1978b, Westermeyer, 1982), about 60% to 75% may manifest severe symptoms at some point in the posthospital period (Harrow et al., 1985; Marengo & Harrow, 1986), and about 40% to 50% are rehospitalized in the first year after discharge (Harrow et al., 1978).

Although most follow-up studies in schizophrenia have examined outcome at one point in time, the long-term life-course of this disorder is extremely important. Life-course implies an analysis of the illness across several years, or much of the life cycle, rather than an episode or instance at one point in time. Recently, there has been great interest in developing life-course typologies for schizophrenia and other types of mental illness (Bleuler, 1978; Carpenter & Kirkpatrick, 1988; Huber, Gross, Schutter, & Linz, 1980; Marengo, Harrow, Benson, Sands, & Galloway, 1987). In contrast to outcome studies at *one point in time,* life-course analyses, based on multi-follow-up designs, may document and compare improvements, declines, episodes, and stability at one point in time with prospective data gathered at earlier points in time. The life histories of Mr. A and Mr. B above illustrate two of several types of *courses* of illnesses.

Bleuler (1978) has provided us with the longest, prospective multi-follow-up study. Although follow-ups were not completed at systematic intervals, he was able to make at least three contacts with 208 schizophrenic patients over a 23-year period. Bleuler suggested that it is only for the first 5 to 10 years that schizophrenics, as a group, may show the deterioration observed by Kraepelin in his classic studies in the first part of the 20th century. After this initial period, Bleuler maintained, gradual improvement may occur for many schizophrenics across the life span.

Bleuler presented four types of "end states," which he defined as outcome plateaus that persist for at least 5 years. These four types are: (a) severe (illustrated by Mr. B above), (b) moderate, (c) mild, and (d) recovery (illustrated by Mr. A above). Bleuler reported that a substantial minority (about 25%) did not achieve a stable "end state" but rather displayed a fluctuating course with outcome changing back and forth. It should be emphasized that the detection of a "fluctuating" group is important and is best revealed by multi-follow-up studies that are not confounded by potential memory distortions. Moreover, in accord with other research on mentally disturbed samples and "normal" samples across the life cycle, such a perspective suggests human adjustment is quite complex and subject to change (Vaillant, 1977; Vaillant & Vaillant, 1990).

Bleuler maintained that the course of schizophrenia had improved in the post-World War II period. For example, he found that the cases of severe chronic conditions had decreased across the life cycle and the proportion of milder cases had increased. Traditional expectations of schizophrenia, based on the older picture seen by Kraepelin, would have predicted a higher proportion of chronic conditions (similar to Mr. B's case above).

In addition, Bleuler presented an original classification of eight types of courses, in an attempt to describe the illness across much of the adult life span rather than to describe outcome at one point in time. Marengo et al. (1987),

Ciompi (1980), and Harding (1988) have applied modified versions of Bleuler's course typologies to various groups of schizophrenics and have found similar results; all report considerable variations in the course of schizophrenia across adulthood. In addition, Marengo et al. (1987) created new constructs for assessing course in schizophrenia and other disorders.

It should be emphasized that multi-follow-up studies also show that some schizophrenics may decline between successive follow-ups (Bleuler, 1978; Westermeyer et al., 1987). For example, Vaillant found that 20 (40%) of 51 schizophrenics who showed a total or complete remission in a 1-to-2-year follow-up later showed repeated rehospitalizations and a chronic course of illness in a 10-year follow-up. Their poor outcomes included work and social impairment (Vaillant, 1978a).

Overall, the power of prospective, long-term, longitudinal research has provided an accurate view of the natural course of schizophrenia. Contrary to previous beliefs, schizophrenics as a group do *not* deteriorate in the posthospital period and changes are ever possible. These changes include both improvements and declines in functioning. Although early onset is associated with a more unfavorable outcome than later onset, individual adolescents experiencing schizophrenia may still show improvement. Most improvement for the group of schizophrenics involves "social" remission, in which patients may be able to reside socially in the community yet still be symptomatic or work-impaired. A group of 15% to 25% of schizophrenics (such as Mr. A) will show total or complete recovery after their first few episodes.

It is not fully understood why time or aging may be associated with improvements for some schizophrenics. It is, however, important to note that prospective longitudinal research has shown improvements across the life span in longitudinal studies of alcoholism (Vaillant, 1983), sociopathy (Robbins, 1966), mental disturbances in childhood and adolescence (Kohlberg, Ricks, & Snarey, 1984), nonpsychotic depressive disorders (Westermeyer et al., 1987), and normal development (Vaillant, 1977). There appears to be a general process of growth or maturation through adulthood (Vaillant & Milofsky, 1980; Weinberger, 1987). Again, this is a complex phenomenon probably influenced by a number of factors. It may be facilitated by the cumulative total of social, play, and work experience over the years, and by the continual emotional and cognitive growth (and, possibly, continual brain myelination) of individuals across the life span.

Information on the course of schizophrenia may set parameters for a plausible etiology of schizophrenia, or may rule out explanations that are not consistent with the developmental unfolding of the illness. For example, Weinberger noted:

Alternately, if schizophrenia is analogous to a metabolic encephalopathy or to a neuro-degenerative disorder, then the pathology should parallel the disease process and become more extensive over time as the process continues. In other words a simple model of schizophrenia being caused by a major, irreversible insult to the brain is not consistent with the long-term course of schizophrenia. (Weinberger, 1987, p. 662)

Similarly, the skills, attitudes, and mental processes that are untouched by schizophrenia also provide information on the nature of this illness. In this regard, Vaillant and Milofsky (1980) commented:

Indeed, schizophrenia—which spares all the developmental functions associated with Piagetian cognitive maturation and interferes with all those associated with psychosocial maturation—provides an arena in which to begin teasing apart Eriksonian and Piagetian concepts of maturation. (Vaillant & Milofsky, 1980, p. 1358)

Piaget's cognitive development and Kohlberg's moral development theories posit invariant sequences of developmental phases that are irreversible and must be traversed in succession before attaining the next stage. One could question some of these "invariant" sequences, even in "normals," but certainly schizophrenic clinical course and adjustment are reversible under some circumstances, and certain types of cognitive processes remain intact in many schizophrenics. Schizophrenia does not always follow an irreversible sequence or an unchanging maturational model toward a favorable or unfavorable outcome. Consequently, the course of schizophrenia, and that of some other major mental disturbances, may best fit other models of the life cycle that emphasize social and emotional development and are less tied to an invariant sequence (Cohler, 1986; Cohler & Boxer, 1984; Erikson, 1963; Neugarten, 1979; Vaillant, 1977).

Despite the possibility of change, the majority of schizophrenics fail to achieve full independence or to be free of treatment/institutional ties. Thus, a large percentage of schizophrenics, such as Mr. B above, do not achieve adequate evolution to Erikson's higher developmental tasks, which include industry versus inferiority, intimacy versus isolation, and generativity versus self-absorption.

Moreover, as with research on normal development and on most other types of psychopathology, changes (improvements or declines) in the course of schizophrenia may occur at any age. Although complete remissions are most likely to occur early in the course of schizophrenia, the illness process is not restricted by a precise time schedule. Again, such a dynamic, open-ended developmental model is not consistent with an invariant model of development or an overarching brain insult in schizophrenia leading to irreversible, steady deterioration.

Despite a variety of courses in schizophrenia and a tendency toward mild improvement across the adult life cycle, it should be noted that the course of schizophrenia appears to be more fixed than the illness course for other types of mental disturbances. For example, schizophrenics show less improvement and more continuity of deficits, malfunctioning, and psychopathology than other nonpsychotic disorders (Westermeyer et al., 1987). In addition, Kohlberg et al. (1984) suggested, in a review of prospective longitudinal studies tracing the course of a variety of mental disturbances from childhood and adolescence through adulthood, that psychotic disturbances showed the greatest continuity through the life cycle in comparison to other types of mental disturbances and normal behavior. Many different types of normals and patient groups benefit over the years by the positive effects of factors associated with the aging process, but schizophrenics may be among the groups showing the least benefit.

SUICIDE AND MORTALITY IN SCHIZOPHRENIA

Recently, suicide and mortality in schizophrenia and other types of mental disorders have been recognized as major problems. The older outcome literature, often based on retrospectively studied samples of older patients, was more likely than prospective studies to neglect or underestimate the true lifetime morbid risk for suicide. These studies initially focused on surviving schizophrenics who were in the middle and later phases of their illness, and so could not assess schizophrenics who died in early phases of their illness. Prospective follow-ups of more representative samples of patients have shown that the suicide rate may range up to 10% among the major mental disorders (Miles, 1977). For schizophrenia, several reviews and follow-up studies suggest the rate of suicide is about 10% (Drake, Osher, & Wallach, 1985; Miles, 1977; Roy, 1986; Westermeyer & Harrow, 1989; Westermeyer, Harrow, & Marengo, 1991).

In an important recent study, Allebeck (1989) reported a 10-year follow-up of 1,190 schizophrenics in Stockholm (Sweden), in which inpatient data bases were computer-linked to national cause-of-death registers, thereby allowing for a detailed analysis of death for a large sample of schizophrenic patients and the general population. Allebeck reported that the overall mortality rate of schizophrenics was more than twice that of the general population and suggested that the excess mortality in schizophrenia is primarily due to suicide and violent death. Allebeck also found that the number of suicides was more than ten times higher in schizophrenia than in the general population.

Current theories on suicide in schizophrenia suggest that it is usually a *nonpsychotic* reaction, often based on discouragement and/or hopelessness about a severe illness or debilitation, rather than a psychotically driven action. Several factors lead to this conclusion. First, suicide in schizophrenia often occurs in persons who would appear to initially have for themselves high expectations, which are dashed by the prospects of a chronic mental illness. Schizophrenics who commit suicide are more likely than nonsuicides to be White males who have high intelligence (Breier & Astrachan, 1984; Drake, Gates, Cotton, & Whitaker, 1984; Roy, 1986; Westermeyer, Harrow & Marengo, 1991; Westermeyer & Harrow, 1989).

Second, as shown above, outcome for schizophrenics is often unfavorable, and schizophrenics often show severe social and work deficits. Such social, work, and symptom difficulties may lead to severe frustration and depression for many schizophrenics, and some of these patients, despairing about the quality of their lives, may choose suicide.

Third, the critical period for suicide among schizophrenics appears to be in its earliest phases, when an individual must come to terms with the implications of the illness and possibly revise his or her expectations for the future (Drake, Gates, Whitaker, & Cotton, 1985; Westermeyer & Harrow, 1989). Because the critical period for schizophrenic suicide is the first 6 to 8 years of the illness (Westermeyer, Harrow & Marengo, 1991), adolescent and young adult male schizophrenics are at special risk for suicide and for depression. Again, in the earliest phases, individuals are most likely to see themselves as "off-time" and to be depressed and frustrated about their illness.

Persons at high risk for suicide may engage in rigid thinking in which they may feel hopeless about their future. Therapeutic efforts with adolescent schizophrenics at high risk for suicide should aim to instill hope regarding their potential for recovery and should point out options for the future.

TREATMENT OF SCHIZOPHRENIA

Malfunctioning and severe symptoms may be manifest across the life cycle of schizophrenics. Treatment has often proved to be time-consuming and expensive, and may take many forms during the person's life. It has been suggested that there are over 100 types or schools of therapy, and many of these have been used in treating schizophrenics.

Neuroleptics

A major advance in the treatment of schizophrenics occurred in the 1950s with the appearance of neuroleptic medications in treating schizophrenics. Neuroleptics tend to diminish more flagrant psychosis, although they do not completely cure schizophrenia. Research on the effectiveness of neuroleptics in reducing acute psychosis has been verified in a number of different investigations (Davis, Schaffer, Killian, Kinard, & Clan, 1980). In addition, Hogarty, Goldberg, Schooler, and Urich (1974) and May, Tuma, and Dixon (1981) have documented the positive effects of neuroleptics on short-term outcome (or as a *prophylactic*) in treating schizophrenics in carefully designed, controlled studies.

Neuroleptics were given much credit for the possibility of allowing schizophrenics to live in the community in the 1970s and 1980s. Psychosis in schizophrenia often manifests itself in flagrant delusions and hallucinations that may be terrifying for the person with schizophrenia as well as for his or her family and acquaintances. A psychotic episode may be quite destructive to individuals and may leave emotional scars and deficit symptoms long after the psychotic symptoms have remitted. Especially in acute phases, neuroleptics have been found to have a beneficial effect in reducing, calming, or eliminating these severe symptoms. Moreover, clozapine, a new medication, offers the hope that some formerly treatment-resistant chronic schizophrenics may show a degree of improvement (Kane, Honingfeld, Singer, Meltzer, & Clozaril Collaborative Study Group, 1989).

Unfortunately, a large number of schizophrenics (20% to 35%) can develop tardive dyskinesia (TD) as a side effect of neuroleptic use, although clozapine may not lead to TD. Tardive dyskinesia is a potentially irreversible neurological disorder characterized by involuntary movements ranging from minor to severe. The tardive dyskinesia problem has left therapists with the agonizing dilemma of risking the reemergence of severe psychosis in some schizophrenics by removing their medications, or maintaining neuroleptic use for prolonged periods and risking tardive dyskinesia (Stein, 1989).

Psychotherapy; Group and Family Therapy

Controlled drug studies have shown that medications augmented with psychotherapy produce better results (Hogarty et al., 1974; May et al., 1981). Several theorists have written extensively on the optimum treatment strategies for schizophrenia (Bleuler, 1978; Grinker & Holzman, 1973). Bleuler (1978) noted that it is best to provide a benign, protective, therapeutic environment for schizophrenics. Others, feeling that schizophrenics do not do well in confrontive types of therapy, have suggested that psychoanalysis would be too intense and involving for most schizophrenics.

The helpful therapeutic effects on schizophrenia have been shown in studies of community support systems (Bond, Miller, Krumwied, & Ward, 1988; Mosher & Keith, 1980; Stein & Test, 1980). A number of different types of community agencies, community programs, and different modalities may be involved in community support systems—therapy and activities groups, medication groups, self-help groups, and work rehabilitation programs. They also include outreach programs such as the Program of Assertive Community Treatment (PACT) and the Bridge Program, which attempt to contact and help patients in their own homes within the community (Bond et al., 1988; Stein & Test, 1980).

Because many schizophrenics experience difficulty in more intense—and, at times, emotionally loaded—relationships, group treatments (usually available in community treatment programs) are often employed with schizophrenic patients. Group therapy may permit the patient to enter a therapeutic modality where he or she is not the single major focus of the therapeutic situation. In group therapy, the schizophrenic can engage in reality testing and obtain support, and even empathy, from other schizophrenics.

The expressed-emotion literature has suggested that family therapy with schizophrenics should avoid an intense, probing exploration of family dynamics, and, instead, focus on family problem solving. Falloon et al. (1985) recommended that the patient's needs be discussed within the context of the family. Together, the family is trained in communication skills and discussion of alternate solutions to a specific problem.

Overall, in terms of treatment for patients with schizophrenia, there have been a number of advances over the past 40 years. These have included (a) neuroleptics, (b) community support programs, such as the Program of Assertive Community Treatment and the Bridge Program; (c) and greater use of group psychotherapy and family treatment, based on principles derived from recent research on expressed emotion (EE). However, May et al. (1981) have reminded us that the effectiveness of current therapies is limited and that outcome for most schizophrenics is far from reassuring, whatever the treatment.

Long-Term Follow-Ups and the Natural Healing Process in Schizophrenia

Research on long-term course and outcome in schizophrenia provides information of value for theory, for public policy, and for general treatment planning, but it is not experimentally designed to pinpoint the effects of various therapies. Long-term outcome studies are "naturalistic" studies that focus on adjustment across the life cycle in a variety of environments. It is difficult to randomly assign a large sample of patients to specific treatments and medications that must be maintained for the duration of long-term study. Even if it were possible, such a sample would hardly be representative of all schizophrenic patients, who are often on and off medications, are sometimes rehospitalized and have their treatment changed at hospitalization, and experience a range of therapies and medications.

In general, in naturalistic outcome studies that focus on the natural course of the illness over many years, the patients who are in therapy and are receiving mediations are the poor-outcome patients. These patients are major consumers of therapy because their more pathological clinical picture demands treatment. The case history of Mr. B above showed that he was continually in treatment. Because poor-outcome patients persistently need and often get treatment, uncontrolled outcome studies usually do not show patients treated with neuroleptics or in treatment as having better outcomes than patients not on medications or not in treatment.

Schizophrenics with favorable outcomes may not need treatment. Such patients may ask to be taken off medications, to avoid undesirable side effects such as the sluggishness and lethargy that are often products of neuroleptic treatment. The case history of Mr. A above showed that he maintained his recovery drug-free and without treatment over a 16-year period. Overall, the follow-up studies present a more optimistic view of human nature for select schizophrenics because outcome for these patients who do not need treatment is generally more benign than outcome for schizophrenics seen in clinical practice. Bleuler (1978), Vaillant (1978b), and Fenton and McGlashan (1987) reported that remitting schizophrenics are not likely to be receiving medications at follow-up, and our own follow-ups are in agreement. Many of the patients who reach complete or total recovery are not major consumers of treatment services and usually do not present themselves at hospital or clinics. Similar trends in treatment utilization have been observed in naturalistic, longitudinal studies of alcoholism and "normal" development (Shapiro et al., 1984; Vaillant, 1977; 1983).

Longitudinal research also suggests that the *duration* of either illness or recovery is one of the key factors for understanding illness course across the adult life cycle. Treatment is important, but there appears to be a natural healing process associated with the passage of time in which some psychotic persons show improvement or even get well, quite apart from the type of treatment or whether there is any treatment. Moreover, there appear to be critical periods for spontaneous psychotic remissions, which often occur early in the course of schizophrenia, as was Mr. A's experience. Persons experiencing *enduring* psychotic states are less likely to subsequently remit completely, although the great majority of them do not remain hospitalized indefinitely. The longer the psychosis endures, as in the case of Mr. B, the less likely the chance for complete recovery. Similarly, a total remission that *endures* over many years decreases the chance of a subsequent episode or a total breakdown; however, such individuals are at significantly greater risk for a new psychotic episode than individuals who have never had a psychotic episode.

The longitudinal perspective allows a dynamic view in which not only the *severity* of the psychotic symptoms is important, but the *duration* of the symptoms as well. Such a perspective supports analyses by Epstein (1979) and Vaillant (1978a) suggesting that the *aggregation* of observations over a greater number of behaviors, and across time, is a key element in increasing predictability. Furthermore, time-limited or cross-sectional events are less important in human development than constant support or persisting strains (Pearlin, 1980). A time-limited event increases in importance if it induces a persisting strain or a persisting support in people's lives.

Applied Social Policy

The suffering and torments of schizophrenia, and the variety of costs of this pernicious illness to society, make this disorder a high priority for policy makers and for therapists treating people with schizophrenia. It is estimated that 80% of schizophrenics will be hospitalized at some point in their lives and most of the approximately 3 million schizophrenics in the United States will experience major work and social difficulties across the life cycle. About 900,000 schizophrenics were served by organized inpatient, outpatient, and partial care programs in 1986 (Rosenstein, Millazzo-Sayre, & Mandersheid, 1989).

In preindustrial America, mentally disturbed persons usually remained with their families in the community. During the 19th century, the mentally ill were gradually removed from the community to asylums, usually located in rural areas. Theoretically, this form of treatment was partly premised on the assumption that societal factors, rather than God's will, were largely responsible for mental disabilities. It was hypothesized that, if chaos in society was creating mental illness, then rest in serene and orderly surroundings would help patients. Through the last part of the 19th century and the first half of the 20th century, asylums and hospitals increased. Large numbers of chronically mentally ill persons were removed from society and hospitalized for years in state mental hospitals, some of which did not emphasize social activities or stimulation for these patients. Long-term hospitalization in this type of nonstimulating environment seemed to be deleterious for many schizophrenics and currently is regarded as "regressive" by many investigators.

The past few decades have seen a process known as "deinstitutionalization," in which the chronically mentally ill have been discharged from long-term institutions to the community. For example, the resident population of state mental hospitals fell from 559,000 in 1955 to 110,000 in 1985 (National Institute of Mental Health, 1985). The deinstitutionalization of the chronically mentally ill over the past few decades was prompted by several factors, including (a) the belief that long-term involuntary incarceration in hospitals, and especially on "back wards" or continuous care treatment units, increased social disability and that patients would receive better care and treatment in the community; (b) the introduction in the 1950s of antipsychotic medications (neuroleptics), which better controlled severe symptoms; and (c) the desire to reduce the rising costs of hospitalization.

The research of Stein, Test, Bond, and others documents the potential effectiveness of carefully planned and assertive community support programs for the chronically mentally ill (Bond et al., 1988; Bond, Witheridge, Setze, & Dincin, 1985; Stein & Test, 1980, 1982; Test, 1981; Test & Stein, 1980). The placement of patients with schizophrenia into the least restrictive community setting, where they are then supported by a variety of treatment programs, can be quite conducive to the natural healing process that has been observed across the course of most mental disorders and, to an extent, in schizophrenia.

Nevertheless, deinstitutionalization may lead to neglect of schizophrenics in the community (Lamb, 1979; Lamb & Goertzel, 1971, 1977), especially young adult or adolescent schizophrenics (Caton, 1981), who may have a particularly severe form of the disease. As noted above, the great majority of schizophrenics have achieved partial but not total remission. Many schizophrenics and other types of psychotic patients experience an episodic or fluctuating course of illness in which there are periodic relapses and rehospitalizations. Thus, a variety of social problems have emerged over the past decade with the deinstitutionalization of the chronically mentally ill. For example, it has been found in recent studies that persons with severe psychoses may account for 20% to 30% of the homeless (Koegel, Burnam, & Farr, 1988). Mentally disturbed persons, including schizophrenics, have been found to be increasing in prison populations (Schock, Chen, & Gross, 1984). Alcohol and drug abuse has been playing a new and destructive role in the cohort under 45 years of age, and some schizophrenics have been found to have alcohol abuse problems (Drake et al., 1989).

This myriad of social problems has placed new demands on social welfare programs, community mental health services, and nonprofit religious and voluntary organizations of all types. Moreover, it has been estimated that about two-thirds of the multibillion-dollar cost of schizophrenia to society is accounted for by lost productivity (or lost work wages) rather than the cost of therapeutic efforts to treat it (Gunderson & Mosher, 1975). Because schizophrenia often strikes at the earliest phases of the life cycle, most of the lifetime of many schizophrenics is spent in underemployment or unemployment. Their condition represents a great productivity loss to society, quite apart from the human suffering caused by this mental illness.

Community Support Systems

The centerpiece of treatment of schizophrenics today is the community support system, which was designed to take the place of long-term institutionalization. Two major assumptions underlie the theory of individualized care for schizophrenia and other types of chronic mental illnesses in the community. First, it was assumed that community-based treatment would be therapeutic for the client and would be conducive to a variety of rehabilitative efforts (Stein & Test, 1982; Test & Stein, 1980). Second, it was assumed that community-based treatment is less costly than institutionally based or hospital treatment (Bond, 1984; Weisbrod, Test, & Stein, 1979).

The first assumption suggests that living in the community rather than in an institution (with most of these long-term institutions located in rural areas) provides debilitated schizophrenics and other types of chronically mentally ill patients with a variety of resources and opportunities that are therapeutic. For example, community living affords a degree of freedom and privacy, an opportunity to interact with family and friends, an opportunity for employment and educational opportunities, and, in general, a chance to live a more "normal" life. It was also felt that patients living in the community would be less likely to assume dependent roles and to be stigmatized by patient roles. In general, this normalization process, in which patients are placed in the least restrictive community environment, is considered important in treating schizophrenics.

The second assumption suggests that community-based treatment is less expensive than institutionalization (Weisbrod, Test, & Stein, 1980). Institutionalization requires buildings and equipment, food service, maintenance, and a staff providing 24-hour care. Over the years, state mental hospitals, which were originally maintained at only modest expense, have become more expensive. This cost increase, and the fact that some community support programs are partly funded by the federal government rather than just the state government, is one among several reasons for state mental hospitals' policy of rapidly discharging chronically mentally ill patients.

Community-based treatment utilizes the productive abilities of the patients themselves, in addition to a variety of natural support groups—religious organizations, volunteer and self-help groups, neighbors, friends, and an assortment of public and private groups. Most importantly, the family is directly involved in care. To the extent former patients may care for themselves, they are relieved of the stigma of the illness, and self-reliance, self-esteem, and independence are fostered.

Many individual schizophrenics discharged to the community cannot function without considerable support. This support, in the form of halfway houses, vocational rehabilitation, outreach programs, continuing therapy, and medication maintenance, has not been forthcoming in many areas. In addition, many service organizations in the therapeutic community (which are greatly dependent on private funds for their existence) often direct their efforts toward patients who can pay for services rather than toward the chronically mentally ill, who often cannot pay for services. Because many of the discharged patients are unemployed and indigent, they sometimes overwhelm social agencies and clinics trying to care for them.

Rather than improving, many discharged patients drift downward in social status and move to geographically impoverished areas, often in the central cities. Many discharged schizophrenics find it difficult to maintain social networks or therapeutic supports in the community. Medication compliance becomes difficult without therapeutic support. Thus, the quality of life for many of the chronically mentally ill has deteriorated, and homelessness, substance abuse, and arrest or imprisonment have increased in this population.

Family Environments in Schizophrenia and Expressed Emotion

The family may provide much of the support and resources discharged schizophrenics need to cope with their illness, thereby preventing the deterioration that many schizophrenics experience in the community. The family may provide a home, a social network, financial resources, and a powerful advocacy for the discharged patient to obtain the legal and medical resources he or she is entitled to. For adolescents, a community placement usually involves living with their parents and other family members.

However, the role of the parents and the family environment in the etiology and treatment of schizophrenia has been a subject of much controversy over the years. Prior to the 1960s, the role of parents, especially the mother (the presumed "schizophrenigenic" mother), in causing schizophrenia was widely discussed in the research literature. Mothers were often thought to play a major role in precipitating schizophrenia in their children. Many of these hypotheses focused on the "double bind" theory in which parents would say one thing but mean another, causing stress or psychotic episodes in their offspring. As genetic and biochemical evidence on the etiology of schizophrenia has increased over the years, and as solid empirical evidence has *not* been found over the years in support of the hypothesis about schizophrenigenic mothers, the stigma associated with being the parents of schizophrenics has decreased. As the illness has been seen as partly biochemical in origin, parents have, to a great extent, been freed of the "blame" many felt for their behavior toward their schizophrenic offspring during his or her childhood (Wahl & Harman, 1988).

In recent years, the issue of the role of the family environment in precipitating schizophrenic episodes has emerged in the research on expressed emotion (EE) (Falloon et al., 1981; Falloon et al., 1985; Vaughn, Snyder, Jones, Freeman, & Falloon, 1984). Expressed emotion in these studies refers to the number of critical comments, expression of hostility, or marked emotional overinvolvement by the schizophrenic's relatives.

Evidence has suggested that criticism or overinvolvement (high expressed emotion or high EE) is predictive of relapse among schizophrenics (Vaughn et al., 1984). Families low in criticism or emotional involvement (low expressed emotion or low EE) are less likely to have their schizophrenic relatives relapse or be hospitalized. In particular, male schizophrenics have been found to do better in emotionally more neutral homes. The data on expressed emotion support other observations that schizophrenics have difficulty handling intensity in general, and intense interpersonal situations in particular. A low EE environment is similar to the benign, accepting, nonthreatening milieu advocated by many in treating schizophrenics.

Some theorists have feared that the EE literature has returned us to the older concepts placing the blame for schizophrenia on the parents. From another perspective, however, it is possible that the schizophrenic's attitude or behavior may be inviting the negative comments, attitudes, or hostility on the part of the parents. The concept underlying this view may be referred to as *reciprocal socialization,* in which the child socializes or influences the parent to behave in particular ways. For example, Mr. B (in the case history above) was quite disruptive in his parents' home. He destroyed furniture and was generally abusive toward his parents. He was placed in hospitals and a long-term halfway house because his family could not tolerate his bizarre behavior.

In general, it is possible that a greater potential to engender negative EE in their parents could be present in those schizophrenics who have a long history of failure in adjustment and frequent psychotic relapses. These schizophrenic patients with a high potential for relapse may continually frustrate their overinvolved parents' expectations or hopes that they will function better, with this increasing EE.

Other Issues in Social Policy

As the problems of the mentally ill have become more visible in our communities, advocates of various social policies have come forth. Haley (1989) objected to the use of neuroleptics and suggested a return to the moral treatment philosophy of the 19th century. Stein (1989) countered that the therapeutic effects of neuroleptics merit their continued use.

Ciompi (1984) and others fundamentally question the concept of schizophrenia. Some argue that it places a stigma on individuals that in itself prohibits recovery. Stigma or labeling is a complex concept (Clausen, 1981), and the specific influences of stigma on outcome is unknown. Whatever the label applied to schizophrenics, it is in good part their behavior in the community that people respond to (i.e., a type of reciprocal socialization), and this response may be quite separate from labels assigned in medical settings.

Others suggest we need to go back to the period of institutionalization to provide greater protection and care for the chronic schizophrenic. Nevertheless, the evidence indicates that, when properly planned and managed, support systems are therapeutically effective in helping people reside in the community, and they are preferable for most schizophrenics to long-term institutionalization (Bond et al., 1988; Stein & Test, 1980; Test, 1981). Moreover, they are *cost-effective* to society and will save funds over the long term (Bond, 1984; Weisbrod et al., 1980).

Education may help people to better understand that most mentally ill persons are not dangerous, and that community-based halfway houses, or rehabilitation or drop-in centers, will not damage neighborhoods. Also needed are greater concentrations of support, activity, therapy, and outreach programs in the community, with efforts to educate concerned relatives and others to prodromal markers of relapse so that individuals can be better treated and psychotic episodes can be prevented. The least restrictive setting requires assertive case management, mobile outreach programs, and better community assessments of schizophrenics to determine when they may need treatment, medication, or hospitalization.

CONCLUSION

Schizophrenia is an often chronic illness characterized by psychotic symptoms (such as delusions, hallucinations, or severe thought disorder); most of those who are afflicted suffer major social, work, and family deficits across the life cycle. Although schizophrenia occurs in only about 1% of the general population, it is a pernicious illness with a relatively unfavorable outcome in comparison to other disorders, and often causes great suffering to individuals and their families and a great financial cost to society in general.

From a more optimistic point of view, long-term follow-ups have established that schizophrenia is not the intractable illness it was once thought to be. About 15% to 25% of schizophrenics eventually remit completely; many others improve from a flagrantly psychotic state at hospitalization to one of moderate impairment after discharge, and they may be able to function socially in the community, with support. Only a small minority of schizophrenics are totally impaired to the point of requiring long-term hospitalization.

Schizophrenia has special relevance for adolescence or the early adult phases of the life cycle:

1. Schizophrenia often becomes apparent in the early phases of the life cycle. The deficits manifested in schizophrenia include abnormalities in the higher cognitive processes, which typically come on-line in human development in adolescence or young adulthood.
2. Early onset or adolescent schizophrenia has a poorer outcome than later-onset schizophrenia.
3. Adolescent schizophrenics are more likely to be male than female, and adolescent (and male) schizophrenics have poorer prehospital adjustment than late-onset (and female) schizophrenics.

For adolescents, schizophrenia strikes at a time in the life cycle in which separation from family and preparations for career and intimacy are major developmental tasks. Difficulty in handling these developmental tasks may impair a mentally disturbed person across the life cycle. The onset of schizophrenia may derail the adolescent and young adult from the successful achievement of many developmental tasks and so may quickly put individuals "off-time" regarding expected life events.

Diathesis-stress, vulnerability, or systems theories are current heuristic models for understanding schizophrenia. These theories usually posit an inherent (often biochemical or genetic) vulnerability that is "triggered" by a stressful event or a life phase such as adolescence. These heuristic models allow for the separate analyses of biological, genetic, developmental, and social factors in contributing to a schizophrenic pathogenesis and natural history and to potential complex interactions among these separate areas. These models are compatible with a life-course analysis of schizophrenia which has revealed considerable heterogeneity, both cross-sectionally, in terms of various symptoms, and longitudinally, in terms of a variety of illness courses. Most importantly, the variety of illness courses observed across the lives of persons with schizophrenia is not compatible with an etiology involving (a) a single, major insult to the brain of all schizophrenics or (b) views of schizophrenia as an irreversible, degenerative disorder.

Although the course of schizophrenia is *more* fixed than that of other mental disorders, most schizophrenics improve to a point where they may live in the community. However, many persons with schizophrenia still experience episodic symptoms requiring rehospitalization, and major deficits in work and social functioning in the community. The use of neuroleptics (or clozapine), especially in those schizophrenics who show vulnerability to flagrant psychoses or thought disorder, is beneficial. In addition, the course of schizophrenia appears to be ameliorated by several similar or converging factors in different contexts:

1. In nonbiological or psychosocial therapies (both inpatient and outpatient), persons with schizophrenia are helped by treatments that are supportive and not confrontive or intense. These therapies can allow a "normalization" process in which persons may develop social skills and self-reliance,
2. In family settings, persons with schizophrenia appear to be helped by environments that are low in critical or hostile comments or emotional overinvolvement,
3. In lesser developed countries (and possibly in preindustrial America), persons with schizophrenia appear to be helped by supportive extended families, which seem to provide a more benign and less stressful environment than nuclear families in modern, developed countries.

Community support programs are central for the care and treatment of persons with schizophrenia and other types of severe mental illnesses. Although the precise etiology of schizophrenia is as yet unknown and therapies and medications are not able to guarantee complete recovery for all schizophrenics, the treatment of persons with schizophrenia in the community has progressed. An expanding system of community care and support, which allows severely mentally ill persons to live a more "normal" life in the community, is conducive to the natural healing processes observed across the life span of many schizophrenics.

REFERENCES

Allebeck, P. (1989). Schizophrenia: A life-shortening disease. *Schizophrenia Bulletin, 15,* 81–90.

American Psychiatric Association. (1968). *Diagnostic and statistical manual of mental disorders, (2nd ed.).* Washington, DC: Author.

American Psychiatric Association. (1980). *Diagnostic and statistical manual of mental disorders (3rd ed.).* Washington, DC: Author.

American Psychiatric Association. (1987). *Diagnostic and statistical manual of mental disorders (3rd ed., rev.).* Washington, DC: Author.

Angermeyer, M. C., & Kuhn, L. (1988). Gender differences in age at onset of schizophrenia: An overview. *European Archives of Psychiatry and Neurological Sciences, 237,* 351–364.

Angermeyer, M. C., Kuhn, L., & Goldstein, J. M. (1990). Gender and the course of schizophrenia: Differences in treated outcomes. *Schizophrenia Bulletin, 16,* 293–308.

Benes, F. M. (1989). Myelination of cortical-hippocampal relays during late adolescence. *Schizophrenia Bulletin, 15,* 585–593.

Bleuler, M. N. (1978). *The schizophrenic disorders: Long-term patient and family studies.* New Haven: Yale University Press.

Bond, G. R. (1984). An economic analysis of psychosocial rehabilitation. *Hospital and Community Psychiatry, 35,* 356–362.

Bond, G. R., Miller, L. D., Krumwied, M. H. A., & Ward, R. S. (1988). Assertive case management in three CMHCs: A controlled study. *Hospital and Community Psychiatry, 39,* 411–418.

Bond, G. R., Witheridge, T. F., Setze, P. J., & Dincin, J. (1985). Preventing rehospitalization of clients in a psychosocial rehabilitation program. *Hospital and Community Psychiatry, 36,* 993–995.

Breier, A., & Astrachan, B. (1984). Characteristics of schizophrenic patients who commit suicide. *American Journal of Psychiatry 141,* 206–209.

Carlsson, A. (1988). The current status of the dopamine hypothesis of schizophrenia. *Neuropsychopharmacology, 1,* 179–186.

Carpenter, W. T., & Kirkpatrick, B. (1988). The heterogeneity of the long-term course of schizophrenia. *Schizophrenia Bulletin, 14,* 645–652.

Caton, C. L. M. (1981). The new chronic patients and the system of community care. *Hospital and Community Psychiatry, 32,* 475–478.

Ciompi, L. (1980). The natural history of schizophrenia in the long term. *British Journal of Psychiatry, 136,* 413–430.

Ciompi, L. (1984). Is there really a schizophrenia? The long-term course of psychotic phenomena. *British Journal of Psychiatry, 145,* 636–640.

Clausen, J. A. (1981). Stigma and mental disorder: Phenomena and terminology. *Psychiatry, 44,* 287–296.

Cohler, B. J. (1986). Adversity, resilience and the study of lives. In E. J. Anthony & B. J. Cohler, *The invulnerable child.* New York: Guilford Press.

Cohler, B. J., & Boxer, A. (1984). Settling into the world: Person, time and context during the middle adult years. In D. Offer & M. Sabshin (Eds.), *Normality and the life cycle.* New York: Basic Books.

Cohler, B. J., & Ferrono, C. L. (1987). Schizophrenia and the adult life-course. In N. E. Miller & G. D. Cohen (Eds.), *Schizophrenia and aging* (pp. 189–199). New York: Guilford Press.

Cooper, J., & Sartorius, N. (1977). Cultural and temporal variations in schizophrenia: A speculation on the importance of industrialization. *British Journal of Psychiatry, 130,* 50–55.

Davis, J. M., Schaffer, C. B., Killian, G. A., Kinard, C., & Clan, C. (1980). Important issues in the drug treatment of schizophrenia. *Schizophrenia Bulletin, 6,* 70–87.

Demos, J., & Demos, V. (1969). Adolescence in historical perspective. *Journal of Marriage and the Family, 31,* 632–638.

Drake, R. E., Gates, C., Cotton, P. G., & Whitaker, A. (1984). Suicide among schizophrenics: Who is at risk? *Journal of Nervous and Mental Disease, 172,* 613–617.

Drake, R. E., Gates, C., Whitaker, A., & Cotton, P. G. (1985). Suicide among schizophrenics: A review. *Comprehensive Psychiatry, 26,* 90–100.

Drake, R. E., Osher, F. C., & Wallach, M. A. (1989). Alcohol use and abuse in schizophrenia: A prospective community study. *Journal of Nervous and Mental Disease, 117,* 408–414.

Elder, G. (1974). *Children of the Great Depression.* Chicago: University of Chicago Press.

Epstein, S. (1979). The stability of behavior: I. On predicting most of the people much of the time. *Journal of Personality and Social Psychology, 37,* 1097–1126.

Erikson, E. H. (1963). *Childhood and society* (2nd rev. ed.). New York: Norton.

Falloon, I. R. H., Boyd, J. L., McGill, C. W., Stang, J. S., & Moss, H. B. (1981). Family management training in the community care of schizophrenia. In M. J. Goldstein (Ed.), *New developments in interventions with families of schizophrenics* (pp. 61–77). San Francisco: Jossey-Bass.

Falloon, I. R. H., Boyd, J. L., McGill, C. W., Williamson, M., Razani, J., Moss, H. B., Gilderman, A. M., & Simpson, G. M. (1985). Family management in the prevention of morbidity of schizophrenia: Clinical outcome of a two-year longitudinal study. *Archives of General Psychiatry, 42,* 887–896.

Fenton, W. S., & McGlashan, T. H. (1987). Sustained remission in drug-free schizophrenics. *American Journal of Psychiatry, 144,* 136–139.

Goldstein, J. (1988). Gender differences in the course of schizophrenia. *American Journal of Psychiatry, 6,* 684–689.

Goldstein, J. M., & Tsuang, M. T. (1990). Gender and schizophrenia: An introduction and synthesis of findings. *Schizophrenia Bulletin, 16,* 179–185.

Gottesman, I. I., & Shields, J. (1982). *Schizophrenia: The epigenetic puzzle.* Cambridge, England: Cambridge University Press.

Gottesman, I. I. (1989). Vital statistics demography and schizophrenia: Editor's introduction. *Schizophrenia Bulletin, 15,* 5–7.

Gove, W. R., & Herb, T. R. (1974). Stress and mental illness among the young: A comparison of the sexes. *Social Forces, 53,* 256–265.

Grinker, R. R., Sr., & Harrow, M. (Eds.). (1987). *Clinical research in schizophrenia: A multidimensional approach.* Springfield, IL: Thomas.

Grinker, R. R., Sr., & Holzman, P. S. (1973). Schizophrenic pathology of young adults: A clinical study. *Archives of General Psychiatry 28,* 168–175.

Grinker, R. R., Sr., & Westermeyer, J. F. (1984). Systems theory in the practice of psychiatry. *International Journal of Family Psychiatry, 6,* 33–43.

Gunderson, J. G., & Mosher, L. R. (1975). The cost of schizophrenia. *American Journal of Psychiatry, 132,* 901–906.

Haas, G. L., Glick, I. D., Clarkin, J. F., Spencer, J. H., & Lewis, A. B. (1990). Gender and schizophrenia outcome: A clinical trial of an inpatient family intervention. *Schizophrenia Bulletin, 16,* 277–292.

Haley, J. (1989). The effect of long-term outcome studies on the therapy of schizophrenia. *Journal of Marital and Family Therapy, 15,* 127–132.

Harding, C. M. (1988). Course types in schizophrenia: An analysis of European and American studies. *Schizophrenia Bulletin, 14,* 633–644.

Hare, Edward. (1988). Schizophrenia as a Recent Disease. *British Journal of Psychiatry, 153,* 521–531.

Harrow, M., Carone, B. J., & Westermeyer, J. F. (1985). The course of psychosis in early phases of schizophrenia. *American Journal of Psychiatry, 142,* 702–707.

Harrow, M., Grinker, R. R., Sr., Silverstein, M. L., & Holzman, P. (1978). Is modern-day schizophrenic outcome still negative? *American Journal of Psychiatry, 135,* 1156–1162.

Harrow, M., & Marengo, J. T. (1986). Schizophrenic thought disorder at followup: Its persistence and prognostic significance. *Schizophrenia Bulletin, 12,* 373–393.

Harrow, M., & Quinlan, D. (1985). *Disordered thinking and schizophrenic psychopathology.* New York: Gardner Press.

Harrow, M., & Westermeyer, J. F. (1987). Process-reactive dimension and outcome for narrow concepts of schizophrenia. *Schizophrenia Bulletin, 13,* 361–368.

Harrow, M., Westermeyer, J. F., Silverstein, M., Strauss, B. & Cohler, B. J. (1986). Prediction of outcome in schizophrenia: The process-reactive dimension. *Schizophrenia Bulletin, 12,* 195–207.

Hogarty, G. E., Goldberg, S. C., Schooler, N. R., & Urich, R. F. (1974). Drug and sociotherapy in the aftercare of schizophrenic patients: II. Two-year relapse rates. *Archives of General Psychiatry, 31,* 603–608.

Holinger, P. C., Offer, D., & Zola, M. A. (1989). A prediction model of suicide among youth. *Journal of Nervous and Mental Disease, 176,* 275–279.

Holzman, P. S., & Grinker, R. R. (1974). Schizophrenia in adolescence. *Journal of Youth and Adolescence, 3,* 267–279.

Huber, G., Gross, G., Schutter, R., & Linz, M. (1980). Longitudinal studies of schizophrenic patients. *Schizophrenia Bulletin, 6,* 592–605.

Kane, J. M., Honingfeld, G., Singer, J., Meltzer, H., & Clozarill Collaborative Study Group. (1989). Clozapine for the treatment-resistant schizophrenic: Results of a U.S. multi-center trial. *Psychopharmacology, 99,* s60–s63.

Koegel, P., Burnam, A., & Farr, R. K. (1988). The prevalence of specific psychiatric disorders among homeless individuals in the inner city of Los Angeles. *Archives of General Psychiatry, 45,* 1085–1092.

Kohlberg, L., Ricks, D., & Snarey, J. (1984). Childhood development as a predictor of adaptation in adulthood. *Genetic Psychology Monographs, 110,* 91–172.

Kraepelin, E. (1919). *Dementia praecox and paraphrenia* (R. M. Barclay, Trans.). Edinburgh: Livingstone.

Lamb, H. R. (1979). The new asylums in the community. *Archives of General Psychiatry, 36,* 129–134.

Lamb, H. R., & Goertzel, V. (1971). Discharged mental patients—Are they really in the community? *Archives of General Psychiatry, 24,* 29–34.

Lamb, H. R., & Goertzel, V. (1977). The long-term patients in the era of community treatment. *Archives of General Psychiatry, 34,* 679–682.

Lamb, H. R., Schock, R., Chen, P. W., & Gross, B. (1984). Psychiatric needs in local jails: Emergency issues. *American Journal of Psychiatry, 141,* 774–777.

Lewine, R., Burbach, D., & Meltzer, H. Y. (1984). The effects of diagnostic criteria on the ratio of male to female schizophrenic patients. *American Journal of Psychiatry, 141,* 84–87.

Lin, K. M., & Kleinman, A. M. (1988). Psychopathology and clinical course of schizophrenia: A cross-cultural perspective. *Schizophrenia Bulletin, 14,* 555–568.

Loyd, D., Simpson, J. C., & Tsuang, M. T. (1985). Are there sex differences in the long-term outcome of schizophrenia? *Journal of Nervous and Mental Disease, 173,* 643–649.

Marengo, J., & Harrow, M. (1986). Thought disorder: A function of schizophrenia, mania, or psychosis? *Journal of Nervous and Mental Disease, 12,* 497–511.

Marengo, J., & Harrow, M. (1987). Schizophrenic thought disorder at followup: A persistent or episodic course? *Archives of General Psychiatry, 44,* 651–659.

Marengo, J. T., Harrow, M., Benson, J., Sands, J. R., & Galloway, C. (1987, August). *European versus United States data on the course of schizophrenia.* Paper presented at the annual meeting of the American Psychological Association, New York.

Marneros, A., Diester, A., Rohde, A., Steinmeyer, E. M., & Junemann, H. (1989). Long-term outcome of Schizoaffective and schizophrenic disorders: A comparative study: I. Definition, methods, psychopathological and social outcome. *European Archives of Psychiatry and Neurological Science, 237,* 264–275.

May, P. R. A., Tuma, A. H., & Dixon, W. J. (1981). Schizophrenia: A followup study of the results of five forms of treatment. *Archives of General Psychiatry, 38,* 776–784.

McGlashan, T. H. (1984). The Chestnut Lodge Followup Study: II. Long-term outcome of schizophrenia and the affective disorders. *Archives of General Psychiatry, 41,* 586–601.

McGlashan, T. H. (1988). A selective review of recent North American long-term followup studies of schizophrenia. *Schizophrenia Bulletin, 14,* 515–542.

McGlashan, T. H., & Bardenstein, K. K. (1990). Gender differences in affective, schizoaffective, and schizophrenic disorders. *Schizophrenia Bulletin, 16,* 319–331.

Miles, C. P. (1977). Conditions predisposing to suicide: A review. *Journal of Nervous and Mental Disease, 164,* 231–246.

Mosher, L. R., & Keith, S. J. (1980). Psychosocial treatment: Individual, group, family and community support approaches. *Schizophrenia Bulletin, 6,* 10–41.

Murphy, G. E., & Wetzel, R. D. (1980). Suicide risk by birth cohort in the United States, 1949 to 1974. *Archives of General Psychiatry, 37,* 519–523.

National Institute of Mental Health. (1985). *Annual survey of patient characteristics—1985 State and county mental hospital inpatient services.* Rockville, MD: NIMH, Division of Biometry and Applied Science.

Neugarten, B. L. (1979). Time, age and the life cycle. *American Journal of Psychiatry, 136,* 887–894.

Opjordsmoen, S. (1988). Long-term course and outcome in delusional disorder. *Acta Psychiatrica Scandinavia, 78,* 576–586.

Pearlin, L. I. (1980). Life strains and psychological distress among adults. In N. J. Smelser & E. H. Erikson (Eds.), *Themes of work in love and adulthood.* Cambridge, MA: Harvard University Press.

Professional Staff of the U.S.–U.K. Cross-National Project. (1974). The diagnosis and psychopathology of schizophrenia in New York and London. *Schizophrenia Bulletin, 2,* 80–102.

Regier, D. A., Boyd, J. H., Burke, J. D., Rae, G. S., Myers, J. K., Kramer, M., Robins, L. N., George, L. K., Karno, M., & Locke, B. Z. (1988). One-month prevalence of mental disorders in the United States. *Archives of General Psychiatry, 45,* 977–986.

Robbins, L. N. (1966). *Deviant children grow up: A sociological and psychiatric study of sociopathic personality,* Baltimore, MD: Williams & Wilkins.

Rosen, B., Klein, D. F., & Gittelman-Klein, R. (1969). Sex differences in the relationship between premorbid asociality and posthospital outcome. *Journal of Nervous and Mental Disease, 149,* 415–420.

Rosen, B., Klein, D. F., & Gittelman-Klein, R. (1971). The prediction of rehospitalization: The relationship between age of first psychiatric treatment contact, marital status, and premorbid social adjustment. *Journal of Nervous and Mental Disease, 152,* 17–21.

Rosen, B., Klein, D. F., Levenstein, S., & Shanian, S. (1968). Social competence and posthospital outcome. *Archives of General Psychiatry, 19,* 165–170.

Rosenstein, M. J., Millazzo-Sayre, L. J., & Mandersheid, R. W. (1989). Care of persons with schizophrenia: A statistical profile. *Schizophrenia Bulletin, 15,* 45–58.

Roy, A. (1986). Suicide in schizophrenia. In A. Roy (Ed.), *Suicide* (pp. 97–112). Baltimore, MD: Williams & Wilkins.

Salokangas, R. K. R. (1983). Prognostic implications of the sex of schizophrenic patients. *British Journal of Psychiatry, 142,* 145–151.

Sartorius, N., Jablensky, A., & Shapiro, R. (1978). Cross-cultural differences in the short-term prognosis of schizophrenic psychoses. *Schizophrenia Bulletin, 4,* 102–112.

Seeman, M. (1983). Interaction of sex, age and neuroleptic dose. *Comprehensive Psychiatry, 24,* 125.

Seeman, M. V. & Lang, M. (1990). The role of estrogen in schizophrenia gender differences. *Schizophrenia Bulletin, 16,* 185–194.

Shapiro, S., Skinner, E. A., Kessler, L. G., Vonkorff, M., German, P. S., Tishler, G. L., Leaf, P. J., Benham, L., Cottler, L. & Regier, D. A. (1984). Utilization of health and mental health services: Three Epidemiologic Catchment Area sites. *Archives of General Psychiatry, 41,* 971–978.

Spitzer, R. L., Endicott, J., & Robins, E. (1978). Research diagnostic criteria: Rationale and reliability. *Archives of General Psychiatry, 35,* 773–782.

Stein, L. I. (1989). The effect of long-term outcome studies on the therapy of schizophrenia: A critique. *Journal of Marital and Family Therapy, 15,* 133–138.

Stein, L. I., & Test, M. A. (1980). Alternative to mental hospital treatment: I. Conceptual model, treatment program, and clinical evaluation. *Archives of General Psychiatry, 37,* 392–396.

Stein, L. I., & Test, M. A. (1982). Community treatment of the young adult patient. In B. Pepper & H. Ryglewicz (Eds.), *New directions for mental health services: The young adult chronic patient* (pp. 57–67). San Francisco: Jossey-Bass.

Stephens, J. H. (1978). Long-term prognosis and followup in schizophrenia. *Schizophrenia Bulletin, 4,* 25–37.

Strauss, J. S., & Carpenter, W. T., Jr. (1977). Prediction of outcome in schizophrenia: III. Five-year outcome and its predictors. *Archives of General Psychiatry, 34,* 159–163.

Strauss, J. S., Kokes, R. F., Carpenter, W. T., & Ritzler, B. A. (1978). The course of schizophrenia as a developmental process. In L. C. Wynne, R. L. Cromwell, & S. Matthysse (Eds.), *The nature of schizophrenia: New approaches to research and treatment* (pp. 617–631). New York: Wiley.

Test, M. A. (1981). Effective community treatment of the chronically mentally ill: What is necessary: *Journal of Social Issues, 37,* 71–85.

Test, M. A., & Stein, L. I. (1980). Alternative to mental hospital treatment: III. Social cost. *Archives of General Psychiatry, 37,* 409–412.

Tolan, P. H. (1988). Delinquent behavior and male adolescent development: A preliminary study. *Journal of Youth and Adolescence, 171,* 413–422.

Tsuang, M. (1978). Suicide in schizophrenics, manics, depressives and surgical controls: A comparison with the general population suicide mortality. *Archives of General Psychiatry, 35,* 153 155.

Tsuang, M. T., Woolson, R. F., & Fleming, J. A. (1979). Long-term outcome of major psychosis: I. *Archives of General Psychiatry, 39,* 1295–1301.

Vaillant, G. E. (1977). *Adaptation to life.* Boston: Little, Brown.

Vaillant, G. E. (1978a). A 10-year followup of remitting schizophrenics. *Schizophrenia Bulletin, 4,* 78–85.

Vaillant, G. E. (1978b). The distinction between prognosis and diagnosis in schizophrenia: A discussion of Manfred Bleuler's paper. In C. L. Wynne & S. Matthysse (Eds.), *The nature of schizophrenia: New approaches to research and treatment.* New York: Wiley.

Vaillant, G. E. (1983). *The natural history of alcoholism.* Cambridge, MA: Harvard University Press.

Vaillant, G. E., & Milofsky, E. (1980). Natural history of male psychological health: IX. Empirical evidence of Erikson's model of the life cycle. *American Journal of Psychiatry, 137,* 1348–1359.

Vaillant, G. E., & Vaillant, C. O. (1990). Natural history of male psychological health: XII. A 45-year study of predictors of successful aging at age 65. *American Journal of Psychiatry, 147,* 31–37.

Vaughn, C. E., Snyder, K. S., Jones, S., Freeman, W. B., & Falloon, I. R. H. (1984). Family factors in schizophrenic relapse. *Archives of General Psychiatry, 41,* 1169.

Wahl, O. F. & Harman, C. R. (1989). Family view of stigma. *Schizophrenia Bulletin, 15,* 131–139.

Weinberger, D. R. (1987). Implications of normal brain development for the pathogenesis of schizophrenia. *Archives of General Psychiatry, 44,* 660–669.

Weinberger, D. R., Berman, K. F., & Chase, T. N. (1988). Mesocortical dopaminergic function and human cognition. *Annals of the New York Academy of Sciences, 537,* 330–338.

Weisbrod, B. A., Test, M. A., & Stein, L. I. (1980). Alternative to mental hospital treatment: II. Economic benefit–cost analysis. *Archives of General Psychiatry, 37,* 400–405.

Weissman, M. M., & Klerman, G. L. (1977). Sex differences and the epidemiology of depression. *Archives of General Psychiatry, 34,* 98–111.

Westermeyer, J. F. (1982). *Factors associated with urban instrumental work performance in young psychiatric patients.* Unpublished doctoral dissertation, University of Chicago.

Westermeyer, J. F., & Harrow, M. (1984). Prognosis and outcome using broad (DSM-II) and narrow (DSM-III) concepts of schizophrenia. *Schizophrenia Bulletin, 10,* 624–637.

Westermeyer, J. F., & Harrow, M. (1986). Predicting outcome in schizophrenics and nonschizophrenics of both sexes: The Zigler–Phillips social competence scale. *Journal of Abnormal Psychology 95,* 406–409.

Westermeyer, J. F., & Harrow, M. (1987). Prognosis in schizophrenia. In R. R. Grinker, Sr. & M. Harrow (Eds.), *Clinical research in schizophrenia: A multidimensional approach* (pp. 299–313). Springfield, IL: Thomas.

Westermeyer, J. F., & Harrow, M. (1988). Course and outcome in schizophrenia. In M. Tsuang & J. C. Simpson (Eds.), *Handbook of schizophrenia: Volume 3. Nosology, Epidemiology and Genetics* (pp. 205–244). New York: Elsevier.

Westermeyer, J. F., & Harrow, M. (1989). Early phases of schizophrenia and depression: Prediction of suicide. In R. Williams & J. T. Dalby

(Eds.), *Depression in schizophrenia* (pp. 153–169). New York: Plenum Press.

Westermeyer, J. F., & Harrow, M. (1990). Prognosis and the natural course of schizophrenia. *Current Opinion in Psychiatry, 3,* 3–7.

Westermeyer, J. F., Harrow, M., & Carone, B. (1987). The clinical course of schizophrenia: Two successive followups. In R. R. Grinker, Sr. & M. Harrow (Eds.), *Clinical research in schizophrenia: A multidimensional approach* (pp. 314–328). Springfield, IL: Thomas.

Westermeyer, J. F., Harrow, M., & Marengo, J. T. (1989, May). *Gender and outcome in schizophrenia and depression.* Paper presented at the annual meeting of the American Psychiatric Association, San Francisco.

Westermeyer, J. F., Harrow, M., & Marengo, J. T. (1991). Risk for suicide in schizophrenia and other psychotic and nonpsychotic patients. *Journal of Nervous and Mental Disease,* 179:259–266.

World Health Organization. (1979). *Report of the international pilot study of schizophrenia,* Geneva: Author.

Zigler, E., Glick, M., & Marsh, A. (1979). Premorbid social competency and outcome among schizophrenics and nonschizophrenic patients. *Journal of Nervous and Mental Disease, 164,* 333–339.

Zigler, E. & Levine, J. (1981). Age on first hospitalization of schizophrenics: A developmental approach. *Journal of Abnormal Psychology, 96,* 458–467.

Zigler, E., & Phillips, L. (1961). Social competence and outcome in psychiatric disorder. *Journal of Abnormal Social Psychology, 63,* 264–271.

Zubin, J., & Spring, B. (1977). Vulnerability–A new view of schizophrenia. *Journal of Abnormal Psychology, 86,* 103–126.

CHAPTER 16

Outpatient Treatment of Mild Psychopathology

MARK A. REINECKE

INTRODUCTION

Psychotherapy with adolescents is of relatively recent origin. It was not until the late 19th century that adolescence came to be seen as a unique developmental period, and not until the early 20th century that psychotherapeutic treatments for emotional and behavioral problems experienced by adolescents were developed. Psychotherapy with adolescents dates to Freud's publication of *Fragment of an Analysis of a Case of Hysteria* (1953), in which he summarized the treatment of Dora, an 18-year-old girl suffering from "low spirits and an alteration in her character," migraine headaches, nervous coughing, social withdrawal, and taedium vitae. Psychoanalytic models and techniques with adolescents were subsequently elaborated by Blos, Fraiberg, A., Freud, Geleerd, Klein, Redl, Anthony, and others. More recently, cognitive, behavioral, family systems, and psychodynamically oriented approaches have been adapted for adolescent problems. The use of medication in treating emotional problems in this age group is of more recent origin, dating to Bradley's use of dexedrine during the late 1930s. The use of medications accelerated during the 1960s, with the development of neuroleptics and tricyclic antidepressants.

This chapter briefly reviews theoretical and empirical work on the treatment of adolescents, examines the status of research on treatment for their mild behavioral and emotional problems, and highlights promising areas for clinical investigation.

The chapter focuses specifically on behavioral and emotional problems that can be effectively handled on an outpatient basis through individual psychotherapy. Psychotherapy might be defined as an interaction specifically designed to produce behavioral, emotional, or cognitive understanding or change on the part of the patients, and so to help them to resolve problems that are primarily emotional or psychological in nature. Although the nature of psychotherapy is poorly understood, it is commonly accepted that the relationship established between the patient and the therapist influences the patient to change his or her behavior and emotional responses. It is generally believed that the development of reflective self-knowledge plays a central role in therapeutic improvement. We will not review the treatment of more serious disorders or the treatment of adolescents after their discharge from psychiatric hospitalizations. An examination of the use of psychotropic medications with children and adolescents is also beyond the scope of this chapter. Excellent reviews of pediatric psychopharmacology have been presented by Greenhill (1985), Koplewicz and Williams (1988), and Werry (1982). The treatment of conduct disorder among adolescents is discussed in a separate chapter.

The strength of any review is limited by both the quality and breadth of the research in the area it sets out to cover. As will be seen, the empirical foundation on which our clinical interventions are based is limited. Although there is a relatively large and detailed literature on psychotherapy with adults (Bergin & Lambert, 1978; Marks, 1978; Wolberg, 1977) and a more limited literature on the treatment of children (Barrett, Hampe, & Miller, 1978; Ross, 1978), controlled outcome studies on the effects of psychotherapy with adolescents are scarce. Longitudinal research into the natural course of mild behavioral and emotional disturbances among this age group is all but nonexistent. Moreover, there is a tendency among researchers to view adolescents as a homogeneous group. Data are frequently combined from individuals of varying ages, backgrounds, and diagnoses, and with problems differing in both severity and chronicity. This heterogeneity of patient characteristics obscures important developmental differences, as well as specific factors mediating improvement in psychotherapy. In short, research on the treatment of adolescents does not compare, in either quality or quantity, with work on adults or children.

Need we conclude, however, as Rachman (1971) did in an early review of research into the benefits of psychotherapy for adults, that "we do not have satisfactory evidence in support of the claim that psychotherapy is effective"? Probably not. A recent meta-analysis by Weisz, Weiss, Alicke, and Klotz (1987), as well as critical reviews of the literature by Kazdin (1985), Tramontana (1980), and Tramontana and Sherrets (1984), suggest that psychotherapy is capable of providing significant, relatively lasting improvement for a range of adolescent groups and problems. Our task will be to examine this literature and to derive general guidelines for conceptualizing and treating mild behavioral and emotional problems among adolescents. Our goal, as such, is practical: to suggest ways of utilizing the limited research available to guide clinical practice, and to suggest potentially useful directions for future exploration. A central thesis of this chapter is that clinical practice and empirical research are mutually supportive. Although one might reiterate criticisms of the empirical literature or bemoan the gap between research and clinical application, this has been done on numerous occasions and has not proven to be an entirely useful endeavor. A goal of this chapter is to step beyond this state of affairs and suggest useful points of contact between the clinical and empirical literatures.

DEVELOPMENTAL CONSIDERATIONS

As this volume attests, there is a general consensus about the importance of adopting a developmental and contextual perspective for describing and treating adolescents. As Tramontana and Sherrets (1984), Kendall and Williams (1986), Weisz et al. (1987), and others have observed, the processes mediating the expression of behavioral and emotional disorders among adolescents may differ from those of both children and adults. Inasmuch as a range of physical, cognitive, emotional, and social changes occurs during adolescence, the developmental characteristics and issues of this period must be considered when conceptualizing the problems of teenagers and developing a treatment plan. The developmental changes include the advent of formal operational thought, an increasing emphasis on peer relationships and autonomy from family influences, the emergence of heterosexual interests, puberty, and the development of an adult identity.

Cognitive Development

Developmental changes in abstract reasoning may influence the effectiveness of psychotherapy with adolescents. As formal operational thought emerges, for example, it may be overapplied by adolescents in an egocentric manner (Elkind, 1967). This leads the adolescent to believe that others are as concerned with his or her behavior and appearance as he or she is (the imaginary audience) and that his or her emotional experiences are entirely unique (the personal fable). Clinically, such thinking can contribute to lability of mood, in that adolescents may feel overwhelmed by emotions and experiences they believe are "more intense" than those experienced by their peers and, certainly, by adults. It can also contribute to a wariness toward others, including their therapist, and a belief that "No one can really understand me."

Autonomy

Adolescents' desires for autonomy or independence from adults and their increasing sensitivity to the norms of the peer culture frequently lead them to become more resistant to the authority of their parents or other adults than during childhood. Disturbed adolescents may, therefore, show little concern for fitting their actions to the norms of adult society and a reduced motivation to participate in psychotherapy. This is exacerbated by a frequent tendency on the part of parents, clinicians, and adolescents to view their problematic behavior as "a normal part of growing up" or "just like everyone else I know" (Jaffe & Tolan, 1989).

As Weisz et al. (1987) have noted, however, adolescents are also more likely than children to appreciate the fact that there are psychological determinants to behavior and to recognize the purpose of therapy. Like adults, they are able to reflect on their behavior and emotions and to process this material verbally. Their developed cognitive capacities make them better able than are children to generate and evaluate alternative perspectives and solutions to problematic situations. This is particularly true of older adolescents.

Asynchronies in the rates of development across domains complicate our understanding of adolescents and our attempts to assist them. An older adolescent male, for example, may have essentially completed his physical growth and, so, may present as a relatively mature individual. His cognitive and social maturation, however, may not have kept pace with his physical development. This heterochronicity of development may lead his therapist to mistakenly assume that the young man is capable of mature introspection and reasoning when, in fact, these are beyond his current ability. As a result, therapeutic progress may be impeded. Therapists are no less liable to such misjudgments, probably, than are parents. Steinberg and Hill (1978) found that parents' reactions to their sons were more closely related to the children's level of physical development than to their level of cognitive maturity—not surprising, given the salience of physical changes during adolescence. Although we can only speculate as to the effects of physical maturation on therapists' perceptions, these findings suggest that it would be prudent to view adolescents' social, physical, emotional, and cognitive development as domains in need of individual assessment.

Calling for a developmental view in understanding and treating adolescents is certainly not new (Achenbach, 1987; Rutter, 1980; Sroufe & Rutter, 1984). Unfortunately, the call has largely been unheard. Diagnostic criteria for disorders of adolescents, such as those promulgated by DSM-III-R, rarely take into account developmental differences in symptom presentation. Similarly, recent cognitive and behavioral treatments for adolescent disorders employ without modification principles and procedures designed for use with adults.

Systematic desensitization and relaxation therapy, for example, have been used with good success in treating a range of anxiety disorders experienced by children, adolescents, and adults. Age-related differences in the effectiveness of these techniques, however, have received little attention. Variations in the effectiveness of these interventions, because of developmental changes in symptomatic presentation, the nature of the anxiety-provoking stimuli, and cognitive concomitants of anxiety disorders, may be obscured in studies combining children and adolescents (Achenbach, 1985a, 1985b; Francis, 1988).

A second example of the way in which development influences the choice of therapeutic interventions comes from the field of cognitive therapy. Cognitive approaches to the treatment of childhood behavior problems typically focus on the remediation of cognitive deficits—specifically, the inability of children to employ self-directed thought and adaptive problem-solving techniques. Cognitive therapy with adults, in contrast, emphasizes the identification and reconstrual of specific thoughts or beliefs. The focus here is on thought content. Developmental factors thus mediate a shift in therapeutic emphasis—from cognitive process to cognitive content—sometime during adolescence. The choice of specific techniques to employ during adolescence, however, is rarely articulated by cognitive therapists. It seems reasonable to conclude, nonetheless, that developmental stage mediates the effectiveness of specific interventions.

In summary, normal developmental processes during adolescence appear to mediate symptom presentation, adolescents' ability to profit from specific interventions, and therapists' perceptions. Although our understanding of the relationship between normal development and the emergence of emotional disturbance during this period is limited, one should remain aware of these processes and the manner in which they affect treatment.

EPIDEMIOLOGY OF MILD BEHAVIORAL AND EMOTIONAL PROBLEMS

Prevalence and incidence rates of mild behavioral and emotional disorders among adolescents vary. These variations stem from differences in the range of disorders included in studies, as well as the specific diagnostic criteria employed, the cut-off points for severity, sample selection criteria, sources of information (self-report, parent ratings, teacher report), and the assessment instruments used. The prevalence of mild behavioral and emotional disorders appears to vary not only with age, but also with gender, socioeconomic status, cultural background, and geographic location.

In the small number of published studies of the prevalence of behavioral and emotional disorders among adolescents in the general population, the results have been reasonably consistent. Surveys completed by Leslie (1974), for example, suggested that between 10% and 20% of adolescents living in urban areas experience some form of psychiatric disorder. A study completed by Langer, Gersten, and Eisenberg (1974) in New York yielded similar results. They reported that 8% to 9% of White children, and 17% to 20% of Black and Hispanic children experienced subjectively severe problems. Unfortunately, however, the authors combined data from subjects between ages 6 and 18, so one cannot know the rates among adolescents specifically. Moreover, they did not report separately the rates for mild and more severe disorders.

The Isle of Wight study (Graham & Rutter, 1973; Rutter, Tizard, Yule, Graham, & Whitmore, 1976) is perhaps the most widely cited investigation in this literature. Over 2,000 adolescents 14 to 15 years old were screened for this study, using both parent and teacher rating scales. More comprehensive diagnostic interviews were then completed on subjects receiving high scores on either measure. Approximately 10% to 15% of adolescents were found to have manifested a diagnosable psychiatric disorder over the course of a year; an additional 5% to 10% experienced subjectively distressing symptoms that were not noted by either their parents or teachers. Most common among the adolescent problems were anxiety disorders, depression, and conduct disorder.

As Graham and Rutter (1985) noted, the specific types of psychiatric disorders found among adolescents differ considerably from those found among younger children. Moreover, psychopathological symptoms among adolescents are relatively common, even though the percentage of adolescents suffering from a specific psychiatric diagnosis at any given time may be relatively low.

Although the occurrence of specific phobias among children has received considerable attention, studies of the rates of anxiety disorders among adolescents are rare. The results of two studies suggest that the prevalence of specific phobias among adolescents is low (Abe & Masui, 1981; Baker & Wills, 1978). The latter authors, for example, reported a prevalence rate of 7.6% for school phobias among 1,300 adolescents referred for counseling. In general, females of all ages tend to report more fears and anxieties than do males. Most commonly, adolescent females report being troubled by lightning and fears of blushing or "being looked at." It is unclear, however, whether these sex differences in the prevalence of anxieties and phobias reflect a higher incidence of anxiety among females or a greater willingness of girls and their parents to acknowledge these anxieties or seek treatment for them.

The prevalence of obsessive-compulsive disorder among adolescents is also low. Flament et al. (1988) conducted one of the few comprehensive surveys of the occurrence of obsessive-compulsive symptoms among this age group. They screened over 5,000 students, then interviewed those who had scored highest on their initial measures. They reported a prevalence rate of .35% in the general adolescent population.

Estimates of the prevalence of depressive disorders among adolescents are varied. Using semistructured interviews, Kashani and his colleagues found the prevalence of major depression and dysthymic disorder to be 4.7% and 3.3%, respectively, in a community sample of 150 14-, 15-, and 16-year-olds (Kashani et al., 1987). In addition to those adolescents meeting DSM-III diagnostic criteria for depression or dysthymic disorder, an additional 33 subjects (22%) reported experiencing subclinical depressive symptoms and 28 (18%) reported having experienced dysphoric mood for 2 weeks to 1 year. These findings are inconsistent, however, with those of other investigators who have reported lower prevalence rates for depression among adolescents. Rutter et al. (1976), for example, reported a prevalence rate of .4% among the 14-year-olds surveyed in the Isle of Wight study. Similarly, Weiner and Del Gaudio (1976) reported only one case of "affective psychosis" in their review of over 1,300 adolescent patients listed in a county case register.

Although completed suicides are uncommon among teenagers, suicide rates increase with age over the course of adolescence (Centers for Disease Control, 1986; Shaffer & Fisher, 1981; Shaffer & Gould, 1987). Annually, there are between 100 and 200 suicides among adolescents 10 to 14 years old, yielding a incidence of approximately 1 per 100,000. This rate increases to 9 per 100,000 for those 15 to 19 years old. As among adults, the frequency of suicide attempts is higher among females than males, and the frequency of completed suicide is higher among males than females in this age group. Approximately five times as many adolescent males commit suicide as females.

A second index of the extent of behavioral and emotional problems among adolescents is the rate at which they are referred for clinical services. After reviewing the literature on the incidence of mental illness among adolescents, Offer, Ostrov, and Howard (1987) concluded that, at any given time, approximately 20% of teenagers were disturbed. Of these, however, only half sought assistance. Thus, as Offer and his colleagues observed, "in the United States . . . 1.8 million adolescents are quietly disturbed and stand in need of mental health care but do not receive it" (p. 87).

Although many childhood disorders, such as school phobias, enuresis, and separation anxiety, decline in frequency and severity with age, others continue into adolescence. Attention Deficit-Hyperactivity Disorder (ADHD) is a case in point. The specific symptoms and concomitants of this disorder appear to vary with age, but ADHD has long-term effects on children's academic, social, and emotional adjustment. Adolescents do not simply outgrow it. Even when primary symptoms, like motoric overactivity and inattentiveness, are resolved, the negative effects of ADHD on adjustment and self-image can continue (Gittelman, Mannuzza, Shenker, & Bonagura, 1985). Not only, then, can problems be manifested in new ways over the course of development, but residual effects can emerge. Similar considerations apply to depression among adolescents.

It may be something of a misnomer to characterize these behavioral and emotional problems experienced by adolescents as "mild," once one recognizes that long-term outcomes for untreated individuals may be significant. A case can be made that even "mild" or relatively common behavioral and emotional problems emerging during developmentally important periods of life should be viewed as significant. Behavioral and emotional problems experienced by adolescents are frequently an extension of emotional difficulties beginning earlier in life (Pichel, 1974). This history of earlier disorders, and the continuation of the stressors and psychosocial risk factors that have maintained them, has been associated with poor long-term outcomes. Longitudinal studies suggest that the mechanisms of development are quite complex. A range of factors, including genetic and biological variables, peer and family relationships, cognitive and social skills, coping capacities, habits, feelings of self-efficacy, and the timing of key experiences, interact in mediating development into adulthood (Rutter, 1984, 1989). Further longitudinal research is needed to determine not only the variables that are predictive of positive versus poor outcomes, but also the mechanisms by which they influence development. It is impossible at the moment to predict the precise impact of mild behavioral and emotional problems on adolescents' later social, academic, work, and emotional adjustment.

A BRIEF HISTORY OF ADOLESCENT PSYCHOTHERAPY

As noted, the application of psychotherapeutic interventions with adolescents dates to Freud's treatment of Dora (Freud, 1953). Even a cursory reading of this case suggests, however, that Freud was not explicitly concerned with Dora's age or developmental status. Rather, his interest centered on exploring the analysis of dream material and on elaborating his model of the libido and defenses against its expression. As Greenberg and Mitchell (1983) observed, Freud's presentation of this case:

illustrates the way in which drives are construed as the sole determinants of an object relationship . . . . The drive/structure model, like other models, by positing a clearly defined hermeneutic system, directs our attention to certain aspects of a situation and away from others. (p. 43)

Freud emphasized the libidinal contributions to object relationships, not the social context of Dora's behavior or how her developmental status may have influenced her behavior or response to treatment. Questions might be raised as to whether Dora was an "adolescent" by today's standards—individuals in her social group may have completed school, married, and raised children at younger ages—but the essential point remains. Developmental variables did not appear to play a central role in Freud's conceptualization of this case.

Traditional psychoanalytic models of personality development and psychopathology continue, nonetheless, to influence strongly the practice of adolescent psychotherapy. Important contributors to the theoretical and clinical elaboration of psychoanalysis for the treatment of adolescents include Blos (1962, 1970, 1979),

A. Freud (1958), Geleerd (1957, 1961, 1964), Josselyn (1952), Pearson (1968), and Solnit (1959). More recently, Elson (1987), Miller (1974, 1981, 1983), Masterson (1985), Marohn, (1980), and others have articulated psychodynamic models for treating such varied emotional disorders as major depression, delinquency, anxiety, eating disorders, and borderline personality disorder among adolescents. Although numerous case reports of the effectiveness of these interventions have been presented, there have been few empirical attempts to document the utility of these approaches.

Behavior therapy developed independently of the psychoanalytic tradition and represents a second important contribution to the treatment of mildly disturbed adolescents. Contingency management programs are frequently used in treating delinquent, oppositional, or hyperactive children and young adolescents (Barkley, 1981; Davidson & Seidman, 1974; Kazdin, 1985) and appear to be effective in improving social skills, reducing shyness, and eliminating tics (Christoff et al., 1985; Finney, Rapoff, Hall, & Christopherson, 1983; Spence & Marzillier, 1981). Treatment typically emphasizes the management of aversive or dangerous behavior, the development of academic or social skills, and the training of the individual in effective problem-solving techniques.

More recently, cognitive conceptualizations and techniques have been developed and applied to the treatment of adolescent emotional disorders (Barth, 1986; Bedrosian, 1981; DiGiuseppe, 1988; Feindler, Ecton, Kingsley, & Dubey, 1986; Grossman & Freet, 1987; Santostefano, 1985; Schrodt & Wright, 1987; Snyder & White, 1979; Stark, Rouse, & Livingston, 1991; Wilkes & Rush, 1988). Although cognitive models have usually been seen as derivative of behavior modification, such a view does not do justice to the contributions made by others, particularly phenomenologists and constructivists, to recent cognitive theory (Guidano & Liotti, 1983).

Cognitive interventions with adolescents are, for the most part, based on work by Luria (1961) and Vygotsky (1962, 1978) on the internalization of language and the socialization of thought processes, and by White (1960), who described mediational models of cognitive development in childhood. The influences of these writers can be seen in the work of Meichenbaum (1977, 1978), who emphasized the reinforcement of adaptive self-statements, and in the methods proposed by Kendall and Braswell (1985) on training of focused attention and adaptive problem solving.

Cognitive approaches show particular promise for handling the problems of adolescent depression, suicide, and anger control. Recent clinical advances with adults in cognitive therapy of depression (Beck, Rush, Shaw, & Emery, 1979), suicide (Freeman & Reinecke, in press), and anxiety disorders (Beck, Emery, & Greenberg, 1985) provide a promising model for understanding the specific cognitive distortions and belief systems characterizing these disorders. They lend themselves to brief, strategic interventions and have been found to be effective in several controlled outcome studies (Beck, Hollon, Young, Bedrosian, & Budenz, 1985; Blackburn, Bishop, Glenn, Whalley, & Christie, 1981; Murphy, Simons, Wetzel, & Lustman, 1984). As noted earlier, their focus on the "content" of one's thoughts is only now being applied to conceptualizing and treating adolescent disorders.

Family therapy has, during recent years, become an important theoretical orientation. The significance of family members in initiating, influencing, and treating the behavioral and emotional difficulties experienced by adolescents is clear (Walsh & Scheinkman, Chapter 7 of this volume). Family therapy techniques for treating adolescents have been the subject of a recent edited volume (Mirkin & Koman, 1985) and is also addressed by Walsh and Scheinkman.

A GENERAL DEVELOPMENT APPROACH TO THERAPY

As this brief review suggests, therapists treating adolescents have developed a range of theories and alternative approaches to psychotherapy. With the possible exception of those committed to radical behaviorism and family therapy, many who treat adolescents would agree to the importance of intrapsychic determinants of behavioral and emotional problems, and would regard the elucidation and resolution of thoughts, feelings, beliefs, and subjective experiences as essential for therapeutic improvement. What distinguishes the different approaches is the relative emphasis given to affective, cognitive, interpersonal, and environmental factors.

The many forms of psychotherapy, then, are founded on similar assumptions. They presume that behavioral and emotional change is contingent on elucidating the individual's personality or beliefs, encouraging the expression of affect, developing insight, and generating and evaluating alternative ways of viewing one's difficulties and of behaving in problematic situations.

With younger adolescents, the format of therapy typically is similar to that practiced with children: there is a greater emphasis on the interpretation of play or other activities than with older adolescents, and verbal discourse is relatively deemphasized.

As numerous authors have noted, the physical, social, and emotional changes accompanying puberty are significant. They play a central role in our understanding of early adolescence (see Richards, Abell, & Petersen, Chapter 2 of this volume; Jaffe & Ryan, Chapter 17 of this volume) and guide our conceptualizations of behavioral problems during this period. With the onset of puberty, for example, concerns about physical appearance become increasingly important to the individual. Given the importance of body image and social acceptance for one's self-image and sense of self-esteem, the psychological consequences of puberty should not be underestimated. Research indicates that there is an increased awareness and attention to one's body during this period (Simmons, Rosenberg, & Rosenberg, 1973), and that a sizable proportion of young adolescents are dissatisfied with their physical appearance (Rosenbaum, 1979; Simmons & Rosenberg, 1975). There appears to be a positive relationship, moreover, among physical maturity, attractiveness, and peer acceptance during adolescence (Walster, Aronson, Abrahams, & Rottman, 1966). Adolescents who are late maturers or who have unattractive physical characteristics, such as acne, are frequently subjected to social criticism or ostracism. Clinically, therefore, it is often useful to explore with young adolescents their feelings about their appearance, peer acceptance and rejection, and the changing nature of their relationships with their family and childhood friends. These recommendations are consistent with the finding that transient feelings of self-doubt, resentment of parents, avoidance of responsibility, and anxiety about relationships with peers peak during early to mid-puberty (Frank & Cohen, 1979).

Physiological maturation continues during middle adolescence and is accompanied by the emergence of a questioning attitude toward social norms and, at times, a rejection of social authority. As Miller (1983) observed, the middle adolescent typically demands to know the reasons for rules set by society and why they should be obeyed. Middle adolescence, then, is characterized by a developing sense of one's identity and personal uniqueness. As a result, there is a tendency at this age to identify with adults outside of the immediate family who possess qualities that the adolescents wish to develop. Similarly, there are preliminary attempts at selecting a career and at identifying life goals. Other challenges during middle adolescence include adjustment to the intensification of sexual drives, toleration of the loss of confidence in one's parents as infallible guides and protectors, and development of social skills and of the ability to deal with strong emotional states.

With middle and older adolescents, the format of the therapy sessions is more similar to that with adults. Verbal expression is encouraged and the patient assumes a relatively greater responsibility for directing the conversation to important issues. By later adolescence, adjustment to physiological and social changes accompanying puberty has declined in importance and is replaced by issues of autonomy from one's family and the consolidation of an adult identity. As Siegel (1982) observed, it is during late adolescence that issues related to defining oneself—morally, politically, sexually, and occupationally—become the focal point of experience. This process of developing an identity independent of the family, while at the same time maintaining a sense of continuity in one's relationships, requires that both adolescents and their parents be open to adjustment and compromise. Closer identification with peers, as well as a developing ability to view one's parents in a nonidealized manner, serves the important function of supporting the adolescent's desire for increased autonomy from his or her family. The peer group provides the older adolescent with a sense of belonging or security at a time when ties to parents are being loosened and alternative values, roles, and long-term goals are being evaluated. The peer group, then, can serve as something of a stabilizer during the transition to adulthood, but peer group values often differ not only from those of the parents, but also from those of the individual teenager. What can result for the adolescent is a confusing and anxiety-ridden conflict that frequently becomes an important therapeutic issue.

Older adolescents are often seen as rebellious, oppositional, or moody—qualities that, at first glance, seem without redemptive value. But conflict is a normal aspect of adolescence. It does not, in and of itself, imply psychopathology and can, in fact, serve to facilitate development. Oppositionality can be adaptive in that it facilitates the developmentally appropriate function of separation or disengagement from one's parents. As Blos (1971) succinctly stated: "Generational conflict is essential for the growth of the self." Despite challenging parental authority with regard to such issues as dress, friends, dating, music, and the like, the majority of older adolescents continue to maintain strong identifications with their parents on more substantive issues and basic values (Kandel & Lesser, 1969). The conflict of older adolescence, then, may serve to maintain the attachment to parents and families, while simultaneously supporting the development of a differentiated, mature sense of self.

An appreciation of the normality of conflict during late adolescence can be quite useful clinically. Parents need to be reassured about the positive functions of mild oppositionality and identification with peers, and advised about helping the teenager to evaluate more realistically the values, attitudes, and behaviors of the peer group and of the parents themselves. The goal of treatment during this period is often not that of "reining in" an adolescent's behavior, but of guiding his or her development. Psychotherapy takes the form of assisting teenagers in their search for a consistent set of values and a life direction, actively encouraging their attempts to make adaptive choices and supporting their developing capacities for committed, intimate relationships.

THE EFFECTIVENESS OF PSYCHOTHERAPY IN TREATING ADOLESCENTS

Relatively few controlled outcome studies have focused specifically on the treatment of adolescents with mild behavioral and emotional problems. The existing studies allow some tentative conclusions, nonetheless, about the effectiveness of psychotherapy with this population. As we will see, one need not be discouraged about clinical work with teenagers.

Weisz et al. (1987) who conducted a comprehensive review and meta-analysis of the literature since 1970 on psychotherapy with children and adolescents, identified over 100 independent investigations. Combining data across outcome measures, they found that the average treated youngster was better adjusted after treatment than about four-fifths of those not receiving therapy. It must be said that the majority of the studies included in their analysis focused primarily on psychotherapy with children or combined data from children and adolescents. Strictly speaking, therefore, one cannot rely on Weisz et al. for conclusions that are specific to the treatment of adolescents. Nonetheless, their findings are encouraging. As they put it, "there is reason for optimism about therapy effects with children and adolescents" (p. 548).

Tramontana (1980) focused specifically on the effectiveness of psychotherapy with adolescents in his critical evaluation of the outcome research completed between 1967 and 1977. The papers included in his review ranged from single case studies to controlled group comparisons of several therapeutic modalities. Treatments included individual, family, and group psychotherapy. Despite the heterogeneity of the studies both as to the populations involved and their methodological sophistication, moderately positive outcomes were found across investigations. The median rate of positive outcome for psychotherapy was approximately 75%, in comparison to about a 40% rate of spontaneous improvement without treatment.

Pooling data across studies of varying quality or making box-score comparisons of studies showing positive treatment effects with those showing no effects can yield artifactual findings. As Tramontana himself observed, of the 33 investigations he reviewed, only 5 were "methodologically sound and sufficiently comprehensive in evaluating outcome" (p. 446). These included studies by Jesness (1975), Massimo and Shore (1963, 1967), Persons (1966, 1967), Redfering (1972, 1973), Ro-Trock, Wellisch, and Schoolar (1977) and Shore and Massimo (1966, 1969, 1980). One cannot dismiss these studies, at least.

Several other methodologically sound studies have been completed during more recent years; again, their findings support the effectiveness of therapeutic interventions. Kolvin et al. (1981), for example, used epidemiological approaches to identify Newcastle school children and adolescents with emotional and behavioral difficulties. The disturbed children were then randomly assigned by class to a range of treatment or control conditions. Outcome was assessed at the completion of therapy, and at 18- and 36-month intervals posttreatment. Individuals who had participated in Rogerian group therapy or behavioral therapy were found to have made greater improvement than those in the no-treatment control groups or those who had received only parent counseling with teacher consultation. These gains were maintained over time.

Snyder and White (1979) investigated the effectiveness of cognitive interventions in improving the adjustment of a small sample of more seriously disturbed adolescents. Their sample included 15 adolescents 14 to 17 years old in residential treatment who had demonstrated only "minimal behavior change in response to an operant behavior modification program" (p. 228). Cognitive self-instruction therapy was associated with significant improvements in class attendance, completion of self-care activities, and reductions in drug use, physical aggression, stealing, and destruction of property. These gains reportedly were maintained over a 6-week follow-up period.

Snyder and White did not, however, assess the stability of these improvements after discharge from the residential treatment program or their effects on their general adjustment. Their findings are, nonetheless, promising in that they suggest that focused, short-term interventions can be useful with adolescents who had been unresponsive to other modes of treatment.

Apparently, then, psychotherapy can be beneficial in ameliorating behavioral and emotional problems among adolescents. In concluding an investigation of the effectiveness of clinic-based psychotherapy with children and adolescents, Weisz and Weiss (1989) observed:

. . . adolescent psychotherapy can be effective when the conditions are carefully arranged, as when the targets of treatment are clearly delineated, when these are well-matched to the type of therapy provided, and when the therapists are well-trained in the approach they use. (p. 746)

In discussing the utility of therapy, however, it is important not only to assess its immediate effects on the individual's mood and functioning at home and at school, but also to examine its effects on his or her long-term adjustment. The data are far from conclusive insofar as the long run is concerned. Our goal, in the larger sense, is not simply to assist the adolescent in resolving immediate concerns, but also to support ongoing development—to assist him or her in developing the capacity to form mature, trusting relationships and to function effectively as an adult—in short, to love and to work. Developing specific competencies and eliminating aversive behaviors is not all that work with adolescents is about. These changes need to be accompanied by meaningful improvements in the individual's overall social, emotional, and vocational adjustment. In evaluating the effectiveness of any form of treatment, then, we should examine not just the effects on specific behaviors, but also the patient's general adjustment. These are clinical truisms, perhaps, but it is distressing to note how often they are overlooked by researchers who employ narrowly focused sets of outcome measures and by clinicians who make too much of too little behavioral change. A better approach in evaluating the effectiveness of one's treatment program is to assess symptomatic improvement on a regular basis during treatment, as well as the patient's mood, relationships, need for additional treatment, and satisfaction with work during the years following termination.

METHODOLOGICAL CONSIDERATIONS

As this brief review suggests, research bearing on the effectiveness of psychotherapy has been plagued by a range of conceptual and methodological shortcomings. While not an indictment of the literature as a whole, these difficulties speak to the need for a more concerted effort to evaluate the effectiveness of psychotherapy with adolescents and to use greater care in the design of studies. It is worth noting that these methodological and conceptual problems are not unique to studies of adolescents, and that it is far easier to critique research than to design and implement a sound program of study in this area. As Samuel Johnson once observed, "It is easier to recognize a bad cake than to bake a good one." It is, in short, quite difficult to do good (let alone superlative) research with this age group. Nonetheless, by identifying common stumbling blocks in the literature, they might more readily be avoided in the future. Common shortcomings in the literature include:

1. A lack of demographic information about patients;
2. A lack of information about patients' academic placement, as well as the presence of learning disabilities or medical problems;
3. Failure to report response to prior therapy or medications;
4. Lack of reliable diagnoses for patients;
5. Use of heterogeneous groups of patients in treatment groups;
6. Failure to report the age of onset and duration of symptoms;
7. Use of retrospective evaluations of patients' problems and response to treatment;
8. Small numbers of subjects in treatment and control groups;
9. Use of small number of therapists;
10. Failure to fully document the type, adequacy, amount, intensity, and duration of the therapy provided;
11. Use of inappropriate outcome measures;
12. Limited scope of outcome measures;
13. Use of inappropriate control groups.

Insofar as is possible and practical, studies of therapy should include relevant descriptions of the patients being treated, what the intervention was like, and whether it was effective.

Patient Descriptions

At a minimum, one needs to include demographic information such as parental marital status, socioeconomic status, and the number of siblings. For adolescents, academic placement and history, including the presence of learning disabilities, are important data.

One needs to know, as well, the patients' psychiatric diagnoses (using RDC, DSM-III-R, or any other classification system of some currency) and how they were established. A number of interview schedules have been developed during recent years, including the K-SADS (Puig-Antich & Chambers, 1978), Interview Schedule for Children (Kovacs, 1982), Diagnostic Interview for Children and Adolescents (Herjanic & Reich, 1982), and Child Assessment Schedule (Hodges, Kline, Stern, Cytryn, & McKnew, 1982). These measures have been reviewed by Edelbrock and Costello (1988) and Orvaschel (1988). Concomitant medical disorders that may affect the patient should be noted. Along the same lines, it is essential to document the nature of onset and duration of the disorders, plus the previous treatment history (including medications). For most studies, it is wisest to work with a well-defined and diagnostically homogeneous sample, if one wishes to test the specificity of action of a given treatment.

Intervention

More and more, refereed journals and funding agencies (not to mention third-party payors) demand detailed documentation of what, in fact, was entailed by the "treatment." This documentation requires some specification of technique (a manual, for example) and evidence, via protocols and time-sampling, that the implementation was along the lines intended by the investigators. That is no small undertaking, so it is not surprising to see it so often lacking. Beyond documenting the "purity" of the intervention—that is, the extent to which the intended treatment was, in fact, provided—it is also useful to assess the "quality" of the intervention or the competence of the therapist.

For these reasons alone, it would make sense for many treatment studies to be collaborative or to come from large centers of research. Supportive funds are needed to mount the studies and document them adequately. Similarly, a research group can provide the person-power for investigations with the requisite number of patients and therapists. Too small a sample size and small numbers of therapists in each treatment condition make it impossible to determine whether treatment effects are generalizable to a range of adolescents or to therapists with differing styles. Moreover, the use of small numbers of subjects tends to reduce statistical power, making it difficult to detect differences between groups when alternative treatments are contrasted (Kazdin & Bass, 1989). Because statistical power is a function of effect size, it can be maximized by increasing the number of patients in each treatment group, selecting homogeneous groups of patients, standardizing assessment procedures, and enhancing the reliability of the treatment protocol. O'Leary and Turkewitz (1978) recommended that a minimum of 3 to 4 therapists be used per treatment condition—or more, when therapist variables are the focus of the study.

Outcome

Ideally, one wishes to measure the impact of treatments prospectively and to test hypotheses concerning the effectiveness or differential impact of specific interventions. Retrospective studies have heuristic value but are plagued with difficulties (Campbell & Stanley, 1963). Wait-list, no-treatment control groups and "placebo" (nontherapeutic) controls are inadequate and have probably led to the underestimation of the effectiveness of psychotherapy. People are not inert, so they very frequently seek help where they can get it, whether the helper is a certified psychotherapist, a bartender, a friend, or the basketball coach. So much for "notreatment" controls. Moreover, meeting with a therapist—even one determined *not* to be psychotherapeutic—can be helpful. Talking about one's concerns with an interested individual can lead people to reflect on their problems, to gain insight into their concerns, and to spontaneously generate alternative solutions. One just can't charge for it. So much for "placebo" controls.

It is important to think broadly about measuring outcome. The choice of dependent measures varies with the specific questions being addressed, the theoretical orientation of the investigator, and the exigencies of the setting. Researchers frequently use a restricted range of outcome measures, or use measures that are similar to treatment procedures. Moreover, self-report scales, parental rating scales, and teachers' reports are all subject to demand effects and are potentially biased. Adolescents often do not, for example, perceive their behavior as problematic and may complete self-report scales accordingly. Similarly, teachers' reports may be biased in that the adolescent may be troublesome in the classroom and quite frustrating for them. Alternatively, teachers may not have the opportunity to observe a range of clinically significant behaviors (such as suicidal statements, theft, or fire setting) that occur only occasionally—and, typically, outside of the school. They may overlook potentially important problems, such as dysphoria, that are not disruptive in the classroom. This potential bias is particularly important when assessing mild problems and internalizing disorders. Parental ratings have been found to be influenced by marital discord, differing (and unrealistic) expectations of appropriate adolescent behavior, and parental psychopathology. Clinically, parents of disturbed adolescents have been observed both to minimize and overestimate the severity of their child's difficulties.

With these concerns in mind, no single outcome measure is sufficient for assessing the effectiveness of a clinical intervention. Rather, each provides unique information that can be useful in evaluating treatment outcomes. A variety of measures, methods, and sources are best used as part of a multidimensional assessment process. Self-report scales in conjunction with interviews or questionnaires completed by parents, teachers, and clinicians should be included.

To make things more complicated, it should be noted that behavioral observations, self-report questionnaires, and behavioral ratings completed by parents and teachers often show little intercorrelation (Herjanic & Reich, 1982; Kazdin, Esveldt-Dawson, Unis, & Rancurello, 1983). The low correlations among measures, while often viewed as "error variance" in the assessment procedures, may, in fact, reflect situational specificity of adolescents' problem behaviors and feelings. The discrepancy between self-report and ratings by others is an area of clinical and theoretical interest in its own right.

As a general conclusion, then, it is best to assess the effects of an intervention over a range of settings, with ratings being completed by independent observers. The stability of improvement should be assessed through the use of repeated measures. It is essential to use measures that are psychometrically sound, but it is equally important that the assessment reflect the presence or absence of clinically meaningful changes in the adolescent's affect, behavior, and overall adjustment. The effects of treatment on adolescents' subsequent social adjustment, ability to maintain a job, contacts with law enforcement, and need for additional therapy, for example, are frequently overlooked. One must also consider seriously the span of time to be covered in determining the benefits of therapy. With adolescents still very much in the process of growth and change, one could argue that long-term effects are unreasonable to demand of any interventions. On the other hand, arguments could be martialed that treatment without substantial endurance over time is only palliative and quite nonspecific. A good rule of thumb is to consider the benefits of interventions in comparison with what the patient would normally be expected to get from his or her family, school, and community. From the point of view of public health, the benefits of treatment are best measured as increments over the currently available resources.

Time is to be considered at every step in evaluating psychotherapy. Improvement in different aspects of behavior may occur at different rates over the course of treatment. In a conduct-disordered adolescent, for example, a change in his or her empathy for others, aggressiveness, problem-solving ability, lying, and fire setting should not be expected to become apparent at the same time. In the same vein, one need not expect that somatic symptoms, such as fatigue, loss of appetite, or insomnia will improve at the same rate as feelings of self-reproach, hopelessness, or anhedonia when treating a depressed adolescent. By comparing alternative treatments as to the differential rates of improvement for specific symptoms, one would be better able to identify which therapeutic interventions will most rapidly yield clinical change. Moreover, the careful assessment of behavioral change over the course of therapy can provide insights into the clinical change process.

SPECIFIC FINDINGS

Even if one accepts the general conclusion that therapy can be beneficial for adolescents, more specific questions remain. Do the different problems experienced by adolescents require different forms of treatment? Are variations in therapeutic technique required because of developmental changes over the course of adolescence? What specific factors contribute to variations in therapeutic improvement? What processes underlie change over the course of psychotherapy with adolescents? As is the case regarding psychotherapy research with adults, we do not as yet have clear answers to these questions. Insights from individual studies, however, permit several suggestions that may be clinically useful.

1. There is a growing consensus that *traditional long-term individual psychotherapy is less effective than briefer and more focused psychotherapeutic interventions* (Rutter, 1983). Although findings are not conclusive, strategic and problem-focused forms of psychotherapy appear to be relatively effective in treating depression (Beck, Hollon, Young, Bedrosian, & Budenz, 1985; Blackburn, Bishop, Glen, Whalley, & Christie, 1981; Blackburn, Eunson, & Bishop, 1987; McLean & Hakstian, 1979; Murphy, Simons, Wetzel, and Lustman, 1984; Rush, Beck, Kovacs, & Hollon, 1977; Shaw, 1977; Teasdale, Fennell, Hibbert, and Amies, 1984; Wilkes & Rush, 1988; Wilson, Goldin, & Charbonneau-Powis, 1983). They have also been found useful in treating panic disorder (Clark, Salkovskis, & Chalkley, 1985), obsessive-compulsive disorder (Emmelkamp, 1987), and eating disorders (Garner, 1986; Wilson, 1986). Their effectiveness is reflected both in the results of meta-analyses and in findings from individual studies. Although few comparative outcome studies have been completed, examinations of the superiority of long-term traditional psychotherapy have not been encouraging. The future—at least the immediate future—appears to belong to the briefer, focused interventions, whether cognitive, behavioral, family systems, or psychodynamically oriented.

As in research with adult populations, no specific model or intervention has consistently been found to be better than the others (Frank, 1973, 1979; Parloff, 1984). Are all forms of short-term therapy, then, equally useful for all problems? Do therapeutic benefits stem merely from the nonspecific effects of providing patients with a supportive relationship or enhancing their expectancy of change? It doesn't seem so.

The results of Weisz et al.'s (1987) meta-analysis, for example, revealed:

> [Behavioral interventions] yielded significantly larger effects than nonbehavioral methods. This finding held up across differences in age level, treated problem, and therapist experience, and was not qualified by interactions with any of these factors. . . . Overall, the findings make a case for the superiority of behavioral over nonbehavioral approaches. (p. 548)

Admittedly, something of an artifact is at work here. The problem-focused nature of the behavioral assessment of therapy outcome works in its own favor. Nonetheless, the findings still obtain, if only because behaviorally oriented therapists have taken greater care to document the utility of their interventions. It might be argued that measurement problems for nonbehaviorally oriented therapists are inherently greater, but these findings highlight the need for careful assessment of therapeutic outcome.

Our inability to identify specific factors mediating therapeutic improvement or to specify which interventions are most useful for specific problems may stem as much from the methodological shortcomings of comparative outcome studies as from the effects of nonspecific treatment factors. As has already been noted, investigations of the relative effectiveness of alternative treatments have most often yielded equivocal results. For the most part, treatments for specific disorders are found to be superior to wait-list or placebo controls, but do not differ significantly among themselves. As Kazdin and Bass (1989) have argued in discussing adult psychotherapy research, however, these results may be misleading. The lack of differences in outcome between alternative treatment groups appears to stem, at least in part, from the use of experimental designs that are not sufficiently powerful to detect the differential effects.

2. *Focused, multimodal interventions can be effective with delinquent adolescents,* particularly when attention is paid to developing their motivation to participate in the treatment program. Cases in point are the studies completed by Massimo and Shore (1963, 1967) and Shore and Massimo (1966, 1969, 1980) with antisocial males. Their treatment program included vocational training, remedial education, and psychoanalytically oriented psychotherapy. Treatment, which began within 24 hours of the boys' dropping out of school or being expelled, was presented as a means of helping them to "get a job." This pragmatic orientation was maintained throughout. Remedial education focused on developing the patients' job readiness and included discussions of their attitudes, expectations, and feelings about work. The program was individually designed in that each boy was responsible for making decisions about the frequency of sessions and the topics to be discussed. Individual therapy sessions also centered on helping the boys to find work and to manage everyday responsibilities. Issues surrounding work were used as a point of departure for discussing more "psychological" topics, such as controlling anger and blaming others for their own difficulties.

Twenty individuals participated in the treatment program, and 20 matched peers were in a no-treatment control group. Evaluations were completed at the conclusion of treatment and longitudinally over the course of the ensuing years. The treated individuals showed a better employment history, less frequent contact with the law, and a higher rate of returning to school than did their nontreated peers.

The work of Massimo and Shore is exemplary in the care taken by the authors to examine clinically meaningful outcome variables over the course of time. Their findings are impressive and have been widely cited. There are some caveats, however. First, they dealt with a relatively small sample of adolescents. Second, they failed to document statistically the significance of the improvements observed and did not control for the nonspecific effect of being seen by a therapist on a regular, and apparently frequent, basis. Nonetheless, the value of these studies remains. They have demonstrated the long-term effectiveness of specific interventions in improving the adjustment of delinquent adolescent males, a group widely viewed as difficult to treat (Kazdin, 1985). An integrated program of psychotherapy and interventions designed to develop problem-solving skills can, it appears, lead to enduring changes in quality-of-life.

3. *Only regular participation in therapy is associated with therapeutic improvement and positive long-term outcomes* (Gossett, Barnhart, Lewis, & Phillips, 1977; Gossett, Lewis, & Barnhart, 1983). Although research suggests that therapy can be of some benefit to troubled adolescents, this presupposes their regular

attendance and participation in the treatment. Several studies have documented the high rates of premature termination among adolescents (Tolan, Ryan, & Jaffe, 1988; Viale-Val, Rosenthal, Curtiss, & Marohn, 1984). The decision to terminate treatment before significant progress has been achieved may reflect the patient's motivation to continue in therapy, the parents' motivation for him or her to continue, factors related to the specific therapeutic approach employed, or a combination of these variables.

Which variables discriminate premature terminators from individuals and families who continue in therapy? Interestingly, *not* demographic variables, therapist age and sex, the nature and severity of the patient's problems, or the parents' perceptions of the effectiveness of therapy (Baekeland & Lundwall, 1975; Garfield, 1989; McAdoo & Roeske, 1973; Weisz, Weiss, & Langmeyer, 1987, 1989). According to Gould, Shaffer, and Kaplan (1985), however, the parents' level of distress and the nature of the referral source may be important factors in premature termination. Children and adolescents referred by the schools were found to be at an increased risk for premature termination. Gould, Shaffer, and Kaplan recommended that the parents' perceptions of the referral and resistances to the treatment be carefully explored. They suggested that self-report parent symptom checklists be part of the intake process, because high levels of parental distress are associated with the risk for discontinuation of treatment.

Because their study included data on patients between 4 and 18 years of age, it is difficult to draw conclusions that are specific to adolescents. Nonetheless, their suggestions are intuitively appealing and lend themselves to simple implementation.

With this in mind, one might add another idea, to facilitate continued involvement in therapy. Asking patients whether they felt they were able to express themselves clearly and whether they believed the therapist was able fully to understand them may be useful in encouraging continued attendance. Viale-Val et al. (1984) retrospectively studied a sample of 102 adolescents who had participated in outpatient psychodynamically oriented individual psychotherapy. Patients' reaction to their initial referral was predictive of premature termination of therapy. Over half of the patients who initially denied their problems, or who did not wish to accept the referral for treatment, failed to keep their initial appointment. An additional one-third terminated before the completion of the initial evaluation. This finding speaks to the importance of attempting, as quickly as feasible, to develop the individual's motivation to participate in treatment. This recommendation is in accord with findings from research with adult outpatients indicating that premature termination, particularly after the initial evaluation or first therapy session, is associated with patients' belief that they were "not really understood" by their therapist. This finding may be applicable to work with adolescents, particularly older adolescents, who seek treatment on their own.

4. *An active, collaborative approach may be useful in treating adolescents.* Meyer and Zegans (1975) conducted one of the few studies of how therapist variables influence the outcome of psychotherapy with adolescents. Twenty-five older adolescent outpatients were interviewed as to their views of their therapists and their feelings about the effectiveness of their treatment. Whereas adolescent girls tended to prefer a male therapist, adolescent boys reported no preference. For the entire group, opinions were mixed as to whether they preferred a younger or older therapist. Common themes, however, included a desire for a therapist who could be a "real person"—relaxed, caring, empathetic, active, and expressing affect spontaneously—yet who remains objective and insightful. The descriptions were similar to the qualities embodied in the "Supershrink" described by Ricks (1974), whose active, responsive, problem-oriented stance and recommendations were positively related to adult outcomes for severely disturbed adolescents. As Ricks (1974) stated:

There seem to be four major ways in which the methods . . . differed. Compared to Therapist B,

Supershrink appeared to allocate his efforts more appropriately, to make more frequent and better planned use of community resources, to handle families with more firmness and directedness, and to set up deeper and more lasting therapy relationships. The main elements in these relationships, in turn, seemed to help the boys in achieving autonomy and in developing competence in school and work. (p. 281)

Ricks was concerned with the treatment of more severely disturbed adolescents and focused primarily on inpatient psychotherapy, but his suggestions were sensible and might readily be applied in working with less severely disturbed adolescents.

5. *Patients' perceptions of personal efficacy or competence and the belief that outcomes may be controllable may also mediate progress in psychotherapy.* There appears to be a developmental change in children's ability to recognize the extent to which they can influence events in their lives. In an interesting study, Weisz (1986) found that positive outcomes over the course of outpatient psychotherapy were strongly associated with (a) the belief that problems are controllable and (b) the perception that one has the ability or competence to solve them. The latter beliefs were not associated with positive outcomes among those 8 to 12 years old in his sample, but were associated with gains achieved by adolescents. Clinically, this suggests that therapeutic progress is fostered by developing the adolescent's belief that desired outcomes can be influenced by his or her behavior and that, with effort, he or she has the ability to control those eventualities. As Weisz (1986) noted, this is particularly important in treating children and adolescents:

> . . . [They] rarely volunteer for therapy, . . . [and] cannot be assumed to believe in its efficacy or in the controllability of their problems that stimulated the therapy. (p. 794)

GUIDELINES FROM THE RESEARCH FOR THE TREATMENT OF ADOLESCENTS

Before effective treatments can be developed, the etiology, course, and factors maintaining problems must be understood. Unfortunately, there is limited consensus as to the factors contributing to behavioral and emotional disorders among adolescents. As a result, the therapeutic techniques now employed depend as much on the theoretical orientation of the therapist as on the nature of a given adolescent's specific concerns. Psychologists tend to look for intrapsychic factors; family therapists examine intrapersonal and systemic contributions; and psychiatrists postulate compromised organic or physiological systems. All of these variables (and others) play an important role in adolescent psychopathology and its treatment. Despite all the confusion and groping, nonetheless, several conclusions or guidelines can be drawn from the literature on adolescence:

1. Treatment should maintain a developmental orientation and stay sensitive to developmental issues and concerns.

2. Structured approaches, including cognitive, behavioral, and psychodynamically oriented interventions, appear to be more effective than longer-term, unfocused treatments.

3. Consistency is essential when employing these approaches. The therapist, parents, and teachers should agree on the specific outcomes and be capable of administering the program consistently.

4. Most "mild problems" are effectively handled by integrated treatment programs. These typically include individual or group therapy, parent guidance sessions or family therapy, and interventions in the school.

5. It is important to develop the adolescents' motivation to participate actively in the treatment process. It is often helpful to focus on their specific goals and concerns as a means of motivating these young people to involve themselves.

6. Progress for adolescents may be dependent on developing their belief that problems are controllable and that they possess the abilities to solve them.

7. Feelings of intimidation or threat should not result from the lability of adolescents'

affect and behavior. It frequently reflects their tendency to misperceive the reactions of others or to exaggerate the seriousness of their predicament. These cognitive or perceptual distortions appear to stem from the egocentric application of formal operational thought—a normal developmental process. Calm, socratic questioning and the development of alternative solutions can be helpful with upset teenagers.

8. With depressed or suicidal adolescents, clinical interventions should initially be directed toward alleviating their feelings of hopelessness and toward enhancing their problem-solving abilities.

CONCLUSION

We have reason for optimism about the effectiveness of psychotherapy in treating mild behavioral and emotional problems experienced by adolescents. The number of available outcome studies, however, is quite limited, as is research into processes mediating psychotherapeutic change among adolescents. Case studies and descriptive analyses are of heuristic value, but they are not sufficient for developing empirically based treatment programs. When applied to adolescents, the utility of treatments designed for use with children or adults must be empirically evaluated by means of controlled outcome studies that use a range of sensitive outcome measures.

Inasmuch as even relatively mild behavioral and emotional problems experienced by adolescents can have pernicious effects, it is important to recognize the value of including long-term follow-up assessments as a regular part of both research and clinical work. Similarly, we should more carefully attempt to ensure that our interventions have the positive effects we desire for adolescents' overall development. Our theories and techniques appear to show promise of providing meaningful support for adolescents' development. We need not require that the interventions made during adolescence ameliorate all of the trials and tribulations of that period or lead to improvements that will be apparent throughout the patients' lives.

With this in mind, we should attempt to keep both the forest and the trees in view. Our interventions may be narrow in the sense that they are designed to ameliorate immediate distress and to prevent negative repercussions for the teenager over the short term. To a significant degree, individuals act in ways that shape their environment and their experiences. As a result, specific interventions may have broader effects on adolescents' social, emotional, academic, and work adjustment, and treatment might be seen as a potential transition point in the adolescent's life. The challenge, then, is to develop interventions that support this growth and to assess the effects of our interventions in broader ways and over a more considerable length of time.

REFERENCES

Abe, K., & Masui, T. (1981). Age-sex trends of phobic and anxiety symptoms in adolescents. *British Journal of Psychiatry, 138,* 297–302.

Achenbach, T. (1985a). Assessment of anxiety in children. In A. Tuma & J. Maser (Eds.), *Anxiety and the anxiety disorders* (pp. 707–734). Hillsdale, NJ: Erlbaum.

Achenbach, T. (1985b). *Assessment and taxonomy of child and adolescent psychopathology.* Beverly Hills: Sage.

Achenbach, T. (1987). *Developmental psychopathology* (2nd ed.). New York: Wiley.

Baekeland, F., & Lundwall, L. (1975). Dropping out of treatment. *Psychological Bulletin, 82,* 738–783.

Baker, H., & Wills, U. (1978). School phobia: Classification and treatment. *British Journal of Psychiatry, 132,* 492–499.

Barkley, R. (1981). *Hyperactive children: A handbook for diagnosis and treatment.* New York: Guilford Press.

Barrett, C., Hampe, I., & Miller, L. (1978). Research on child psychotherapy. In S. Garfield & A. Bergin (Eds.), *Handbook of psychotherapy and behavior change* (2nd Ed.) (pp. 411–435). New York: Wiley.

Barth, R. (1986). *Social and cognitive treatment of children and adolescents*. San Francisco: Jossey-Bass.

Beck, A., Emery, G., & Greenberg, R. (1985). *Anxiety disorders and phobias*. New York: Basic Books.

Beck, A., Hollon, S., Young, J., Bedrosian, R., & Budenz, D. (1985). Treatment of depression with cognitive therapy and amitryptyline. *Archives of General Psychiatry, 42,* 142–148.

Beck, A., Rush, A., Shaw, B., & Emery, G. (1979). *Cognitive therapy of depression*. New York: Guilford Press.

Bedrosian, R. (1981). The application of cognitive therapy techniques with adolescents. In G. Emery, S. Hollon, & R. Bedrosian (Eds.), *New directions in cognitive therapy* (pp. 68–83). New York: Guilford Press.

Bergin, A., & Lambert, M. (1978). The evaluation of therapeutic outcome. In S. Garfield & A. Bergin (Eds.), *Handbook of psychotherapy and behavior change* (2nd Ed.) (pp. 139–189). New York: Wiley.

Blackburn, I., Bishop, S., Glenn, A., Whalley, L., & Christie, J. (1981). The efficacy of cognitive therapy of depression: A treatment trial using cognitive therapy and pharmacotherapy, each alone and in combination. *British Journal of Psychiatry, 139,* 181–189.

Blackburn, I., Eunson, K., & Bishop, S. (1987) A two-year naturalistic follow-up of depressed patients treated with cognitive therapy, pharmacotherapy, and a combination of both. *Journal of Affective Disorders, 10,* 67–75.

Blos, P. (1962). *On adolescence: A psychoanalytic interpretation*. New York: Free Press.

Blos, P. (1970). *The young adolescent: Clinical studies*. New York: Free Press.

Blos, P. (1971). The generation gap: Fact and fiction. In F. Feinstein, P. Giovacchini, & A. Miller (Eds.), *Adolescent psychiatry: Vol. 1* (pp. 5–13). New York: Basic Books.

Blos, P. (1979). *The adolescent passage*. New York: International Universities Press.

Campbell, D., & Stanley, J. (1963). Experimental and quasi-experimental designs for research on teaching. College Publishing Co. Chicago: Rand McNally.

Center for Disease Control. (1986). Youth suicide in the United States, 1970–1980. Washington, DC: Department of Health and Human Services.

Christoff, K., Scott, W., Kelley, M., Schlundt, D. Baer, G., & Kelly, J. (1985). Social skills and social problem solving training for shy young adolescents. *Behavior Therapy, 16,* 468–477.

Clark, D., Salkovskis, P., & Chalkley, A. (1985). Respiratory control as a treatment for panic attacks. *Journal of Behavior Therapy and Experimental Psychiatry, 16,* 23–30.

Davidson, W., & Seidman, E. (1974). Studies of behavior modification and juvenile delinquency: A review, methodological critique and social perspective. *Psychological Bulletin, 81,* 998–1011.

DiGiuseppe, R. (1988). A cognitive-behavioral approach to the treatment of conduct disorder children and adolescents. In N. Epstein, S. Schlesinger, & W. Dryden (Eds.), *Cognitive-behavioral therapy with families* (pp. 183–214). New York: Brunner-Mazel.

Edelbrock, C., & Costello, A. (1988). Structured psychiatric interviews for children. In M. Rutter, A. Tuma, & I. Lann (Eds.), *Assessment and diagnosis in child psychopathology* (pp. 87–112). New York: Guilford Press.

Elkind, D. (1967). Egocentrism in adolescence. *Child Development, 38,* 1025–1034.

Elson, M. (Ed.). (1987). *The Kohut seminars on self psychology and psychotherapy with adolescents and young adults*. New York: Norton.

Emmelkamp, P. (1987). Obsessive-compulsive disorders. In L. Michelson & L. Ascher (Eds.), *Anxiety and stress disorders* (pp. 310–331). New York: Guilford Press.

Feindler, E., Ecton, R., Kingsley, D., & Dubey, D. (1986). Group anger control training for institutionalized psychiatric male adolescents. *Behavior Therapy, 17,* 109–123.

Finney, J., Rapoff, M., Hall, C., & Christopherson, E. (1983). Replication and social validation of habit reversal treatment for tics. *Behavior Therapy, 14,* 116–126.

Flament, M., Whitaker, A., Rapoport, J., Davies, M., Berg, C., Kalikow, K., Sceery, W., & Shaffer, D. (1988). Obsessive compulsive disorder in adolescence: An epidemiological study. *Journal of the American Academy of Child and Adolescent Psychiatry, 27,* 764–771.

Francis, G. (1988). Assessing cognitions in anxious children. *Behavior Modification, 12,* 267–280.

Frank, J. (1973). *Persuasion and healing.* Baltimore, MD: Johns Hopkins University Press.

Frank, J. (1979). The present status of outcome studies. *Journal of Consulting and Clinical Psychology, 47,* 310–316.

Frank, R., & Cohen, D. (1979). Psychosocial concomitants of biological maturation in preadolescence. *American Journal of Psychiatry, 136,* 1518–1524.

Freeman, A., & Reinecke, M. (in press). *Cognitive therapy of suicide.* New York: Springer.

Freud, A. (1958). Adolescence. *Psychoanalytic Study of the Child, 13,* 255–278.

Freud, S. (1953). A case of hysteria. In J. Strachey (Ed. and Trans.). *The standard edition of the complete psychological works of Sigmund Freud* (Vol. 7, pp. 1–122). London: Hogarth Press.

Garfield, S. (1989). Giving up on child psychotherapy: Who drops out? Comment on Weisz, Weiss, and Langmeyer. *Journal of Consulting and Clinical Psychology, 57,* 168–169.

Garner, D. (1986). Cognitive therapy for anorexia nervosa. In K. Brownell & J. Foreyt (Eds.), *Handbook of eating disorders* (pp. 301–327). New York: Basic Books.

Geleerd, E. (1957). Some aspects of psychoanalytic technique in adolescents. *Psychoanalytic Study of the Child, 12,* 263–283.

Geleerd, E. (1961). Some aspects of ego vicissitude in adolescence. *Journal of the American Psychoanalytic Association, 9,* 394–405.

Geleerd, E. (1964). Adolescence and adaptive regression. *Bulletin of the Menninger Clinic, 28,* 302–308.

Gittelman, R., Mannuzza, S., Shenker, R., & Bonagura, N. (1985). Hyperactive boys almost grown up. *Archives of General Psychiatry, 42,* 937–947.

Gossett, J., Barnhart, D., Lewis, J., & Phillips, V. (1977). Follow-up of adolescents treated in a psychiatric hospital: Predictors of outcome. *Archives of General Psychiatry, 34,* 1037–1042.

Gossett, J., Lewis, J., & Barnhart, D. (1983). *To find a way: The outcome of hospital treatment of disturbed adolescents.* New York: Brunner-Mazel.

Gould, M., Shaffer, D., & Kaplan, D. (1985). The characteristics of dropouts from a child psychiatry clinic. *Journal of the American Academy of Child Psychiatry, 24,* 316–328.

Graham, P., & Rutter, M. (1973). Psychiatric disorder in the young adolescent: A follow-up study. *Proceedings of the Royal Society of Medicine, 66,* 58–61.

Graham, P., & Rutter, M. (1985). Adolescent disorders. In M. Rutter & L. Hersov (Eds.), *Child and adolescent psychiatry: Modern approaches* (2nd ed.) (pp. 351–367). Oxford: Blackwell Scientific.

Greenberg, J., & Mitchell, S. (1983). *Object relations in psychoanalytic theory.* Cambridge, MA: Harvard University Press.

Greenhill, L. (1985). Pediatric psychopharmacology. In D. Shaffer, A. Ehrhardt, & L. Greenhill (Eds.), *The clinical guide to child psychiatry* (pp. 493–518). New York: Free Press.

Grossman, R., & Freet, B. (1987). A cognitive approach to group therapy with hospitalized adolescents. In A. Freeman & V. Greenwood (Eds.), *Cognitive therapy: Applications in psychiatric and medical settings* (pp. 132–151). New York: Human Sciences Press.

Guidano, V., & Liotti, G. (1983). *Cognitive processes and emotional disorders.* New York: Guilford Press.

Herjanic, B., & Reich, W. (1982). Development of a structured psychiatric interview for children: Agreement between child and parent on individual symptoms. *Journal of Abnormal Child Psychology, 10,* 307–324.

Hodges, K., Kline, J., Stern, L., Cytryn, L., & McKnew, D. (1982). The development of a child assessment interview for research and clinical use. *Journal of Abnormal Child Psychology, 10,* 173–189.

Jesness, C. (1975). Comparative effectiveness of behavior modification and transactional analysis programs for delinquents. *Journal of Consulting and Clinical Psychology, 43,* 758–779.

Josselyn, I. (1952). *The adolescent and his world.* New York: Family Service Association of America.

Kandel, D., & Lesser, G. (1969). Parent–adolescent relationships and adolescent independence in the United States and Denmark. *Journal of Marriage and the Family, 31,* 348–358.

Kashani, J., Carlson, G., Beck, N., Hoeper, E., Corcoran, C., McAllister, J., Fallahi, C., Rosenberg, T., & Reid, J. (1987). Depression, depressive symptoms, and depressed mood among a community sample of adolescents. *American Journal of Psychiatry, 144,* 931–934.

Kazdin, A. (1985). *Treatment of antisocial behavior in children and adolescents.* Homewood, IL: Dorsey Press.

Kazdin, A., Esveldt-Dawson, K., Unis, A., & Rancurello, M. (1983). Child and parent evaluations of depression and aggression in psychiatric inpatient children. *Journal of Abnormal Child Psychology, 11,* 401–413.

Kazdin, A., & Bass, D. (1989). Power to detect differences between alternative treatments in comparative psychotherapy outcome research. *Journal of Consulting and Clinical Psychology, 57,* 138–147.

Kendall, P., & Braswell, L. (1985). *Cognitive behavioral therapy for impulsive children.* New York: Guilford Press.

Kendall, P., & Williams, C. (1986). Therapy with adolescents: Treating the "maginal man." *Behavior Therapy, 17,* 522–537.

Kolvin, I., Garside, R., Nicol, A., Macmillan, A., Wolstenholme, F., & Leitch, I. (1981). *Help starts here: The maladjusted child in the ordinary school.* London: Tavistock.

Koplewicz, H., & Williams, D. (1988). Psychopharmacological treatment. In C. Kestenbaum & D. Williams (Eds.), *Handbook of clinical assessment of children and adolescents: Vol. 2* (pp. 1084–1110). New York: New York University Press.

Kovacs, M. (1982). *The Interview Schedule for Children* (ISC). Unpublished. Department of Psychiatry, University of Pittsburgh.

Langer, T., Gersten, J., & Eisenberg, J. (1974). Approaches to measurement and definition in epidemiology of behavior disorders: Ethnic background and child behavior. *International Journal of Health Services, 4,* 483–501.

Leslie, S. (1974). Psychiatric disorder in the young adolescents of an industrial town. *British Journal of Psychiatry, 125,* 113–124.

Luria, A. (1961). *The role of speech in the regulation of normal and abnormal behavior.* New York: Liveright.

Marks, I. (1978). Behavioral psychotherapy of adult neurosis. In S. Garfield & A. Bergin (Eds.), *Handbook of psychotherapy and behavior change* (2nd ed.) (pp. 493–547). New York: Wiley.

Marohn, R., Dalle-Molle, D., McCarter, E., & Linn, D. (1980). *Juvenile delinquents: Psychodynamic assessment and hospital treatment.* New York: Brunner-Mazel.

Massimo, J., & Shore, M. (1963). A comprehensive, vocationally oriented psychotherapeutic program for delinquent boys. *American Journal of Orthopsychiatry, 33,* 634–642.

Massimo, J., & Shore, M. (1967). Comprehensive vocationally oriented psychotherapy: A new treatment technique for lower-class adolescent delinquent boys. *Psychiatry, 30,* 229–236.

Masterson, J. (1985). *The treatment of the borderline adolescent: A developmental approach.* New York: Brunner-Mazel.

McAdoo, W., & Roeske, N. (1973). A comparison of defectors and continuers in a child guidance clinic. *Journal of Consulting and Clinical Psychology, 40,* 328–334.

McLean, P. & Hakstian, A. (1979) Clinical depression: Comparative efficacy of outpatient treatments. *Journal of consulting and Clinical Psychology, 47,* 818–836.

Meichenbaum, D. (1977). *Cognitive-behavior modification: An integrative approach.* New York: Plenum Press.

Meichenbaum, D. (1978). Teaching children self-control. In B. Lahey & A. Kazdin (Eds.), *Advances in child clinical psychology: Vol. 2.* New York: Plenum Press.

Meyer, J., & Zegans, L. (1975). Adolescents perceive their psychotherapy. *Psychiatry, 38,* 11–22.

Mirkin, M., & Koman, S. (Eds.). (1985). *Handbook of adolescents and family therapy.* New York: Gardner Press.

Miller, D. (1974). *Adolescence: Its psychology, psychopathology, and psychotherapy.* New York: Aronson.

Miller, D. (1981). Adolescence: Etiology and treatment of suicide. In S. Feinstein, J. Looney, A. Schwartzberg, & A. Sorosky (Eds.), *Adolescent psychiatry: Developmental and clinical studies: Vol. 9* (pp. 327–342). Chicago: University of Chicago Press.

Miller, D. (1983). *The age between: Adolescence and therapy*. New York: Aronson.

Murphy, G., Simons, A., Wetzel, R., & Lustman, P. (1984). Cognitive therapy and pharmacotherapy: Singly and together in treatment of depression. *Archives of General Psychiatry, 41,* 33–41.

O'Leary, K., & Turkewitz, H. (1978). Methodological errors in marital and child treatment research. *Journal of Consulting and Clinical Psychology, 46,* 747–758.

Offer, D., Ostrov, E., & Howard, K. (1987). Epidemiology of mental health and mental illness among adolescents. In J. Noshpitz (Ed.), *Basic handbook of child psychiatry: Vol. 5* (pp. 82–88). New York: Basic Books.

Orvaschel, H. (1988). Structured and semistructured psychiatric interviews for children. In C. Kestenbaum & D. Williams (Eds.), *Handbook of clinical assessment of children and adolescents: Vol. 1* (pp. 31–92). New York: New York University Press.

Parloff, M. (1984). Psychotherapy research and its incredible credibility crisis. *Clinical Psychology Review, 4,* 95–109.

Pearson, G. (1968). *A handbook of child psychoanalysis*. New York: Basic Books.

Persons, R. (1966). Psychological and behavioral change in delinquents following psychotherapy. *Journal of Clinical Psychology, 22,* 337–340.

Persons, R. (1967). Relationship between psychotherapy with institutionalized delinquent boys and subsequent community adjustment. *Journal of Consulting Psychology, 31,* 137–141.

Pichel, J. (1974). A long-term follow-up study of 60 adolescent psychiatric outpatients. *American Journal of Psychiatry, 131,* 140–144.

Puig-Antich, J., & Chambers, W. (1978). *The Schedule for Affective Disorders and Schizophrenia for School-Aged Children*. Unpublished. New York: New York State Psychiatric Institute.

Rachman, S. (1971). *The effects of psychotherapy*. Oxford, England: Pergamon Press.

Redfering, D. (1972). Group counseling with institutionalized delinquent females. *American Corrective Therapy Journal, 26,* 160–163.

Redfering, D. (1973). Durability of effects of group counseling with institutionalized delinquent females. *Journal of Abnormal Psychology, 82,* 85–86.

Ricks, D. (1974). Supershrink: Methods of a therapist judged successful on the basis of adult outcomes of adolescent patients. In D. Ricks, A. Thomas, & M. Roff (Eds.), *Life history research in psychopathology: Vol. 3* (pp. 275–297). Minneapolis: University of Minnesota Press.

Rosenbaum, M. (1979). The changing body image of the adolescent girl. In M. Sugar (Ed.), *Female adolescent development*. New York: Brunner-Mazel.

Ross, A. (1978). Behavior therapy with children. In S. Garfield & A. Bergin (Eds.), *Handbook of psychotherapy and behavior change* (2nd ed.) (pp. 591–620). New York: Wiley.

Ro-Trock, G., Wellisch, D., & Schoolar, J. (1977). A family therapy outcome study in an inpatient setting. *American Journal of Orthopsychiatry, 47,* 514–522.

Rush, A., Beck, A., Kovacs, M., & Hollon, S. (1977). Comparative efficacy of cognitive therapy and pharmacotherapy in outpatient depressives. *Cognitive Therapy and Research, 1,* 17–37.

Rutter, M. (1980). Introduction. In M. Rutter (Ed.), *Scientific foundations of developmental psychiatry* (pp. 139–164). London: Heinemann.

Rutter, M. (1983). Psychological therapies: Issues and prospects. In S. Guze, F. Earls, & J. Barrett (Eds.), *Childhood psychopathology and development*. New York: Raven Press.

Rutter, M. (1984). Psychopathology and development: I. Childhood antecedents of adult psychiatric disorders. *Australian and New Zealand Journal of Psychiatry, 18,* 225–234.

Rutter, M. (1989). Pathways from childhood to adult life. *Journal of Child Psychology and Psychiatry, 30,* 23–51.

Rutter, M., Tizard, J., Yule, W., Graham, P., & Whitmore, K. (1976). Research report: Isle of Wight studies, 1964–1974. *Psychological Medicine, 6,* 313–332.

Santostefano, S. (1985). *Cognitive control therapy with children and adolescents*. New York: Pergamon Press.

Schrodt, G., & Wright, J. (1987). Inpatient treatment of adolescents. In A. Freeman & V. Greenwood (Eds.), *Cognitive therapy: Application in psychiatric and medical settings* (pp. 69–82). New York: Human Sciences Press.

Shaffer, D., & Fisher, P. (1981). The epidemiology of suicide in children and young adolescents.

Journal of the American Academy of Child and Adolescent Psychiatry, 20, 545–565.

Shaffer, D., & Gould, M. (1987). *Study of completed and attempted suicides in adolescents.* Progress report: National Institute of Mental Health.

Shaw, B. (1977) Comparison of cognitive therapy and behavior therapy in the treatment of depression. *Journal of Consulting and Clinical Psychology, 45,* 543–551.

Shore, M., & Massimo, J. (1966). Comprehensive vocationally oriented psychotherapy for adolescent delinquent boys: A followup study. *American Journal of Orthopsychiatry, 36,* 609–615.

Shore, M., & Massimo, J. (1969). Five years later: A followup study of comprehensive vocationally oriented psychotherapy. *American Journal of Orthopsychiatry, 39,* 769–773.

Shore, M., & Massimo, J. (1980). Contributions of an innovative psychoanalytic therapeutic program with adolescent delinquents to developmental psychology. In S. Greenspan & G. Pollock (Eds.), *The course of life: Psychoanalytic contributions toward understanding personality development: Vol. II. Latency, adolescence, and youth* (pp. 445–462). Washington, DC: NIMH.

Siegel, O. (1982). Personality development in adolescence. In B. Wolman (Ed.), *Handbook of developmental psychology* (pp. 537–548). Englewood Cliffs, NJ: Prentice-Hall.

Simmons, R., Rosenberg, F., & Rosenberg, M. (1973). Disturbance in the self-image at adolescence. *American Sociological Review, 38,* 553–568.

Simmons, R., & Rosenberg, F. (1975). Sex, sex roles, and self-image. *Journal of Youth and Adolescence, 4,* 225–258.

Snyder, J., & White, M. (1979). The use of cognitive self-instruction in the treatment of behaviorally disturbed adolescents. *Behavior Therapy, 10,* 227–235.

Solnit, A. (1959). Ego vicissitudes of adolescence. *Journal of the American Psychoanalytic Association, 7,* 523–535.

Spence, S., & Marzillier, J. (1981). Social skills training with adolescent male offenders—II. Short-term, long-term, and generalized effects. *Behavioral Research and Therapy, 19,* 349–368.

Sroufe, L., & Rutter, M. (1984). The domain of developmental psychopathology. *Child Development, 55,* 17–29.

Steinberg, L., & Hill, J. (1978). Patterns of family interaction as a function of age, the onset of puberty, and formal thinking. *Developmental Psychology, 14,* 683–684.

Teasdale, J., Fennell, M., Hibbert, G. & Amies, P. (1984) Cognitive therapy for major depressive disorder in primary care. *British Journal of Psychiatry, 144,* 400–406.

Tolan, P., Ryan, K., & Jaffe, C. (1988). Adolescents' mental health service use and provider, process, and recipient characteristics. *Journal of Clinical Child Psychology, 17,* 228–235.

Tramontana, M., & Sherrets, S. (1983). Assessing outcome in disorders of childhood and adolescence. In M. Lambert, E. Christensen, & S. DeJulio (Eds.), *The measurement of psychotherapy outcome in research and evaluation: A handbook* (pp. 285–303). New York: Wiley.

Tramontana, M., & Sherrets, S. (1984). Psychotherapy with adolescents: Conceptual, practical, and empirical perspectives. In P. Karoly & J. Steffen (Eds.), *Adolescent behavior disorders: Foundations and contemporary concerns.* Lexington, MA: Heath.

Viale-Val, G., Rosenthal, R., Curtiss, G., & Marohn, R. (1984). Dropout from adolescent psychotherapy: A preliminary study. *Journal of the American Academy of Child Psychiatry, 23,* 562–568.

Vygotsky, L. (1962). *Thought and language.* Cambridge, MA: MIT Press.

Vygotsky, L. (1978). *Mind in society.* Cambridge, MA: Harvard University Press.

Walster, E., Aronson, V., Abrahams, D., & Rottman, L. (1966). Importance of physical attractiveness in dating behavior. *Journal of Personality and Social Psychology, 4,* 508–516.

Weiner, I., & Del Gaudio, A. (1976). Psychopathology in adolescence: An epidemiological study. *Archives of General Psychiatry, 33,* 187–193.

Weisz, J. (1986). Contingency and control beliefs as predictors of psychotherapy outcomes among children and adolescents. *Journal of Consulting and Clinical Psychology, 54,* 789–795.

Weisz, J., & Weiss, B. (1989). Assessing the effects of clinic-based psychotherapy with children and adolescents. *Journal of Consulting and Clinical Psychology, 57,* 741–746.

Weisz, J., Weiss, B., Alicke, M., & Klotz, M. (1987). Effectiveness of psychotherapy with children and adolescents. *Journal of Consulting and Clinical Psychology, 55,* 542–549.

Weisz, J., Weiss, B., & Langmeyer, D. (1987). Giving up on child psychotherapy: Who drops out? *Journal of Consulting and Clinical Psychology, 55,* 916–918.

Weisz, J., Weiss, B., & Langmeyer, D. (1989). On dropouts and refusers in child psychotherapy: Reply to Garfield. *Journal of Consulting and Clinical Psychology, 57,* 170–171.

Werry, J. (1982). An overview of pediatric psychopharmacology. *Journal of the American Academy of Child Psychiatry, 21,* 3–9.

White, R. (1960). Competence and psychosexual stages of development. In M. Jones (Ed.), *Nebraska symposium on motivation* (pp. 97–144).

Wilkes, T., & Rush, A. (1988). Adaptations of cognitive therapy for depressed adolescents. *Journal of the American Academy of Child and Adolescent Psychiatry, 27,* 381–386.

Wilson, G. (1986). Cognitive-behavioral and pharmacological therapies for bulimia. In K. Brownell & J. Foreyt (Eds.), *Handbook of eating disorders* (pp. 450–475). New York: Basic Books.

Wilson, P., Goldin, J. & Charbonneau-Powis, M. (1983) Comparative efficacy of behavioural and cognitive treatment of depression. *Cognitive Therapy and Research, 7,* 111–124.

Wolberg, L. (1977). *The technique of psychotherapy.* New York: Grune & Stratton.

CHAPTER 17

The Adolescent Psychotherapist: Research Consumer and Producer

CHARLES M. JAFFE and KATHERINE RYAN

INTRODUCTION

The purpose of this chapter is to examine some aspects of the psychodynamically oriented adolescent psychotherapist's relationship with adolescent research. We address two distinct yet intimately related issues. The first concerns the psychotherapist's relationship with the large body of available research on adolescent development and psychopathology. We elaborate the position that most adolescent psychotherapists can freely and productively use research in clinical practice; they can be good "research consumers." We support this position through a discussion of the elements of empathy and some problems that arise from confusions about its use and scope. The second issue addresses a few points related to the psychotherapist as clinical researcher.[1] We elaborate the position that there is ample justifiable room for adolescent psychotherapists to function as researchers in areas concerning the psychotherapeutic process, normal adolescent development, and psychopathology; that is, to be effective "research producers." To this end, we refer to some issues of theory formation and scientific philosophy that currently influence the thought of many analytically oriented psychotherapists.

Before proceeding, it should be clearly noted that our approach to adolescent psychotherapy is based on psychoanalytic principles; that is, we hold the essence of the psychotherapeutic process to be a dialogue that results in the increasingly accurate understanding of the adolescent's affectively toned, often unconscious internal world. The psychotherapist's understanding is used to facilitate the patient's optimal competence and adaptation. Despite the psychoanalytic basis of our thinking, we believe that the issues discussed in this chapter are generally applicable to psychotherapy in general. In other words, although a psychotherapist may proceed to understand a patient using knowledge derived from psychoanalysts practicing psychoanalysis, the therapist may employ his or her understanding of the patient in a variety of ways that are not limited to psychoanalytic technique. We might also note that other modes of

---

[1]The current examination is not a statement about evaluating the methodology of any given study. We assume that a serious consideration of the source of the data precedes a clinician's considering a bit of information about adolescent behavior to be worth noting. It is also not an effort to critique particular contributions of developmental research that presume to validate or refute psychoanalytic theories of adolescence or, for that matter, contributions from clinical practice that bear on the findings of formal developmental research.

psychotherapy, such as behavioral, cognitive, or social skills training, rely more heavily on the yield of formal research for their techniques and are not essentially concerned with the patient's unconscious affects. For this reason, the issues of use of research in these treatments may in fact be less problematic. However, even with research-driven components of psychotherapy, the relationship aspect of most approaches to treatment has not seen much influence of research on the clinician's activities.

USING RESEARCH IN A PSYCHOTHERAPY

Psychotherapists (Aichorn, 1925; Blos, 1962; A. Freud, 1958; Freud, 1905) have provided rich clinical theories about adolescent development and psychopathology. Within psychoanalysis, the more recent emphasis on the centrality of self-transformation in adolescence has increased our ability to understand and to form relationships with adolescents and to manage the particular problems faced by clinicians in the therapeutic encounter (Goldberg, 1978; Marohn, Dalle-Molle, McCarter, & Linn, 1980; Wolf, 1982; Wolf, Gedo, & Terman, 1972). Despite the lively and useful ferment within psychoanalysis, the psychoanalytic perspective of adolescent development and psychopathology has faced well-placed criticism as being too narrow to account for the variety and complexity of adolescent experience in and out of the treatment setting. Integrating the growing body of research into a psychotherapy is, however, not always straightforward. The accumulated facts about adolescence as a phase of life described along physiological, cognitive, and social role or status dimensions may not be readily transposed into a psychotherapy where the ultimate interest lies in the patient's subjective experience.

How does one approach the accumulated data from research in a psychotherapy? Ordinarily, one simply does not, at least not with any conscious intent. Perhaps a reasonable approximation of the therapist's use of information is that he or she achieves understanding through totaling bits of information that have been accumulated about adolescents from sources that span the range from Anna Freud to ZZ Top. This knowledge summation is then processed, along with the affect and context of the current moment, in the crucible of models of normal development and the results of deviations from the norm. At these moments, one does not usually pause to make discriminations about the source of the information or the methods used to gather and assess it. Equal weight may be assigned to such diverse sources of information as developmental research demonstrating varied routes through adolescence (Offer & Offer, 1975); classifications of delinquents' character pathology (Marohn et al., 1980); epidemiological data, such as the fact that 20% of teenagers demonstrate clinical levels of stress, anxiety, and/or depressive symptoms (Rutter, Graham, Chadwick, & Yule, 1976); the Self Psychology finding that adolescent grandiosity often defends against confusion and shame (Basch, 1984); or the therapist's own emotional experience with that particular patient or similar patients. In other words, in ordinary clinical thought, one uses knowledge derived from research in much the same way as any information gathered to help understand patients; together, these bits of phenomenology form a picture of the adolescent's current and past experiences.

This process occurs at every phase of therapy, although it may be employed in various ways throughout. The earliest connection with a patient, before any opportunity for more personal resonance has occurred, includes locating that person within some generally identifiable context. From the first moment of contact with an adolescent, one immediately makes judgments based on placing him or her in the context of the child's roles in the family, in school, in the community, or in comparison to the normative model of development called "adolescence." Although the therapist often emphasizes his or her own or others' (often, other patients') adolescence as referents, it is our contention that a major information source is the context supplied by research, which contributes, consciously or unconsciously, to a general framework within which to view a given adolescent.

Data that supply a context for further appreciation of a particular patient may not be accumulated through studying the literature in any formal sense. In recent years, a great deal of attention has been paid to the travails of adolescents, especially in the areas of suicide, drug abuse, and delinquent behaviors. This information, particularly as it is conveyed by the media in news reports and television dramas, creates a picture of the adolescent years that becomes a filter through which any given teenager is perceived. In reciprocal fashion, adolescents use the same general information to place themselves and their therapists in a context that then significantly influences their interactions. Ubiquitous questions posed by adolescents about their need for treatment—whether they really have more serious problems than their peers, whether their feelings are temporary and normal or indicative of severe mental illness—are all related to the adolescents' own sense of themselves as individuals in relation to a context derived from large "normative samples."

Research about normal development and psychopathology may be useful to enhance the development of treatment. It is a rare adolescent who is not interested in (and anxious about) the extent to which others share his or her feelings. Conveying appropriate concern and information about the reason for concern can be an important first step in developing a dialogue that is a requisite of clinical effectiveness. Furthermore, the introduction of this information enables discussion of important parameters such as probable length, frequency, and modality of treatment. Answering these questions is often the first step in helping patients feel understood. In turn, their reaction to this information is very helpful in developing an understanding of their self-perception and overall adjustment—an essential component of empathic resonance with their feeling state.

During the diagnostic phase, the clinician's understanding of the meaning of the adolescent's complaints and his or her feelings about the difficulties being experienced is most certainly enhanced by a command of prevalence rates and their correlates. For example, an adolescent who considers it disturbed behavior to feel anxiety about his or her future is underestimating how common the feeling is among his or her age group. Similarly, the adolescent who dismisses illogical thoughts and serious problems in social relations may be overestimating the commonality and underestimating the stability and prognosis of these issues. A clinician aware of the pertinent epidemiological findings can process the immediate emotions of the adolescent in a context enriched by a social-reference understanding of the symptoms' commonality and prognostic implications.

Beyond the diagnostic phase and throughout the treatment process, clinicians typically focus their attention on efforts to establish some shared affective experience with their patients, in the service of highlighting a relationship that serves as the fulcrum for change (Peterfreund, 1983). This process, variably referred to as narcissistic contact (Gittelson, 1948), the fragile alliance (Meeks, 1971), idealizing transference (Wolf et al., 1972), and the development of a shared meaning (Goldberg, 1987), presumes reciprocal error-correcting feedback between the involved parties. For reasons of impaired development, cognitive limitations, resistance, or response to coercive referral for treatment, teenagers often do not verbalize their thoughts clearly, leaving their therapists to struggle with their nonverbal or distorted communications (Jaffe & Offer, 1980). When a teenager does not participate with the therapist in a rigorous examination of the meaning of his or her communications, the therapist is precluded from feeling comfortably in tune with the patient. Not infrequently, the problems in communication are so great that the therapist is left only with a profound sense of being unrelated to the patient. To put it simply, this means having no idea where to start to understand the patient. In these commonly encountered situations, finding some initial point of contact becomes important. It is at this point that one may look to extraclinical information to get some orientation toward the adolescent's internal experience.

The psychotherapist, perhaps best described as a consumer of research, may be perfectly comfortable using every available resource to understand patients, but is such free-wheeling mixing and matching justifiable? Questions arise when one looks more carefully at such activities. Is the therapist combining theories of adolescence based on incompatible assumptions, translating concepts as if they were synonyms when they are not, assuming accumulated subjective (that is, biased) folk knowledge to be true and on the same plane as knowledge derived from rigorous controlled study? The therapist may be concerned about abandoning an empathic stance when thinking of research findings. Are thoughts about research studies in the midst of a psychotherapy a countertransference retreat to an intellectual, exterospective position? Is some nonverbal communication or the repetition of preverbal transactions being overlooked? Does thinking about research signal a defensive retreat to a descriptive view of the patient?

Because at any given moment any of these concerns may in fact be the case, how is one to feel justified in using material from any available source? How does one evaluate and integrate research in a direct application in psychotherapy? A brief review of a central component of the psychotherapeutic process, empathic understanding, gives reassurance on the presence of ample evidence that there is nothing antithetical about using research data in a psychotherapeutic process that includes, as its essence, the understanding of the adolescent's internal world.

The Task of Integration— Empathic Understanding

The so-called "how-the-therapist-thinks" or "mind-of-the-therapist" process has been approached in a number of ways. The question addressed is: What enables one person to know another's internal experiences? Essays on psychoanalytic theories of adolescent development such as character synthesis (Gitelson, 1948) and the transformation of ideals (Wolf et al., 1972) have emphasized the relationship of development to the patient's subjective experience, known to the therapist through his or her immersion into the adolescent's affective world. These explorations in adolescence have paralleled the general issues of coming to know another person through freely hovering attention (Freud, 1912), trial identification and the therapist's "work ego" (Fleiss, 1942), the therapist's cognitive processes (Heimann, 1977), and, most recently, empathy.[2]

It has not been easy to explain this process. Reed (1984), for example, summarized the various definitions of empathy as a form of knowledge and communication (Modell, 1979), a capacity to feel instinctively, a process of the ego, an emotional ego expression (Olden, 1953), an ability to sample others' affects (Easser, 1974), a mode of prolonged data gathering and a method for discerning complex mental states in a single act of recognition (Kohut, 1966), an experience of sharing a mental state with another (Schafer, 1959), a special mode of perceiving (Greenson, 1960/1978), and a means of communication and of nonrational understanding (Karush, 1979).

Recent efforts that operationalize empathy serve to demystify and legitimize it as an observational tool. A number of statements illustrate this perspective. Empathy is not direct knowledge of another person. It is, instead, a set of inferences based on the assumption that we have within our minds something similar to the mental state of another person. These inferences may derive from the therapist's personal memories, contagion of the patient's affect, imitation, and a general knowledge of human functioning (Buie, 1981). Inferences are made from vantage points within and outside the patient's frame of reference (Lichtenberg, 1984).

---

[2]For a review of empathy and an extensive bibliography, see Lichtenberg, Bornstein, and Silver (1984).

These various vantage points should strike a balance between receptivity and a more theoretical, or experience-distant, perspective (Agosta, 1984).

Empathic understanding is achieved through interaction, a reciprocal process between participants. The essential sequence is: (a) the psychotherapist's affects are stimulated by the patient's verbal and behavioral communications; (b) the psychotherapist interprets the stimulated affects within his or her personal experience; (c) the psychotherapist subjects his or her personal meaning of the patient's communications to an evaluation in the total context that includes but is not limited to the patient's life circumstances and developmental functioning, and the therapeutic process; (d) the therapist's synthesis is communicated to the patient (Basch, 1983). The patient is engaged in a reciprocal process of understanding and, in turn, communicates his or her own synthesis to the therapist. Each time this interaction is repeated, with special attention to the feelings associated with areas of resonance or dissonance, two people may come closer to mutual understanding.

Interference with empathy may occur if any part of the synthesis is precluded. In this regard, it is useful for the clinician to understand that empathic understanding does not of necessity start with affective resonance and lead to interpretation and evaluation. Rather, a thought experiment may provide the stimulation for engaging affective-laden issues for the patient. Such an experiment may be simply the often repeated process wherein the therapist thinks, or even says, "If I were in your place I know I would be feeling . . . ."

Basch (1983) made a crucial point for the psychotherapist using research when he noted that the helical process of empathic understanding need not begin with the affective component but can be entered at the interpretive or experimental phase of the process:

In the case of analyst and analysand, the greater the biological, cultural, and psychological similarity between the two, the more likely it is that, from the very beginning, the analyst's unconscious will be receptive to and understand the significance of his patient's unspoken, disguised, affective communications. Such an experience . . . should not be taken as a paradigmatic for the empathic process in psychoanalysis. Often as not, such mutuality does not exist and there is no immediate feeling of affective communication and recognition between analyst and patient. Under these circumstances it often requires from us a long period of listening to what the patient is saying (or not saying), examining our own reactions to this material analytically, and then bridging the gap between ourselves and the patient by constructing suitable analogies between his associations and our own experience, before we finally may find ourselves attuned to the patient's affective communications. (p. 112)

The essence of these statements is that thorough empathic understanding and successful treatment of adolescents necessarily involve a reciprocal process of integrating information about adolescents as a group and resonance with the individual's affective tone. However, the psychodynamically oriented psychotherapist may be resistant to including the full range of available information from research in the empathic process.

Reed (1984) elaborated a structure of opposite views that has emerged toward empathy in psychoanalysis and that may be useful to understand some resistances to the full integration of information:

First, there are the active and passive versions of the clinical experience of empathy—the former associated with grasping meaning, understanding, and interpreting; the latter with resonating, sudden illumination, losing the self. Second, there are the rational and mystical sides to the concept of empathy— the first associated with concepts such as perceptual scanning, organization of derivatives, and inference; the second, usually rejected, with telepathy and the uncanny. Third, there is an opposition between science and art, in which the dispassionate observation of data that leads to uncontaminated understanding contrasts with the creative resynthesis of data. Recognizing that in practice these oppositions are combined in various ways and quantities, we may still note the dichotomy between, on the one hand, an active mode involving scientific observation, which grasps unconscious meaning and finds rational explanations for apparently mysterious data, and, on the other hand, a passive mode, which involves losing the self, mystery, merger, oneness, ineffable experience, and creative participation. (p. 16)

Reed embodied the qualities of the active, rational, scientific approach in the figure of a mythical "rational scientist of 'calibrated ego.'" The qualities of the passive, mystical, artistic, creative person with special access to the earliest emotional moments in the mother–infant bond were embodied in the figure of the "perfectly attuned, resonating, responsive mother" (p. 16).

Misunderstandings of the therapeutic process and resistance to using a full range of information may certainly result from subscribing to such myths. As for the myth of the perfectly attuned mother, it was noted earlier that empathy may be precluded if any part of the resonance, interpretation, or evaluation process is blocked. Such a problem usually is thought to result from anxiety associated with the meaning of a particular affective response from one's past that is restimulated during interaction with a patient (Basch, 1983). However, it may also result from an inability to consider all sources of available information, such as thought experiment, because that would generate some anxiety over an aspect of professional identity involved with efforts to distinguish oneself as an "empathic olympian."

Perhaps the myth of the perfectly attuned mother has had an unwitting contributor in Kohut's (1959) statement that psychological information is derived from affective resonance through introspection and empathy and that the appreciation of another person from an external perspective is nonpsychological. This position deemphasizes the importance of information about the context of the person's communications (whether an extra- or intra-analytic context) and of the process of validation of those communications. The clinician's personal ethos may be affected by misconceptions that arise from the view that information about a person's emotional life is derived from a different process than information about the rest of the world. The distinction between psychological and sociological information tends to become that which distinguishes clinicians from social scientists; that is, the "caring" from the "calibrated." The result is that the clinician may discount as nonpsychological a process of understanding that does not begin with affect resonance.

A short vignette about one of the authors' (C.M.J.) experiences with a supervisee illustrates the problem. The situation was familiar: a patient was not forthcoming with much information about herself and the resident had no idea what was going on. During supervision, the resident revealed that, in truth, he had a number of ideas about the patient's experiential state, derived from his own history as well as from the literature on adolescent development and pathology that he had been reviewing for a class, but he quickly dismissed them as "putting words in her mouth—only guesswork." He felt that, as a person interested in psychodynamic thinking, he could take seriously only his emotional state in response to the patient's communications. To relate to the patient as an outside observer evaluating her current status carried a number of negatively charged connotations including "unempathic" and "experience-distant." To use his own life and impose it on the patient carried the further negative connotations of "intrusiveness" and "using the patient as an extension of myself." Because he had no identifiable emotional response, this left him, if not altogether a failure, at best all dressed up with no place to go.

THE ADOLESCENT PSYCHOTHERAPIST AS RESEARCHER

Let us now shift from the vantage point of the psychotherapist as a research consumer to the psychotherapist as a research producer. The first section of this chapter acknowledged and elaborated the obvious fact that, in everyday psychotherapeutic practice, the clinician uses the accumulated yield of research in adolescence in a variety of ways throughout the treatment process. The argument was made that the integration of information from the broadest reaches is an integral part of the empathic process. Reluctance to make the fullest use of research in the clinical setting may result from misunderstandings about empathy or professional identity conflicts.

Still, merely using science does not make one a scientist. After all, writers of science fiction make liberal use of science fact. A second consideration here, then, concerns the adolescent psychotherapist as researcher and addresses a few difficulties for the psychotherapist envisioning himself or herself in this role. Again, our focus is not so much on specific design as it is on the possibility of employing one's clinical experience in the broadest sense.

Where is the place for the clinician as researcher? A rich and varied literature now elaborates developmental (Chapters 2 through 6 of this volume; Offer & Offer, 1975; Offer, Ostrov, & Howard, 1981), family systems (Haley, 1980; Tolan, Cromwell, & Brasswell, 1986; Walsh & Scheinkman, Chapter 7 of this volume), social (Ckszentmihalyi & Larson, 1984), cultural (Havinghurst, 1987; Watts, Machabanski, & Karrer, Chapter 10 of this volume), political (Gallatin, 1980), cognitive (Dulit, 1972; Inhelder & Piaget, 1958), and biological (Petersen & Taylor, 1980; Richards, Abell, & Peterson, Chapter 2 of this volume) aspects of adolescent development and psychopathology. The many maps of the landscape of adolescence include studies elaborating rates of symptomatology in clinical and nonclinical settings, prevalence of specific syndromes within adolescence, and comparisons of data from adolescent populations with those from adults and children (Tolan, Jaffe, & Ryan, 1988). In addition, there is a growing literature on the outcome of psychotherapy with adolescents (Reineke, Chapter 16 of this volume).

Qualified clinical and nonclinical professionals certainly may participate in studies of all these aspects of adolescence, but we feel that there are two areas of research to which the psychotherapist brings special expertise: (a) the elaboration of nuances of subjective experience that may point to more accurate and useful study of development; and (b) studies of the intersubjective processes that influence the course and outcome of treatment.

The first area, the contribution of psychotherapists to developmental research, is illustrated by a recent collaboration of two psychotherapists with developmental researchers. Jaffe and Barglow (in press) studied the continuity of infant experience and adolescent psychopathology from multiple perspectives, emphasizing the mutual contributions of clinical insights and attachment research.[3] The collaboration was stimulated by questions left unanswered by a study of the effects of mothers' working away from home on the attachment of their infant children (Barglow, Vaughn, & Molitor, 1987). The concurrent unfolding of two treatments—a psychotherapy of a teenager, and the mother's psychoanalysis—provided a special opportunity to make use of multiple perspectives to understand the infant–mother interaction of this now adolescent–mother pair, and to shed new light on the research findings. Specifically, an understanding of the adolescent's subjective world through psychotherapy and reconstructions from the mother's psychoanalysis enabled the attachment researchers to formulate questions that more precisely delineated the factors influencing the infants' behavior.

---

[3]The emphasis in Jaffe and Barglow (in press) on the mutual contributions of adolescent psychotherapy and attachment research represents part of a larger study (Barglow, Jaffe, & Vaughn, 1989) that examines the contributions of research to validating psychoanalytic reconstructions.

Barglow et al. (1987) used the Ainsworth Strange Situation (Ainsworth, Blehar, Waters, & Wall, 1978) to study the effects of mothers' working out of the home on their infant children.[4] Barglow demonstrated that avoidance scores of the group of infants of full-time working mothers who returned to work in the first 3 months postpartum were significantly greater than those for the group of infants whose mothers remained at home as primary caretakers. Specifically, 71% of the infants in the at-home group were securely attached, compared to 54% of the infants in the at-work group. The interpretation of the results was that many infants of mothers who return to full-time employment during the first year experienced the repeated, daily separations from the mother as a rejection, leading to avoidance of her in the strange situation.

Despite these findings, important questions went unanswered in the study. What psychological factors could explain the finding that a little more than half of the infants in the at-work group were securely attached to their mothers despite the repeated daily separations they experienced? Why did contrasts between personality factors in working and nonworking mothers not show any major statistical differences?

Data from the teen's psychotherapy and developmental history, and reconstructions derived from the mother's analysis, suggested an "anxious avoidant attachment" relationship. The mother had worked full-time at an outside job since the second month of her child's life, a social variable associated statistically with this kind of avoidant infant response to separation. However, review of the clinical material obtained from the treatments suggested that the mother's response to separation from her infant might be a crucial contributing factor that would explain the increase of avoidant attachment in infants of working mothers. This hypothesis led the research team to administer a psychological test that had been designed specifically to measure the mother's separation anxiety upon leaving her infant. The findings from the new measures were consistent with the hypotheses originating in the psychotherapies: The mother's avoidance was causally related to her child's avoidance of her. The infant's avoidance was related not only to the repeated daily fact of separation from the mother because of her work, but was also related to the psychopathology of the mother, manifested by her need to flee the baby and the demands of the infant–mother relationship that she experienced as intrusive.

The insights from these dual clinical experiences made more comprehensible and meaningful the empirical generalizations derived from infant observation. The research finding that many infants of working mothers were securely attached, although significantly fewer than those of nonworking mothers, was more clearly appreciated. The perspective derived from the psychotherapies provided a direction for a fruitful search for factors aside from maternal work status that affected the quality of infant attachment.

The second area for special contribution by psychotherapists concerns studies of the factors influencing the evolution and outcome of the clinical process. For example, Tolan et al. (1988) studied over 500 successive referrals to an outpatient clinic, to determine how client characteristics, diagnosis, referral sources, service delivery procedures, and therapist characteristics related to outcome. Various outcome indicators included return after the first visit, successful progress through the clinic intake and diagnostic procedures, and the total number of visits. The presence of a single therapist throughout was most crucial. Something was happening in the process that went beyond the variety of other variables examined, such as demographic, referral, and diagnostic factors that would seem to argue against or in favor of patient follow-through, but the data collected were not suitable to pursue the vicissitudes of the patients' experiences that led to this result.

---

[4]For a review of attachment research in general and the Strange Situation in particular, the interested reader is referred to Joffe and Vaughn (in press).

Other similar studies examining referrals for psychotherapy (Kellam, Branch, Brown, & Russell, 1981), outcome (Lessing, Black, Barbera, & Siebert, 1976; Novick, Benson, & Rembar, 1981; Vaile-Val, Rosenthal, Curtiss, & Marohn, 1984) and the overall value of psychotherapy for adolescents (Reineke, Chapter 16 of this volume; Taramontana, 1980) have left similar questions unanswered. No studied offered a detailed examination of issues in the process that would allow a more precise understanding of an adolescent's course through treatment and the therapeutic outcome.

What questions might one ask to make the data from these studies more meaningful to the practitioner? As Galatzer-Levy (1989) noted, clinicians are interested in studies that explore theory and that yield practical information about the treatment process. Questions of practical significance to the therapist in the above mentioned studies might include: How does the alliance develop? What is the relationship of "narcissistic contact," idealization, or a positive alliance with change? Is the establishment of the alliance the core of treatment with adolescents? The alliance is generally considered a central issue with adolescents, more so than with adults (Gittelson, 1948; Masterson, 1958; Meeks, 1971). Why do some therapists seem better able to establish contact than others? Do successful adolescent psychotherapists respond differently than less successful therapists? How does the alliance vary in character with various diagnostic categories, phases of treatment, or phases of adolescence?

In terms of theory, one might ask: Do the usual distinctions between adult and adolescent therapeutic alliances still apply when a self psychological rather than an ego psychological perspective is employed? Adolescent psychotherapists have always applied general psychoanalytic principles to adolescent development (Jaffe, in press). In that regard, the fragility of the alliance with adolescents has been described in terms of anxiety over oedipal wishes (A. Freud, 1958; Blos, 1962), merger with the archaic mother (Masterson, 1972), and the deidealization of parental imagoes (Wolf et al., 1972). In recent years, the trend has been toward theories that are based on the development over time of an internal world through the progressive integration of affectively meaningful experiences within the context of cognitive development and an appropriate empathic matrix (Basch, 1988; Bowlby, 1969; Gedo, 1988; Lichtenberg, 1982; Stern, 1985). Separate parameters of biology, cognitive development, or social expectations in adolescence are important only insofar as they are perceived to be so by the individual (Gedo, 1979). Consistent with this view, Gedo (1988) offered developmental diagnoses made through the therapeutic process that are based on an epigenetic hierarchy of behavioral organization. He then correlated many vicissitudes of the psychoanalytic process that have been subsumed under the rubric alliance with this hierarchy of organization.[5] Is this a more useful way to measure the alliance? Does such an approach call for a reappraisal of the supposed differences between adult and adolescent therapeutic relationships?

Good data that would answer these questions can be gathered only through the systematic study of the intersubjective process as it occurs between patient and therapist. Psychotherapists, of course, have unique access to these data, for they include not only the patient's and therapist's verbal and nonverbal communications but also the therapist's reports of his or her subjective experience as a participant in the interaction.[6] Unfortunately, we have not seen these studies in the adolescent psychotherapy literature. Perhaps Masterson's (1972, Masterson & Costello, 1980) work with borderline adolescents comes the closest, but his approach

---

[5]Gedo's epigenetic schema of behavioral organization includes tension regulation, the ability to form an overall plan of action, acceptance of reality, and appropriate avenues for the expression of desire.

[6]Merely posing these questions does nothing to assuage concerns about the methodological complexities of such studies. The considerable problems involved in psychotherapy research, including definition of terms, standardization of treatment, methods of data collection that capture the subjective experiences of both patient and therapist, and evaluation strategies, have all been widely noted and are not the present focus.

is to study the effects of the application of a particular theoretical orientation (i.e., object relations theory) rather than to use the data from the psychotherapeutic process to study the theory itself. Examples of this type of work do exist in the adult psychoanalytic research literature, as exemplified by Weiss and Sampson (1986) and Gill (1982; Gill & Hoffman, 1982).

It is our position, then, that psychotherapists are especially well suited to conduct studies that emphasize the patient's subjective experiences, but that misperceptions about the criteria for scientific research have hampered their involvement. Why might this be so? To return for a moment to the myth of the "calibrated scientist," one argument against the continuity of social science and psychoanalytic theories is that social science observation views "reality" with sense data while psychoanalysis makes hypotheses about self-reports (i.e., demands, dreams, fantasies) of questionable reliability. Observations and theory derived from the psychoanalytic process, while seeming to convey something rich and in-depth about a person, are presumed bias-laden, idiosyncratic, and simply confirming of preconceived ideas; social science, with its many methodologic controls, is supposed to be free of bias and purely observation based.

This mentality pervades adolescent research and has, to some extent, defined the research priorities for adolescence. For example, Blotcky and Looney (1980), in reviewing the sources of information about normal male and female adolescent development, made the following statement: "The first [source of information] is theory and encompasses what we *think* we know—our hypotheses and working formulations supported largely from clinical experience with patients. The second perspective represents what we *do* know—that is, what research data reveals" (p. 184, emphasis added). In a second paper 5 years later, Looney (1985) detailed the report of the Committee on Research of The American Society for Adolescent Psychiatry. Although a plea was made for involving clinicians in research, the work of clinicians was again relegated to the status of unreliable trial-and-error hypotheses. Beyond outcome and comparing various treatment modalities, no priority is given to research on the psychotherapeutic process itself.

The absence of this type of study may relate in two ways to the myth of the calibrated scientist. The first may be another form of resistance. Clinical research may not be of interest to many psychotherapists because they identify themselves as special in regard to empathic abilities and enjoy the mantle of the "attuned mothers." Related to this may be psychotherapists' reluctance to supply the necessary recorded data for study, usually on the grounds of the patient's confidentiality but probably mostly for the sake of their own. Second, the psychotherapists' reluctance may relate not so much to resistance as to confusion about the types of theories formed in a psychotherapy and therefore the legitimate possibility of using the treatment itself for research on the intersubjective process.

Theory Formation

A long-standing confusion has resulted from the typical division of psychoanalytic theory into two theories—specifically, a clinical theory that includes such issues as repetitions, symptom formation, and defenses, and a metapsychology that is concerned with issues of instinct and the flow and transformation of psychic energy. Typically, the clinical theory has been considered to be empirical-inductive and the metapsychology has been considered to be speculative-deductive.[7] In contrast, theory in other areas of science is seen as empirical only (Basch, 1973).[8] A clearer representation of the state of affairs is achieved if psychoanalytic

---

[7]More recently, similar discussion has focused on so-called "experience-near" and "experience-distant" psychoanalytic theories (Atwood & Stolorow, 1984; Basch, 1986a, 1986b; Goldberg, 1988).

[8]Although the reference to Basch's paper on theory formation appears only once, all the related ideas in this section are his.

theory is understood as inductive theory, that is, as theory based on perceptual evidence from sensation or introspection that includes inductive and deductive inferences. Rather than some theories being derived inductively and others deductively, any inductive theory contains inferences that lead to statements that are abstractions from the sense data (inductive inferences) as well as hypotheses about relations between statements in a framework (deductive inferences).[9] In other words, the need to seek new observations presumes a hypothesis that reality is not being addressed adequately by current theory, as well as some speculation about what observations would comprise a more useful description. In addition, because one always integrates new information with previous experience, one cannot say that any observations are completely devoid of assimilation according to some prior conceptual frames of reference (Popper, 1968; Tolan, Keys, Chertok, & Jason, in press).

Various psychoanalytic theories, then, are better subclassified as classificatory, descriptive explanatory, or causal explanatory. Classificatory theory organizes and systematizes data through an interlocking hierarchy of definitions. Its usefulness depends on the accuracy of observation and its proof is that its premises may be traced back to observation. Classifications of observed data are theories of this type, whether they are biological ("vertebrate"), epidemiologic ("20% of adolescents show depressive symptoms"), or psychoanalytic ("infantile sexuality," "primary and secondary process," "transference," "early adolescent behavior concomitant with an increase in ambivalent relations to mother").

Explanatory theory may address the descriptive or causal aspect of an explanation.

Descriptive explanatory theories, then, are arbitrary ways of looking at relationships for the purpose of postulating the relations between systems and making predictions involving only those relationships. Descriptive explanatory theory may be thought of as a means of tracing the outlines, finding clarifying connecting threads that makes what happens comprehensible. Causal explanatory theory, on the other hand, explains why what happens *happens*. Examples of descriptive explanatory theory in social science are the postulates that socioeconomic status or certain childhood symptoms predict adolescent disturbance. The dynamic and genetic points of view serve as examples from psychoanalysis. Both establish some operational laws through which specific behavior may be more fully appreciated.

It is our position that the confusion over psychoanalytic theory formation has contributed to the polarization of psychotherapists into "humanist" or "scientist" camps. Although the current fashion of psychotherapists is toward underemphasizing the scientific possibilities of their work, psychotherapists in the past contributed to the distancing of psychoanalysis from other areas of science by identifying themselves as "calibrated" and overrepresenting what may be learned from the psychoanalytic process. As Basch succinctly noted, events in the psychoanalytic situation that may be understood (classified) and explained dynamically or genetically (described) have then been assumed to represent some connection to the process of mental functioning itself (causal explanatory theory). Such is the case with theories of instinct, psychic energy, and the mental apparatus. These untestable theories have been used to explain the fundamental cause of observed behavior; at the same time, observed behavior has been cited as evidence for the existence of these entities. The confusion that has resulted from the emphasis on metapsychology has drawn attention away from the valuable classificatory and descriptive theories that predominate in psychoanalytic thinking.

---

[9]Both systems of inference are valuable in that they provide useful predictions; neither is a statement of truth in any larger sense. The proof of inductive inferences is that they accurately describe some perception; deductive inferences are proved by demonstrating that the conclusions are properly derived from the premise, i.e., that the conclusions follow the rules of the system.

We believe that the overrepresentation of the yield of psychoanalysis by psychotherapists has had no less an impact on studying, within the clinical setting, the adolescent's subjective world and development. The controversy over adolescent turmoil provides an example of the confusion that results from such misrepresentations. The challenge, as is well known, has been to Anna Freud's (1958) assertion that adolescence is a period of normative psychic disruption secondary to instinctual upsurge and that an absence of symptoms is indicative of psychopathology. This challenge has been decisively met. There is no question that the exploration of behaviors within the range of normal adolescent development, led by Offer (Offer & Offer, 1975; Offer, Ostrov, & Howard, 1981), Masterson (1965), Golombek, Marton, Stein, and Korenblum (1978), and others, has had enormous impact on our view of the adolescent process. The clinical object lesson of crucial value has been that persistent problems in adolescents are indeed problems; they are to be taken seriously as evidence of developmental disruption and not dismissed as part of a normative regression. In a more subtle way, however, the challenge goes beyond the idea that psychoanalysis cannot provide a normal adolescent developmental psychology by studying psychopathology. It goes to the problem of psychoanalysis providing a causal explanatory theory at all. Because of the usual co-occurrence of physiologic and psychology transformations during the second decade of life, adolescence has been offered as the most direct evidence for the theory of psychic energy or instinct. The untestable nature of this assumption has, we believe, contributed to the idea that classificatory and descriptive theory derived from the empathic method of study in the clinical setting is also of questionable value. In other words, the failure of psychoanalysis as an adequate arena to provide and test theories of instinct, as well as such mental operations as cognition, memory, and learning, has cast doubt on the possibility of using clinicians' observations in the treatment situation to prove any psychoanalytic hypotheses.

Scientific Investigation of the Clinical Process

Even when one confronts the limits of what may be ascertained in the clinical situation by realizing that one cannot prove hypotheses about mentation or normal development using only the data from the clinical setting, there is still an important yield from applying scientific method to the primary data of the intersubjective process. Essentially, the issue of the scientific value of clinical data revolves around the argument that the study of meanings to an individual places psychoanalysis within the humanities, not within the sciences, where causality is in question (Wallerstein, 1986). One position holds that psychoanalysis is not a science and cannot provide valid statements about human mental functioning (Grunbaum, 1984). Two main reasons justify this position. The first is the criticism of Freud's claim that ". . . conflicts will only be successfully solved and resistances overcome if the anticipatory ideas he is given [i.e., interpretations] tally with what is real to him" (1917, p. 452). Freud's position was meant to counter the claims that psychoanalytic change resulted from suggestion rather than an alteration in psyche due to interpretation of unconscious motive. This so-called Tally argument has been proven untenable because we now know that outcome of a treatment does not establish the validity of a theory. Cures from other methods, spontaneous recovery, and failure of outcome studies to establish superiority of one intervention over another argue against Freud's position that clinical change validates the theory. The second criticism of psychoanalysis as a science relates to the first. If the Tally argument fails, then psychoanalysis cannot be separated from suggestion and all data obtained in the clinical setting are contaminated by the therapist's investment in the outcome.

A second position is that psychoanalysis is a science, but of a different kind that requires a different kind of proof. This position holds that the criteria for proof should lie "in the articulation of the entire network: theory, hermeneutics, therapeutics, and narration" (Ricoeur, 1977, p. 865). Lawlike patterns of behavior among people are not as important as the ". . . harmony of coherence, consistency, and configuration" (Steele, 1979). In its extreme, this position holds that no validity of historical data is possible, but that only a narrative truth is obtained (Spence, 1982).

Neither of these positions is particularly satisfying. One simply denigrates repeated observations by dismissing all observers as hopelessly cursed with the tragic flaw of good intentions. The other has considerable appeal in that it accurately captures certain observed phenomena, especially those interpersonal transactions that are associated with coming to know someone through a sense of resonant interaction. However, it seems to be isolating in its claim to use a different method of understanding and validation and in its overvaluation of coming to know someone solely through the use of affective resonance without the context of prior expectations.

More congenial are the rebuttals to these positions that sum, in essence, to the idea that science is defined by a method of study rather than by a subject (Holt, 1961). The study of subjective human emotion is therefore as legitimate a field of pursuit as any, and the method of study is essentially the same in what we think of as science proper, the humanities, or literature. Convincing arguments have been made that so-called hermeneutic–natural science distinctions refer to no more than different realms of inquiry approached with similar methods (Holt, 1981; Holzman, 1985; Wallerstein, 1986). For example, the hermeneutic test of internal consistency is not different from prediction as a truth criterion in different sciences. "[T]he test of predictive validity is nothing more than establishing the degree of internal consistency within the combined body of (1) the data (and theory) and (2) the newly obtained data" (Holt, 1961, p. 52).

In psychoanalysis, the data for study are subjective mental phenomena ascertained through introspection and empathy, which are not beyond scientific scrutiny by virtue of being private (Goldberg, 1983). In this regard, subjective merely means within, not biased, and empathy is simply a way to find out about people. Like any assessment method, empathy combines inferences made about observations as well as guiding theoretical preconceptions. The data supplied by empathy must be subjected to the same criteria for reliability and validation as any other piece of evidence. Although it is beyond the scope of this presentation, recent work suggests that the single case study may indeed offer, with proper methodologic attention, the opportunity for just such validation (Edelson, 1988).

CONCLUSION

We have tried to visit a few issues related to adolescent psychotherapists' relationship with research in adolescence, as well as adolescent researchers' relationship with the psychotherapeutic process. As research consumers, adolescent psychotherapists do, and in our view should, use the widest variety of information available in order to understand and intervene with troubled young people. As research producers, adolescent psychotherapists and adolescent researchers must deal with a variety of limitations about the scope of what may be demonstrated within the therapeutic process, but ought not to be deterred by professional identity allegiances, confused by theory, or intimidated by issues of scientific philosophy from considering useful questions related to adolescents in psychotherapy.

REFERENCES

Agosta, L. (1984). Empathy and intersubjectivity. In J. Lichtenberg, M. Bornstein, & D. Silver (Eds.), *Empathy I*. Hillsdale, NJ: Analytic Press.

Aichorn, A. (1925) *Wayward youth*. New York: Viking Press.

Ainsworth, M., Blehar, M., Waters, E., & Wall, S. (1978). *Patterns of attachment: A psychology* study of the strange situation. Hillsdale, NJ: Erlbaum.

Atwood, G., & Stolorow, R. (1984). *Structures of subjectivity: Explorations of psychoanalytic phenomenology.* Hillsdale, NJ: Analytic Press.

Barglow, P., Vaughn, B., & Molitor, N. (1987). Effects of maternal absence due to employment on the quality of infant–mother attachment in a low-risk sample. *Child Development.*

Barglow, P., Jaffe, C., & Vaughn, B. (1989). Psychoanalytic reconstructions and empirical data: Reciprocal contributions. *Journal of the American Psychoanalytic Association, 37,* 401–435.

Basch, M. F. (1973). Psychoanalysis and theory formation. *Annals of Psychoanalysis. 1,* 9–52.

Basch, M. F. (1983). Empathic understanding: A review of the concept and some theoretical considerations. *Journal of the American Psychoanalytic Association, 31,* 106–126.

Basch, M. F. (1984). *Doing psychotherapy.* New York: Basic Books.

Basch, M. F. (1986a). Clinical theory and metapsychology: Incompatible or complementary? *Psychoanalytic Review, 73,* 261–271.

Basch, M. F. (1986b). How does analysis cure: An appreciation. *Psychoanalytic Inquiry, 6,* 403–428.

Basch, M. F. (1988). *Understanding psychotherapy.* New York: Basic Books.

Blos, P. (1962). *On adolescence.* New York: Free Press.

Blotcky, M., & Looney, J. (1980). Normal female and male psychological development: An overview of theory and research. *Adolescent Psychiatry: Developmental and Clinical Studies, 8,* 184–199.

Bowlby, J. (1969). *Attachment and loss: Vol. 1. Attachment.* New York: Basic Books.

Buie, D. (1981). Empathy: Its nature and limitations. *Journal of the American Psychoanalytic Association, 29,* 281–307.

Ckszentmihalyi, M., & Larson, R. (1984). *Being adolescent.* New York: Basic Books.

Dulit, E. (1972). Adolescent thinking à la Piaget: The formal state. *Journal of Youth and Adolescence, 4,* 281–301.

Easser, R. (1974). Empathic inhibition and psychoanalytic technique. *Psychoanalytic Quarterly, 43,* 557–580.

Edelson, M. (1988). *Psychoanalysis: A theory in crisis.* Chicago: University of Chicago Press.

Fleiss, R. (1942). The metapsychology of the analyst. *Psychoanalytic Quarterly, 2,* 211–227.

Freud, A. (1958). Adolescence. *Psychoanalytic Study of the Child, 13,* 255–278.

Freud, S. (1905). Three essays on the theory of sexuality. In J. Strachey (Ed. and Trans.). *The standard edition of the complete psychological works of Sigmund Freud* (Vol. 7, pp. 125–245). London: Hogarth Press.

Freud, S. (1912). Recommendations to physicians practising psycho-analysis. In J. Strachey (Ed. and Trans.). *The standard edition of the complete psychological works of Sigmund Freud* (Vol. 12, pp. 111–120). London: Hogarth Press.

Freud, S. (1917). Introductory lectures on psychoanalysis: Lecture 28. In J. Strachey (Ed. and Trans.). *The standard edition of the complete psychological works of Sigmund Freud* (Vol. 28, pp. 448–463). London: Hogarth Press.

Galatzer-Levy, R. (1989). *What analysts want to know.* Paper presented to the University of Chicago Graduate Program in Human Development.

Gallatin, J. (1980). Political thinking in adolescence. In J. Adelson (Ed.), *Handbook of adolescent psychology* (pp. 344–382). New York: Wiley.

Gedo, J. (1979). *Beyond interpretation.* New York: International Universities Press.

Gedo, J. (1988). *The mind in disorder.* Hillsdale, NJ: Analytic Press.

Gill, M. (1982). *Analysis of transference: Studies of nine audio-recorded psychoanalytic sessions: Vol. 1.* (Psychological Issues Monograph 53.) New York: International Universities Press.

Gill, M., & Hoffman, E. (1982). *Analysis of transference: Studies of nine audio-recorded psychoanalytic sessions: Vol. 2* (Psychological Issues Monograph 53.) New York: International Universities Press.

Gittelson, M. (1948). Character synthesis: The psychotherapeutic problem of adolescence. *American Journal of Orthopsychiatry, 18,* 422–431.

Goldberg, A. (1978). A shift in emphasis: Adolescent psychotherapy and the psychology of the self. *Journal of Youth and Adolescence, 7,* 119–134.

Goldberg, A. (1983). The scientific status of empathy. *Annals of Psychoanalysis, 11,* 155–169.

Goldberg, A. (1987). Psychoanalysis and negotiation. *Psychoanalytic Quarterly, 56,* 109–129.

Goldberg, A. (1988). Experience near, distant, and absent. In *A fresh look and psychoanalysis: The view from self psychology.* Hillsdale, NJ: Analytic Press.

Golombek, H., Marton, P., Stein, B., & Korenblum, M. (1987). Personality functioning status during early and middle adolescence. *Adolescent Psychiatry: Developmental and Clinical Studies, 14,* 365–393.

Greenson, R. (1978). Empathy and its vicissitudes. In *Explorations in psychoanalysis* (pp. 147–161). New York: International Universities Press. (Original work published 1960)

Grunbaum, A. (1984). *The foundations of psychoanalysis: A philosophical critique.* Berkeley: University of California Press.

Haley, J. (1980). *Leaving home.* New York: McGraw-Hill.

Havinghurst, R. (1987). Adolescent culture and subculture. In V. B. Van Hasselt & M. Hersen (Eds.), *Handbook of adolescent psychology* (pp. 401–412). New York: Pergamon Press.

Heimann, P. (1977). Further observations on the analyst's cognitive process. *Journal of the American Psychoanalytic Association, 25,* 313–333.

Holt, R. (1961). Clinical judgment as a disciplined inquiry. *Journal of Nervous and Mental Disease, 133,* 369–382.

Holt, R. (1981). The death and transfiguration of metapsychology. *International Review of Psychoanalysis, 8,* 129–143.

Holzman, P. (1985). Psychoanalysis: Is the therapy destroying the science? *Journal of the American Psychoanalytic Association, 33,* 725–770.

Inhelder, B., & Piaget, J. (1958). *The growth of logical thinking from childhood to adolescence.* New York: Basic Books.

Jaffe, C. (in press). Theories of adolescent psychology. In M. Slomowitz (Ed.), *Adolescent psychotherapy.* Washington, DC: APA Press.

Jaffe, C., & Barglow, P. (1989). Adolescent psychopathology and attachment research: Mutual contributions. *Annals of Adolescent Psychiatry, 16,* 350–372.

Jaffe, C. & Offer, D. (1980). Psychotherapy with adolescents. In A. Sholvar, R. Benson, & B. Blinder (Eds.), *Emotional disorders in children and adolescents.* New York: Spectrum.

Joffe, L., & Vaughn, B. (in press). Infant–mother attachment: Theory, assessment, and implications for development. In B. Wolman (Ed.), *Handbook of developmental psychology.* Englewood Cliffs, NJ: Prentice-Hall.

Karush, A. (1979). Introductory remarks on the role of empathy in the psychoanalytic process. *Bulletin of the Association of Psychoanalytic Medicine, 18,* 62–63.

Kellam, S. G., Branch, J. D., Brown, C. H., & Russell, G. (1981). Why teenagers come for treatment: A ten-year prospective epidemiological study in Woodlawn. *Journal of the American Academy of Child Psychiatry, 20,* 477–495.

Kohut, H. (1959). Introspection, empathy, and psychoanalysis. *Journal of the American Psychoanalytic Association, 7,* 459–483.

Kohut, H. (1966). Forms and transformations of narcissism. *Journal of the American Psychoanalytic Association, 14,* 243–272.

Lessing, E., Black, M., Barbera, L., & Siebert, F. (1976). Dimensions of adolescent psychopathology and their prognostic significance for treatment outcome. *Genetic Psychology Monographs, 93,* 155–168.

Lichtenberg, J. (1982). Continuities and transformations between infancy and adolescence. *Adolescent Psychiatry, 10,* 182–198.

Lichtenberg, J. (1984). The empathic mode of perception and alternative vantage points for psychoanalytic work. In M. Bornstein, D. Silver, & J. Lichtenberg (Eds.), *Empathy II*. Hillsdale, NJ: Analytic Press.

Looney, J. (1985). Research priorities in adolescent psychiatry: Report of the Committee on Research of the American Society for Adolescent Psychiatry. *Adolescent Psychiatry: Developmental and Clinical Studies, 12,* 104–114.

Marohn, R., Dalle-Molle, D., McCarter, E., & Linn, D. (1980). *Juvenile delinquents: Psychodynamic assessment and hospital treatment.* New York: Brunner-Mazel.

Masterson, J. (1958). Psychotherapy of the adolescent: A comparison with psychotherapy of the adult. *Journal of Nervous and Mental Disease, 127*, 511–517.

Masterson, J. (1965). *Psychiatric dilemma of adolescence.* Boston: Little, Brown.

Masterson, J. (1972). *Treatment of the borderline adolescent: A developmental approach.* New York: Wiley.

Masterson, J., & Costello, J. (1980). *From borderline adolescent to functioning adult: The test of time.* New York: Brunner/Mazel.

Meeks, J. (1971). *The fragile alliance.* Baltimore, MD: Williams & Wilkins.

Modell, A. (1979). Empathy and the failure of empathy. *Bulletin of the Association of Psychoanalytic Medicine, 18*, 70–75.

Novick, J., Benson, R., & Rembar, J. (1981). Patterns of termination in an outpatient clinic for children and adolescents. *Journal of the American Academy of Child Psychiatry, 20*, 834–844.

Offer, D., & Offer, J. (1975). *From teenage to young manhood: A psychological study.* New York: Basic Books.

Offer, D., Ostrov, E., & Howard, K. I. (1981). *The adolescent: A psychological self-portrait.* New York: Basic Books.

Olden, C. (1953). On adult empathy with children. *Psychoanalytic Study of the Child, 8*, 111–126.

Peterfreund, E. (1983). *The process of psychoanalytic therapy: Models and strategies.* Hillsdale, NJ: Analytic Press.

Peterson, A., & Taylor, B. (1980). The biological approach to adolescence. In J. Adelson (Ed.), *Handbook of adolescent psychology* (pp. 117–157). New York: Wiley.

Popper, K. (1968). *The logic of scientific discovery.* New York: Harper & Row.

Reed, G. (1984). The antithetical meaning of the term "empathy" in psychoanalytic discourse. In J. Lichtenberg, M. Bornstein, & D. Silver (Eds.), *Empathy I.* Hillsdale, NJ: The Analytic Press.

Ricoeur, P. (1977). The question of proof in Freud's psychoanalytic writings. *Journal of the American Psychoanalytic Association, 25*, 835–871.

Rutter, M., Graham, P., Chadivich, D. F. D., & Yule, W. (1976). Adolescent turmoil: Fact or fiction. *Journal of Child Psychology and Psychiatry, 17*, 35–36.

Schafer, R. (1959). Generative empathy in the treatment situation. *Psychoanalytic Quarterly, 28*, 342–373.

Spence, D. (1982). *Narrative truth and historical truth: Meaning and interpretation in psychoanalysis.* New York: Norton.

Steele, R. (1979). Psychoanalysis and hermeneutics. *International Review of Psychoanalysis, 6*, 389–412.

Stern, D. (1985). *The interpersonal world of the infant.* New York: Basic Books.

Taramontana, M. (1980). Critical review of research on psychotherapy outcome with adolescents: 1967–1977. *Psychological Bulletin, 88*, 429–450.

Tolan, P. H., Cromwell, R., & Brasswell, M. (1986). The application of family therapy to juvenile delinquency: A critical review of the literature. *Family Process, 25*, 619–649.

Tolan, P., Jaffe, C., & Ryan, K. (1988). *The epidemiology of adolescent psychopathology: An integrative review of the literature.* Unpublished manuscript.

Tolan, P., Ryan, K., & Jaffe, C. (1989). Adolescents' mental health service use and provider, process, and recipient characteristics. *Journal of Clinical Child Psychology, 17*, 228–235.

Viale-Val, G., Rosenthal, R. H., Curtiss, G., & Marohn, R. C. (1984). Dropout from adolescent psychotherapy: A preliminary study. *Journal of the American Academy of Child Psychiatry, 23*, 562–568.

Wallerstein, R. (1986). Psychoanalysis as a science: A response to the new challenges. *Psychoanalytic Quarterly, 55*, 414–451.

Wallerstein, R. (1988). Psychoanalysis, psychoanalytic science, and psychoanalytic research—1986. *Journal of the American Psychoanalytic Association, 36*, 3–30.

Weiss, J., & Sampson, H. (1986). *The psychoanalytic process: Theory, clinical observations, and empirical research.* New York: Guilford Press.

Wolf, E. (1982). Adolescence: Psychology of the self and self-objects. *Adolescent Psychiatry, 10*, 171–181.

Wolf, E., Gedo, J., & Terman, D. (1972). On the adolescent process as a transformation of the self. *Journal of Youth and Adolescence, 1*, 257–272.

CHAPTER 18

Alternative and Preventive Interventions

LESLIE DAVIS and PATRICK H. TOLAN

INTRODUCTION

This chapter focuses on describing existing alternative interventions for youth which, while relevant to mental health's purview, are not widely recognized by the field's professionals as viable for treatment and prevention. Although overlooked in this way, they are still quite common and possess immense potential for enhancing mental health in youth. The discussed approaches are selected for review here on the basis of their promise. Most require further research and more systematic implementation to allow confident evaluation of their worth.

In distinguishing these mental health interventions from the more conventional approaches presented in the other chapters, we are, as suggested in the Introduction, working with a broad definition of mental health. We assume mental health interventions need to be concerned with more than diminishment of symptoms of psychological disturbance. The interventions discussed here, then, are concerned with remediation, prevention, and the promotion of competencies and general health. They tend to recognize the multivariate influence of economic, educational, physical health, and emotional support conditions on mental health. These interventions also differ in terms of service delivery. They tend to shift services from a referral-based, one-to-one professional–client contact conducted in a treatment facility to proactive outreach services, often with groups and often using nonprofessionals and/or paraprofessionals for service delivery. These services are frequently provided to youth in their natural environment (e.g., school or neighborhood).

The general rationale for exploring and implementing alternative interventions has been that the problems faced by today's youth are vast and complex and their mental health implications are profound. Many psychological difficulties represent the impact of "ill-structured" social problems; problems that are not ameliorated universally to reach a single final solution, but rather require repeated, ecologically specific solutions (Mitroff, 1983; Seidman, 1983; Tolan, Keys, Chertok, & Jason, 1990). Because such problems require recurrent efforts at changing social structures and a focus on the impact of social structures rather than individuals, they are not satisfactorily resolved via the traditional mental health methods, services, and personnel. The initiatives that are the focus of this chapter are seen as addressing the social structure level of cause. We do not believe that these interventions are necessarily always preferable or even contradictory to use of traditional services, conceptually or in practice. However, they can contribute uniquely in several important ways. For example, they not only augment traditional services to adolescents, a population that is disproportionately underserved in the formalized mental health service system (Lewis, Dlugokinski, Caputo, & Griffin, 1988; Weiner, 1970), but also provide services that may be better suited to some adolescent needs.

These alternative interventions extend the service base to include segments of the youth population often missed by the traditional mental health and social service institutions—rural youth, those living in neighborhoods of concentrated poverty in the inner city (Youth and America's future, 1988a), and minority youth (Gibbs, 1984). Because they also expand the sites of provision of services to natural contexts, they help to reach the large percentage of adolescents with psychological problems who are unlikely to approach the mental health system (Elmen & Offer, Chapter 1 in this volume). Schools, neighborhood centers, and other similar settings are more accessible to and are used by more youth than are mental health clinics and hospitals. They are geographically proximal and may also be more "usable" because of the settings' social value (they are viewed positively and part of the community). Using clinic-based services may require behaviors that are incompatible with the youth's or family's value systems, exceed their sophistication in accessing formalized services, or demand scheduling that is implausible (Cowen & Gesten, 1978). Thus, alternative services provide a wide-reaching, potent force in mental health. By emphasizing competencies and working within the adolescents' natural contexts, these programs are potentially less stigmatizing than traditional mental health interventions.

The existence of these intervention alternatives is also important because of their congruency with a life-span perspective (Tolan, Pentz, Aupperle, & Davis, 1990). This view emphasizes that human behavior continues to transform and be modifiable into adolescence and adulthood. As Hobbs and Robinson (1982) pointed out, at the heart of much of this country's youth service delivery initiatives has been a fundamental assumption that early experience shapes the development of the individual irrevocably. It is then concluded that little can be gained by compensatory or enhancing interventions after childhood. Subsequently, public resources have been heavily concentrated in programs for young children, with relatively little investment in developing competencies of adolescents and young adults. The alternative interventions discussed here recognize that such a view is short-sighted and unnecessarily narrow (see Chapter 1).

The developmental/life-span perspective is also often evident in the extent to which these interventions coincide, at least in principle, with the fundamental developmental needs of adolescents. As outlined by Costello (1980), in addition to the development of identity, adolescence is a time of development of a sense of physical vitality, an ability to sustain caring relationships, a sense of resourcefulness, and a sense of social connection. In general, the interventions summarized here foster these developmental progressions. Most expand youths' social connection to peers and to nonparental adults. Often, this occurs by supplementing social roles for adolescents outside those of student and family member. In more specific ways, the programs may promote athletic, social, or academic skills, each of which contributes importantly to a developing adolescent's sense of competency.

Finally, the interventions discussed here are valuable because they benefit not only the targeted youth but those around them and, often, general society as well. For example, programs designed to circumvent the incidence of crime may also promote the young participants' future financial success and hence their contribution as citizens of their community, while decreasing victimizing of others as well. These alternative mental health interventions recognize the youths as assets (Combrinck-Graham, 1989).

Our contention, in this chapter, is that the reach, impact, and viability of these interventions are such that an integration of alternative interventions into mental health services for adolescents is needed. The research and practice development of a knowledge base for how to do so should be a priority. Ultimately, this integration should occur at the administrative level, but it also depends on the efforts of individual demonstrations (Tuma, 1989). Practitioners can assume an increased responsibility for coordinating their casework with non-mental-health resources and for introducing alternative programs to their agencies. Researchers can form partnerships with service agencies, contributing their scientific skills to help implementation and evaluation efforts. Such a partnership can advance the scientific knowledge base as well as the impact of existing agencies (Kelly, 1988; Rappaport, 1987).

Five types of alternative interventions have been identified in the literature and are discussed here: (a) social-skills training; (b) community-based alternatives; (c) health promotion; (d) academic enhancement; and (e) delinquency alternatives. Family- and policy-level interventions pertaining to youth are no less important and, while overlapping extensively with this chapter's interest, will be excluded since they are covered specifically in previous chapters (see Chapters 7, 20, and 21).

The present chapter is not intended to provide the reader with an in-depth literature review but rather with an overview of the range of existent youth mental health service alternatives, a highlighting of some exemplary interventions, and an evaluation of their promise and demonstrated utility. More comprehensive reviews, when available for specific types of interventions, are cited for reference.

SOCIAL SKILLS TRAINING

Social skills training is the alternative to traditional mental health approaches with adolescents that has had the most impact on clinical services (Curran & Monti, 1982; L'Abate & Milan, 1985; Sundberg, Snowden, & Reynolds, 1978). It is distinguishable from conventional treatment in its broadening of the definition of mental health beyond the presence or absence of symptoms, its emphasis on competence enhancement, its prominence as a preventive method, and its reliance on nonprofessionals (Tolan et al., 1990).

Social skills training initiatives with adolescents have largely focused on self-expression skills such as verbal skills, support utilization, perspective taking, other-enhancement, assertion, and communication (Hansen, Watson-Perczel, & Christopher, 1989; Marziller, 1979; Rinn & Markle, 1979). Social skills training has also been elaborated for use in specific life domains. Skills training in refusal or peer-pressure resistance strategies, for example, has become common in substance abuse prevention (Pentz et al., 1989). Social skills training has also been applied to pregnancy prevention efforts (Hayes, 1987).

The chapter's authors recently collaborated on an extensive review of the status of and trends in social skills training with adolescents (Tolan et al., 1990). Content-oriented reviews are also available (Bierman, 1986; Gilchrist, 1981; Goldstein & Pentz, 1984; Goldstein, Sprafkin, Gershaw, & Klein, 1979; Hansen et al., 1989; Rotheram & Armstrong, 1980; Schinke, 1981). A total of 164 independently published studies were located and evaluated in our review. Overall, studies evidenced that social skills training is effective for a variety of adolescents' problems. The training applied in the field is impressive in that most studies focused on developing positive behaviors, rather than on reducing negative behavior. The interventions included several skills components and techniques and used sophisticated methodology, and the research reported a positive outcome. The prominence of general and at-risk populations, the inclusion of positive skills in almost all of the interventions, and the greater emphasis on a situational skills focus (rather than skills training separate from a context) suggest that the primary orientation of social skills training is preventive and ecological. This orientation's preferability is supported by the finding that studies of interventions in schools and community settings had positive outcome more often than those in clinical settings. Commonly, studies would focus on training students in social problem-solving techniques, rehearsing assertive, prosocial statements, and imitating modeling of such skills. The goal of the training would be to increase the ability to negotiate stressful interpersonal situations with parents, peers, or others.

Five studies were cited as exemplary in terms of their individual characteristics and overall approach to social skills training: Biglan, Severson, Ary, & Faller (1987); Filipczak, Archer, and Friedman (1980); Pentz (1980); Sarason and Sarason (1981); and Bierman and Furman (1984). Each of these studies was strong in its prevention orientation, intervention comprehensiveness, and methodological rigor. The study by Bierman and Furman (1984) exemplifies these characteristics. Fifty-six preadolescents, identified as both disliked by peers and deficient in conversational skills, were randomly assigned to one of four conditions: (a) conversational skill training through individual coaching; (b) peer involvement through supervised group experience; (c) conversational skill coaching combined with supervised group peer involvement; and (d) no intervention. At posttest and follow up, skill training resulted in sustained increases in conversational skill. Peer involvement did not significantly affect conversational skill but produced improvements (temporary) in classroom sociometric status, lunchtime rates of peer interaction, and feelings of self-efficacy. The combined condition produced an additive effect, yielding improvements in both areas.

Beyond the characteristics of individual studies and the trends identified in the analyses, a question remains as to the overall efficacy of social skills training when compared to other interventions with adolescents. Reviews of adolescent psychotherapy research (Reinecke, Chapter 16 of this volume; Tramantona, 1980; Weisz, Weiss, Alicke, & Klocke, 1987) have noted its overall efficacy but the relative lack of comparisons to other interventions. In our review, only three studies were located that made direct comparisons of social skills training and psychotherapy (Fiedler, Ornstein, Chiles, Fritz, & Breitt, 1979; Jesness, 1975, 1976; Robin, 1981). Of these, only one utilized an experimental design (Robin, 1981) and all three obtained differential effects depending on the measures used, suggesting that training was confounded with type of measure. The social skills training field provides an example of how a relatively sound theoretical and empirical base for alternative interventions can be provided. The competence orientation, the broader definition of mental health, the ecological sensitivity of intervention designs, and the careful evaluation of outcome provide good evidence that alternative interventions can be significant contributors to adolescent mental health.

COMMUNITY-BASED ALTERNATIVES

Recently, three distinguished commissions/panels independently concluded that there is a strong need for private and public community agencies to align themselves with families and schools as primary fosterers of youth development (Carnegie Council on Adolescent Development, 1989; Wynn et al., 1987; Youth and America's Future, 1988a). These "community supports" are being called on to relieve the increasing burden on families and schools for rectifying problems of today's youth that are beyond family and school control. This push for shared responsibility for raising the next generation is predicated on the assumption that an array of community-based efforts is needed and that these efforts can be important contributors.

This section highlights some of the more prominent types of community-based initiatives already in place. The interested reader is encouraged to consult the W. T. Grant Foundation Commission (Youth and America's Future, 1988a,b) and the Carnegie Council on Adolescent Development (1989) reports for more extended discussions of the initiatives and the attendant issues.

Youth Organizations

There exists a multitude of youth organizations. They vary widely in the comprehensiveness and sophistication of their programming, which ranges from building-based and daily programming to less frequent after-school meetings. They also vary substantially in their emphasis. Although most organizations are largely recreational, some are career- or avocation-oriented (e.g., Junior Achievement and 4-H), some are "character-building" (e.g., Boys and Girls Clubs of America; Boy Scouts and Girl Scouts), some are politically oriented (e.g., Young Democrats, Young Republicans), some instill ethnic pride (e.g., Ukrainian Youth Organization), and some are religiously oriented (e.g., Young Life) (see Erickson, 1983). The Boys and Girls Clubs, in particular, outreach to minority youth who might otherwise not receive services. Over 400 youth organizations exist nationally. They range in membership size, with some (e.g., Boy Scouts and 4-H) as high as 4.4 million (Erickson, 1986). National surveys of randomly selected samples of adolescents between the ages of 11 to 18 have revealed that at least 20% are enrolled in a community youth organization (Erickson, 1982; LaBelle, 1981).

The widespread participation of youth in these organizations has spurred recent interest among educators and policy makers in this "burgeoning social movement in modern society" as a means for promoting youth mental health (Stephens, 1983). Proponents of youth organizations frequently contend that the current formal education process emphasizes competition and individual academic achievement, insulates young people from the concerns and values of the adult world, and ultimately constrains them into passive–dependent roles. They argue that youth get little opportunity to assume responsibility, act independently, or feel vital (Erickson, 1986). The youth organizations, in contrast, are valued for promoting these presumably more healthy attitudes. To illustrate, Boys and Girls Clubs of America program components often include youth serving in the role of junior staff helping younger children, and team building among youth and with senior staff.

Analytic and empirical analyses of youth organizations' impact on the lives of adolescents are strikingly absent from the professional literature within the field of mental health. The organizations themselves have rarely undertaken any research on their effects. As the W. T. Grant Commission pointed out (Youth and America's Future, 1988a), this lack of data is all too often interpreted as evidence of ineffectiveness when actually it is more a matter of lacking the funds or appreciation of the need to produce evaluation data.

The bulk of the existent data on youth organizations is devoted to describing membership patterns. One particularly notable trend is the sharp drop-off in membership after the ages of 12 to 14 years. Although this can be explained, in part, by adolescents' diversion to other interests during these years, it seems that many drop out because the program activities are no longer relevant (Konopka, 1976; Youth and America's Future, 1988a). For example, a recent 4-H alumni survey conducted by Ladewig and Thomas (1987) revealed that 59% dropped out while still eligible, and, of these, 44% had decided that the program no longer met their needs and interests as older teens. Other common reasons given for premature drop-out included a perception that involvement was of no benefit and a lack of funds to support participation. Importantly, all of the survey respondents reported that they would have preferred more leadership opportunities rather than the adult-directed activities that predominated.

Other research described differences between members and nonmembers. Members are more likely to have higher academic achievement, career aspirations, and political and civic awareness during adolescence (Erickson, 1982) and greater educational attainment and political and civic involvement in later adulthood (Ladewig & Thomas, 1987). As Wynn et al. (1987) concluded in their review, these data suggest valuable differences, but it cannot be discerned whether they reflect differences participants bring to the program or are a direct result of involvement.

Most of the remaining reports are of programs that did not analyze participation in community-based youth organizations exclusively but lumped it together with participation in extracurricular school activities. Several important trends, discussed extensively by Wynn et al. (1987), can be extracted. First, a relationship between participation and level of educational aspiration and accomplishment among adolescents has been repeatedly documented, even when the researchers control for socioeconomic status, intellectual ability, and academic performance (Hanks & Eckland, 1978; Otto, 1975; Otto & Featherman, 1975). Second, longitudinal studies (Hanks, 1981; Otto, 1976) point to a relationship between adolescent participation in community and school-based activities and later membership in voluntary organizations and political activity in adulthood (again, even more so than later involvement was related to education, occupation, or income). Third, it appears that this effect is relatively specific to the type of community involvement emphasized by the organization. For example, Hanks (1981) found that participation in organizations designed to achieve a social objective was more predictive of later political involvement than was participation in organizations in which recreational and other "expressive" activities were emphasized.

A few researchers have attempted more process-oriented analyses of youth organizations. Kleinfeld and Shinkwin (1982) explored some of the assumptions about the value of these organizations through a series of extensive interviews with staff, youth members, and their parents, as well as through participant observations of multiple Scout troops and 4-H clubs. They concluded that these organizations attract only a small fraction of youth—primarily those whose families and backgrounds support the ideology of that particular group. Nevertheless, well-functioning chapters provide adolescent constituents with valuable learning experiences that they do not receive in schools. Most notably, participants obtained increased familiarity with practical skills, experience with leadership and other organizational roles, and greater feelings of community responsibility. Family involvement in teaching and values socialization was more likely.

Kleinfeld and Shinkwin (1982), in the same report, identified several key features that promote the youth involvement and the positive impact of youth groups: (a) an emphasis on the youth group as fun and social (versus achievement-based); (b) a wide variety of activities and organizational roles available to youth; and (c) the reflection of local cultural patterns. With respect to the importance of cultural reflection, the report by Kleinfeld and Shinkwin (1982) included a description of a youth organization in an Eskimo village. Apparently, it succeeded in great part by adapting the activities to reflect local culture. To illustrate, the group deemphasized the meetings, awards, and ceremonies that are central features of most established youth groups but did not fit with the culture's values. Instead, they emphasized recreation, which was critically lacking in availability, and the carrying out of community projects through cooperative groups. The cooperative orientation was a traditional organizational structure for this community.

Youth organizations are hampered by the instability of program design and the high staff turnover (Stephens, 1983). Additional problems include frequent loss of funding; staff burnout (little salary and little career stake); a common occurrence of loss of an inspirational leader, causing the organization to essentially die out; and failure to create the conditions for youth commitment to the program. Intensive staff training and the establishment of merit and reward systems for youth are among the strategies proposed for decreasing such problems.

In sum, the research on the process and effectiveness of youth organizations has not begun to match their prevalence or the enthusiasm they generate. However, the natural fit of the programs with the goals of adolescent development, especially social responsibility; the programs' accessibility to many otherwise unreachable youth; and the positive impact found among the few evaluated programs suggest that they deserve carefully designed programming and evaluations. Their enhancement effects may provide one of the most effective means for primary prevention.

Organized Youth Sports

Organized youth sports, orchestrated out of youth organizations, schools, and other community settings, represent another major ecological context for youth development—and another that has been largely neglected by mental health researchers. Reppucci (1987) reviewed the psychological literature and found that our field has paid little to no attention to the role of organized sports in youth development and mental health. As in the case of youth organizations, the widespread societal presumption of organized sports' positive effect on youth development has not been tested. Similarly, the deliberate use of youth sports as a mental health intervention has not been seriously examined (Reppucci, 1987). Attention to sports and exercise programs' contributions to social development has come from within the physical education field and, to some extent, from among sociologists, although virtually no objective empirical data have been generated in either field. In a review of the literature, Reppucci (1987) identified a split. Youth sports proponents, particularly physical education professionals, in effect mirror our culture's heavy value on organized competitive sports. In addition to their physical health effects, sweeping claims about the benefits of competitive sports include: they keep youth "out of trouble," promote self-confidence and self-discipline, and provide a needed context for the expression of natural aggressive tendencies.

The claim for keeping youth "out of trouble," that is, serving as a deterrent to delinquency, is one of the few that has been subjected to empirical scrutiny. Among lower-income male youth, those involved with sports display significantly less delinquent activity than their nonathletic counterparts (Schafer, 1969; Segrave & Chu, 1978). Apparently, this did not hold true for middle-class adolescent male samples. These findings have spurred Hellison and colleagues (DeBusk & Hellison, 1989; Hellison, 1989) to develop and evaluate a physical education intervention program for "teaching self-responsibility to delinquency-prone youth." In an initial project involving fourth-grade delinquency-prone boys, classroom teachers' behavioral observations, students' self-reports, and the investigator's anecdotal data on the youths' affective behavior all evidenced positive changes (DeBusk & Hellison, 1989). Implementation and evaluation with older youth are ongoing (Hellison, 1989).

On the other side of the debate are those who conclude that there is little, if any, valid evidence that sports participation is a valuable or unique socialization experience. Some go on to charge that sports place an unhealthy emphasis on winning, resulting in excessive levels of stress and overcompetitiveness, and that high structure undercuts creativity and spontaneity in youth. Another cause for concern is that some children are pushed into sports to benefit eager adults rather than themselves.

As Reppucci (1987) concluded, the issues of the impact of sports experiences are undoubtedly complex. Differential effects are likely, depending on the type of sport, individual youth characteristics, and other parameters. The sheer numbers of youth participating in organized sports, their potential for impact on a wide range of adolescents, the social value given to participants, and their ready convenience as an intervention modality all cry for scientific study of them. These characteristics also argue for increased consideration for the use of sports intervention by mental health practitioners.

Youth Volunteer Service Opportunities

Mobilizing youth to take on service functions in their community and to become direct helpers of others—companions for the aged, tutors, counselors, or mentors for other children and youth—has recently attracted increased attention from community-oriented professionals. This approach, based on viewing youth as *assets* to society and as viable citizens who have and can extend considerable energy in serving others, is a particularly attractive alternative to the view that underlies much of this country's current youth service initiatives: young persons are problems and need something done *for* or *to* them (Youth and America's Future, 1988a). Thus, these youth service activities have "double social utility" (Wynn et al., 1987). Youth are tapped to contribute to others and, in turn, are afforded an opportunity that is unfortunately rare for many youth: to feel important and useful (Nightingale & Wolverton, 1988; Youth and America's Future, 1988a).

Some of the many youth initiatives are currently in place in colleges and high schools that encourage, or even require, students to complete unpaid service hours (Youth and America's Future, 1988a). Other youth service efforts include youth corps membership; the VISTA program is probably the best known. The attraction of such programs is exemplified by the current consideration within the U.S. Congress to establish a National Youth Conservation Corps as a means for enhancing youth citizenship consciousness.

With regard to relevant research, the Youth and America's Future report (1988a) and a review paper by Wynn et al. (1987) cited a few unpublished studies that uniformly support the psychological value of service in young people's lives. Most studies involve college students and consist of anecdotal accounts (Branch & Freedman, 1986; Levine, 1988). A small number used pre- and posttests or comparison groups (Hamilton & Fenzel, 1987; Newmann & Rutter, 1983) and suggested that voluntary service involvement relates to reduced feelings of alienation and isolation, an increased understanding of and desire to get involved in the community, and a sense of competence and worth. Service experiences appear to be most valuable when they are coupled with opportunities for discussion and reflection on the experiences (Wynn et al., 1987). None of this literature has, however, included adequate attempts to rule out other factors such as motivation and self-selection, which may account for differences between experience effects on youth volunteers and their comparison peers. Another needed evaluation component is the effect of such organizations on the community's attitudes about adolescents.

Peer Helping Programs

The installation of youth as helpers of their peers (as mentors, "big brothers/sisters," and/or advocates and tutors for their peers and younger children) is a form of youth service that is being applied because it benefits the helpers as well as the help recipients. Peer helping programs are being hailed by some advocates as *the* human services paradigm of the 1990s because they restructure the help relationship. The helped recipient or consumer becomes the producer of help (Reissman, 1989). The benefits said to accrue from this approach include (a) a vast expansion of helping resources; (b) conversion of peer interactions into informed, positive help; (c) communication in their own vocabulary among target populations; and (d) promotion of helper strengths and their sense of meaningfulness and community. The view is that tapping strengths in order to enhance mental health is better than targeting and removing inadequacies.

The youth-helping-youth approach has received relatively more empirical scrutiny than other community-based interventions. The research has, however, been conducted mostly on one topic: the enlistment of older youth to serve as academic tutors. In other peer helping interventions, adolescents have been placed in the roles of community-based advocates for other in-trouble youth (e.g., Rehabilitation Services Administration, 1974) and peer mediators in youth conflict situations in schools (e.g., LeFlore, 1989), and in the general capacity of mentors (e.g., Mason, 1979). Overall, the evaluations of tutoring suggest a reciprocal effectiveness for elementary and secondary school recipients as well as for the teen providers. All show small but significant gains in academic and personal functioning (Devin-Sheehan, Feldman, & Allen, 1976; Gerber & Kaufman, 1981; Hedin, 1987). In fact, in a meta-analysis, Cohen, Kulik, and Kulik (1982) found that in 33 of the 39 studies, students who served as tutors performed better academically than did control students.

Impressively, the favorable results of adolescent tutoring have been replicated where the older youth themselves had evidenced problems. Two studies are particularly informative on this issue. Maher (1982) randomly assigned 18 high school students who were administratively classified as emotionally disturbed (all had displayed conduct problems) to one of three conditions: provision of peer tutoring to elementary school-age children; reception of peer tutoring; and reception of group counseling. In comparison to the two contrast groups, the peer tutors made significant improvement on all dependent measures: increased social science and language arts grades and significantly reduced rates of absenteeism and disciplinary referrals. Another application targeted 13 youth with high external locus of control, low academic achievement, and nomination by the school counselor as hating school (Maher, 1982). They were assigned as tutors to second- and third-grade students, with matches made according to similarity in academic and behavioral problems. Among 10 of the 13 tutors, at a 3-month follow-up, significant differences resulted in locus of control (there was increased internality). Additionally, 81% of the students were reported by their respective teachers (most of whom had not been aware of the program) to have improved "some" to "very much" in their classroom work and in attitude toward school and/or self. These two studies suggest that a competence-based peer-helping-peer model is very promising. Hedin (1987), who reviewed studies of factors that facilitate tutoring effects, found no systematic differences by gender pairings, although there was a decided preference among young people to work with tutors of the same sex. The data are mixed as to optimal program length. However, structured tutoring and regular adult supervision were consistently found to be helpful.

These results suggest that, at least in the important realm of psychosocial development, students with problems can be helped by being positioned to help others. The extension of the peer helping paradigm to nonacademic domains is more recent and only a few anecdotal reports are available. For example, Mason (1979) found high self-reported satisfaction among high school students who had been trained in helping skills and then matched to work with small groups of middle school students.

Mentor Programs

A contrasting approach to youth being helped by helping is intervention by increasing contact with an adult "identification" figure. The concept of "one-on-one mentoring" is increasingly being promoted as an intervention with youth, especially those from impoverished, inner-city areas, and generally refers to a successful adult helping a younger one in an individual relationship. Mentors try to help adolescents succeed in school and in roles such as parenting. These initiatives are being organized through public and private efforts (e.g., schools and corporations) and via private and public sector partnerships. The mentor-volunteers are solicited through universities, youth organizations, schools, church congregations, and, most often, businesses that encourage their employees to participate.

The effect of mentoring as a mental health intervention for youth recipients is unknown. Evidence suggests that mentor relationships were present in the early lives of a substantial number of successful businessmen (Roche, 1979) and that their presence is significantly related to greater psychosocial competence in inner-city minority adolescents (Valentin, 1984). Despite the hoped-for benefits of a mentor relationship, available analyses of the short-term impact of formalized mentor programs are discouraging. For example, in a current joint public and private citywide mentoring venture in Milwaukee, 300 high-risk middle school students were identified on the basis of economic conditions and behavioral problems such as underachievement and absenteeism. They were then matched with civic and private-sector adult mentors. On the average, grades *decreased* during the first year; substantial grade increases occurred in only one of the participating schools. A particular problem was that many students failed to attend their appointments and there was little outreach effort. It may be that the program effects were not seen because of limited implementation (Kazdin, 1990). Another possibility is that the implemented intervention depended on identification as the impact process rather than competence building. Competence development may be a necessary component for mentoring to have a positive effect.

One closely examined application of a mentoring approach is the Community Woman component of Project Redirection, a teen pregnancy and parent support project designed and evaluated by Manpower Demonstration Research Corporation (MDRC). The mentoring part of this multicomponent intervention involved matching low-income teen mothers with women mentors. In addition to mentoring, this program included regularly scheduled peer group sessions, workshops, counseling, and individualized brokering for health, education, employment, and employability development. Recreational activities, transportation, and child care assistance were also made available.

The project was implemented in seven cities. Turnover of mentors was high, and, even when replacements were secured, the teenagers reported great difficulty in transferring loyalties. The evaluation did not distinguish the mentoring program's impact from the overall effects. Also, partialing out the impact of those mentors who persisted in the program would seem to be important. Only results for the overall program are available. Follow-up interviews were conducted at 1, 2, and 5 years after implementation on the intervention group and a matched comparison group. The 1- and 2-year follow-up interviews were discouraging. However, at 5 years, the results were quite impressive. Statistically significant differences, favoring the intervention group, were found in mean weekly earnings, number of hours per week and number of weeks worked at a job, percent receiving Assistance for Dependent Children (AFDC) benefits, mean number of subsequent live births, home environment scores, percent enrolled in Head Start, and children's mean vocabulary score. Although not reaching statistical significance, a higher percentage of the Project Redirection participants had received a diploma or graduation equivalency diploma (GED) and were employed (Polit, Quint, & Riccio, 1988; Rappoport, 1987). From this general evaluation, several conclusions were drawn specifically about Project Redirection's mentoring component (Rappoport, 1987). Reports from teen participants, mentors, and project staff confirmed that the mentoring component was a vital element in the program. The matches were more successful when the mentors and the teens shared the same racial and class characteristics and the volunteers lived in the same community. The matches were enhanced when the mentor took active steps to involve the teen's family.

These qualitative findings suggest that mentoring can be valuable but that its applications must be done with care and sophistication. Congruence in matching and the process of the mentors' building a relationship with the teens' families seem most important. Building these factors into programs and studying other factors that facilitate the impact of mentors are vital to establishing the overall value of this popular approach and providing specific directions.

Work Training Programs

Commissions and panels on the status of adolescents (e.g., W. T. Grant Commission, and Carnegie Council on Adolescent Development) have endorsed the adolescent work experience as an integral and effective means of easing the transition into adult roles because it helps adolescents develop a sense of independence, brings them into closer contact with adults, and teaches them skills that they will need as adults. They suggest that the workplace is an important educational environment.

Schools and other institutions have been criticized for segregating work from the rest of the adolescent's life, and adolescent work from the adult workplace (Steinberg, Greenberger, Garduque, Ruggerio, & Vaux, 1982). Thus, better work options and training opportunities for youth are being called for as supplements to schooling. Work that can function as an education alternative to schooling for drop-outs, non-college-bound, and impoverished youth is also needed (e.g., Youth and America's Future, 1988b).

One increasingly popular youth employment initiative is through formalized partnerships of private employers, schools, and government (e.g., through internships and apprenticeships). The National Job Corps, now 23 years old, represents one of the better known partnerships between private contractors and federal, state, and local government agencies. It is designed to provide intensive, residentially based job training programs. Comparisons of nonparticipants with participants who complete these programs yield impressive findings. In a synthesis of the results of various programs, graduates were found to be: earning an average of $567 more per year; relying on welfare 2 weeks less and on unemployment compensation benefits 1 week less, over the course of a year; and five times more likely to have received a GED or high school diploma (Commission on Youth Employment Programs, 1985). There was a $1.46 net return for every tax dollar invested in these programs. However, the attrition rates in these programs are high. For example, a recent evaluation of the California Conservation Corps revealed that the average length of stay was 5.1 months and that only one in five participants completed the full 12-month program (Wolf, Leiderman, & Voith, 1987).

The optimism for these youth employment programs must be taken within the context of some recent results that challenge the widely held belief that early work experience is always positive (for an excellent review, see Steinberg, 1989). Steinberg et al.'s (1982) series of investigations into the developmental significance of youth employment has found both negative and positive results. Notably, these authors believe that the constraining work experience that adolescents typically have is a key limitation. Most adolescents have petty jobs at fast-food restaurants and similar workplaces. They are segregated from adult workers, and there is limited transferability of skills to adult jobs. Because of these constraints, Steinberg and colleagues have suggested that the benefits have been overrated and the costs underestimated. Specifically, they have found that, although the development of self-management and autonomy appears to be facilitated by paid employment experiences, social responsibility and commitment to personal relationships with family and friends are not (Greenberger & Steinberg, 1986). They also found that teenage workers were less likely to develop close relationships with adults at work (Greenberger & Steinberg, 1981). The development of cynical attitudes toward work and the ethics of work practices, and increased use of cigarettes and marijuana were also related to having a job. Another study found that working did not deter delinquency among high-risk inner-city youth (Gottfredson, 1985). More general samples of youth netted the finding that employment was, in fact, associated with increased delinquent behavior, especially when the working hours were long (Bachman, Bare, & Frankie, 1986; Greenberger & Steinberg, 1986).

Employment per se, especially among middle-class adolescents, may not determine effects; learning about being a worker may be more significant (Tolan, 1988). Just as the mentoring impact seems to be related to identification with a competent adult as a base for developing competence positive employment effects may be dependent on access to adult identification figures and opportunity to develop a sense of competence. More careful evaluation of these components' importance is warranted.

HEALTH-RELATED INTERVENTIONS

As part of the overall focus on health promotion as prevention, youth have been frequently targeted. The mounting evidence that life-style patterns determine a substantial portion of risk for disease and psychopathology, and that these patterns often gel in childhood and adolescence, has led to increasing primary prevention efforts aimed at youth. This attention has been particularly strong in efforts to prevent chronic diseases, including AIDS/HIV, alcohol and substance abuse, and teenage pregnancy.

Disease Prevention

Cardiovascular disease (CVD) has received particular attention in health promotion with youth because of its pervasiveness, the importance of life-style in determining risk, and the long period before its effects are evident. Primary prevention of CVD is seen to hinge on teaching youth healthy life-styles that, if maintained, will lessen the likelihood of the development of risky behaviors and the disease sequelae.

The Minnesota Heart Health Program (MHHP) stands out as an exemplary approach to CVD prevention. It is a populationwide, community-based CVD prevention program developed by researchers at the University of Minnesota (Blackburn et al., 1984; Perry, Klepp, & Schultz, 1988). The entire populations in three participating cities in the north-central United States have been targeted in a 5-year educational program aimed at encouraging healthy habits in eating, exercise, and control of smoking and high blood pressure. The multiple strategies employed include multimedia educational campaigns, family risk-screening clinics, health professionals' education, and educational and other intervention programs specifically targeting youth.

Youth are actively integrated into each of the project components, but the primary educational intervention for them is accomplished within the schools. Developmentally appropriate interventions have been designed for youth in the third to tenth grades; they range from healthy eating/exercise promotion to smoking/substance abuse prevention. Because the programs are long-term, only preliminary results are available, but these are promising. Results have indicated that participants ($n = 1,500$) significantly reduced their fat and sodium intake and smoking onset rates, when compared to same-age students from a reference community (Perry et al., 1987; Perry, Mullis, & Maile, 1985; Perry, Murray, & Klepp, 1987).

The prevention of AIDS and HIV infection represents a newer challenge for pediatric and adolescent disease prevention and health promotion. Prevention strategies are being introduced to increasingly younger children and are primarily incorporated into school curricula; they focus on drug use prevention and sex education (Klitzner, 1989). These are overviewed below. Unfortunately, as the reader will find, the impact of drug prevention programs has barely been established, and the evaluation of pregnancy prevention programs is negligible. The further step of linking these interventions to AIDS and HIV infection incidence and prevalence rates has not occurred.

Substance Abuse Prevention

The adolescent substance abuse prevention literature is vast, and to thoroughly describe and evaluate it would obviously be beyond the capability of this section. Our interest here is in interventions that are preventive in intent and/or use methods other than therapy or A.A. models (Tolan et al., 1990). Many of the implications of drug prevention efforts can be summarized based on two recent independent meta-analyses conducted by Tobler (1986) and Bangert-Drowns (1988). Their results yield differing but not irreconcilable pictures.

Tobler (1986) evaluated 143 adolescent drug prevention programs. Across the programs, she discerned five program modalities that address drug problems. Two take *indirect* approaches: affective enhancement (aimed at interpersonal and social growth) and alternatives programs (focused on community and leisure or physical activities, remedial skills, and one-on-one relationships). She classified the remaining three modalities as *direct* approaches to substance abuse prevention: knowledge and education, peer programs focused on refusal and social life skills, and combination of affective and knowledge approaches. Tobler defined program success through five outcome measures: (a) increased knowledge about drugs and their effects; (b) changes in attitudes toward drugs and deviant behavior; (c) enhanced personal and interpersonal skills; (d) decreased negative behavior as gathered by collateral records or contacts (police, parents, teachers); and (e) decreased or noninitiated drug use, as evidenced by self-reports with or without physiological measures.

Tobler found that peer programs and alternative programs were effective modalities. Peer programs produced the only actual reductions of drug-abusing *behaviors* among general school-based populations. This effectiveness held true across alcohol, drug, and smoking behavior outcomes. The alternatives programs were equally successful for special "at-risk" adolescent populations, such as drug abusers, juvenile delinquents, and those with other school difficulties. In general, the other three program approaches (knowledge, affective, and knowledge–affective) had little effect on any outcomes with any population. In fact, Tobler found that such approaches were sometimes followed by *increased* drug use.

Bangert-Drowns (1988) completed a smaller-scale meta-analysis of 33 school-based substance prevention program evaluations. A far more pessimistic conclusion than Tobler's was drawn. Using a more stringent methodological criterion for selection and attempting to avoid statistical problems inherent in the classic meta-analysis techniques as applied by Tobler, Bangert-Drowns concluded that substance abuse education had positive effects on knowledge and attitudes but was wholly unsuccessful in demonstrating change in students' drug use. Thus, the results of efforts to date are most helpful in indicating what does not work (Botvin, 1985). Along with early efforts of moral exhortations ("Just Say No" equivalents), scare tactics, and drug education initiatives, it appears that providing information alone is proving not sufficient to change drug attitudes or behaviors. In fact, it may have the paradoxical result of arousing interest in trying substances (Falco, 1988). Nevertheless, drug education continues to be the most widely used approach (Botvin, 1985).

Affective education or skills-based strategies represent a newer approach. This model rests on the assumption that young people use drugs not out of ignorance about their effects but rather to compensate for a lack of self-esteem or because they do not know how to make healthy decisions. The programs share a fundamental goal of reducing substance abuse by promoting skills in problem solving, decision making, values awareness, stress reduction, and interpersonal communications. The approach also assumes a gateway model of drug use. Primary prevention to impede onset of use of tobacco, alcohol, and marijuana is considered the best way to prevent later, more serious drug use. Often, the skill training is presented without reference to drugs themselves. The Social Assertiveness Skills Training model, developed by Pentz et al. (1986), and the Cognitive-Behavioral Skills Training model (Schinke & Gilchrist, 1984) are among the most prominent of these. They have shown mixed results with moderate levels of change in problem-solving skills of limited duration but have had no significant effects on drug use.

A more recent effort, targeting elementary school-age children, views substance and alcohol use as a socially learned, functional behavior resulting from a complex interaction of environmental and personal factors. The emphasis is on teaching techniques to resist peer and media pressure to use drugs. In addition, socialization and coping skills training, decision making, and drug education are provided. Very often, peer leaders and teachers are utilized to deliver the prevention programs. The success of this new prevention strategy appears to be greater than earlier approaches. For example, in follow-up studies of the Life-Skills Training Program developed out of Cornell University Medical College (Botvin, 1985), participating students, who received additional "booster sessions" in the second year of the study, showed an 87% reduction in new smoking compared to students in nonparticipating schools.

The Midwestern Prevention Project (Pentz et al., 1989), apparently the most effective approach to date, combines individual-level skills training and education aimed at youth with efforts to simultaneously promote wider community norms for not using drugs. Mass-media campaigns (radio and television broadcasts and newspaper articles) designed to modify community norms were combined with homework assignments to the participating youth (as companions to the school-based training). Students were required to interview their family and peers about family drug use rules, and were given training in techniques for avoiding drug use and education about methods for family counteraction of media and community pressures to use drugs. Initial effects reported are: a decrease in the prevalence rates of use of cigarettes, alcohol, and marijuana, even when race, grade, socioeconomic status, and urbanicity are controlled (e.g., 17% vs. 24% for cigarette smoking, 11% vs. 16% for alcohol use, and 7% vs. 10% for marijuana use). Further analyses are needed, but this integrated approach seems most promising.

Sexuality and Adolescent Pregnancy Prevention

Teenage pregnancy is no less a problem than drug abuse in terms of the great compromises it imposes on the future of the young mothers and their offspring (Furstenberg, Brooks-Gunn, & Chase-Lansdale, 1989). Premature school drop-out, which is very prevalent among teen mothers; poor basic academic skills; low employability and ensuing poverty are the foremost damaging sequelae (Schorr, 1988). These facts are of even greater concern when the pervasiveness of teenage pregnancy is considered: 19% of White females and 41% of Black females will become pregnant by the age of 18 (Moore, 1985). Consequently, programs that prevent teenage pregnancy *and* those that provide ameliorative care for pregnant and parenting teenagers can both be important mental health interventions.

The Panel on Adolescent Pregnancy and Childbearing of the National Academy of Sciences, in a two-volume report, recently overviewed the teenage pregnancy programs available across the country (Hayes, 1987; Hofferth & Hayes, 1987). They noted two types of interventions: those aimed at preventing pregnancy, and those aimed at enhancing the well-being of adolescent parents and their children. The panel concluded that primary prevention efforts (i.e., those that aim to prevent the occurrence of teenage pregnancy) should be a foremost social priority. Without recommending that ameliorative programs be abandoned, the panel suggested that the cost and the difficulty in implementing them effectively argue against their emphasis.

Adolescent Pregnancy Prevention

Alternative intervention efforts in the pregnancy prevention vein have generally followed one of three approaches: educating teens about sexuality and contraception; changing attitudes about early sexual intercourse ("saying no"); and providing contraceptive and family planning services. Usually, these are done through school clinics. At recent count, comprehensive school-based health clinics, in which family planning counseling is offered as a means of pregnancy prevention, numbered 138 across the country. This is a remarkable figure, given the immense opposition by right-to-life groups and others (Dryfoos, 1988).

Kirby (1985) evaluated 15 education programs for adolescents, including a school-based clinic, each of which he selected as exemplary and representative of different approaches. Notably, he was able to randomly assign youth to experimental groups but at several sites secured no-treatment matches. Kirby found that, overall, there was an increase in knowledge about sexuality but little measurable impact on values, attitudes, self-esteem, relationship satisfaction, decision making, or communication skills. Most programs did not succeed in altering the participants' sexual activity or contraceptive usage. The exception was one school health clinic program which not only significantly altered birth-control usage but yielded a decrease in the unintended birth rate (Zabin, Street, & Hardy, 1983). The clinic component of this program entailed individual education and counseling about contraceptive methods, gynecological examinations, referrals to a hospital teen program for prescriptions, and follow-up.

Kirby's results demonstrate greater effectiveness when programs incorporate what he calls a relevant "experiential" component—directly facilitating desired behavior, not just talking about it. Two examples he considered most powerful are a parent–child model, which fostered parent–child dialogue right in the classroom, and a school-based clinic that provided comprehensive services.

Teen Parent Interventions

Hayes (1987) described several general types of interventions to assist pregnant teens and teen parents and their children: those that provide abortion services; those that provide prenatal and perinatal health care services; those that provide economic support; those that promote the emotional well-being and education of the children; and those that promote the educational/occupational advances and the "life options" of the teen parents. More specifically, among strategies for intervening psychosocially with the teen mothers are employment programs and mentoring programs (described elsewhere in this chapter). Another approach that intends to directly enhance the emotional well-being of the adolescent is life-skills training. Instruction about basic aspects of daily life, such as budgeting, consumer awareness, and homemaking skills, is incorporated into alternative school programs to provide information, skills, and support (see Hayes, 1987). Life planning, specifically goal setting and decision making, has also received special attention in several programs, including Project Redirection (Polit et al., 1988). Alternative schools for teen parents, established within regular schools or in separate facilities, also often build social service and support components into the academic curriculum. Another approach is to include counseling and support activities for the families of pregnant and parenting teenagers, to aid in this transition (Klerman, 1983).

Each of these approaches has potential to help combat the negative social, economic, and health consequences of early childbearing, and programs that combine strategies are appealing. Unfortunately, very little is known about the effectiveness and feasibility of multicomponent programs or about the impact of specific components (Hayes, 1987; Hofferth & Hayes, 1987). The outcome information available indicates positive effects, but the improvements are specific to the targeted goals and are short-term. For example, abortion services have prevented childbearing, education improves the teens' developmental knowledge, and alternative school programs enable student parents to stay in school (Hayes, 1987). The programs' longer-term effects, however, especially delay in subsequent pregnancy and educational/occupational outcomes, have yet to be demonstrated (Furstenberg et al., 1989; Hofferth & Hayes, 1987).

Adolescent Medicine/Health Centers

A fourth health-related intervention is the establishment of adolescent health centers/clinics. Adolescent medicine has been identified as the remaining frontier of pediatrics (Haggerty, 1987). Postdoctoral subspecialty training programs and research activities in adolescent medicine are growing in number, as are the numbers of professional conferences and journals devoted to adolescent medicine. (The interested reader is encouraged to consult the Carnegie Council report (Hein, 1988) for an overview of the history and programmatic directions of adolescent health care.) The potential contributions of this approach to adolescent mental health can be enormous.

A particularly popular model for the delivery of adolescent health care services is the school-linked center. The background, characteristics, and evaluation results of these school-linked programs are reviewed comprehensively by Millstein (1988) in another Carnegie Council report that is summarized in this section. The first school-linked health centers began in 1970; by March 1988, 125 were located either within schools proper or in adjacent buildings. The majority were servicing high schools, although 13 served middle and junior high school students. Most clinics were located within economically disadvantaged areas, where there were high concentrations of minority students and high rates of drop-out.

The establishment and evaluation of the effects of the school-linked centers have been impeded. Variation in levels and low stability of funding resources have led to unreliability in the type and intensity of services provided. At present, "drop-in" care during school hours is the most common form of contact. Physical and mental health services, usually including reproductive health services, are common. Most centers provide at least gynecological screening and reproductive health service referral; 48% prescribe contraceptives and 21% distribute them. Of the services used, 25% are for reproductive health care.

Program effectiveness has been measured in a number of ways. Where program utilization has been selected as the criterion, Millstein (1988) concluded that the programs appear to be quite successful. The average enrollment at the health centers is 71% of the student body, with 32% to almost 50% actually using them (self-referred). In one health center, 38% of the users reported they would not have otherwise sought care and 26% said they had no other source of non-emergency-room health care (probably because they have no health insurance); and 30% of enrollees became regular users. A cost–benefit analysis showed that the average cost of a routine physical examination at a school-linked center was $11.25, in comparison to $45 at a private physician's office within the same community. The preventive cost benefits are likely to be geometrically larger, given that more adolescents were getting regular and preventive health care and many of them were otherwise unlikely to get such care. For example, otherwise undetected conditions, such as diabetes, heart disease, seizure disorders, depression, and sexual abuse have been reported in as many as 25% of a center's utilizers (Dryfoos, 1988).

Satisfaction surveys collected from enrolled students, their parents, and community residents have likewise been highly favorable. Measurements of the school-linked centers' impact on problem behaviors have shown better school attendance, lower substance abuse and mental health problem incidence, and lower sexual activity and teen pregnancy. However, these findings were not based on comparison schools or participants. The other important question regarding effectiveness, which has lacked any attention altogether, is the comparison of school-linked centers' impact to that of other adolescent health care delivery models. Several evaluation efforts are currently under way and should be expected to be more rigorous methodologically; for example, one by the Robert Wood Johnson Foundation, begun in 1987, includes a 5-year longitudinal evaluation of several school-linked clinics (Millstein, 1988).

ACADEMIC-RELATED INTERVENTIONS

Schools are potentially a powerful social context for promoting healthy psychosocial development as well as achievement outcomes; yet, all too often, the school experience may exacerbate, if not directly foster, a wide variety of problematic behavior (Linney & Seidman, 1989; Trickett & Schmid, Chapter 8 of this volume). Poor grades, chronic truancy, and other school difficulties have been found to be related to later school failure and premature school drop-out (U.S. Department of Health, Education, and Welfare, 1975), delinquency, teen pregnancy, and substance abuse (Hawkins, Lishner, & Catalano, 1985). Peer difficulties at school and the concomitant risk for later maladjustment have also been widely documented (Parker & Asher, 1987).

In an earlier chapter, Trickett and Schmid outlined an ecological perspective on schools which is valuable both in terms of its elaboration of the school as a "social context" influencing adolescents psychosocially and as a framework from which mental health professionals can conceptualize and plan meaningful school interventions. The present chapter augments their perspective and examples by describing some additional academic interventions for adolescents that are particularly promising for mental health promotion.

Several of the key aspects of an effective school context have been isolated in research (Linney & Seidman, 1989; Rutter, 1983; Trickett & Schmid, Chapter 8 of this volume). These include a smaller school size; opportunities for peer interaction; an orderly and nonoppressive school atmosphere; an emphasis on academics; teacher expectations for student mastery; and classroom management strategies.

As noted by Trickett and Schmid, the extant research on school effects is limited less in terms of the range of independent variables considered than in its overreliance on too narrow a criterion of effectiveness, that is, standardized group-administered achievement scores. The prevention of drop-out, the improvement of classroom performance, and the promotion of various aspects of psychosocial development are examples of outcomes that are now considered valuable effectiveness criteria. Another important shift is the emphasis on exploration of the impact of various "school regularities" (Linney & Seidman, 1989), such as the practices of age grouping, "tracking" (the process of separating students according to level of ability), racial desegregation, and the transition process from junior to senior high school (Steinberg, 1989). This shift away from the individual student represents a broadening of the understanding of school's impact on adolescent mental health.

Another thrust of the literature, exemplified by the work of the Carnegie Council on Adolescent Development (1989), emphasizes the middle school period as critical in adolescent development. With that concern guiding them, the report committee recommended the creation of smaller learning environments: "houses" or "schools within schools," teacher–student teams, assignment of adult advisers to each student, instruction of a core of common knowledge such as critical thinking, citizenship, and the *process* of learning.

Such an effort has been carried out in STEP (School Transitional Environmental Program) by Felner and colleagues (Felner & Adan, 1988; Felner, Ginter, & Primavera, 1982). STEP is designed to ease the transition of youth from junior high school to high school. Recent research has indicated that this normative transition is often accompanied by significant decreases in academic performance and psychological well-being and by increases in absenteeism and the potential for delinquency, substance abuse, and other social and behavioral problems (Felner et al., 1982; Felner, Primavera, & Cauce, 1981) similar to the adverse effects documented for the transition to junior high school (Blyth, Simmons, & Carlton-Ford, 1983; Hirsch & Rapkin, 1987).

STEP students take all primary academic subjects and homeroom only with other STEP students. Distance between nonhomeroom classes is minimized, and the homeroom teacher serves as the primary administrative and counseling link between the students and their parents, or the students and the rest of the school. STEP teachers are initially given additional training in counseling skills and an opportunity for team building as well as ongoing support meetings. The reorganizational measures are intended to cut down on the degree of flux and the complexity of the setting the student confronts and to facilitate increased peer interaction and teacher support.

A 4-year follow-up of ninth graders in a large urban high school in Chicago, where students were from primarily low socioeconomic and minority background, compared 59 STEP students with 113 control students. The STEP students evidenced higher academic test scores and adjustment to school and lower levels of psychological dysfunction. The most striking finding was the differential drop-out rate: 21% compared to 43% among control students (Felner & Adan, 1988). Similar findings were replicated in two high schools and three junior high schools in rural and suburban communities (Felner & Adan, 1988).

Another academic strategy with significant potential mental health implication is the promise of college sponsorship to economically disadvantaged youth. The recent burst of enthusiasm for this movement can be credited, to a large extent, to Eugene M. Lang, a wealthy New York City businessman who, in 1981, promised 61 graduating sixth-grade students from East Harlem that he would pay their way through college if they would stay in school long enough to take up his offer. Throughout their adolescent years, Lang met regularly with these students. Considering the estimated 40% to 75% drop-out rates in Manhattan's poorest areas, the findings are impressive. Of Lang's original 61 students, the whereabouts of which 52 are still known, 34 are enrolled in colleges and another 15 have at least completed the 10th grade on time if not graduated from high school (Berger, 1989). Since the inception of his program, Lang has set up the I Have a Dream Foundation, through which he advises 130 sponsors across 31 cities in implementing similar programs. The model is, in fact, scheduled to be implemented at a statewide level in Rhode Island, with all low-income pupils being promised full state-college scholarships upon completing high school and being provided mentors in the meantime (Berger, 1989).

DELINQUENCY INTERVENTION ALTERNATIVES

The traditional tertiary handling of juvenile delinquency through the juvenile justice and mental health systems has long been viewed as ineffective (Tolan & Loeber, Chapter 13 of this volume; Lorion, Tolan, & Wahler, 1987). Therefore, substantial attention has been directed toward alternate approaches, specifically secondary prevention and diversion of youth-in-trouble from the juvenile justice system. As mentioned in the chapter by Loeber and Tolan, the literature is vast, and overall evaluations, to date, have been pessimistic. However, a more careful and sophisticated evaluation by Lipsey (1989) suggests the pessimism is exaggerated because of weak and simplistic evaluation. The final results of this meta-analysis, when disseminated, should be consulted for guidance on delinquency intervention design. The following material augments summaries of Lorion et al. (1987) and Loeber and Tolan (Chapter 13 of this volume) by focusing on the current conceptual status of alternative interventions in the field.

Delinquency Prevention

Rigorous evaluation of prevention efforts is rare. Those available present ambiguous results at best (National Council on Crime and Delinquency, 1981). In some instances, unintended negative results have been reported (Gottfredson, 1985; McCord, 1978). However, there is evidence that community-based programs and ecologically sound social programs are effective (Gottschalk, Davidson, Gensheimer, & Mayer, 1987; Lorion et al., 1987).

Well-deserved criticisms of the delinquency prevention field are that, despite some evidence of effectiveness, it has lacked a conceptual foundation (Lorion et al., 1987) and there has been a failure to base the efforts on the best available theories and empirical evidence (Hawkins & Weis, 1985; National Task Force to Develop Standards and Goals for Juvenile Justice and Delinquency Prevention, 1977). Whether prevention efforts are best targeted at individual risk factors (e.g., early intellectual enrichment; Farrington, 1985) *or* environmental risk factors (e.g., the family; Johnson, Bird, Little, & Beville, 1981; Tolan, Cromwell, & Brasswell, 1986; Tolan & Mitchell, 1990) has been a matter of lively debate. An ever increasing body of data attests to the multivariate basis of delinquency; nevertheless, few interventions consider both the individual and the environmental factors (Lorion et al., 1987; Tolan & Lorion, 1988).

Lorion et al. (1987) suggested that a transactional model is most viable for prevention because it is able to consider both environmental and individual factors *and* the dynamic nature of these influences. They further suggested that not only are program components that correspond to identified predictors important but prevention that is ecological (e.g., in and of the natural settings of adolescents) is most advantageous. They cited, as an example of this type of program, interventions aimed at increasing the management skills of parents, peers, and/or teachers of antisocial children and adolescents. For example, Alexander and Parsons (1973) and Alexander, Barton, Schiavo, and Parsons (1976) significantly improved communication exchanges and formal contingency contracts between parents and their antisocial children. Hawkins and Weis (1985) made an argument similar to that of Lorion et al. (1987) by suggesting, for example, that changes in school settings can reduce delinquency as well as have other general positive effects.

Diversion Practices

Diversion practices gained considerable momentum in the 1950s and 1960s with the advent of labeling theory (Guerra, 1988), which proposed that the justice system's practices were not only stigmatizing but actually iatrogenic. In 1967, the Presidential Commission on Law Enforcement and Administration of Justice instituted policy mandates encouraging diversion practices. These quickly caught on, and there was a rapid proliferation of such programs. Ironically, diversion was the original intent of the juvenile justice system (Gottschalk et al., 1987).

As Guerra (1988) articulated, a wide range of efforts have been implemented under the rubric of diversion. Some have essentially constituted an abandonment of any formal sanctions; others have viewed diversion as a channeling of cases to noncourt institutions. The impact of diversion programs has been assessed from two standpoints. One question related to impact (reviewed by Guerra (1988) and Gensheimer, Mayer, Gottschalk, and Davidson (1986) has to do with whether these programs have not actually served to "widen the net" of social control, for example, by providing services for youth who would ordinarily have been released at the intake or arrest stage. The other important impact question is how successful diversion programs have been in altering delinquent behavior and reducing future delinquent behavior.

The most recent and comprehensive assessment of diversion programming was conducted by Gensheimer et al. (1986). These researchers conducted a meta-analysis of 44 outcome studies of interventions with officially delinquent youth reportedly diverted from formal juvenile justice from 1967 to 1983. The diversion interventions included casework approaches, behavioral interventions, group psychotherapy, individual psychotherapy, educational/vocational guidance, and "nonspecific" interventions (almost 40% were nonspecific because of ambiguous services or the failure of investigators to document pertinent information). Based on both quantitative impact measures and qualitative effectiveness ratings, the overall impact is "no effect." Younger clients benefited more from diversion and the number of contact hours was related positively to outcome. The authors were unable to disentangle any differential impact of intervention modality because the majority were "unspecific." This conclusion was modified when only community-oriented programs were considered (Gottschalk et al., 1987); apparently, they show a small positive effect. In both cases, they echo the commonplace and correctly placed criticism that more comprehensive documentation of service consent and more rigorous evaluation methodology are needed.

CONCLUSION

We have summarized the status of alternative interventions for adolescents. Because they are new, the variations in how they have been implemented, their frequent establishment by persons interested in social service rather than rigorous evaluation, and other imposing political factors, many of these interventions are presently more notable for their promise and their compelling logic than their demonstrated effects. Many are, however, resisted by mental health profession circles because their assumptions about causes, effects, change components, and intervention delivery methods (and service persons) run counter to the predominant mental health service systems and professionals' training. The interventions tend to acknowledge the political and economic as well as the psychological influences on adolescent problems, all of which can impede their consideration. It is not certain whether any or all of these alternatives are viable and, if so, for what adolescents and what problems. Also, it is unclear to what extent they complement, conflict with, or are preferable to traditional psychotherapeutic interventions. At least, they serve to broaden and stimulate thinking about clinical work with adolescents. The alternatives presented are rich in ideas and are usually put forth with enthusiasm. They deserve careful consideration as mental health interventions, and they deserve and need careful scientific study.

REFERENCES

Alexander, J. F., Barton, C., Schiavo, R. S., & Parsons, B. V. (1976). Systems-behavioral intervention with families of delinquents: Therapist characteristics, family behavior and outcome. *Journal of Consulting and Clinical Psychology, 44,* 656–664.

Alexander, J. F., & Parsons, B. V. (1973). Short-term behavioral intervention with delinquent families: Impact on family process and recidivism. *Journal of Abnormal Psychology, 81,* 219–225.

Bachman, J., Bare, D., and Frankie, A. (1986). *Correlates of employment among high school seniors.* Paper available from the Institute for Social Research, University of Michigan, Ann Arbor.

Bangert-Drowns, R. L. (1988). The effects of school-based substance abuse education: A meta-analysis. *Journal of Drug Education, 18,* 243–264.

Berger, J. (1989, August 27). East Harlem students clutch a college dream. *New York Times,* pp. 1 and 21.

Bierman, K. (1986). Process of change during social skills training with preadolescents and its relation to treatment outcome. *Child Development, 57,* 230–240.

Bierman, K. L., & Furman, W. (1984). The effects of social skills training and peer involvement on the social adjustment of preadolescents. *Child Development, 55,* 151–162.

Biglan, A., Severson, H., Ary, D. V., & Faller, E. A. (1987). Do smoking prevention programs really work? Attrition and the external and internal validity of an evaluation of a refusal skills training program. *Journal of Behavioral Medicine, 10,* 159–171.

Blackburn, H., Luepker, R. V., Kline, F. G., Bracht, N., Carlaw, R., Jacobs, D., Mittelmark, M., Stauffer, L., & Taylor, H. L. (1984). The Minnesota Heart Health Program: A research and demonstration project in cardiovascular disease prevention. In J. D. Matarazzo, S. M. Weiss, J. A. Herd, N. E. Miller, & S. M. Weiss (Eds.). *Behavioral health: A handbook of health enhancement and disease prevention* (pp. 1171–1178). New York: Wiley.

Blyth, D. A., Simmons, R. G., & Carlton-Ford, S. (1983). The adjustment of early adolescents to school transitions. *Journal of Early Adolescents, 3,* 105–120.

Botvin, G. J. (1985). The Life Skills Training Program as a health promotion strategy: Theoretical issues and empirical findings. *Special Services in the Schools, 1*(3), 9–23.

Carnegie Council on Adolescent Development (1989). *Turning points: Preparing youth for the 21st century.* New York: Carnegie Corporation.

Cohen, P. A., Kulik, J. A., & Kulik, C-L. C. (1982). Educational outcomes of tutoring: A meta-analysis of findings. *American Educational Research Journal,* 237–248.

Combrinck-Graham, L. (1989). *Children in family contexts.* New York: Guilford.

Commission on Youth Employment Programs, National Research Council (1985). *Youth employment and training programs: The YEDPA years.* Washington, DC: National Academy Press, p. 111 ff.

Costello, J. (1980). *Criteria for evaluating and planning public policies for children.* Unpublished. Chicago: University of Chicago.

Cowen, E. L., & Geston, E. L. (1978). Community approaches to intervention. In B. B. Wolman, J. Egan, & A. O. Ross (Eds.). *Handbook of treatment of mental disorders in childhood and adolescence.* Englewood Cliffs, NJ: Prentice-Hall.

Curran, J. P., & Monti, P. M. (Eds.). (1982). *Social skills training: A practical handbook for assessment and treatment.* New York: Guilford Press.

DeBusk, M., & Hellison, D. (1989). Implementing a physical education self-responsibility model for delinquency-prone youth. *Journal of Teaching in Physical Education, 8,* 104–112.

Devin-Sheehan, L., Feldman, R. S., & Allen, V. L. (1976). Research on children tutoring children: A critical review. *Review of Educational Research,* 355–385.

Dryfoos, J. G. (1988). School-based health clinics: Three years of experience. *Family Planning Perspectives, 20,* 193–200.

Erickson, J. B. (1982). *A profile of community youth organization members, 1980.* Boys Town, NE: Boys Town Center for Youth Development.

Erickson, J. B. (1983). *Directory of American youth organizations* (2nd ed.). Boys Town, NE: Communications and Publications Service Division, Boys Town.

Erickson, J. B. (1986). Non-formal education in organizations for American youth. *Children Today,* January–February, 17–23.

Falco, M. (1988). *Preventing abuse of drugs, alcohol, and tobacco by adolescents.* Report prepared by the Carnegie Council on Adolescent Development, Carnegie Corporation, New York.

Farrington, D. P. (1985). Delinquent prevention in the 1980s. *Journal of Adolescence, 8,* 3–16.

Felner, R. D., & Adan, A. A. (1988). The school transitional environmental project: An ecological intervention and evaluation. In R. H. Price, E. L. Cowen, R. P. Lorion, I. Serrano-Garcia, & J. Ramos-McKay (Eds.), *14 ounces of prevention: A casebook for practitioners.* Washington, DC: American Psychological Association.

Felner, R. D., Ginter, M., & Primavera, J. (1982). Primary prevention during school transitions: Social support and environmental structure. *American Journal of Community Psychology, 10,* 277–290.

Felner, R. D., Primavera, J., & Cauce, A. M. (1981). The impact of school transitions: A focus for preventive efforts. *American Journal of Community Psychology, 9,* 449–459.

Fiedler, P. D., Ornstein, H., Chiles, J., Fritz, G., & Breitt, S. (1979). Effects of assertive training on hospitalized adolescents and young adults. *Adolescence, 14,* 523–538.

Filipczak, J., Archer, M., & Friedman, R. M. (1980). School social skills training: Use with disruptive adolescents. *Behavior Modification, 4,* 243–263.

Furstenberg, F. E., Brooks-Gunn, J., & Chase-Lansdale, L. (1989). Teenaged pregnancy and childbearing. *American Psychologist, 44,* 313–320.

Gensheimer, L. K., Mayer, J. P., Gottschalk, R., & Davidson, W. S. (1986). Diverting youth from the juvenile justice system: A meta-analysis of intervention efficacy. In S. P. Apter & A. P. Goldstein (Eds.), *Youth violence: Programs and perspectives* (pp. 39–57). New York: Pergamon Press.

Gerber, M., & Kaufman, J. M. (1981). Peer tutoring in academic settings. In P. S. Strain (Ed.), *The utilization of classroom peers as behavioral change agents.* New York: Plenum Press.

Gibbs, J. T. (1984). Black adolescents and youth: An endangered species. *American Journal of Orthopsychiatry, 54,* 6–21.

Gilchrist, L. D. (1981). Social competence in adolescence. In S. P. Schinke (Ed.), *Behavioral methods in social welfare.* New York: Aldine.

Goldstein, A. P., & Pentz, M. A. (1984). Psychological skill training and the aggressive adolescent. *School Psychology Review, 13,* 311–323.

Goldstein, A. P., Sprafkin, R. P., Gershaw, N. J., & Klein, P. (1979). *Skill-streaming the adolescent: A structured learning approach to teaching prosocial behavior.* Champaign, IL: Research Press.

Gottfredson, D. (1985). Youth employment, crime, and schooling: A longitudinal study of a national sample. *Developmental Psychology, 21,* 419–432.

Gottschalk, R., Davidson, W. S., Gensheimer, L. K., & Mayer, J. P. (1987). Community based interventions. In H. C. Quay (Ed.), *Handbook of juvenile delinquency* (pp. 266–289). New York: Wiley.

Greenberger, E., & Steinberg, L. (1981). The workplace as a context for the socialization of youth. *Journal of Youth and Adolescence, 10,* 185–210.

Greenberger, E., & Steinberg, L. (1986). *When teenagers work: The psychological and social costs of adolescent employment.* New York: Basic Books.

Guerra, N. G. (1988). *Psychological interventions with delinquent youth: I. A review of community-based programs.* Unpublished manuscript, University of Illinois at Chicago.

Haggerty, R. J. (1987). Ensuring a better future for youth and America. *Developmental and Behavioral Pediatrics, 8,* 341–348.

Hamilton, S. F., & Fenzel, L. M. (1987). *The effect of volunteer experience on early adolescents' social development.* Paper presented at an American Educational Research Conference. Cited in Wynn, et al. (1987).

Hanks, M. (1981). Youth voluntary associations and political socialization. *Social Forces, 1,* 211–223.

Hanks, M., & Eckland, B. (1978). Adult voluntary associations and political socialization. *Social Forces, 1,* 223–231.

Hansen, D. J., Watson-Perczel, M., & Christopher, J. S. (1989). Clinical issues in social skills training with adolescents. *Clinical Psychology Review, 9,* 365–391.

Hawkins, J. D., Lishner, D. M., & Catalano, R. F. (1985). Childhood predictors and the prevention of adolescent substance abuse. In C. L. Jones & R. J. Battjes (Eds.), *Etiology of drug abuse: Implications for prevention* (pp. 75–126). Rockville, MD: National Institute on Drug Abuse.

Hawkins, J. D., & Weis, J. G. (1985). The social development model: An integrated approach to delinquent prevention. *Journal of Primary Prevention, 6*(2), 73–97.

Hayes, C. D. (Ed.), (1987). *Risking the future:* (Vol. 1). Washington, DC: National Academy Press.

Hedin, D. (1987). Students as teachers: A tool for improving school. *Social Policy,* Winter, 42–47.

Hein, K. (1988). *AIDS in adolescence: A rationale for concern.* A report prepared for Carnegie Council on Adolescent Development, Carnegie Corporation, New York.

Hellison, D. (1989). The physical education at-risk youth program at UIC. *Department of Physical Education Newsletter* (1). Chicago: University of Illinois at Chicago.

Hirsch, B. J., & Rapkin, B. D. (1987). The transition to junior high school: A longitudinal study of self-esteem, psychological symptomatology, school life, and social support. *Child Development, 58,* 1235–1243.

Hobbs, N., & Robinson, S. (1982). Adolescent development and public policy. *American Psychologist, 37,* 212–223.

Hofferth, S. L., & Hayes, C. D. (Eds.). (1987). *Risking the future* (Vol. 2). Washington, DC: National Academy Press.

Jesness, C. (1976). Transactional analyses and behavior modification programs for delinquents. *Behavioral Disorders, 1,* 27–36.

Jesness, O. F. (1975). Comparative effectiveness of behavior modification and transactional analysis programs for delinquents. *Journal of Consulting and Clinical Psychology, 6,* 758–779.

Johnson, G., Bird, T., Little, J. W., & Beville, S. L. (1981). *Delinquent prevention: Theories and strategies.* Washington, DC: Department of Justice, Office of Juvenile Justice and Delinquency Prevention.

Kazdin, A. E. (1990, June). *Prevention of conduct disorder.* Paper presented at the National Conference on Prevention Research. National Institute of Mental Health, Washington, DC.

Kelly, J. G. (1988). A guide to conducting prevention research in the community: First steps. *Prevention in Human Services, 6,* 1–8.

Kirby, D. (1985). The effects of selected sexuality education programs: Toward a more realistic view. *Journal of Sex Education Therapy, 11,* 28–37.

Kleinfeld, J., & Shinkwin, A. (1982). *Youth organizations as a third educational environment particularly for minority youth.* Final report to the National Institute of Education. Washington, DC: Educational Resources Information Center. (ERIC Document Reproduction Service No. ED 240 194.)

Klerman, L. V. (1983). *Family home care: Critical issues for services and policies.* New York: Haworth Press.

Klitzner, M. D. (1989). AIDS prevention and education. *Journal of Adolescent Health Care, 10,* 45S–47S.

Konopka, G. (1976). *Young girls: A portrait of adolescence.* Englewood Cliffs, NJ: Prentice-Hall.

L'Abate, L., & Milan, M. A. (Eds.) (1985). *Handbook of social skills training and research.* New York: Wiley.

LaBelle, T. J. (1981). An introduction to the nonformal education of children and youth. *Comparative Education Review, 25,* 313–329.

Ladewig, H., & Thomas, J. K. (1987). *Does 4-H make a difference?* Washington, DC: Educational Resources Information Center. (ERIC Document Reproduction Service No. ED 282 682.)

LeFlore, F. (1989, December 10). Pat on the back: Educators, students join in positive approach. *Milwaukee Journal,* p. 2.

Levine, M. D. (1988). *The difference that differences make: Adolescent diversity and its deregulation.* Washington, DC: Youth and America's Future.

Lewis, R. J., Dlugokinski, E. L., Caputo, L. M., & Griffin, R. B. (1988). Children at risk for emotional disorders: Risk and resource dimensions. *Clinical Psychology Review, 8,* 417–440.

Linney, J. A., & Seidman, E. (1989). The future of schooling. *American Psychologist, 44,* 336–340.

Lipsey, M. (1989, November). *The efficacy of intervention for juvenile delinquency: Results from 400 studies.* Paper presented at the annual meeting of the American Society of Criminology, Reno, NV.

Lorion, R. P., Tolan, P. H., & Wahler, R. G. (1987). Prevention. In H. C. Quay (Ed.), *The handbook of juvenile delinquency* (pp. 383–416). New York: Wiley.

Maher, C. A. (1982). Behavioral effects of using conduct problem adolescents as cross-age tutors. *Psychology in the Schools, 19,* 360–364.

Marziller, J. (1979). Outcome studies of skills training: A review. In P. Trower, B. Bryant, & M. Argyle (Eds.), *Social skills and mental health* (pp. 13–41). London: Metheun & Co.

Mason, B. C. (1979). *An experiment in cross-age peer interaction.* Washington, DC: Educational Resources Information Center. (ERIC Document Reproduction Service No. ED 185 492.)

McCord, J. (1978). A thirty-year follow-up of treatment effects. *American Psychologist, 33,* 284–289.

Millstein, S. G. (1988). *The potential of school-linked centers to promote adolescent health and development.* Report prepared for the Carnegie Council on Adolescent Development, Carnegie Corporation, New York.

Mitroff, I. I. (1983). Beyond experimentation: New methods for a new age. In E. Seidman (Ed.), *Handbook of social intervention* (pp. 163–178). Beverly Hills, CA: Sage.

Moore, K. A. (1985). *Facts at a glance.* Unpublished manuscript. Washington, DC: Child Trends, Inc. Cited in Furstenberg et al. (1989).

National Council on Crime and Delinquency (1981). *The national evaluation of delinquency prevention.* San Francisco: National Council on Crime and Delinquency Research Center.

Newmann, F. M., & Rutter, R. A. (1983). *The effects of high school community service programs on students' social development.* Final report to the National Institute of Education. Madison, WI: Wisconsin Center for Education Research, University of Wisconsin.

Nightingale, E. O., & Wolverton, L. (1988). *Adolescent rolelessness in modern society*. Report prepared by the Carnegie Foundation Council on Adolescent Development, Carnegie Corporation, New York.

Otto, L. B. (1975). Extracurricular activities in the educational attainment process. *Rural Sociology, 40*, 162–176.

Otto, L. B. (1976). Social integration and the status-attainment process. *American Journal of Sociology, 81*, 1360–1383.

Otto, L. B., & Featherman, D. L. (1975). Social structural and psychological antecedents of self-estrangement and powerlessness. *American Sociological Review, 40*, 701–719.

Parker, J. G., & Asher, S. R. (1987). Peer relations and later personal adjustment: Are low-accepted children at risk? *Psychological Bulletin, 102*, 357–389.

Pentz, M. A. (1980). Assertion training and trainer effects on unassertive and aggressive adolescents. *Journal of Counseling Psychology, 27*, 76–83.

Pentz, M. A., Dwyar, J. H., MacKinnon, D. P., Flay, B. R., Hansen, W. B., Wang, E. Y. I., & Johnson, A. (1989). A multicommunity trial for primary prevention of adolescent drug abuse: Effects on drug use prevalence. *Journal of the American Medical Association, 261*, 3259–3266.

Perry, C. L., Klepp, K. I., Halper, A., Dudovitz, B., Golden, D., Griffin, G., & Smyth, M. (1987). Promoting healthy eating and physical activity patterns among adolescents: Slice of life. *Health Education Research: Theory and Practice, 2*, 93–104.

Perry, C. L., Klepp, K. I., & Schultz, J. M. (1988). Primary prevention of cardiovascular disease: Community wide strategies for youth. *Journal of Consulting and Clinical Psychology, 56*, 358–364.

Perry, C. L., Mullis, R. M., & Maile, M. C. (1985). Modifying the eating behavior of young children. *Journal of School Health, 55*, 399–402.

Perry, C. L., Murray, D. M., & Klepp, K. I. (1987). Predictors of adolescent smoking and implications for prevention. *Morbidity and Mortality Weekly, 36*, 415–455.

Polit, D., Quint, J. C., & Riccio, J. A. (1988). *The challenge of serving teenage mothers; Lessons from Project Redirection*. New York: Manpower Demonstration Research Corporation.

Rappoport, R. N. (1987). *New interventions for children and youth*. Cambridge, England: University of Cambridge.

Rehabilitation Services Administration. (1974). *Teens helping other teens get together: An evaluation of the Baltimore Youth Advocate Project Final Report*. Washington, DC: Educational Resources Information Center. (ERIC Document Reproduction Service No. ED 134 658.)

Reissman, F. (1989, August 12). *Restructuring help: A paradigm for the 1990s*. Invited address: Award for Distinguished Practice of Community Psychology, Division of Community Psychology, American Psychological Association, Washington, DC.

Reppucci, N. D. (1987). Prevention and ecology: Teen-age pregnancy, child sexual abuse, and organized youth sports. *American Journal of Community Psychology, 15*, 1–22.

Rinn, R. C., & Markle, A. (1979). Modification of social skills deficits in children. In A. S. Bellack & M. Hersen (Eds.), *Research and practice in social skills training*. New York: Plenum Press.

Robin, A. L. (1981). A controlled evaluation of problem-solving communication training with parent–adolescent conflict. *Behavior Therapy, 12*, 593–609.

Roche, G. R. (1979, January–February). Much ado about mentors. *Harvard Business Review, 57*, 14–16.

Rotheram, M. J., & Armstrong, M. (1980). Assertiveness training with high school students. *Adolescence, 15*, 267–276.

Rutter, M. (1983). School effects on pupil progress: Research findings and policy implications. *Child Development, 54*, 1–29.

Sarason, I. G., & Sarason, B. R. (1981). Teaching cognitive and social skills to high school students. *Journal of Consulting and Clinical Psychology, 6*, 908–918.

Schafer, W. E. (1969). Participation in interscholastic athletics and delinquency: A preliminary study. *Social Problems, 17*, 40–47.

Schinke, S. P. (1981). Interpersonal-skills training with adolescents. In M. Hersen, R. M. Eisler, & P. M. Miller (Eds.), *Progress in behavior modification* (Vol. II). New York: Academic Press.

Schincke, S. P., & Gilchrist, L. D. (1984). *Life skills counseling with adolescents*. Baltimore: University Park Press.

Schorr, L. B., with Schorr, D. (1988). *Within our reach: Breaking the cycle of disadvantage.* New York: Doubleday.

Segrave, J. O., & Chu, D. B. (1978). Athletics and juvenile delinquency. *Review of Sport and Leisure, 3,* 1–24.

Seidman, E. (1983). Unexamined premises of social problem solving. In E. Seidman (Ed.), *Handbook of social intervention* (pp. 48–68). Beverly Hills, CA: Sage.

Steinberg, L. (1989). *Adolescence* (2nd ed.). New York: Knopf.

Steinberg, L., Greenberger, E., Garduque, L., Ruggerio, M, & Vaux, A. (1982). Effects of working on adolescent development. *Developmental Psychology, 18,* 385–395.

Stephens, W. (1983). *Explanations for failures of youth organizations.* Washington, DC: Educational Resources Information Center. (ERIC Document Reproduction Service No. ED 228 440).

Sundberg, N., Snowden, L., & Reynolds, W. (1978). Toward assessment of personal competence and incompetence in life situations. *Annual Review of Psychology, 29,* 179–222.

Tobler, N. S. (1986). Meta-analysis of 143 adolescent drug prevention programs: Quantitative outcome results of program participants compared to a control or comparison group. *Journal of Drug Issues, 16,* 537–568.

Tolan, P. H. (1988). Delinquent behaviors and male adolescent development: A preliminary study. *Journal of Youth and Adolescence, 17,* 413–427.

Tolan, P. H., Cromwell, R. E., & Brasswell, M. (1986). The application of family therapy to juvenile delinquency: A critical review of literature. *Family Process, 25,* 619–649.

Tolan, P. H., Keys, C., Chertok, F., & Jason, L. A. (1990). Introduction: conversing about theories, methods, and community research. In P. H. Tolan, C. Keys, F. Chertok, & L. Jason (Eds.), *Researching community psychology: The integration of theories and method* (pp. 3–8). Washington, DC: American Psychological Association.

Tolan, P. H., & Lorion, R. P. (1988). Multivariate approaches to the identification of delinquency-proneness in males. *American Journal of Community Psychology, 16,* 547–561.

Tolan, P. H., & Mitchell, M. (1990). Families and antisocial and delinquent behavior. *Journal of Psychotherapy and the Family, 6,* 29–48.

Tolan, P. H., Pentz, M. A., Aupperle, D., & Davis, L. (1990). *Social skills training with adolescents: A critical review of trends, dimensions, outcome for prevention utility, 1972–1987.* Manuscript submitted for review.

Tramontana, M. G. (1980). Critical review of research on psychotherapy outcome with adolescents: 1967–1977. *Psychological Bulletin, 88,* 429–450.

Tuma, J. M. (1989). Mental health services for children: The state of the art. *American Psychologist, 44,* 188–199.

U.S. Department of Health, Education, & Welfare. (1975). *Dropout prevention.* Washington, DC: Educational Resources Information Center (ERIC Document Reproduction Service No. ED 105 354).

Valentin, C. (1984). The mentor and the dream: Facilitators of psychosocial competence in inner-city adolescents. *Dissertation Abstracts International, 45,* 2705B.

Weiner, I. B. (1970). *Psychological disturbance in adolescence.* New York: Wiley.

Weisz, J., Weiss, B., Alicke, M., & Klotz, M. (1987). Effectiveness of psychotherapy with children and adolescents. *Journal of Consulting and Clinical Psychology, 55,* 542–549.

Wynn, J., Richman, H., Rubenstein, R. A., Littell, J., with Britt, B., & Yoken, C. (1987). *Communities and adolescents: An exploration of reciprocal supports.* Report prepared for the William T. Grant Foundation Commission on Work, Family, and Citizenship, Washington, DC.

Youth and America's Future. (1988a). *The forgotten half: Pathways to success for America's youth and young families.* Washington, DC: William T. Grant Foundation Commission on Work, Family, and Citizenship.

Youth and America's Future. (1988b). *The forgotten half: Non-college youth in America.* Washington, DC: William T. Grant Foundation Commission on Work, Family, and Citizenship.

Zabin, L., Street, R., & Hardy, J. (1983, July). *Research and evaluation in a university, clinic and school-based adolescent pregnancy prevention program.* Paper delivered to the American Public Health Association meetings, Dallas, TX.

CHAPTER 19

Residential Services

RICHARD C. MAROHN

INTRODUCTION

Residential treatment services and psychiatric hospital programs for adolescents are important, costly, and widely used therapeutic modalities. Such approaches can be fertile environments for studying adolescent development and psychopathology, especially clinical phenomena such as primitive transferences. A strong research commitment by the leadership of these programs enhances staff esteem and treatment efficacy by fostering staff personal and professional growth. This chapter demonstrates the enrichment that can be derived from integrating treatment and clinical research. As part of that demonstration, the difficulties often encountered and some suggestions for future work are presented.

Essential to such a presentation is an explanation of the contextual influences on how and why residential care of adolescents occurs. Many severely emotionally disturbed adolescents who could profit from residential treatment are not receiving it (President's Commission on Mental Health, 1978). Yet, some studies suggest that as many as 40% of those in residential placement do not need it (Knitzer, 1982). Apparently, economic and procedural factors strongly influence when and how such services are applied (Myers, 1986).

Although formal diagnostic categories are unable to capture the multiplicity of problems that adolescents in residential placement have, most are exhibiting significant antisocial behavior, including drug abuse, psychotic symptoms, and/or serious depression (Kahn & Boyer, 1980). The distribution and overlap of diagnoses vary from setting to setting and change over time. A survey of residential facilities for adolescents by Kahn and Boyer (1980) indicated that 23% of admissions were diagnosed as behavior problems, 32% as borderline personality or schizophrenia, 14% as affective disorders, and 13% as drug and alcohol use. Surprisingly, 25% had adjustment reaction diagnosis. (Interested readers can consult Kahn and Boyer (1980) for a more specific breakdown of distributions of diagnosis by facility type.) Because our experience has been more with behavior-disordered adolescents, most of the discussion in this chapter focuses on this group. However, the issues usually apply to adolescents with other problems as well.

Although comparisons of conceptual approaches have been made, none has provided analyses that are sophisticated enough to direct treatment. In fact, trying to provide an overall direction may not be a useful focus for research. The programming and process factors are often as influential as the particular theoretical approach, and, in practice, they are common across conceptual approaches (Kahn & Boyer, 1980). Their impact is so complex as to elude simple classification. At present, it is sufficient to say that demonstrations of effectiveness for a variety of conceptual approaches can be found in the literature (Fineberg, Sowards, & Kettlewell, 1980; Steinberg, 1987).

Natural History of Adolescent Problems

Compared to most adolescent disorders, serious behavior problems are rarely unrecognized and are often treated (Offer, Ostrov, & Howard, 1984). The police, the school, neighborhood members, and even the juvenile court intercede often, albeit independently. Involvement of so many separate systems convolutes research efforts in this area: in addition to multiplying the variables to be studied, interpretation of treatment and outcome studies becomes more difficult. For example, in many states, a person's juvenile delinquency record and treatment history do not follow him or her into adulthood (Maltz, 1984). As a result, when arrested for their first adult crime, many adult criminals are characterized as "first offenders." Consequently, a researcher conducting a follow-up study cannot assume valid juvenile data in adult records.

The variation in tolerance for adolescent behavior by individuals in these systems also complicates research. For example, the classroom teacher's tolerance for disruptive behavior, the school counselor's empathic skills, the disciplinary dean's personal preferences, the principal's preoccupations, police discretion on the street, a caseworker's judgment in preparing the case study, the biases of the juvenile officer who investigates, and the options and predilections of the juvenile court judge or referring physician all influence a given adolescent's likelihood of being referred for residential care. Because these factors cannot be controlled or easily measured, they increase the variability and error of data. Further, girls are often "excused" informally for behavior, so that when they finally come to the attention of authorities, they may be more seriously disturbed (Offer, Ostrov, & Howard, 1984). Ethnic and racial bias, in reasons for referral and judgment about the meaning of behavior problems, also occurs. For example, minority violence may be viewed as less serious or as a criminologic problem while nonminority violence is considered a manifestation of an underlying psychopathology. Thus, comparisons of intervention effects are proportionately more difficult, to the point of reaching impossibility.

A second issue is that the application of clinical interventions often changes as a person moves into adolescence. Many children who are treated for behavior problems later appear in correctional and juvenile justice systems. At this point, however, they are seen as needing punishment rather than treatment. The adolescent's problems are considered unrelated to childhood behavior problems. Thus, some adolescents' behavior problems are handled too severely, and others' are neglected. This result is particularly likely when dealing with violent adolescents (Lewis & Shanok, 1980). Because adolescents are bigger and more active than children, they often elicit anxiety in parents or other authorities. As a result, such adults frequently react in the extreme, using overly restrictive and intrusive interventions or ignoring the behavior completely, hoping it is a single episode. Not surprisingly, adults' emotional reactions to adolescents influence their clinical work with them. Many adults feel hostility toward teenagers in general (Marohn, 1984). Therefore, close supervision of and consultation for the psychotherapist and treatment staff are crucial.

Residential treatment of the adolescent also differs from the treatment of adults because it must include parents and the family, must attend to school and recreational activities, and requires an integration of various, and sometimes diverse, treatment modalities. As a result of the involvement of recreational therapists, teachers, and others in treating the adolescent, the individual psychotherapist of an adolescent cannot become isolated from other staff, as the adult therapist might. Some theorists have gone so far as to claim that "therapist-oriented" administrative formats foster most clinical/administrative splitting (Kahn & Boyer, 1980).

Treating adolescents also differs from treating children. There are crucial differences between the child and adolescent developmentally and in presentation of psychopathology, and these differences result in a different character of treatment interventions. Unfortunately, a tradition remains in American mental health to cluster "child" and "adolescent" together. This convention blurs important distinctions. As a result, many clinicians, in effect, ignore the significant influence of adolescent development on symptomatology. It could well be that many child therapists work poorly with adolescents and, as a result, shunt them, unknowingly, into less therapeutic systems.

One can see that how and for whom residential care is applied to adolescents is a precarious and complex formulation. Although some empirical studies on outcome exist (Fineberg et al., 1980; Gossett, Barnhard, Phillips, & Lewis, 1979; Marohn, Dalle-Molle, McCarter, & Linn, 1980), empirical guidance available presently has limited reliability. The issues are far more complicated than whether such treatment works or whether the "right" adolescents are receiving it. There is a need for better descriptive and survey analyses of the contextual factors influencing use of such services. However, the important of such research in illuminating residential treatment processes is often not understood. An extended example from our own work illustrates this point.

The Clinical Implications of Research on Residential Treatment

Nowhere in the treatment lore are there more aphorisms than in adolescent hospital or residential treatment. Each treatment culture develops its unique way of conveying the nuances of its efforts to work with the patient or resident. Redl's "life space" interview (Redl, 1966) is one such example. Many have thrilled to the insights and maxims of Fritz Redl about providing external ego to the adolescent in action, just as Viennese students were stimulated by Aichhorn's understanding of the unfolding transference (1925/1935), especially the idealizing transference and other narcissistic problems in the delinquent adolescent (Marohn, 1977). These mottos eventually take on a dignity and reality that may exceed their validity, and newcomers to a treatment unit may need time to decipher the nuances of the culture. For example, one frequently heard truism is the importance of helping patients express their anger. An underlying psychodynamic belief assigns therapeutic value to the conversion of adolescent motor behavior into verbal behavior. Yet, clinicians are also aware of the risks involved in working with potentially violent adolescents, whose behavior may escalate into riot or contagion (Marohn, 1974; Marohn et al., 1973). A useful way of teaching others about these complex matters is to share clinical impressions, particularly when they resonate with the others' own treatment experience. Carefully drawn case studies can be quite helpful. Not every treatment principle can be readily validated by a quantitative research study.

Occasionally, however, one can study certain behaviors and interventions in a way that tests a well-accepted treatment slogan. One such episode occurred in our work with hospitalized juvenile delinquents at the Illinois State Psychiatric Institute (ISPI) several years ago (Marohn et al., 1980). Staff had begun to recognize intuitively that deterioration of or damage to property on the unit seemed to have something to do with outbreaks of physical violence. Staff closely monitored property damage or abuse and tried to anticipate personal assaults before they materialized. We were uncertain, however, about the relation of verbal expressions of angry feelings to property damage. We all subscribed to the idea that expressing one's feelings, especially angry feelings, would obviate future physical violence. Yet, there was the problem of escalation. Some patients get "worked up" by efforts to help them express violent feelings and become violently disorganized. When we opened the program, we had been told that cathartic physical outlets for adolescent "aggression" were therapeutic for juvenile delinquents and enabled them to discharge violent tendencies. Like many treatment programs, we thought we might exhaust adolescents with athletics. We thought putting a punching body bag on the unit would help adolescents "work off" anger. The actual results, however, were greater disorganization and escalation to more frequent and severe violent behavior. These activities proved taxing to the staff and overstimulating to the residents, rather than tiring and calming. Patients began writing "hated" staff members' names on the bags. Sometimes they did so in their own blood, after scratching themselves, then began punching the staff member/bag. They did not derive any therapeutic benefit from such experiences. The pathology of the adolescents so affected resembled closely the "borderline" end of the psychopathology spectrum. We concluded that psychologically deficient individuals, those who lack *internal* regulating structures, do not "learn" from these experiences and, instead, escalate and become more disruptive.

These observations were not reported originally in our research monograph (Offer, Marohn, & Ostrov, 1979) because we could see only trends that did not reach statistical significance. That report focused on describing a typology of acting-out adolescents, which we thought was useful for residential treatment. At a later date, we again reviewed our data more carefully. These analyses revealed association between *violence to property* and *violence to person* on the Antisocial Behavior Check List (ABCL) (Ostrov, Marohn, Offer, Curtiss, & Feczko, 1980). Those impulsive adolescents who damaged property also assaulted other people. Furthermore, threats of verbal assault (e.g., "Get out of my face, or I'll beat the crap out of you.") clearly correlated with physical assault, while "cathartic" verbal expressions of anger (e.g., "I'm so mad at you; I *feel* like hitting you.") did not correlate with a higher incidence of physical assault. These findings clearly validated the staff's impression that it was correct to help patients verbally express angry feelings while interfering with tendencies to displace anger onto objects in the environment. The empirical validation increased staff confidence and therapeutic efficacy. Given this fining, it might be useful, as a further step, to determine whether the same principle applies to the sense generally held in residential programs (and in communities) that there is something dangerous about graffiti and that it is important to clean it up as soon as possible.

This all-too-infrequent example of research informing a clinical intervention underlines how important a research and questioning culture is to a treatment program. The impact extends beyond merely guiding or confirming therapeutic approaches, to focus staff gratification on learning and professional attitudes. If staff gratification comes from patient improvement, many adolescents and staff will suffer demoralization, because of the recalcitrant nature of the psychopathology. If their gratification can instead be derived from personal and professional growth, then staff members are less likely to be overreactive to therapeutic setbacks and the adolescent patient is freed to focus on self-direction. Furthermore, intrastaff relationships are very important. Fineberg et al. (1980) summarized the relevant clinical research as indicating that adolescents project family conflicts onto staff. This necessitates healthy intrastaff and staff–adolescents interactions, to allow patients to successfully work through their struggles. Satisfactory intrastaff relationships also reduce the likelihood that staff will attempt to meet their social needs through interactions with adolescents. A useful research focus would be a careful description of staff coherence building methods.

MAJOR ISSUES IN TREATMENT PROGRAMMING

The remainder of this chapter describes major issues in residential treatment planning. Where appropriate, needed research is suggested.

Our basic treatment philosophy attempts to integrate dynamic psychotherapy with accredited schooling and recreational activities. Researchers have found these components in most "good" inpatient programs, along with family therapy, group psychotherapy, multiple family therapy, and recreational/occupational therapy (Kahn & Boyer, 1980; Steinberg, 1987). Many treatment cultures are conceptualized along behavior modification principles. The author believes that treatment of adolescents can be better understood and implemented psychodynamically by relying on the discoveries of classical psychoanalysis, revised by the later modifications of ego psychology, object relations theories, and Self Psychology (see Marohn et al., 1980, for more specific discussion). In the not-too-distant past, hospital treatment of adolescents was invariably long-term and psychodynamic, and closely resembled residential treatment. Today, however, because of health insurance changes and other economic pressures, hospital treatment has become more short-term and medication-oriented. Thus, although some differences in hospital and residential care are emerging, most of the issues mentioned here apply to both.

Indications and Contraindications of Residential Treatment

Adolescents who come to residential treatment centers and hospitals are often from dysfunctional families. Many children have already been removed from their parents and homes before they are institutionalized, and most have failed in some other kind of mental health treatment. Studies have shown that these young people are usually academically retarded, do not comply with others' expectations, are immature and aggressive, but are not usually substance abusers or psychotic (Wurtele, Wilson, & Prentice, 1983).

The purpose of hospital or residential treatment is quite similar to that of other psychodynamic psychotherapy. The aim of treatment is to "restructure" the personality; "missing" or defective psychological functions are provided by the treatment team and therapist. Transferences to team and therapist are given primary focus because they represent the struggles of the self to heal and are replicated in the attachment to the therapist. As inevitable disruptions in treatment arise, the nature of the transference wishes is evidenced. Thus, what is often limited to within-session exchanges between therapist and patient in psychodynamic therapy, is applied to the entire milieu and array of relationships in residential treatment.

In most psychodynamically oriented treatment ventures, the emergence of transference—its unfolding, interpretation, and resolution—is viewed as an important stage in therapy. Unlike classical psychoanalysis, the transference manifestations of adolescents in residential treatment are not confined to the consultation room or session. They frequently appear in the school, in activities, or in other interactions in the milieu. They usually occur as behavior rather than verbal expression, and they usually are not reported by the patient to the therapist. The therapist in a treatment center must rely on staff and colleagues to inform him or her about the patient's conduct, in order to evaluate whether and how it manifests the transference. Then the therapist brings such behavior to the patient's attention and tries to understand it and interpret it, in the same way that other associative material would be dealt with. These adolescents "bring" their dynamics and pathology to their therapists' attention, but do so through their behavioral associations and not necessarily through their verbal associations. Symptomatic or simple behavioral change is not sufficient, from this view, unless related to change in the personality structure.

The therapeutic process always begins with an assessment that is psychosociobiological scope and multidisciplinary in execution (Marohn et al, 1980; Steinberg, 1983, 1987). As Easson (1969) described, the decision to admit or not to admit to a residential setting should be based on that person's ability to utilize others for support while in the throes of psychotherapy. How this might be quantified, for example, in terms of peer and family relationships, remains to be studied. We know that adolescents who maintain significant relationships with both peers and their mother function most competently (Stein, Golombeck, Marton, & Korenblum, 1987). Whether these factors are sufficiently protective to mitigate against hospitalization by themselves, or whether they might be better viewed as components of a system of various relationships that could be given weighted values in determining whether hospital admission might be indicated, also remains to be evaluated.

Steinberg (1983) presented three questions that need answering in preparing residential care. Each seems to provide a rich research focus for evaluating how appropriately residential placement is applied:

1) Given that the case for psychiatric treatment has been made, can it be provided with the adolescent living at home? 2) What are the *positive* reasons for admission? and 3) If an adolescent must be away from home, what are the alternatives available? (pp. 311–314)

Many children and adolescents live in the midst of supportive and nurturing relationships in their families, nuclear or extended, or in their peer and friendship circles. These relationships will perform important self-object functions, given the patient's current capacity to use others for such functions. So supported, many children and adolescents will be able to tolerate the intense stimulations and challenges of a psychotherapy relationship without needing a partial or complete therapeutic milieu. Others, however, will do better, and some *only* will do well enough, when they are supported and their development is facilitated in a more extended therapeutic milieu, such as a hospital or residential facility.

Treatment Planning

Just as it is important to assess the level at which the adolescent is functioning in order to determine the appropriate treatment (outpatient, day, hospital, or residential), so too it is important to use this assessment in treatment planning. Specifically, one assesses the patient's psychological and developmental level and identifies opportunities that can allow the adolescent to use possessed skills to meet appropriate psychological challenges and to master currently difficult situations. At the same time, the therapist identifies and provides missing or underdeveloped psychological functions, which creates opportunities for the development of internal psychological structure.

A general goal of psychodynamic treatment of the disturbed adolescent is to convert symptomatic behaviors into an internal psychological experience and therefore eliminate their destructiveness. The behaviors may be the result of the classically described neurotic conflict or of psychological deficits, especially in self-regulation. Patients can express their pathology in an autoplastic manner (as symptoms) or in an alloplastic manner (as behavior). Usually, adolescents, especially delinquents and behaviorally disordered adolescents, express through action rather than experience symptoms. These behavioral problems have been incorrectly described as "acting out." Many behaviorally disordered adolescents function at a regressed level and do not distinguish a psychological inner world and an external world of behavior and reality. Both merge and mix together such that thought and feeling are interchangeable with activity and behavior. "Inside" and "outside" (essential to formulating the concept of "acting out") are abstractions of the observer, rather than the subject's own personal experience. A relatively simple study, once clinically relevant operational definitions are established, would involve comparing the kind and frequency of impulsive behavior in a treatment setting with patients' capacity to test reality, to distinguish an "inside" from an "outside," and to establish boundaries between self and other.

When treatment staff help the patient delineate an inner psychological world and begin to understand the meaning of his or her behavior, they do several things. They refuse to permit the kind of immature, self-defeating gratification that comes from the symbolic expression of wish, need, or conflict. They make themselves available as supportive and therapeutic self-objects by trying to provide a milieu in which all behavior can be understood. They facilitate transforming motor expressions into verbal expression, and thus enhance the establishment of internal psychological structure. However, it is important to understand that this change from behavior to verbalization is a treatment goal rather than a prerequisite. Mental health professionals who ignore or will not treat delinquent and behaviorally disordered adolescents will miss and fail the vast bulk of disturbed teenagers.

Important Program Components

Another important clinical concern that is ripe for research study and evaluation is the necessary and sufficient components of a therapeutic program. Treatment programs are usually organized around school and activities, not around the individual psychotherapy situation, even though the individual psychotherapy is the central factor in helping the patient change.

School

School is the "work" and life task of the adolescent; consequently, regular schedules including school attendance are typical in most treatment centers. The integration of school into the overall program has varied from a minor problem to a major nuisance for residential programs (Kahn & Boyer, 1980). Teachers may feel pressured by a mental health philosophy to forsake their educator identities and think of themselves as psychotherapists or "educational therapists." It is important for teachers to remain teachers. Although they should understand psychodynamics, psychopathology, and treatment planning and implementation, their work emphasizes the relatively healthy and conflict-free area of the patient's psyche. The therapist and treatment staff supply missing psychological functions and shore up defective functions so that the student can separate his/or her psychological problems from school work and classroom activities. Teachers who become enamored of psychodynamics and act as therapists can interfere significantly with the student's education. Those students who would require extreme modification of the school setting are best withheld from the classroom so as not to encounter further failure or disrupt the learning of others (Kahn & Boyer, 1980). A careful study of the personality pressures and changes the special educator experiences in the mental health treatment environment would be welcome.

Recreational Activities

Crafts and manual arts, gym and sports, exercise, outings, and trips to the community are important parts of the treatment program. They promote socialization, age-appropriate pursuits, and grist for the psychotherapeutic mill. As we noted above, such activities will not "burn off" energy or "tire them out," but should be carefully designed and monitored to provide the adolescent with growth-promoting experiences. Simple catharsis or affect discharge is not successful treatment, but facilitating verbalization and introspection is. The particular effects of recreational activities and articulation of the processes of such effects are needed.

Limit Setting

Limit setting is a major treatment issue and component of residential treatment. Treatment staff perform many important psychological functions that the behaviorally disordered adolescent cannot provide; these eventually will become internalized functions. Limit setting is an important part of these functions (Marohn et al., 1980). The curbs should correspond to a balancing of the adolescent developmental stage of the patient and the psychological and emotional functioning the patient manifests at any particular moment. Thus, one can conceptualize a hierarchy or spectrum of limit-setting interventions, from something as simple as being with the patient or talking with the patient, to the use of physical restraints or seclusion. The latter two interventions, although often used appropriately in a psychiatric hospital setting, are usually not seen in a residential treatment setting, because they involve medical and nursing supervision and monitoring. Often, however, disturbed and disruptive patients can be helped to reintegrate or to grow by spending time in their individual private rooms, with or without help, thinking about their behavior and learning how to introspect about its meaning. Engaging the child or adolescent in activities should not simply divert attention, but should serve to limit behavior, rechannel it, and provide a growth experience. Medication provides appropriate limit setting by helping a patient regulate his or her inner psychological world. A pilot study of how the treatment staff intervene to pacify a patient unwittingly revealed a correspondence to how the patient's parents originally calmed their child (Goldberg & Rubin, 1970). It could be readily expanded to a larger sample and studied in a more controlled manner.

One problem in setting limits is that they frequently can be applied because of a staff member's discomfort or countertransference instead of in response to patients' needs. Truly, staff need to employ their own emotional reactions to patients' behavior as clues about what the patient is experiencing and how to intervene. This "use of the self" is frequently emphasized in training mental health personnel. Such skills must be refined into an empathic capacity that enables the staff member to "taste" what the patient is experiencing, but then to differentiate the self, achieve some emotional distance, and use the experience to chose an appropriate treatment intervention. One study found that seclusion was used more frequently with younger children and with those who show delayed or retarded development (Cates & Cooper, 1983), demonstrating the hypothesized tendency to employ limits for staff's convenience or comfort, rather than, appropriately, as an intervention to meet the client's needs. More careful studies of how and why limit setting is applied accurately (or not) would aid staff training greatly.

Staff Training

The success of any treatment program depends on the ability of the staff to understand, assess, and respond to patient psychopathology therapeutically. Such understanding includes an awareness of social systems, group psychology, family dynamics, and individual psychology. Supervision and teaching of staff members by competent mental health professionals are fundamental to this process. As mentioned earlier, staff gratification best comes from learning and self-growth, and not from patients' improving. Such demands on patients to improve for the sake of staff or therapist will frequently interfere with the patients' ability to find their own way and to move toward health. Patients respond negatively when they reexperience the frequently seen family constellation of the children being responsible for the parents' sense of self-worth. Staff professional development is seen as the healthier option for gratification. Thus, providing excellent service to patients depends on the staff's being given opportunities for personal and professional growth. To achieve this goal, clinical administration must create a healthy teaching and research environment so that staff have opportunities to learn. Personal psychotherapy for staff should be not only permitted but encouraged.

Ongoing teaching and learning opportunities, as well as a general agreement that learning is important, are essential to the success of any residential or day treatment program.

Clinical administration must support these educational alliances and several other basic principles as well: that introspection and self-understanding are important; that staff members must change in order to effect change in patients; that adequate supervision, consultation, training, and, sometimes, personal therapy are necessary to achieve such change; that there must be reliable and consistent administrative support to discharge incompetent and training-resistant staff; that there must be administrative support to hire or fill staff vacancies according to qualifications rather than seniority; that there must be administrative support to control disruptive outside pressures; and that administration recognizes that tensions and struggles persist and are continuous among all relationships within the treatment milieu. Just as patient change emerges from self-awareness in the context of a treatment alliance, so too does staff and professional growth develop from an understanding of the self, and of how to use oneself, in the holding environment of a supervisory relationship. Without these essential ingredients, one is not treating patients, but only processing patients; one is not nurturing staff, but only occupying staff.

These tensions and potentials for disruption are probably more acute in adolescent than in adult programs. Working with adolescent patients usually presents the trainee or new staff member with unique developmental challenges; most adults carry "unresolved" or unfinished adolescent tasks into adulthood. An alternative view is that the so-called developmental tasks of adolescence persist normatively well into adulthood, as part of ongoing, expectable transformations. Nonetheless, working with adolescents challenges us by confronting us with such unresolved developmental tasks. An interesting study could be designed to evaluate the interaction of the development and maturation of the therapist-trainee and the first confrontation with an adolescent patient in psychotherapy. One could use trainee and supervisor reports, as well as some assessment of the patient's focal dynamics, to accomplish such an inquiry.

Staff Leadership

An issue of particular importance is the impact of administrative leadership. Studies have confirmed clinical impressions that leadership is essential to the clinical process, and that successful clinical administration affirms the worth of the group and exemplifies the group's ideals (Diamond, 1984). Leaders should be available and present, empathic and interested, confident and secure, ethical and professional, and clinically focused on a therapeutic approach. The leader emphasizes and exemplifies team collaboration and open communication and espouses the importance of understanding the psychological meaning of behavior. In residential treatment of adolescents, to lead is not to dictate but to be involved in a process with others, to be sensitive to others' wishes and ideas but capable of articulating one's own informed views. An idealized leader can readily lose touch with the ideas and feelings of others, which may affect their ability to speak openly. As a result, some "followers" so rigidly adhere to treatment principles and practices that the program becomes inflexible, instead of constantly being refined and modified. New staff members and rotating trainees can provide the system with new ideas and viewpoints; leadership must accept and promote these contributions to incorporate them in the milieu. An organizational analysis of treatment leadership styles that are most effective in maintaining staff interest, and their therapeutic effect, would be valuable.

Token Economies

Many treatment programs, especially in the correctional field, are conceptualized along behavior modification lines, with token economies and clients earning various privileges and levels of freedom of movement. Although such programs are easy to construct and to teach and although they may readily change behavior in some young people, they do not necessarily address underlying personality or psychological difficulties. Many mental health professionals consider them too superficial unless tied to therapeutic planning and careful use of limit setting (Steinberg, 1987). Nonetheless, much of what occurs in the day or residential milieu can be understood in terms of learning or behavior modification theories. For example, patients in psychotherapy are "taught" how to introspect and to talk about their feelings, and they receive rewards for such activity. Yet, we know that, developmentally, such learning and modification of behavior occur only in the context of an enriching and affirming self–object relationship and environment. Adolescents can be made to conform and taught how to get along, survive, obey the rules, and reap rewards, but therapeutic change involves much more than simple conformity, and persistent change depends on internal restructuralization and help in finding one's own way in healing the self. Many young people are able to navigate the demands, for example, of a token economy because they are healthy enough to do so or because they have changed sufficiently in their therapy. Change often facilitates movement in a token economy, rather than being achieved by it. An interesting investigation would be whether a combination of projective testing and behavioral measurement could be used to assess this contention of the order of change and the necessity of developmental readiness to use behavioral techniques, and to delineate the change process. It may also be that "levels" or "points" effects reflect the positive peer culture often promoted in residential treatment as part of the behavior modification. The specific effects of token economies versus structure per se need comparison.

Peer Culture

The peer culture of the residential or day treatment center exerts powerful, subtle, and pervasive influence on patients; it can support or undermine the therapeutic values and goals of staff (Schaefer, 1980). Community meetings are important in verbalizing and consolidating protreatment goals and values. Probably most important in helping residents acquire unit norms are the minute and subtle interactions between people in the milieu. Consistent routines, rules, and policies, and learning traditions of the unit are also major components (Tuss & Greenspan, 1979). The effect of peer culture is a rich focus for research.

Coeducational Units

A good deal of clinical experience suggests that coeducational living units and treatment programs are beneficial. This arrangement provides the child or adolescent with a more open and realistic appreciation of the opposite sex, does not lead to overstimulation or sexual delinquency if properly managed (James & James, 1980), and decreases the likelihood of emotional contagion that leads to riot (Levinson & Crabtree, 1979; Marohn, Dalle-Molle, Offer, & Ostrov, 1973). As part of this coeducational atmosphere, a proper balance of male and female staff, serving as paternal and maternal surrogates and older brothers and sisters, is also crucial.

LIMITATIONS AND COMPLICATIONS—A REITERATION

Treatment is, ideally, a supportive, growth-promoting experience; but it can also be stimulating, demanding, and stressful. It often leads to pain and personal disruption before benefits are clearly felt. Research is intended to further treatment effectiveness and efficiency. Residential clinical phenomena are not simple to effect or to study. However, good analysis can occur and be very useful.

Study of a riot or assaultive behavior in an adolescent hospital setting (Marohn, 1974; Marohn et al., 1973), for example, demonstrated that the overstimulation of intense affectionate (not hostile) feelings spurred many disturbed adolescents to commit violent acts. Indeed, violence is a common problem in working with behaviorally disordered adolescents (Marohn, 1980). Not only are these teenagers more likely to experience violent death—such as through homicide, suicide, or trauma such as an auto accident—but they also behave violently, and their violent feelings and behaviors are common occurrences in their therapy. A treatment program that purports to experience no violence in working with this kind of patient is either suppressing the violence or causing it to be displaced, for example, onto the environment through the destruction of property and furniture, the defacing of walls, and similar actions. However, the problem is not one of merely delineating the negative events and feelings that bring on violence.

Feelings of hostility and destructiveness are an ongoing part of residential psychotherapeutic work with most adolescents. In many instances, such feelings are not simple expressions of resistance, but rather lie at the very core of the psychopathology. Negativism is frequently seen in working with behaviorally disordered adolescents and is not to be confused with the absence of the therapeutic alliance; defiance can be as much an indication of a bond as is obedience (Marohn, 1980). Many treatments fail because the negative transference is never acknowledged and never processed.

The delinquent adolescent frequently manifests a negative transference. Sometimes, negativism is not a true transference but a defense against the emergence of positive transference feelings. Often there are tendencies to idealize the therapist or expressions of a search for an idealized parent. As part and parcel of this tendency to idealize, there is a tendency to deidealize or depreciate the therapist. Such depreciation or deidealization may express a defense against the emergence of intense primitive longings for a perfect parent. Other such expressions of hostility may, indeed, represent the disillusionment that the adolescent has experienced time and time again: the hoped-for parent has failed to materialize. The adolescent may be reexperiencing with the new therapist the conflict of the two feelings: the search for the wished-for parent and the expectation that this therapist, like other parents in the past, will fail him. In addition, upon noticing some "defect" in this therapist, the adolescent may immediately experience the disillusionment that the hoped-for idealized parent has once again failed to materialize. It is important to remember that, in all of these instances, the negativism and hostility in no way indicate that a therapeutic alliance is absent or impossible. In fact, the very expression of this core pathology of the patient indicates that an attachment does exist, an attachment that needs to be understood and worked through in the same way that a positive attachment needs to be worked through (Marohn, 1977, 1980).

The author's previous study of the negative transference rescued him from a difficult and uncomfortable clinical situation, encountered in the following case:

Karl was 16 when he presented himself for an evaluation. In his arrogant and haughty manner, he claimed to have significant career plans which he knew he would realize, despite his failing grades at a private high school. He seemed to be bright, but was not doing well academically, much to the chagrin of his academically oriented and financially successful parents. There had been a number of attempts to treat his depressions and his behavioral problems over the years, and all these attempts at psychotherapy failed. During one diagnostic interview, when he and his parents were talking about the previous attempts to help him with his problems, he turned to the psychiatrist and talked with sarcasm about the "fool" who had treated him before, and how playing with puppets was really a waste of his parents' time and money. The psychiatrist was taken aback by Karl's sudden assault, thought for a moment, and then pointed out that he must have been terribly disappointed in the past in someone whom he had looked up to and was quite angry and disillusioned with, whoever that was. He was silent for a moment and then went on talking about other things. The next day, his mother called to say that Karl had talked with her at length the night before about how at times he did feel disappointed in people and how disappointed he was in his father. When she suggested that that might be something he could discuss with the psychiatrist in a further session, he latched onto the idea willingly and returned a few days later. During that session, he talked about how often his father was unavailable to him, but at the same time how difficult it was for him to reach out to his father.

Only careful dissection of the clinical material, coupled with an appreciation of transference, defense and resistance, and narcissistic idealizing tendencies, can help the investigator recognize that a "no" in a structured interview or a "false" on an inventory question about a prosocial attitude may hide positive, affectionate, or adoring feelings. Thus, the researcher of the adolescent confronts another problem: Things are not always what they seem to be or are said to be (Marohn, 1980). As well as asking complex enough questions, establishing an adequate research alliance is important in obtaining reliable and useful results (Offer et al., 1979). This same problem confounds the work of the civil libertarian: Adolescents who say they do not want treatment and do not need help often hunger for it and try to provoke more and more significant interventions.

UNRESOLVED PROBLEMS AND NEEDED RESEARCH

Elsewhere, we have noted that our residential patients, once discharged, did not usually continue in outpatient psychotherapy for more than 6 months (Viale-Val, Rosenthal, Curtiss, & Marohn, 1984). We generally viewed this as a failure of the follow-up treatment and a defective psychotherapy alliance. Yet, vignettes and impromptu contacts with our alumni suggested that they were doing well. We began to question whether we were judging the success of adolescent treatment by inappropriate standards. In an unpublished series of interviews and behavior inventories of the patients at 18 months postdischarge, we found that, indeed, most of them were doing well (Bowes, Marohn, Offer, & Ostrov, 1975). What we had failed to recognize was that leaving therapy and the psychotherapist was an integral part of the continuing adolescent maturation process. A period of turmoil may ensue for as long as a year past discharge, but, later, the adolescent speaks positively about the usefulness of the treatment experience.

Follow-up and outcome research, as mentioned at the beginning of the chapter, are difficult, especially if one seeks the precision inherent in a control group design. What should one measure? Should one look at changes in symptoms and behavior? Or should one emphasize internal psychological and emotional shifts? Probably, the most valuable approach is to try to do both, relying on various tests and measurements to validate behavioral change, and other tests and in-depth interviews to gauge internal shifts. Most studies usually demonstrate that healthier patients derive more from treatment and do better at follow-up. However, the results of most studies are suggestive rather than definitive. For example, Velasquez and Lyle (1985) compared adolescent delinquents in residential and intensive day treatment. At 6- and 12-month follow-ups, no differences were found in the nature of the placement, attendance at school, frequency of status offenses, or impact of treatment. However, residential subjects committed significantly fewer misdemeanors.

Nonetheless, engaging in a research endeavor can sharpen the clinician's acumen and often help him or her to realize something that had been ignored, denied, or omitted. For example, when we decided to study the outpatient psychotherapy dropout rate, wondering which patients did not "take" with which psychotherapy trainees and why, we found that those patients who were being seen at least twice a week continued in therapy, and those seen less than twice a week tended to drop out (Viale-Val et al., 1984). There are many ways to consider these data, but we were amazed to find that we who, as psychoanalytically oriented therapists, all committed to a system of more frequent sessions, had not structured the outpatient experience in that fashion! This realization helped us to examine not only our countertransferences, but also the reasons we anticipated difficulties with our trainees and their patients if we were to plan for more numerous therapy sessions. Had we not embarked on this study, we might have never have had the opportunity for such self-scrutiny and repair. At a policy level, such research can enable clinicians to move from aphorisms about residential treatment to incorporation of scientific evidence to better fit the provision of services to the needs of adolescents (Kahn & Boyer, 1980).

CONCLUSION

Residential therapeutic work with disturbed and behaviorally disordered adolescents has a long, rich history. Often, it has been informed by intuitive understandings rather than key systematic and empirically derived interventions. The interventions applied need to be continually challenged and rethought. More formally organized clinical research can enhance the psychological animation of these strategies. Writing about one's work forces one to think about one's work. Adolescents benefit and so do their families.

REFERENCES

Aichhorn, A. (1935). *Wayward youth.* New York: Viking Press. (Original work published 1925.)

Bowes, P., Marohn, R. C., Offer, D., & Ostrov, E. (1975). *Eighteen-month followup study.* Unpublished.

Cates, J. A., & Cooper, G. D. (1983). Characteristics of secluded children in a residential treatment center. *Residential Group Care and Treatment, 1,* 43–54.

Diamond, A. (1984). Administrative impact on the treatment of children and adolescents in residential settings. *Residential Group Care and Treatment, 1,* 43–54.

Easson, W. M. (1969). *The severely disturbed adolescent.* New York: International Universities Press.

Fineberg, B. L., Sowards, S. K., & Kettlewell, P. W. (1980). Adolescent inpatient treatment: A literature review. *Adolescence, 15,* 915–925.

Goldberg, A., & Rubin, B. (1970). A method of pacification of the psychotic excited state: The use of the hospital as a transitional object. *Comprehensive Psychiatry, 2,* 450–456.

Gossett, J. T., Barnhard, F. D., Phillips, V. A., & Lewis, J. M. (1979). Follow-up of adolescents treated in a psychiatric hospital. *Archives of General Psychiatry, 34,* 1037–1042.

James, K. L., & James, D. (1980). Coed residential milieu. *Child Care Quarterly, 9,* 32–40.

Kahn, D. G., & Boyer, D. N. (1980). Inpatient hospital treatment of adolescents. *Psychiatric Clinics of North America, 3,* 513–545.

Knitzer, J. (1982). *Unclaimed children: The failure of public responsibility to children and adolescents in need of mental health services.* Washington, DC: The Children's Defense Fund.

Levinson, D. F., & Crabtree, L. H. (1979). Ward tension and staff leadership in a therapeutic community for hospitalized adolescents. *Psychiatry, 42,* 220–240.

Lewis, D. O., & Shanok, S. F. (1980). The use of a correctional setting for follow-up care of psychiatrically disturbed adolescents. *American Journal of Psychiatry, 137,* 953–955.

Maltz, M. D. (1984). *Recidivism.* New York: Academic Press.

Marohn, R. C. (1974). Trauma and the delinquent. *Adolescent Psychiatry, 3,* 354–361.

Marohn, R. C. (1977). The "Juvenile Imposter": Some thoughts on narcissism and the delinquent. *Adolescent Psychiatry, 5,* 186–212.

Marohn, R. C. (1980). Adolescent rebellion and the task of separation. *Adolescent Psychiatry, 8,* 173–183.

Marohn, R. C. (1984). Disappointing and deviant youth and the rage of the elders. *Children and Youth Services Review, 6,* 367–373.

Marohn, R. C., Dalle-Molle, D., McCarter, E., & Linn, D. (1980). *Juvenile delinquents: Psychodynamic assessment and hospital treatment.* New York: Brunner/Mazel.

Marohn, R. C., & Dalle-Molle, D., Offer, D., & Ostrov, E. (1973). A hospital riot: Its determinants and implications for treatment. *American Journal of Psychiatry, 130,* 631–636.

Myers, J. (1986). How public policy affects the role of residential psychiatric care for children and youth. In K. Wells (Chairman), *Division 37 task force on residential treatment* report. Symposium conducted at the meeting of the American Psychological Association, Washington, DC.

Offer, D., Marohn, R., & Ostrov, E. (1979). *The psychological world of the juvenile delinquent.* New York: Basic Books.

Offer, D., Ostrov, E., & Howard, K. I. (1985). Epidemiology of mental health and mental illness among adolescents. In J. Call (Ed.), *Significant advances in child psychiatry.* New York: Basic Books.

Ostrov, E., Marohn, R. C., Offer, D., Curtiss, G., & Feczko, M. (1980). The Adolescent Antisocial Behavior Check List, *Journal of Clinical Psychology, 36,* 594–601.

President's Commission on Mental Health (1978). *Report to the President:* Vol. 1. Commission Report); Vol. 3. Task Panel Reports. Washington, DC: U.S. Government Printing Office.

Redl, F. (1966). The life space interview—strategy and techniques. In *When we deal with children* (pp. 35–67). New York: Free Press.

Schaefer, C. (1980). The impact of the peer culture in the residential treatment of youth. *Adolescence, 15,* 831–845.

Stein, B., Golombeck, H., Marton, P., & Korenblum, M. (1987). Personality functioning and change in clinical presentation from early to middle adolescence. *Adolescent Psychiatry, 14,* 378–393.

Steinberg, D. (1983). Aspects of residential treatment. In D. Steinberg, *The clinical psychiatry of adolescence* (pp. 308–323). New York: Wiley.

Steinberg, D. (1987). *The adolescent unit.* New York: Wiley.

Tuss, C. J., & Greenspan, B. (1979). The transmission and acquisition of values in the residential treatment of emotionally disturbed adolescents. *Adolescence, 14,* 471–480.

Velasquez, J. S., & Lyle, C. G. (1985). Day versus residential treatment for juvenile offenders: The impact of program evaluation. *Child Welfare, 64,* 145–156.

Viale-Val, G., Rosenthal, R. H., Curtiss, G., & Marohn, R. C. (1984). Dropout from adolescent psychotherapy: A preliminary study. *Journal of American Academy of Child Psychiatry, 23,* 562–568.

Wurtele, S. K., Wilson, D. R., & Prentice, D. S. (1983). Characteristics of children in residential treatment programs: Findings and clinical implications. *Journal of Clinical Child Psychology, 12,* 137–144.

PART FOUR
Policy Issues

CHAPTER 20

Enhancing Adolescent Development Through Social Policy

JAMES GARBARINO

INTRODUCTION

This chapter sets out to examine the interplay of culture, social change, and the intrinsic processes of adolescence in setting the policy agenda for addressing the clinical needs of adolescents. It begins with an overview of the meaning of social policy as an effort to integrate and advance values with an understanding of the psychological, social, cultural, and biological realities of adolescents living in late 20th-century North America. One way of approaching social policy and the clinical needs of adolescents is to pose a series of metaphorical dichotomies that capture the issues faced in efforts to service important values. One of these metaphors is "icebergs vs. ice cubes." The former suggests that the root of adolescent clinical problems lies beyond the individual, below the surface, in broad social and cultural forces (e.g., racism and poverty). The latter indicates a model that treats adolescent problems as idiosyncratic to individual development (i.e., deficiencies of individual youth and their families) rather than expressing fundamental flaws in the social structure. This series of metaphors provides a perspective from which to view adolescent issues.

The chapter next examines social stereotypes and realities relevant to understanding the role played by abuse and neglect as a focal point for evaluating the clinical needs of adolescents. This examination in turn provides the basis for formulating a concept of the "good society" with respect to meeting the developmental needs of adolescents in ways that minimize psychological costs to the individual and social costs to the community. The chapter concludes with a series of hypotheses about adolescent maltreatment as a case study for assessing the relationship between social policy and the clinical needs of adolescents.

SOCIAL POLICY: WHAT IS IT?

Social policy is a slippery subject, particularly when it involves adolescents. Some of us are inclined to take the easy way out and say, in effect, "Our social policy ought to be 'End poverty, racism, violence, and sexism, period.' Now let's go home." When people talk about social policy, they may have in mind something more specific. I recall an incident from the first years of the Reagan Administration, when issues of child and family services and support had become highly politicized, in the sense of becoming very much a partisan political issue. The incident occurred during a seminar presented by a researcher who had worked for many years in Latin America. He presented his research on the impact of early nutrition on child development—a very sophisticated, technical exposition of the results of his studies on early nutritional supplement programs and their effects on birth weight and brain growth. At the end of this very technical presentation, during the question period, someone asked, "Well, professor, what would you say is the major public policy implication of your work?" He thought for a moment and said, "Vote Democratic." Our concern here is with social policy in the broader sense, beyond narrow political orientation.

When we talk about policy, we are talking about what we think is simultaneously desirable and attainable: a statement of will, a statement of goals, and the social maps that we see giving us the route to attain these goals.

Social policy informs clinical practice and it indirectly sets the agenda for clinical practice. Social policy offers a definition of what the issues are, and it shapes the means available to address those issues. Social policy regarding social problems and adolescents rests on fundamental assumptions or conclusions about the nature of both social reality and adolescence. One way to understand social policy is to examine some of these assumptions and conclusions.

Icebergs vs. Ice Cubes

One of the underlying forces shaping social policy lies in two contrasting views of the origins of adolescent problems: the "iceberg" view and the "ice cube" model. To what extent are adolescent problems simply the result of problem people? To what extent do the experiences and behaviors of problem adolescents reflect something wrong in the social structures of the community? The answers we give to those questions have many implications for the policy and practice of adolescent services, particularly when we are dealing with prevention.

Are problem adolescents simply the manifestation of basic social problems, of culture gone awry, of corruption in the social order, of fundamental injustices and deficiencies in the social fabric? Put another way, are adolescent problems just the tip of an iceberg of institutionalized social pathology? Or, are problem adolescents simply deficient individuals or bad people, like ice cubes floating on the surface of a basically good, sound, and just society? How we answer these questions provides direction for our policies and, ultimately, for clinical services.

Total Reform vs. Patchwork Prevention

One approach to preventing adolescent problems says that there is no programmatic approach that makes any sense. From this perspective, the only way to think about preventing adolescent problems is to think about total social reform: We aren't going anywhere unless we end poverty, racism, sexism, and other forms of institutionalized oppression by uprooting those problems from the heart of the society. We could call this perspective total reform prevention policy.

The other view says that we need not engage in total social reform to prevent adolescent problems, but can instead do something that might be called "patchwork prevention." Following this metaphor, if we're faced with a cold night, a stack of pieces of cloth won't keep us warm. But if we somehow stitch them together into a quilt, then we can put that over us and stay warm. Patchwork prevention implies that we can find a set of programs, no one of which produces total social reform, which, when put together in a coherent package, will prevent most adolescent problems. When the community stitches together all of the elements of a comprehensive program, the result is sufficient social influence to achieve prevention.

Deciding between a total social reform orientation and a patchwork prevention approach presents a troublesome and challenging dichotomy. There are many pressures—political pressures, pressures in our culture—that would make some of us want to believe in a patchwork prevention approach. It doesn't rock the big boat. It doesn't put us in conflict with powerful, entrenched economic interests. It makes it possible for corporations to support prevention efforts because such programs "do good" but don't threaten the fundamental status quo. This approach extends beyond prevention to treatment efforts: teaching the adolescent to adapt to existing structures is an easier sell. What is more, such efforts can and do produce significant clinical results for adolescents in trouble—at least for some kids, under some circumstances, some of the time. For some of us, total social reform prevention is appealing precisely because it resonates with some personal or collective sense of injustice or personal need to rationalize inaction on the programmatic level.

Whatever our political orientation, we can't lose sight of the fact that total social reform may be what it takes to change some of the big problems. For example, recent research documents that most (up to 85%) kids in inner city neighborhoods witness severe acts of violence (Garbarino, Dubrow, Kostelny, & Pardo, 1992). Will programming deal with that awesome fact? Can social reform be enough to cope with the consequences (and the origins) of widespread violence? That dichotomy puts a lot of pressure on us, as people interested in adolescent development, because it forces us to live in a kind of schizophrenic state. Indeed, years ago, a colleague once concluded, "To get along in the 20th century, you really must manage as an ambulatory schizophrenic." He meant that we're constantly faced with the fact that some of the things that need doing are awesome—if we really think about them. We have to get up every morning knowing that there are enough nuclear weapons in the world to target every community of 1,500 people or more with its own thermonuclear weapon. We have to be aware that the ozone layer is eroding and the ice cap may be melting. We have to recognize that massive economic inequality continues and racism persists. We have to acknowledge that many teens are in desperate trouble. We have to know all of this and yet get up in the morning, brush our teeth, give our kids breakfast, send them off to school, do the laundry, and go to our jobs—perhaps in the field of delivering clinical services to adolescents.

We have to live as ambulatory schizophrenics if we are to wrestle with adolescent problems. That's the way the world comes to us. We must neither forget the impulse to achieve total social reform while we do small good works nor simply sit back saying, "I'll wait to do my program until reform comes."

Pudding vs. Salad

Assuming we see our way clear to proceed with a patchwork approach to adolescent problems (at least as part of our campaign to make the world a better place for youth), how do we decide how, specifically, to target our programs? A group of Canadian government policy makers couched this issue as one of "pudding" vs. "salad." They explained that the pudding approach meant mixing together all adolescent clinical efforts into one homogeneous approach. The salad model meant keeping each programmatic element distinct, although the elements might operate under the umbrella of some large agency. A pudding approach makes a lot of sense for preventing many adolescent problems, where the goal is a few powerful homogeneous prevention programs that reach a broad audience and do a lot of things at once. Home health visitors for teen mothers, for example, can simultaneously do good on many fronts, including dealing with the teen mother's problems as an adolescent. However, some adolescent problems, particularly those that are more severe, probably need specialized services, as in cases of intrafamilial and extrafamilial sexual abuse. A policy issue that we have to face involves puddings and salads, or finding the best balance of generic and specialized programs.

Skimming vs. Program Reach

Another policy issue presents us with "skimming" versus "program reach." We have known for many years that, when agencies offer programs, particularly prevention programs, the easiest people to get hold of are the people who have a little bit of an edge already. Twenty years ago, the early Head Start intervention programs demonstrated that "Those who have the most, gain the most."

This principle becomes important when thinking about policy for adolescent clinical services because it is very tempting to simply lay out the program and skim off the cream of the crop, even the cream of the troubled crop or the high-risk crop. Thus, one measure for evaluating the soundness of clinical programs (and the policies that sustain and justify them) has to be: "Do they reach down and out to the down-and-out in the society?" How far do they reach now? How far could they reach? What does it take to participate in a program? How does policy motivate and reward program reach, and discourage skimming?

Enhancement vs. Prevention

A related question is: Do our program activities really involve prevention or simply involve enhancement? Enhancing already adequately functioning adolescents can certainly be a route to prevention, and it is a worthwhile endeavor on ethical and political grounds. However, we face the real risk that programs will present themselves as prevention or clinical treatment programs but may in fact only be enhancement programs. Such programs only reach people who are not at significant risk for serious development malfunction or social pathology, but they do succeed in enhancing their functioning. This is a laudable goal, but we shouldn't confuse it with prevention or clinical treatment. If we know that the vast proportion of serious adolescent problems occurs among 10% to 20% of our youth population, and if our programs don't reach that 10% to 20%, then we aren't meeting the policy goal of adolescent clinical services in any significant way. If we only reach the people "above" them—enhancing their functioning and making them better students and citizens—we may be doing great good, but we are not meeting the goals set by a policy aimed at high-risk youth. For example, we now recognize that programs aimed at inner-city high school seniors may fall victim to the skimming–enhancement problem by virtue of the fact that most of the highest-risk kids are long gone by the time twelfth grade arrives.

This problem with enhancement and skimming is a particular concern in the United States, because our strategy of choice is always "voluntarism," with its emphasis on educational efforts to help youth fit into "the system." We ask: "Who would like to be part of this prevention program?" We should be asking: "How do we make sure that everyone who needs this prevention program gets it?"

Allocating Costs: Categorical or Generic Programming

Another policy issue we face involves how to allocate the costs of adolescent clinical services. One of our persistent problems is that we attempt to allocate the costs of prevention too narrowly, on a categorical basis. Going back to the pudding and salad metaphor, if we indeed adopt a pudding approach to prevention, we must think of a few key preventive interventions that will succeed with respect to a wide range of adolescent problems. Therefore, we must insist that the costs of those programs be understood in terms of all the various things they might prevent. This produces a lower "cost per success" than does conventional categorical accounting.

A good example comes from the Home Health Visitor Program, conducted by David Olds and his colleagues (1986) in Elmira, New York. Olds's project is cited often because it is one of the few that combines both a strong intervention and a strong research design. Home health visitors (registered nurses) in the primary experimental condition began visiting high-risk teen parents prenatally, and continued for as long as 2 or 3 years after the birth of a child. That intervention was contrasted with three other conditions: home health visitors whose visits began after the child was born; families who didn't get a home health visitor at all but simply had access and transportation to a regular clinic; and households whose only extra service was routine developmental screening of the children.

Olds found that the poor, unmarried teenage mothers who got the prenatal and continuing home health visitor evidenced dramatic and significant preventive effects, in contrast to the other groups. What were the effects of the home health visitor, which cost about $2,500 per family (in 1980 dollars)?

One effect was reduced child abuse in the first 2 years of newborns' life. In contrast to the comparison groups receiving other services, among this high-risk group of mothers, about 4% ended up being reported for abuse and neglect in the first 2 years of their children's life, as opposed to about 19% among the groups who got no home health visitor prenatally. If the only justification for the program's cost was its prevention of child abuse, it might look like a expensive program to run: $21,000 per case of child abuse prevented in the first 2 years of life.

Every time we prevent a serious case of physical abuse, the financial impact may be great. If we prevent the permanent placement of a child or the permanent hospitalization of a child, hundreds of thousands of dollars are involved.

Indeed, a home health visitor program conducted in Denver in the 1970s offered just such a cost-effectiveness rationale. The program was able to prevent five cases of serious hospitalization (out of 100 families served), one of which called for lifelong nursing care. Even at $2,000 a family, preventing one $200,000 bill is doing a lot of good—and doing it cost-effectively.

However, the key to Olds's study, and the beauty of it, lies in the fact that he didn't stop with cost-effectiveness as a rationale for preventing cases of child abuse. He found that the same program reduced a whole series of problems particularly salient for teen parents. The program resulted in lowered prematurity rates, increased birth weight, decreased smoking during pregnancy, decreased accidental ingestions of poison in the first years of life, and improved maternal attitude and perception of the child.

One of the most important findings was dramatic. The likelihood of a second pregnancy within 13 months of the first birth was reduced from approximately 60% in the comparison group to about 20% in the group who got the home health visitor starting prenatally. This program permits a strong statement about policy regarding clinical services to adolescents:

If we allocate the cost of the home health visitor across all of those areas—and probably even delinquency, teenage years, illiteracy, and school failure—we begin to see an intervention that more than pays for itself.

The policy questions then become: Who pays? When do they pay? Assuming that the "who" doing the paying is the public treasury: From whose budget do we fund prevention programs? One of our advocacy efforts has to be to insist that key prevention programs aimed at adolescents, like prenatal home health visitors for teen parents, ought to be paid for by many different budgets because they have their effects across the board, not just in one category of problem or need. We recognize and we have to point out to policy makers that the same teen parents who "produce" child maltreatment are linked to delinquency, infant mortality, and illiteracy. These same adolescents are often victims of the problems themselves (Garbarino, et al., 1986).

If one works in a small community, one knows that case management meetings often include the refrain, "Oh yes, here come the Joneses again. And, oh yes, the Smiths. My mother dealt with the Smiths when she was a social worker." If one works in a big city, one sometimes loses track of that constancy because of agency specialization and sampling from a much bigger pool of families. "We deal with 100 teenage runaways; you deal with 100 abused teenagers. We deal with 100 cases of infant mortality among the children of teen parents; you deal with 100 cases of child abuse inflicted by teen parents." Upon closer inspection, the 400 "cases" turn out to be 200 teens or 150 families. The multiple cases are often the same people—if not concurrently, then at least sequentially (and across generations). The need for a policy of comprehensive core services addressed to adolescents in trouble flows from the nature of adolescent problems themselves.

A TEEN IN TROUBLE IS A TEEN WHO HAS BEEN HURT

A wide range of adolescent problems are linked dynamically—delinquency, parricide, running away, and prostitution, to name but four that are mentioned frequently in research and clinical reports (Garbarino, Schellenbach, Sebes, et al. 1986). The common theme lining these problems appears to be abuse and neglect in the family, with the degree of coincidence between maltreatment and the four youth problems noted above being in excess of 65% in some samples. These links provide an important aspect of the context within which we must understand efforts to deal with adolescent maltreatment as a core issue for social policy regarding adolescent clinical services. A second aspect of that context is public and professional stereotypes about adolescents.

Stereotypes of Adolescents: The Myth That Adolescents' Behavior Is a "Phase"

Some of the most prominent observers of adolescence in the 1950s and 1960s saw negative stereotypes of youth as both the cause and effect of adolescent alienation from the adult world. Classics such as Paul Goodman's *Growing Up Absurd* (1956) and Edgar Friedenberg's *The Vanishing Adolescent* (1959) and *The Dignity of Youth and Other Atavisms* (1965) explored this theme. Goodman's title is self-explanatory. Friedenberg emphasized the way adults often regard adolescents in general: with fear and contempt. High schools are the principal arena in which adult society plays out this theme:

They are problem-oriented and the feelings and needs for growth of their captives and unenfranchised clientele are the least of their problems; for the status of the "teenager" in the community is so low that even if he rebels, the school is not blamed for the conditions against which he is rebelling. What high school personnel become specialists in, ultimately, is the *control* of large groups of students. (Friedenberg, 1965, pp. 92–93)

Twenty-five years later, as controlling school crime and meeting basic scholastic requirements have become dominant issues, Friedenberg's analysis remains timely. What is more, as public sympathy for troubled adolescents turns to public support for "getting tough" (e.g., through "Tough Love" programs), Friedenberg's words may come to be applied with equal validity to families and the models for parents.

In *Children Without Childhood* (1983), Marie Winn speaks of "The Myth of the Teenage Werewolf":

A pervasive myth has taken hold of parents' imagination these days, contributing to their feeling of being powerless to control the fates of their children: the myth of the teenage werewolf. Its message is that no matter how pleasant and sweet and innocent their child might be at the moment, how amiable and docile and friendly, come the first hormonal surge of puberty and the child will turn into an uncontrollable monster. (p. 14)

These images of adolescence contribute to the context in which the dynamics of adolescent problems take place, *and in which those who would respond clinically and/or in the policy domain must operate*. These images find their professional parallel in the widely held image of adolescence as necessarily "stormy and stressful" (*"sturm and drang"*) (Garbarino, et al., 1986). In this view, adolescents experience conflict and turmoil as a normal part of their development. Many who hold this view most strongly have studied or worked professionally with disturbed adolescents engaged in deviant behavior.

Along these lines, Anna Freud (1958) wrote of the difficulty of distinguishing normality from psychopathology in adolescence:

... adolescence constitutes by definition an interruption of peaceful growth which resembles in appearance a variety of other emotional upsets and structural upheavals. The adolescent manifestations come close to symptom formation of the neurotic, psychotic or dissocial order and merge almost imperceptibly into borderline states, initial, frustrated or fully fledged forms of almost all the mental illnesses. Consequently, the differential diagnosis between the adolescent upsets and true pathology becomes a difficult task. (p. 267)

This "period of upheaval" is a healthy, normal expression of development, but, during its term, adolescents will reject their parents (in response to the unacceptable desire to possess the opposite sex parent) and enter into a series of intense but brief romantic involvements with their peers (as they learn to accept and adapt to their new found sexuality).

This behavior will be perceived as "rebellion." It provides a theoretical explanation for the stereotyped view of adolescents as being necessarily "rebellious." Indeed, we should recall that Anna Freud (1958) saw the absence of such "structural upheavals" and "rebellious" activities as a serious indicator of pathology, as an adolescent problem that required clinical intervention.

Empirical surveys of the normal adolescent population have challenged the "teenagers are crazy" model, and consistently report that only about 20% of nonpatient adolescents report experiencing serious turmoil as they grow up (Balswick & Macrides, 1975; Bandura & Walters, 1959; Elmen & Offer, Chapter 1 of this volume). This is far short of the majority predicted by storm and stress theorists, and it tells us that we should be alert to families that are experiencing a high level of conflict, for it is not typical or "normal" to do so.

In their study of middle-class families of adolescent boys, Bandura and Walters (1959) found little evidence of storm and stress. When teenagers did exhibit aggressive behavior, such as fighting physically with their parents, it was found that these kids had presented the same problems as children; only when they became bigger and stronger could they overpower their parents (a finding to which we will return). Bandura and Walters concluded: "Our findings suggest . . . that the behavioral characteristics exhibited by children during the so-called adolescent stage are lawfully related to, and consistent with, pre-adolescent behavior" (Bandura, 1963, p. 196). Subsequent research tends to confirm this conclusion (Ebata, 1986).

The general conclusion that profound conflict and turmoil across all life's domains is not the typical pattern of development for adolescents receives support from other studies of nonclinical populations (Grinker, Grinker, & Timberlake, 1962; Hamburg, Coelho, & Adams, 1964; Oldham, 1978;). The data seem to fairly well establish that the typical adolescent is *not* one who is experiencing far-reaching psychic disturbance as a matter of predetermined developmental course. No period in the human life-course is totally free from stress and conflict; adolescents have no monopoly on storm and stress, any more than toddlers or middle agers do.

All of this tells us that seriously troubled youth should be taken seriously, and that the behaviors that give rise to concern among sympathetic adults and peers are usually indicators of genuinely serious problems, often problems of family breakdown associated with the special challenges of adolescence (Jaffe & Tolan, 1989). It also tells us that social policy should insist on a "nonpathological" model for understanding and responding to "political" conflicts between adults and adolescents, that is, social policy should recognize these as conflicts over power and treat them accordingly. Negotiation, not incarceration or therapy, is the appropriate response when families are in conflict over substantive value issues. Similarly, clinical services may be an inappropriate response to many situations to which we as a society currently apply them (e.g., conflicts between adolescents and parents about housekeeping rules and standards for sexual conduct). This is the rationale for growing concern that psychologically normal adolescents involved in power struggles with parents or other adults are being inappropriately dealt with in the mental health system. A parallel approach was applied to adults in the Soviet Union, where professionals were all too ready to go along with the idea that to oppose the government was an indication of psychopathology.

Why Do Negative Stereotypes of Adolescence Persist?

Why is the myth of the teenage werewolf so durable? Why do negative stereotypes of adolescence continue? We do not know for sure, but several hypotheses are plausible. From a psychoanalytic perspective, we can hypothesize that the negative stereotype serves an important function for adults. It may act as a kind of defense mechanism by transferring onto adolescents responsibility for the envy that the no-longer-young feel for the sexuality and freedom of the young. It may also serve to justify the structures of social control that adults impose in schools and in families.

From an ecological perspective, these negative stereotypes are part of the larger macrosystems that legitimize and organize social relations (Bronfenbrenner, 1979; Garbarino et al., 1985). In this view, negative stereotypes of adolescence reflect a combination of factors: resistance to change in generational power distribution, naïve overgeneralization from the behavior of the "tumultuous" minority to the "continuous" majority of teenagers, and lack of empathy and absence of self-understanding on the part of adults who do not see the parallels between adolescent and adult behavior and who dismiss the "vulgarity" of adolescent portrayals and exhibitions of adult roles and behavior.

Whatever the source of these negative stereotypes, they do exist and they contribute to the problems of troubled youth in troubled families. They justify unresponsive parenting and exacerbate family conflict that is already serious. They also color and interpret the normal challenges to the family system that inhere in adolescence in modern societies. All told, they seriously complicate the task of developing and implementing appropriate policies for adolescent clinical services. To overcome this obstacle, we must see clearly the essential challenges faced by parents dealing with adolescents.

THE CHALLENGE OF BEING PARENT TO AN ADOLESCENT

What does adolescence mean for the family as a whole? For one thing, it means adjusting patterns of authority and interaction to incorporate a new person. Developmental psychologist John Hill (1980) looked at the research on this matter and concluded that studies where family interaction is directly observed suggest that there may be a period of temporary disequilibrium in early adolescence while the family adjusts to having a "new person" in the household—"new" in stature, "new" in approaching reproductive capability, "new" in cognitive competence. However, this disequilibrium in no way approaches the "shoot-out" that many parents are led to expect from media reports. Instead, in most families, there appears to be a period of adaptation to the primary changes, a period when both parents and their newly adolescent children work out, often not consciously, what these changes mean for their relationships (Hill, 1980, p. 33).

At its heart, the process of being parent to an adolescent (and adolescent to a parent) is substantially different from the parent–child relationship, in ways that have implications for policies regarding clinical services to adolescents (Garbarino et al., 1986; Garbarino & Gilliam, 1980). Adolescents are more powerful than children and this demands important (and often difficult) changes in parental behavior and attitude, away from measuring power in terms of simple obedience and toward measuring it in terms of internalized motivation to emulate the parent and seek desired behavior.

The adolescent's power is much greater than the child's. This includes physical power, of course, including the capability for physical retaliation if assaulted by a parent. The enhanced power that comes with adolescence accompanies that need to redefine family roles and is often a destabilizing force, particularly when parents and/or adolescents have little motive or facility for flexible negotiation and compromise. These changes in power and role set in motion challenges to the family. A family's success or failure in meeting these challenges depends in large measure on the character of the human ecology within which that family is embedded. Practitioners have long recognized that the service needs of children and adults differ markedly, with respect to issues of informed consent, placement, verbally mediated therapy, and other aspects of intervention. Placing adolescents on this continuum of maturity has proven even more difficult. This is particularly evident in our efforts to understand and deal with abuse and neglect. Most approaches differentiate between child abuse and spouse abuse but, until recently, few researchers, practitioners, or policy makers have addressed the differentiation of child abuse and neglect from adolescent maltreatment. However, both policy and services should reflect changes in the meaning, causes, correlates, and effects of mistreatment as a function of development and maturation (Cicchetti & Rizley, 1981; Garbarino et al., 1986).

The issues for school-age children differ from those for infants, or even for 3-year-olds, for that matter. The infant is a perfect victim, in two senses. First, the infant can do virtually nothing to protect itself from abuse and is totally defenseless against neglect. The battered baby is victimized in direct proportion to the parent's impulses and the presence of internal and external constraints (which are often few). The infant experiences neglect in exact proportion to the parent's failure to provide care, thus being liable to nonorganic failure to thrive. What is more, the infant's capacity to signal its plight to others is limited and largely unconscious. Second, the infant is perfectly blameless when victimized. There is no issue of culpability raised, as there often is when the victim of assault is a spouse or an adolescent.

In contrast to infants, school-age children have better resources. They can adapt to the parent, to minimize abuse, by assuming whatever role will appease the parent, for example, by being extremely compliant, innocuous, or responsible. They can counteract neglect by fending for themselves to some degree. Their ability to communicate their plight is greater because of language skills, and attending school offers many opportunities to do so. Finally, they are likely to have larger independent social networks from which to draw nurturance, support, and protection. However, what they gain in power, they lose in credibility as a victim. This sort of developmental contrast is essential when we consider adolescent maltreatment. Developmental shifts and changes in social expectations for caregiving and socialization come together to displace the standards that guide appropriate behavior in family relationships when a child reaches adolescence. Some forms of behavior by parents toward their offspring, which were appropriate (if not particularly wise) in childhood, may become abusive in adolescence. For example, the psychological connotations and behavioral response to spanking a 3- or 4-year old ("control through force") are usually different from those of spanking a 15-year-old. Likewise, a permissive policy of "control through indulgence" that is possible in response to the child's relatively benign impulses may become untenable in adolescence, when even the most permissive parent cannot fully indulge the more powerful impulses of the adolescent. Managing every detail of a 4-year-old's daily existence ("control through intrusion") may be acceptable, but the same intrusiveness with a teenager would be entirely inappropriate and is likely to produce a strong adverse reaction leading to family conflict.

Adolescents typically demand a more nearly equal role in family decision making. Observational research presents a picture of the youth challenging the parents (particularly the father) and aspiring to a more active role in leading family discussions and decision making (Steinberg & Hill, 1980).

These factors, combined with differences in our culture's suspicious view of adolescents and in our institutional treatment of them with little compassion, suggest that the phenomenon of adolescent maltreatment will differ from child abuse. In fact, in their interpersonal dynamics and cultural interpretation, such destructive relations may more closely resemble spouse abuse than the mistreatment of children. Efforts to understand adolescent maltreatment may serve as a bridge to constructing a much needed, general life-course theory of domestic violence, one that can integrate policy and services in this area.

A Life-Course Perspective

Figure 20.1 places abused adolescents on a circular continuum relating abused wives, mistreated children, and abused elders. The central issue is power, the ability to determine one's own behavior and influence the actions of others. Children and the frail elderly are nearly powerless (although their behavior can have a significant effect on what happens to them). Teenagers gain power because adolescence brings increases in the ability to think, argue, and act. Just as wives in a patriarchal and sexist society can be powerful enough to threaten the authority of husbands, teenagers can challenge parental authority. Paradoxically, because children and the elderly are powerless, they are "perfect" victims, for two reasons: they are easily victimized, and

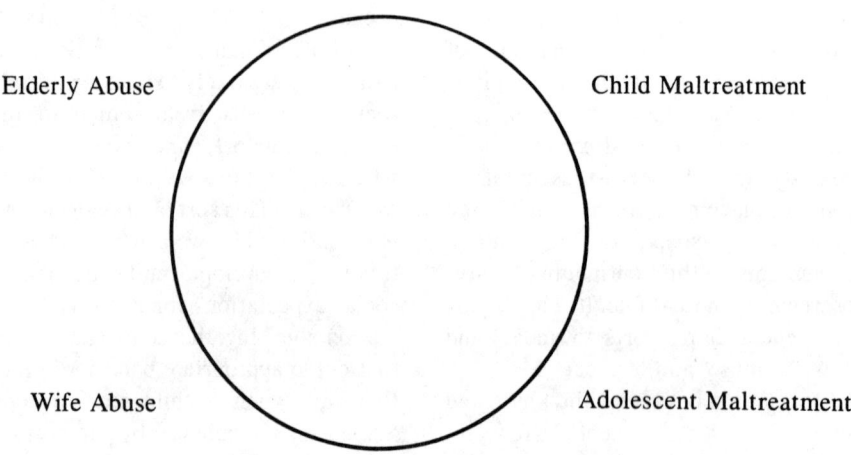

Figure 20.1 A life-course continuum of maltreatment.

they elicit sympathy once they are abused. Teenagers are closer to wives in being imperfect victims, in both respects.

One evidence of the greater power of abused teens and wives is the fact that they sometimes are involved in reciprocal assault (Browne, 1987; Post, 1982). Children and the elderly cannot match the strength of the parent generation, but abuse has been identified as a contributing factor in many assaults by adolescents, from relatively minor incidents to parricide (Garbarino & Gilliam, 1980). Wives who kill their husbands are often retaliating for abuse, usually as the culmination of a long period of mutual assault in which wives are the chronic losers. Straus, Gelles, and Steinmetz (1980) reported assault by youth against their parents in some 10% of American families. The likeness between adolescent and wife abuse extends beyond these power dynamics. The two groups are likely to face similar psychodynamic issues, including ambivalence about dependency and separation in their relationships with family authority figures. For example, both may engage in repeated attempts to flee the home, only to return when the challenges of independent living and/or the pain of separation is too great.

The Role of Social Context in Precipitating Adolescent Problems

Being a child in a highly stressful environment can lead to long-term mental health concerns, even when the child has access to parental protection in the short term. For example, Elder (1980) found that the effects of having been a child during the Great Depression of the 1930s in the United States were often seen decades later in the life-course of adults.

What is more, children forced to cope with chronic danger may adapt in ways that are dysfunctional in any "normal" situations in which they are expected to participate, such as in school. Being tough and belligerently aggressive may be adaptive on the playground of a gang-dominated school, but it may be maladaptive inside the classroom, where a cooperative and obedient approach is the best route to success. What is more, youth in situations of chronic threat of violence may find they can best defend themselves by becoming hyperaggressive; however, in so doing, they become a danger to the next generation of children and psychologically diminished individuals (a social cost that transcends the cost to the community of being plagued with overtly and uncontrollably violent individuals in its midst).

The same can be true of parents. Their adaptations to dangerous environments may produce child-rearing strategies that impede normal development, as in the case of a mother who doesn't allow her child to play on the floor because there is poison on the floor to kill the rats that infest the apartment, but who, in doing so, may deprive the child of important opportunities for exploratory play. The parent who prohibits the child from playing outside, for fear of shooting accidents, may be denying the child a chance to engage in social and athletic play, as an undesirable side effect of protecting the child from assault. Or, the parent of an adolescent in a dangerous environment may feel the need to resort to draconian measures of discipline and control, to keep the teenager from falling prey to the drugs, violence, exploitative and irresponsible sex, and crime that lie just outside the door. In all three of these examples, the adaptation is well intentioned, but its side effects may be detrimental in the long run. The onus here, of course, is on the social forces that create and sustain danger in the family's environment.

In addition, early adaptation may lead to a process of "identification with the aggressor," in which children model themselves and their behavior on those powerful aggressive individuals and groups in their environment who cause the danger in the first place (e.g., gangs in public housing projects and enemy soldiers under conditions of occupation). Children and youth exposed to the stress of extreme violence (such as was the case in Cambodia) may reveal mental health disturbances years after the immediate experience is over (Goleman, 1986). Recent longitudinal analyses of the impact of divorce on children reveal a similar "sleeper effect," with life adjustment problems emerging 10 or more years after family dissolution (Wallerstein, 1989).

ADOLESCENTS AS SOCIAL WEATHER VANES: THE ROLE OF IDEOLOGY

The quality of life for young children—and their reservoirs of resilience—is a "social indicator" of the balance of social supports for parents and parental capacity to buffer social stress in the lives of children (Guttman & Seeley, 1986). This hypothesis emerges from a wide range of research and clinical observation, including Anna Freud's work with children in England during World War II. It finds validation in other studies of World War II, where the level of emotional upset displayed by adults in a child's life, not the war situation itself, was most important in predicting the child's response (Garbarino, Kostelny, & Dubrow, 1991).

Some observers point to the importance of ideological factors in sustaining the ability to function under extreme stress. In his observations of life in Nazi concentration camps, Bettelheim (1943) notes that those who bore up best were those with intense ideological commitments (most notably, the ultrareligious and the communists), commitments that offered meaning impervious to day-to-day brutalization. Contemporary research has offered further documentation of this finding; a recent study in Israel reported that ultra-orthodox Jews were suffering less from stress as a result of the current Palestinian uprising than were most secular Jews (Pines, 1989). Ideology is a psychological resource, even while it may be an impediment to political settlement.

This ideological dimension emerges repeatedly in accounts of families under stress. Political and religious interpretation can play an important role in shaping the consequences of experience, particularly when held to with "fanatic" intensity, which is often required to defend against the crushing weight of reality in a concentration camp, a prison, or a refugee camp.

Punamaki (1987) saw exactly this process at work among Palestinians under occupation and in refugee camps, where every feature of day-to-day stress and physical deprivation is met with a process of ideological response that mobilizes social and psychological resources:

[T]he psychological processes of healing the traumatic experiences drew strength from political and ideological commitment. Nationalistic motivation was present at all stages of the stress process: The meaning and harmfulness of an event as well as sufficiency of one's own resources to cope with stressors were approached in the wider social and political context of a victimized and struggling nation. (Punamaki, 1987, pp. 82–83)

The concept of determined struggle to persist (*"sumud"*) figures prominently in analyses of Palestinian culture and community life (Grossman, 1988), and in the resilience of children in the face of awesome stress, such as was experienced by Palestinian families under siege in the refugee camps in Lebanon (Cutting, 1988).

This is evident even more clearly with respect to the psychosocial development of adolescents because as development proceeds, the child is less and less dependent on the narrow confines of the parent–child relationship. More and more, the child lives in response to the world beyond the family.

A hypothesis that emerges from a review of the available evidence suggests that adolescents function as a kind of "social weather vane." The normal issues of adolescence, particularly as they are played out in identity formation, get bound up in the ideological events of the society in which those young people are growing to maturity. There is increasing recognition among developmental psychologists that where one is developmentally has a lot to do with how and how much historical events in the society and the community influence one's personal development. For example, Stewart and Healy

(1989) found that the effects of changed roles for American women during World War II "took" for women who "came of age" during the war, to a larger degree than for their younger or older counterparts.

This leads to the idea that social history is more important for adolescents than for other age groups because developmental outcomes for adolescents depend on the ideologically driven activities available in the community and the larger society, as well as the day-to-day character of the infrastructure for families. It suggests that adolescents encounter social conditions and culture more directly than do young children and that adolescents incorporate social events into their repertoire of "identity alternatives" and then use them as resources in forming a coherent identity in early adulthood (Stewart & Healy, 1989).

The openness to social redefinition that accompanies role changes at the heart of normal adolescence makes adolescents acutely susceptible to ideology as an influence on development and identity—and specially able to make use of it as a personal resource and as a source of resilience (Elder, 1980). This is evident over and over again, as young people are the vehicles for social movements. We have seen this in the United States, for example, in the civil rights movement, where Black youth (and, to some degree, their White peers) found personal meaning through social action. Discussions held with mental health professionals dealing with Palestinian adolescents suggest a diminution of mental health problems being expressed in delinquent behavior when political activities provide a socially legitimate role for rebellion as an expression of positive identity (Garbarino, Kostelny, & Dubrow, 1991).

We think of adolescence as being a time for focusing on the here and now, on the present; yet, the relation of the present to the future is very important to most adolescents (Garbarino et al., 1985; Tolan, 1988). In social movements and ideology, they seek to find a path to meaningfulness that fits into individual identity. Thus, one measure, perhaps *the* measure, of a "good society" for adolescents lies in its capacity to provide constructive social movements—movements that assist young people in developing identity without exploiting that need, to serve narrow political or economic interests.

Evaluation of the legitimacy of the social movements to which adolescents are attracted is a matter for students of social policy, historians, political scientists, and moralists. Nonetheless, the psychological dynamic seems clear. Ideology plays to identity, and adolescent energy is mobilized through dramatic action that engages the critical process of identity formation. This returns our attention to the importance of community context in understanding the role and significance of social policy as it affects the need for and direction of adolescent clinical services.

A COMMUNITY ORIENTATION

We must recognize the policy issues that arise from community variations in adolescent experience. A colleague was fond of saying, "No one lives in the United States. People live in Omaha, or Louisville, or the South Side of Chicago . . . ." He meant that, although there are some national effects, the actual experience of adolescents comes from the community they live in. Some effects come from the state, and some even come from the neighborhood.

As an example of how dramatic those community effects can be, it is often reported that identical twins grow up with very similar IQ scores. What often isn't reported is that identical twins growing up in very dissimilar communities end up much less similar than identical twins growing up in similar communities. The correlation between their IQ scores is more like .2 or .3 (not a strong relationship) than .8 or .9 (a very strong relationship) (Bronfenbrenner, 1979). Even something as fundamental as how one's genetic heritage is expressed in IQ can appear quite different between people who grow up in different communities.

In a sense, we live in one world; we live in one society; we live in 50 states. But we really live in over 3,000 communities because there are more than 3,000 counties in the United States. Those community variations are important, particularly in the area of clinical services to adolescents, where county-based systems dominate the scene (even when formal authority lies with a statewide system).

When we move beyond these issues, we come up against some policy questions. The number-one policy question is: Where shall we set the minimum standard of care for adolescents? The process of setting that standard is a negotiation between professional expertise and scientific knowledge, on one hand, and community standards, values, or culture, on the other. We are constantly renegotiating that statement.

The second policy question is related to the first: Will we allow social class (or, more properly, poverty/low income) to determine basic life prospects? The power of low income in predicting infant and child morbidity, child abuse, and other forms of developmental pathology is not a given fact (Garbarino, Dubrow, Kostelny, & Pardo, 1992). In some communities and societies, it is a much more powerful predictor than in others. In most European countries, low income is a much less powerful predictor of child outcome than it is in the United States. In our research of child abuse rates, for example, we found that social class/low income is a very powerful predictor of the amount of child abuse and neglect in neighborhoods within American cities.

Why? One key is whether having a low income means lack of access or lack of utilization of basic prenatal and postnatal health care. Many observers have reported that the link between low income and access to services is much stronger here than it is in other "modern industrial" societies (Garbarino, Dubrow, Kostelny, & Pardo, 1992).

The question of policy then becomes: Will we allow low income to be a powerful predictor of child mortality, morbidity, and pathology? It is quite one thing to say social class is a powerful predictor of life-style—whether one drinks white wine, watches PBS, or eats brie, for example. It's acceptable to have those kinds of cultural differences linked to socioeconomic differences. But the policy question we have to face is this: Should those same socioeconomic differences predict the odds of having a child die in the first year of life, having a child be born with a disability, having a child who fails in school, and having a child who is likely to be the victim of child maltreatment?

WHAT IS OUR COMMITMENT TO SOLVING ADOLESCENT PROBLEMS?

What is our commitment toward adolescent problems, particularly those linked to abuse and neglect? This statement of commitment, and the policy it represents, may serve as a kind of litmus test for policy makers. Some say: "We would like to prevent a lot of abuse, but preventing all child abuse would require living in a prison-like society, and we don't want that." The irony here is that all the settings in America that are the most abusive most resemble our prisons (which are the most abusive environments in our society). Is the prison the model for a preventive society? Is it such an invasion of privacy to say that every pregnant person in America—particularly every pregnant teenager—should have a home health visitor who is acting in a supportive role and who represents the community? An alternative to this regulatory orientation is to focus on promoting the social and familial supports that enhance family and adolescent development and coping (Combrinck-Graham, 1989).

What Is a Support System?

This leads to another policy question: Do we have the will to implement full-fledged family support systems to protect children from becoming problematic adolescents? When we say "support systems," we go back to Gerald Caplan's formulation, in the mental health movement 30 years ago, that a support system combines nurturance and feedback. It is not simply the giving of resources, of strokes, or nurturance; they must be coupled with feedback, guidance, and information.

In David Olds's study, those same home health visitors who were providing nurturance and support to teen parents were also providing feedback. In several cases, they persuaded young pregnant women that there was no way on Earth that they would be able to care adequately for their child, and they negotiated a settlement that led to an adoptive placement at birth for some of those newborns as a way of preventing later harm. These are really support systems: they provided nurturance and feedback in the same relationship.

The villain is social isolation, in the form of isolation from prosocial support systems. Some of those support systems are the natural corrective mechanisms of day-to-day life that one has in relationship with people; others require deliberate intervention to produce.

The Price of Privacy

Decades ago, people said that the idea that the state could compel people to register their children for school or could set a minimum age for leaving was an intrusion on family privacy. It was un-American, and it threatened the fabric of our society. Each policy issue must be evaluated in regard to its perceived threat to privacy. For example, the AIDS crisis brings up the same questions again.

We are in a helpless, hopeless crunch until we develop an ideology that says the community is really responsible for all children and adolescents. That ideological bind comes into focus as we look closely at the problem of adolescent maltreatment, a problem that is correlated with most of the clinical problems facing adolescents in contemporary North America (Garbarino et al., 1986).

POLICY CONSIDERATIONS IN DEVELOPING CLINICAL SERVICES FOR ADOLESCENTS IN TROUBLE

Drawing on the available research, we are now in a position to put forth a series of proposals concerning the direction for clinical services to adolescents in trouble, particularly where that trouble is linked dynamically to maltreatment. Each proposal is based on an attempt to synthesize existing findings.

1. Programs should target adolescent maltreatment because adolescent maltreatment figures prominently in the dynamics of troubled youth. Troubled youth are disproportionately likely to become future perpetrators (if they are not already, as teen parents). We cannot justify the current disregard for adolescent victims that is evident in service delivery systems. Adolescent victims are numerous, and they exhibit many signs of harm (Burgdorff, 1980).

2. Some adolescent problems are simply a continuation of problems (like abuse and neglect) begun in childhood; others represent the deterioration of unwise childhood patterns or the inability of a family that functioned well in childhood to meet new challenges in adolescence. The proportion of adolescent problems in the two categories (child vs. adolescent onset) varies from study to study (based in part, it seems, on difference in definition and/or sampling). This is evident with respect to abuse and neglect. Lourie (1977) concluded that 90% of adolescent abuse cases begin in adolescence. In Libby and Bybee's study (1979), 80% were so described. Garbarino and Gilliam (1980) reported a 50-50 split. Pelcovitz, Kaplan, Samit, Krieger, and Cornelius (1984) reported a 57% adolescent onset. According to Farber and Joseph (1986), 29% displayed adolescent onset, and 51% began in childhood but became qualitatively more severe in adolescence (21% were severe through childhood into adolescence). Berdie, Berdie, Wexler and Fisher (1983) concluded that 24% of their adolescent cases began in adolescence.

Taken together, the existing studies tell us that there is a distinctly adolescent genesis in a significant number of adolescent problems linked to family dysfunction. This means that our preventive efforts must not be limited to programs and policies aimed exclusively at infancy and early childhood. They should address the special issues that are involved in the transition from childhood to adolescence (e.g., negotiated role transitions in families). Thus, for example, the late elementary and early junior high school period is a high-priority period for interventions that teach nonviolent conflict resolution skills to both parents and youth.

3. Adolescents at high risk for maltreatment and other family problems linked to clinical intervention are less socially competent and exhibit more developmental problems than their peers. Therefore, prevention programs must respond to the additive and interactive nature of adolescent maltreatment (i.e., that adolescence may be precipitating and/or exacerbating patterns of difficulty rooted in childhood). Most studies comment on the aversive and/or dysfunctional character of the adolescent victim of maltreatment. Libby and Bybee (1979) reported that, in more than 90% of the cases they studied, specific abusive incidents were preceded by negative adolescent behavior (such as disobeying or arguing). Was this negative behavior the result of earlier maltreatment? The studies do not provide clear evidence on this score; none offers the kind of prospective, longitudinal design that would be necessary. In a general way, parents are responsible for the outcomes evidenced by their children. However, it is undeniable that maltreatment is not the sole source of problematic development in children. Temperamental problems, parent–child mismatches, negative extrafamilial influences, and genetic predisposition to pathology all play a role. Although we cannot be confident about the pattern of causation, the pattern of association is evident. Preventing adolescent maltreatment involves helping parents (and other adults) work effectively and nonabusively with troubled and troublesome teenagers.

Berdie et al. (1983) reported that 49% of their adolescent maltreatment victims exhibited significant clinical indicators of depression. Problems such as nervous habits, isolation, poor social skills with peers, lethargy, low self-esteem, low frustration tolerance, temper outbursts, and stubbornness characterized from 45% to 70% of the adolescents (depending on which problem is being considered in the analysis).

Garbarino et al. (1986) used the Child Behavior Checklist to assess the presence of problems in abused adolescents. Having selected a sample to maximize the presence of such problems (the overall group's score is at the 85th percentile on such problems), the important finding is in the contrast between maltreated and nonmaltreated youth. The abused group was significantly more problem-ridden (the 90th versus the 80th percentiles), evidencing between 50% and 100% more problems (depending on the type of problems being considered and the source of the report). The difference was greater for externalizing problems (acting out) than for internalizing problems (e.g., somatic complaints, obsessive-compulsive behavior, withdrawal). Programming and policy that are aimed at adolescent maltreatment should be a high priority for institutions serving adolescents who evidence developmental problems. These youth are the principal high-risk group to be targeted for preventive and protective intervention.

4. Families most likely to generate adolescent problems such as maltreatment are characterized as being at high risk on the dimensions of adaptability, cohesion, support, discipline, and interparental conflict. Therefore, prevention programs and clinical services should adopt a broadly based approach to supporting and redirecting family systems. However, these programs should recognize that, in some cases, servicing the family may be untenable, and direct services to support the adolescent as an independent individual may be the most practical approach.

Libby and Bybee (1979) reported that 13 of their 25 cases of adolescent maltreatment could be characterized as "reasonably well-functioning families who had recently been under stress." The other 12 cases were characterized by "psychopathology or disturbed behavior by either the adolescent or parents." Few cases seemed to be attributable to the high stress/social isolation syndrome that is characteristic of many child maltreatment families. In contrast, Berdie et al. (1983) concluded that "adolescent maltreatment families, like many child maltreatment families, are multi-problem families with high rates of divorce and separation, financial stresses and family conflict." Farber and Joseph (1986) omitted direct comment on family functioning, but reported that an analysis of adolescent problems did not find differences based on Lourie's classification of maltreatment types (with its implicit classification of families).

Pelcovitz et al. (1984) conducted a clinical analysis of their 22 adolescent maltreatment families. They classified cases into childhood and adolescent onset. The 8 childhood-onset families (14 adolescents) were characterized in the multiproblem child abuse mode; that is, they manifested intergenerational abuse, spouse abuse, and developmentally inappropriate demands—all elements of what Helfer and Kempe (1976) termed "the world of abnormal rearing." The 14 adolescent-onset families (19 adolescents) fell into two categories on the basis of multiple, independent clinical assessments: 7 "authoritarian" and 7 "overindulgent."

The authoritarian families were characterized by paternalistic, harsh, rigid, domineering styles of child rearing. This was coupled with denial of parental feelings toward each other and about the family system. Abuse typically arose from adolescent challenge (acting out and testing behavior), which was met with overwhelming force. The high priority placed on control provided the foundation for high levels of force.

In contrast, the overindulgent families were characterized by parental efforts to compensate for the emotional deprivation that they had experienced in their own childhood (12 of the 14 parents had lost one or both of their parents during childhood). These families made few demands on their children, set few limits, and desired a high level of emotional gratification from them. When the children reached adolescence and sought to form primary attachments outside the home or began to act impulsively in important social settings, the overindulgent parents reacted with excessive force.

Garbarino et al., (1986) contrasted the family system of families judged to be abusive with that of families judged to be nonabusive. They used an assessment of family adaptability and cohesion (FACES) to evaluate the overall interaction. Abusive families tended to score in the "chaotic" and "enmeshed" categories (on adaptability and cohesion, respectively). Nonabusive families' lower scores on these scales put them in the more normal "flexible" and "connected" range. On a measure of interparental conflict, adolescents in the abusive families tended to rate their parents as evidencing more conflict. However, the average difference masks the fact that some abusive families evidenced extremely high conflict while others evidenced extremely low conflict. This pattern was evident in a 2-year follow-up in which it appeared that some families dealt with conflict by expelling the adolescent, and others simply suppressed all manifestations of conflict through a conspiracy of silence.

Adolescents in the abusive families tended to describe their parents as being much more punishing. This tendency was also found in an assessment of attitudes and values concerning punishment, the Adolescent Abuse Inventory (AAI), which measures risk for abuse (Sebes, 1983) and taps parental commitment to abusive versus nonabusive responses toward adolescent behavior. An analysis that defined any family with at least one parent in the top quartile of risk (based on AAI score) correctly classified as abusive or nonabusive 100% of the families that had been so described on the basis of the adolescent's comparable description of self (Sebes, 1983). It correctly identified 85% using the descriptions of outside observers. An assessment of stressful life changes indicated 50% more recent changes in the lives of adolescents in abusive families than in nonabusive families.

Adolescent maltreatment is most likely to arise when troubled youth lives within a high-risk family. In part, we should direct our efforts toward identifying family patterns in childhood that bode ill for effective adjustment to adolescence. Overindulgence and authoritarianism are the two patterns that appear most frequently in the existing research. Parent education programs should seek to identify these high-risk patterns in childhood and redirect them toward more adaptive patterns that cast neither the child nor the parent in a dictatorial role, but rather establish norms and practices of reciprocal negotiation that evolve from appropriate use of parental authority. This will help to pave the way for an effective transition to adolescence. In part, also, intervention programs should focus on the adolescent period itself. They should stress the normal demands for adaptation that adolescence brings for youth and adults alike. Effective conflict resolution and communication skills will provide the foundation for accomplishing this important process of adaptation and preventing the deterioration of parent–child relations that results in adolescent maltreatment.

These are the keys to a social policy approach that can prevent adolescent problems: effective intervention in child abuse, to stop developmental deterioration into adolescence; effective intervention with troubled adolescents, to prevent them from exceeding parental coping capacity; and promulgation of nonviolent conflict resolution skills, as part of a broad campaign to improve family functioning in adolescence.

REFERENCES

American Humane Association. (1982). *Annual report of the national study of child abuse and neglect reporting.* Denver, CO: Author.

Balswick, J. O., & Macrides, C. (1975). Parental stimulus for adolescent rebellion. *Adolescence, 10,* 253–266.

Bandura, A. and Walters, R. (1959). *Adolescent aggression.* New York: Ronald.

Bandura, A. (1973). Aggression: A social learning analysis. Englewood Cliffs, N.J.: Prentice Hall.

Berdie, J., Berdie, M., Wexler, S., & Fisher, B. (1983). *An empirical study of families involved in adolescent maltreatment.* San Francisco: URSA Institute.

Bettelheim, B. (1943). Individual and mass behavior in extreme situations. *Abnormal & social psychology, 38,* 417–452.

Bronfenbrenner, U. (1979). *The ecology of human development.* Cambridge, MA: Harvard University Press.

Browne, A. (1987). *When battered women kill.* New York: Free Press.

Burgdorff, K. (1980, December). *Recognition and reporting of child maltreatment: Findings from the national incidence and severity of child abuse and neglect.* Prepared for the National Center on Child Abuse and Neglect, Washington, DC.

Burgess, B., & Garbarino, J. (1983). Doing what comes naturally? An evolutionary perspective on child abuse. In D. Finkelhor, R. Gelles, G. Hataling, & M. Straus (Eds.), *The dark side of families* (pp. 88–101). Beverly Hills, CA: Sage.

Caplan, G. (1974). *Support systems and community mental health.* New York: Behavioral Publications.

Cicchetti, D., & Rizley, R. (1981). Developmental perspectives on the etiology, intergenerational transmission, and sequelae of child maltreatment. *New Directions for Child Development, 11,* 31–52.

Combrinck-Graham, L. (Ed.) (1989). *Children in family contexts.* New York: Guilford Press.

Daly, M., & Wilson, M. (1981). Child maltreatment in sociobiological perspective. *New Directions for Child Development, 11,* 93–112.

Douvan, E., & Adelson, J. (1966). *The adolescent experience.* New York: Wiley.

Ebata, A. (1986). *Stability of depression in early adolescence.* Unpublished doctoral dissertation, Pennsylvania State University.

Elder, G. (1980). Adolescence in historical perspective. In J. Adelson (Ed.) *Handbook of adolescent psychology.* (pp. 3–46). New York: John Wiley.

Farber, E., & Joseph, J. (1986). The maltreated adolescent: Patterns of physical abuse. *Child Abuse and Neglect, 10,* 211–221.

Farber, E., McCoard, W. D., Kinast, C., & Falkner, D. (1984). Violence in the families of adolescent runaways. *Child Abuse and Neglect, 8,* 295–300.

Finkelhor, D. (1979). *Sexually victimized children.* New York: Free Press.

Friedenberg, E. Z. (1959). *The vanishing adolescent.* Boston: Beacon Press.

Friedenberg, E. Z. (1965). *The dignity of youth and other atavisms.* Boston: Beacon Press.

Freud, A. (1958). Adolescence. *Psychoanalytic Study of the Child, 13,* 255–278.

Garbarino, J., Dubrow, N., Kostelny, K. & Pardo, C. (1992). Children in danger: Coping with the consequences of community violence. San Francisco: Jossey-Bass Publishers.

Garbarino, J., & Gilliam, G. (1980). *Understanding abusive families.* Lexington, MA: Lexington Books.

Garbarino, J., Kelley, A., & Schulenberg, J. (1985). Adolescence: An introduction. In J. Garbarino & Associates (Eds.), Garbarino, J., Abramowitz, R., Ebata, A., Galambos, N., Gamble, W., Garbarino, A., Kaus, C., Kelly, A., Schellenbach, C., Schulenberg, J., Sebes, J., Vondra, J. *Adolescent development: An ecological perspective* Columbus, OH: Merrill.

Garbarino, J., Kostelny, K. & Dubrow, N. (1991). *No place to be a child: growing up in a war zone.* New York: Lexington (Free Press).

Garbarino, J., Schellenbach, C., Sebes, J., & Associates. (1986). *Troubled youth, troubled families.* New York: Aldine.

Helfer, R., & Kempe, C. H. (1976). *Child abuse and neglect: The family and the community.* Cambridge, MA: Ballinger.

Hill, J. P. (1980). The family. In M. Johnson (Ed.), *Seventy-ninth yearbook of the National Society for the Study of Education.* Chicago: University of Chicago Press.

Jaffe, C., & Tolan, P. H. (1989). Research and the adolescent psychotherapist. Manuscript submitted for publication. (Available from Tolan at Department of Psychology, DePaul University, 2219 N. Kenmore, Chicago, IL 60614.)

Kalter, N. (1977). Children of divorce in an outpatient psychiatric population. *American Journal of Orthopsychiatry, 47,* 40–51.

Libby, P., & Bybee, R. (1979). The physical abuse of adolescents. *Journal of Social Issues, 35,* 101–126.

Lourie, I. (1977). The phenomenon of the abused adolescent: A clinical study. *Victimology, 2,* 268–276.

Morgan, R. (1977). The battered adolescent: A developmental approach to identification and intervention. *Child Abuse and Neglect, 1,* 343–348.

Offer, D. (1969). *The psychological world of the teenager: A study of normal adolescent boys.* New York: Basic Books.

Offer, D., & Offer, J. (1973). Normal adolescence in perspective. In J. C. Schoolar (Ed.), *Current issues in adolescent psychiatry.* New York: Brunner/Mazel.

Offer, D., & Offer, J. D. (1974). Normal adolescent males: The high school and college years. *Journal of the American College Health Association, 22,* 209–215.

Offer, D., & Offer, J. D. (1975). *From teenager to young manhood: A psychological study.* New York: Basic Books.

Oldham, D. G. (1978). Adolescent turmoil: A myth revisited. In S. C. Feinstein & P. L. Gioracchini (Eds.), *Adolescent Psychiatry, 6,* 10–21.

Olds, P. et. al. (1986). Preventing child abuse. *Pediatrics, 78*(1), 65–78.

Olsen, L., & Holmes, W. (1983). *Youth at risk: Adolescents and maltreatment.* Boston, MA: Center for Applied Social Research.

Pelcovitz, D., Kaplan, S., Samit, C., Krieger, R., & Cornelius, P. (1984). Adolescent abuse: Family structure and implications for treatment. *Journal of Child Psychiatry, 23,* 85–90.

Pines, R. (1989). Why do Israelis burn out? Paper presented at the International Conference on

Psychological Stress and Adjustment. Tel Aviv, Israel.

Post, S. (1982). Adolescent parricide in abusive families. *Child Welfare, 61,* 445–455.

Punamaki, R. (1987, April). Psychological stress responses of Palestinian mothers and their children in conditions of military occupation and political violence. *Quarterly newsletter of the Laboratory of Comparative Human Cognition.* 9(2), 76–84.

Reid, J. (1986). Social interactional patterns in families of abused and non-abused children. In C. Waxler & M. Radke-Yarrow (Eds.), *Social and biological origins of altruism and aggression.* Cambridge, England: Cambridge University Press.

Rutter, M., Graham, P., Chadwick, O. F. D., & Yule, W. (1976). Adolescent turmoil: Fact or fiction? *Journal of Child Psychology and Psychiatry, 17,* 35–36.

Sebes, J. M. (1983). *Determining risk for abuse in families with adolescents: The development of a criterion measure.* Unpublished doctoral dissertation, Pennsylvania State University.

Steinberg, L., & Hill, J. (1980). Family interaction patterns during early adolescence. In R. Muuss (Ed.), *Adolescent behavior and society: A book of readings* (3rd ed.). New York: Random House.

Stewart, A., & Healy, J. (1989). Linking individual development and social change. *American Psychologist, 44,* 30–43.

Straus, M., & Gelles, R. (1986). Societal change and change in family violence from 1975–1985 as revealed in two national surveys. *Journal of Marriage and the Family, 48,* 465–479.

Straus, M., Gelles, R., & Steinmetz, S. (1980). *Behind closed doors.* New York: Doubleday.

Tolan, P. H. (1988). Delinquent behaviors and male adolescent development: A preliminary study. *Journal of Youth and Adolescence, 17,* 413–427.

Trainor, C. (1984). *A description of officially reported adolescent maltreatment and its implications for policy and practice.* Denver, CO: American Humane Association.

Vondra, J. (1986). Socioeconomic stress and family functioning in adolescence. In J. Garbarino, C. Schellenbach, J. Sebes, Ebata, A., Garbarino, A., Guerncy, L., Guttmann, E., Kelly, A., Krejei, M., Mikesell, J., Plants, M., Wilson, J., & Vondra, J. (Eds.), *Troubled youth, troubled families* (pp. 191–234). New York: Aldine.

Weiner, I. B. (1970). *Psychological disturbance in adolescence.* New York: Wiley.

Westley, W. A., & Elkin, F. (1956). The protective environment and adolescent socialization. *Social Forces, 35,* 243–249.

Winn, M. (1983). *Children without childhood.* New York: Penguin.

CHAPTER 21

Tomorrow's Adolescent: Life-Course, Psychopathology, and Prevention

BERTRAM J. COHLER and PATRICK H. TOLAN

Over three decades ago, the British novelist and social philosopher C. P. Snow (1959) wrote of his concerns regarding the two cultures of science and the humanities, and of escalating problems in relating science to everyday affairs. Snow's concerns were focused particularly on the physical sciences, but a similar problem may be observed in the human sciences, where professional practice has become increasingly remote from the systematic study of lives over time. Those concerned with intervening with troubled persons often maintain that available systematic studies are of little immediate value in the effort to understand and intervene in personal distress. The practitioner's interest in findings that are clinically relevant is often greeted with skepticism by the scholar concerned with normative study of adjustment across the course of life.

These perceived conflicts, together with the assumption that systematic inquiry has little relevance for assessment and intervention, have led at least some investigators to turn away from concern with important clinical issues in the study of personality and mental health. Those involved in normative study sometimes maintain that study of personal psychopathology has little to do with understanding the course of life; too often distress is seen as extraordinary and little able to provide information regarding the expectable course of personality development. The present volume has attempted to realize enhanced integration of research and clinical intervention in the study of adolescence and psychological intervention across the adolescent decade. This volume shows that clinical and research issues mutually inform each other; systematic study of the adolescent decade both enhances understanding of troubled adolescent lives and, reciprocally, is enriched by study of troubled lives. Ultimately, this integration of clinical and normative study will be important both in enhanced understanding of the adolescent decade and the place of adolescence within the course of life, (Hogan & Astone, 1986; Modell, 1989; Modell, Furstenberg & Hershberg, 1978) and in providing additional modes of intervention in personal distress across the adolescent decade, which will be of particular value in working with tomorrow's adolescent as we move toward an increasingly complex and diverse society in the 21st century.

ADOLESCENCE, GENERATION, AND LIFE-COURSE

Concepts of development and change in personality over time have been central in the systematic study of adolescence since G. Stanley

Hall's (1904) text first highlighted this phase of life. However, only within the past two decades has the study of adolescence been placed in a historical context emphasizing integration of life time and historical time (Dragastin & Elder, 1975; Elder, 1975a, 1980, 1990; Elder & Caspi, 1990; Boxer, Gershenson & Offer, 1984; Hareven, 1986). This study has shown that it is important to recognize variation in the impact of history on the course of development (Keniston, 1971).

Elder (1975b) emphasized the significance of the shift from the concept of life span to that of life-course in developmental social science: life span implies an ordered, cyclical sequence, and life-course reflects an open system. The life-course perspective acknowledges the significance of social and historical change, understanding lives over time within the context of expectable and eruptive life changes that are important in comprehending both personal adjustment and the onset of distress. A life-course emphasis is consistent with contemporary study of personality and psychological development, which emphasizes the importance of studying change rather than continuity in personality over time. This emphasis is also consistent with contemporary social science perspectives regarding the extent to which socially determined factors are important in the construction of the life story or personal narrative (Cohler, 1982a, 1988/1989, 1991).

The Concept of Generation and Realization of Social Change

Across the past two decades, there has been a dramatic change in the manner in which lives may be understood over longer periods of time (Eichorn, Clausen, Haan, Honzik, & Mussen, 1981; Jones, Bayley, MacFarlane, & Houzik, 1971). Partially as a result of (a) findings from a number of longitudinal studies reporting on personality and adjustment from childhood to adulthood and showing few demonstrable relationships over time, other than those reflecting biological rhythm or tempo (Kagan & Moss, 1962), and (b) findings from longitudinal studies showing important insights regarding the interplay of life history and history (Elder, 1974, 1979), the longitudinal method has yielded to recognition of the need for more complex cross-sequential designs.

In what may be the most dramatic example of the significance of this cross-sequential design, Schaie (1984) and Schaie, Labouvie, and Buech (1973) reported on findings from a continuing study of aging and intelligence. Reviewing intelligence test findings from successive birth cohorts, Schaie reported little association between aging and decrement in intellectual functioning. Expected decrement in intellectual functioning, which had been previously reported across the second half of life, appears to be restricted to persons beginning with the eighth decade of life; the previously reported association of decline in intellectual ability with age appears to have been largely a consequence of early educational experiences combined with adult occupational attainments requiring little intellectual effort. More recent cohorts of better educated older adults continued to read and to talk about ideas in ways that demanded continued use of intellectual abilities.

Schaie's work pointed to the importance of including early-life educational attainment within particular birth cohorts for understanding later adult intellectual functioning; this cohort-linked study also showed the importance of cohort in the study of personality change in adulthood and aging. Schaie's work has pointed to the significance of sociohistorical events as defining characteristics shaping personality and adjustment across the life span. Schaie's conclusions from psychometric studies have been supported by intensive study of adults followed from early childhood in the several longitudinal studies later combined into a single study at the Institute of Human Development, The University of California at Berkeley.

Studying two cohorts of men and women who were preschoolers or teenagers at the time of the Great Depression, and whose families varied in income loss, Elder (1974) was able to relate this particular sociohistorical event to lifelong patterns of personality and adjustment. Particularly among men who were preschoolers at the time of the Great Depression, whose families experienced at least a one-third drop in income, and whose fathers subsequently left the family, the problems posed for adjustment continued into adulthood (Elder & Rockwell, 1979). Boys who lost their fathers had particular adjustment problems; girls who were preschool age at the time of the Great Depression showed fewer problems because their mothers remained within the family; teenagers at the time of the Great Depression seem to have been less affected than children who were of preschool age.

Life-course studies have shown that assumptions regarding intellectual and personality development must be qualified in terms of factors related to particular sociohistorically defined cohorts. Elder's continuing concern with the course of personality and adjustment over several decades represented a natural experiment showing that both particular historical circumstances and such unanticipated adversity as the Great Depression have an impact on personality; particularly among boys who were preschool age at the time when their parents suffered at least a one-third loss of income, and whose fathers subsequently left the family, there was a long period of turmoil before attaining settled adulthood. Indeed, the fortuitous timing of the opportunity for these boys to enter military service in the Second World War may have led them to overcome childhood adversity and to succeed in adulthood.

Elder's studies of the Great Depression and, subsequently, the Second World War as cohort-defining events affecting the course of life show that personality and adjustment across the course of life are impacted by sociohistorical events experienced in common by persons of a particular age. The combined influence of the civil rights and antiwar movements had particular impact on youth who were of high school and college age during the late 1960s and affected persons of different ages in quite different ways; parents of involved youth experienced these social movements to a higher degree than parents of less involved youth. Taking place at a time of widespread personal and social experimentation, problems of substance abuse with marijuana and LSD had somewhat different implications for mental health among young people in the 1960s, as contrasted with the appearance of these problems two decades later. At the present time, although alcohol abuse in many high schools and colleges has returned to levels not seen since the early 1960s, it is largely the most psychologically and socially marginal adolescents and youth who continue to experiment with these recreational drugs.

Social changes taking place across the past three decades have been associated with marked changes in what is expected by and for adolescents. Although there are problems in claiming distinctive role strain and overload for any particular cohort, changes taking place in contemporary Western middle-class society may be without parallel in this century. Hogan (1981) has shown that an expectable sequence of life transitions has traditionally characterized attainment of an adult role portfolio in American society. School leaving is followed by entrance into the workplace and, somewhat later, courtship, marriage, and the advent of parenthood. The experience of continued personal well-being is associated with remaining congruent or "on time" with this socially defined, expectable, life-course trajectory (Cohler & Boxer, 1984). For example, the lowered morale reported among adult women in virtually every survey study of contemporary American society (Cohler, 1984; Klerman & Weissman, 1980; Weissman & Klerman, 1977) may be largely accounted for by the less continuous sequence of transitions among women, who are more likely than their male counterparts to interrupt schooling or career for marriage or parenthood, and who realize expectable career attainments much later in life than is characteristic among the men (Hogan, 1981; Marini, 1981; Rossi, 1985).

Two interrelated social timing phenomena have had an impact on morale and adjustment across the period of adolescence and youth. In the first place, the traditional, shared "timetable" (Roth, 1963) for expectable role transitions (Neugarten, 1979; Neugarten & Hagestad, 1976) has been disrupted across the past few decades by such adversity as social turmoil, economic dislocation, continuing recession, and war. The Vietnam conflict disrupted the lives of large numbers of youth and was accompanied by continuing domestic recession, which posed employment problems for veterans returning home from military service.[1] In this regard, the impact of the Vietnam conflict on the transition into adulthood was markedly different from that of the Second World War. Accompanying social conflict, regarding the legitimacy and value of the Vietnam conflict, fostered additional social dislocation for youth not serving in the military. The Vietnam controversy, in conjunction with other social disruptions of the 1960s and 1970s, and the problem of finding work in a continuing-weak domestic economy led to postponement of such expectable young adult role transitions as entering into career or family formation.[2]

This postponement of expectable role transitions has been compressed into a very foreshortened period of time, typically in the late 20s or early 30s (Modell & Goodman, 1990). The significance of this dilemma was well illustrated by the television program "ThirtySomething," which enjoyed enormous popularity among middle-class young adults and which dramatically portrayed the nature of the struggles that young adult men and women confront in contemporary society.

The impact on middle-class women entering into careers has been particularly marked. Just at the time when they are able to realize initial career success within business, law, or medicine, women in their late 20s or early 30s are forced to consider issues of courtship and marriage. The reality of the biological clock for fertility and its threat to disrupt career advancement require a decision on election of parenthood more rapidly following entrance into career and marriage than in past times. Because a very small number of couples elect to remain voluntarily childless (Veevers, 1979), most women entering into careers are faced with the burden of making a large number of role transitions within a brief period of time.

This event-based concept of cohort represents one use of the term *generation* within the

---

[1] In addition, across the decade of the 1980s, the disparity between unusually privileged and underprivileged youth became ever more pronounced; youth headed for elite liberal arts colleges are often not sufficiently aware of the plight of their less privileged consociates. As a small number of college-bound youth attain ever greater levels of sophistication in literacy and computational skills, counterparts at lower socioeconomic levels appear not to be benefiting from these advances; 20% of adults in America are unable to read, and, of an entering cohort in urban public schools, only a small proportion remain in school through high school graduation. With a smaller number of increasingly complex jobs available, as in so many aspects of life, late off-time transition may work to a student's advantage, particularly if delayed entry into the work force fosters enhanced work skills. The lifecourse and life chances of advantaged and disadvantaged students are becoming ever more discrepant in ways that may threaten the social fabric of our democratic society over the next several decades.

[2] The problem of entrance into the labor market has markedly affected the morale and mental health of a generation of young adults over the past several decades.

Among both working-class and middle-class youth, problems of entrance into the labor market have become increasingly serious. The "downsizing" of the American factory means that offspring no longer can assume the possibility of work along with their father in the same factory (Frank, 1988); even recent doctorate recipients cannot assume the possibility of academic employment. Havighurst and Gottlieb (1975) and Greenberger and Steinberg (1986) called into question the assumptions of Coleman (1974) that entry-level job experiences are essential in developing a work ethic. Poorly paid entry-level positions expose youth to workers already demoralized with a poor work attitude and, at least among teenagers still in school, seriously detract from time and effort available for school and for homework. Findings from these studies show that it is far better for students to complete schooling before taking on work responsibility. Again, the contributions of social science to the study of mental health and psychological impairment become relevant in studying issues of work and mental health.

contemporary social sciences (Eisenstadt, 1956; Mannheim, 1952; Troll, 1970). Viewed from the perspective of the cross-sequential research design (Baltes, 1968) cohort as generation represents a group of persons (particularly of the same chronological age or place in the course of life) who have experienced some notable sociohistorical event in common. Used in this sense, we can speak of the Vietnam generation, referring to persons who were of college age and susceptible to the draft at the time of the Vietnam conflict, just as we can speak of the Depression generation, referring to persons who were young during the time of the Great Depression. However, Rosow (1978) cautioned that any event may be seen as cohort-defining when looked at from a particular perspective. Events may only be cohort-defining when viewed in retrospect; few realized during the late 1960s the fateful significance of the events of this time (the Kennedy and King assassinations, the Vietnam draft and war, the Woodstock concert, the Mississippi slaughter of three civil rights workers, and so on).

A second use of the term generation refers to place within ranked descent groups passing through society at any one time. Persons of a particular age exist within a multilayered population stratified in terms of age. Infants are the youngest age group, and the oldest of the old are the most aged group within society. Often, specific attributions of personality and attitude are based simply on place within this multilayered age structure: place within ranked descent group is assumed to have certain "causative" explanatory power, in the sense that being at a particular point in the age distribution has its own capacity to evoke particular attitudes or actions. For example, it is often assumed that youth are liberal and that older adults may be particularly conservative in their political and social views. Too often, based on findings regarding a previous generation of less well educated, often foreign-born persons, older adults are assumed necessarily to be personally and socially rigid.

A third use of the term generation within the social sciences refers to phase or stage within the life cycle, as based on the concept of developmental task. From this perspective, there is an interplay between age and socially constructed or expectable socialization demand or "task." For example, childhood is a time of learning socially valued knowledge (with school and socialization central to this role learning); adolescence is a time of definition of self within the cycle of generations, and construction of defined goals for the future, including career or occupation; young adulthood is a time of establishing with another person intimate ties of long duration, preparatory for marriage and parenthood; and the stable adult years prior to middle age are a time of generativity characterized both by the advent of parenthood and the care of younger members of society in such aspects of one's life as mentoring or teaching.

This developmental-task perspective on generation was perhaps best portrayed by Erikson's (1950/1963) discussion of psychosocial epigenesis, which posited that the developmental task of adolescence concerns the connection between the presently experienced past and present and the anticipated future (the so-called identity guest), and the developmental task of young adulthood is finding and maintaining an intimate tie with another within the context of a relationship of some duration. This perspective on generation assumes a complex interplay of personal experiences in the context of shared understandings of the expectable course of life. Such concepts as the "adolescent passage" (Blos, 1979) assume that the particular psychosocial problems posed for adolescents are similar among persons at this point in the life-course, and different from persons at other points in the course of life, who confront different developmental tasks.

This perspective, in which lives are socially organized, assumes shared understanding of expectable role transitions. Across otherwise diverse groups within society, there is fairly strong agreement regarding such expectable transitions as school leaving, marriage, advent of parenthood, and retirement (Neugarten &

Hagestad, 1976). Persons may be portrayed as early or late in the course of life in terms of realization of these expectable transitions (Roth, 1963). Although the meaning of particular events may vary for diverse groups (Watts, Machabanski, & Karrer, Chapter 10 of this volume), Cohler and Boxer (1984) suggested that morale may be largely determined by a sense of being on-time for expectable events. In general, being off-time at an early age has more malignant impact than being off-time in later years. Adolescent pregnancy, premature retirement, or early death of spouse are among the life changes that pose particular problems because they are taking place off-time and early across the course of life (Pearlin, 1975, 1983; Pearlin, Menaghan, Lieberman, & Mullan, 1983).

This life-course perspective differs from a conception of lives based on life-span or life-cycle approaches, which assumes a series of sequentially negotiated stages or phases of personality development emerging within an epigenetic program in which personal and social forces combine to shape individual development (Cain, 1964; Riles 1973, 1976, 1981, 1986; Neugarten & Hagestad, 1976). Such formulations as those of Erikson (1950/1963) or Havighurst (1953) fail to consider the interplay between sociohistorical context and developmental process. Recognition of the place of history in the study of particular lives has important consequences for theory, method of study, and clinical intervention. In evaluating the findings reported in this book, and in understanding implications for intervention, it is important to maintain a life-course perspective that includes all three conceptions of generation.

The life-course perspective emphasizes the extent to which larger social changes qualify previous conclusions, including implication for intervention. For example, assumptions regarding the significance of particular personal distress may be characteristic more generally of other members of the same generation, understood as persons experiencing sociohistorical events in common (Clausen, 1972; Elder, 1975b). The decision to take a year off from college and spend it working on a tramp steamer or hitchhiking across country was a common experience among youth attending elite liberal arts colleges in the 1960s (Keniston, 1960/1965). The introduction of the Vietnam draft for young persons not in college ended this tradition. A decade later, it was as uncommon to take a year off as it had been common a decade earlier. In the 1980s, economic uncertainty led young people to remain in college without a break, in order to obtain the best possible education and maximize later economic security.

Issues of timing are inextricably interrelated with the issue of cohort. As Keniston (1965) observed, the concept of youth as a time between adolescence and young adulthood is unique to our own time. Formerly, young people leaving school would begin to work; at the present time, particularly among middle-class college graduates, there is a time of uncertainty and delay between college and either graduate school or career. Being age 25, with no clear career line or employment, would have been viewed as off-time late for expectable course of work life prior to about 1970; at the present time, taking a few years out, returning home to live after college, and underemployment are characteristic of those in their early 20s.

Particular sociohistorical events have contributed to the present experience of youth as a time between college and work. In the first place, continuing recession and underemployment across more than a decade have made it difficult for young people to find work. The downsizing of the American work force and the realization of automation of industry, feared for the preceding several decades, have finally begun to take their toll on employment among both blue- and white-collar workers. Further, these reductions in employment opportunities took place at a time when the largest birth cohort in history was growing to adulthood and searching for work. Membership in a birth cohort of unprecedented size has taken its toll on a generation (Easterlin, 1987; Guttentag & Secord, 1983). Members of a large birth cohort face greater competition for place in college, acceptance at graduate and professional schools, marital partners, and jobs than members of smaller birth cohorts. Birth cohort size is another of those sociohistorical characteristics that have fateful consequences for the adjustment of particular members of a generation of sociohistorical cohort.

Social Timing, Life-Course, and Mental Health

The concepts of generation (viewed as cohort) and life-course have particular relevance for the study of mental health and illness, precisely because adolescence and youth are unique life-course points that make particular contact with social change and experimentation. Nowhere in the course of life is the impact of cohort or generation more visible in determining adjustment or more important for understanding psychological distress and intervention.[3] Two particular factors, anticipatory socialization and role convoy, are associated with the distress of being off-time early. Much of the content associated with enacting particular social roles is learned from others.

Beginning with earliest infancy, persons are taught the particular reciprocal expectations or obligations that are associated with such cardinal roles as childhood or becoming a student. This teaching is often implicit and usually informal; it is reflected in the series of encounters that make up the daily round. The bundle of roles assumed for young children is fairly limited, but, across adolescence and youth, there is a change both in the number of new roles to be learned and the manner in which these roles are to be enacted. The role of the elementary school child is much less complex than that of the high school student, who moves from class to class within a multitude of expectations from different teachers. Much of the learning of these social roles is indirect and informal, and occurs in advance of enactment, through observation of others. For example, a child may learn from an older brother or sister about the role of high school student, the role of worker, and, given an opportunity to visit a brother or sister at college, the role of a student in a residential college. This learning is in anticipation of the child's own movement into these roles.

Role transitions are made less difficult not only through anticipatory socialization, which prepares a person in advance for the realization of a new role in society, but also through a "convoy of consociates"—other members of the same cohort-generation who assume particular new roles at about the same time (Kahn & Antonucci, 1980, 1981; Antonucci, 1985; Antonucci & Akiyama, 1987; Plath, 1980). Young adolescents making the transition from junior high school to high school reflect this concept of role convoy; orientation meetings have a clear socialization function but are also designed to create a cohort of consociates, or persons sharing the same role transition at the same time.[4] A young person who enters high school in the middle of the year lacks this convoy or group of persons undergoing the same role transition at the same time, even though the benefit of anticipatory socialization, through observation of brothers and sisters making the transition to high school, may have been present.

---

[3] Erikson (1958, 1963) expressed this position with particular clarity in his discussion of the young people at the Austen Riggs Center, whose serious psychopathology may have been more the result of being adolescent at a time of social change than of enduring, more malignant, underlying psychopathology. Cohler and Boxer (1984) suggested that the experience of being "on-time" in terms of the social timetable fosters a sense of personal well-being.

[4] The point at which the transition to high school is made has consequences for psychological development. Hill (1980; Blyth, Simmons and Carlton-Ford, 1983; Entwisle, 1990) and Simmons and Blyth (1987) have shown that different consequences are attached to adolescent socialization when communities make a transition after the sixth grade (into a junior high school), after the eighth grade, or after the ninth grade. Students "sheltered" from contact with older adolescents through a junior high school experience appear to grow up less rapidly, but they "catch up" once they make the transition to high school in the tenth grade.

Early off-time role transitions are particularly difficult because of the failure of anticipatory socialization and the lack of consociates who are able to provide a social support system. For example, advent of widowhood in our society is expectable sometime during the middle-to-late 70s. A woman in her 70s has had long experience with friends who have lost their spouses and has observed how they have dealt with this loss. Further, a woman in her mid-70s knows many other women who are widows and who are available to help the new widow with the tasks of everyday life and the process of grieving. A 40-year-old woman who becomes a widow has few of these benefits of anticipatory socialization and role convoy. With much less observation of the transition to widowhood and few other widows able to provide a support system, the 40-year-old widow is at increased risk for personal distress beyond that of her on-time counterparts. Late off-time role transitions pose fewer risks than early off-time role transitions, both because of the lengthy period of preparation prior to this transition, and because of the presence of consociates already making this transition and able to provide social support. On the other hand, the fact that most consociates have already made this role transition makes it somewhat more difficult to find others willing to be of assistance: late off-time role transitions pose greater mental health risks than those made on-time.

Cohort factors are clearly associated with the timing of role transitions. For example, in earlier times, the transition between college and work was relatively automatic; over the past 30 years, there has been increasing delay between college graduation and a next step in assumption of an adult role portfolio. Particularly among middle-class youth, a lengthy period of time spent working or traveling before assuming expectable career is now common, with the role transitions of career, courtship and marriage, and advent of parenthood all compressed into a relatively brief period of time during the late 20s or early 30s. Such cohort-related factors as economic recession or required military service shape the particular manner in which role transitions are realized within particular cohorts.

Evaluation of the significance of personal distress within the adolescent decade depends on knowledge of the experiences of a cohort. For example, experimentation with recreational drugs had somewhat different diagnostic significance when high school students during the early 1970s tried such drugs, as compared with the early 1990s, when far fewer students are involved in recreational drugs and alcohol abuse is once again more common than drug abuse. At the present time, drug abuse seems to be associated with particularly malignant psychopathology. The psychotherapist evaluating a young person expressing frustration with education and the social order during the early 1960s might have approached understanding the meaning of this concern in quite different ways from the psychotherapist working with adolescents three decades later.

ADOLESCENCE AND SOCIAL CHANGE

Adolescence and youth represent distinctive points across the course of life: at no other point is the combined influence of generation, history, and socially defined expectation of person and action so powerful in governing individual conduct. Indeed, adolescence and youth have become the major entry point into social change other than that specifically related to technological change in the workplace. It is well appreciated that important advances in mathematics and science are the consequence of early career attainments, often during college or graduate school. In the same manner, changes ranging from life-style to literature and politics have been the realization of youthful accomplishments. From the Beatles, to the Provos, to the antiwar movement of the late 1960s, youth has been responsible for institutionalizing these changes within the larger social order.

First adherents for every significant political or social revolution are drawn from among the ranks of adolescents and youth, and not simply because adolescents are more "impressionable." At the same time, particular burdens may accompany this responsibility for realization of social change. Social change is difficult not only for those coping with its consequences, but also for the innovators who are responsible for this change. Innovators encounter additional problems stemming from failure of anticipatory socialization; for example, contemporary youth are the social pioneers of a new approach to intimate relations and sexuality, and they are moving into new realms of behavior without the guidance and support of those who have been through this transition.

Foundations of Social Change in Youth

Three factors—education, group relations, and the place of the adolescent generation in terms of expectable role transitions across the course of life—all play a part in featuring adolescence and youth as the leading edge of social change. School and homework consume much of the day for most high school and college students. Classroom instruction fosters new learning beyond the contributions of particular classes or teachers. All aspects of education, taken together, provide a unique opportunity for integrating learning of important social and technological innovation. Indeed, instructors may not always be aware of the significance of the curriculum they are teaching.

The very nature of high school and college education further highlights issues of social change and the place of the young person within the course of life; students are taught the latest technology and come into contact with the leading ideas of the time. Intense group involvement outside of class enriches and extends ideas learned in class; discussion of political involvement in other places and times, redefinition of the expectations of men and women toward each other, or introduction of new technology extends and enhances classroom discussion (Katz, 1962; Sanford, 1966). The "bull sessions" outside of the classroom are viewed by students as perhaps more important in their education than the formal classroom instruction; bull sessions are effective largely because they extend and enlarge on issues first raised in the classroom (Cohler, 1992b; Cohler & Taber, 1993).

Together, formal instruction and group formation foster increased learning and social changes through mutual discussion and support of new trends in both idea systems and lifestyles. Adolescents spend far more time in group situations than persons at any other point in the course of life. Grade school children are generally expected to "come home" after school, perhaps in the company of a friend, but high school students have much greater personal and social freedom. After-school hours are most often spent in groups, participating in organized athletic events or other activities or "hanging out" (Berndt & Savin-Williams, Chapter 9 of this volume; Csikszentmihalyi & Larson, 1984; Deutsch, 1967; Sullivan, 1953). Informal peer-sponsored group activities outside of the classroom support and enhance formal instruction.

Within American society, groups become effective means for fostering social change not possible through individual action.[5] Through activities as varied as a rock concert or a Boy Scout jamboree, adolescents learn and grow in groups, which then become an important source of social change for the larger society. The 1969 Woodstock concert may have been responsible for grater social change than any other informal gathering in recent times! At no other point in the course of life do persons spend as much

---

[5] Lewin (1936), echoing earlier sentiments of Tocqueville (1832/1969), expressed considerable surprise regarding the American preoccupation with group membership. It is significant that much of American social psychology, from Lewin and Ash to Festinger and Milgram, has focused on issues of autonomy and conformity within groups.

time participating in groups as during adolescence and youth, and at no other point is there the possibility of such intense reflection within the context of a group discussion.

The third factor accounting for youth as the generation that determines social change concerns the relatively greater normlessness of persons at this point, as contrasted with other points, across the course of life. Adolescence, a point between protected and supervised childhood and the assumption of adult responsibilities, is characterized by relative normlessness; problems distinctive of the adolescent epoch both offer possibilities and pose problems for those working in clinical situations. Across the adolescent decade, teens gradually acquire many of the roles characteristic of adulthood; beginning with expected changes at home and at school, adolescents learn work skills through at least part-time work, make friendships that will endure across decades, and form their first intimate ties with a significant other.[6] At the same time, as Erikson (1958, 1963) observed, a major problem of the adolescent decade is learning the concept of "for keeps" or "meaning it." The very concept of identity crisis or conflict (Erikson, 1950/1963, 1958) refers to a time when it is still possible to try out new ways of being and doing without the constriction of predefined roles.

Erikson (1958) applied an analogy of joining a monastery in the high Middle Ages to the contemporary experience of the adolescent. The novice was quite literally between the monastery walls, separated from the profane outside world and from the sacred world within. The novice was only admitted to the inner monastery, to begin to learn the role of the monk, after a time of personal reflection, partial participation, and increasing sense of vocation. The process of becoming an adult in our society is very much like the novice's entry into the monastery. Adolescence and youth is a time "between the walls," no longer children and yet not fully adult—a time that permits exploration in wide areas of life, including life-style, relations with other family members, interests and hobbies, areas of academic specialization, and even sexual orientation.[7]

Freedom to innovate, which is uniquely possible across adolescence and youth, allows experimentation in life-styles, technology, and ideas. However, it should be noted that innovation may come at some cost to adolescents caught in the midst of social change. Experiments with both idea systems and life-styles may lead to increased conflict with both parents and society; the freedom to innovate may intensify the moratorium associated with identity conflict, thereby postponing resolution and leading to diffusion or a negative identity most explicitly concerned with *not* being like such formerly idealized persons as parents, teachers, or other significant adults. Erikson has portrayed "identity foreclosure" as another possible means for avoiding the danger of experimenting with trial identities; early decisions regarding such issues as career or political and social values make it difficult for the adolescent to engage in that very experimentation which, optimally, fosters consolidation of adult identity and the possibility of accepting or "owning" who and what one is as an adult.

Innovations created by youth are taught to parents and other adults through the process

---

[6] Although Coleman et al. (1974) recommended increased commitment of adolescents to at least part-time work as the foundation for adult work attitudes and skills, Greenberger and Steinberg (1986) provided findings that challenge this view. Working at largely semiskilled or unskilled jobs, adolescents meet older co-workers who have not been successful and may learn work attitudes that are not adaptive for later attainments. Further, part-time work interferes with school performance and fosters an attitude toward class and homework that conflicts with the expectations of the school. These findings cast serious doubt on the received view that work is important in fostering personal growth across the adolescent epoch.

[7] At least part of the popularity among adolescents of such role-playing games as "Dungeons and Dragons" may be the possibility for constructing a variety of roles and for remaking these roles over time, changing such attributes as power and attractiveness. At least to some extent, adolescence enjoys the same role ambiguity as the role-playing game; roles are constructed and remade as adolescents attempt to work through the issue of their own identity (Erikson, 1958, 1963).

of "backward" socialization. The concept of socialization provides important explanatory power within the social sciences (Brim, 1968; Cook and Cohler, 1986). Successfully, across the course of life, induction into new roles is fostered by observation and coaching or "mentored" participation. Elementary school children are socialized into the role of high school student both through watching older brothers and sisters already in high school and through more formal teaching by parents, teachers, and other adults who are important in the lives of early adolescent children. Widows are socialized into their role both through long-term observation of the manner in which other widows have dealt with the transition into their new status, and through continuing support and more formal preparation by others who have already become widows.

It is less often realized that socialization is a reciprocal, forward-and-backward process in which, from earliest infancy to oldest age, each generation tries to influence the other (Bell, 1977; Cook & Cohler, 1986; Harper, 1975; Lerner & Spanier, 1978). Forward socialization has been well portrayed in the child development literature, but backward or reverse socialization has been less well understood, although it is equally relevant in understanding socialization across the course of life. Just as parents attempt to teach offspring new roles, offspring attempt to teach parents new roles. Although there has been little systematic study of the course of reciprocal socialization among children and parents, it is clear that, as early as elementary school, while parents are inducting children into new roles and values, the children are influencing parental conceptions of their present understandings of self and place in the course of life.

A college-student daughter, returning home to find that her "empty-nest" mother is still searching for personal fulfillment, may encourage the mother to go to work or to resume her education. Brought up in a time when the role of women in society was defined in a more traditional manner, the mother may have a difficult time making this decision on her own. However, influenced by the daughter's encouragement, the mother may now set about to realize her own goals (Hagestad, 1974). Men in college similarly influence their fathers to adopt a more flexible attitude toward work and relationships than the father may have believed possible.

As Hagestad (1974) initially observed, contact with leading ideas and technology is an important factor in "reciprocal socialization" within the family. Across the past decade, it has not been unusual for children from the elementary school grades to teach their parents how to work computers. The phenomenon of an eighth grader teaching his or her parents how to program in BASIC has become commonplace in many households. An association of adolescence and youth with "computer hacking" frequently appears in the media. Young people seem to have a natural affinity for making electronic machines work. Again, a combination of factors, including formal instruction in school, group activities such as writing a composite computer game program, or "hanging out" in a video arcade, all foster increased mastery and transmission of technology across generations. Group activity enhances formal classroom learning and consequent social change.

The tensions created by the exposure of adolescents and young adults to the leading edge of knowledge have been acknowledged in the study of young people and their families. For example, from the time of the "new immigration" of the post-Civil War period in the United States, successive waves of immigrant families have experienced their children's attendance at American schools, where they rapidly became English-speaking and learned values that conflicted with the home culture (Covello, 1944/1972).[8] While grandparents and parents tried

---

[8] In all the controversy that has erupted regarding the performance of public education in contemporary American society, the role of the school in the education of immigrant groups is often neglected. No system of public education has ever succeeded in educating such a large number of immigrant children as participating citizens. With immigration in most states (excepting the West Coast) no longer a problem with which schools must reckon, the mission

to maintain traditions that provided the foundations of ethnicity, young people became restive and attempted to break away from the family (Spiegel, 1971). Conflicts increased as young people attempted to induct their parents and grandparents into American culture and to teach them English. This conflict has surfaced again with the new East Asian immigration. Along with English, adolescents learn an individualism that is in sharp contrast with the familistic orientation of both Korean and Japanese cultures. This conflict intensifies when offspring begin relationships with American young people, posing the threat that the young person may marry outside of the traditional culture.

An increasing emphasis within American culture, valuing what is current more than historical family beliefs and practices, may be one reason for the continuing prominence of the youth culture and the extent of struggles among immigrating families. The findings that peer influences are preeminent explanations of antisocial behavior may reflect this youth culture value.

Social Change and Adolescent Mental Health: The Legacy of the 1960s

It is critically important that clinical research and practice focused on the adolescent decade be informed by social science perspectives regarding the impact of life-course and historical perspectives for understanding psychological development. Too often, we assume that a present adjustment problem is a fundamental characteristic of adolescence over time. For example, European and American concern with

---

of the school in society may show dramatic change. Rather than socializing children into American values and attitudes necessary for achievement in a workplace with several levels of management, there may be additional pressure to provide the technological innovation necessary for success in the international marketplace of the next century. Changed expectations for the schools are inconsistent with administration designed to promote literacy and transmit values to immigrant groups.

---

identity struggle as a part of adolescence may be unique to the modern West and is hardly intrinsic to becoming an adult in other cultures and other times (Demos & Demos, 1969). Such pressing adjustment problems as eating disorders associated with adolescence, while certainly known in previous times, have taken on increased urgency as a consequence of pressures experienced by young women at home and at school (Schwartz & Thompson, 1981, 1982). In the same way, concern with the effects of redundancy in employment and lack of apprenticeship poses problems for boys, expressed in ways such as psychosomatic disorders and substance abuse, masking underlying depression.

Particular problems have been posed for understanding clinical intervention in the light of the significant social change of the past decade. Expectable adolescent experimentation may be viewed as heralding serious psychopathology. Writing in *Young Men Luther,* Erikson (1958) discussed the problems of differentiating between the malignant psychopathology reflected in adult psychosis and the intense personal distress expressed by adolescent patients seen at the Austen Riggs Foundation. Erikson suggested that adolescent psychopathology might not be continuous with that observed in adulthood. The so-called "identity crisis" of the adolescent might be phenotypically congruent with the disordered thinking and troubled interpersonal relationships characteristic of borderline adult patients, but might not show the same stability over time, or might not show the same resistance to efforts at understanding and intervention.

Two additional problems are posed by adolescent psychopathology for the study of lives: social change may be most apparent in adolescence and young adulthood, and may be most burdensome for young people who are the carriers of this social change. Exposure to social change leads to particular problems in understanding the significance of psychopathology for clinical intervention across the adolescent decade. At the same time, the implications of immediate distress for long-term outcome may be more difficult to predict during adolescence than at other points in the course of life (Livson & Peskin, 1980). For example, although alcohol abuse during adolescence appears predictive of a substance-abusing habit and alcoholism across the adult years, experimental use of marijuana during adolescence may be less predictive of later chemical dependence than use of marijuana during adulthood. Further, marijuana use among adolescents during the 1970s may have had different significance for adult mental health and chemical dependency than at the present time. Both the meaning and expression of symptoms shift as a consequence of place in the course of life, including expectable changes over time and with age.

Historians might challenge the claim that the decade of the 1960s was one of unusual turmoil, particularly when viewed from a longer-term historical perspective. However, within the more limited perspective of present generations, the last half of the 1960s marked a period of more rapid shift in values and life-style than at any time since the advent of the Great Depression. The social sciences have had great difficulty understanding the sources of this social change. Although capable of portraying the place of particular institutions such as school and family for the present social order, the structural-functional approach characteristic of social theory across the past half-century has been little able to account for change over time (Parsons, 1966).

The eruptive social changes of the 1960s posed a challenge to traditional modes of social science study. Within a period of about 5 years, from 1965 to 1970, American young people recast their lives and altered their values, in ways different from both their parents and their older brothers and sisters. Intensification of the civil rights struggle, particularly in the American South, together with advent of opposition to the Vietnam war and, somewhat later, response to the assassinations of Martin Luther King, Jr. and Robert Kennedy, all fostered a restive attitude.[9] The cumulative impact of these changes was a dramatic shift in political and social attitudes, together with revision of norms regarding acceptable behavior in realms as different as sexuality and smoking. The "pill" removed much of the worry regarding unplanned pregnancy. However, ever decreasing age of first intercourse, even among middle-class adolescents, between 1960 and 1970, reflected changed views regarding mode of expression of sexual desire across the adolescent decade. Increased concern about such social issues as health and smoking, or the environment, together with increasing acceptance of deviant and unusual life-styles, reflected in the concept of "punk," all were part of the social change taking place across the late 1960s.

Precisely because youth is so close to the leading edge of social change, when such change occurs, it is almost always first evident among adolescents and young adults. Youthful opposition to the war sparked a national protest that led to significant political

---

[9] Those participating in the social movements of the late 1960s are familiar with the intense sense of participation and with the power of the group to inspire conduct less likely to occur among persons in small groups. The Woodstock concert of 1969 is perhaps the ideal type of such an event. Mass behavior is associated with increased normlessness, from the initiation rites of the Australian aborigine to the late adolescent group behavior of the rock concert audience. Increased substance abuse and sexuality were characteristic of these large events. However, even within smaller groups, canvassing on such issues as improved housing, the intensity of the effort and the long hours spent together fostered a unique intimacy in which personal experimentation with sexual expression and drugs was accepted. This tolerant interpersonal climate also attracted some persons less socially committed than troubled. While apparently committed to group goals, the acceptant and tolerant climate of these political and social action groups permitted these young people to satisfy their own desires at the expense of the group. As Haan, Smith, and Block (1968) showed, these social movements phenotypically characterized as radical and motivated toward social change included both those genuinely committed to such change and those, less well organized, who used the group for their own ends and tended to be divisive and a continuing source of tension.

opposition and, ultimately, change in national policy. Working together in political change projects, often in an intense manner and in circumstances supporting increased questioning of traditional values and ways of relating, men and women began to evaluate anew accepted concepts of gender relations. Often, in quite different ways, women emerged as important leaders in these social action movements and men encountered the unique experience of working for these women leaders.

This coeducational political and social action both hastened and was supported by such other changes as the emergence of the coeducational college dormitory (Komarovsky, 1985; Levine, 1980). Over a period of less than 5 years, liberal arts colleges shifted from a policy of tight restrictions on relations between men and women in social life and college housing to complete elimination of such rules. Indeed, across this brief period of time, many college dormitories included men and women living on the same floors and in adjoining rooms, and sharing common bathrooms.[10] A few years earlier, these living arrangements would have been unthinkable. College officials encouraged the creation of coeducational dormitories because the effect of women living in formerly all-male houses was marked reduction in wild and destructive group activity!

Enhanced personal freedom posses particular challenge to efforts at providing clinical intervention for young people. In the first place, there has been inevitable conflict between the values of therapists and those of their troubled adolescent patients, who are growing up in a culture markedly at odds with the therapist's own adolescence. Therapists sometimes find it difficult to understand the so-called permissiveness of contemporary adolescent culture, protesting that contemporary liberal attitudes of family and school threaten adolescents' need for control (Bettelheim, 1967; Hendin, 1977). Psychoanalytically oriented therapists maintain an image of adolescence as inevitably a decade of turmoil and struggle over control of biologically based passions, requiring restraint only possible through external control. They have decried social changes taking place in American and Western European society (Blos, 1979) as posing a danger to the adolescent's need for external structure as the foundation of personal control.

Even when evidence from biological study questions the significance of pubertal change for effective personal control (Petersen & Taylor, 1980; Richards, Abell, & Petersen, Chapter 2 of this volume), it has been difficult to reshape thinking regarding issues of personality development and psychopathology across the adolescent decade. Psychodynamically oriented theorists have continued to stress the conflict between the young person and the family as an inevitable aspect of adolescent development (Blos, 1962, 1967, 1979; Stierlin, 1974). This position has been maintained even as a number of studies have raised questions regarding the inevitable character of this conflict between adolescent and family, including the significance of the concept of a "generation gap," which is reflected by this conflict. Flacks (1967, 1971) has shown that the new left is comprised largely of the children of the old left.

At the same time, the attitudes and values of same-generation consociates have affected the mode in which these values are expressed. Political and social attitudes of youth are likely to be consistent with those of their parents (Bengtson & Black, 1973; Thomas, 1974) but are expressed in the terms common

---

[10] It has been assumed that group norms similar to an incest taboo function to reduce sexual intimacies among students on the same floors or within college houses. First-person accounts and observation by those supervising college housing do not support this assumption! At the present time, changed norms regarding sexual expression across late adolescence and early adulthood have led to complete acceptance of a variety of forms of sexual expression in which there may be sexual encounters among students living together in college houses. The open manner in which students discuss issues related to sexuality and their own wishes and preferences is evidence that a dramatic shift has taken place in American society regarding issues that were considered unacceptable even to think about in their parents' generation.

to other members of the same generation. Liberal parents are most likely to have liberal offspring, and conservative parents are most likely to have conservative offspring, but the issues in terms of which these views are expressed will most likely reflect the political and social views and issues of the newer generation. Studies of the transition from youth to young adulthood have emphasized the adolescent's intrinsic need to separate from parents, and the inevitable conflict with parents that is required in order for young people to differentiate themselves. These studies suggest the importance of differentiating subgroups of adolescents and their parents, including those families in which the young person was comfortably able to separate, and those in which the young person was either delegated to achieve in order to enhance the status of the family or bound to the family in order to maintain a threatened solidarity (Grotevant, 1983; Hauser et al., 1984).[11]

Social Change and Sexuality in Adolescence and Youth

Between 1960 and 1970, a dramatic change occurred in both values and practices regarding sexuality. Sexual activity took place at an earlier age in 1970 than a decade previously: both opportunity and frequency of sexual activity showed a dramatic increase over this period of rapid social change in American society. The coed dormitory in the liberal arts college became a symbol of this change, but, as Modell (1989) has suggested, there was a significant change in the concept of men's and women's roles accompanying this shift. If the sexuality active girl was no longer a "bad" girl, then boys had responsibilities within relationships; they had to understand the point of view of girls and could not simply take girls for granted as part of a fast crowd willing to grant sexual favors. This changed attitude toward sexuality influenced men's understanding not only of women's roles but also of their own attitudes toward women and sexuality.

Among men, the possibility of more open expression of feelings became acceptable; among women, adoption of such nontraditional careers as law and business, together with the decision to postpone marriage, became the rule rather than the exception within middle-class families. Cross-sequential findings reviewed by Modell (1989) suggest that the new androgyny, once the stuff of futurists, has become nearly the norm among younger adults in American society. The present generation of younger men and women emphasizes similarities rather than differences in the roles of men and women and has a better ability to talk about their feelings within relationships, as compared to men and women in past time.

At the time when adolescents became more sexually active, they also became more introspective regarding the significance of sexuality for the roles of both men and women. The adolescent not yet ready for encounter with sexuality finds it increasingly difficult to avoid this issue because it is so much the basis for discussion at school, among friends, and in the media. At the same time, there is marked uncertainty regarding what is appropriate sexual behavior. Concern with the issue of "date (acquaintance) rape" is paramount on American college campuses at the present time. Men complain that it is difficult to read the wishes of women who still proffer the ritual "no" but signal other intentions by their actions. Women complain that men fail to show them respect, to acknowledge their saying "no" to increased sexual involvement, or to recognize their role and responsibilities in sexual and other intimate

---

[11] The capacity to realize comfortable separation is perhaps best understood as comfortable interdependence. Across the course of life, family members continue to look to each other as sources of solace and support and to affirm their own identity within the context of the family (Cohler, 1983; Cohler & Stott, 1987; Cooper, Grotevant and Condon, 1983; Leichter & Mitchell, 1967; Mitchell, 1978; Pruchno, Blow, & Smyer, 1984; Rudolph & Rudolph, 1978). Continuity and interdependence rather than conflict are most characteristic of relations among members of the modified extended middle-class family of the modern West. The question is whether family members are able to feel comfortable with this interdependence (Galatzer-Levy & Cohler, Chapter 4 of this volume).

communication.[12] Living together on a coed floor, often sharing a common bathroom, college-age men and women have more opportunities for sexual experimentation than were possible in the past, when college men and women lived in separate dorms (Komarovsky, 1976, 1985). Lacking the control on physical intimacy resulting from such regulations as single-sex dormitories and parietal hours (restricted visiting times), men and women are forced to deal with these issues on their own. At the present time, many young men and women are uncertain how to respond when invited into an intimate relationship.

Changes in living arrangements were hastened by a shift away from the single-sex college, particularly in New England, and toward the inclusion of both men and women on campus.[13] With college-age men and women living together, and with the new reproductive technology that makes possible nonobtrusive contraception, problems of sexuality and its control shifted from external authority to students' own preferences and desires (Modell, 1989). Sex without guilt, but also without necessary commitment to long-term intimacy, became the rule rather than the exception from the late 1960s onward; this new view regarding gender identity, intimacy, and sexuality continues into the present time (Moffat, 1989).

Accompanying the dramatic change in values regarding sexuality that began in the late 1960s, there has been a new focus on the definition of sexual orientation. Social acceptance of a homosexual orientation has become a possibility within American and Western European society in ways not conceived of in previous cohorts. Herdt (1989) suggested that the 1967 resistance by homosexual patrons to a police raid at the Stonewall Bar in New York marked a turning point in making the possibility of sexual attraction among members of the same gender a reality that could be openly acknowledged. The generation coming of age after the "Stonewall riots," an open resistance to this police action, thought of themselves as gay and lesbian rather than homosexual, and were able to adopt an honest life-style rather than one marked by duplicity. Terms such as "coming out" and being "out" reflected this new honesty, which was contrasted with being "in the closet."[14]

---

[12] The issue of saying "no" to the bid for sexual intimacy, typically made by the man, is an important and urgently needed area of study. Some women complain that men still fail to respect their refusal to become intimate, and that men too often attempt intimidation and coercion in an effort to entreat them into a relationship. Other women complain that men fail to understand the subtleties of the conventional and expected "no" and tend to be too easily inhibited. Young men complain that it is difficult to interpret the many meanings of "no" and that women send "mixed signals" regarding their wishes. Both men and women attending an elite liberal arts college may agree regarding relationships that become coercive, but they find it more difficult to determine how to proceed when either or both members of the couple are uncertain of their own wishes and sentiments. The problem of communication regarding extent of sexual intimacy between members of a couple, particularly when first becoming acquainted, appears to be particularly troubling among young men and women in contemporary society.

[13] Undoubtedly, the decision to move to coeducation was hastened by the declining "pool" of eligible 18-year-olds able to pay the increasingly outrageous costs of private higher education. Marketing has become a dominant force in higher education, with glossy picture books and recruiting visits essential for most private colleges and universities in attracting clientele. For students, higher education has become a "buyer's market," reducing much of the anxiety attendant on being selected by an appropriate college, which was a major factor in adolescents of the previous two decades. At the same time, the benefits of single-gender college education have been lost as women's colleges have become coeducational. There is some evidence that women in single-gender colleges were able to develop greater self-esteem when not having constantly to compete with men. The women faculty in these colleges served as important role models, showing that it is possible for women to realize intellectual distinction and also attain the roles of wife and mother, so essential to the concept of being an adult in contemporary society.

[14] There has been little systematic study of the life-course of gay men and lesbian women following college. Anecdotal accounts suggest that, among men who have come out, a gay life-style becomes an enduring sexual orientation; particularly as a result of the AIDS epidemic, gay men are increasingly adopting a monogamous life-style, in contrast with the frequent change in sexual partners that characterized gay men in times past. There is still little information regarding the life-course of middle-aged or older gay men; a monogamous life-style may

Emergence of gay and lesbian social activism, reflected in such terms as "gay pride," led to extension of antidiscrimination laws to sexual orientation in many cities; acceptance of neighborhoods containing proportionately larger numbers of gay and lesbian men and women; the emergence of an openly gay press; stores and services providing for the particular needs of the homosexual community; and community centers and health centers explicitly designed to provide appropriate support services. With the terrible outbreak of AIDS in the early 1980s, these centers became particularly important in raising money for the support of ill members of the community and for the creation of health education and prevention programs. Community centers were also important in providing support programs for gay adolescents coming out into the world of same-gender sexual orientation. Study of these adolescents has suggested that same-gender sexual orientation was not associated with increased psychopathology in adolescence, except as the consequence of discrimination and prejudice (Boxer, Cohler, Herdt, & Irwin, Chapter 11 of this volume).

Recognition of possible variation in sexual orientation as expectable among high school and college youth led to increased acceptance of homosexuality as but another mode for the expression of sexual desire. Although it has been argued that adolescents, unsure of their own identity, would be particularly threatened by the possibility of a gay or lesbian life-style, high school youth appear to be at least as acceptant of diversity of sexual orientation as their college-age brothers and sisters. Concomitantly, the whole question of sexuality and sexual orientation was introduced, with increased recognition of variation in modes of preferred sexual expression and open acknowledgment of such nontraditional modes as gay and lesbian sexuality. These changes, in turn, have had important implications for clinical practice: on the one hand, we now recognize that the gay or lesbian adolescent need not necessarily be troubled, except to the extent that "coming out" may lead to conflict with family and friends. On the other hand, many adolescents, troubled in other areas, find the more overt expression of sexual wish and preference to evoke additional turmoil. A more "open" attitude toward sexuality may be helpful overall, but both the temptations and the risks imposed for many teenagers pose a significant risk for adjustment problems.[15]

Social Change, Adolescence, and the Transition into Parenthood

Particularly among girls, social changes across the past two decades have led to the view that marriage and parenthood are much more an individual choice than an expected responsibility. Adolescent pregnancy, while by no means the norm, has become accepted; in the past 20 years, most public high schools have implemented programs that permit pregnant adolescent girls and adolescent mothers to continue with their education within the "mainstream" of the high school. Study of the social context of adolescent pregnancy is particularly difficult because open acknowledgment of sexual relations prior to marriage, especially with pregnancy as an outcome, was seldom discussed in former times.

---

mean long-lasting relationships enduring into middle and later life. The lesbian life-style may be more political than sexual-social. Particularly among women in Eastern elite liberal arts colleges, it is more common for lesbian women subsequently to marry and have children. The life-course of these formerly lesbian women through middle and old age may be less different from their heterosexual counterparts than is characteristic of gay men at midlife.

[15] Working with a group of gay adolescent boys, Boxer (personal communication) found that these young people believe they are hardly at risk for AIDS, which is presumed to afflict older men. They believe that they and their agemates have not yet had sufficient sexual contact to have come into contact with HIV-positive gay men and that they are sufficiently healthy to resist the ravages of the virus. Health instruction is a particularly difficult task among both gay and straight teenagers, who believe themselves to be more invincible than their elders. This belief may stem from either the place of adolescents within the generations making up society at any given time (they have had less contact with death and issues of finitude) or from a developmental task of the adolescent epoch.

The Crittendon Home, a charitable organization of shelters for unwed mothers, provides both a social support system for unwed teen mothers and a means for legitimate entry into an adoption system that protects both natural mothers and adoptive parents. At least to some extent, the "pill" has reduced the need for group homes for pregnant girls and new teenage mothers. Legalization of abortion, which replaced the dangerous methods of the past with the sanitary environment of a clinic or hospital procedure, has become an increasingly widespread alternative to keeping a baby. At the same time, particularly in much of the current debate regarding freedom of choice, there has been little concern with the psychological impact of the decision for or against abortion on the women and on the morale of the entire medical community carrying out these procedures. The "morning after" pill, currently accepted as legal only in New Hampshire, will have important implications for the issue of reproductive freedom and sexuality among adolescent women. At the same time, significant retrenchment regarding the guarantee of legal rights for these women has been taking place (see Crosby & Reppucci, Chapter 12 of this volume).[16]

As Caldwell (1980) noted, much of the study of adolescent parenthood has assumed, in common with other longitudinal study, that earlier effects have a single, unitary, continuous impact on later life. As Furstenberg's (1987) and other recent findings show, this assumption is hardly warranted (East and Felice, 1990). Indeed, although comparative findings are lacking and the group of mothers studied was a homogenous group of disadvantaged Black women, Furstenberg's findings suggest little continuity in the development of either mothers or children across his 17-year period of study.

Social status, later life experiences, and even chance phenomena all affect the later psychosocial outcome for men and women who assume the parental role off-time and off-sequence in the expectable course of life. When early off-time parenthood is combined with the impact of poverty and social disorganization, as in the urban African American family, the impact of early off-time advent of parenthood magnifies the impact of poverty and social disorganization. Being off-time early has a marked negative impact on maternal self-concept. Poverty magnifies the impact of disorganized sequencing (Hogan, 1981), makes it more difficult for mother and baby to get good medical care, and is accompanied by uncertainty regarding the social resources available to assist the family.

Particularly within stable working-class families, where age at first marriage and pregnancy is lower than within middle-class families, unmarried teen pregnancy is not uncommon. Most often, the adolescent mother continues to live at home, assisted in child-care by her mother and other women relatives (Furstenberg, 1987, 1990). Their care and support make it possible for the teenage mother to work or to continue with her education. Age at first pregnancy is therefore less of an issue than the nature of social supports provided for adolescent mothers within family and community (Field, Widmayer, & Adler, 1990; Gershenson, 1983). Two major sources of

---

[16] Changes in birth control technology and values among prospective adolescent parents have taken place even as couples seeking to adopt encounter ever greater problems in arranging for an adoption. Women have been marrying at later ages; for a woman in her 30s, the biological clock of fertility exerts particular pressures. Fertility problems discovered at such a late age may provide little possibility for intervention in time to have a child, and adoption is even less a possibility. Ironically, the new birth control technology has reduced the possibility of adoption at a time when many middle-aged couples are desperate to adopt a baby. Further, across the past decade, the issue of adolescent pregnancy has become charged with increasing political tensions. Unmarried pregnancy remains high among impoverished African American families, where more than half of all pregnancies may be attributed to unmarried teen mothers. With most of these adolescent mothers welcoming the advent of parenthood and committed to caring for the baby, albeit in difficult circumstances, the magnitude of this problem has posed a burden for welfare resources. Persons of African American descent comprise less than 12% of the population. Most teen mothers are from more affluent and advantaged families.

distress associated with early off-time role transitions—lack of anticipatory socialization, and lack of a role convoy of others experiencing this transition—are minimal issues within working-class families in which at least some other members of the extended family have experienced adolescent pregnancy.[17]

Problems for the course of the child's development are most likely to arise when the advent of adolescent parenthood appears in the context of poverty and social disorganization, such as in urban high-rise housing projects (Christ et al., 1990). Most studies focusing on this "at risk" group have shown a deleterious impact on infant and child development among children of adolescent mothers (Baldwin & Cain, 1980; Furstenberg, 1976; Field, 1981). Pregnant women living in poverty have reduced opportunity for good prenatal care and are more likely to deliver low-birth-weight babies who are particularly at risk in terms of later development.

There has been little comparative study of the ecology of adolescent parenthood (Bronfenbrenner, 1979). However, when adolescent parenthood takes place within the context of a stable modified-extended family able to provide support and assistance, there is little reason to suppose that age at advent of parenthood, from midadolescence onward, necessarily increases the risk for impairment in the child's cognitive or behavioral development. Where medical care has been adequate and where there is a good relationship between mother and baby (Osofsky & Osofsky, 1970), there is little evidence of increased risk for the psychological development or the growth and maturation of the children of teenage mothers, based on age alone (Broman, 1981; Cohler, 1992a; Field, Widmayer, Stringer, & Ignatoff, 1980).

There has been little study of the father in these early off-time births. The transition to parenthood is made by a couple, even if that couple is not married (McCluskey, Killarney, & Papini, 1983). For example, Cohen and Weissman (1984) discussed the concept of the parenting alliance, which permits divorced couples to maintain continuing contact with each other in the best interests of the child. It is likely that teenage parents maintain a similar parenting alliance, and that parents continue some sort of contact in the best interests of the child. However, discussion of the quality of the parental alliance has been overlooked in most studies to date. Study of the father–child relationship, seldom considered in much of the larger literature on the transition to parenthood, is even less studied in early off-time parenthood. The father is a nearly invisible participant in this research, a problem accentuated in studies of early off-time transition to parenthood among Black teenagers.

There has been some effort to understand the father's contribution to on-time parenthood (Lamb, Pleck, Charnov, & Levine, 1987; Parke, 1986), but there has been much less explicit concern with the father's role within the family characterized by assumption of the parental role during adolescence (Parke, Power, & Fisher, 1980). Particularly within families headed by Black adolescent mothers, it has been difficult to study the life-course of socially disadvantaged Black men (Gary, 1981) and even more difficult to study socially disadvantaged Black adolescent fathers (Hendricks, 1981). It is important for those studying early off-time parenthood to refer to the larger literature on the transition to parenthood, in terms of what is known more generally regarding the significance of parenthood for parents and family. They should also study the determinants and consequences of early off-time parenthood, using cross-sequential research designs that provide information regarding both change over

---

[17] It should be noted that there is very little information contrasting the development and subsequent adjustment of children of teenage parents with children born to parents making the transition to parenthood in their 20s, or children born to late off-time parents. Demographic perspectives provide some understanding of the scope of the problem of early off-time parenthood, but must be complemented by increased understanding of the significance of this off-time transition for parents, child, and other family members.

time and the impact of sociohistorical events on the consequent course of life.

In most studies to date, information regarding transition to parenthood and living arrangements postpartum for teenage mothers is much more detailed than is information regarding marital ties. Furstenberg (1987) reported that about two-thirds of the group had married, but more than half of these marriages had dissolved within the 5-year period of the study, with marked marital strain among remaining married couples.

Reporting on data from a national survey study, McCarthy and Menken (1981) indicated that more than four-fifths of White teenage women and two-fifths of Black teenage women marry by the time a baby is born to them. By the end of 4 years after a first birth, virtually all White women and four-fifths of Black women have married. Twenty years after the initial study, more than four-fifths of the women had married; however, these marriages had been unstable and the subsequent marital history of women entering parenthood during their teen years revealed markedly less stable marital ties than among counterparts who had not entered parenthood during their teen years. Similar findings have been reported on a national survey study by Morgan and Rindfuss (1985). Duration of marriage among parents giving birth out of wedlock varies, with Black women more likely to attain separation than White counterparts. Informal separation, rather than formal divorce, was the most characteristic means for the dissolution of the marriage.

Although national attention regarding the problem of adolescent pregnancy has increased over the past two decades, there still is much less long- than short-term study regarding the impact of adolescent parenthood on mother, father, and children. Many factors enter into the subsequent development and adjustment of the children of adolescent parents. Largely as a result of an accelerated role transition into parenthood, marital disruption and reduced level of education attainment are often associated with teenage parenthood. Timing and sequence of parenthood prior to marriage both contribute to the problems in maintaining these early off-time role transitions across the course of later life. Findings from a number of studies have shown that, particularly within Black families, women who become parents in their teenage years do not differ in later-life educational and occupational attainments from counterparts with similar social position who become parents in young adulthood (Bacon, 1974; Hofferth & Moore, 1979; Howell & Frese, 1982).[18] However, Black teenage fathers do show markedly reduced levels of educational attainment (Howell & Frese, 1982).

Waite and Moore (1978) and Hofferth and Moore (1979) maintained that women who are early off-time for parenthood never build up the "human capital," in terms of early work experience that would permit them to increase their earning potential (Card & Wise, 1978). However, Furstenberg's (1987) longitudinal study showed that women leaving school during high school often return to complete their education. Further, although the advent of early off-time parenthood has short-term costs for adolescent mothers, these women have completed much of their active parenthood by their mid- to late 20s, and are able to return to school or to the labor force as full-time employees at about the time when their counterparts, becoming parents at a more expectable time, are at home caring for children. A sense of well-being among these early off-time adolescent parents increases as their children become independent, freeing parental time and energy to return to work.

Furstenberg's (1987) 25-year follow-up study showed that nearly 90% of adolescent mothers had returned to work. Although the nature of their present role portfolio and life attainments did not differ greatly from those of counterparts realizing the advent of on-time

---

[18] Card and Wise (1978) reported an adverse impact on later educational attainment as a consequence of teenage parenthood, but their findings are based on a national probability sample, which did not disaggregate Black from White teenagers in reported level of later educational attainment.

parenthood, women who had become parents during adolescence continued to struggle with their life and usually lacked family and social supports that were more readily available to on-time, on-sequence counterparts.[19] Problems posed by off-time election of parenthood prior to marriage are mitigated to some extent by family supports available to these women as they negotiate the tasks of parenthood. Black adolescent parents are particularly likely to move in with an extended family, receiving greater support than their White counterparts (Stack, 1974; Waite & Moore, 1978). Furstenberg's (1981, 1987) continuing follow-up study of teenage parents in Baltimore showed that nearly two-thirds of teenage parents still live with their parents more than 2 years after a first birth; nearly half (46%) of these teenage parents continue to live with parents 5 years after a first teenage birth.

At the same time, teenage parenthood encourages women to move out of the parental home in greater numbers than counterparts who did not experience early parenthood (Furstenberg & Crawford, 1978). More than a decade later, only 10% of these former adolescent parents were still living with their own parents. In the Baltimore study, the definitive study to date of early off-time parenting and its aftermath in terms of the adult life-course, most women maintained good relations with their family; movement out of the household took place most often when there was conflict between generations. Even when the offspring established separate residence, their parental family continued to provide assistance and emotional support.

Findings to date regarding the transition to parenthood among adolescent men and women leave many questions unanswered. First, as Furstenberg (1987) has recognized, social change over the past 20 years means that many of the conclusions from his study must be replicated with subsequent cohorts of adolescent parents. Second, most study to date has been concerned primarily with structural characteristics. Taking a social problems approach, these studies reveal what is generally accepted: early off-time, unevenly sequenced parenthood leads to somewhat lower economic attainment and to family instability.

Placed within this life-course perspective, these findings present a complex picture of adolescent development. Asocial and antisocial behavior in adolescence appears to predict serious adult psychopathology (Caspi, Elder, & Herbener, 1990; Cohen, Brook, Cohen, Velez, & Garcia, 1990; Newcomb & Bentler, 1990), but it is important to focus not only on psychopathology, but also on protective factors that might be associated with increased resilience, even when confronted with circumstances that might otherwise be associated with increased psychopathology.

CLINICAL RESEARCH AND INTERVENTION: TOWARD THE 21st CENTURY

Placed within a life-course perspective, these findings provide a complex picture of adolescent development. Diverse pathways and diverse outcomes from a particular pathway are common, but several basic developmental concerns remain consistent for adolescents. Further, although accumulating evidence is leading to greater appreciation regarding the resilience of the more troubled adolescent, problems presented by adolescents are increasingly being identified as serious psychopathology rather

---

[19] Furstenberg observed:

. . . many teenage parents seem to stage a recovery of sorts in later life. Most do not fit the popular image of the poorly educated, unemployed woman with a large number of children living on public assistance. Nonetheless, early childbearing extracts a price for many women. Premature parenthood diminishes the chance of economic mobility, in part by restricting educational and occupational opportunities, but also in large measure because it decreases the likelihood of marriage and marital stability. A strong implication of these findings is that teenage childbearers do worse because they are much more likely in later life to become female heads of households, primarily or exclusively dependent on their own earning ability. (1987, p. 131)

than as the inevitable conflict accompanying characteristic adolescent development.

Our goals in the present volume have been to find ways of bringing together these two cultures of intervention and study of the adolescent decade, to provide an integration of clinical and systematic normative perspectives, and to identify promising areas for future normative and clinical collaboration. As this volume has shown, collaborative study enjoys the dual benefits of improved care and enlivened scholarship regarding adolescence and youth. This book has identified important areas of study relevant to issues of intervention and change; clinically focused study of intervention provides important understandings of adolescence, which are particularly significant as the foundation for future study. Many of the problems posed for mental health intervention and social policy by the adolescent decade may be understood in terms of life-course, cohort, and generation.

From sexuality and early off-time pregnancy to substance abuse and status offenses, problems are created both for the adolescent and the larger society by the accentuated normlessness associated with this time between childhood and adulthood, by the particular sensitivity of adolescents and youth to social change, by the role of youth as the generation most responsible for social change, and, at least in contemporary society, by the compression of major life-course transitions. This compression reflects the continuing effort on the part of society to provide normative structure for what is commonly recognized as a time of relative normlessness. For example, reviewing the findings of the Carnegie Council Report on adolescent development, Davis and Tolan (Chapter 18 of this volume) noted the impact of achievement-tracking in schools. This tracking system reflects the effort to provide normative structure through enhanced sense of regularity, but at the cost of limiting opportunity and a sense of worthwhile endeavor.

Perspectives of clinical intervention across the adolescent decade have found it difficult to keep pace with changing formulations of personality development and family relations based on systematic study of large groups of adolescents. Normative study of adolescence has sometimes failed to appreciate the diversity of pathways through adolescence and has largely neglected systematic study of the determinants and course of personal distress and psychopathology across the adolescent epoch. Most significantly, normative study of the adolescent decade has not always appreciated the significance of reports founded on detailed study of particular lives over time as a means of understanding variation in adolescent development (Blos, 1962, 1967, 1971, 1979).

Concepts of cohort and social timing also have an impact on our understanding of the origins and course of major psychiatric disorder. Epidemiological findings (Westermeyer & Harrow, Chapter 15 of this volume) show that late adolescence represents a particular risk point for the onset of schizophrenia. Although the foundation of this increased risk is not clearly understood, the combination of expectation for enhanced performance within a role portfolio that is more complex and personally demanding than earlier in adolescence, interacting with maturational processes such as changes in brain chemistry, which enhance the sensitivity of the dopamine uptake receptors, may contribute to the particular risk associated with the onset of schizophrenia in late adolescence. Changes in the management of schizophrenia, including aggressive use of such second-generation antipsychotic medications as clozapine, may alter, in ways quite different from earlier generations of seriously troubled adolescents, the pattern of illness and consequent hospitalization for persons first succumbing to episodes of schizophrenia during adolescence.

Contributions of improved forms of treatment—prevention of the formation of negative symptoms of apathy and social withdrawal, treatment of the positive symptoms of hallucinations and delusions, and avoidance of the side effects that play a significant role in stigmatizing schizophrenics—all may play an important part in shaping a quite different life-course for schizophrenic patients within future generations of adolescents and youth. Fundamental shifts in understanding the major psychiatric disorders, including increasing concern with differentiation of a number of life-course patterns of episode and response to treatment, will further clarify our understanding of the impact of serious psychiatric illness on lives over time, form adolescence through the adult years.

Study of troubled lives is important in providing increased understanding of the origin and course of psychopathology and, through study of extreme cases, the impact of life experiences on personality development across the adolescent decade. Working with troubled adolescents within the context of psychotherapy provides particularly rich detail regarding issues that may be relevant more generally in understanding adolescence. The clinical setting provides an important avenue for study of the impact of social change on adjustment and for observation of those values and life-styles that are directly linked to a particular cohort or sociohistorically defined generation.

For example, many of the problems presently associated with the adolescent decade are a reflection of the large size of recent adolescent cohorts relative to the population pyramid as a whole (Easterlin, 1987; Guttentag & Secord, 1983). Reviewing findings regarding adolescent suicide, Clark and Mokros (Chapter 14 of this volume) observed that youth suicide rates will drop as the older adult population increases relative to the adolescent generation. The findings these authors reviewed show that, at least to some extent, adverse mental health outcomes represent a response to the increased competition for jobs and marital partners presented by a large birth cohort, particularly when society is unable to create sufficient jobs or to respond to an enlarged demand for educational resources, which accompanies a large birth cohort.

Problems posed by pubertal change and personal control of sexuality also show a clear effect of cohort and place of the adolescent decade in the course of life. Findings reported by Brooks-Gunn, Petersen, and their colleagues (Brooks-Gunn & Petersen, 1984; Brooks-Gunn, Petersen, & Eichorn, 1985; Petersen, 1988) have been particularly instructive in showing the interplay of cohort change and developmental process in the study of the transition to early adolescence. Following up on earlier findings by Mussen and Jones (1957), these investigators have studied the personality and pubertal development of early and later maturing boys and girls.

In findings that are particularly significant for clinical intervention, early maturing girls and late maturing boys appear to be at greater risk for personal distress, although virtually all adolescents in these studies were preoccupied by changes taking place in their bodies. Richards, Abell, and Petersen (Chapter 2 of this volume) have discussed the implications for clinical intervention. These findings are among the first to systematically report on the personal significance, for girls, of breast development and first menarche, and, for boys, of change in shape and size of genitals, pubic hair growth, and first ejaculation. These studies show the importance of the interplay between life-course and psychological perspectives in understanding the manner in which adolescents experience self- and pubertal-change across the years of early to middle adolescence.

Miller and Dyk (Chapter 5 of this volume) reviewed findings showing a dramatic increase in the number of adolescent girls reported being sexually active across the past two decades. Changes in norms for sexuality pose particular problems for young persons coming of age in the era of AIDS, when important issues are being raised regarding the role of young men and women in the decision for sexual intimacy. Significantly, enhanced use of condoms form first intercourse (Miller & Dyk), which should reduce the rate of adolescent pregnancy, is one positive outcome of concern with this near-epidemic and life-threatening sexually transmitted disease.

Increased awareness of the importance of male contraception for prevention of disease will have the associated consequence of reduced teenage pregnancy (although there is still some question whether teens living in the midst of urban poverty are as aware as their less impoverished counterparts regarding the importance of contraception). Teenagers from families of marital discord, particularly girls living with their mothers, may have more liberal sexual attitudes than their counterparts in intact marriages. Frequently, they see their mothers with lovers and are early introduced to awareness of nonmarital sexuality. Teenage girls living in single-parent households also have earlier sexual intercourse. With present trends showing acceleration rates of divorce, there will be fewer such single-parent households and less modeling of nonmarital sexuality on the part of adults.

Contemporary social problems have compounded the problems of many teenagers regarding the expression of sexual desire. The anxiety young men experience regarding their sexual adequacy has been compounded by fear that their female partner may later file a criminal charge of date rape. The anxiety women experience regarding their adequacy as a sexual partner has been compounded by concern that their sexual partner may leave them with a sexually transmitted disease. Conflicting values regarding sexuality have led to the fundamentalist claim that the scourge of AIDS has been visited on a profligate population given to sexual license. As a society, we are still in the process of dealing with the changed norms and practices associated with adolescent sexuality, which is a legacy of the 1960s. Middle-age adults, representing a more conservative generation than the present generation of adolescents and young adults, clearly have difficulty with this social change.

The area of substance abuse is one in which life-course perspectives will be important in informing subsequent intervention. The unprecedented social experimentation permitted for adolescents across the past two decades has been reflected in use of recreational drugs. Over the next half-century, as adolescents represent an every declining proportion of the population at any point in time, many of the present social ills associated with adolescence will also diminish. Further, smaller birth cohorts of adolescents will lead to a lessened sense of role strain and overload, which should further reduce such mental health risks associated with this point in the course of life as chemical dependence or substance abuse. To the extent that reliance on drugs or alcohol is a response to a world experienced as overwhelming, lessened pressure on members of a birth cohort should lead to reduced drug and alcohol use.

Larson and Kleiber and Berndt and Savin-Williams (Chapters 6 and 9 of this volume) have suggested that recreational drugs are used, at least partly, in order to deal with feelings of boredom and anxiety engendered by the American high school. Use of the drugs is a response to a world felt as overwhelming, particularly among underprivileged adolescents. Remediation of substance abuse problems depends, at least in part, on the ability of the schools to respond more effectively to adolescents' developmental and educational needs. In the construction of its curriculum, the American high school must attend more effectively than at present to the psychological needs of adolescent students from diverse social backgrounds. More explicit concern with the transition from school to work, including formalization of an apprenticeship program for youth not planning to attend college, is important if we are to respond more effectively to the distinctive place of adolescence within the course of life. European society has long formalized apprenticeship programs that lead both to learning a trade and to reasonable certainty that there will be employment following satisfactory completion of the apprenticeship program.

Tomorrow's adolescent is likely to encounter the mental health system as a more empowered consumer than in the past, according to Jaffe and Ryan, and Garbarino (Chapters 17 and 20 of this volume). Although recent court cases have been ambiguous regarding the rights of adolescents to seek abortion without parental consent, most states recognize the right of adolescents to obtain mental health services. This trend is likely to continue as the health and mental health needs of adolescents are more explicitly recognized. At the same time, there is likely to be a shift away from the traditional model of individual, long-term, outpatient psychotherapy. As Watts, Machabanski, and Karrer (Chapter 10 of this volume) have shown, a majority of the nation's adolescents in the 21st century will be from minority groups. Among these adolescents, the question of what are the most comfortable and valued modes of treatment is in urgent need of study.

Traditional psychotherapeutic approaches may inform the understanding of the world of the inner-city adolescent, but it is not clear that individual psychotherapy is always the treatment of choice. Rather, some sort of activity therapy or a more ecologically congruent intervention, as recommended by Davis and Tolan (Chapter 18 of this volume), may provide the most comfortable setting—a context in which it may be possible for troubled adolescents to discuss their distress. This approach, pioneered by Knopka (1949/1965) has proven effective in working with children and adolescents in the school setting. Just as is true among inner-city youth, teenagers from diverse cultures may not feel comfortable talking with an "Anglo" therapist of obviously middle-class background, especially regarding personal distress. Within cultures in which the role of privacy and distress has been differently constructed from that of the middle-class West, psychotherapeutic services must be tailored to particular cultural expectations.

It is important to take cultural context into account, not only in determining the most appropriate mode of intervention, but in tailoring specific interventions. Walsh and Scheinkman (Chapter 7 of this volume) have dealt with the problems of working with dysfunctional families differing in cultural context; their recommendations show particular clarity and sensitivity. Issues of identity, sexuality, and separation, all possible sources of conflict between the adolescent and the family, must be considered in both a developmental and a cultural context. The immigrant experience may pose particular problems for the adolescent attempting to resolve issues of "Who and what am I?", and the construction of closeness and separation within the multigeneration Pacific Rim family is quite different from that of the West (Watts, Machabanski, & Karrer, Chapter 10 of this volume).

The striking record of academic accomplishment among some Asian American immigrant groups is a reflection of their very close family ties, which ensure compliance with demands for homework. However, this same ethos of close family ties may make it particularly difficult for the adolescent to separate from the family. The Anglo-American ethos of individuality (MacFarlane, 1987; Parker, 1972) is in marked contrast with the emphasis on harmony and collectively characteristic of most cultures. Adolescents from other cultures largely define their identity in terms of the larger family group; even when there is conflict with the family, it is still important to recognize that intergenerational struggles appear quite different within corporate than within individually oriented cultures (Jenkins, 1984; McGoldrick, Pearce, & Giodarno, 1982; Spiegel, 1971).

Recognition of the significance of ethnicity for psychological development also poses problems for hospital or residential treatment, from admission of the troubled adolescent, through family and hospital issues during the period of inpatient stay, to planning for discharge and posthospital aftercare. The relationship between the family and the psychiatric hospital has received little study (Riess, Costell, Jones, & Berkman, 1980). As complex as it may be to close the gap between the different perceptions of personal significance of treatment and posthospital adjustment within middle-class American families, ethnicity poses additional problems in understanding the place of the adolescent within the family, in helping the family to receive the adolescent home from the hospital, and in planning posthospital aftercare (Marohn, Chapter 19 of this volume). Issues such as indications for residential treatment or psychiatric hospitalization, or planning for aftercare, may vary dramatically across ethnic groups. Study of the association of ethnicity and expression of hostility and resentment regarding disruptive patient behavior following discharge from the hospital (the so-called phenomenon of "expressed emotion") has shown that American and English families are likely to be less tolerant and more critical of deviant role performance than families from other cultures, who are better able to accept and support more troubled family members (Jenkins, 1984; Jenkins et al., 1986; Karno, Jenkins, de la Selva, & Santana, 1987; Kleinmann, 1988; Lefley, 1985).

American parents are particularly harsh critics of their own child-rearing (Minturn & Lambert, 1964) and tend particularly to believe that personal distress in their offspring is a consequence of their personal failure within this role. Parental feelings of guilt and responsibility, which make aftercare additionally difficult, may be less significant among other ethnic groups than among those identified with the tradition of the Western middle-class family. On the other hand, particularly among Korean and Japanese families, shame attendant on having to publicly acknowledge family problems may impede plans for aftercare or for managing medication compliance.

With dramatic escalation in migration from the Pacific Rim, intervention with adolescents must once again focus on issues of acculturation and the problems posed for adolescents who live between two worlds. More than a half-century ago, Covello (1944/1972) wrote of the problems of the Italian immigrant child facing New York City public schools, where adolescents were expected to take high school courses designed to prepare for the future, even though the concept of preparation for the future was much less relevant within traditional Southern Italian culture than within the United States. Southern Italian immigrant parents actively discouraged their teenage children form homework in subjects perceived as of little present relevance. Covello's work highlighted the problems posed for immigrant children caught between two worlds. Precisely because they are the principal carriers of social change within the family, adolescents within immigrant families are responsible for induction of parents into the "American way of life," teaching English to other family members or helping other family members learn about Western customs.

Maintaining traditional respect and demeanor while inducting older family members into American culture is a task that poses potential conflict for the extended family as a whole. The precarious role of the adolescent within the immigrant family often leads to tensions. These tensions are particularly significant among Japanese, Chinese, and Korean immigrant families, who are understandably wary of intergroup dating and marriage. It is inevitable that Asian American adolescents will date and become seriously involved with American boys and girls. As Larson and Kleiber (Chapter 6 of this volume) have shown, involvement with peers is a major source of support and morale for adolescents, and an important way of avoiding feelings of boredom or alienation.

The generality of these findings for adolescents within Pacific Rim immigrant groups is still not known, but it is likely that these immigrant adolescents will feel intense conflict between peer group enjoyment/loyalty within the peer group, and family obligations and responsibilities, which are likely to be more pronounced and significant than those imposed on American adolescents. Inevitably, parents object to increased participation within the peer group and intense family conflict ensues. Intervention within the family system of an immigrant adolescent requires particular familiarity with the culture, including values regarding family structure and process (McGoldrick et al., 1982; Spiegel, 1971). Within those cultures in which interdependence is understood as central to effective family functioning, the task of the therapist may be to restore comfortable harmony between parents and offspring rather than, as within the Western middle-class family, to foster enhanced autonomy and independence (Blos, 1979; Stierlin, 1974).

CONCLUSION

We are in the midst of important changes in the manner in which adolescence is understood within the context of life-course and culture. The social changes of the past three decades are without precedent in our own time. They have accentuated cohort differences, making it particularly difficult to understand the place of adolescence and youth in the course of life or the conflicts taking place between the generations within contemporary society. It is not clear whether parent–youth conflict is inherent and an inevitable consequence of the different place of parents and adolescents (in terms of position within society and access to valued resources and rewards), or a particular conflict induced by the dramatic social changes taking place within contemporary society, or some combination of these factors. At least as presently remembered, the parents of today's adolescents, growing up in the late 1950s and early 1960s, represented the last cohort before the sequence of civil rights and antiwar protest changed the social landscape of adolescence within our society. These presently middle-aged adults often have difficulty understanding the life-style and value choices of their offspring, even when there is intergenerational consistency in political attitudes.

The social changes of the past three decades have been without precedent in our own time. The social sciences have great difficulty understanding social change; they are better equipped to study the function of social institutions at any one point in time than to understand changes within these institutions over time. Social change is easier to recognize in retrospect than as it is taking place. At the same time, one of the most fascinating aspects of the youth movement of the 1960s was the clear recognition, even as it was taking place, that fundamental changes were occurring in American society.

Clarification of the concept of generation, and introduction of the concept of cohort, has significant impact on the social sciences, reflected not only in method of study (cross-sequential longitudinal designs), but also in the emergence of new modes of understanding structure and change in social life. Pioneering studies by Elder (1974), Schaie (1984), and their colleagues have dramatically changed our ability to study social life over time and across generations. Concurrently, there has been less appreciation of these innovative contributions among those concerned with troubled lives, both as a subject of systematic study and as having relevance to intervention with particular adolescents or young adults, the family, and such developmentally significant social institutions as the school and the workplace. Life-course social science perspectives focus not only on issues of continuity, but also on change over time. They frame particular issues in individual, family, and group psychotherapy, and in social system interventions, such as those occurring within the school (see Trickett & Schmid and Davis & Tolan, Chapters 8 and 18 of this volume), or the legal system (Crosby & Repucci, Chapter 12 of this volume).

Relying on clues provided by life-course demographic study (Easterlin, 1987; Hogan, 1981; Modell, 1989), the adolescent of the 21st century will encounter a smaller cohort than in years past. Situated within a society in which a changing age pyramid will include proportionately a much larger number of older than younger adults, including large numbers of persons expecting benefits from social security, full employment of younger adults is essential if older adults are to receive their benefits. Jobs will be increasingly technologically demanding, which will require a strong educational preparation. As a society, we can ill afford any kind of discrimination, in school or in the work force, that will deter from maximum productivity as we move into the 21st century. From apprenticeship work programs to increased use of such school-based counseling as group therapy, the school will be in a unique position to assist tomorrow's adolescent to realize the potential contribution of this generation within a society ever more dependent on youth as the foundation of economic and social productivity.

The proportion of immigrants, particularly from Pacific Rim and Latin American countries, relative to the population as a whole, will be larger, and their offspring will contribute significant numbers of younger and better educated workers. New values regarding both distinctive contributions and equality of men and women will foster ever greater collaboration in the workplace and increasing expectations of shared contribution of husband and wife at home. Sharing of child-care between husband and wife and the presence of child-care within the workplace are both likely to become more common. Accentuation of present trends toward dual-career families also means that an ever larger proportion of adolescents will have been involved in day-care and other group-rearing situations, and may be more comfortable in group than in individual settings, including group (rather than individual) psychotherapy, which places less emphasis on the formation of an intense tie between two people (Bettelheim, 1967).

Norms regarding the age at which first sexual intimacy may be appropriate will shift toward younger ages; much of the present stigma regarding unusual life-styles and differences in sexual orientation may disappear. Recognition of a larger number of self-acknowledged gay and lesbian adolescents and young adults, who will be more comfortable with their sexual orientation than in past time, will make increasing demands on the self-reflective quality of the therapist to recognize distress and assist adolescents in maintaining their sense of self and enhanced morale (Boxer, Cohler, Herdt, & Irwin, Chapter 11 of this volume). Issues of sexuality must be more explicitly acknowledged; tomorrow's adolescent may be more comfortable talking about body and sexuality than any member of past generations. Issues of early off-time adolescent pregnancy will likely diminish as a consequence both of smaller cohort size and new, less obtrusive forms of contraception. Increasingly effective education in the use of contraception should also reduce the incidence of sexually transmitted diseases.

With divorce somewhat less common than at present (Glick, 1977, 1979), treatment may focus increasingly on issues stemming from relationships expected to last over some duration.

Most significantly, tomorrow's adolescent will be a particularly demanding consumer of mental health services; therapists will be expected to be both savvy regarding population trends and empathic regarding stress emanating from social pressures to grow up ever more rapidly and to become a part of a productive society. Compression of a number of significant role transitions within a constantly shortening period of time (Modell & Goodman, 1990) will become accentuated; pressure for adolescents to begin work ever earlier in life may be particularly intense, in order to help support an aging population. Given these constraints, concern with identity may become a social luxury that is no longer affordable.

Socially allocated time "between the walls" of childhood and adulthood may become foreshortened when compared with the present generation of adolescents, and identity conflict may yield to premature foreclosure (Erikson, 1968) under this press to join the work force. Expectation of productive activity ever earlier in the course of life will require new apprenticeship programs much along the lines presently attempted in Europe, where there is a clear alternative to university education for those young people seeking to join the work force in late adolescence. Mental health interventions for troubled adolescents will also have to be more explicitly job-focused. It is still difficult to realize effective mental health intervention within the school; concepts of primary prevention will have to be extended to the workplace as well, with particular attention paid to problems induced by rapid transition from school to work, perhaps accompanied by accelerated transition to marriage and parenthood as well.

In order to meet the mental health needs of tomorrow's adolescent, we must become increasingly appreciative of cultural diversity and increasingly helpful to the public schools, which will have to face the educational challenge of the 21st century. The significance of recognizing this diversity has been well portrayed by Watts, Machabanski, and Karrer (Chapter 10 of this volume). Mental health intervention will require continuing a dual perspective on the subjective world of adolescents growing to adulthood within sociopolitical systems in multicultural communities far more complex than at present. Indeed, many of the problems presently found in Southern California will become common nationwide. Recognition of the contribution of culture and ethnicity to certain aspects of development—means for control of emotions, or a desired mode of relationships within the family—will become increasingly significant in realizing therapeutic success with adolescents who are far more diverse in their ethnic background than those from the Western European and American middle-class families who have most often been served by present mental health services.

Additional problems will be presented for those working with adolescents and their families within residential inpatient settings (Marohn, Chapter 19 of this volume). Study of the interplay between family and response to psychiatric services is among the most complex and neglected areas of study. Beyond pioneering study of pathways into and out of hospitalization, represented by the study of recurrent adult psychiatric illness, and the studies of David Riess and his colleagues regarding the family's initial encounter with the psychiatric inpatient setting, little is known about the manner in which hospitalization, aftercare, and recurrent psychiatric illness impact family process among adolescents and their families.

The introduction of the complex extended family represented by Pacific Rim, South Asian, and Latin American cultures will require both reconsideration of the relevant family unit in inpatient and outpatient family therapy, and new modes of intervention designed to assist the more troubled adolescent within an extended family whose values may diverge in significant ways from those of the Western middle-class family. As many of the chapters in the present volume have emphasized, it is important to develop alternative modes of intervention that recognize and support the ethnic diversity of today's and tomorrow's adolescents, such as the significance of extended family ties, which are particularly characteristic among recent immigrant groups from Latin America and the Pacific Rim, and to support culturally significant factors that mitigate against psychopathology and foster enhanced well-being.

There is growing appreciation of the diverse developmental pathways across the adolescent decade. At the same time, certain more general developmental tasks are presented for the family, the community, and society. Attaining a balance between the general and the specific in the study of adolescent development and psychopathology continues to require our consideration. Increased attention to the integration of research and practice will foster greater understanding of the multiple influences on adolescent behavior. As Garbarino (Chapter 20 of this volume) has emphasized, the adolescent decade presents problems conceived as "icebergs" rather than "ice cubes."

As noted in several chapters of this volume, it is important to develop a research-based approach to the varied repertoire of interventions required in the treatment of the more troubled adolescents living in the ethnically diverse community of the 21st century, which will present particular developmental challenges and opportunities. Understanding particular conceptions of adolescence and the social and cultural context of adolescence will contribute to enhanced intervention across the years of adolescence and young adulthood. In sum, research *and* clinical observation contribute to our understanding of both expectable adolescent development and the emergence, course, treatment, and later outcome of serious psychopathology. Our hope is that this volume will be able to contribute to enhanced understanding and increased success in fostering psychological well-being among tomorrow's adolescents.

REFERENCES

Antonucci, T. (1985). Personal characteristics, social support, and social behavior. In R. Binstock & E. Shanas (Eds.), *Handbook of aging and the social sciences* (2nd ed.) (pp. 94–128). New York: Van Nostrand Reinhold.

Antonucci, T., & Akiyama, H. (1987). Social networks in adult life and a preliminary examination of the convoy model. *Journal of Gerontology, 42,* 519–527.

Bacon, L. (1974). Early motherhood, accelerated role transition, and social pathologies, *Social Forces, 52,* 333–341.

Baldwin, W., & Cain, V. (1980). The child of teenage parents, *Family Planning Perspectives, 12,* 34–45.

Baltes, P. B. (1968). Longitudinal and cross-sectional sequences in the study of age and generation effects. *International Journal of Aging and Human Development, 11,* 145–171.

Bell, R. Q. (1977). Socialization findings reexamined. In R. Q. Bell & L. Harper (Eds.), *Child effects on adults* (pp. 53–84). Hillsdale, NJ: Erlbaum.

Bengtson, V., & Black, K. D. (1973). Intergenerational relations and continuities in socialization. In P. B. Baltes & K. W. Schaie (Eds.), *Life span developmental psychology: Personality and socialization* (pp. 207–234). New York: Academic Press.

Bengtson, V., & Kuypers, J. (1971). Generational differences and the developmental stake. *International Journal of Aging and Human Development, 2,* 249–260.

Bettelheim, B. (1963). The problem of generations. In E. H. Erikson (Ed.), *Youth: Change and challenge* (pp. 64–92). New York: Basic Books. (Original work published in 1961.)

Bettelheim, B. (1967). Psychoanalysis and education. *School Review, 77,* 73–86.

Bettelheim, B. (1969). *Children of the dream.* New York: Macmillan.

Blos, P. (1962). *On adolescence.* New York: Free Press.

Blos, P. (1967). The second individuation process of adolescence. *Psychoanalytic Study of the Child, 22,* 162–186.

Blos, P. (1971). The child analyst looks at the young adolescent. *Daedalus, 100* (4), 961–978. (Special issue: Twelve to Sixteen: Early Adolescence.)

Blos, P. (1979). *The adolescent passage.* New York: International Universities Press.

Blyth, D., Hill, J., & Smyth, C. (1981). The influence of older adolescents on younger adolescents: Do grade-level arrangements make a difference in behaviors, attitudes, and experiences? *Journal of Early Adolescence, 1,* 85–110.

Blyth, D., Hill, J., & Thiel, K. (1982). Early adolescents' significant others: Grade and gender differences in perceived relationships with familial and nonfamilial adults and young people. *Journal of Youth and Adolescence, 11,* 435–450.

Blyth, D., Simmons, R. G., & Carlton-Ford, S. (1983). The adjustment of early adolescents to school transitions. *Journal of Early Adolescence, 3,* 105–120.

Boxer, A., Gershenson, H., & Offer, D. (1984). Historical time and social change in adolescent experience. In D. Offer, E. Ostrov, & K. Howard (Eds.), *Patterns of adolescent self-image* (pp. 83–92). San Francisco: Jossey-Bass.

Brim, O. G., Jr. (1968). Socialization through the life cycle. In O. G. Brim, Jr. & S. Wheeler, *Socialization after childhood: Two essays* (pp. 3–48). New York: Wiley.

Bronfenbrenner, U. (1979). *The ecology of human development.* Cambridge, MA: Harvard University Press.

Brooks-Gunn, J., Petersen, A., & Eichorn, D. (1985). The study of maturational timing effects in adolescence. *Journal of Youth and Adolescence, 14,* 149–162.

Brooks-Gunn, J., & Petersen, A. (1984). Problems in studying and defining pubertal events. *Journal of Youth and Adolescence, 13,* 181–196.

Brooks-Gunn, J., & Reiter, E. O. (1990). The role of pubertal processes. In S. Feldman & G. R. Elliott (Eds.), *At the threshold: The developing adolescent* (pp. 16–53). Cambridge, MA: Harvard University Press.

Brooks-Gunn, J., & Ruble, D. (1983). The experiences of menarche from a developmental perspective. In J. Brooks-Gunn & A. Petersen (Eds.), *Girls at puberty: Biological and psychosocial perspectives* (pp. 155–178). New York: Plenum.

Brooks-Gunn, J., & Warren, M. (1985). Measuring physical status and timing in early adolescence: A developmental perspective. *Journal of Youth and Adolescence, 14,* 163–190.

Cain, L. (1964). Life course and social structure. In R. L. Faris (Ed.), *Handbook of modern sociology* (pp. 272–309). Chicago: Rand McNally.

Caldwell, S. (1980). Life-course perspectives on adolescent parent research. *Journal of Social Issues, 36,* 130–144.

Card, J., & Wise, L. (1978). Teenage mothers and teenage fathers: The impact of early childbearing on the parents' personal and professional lives. *Family Planning Perspectives, 10,* 199–207.

Caspi, A., Elder, G., & Herbener, E. (1990). Childhood personality and the prediction of life-course patterns. In L. Robins & M. Rutter (Eds.), *Straight and devious pathways from childhood to adolescence* (pp. 13–35). New York: Cambridge University Press.

Christ, M. A., Lahey, B., Frick, P., Russo, M., McBurnett, K., Loeber, R., Stouthamer-Loeber, M., & Green, S. (1990). Serious conduct problems in the children of adolescent mothers: Disentangling confounded correlations. *Journal of Consulting and Clinical Psychology, 58,* 840–844.

Clausen, J. (1972). The life-course of individuals. In M. Riley & A. F. Foner (Eds.), *Aging and society: III. A sociology of age stratification* (pp. 457–514). New York: Russell Sage.

Cohen, P., Brook, J., Cohen, J., Velez, N., & Garcia, M. (1990). Common and uncommon pathways to adolescent psychopathology and problem behavior. In L. Robins & M. Rutter (Eds.), *Straight and devious pathways from childhood to Adolescence* (pp. 242–258). New York: Cambridge University Press.

Cohen, R., & Weissman, S. (1984). The parenting alliance. In R. Cohen, B. Cohler, & S. Weissman (Eds.), *Parenthood: A psychodynamic perspective* (pp. 33–49). New York: Guilford Press.

Cohler, B. (1982a). Personal narrative and life-course. In P. B. Baltes & O. G. Brim, Jr. (Eds.), *Life-course development and behavior: Vol. 4* (pp. 205–241). New York: Academic Press.

Cohler, B. (1982b). Stress or support: Relations between older women from three European ethnic groups and their relatives. In R. Manuel (Ed.), *Minority aging: Sociological and social psychological perspectives* (pp. 115–120). Greenwich, CT: Greenwood Press.

Cohler, B. (1983). Autonomy and interdependence in the family of adulthood: A psychological perspective. *The Gerontologist, 23,* 33–39.

Cohler, B. (1984). Parenthood, psychopathology, and childcare. In R. Cohen, B. Cohler, & S. Weissman (Eds.), *Parenthood: A psychodynamic perspective* (pp. 119–147). New York: Guilford Press.

Cohler, B. (1988/1989). The human studies and the course of life. *Social Service Review, 62,* 552–576.

Cohler, B. (1991). The life story and the study of resilience and response to adversity. *Journal of Narrative and Life History, 1,* 169–200.

Cohler, B. (1992a). Becoming adolescent parents: Strain in the off-time transition to parenthood. In A. Greene & A. Boxer (Eds.), *Adolescence*. Hillsdale, NJ: Erlbaum.

Cohler, B. (1992b). Psychoanalysis and the classroom: Intent and meaning in learning and teaching. In N. Szajnberg (Ed.), *Education and the emotions: Psychoanalysis in American culture*. New York: Plenum Press.

Cohler, B., & Boxer A. (1984). Middle adulthood: Settling into the world—Person, time and context. In D. Offer & M. Sabshin (Eds.), *Normality and the life course: A critical integration* (pp. 145–203). New York: Basic Books.

Cohler, B., & Stott, F. (1987). Separation, interdependence, and social relations across the second half of life. In J. Bloom-Feshbach & S. Bloom-Feshbach (Eds.), *The psychology of separation and loss* (pp. 165–204). San Francisco: Jossey-Bass.

Coleman, J. and Associates (1974). *Youth: Transition to adulthood*. Chicago: University of Chicago Press.

Cook, J., & Cohler, B. (1986). Reciprocal socialization and the care of offspring with cancer and with schizophrenia. In N. Datan, A. Greene, & H. Reese (Eds.), *Life-span developmental psychology: Intergenerational relations* (pp. 223–244). Hillsdale, NJ: Erlbaum.

Cooper, C., Grotevant, & Condon, S. (1983). Individuality and connectedness in the family as a context for adolescent identity formation and role-taking skill. In H. Grotevant & C. R. Cooper (Eds.), *Adolescent development in the family* (pp. 43–60). San Francisco: Jossey-Bass.

Costello, R., Reiss, D., Berkman, H., & Jones, C. (1981). The family meets the hospital: Predicting the family's treatment program from its problem solving style. *Archives of General Psychiatry, 38,* 569–577.

Covello, L. (1972). *The social background of the Italo-American school child in New York.* Totowa, NJ: Rowman and Littlefield. (Original work published in 1944).

Csikszentmihalyi, M., & Larson, R. (1984). *Being adolescent: Conflict and growth in the teenage years.* New York: Basic Books.

Demos, J., & Demos, V. (1969). Adolescence in historical perspective. *Journal of Marriage and the Family, 31,* 632–638.

Deutsch, H. (1967). *Selected problems of adolescence. With emphasis on group formation.* (Psychoanalytic Study of the Child Monograph 3). New York: International Universities Press.

Dragastin, S., & Elder, G. (1975). *Adolescence in the life-cycle.* Washington, DC: Hemisphere.

East, P., & Felice, M. (1990). Outcomes of parent–child relationships of former adolescent mothers and their 12-year-old children, *Journal of Developmental and Behavioral Pediatrics, 11,* 175–183.

Easterlin, R. (1987). *Birth and fortune: The impact of numbers on personal welfare* (2nd ed.). Chicago: University of Chicago Press.

Eichorn, D., Clausen, J., Haan, N., Honzik, M., & Mussen, P. (1981). *Present and past in middle life.* New York: Academic Press.

Eisenstadt, S. N. (1956). *From generation to generation: Age groups and social structure.* New York: Free Press.

Elder, G. (1974). *Children of the Great Depression.* Chicago: University of Chicago Press.

Elder, G., Jr. (1975a). Adolescence in the life-cycle: An introduction. In S. Dragastin & G. H. Elder, Jr. (Eds.), *Adolescence in the life-cycle* (pp. 1–24). New York: Wiley.

Elder, G. (1975b). Age differentiation and the life course. *Annual Review of Sociology, 1,* 165–190.

Elder, G. (1979). Historical change in life patterns and personality. In P. Baltes & O. G. Brim, Jr. (Eds.), *Life-span development and behavior:* Vol. 2 (pp. 117–159). New York: Academic Press.

Elder, G., Jr. (1980). Adolescence in historical perspective. In J. Adelson (Ed.), *Handbook of adolescent psychology* (pp. 3–46). New York: Wiley.

Elder, G. (1984). *Studying women's lives: Research questions, strategies and lessons.* Unpublished manuscript. Cambridge MA: Henry A. Murray Research Center.

Elder, G. (1990). The life course. In E. F. Borgatta & M. L. Borgatta (Eds.), *The encyclopedia of sociology.* (In Preparation)

Elder, G., & Caspi, A. (1990). Studying lives in a changing society: Sociological and personological explorations. In A. I. Rabin, R. A. Zucker, & S. Frank (Eds.), *Studying persons and lives* (pp. 201–247). New York: Springer.

Elder, G., & Rockwell, R. (1979). The life-course and human development: An ecological perspective. *International Journal of Behavioral Development, 2,* 1–21.

Elster, A., & Lamb, M. (1986). Adolescent fathers: The understudied side of adolescent pregnancy. In J. B. Lancester & B. Hamburg (Eds.), *School age pregnancy and parenthood* (pp. 177–190). New York: Aldine.

Entwisle, D. (1990). Schools and the adolescent. In S. Feldman & G. R. Elliott (Eds.), *At the threshold: The developing adolescent* (pp. 197–224). Cambridge: MA: Harvard University Press.

Erikson, E. (1963). *Childhood and society.* New York: Norton. (Original work published 1950)

Erikson, E. (1958). *Young-man Luther.* New York: Norton.

Erikson, E. H. (1963). Youth: Fidelity and diversity. In E. H. Erikson (Ed.), *Youth: Change and Challenge* (pp. 1–23). New York: Basic Books. (Original work published 1961)

Erikson, E. (1968). *Identity, youth and crisis.* New York: Norton.

Field, T. (1981). Early development of the preterm offspring of teenage mothers. In K. G. Scott, T. Field, & E. G. Robertson (Eds.), *Teenage parents and their offspring* (pp. 147–175). New York: Grune & Stratton.

Field, T., Widmayer, S., Adler, S., & de Cubas, M. (1990). Teenage parenting in different cultures, family constellations, and caregiving environments: Effects on infant development. *Infant Mental Health Journal, 11,* 158–174.

Field, T., Widmayer, S., Stringer, S., & Ignatoff, E. (1980). Teenage, lower class Black mothers and their preterm infants: An intervention and developmental follow-up. *Child Development, 51,* 426–436.

Fischer, J., & Fischer, A. (1963). The New Englanders of Orchard Town. In B. Whiting (Ed.), *Six cultures: Studies of childrearing* (pp. 869–1010). New York: Wiley.

Flacks, R. (1967). The liberated generation: An exploration of the roots of social protest. *Journal of Social Issues, 23,* 52–75.

Flacks, R. (1971). *Youth and social change.* Chicago: Markham.

Frank, D. (1988). *The work of unemployment: Mourning for work and the meaning of job loss in an age of industrial decline.* Unpublished doctoral dissertation, University of Chicago.

Furstenberg, F. (1976). *Unplanned parenthood: The social consequences of teenage childbearing.* New York: Free Press.

Furstenberg, F. (1980). Burdens and benefits: The impact of early childbearing on the family. *Journal of Social Issues, 36,* 64–87.

Furstenberg, F. (1981). The social consequences of teenage parenthood. In F. Furstenberg, R. Lincoln, & J. Menken (Eds.), *Teenage sexuality, pregnancy, and childbearing* (pp. 184–210). Philadelphia: University of Pennsylvania Press.

Furstenberg, F. (1987). *Adolescent mothers in later life.* New York: Cambridge University Press.

Furstenberg, F. (1990). Coming of age in a changing family system. In S. Feldman & G. R. Elliott (Eds.), *At the threshold: The developing adolescent* (pp. 147–170). Cambridge, MA: Harvard University Press.

Furstenberg, F., & Crawford, A. (1978). Family support: Helping teenage mothers to cope. *Family Planning Perspectives, 10,* 322–323.

Gary, L. (1981). A social profile. In L. Gary (Ed.), *Black men* (pp. 21–46). Beverly Hills, CA: Sage.

Gershenson, H. (1983). *The ecology of childrearing in White families with adolescent mothers.* Unpublished doctoral dissertation, University of Chicago.

Glick, P. (1977). Updating the life cycle of the family. *Journal of Marriage and the Family, 39,* 5–13.

Glick, P. (1979). The future of the American family, *Current Populations Reports,* Series P-23, No. 78, 1–6.

Greenberger, E., & Steinberg, L. (1986). *When teenagers work: The psychological and social costs of adolescent employment.* New York: Basic Books.

Grotevant, H. (1983). The contribution of the family to the facilitation of identity formation in early adolescence. *Journal of Early Adolescence, 3,* 225–237.

Guttentag, M., & Secord, P. (1983). *Too many women: The sex ratio question.* Beverly Hills, CA: Sage.

Haan, N., Smith, M. B., & Block, J. (1968). Moral reasoning of young adults: Political-social behavior, family background, and personality correlates. *Journal of Personality and Social Psychology, 10,* 183–201.

Hall, G. S. (1904). *Adolescence: Its psychology and its relations to anthropology.* New York: Appleton.

Hagestad, G. (1974). *Middle-aged women and their children: Exploring changes in a role relationship.* Unpublished doctoral dissertation. University of Minnesota.

Hareven, T. (1986). Historical changes in the social construction of the life course. *Human Development, 29,* 171–180.

Harper, L. (1975). The scope of offspring effects: From caregiver to culture, *Psychological Bulletin, 82,* 784–801.

Hauser, S., Liebman, W., Houlihan, J., Powers, S., Jacobson, A., Noam, G., Weiss, B., & Follansbee, D. (1984). Family contexts of pubertal timing. *Journal of Youth and Adolescence, 14,* 317–338.

Havighurst, R. (1953). *Human development and education.* New York: Longman.

Havighurst, R., & Gottlieb, D. (1975). Youth and the meaning of work. In R. Havighurst & P. Dreyer (Eds.), *Youth: The seventy-fourth yearbook of the National Society for the Study of Education* (pp. 145–160). Chicago: University of Chicago Press.

Hendin, H. (1977). *The age of sensation.* New York: McGraw-Hill.

Hendricks, L. (1981). Black unwed adolescent fathers. In L. Gary (Ed.), *Black men* (pp. 131–138). Beverly Hills, CA: Sage Publications.

Herdt, G. (1989). Introduction: Gay and lesbian youth, emergent identities, and cultural scenes at home and abroad. *Journal of Homosexuality, 17,* 1–42.

Hill, J. (1980). The family. In M. Johnson (Ed.), *Toward adolescence: The middle school years.* Chicago: University of Chicago Press.

Hoffreth, S., & Moore, K. (1979). Early childbearing and later economic well being. *American Sociological Review, 44,* 784–815.

Hogan, D. (1981). *Transitions and social change: The early lives of American men.* New York: Academic Press.

Hogan, D. (1987). Demographic trends in human fertility, and parenting across the life span. In J. Lancaster, J. Altman, A. Rossi, & L. Sherrod (Eds.), *Parenting across the life span: Biosocial perspectives* (pp. 315–349). New York: Aldine.

Hogan, D., & Astone, N. (1986). The transition to adulthood. *Annual Review of Sociology, 12,* 101–130.

Howell, F., & Frese, W. (1982). Adult role transitions, parental influence, and status aspirations early in the life course. *Journal of Marriage and the Family, 44,* 35–49.

Jenkins, J. (1984). Schizophrenia and the family: Expressed emotion among Mexican-Americans and Anglo-Americans. *Dissertation Abstracts International, 45,* (6-A), 1806.

Jenkins, J., Karno, M., de la Selva, A., Santana, F., Telles, C., Lopez, S., & Mintz, J. (1986). Expressed emotion, maintenance pharmacotherapy and schizophrenic relapse among Mexican-Americans. *Psychopharmacology Bulletin, 22,* 621–627.

Jones, M. C., Bayley, N., MacFarlane, J., & Honzik, M. (Eds.). (1971). *The course of human life.* New York: Wiley.

Kagan, J., & Moss, H. (1962). *Birth to maturity.* New York: Wiley.

Kahn, R. (1979). Aging and social support. In M. Riley (Ed.), *Aging from birth to death* (pp. 77–91). Boulder, CO: Westview Press.

Kahn, R., & Antonucci, T. (1980). Convoys over the life course: Attachment, roles, and social support. In P. Baltes & O. G. Brim, Jr. (Eds.), *Life-span development and behavior: Vol. 3* (pp. 353–386). New York: Academic Press.

Kahn, R., & Antonucci, T. (1981). Convoys of social support: A life-course approach. In S. Kiesler, J. Morgan, & V. Oppenheimer (Eds.), *Aging: Social change* (pp. 383–405). New York: Academic Press.

Karno, M., Jenkins, J., de la Selva, A., & Santana, F. (1987). Expressed emotion and schizophrenic outcome among Mexican-American families. *Journal of Nervous and Mental Disease, 175,* 143–151.

Karno, M. (1987). Mental disorder among Mexican Americans and non-Hispanic Whites in Los Angeles. In M. Gaviria & J. D. Arana (Eds.), *Health and behavior: Research agenda for Hispanics.* Chicago: University of Illinois/Simon Bolivar Hispanic Research Program.

Katz, J. (1962). Personality and interpersonal relations in the college classroom. In N. Sanford (Ed.), *The American college: A psychological and social interpretation of higher education* (pp. 365–395). New York: Wiley.

Katz, J. (1968). *No time for youth: Growth and constraint in college students.* San Francisco: Jossey-Bass.

Keniston, K. (1971). Psychological development and historical change. In T. K. Rabb & R. I. Rotberg (Eds.), *The family in history: Interdisciplinary essays* (pp. 141–158). New York: Harper.

Keniston, K. (1963). Inburn: An American Ishmael. In R. W. White (Ed.), *The study of lives: Essays in honor of Henry A. Murray* (pp. 43–71). New York: Aldine.

Keniston, K. (1965). *The uncommitted: Alienated youth in American society.* New York: Dell. (Original work published 1960)

Keniston, K. (1968). *Young radicals.* New York: Harcourt.

Kleinmann, A. (1988). *Rethinking psychiatry: From cultural category to personal experience.* New York: Free Press.

Klerman, G., & Weissman, M. (1980). Depressions among women: Their nature and causes. In M. Guttentag, S. Salasin, & D. Belle (Eds.), *The mental health of women.* New York: Academic Press.

Knopka, G. (1965). *Therapeutic group work with children.* Minneapolis: University of Minnesota Press. (Original work published 1949)

Kohli, M., & Meyer, J. (1986). Social structure and social construction of life stages. *Human Development, 29,* 145-149.

Komarovsky, M. (1976). *Dilemmas of masculinity: A study of college youth.* New York: Norton.

Komarovsky, M. (1985). *Women in college: Shaping new feminine identities.* New York: Basic Books.

Lamb, M. (1986). The changing roles of fathers. In M. Lamb (Ed.), *The father's role: Applied perspectives* (pp. 3-27). New York: Wiley.

Lamb, M., & Lamb, J. (1976). The nature and importance of the father-infant relationship. *The Family Coordinator, 20,* 379-385.

Lamb, M., Pleck, J., Charnov, E., & Levine, J. (1987). A biosocial perspective on paternal behavior and involvement. In J. B. Lancaster, J. Altman, A. Rossi, & L. Sherrod (Eds.), *Parenting across the life-span: Biosocial dimensions* (pp. 111-142). New York: Aldine.

Lefley, H. (1985). Families of the mentally ill in cross-cultural perspective. *Psychosocial Rehabilitation Journal, 8,* 57-75.

Leichter, H., & Mitchell, W. (1967). *Kinship and casework.* New York: Russell Sage.

Lerner, R., & Spanier, G. (Eds.) (1978). *Child influences on marital and family interaction.* New York: Academic Press.

Levine, A. (1980). *When dreams and heros died: A portrait of today's college student.* San Francisco, CA: Jossey-Bass.

Lewin, K. (1936). Some social-psychological differences between the United States and Germany. *Character and Personality (Journal of Personality), 4,* 265-293.

Livson, N., & Peskin, H. (1980). Perspectives on adolescence from longitudinal research. In J. Adelson (Ed.), *Handbook of adolescent psychology* (pp. 47-98). New York: Wiley.

McCluskey, K., Killarney, J., & Papini, D. (1983). Adolescent pregnancy and parenthood: Implications for development. In E. Callahan & K. McCluskey (Eds.), *Life-span developmental psychology: Normative life-events* (pp. 69-113). New York: Academic Press.

McGoldrick, M., Pearce, J., & Giordano, J. (1982). *Ethnicity and family therapy.* New York: Guilford Press.

MacFarlane, A. (1987). *The culture of capitalism.* Oxford, England: Basil Blackwell.

Mannheim, K. (1952). The problem of generations. In K. Mannheim, *Essays on the sociology of knowledge* (pp. 276-322). London: Routledge and Kegan Paul.

Marini, M. (1981). *Age and sequencing norms in the transition to adulthood.* Paper presented at the annual meetings, American Sociological Association, Toronto, Ontario, Canada.

Minturn, L., & Lambert, W. (1964). *Mothers of six cultures: Antecedents of childrearing.* New York: Wiley.

Mitchell, W. E. (1978). *Mishpokhe: A study of New York City Jewish family clubs.* New York: Aldine.

Modell, J. (1989). *Into one's own: From youth to adulthood in the United States, 1920-1975.* Berkeley: University of California Press.

Modell, J., Furstenberg, F., & Hershberg, T. (1978). Social change and transitions to adulthood in historical perspective. In M. Gordon (Ed.), *The American family in social-historical perspective* (2nd ed.) (pp. 192-219). New York: St. Martin's Press.

Modell, J., & Goodman, M. (1990). Historical perspectives. In S. Feldman & G. R. Elliott (Eds.), *At the threshold: The developing adolescent* (pp. 93-122). Cambridge, MA: Harvard University Press.

Moffat, M. (1989). *Coming of age in New Jersey: College and American culture.* New Brunswick, NJ: Rutgers University Press.

Morgan, S., & Rindfuss, R. (1985). Marital disruption: Structural and temporal dimensions. *American Journal of Sociology, 90,* 1055-1077.

Mussen, P. H., & Jones, M. C. (1957). Self-conceptions, motivations, and interpersonal attitudes of late- and early-maturing boys, *Child Development, 28,* 243-256.

Neugarten, B. (1969). Continuities and discontinuities of psychological issues into adult life. *Vita Humana (Human Development), 12,* 121-230.

Neugarten, B. (1973). Personality change in late life: A developmental perspective. In C. Eisdorfer & M. P. Lawton (Eds.), *The psychology of adult development* (pp. 311-338). Washington, DC: American Psychological Association.

Neugarten, B. (1979). Time, age, and the life-cycle. *American Journal of Psychiatry, 136,* 887-894.

Neugarten, B., & Hagestad, G. (1976). Age and the life-course. In R. Binstock & E. Shanas

(Eds.), *Handbook of aging and the social sciences* (pp. 35–55). New York: Van Nostrand Reinhold.

Newcomb, M., & Bentler, P. (1990). Antecedents and consequences of adolescent cocaine use: An eight-year study from early adolescence to young adulthood. In L. Robins & M. Rutter (Eds.), *Straight and devious pathways from childhood to adolescence* (pp. 158–181). New York: Cambridge University Press.

Osofsky, J., & Osofsky, H. (1970). Psychological and developmental perspectives on expectant and new parenthood. *Review of child development research: Vol. 7: The family* (pp. 372–397). Chicago: University of Chicago Press.

Parke, R. D. (1981). *Fathers.* Cambridge, MA: Harvard University Press.

Parke, R. (1986). Fathers: An intra-familial perspective. In M. Yogman & T. B. Brazelton (Eds.), *In support of families* (pp. 59–68). Cambridge, MA: Harvard University Press.

Parke, R., Power, T., & Fisher, T. (1980). The adolescent father's impact on the mother and child. *The Journal of Social Issues, 36,* 88–106.

Parker, B. (1972). *A mingled yarn: Chronicle of a troubled family.* New Haven, CT: Yale University Press.

Parsons, T. (1966). *Societies; Evolutionary and comparative perspectives.* Englewood Cliffs, NJ: Prentice-Hall.

Pearlin, L. (1975). Sex roles and depression. In N. Datan & L. Ginsberg (Eds.), *Life-span developmental psychology: Normative life crises* (pp. 191–207). New York: Academic Press.

Pearlin, L. (1983). Role strains and personal stress. In H. B. Kaplan (Ed.), *Psychological stress: Trends in theory and research.* New York: Academic Press.

Pearlin, L., Menaghan, E., Lieberman, M., & Mullan, J. (1981). The stress process. *Journal of Health and Social Behavior, 22,* 337–356.

Petersen A. (1988). Adolescent development. *Annual Review of Psychology, 39,* 583–607.

Petersen, A., & Crockett, L. (1985). Pubertal timing and grade effects on adjustment. *Journal of Youth and Adolescence, 14,* 191–206.

Petersen, A., & Taylor, B. (1980). The biological approach to adolescence. In J. Adelson (Ed.), *Handbook of adolescent psychology* (pp. 117–155). New York: Wiley.

Plath, D. (1980). Contours of consociation: Lessons from a Japanese narrative. In P. Baltes & O. G. Brim, Jr. (Eds.), *Life-span development and behavior* (pp. 287–307). New York: Academic Press.

Pruchno, R., Blow, F., & Smyer, M. (1984). Life-events and interdependent lives. *The Gerontologist, 27,* 31–41.

Reinecke, B., Ellicott, A., Harris, R., & Hancock, E. (1985). Timing of psychosocial changes in women's lives. *Human Development, 28,* 259–280.

Reiss, D., Costell, R., Jones, C., & Berkman, H. (1980). The family meets the hospital: A laboratory forecast of the encounter. *Archives of General Psychiatry, 37,* 141–154.

Riley, M. W. (1973). Aging and cohort succession: Interpretations and misinterpretations. *Public Opinion Quarterly, 37,* 35–49.

Riley, M. W. (1976). Age strata in social systems. In R. Binstock & E. Shanas (Eds.), *Handbook of aging and the social sciences* (pp. 189–217). New York: Van Nostrand Reinhold.

Riley, M. W. (1981). Aging and social change. In M. W. Riley and (Eds.) Boulder, CO: Westview Press, 11–26.

Riley, M. (1986). The dynamisms of life stages: Roles, people, and age. *Human Development, 29,* 150–156.

Rosow, I. (1978). What is a cohort and why? *Human Development, 21,* 65–75.

Rossi, A. (1985). Gender and parenthood. In A. Rossi (Ed.), *Gender and the life-course.* New York: Aldine.

Roth, J. (1963). *Timetables: Structuring the passage of time in hospital treatment and other careers.* Indianapolis, IN: Bobbs–Merrill.

Rudolph, S., & Rudolph, L. (1978). Rajput adulthood: Reflections on the Amer Singh diary. In E. Erikson (Ed.), *Adulthood* (pp. 149–172). New York: Norton.

Sanford, N. (1966). *Self and society: Social change and individual development.* New York: Aldine.

Schaie, K. W. (1984). The Seattle longitudinal study: A 2-year exploration of the psychometric intelligence of adulthood. In K. W. Schaie (Ed.), *Longitudinal studies of personality* (pp. 64–135). New York: Guilford Press.

Schaie, K. W., Labouvie, G., & Buech, B. (1973). Generational and cohort-specific differences in adult cognitive behavior: A fourteen-year study of independent samples. *Developmental Psychology, 9,* 151–166.

Schwartz, D., & Thompson, M. (1981). Do anorectics get well? Current research and future needs. *American Journal of Psychiatry, 138,* 319–323.

Schwartz, D., Thompson, M., & Johnson, C. (1982). Anorexia nervosa and bulimia: The sociocultural context. *International Journal of Eating Disorders, 1,* 20–36.

Seltzer, M. (1976). Suggestions for examination of time-disordered relationships. In J. Gubrium (Ed.), *Time, roles, and self in old age* (pp. 111–125). New York: Human Sciences Press.

Simmons, R., & Blyth, D. (1987). *Moving into adolescence: The impact of pubertal change and school context.* New York: Aldine.

Simmons, R., Burgeson, R., Carlton-Ford, S., & Blyth, D. (1987). The impact of cumulative change in adolescence. *Child Development, 58,* 1220–1234.

Simmons, R., Carlton-Ford, S., & Blyth, D. (1987). Predicting how a child will cope with the transition to junior high school. In R. M. Lerner & T. T. Foch (Eds.), *Biological-psychosocial interactions in early adolescence* (pp. 325–376). Hillsdale, NJ: Erlbaum.

Snow, C. P. (1959). *The two cultures and the scientific revolution.* New York: Cambridge University Press.

Spanier, G., Sauer, W., & Larzelere, R. (1979). An empirical evaluation of the family life cycle. *Journal of Marriage and the Family, 20,* 27–38.

Spiegel, J. (1971). *Transactions: The interplay between individual, family, and society.* (Ed. J. Papajohn). New York: Aronson.

Stack, C. (1974). *All our Kin: Strategies for survival in a Black community.* New York: Harper & Row.

Stierlin, H. (1974). *Separating parents and adolescents.* New York: Quadrangle Books/New York Times.

Sullivan, H. S. (1953). *The interpersonal theory of psychiatry.* New York: Norton.

Thomas, L. E. (1974). Generational discontinuity in beliefs: An exploration of the generation gap. *Journal of Social Issues, 30,* 1–22.

Tocqueville, A. de (1969). *Democracy in America.* Travis G. Lawrence, Ed. J. P. Mayer and M. Lerner. New York: Anchor Books. 1969. (Original work published 1832).

Troll, L. (1970). Issues in the study of generations. *International Journal of Aging and Human Development, 9,* 199–218.

Uhlenberg, P. (1974). Cohort variations in family life cycle experiences of U.S. females. *Journals of Marriage and the Family, 20,* 284–292.

Valliant, G. (1977). *Adaptation to life.* Boston: Little, Brown.

Veevers, J. (1979). Voluntary childlessness; A review of issues and evidence. *Marriage and Family Review, 2,* 1–26.

Waite, L., & Moore, K. (1978). The impact of an early first birth on young women's educational attainment. *Social Forces, 56,* 845–865.

Weissman, M., & Klerman, G. (1977). Sex differences in the epidemiology of depression. *Archives of General Psychiatry, 34,* 98–111.

Zeits, C., & Prince, R. (1982). Child effects on parents. In R. Wolman & Associates (Eds.), *Handbook of developmental psychology* (pp. 751–770). Englewood Cliffs, NJ: Prentice-Hall.

Author Index

Abe, K., 391
Abel, G.G., 115
Abel, R.L., 282
Abell, R., 394, 417, 502, 511
Abelson, R., 54
Aber, J.L., 321
Aber, M., 301
Abrahams, D., 394
Abrams, N., 319
Achenbach, T., 45, 335, 389–390
Ackerman, N., 151
Adams, G., 152, 475
Adan, A.A., 443–444
Adan, R.D., 444
Adelman, H.S., 292, 299
Adelson, J., 7, 9–10, 31, 133, 258, 265, 270
Adler, N.W., 118
Adler, S., 506
Ageton, S.S., 111, 114, 309–311, 314–315, 323
Agnew, R., 314
Agosta, L., 415
Aichorn, A., 80, 412, 455
Ainsworth, M., 418
Akiyama, H., 495
Albee, G., 224–225, 236
Albert, N., 336–337
Albrecht, H., 30
Albrecht, R., 33–35, 40
Alessi, N.E., 339–340
Alexander, J., 10, 168, 287, 321, 445
Algozzine, B., 177
Alicke, M., 341, 388, 430
Allan, M.J., 346, 348
Allebeck P., 371

Allen, C.F., 134
Allen, J.P., 321
Allen, N., 319
Allen, V.L., 435
Allman, C.J., 348–349, 351–352
Alwin, D., 129, 131
Amborsini, P., 334, 338, 340–341
Ambuel, B., 291
Ames, M.A., 98
Amies, P., 400
Anderson, C., 152, 157
Anderson, E., 36
Anderson, J.C., 337
Anderson, J.D., 337
Andersson, T., 318
Andrews, K., 207
Angermeyer, M.C., 365
Anolik, S.A., 50
Anson, R., 139
Anthony, E.J., 9, 263, 387
Anthony, J., 9, 84, 318, 322–323
Antogini, F., 163
Antonucci, T., 495
Aponte, H., 344
Appelboom-Fondu, J., 340
Arbuthnot, J., 52, 287, 320
Archer, M., 430
Argyle, M., 133
Argyris, C., 194
Armstrong, M., 429
Arnold, G.S., 29
Arnold, W.R., 288
Aronson, V., 394
Ary, D.V., 430

Asher, S., 134, 203, 211–214, 314, 443
Ashway, J.A., 80
Asnis, L., 334
Astone, N., 489
Astrachan, B., 372
Attie, I., 34
Atwood, G., 67, 420
Aultman, M.G., 232
Aupperle, D., 313, 318–319, 428
Avalon, A., 81
Ayalah, D., 33

Bachman, J., 311, 313, 438
Bachorowski, J., 54
Bachrach, C., 105
Back, L., 254
Bacon, L., 508
Baekeland, F., 402
Baer, D.J., 287
Baer, G., 393
Baker, H., 391
Baker, L., 161, 162
Baker, R., 79
Baker, S.A., 110
Baldwin, A., 69
Baldwin, J., 48
Baldwin, W., 101, 507
Ball, S.J., 206
Balswick, J.O., 475
Balter, M.B., 8
Baltes, P.B., 259, 267, 269, 493
Bandura, A., 7, 9–10, 46, 54–55, 475
Bangert-Drowns, R.L., 439
Bank, L., 310, 312, 321

Barbera, L., 419
Bardenstein, K.K., 365
Bare, D., 438
Barenboim, C., 50
Barglow, P., 417–418
Barker, R., 134, 174, 183, 229, 265
Barkley, R., 393
Barnett, J., 37
Barnhard, F.D., 455
Barnhart, D., 401
Barone, C., 183
Barrett, C., 388
Barrett, M.J., 161
Barrett, M.W., 215
Barth, R., 393
Bartholomew, K.,1 88
Barton, C., 168, 287, 445
Basch, M., 69, 81, 412, 415–416, 419–421
Bass, D., 312, 321, 398, 401
Baumann, K.E., 206, 208
Bayley, N., 31, 263, 490
Beach, F.A., 95
Bear, G.G., 51
Beardslee, W., 334, 338–339
Beavin, J., 150
Beck, A., 333, 335–337, 393, 400
Beck, N., 337–338, 391
Becker, J.V., 115–116
Beckner, C., 347
Bedrosian, R., 393, 400
Begel, D.M., 71
Behar, L., 286, 301
Belenky, M., 235
Bell, A.P., 98, 99, 102, 262
Bell, R.Q., 251, 499
Bell, T., 101, 118
Bellur, S.N., 334, 340
Belter, R.W., 292
Bemporad, J., 339
Benedict, R., 7
Benes, F.M., 363, 367
Bengston, V., 252, 502
Benham, L., 374
Bennett, E.M., 174
Bennett, M., 224
Bennett, R., 194
Benson, J., 369–370
Benson, R., 419
Bentler, F.M., 318

Bentler, P., 308, 319, 509
Berdie, J., 483–484
Berdie, M., 483–484
Berg, C., 391
Berger, J., 444
Berger, P.L., 224
Berger, R.M., 263, 268
Bergin, A., 388
Bergman, A., 70, 83
Berk, R., 139
Berkman, H., 513
Berman, A.L., 345
Berman, J.S., 341
Berman, K.F., 362
Berndt, T.J., 49, 203–205, 207–210, 214–215, 497, 512
Bernfeld, S., 64, 78
Bernstein, D., 13
Bernstein, I., 79
Bernstein, R.M., 50, 58
Berry, G., 232
Berry, J., 222, 227, 231–235
Bersoff, D., 293
Betsey, C.L., 107
Bettelheim, B., 68, 480, 502, 516
Beville, S.L., 445
Beyer, J.M., 224
Bhattacarya, 81
Bieber, I., 251, 256
Bieber, T., 251, 256
Bierman, K., 49, 203, 210, 429–430
Bifulco, A., 339
Biglan, A., 430
Biklen, D.,1 83
Billy, J.O.G., 106, 110, 111, 205, 208
Binder, A., 225
Bingham, C.R. 108
Bird, T., 445
Birelson, P., 335
Birman, D., 174, 184, 198, 238, 240
Biron-Meisels, S., 48
Bishop, S., 393, 400
Bjornsson, S., 8
Black, D.W., 350
Black, K.D., 502
Black, M., 419
Blackburn, H., 438
Blackburn, I., 393, 400
Blackman, G., 10

Blehar, E., 418
Bleuler, M.N., 369–370, 373–374
Blitz, C., 313–314, 316, 320
Block, C.B., 229
Block, J., 251, 269, 339, 501
Blom, G.E., 55
Blood, L., 10
Bloom, B., 136
Blos, P., 6, 9, 63, 78, 258, 261, 387, 392, 395, 412, 419, 493, 502, 510, 514
Blotcky, M., 420
Blow, F., 503
Blue, J.H., 22, 25, 29
Blum, H.P., 84
Blumenthal, R., 225
Blumstein, A., 308, 317
Blyth, D., 45, 31, 33–34, 36, 95, 260, 444
Bock, R.D., 23
Boileau, H., 318, 321–322
Bolton, F.G., Jr., 116
Bonagura, N., 392
Bond, G.R., 373, 375–376, 378
Bonstrom, O., 182, 191
Bordie, S.K., 34
Bornstein, P.H., 45
Boruin, C.M., 321
Botvin, G., 183, 191, 439–440
Botwinick, J., 267
Boumil, M.M., 295
Bouterline-Young, H., 31
Bowen, R., 51
Bowes, P., 464
Bowlby, T., 419
Boxer, A., 31–35, 38, 80, 249–251, 253–254, 256–258, 260–263, 265–266, 268–269, 271–272, 363, 367, 371, 490–491, 494–495, 505, 516
Boyd, J., 9, 338, 344, 361, 373, 377
Boyer, C.B., 117
Boyer, D., 258, 453–455, 457, 459, 465
Boyer, E., 176
Boyer, L.B., 84
Boyle, M.R., 310–312, 316
Bozigar, J., 346
Bracht, N., 438
Bradlow, P., 79

Braiman, S., 9
Branch, J.D., 419, 434
Brandcraft, B., 67, 77
Brasswell, M., 167, 314, 321, 417, 445
Braswell, L., 393
Breier, A., 372
Breitt, S., 430
Bremner, R.H., 259
Brendtro, L.K., 215
Brennan, T., 318
Brent, D.A., 346–352
Breuer, J., 71
Breunlin, C., 167
Breunlin, D., 167
Brim, O., 253, 499
Brink, K.L., 288
Brion-Meisels, S., 52
Britt, B., 430, 432, 434
Brodsky, G., 167
Broman, R., 507
Bromet, E.J., 350
Bronfenbrenner, U., 174, 188, 204, 239, 265, 312, 476, 481, 507
Brook, C.G., 23
Brook, J., 509
Brooks-Gunn, J., 29, 33–34, 37, 39, 63, 117, 261, 440, 442, 511
Brophy, J., 173
Brown, B.B., 134, 204, 206–207, 213
Brown, C.H., 318, 322-323, 419
Brown, E.J., 115
Brown, G.L., 313
Brown, G.W., 339
Browne, A., 114, 479
Browning, M.M., 35
Bruch, H., 160
Bruner, J., 125
Bryant, C., 237
Buckley, P., 71
Budenz, D., 393, 400
Buech, B., 490
Bugental, D.P., 252
Buhrmester, D., 208
Buie, D, 414
Buiel, R., 234
Bulhan, H., 224–225
Burbach, D., 365
Burch, P.R., 321

Burchard, J., 286, 322
Burchard, S., 286, 322
Burgdorff, K., 483
Burgeson, R., 25
Burgess, A.W., 111, 114
Buriel, R., 222, 239, 240
Burke, J., 9, 338, 361
Burke, N., 84
Burke, P.M., 334
Burnam, A., 375
Burns, B.J., 15
Burns, T.L., 350
Burroughs, J., 334
Bursik, R.J., Jr., 315
Burt, M.R., 111–112
Burton, N., 333
Burton, R.V., 267
Burts, D., 136
Busch-Rossnagel, N., 127
Buser, R., 135
Bush, D.M., 31, 34, 260
Bushwall, S.J., 109
Buss, A., 126
Butler, R., 254
Butts, J.D., 106
Bybee, R., 484–485
Byrne, D., 48, 105

Cadoret, R.J., 313
Caes, P., 213
Cage, R., 288
Cain, L., 494
Cain, V., 507
Cairns, C., 313
Cairns, R.B., 313
Calabrese, R., 136
Caldwell, S., 506
Camburn, D., 108–109
Camp, B.W., 55
Campbell, D., 398
Campbell, E., 152
Campbell, J.D., 267
Campbell, M., 340–341
Campbell, S.B., 290
Cance, A., 183
Capaldi, D., 310, 312, 317, 320–321
Caplan, G., 175, 482
Caplan, N., 224
Caplinger, T.E., 320
Caputo, L.M., 428
Card, J. 118, 508

Carins, R.B., 320
Carlaw, R., 438
Carlsmith, J.M., 37, 106, 109
Carlson, G., 336–338, 391
Carlsson, A., 362
Carlton-Ford, S., 25, 34, 444, 495
Carone, B., 368–369, 371
Carpenter, W.T., 367, 369
Carrier, J., 265
Carrigan, S., 347
Carstensen, L.L., 345
Carter, E., 151
Carter, R.T., 235
Carver, C.S., 50, 181
Casey, A., 182, 191
Casey, P., 283, 287–288
Casey, R.J., 341
Cashman, M.A., 339
Casper, R.C., 34, 40
Caspi, A., 490, 509
Cass, V.C., 262, 268
Castro, J., 177
Catalano, R.F., 443
Cates, J.A., 460
Caton, C.L.M., 375
Cauce, A.M., 214, 210, 215, 444
Cavallo, D., 129
Cernkovich, S.A., 210
Chadwick, D.F., 1, 37, 412
Chadwick, O., 8, 10, 13
Chaiken, J.M, 317–318
Chaiken, M.R., 318
Chalip, L., 129
Chalkley, A., 400
Chambers, W.J., 335, 398
Chan, S.Q., 222, 234, 239–240
Chandler, M., 49, 51–52
Chang, J., 251
Charbonneau-Powis, M., 400
Charlebois, P., 310, 318, 321–323
Charnov, E., 507
Chase, T.N., 362
Chase-Lansdale, L, 440, 442
Chassin, L., 206–208
Cheek, N.H., 204
Chen, C., 375
Cherlin, D., 174
Cherniss, C., 182, 192
Chertok, F., 421, 427, 429, 439
Chesler, J., 189
Chiaken, M.R., 317

Chiles, J., 430
Chilman, C.S., 108
Chisin, I.H., 8
Chodorow, N., 252, 267
Chouros, G.P., 22, 25, 26
Christ, M.A., 507
Christensen, O.V., 251
Christensen, R., 107–108
Christie, J., 393, 400
Christie, K.A., 338
Christoff, K., 393
Christopher, J.S., 429
Christopherson, E., 393
Chu, D.B., 433
Cicchetti, D., 335, 477
Ciompi, L., 370, 378
Circk, N.R., 45
Clan, C., 372
Clark, B.R., 259
Clark, D., 400, 511
Clark, D.C., 342, 345–347
Clark, L.A., 210
Clark, L.V., 47
Clark, S., 37
Clark, S.M., 109
Clarke, A., 259
Clarke, G., 45
Clarkin, J.F., 365
Clarkson, S.E., 337
Clasen, D., 134, 206–207
Clausen, J., 30, 260, 261, 378, 490, 494
Clinchy, B., 235
Clingempeel, W., 36
Clinthorne, J., 8
Cloninger, C.R., 313
Coates, T.J., 360
Coats, K.I., 45, 341
Cochrane, D.B., 52
Coelho, R., 475
Coen, S., 79
Cogswell, K.A., 45
Cohan, P., 13
Cohen, D., 394
Cohen, H.L., 287
Cohen, J., 205–206, 311, 509
Cohen, L., 173, 288
Cohen, M.I., 117
Cohen, P., 435, 509
Cohen, R., 507
Cohler, B., 63–64, 66–67, 70–71, 73–74, 77, 80, 84,
153, 251–254, 259, 262–263, 269, 359, 361, 363, 366–367, 371, 490–491, 494–495, 497, 499, 503, 505, 507, 516
Coie, J.D., 54, 211–212, 323
Cole, M., 230
Coleman, E., 258
Coleman, J., 131, 137, 204, 206, 259, 260, 492, 498
Coleman, S., 165
Coles, R., 108
Colfer, M.V., 339–340
Colletti, J., 137–138
Collins, J.K., 101
Combrinck-Graham, L., 150, 153, 155, 168, 429, 482
Condon, S., 503
Condry, J., 207
Conger, J.J., 259
Conger, R., 167
Conlin, M., 282, 283
Connor, P., 317, 319
Conrad, D., 136
Conroy, R.C., 345
Constantino, G., 225
Constanzo, P.R., 30
Conte, F.A., 22
Cook, J., 249–252, 265, 271, 499
Cooley, C.H., 251
Coons, N., 259
Cooper, C., 503
Cooper, G.D., 460
Cooper, J., 364
Cooper, M., 54
Cooper, T.B., 334
Coppotelli, H., 211–212
Corbett, H., 193
Corcoran, C., 337–338, 391
Cornelius, P., 483, 485
Coryell, W., 346–347
Costa, F., 107
Costantino, G., 237
Costell, R., 116, 513
Costello, A., 335, 398
Costello, J., 419, 428
Cote, G., 309
Cottey, 351
Cottler, L., 374
Cotton, P.G., 372
Covello, L., 499, 514
Covelman, C., 163, 164
Covington, J., 232
Cowen, E.L., 320–321, 428
Cowles, K.V., 347
Crabtree, L.H., 462
Crawford, A., 509
Crick, N.R., 56
Crockett, L., 32, 34, 36, 39, 203, 261
Cromwell, C., 417
Cromwell, R., 167, 314, 321, 445
Crosby, 515
Cross, C.E., 260
Croughan, J., 337
Crouse-Novak, M.A., 334
Crowe, R.R., 313
Crowfoot, D., 189
Csikszentmihalyi, M., 1, 63, 125–129, 132, 134, 138–140, 203, 212–213, 216, 261, 270, 337, 417, 497
Cunningham, M., 139
Cunningham-Rathner, J., 116
Curran, J.P., 429
Currier, R.L., 95
Curry, J.F., 321
Curtis, H., 73
Curtis, J., 83
Curtiss, G., 402, 419, 456, 464
Cusick, P., 173, 176
Cutler, G.B., 22, 25, 26, 29
Cytryn, L., 319–320, 335, 337, 398

Dahlgren, K.G., 342
Dain, H., 251
Daives, M., 208
Dalle-Molle, D., 412, 455, 457–458, 460, 462
Damon, W., 45–47, 50–51
Danforth, H., 334
D'Angelo, R., 10
Danish, S., 130–131
Dank, B., 263, 268
Dannefer, D., 288
D'Antonio, M., 182, 192
Datan, N., 36
D'Augelli, A., 224, 260
D'Augelli, J., 260
Davidson, J., 191

Davidson, W.S., 320, 322, 393, 445–446
Davies, M., 9, 314, 336, 337, 339, 391
Davies, S., 334
Davis, G., 53, 115–116
Davis, J.B., 259
Davis, J.M., 372
Davis, K., 96
Davis, L., 313–316, 317, 318–320, 428, 510, 513, 515
Davis, M., 334
Davis, S.M., 282, 284
Dawes, R., 181
Dawson, R.E., 252
Deandreis, A., 183
DeBusk, M., 433
Decker, H.S., 71
Deisher, R., 115, 268, 270
DeJesus, S., 339
Delacour, S., 71
Del Gaudio, A., 9, 391
DeLamater, J., 96, 100
De la Selva, 514
DeLong, G.R., 334
DeMartini, J., 136
Demilio, J., 96
Demorest, A., 52
Demos, J., 364, 500
Demos, V., 364, 500
Dennis, W., 259
DePaulo, B.M., 54
Depue, R.A., 334
Derogatis, L., 14
Derrick, A., 347
Deutsch, F., 63, 71
Deutsch, H., 497
Devin-Sheehan, L., 435
DeVries, M., 141
Dew, M.A., 350
Deykin, E.Y., 337–338
Diamond, A., 461
Diaz-Guerrero, R., 237
DiClemente, R.J., 118
Diepold, J., Jr., 95
Diester, A., 368
DiGiuseppe, R., 393
Dince, P., 251
Dincin, J., 375
Dishion, T.J., 207, 312–315
Dittmann-Kohli, F., 127

Dixon, W.J., 372–373
Dlugokinski, E.L., 428
Dobson, W., 152
Dodge, K.A., 45, 46, 53–54, 56–57, 211–212, 313–314, 316, 317
Doering, Z.B., 259
Dolan, L.J., 322–323
Dolgin, K.G., 56
Dolinsky, A., 9
Donaldson, G., 267
Donovan, J.E., 107, 313, 318
Dorer, D.J., 334, 338
Dorn, L.D., 22, 25, 26, 29
Dornbusch, S., 37, 63, 109
Douvan, E., 7, 9–10, 14, 31, 133, 265, 270
Dovidio, J.F., 225
Downey, G., 260, 345
Downs, W.R., 204, 206
Doyle, A.B., 203, 212
Dragastin, S., 490
Drake, B.E, 372
Drake, R.E., 371, 376
Draper, R., 222
Dreher, D., 134
Drellich, M.,2 51
Dreyer, P., 95, 260
Dryfoos, J.G., 441–442
Dubey, D., 55–56, 393
DuBois, W.E., 234
Dubrow, N., 471, 480–482
Duckett, E., 132–133
Duda, J., 130
Duke, P., 32, 37, 106
Dulcan, M.K., 335
Dulit, E., 417
Dumas, J., 316, 321
Duner, V., 318
Dunford, F.W., 311–312
Dunphy, D., 204, 214
Dusenbury, L., 183, 191
Dwyar, J.H., 319, 334, 429, 440
Dyk, 204, 511
D'Zurilla, T.J., 53

Earls, F., 312–313, 317
Easser, R., 414
Easson, W.M., 458
East, P., 211–212, 506
Easterlin, R., 511, 515
Ebata, A., 25, 475

Eckland, B., 131, 134, 136, 432
Ecton, R., 55–56, 393
Edelbrock, C., 45, 335, 398
Edelsohn, G., 322–323
Edelson, M., 66, 423
Eder, D., 209, 213–215
Edgar, E., 178
Edind, E., 134
Edmonds, R., 186
Edwards, H., 131
Egeland, J.A., 346
Eicher, S., 134, 206–207
Eichorn, D., 23, 259–261, 490, 511
Einstein, Albert, 134
Eisen, M., 50
Eisenberg, J., 389
Eisenberg-Berg, N., 51
Eisenstadt, S.N., 493
Eitzen, D.S., 131
Elardo, P.T., 54
Elde, G., 364, 479, 481, 490–491, 494, 509, 515
Elder, G.H., 260, 267–269
Elkind, D., 46, 51, 133, 389
Elliot, D.S., 308–312, 314–315, 317–319, 321, 323
Ellis, L., 98
Elmen, R., 428, 475
Elson, M., 71
Emde, R., 263
Emery, G., 393
Emmelkamp, P., 400
Endicott, J., 346–347, 360
Ennis, D., 293
Ensminger, M.E., 318
Entwisle, D., 495
Epstein, J., 183, 205–206, 208, 374
Epstein, S., 374
Erickson, J.B., 431–432
Erickson, M.L., 314
Erikson, E., 6, 9, 45, 71, 76, 80, 113, 125, 257, 260, 264, 371, 493–495, 498, 500, 516
Erikson, J., 260
Eron, L., 45, 313–318, 320, 322–323
Esterlin, R., 494
Esvedlt-Dawson, K., 399
Eunson, K., 400
Evans, A.C., 185

Evans, D.L., 334
Eveland, L.K., 308
Eyferth, K., 127, 140

Fairchild, H., 242
Fairweather, G., 227
Falco, M., 439
Falk, J., 253
Fallahi, C., 337–338, 391
Faller, E.A., 430
Falloon, I.R.H., 373, 377
Fanon, F., 81
Farber, E., 483, 485
Farberow, N.L., 346
Farley, J., 222
Farmer, F.L., 109
Farnsworth, M., 311
Farr, R.K., 375
Farrington, D.P., 308–313, 315, 317–318, 322–323, 445
Fasick, F.A., 229, 232
Faust, D., 52
Faust, M.S., 33
Faust, R., 164, 318
Fawcett, J., 339–340, 345–347
Fay, R.E., 97
Featherman, D.L., 432
Feczko, M., 456
Federn, P., 68
Feffer, M., 51
Fehrenbach, P.A., 115
Feiguine, R.J., 334, 341
Feinberg, T.L., 334
Feindler, E., 45, 55–56, 393
Feinichel, O., 78
Feldman, D.A., 271
Feldman, R.S., 209, 213, 226–227, 435
Felice, M., 506
Felner, R., 183
Feltham, R.F., 203, 213
Fenichel, O., 80
Fenigstein, A., 50
Fennell, M., 400
Fenton, W.S., 374
Fenzel, L.M., 434
Feraios, A., 80, 250
Ferguson, R., 235
Ferguson, T.J., 47
Fernandez, T., 234, 238
Ferris, J.A., 344–345
Ferrono, C.L., 359, 361, 363

Fick, P., 507
Fiedler, R.D., 430
Field, T., 506–507
Figlio, R.M., 309, 311
Filby, N., 173
Filipczak, J., 287, 430
Finch, A.J., 55
Fine, M., 38
Fineberg, B.L., 454–456
Fingerhut, L.A., 343
Finkelhor, D., 111, 113–114
Finkelstein, R., 334
Finnegan, T.A., 309, 317
Finney, J., 393
Firestone, W., 193
Fisher, A., 313–316, 320
Fisher, B., 483–484
Fisher, L.A., 206, 308
Fisher, P., 338, 343, 391
Fisher, S., 65
Fisher, T., 110, 507
Fisher, W.A., 105
Fishman, H.C., 167
Flacks, R., 502
Flament, M., 391
Flanagan, T.J.,115
Flavell, J.H., 47, 56
Flay, B.R., 319, 440
Fledman, R.A., 320
Fleiss, R., 414
Fleming, J.A., 368
Fleming, J.P., 318
Flener, R.D., 443–444
Flitcraft, A., 225
Flora, J.A., 117
Fogg, L., 346–347
Foley, C., 340
Follansbee, D., 152, 503
Foote, F.H., 319
Ford, C.S., 95
Ford, K., 107–108
Ford, M.E., 213
Forrest, J., 105
Forste, R.T., 108
Foster, B., 139
Fountain, C.D., 129
Fowler, R.C., 348, 350
Fox, G.L., 109–110
Fraiber, A., 387
Frame, C.M., 54, 313, 317
Frances, A., 12
Francis, G., 390

Francis, J., 79
Frank, D., 492
Frank, J., 400
Frank, R., 394
Frankie, A., 438
Frealy, M.J., 23
Frechette, M., 322
Freedman, E., 96, 434
Freeman, A., 393
Freeman, H.P., 224
Freeman, L.N., 335
Freeman, M., 139
Freeman, R., 334
Freeman, W.B., 377
Freet, B., 393
French, D.C., 212
Frese, W., 508
Fretwell, E., 134
Freud, A., 6, 9–10, 25, 63, 72, 79, 257, 261, 270, 392–393, 412, 419, 422, 475
Friedenberg, E., 474
Friedman, R.M., 301, 430
Friesen, J., 150, 162
Fritz, G., 430
Fuast, R., 319
Fuhr, R., 187
Furman, W., 208, 430
Furstenberg, F., 103, 107, 109, 440, 442, 489, 506–509

Gabel, S., 71
Gabrielli, W.E., 313
Gaertner, J.L., 225
Gagnon, C., 310, 318, 321–323
Gagnon, J.H., 95, 97, 251
Gailly, A., 254
Galambos, N.L.,2 59
Galatzer-Levy, R., 63–64, 66, 71, 73–75, 77, 83, 491, 503
Gallatin, J., 417
Galloway, C., 369–370
Gammon, C.D.,3 34
Ganzer, V.J., 57
Garbarino, J., 471, 474–477, 479–485, 517
Garber, J.,3 19
Garcia, M. 509
Garcia-Preto, N., 151–154
Gardner, R., 65
Gardner, W., 289, 290
Garduque, L., 437

Garfield, S., 402
Garfinkel, P., 162
Garland, A., 350
Garner, D., 162, 400
Garside, R., 396
Gary, L., 232, 507
Gassner, S., 347
Gates, C., 372
Gatsonis, C., 334
Gauthier, W., 134
Gebhard, P.H., 251, 262
Gedo, J., 68–69, 73, 85, 412–414, 419
Geertz, C., 254
Gehring, T.M., 226, 227
Gelb, S., 178
Geleerd, E., 387, 393
Gelinas, D.J., 114
Geller, B., 334
Gelles, R., 479
Gensheimer, L.K., 320, 322, 445–446
George, L.K., 361
Gerber, M., 183, 435
Gerdt, G., 264
Gergen, K., 222, 253–254
German, R.S., 374
Gershaw, N.J., 429
Gershenson, H., 269, 490, 506
Gershoni, R., 208
Gerson, R., 156
Gerstel, C., 80, 250
Gersten, J., 317, 389
Gesten, E.L., 428
Geyer, E.S., 153, 251
Giarrusso, R., 111, 112
Gibbons, R.D., 345
Gibbs, J.T., 230, 231, 428
Gibson, M.J., 195
Gibson, P., 270
Gibson, R., 182
Gilbert, M., 110
Gilchrist, L.D., 429, 440
Gilderman, A.M., 373, 377
Gill, M., 56, 64, 66, 71, 420
Giller, H., 139, 312, 315, 320, 323
Gilliam, G., 477, 479
Gilligan, C., 48, 51, 72, 152, 252, 267
Ginsberg, D., 72
Ginter, M., 176, 443–444

Giodarno, J., 513–514
Giordano, P., 210
Gitelson, M., 414
Gittelman, R., 333
Gittelman-Klein, R., 366
Gittelson, M., 413, 419
Gittleman, R., 392
Giudano, V., 393
Gjerde, P., 339
Glaser, K., 335
Glass, G., 173
Glenn, A., 393, 400
Glenn, J., 71, 79
Glick, I.D., 365
Glick, M., 366–367
Glick, P., 516
Glover, E., 73
Godbey, G., 126
Goertzel, V., 375
Goetz, R., 334
Gold, M., 214
Goldberg, A., 69, 80, 84, 412–413, 420, 423, 460
Goldberg, S.C., 372–373
Goldberger, N., 235
Goldenberg, I.I., 174
Goldfried, M.R., 53
Goldin, J., 400
Goldman, J., 95
Goldman, R., 95
Goldner, V., 152
Goldsmith, M., 117
Goldstein, A.P., 429
Goldstein, C., 346, 348
Goldstein, J.M., 365
Goldston, S., 130
Goleman, 479
Golombeck H., 422, 458
Gonso, J., 55
Gonzales, N., 215
Good, B.J., 233
Good, M.D., 233
Good, T., 173
Goodale, T., 126
Goodchilds, J., 111, 112
Goodlad, J., 176
Goodman, G.S., 301
Goodman, J., 55
Goodman, M., 492, 516
Goodman, P., 474
Goossens, F.A., 213
Gordon, D.A., 52, 287, 320

Gorman-Smith, D., 313
Gossett, J., 401, 455
Goswick, R.A., 213
Gottesman, I.I., 359, 361–362
Gottfredson, D., 437, 445
Gottfredson, G.D., 314
Gottlieb, B., 177
Gottlieb, D., 492
Gottman, J., 55, 72, 133
Gottschalk, R., 320, 322, 445–446
Gould, M., 345, 391, 402
Gove, W.R., 366
Graden, J., 182, 191
Graef, R., 132, 261
Graham, D., 334
Graham, P., 1, 8–10, 13, 37, 390–391, 412
Grand, H., 251
Granovetter, M., 183
Grave, G.D., 21
Green, A., 71
Green, J., 336
Green, R., 80, 250–252, 258
Green, S., 507
Green, T., 10, 37
Greenberg, J., 392
Greenberg, R., 65, 393
Greenberger, E., 50, 437–438, 492, 498
Greene, A.L., 253, 260, 268, 272
Greenhill, L, 388
Greenhouse, J.B., 350
Greenson, R., 414
Greenspan, B., 462
Griffin, R.B., 428
Grigg, D., 150, 162
Griliches, Z., 259
Grimson, R.C., 337
Grinker, R.E., 9, 363, 475
Grinker, R.R., 9, 362, 366, 368–369, 373, 475
Grisso, T., 282–284, 287–288, 290, 292
Gross, G., 369, 375
Gross, R., 32, 37, 106, 109
Grossman, R., 393, 480
Grotevant, H., 503
Groth, N.A., 115–116
Grumbach, M.M., 21, 22
Grunbaum, A., 422

Guerra, N., 45–46, 54–57, 308–309, 311, 313–316, 318, 320–323, 445
Gump, P., 134
Gunderson, J.G., 376
Gundlach, R., 251
Gurber, J., 176
Gurman, A., 167
Gutstein, S., 166
Guttentag, M., 494, 511
Guttman, R., 480
Guze, S.B., 313
Gysbers, N., 182

Ha, H., 340
Haaertel, G.D., 205
Haan, N., 260, 490, 501
Haas, G.L., 365
Haertel, G.D., 206
Haffner, D., 117
Hagestad, G., 251, 492, 494, 499
Haggerty, G.G., 334
Haggerty, R.J., 442
Hains, A.H., 45
Hakstian, H., 400
Haley, J., 151, 165, 378, 417
Halikas, J., 9
Hall, C., 393
Hall, E.T., 229–231, 238
Hall, G. S., 6, 261, 490
Hall, H., 130
Hall, J., 10
Hallinan, M.T., 208–209, 215
Halpert, E., 79
Ham, M., 128–129, 132
Hamape, I., 388
Hamilton, M., 335
Hamilton, S.F., 434
Hammer, T., 152
Hammersmith, S.K., 97, 99, 102, 252, 262
Hanks, M., 131, 134, 136, 432
Hann, N., 269
Hansen, D.J., 429
Hansen, W.B., 319, 429, 440
Hansley, P., 134
Hanson, C.L., 321
Hanssen, C., 232
Harding, C.M., 370
Hardy, J., 106–107, 441
Hare, E., 364–365

Hareven, T., 490
Hare-Mustin, R.T., 71, 222, 234
Harlter, S., 50
Harman, C.R., 377
Harper, L., 251, 499
Harris, G., 181
Harris, L., 104, 110
Harris, T.O., 339
Harrison, A.O., 222, 234, 239–240
Harrow, M., 361–363, 365–372, 510
Harry, J., 252
Hart, D., 46, 50
Harter, S., 339
Hartmann, H., 68–69, 73
Hartup, W.W., 208
Hastorf, A.H., 109
Hauser, S., 152, 503
Havighurst, R., 127, 417, 492, 494
Hawkins, J.D., 312, 317–318, 443, 445
Hayden, A., 178
Hayden, B., 54
Hayes, C.D, 101, 108, 429, 440–442
Hazard, W., 222
Hazel, J.S., 287
Healy, J., 480–481
Heaton, T.B., 108
Hebert, F., 55
Hedeker, D., 342
Hedin, D., 132, 135–136, 435
Heiman, J., 96
Heimann, P., 414
Hein, K., 101, 117–118, 442
Helfer, R., 485
Hellison, D., 433
Helmreich, R., 257
Helms, J.E., 234–237
Helzer, J.E., 337
Hendin, H., 502
Hendricks, L., 507
Hendry, L., 131, 134–135, 137, 139
Henggeler, S.W., 210, 312, 314, 316, 320–322
Hepburn, E.H., 110
Herb, T.R., 366
Herbener, E., 509

Herdt, G., 80, 97, 249–250, 252, 255–256, 259–260, 263, 265–266, 268, 504–505, 516
Herjanic, B., 335, 398–399
Hernandez, M., 237
Herot, G., 271
Hershberg, T., 489
Hertzog, C., 269
Hervis, O., 319
Herzog, J., 74
Hess, L.E., 211–212
Hess, R., 174, 191, 196
Heterington, E., 36
Hetherington, M., 159
Hetrick, E., 80–81, 237
Hibbert, G., 400
Higgins, A., 216
Higgins, R., 182
Higham, J., 95
Hildreth, G., 136
Hill, J., 5, 10, 31, 36–37, 261, 389, 478, 495
Hill, J., 476–477
Hill, M.K. 31
Hill, P., 131
Hindelang, M.J., 311
Hindmarsh, D., 339
Hirsch, B.J., 210, 444
Hirsch, M.B., 106–107
Hirschi, T., 311
Hobbs, N., 428
Hodges, K., 398
Hoeper, E., 337–338, 391
Hofferth, S., 101, 104, 440–441, 508
Hoffman, B.D., 295
Hoffman, E., 420
Hoffman, J.W., 208
Hoffman, L., 151
Hogan, D., 108–109, 489, 491, 506, 515
Hogarty, G.E., 372–373
Holeman, R.E., 251
Holinger, P.C., 343, 364
Hollon, S., 393, 400
Holmbeck, G., 31, 36–37
Holmbeck, T., 10
Holmes, K.A., 114
Holmstrom, L.L., 114
Holstein, C.B., 48, 51
Holt, R., 423
Holzen, C., 9

Holzman, P., 65–66, 363, 368–369, 373, 423
Hong, G.K., 336–337
Honingeld, G., 373
Honzik, M., 260, 263, 490
Hooker, E., 254
Hopkins, T., 81
Horn, J.L., 267
Horn, M., 105
Houlihan, J., 503
Houzik, M., 490
Howard, K., 1, 8, 11, 14, 16, 63, 270, 391, 417, 422, 454
Howell, F., 508
Hoyle, S.G., 209
Hsu, G.L., 339
Huba, C.G., 308
Huber, G., 369
Hubley, P., 67
Huebner, E.S., 178
Huesmann, L.R., 38, 45–46, 54, 315–317, 321–322
Huesmann, R., 313–321, 323
Huizinga, D., 308–312, 314–315, 317, 319, 323
Humphreys, L., 262
Husemann, L.R., 314
Hutchings, B., 313

Ide, J.K., 205–206
Ifekwunigue, M., 291
Ignatoff, E., 507
Inazu, J.K., 109
Inhelder, B., 72, 417
Inoff-Germain, L.D., 22, 25, 26, 29
Inouye, D.K., 301
Irvin, F.S., 266, 505, 516
Irwin, C.E., 118
Isay, R., 79–80, 252
Iscoe, E., 185
Iscoe, I., 237
Iso-Ahola, S., 126
Iwata, M., 55
Iyengar, S., 334, 338
Izard, E.E., 333, 335, 339

Jablensky, A., 364
Jackson, D., 150
Jackson, M., 135
Jackson, S., 64
Jacobs, D., 438

Jacobsen, A., 152, 503
Jacobson, E., 69
Jacobson, F.M., 237
Jaffe, C., 1, 9, 11, 13, 389, 394, 402, 413, 417–419, 476
Jahoda, G., 227
James, D., 462
James, K.L., 462
Janet, P., 254
Janowitz, M., 251
Jarcho, H., 31
Jason, L.A., 429, 439
Jason, L.H., 421, 427
Jenkins, J., 153, 514
Jenkins, R.R., 106
Jennings, D., 106
Jennings, L., 71
Jensen, G.E., 314
Jesness, C., 396, 430
Jessor, R., 107, 308, 313, 317–318
Jessor, S.L., 107, 308, 317
Jewell, L., 129, 132
John, K., 334
Johnson, A., 319, 429, 440
Johnson, C., 10, 160
Johnson, G., 445
Johnson, J., 9
Johnson, P.B., 111, 112
Johnson, Samuel, 397
Johnston, J., 311, 313
Johnston, L.D., 308
Jolly, A., 125
Jones, C., 513
Jones, E., 105
Jones, H., 259–260, 269
Jones, J.M., 225, 229, 237
Jones, M.C., 31, 259–260, 263, 490, 511
Jones, R., 167, 242
Jones, S., 377
Jones, W.H., 213
Jorgensen, S.R., 108
Joseph, J., 483, 485
Josselyn, I., 393
Junemann, H., 368
Jurkovic, G.J., 287

Kagan, J., 251, 253, 259, 262–263, 490
Kahn, D.G., 453–455, 457, 459, 465
Kahn, J.R., 101, 109

Kahn, R., 495
Kahneman, D., 54
Kalikow, K., 9, 391
Kandel, E., 164, 205–207, 265, 270, 311–312, 314, 318–319, 336, 338–339, 395
Kander, D.B., 337
Kane, J.M., 373
Kanner, A.D., 213
Kanzer, M., 71
Kaplan, B.H., 337
Kaplan, D., 402
Kaplan, M.S., 116
Kaplan, S., 22, 64, 67, 69, 71, 336–337, 340, 483, 485
Kaplan, T., 334
Kappel, M., 115
Karabenick, S.A., 31
Karno, M., 361, 514
Karrer, B., 236, 494, 513, 517
Karush, A., 414
Kaser-Boyd, N., 292, 299
Kashani, J., 337–338, 391
Kaslow, N.J., 335
Katlin, R., 222
Katz, J., 224, 235, 240, 497
Katz, P., 37
Kauffman, J., 183
Kaufman, J.M., 435
Kavrell, S.M., 31
Kayes, J., 347
Kazdin, A., 46, 312, 316, 318, 320–323, 388, 393, 398–399, 401
Kearns, D., 167
Keasey, C.B., 47
Keating, D.P., 47
Keesing, R.M., 229
Kegeles, S.M., 118
Kehoe, M., 268
Keith, P., 196
Keith, S.J. 373
Kellam, S.G., 318, 322–323, 419
Keller, M.B., 334, 338–339
Kellerman, A.L., 344–345
Kelley, A., 476, 481
Kelley, M., 393
Kelly, F.J., 287
Kelly, J., 126, 174, 181, 188, 190–192, 196, 224, 239, 263, 393, 429

Kempe, C.H., 114, 485
Kempe, R.S., 114
Kendall, P., 52, 57, 388, 393
Kendell, R., 12
Keniston, K., 232, 490, 494
Kerkhofs, M., 340
Kernberg, O.F., 68–69, 79, 84
Kerr, M.M., 346
Kertzer, D.I., 269
Kessler, L., 15, 374
Kessler, M., 222
Kessler, R., 338, 345
Kestenberg, J., 25
Kett, J., 72, 76, 259
Kettlewell, P.W., 454–456
Kety, S.S., 346
Keys, C., 421, 427, 429, 439
Khan, M., 64, 68, 70–71
Killarney, J., 507
Killian, G.A., 372
Kim, L.C., 234
Kim, U., 232, 235
Kimmel, D., 224, 259, 263, 268
Kinard, C., 372
King, L., 224
King, O., 233
Kingsley, D., 55–56, 393
Kinsey, A., 95, 97, 261
Kirby, D., 4 41
Kirkpatrick, B., 369
Kirshnet, C., 129
Kitagawa, E.M., 108–109
Kivnick, H., 260
Klassen, A.D., 97
Kleiber, D., 128–131, 134, 512, 514
Klein, D.F., 365–366, 387
Klein, D.N., 334
Klein, G., 64–69, 71
Klein, M., 81, 309–312, 318
Klein, P., 429
Klein, R., 259
Kleinfeld, J., 432
Kleinman, A.M., 363–365, 514
Kleinman, J.C., 343
Kleinman, M., 345
Klepp, K.I., 438
Klerman, G., 334, 338–339, 343, 365, 491
Klerman, L.V., 441
Kline, F.G., 438
Kline, J., 398

Klitzner, M.D., 438
Klocke, M., 430
Klotz, M., 341, 388
Kluckhohn, C., 228
Kluegel, J., 288
Knight, F., 223, 228
Kniskern, D., 167
Knitzer, J., 301, 453
Knoff, H., 178
Knopka, G., 513
Knowles, B.A., 318
Kochman, T., 238
Koegel, P., 375
Koff, E., 32–33, 38
Kohlberg, L., 46–48, 72, 216, 259, 370–371
Kohon, G., 71
Kohut, H., 64, 66–70, 73–75, 77, 79, 81, 414–415
Kokes, R.F., 367
Kolko, D.J., 348
Kolvin, I., 396
Koman, R., 393
Komarovksy, M., 502, 504
Konopka, G., 431
Koplewixz, H., 388
Korenblum, M., 422, 458
Koss, M.P., 111
Kostelny, K., 471, 480–482
Kourany, R.F.C., 270
Kovacs, M., 333–335, 398, 400
Kracke, B., 30
Kraepelin, E., 359
Kramer, A.D., 334, 341
Kramer, M., 9, 361
Kramer, R.B., 48
Krasnor, L.R., 46
Kravitz, H., 339–340
Kremer, M., 251
Krepelin, R., 369
Krieger, R., 483, 485
Kroeber, A., 228
Krohn, A., 71
Krohn, J., 71
Krohn, M.D., 311
Kruger, L., 194
Krumweid, M.H.A., 373, 375, 378
Ku, L.C., 105
Kubey, R., 137–139
Kuhn, D., 51
Kuhn, L., 365

Kulik, C., 435
Kulik, J.A., 435
Kulka, R.A., 14
Kunjufu, J., 235
Kuperman, S., 350
Kurdek, L.A., 51, 209
Kurpius, D., 189
Kurtines, W., 234, 238, 319, 321
Kutcher, S., 340

L'Abate, L., 429
LaBelle, T.J., 431
Labouvie, G, 490
Lacan, J., 74
Ladd, G.W., 216
Ladewig, H., 431–432
Lahey, B, 507
Lahmeyer, H.W., 334, 340
Lam, T., 318
Lamabert, M., 388
Lamb, H.R., 375
Lamb, M., 507
Lambert, M.C., 223, 228
Lambert, W., 514
Lampert, C., 334
Lampron, L.B., 321
Landau-Stanton, J., 166
Landers, D., 131
Lando, M.A., 31
Lang, E.M., 444
Lang, M., 335, 366
Langer, T., 317, 390
Langfeldt, T., 95
Langmeyer, D., 388–389, 395–396, 400, 402
Langs, R., 71
Laplanche, J., 68
Lappin, J., 163, 164
Laqueur, W., 76
Larrivee, S., 310, 318, 321–323
Larson, R., 1, 34, 40, 63, 125, 128–129, 132, 134, 137–140, 203, 212–213, 216, 261, 270, 337, 417, 497, 512, 514
Larson, S., 51
Lasch, C., 72
Latham, G., 130
Laub, J.H., 317
Laudolff, J., 322–323
Laufer, M.E., 71, 78–79
Lavin, D., 52

Lavori, P.W., 334, 338
Lawler, E., 189
Leadbeater, B., 321
Leak, P. 9, 374
LeBlanc, M., 308–312, 317–318, 321–323
Ledingham, J.E., 203, 212
Lee, J.A., 263, 265, 271
Lee, L.C., 48
Lee, P.A., 22–24
Lee, S., 339
Lefkowitz, M.M., 314, 316–317, 333, 335
Lefley, H., 514
LeFloe, F., 435
Lehman, W.E., 215
Leichter, H., 503
Leiderman, H., 109, 437
Leigh, G.K., 259
Leitch, I., 396
Leitenberg, H., 115–116
Leming, J., 139
Lennenberg, E., 259
Lens, W., 254
Leone, P., 181
Lerner, R., 31, 31, 127, 211–212, 259, 499
Leslie, S., 8, 390
Lesser, G., 265, 270, 395
Lessing, E., 419
Levenstein, S., 365–366
Levin, S., 79
Levine, A., 502
Levine, J., 366, 507
Levine, M., 174, 434
Levine, R.H., 265
Levinson, D.F., 462
Levinson, R.A., 249, 261
Levy, J.C., 337–338
Lewin, K., 71, 265, 497
Lewine, R., 365
Lewis, A.B., 365
Lewis, C.E., 237, 291
Lewis, D.O., 454
Lewis, J., 401, 455
Lewis, M.A., 291
Lewis, R.A., 319
Lewis, R.J., 428
Libby, P., 484–485
Lichtenberg, J., 414, 419
Lidz, C.W., 289, 290
Lieberman, M., 253, 494

Liebman, R., 161
Liebman, W., 503
Lightfoot, S., 176, 181, 184
Lin, K.M., 363–365
Lin, T., 232
Linehan, M., 342
Linn, D., 412, 455, 457–458, 460
Linney, J., 173, 282–283, 443
Linton, H., 65
Linz, M., 369
Liotti, G., 393
Lipsey, M., 318, 320–321, 444
Lishner, D.M., 443
Littell, J., 430, 432, 434
Little, B., 135
Little, J.W., 445
Livingston, R., 393
Livson, H., 253, 263
Livson, M., 30
Livson, N., 260, 501
Lizotte, A.J., 311
Lochman, J.E., 321
Locke, B.Z., 338, 361
Locke, G., 130
Loeber, R., 287, 307–310, 312–315, 317–319, 322–323, 444, 507
Loftin, T., 351
Lohr, J., 213, 339
Long, R., 135
Longo, R.E., 115
Looney, J., 420
Lopez, S., 514
LoPiccolo, J., 96
Loriaux, D.L., 22, 25, 26, 29
Lorimer, A., 291
Lorion, R., 307–310, 312–313, 315–316, 320–322, 444–445
Losoff, M., 203
Lourie, I., 483
Lowe, B., 131
Loyd, D., 365
Lozoff, M., 83
Lu, L.C., 118
Luafer, M., 71
Luckmann, T., 224
Luepker, R.V., 438
Lull, J., 139
Lunde, I., 346
Lundwall, L., 402
Lupkowski, A., 134

Luria, A., 393
Lustman, P., 393, 400
Luttge, W.G., 23
Lyle, C.G., 464
Lynch, F.R., 268
Lynch, M., 10, 31, 37
Lyons, N., 152
Lystad, M., 111

MacCorquodale, P., 100
MacEachron, A.E., 116
MacFarlane, A., 513
MacFarlane, J., 263, 490
MacKinnon, D.P., 319, 429, 440
Machabanski, 417, 494, 513, 517
Mack, J., 286
Macmillan, A., 396
Macrides, C., 475
Magnusson, D., 318
Maher, C., 194, 435
Mahle, M., 83
Mahler, M., 70
Maile, M.C, 438
Malgady, R., 225, 237
Malkin, A., 340
Malkin, D., 340
Malmisur, M., 131
Malson, L., 293
Maltz, M.D., 454
Mandersheid, R.W., 375
Manely-Casimir, M., 52
Mannarino, A.P., 209–210
Manneheim, P. 493
Mannuzza, S., 392
Mantilla, Y., 185
Marcia, J., 45, 131
Marcoen, A., 213
Marecek, J., 222, 234
Marengo, J.T., 362, 365, 369–372
Marini, M., 491
Markle, A., 429
Marks, A., 117
Marks, I., 388
Marlow, L., 10, 37
Marneros, A., 368
Marohn, R., 393, 402, 412, 419, 454–458, 460, 426–464, 513, 517
Marriott, S.A., 55
Marsh, A., 366–367
Marsh, D.T., 53, 58

Martin, A.D., 80–81, 95, 97, 270
Martin, C.E., 95, 97, 261–262
Martin, J.A., 106
Martin, R., 253
Martinson, F.M., 95
Marton, P., 340, 422, 458
Marziller, J., 393, 429
Mas, C., 168
Mason, B.C., 435
Massimo, J., 321, 396, 401
Masten, A.S., 319
Masterson, J., 8–9, 13, 393, 419, 422
Masui, T., 391
Matthews, W.S., 37
Mattison, A.M., 271
Matute-Bianchi, M., 179, 180
Maughan, B., 173
May, F.R.A., 372–373
Mayer, F.E., 21
Mayer, J.P., 320, 322, 445–446
Mayer, L.S., 322–323
Mays, J.M., 259
McAdoo, W., 402
Mcallister, J., 337–338, 391
McBride, A., 117
McBurnett, 507
McCabe, M.P., 101
McCall, G., 263
McCarter, E., 412, 455, 457–458, 460
McCarthy, 33, 508
McCauley, E., 210, 334
McClure, J., 9
McCluskey, K., 507
McCluskey-Fawcett, K., 36
McCombs, H.G., 334
McConahay, J., 176
McCord, C., 224
McCord, J., 312, 317, 318, 320–322, 445
McCormack, J., 139
McCoy, J.K., 110
McCracken, H.W., 209
McCubbin, J., 10
McDill, E., 187
McDonald, G.J., 262
McDowall, 351
McDuff, P., 310, 323
McEvoy, L., 317
McFadin, J.B., 115
McFall, R.M., 54

McGee, R., 312, 337, 339, 377
McGill, C.W., 373, 377
McGlashan, T.H., 365, 368, 374
McGoldrick, M., 150–152, 156–157, 513–514
McGrew, J., 206, 208
McGuire, K., 203, 209–210, 214
McKenry, P., 10
McKinney, K.L., 33
McKnew, D., 319–320, 335, 337, 398
McLean, P., 400
McLeod, M., 115
McWhirter, D.P., 271
Mead, G., 69, 211
Mead, G. H., 48
Mead, M., 227
Mednick, S.A., 313
Medway, F., 175, 182
Meeks, J., 413, 419
Meichenbaum, D., 55, 393
Meisel, A., 289–290
Meissner, W., 69
Mellinger, G.D., 8
Melton, G.B., 294, 299–301
Meltzer, H., 365, 373
Menaghan, E., 494
Menard, S., 308–309, 311–312, 317, 319
Mendelson, M., 339
Menken, M. 508
Menlewicz, J.A., 340
Merick, W., 132
Merikangas, K., 334
Merrick, W., 129, 137
Messick, S., 65
Mettetaal, G., 72
Meyer, J., 30, 402
Meyer, M., 117
Meyers, J., 150
Michelson, L., 320
Miessner, W., 68, 71
Milan, M.A., 429
Milavasky, J.R., 345
Miles, C., 371
Miles, P., 342, 347
Millan, G., 271
Millazzo-Sayre, L.J., 375
Miller, B., 107–108, 110, 118, 262
Miller, D., 393–394
Miller, F.T., 337

Miller, J., 183
Miller, K.E., 204, 210
Miller, L., 46, 373, 375, 378, 388, 511
Miller, L.E., 224
Miller, L.S., 321
Mills, R., 174
Millstein, S.G., 442–443
Milofsky, E., 370
Minton, H.L., 262
Minturn, L., 514
Mintz, J., 514
Minuchin, S., 150, 161–162
Mirkin, M., 163, 393
Mitchell, J., 334, 338
Mitchell, M., 167, 182, 314, 316, 321, 445
Mitchell, R., 174
Mitchell, S., 392
Mitchell, W,. 503
Mitroff, I.I., 427
Mittelman, M., 115
Mittelmark, M., 438
Mize, J., 216
Mizokawa, D., 178
Modell, A., 414
Modell, J., 489, 492, 503–504, 515–516
Moffat, M., 504
Moffitt, T.E., 309, 311–313, 316–317, 319
Moghaddam, F.M., 239
Moiss, H., 490
Moitra, S., 308, 317
Mokros, H.B., 335, 339–340, 511
Molcan, K., 339
Molitor, N., 417–418
Monahan, J., 301
Monasterky, C., 115
Montello, D., 206–208
Montemayer, R., 10, 37, 50, 156, 253
Monti, P.M., 429
Moody, S.,2 24
Moore, E., 182
Moore, K., 103, 105, 107, 109, 113, 117, 440, 508–509
Moos, R., 174, 177, 186–187
Moos, S.J., 334
Morgan, S., 103, 107, 508
Morgan, W., 130
Morin, S.F.,2 50

Moritz, G.M., 351–352
Morrell, W., 334
Morris, N., 26, 29, 106
Morrison, D.M., 110
Morrissey, R., 234
Mortimore, P., 173
Moscicki, E.K., 344
Mosher, L.R., 373, 376
Mosher, W., 105
Moss, H., 251, 263, 373, 377
Muller, R., 271
Mullis, R.M., 438
Mulvey, E.P., 287–288, 309, 321
Murphy, G., 343, 347, 393, 400
Murphy, J., 181
Murphy, R.D., 364
Murray, C., 242
Murray, D.M., 438
Murray, H., 176
Murray, J., 23
Murray, S.O., 249, 268–269
Musen, P.A., 511
Muslin, H., 71, 82
Mussen, P., 31, 260, 490
Mustin, H., 152
Myers, J., 9, 453
Myers, L.K., 361
Myrdal, 236

Naditch, M., 234
Nagle, R., 175, 182
Nasby, W., 54
Naylor, K.E., 112
Natriello, G., 187
Neckerman, K.J., 320
Needle, R., 10
Nelson, B., 334, 338, 340–341
Nelson, P., 292, 299
Nelson, S., 224
Nelson, W.M., 55
Nemeroff, C.B., 334
Nesselroade, J., 269
Neugarten, B., 29, 249, 253, 268, 371, 492–494
Newcomb, M., 318–319, 509
Newcomer, S., 108–110
Newell, A., 53
Newman, B., 183
Newman, J.P., 54
Newman, P., 183
Newmann, F.M., 434
Nicol, A., 396

Nieva, N., 189
Nightingale, E.O., 434
Nixon, H., 131
Noam, G., 152, 503
Noel, D.L., 239
Nord, C.W., 113
Nottelmann, E.D., 22, 25, 26, 29
Novacenko, H., 334, 340–341
Novick, J., 79, 419
Novick, K., 79
Novoco, R., 10
Nydegger, C., 269
Nye, F., 14

O'Brien, S.F., 49, 203
O'Leary, K., 398
O'Malley, P., 308, 311, 313
O'Neill, P., 175, 185, 192
Ochberg, F., 189
Oerter, R., 127, 134
Offer, D., 1, 7–12, 14, 16, 56, 63, 78, 261, 265, 269–270, 343, 364, 391, 412–413, 417, 422, 428, 454–456, 462, 464, 475, 490
Offer, J., 7–9, 63, 310, 412, 417, 422
Offord, D.R., 310–312, 316, 319
Ogbu, J.U., 222
Ogden, D., 293
Ohlin, L.E., 311–313, 315, 322–323
Olden, C., 414
Oldham, D.G., 475
Olds, D., 473, 483
Oler, C., 235
Olmedo, E.L., 231–234
Olson, D.H., 154
Olson, T.D., 107–108, 110
Olvier, W., 235
Olweus, D., 212, 316–317
Opjordmoen, S., 368
Opler, M.K., 30
Oremland, J., 77
Ornstein, H., 430
Oros, C.J., 111
Ortiz, D.E., 288
Ortman, J., 346
Orvaschel, H., 348
Orvaschel, M., 9
Osher, C., 371
Osofsky, H., 507

Osofsky, J., 507
Ostrov, E., 1, 8, 11, 14, 16, 63, 270, 334, 391, 417, 422, 454–456, 462, 464
Otto, L., 129, 131, 432
Ouston, J., 173

Paige, K.M., 30
Paight, D.J., 345
Pallas, A., 187
Palmer, B., 291
Panella, D., 210
Papini, D., 36–37, 109, 507
Pardo, C., 471, 482
Parham, T., 228, 235
Paris, A.E., 45
Parke, R., 507
Parker, B., 513
Parker, J., 133–134, 203, 211–214, 314, 443
Parkerson, J., 205–206
Parkoff, R.L., 118
Parloff, M., 400
Parson, R.J., 227
Parsons, B.V., 321, 445
Parsons, D., 168
Parsons, R., 175
Parsons, T., 9, 501
Paton, S., 338
Patrick, H., 137, 139
Patterson, G.R., 167, 207, 310, 312–314, 316–317, 320–321
Paulauskas, S.A., 334
Paulson, M.J., 232
Paykel, E.S., 342
Payot, J., 131
Pearce, J., 513–514
Pearlin, L., 374, 494
Pearson, G., 393
Pederson, C.A., 334
Peevers, B., 50
Pelcovitz, D., 483, 485
Pendergrass, M., 222
Pentz, M.A., 313, 318–319, 428–430, 440
Peplau, L.A., 213
Percy, F.P., 319
Perez-Vidal, A., 319
Perkins, N., 189
Perlman, D., 213
Perper, J.A., 348–349, 351–352
Perry, C., 260, 438

Perry, D.G., 46
Perry, L.L. 46
Perry, T.B., 209–210
Persons, R., 396
Peskin, H., 30, 253, 260, 263, 501
Peterfreund, E., 413
Petersen, A., 7, 10, 21, 23, 25, 29–36, 38–40, 63, 203, 249, 259–261, 268, 394, 417, 502, 511
Petersen, G.W., 259
Peterson, C., 50, 339, 417
Peterson, G., 320
Peterson, J., 103, 105, 107, 109, 113, 117–118
Peterssen, D., 183
Pettigrew, T., 231
Phelps, P., 287, 309, 321
Phillips, D., 176, 345, 366–367
Phillips, V., 401, 455
Phinney, J., 222, 235
Phye, G., 182
Piaget, J., 46–47, 72, 125, 417
Pichel, J., 392
Pike, K., 227
Pine, C.J., 234, 239, 240
Pine, F., 69–70, 83
Pine, L.J., 222
Pines, R., 480
Pinsof, W., 167
Pirce, J.M., 54
Pitts, F., 346
Plath, D., 495
Platt, J.J., 53
Play, B.R., 429
Pleck, J., 105, 118, 507
Plummer, K., 264, 268
Polit, D., 436, 441
Pomeroy, W.B., 95, 97, 251, 261
Ponse, B., 234, 252
Pontalis, J.B., 68
Popper, K., 64, 421
Post, S., 479
Power, T., 188, 507
Powers, S., 152, 503
Poznanski, E.O., 334–335, 339–340
Pratt, W., 105
Prentice, D.S., 457
Presson, C.C., 206–208
Prestby, J.E., 2 40

Prewitt, K., 252
Price, R.H., 320–321
Prilletensky, I., 223–224
Primavera, J., 183, 443–444
Prinz, R., 134, 317, 319
Prosen, H., 253
Pruchno, R., 503
Prusoff, B., 334
Pugach, M., 178
Pugh, M.D., 210
Puig-Antich, J., 320, 333–335, 338–341, 348, 398
Pulkkinen, L., 317
Pullen, D., 173
Punammaki, R., 480
Putallaz, M., 213–214

Quay, H.C., 312–313
Quinlan, D., 363
Quint, J.C., 436, 441

Rabichow, H., 10
Rabinovich, H., 334, 338, 340–341
Rachman, S., 388
Racker, H., 84
Rae, D.S., 338
Rae, G.S., 361
Raffaelli, M., 128–129, 132–133
Ramirez, M., 230, 233, 235–237
Ramos-McKay, J., 320–321
Rancurello, M., 399
Rants-Rodriguez, D., 112
Rapaport, D., 64–65
Rapkin, B.D., 444
Rapoff, M., 393
Rappaport, R.N., 429, 436
Rappoport, J., 9, 226–227, 291, 391
Raskin, P., 163
Rasmussen, P.R., 46
Ratcliff, K.S., 308, 337
Razani, J., 373, 377
Read, P.E., 335, 339
Reay, D.T., 344–345
Rebok, G.N., 322–323
Redfering, D., 396
Redl, F., 387, 455
Reed, G., 414–415
Regier, D.A., 361, 374
Rehm, L.P., 335
Reich, T., 313

Reich, W., 78, 80, 335, 398
Reid, J., 167, 337, 391
Reiger, D.A., 338
Reimer, J., 139
Reinecke, M., 341, 393, 419, 440
Reinharz, S., 189
Reishl, T.M., 211
Reiss, D., 158
Reissman, F., 434
Reld, J.C., 338
Rematedi, G., 97, 270
Rembar, J., 419
Reppucci, N.D., 287–288, 292–293, 301, 433, 515
Reschly, D., 177, 182
Rest, J.R., 52
Revere, V., 254
Reynolds, W., 45, 335–337, 341, 429
Riccio, J.A., 436, 441
Rich, C.L., 348, 350
Richard, B.A., 53, 54
Richard, S., 136, 394, 417, 502, 511
Richards, A., 68
Richards, H.C., 51
Richards, H.E., 22
Richards, M., 21, 33–34, 39, 125, 128, 132, 134
Richards, P., 139
Richman, H., 430, 432, 434
Ricks, D., 259, 370–371, 402
Ricoeur, P., 65, 254, 423
Rie, H.E., 333
Riech, W., 399
Rierdan, J., 32–33, 38
Riess, B., 513
Riess, D., 517
Rifkin, A., 251
Riley, M.W., 494
Rimmer, J., 9
Rindfuss, R., 508
Rinn, R.C., 429
Ritter, P.L., 109
Ritvo, L., 64
Ritzler, B.A., 367
Rivera, F.P., 344–345
Rivlin, H., 222
Rizley, R., 477
Robbins, D.R., 339–340, 345
Robbins, L.N., 370
Roberson, M.K., 288

Roberts, E.J., 109
Roberts, G., 129, 131, 134
Robin, A., 10, 430
Robins, A.J., 337
Robins, E., 347, 360
Robins, L., 308, 312–313, 317–318, 337, 361
Robinson, D., 334, 338, 340–341
Robinson, M.K., 263, 268
Robinson, S., 428
Robin-Richards, M.H., 34, 35
Roche, A.F., 23
Roche, G.R., 436
Rockwell, R.W., 260, 491
Rodgers, J.L., 108, 111
Rodick, J.D., 321
Roe, K., 139
Roemer, J., 134
Roesch, R., 287
Roeske, N., 402
Roesler, T., 270
Rogler, L., 225, 237
Rogow, A.A., 71
Rohde, A., 368
Rosen, B., 365–366
Rosen, E., 96
Rosenbaum, M., 33, 394
Rosenberg, A., 37, 106
Rosenberg, F., 31, 394
Rosenberg, M., 261, 394
Rosenberg, T., 337–338, 391
Rosenblatt, B., 69
Rosenblatt, P., 139
Rosenstein, M.J., 375
Rosenthal, D., 346
Rosenthal, R., 402, 419, 464
Rosman, B., 161, 162
Rosow, I., 269, 493
Ross, A., 388
Ross, M.W., 267, 271
Rossi, A., 37, 491
Rossman, G., 193
Roth, J., 492, 494
Roth, L.H., 289–290
Rothbaum, F., 45–46
Rotheram, M.J., 429
Rottman, L., 394
Rouse, R., 393
Rowe, D.C., 312, 318
Rowe, K., 291
Roy, A., 346, 371–372
Royal, J., 185

Ro-Trock, G., 396
Rubenstein, E., 139
Rubenstein, J.L. 209
Rubenstein, R.A., 430, 432, 434
Rubin, B., 318, 460
Rubin, C., 209
Rubin, K.H., 46
Ruble, D.N., 39
Rudinger, G., 127, 140
Rudolph, L., 503
Rudolph, S., 503
Ruggerio, M., 314, 437
Rule, B.G., 47
Runeson, B., 349–350
Rush, A., 45, 393, 400
Russell, B., 134
Russell, G., 419
Russell, W., 167
Russo, M., 507
Rutter, M., 1, 8–10, 13, 37, 139, 173, 211, 259, 263, 312, 315, 319–320, 323, 333, 335, 339, 389–392, 400, 412, 434, 443
Ryan, K., 9, 11, 13, 394, 402, 417–418
Ryan, N.D., 334, 338, 340–341
Ryder, N.B., 259, 269

Saba, G., 161
Sabshin, M., 12, 269–270
Sabshin, S., 78
Sackett, G.P., 313
Sage, G., 131
Salkovskis, P., 400
Salokangas, R.K.R., 365
Sameroff, A.J., 313
Samit, C., 483, 485
Sampson, H., 420
Sampson, R.J., 317
Samuelson, H., 334, 338
Sander, L., 64, 67, 70
Sandler, J., 69
Sands, J.R., 369–370
Sanford, N., 497
Santana, F., 514
Santostefano, S., 393
Sarason, B.R., 340
Sarason, C.W., 57
Sarason, I.G., 430
Sarason, S., 174, 179, 188
Sargent, J.,1 611

Sarrel, L.J., 98, 99, 100
Sarrel, P.M., 98, 99, 100
Sarri, L., 130
Sartorius, N., 364
Savage, C., 37
Savin, R.C., 203
Savin-Williams, R., 31, 49, 207, 212–214, 265, 497, 512
Savin-Williams, T.J., 208
Scarpitti, R., 288
Sceery, W., 391
Schachar, R., 319
Schaefer, C., 462
Schafer, H., 414
Schafer, R., 65, 68
Schafer, W.E., 433
Schaffer, C.B., 372
Schaffer, R., 259
Schaffner, P., 177
Schaie, K.W., 267, 269, 490, 515
Schank, R.C., 54
Schatz, C., 181
Scheftner, W.A., 346–347
Scheier, M.F., 50
Scheinkman, 393, 417, 513
Schellenbach, C., 474–475, 477, 483–485
Schenck, E., 10
Schenck, Q., 10
Scherer, D., 289, 290, 292–293
Schiavo, R., 168, 445
Schinke, S.P., 429, 440
Schlundt, D., 393
Schmaling, K.B., 317
Schmid, K., 181, 239, 443, 515
Schneider, A., 287
Schneider, M., 80, 265
Schneider-Rosen, K., 335
Schoenbach, V.J., 337
Schofield, J.W., 213
Schonberg, S.K., 117
Schooler, N.R., 372–373
Schorr, L.B., 440
Schrodt, G., 393
Schuckit, J., 9
Schulenberg, J., 476, 481
Schuler, P., 55
Schulsinger, F., 313, 346
Schultz, J.M., 439
Schumaker, J.B., 287
Schumer, H., 136
Schwab-Stone, M., 13

Schwartz, D., 500
Schwartz, J., 315
Schwartz, L., 313–314, 316, 320
Schwartz, M., 342
Schwartz, R., 161
Schwartzman, A.E., 203, 212
Scopetta, M., 233
Scott, E., 293–295, 301, 503
Scott, W., 393
Scribner, S., 230
Sebby, R.A., 36–37
Sebes, J., 474–475, 477, 483–486
Secord, P., 50, 494, 511
Sedlak, M., 173
Seeley, R., 480
Seeman, M.V., 366
Segal, H., 81
Segrave, J.O., 433
Seidman, E., 173, 314, 393, 427, 443
Seligman, M., 226, 339
Sellin, T., 309, 311
Selman, R., 45–46, 48
Seltze, P.J., 375
Serbin, L.A., 203, 212, 287
Serna, L.A., 287
Settlege, C., 83
Severson, H., 430
Sgroi, S.M., 115
Shaffer, D., 9, 338, 343, 345, 348, 350, 391, 402
Shafii, M., 347, 350
Shah, F.K., 103–105, 118
Shane, E., 77
Shanian, S., 365–366
Shanok, S.F., 454
Shapiro, R., 364
Shapiro, S., 374
Sharabany, R., 208
Shaw, B., 393, 400
Shaw, K., 130
Shaw, M.E., 30
Shcoolar, J., 396
Shcutter, R., 369
Sheldon, J.B., 287
Shenker, R., 392
Shennum, W.A., 252
Sherif, C., 133, 140
Sherif, M., 133, 140
Sherman, S.J., 206, 208
Sherrets, S., 388

Shidla, M., 181
Shields, J., 361–362
Shinkwin, A., 432
Sholomskas, D., 334
Shore, M., 321, 396, 401
Short, J., 14
Shrum, W., 204
Shure, M.B., 46, 53
Siebert, F., ,419
Siegel, A.W., 335
Siegel, J., 130
Siegel, O., 395
Siegel, T., 312, 321
Siegler, R., 55
Siever, L., 13
Silbereisen, R., 30, 140
Silberman, A., 10
Silberschatz, G., 83
Silva, P.A., 312–313, 316–317, 337
Silver, M., 161
Silverberg, J., 206, 340
Silverberg, S.B., 204, 207–208, 253
Silvereisen, R.K., 127
Silverstein, C., 252, 271
Silverstein, M.L., 366, 368–369
Siman, M.L., 207
Simburg, E., 83
Simcha-Fagan, O., 315, 317
Simmons, C.H., 227
Simmons, R., 25, 31, 33–34, 36, 260–261, 394, 444, 495
Simms, M.C., 107
Simon, D.R., 232
Simon, H.A., 53
Simon, M.D., 346
Simon, P., 131, 135
Simon, W., 95
Simons, A., 393, 400
Simons, J., 263
Simpson, D.D., 215
Simpson, G.M., 373, 377
Simpson, J.C., 365
Sinclair, R.J., 209
Singer, J., 373
Single, E., 164
Skandsky, M., 10
Skinner, E.A., 374
Sklansky, M., 79
Skolnikoff, A., 84

Slaby, R.G., 45–46, 54–57, 313, 318, 321
Sladkin, R., 256
Slater, T.F., 334
Sleman, R., 49, 52
Slipp, S., 71
Sloan, J.H., 344–345
Smetana, J., 10
Smith, A., 173, 319
Smith, E., 26, 101, 106–107
Smith, K.W., 109
Smith, L., 196
Smith, M., 173, 501
Smith, R.S., 313
Smith, W., 115
Smollar, J., 132–133
Smyer, M., 503
Snapp, M., 191
Snarey, J., 259, 370–371
Sneesby, K.R., 108
Snell, W.E., 109
Snow, C.P., 489
Snowden, L., 429
Snyder, H.S., 309, 317
Snyder, J., 207, 393, 396
Snyder, K.S., 377
Socarides, C., 80
Solnit, A., 393
Solomon, B., 151, 227
Somberg, D.R., 313
Sommerfeldt, L., 342
Sonenstein, F., 105, 118
Sophie, J., 252
Sorenson, R.E., 118
Sosin, M., 287–288
Sowards, S.K., 454–456
Spacks, P.M., 259
Spady, W., 131, 136
Spanier, G., 267, 499
Spence, D., 65, 423
Spence, J.T., 257
Spence, S., 393
Spencer, E.K., 340–341
Spencer, J.H., 365
Spiegel, J., 500, 513–514
Spiro, R.P., 9
Spitzer, R.L., 360
Spivack, G., 46, 53
Sprafkin, R.P., 429
Sprenkle, D.H., 319
Spring, B., 362
Sroufe, L., 389

Stack, C., 509
Stanley, J., 398
Stanton, M.D., 164–166
Stark, E., 225, 393
Stattin, H., 318
Stauffer, L., 438
Stechler, G., 64, 67, 69, 71
Steele, R., 423
Stein, B., 422, 458
Stein, L.I., 373, 375–376, 378
Steinberg, D., 454, 457–458, 462
Steinberg, L., 10, 31, 36–37, 151, 154, 204, 206–208, 253, 259, 261, 389, 437–438, 443, 478, 492, 498
Steinmetz, S., 479
Steinmeyer, E.M., 368
Steltz-Lenarsky, J., 347
Stengel, E., 64, 342
Stent, M., 222
Stephens, J.H., 368
Stephens, W., 431–432
Stephenson, R., 288
Stern, D., 64–67, 70–71
Stern, L., 398
Stern, S., 419
Stewart, A., 480–481
Stewart, C.S., 100
Stien, L.I., 373
Stierlin, H., 155, 502, 514
Stipp, H., 345
Stokes, G., 108
Stolorow, R., 67, 420
Stolz, H., 259
Stolz, L.M., 259
Stolzman, R., 9
Stouthamer-Loeber, M., 310–315, 317–318, 322, 507
Strachey, J., 68
Straus, M., 479
Strauss, A., 251
Strauss, B., 366
Strauss, J.S., 367
Street, R., 441
Stringer, G.M., 112
Stringer, S., 507
Strober, M., 334, 336
Stuart, R., 167
Stubbs, M., 32, 38
Sue, S., 230
Sujomi, S.J., 313

Sullivan, H., 69, 203, 208, 210, 497
Sullivan, K., 319
Sulloway, F., 64
Sundberg, N., 429
Sundstrom, J., 322
Susman, E.J., 22, 25, 26, 29, 263
Sussex, J.N., 346
Sutton, R.G., 222
Swanson, D., 63
Swedo, S., 11
Sylva, K., 125
Szapocznik, J., 233–234, 238, 319, 321

Taber, S., 497
Tabrizi, M., 335
Talbert, L., 26, 29, 106
Tanner, J.M., 22–23, 261
Tarule, J., 235
Taube, C.A., 15
Taylor, B., 21, 25, 29, 30, 63, 261, 417, 502
Taylor, D., 222
Taylor, H.L., 438
Taylor, L., 292, 299
Teasdale, J., 400
Telles, C., 514
Temoshok, L., 118
Teri, L., 336–337
Terman, D., 73, 412–414, 419
Terry, P., 134
Tesiny, E.P., 335
Test, M.A., 373, 375–376, 378
Tester, M., 289, 290
Thalberg, S.P., 110
Thissen, D., 23
Thomas, C., 288, 312, 321
Thomas, J.K., 431–432
Thomas, L.E., 502
Thomas, P., 308–310, 312–314, 316, 320
Thomas, T., 339
Thompson, M., 500
Thompson, O., 224
Thoresen, C.E., 117
Thornberry, T.P., 311
Thornton, A., 108–109
Timberlake, I., 9, 475
Tischer, G., 9
Tisher, M., 335

Tishler, G.L., 374
Tizard, J., 390–391
Tobin, S., 254
Tobin-Richards, M., 31–33, 38, 268
Tobler, N.S., 439
Todd, D., 174, 224, 239
Todd, T., 164–166
Tolan, P., 1, 9, 11, 13, 112, 140, 167, 287, 307–323, 339, 366, 389, 402, 417–418, 421, 427–429, 438–439, 444–445, 476, 481, 510, 513, 515
Tolpin, M., 69
Tolpin, P., 77
Tolsdorf, C., 185
Tomkins, A., 283, 287–288
Tomlinson-Keasey, C., 47
Tonry, M., 311–313, 315, 322–323
Torrance, E., 183
Townsend, M.A.R., 209
Tracy, K., 182, 192
Tramontana, M., 388, 396, 419, 430
Travis, D., 151–153
Treinman, R., 164
Tremblay, R.E., 310, 312, 318, 321–323
Trepper, T.S., 319
Trevarthaan, C., 67
Trickett, E., 175–177, 181–186, 189, 191–192, 195, 198, 224, 239–240, 443, 515
Trimbel, J.E., 231–234
Tripp, C.A., 262
Troiden, R., 80, 262–265, 267–268
Troll, L., 252, 493
Tsuang, M., 346, 365, 368
Tucker, J., 178
Tuma, A.H., 372–373, 429
Turiel, E., 46
Turkewitz, 398
Turner, C.F., 97
Turner, C.W., 287
Tuss, C.J., 462
Tversky, A., 54
Twomey, J., 334
Twomey, S., 338
Tyson, R.L., 84

Udry, J.R., 26, 29, 101, 106, 108–111, 205, 308
Uhlenhuth, E.H., 8
Ullman, C. 10
Unger, R., 222
Unis, M., 399
Urbain, E.S., 52, 57
Urey, J.R., 321
Urich, R.F., 372–373
Urphy, R., 364

Vaile-Val, G., 419
Vaillant, C.O., 369
Vaillant, G., 77, 318, 368–371, 374
Valentin, C., 436
Van Acker, R., 313–316, 318, 320, 322–323
Van Cleave, E.F., 31, 31, 260
Van Doorninck, W.J., 55
Van Gennep, A., 76, 264
Van Kammen, W.B., 317–319
Van Ness, R., 116
Vaughn, B., 417–418
Vaughn, C.E., 377
Vaux, A., 183, 185, 314
Vaux, H., 437
Veevers, J., 492
Velasquez, J.S., 464
Velez, C., 13
Velez, N., 509
Vener, A.M., 100
Verhoff, J., 14
Viale-Val, G., 402, 464
Vidyarnave, 81
Vierling, L., 290
Vincent, D.T., 181
Vincent, T., 174, 184
Voeth, S., 437
Von Bertallanfy, L., 186
Vonkorff, M., 374
Vorrath, H.H., 215
Vygotsky, L., 393

Waas, G.A., 212
Wadlington, W., 282, 284, 289
Wagner, E.H., 337
Wahl, O.F., 377
Wahler, R.G., 307, 310, 316, 320–322, 444–445
Wainer, H., 23
Waite, L., 508–509

Walberg, H.J., 205–206
Walder, L.O., 314, 316–317
Waldron, H., 168, 287
Walker, L., 52, 301
Wall, S., 418
Wallace, C.M., 110
Wallach, M.A., 371
Wallenstein, S., 345
Wallerstein, R., 63, 65–66, 422–423, 480
Wallston, B.S., 224, 236
Walsh, B.T., 9, 393, 417, 513
Walsh, F., 150–154, 156–160, 166–167
Walster, E., 394
Walter, L., 10
Walter, M., 181
Walters, P., 9
Walters, R., 7, 475
Walton, L.A., 337
Wandersman, A., 240
Wang, E.Y.I., 319, 429, 440
Wanlass, R., 134
Warburton, J., 287
Ward, R.S, 373, 375, 378
Warfield-Coppock, N., 235
Warner, V., 334
Warren, M., 29, 33
Wartella, M., 346, 351–352
Wasserman, F., 115
Watel, L., 342
Waters, E., 418
Watson, D., 210
Watson, S.M., 321
Watson-Perczel, M., 429
Watters, A.T., 250
Watts, R., 73, 235, 239, 417, 494, 513, 517
Watzlawick, P., 150, 222
Weinberg, M.S., 98–99, 102, 262–263
Weinberg, T.S., 253, 268
Weinberger, D.R., 213, 362–363, 366, 370
Weiner, I.B., 9, 391, 428
Weiner, J.B., 259
Weinhold, C., 337
Weinstein, E., 96
Weinstein, R., 173, 181–182
Weinstock, I.J., 33
Weis, J.G., 311, 322, 445
Weisbrod, B.A., 376, 378

Weiss, B., 152, 341, 388–389, 395–396, 400, 402, 430, 503
Weiss, J., 420
Weiss, R.M., 224
Weissman, M., 9, 334, 342, 365, 491
Weissman, S., 507
Weisz, J., 45–46, 203, 209–210, 214, 223, 228, 388–389, 395–396, 400, 402–403, 430
Weithorn, L.A., 289–290, 300–301
Wellford, C.F., 232
Wellisch, D., 396
Wellman, H.M., 56
Wells, J., 334
Wells, V., 337–338
Wender, P.H., 346
Wermer, H., 79
Werner, E.E., 313
Werry, J., 388
Werthamer-Larsson, L., 322–323
West, D.J., 309–312, 317
Westendorp, F., 288
Westermeyer, J.E., 361–362, 365–372
Westney, O.E. 106
Wetzel, G.E., 364
Wetzel, R., 343, 393, 400
Wexler, S., 483–484
Whalley, L., 393, 400
Wheeler, C., 173
Wheeler, V.A., 212
Whitaker, A., 9, 372, 391
White, J., 228, 312–313, 317
White, M., 393, 396
White, R., 70, 393
Whitebread, C.H., 282, 284
Whitley, J., 9
Whitmore, K., 390–391
Whittinghill, J.R., 347
Whittle, B., 350
Wicklund, R.A., 50
Widiger, T., 12
Widmayer, S., 506–507
Widmer, K., 318
Wiersema, R., 351
Wilbur, C., 251
Wilen, J.B., 38
Wilkes, T., 45, 393, 400
Wilkinson, R.H., 347

William, I., 106
Williams, C., 262–263, 388
Williams, D., 388
Williams, J.E., 114
Williams, S., 312, 337, 339
Williams, T.J., 203
Williamson, M., 373, 377
Williamson, P., 340
Willliams, S., 337
Wills, T., 317
Wills, U., 391
Wilson, C., 317, 319
Wilson, D.R., 457
Wilson, G., 400
Wilson, M., 10, 112, 222, 234, 239–240
Wilson, P., 400
Wilton, K.M., 209
Winn, M., 474
Winnett, R.L., 45
Winnicott, D., 64, 67–71
Winokur, G., 251, 346
Winterdyk, J., 287
Wise, L., 508
Wish, E., 317
Witheridge, T.F., 375
Witkin, H., 230

Wittes, G., 189
Wodarski, J.S., 320
Wohl, R., 76
Wolberg, L., 388
Wolf, E., 64, 67, 69–70, 73, 412–414, 419, 437
Wolfgang, M.E., 309, 311
Wolstenholme, F., 396
Wolverton, L., 434
Wood, J., 185
Wood, M.E., 50
Woolson, R.F., 368
Worrell, C., 282
Wright, J., 393
Wullivan, H.S., 214
Wunder, J., 334, 338
Wurtele, S.K., 457
Wynn, J., 430, 432, 434

Yagmuchi, K., 318
Yanchysyn, G.W., 339–340
Yanof, D.S., 214
Yarmouth, J., 134
Yarrow, M.R., 267
Yinger, J.M., 231
Yoken, C., 430, 432, 434
Young, D., 348, 350, 393, 400

Young, M.A., 346–347
Young, R.D., 95
Youniss, J., 132–133, 203, 205, 208, 214–215
Ysseldyke, J., 177
Yu, K.H., 234
Yule, W., 1, 8, 10, 13, 37, 390–391, 412

Zabin, L., 106–107, 441
Zakin, D.F., 34, 36
Zane, N., 230
Zayas, L., 237
Zegans, J., 402
Zelenak, J.P., 351–352
Zelli, A., 46, 318, 321
Zellman, G.L., 111, 112
Zelnak, J.P., 348
Zelnik, M., 103, 104, 105–108, 118
Zigler, E., 366–367
Zilbergeld, B., 38
Zimmerman, M., 226, 227
Zola, M.N., 364
Zorn, J., 118
Zuboin, J., 362

Subject Index

Abandonment, fears of, 153
Abortion:
   future research, 512
   parental consent, 295–296
   parental notification, 295–298
   restrictions, 295
   waiting period, 297
Absence-of-pathology model of normality, 12
Acculturation:
   adjustment reaction to, 233
   conflicts, 232
   cultural identity and, 233–234
   defined, 231
   future research, 514
   stress, 232–233
Achievement, importance of, 5
Acne, 394
Acquaintance rape, 111–112, 114, 503–504
Action(s):
   defensive operations, 83
   environmental response, 83
   need for, 78
   therapist's reaction to, 82–84
Addiction, family dysfunction, 164–166
Adjustment reaction to acculturation, 233
Adolescent Abuse Inventory (AAI), 485–486
Adolescent Growth Study, 259–260
Adolescent maltreatment:
   causes of, 484, 486
   child abuse, differentiated from, 477–478
   clinical problems, 484
   environmental influences, 478–480
   family adaptability and cohesion assessment, 485
   life-course perspective, 478–479
Adolescent medicine/health centers, 442–443

Adolescent psychotherapist:
   clinical process and, 422–423
   empathic understanding, 414–416
   as researcher, 416–420
   theory formation, 420–422
Adolescent psychotherapy:
   developmental considerations, 388–390
   effectiveness of, 395–397, 404
   evaluation of, 399–400
   format of, 394
   future research, 511, 513
   guidelines, 403–404
   intervention, 398
   methodological considerations, 397–400
   origin of, 387, 392–393
   outcome, 398–400
   patient descriptions, 397–398
   research:
      lack of, 388
      significance of, 411–414, 423
      studies of, 397
      therapeutic improvement, 400–402
   therapist, see Adolescent psychotherapist
Adolescent turmoil:
   cross-cultural studies, 7
   cross-generational studies, 9
   defined, 10
   homosexuality, 250
   normality of, see Normality
   parent-adolescent conflict, see Parent-adolescent conflict
   psychiatric symptoms, 9
   psychoanalytic theory of, 10–11
   reasons for, 7
   role of, 5, 10–13, 16
   separation and identity development and, 6

Adolescent turmoil *(Continued)*
  studies of:
    Isle of Wight study, 13
    psychiatric symptoms, degree of, 7–9
    self-image, cross-generational, 9
    "sturm and drang" theory, 156, 475
  theories of:
    biogenetic, 6
    psychoanalytic, 6
  treatment of, 9
Adrenal androgens, effects of, 22–23, 29
African psychology, 236. *See also* Minorities
Ageism, 224
Aggression:
  information-processing and, 56
  as motivational factor, 313
  peers and, 211
  problem-solving skills, 54–55
  sexual behavior and, 116
AIDS:
  coming out and, 266
  educational programs, 259
  prevalence and potential of, 117–118
  prevention of, 438
  psychosocial impact, 271–272
Alcohol abuse:
  depression and, 338
  multigenerational, 165
  schizophrenia, 376
Alcohol use:
  as free time activity, 139
  incidence of, 311
  peer influence and, 205–206
  prevention programs, 439–440
  suicide and, 349
Alcoholism, suicide and, 347
Alienation, acculturation and, 232
Alternative intervention:
  academic-related interventions, 443–444
  benefits of, 428
  community-based alternatives, 430–438
  delinquency intervention, 444–446
  developmental/life-span perspective, 428
  future research, 516–517
  health-related intervention, 438–443
  integration of, 429
  purpose of, 427–428, 446
  significance of, 428, 446
  social skills training, 429–430
  types of, 429

Anger:
  hormonal influence on, 29
  problematic, criteria, 10
Anorexia nervosa:
  off-time maturation and, 32
  as suicidal behavior, 342
  See also Eating disorders
Antisocial behavior:
  chronicity, 309, 316
  co-morbidity, 319–320, 323
  conduct disorder, 308
  defined, 308
  delinquency, *see* Delinquency
  depression and, 323
  developmental parameters, 309–310
  drug use as, 308, 311, 317, 319, 323
  duration of, 309
  explanatory model, 315–316
  genetic correlation, 313
  incidence of, 310–312
  involvement in, 308, 311, 323
  moral reasoning development and, 51–52
  onset of, 309, 317
  patterns of:
    aggressive/versatile path, 317–318, 323
    exclusive substance use path, 318, 323
    nonaggressive path, 318, 323
    peer influence and, 206–207, 308, 314
    perspective-taking skills and, 52
  prevalence rates, 310–312
  prevention of, 320–322
  progression:
    patterns, 309–310
    rate, 310, 317
  predictive variables:
    constitutional, 312–313
    familial, 314
    peer group/relations, 314
    psychological, 313
    social/community, 314–315
  prevention of, 316, 323
  research methods, 323
  self-reports, 310–311, 314
  social information-processing skills deficits, 56
  syndrome orientation research, 307
  treatment of, 320–321, 323, 456
Antisocial Behavior Check List (ABCL), 456
Anxiety:
  adolescent psychotherapy models, 393
  cognitive therapy, 393
  normality of, 13, 16
Art, participation in, 134–136

Ash, 497
Athlete identity, 131
Attention Deficit Disorder (ADD):
  antisocial behavior and, 319–320
  familial risk factors, 317
  treatment of, 392
Attention Deficit-Hyperactivity Disorder (ADHD), 392
Attractiveness, importance of, 31
Authoritarian parents, 485–486
Autonomy:
  behavioral, 232
  eating disorders and, 161
  psychotherapy effectiveness and, 389–390
  self-destructive behavior and, 158
  significance of, 395
  See also Empowerment
Axis II diagnosis, personality dysfunction pattern, 13

Beck Depression Inventory, 335–336
Behavior, influences on, *see specific types of behavior*
Behavioral autonomy, 232
Beliefs:
  behavioral standards and, 46
  causality, 46
  consequences of action, 46
  imaginary audience, 50, 57
  personal fable, 50, 57
  social information processing and, 54–55
Biological changes, *see* Puberty
Black adoloscents, 242
Body image:
  pubertal development and, 31–32, 39–40
  significance of, 394, 511
  weight and, 33
Borderline personality disorder:
  adolescent psychotherapy models, 393
  suicide and, 349
Boy Scouts, involvement in, 126, 431
Boys Clubs of America, involvement in, 431
Breast development:
  early maturation and, 32, 33
  hormonal changes and, 23
  as secondary sex characteristic, 97
  self-definition and, 33
  sexualized meaning of, 33
Bridge Program, schizophrenia treatment, 373

Cardiovascular disease, prevention of, 438
Carnegie Council on Adolescent Development, 430–431, 442–443

Catatonic behavior, 360
Celibacy, 99–100
Centers for Disease Control, 343, 345, 352, 391
Cheating, 206
Child Assessment Schedule, 398
Child Behavior Checklist, 484
Childhood, as biogenetic theory stage, 6
Childhood disorders, pathways of, 9
Children of the Great Depression, 260
Children Without Childhood, 474
Children's Depression Rating Scale, revised, 335
Children's Depression Scale, 335
Chlamydia, 118
Chronological age, hormonal interaction and, 29
Cigarette smoking:
  increase, 437
  peer influence and, 205–207
  prevention programs, 439–440
  as life-endangering behavior, 342
Classroom Environment Scale, 177, 186–187
Classroom behavior, norms, 177–178
Clinical practice:
  description, 1
  vs. research, 1
Cliques, 204
Clozarill Collaborative Study Group, 373
Cognitive "scripts," *see* Scripts
Cognitive development:
  identity and, 45–46
  moral reasoning, 47–48
  psychotherapy effectiveness and, 389–390
  self-understanding, 49–51
  social perspective taking, 48–49
  substages of, 47
  See also Social-cognitive development
Cognitive self-control, 55
Cognitive self-instruction therapy, 396
Cognitive therapy, developmental factors, 390
Collaborative intervention, style development, 175
Coming out, *see* Homosexuality, coming out
Committee on Research of the American Society for Adolescent Psychiatry, 420
Communication:
  collaborative relationship, 175
  families and, 156, 167
  parent-teen, 109–110
  sex-related topics, 109
Community influence, pubertal development and, 34–36, 84
Community Orientation Program, 177
Community support systems, schizophrenia treatment, 373, 375–376

Community transference, 84
Concrete operational period of Piaget's cognitive development model 46–47
Condoms, 105, 118
Conduct disorder, defined, 308
Conflict:
    between friends, 208–209
    normality of, 395, 475
    See also Adolescent turmoil
Conformity:
    importance of, 207
    pubertal development, timing of, 30
    peer pressure and, 134
Contraception:
    availability of, 104–106, 118, 501, 506
    disease prevention, 511
    legal rights, 294–295
Control, see Empowerment
Conventional reasoning, moral reasoning development, 48
Coping skills, lack of, 313
Countertransference, 84–85
Creativity, reciprocity and, 67
Crime, antisocial development pattern, 318
Crittendon Home, 506
Cross-cultural studies:
    inappropriate conclusions, 7
    schizophrenia, 364
Cuento therapy, 237
Cultural identity:
    development of, 222–223
    significance of, 233–235
Cultural influences:
    rites of passage, 39, 76, 240
    sexuality, 95–96, 107, 109–110
Culture:
    acculturation, 231
    defined, 228–229
    high-context, 229–230
    influence of, see Cultural influences
    low-context, 229–230
    status and, 230
    stress and, 231
Culture of narcissism, 72

Daily experience:
    art/hobbies/organizations, 134–136, 141
    deviant activities, 139–141
    leisure activities, 126–128
    music, 137–139
    reading, 137
    study of, 128
    sports, 129–131
    television watching, 136–137, 141
Dating behavior, pubertal development and, 37
Death, of family member, 165
Defense mechanisms, self protection and, 77–85
Delinquency Checklist (DCL), 14
Delinquency:
    adolescent psychotherapy models, 393
    behavior, see Delinquent behavior
    defined, 283, 308
    depression and, 319–320
    intervention programs:
        diversion practices, 445–446
        prevention, 444
    marginalization and, 231–232
    multimodal interventions, 401
    peers and, 211
    perspective-taking skills and, 49, 51–52
    record of, 454
    social information-processing skills deficits, 56
    sports participation and, 433
Delinquent behavior:
    aggression, 54
    imaginary audience and, 50
    self-control skill development programs, 56–57
    truancy, 45
Delusions, 360
Dementia Praecox, 359, 369
Dependence, maladaptive, 83
Depression:
    age of onset, 338
    antisocial behavior, correlation of, 319–320
    assessment of:
        case identification, 335–336
        cut-off scores, 335–336
        interview, 335
        self-report, 335–336
    biological markers:
        cognitive-behavioral intervention, 45
        Dexamethasone Suppression Test (DST), 339–340
        growth hormone secretion, 340
        research of, 339
        sleep studies, 340
    comorbidity, 338–339
    continuity assumption, 334–335
    diagnostic criteria, 334
    DSM-III diagnosis, 336, 338
    epidemiology:
        demographic correlates, 337–338
        incidence rates, 336

severity, 336
misconceptions, 341
mood disturbances, 334
psychosocial markers, 339
recurrence of, 338
research, 334
risk of, 334
severity of, 341–342
suicide and, *see* Suicide
survey, 333–335
symptoms of, 334–335
information-processing and, 56
incest and, 114
learned helplessness, 226
normality of, 13, 16
self-awareness and, 50
treatment:
adolescent psychotherapy models, 393
cognitive therapy, 393
pharmacotherapy, 341
psychotherapy, 340–341, 393
survey of, 340
Depressive disorders, prevalence of, 391
Developmental research, method problems, 268–270
Deviance hypothesis, pubertal development and, 29–30
Deviant activities:
developmental value, 140
types of, 139–140
Deviant adolescents:
generalizations based on, 7
hormonal influence on, 29
Dexamethasone Suppression Test (DST), depression and, 339–340
Diagnostic Interview for Children and Adolescents, 335, 398
Diagnostic Interview Schedule, 337
Dignity of Youth and Other Atavisms, 474
Dilemma discussions, moral reasoning education programs, 52
Direct Effects Model of pubertal changes, 25–26, 29
Discipline:
antisocial behavior and, 314
consistency of, 321
Discrimination, 224–225, 239
Disease prevention, 438
Divorce, effect of, 159–160
Drug abuse:
family relations conflict level and, 10
intervention programs, peer's influence on, 215
systemic homeostatic model of addiction, 165–166
Drug use:
aggressive/versatile delinquents and, 317
antisocial behavior and, 308
incidence of, 139, 311
marijuana, *see* Marijuana use
peer influence, 314
therapy for, 319
DSM-II diagnostic systems, schizophrenia, 360–361
DSM-III-R diagnostic systems:
adolescent disorders and, 389
psychotherapy, 398
schizophrenia, 360–362, 365

Early maturation, effect of:
family relations and, 37
females, 25, 30–33
males, 25
Eating disorders:
adolescent psychotherapy models, 393
anorexia nervosa, 160–161
family and, 160–162
females, risk of, 34–35
treatment of, 161
Ecological psychology:
exosystem, 239
mesosystem, 239–240
microsystem, 240
vs. population-specific psychologies, 240
theory of, 224, 239–240
Ecological-structural family therapy, 233
Education:
extension of, 76
peers, influence on, 205
See also Schools
Effective Schools Program, 186–187
Ego psychology, 65
Ego:
development of, 72
psychoanalytic definition, 68
Egocentrism:
shift from, 47, 58
social perspective taking, 49, 58
Emic research, 227–228
Emotional adjustment, pubertal development and, 29–30
Emotional liability, 1
Emotional problems, *see* Mild behavioral and emotional problems
Emotional support, sources of, 15

Emotional vitality, 228
Emotionally disturbed youths:
  friendships, 210
  perspective-taking skills, developmental lags, 49
Empathy:
  development of, 67, 73
  understanding, 414–416
Employment:
  full-time employment, 72
  significance of, 76. *See also* Work training programs
Empowerment:
  challenge of, 477–478
  cultural influence on, 228
  intervention, 175–176
  significance of, 35
  strategies of, 226–227
  struggle for, 153
Empty nest syndrome, 153, 499
Enuresis, 392
Environmental assessment:
  adaptive/maladaptive behavior, 180–181
  adolescent adaptation 179
  individual adaptation, 176–179
  sociocultural embeddedness, 179
Estradiol, 23, 26, 29
Estrogens:
  functions of, 23
  increase of, 26, 29
Ethics, principles development, 48
Ethnic identity, *see* Cultural identity
Ethnicity, future research, 513
Etic research, 227–228
Evidence of choice, competency standard, 290
Extracurricular activities, importance of, 134–136, 183

Family:
  adaptability, 154, 485
  addiction, 164–166
  alcohol abuse, multigenerational, 165
  belief systems, 158–159
  bio-psycho-social perspective, 149
  cohesion, 154, 485
  communication processes, 110, 156
  conflict avoidance, 161, 163
  death and, 165
  dimensions of, 154–160
  divorce and remarriage, 159–160, 164
  dysfunctional patterns, 150–151
  enmeshment, 161
  emotional autonomy from, 134, 153
  family-community boundaries, 155–156
  future research, 517
  generational boundaries, 155
  importance of, 150
  independence from, 99, 134
  individual boundaries, 155
  intergenerational patterns, 156–159
  life cycle, *see* Family life cycle
  marital dysfunction, effect of, 149
  mistreatment risk factors, 484–485
  overprotectiveness, 161
  parental causal role, 149
  patterns of, 154
  as primary resource system, 168–169
  relationships within, *see* Family relationships
  rigidity, 161
  school interaction, 188
  sexuality influences, 96
  stress, sources of, 151, 154
  substance abuse and, 164–166
  as support system, 503
  temporary disequilibrium, 476–477
  therapy, *see* Family therapy
Family History Questionnaire (FHQ), 237
Family life cycle:
  identity clarification, 151–153
  multigenerational:
    current stress in, 156–157
    family belief systems, 158–159
    legacies, 153, 157–158
  process of, 150–151
  tasks of adolescence, 151, 154
Family relationships:
  conflict levels of, 10
  father, influence of, 37, 149
  maturation rate and, 37
  pubertal development, effect of, 31, 36–38, 40
  turmoil and, *see* Parent-adolescent conflict
  See also specific relationships
Family systems theory, evolution of, 149
Family therapy:
  antisocial behavior treatment, 321
  communication, 167
  eating disorders, 161–162
  functional family therapy, 168
  goals of, 167
  need for, 168
  parental conflict, 161–162
  positivism, 168
  structural-strategic approach, 167

substance abuse, 166
suicide, 167
Father-daughter relationship:
  changes in, 153
  lesbianism and, 271
Father-son relationship:
  changes in, 157–158
  homosexuality and, 252, 271
Females:
  antisocial behavior, 311
  anxieties, 391
  appearance, importance to, 35
  body image satisfaction, 31–33, 35
  career and, 491–492
  communication processes, 133
  contraceptive use, 105
  depression rates, 33, 337, 339
  drug use, 311
  early maturation, effect on, 25, 30–33
  eating disorders in, *see* Eating disorders
  emotional disturbance, prevalence of, 14
  empowerment, sense of, 38
  fears, 391
  first sexual intercourse experience, 103–104
  friendships, 16, 207–209
  growth patterns, 23
  hormonal influence on:
    behavioral problems, 29, 106
    sexual behavior, 26
  imaginary audience, importance of, 50
  morality reasoning development, 48, 51
  mental health care, utilization of, 15
  peer pressure, 110
  puberty, in:
    menarche, 23, 31, 39, 97
    onset, 22, 24, 97
    physiological changes, 22–23, 97
    secondary sex characteristics, 97
    sequence of, 23
  psychology of, 235
  runaways, 163
  schizophrenia, 359, 365–366
  sexuality issues in, 38
  sexual orientation of, 97–98
  timing, effect of, 31, 35–36
  weight issues, 33–34, 40
Formal operational period of Piaget's cognitive development model, 46–47
4-H Club, 431
Fragment of an Analysis of a Case of Hysteria (Freud), 387

Free time activities, 125–126. *See also* Deviant activities; Leisure activities
Friends:
  choice of, 205–206
  conflict between, 208–209
  development of, 46
  as emotional support, 15
  influence of, 216
  loyalty, 209
  one-one talk, 133
  similarities between, 205–206
  See also Peer relationships
Freud, S.:
  adolescents and puberty, 71
  conflict theory, 422
  countertransference, 85
  Dora, 63, 71, 387, 392
  hysteria studies, 71
  language and, 68
  latency stage, 95
  life histories, influence of, 252–253
  Nirvana principle, 81
  Oedipal phase, 78–81
  sexual orientation, 257
  superego, 134
  Tally argument, 422
  "Three Essays on the Theory of Sexuality," 63
  therapy and, 414
  transference, 85
Functional family therapy, 168

Gangs:
  marginalization and, 231–232
  membership in, 51
Gay youth:
  acceptance model, 264
  clinical services, 270–271
  coming out, 254–256, 263–264, 266–268
  definition of, 254
  development of, 270–271
  friendship and, 257
  future research and, 265–268, 271–272
  heterosexual experimentation, 263–264
  longitudinal studies, 267
  psychological distress, 272
  resilience of, 262–263, 271
  same-sex fantasies, 256
  stereotyping of, 257–258
Girl Scouts, involvement in, 126, 431
Girls Clubs of America, involvement in, 431
Gonadotropins, effects of, 22, 29
Gonorrhea, 118

Great Depression, effect of, 491, 493, 501
Group membership, perspective-taking skill development, 49
Group therapy, schizophrenia and, 373
Growing Up Absurd, 474
Growth hormone secretion, depression and, 340
Guidance counselors, as student resource, 182
Gun control, suicide and, 343–345, 351–352

Hallucinations, 360
Hamilton Rating Scale for Depression, 335
"Hanging out," *see* Socializing
Havighurst's developmental tasks, 127
Head Start, 472
Hedonism, cognitive development and, 45
Hispanic children, *see* Minorities, hispanics
HIV infection, prevention of, 438. *See also* AIDS
Hobbies, participation in, 134–136
Homophobia, 80, 224, 270
Homosexuality:
  acceptance model, 264
  adolescent sexuality and, 255–257
  coming out, 254–256, 263–264, 266–268, 505
  developmental perspective, 250–258
  first experience, 256
  friendships, 257
  gender differences and, 257
  identity and, 263
  life-style, 258, 263–264
  longitudinal studies:
    "coming out," 254–256
    life-course, 253–254
    method problems, 268–270, 273
    past and present, 252–253
    personal narrative, 253–254
    significance of, 259
  prostitution, 258
  psychoanalytic theory of, 257–258
  pubertal changes and, 261
  religious perspective, 96
  same-sex fantasies, 256, 258
  self-definition and, 254
  self-identity problems, 80
  sexual orientation emergence, 250–252
  social change and, 504–505
  sociohistorical events, effect on, 254–255
  statistics of, 97
  stereotypes, 257–258
  Stonewall raid, 254–255, 269, 504
  transition to, 263–264
  See also Gay youth; Lesbian youth
Hopkins Symptom Checklist, 336

Hormonal changes:
  behavior problems associated with, 29
  effects of, 22
  estrogen, 366
  sexual behavior and, 26
Hostility:
  information-processing and, 56
  problem-solving skills and, 54
Human diversity:
  adolescent research and, 240, 242
  cross-cultural perspective, 224, 227–235, 242–243
  cultural identity development, 222–223
  discrimination, 224–225
  ecological psychology, 224, 239–243
  future research, 517
  human relativism, 222
  key paradigms, 223–224, 243
  philosophy and values, 222–223
  pluralism, 222, 242
  population-specific psychologies, 223–224, 235–239, 242–243
  professional practice, 242–243
  psychology, development of, 221
  sociopolitical approach, 223–227
Human relativism, 222
Hyperactivity:
  antisocial behavior and, 318
  peers and, 211

I Have a Dream Foundation, 444
Identity:
  clarification, *see* Identity clarification
  formation, 394
  psychoanalytic definition, 68
  search for, 45
  significance of, 234
Identity clarification:
  process of, 151–152
  separation, 153, 155
  sexuality, 152–153
Ideology, 224–226
Imaginary audience, 50, 57
Impotence, 99
Incoherence, 360
Independence:
  establishment, 5
  pseudo-autonomy, 155–156
  See also Autonomy
Individualism, personality development and, 70–71
Infancy, as biogenetic theory stage, 6
Inference, competency standard subscale, 290

Informed consent:
  homosexuality and, 268
  legal rights, 289
  voluntariness, 292
Intercourse, first experience, 103–104
Interdependence principle, school and:
  adolescent-school transactions, 186–188
  congruence of connections, 186–187
  feedback, monitoring process development, 194–195
  nature and strength of connections among component parts, 186
  proposed intervention and school, 193–194
  side effects, search for, 194
International Pilot Study of Schizophrenia, The, 364
Interpersonal cognitive problem solving, 53–55
Interpersonal problems, solution processes, 46
Intersubjectivity, 67
Intervention, alternative, *see* Alternative intervention
Interview schedule for children, 335
Involuntary commitment, legal rights, 299–301
Involuntary sterilization, legal rights, 293–294
IQ, 481

Junior Achievement, 431
Just Communities, 216
Juvenile delinquency, *see* Delinquency
Juvenile justice system:
  adjudication, 283
  capital punishment, 285–286
  constitutional protections, 284
  delinquent, defined, 283
  disposition, 283
  diversion, 282
  history of, 282
  legal rights of adolescents in, 283–286, 301
  Miranda rights, 284–285
  order of waiver or transfer, 283
  philosophy of, 282
  pretrial detention, 282, 285
  psychological research:
    justice decision-making discretion, 287–288
    purpose of, 286
    treatment effectiveness, 286–287
  right to trial by jury, denial of, 285
  status offender, defined, 283
  structure of, 282–283

Kinsey Institute for Sex Research, sexual orientation study, 97

Kohlberg's moral reasoning development theory, 47–48
K-SADS Interview Schedule for Children, 398

Labeling, 7, 378
Language development, deficit in, 55
Learning disabilities, 177–178
Leaving home, addiction and, 165
Legal system, *see* Juvenile justice system
Leisure activities:
  art/hobbies/organizations, 141
  benefits of, 127, 134–135. 141
  evaluation criteria:
    challenge, 127
    enjoyment, 126–127
    instrumentality, development of, 127–128
    operationalizing, 128
    problem of leisure, 126
  extracurricular activities, 134–136
  historical perspective, 126
  importance of, 140–141
  longitudinal research, 136
  media, 136–140
  socializing, 131–133
  sports, 128–131
  substance use, 139–141
  structure of, 127
  television, 136–139
Lesbian youth:
  acceptance model, 264
  clinical services, 270–271
  coming out, 254–256, 263–264, 266–268
  definition of, 254
  development of, 270–271
  friendship and, 257
  future research and, 265–268, 271–272
  heterosexual experimentation, 263–264
  longitudinal studies, 267
  marriage and, 257
  psychological distress, 272
  resilience of, 262–263, 271
  same-sex fantasies, 256
  social change and 504–505
  stereotyping of, 257–258
Life story:
  continuity/discontinuity and, 262–263
  homosexual life-style, transition into, 263–264
Life-course development:
  continuities and discontinuities, 262–263
  historical overview, 268
  longitudinal studies, 259–262
  outcome of, 259–260

Life-course development *(Continued)*
  pubertal development studies, 260–262
  research and, 265–268, 271–272
  significance of, 258–259
Life-Skills Training Program, 440
Loneliness, effect of, 212–213
Loyalty, between friends, 208–209

Males:
  antisocial behavior, 311–312
  anxieties, 391
  career and, 491
  contraceptive use, 105
  depression and, 337, 339
  drug use, 311
  early maturation, effect on, 25
  emotional disturbance, prevalence of, 14
  fears, 391
  first sexual intercourse experience, 103–104
  friendships, 16, 207–209
  growth patterns, 23, 25
  homosexuality, 97, 263–264
  imaginary audience, importance of, 50
  morality reasoning development, 48, 51
  mental health care, utilization of, 15
  peak sexual behavior, 261
  puberty, in:
    concerns of, 38
    onset, 22, 24
    physiological changes, 22–23
    schizophrenia, 365–366
    secondary sex characteristics, 96–97
    sequence of, 23
  peer pressure, 110
  runaways, 163
  sexual behavior:
    homosexuality, *see* Homosexuality
    hormonal influence on, 26, 106
    issues of, 38
Marijuana use:
  increase in, 437
  peer influence and, 207
  prevention programs, 439–440
  reasons for, 139
  social change and, 501
Marital dysfunction:
  effect of, 149–150
  runaways, 162
Marriage:
  self-development and, 72
  social change and, 503

Mass media, sensationalism, as source of turmoil, 7
Masturbation:
  discouragement of, 99
  religious perspective, 96
  sexual fantasies and, 79
Mediated effects models of pubertal changes, 29–31
Medical decision making:
  autonomy, 293
  competence:
    dimensions of, 291
    legal rights and, 288
    mental health services and, 298–301
    reproductive rights, 293–298, 301
  research, 289–293
  standards of, 290
Menarche:
  onset of, 23, 31, 39, 97, 106
  perception of, 38
  sexual behavior and, 106
Mental health care, utilization of, 15
Mental health intervention, alternatives, *see* Alternative intervention
Mental health professionals, as student resource, 182
Mental Health Utilization Questionnaire (MHUQ), 14
Mentor programs, 435–437
Mestizo psychology, 236
Metapsychology, 64–66
Middle school, as development period, 443
Midwestern Prevention Program, The, 440
Mild behavioral and emotional problems, epidemiology, 390–392
Milgram, 497
Minnesota Heart Health Program (MHHP), 438
Minorities:
  blacks:
    adolescent mothers, 507–508
    behavioral/emotional problems, 390
    depression and, 337
    idealization of figures, 75
    teenage parenthood, 507–509
  cultural influence, 222
  discrimination of, 224–225, 239
  hispanics, 235, 390
Miranda rights, study of, 284–285
Moral reasoning:
  development of, 46–48, 58
  education programs, 52
  limited skills, 313

Mother(s):
 influence of, 37, 149, 151
 schizophrenia and, 377
 relationships, *see specific relationships*
 working, *see* Working mothers
Mother-daughter relationship:
 communication, sex-related topics, 109
 conflict, physical maturation and, 37
 lesbianism and, 271
 sexual experience correlation, 108
 sexuality and, 158
Mother-son relationship, homosexuality and, 271
Mourning, unresolved, 164, 167
Multiple Autobiography in a Single Family, The (MASF), 236–237
Multiple Autobiography in aa Single Family (MASF), 236
Music:
 as leisure activity, 137–139
 participation in, 134–136

Narcissism:
 eroticization of, 79
 rage, 81–82
National Adolescent Perpetrator Network, 115, 117
National Center for Health Statistics, 343
National Coaltity of Advocates for Students, 178
National Council on Crime and Delinquency, 445
National Crime Survey, 111, 113
National Institute of Mental Health, 375
National Task Force to Develop Standards and Goals for Juvenile Justice and Delinquency Prevention, 445
National Youth Conservation Corps, 434
National Youth Survey, The, 310
Network orientation, 185
Neuroleptics:
 schizophrenia treatment, 372–373
 treatment trends, 387
NIMH Epidemiologic Catchment Area Program (ECA), schizophrenia and, 361
Noble, 236
Nocturnal emissions, 97
Nonconformity, as source of turmoil, 7
Nonconsensual sex:
 acquaintance rape, 111–112, 114, 512
 defined, 111
 incest, 114
 revictimization, 114
 sexual assault, 111–113
 sexual victimization, 111–113, 114–115

 victim response:
  developmental implications, 113
  patterns of, 113–114
  rape trauma syndrome, 114
Normality:
 absence-of-pathology model, 12
 definition of, 5, 12
 distinguished from psychopathology, 475
 generalizations, 11, 78, 86
 individual uniqueness factor, 12
 models of, 12
 psychoanalytic theory, 10–11
 pragmatic model, 12
 statistical model, 12
 studies of:
  mental health professional perspectives, 11
  pediatricians' conceptions, 11
 systems model, 12
 utopia model, 12

Obsessive-compulsive behavior:
 peers and, 211
 prevalence, 391
Oedipal phase, 71, 74, 78, 257–258
Offer Self-Image Questionnaire (OSIQ), 14
Oppression, 225–226
Organizational patterns, 154–156
Orgasm, lack of, 99
Overprotectiveness, 161

Pacific Rim immigrants, acculturation, 514, 516
Parens patriae, 288
Parental rating scales, 399
Parenthood, teenage, *see* Teenage parenthood
Parenting:
 challenge of, 476–480
 educational programs, 259, 436
 types of, *see specific types of parenting*
Parents:
 adolescent psychotherapy and, 402
 as adversaries, 7
 attitude toward, 7, 253
 authority of, 152, 155
 conflict, *see* Parent-adolescent conflict
 educational level of, 108
 empty nest syndrome and, 153
 midlife crisis, 156–157
 permissive, 207
 prohibitions set by, 82–83
 relationship with, 264
 separation from, 395
 as supportive influence, 7, 15–16, 83

Parent-adolescent conflict:
　anger, problematic criteria, 10
　detouring, 162
　duration of, 37
　effect of, 163
　exaggeration of, 7
　father, role in, 37, 149, 151
　mother, role in, 37, 149, 151
　physical appearance, 36
　psychoanalytic theory of, 9–10
　runaways and, 163
　severity of, 10
　source of, 6
　stable parent-child coalition, 161–162
　studies, 10
　transpuberty, 37
　triangulation, 161, 163
Parent-child relationship, independence from, 480
Patient-therapist relationship, transference, 463–464
Pediatricians, normality conceptions, study of, 11
Peer helping programs, benefits of, 434–435
Peer Nomination Inventory, 335
Peer relationships:
　acceptance of, 203, 211, 394
　adjustment and, 209–210, 214–216
　behavior toward, 208
　characteristics, influence of, 205–208
　choice of, 205
　cliques, 204
　conflict, 208–209
　effect of, 204–211
　features of, 209–211
　influence of, 110–111, 133
　leadership and, 207
　mutual process of, 206–207
　negative effect, 210
　neglect of, 212–213
　rejection by, 211–213, 314, 320
　relationship anxiety, 394
　research strategies, 214–216
　residential services, see Residential services
　as security system, 395
　sex differences and, 207–208
　sexual behavior and, 110–111
　significance of, 203, 216
　social status categories, 211, 213–214
　substance abuse prevention programs, 438
　support from, 208–209
　time spent with, 203
Pelvic inflammatory disease, 118
Permissive parents, 207, 485–486

Personal fable, 50, 57
Personality development, as life-span process, 7
Petting, 100–101
Pharmacotherapy, depression treatment, 341
Phobias, prevalence, 391
Piaget's stage model of cognitive development:
　concrete operational period, 46
　formal operational period, 46–47
　preoperational period, 46–47
　sensorimotor period, 46
　structural developmental competencies, 45–46, 57
Planned Parenthood, 294–295
Pluralism, 222, 242
Poisson mixture model, suicide cluster assessment, 345
Population-specific psychologies:
　creativity, 236–237
　critique, 236
　personal experience, 237
　theory of, 223–224, 236, 242–243
　time perspective, 238
Postconventional morality, moral reasoning development, 48
Pragmatic model of normality, 12
Preconventional thinking, moral reasoning development, 48
Pregnancy:
　educational programs, 259, 436
　prevention of, 105, 440–441
　self-development and, 72, 76
　social change and, 505–509
　unwanted, 117–118
Premarital intercourse, 96, 107
Premature ejaculation, 99
Preoperational period of Piaget's cognitive development model, 46–47
President's Commission on Mental Health, 453
Prisoner's Dilemma Game, 210
Problem-solving skills, development, 53–55
Progestins, effects of, 22
Program of Assertive Community Treatment, schizophrenia treatment, 373
Project Redirection, Community Woman, 436, 441
Prostitution, homosexual, 258
Psychiatric disorders, family relations conflict level and, 10
Psychoanalytic theory:
　adolescent psychotherapy, 392
　adolescent turmoil, 6, 9–10
　"clinical theory":

empathy, 66–67
intersubjectivity, 67
defense mechanisms:
  projection, 69
  splitting, 69
  motivation and, 65–66
homosexuality, 257–258
motivational theory:
  clinical, 66–67
  ego psychology and, 65–66
  "experience" perspectives, 65–67, 71
  metapsychology, 64–67
  neuroscience influence, 64, 66
normality, 12
object relationships, 392
parent-adolescent conflict, 9–10
self:
  contemporary perspectives, 68–70
  defined, 68–69
  ego development and, 68–69
  identity and, 68-69
sexuality drives, 79
self psychology, *see* Self psychology
types of, 421
Psychodynamic psychotherapy, 66
Psychological adjustment, pubertal development, effects of, 25
Psychopathology:
  normality, empirical link between, 13
  persistence of, 9
  rate of, 8
  treatment of, 9
Psychosocial development:
  puberty and, 260–262
  sexuality and, 98–100
Psychosocial issues, importance of, 5
Psychotherapy:
  adolescents, *see* Adolescent psychotherapy
  childhood disorders, 8–9
  competence and, 292
  defined, 387
  depression treatment, 340–341
  family, 373
  group, 373
  patient-therapist relationship, 387
Puberty:
  breast development, *see* Breast development
  clinical implications, 38–40
  dealing with, 5
  Direct Effects Model, 25–26, 29
  deviance hypothesis, 30
  discussion groups, 39

early/late maturation, 394
family relations and, 36–38, 151
female concerns, *see* Females
Freudian theory and, 71–72
grade in school and, 36
homosexuality and, *see* Homosexuality, pubertal changes and
Indirect Effects Model, 29–31
longitudinal studies, 260–262
male concerns, *see* Males
maturation, duration of, 24
Mediated Effects Models, 29–31
nature of changes, 21–25
neuroses and, 78
off-time maturation, 31–33
onset of, 22, 24, 96
perceptions of, 38
physical changes, 249
psychoanalytic theory and, 6
psychological adjustment, effect on, 25, 29–30, 40
psychosocial development studies, 260–262
rites of passage, 39, 76
secondary sex characteristics, development of, 23, 96–97
sexual behavior, influence on, 106
simultaneous transitions during, 34, 39–40
social status and, 30–31, 38–40
theories of:
  biogenetic, 6
  psychoanalytic, 6
  universality of, 25
timing of, 29, 31–33, 35–36, 262

Racism, 224–225
Radical behaviorism, 394
Rape trauma syndrome, 114
Rational Reasons, competency standard, 290
Reading, as leisure activity, 137
Reasonable Outcome, competency standard, 290
Rebellion:
  clinical confusion, 7
  cognitive development and, 45
  information-processing and, 56
  self-awareness and, 51
  stereotypical view, 475
Reciprocal socialization, 377
Rehabilitation Services Administration, 435
Rejection, behavioral patterns of, 212
Relationships:
  formation, 5, 203
  perspective taking development, 48–49

Relationships *(Continued)*
  role in personal development, 75
  see also specific relationships
Relative Improvement over Chance Index (RIOC),
  antisocial behavior and, 315–316
Relaxation therapy, 389
Religion:
  cults, 10
  sexual behavior and, 96, 107–108
REM, study of, 340
Remarriage, effect of, 159–160
Research Diagnostic Criteria, schizophrenia,
  360–361, 398
Research as intervention, 196
Residential services:
  alumni, 464
  complications, 462–464
  future research, 513–514
  intrastaff relationships, 456
  limitations, 462–464
  outcome, 455
  patient-therapist relationship, 463–464
  referral and judgment for, 454
  research of, 455–456, 464–465
  significance of, 453–454
  treatment programming:
    coeducational units, 462
    contraindications of, 457–458
    indications of, 457–458
    limit setting, 459–460
    planning of, 458–459
    peer culture, 462
    recreational activities, 459
    school, 459
    staff leadership, 461
    staff training, 460–461
    token economies, 461–462
  unresolved problems, 464
Reynolds Depression Rating Scale, 335
Ridicule, effect of, 213
Risk-taking, information-processing and, 56
Rites of passage, cultural influence, 39, 76, 240
Rod and Frame Test, 230
Role playing:
  moral reasoning education programs, 52
  social information-processing skills, 56–57
Role transitions, 495–496
Romeo and Juliet, example of self-object
  functions, 82–83
Rote Recall, competency standard subscale, 290
Runaways:
  parental collusion, 163–164

  family dysfunction and, 10, 162–164
  identity search and, 45
  life-style stereotypes, 258

Schizophrenia:
  aging, 370
  case histories, 367–368, 374
  cross-cultural studies, 364, 379
  definitions, 360
  deinstitutionalization, 375
  end states, 369
  epidemiological data, 359–362
  etiology, 362–363, 370, 375–377
  expressed emotion, 377–378
  family environment, 377–379
  follow-up studies, 369–371, 378
  gender differences, 365–366
  heuristic models, 379
  historical differences, 364–365, 375
  hospitalization, 366–368, 378
  International Pilot Study of Schizophrenia, The,
    364
  labeling, 378
  longitudinal research, 373–374
  mortality, 371–372
  natural course of, 368–371, 379–380
  off-time events, 363
  onset, 361–362, 365–366, 510
  outcome, 365, 368–369, 374, 379
  prevalence of, 361, 363
  prognosis, 366–368
  reciprocal socialization, 377
  relapse, 371, 374, 378–379
  social policy, 375–376, 378
  stress and, 362, 366–368, 377, 379
  suicide, suicide and, 347, 349, 371–372
  symptoms, 360, 378
  time schedule, 371
  thought disorder, 363
  treatment of:
    community support systems, 373, 375–376,
      379
    family therapy, 373
    future research, 510
    group therapy, 373
    long-term follow-up, 373–374
    natural healing process, 373–374
    neuroleptics, 372–373, 379
  vulnerability to, 362, 379
School:
  change of, pubertal development and, 34, 39–40
  dropouts, *see* School dropouts

environmental influence of, 191–192
  as future support system, 515
  grade in, influence of, 36
  host environment and intervention, 190–191
  resource conservation and management, 192
  searching for resources, 192–193
  as social context:
    adaptation principle, 179–181
    attitudes, 178
    ecological metaphor:
      collaborative intervention style, 175
      empowering intervention, 175–176
      environmental assessment, *see* Environmental assessment
      intervention, example of, 196–198
      host environment, coupling with, 190–191
      individually defined problems, systemic implications, 191–192
      underlying assumptions, 174
    importance of, 173
    norms, 177–178
    organizational structure, 176–177
    policies, 178–179
    student resources:
      events, 184
      mental health professionals, 182
      network orientation, 185
      people as resources, 181
      peers, 183
      principal, role of, 181
      school personnel, 182
      setting as, 183–184
      teachers, 181–182
      "weak ties," 182–183
  succession, 188–189
  truancy, 45
School dropout:
  prevention of, 443
  self-development and, 72
School events, as student resource, 184
School failure, educational programs, 259
School personnel, as student resource, 182
School principal, role of, 181
School Transitional Environmental Program (STEP), 443–444
Scripts, 54
Secondary sex characteristics, development of, 23, 96–97
Self:
  buildings romans, 72
  discovery and understanding of, 5
  exploration for, 71
  preoccupation with, 72
  psychoanalytic definition, 68
  psychoanalytic psychotherapy, 77–85
  psychology of, *see* Self psychology
  theoretical perspectives:
    developmental, 70–71
    psychoanalytic, 68–70
Self-consciousness:
  experience of self and, 81
  imaginary audience, 50
  increase in, 50
  personal fable, 50
  private, 50–51
Self-control, processes of, 55–56
Self-definition:
  homosexuality and, 250, 254
  search for, 50, 57
Self-destructive behavior:
  autonomy and, 158
  incest and, 114
Self-esteem:
  adolescent sex offenders, 116
  body image and, 394
  incest and, 114
  peer's influence on, 209–210
  pubertal development, effect on, 30, 32
  sexual intercourse experience and, 107
Self-identity, family interaction and, 152
Self-image:
  body image and, 394
  cross-generational studies, 9
  pediatricians' conceptions of, 11
Self-knowledge, therapy and, 387
Self objects:
  failure of, 82
  parents and, 84
  role of, 73–74
  transference, 85
Self-perception, maturation rate and, 32
Self-protection, 77–85
Self psychology:
  application of, 72–73
  defense mechanisms and, 77
  development of, 70–71
  empathy, 73
  "experience" perspectives, 65–67, 71, 77
  parents' role and, 84
  self objects:
    defined, 73
    development of, 75
    developmental assistance, 75
    environmental influences, 74–75

Self psychology *(Continued)*
    finding, 74–75
        superfly figures, 75
    social roles, 76
    transmuting internalization, 73
    treatment and, 86, 412
Self-reflection, significance of, 51
Self-regulation, reciprocity and, 67
Self-report scales, 399
Self-system, studies of, 50
Self-understanding, development of, 46, 49–51, 57
Sensorimotor period of Piaget's cognitive development model, 46–47
Separation anxiety, 392
Sex offenders:
    characteristics of, 115–117
    defined, 115
    male, 115
Sexism, 224–225
Sexual activities:
    childhood inhibitions and, 99
    communication and, 99
    dysfunctions, 99
    single parent homes and, 108–109
Sexual assault:
    acquaintance rape, 111–112, 114, 503–504
    gender differences, 112
    offender, 111–112
    physical force, 112
    prevention of, 112–113
    rape knowledge and, 112
    statistical data, 113
Sexual behavior:
    family influence on, 108–110
    future research of, 512
    nature of, 100–101
    peak, 261
    peer influence and, 205
    religion and, 107–108
    rural-urban factors, 108
    social change and, 503–506, 511, 516
    See also Nonconsensual sex
Sexual development:
    biological changes, 96–97
    psychosocial development, 98–100
    sexual behavior, nature of, 100–101
    sexual orientation, 97–98
    See also Puberty
Sexual dysfunctions, 99
Sexual fantasies, 79–80
Sexual intercourse:
    antecedents of:
        biological factors, 106
        culture, 107–108, 116
        family and, 108–110
        individual factors, 106
        peers, 110–111
        psychosocial factors, 107
        social factors, 107–108
    contraception, 104–106, 118
    first experience, 103–104, 107, 118, 501
    frequency of, 104, 116–117
    number of partners, 104, 116
    "playing at," 76
    prevalence and trends, 101–102, 105, 116
    transition to, 102–104, 106
Sexuality:
    biological determination of, 7
    development of, *see* Puberty
    emergence of, 95
    eroticization of narcissism, 79
    family influence on, 153
    fantasies, 79–80
    homosexuality, *see* Homosexuality
    hormones and, 95
    identity and, 80
    inhibitions, 80
    masturbation, 79, 96, 99
    norms and taboos, 96
    psychoanalytic drive theory, 79
    psychological development and, 79
    responsibility and, 100
    sex and love, fusion of, 100
    sociocultural factors, 95
    value of sex, 99–100
    see also Sexual behavior
Sexually transmitted diseases (STDs), 117–118
Sexual orientation:
    conflict and confusion, 99
    development of, 97–98
Sexual permissiveness, 107, 110
Sexual relationships, early involvement in, 319
Sexual unfolding, 98–99
Sexual victimization:
    behavioral indicators of, 114–115
    incidence of, 111–113
    victim characteristics, 115, 117
Shyness, peer influence on, 212
Siblings:
    as emotional support, 15
    substance abuse therapy and, 166
Sleep studies, depression and, 340
Social Assertiveness Skills Training Model, 440

Social changes:
  adolescent mental health, 1960s influence, 500–503
  life-course perspective:
    conflict, 500, 502
    defined, 490
    education and, 497–498
    foundations of, 497–500
    future research, 509–514
    generation and, 490–495, 497, 515
    mental health, 495–496
    normlessness, 498, 501
    role transitions, 495–496, 498, 503
    sexuality and, 503–505
    social changes, effect of, 491–495
    socialization, 498–499
    social timing, 495–496
Social clock theory of pubertal development, 30–31
Social cognition:
  cognitive-behavioral interventions and, 51–53
  development of, 45
  social information-processing skills, 45
  stage models, critique of, 51
  structural developmental competencies, 45, 57
Social competency, development of, 56, 58
Social consensus process, 222
Social information-processing skills:
  age-related differences in, 56
  cognitive-behavioral interventions, 56–57
  deficits in, 56
  development of, 58
  five step sequential model of, 54, 57
  interpersonal cognitive problem solving, 53–55
  models of, critique of, 55–56
  self-control, 55, 58
  social behavior, 56
  social competency, 53, 56, 58
Social isolation, 134, 213
Socialization, 498–499
Socializing:
  benefits of, 132
  importance of, 131–132
  peers and, 133
Social norms theory of pubertal development, 29, 31
Social perspective taking, theories of, 48–49, 52
Social policy:
  adolescent behavior as "phase," 474–476
  clinical services development proposals, 483–486
  commitment to, 482–483
  community orientation, 481–482
  cost allocation, 472–474
  enhancement vs. prevention, 472
  icebergs vs. ice cubes model, 470
  ideology, 480–481
  keys to, 486
  metaphors and, 469
  negative stereotypes, 476
  nonpathological model, 476
  privacy, 483
  pudding vs. salad approach, 471–472
  skimming vs. program reach, 472
  social history and, 481
  support system, 482–483
  total reform vs. patchwork prevention approach, 470–471
Social rules and conventions, development of, 46
Social skills, low, 313, 318
Social status, pubertal development and, 29–318
Sociocultural embeddedness, 179–181
Solitude, 212
Sports:
  benefits of, 129–131
  identity development and, 131
  organized, 433–434
  psychology, 130
  social integration, 131
  transitional activities, 128, 131
Spousal abuse, 479
Stage termination theory of pubertal development, 30–31
Statistical model of normality, 12
Stereotypes, negative, 476
Stonewall raid (New York City), 254–255, 504
Stress:
  acculturation, 232–233
  culture, 231
  family as source of, 151, 154, 156–157
  peer influence, 212
  schizophrenia and, 362, 366–368, 377, 379
  suicide, 347
Student behavior, resource perspective, 185
"Sturm and drang" theory, adolescent turmoil, 156, 475
Substance abuse:
  depression and, 338
  direct approaches, 439
  educational programs, 259
  family dysfunction, 164–166
  future research, 512
  identity search and, 45
  indirect approaches, 439

Substance abuse *(Continued)*
  incest and, 114
  marginalization and, 232
  prevention of, 439–440
  schizophrenia, 376
  sexual assault and, 112
  suicide and, 347
  therapy, as treatment, 166
Substance use, depression and, 342
Succession principle:
  adolescent and, 189–190
  generally, 188
  intervention:
    interventionist-school relationship, longitudinal time perspective, 195–196
    prior efforts assessment, 195
    school and, 188–189
Suicidal behavior, factors of, 342
Suicide:
  antisocial behavior and, 320
  attempted, 342
  cognitive therapy, 393
  clusters, 345–346
  completed, 342, 391
  epidemiology:
    demographic correlates, 343–343
    guns and, 344–345, 351
    statistical rates, 343
  family dysfunction and, 166–167
  family history of, 346–347
  life-endangering behavior, *see* Suicidal behavior
  mood disorders, 348–349
  prevention of, 350–351
  psychological autopsy studies, 347–350
  psychosocial factors, 345–347
  rate of, 338, 343, 391
  risk factors, 350
  schizophrenia and, 371–372
  stress, 347
  victims, overview, 348–349
Symptom Checklist (SCL-90), 14
Syphilis, 118
Systemic desensitization, 389
Systems model of normality, 12

Teacher's reports, 399
Teachers:
  as emotional support, 15
  as student resource, 181–182
Teasing, effect of, 213

Teenage parenthood:
  father, 506–507
  intervention programs, 441–442
  mother, 506–508
  transition into, 505–509
Television watching, as leisure activity, 136–137, 141
Testosterone, function of, 23
The Ecology of Human Development, 188
Therapists:
  misjudgments by, 389
  relationship with patient, 78
  as transference selfobjects, 75
Transference, negative, 463
Transitional activities, 128, 131
Treatment, epidemiology study:
  emotional support from nonprofessionals, 15–16
  mental health care, utilization of, 14–16
  methodology, 13–14
  need for, recognition of, 7
  objectives, 13
  prevalence of, 9
Tricyclic antidepressants, 387
TRIOS theory of black personality, 237

Understanding, competency standard, 290
U.S. Bureau of the Census, 221
U.S. Department of Health, Education, and Welfare, 177, 443
U.S.-U.K. Cross-National Project, 360
Utopia model of normality, 12

Vandalism:
  onset of, 317
  peer influence, 206
Vanishing Adolescent, The, 474
VCR, use as leisure activity, 137
Video games, 137
Violence:
  crimes, involvement in, 317
  narcissistic rage, 81–82
  role of, 81
  theories of, 79
Vitality, reciprocity and, 67
Voluntary mental health services, legal rights, 298–299
Volunteer service opportunities, benefits of, 434

Weight:
  pubertal development and, 33–34, 40
  thinness standards, 33–35

Withdrawal, peer influence on, 212
Work, significance of, *see* Employment
Work Environment Scale, 187
Working mothers, effects of, 418
Work training programs, 437–438
World Health Organization, International Pilot Study of Schizophrenia, The, 364

YMCA, creation of, 126
Young Democrats, 431
Young Men Luther, 500
Young Republicans, 431
Youth and America's future, 430, 431, 434, 437
Youth organizations:
    participation in, 134–136
    process and effectiveness of, 431–433
YWCA, creation of, 126